....Crafted

Quality, Value and A Name You Trust

RESCUE POD-4®

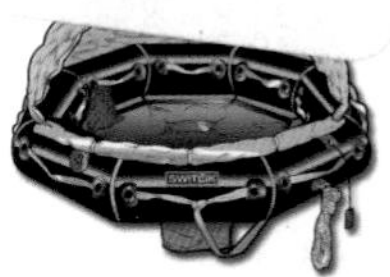

The RESCUE POD-4 is a very high quality inflatable flotation platform with canopy that supports four people and offers basic protection from the elements. The compact sizes of its fiberglass container or soft valise allow it to be carried aboard the smallest open sport fishing boat, day cruiser or sail boat. Although small in packed size, the RESCUE POD-4 is extremely tough and durable.

- Capacity: 4 persons
- Buoyancy: 205 lbs./person
- Floor Area: 3.0 sq. ft./person
- Container Size: 24" x 13" x 12.5" · Wt.: 44 lbs.
- Soft Valise Size: 24" x 12" diam. · Wt.: 33 lbs.

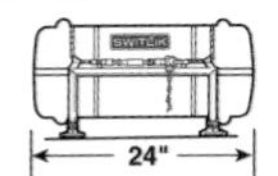

MD-2 6 PERSON LIFE RAFT

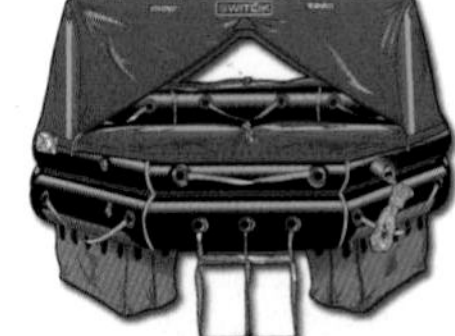

Designed for offshore use, the MD-2 Life Raft includes extended survival equipment and a twin tube configuration, allowing this raft to meet the requirements of the Offshore Racing Council (ORC). Two large canopy entrances and its unique single arch tube geometry provide more ventilation, lookout capability, and occupant headroom than any other raft in this class.

- Capacity: 6 persons
- Buoyancy: 217 lbs./person
- Floor Area: 4.0 sq. ft./person
- Container Size: 31" x 21" x 14" · Wt.: 94 lbs.
- Soft Valise Size: 34" x 18" x 16" · Wt.: 75 lbs.

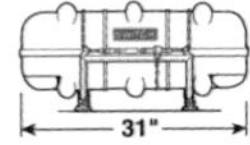

MD-3 6 PERSON LIFE RAFT

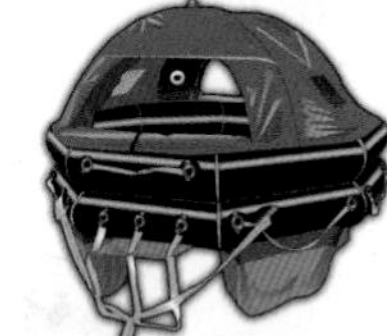

NEW MD-3 Life raft is an advanced design conforming to ISO-9690-1 and all US SAILING & ISAF requirements for Cat.1&2 races. It's Canopy with the dual arch tubes offers full and complete head room for all occupants. two fixed urethane port lights allow all occupants to see the horizon, even with both canopy doors completely closed.

- Capacity: 6 persons (115lbs.)
- Buoyancy: 217 lbs./person (97lbs.)
- Floor Area: 4.0 sq. ft./person
- Container Size: 31" x 21" x 15.5" · Wt.: 94 lbs.
- Soft Valise Size: 34" x 18" x 16" · Wt.: 75 lbs.

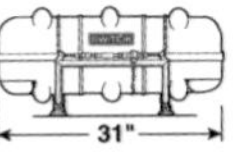

SEARCH AND RESCUE MK-II 6 PERSON LIFE RAFT

Our Search & Rescue MK-II Life Raft is based on the original Military Specification configuration with an updated canopy design, which allows easier boarding from higher freeboard vessels. The Toroidal Stability Device (TSD), rigid boarding step, and Standard Survival Kit are included.

- Capacity: 6 persons
- Buoyancy: 257 lbs./person
- Floor Area: 4.0 sq. ft./person

Container Size: 37" x 24" x 14"	Wt.: 121 lbs.	Standard Kit
Soft Valise Size: 36" x 24" x 15"	Wt.: 102 lbs.	Standard Kit
Container Size: 37" x 24" x 17"	Wt.: 135 lbs.	Extended Kit
Soft Valise Size: 36" x 24" x 17"	Wt.: 116 lbs.	Extended Kit

37"

USCG APPROVED/CLR-6 MK-II 6 PERSON LIFE RAFT

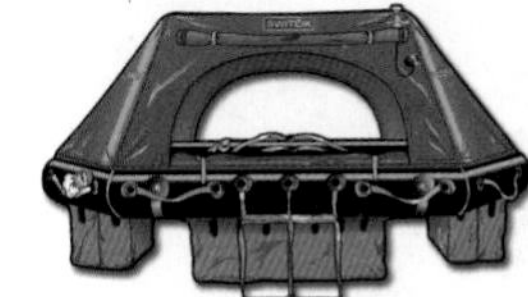

Approved by the USCG and the same basic configuration as our 6 person capacity SOLAS Life Raft,the CLR Life Raft's unique design is substantially better than many non-approved twin tube "Offshore" life rafts. With its buoyancy chamber inner-sleeves, it is the only single tube raft that meets the Offshore Racing Council's (ORC) requirements. It features a self-erecting canopy with two canopy support arch tubes, two large canopy entrances, and the largest occupant space of any raft in this class.

- Capacity: 6 persons
- Buoyancy: 225 lbs./person
- Floor Area: 4.0 sq. ft./person
- Container Size: 31" x 21" x 14" · Wt.: 115 lbs.
- Soft Valise Size: 30" x 20" x 16" · Wt.: 93 lbs.

31"

USCG APPROVED/CLR-10 MK-II 10 PERSON LIFE RAFT

The CLR-10 MK-II Life Raft is identical to our 10 Person Capacity U.S.C.G. Approved/ SOLAS MK-II Life Raft except the SOLAS equipment is replaced with a U.S.C.G. Approved Coastal Service equipment pack. This allows the CLR-10 to be packed into a smaller, lower profile, flat fiberglass container. Additional survival equipment appropriate to your vessel, crew, and area of operation should be packed in a separate Abandon Ship Bag. Twin "Gull-Wing" doors facilitate boarding from higher freeboard vessels and two counter-opposed canopy support arch tubes provide generous head and shoulder room for all occupants.

- Capacity: 10 persons
- Buoyancy: 218 lbs./person
- Floor Area: 4.0 sq. ft./person
- Container Size: 37" x 24" x 17" · Wt.: 145 lbs.

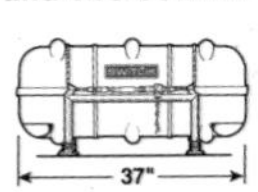

USCG APPROVED/SOLAS MK-II 6 PERSON LIFE RAFT

Based on our USCG Approved CLR life raft design (described above), this configuration also includes a rigid boarding step, two double storm doors, double canopy and SOLAS "A" or "B" equipment. Inflatable floor, deck mounting cradle and USCG approved hydrostatic release are included as standard equipment.

- Capacity: 6 persons
- Buoyancy: 225 lbs./person
- Floor Area: 4.0 sq. ft./person
- Flat Container Size: 37" x 24" x 17"
- Round Container Size: 44" x 21"
- Refer to Brochure for Weights

44"

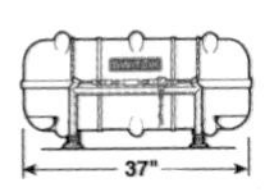

USCG APPROVED/SOLAS MK-II 8,10,15,20,&25 PERSON LIFE RAFTS

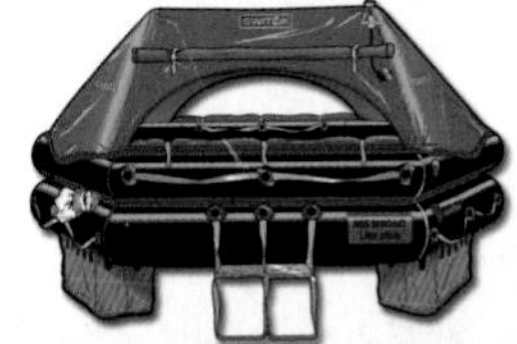

There is no better life raft available for offshore use than one approved by the United States Coast Guard and meeting international SOLAS standards. The configuration shown to the right is available in 8, 10, 15, 20, and 25 person capacities.

- Capacity: 8, 10, 15, 20, & 25 persons
- Buoyancy: 217 lbs./person
- Floor Area: 4.0 sq. ft./person
- Container Sizes: 54" x 24" diam. (8, 10, & 15 person)
  56" x 26" diam. (20 & 25 person)
- Refer to Brochure for Weights

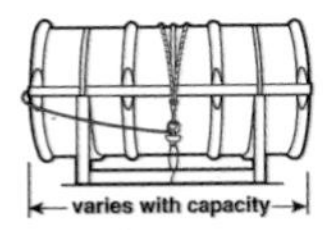

Please Ask Your Dealer for Additional Information

Specifications Subject to Change Without Notice

Established 1920

SWITLIK PARACHUTE COMPANY, INC.
1325 East State Street, Trenton, N.J. 08609, Phone: (609) 587-3300, Fax: (609) 586-6647 www.switlik.com

FOUNDED IN 1947

EDITORIAL OFFICES
York Associates, LLC
326 First Street, Suite 400
Annapolis, MD 21403
All Correspondence to: P.O. Box 4219
Annapolis, MD 21403, 443-482-9377
Book Sales: www.WaterwayGuide.com
800-233-3359

CORPORATE OFFICES
Waterway Guide/Skipper Bob Publications
Dozier Media Group
P.O. Box 1125, Deltaville, VA 23043

On the cover: Kennebunkport, Maine (WATERWAY GUIDE PHOTOGRAPHY). Inset: Pemaquid Point Lighthouse, Maine (©IstockPhoto/wbritten).

Price per copy: $39.95. When ordering by mail or telephone, add shipping and handling charges. Direct all orders to: Waterway Guide, P.O. Box 1125, Deltaville, VA 23043; or call 800-233-3359, fax 804-776-0889.

To provide the most complete and accurate information, all facilities have been contacted within the past year. Although facility operators supplied this data, we cannot guarantee accuracy or assume responsibility for errors. Entrance and dockside soundings tend to fluctuate. Always approach marinas carefully. Reference numbers on spotting charts indicate marina locations. Aerial photos are for general overview only and are not to be used for navigation.

Member of National Marine Manufacturers Association – Printed In China

Navigating Your Guide

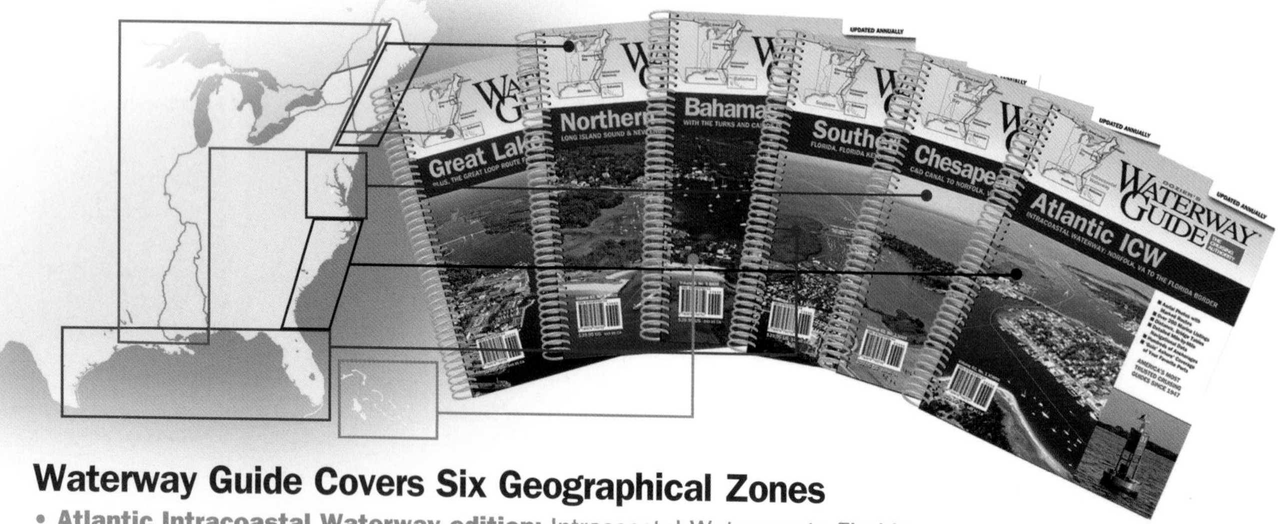

Waterway Guide Covers Six Geographical Zones

- **Atlantic Intracoastal Waterway edition:** Intracoastal Waterway to Florida
- **Chesapeake Bay edition:** Delaware Bay and Chesapeake Bay through Norfolk, VA
- **Southern edition:** Florida and the Gulf Coast to the Mexican border
- **Bahamas edition:** The Bahamas and Turks and Caicos Islands
- **Great Lakes edition:** Great Loop Cruise and the Great Lakes
- **Northern edition:** New Jersey through Maine

1. Section Contents

Sections focus on smaller areas of geographical coverage within the regions. Sections feature:

- ***Color-coding for Easy Reference***
- ***Detailed, Smaller-scale Maps***
- ***A List of Chapters Within Each Section***

2. Chapters

Chapters focus on even smaller coverage areas within the sections. Chapter information includes:

- ***Aerial Photos With Marked Routes***
- ***Navigational Reports***
- ***Dockage and Anchorage Information***
- ***Goin' Ashore Features for Towns Along the Way***

Marina Listings and Locator Charts

The Northern Guide covers hundreds of marinas with the following information:

- *Clearly Labeled Charts*
- *Marina Locator Arrows*
- *Marina Amenities*
- *Phone Numbers*
- *Internet and Wirelsss Internet Capabilities*
- *Fuel, Services and Supplies*
- *GPS Coordinates and Bold Type for Advertising Sponsors*

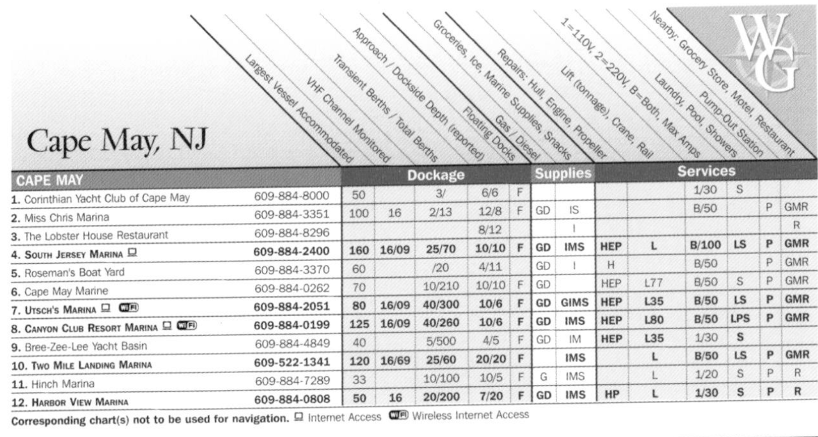

Cape May, NJ

CAPE MAY		Largest Vessel Accommodated	VHF Channel Monitored	Transient Berths / Total Berths	Approach / Dockside Depth (reported)	Floating Docks	Gas / Diesel	Groceries, Ice, Marine Supplies, Snacks	Repairs: Hull, Engine, Propeller	Lift (tonnage), Crane, Rail	1=110V, 2=220V, B=Both, Max Amps	Laundry, Pool, Showers	Pump-Out Station	Nearby: Grocery Store, Motel, Restaurant
		Dockage					Supplies		Services					
1. Corinthian Yacht Club of Cape May	609-884-8000	50		3/	6/6	F					1/30	S		
2. Miss Chris Marina	609-884-3351	100	16	2/13	12/8	F	GD	IS			B/50		P	GMR
3. The Lobster House Restaurant	609-884-8296				8/12			I						R
4. South Jersey Marina 🖳	**609-884-2400**	**160**	**16/09**	**25/70**	**10/10**	**F**	**GD**	**IMS**	**HEP**	**L**	**B/100**	**LS**	**P**	**GMR**
5. Roseman's Boat Yard	609-884-3370	60		/20	4/11		GD	I	H		B/50		P	GMR
6. Cape May Marine	609-884-0262	70		10/210	10/10	F	GD		HEP	L77	B/50	S	P	GMR
7. Utsch's Marina 🖳 WiFi	**609-884-2051**	**80**	**16/09**	**40/300**	**10/6**	**F**	**GD**	**GIMS**	**HEP**	**L35**	**B/50**	**LS**	**P**	**GMR**
8. Canyon Club Resort Marina 🖳 WiFi	**609-884-0199**	**125**	**16/09**	**40/260**	**10/6**	**F**	**GD**	**IMS**	**HEP**	**L80**	**B/50**	**LPS**	**P**	**GMR**
9. Bree-Zee-Lee Yacht Basin	609-884-4849	40		5/500	4/5	F	GD	IM	**HEP**	**L35**	1/30	**S**		
10. Two Mile Landing Marina	**609-522-1341**	**120**	**16/69**	**25/60**	**20/20**	**F**		**IMS**		**L**	**B/50**	**LS**	**P**	**GMR**
11. Hinch Marina	609-884-7289	33		10/100	10/5	F	G	IMS		L	1/20	S	P	R
12. Harbor View Marina	**609-884-0808**	**50**	**16**	**20/200**	**7/20**	**F**	**GD**	**IMS**	**HP**	**L**	**1/30**	**S**	**P**	**R**

Corresponding chart(s) not to be used for navigation. 🖳 Internet Access WiFi Wireless Internet Access

Marina and Contact Information (advertising sponsors are in bold) — *Dockage* — *Supplies* — *Services*

🖳 *Internet Icons for Marinas with Web access*

WiFi *WiFi Icons for Marinas with Wireless Internet access*

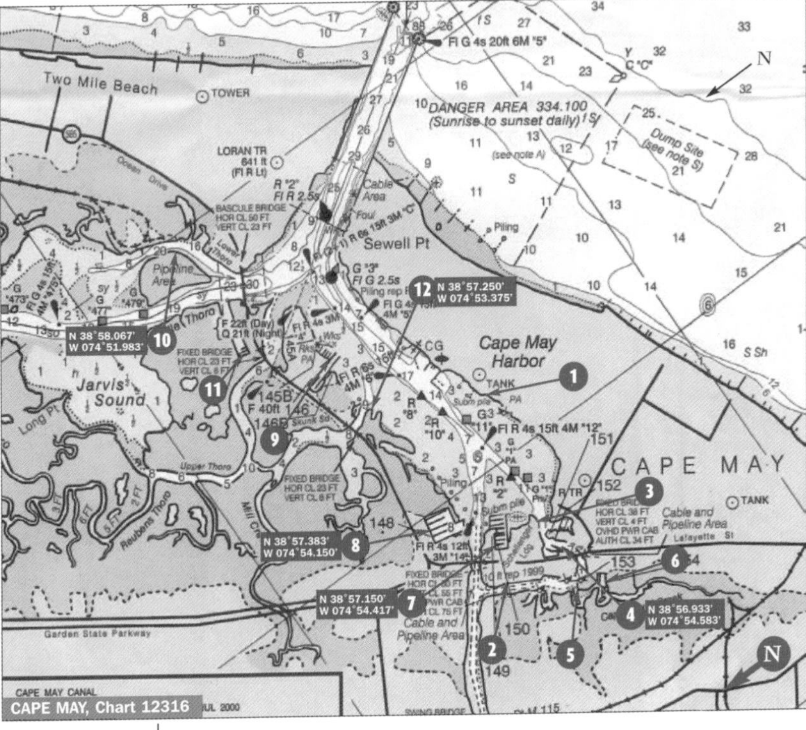

Clearly labeled marina locator charts help tie it all together.

Skipper's Handbook

A whole section with useful boating references

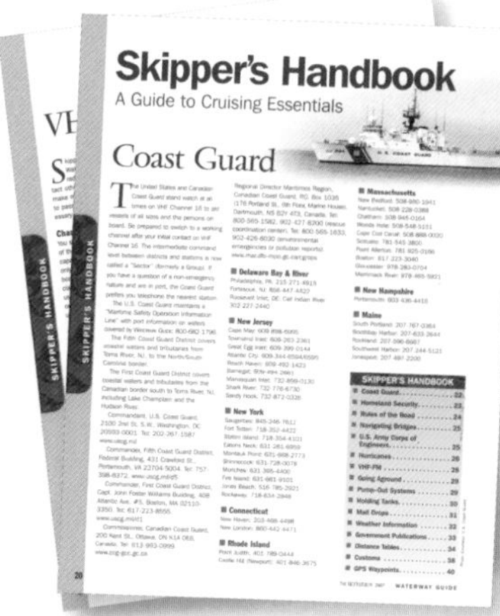

Distances

Tables give you opening times and mileage between points.

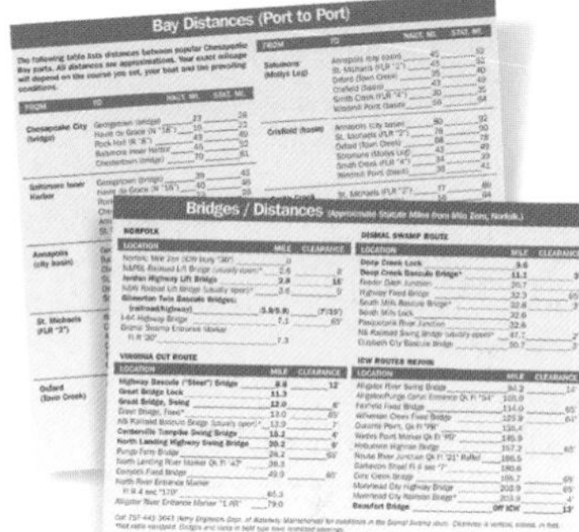

Goin' Ashore

Quick-read features on ports and towns you will visit along the way.

Northern Coverage

PAGE 383
PAGE 332
PAGE 291
PAGE 158
PAGE 93
PAGE 42

Eastport
Camden
Rockland
Boothbay
Seguin I.
Cape Small
Portland
Kittery
Portsmouth
Gloucester
Boston
Nantucket
Martha's Vineyard
Block I.
Montauk
Niantic
Greenwich
Long I.
Waterford
Albany
Manasquan
Cape May
Montreal
Oswego
Buffalo

NOVA SCOTIA
MAINE
NEW HAMPSHIRE
VERMONT
MASSACHUSETTS
CONNECTICUT
NEW YORK
NEW JERSEY
DELAWARE
PENNSYLVANIA
WASHINGTON D.C.
CANADA

Gulf of Maine
Penobscot Bay
Penobscot R.
Kennebec R.
Cape Cod
Buzzards Bay
Massachusetts Bay
Sandy Hook Bay
Barnegat Bay
Delaware Bay
C&D Canal
ATLANTIC OCEAN
St. Lawrence Seaway
Richelieu R.
Lake Champlain
Champlain Canal
Hudson R.
Erie Canal
Oneida Lake
Lake Ontario
Lake Erie

N

Contents

VOLUME 63, NO. 5

Introduction

6 Navigating Your Guide
13 Publisher's Letter
14 Cruising Editors
17 Things to Know Before You Go

Skipper's Handbook

22 Coast Guard
24 Port Security
26 Rules of the Road
27 Bridge Basics
28 Hurricanes
30 VHF-FM
31 Going Aground
32 No-Discharge Zones
33 Weather
34 Getting Mail/Paying Bills
35 Charts and Publications
37 Distance Tables
40 Customs

Planning

521 Tide Tables
532 GPS Waypoints

Extended Cruising Marinas

536 Chesapeake Marinas
538 Southern Marinas

Index

540 Advertising Sponsor/Marina Index
546 Subject Index

C&D Canal to New York

1. Cape May to Barnegat Bay 42
2. Barnegat Bay to Manasquan 66
3. Sandy Hook Bay, Twin Rivers 82

New Jersey offers the mariner a diverse mix of both open water and protected cruising grounds. The Jersey coast, while open ocean, offers all-weather inlets spaced close enough to be convenient for even slower craft seeking protection, with full amenities just inside the jetties. In comparison, the New Jersey Intracoastal Waterway is protected and offers a plethora of intriguing and convenient ports to visit for those able to navigate its shallow depths.

F.J. Duffy/Granard Associates

CHAPTER 1

Cape May to Barnegat Bay

CHARTS 12304, 12316, 12317, 12318, 12323, 12324

NEW JERSEY ICW —MILE 114 TO MILE 26

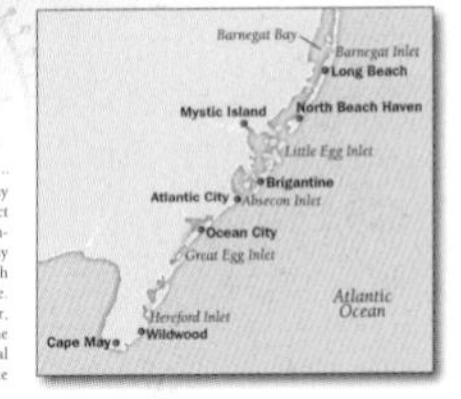

Cape May—Mile 114

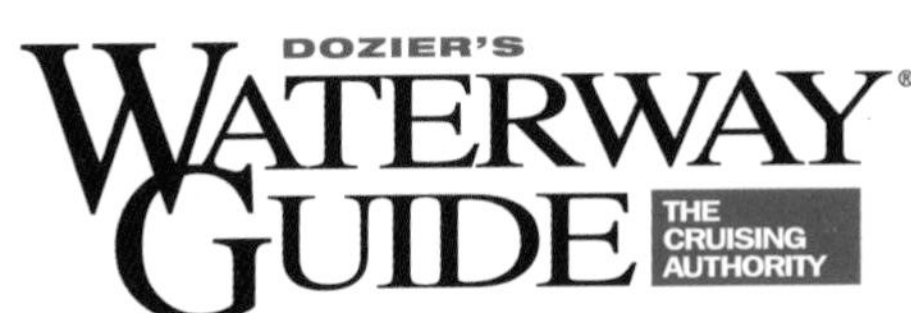

A DOZIER MEDIA GROUP PUBLICATION

CONTENTS

Contents

New York Waters

Introduction 93
4. New York Bay, Hudson River 96
5. East River to Long Island Sound 126
6. South Shore—Western End 132
7. South Shore—Eastern End 142

At Sandy Hook, the skipper can turn the helm in any direction and head for a wide choice of destinations. To the west across Raritan Bay are the sheltered industrial canals of Arthur Kill and Perth Amboy, seldom visited by yachts going north or south. To the east lies Long Island, Rockaway Inlet and the entrance to the inside passage along the South Shore.

F.J. Duffy/Granard Associates

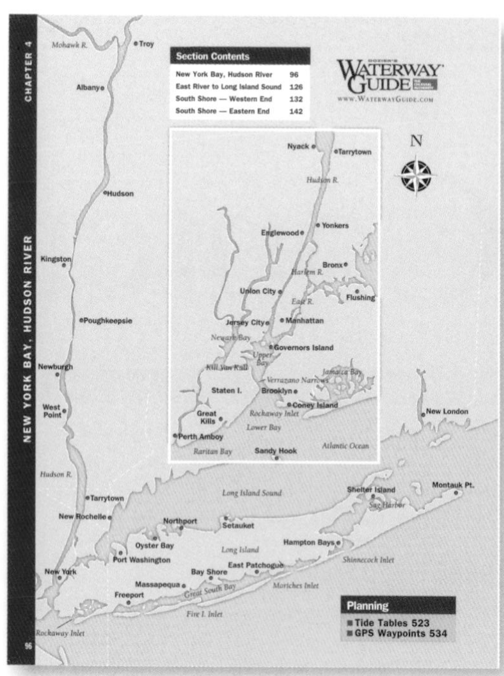

Long Island Sound

Introduction 158
8. City Island to Port Chester 162
9. Greenwich to Bridgeport 174
10. Stratford to Westbrook 189
11. The Connecticut River 204

Long Island Sound, a popular inland sea, lies between New York City and Block Island, RI. It is 90 nautical miles long, up to 20 miles wide and narrower at both ends. The Sound, as it is commonly known, is a major commercial artery, an important fishing and lobstering ground and one of the great cruising areas in the United States.

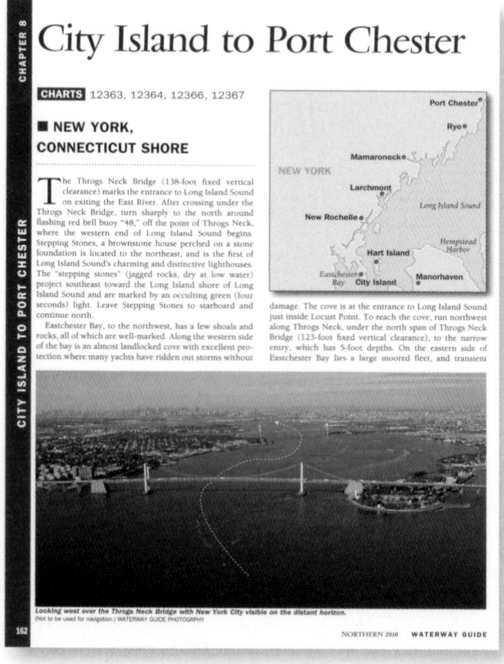

CHAPTER 8

CITY ISLAND TO PORT CHESTER

City Island to Port Chester

CHARTS 12363, 12364, 12366, 12367

■ NEW YORK, CONNECTICUT SHORE

The Throgs Neck Bridge (138-foot fixed vertical clearance) marks the entrance to Long Island Sound on exiting the East River. After crossing under the Throgs Neck Bridge, turn sharply to the north around flashing red bell buoy "48," off the point of Throgs Neck, where the western end of Long Island Sound begins. Stepping Stones, a brownstone house perched on a stone foundation is located to the northeast, and is the first of Long Island Sound's charming and distinctive lighthouses. The "stepping stones" (jagged rocks, dry at low water) project southeast toward the Long Island shore of Long Island Sound and are marked by an occulting green (four seconds) light. Leave Stepping Stones to starboard and continue north.

Eastchester Bay, to the northwest, has a few shoals and rocks, all of which are well-marked. Along the western side of the bay is an almost landlocked cove with excellent protection where many yachts have ridden out storms without damage. The cove is at the entrance to Long Island Sound just inside Locust Point. To reach the cove, run northwest along Throgs Neck, under the north span of Throgs Neck Bridge (123-foot fixed vertical clearance), to the narrow entry, which has 5-foot depths. On the eastern side of Eastchester Bay lies a large moored fleet, and transient

Looking west over the Throgs Neck Bridge with New York City visible on the distant horizon.
(Not to be used for navigation.) WATERWAY GUIDE PHOTOGRPHY

162 NORTHERN 2010 WATERWAY GUIDE

Long Island Sound (Continued)

12. Niantic to Watch Hill 220
13. Little Neck Bay to Cold Spring Harbor 240
14. Huntington Bay to Plum Gut 253
15. The Fishtail 266

Many mariners based on Long Island Sound never leave it, although they cruise all season long, year after year. Crisscrossing between Connecticut's rocky shore and Long Island's sandy beaches, they cruise the summer away—anchoring in isolated coves, visiting luxurious mari-na-cities, racing under sail, fishing, taking long side trips up navigable rivers and exploring big bays.

CHAPTER 12

NIANTIC TO WATCH HILL

Niantic to Watch Hill

CHARTS 13205, 13211, 13212, 13213, 13214, 13215, 12354, 12358, 12372, 12373, 12374, 12375

CONNECTICUT
Norwich
Thames R.
New London
Mystic
Westerly
Stonington
Niantic
Groton
Pleasure Beach
Fishers Island Sound
Watch Hill
Long Island Sound
Fishers I.
Plum I.
Block Island Sound

■ CONNECTICUT, RHODE ISLAND SHORE

NAVIGATION: Use Charts 12372 and 13211. Six miles east of the Connecticut River is big and open Niantic Bay, with Black Point on the western headland and a prominent power plant on the eastern shore, noted on the chart simply as "STACK 389 ft."

The only hazard along the way is the well-marked and well-charted Hatchett Reef. The only shelter between the Connecticut River and Niantic Bay is in the Giants Neck area in the lee of Long Rock and Griswold Island. If you enter, do so with caution; the rocks in this area are charted but numerous.

You will find better protection in the Niantic River, located at the northern end of the bay, which is accessible through a well-marked, narrow (50-foot-wide) dogleg channel, leading through an Amtrak railroad bridge (11-foot closed vertical clearance) and the Route 156 Highway Bridge (32-foot closed vertical clearance) beyond. It is best to enter the river at slack water or against the current to maintain control while negotiating the bridge passages and turns in the channel beyond.

Departing Niantic Bay, eastbound mariners should give a wide berth to flashing red bell buoy "6" to avoid the shoals in the vicinity of White and Little rocks. South of Bartlett Reef (clearly marked by a 35-foot-high lattice tower with two international orange diamonds on its face) strong currents funneling through The Race (farther south) begin to make themselves evident on either tide.

Currents south of Bartlett Reef are the strongest in Long Island Sound, and the waters are also the deepest (more than 300 feet in spots). Opposing winds and current can create sloppy conditions here. In a southwest breeze, an eastbound cruiser can stay in the lee of Twotree Island and Bartlett Reef by running the Twotree Island Channel to Goshen Point. Reefs and rocks are adequately marked, but be aware of your location at all times because visibility can drop suddenly on the Sound and currents can set you far from your intended course. If entering New London Harbor, leave green can buoys "3," "5" and "7" to port.

This is also submarine territory. These partially submerged vessels can be seen slicing the surface with their "sails," often startlingly close to shore. Don't be surprised if one breaks the surface near you. Be on the lookout, as well, for frequent ferry crossings in this area, as it bisects a major route between Orient Point and New London.

Niantic

Niantic is a harbor of refuge and a commodious layover for cruisers in search of rest and provisions. Ample dock space and quiet anchorages are within walking distance, and boat repairs, marine services, reprovisioning and restaurants are nearby.

NAVIGATION: Use Charts 12372 and 13211. Use New London tide tables. For high tide, add 52 minutes; for low tide, add 57 minutes. Two closely spaced bridges cross the curving entrance channel of the Niantic River. With little maneuvering room and tidal currents approaching 4 knots on either tide, full attention is recommended on this passage.

The first bridge, a railroad bascule (11-foot closed vertical clearance), opens on signal as long as oncoming trains are not within range. It is best to contact the bridge tender on VHF Channel 13 before you approach. The second is the Niantic River Bridge carrying Route 156 (32-foot closed vertical clearance at mean low water), which is closed to accommodate rush-hour traffic between 7 a.m. and 8 a.m., and then again between 4 p.m. and 5 p.m. For boats with high vertical clearance requirements, approach only when your signal is acknowledged; it is best to coordinate your passage with the tenders of both bridges via VHF. Contact the highway bridge tender on VHF Channels 13 or 16. It is advisable to make this passage during slack water on either tide. The beauty of the Niantic River and the amenities available make this transit well worth the modest effort required. Current charts refer to all

220 NORTHERN 2010 WATERWAY GUIDE

Block Island And Narragansett Bay

Introduction 291
16. Block Island, Point Judith 293
17. Narragansett Bay 303

After exiting Long Island Sound through the current-washed Race, mariners enter the varied cruising grounds of southern New England—Block Island Sound, the Atlantic coast of Rhode Island and the justly famous waters of Narragansett Bay, including Newport.

After covering Block Island, Waterway Guide crosses Block Island Sound to Point Judith, cruises up both passages of Narragansett Bay, into the yachting mecca of Newport and on up to Providence and Mount Hope Bay. The Sakonnet River, the easternmost part of Narragansett Bay, is covered last in the "Narragansett Bay" section.

Introduction

CHAPTER 16

BLOCK ISLAND, POINT JUDITH

Block Island & Narragansett Bay

After exiting Long Island Sound through the current-washed Race, mariners enter the varied cruising grounds of southern New England—Block Island Sound, the Atlantic coast of Rhode Island and the justly famous waters of Narragansett Bay, including Newport.

After covering Block Island, Waterway Guide crosses Block Island Sound to Point Judith, cruises up both passages of Narragansett Bay, into the yachting mecca of Newport and on up to Providence and Mount Hope Bay. The Sakonnet River, the easternmost part of Narragansett Bay, is covered last in the "Narragansett Bay" section.

Although highly industrialized, Rhode Island is completely water-oriented. Narragansett Bay, cutting 25 miles inland, gives the state a very long shoreline, considering its diminutive size. Rhode Island's seafaring tradition dates back more than 300 years and survives all along the shores of Narragansett Bay. Fishermen still make a living from the sea, yachts from around the world converge on Newport and visiting mariners tie up at guest moorings maintained by the state, or at the many marinas in the maze of harbors here.

Rhode Island waters can be demanding. To reach Block Island in a small boat is to venture across an open ocean, out of sight of land on all but the clearest days. You should review your boat's safety and navigational gear and the crew's preparedness before you set out.

Cruising Characteristics

You can expect fog, with or without warning. Many days will have at least some, and you might be in and out of fog all day. It may be thick "Down East" fog, the sort rarely seen farther south and west. At this point on the coast, serious cruisers consider radar as a standard aid to navigation. From here to the north and east, fewer and fewer boats of more than 30 feet can be seen without their domed or discus-shaped radar antennas mounted on a mast or atop a stern pole or pilot house. At the least, boats in these waters should carry high-mounted radar reflectors to improve their visibility to others.

Seas may seem calm, but with a change of tide or wind, they might suddenly become choppy. You will encounter strong currents and big tidal ranges. Keep an eye out for lobster pots, rocks and ledges.

A watchful eye on the chart, the compass and the weather is always necessary. These waters are among the most beautiful on the East Coast, but under poor conditions, they can be dangerous indeed. Tugs with barges far astern, stealthy submarines operating at full speed and crisscrossing recreational boat traffic should keep the skipper and crew alert. ■

291

CONTENTS

Contents

Buzzards Bay and The Islands

Introduction 330
18. Buzzards Bay 332
19. Cape Cod South Shore 352
20. The Islands 364

The big, crooked arm of Cape Cod and its island neighbors represent some of the most famous and beloved summer communities in the United States. Much of the charm of the whole area—bound by Buzzards Bay on the west, Vineyard and Nantucket sounds on the south, the Atlantic Ocean on the east and Cape Cod Bay on the north—comes from the dominating influence of the Atlantic Ocean, always nearby in one form or another.

Joseph R. Melanson of www.skypic.com

CHAPTER 18

Introduction

Buzzards Bay & The Islands

The big, crooked arm of Cape Cod and its island neighbors represent some of the most famous and beloved summer communities in the United States. Much of the charm of the whole area—bound by Buzzards Bay on the west, Vineyard and Nantucket sounds on the south, the Atlantic Ocean on the east and Cape Cod Bay on the north—comes from the dominating influence of the Atlantic Ocean, always nearby in one form or another. Tiny, deep harbors, such as Falmouth or Oak Bluffs on Martha's Vineyard, all thick with boats, could not be more different from the big, sprawling harbors like Nantucket and Edgartown, or the little secluded hideaways, such as Katama Bay. The variety of nautical scenery is part and parcel of the area's charm.

Businesslike commercial harbors like New Bedford, with its huge fishing fleet, and Woods Hole, with its oceanographic fleet, contrast with the elegant yacht harbors of Quissett, with its local small-boat fleet, and Padanaram, across Buzzards Bay, with its traditional wooden-boat fleet.

Dockage

Finding a dockside slip for an overnight stay around Cape Cod might prove difficult in the peak season during July and August. Skippers accustomed to tying up every night and plugging into shore power might have a tough time finding that kind of dockage. Large local boats, power and sail alike, usually ride to moorings, and slips are rare in many popular harbors. Make reservations where possible, but often marinas in this area will not take any advance reservations. The rule is generally first-come, first-served. You should call the marina of your choice on VHF radio as you come within range, or try calling them via cellular phone if you have one. If slips are not available, ask for a mooring of suitable size. If that fails, be prepared to anchor or, at worst, move on to the next harbor. To avoid end-of-day disappointment, plan to arrive early in the afternoon of the day you need accommodations, particularly in crowded harbors such as Hyannis and Nantucket.

Cruising Conditions

Cape Cod is full of good harbors, delightful gunkholes, clear water for swimming, good eating and sightseeing ashore. But the weather changes continually and deserves constant attention. Adverse conditions can be tough on inexperienced navigators. Study up on navigational skills if in doubt, and do not hesitate to stay comfortably tied up in port if weather conditions are not to your liking.

Distances

This table lists both point-to-point and cumulative distances for Buzzards Bay, Cape Cod and the offshore Islands. All measurements are given in approximate nautical miles.

LOCATION	BETWEEN POINTS	CUMULATIVE
BUZZARDS BAY—WESTERN SHORE		
Buzzards Bay Tower	0	0
Padanaram, breakwater	10	10
New Bedford, breakwaters	4	14
Marion, Bird Island	12	26
Cape Cod Canal, Hog I. Ch.	2	28
BUZZARDS BAY—EASTERN SHORE		
Cape Cod Canal	0	0
Phinneys Harbor	3	3
Pocasset Harbor	4	7
West Falmouth	5	12
Quissett Harbor	5	17
Woods Hole	3	20
Quicks Hole	9	29
Cuttyhunk Harbor	4	33
CAPE COD—SOUTH SHORE		
Woods Hole	0	0
Falmouth Inner Harbor	5	5
Waquoit Bay	4	9
West Bay/Osterville	10	19
Hyannis	8	27
Bass River	9	36
Wychmere Harbor	9	45
Stage Harbor, Chatham	5	50
FROM WOODS HOLE		
Woods Hole	0	0
Buzzards Bay Tower	18	18
Menemsha Bight	12	30
Vineyard Haven	14	44
Oak Bluffs	3	47
Edgartown	5	52
Nantucket breakwaters	21	73
Great Point	5	78

Warning

Laws in Massachusetts prohibit the carrying of handguns on vessels in state waters without a permit. Permits must be applied for in person. Jail sentences and stiff fines await offenders. For more information, contact the Massachusetts State Police at 617-566-4500. ■

BUZZARDS BAY AND THE ISLANDS 330 NORTHERN 2010 WATERWAY GUIDE

Above Cape Cod

Introduction 380
21. Cape Cod Bay to Boston 383
22. Massachusetts Bay to Portsmouth 406
23. Kittery to Cape Small 431
24. Seguin Island to Pemaquid Point 451
25. Muscongus Bay to Rockland 467
26. Penobscot Bay to Eastport 482

The passage through or around the crooked elbow of Cape Cod marks a major step for most coastal cruising plans—and the entrance into an endless mariner's paradise. WATERWAY GUIDE covers the waters from Cape Cod Bay to Eastern Maine in the above six chapters.

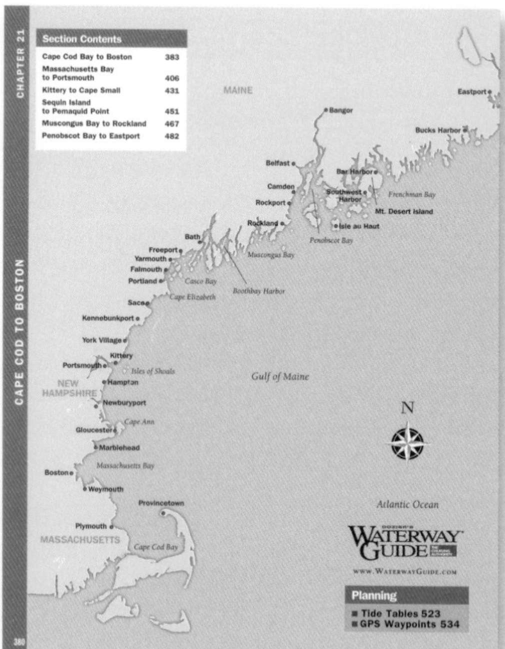

Joseph R. Melanson of www.skypic.com

Weathering Storms

Throughout the ages, storms have consistently been a force to deal with, and frustratingly, a force out of anyone's control. For mariners, they have always been a major factor in formulating plans and routes, selection of ports, scheduling of voyages, hull designs and fitting out. Navigating through storms in uncharted waters presented the greatest challenges of all. Fears and myths, often unfounded, spread throughout the seafaring community with speculation running rampant. The end of the world was thought by many to be just over the horizon. The unknown was the sailor's greatest enemy. Conditions that no one was accountable for often triggered events that changed the lives of individuals, or even whole populations.

It took brave men, men of vision and wisdom, to challenge and succeed against this backdrop of storms and fear. Men who were optimistic and opportunistic who had the confidence to continue on through uncharted territory, regardless of the ferocity of the conditions surrounding them.

Today, throughout the world, sailors (collectively including modern-day power boaters) are navigating through a storm of a different description, but with similar challenges and potential consequences. The current economic tsunami has had a life-changing effect on many throughout the world, and those effects are being felt strongly throughout the boating community. The loss of personal assets and security along with the fear of the unknown as market conditions and the government move us into uncharted territory is changing cruising plans, purchasing plans, goals and lifestyles.

However, just as a hurricane has both a bad side and a (relatively) good side, so does the current economic storm. News reports, of course, focus on the bad side with reports on boat manufacturing plants being shuttered and their employees being laid off, dealerships overflowing with boats but few buyers, and some boat owners forced to walk away from their boats and the attendant lifestyle. This unfortunately is all true.

However, there is a relatively good side to this storm, albeit still a storm and not the calm days we would prefer. What do we hear about the vast majority of boaters who are still cruising and enjoying their boats, those still purchasing boats and marine businesses that continue to thrive in this climate? What do we hear about boaters now finding slips and services more available and affordable? Rapidly disappearing is the attitude of "we've got all the business we need and don't need you." Communities and businesses are opening their arms and welcoming boaters. As always, families are enjoying the water together, finding the relaxation and fun it provides is an important diversion from the dismal, biased television reports. You're not likely to hear about these positive things from news reporters.

As someone in the trenches (marina owner, cruiser and marine publisher), I can assure you that life goes on in the boating community. Weekend cruisers are on the water in abundance alongside the expected dedicated long distance cruisers, evidenced at my marinas and the many others we regularly call on. Cruising plans, both long duration as well as short term, are being made and carried out, evidenced by our increased Guide sales and correspondence with boaters. Maintenance and upgrades on existing boats is strong. Boat sales, although certainly down, are still occurring, especially in the traditionally stable sectors of the market, and this will rebound as credit markets recover and pent up demand takes hold. Manufacturers will restart as speculative excess inventory is sold and new orders come in. As our future course becomes clearer and confidence returns, a similar recovery will occur throughout the economy.

Pictured (from left): John Dozier, Ned Dozier, Associate Publisher Craig Dozier and Publisher Jack Dozier, with Scooter and Molly.

There is an interesting but not surprising attitude we see among those we cruise with and other cruisers we meet. On our boats we are all upbeat, positive and thoroughly enjoying ourselves. Although we all share in the hardships and concerns brought on by the current storm, you rarely sense it in conversations or activities around the docks and on the water. Unless someone pointedly brings up the issue causing us to diverge momentarily, our thoughts and conversations are on the more pleasant surroundings that bring us to boating in the first place: bonding with family and friends, fun, relaxation, planning and preparing for the next cruise.

Inside all of us is the driving spirit and sunny sky emotion we all feel when on, or even thinking about being on, the water. A spirit and emotion inspired by the freedom and confidence to chart our own course and determine our own destination. This is the spirit that will overcome this storm.

See you on the water!

Jack Dozier,
Publisher

Cruising Editors

Janice Bauer Callum

Janice Bauer Callum

Janice Bauer Callum and her husband, George, have been sailing together for 45 years. George has a much longer sailing history. In his youth, he sailed the eastern seaboard with his family onboard their 8-meter *Gracious,* and crewed for numerous Chicago to Mackinac races, as well as taught sailing for the Michigan City Yacht Club. Over the years, Janice and George have cruised and raced the Great Lakes, the East Coast, the Caribbean and the Bahamas. When they weren't cruising or racing their sloop *Morning Glory* with their three children, Treavor, Heather and Dayne, they were racing windsurfers. Janice was a District Chairperson for the International Windsurfing Class Association for whom she organized races for thousands of sailors and qualified them for the first Olympic sail boarding competition in Los Angeles.

Since their retirement in 2000, Janice and George have boon docked on the beaches of Mexico and sailed their Hallberg-Rassy Rasmus, *Calamus,* from the Tennessee-Tombigbee Waterway up and down the eastern seaboard and the ICW to the Bahamas, where they sail several months every year. For the short time that they are not onboard *Calamus*, they are at their small ranch on Lake Calamus in Burwell, Nebraska—home of the oldest (and only) Windsurfing Rodeo.

Jim and Lisa Favors

Jim and Lisa Favors

Jim and Lisa Favors, having been avid boaters in the Great Lakes for over 20 years, spent their first year of retirement traveling the 6,000-mile-long Great Loop Route on their boat, *Kismet*. Jim, who holds a USCG captain's license, retired from Merrill Lynch's Traverse City office in 2007 where he had been the branch manager and a financial consultant. Lisa retired in 2000, from Knorr Marketing, as an art director/designer.

The Favors have recently published their first book, "When the Water Calls... We Follow," which gives 27 different perspectives on experiencing the Great Loop trip (www.favorsventures.com/wwg.html). Currently on their second, two-year Loop, the Favors are writing a twice-monthly log for BoatUS online edition (http://www.boatus.com/cruising/kismet/log.asp). These articles strive to share the many aspects of doing the Loop with those who have an interest in taking this trip or are just curious about it. They provide photography to many boating magazines and also maintain a popular blog (www.favorsgreatloopblog.com) that is more a visual depiction of doing the Loop.

George E. Danner

George Danner

An avid boater whose home port is Galveston Bay, TX, George Danner is Waterway Guide's cruising editor for the ICW from Mississippi to Brownsville, TX. He began serious cruising several years ago by trailering his 26-foot Monterey express cruiser to Chesapeake Bay, Key West, Destin, FL and the Carolina coast from Charleston to Hilton Head Island. Now with a 2006 Silverton 34C, *La Mariposa*, recently added to the fleet, George focuses on Gulf excursions from Galveston to Mississippi and southern trips to Corpus Christi and South Padre Island. The western Gulf region is home to some of the finest cruising grounds in the country and the Danner family frequently explores its coastal waters for new land and sea-based adventures. Out of the water, George is president of a corporate strategy consulting firm in Houston.

Bob and Carol Kunath

Bob and Carol Kunath

Bob and Carol Kunath have owned about a dozen sail and powerboats over the past 40 years. They've ranged from small-lake open boats to those equipped for offshore shark and tuna fishing, to sail and powerboats on Lake Michigan, where they have been cruising for the past 15 years. During those years they have cruised extensively throughout Lake Michigan and the North Channel of Lake Huron. Both are past commodores of the Bay Shore Yacht Club in Illinois and members of the Waukegan, IL, Sail and Power Squadron, where Bob has served as an officer and instructor. He has also contributed to the U.S. Power Squadron national magazine, Ensign, and holds a U.S. Coast Guard Master's license.

During 2005, Bob and Carol completed a two-year cruise of the Great Loop in their Pacific Seacraft 38T trawler, *Sans Souci,* logging 9,000 miles on the Loop and many of its side trips. Recently they have resumed cruising all of Lake Michigan, but have plans to expand that area, perhaps back into the rivers of the Midwest or canals of Canada. Bob has also been a seminar presenter at Passagemaker Trawler Fests over the past four years, sharing his knowledge of Lake Michigan. For 2010, Bob and Carol cover Lake Michigan for WATERWAY GUIDE, including Green Bay and Door County.

Elbert S. (Mack) Maloney

Mack and Florine Maloney

Elbert S. (Mack) Maloney is the author of "Chapman Piloting and Seamanship," which he has continued to update regularly; he also wrote the last two editions of "Dutton's Navigation and Piloting." A retired United States Marine, he lives with his wife, Florine, in Pompano Beach and aboard their 38-foot Present trawler. He began writing about his avocation in 1959, publishing a series of articles in MotorBoating magazine. He first contributed to WATERWAY GUIDE in 1965, when he covered the Okeechobee Waterway. The Maloneys have owned several boats throughout the years, including a 47-foot Chris-Craft Commander and a 36-foot Willard trawler, pausing to stay ashore only twice, once so that Mack could serve a small college as its president and again so that he could write books for the Naval Institute in Annapolis. "I have never been happy very far from saltwater," he explains. Still actively involved with the U.S. Power Squadron, he has been a member since 1954 and served as national Director of Education between 1971 and 1976. He also served as Chief of the Department of Education, National Staff, of the U.S. Coast Guard Auxiliary for several years.

Wally Moran

Wally Moran

Wally Moran, WATERWAY GUIDE'S cruising editor for Georgian Bay, the North Channel, the St. Marys River and Lake Huron, is a former newspaper publisher who has sailed these favored cruising grounds since honeymooning there in 1978. His more recent travels have taken him from Chesapeake Bay to Tampa Bay, then back to Canada via Lake Huron and Lake Erie, the Erie Barge Canal, the Hudson River, Chesapeake Bay, the Intracoastal Waterway and offshore. Wally's next planned cruise will see his completion of the Great Loop into the Gulf of Mexico and on into the Caribbean, before returning to Canada. Wally sails his Dufour 34 *Gypsy Wind* throughout the Georgian Bay area, which he assures WATERWAY GUIDE readers is the "best freshwater boating in the world" and encourages all boaters to visit.

Larry and Ruth Smithers

Larry and Ruth Smithers

Larry and Ruth Smithers are cruising editors for WATERWAY GUIDE'S Northern edition from Cape Cod through Maine. They have boated in various capacities since the early 1970s. Serious passionate boating gripped them with the acquisition of *Back Dock,* their 56-foot Vantare pilothouse motoryacht. They quickly discovered that work got in the way of boating. Bidding their land life adieu they sold their practice, leased out their home in Wisconsin, packed up and moved aboard to cruise full time in pursuit of high adventure and sunsets worthy of the nightly celebratory conch horn serenade. The Smithers have completed the Great Loop, cruised the Bahamas and, as always, look forward to continue exploring new territories.

Larry spent the first half of his working career in the international corporate world and the last as a chiropractor. He is now retired, a U.S. Coast Guard-licensed captain and can proudly recite the pirate alphabet. Ruth's career was in public accounting. She retired to become a stay-at-home mother, which ultimately evolved into being a professional volunteer and dilettante. She enjoys basket making and her role as "Admiral."

Audrey and Ted Stehle

Audrey and Ted Stehle

Audrey and Ted Stehle are WATERWAY GUIDE'S cruising editors for the inland rivers and the Tenn-Tom Waterway, from Chicago to Mobile Bay, for the Great Lakes 2010 Guide.

They began boating as sailors in the early 1970s on the Chesapeake Bay, and then switched to power after retirement. In addition to extensive cruising of Chesapeake Bay and its tributaries, they have traveled the ICW to Florida many times, completed the Great Loop, cruised the Ohio, Tennessee and Cumberland rivers and made six trips on the Tenn-Tom Waterway. Their Californian 45 is presently on Chesapeake Bay, but plans call for returning it to Kentucky Lake to resume cruising the Cumberland and Tennessee rivers. When not cruising, the Stehles reside in Cincinnati, OH, to be near their children and grandchildren and engage in volunteer work.

Robert Wilson

Robert Wilson

Robert Wilson has been cruising the Bahamas from his homeport in Brunswick, GA, for the past nine years. He and his wife, Carolyn, began sailing on Lake Lanier, just north of Atlanta, GA, shortly after they met 25 years ago. Robert is a former employee benefits consultant, and is a Past Commodore of the Royal Marsh Harbour Yacht Club in Abaco. Together they have written extensively about their sailing adventures throughout the Bahamas on their 38-foot Island Packet, *Gypsy Common.* Their current boat, *Sea Island Girl*, is a North Pacific 42 pilothouse trawler, which they cruised in the Pacific Northwest along the coast of British Columbia, before shipping the boat to Florida to continue cruising throughout the Bahamas aboard their new trawler.

When not cruising, the Wilsons reside in Atlanta, GA, where Carolyn teaches pre-school, and Robert continues consulting and writing. Robert is Waterway Guide's cruising editor for the northern Bahamas. ■

Things To Know Before You Go

There are many reasons we go cruising, but they can all be summed up in one word—adventure. The thought of casting off the dock lines with a fully provisioned boat and a reasonably blank calendar is intoxicating indeed. Exploring our northern U.S. waters can take a lifetime. Luckily, we have that.

The ultimate experience is the long-range cruise—the one that continues through several seasons, allowing you to follow the fair weather, from north to south and back again. (Boaters lucky enough to enjoy this lifestyle are often referred to as "snowbirds.")

Many skippers plan their travels to get back to Florida in time for a leisurely return trip to summer grounds in New England or the Great Lakes. Many marine insurers reinforce the migration pattern by requiring their customers to be north of the Florida border by early hurricane season.

The Time Factor

A trip through northern waters can last a week, a month or as long as you choose. It all depends on how fast you go, which route you choose and how long you decide to linger along the way. In about three weeks, you can run from Delaware Bay to Maine; in one week you can run from New York to Long Island Sound and along the New England islands.

It is smart to allow time along the way for sightseeing, resting, waiting out bad weather or making repairs to the boat. Of course, the boat's features and the skipper's temperament will determine whether the pace is fast or slow. Sailboats averaging 5 to 8 knots can cover the same number of miles on a given day as a powerboat that cruises at 20 to 25 knots. The only difference is that the sailboat's crew will have a much longer day under way.

First-Aid Basics

A deep cut from a filet knife is normally not a big deal at home where medical help is close at hand, but on rural waterway stretches (where you may be a long way from help), you'll need to be able to patch yourself up until you can get to an emergency clinic or hospital emergency room. Adequate first-aid kits are essential, along with a medical manual that you can understand quickly; the standard reference is "Advanced First-Aid Afloat" by Dr. Peter F. Eastman. Good first aid kits can be found at most marine supply stores and better pharmacies or drug stores.

Cruisers who take medication should make sure their current prescription has plenty of refills available so supplies can be topped off along the way. Additionally, make sure crew members are aware of any medication you are on in case you become injured and unable to answer questions regarding your health.

All safety equipment—harnesses, life preservers, jack lines, medical kit, etc.—should be in good working condition, within easy reach and ready at a moment's notice. All aboard—crew and guests—should know where to find the emergency equipment. In addition to having the proper first-aid gear aboard, all aboard should be versed in basic "first responder" procedures including CPR and making a May-Day call on the VHF radio.

Check out our Goin' Ashore sections of this Guide; they are equipped with contact information for local hospitals and emergency clinics. Most importantly, if someone's life is in imminent danger, make a May-Day call on VHF Channel 16. This is the best way to get quick help. Making a 911 call on your cell phone is also an option, but not one you should count on because of variable coverage by cellular providers.

A Note on Clean Marinas

The next time you pull into your favorite marina, you might want to look around for some indication of it being a designated Clean Marina. Many states around the country— including those covered in this edition of WATERWAY GUIDE— have launched programs in recent years aimed at making marina owners and boaters more aware of how their activities affect the environment. In order for one's marina to be designated a "Clean Marina," the facility's owner has to take a series of steps prescribed by that state's respective program, anything from making sure tarps are laid down when boat bottoms are worked on, to providing pump-out facilities. (The steps were derived from an Environmental Protection Agency document presented to states across America.)

The underlying principle behind these voluntary, incentive-based programs is this: If the waters we cruise are not clean, then we'll cruise elsewhere and the marine businesses in the polluted areas will suffer. The programs represent a nice coupling of economics and environmental management that is catching on with marina owners and boaters alike. So if you see the Clean Marina designation at your favorite facility, rest assured they are doing the right thing for the environment; if not, ask why.

THINGS YOU WILL NEED

To minimize time spent waiting for spare parts, WATERWAY GUIDE recommends that cruising boaters take along certain equipment.

Spare Parts

For the engine, bring spare seals for the raw-water pump and an extra water-pump impeller, along with V-belts, points and plugs for gas engines (injectors for diesel engines), a fuel pump and raw-water strainer, a distributor cap, fuses, lube oil and filter cartridges. Also, carry a list of service centers for your type of equipment, and bring the engine manual and the parts list.

Other things to bring: spare deck cap keys, a head-repair kit, fresh water pump repair kit, spare hose clamps, lengths of hose and an extra container of fuel. (Keep in mind that, if you want to anchor out, fueling up during the day when there are no crowds at the fuel docks is a good idea.)

Carry a good tool kit with varying sizes of flat- and Phillips-head screwdrivers, socket wrenches (metric and standard), pliers, etc. Remember that all the spare parts in the world are fairly useless without a proper bag of tools aboard to install them with.

For Docking and Anchoring

Your docking equipment should include a minimum of four bow and stern lines made of good, stretchy nylon (each about two-thirds the length of your boat—longer if you would like an extra measure of convenience), and two spring lines (1.5 times the length of your boat) with oversized eyes to fit over pilings. If you have extra dock lines, consider bringing them along with your shore power cord and a shore power adapter or two.

For anchoring, the average 30-foot boat needs 150 to 200 feet of 7/16- to 1/2-inch nylon line with no less than 15 feet of 5/16-inch chain shackled to a 20- to 30-pound plow-type or Bruce anchor – or a 15-pound Danforth-type anchor. Storm anchors and a lunch hook are also recommended. Larger yachts should use 7/8-inch nylon and heavier chain. While one anchor will get you along, most veteran cruisers carry both a plow and fluke-type anchor to use in varying bottom conditions.

Consult a good reference like Chapman's Piloting or West Marine's "West Advisor" articles (available online) if you are unsure about proper anchoring techniques, and make sure that you master them before setting off on the Waterway.

Tenders and Dinghies

A dinghy is needed if you plan to anchor out, gunkhole or carry an anchor to deeper water when kedging off a shoal. Inflatable dinghies are popular, but they require an outboard motor to get them around easily. On the other hand, rowing a hard dinghy is excellent exercise. Check registration laws where you plan to spend any length of time, as certain states have become very strict in enforcing dinghy registration.

Always chain and lock your dinghy when you leave it unattended – even if it is tied off to your boat, as more than one Waterway cruiser has woken to a missing dinghy while at anchor. Outboard engines should always be padlocked to the transom of your dinghy or on a stern rail, as they are often targets of thieves.

Keeping Comfortable

Another consideration when equipping your boat for a cruise is temperature control inside the cabin. Many powerboats—particularly trawlers—are equipped with an air conditioner for those hot, steamy nights. Others can get away with fans and wind socks. When considering heating options for your boat, select something that is not going to suck your batteries dead—and, even more important, something that is safe. Many reliable and safe marine propane heaters are available nowadays for those cruising late into the fall season. Many late-model air conditioning units also feature a reverse cycle heating option as well, but these require a generator while anchored out or shore power while tied up.

Battling the Sun and Bugs

The same cockpit and fly bridge enclosures that deflect the chill breeze also protect against the potentially carcinogenic rays of the sun. Outside it is prudent to wear sunscreen, a hat and, if your skin is particularly sensitive, long sleeves and pants of baggy cotton.

And don't forget the bug spray if you have any intention of enjoying the topside portion of your boat. Bug screens for hatches, ports and companionways are a must, as you'll want to have the boat open for adequate cross ventilation in warm weather.

Glare off the water can be a major contributor to fatigue. Consider purchasing a quality pair of sunglasses, and make sure that they are polarized, as this feature removes annoying reflected light from your view.

Navigating Essentials

Many cruisers are now equipping themselves with the latest GPS chart plotters and computer-driven electronic gizmos. Radar, too, is a wonderful aid, not only to "see" markers and other vessels, but also to track local storms; perhaps half of all boats have it. Single-Sideband (SSB) and amateur (ham) radio are excellent for long-range communications, but you can get by without either one on inland waters. You will not want to cruise the inland waterway passages without a depth sounder, however; this item is essential.

Once you get offshore to the islands the advantages of chart plotters and radar become more apparent. As you cruise beyond the limits of National Weather Service radio broadcasts, the benefits of long range SSB equipment come to the fore, though satellite telephones are an increasingly popular alternative for downloading weather forecasts.

You should learn how to operate all of your electronics inside and out before you rely them it for navigation. A blinding rain squall is no place to figure out how your navigation equipment works. As always, you should have paper charts available as backup in case your electronic unit malfunctions, plus charts really do give you a better grasp of the big picture simply because they are bigger than a display screen.

A VHF marine radio is the cruiser's lifeline to the Coast Guard, marinas and other boats and is also necessary for contacting bridges. Mount yours at the helm or keep a handheld unit there. Many manufacturers now offer a RAM (remote access microphone) option, which allows the skipper to use the hand unit and control the radio from the helm. This is a particularly good option for sailors—better than having a handheld VHF—because it lets the helmsman benefit from the higher power of a fixed-mount radio and an antenna at the top of his mast.

If you are planning any coastal or offshore passages, it would be folly not to carry an Emergency Position Indicating Radio Beacon (EPIRB). Whether it's a MAYDAY situation or a medical emergency, activating the EPIRB is like making a 911 call back home. These satellite-linked EPIRBs broadcast a unique, repeating SOS signal that can be detected from virtually any point on earth. When properly registered, the signal includes a description of the vessel and its location. An activated EPIRB will send critical information via satellite that is routed directly to rescue units, greatly reducing search time.

Most cruisers carry mobile (cellular) telephones, but you cannot count on coverage everywhere, as these systems are optimized for land users. Increasingly cruisers are also using cellular service to connect to the internet, though many marinas now offer free wireless Internet connections for those with computers capable of wireless networking.

We have become an electronic world. For mariners that is a good thing, but electronics come with their own vulnerabilities, so it is good to have a navigation device aboard that will never fail you—a so-called "wet" compass. Have a compass adjuster swing (calibrate) your compass before departure so you can run courses with confidence.

Also carry a good hand-bearing compass or binoculars with a built-in compass for getting bearings to fixed marks or points ashore. Practicing old-school navigation will give you a measure of satisfaction and the confidence to make passages.

Many veteran cruisers prefer to use the spiral bound chart "kits" that feature small-scale charts laid out in order according to regions. Since the local conditions change constantly, use only the latest charts and keep them updated with the U.S. Coast Guard's Local Notice to Mariners, which are available online at www.navcen.uscg.gov/lnm. For planning, many charts and nautical publications (Coast Pilots, light lists, tide tables) can be downloaded free of charge via the Internet. See our Skipper's Handbook section for more detail on how to access this valuable information with your computer.

Looking northeast over East Rockaway Inlet.
(Not to be used for navigation.) WATERWAY GUIDE PHOTOGRAPHY

The Money Issue

Everyone is concerned about money, but when you are a long-range cruiser, the issue becomes a bit more complicated. Luckily, cruisers today can get by with much less cash than in the past. Almost all banks have ATMs. Many grocery stores and drugstores accept ATM and Visa or MasterCard check cards. Remember that most banks will honor the cash-advance feature of Visa cards and MasterCard. In addition, American Express offices will accept a cardholder's personal check in payment for traveler's checks and will also dispense cash to cardholders.

Most marinas, especially the large ones, accept major credit cards and oil-company credit cards for dockage, fuel and marine supplies. Most restaurants, motels and grocery stores will also accept major credit cards. Credit-card statements also serve as excellent records of expenses while traveling.

A majority of banks now offer online banking services that allow you to pay your bills remotely via the Internet. With online banking, you can pay bills, set up new payees, transfer funds, check your balances—and much more. You can also set up recurring payments on an "auto-pay" system that pays your bills automatically every month, or when your payee sends your bank an "e-bill."

Do be careful where you conduct your online banking sessions from, however. Many public marina computers "remember" passwords and forms (handy for a thief looking to steal your identity or your money), and many marina Internet Wi-Fi (wireless) connections are not totally secure. Though rarely convenient and often impossible, it is best to use your own computer hooked up to a terrestrial network with your own secure firewall running.

Getting Your Mail

Your incoming mail can be sent to General Delivery in towns where you plan to put in and stay awhile. Many cruising veterans have friends or family at home check their mail and occasionally forward it to them in the next town they plan to pull into. Tell the sender to write "Hold for Arrival" on the envelope, along with your name and your boat's name. Notify the post office that you want your mail held. They will hold first-class mail or forward it to another post office on receipt of a change-of-address card.

The United States Postal Service is now offering a service called Premium Forwarding that is designed to work in tandem with their Priority Mail program. There are also many companies that specialize in forwarding mail and paying bills for cruisers. Simply enter "mail forwarding, bill services" into your favorite Internet search engine, and many choices should show up for you.

Check the Skipper's Handbook section following this one for mail-drop locations along the coast, as well a compliment of specific details on getting your mail and paying bills.

Waterway Guide Web Updates

WATERWAY GUIDE has recently upgraded its Web site (www.waterwayguide.com) to provide boaters with the most up-to-date cruising information available. These Web site upgrades strongly focus on reader interaction. WATERWAY GUIDE offers cruisers two portals to help plan their trips or report back on what they've just experienced: "Navigation Updates" offers the most up-to-date information available on such items as Waterway conditions, changing bridge schedules and hazards to navigation; "Cruising News" reports events, marina updates and general ICW information, much of it posted by boaters themselve. These two portals are organized into easy-to-follow regions, so navigating WATERWAY GUIDE's Web site is even easier than navigating the Waterway. Our newest feature is a Waterway Forum, which allows members of the cruising community to post their own observations and experiences from the Waterway. Registering to use the forum is simple, free and privacy protected.

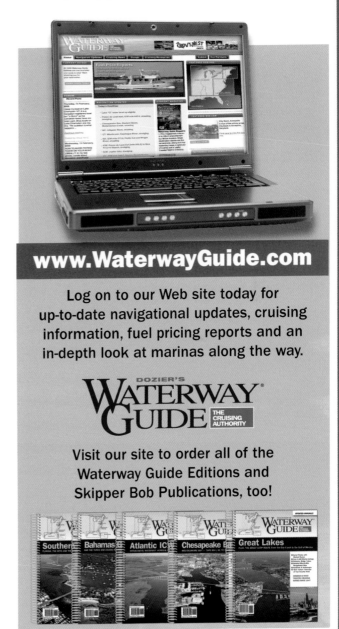

Skipper's Handbook

A Guide to Cruising Essentials

Coast Guard

The U.S. Coast Guard is on duty 24 hours a day, seven days a week to aid recreational boaters and commercial vessels alike. They have search and rescue capabilities and may provide lookout, communication or patrol functions to assist vessels in distress. Although this page contains a complete list of stations for the area that this Guide covers, you can and should seek immediate help by placing an emergency call (see our VHF radio page in this section for more details) on your VHF radio using Channel 16 if your vessel or anyone on board is in immediate danger.

U.S. Coast Guard Contact Information: Commandant, U.S. Coast Guard, 2100 2nd St. S.W., Washington, D.C. 20593. Telephone: 202-372-4411. www.uscg.mil

Fifth District Coast Guard Stations

Fifth Coast Guard District: The Fifth Coast Guard District covers coastal waters and tributaries from Toms River, NJ, to the North/South Carolina border. **Contact Information**: Commander, Fifth Coast Guard District, Federal Building, 431 Crawford St., Portsmouth, VA 23704. 757-398-6390. www.uscg.mil/d5

■ Pennsylvania (Sector Delaware Bay)

Sector Delaware Bay Command Center: 215-271-4800

■ Delaware (Sector Delaware Bay)

Station Roosevelt Inlet (Lewes):
Call Station Indian River Inlet 302-227-2440

■ New Jersey (Sector Delaware Bay)

Station Fortescue: 856-447-4422
Station Cape May: 609-898-6995
Station Townsend Inlet: 609-263-2361
Station Great Egg (Inlet): 609-391-0378
Air Station Atlantic City: 609-677-2225
Station Atlantic City: 609-344-6594
Station Beach Haven: 609-492-1423
Station Barnegat Light: 609-494-2661
Station Manasquan: 732-899-0130

First District Coast Guard Stations

First Coast Guard District: The First Coast Guard District covers coastal waters and tributaries from the Canadian border south to Toms River, NJ, including Lake Champlain and the Hudson River.

Contact Information: Commander, First Coast Guard District, Capt. John Foster Williams Building, 408 Atlantic Ave. #5, Boston, MA 02110. 800-848-3942. www.uscg.mil/d1

■ New Jersey (Sector New York)

Station Manasquan Inlet (Shark River:) 732-776-6730
Station Sandy Hook: 732-872-3428

■ New York (Sector New York)

Station Kings Point: 516-466-7136
Station New York (Staten Island): 718-354-4101
Station Saugerties: 845-246-7612

SKIPPER'S HANDBOOK

- Coast Guard 22
- Port Security Procedures 24
- Rules of the Road 26
- Bridge Basics 27
- Hurricanes 28
- VHF 30
- Going Aground 31
- Onboard Waste and No-Discharge Zones 32
- Keeping A Weather Eye. 33
- Getting Mail and Paying Bills . 34
- Charts and Publications 35
- Distance Tables 37
- Customs 40

■ New York (Sector Long Island Sound)

Station Eatons Neck (Huntington Bay): 631-261-6959
Station Fire Island: 631-661-9101
Station Jones Beach: 516-785-2921
Station Shinnecock: 631-728-0078
Station Montauk Point:.....................................631-668-2773

■ Connecticut (Sector Long Island Sound)

Station New Haven: 203-468-4498
Station New London: 860-442-4471

■ Rhode Island (Sector Southeastern New England)

Station Point Judith: 401-789-0444
Station Castle Hill (Newport): 401-846-3675

■ Massachusetts (Sector Southeastern New England)

Station Cape Cod Canal: 508-888-0020
Station Woods Hole: 508-457-3254
Station Brant Point (Nantucket): 508-228-0388
Station Menemsha (Martha's Vineyard): 508-645-2661
Station Chatham: 508-945-3830
Station Provincetown: 508-487-0077

■ Massachusetts (Sector Boston)

Station Scituate: 781-545-3801
(Only open in Summer, calls go to Point Allerton all other times)
Station Point Allerton (Hull): 781-925-0166

Station Boston:...617-227-0207
Station Gloucester: 978-283-0704
Station Merrimack River: 978-465-5921

■ New Hampshire (Sector Northern New England)

Station Portsmouth/Harbor: 603-436-4415

■ Maine (Sector Northern New England)

Station South Portland: 207-767-0364
Station Boothbay Harbor: 207-633-2661
Station Rockland: 207-596-6667
Station Southwest Harbor: 207-244-4270
Station Jonesport: 207-497-2200
Station Eastport: 207-853-2845

Canadian Coast Guard Contact Information:

Commissioner, Canadian Coast Guard, 200 Kent St., Ottawa, ON K1A OE6, Canada. Tel: 613-993-0999 www.ccg-gcc.gc.ca

Regional Director Maritimes Region, Canadian Coast Guard, P.O. Box 1035 (176 Portland St., 6th Floor, Marine House), Dartmouth, NS B2Y 4T3, Canada. Tel: 800-565-1582, 902-427-8200 (rescue coordination center). Tel: 800-565-1633 (environmental emergencies or pollution reports).

Photo Courtesy: U.S. Coast Guard

Additional Resources

U.S. Coast Guard *www.uscg.mil*

Port Security Procedures

Since September 11, 2001, the U.S. Coast Guard and other law enforcers have increased their presence at ports, near military vessels and throughout the length of the U.S. coastline. The Coast Guard—now a division of the U.S. Department of Homeland Security—requires that all recreational boaters make themselves aware of local security zones, permanent and temporary, before leaving the dock. Cruise ships, military vessels and tankers carrying hazardous materials constitute temporary security zones, and what's more the rules apply whether they are dockside or under way.

Any violation of the security zones is punishable by civil penalties of up to $27,500 per violation, while criminal penalties call for imprisonment for up to six years and fines reaching $250,000. Ignorance of the security zones is no excuse. Having said that, because the regulators could not foresee every eventuality when mandating an 100-yard no-enter zone around moving vessels, law-abiding boaters sometimes find themselves unable to comply with the letter of the law, without, say, hitting a jetty. In such cases, common sense and good communication should prevail.

As this book is prepared for production, Homeland Security officials were considering further measures to better protect maritime targets. Federal agencies are seriously considering a national scheme to license all boaters as well as mandating the onboard installation of expensive identification transponders called AIS or automatic identification systems. It should be no surprise that boaters have responded negatively, ridiculing the proposal as an expensive and ineffective burden.

Government officials view the recreational boating community as an ally. We can do our part—and perhaps stave off draconian licensing and surveillance measures—by become familiar with a Coast Guard program called America's Waterway Watch. Think of if as a neighborhood watch program for the waterways.

It is not the intent of America's Waterway Watch to spread paranoia or to encourage spying on one another, and it is not a surveillance program. Instead, it is a simple deterrent to potential terrorist activity. The purpose of the program is to allow boaters and others who spend time along the water to help the authorities counter crime and terrorism.

To report suspicious behavior, call the National Response Center at 877-24-WATCH. For immediate danger to life or property call 911, or call the Coast Guard on VHF-FM Channel 16. To learn more about the program, visit www.americaswaterwaywatch.org.

At the end of this section are listed the ports and places that require a little forethought and vigilance on your part. Following the steps in the action plan below will help ensure a trouble-free journey and keep you and your crew out of the headlines.

Prepare:

- Before you leave, check the current charts for the area you will be traveling in and identify any security areas. Security zones are highlighted and outlined in magenta with special notes regarding the specific regulations pertaining to that area.
- The Coast Guard Maritime Safety Operation Hotline, 800-682-1796, has information from more than 30 Coast Guard Port Captains from the Mississippi River to the Atlantic Ocean. This toll-free hotline line has up-to-date information on local waterways and ports openings, closures, and restrictions.
- Check the latest Local Notice to Mariners (available online at www.navcen.uscg.gov/lnm/default.htm - posted at some marinas) and identify any potential security areas that may not be shown on the chart.
- Listen to VHF Channel 16 for any Sécurité alerts from the Coast Guard for the area you will be cruising (departing cruise ships, Naval vessels, fuel tankers, etc.) prior to departure.
- Talk to boaters in your anchorage or marina that just came from where you will be traveling. They will most likely have tips and suggestions on any potential security zones or special areas they encountered on their way.

Stay Alert While Underway:

- Mind the aforementioned outlined magenta security areas noted on your charts.
- Look for vessels with blue or red warning lights in port areas, and if approached, listen carefully and strictly obey all instructions given to you.
- Keep your VHF radio switched to Channel 16 and keep your ears tuned for bulletins, updates and possible requests to communicate with you.
- Avoid commercial port operation areas, especially those that involve military, cruise-line or petroleum facilities. Observe and avoid other restricted areas near power plants, national monuments, etc.
- If you need to pass within 100 yards of a U. S. Naval vessel for safe passage, you must contact the U. S. Naval vessel or the Coast Guard escort vessel on VHF Channel 16.
- If government security or the U.S. Coast Guard hails you, do exactly what they say, regardless of whether or not you feel their instructions have merit.

Sensitive Northern Port Areas

New York Harbor – Area with heavy commercial traffic including fast-moving ferryboats. Steer clear of large freighters and other commercial vessels. Also be aware of security restrictions around landmarks such as the Statue of Liberty, Ellis Island and also, landmark bridges. Vessels seen lagging about in secure areas are often subject to inspection. When in doubt, refer to the charted magenta security areas on your chart for details.

Boston Harbor – Another area with heavy commercial freight traffic. Keep clear and give plenty of room to freighters, tankers, vessels under tugboat assist and other large craft.

Groton, CT – Homeport to over 18 Los Angeles-, Seawolf- and Virginia-class submarines. Security zone around berthed vessels with usual security rules for naval vessels underway.

Portsmouth Naval Shipyard – Major refit and repair facility for Los Angeles-class attack submarines. Keep clear of secure berthing areas and maintain at least 100 yards of distance from any submarines underway, also maintaining slow/idle speed if within 500 yards.

Bath, ME – Home of Bath Iron Works, a company that builds the latest and greatest naval warships. Secure area around dry docks and berthed vessels, as well as the usual security rules around moving or anchored naval vessels.

Delaware Bay – Area with heavy commercial freight traffic. Keep clear and give plenty of room to freighters, tankers, vessels under tugboat assist and other large craft.

Newport, RI – Occasional use by cruise ships to embark and disembark passengers. Keep clear and maintain a safe distance from cruise ships—both underway and anchored. Cruise ships may sometimes be under Coast Guard escort.

Kennebunkport, ME – Security Zone off Walker Point.

Portland, ME - Area with heavy commercial freight traffic. Keep clear and give plenty of room to freighters, tankers, vessels under tugboat assist and other large craft.

Additional Resources

Department of Homeland Security www.dhs.gov

U.S. Coast Guard www.uscg.mil

Local Notice to Mariners
www.navcen.uscg.gov/lnm

Atlantic Intracostal Waterway Association
www.atlintracoastal.org

America's Waterway Watch
www.americaswaterwaywatch.org

Waterway Guide www.waterwayguide.com

Courtesy: U.S. Army Corps of Engineers

Rules Of The Road

It's all about courtesy. Much like a busy highway, our waterways can become a melee of confusion when people don't follow the rules of the road. But unlike Interstate 95 and its byways, rivers, creeks, bays and inlets aren't fitted with eight-sided stop signs or the familiar yellow, green and red traffic lights. You'll need to rely on your own knowledge to safely co-exist with fellow boaters and avoid collisions.

Most heated Waterway encounters can be avoided by simply slowing down, letting the other boat go first, and biting your tongue, regardless of whether you think they are right or wrong. Pressing your agenda or taking out your frustrations with the last bridge tender you encountered normally leads to unpleasantness. When in doubt, stand down and get out of the other guy's way. The effect on your timetable will be minimal.

Anyone planning to cruise our waterways should make themselves familiar with the rules of the road. Chapman Piloting: Seamanship and Small Boat Handling and The Annapolis Book of Seamanship are both excellent on-the-water references with plentiful information on navigation rules. For those with a penchant for the exact regulatory language, the Coast Guard publication Navigation Rules: International-Inland covers both international and U.S. inland rules. (Boats over 39.4 feet are required to carry a copy of the U.S. Inland Rules at all times.) These rules are also available on the Web: www.navcen.uscg.gov/mwv/navrules/navrules.htm.

The following is a list of common situations you'll likely encounter on the waterways. Make yourself familiar with them, and if you ever have a question as to which of you has the right-of-way, let the other vessel go first.

Passing or being passed

■ If you intend to pass a slower vessel, try to hail them on your VHF radio to let them know you're coming.

■ In close quarters, BOTH vessels should slow down. Slowing down normally allows the faster vessel to pass quickly without throwing a large wake onto the slower boat.

■ Slower boats being passed have the right-of-way and passing vessels must take all actions necessary to keep clear of these slower vessels.

At opening bridges:

During an opening, boats traveling with the current go first and generally have the right-of-way.

■ Boats constrained by their draft, size or maneuverability (dredges, tugs, barges) also take priority.

■ Standard rules of the road apply while circling or waiting for a bridge opening.

Tugs, freighters, dredges, naval vessels:

These beasts are usually constrained by draft or their inability to maneuver nimbly. For this reason, you'll almost always need to give them the right-of-way and keep out of their path.

■ You must keep at least 100 yards away from any Navy vessel. If you cannot safely navigate without coming closer than this, you must alert the ship of your intentions over VHF radio (Channel 16).

■ Keep a close watch for freighters, tugs with tows, and other large vessels while offshore or in crowded ports. They often come up very quickly, despite their large size.

■ It's always a good practice to radio larger vessels (VHF Channel 13 or 16) to notify them of your location and your intentions. The skippers of these boats are generally appreciative of efforts to communicate with them. This is especially true with dredge boats on the Intracoastal Waterway (ICW).

In a crossing situation:

■ When two vessels under power are crossing and a risk of collision exists, the vessel that has the other on her starboard side must keep clear and avoid crossing ahead of the other vessel.

■ When a vessel under sail and a vessel under power are crossing, the boat under power is usually burdened and must keep clear. The same exceptions apply as per head-on meetings.

■ On the Great Lakes and western rivers (Mississippi River system), a power-driven vessel crossing a river shall keep clear of a power-driven vessel ascending or descending the river.

Power vessels meeting one another or meeting vessels under sail:

■ When two vessels under power (sailboats or powerboats) meet "head-to-head," both are obliged to alter course to starboard.

■ Generally, when a vessel under power meets a vessel under sail (not using any mechanical power), the powered vessel must alter course accordingly.

■ **Exceptions are:** Vessels not under command, vessels restricted in ability to maneuver, vessels engaged in fishing (and by that the rules mean commercial fishing) or those under International Rules, such as a vessel constrained by draft.

Two sailboats meeting under sail

■ When each has the wind on a different side, the boat with the wind on the port side must keep clear of the boat with the wind on the starboard side.

■ When both have the wind on the same side, the vessel closest to the wind (windward) will keep clear of the leeward boat.

■ A vessel with wind to port that sees a vessel to windward but cannot determine whether the windward vessel has wind to port or starboard will assume that windward vessel is on starboard tack and keep clear.

Resources

The Coast Guard publication "Navigation Rules – International-Inland" is available at most well-stocked marine stores, including West Marine (www.westmarine.com) and Bluewater Books and Charts (www.bluewaterweb.com).

These establishments normally stock the aforementioned Chapman's and Annapolis Seamanship books also.

Bridge Basics

The rhythm of life on inland waterways is often determined by bridge openings, and with more than a few opening bridges between Delaware Bay and the Canadian border, you'll be likely to encounter at least one at some point when cruising northern waters. A particular bridge's schedule can often decide where you tie up for the evening or when you wake up and get under way the next day.

Because many bridges restrict their openings during morning and evening rush hours to minimize inconvenience to vehicular traffic, you may need to plan an early start or late stop to avoid getting stuck waiting for a bridge opening. Take a few minutes before setting out to learn whether bridge schedules have changed; changes are posted in the Coast Guard's Local Notice to Mariners reports, which can be found online at www.navcen.uscg.gov/lnm.

The easiest way to hail a bridge is via VHF radio. While some boaters improperly hail bridges on Channel 16, the bridges covered in this Guide respond on Channel 13, and this is the only channel you should hail them on. Keep in mind that bridge tenders are just like the rest of us—everyone has their good and bad days. The best way to thwart any potential grumpiness is to follow the opening procedures to the letter and act with professionalism. This will almost always ensure a timely opening.

Bridge Procedures:

- First, decide if it is necessary to have the drawbridge opened. You'll need to know your boat's clearance height above the waterline before you start your passage. Drawbridges have "Clearance Gauges" to show the closed vertical clearance with changing water levels, but a bascule bridge typically has 3 to 5 feet more clearance than what is indicated on the gauge at the center of its arch at mean low tide. Bridge clearances are also shown on NOAA charts.
- Contact the bridge tender well in advance (even if you can't see the bridge around the bend) by VHF radio or phone. Alternatively, you can sound one long and one short horn blast to request an opening. Tugs with tows and U.S. government vessels may go through bridges at any time, usually signaling with five short blasts. A restricted bridge may open in an emergency with the same signal. Keep in mind bridge tenders will not know your intentions unless you tell them.
- If two or more vessels are in sight of one another, the bridge tender may elect to delay opening the bridge until all boats can go through together.
- Approach at slow speed and be prepared to wait, as the bridge cannot open until the traffic gates are closed. Many bridges are more than 40 years old, and the aged machinery functions slowly.
- Once the bridge is open, proceed at no-wake speed. Keep a safe distance between you and other craft, as currents and turbulence around bridge supports can be tricky.
- There is technically no legal right-of-way (except on the Mississippi River and some other inland rivers), but boats running with the current should always be given the right-of-way out of courtesy. As always, if you are not sure, let the other guy go first.
- When making the same opening as a commercial craft, it is a good idea to contact the vessel's captain (usually on VHF Channel 13), ascertain his intentions and state yours to avoid any misunderstanding in tight quarters.
- After passing through the bridge, maintain a no-wake speed until you are well clear and then resume normal speed.

Bridge Types

Swing Bridges:

Swing bridges have an opening section that pivots horizontally on a central hub, allowing boats to pass on one side or the other when it is open.

Lift Bridges:

Lift bridges normally have two towers on each end of the opening section that are equipped with cables that lift the road or railway vertically into the air.

Pontoon Bridges:

A pontoon bridge consists of an opening section that must be floated out of the way with a cable to allow boats to pass.

Bascule Bridges:

This is the most common type of opening bridge you will encounter. The opening section of a bascule bridge has one or two leaves that tilt vertically on a hinge like doors being opened skyward.

Hurricanes

With images of hurricanes Ike, Fay, and Gustav still fresh in the country's collective memory, more folks are tuned into turbulent tropical weather than ever. Hurricanes can create vast swaths of devastation, but ample preparation can help increase your boat's chances of surviving the storm.

While all coastal areas of the country are vulnerable to the effects of a hurricane (especially from June to November), the Gulf Coast, Southern and Mid-Atlantic states typically have been the hardest hit. But northern locales aren't immune—several destructive hurricanes have hit or dealt a glancing blow to areas in New England over the last 100 years. And even cities far from the ocean such as Annapolis, MD, are subjected to the damage these storms cause—WATERWAY GUIDE'S offices were inundated with more than 4 feet of water from Hurricane Isabel in September 2003.

Hurricane Conditions

■ According to the National Weather Service (NWS), a mature hurricane may be 10 miles high with a great spiral several hundred miles in diameter. Winds can be well above the 74 mph required to classify as hurricane strength. The most extreme devastation of the storm is usually confined to a core that is 50 miles or less in diameter with squalls extending outward up to 500 miles.

■ Hurricane damage is produced by four elements: tidal surge, wind, wave action and rain. Tidal surge is an increase in ocean depth prior to the storm. This effect, amplified in coastal areas, may cause tidal heights in excess of 15 feet above normal. A negative tidal condition may occur, dropping water levels far below normal, particularly in bays and rivers.

■ The most damaging element of a hurricane for boaters is usually wave action. The wind speed, water depth and the amount of open water determine the amount of wave action created. Storm surge can transform narrow bodies of water into larger, deeper waters capable of generating extreme wave action.

■ Rainfall varies; hurricanes can generate anywhere from 5 to 20 inches, or more, of rain. If your boat is in a slip, you have three options: If it is in a safe place, leave it where it is; move it to a refuge area; or haul it and put it on a trailer or cradle.

■ The National Weather Service reports that wind gusts can exceed reported sustained winds by 25 to 50 percent. So, for example, a storm with winds of 150 mph might have gusts of more than 200 mph.

■ Some marinas require mandatory evacuations during hurricane alerts. Check your lease agreement and talk to your dockmaster if you're uncertain. After Hurricane Andrew, Florida's legislature passed a law prohibiting marinas from evicting boats during hurricane watches and warnings. Boaters may also be held liable for any damage that their boat does to marina piers or property; check locally for details.

■ Rivers, canals, coves and other areas away from large stretches of open water are best selected as refuges. Your dockmaster or fellow mariners can make suggestions. Consult your insurance agent if you have questions about coverage.

■ Many insurance agencies have restricted or cancelled policies for boats that travel or are berthed in certain hurricane-prone areas. Review your policy and check your coverage, as many insurance companies will not cover boats in hurricane-prone areas during the June through November hurricane season. Riders for this type of coverage are notoriously expensive.

Preparing Your Boat

■ Have a hurricane plan made up ahead of time to maximize what you can get done in amount of time you'll have to prepare (only 12 hours in some cases). You won't want to be deciding how to tie up the boat or where to anchor when a hurricane is barreling down on you. Make these decisions in advance.

■ Buy hurricane gear in advance (even if there is no imminent storm). When word of a hurricane spreads, local ship stores run out of storm supplies (anchors and line, especially) very quickly.

■ Strip every last thing that isn't bolted down off the deck of the boat (canvas, sails, antennas, bimini tops, dodgers, dinghies, dinghy motors, cushions, unneeded control lines on sailboats—everything), as this will help reduce windage and damage to your boat. Remove electronics and valuables and move them ashore.

■ Any potentially leaky ports or hatches should be taped up. Dorades (cowls) should be removed and sealed up with their deck cap.

■ Make sure all systems on board are in tip-top shape. Fuel and water tanks should be filled, bilge pumps should be in top operating condition, and batteries should be fully charged.

■ You will need many lengths of line to secure the boat—make certain it's good stretchy nylon (not Dacron). It's not unusual to string 800 to 1000 feet of dock line on a 40-foot boat in preparation for a hurricane.

■ If you can, double up your lines (two for each cleat), as lines can and will break during the storm. Have fenders and fender boards out and make sure all of your lines are protected from chafe.

■ If you are anchored out, use multiple large anchors; there's no such thing as an anchor that is too big. If you can, tie to trees with a good root system, such as mangroves or live oaks. Mangroves are particularly good because their canopy can have a cushioning effect. Be sure mooring lines include ample scope to compensate for tides 10 to 20 feet above normal. Keep in mind that many municipalities close public mooring fields in advance of the storm.

■ Lastly, do not stay aboard to weather out the storm. Many people have been seriously injured (or worse) trying to save their boats during a hurricane.

Returning Safely After the Storm

■ Before hitting the road, make sure the roads back to your boat are safe for travel. Beware of dangling wires, weakened docks, bulkheads, bridges and other structures.

■ Check your boat thoroughly before attempting to move it. If returning to your home slip, watch the waters for debris and obstructions. Navigate carefully, because markers may be misplaced or missing. If your boat is sunk, arrange for engine repairs before floating it, but only if it's not impeding traffic. Otherwise, you will need to remove it immediately.

Storm Intensity

Saffir-Simpson Categories

■ **Category 1**	74–95 mph
■ **Category 2**	96–110 mph
■ **Category 3**	111–130 mph
■ **Category 4**	131–155 mph
■ **Category 5**	155+ mph

Hurricane Tracker

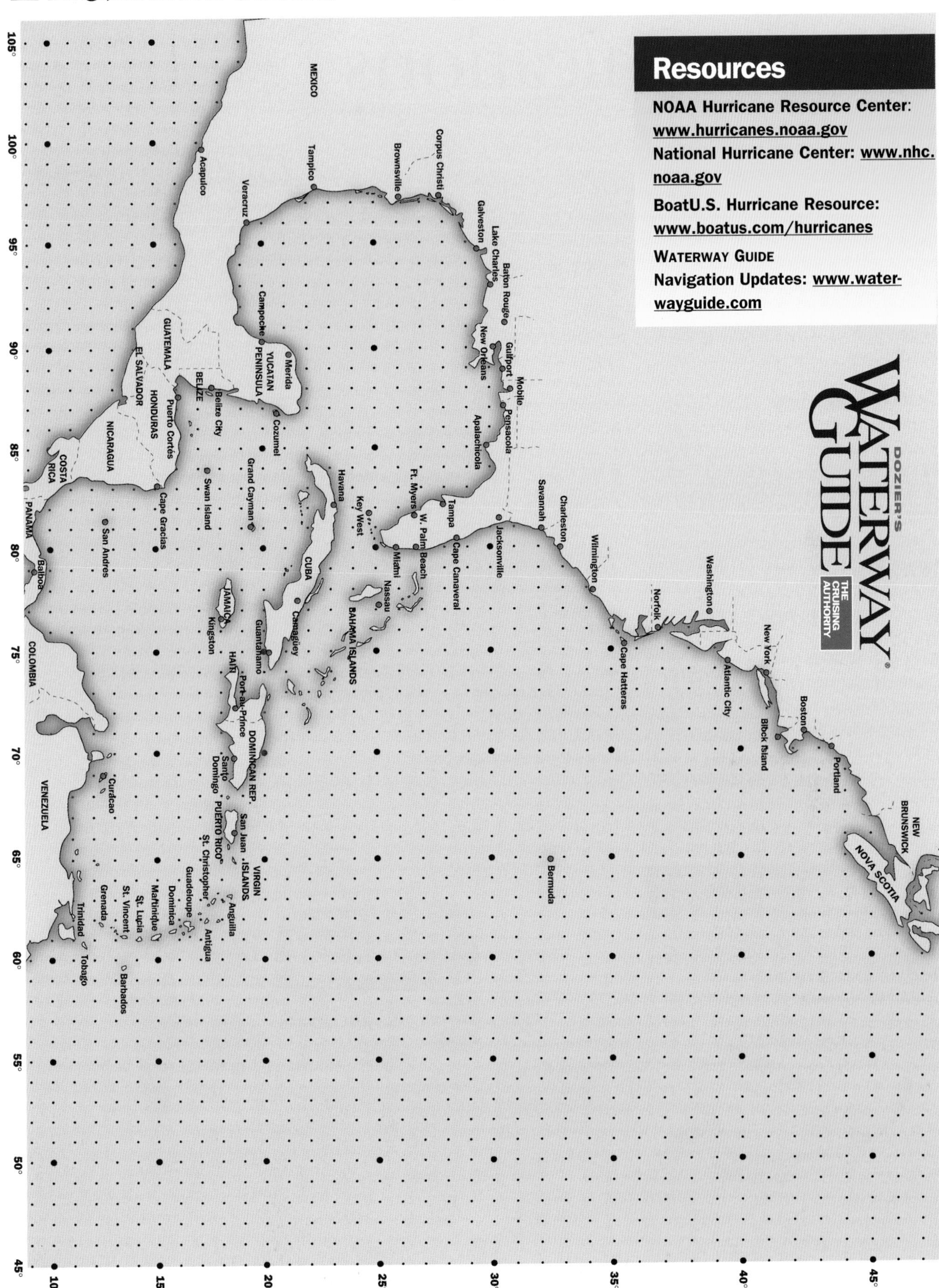

Resources

NOAA Hurricane Resource Center: www.hurricanes.noaa.gov

National Hurricane Center: www.nhc.noaa.gov

BoatU.S. Hurricane Resource: www.boatus.com/hurricanes

WATERWAY GUIDE Navigation Updates: www.waterwayguide.com

VHF Communications

Skippers use their VHF radios almost every day to contact other vessels and bridge tenders, make reservations at marinas, arrange to pass other vessels safely and conduct other business. WATERWAY GUIDE has put together the following information to help remove any confusion as to what frequency should be dialed in to call bridges, marinas, commercial ships or your friend anchored out down the creek.

Channel Usage Tips

■ VHF Channel 16 (156.800 MHz) is by far the most important frequency on the VHF-FM band. It is also the most abused. Channel 16 is the international distress, safety and calling frequency.

■ The Coast Guard recommends that boaters normally keep tuned to and use Channel 16, but no conversations of any length should take place there–its primary function is for emergencies only.

■ VHF Channel 09 is mostly used as a hailing channel and is intended to keep traffic off of Channel 16.

■ FCC regulations require boaters to maintain a watch on either Channel 09 or 16 whenever the radio is turned on and not being used to communicate on another channel.

■ Since the Coast Guard does not have the capability of announcing an urgent marine information broadcast or weather warning on Channel 09, its use is optional. The Coast Guard recommends that boaters normally keep tuned to and use Channel 16.

■ Recreational craft typically communicate on Channels 68, 69, 71, 72 or 78A. Whenever possible, avoid calling on Channel 16 altogether by prearranging initial contact directly on one of these channels. No transmissions should last longer than three minutes.

■ The radio-equipped bridges covered in this edition generally use Channel 13.

■ The Coast Guard's main working channel is 22A and both emergency and non-emergency calls generally are switched to it in order to keep 16 clear. Calling the Coast Guard for a radio check on Channel 16 is prohibited.

■ The Bridge-to-Bridge Radio Telephone Act requires many commercial vessels, including dredges and tugboats, to monitor Channel 13.

■ The Coast Guard has asked the FCC to eliminate provisions for using Channel 09 as an alternative calling frequency to Channel 16 when it eliminates watch keeping on Channel 16 by compulsory-equipped vessels.

VHF Channels

09 – Used for radio checks and hailing other stations (boats, shore side operations).

13 – Used to contact and communicate with commercial vessels, military ships and drawbridges.

16 – Emergency use only. May be used to hail other vessels, but once contact is made, conversation should be immediately switched to a working (68, 69, 71, 72, 78A) channel.

22 – Used for U.S. Coast Guard safety, navigation and Sécurité communications.

68, 69, 71, 72, 78A – Used primarily for recreational ship-to-ship and ship-to-shore communications.

VHF Channel 16 — In Case of Emergency

MAYDAY—The distress signal MAYDAY is used to indicate that a station is threatened by grave and imminent danger and requests immediate assistance.

PAN PAN—The urgency signal PAN PAN is used when the safety of the ship or person is in jeopardy.

Sécurité—The safety signal Sécurité is used for messages about the safety of navigation or important weather warnings.

Resources

U.S. Coast Guard VHF Channel Listing:
www.navcen.uscg.gov/marcomms/vhf.htm

FCC VHF Channel Listing:
http://wireless.fcc.gov/marine/vhfchanl.html

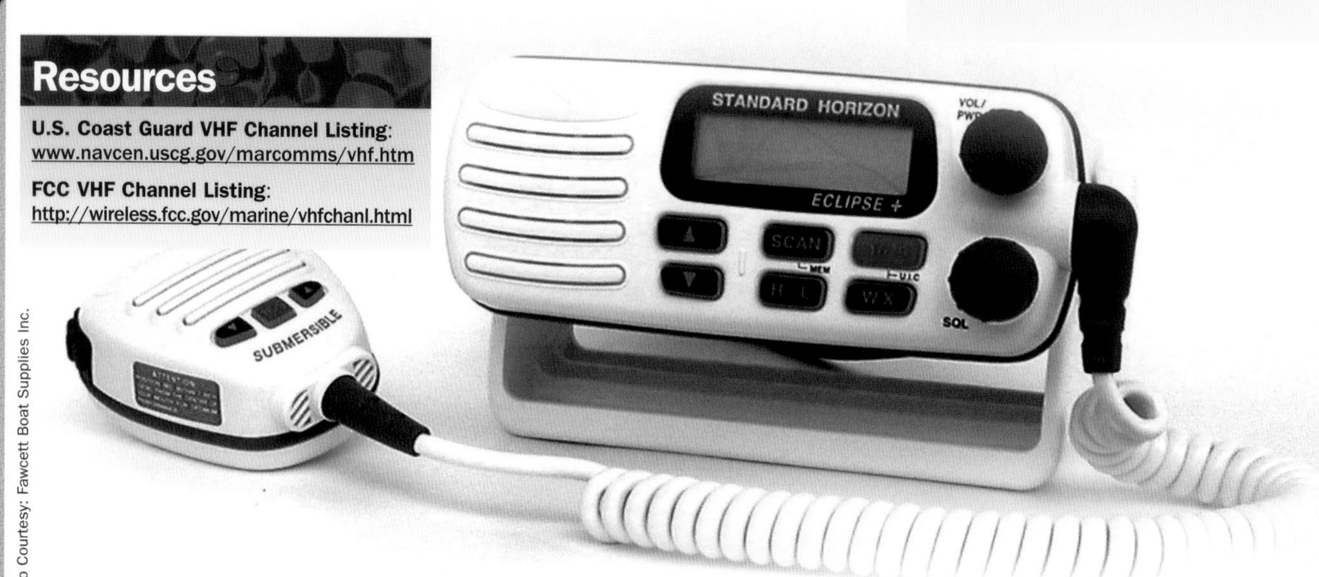

Radio Courtesy: Fawcett Boat Supplies Inc.

Going Aground

"Either you've gone aground or you lie," say the old salts, meaning that sooner or later every boat touches bottom. Of late, cruisers transiting the Intracoastal Waterway (ICW) have found this to be particularly true because of chronically insufficient government funds for dredging.

That said, most of the Waterway is lined with soft, forgiving mud (save for some rocky areas in New England), so going aground may be an inconvenience but it is rarely dangerous, let alone life-threatening. Still, it is wise to have a plan of action and basic familiarity with the tried-and-true techniques for getting unstuck from the muck.

To avoid trouble, a prudent mariner will invest a few minutes in research before leaving the dock. For the latest updates on dredging and shoaling, visit www.waterwayguide.com and click on the "Navigation Updates" and "Cruising News" sections. These pages are updated daily with the latest shoaling and dredging updates, which are fed to our main office by WATERWAY GUIDE'S intrepid cruising editors and cruisers like yourself.

What to do First

■ Throttle back immediately and put the engine into neutral. If under sail, douse and properly stow all sails to avoid being blown farther onto the shoal.

■ Assess the situation. Look back where you came from (it had to be deep enough or you wouldn't be here) and in all other directions for landmarks that might tell you exactly where you are.

■ Determine next the direction to deeper water so you can plan your escape. A quick glance at the GPS and a chart often reveals where you've gone wrong and where the deepest water is relative to your location.

■ When all else fails, it is not a bad idea to sound around the boat with your boat hook (or a fishing rod in a pinch) to determine which side of the boat the deeper water is on. Some skippers carry a portable depth sounder that can work from the dinghy during occasions like this.

■ Determine the state of the tide, especially if you are in an area with a wide range. If it is dropping, you must work fast. If it is rising, you will have some help getting the boat off.

How to Break Free

■ In less severe situations, you may be able to simply back off the bar, but begin gently to avoid damaging the propeller(s).

■ If the tide is low and rising, it may be best to simply set an anchor on the deep side and wait to be floated free. If it is falling and you have a deep-keel boat, be sure that the hull will lie to the shallower side of the shoal so the incoming tide does not fill the cockpit.

■ Sailboats usually come off after turning the bow toward deep water and heeling over to reduce the draft. Placing crewmembers out on the rail works, too. Leading a halyard to the dinghy and pulling gently can provide tremendous leverage for heeling the boat also.

■ Keeping wakes to a minimum is common courtesy on the Waterway, but a boat aground can actually benefit from the rising motion of a good wake to free itself from the bottom. One commonly used technique is to radio a passing power boater and actually request a wake. As the waves lift the boat aground, the helmsman should apply throttle and turn toward deeper water. (Passing power boats should never create wake without a request for assistance from the vessel aground.)

■ A powered dinghy can also be used to tow a boat off a shoal. If you know where the deep water is, you can tie a line off to the bow and pivot the boat into deeper water.

■ Kedging, or pulling off with an anchor, is the next logical step. Use the dinghy to carry an anchor (or float it on a life jacket and push it ahead of you while wading – wearing one yourself) as far into deep water as possible. Then use a winch, windlass, or your own muscle to pull the boat into deeper water. You may need to repeat the process a few times, resetting the anchor in progressively deeper water until the boat is free of the bottom.

■ The U.S. Coast Guard long ago ceased towing recreational vessels, but if you are aground and in imminent danger (e.g. aground in a dangerous inlet and taking on water), you may make an emergency request for assistance. Simple ICW groundings in calm weather with no immediate danger do not warrant a call to the Coast Guard.

■ If you need outside help from a commercial towboat or Good Samaritan, be sure both of you understand in advance exactly what you plan to do. Fasten the towline to a secure cleat at the bow and stand well clear of the end when it comes taut, as it can snap with dangerous force.

Onboard Waste and No-Discharge Zones

No-Discharge Zones

New Jersey: Barnegat Bay, Shark River, Manasquan River, Shrewsbury River, Navesink River.
New York: Mamaroneck Harbor, various portions of the Hudson River, East Hampton area, Greater Huntington, Port Jefferson Harbor, Peconic Estuary.
Connecticut: Pawcatuck River, Little Narragansett Bay, portions of Fishers Island Sound, Stonington Harbor, Mystic River and Pine Island, Eastern Point in Groton to Hoadley Point in Guilford, the Connecticut River, and navigable reaches for the Hammonasset, Menunketesuck, Niantic, and Thames rivers, Branford, East Haven, New Haven, West Haven, Orange, Milford, Stratford, Bridgeport, Fairfield, Westport, Norwalk, Darien, Stamford, Greenwich, Housatonic River from Derby Dam and the Quinnipiac River from the southern border of North Haven.
Rhode Island: Great Salt Pond, Block Island and all navigable waters within the three-mile limit.
New Hampshire: All coastal waters.
Maine: Casco Bay
Massachusetts: Barnstable, all of Buzzards Bay, Chatham/Stage Harbor, Harwich, Nantucket, Plymouth-Kingston, Waquoit, Wareham, Wellfleet and Westport.

Resources

BoatU.S. Guide to Overboard Discharge:
www.boatus.com/foundation/toolbox

BoatU.S. Listing of No-Discharge Zones:
www.boatus.com/gov/f8.asp

EPA Listing of No-Discharge Zones:
www.epa.gov

Federal Clean Vessel Act Information:
http://federalaid.fws.gov/cva/cva.html

Up until the late '80s, many boaters simply discharged their untreated sewage overboard into the water. After a revision to the Clean Water Act was passed in 1987, the discharge of untreated sewage into U.S. waters within the three-mile limit was prohibited. Shortly thereafter, pump-out stations became a regular feature at marinas and fuel docks along the waterways covered in this Guide.

Simply stated, if you have a marine head installed on your vessel and are operating on coastal waters within the U.S. three-mile limit (basically all of the waters covered in the guide you are now holding), you need to have a holding tank, and you'll obviously need to arrange to have that tank pumped out from time to time.

Government regulation aside, properly disposing of your waste is good karma. While your overboard contribution to the Waterway may seem small in the grand scheme of things, similar attitudes among fellow boaters can quickly produce unsavory conditions in anchorages and small creeks. The widespread availability of holding tank gear and shore side pump-out facilities leaves little excuse for not doing the right thing.

No-Discharge Zones

No Discharge means exactly what the name suggests. No waste, even waste treated by an onboard Type I marine sanitation device (MSD) may be discharged overboard. All waste must be collected in a holding tank and pumped out at an appropriate facility.

There are dozens of No Discharge Zones in the coastal waters that this guide covers. Reference the table to the left to see if the area you will be cruising is a No-Discharge Zone.

If you plan to travel outside the coverage area for this Guide, keep in mind that there are some areas (e.g. Lake Champlain, Ontario municipalities) that forbid overboard discharge of any waste, including gray water from showers or sinks. Familiarize yourself with local regulations before entering new areas to ensure you don't get hit with a fine.

The Law

If you have a marine head onboard and are operating on coastal waters within the U.S. three-mile limit, you need to have an approved holding tank or Type 1 MSD.

All valves connected to your holding tank or marine head that lead to the outside (both Y-valves AND seacocks) must be wire tied in the closed position. Simply having them closed without the wire ties will not save you from a fine if you are boarded.

You may discharge waste overboard from a Type 1 MSD (Lectra-San, Groco Thermopure) in all areas except those designated as No-Discharge Zones. A Type I MSD treats waste by reducing bacteria and visible solids to an acceptable level before discharge overboard.

While small and inconvenient for most cruisers, "Port-A-Potties" meet all the requirements for a Type III MSD, as the holding tank is incorporated into the toilet itself.

Pump-Out Station and Holding Tank Basics

Many marinas along the Atlantic and Gulf Intracoastal waterways are equipped with pump-out facilities, normally located at the marina's fuel dock. Check the included marina listing tables throughout this Guide – they list the availability of pump-out services at each facility. Most marinas charge a fee for the service.

Many municipalities and local governments have purchased and staffed pump-out boats that are equipped to visit boats on request, especially those at anchor. Radio the local harbormaster to see if this service is available in the area you are visiting. There is normally a small fee involved.

You'll want to keep an eye out on your holding tank level while you are transiting the Waterway, especially if you are getting ready to enter an area where you many not have access to proper pump-out services for a few days. Plan a fuel stop or marina stay to top off the fuel tank and empty waste before you set out into the wild.

Keeping A Weather Eye

While large portions of the Intracoastal Waterway are protected from harsh weather, skippers should always check the latest forecasts before casting off their lines or weighing anchor (especially if hopping offshore).

Staying out of bad weather is relatively easy if you plan ahead. The National Weather Service (NWS) provides mariners with continuous broadcasts of weather warnings, forecasts, radar reports and buoy reports over VHF-FM and Single Side Band (SSB) radio. Reception range for VHF radios is usually up to 40 miles from the antenna site, though Florida stations are frequently heard in the near Bahamas. There are almost no areas on the U.S. coast where a good quality, fixed-mount VHF cannot pick up one or more coastal VHF broadcasts.

Most late-model VHF radios can pick up all seven frequencies; some older radios may not. Most VHF radios sold in the United States have a special weather selection switch for these channels. Broadcasts are continuous and are updated approximately every four hours. Urgent weather warnings may be broadcast at any time as needed. If the weather looks threatening, stay tuned for the latest updates.

The U.S. Coast Guard also broadcasts special forecasts and warnings on VHF-FM. The broadcasts will first be announced on Channel 16, with the actual forecast usually being given on Channel 22A.

SSB Offshore Weather

Single Side Band (SSB) reports are broadcast from station NMN Chesapeake, VA, and from station NMG, New Orleans, LA. The broadcasts are not continuous, so refer to the latest schedules and frequency lists (see below) to catch them. SSB reports provide the best source of voice offshore weather information. Two major broadcasts alternate throughout the day. The High Seas Forecast provides information for mariners well offshore, including those crossing the North Atlantic Ocean. Coastal cruisers will be more interested in the Offshore Forecast, which includes information on waters more than 50 miles from shore. The forecast is divided into various regions. Mid-Atlantic cruisers will be most interested in Hudson Canyon to Baltimore Canyon, Baltimore Canyon to Hatteras Canyon, Hatteras Canyon to 31N Latitude, and the southwest North Atlantic south of 31N latitude and west of 65W longitude.

For those with weatherfax equipment, a complete menu of products is available from the U.S. Coast Guard broadcasting from Belle Chase, LA. See related text for more information.

- USCG Communications Area Master Station Atlantic, Chesapeake, VA. Call sign: NMN.
- USCG Communications Station New Orleans, LA. Call sign: NMG.
- USCG Weather Fax, Belle Chase, LA. Call sign: NMG Weatherfax broadcasts are on 4317.9 kHz, 8503.9 kHz and 12789.9 kHz continuously. Weatherfax schedules are broadcast at 1315 UTC.
- USCG Weather Fax, Marshfield, MA. Call sign: NMF. Weatherfax broadcasts are on 4235 kHz from 0230 UTC to 1028 UTC, on 6340.5 kHz and 9110 kHz continuously, and on 12750 kHz from 1400 UTC to 2228 UTC. Weatherfax schedules are broadcast at 0243 UTC and 1405 UTC. (Select a frequency 1.9 kHz below those listed when using an SSB radio in the USB mode.)
- Real-time weather on your laptop or chart plotter, including radar images of approaching fronts and squalls, is available through the WxWorx and Sirius Marine Weather, which use satellite radio satellites to beam forecast data and images down to your boat.

On the Web:

- NOAA National Weather Service: www.nws.noaa.gov. This site provides coastal and offshore forecasts for the continental United States and nearby waters, including Puerto Rico and the U.S. Virgin Islands, weather maps, station reports and marine warnings.
- NOAA Marine Weather Radio: www.weather.gov/om/marine/home.htm. Provides coverage areas and frequencies for VHF weather radio products in all 50 states.
- National Hurricane Center: www.nhc.noaa.gov. Tropical warnings, advisories and predictions are available here. There is also access to historical data relating to hurricanes and tropical weather. Weatherfax schedules are available online.
- National Data Buoy Center: http://seaboard.ndbc.noaa.gov. This site provides near-real-time weather data from buoys and light stations.
- OCENS: www.ocens.com. Ocens is a leading provider of satellite based communications for mariners, including downloadable GRIB files and area forecasts from both government and private sources.
- WxWorx: www.wxworx.com. A national aviation forecaster partners with XM satellite radio to deliver subscription based forecasting to boaters.
- Sirius Marine Weather: http://onboard.weather.com. Cable television's Weather Channel partners with Sirius satellite radio to deliver subscription based forecasting to boaters.

Weather Frequencies

UTC	NMN FREQUENCIES (kHz)	NMG FREQUENCIES (kHz)
0330 (Offshore)	4426.0, 6501.0, 8764.0	4316.0, 8502.0, 12788.0
0500 (High Seas)	4426.0, 6501.0, 8764.0	4316.0, 8502.0, 12788.0
0930 (Offshore)	4426.0, 6501.0, 8764.0	4316.0, 8502.0, 12788.0
1130 (High Seas)	6501.0, 8764.0, 13089.0	4316.0, 8502.0, 12788.0
1600 (Offshore)	6501.0, 8764.0, 13089.0	4316.0, 8502.0, 12788.0
1730 (High Seas)	8764.0, 13089.0, 17314.0	4316.0, 8502.0, 12788.0
2200 (Offshore)	6501.0, 8764.0, 13089.0	4316.0, 8502.0, 12788.0
2330 (High Seas)	6501.0, 8764.0, 13089.0	4316.0, 8502.0, 12788.0

(UTC, or Coordinated Universal Time, is equivalent to Greenwich Mean Time)

VHF-FM Broadcasts/NOAA Weather Radio VHF Frequencies

WX1	162.550 MHz
WX2	162.400 MHz
WX3	162.475 MHz
WX4	162.425 MHz
WX5	162.450 MHz
WX6	162.500 MHz
WX7	162.525 MHz

SKIPPER'S HANDBOOK

Getting Your Mail and Paying Bills

One of the most anxiety-inducing issues cruisers face is how to keep their financial life in order while on an extended journey. Luckily, most banks today offer some sort of online banking that allows you to pay your bills with simple Internet access, and post offices will usually hold forwarded mail for transient boaters. With the advent of online banking and new forwarding services from the United States Postal Service (USPS), keeping on top of your bills and important mail need not be a huge hassle.

Resources

United States Postal Service: www.usps.com

St. Brendan's Isle: www.boatmail.net

Options for Mail

General Delivery

■ Use general delivery when you have a person ("mail forwarder") collecting the mail for you at home while you are away.

■ Works best when you are on the move. Your mail forwarder can send bundles of your mail to different post offices ahead of your arrival as you move along the coast. The post office will generally hold these for 10 days.

■ The mail should be addressed as follows:

Your Name
Boat Name
General Delivery
City, State, ZIP Code

"Hold for Arrival" printed on both sides

Premium Forwarding Service

The USPS is now offering a new service called Premium Forwarding that is designed to work in tandem with their Priority Mail program.

■ Once a week, normally on Wednesday, all of your mail is bundled in Priority Mail packaging and sent to you at a single specified temporary address.

■ Premium Forwarding includes most mail that standard forwarding does not normally include like magazines, catalogs, and yes, junk mail.

■ Mail can be sent to a general delivery address (as long as that post office accepts general delivery mail, of course).

■ There is an enrollment fee of $15, and each subsequent weekly Priority Mail shipment costs $13.95. The USPS bills a credit or debit card for each week's delivery fee.

■ Once you pick a temporary forwarding address it cannot be changed as you and your boat move around. Premium Forwarding is designed for people who will be at a fixed temporary address for at least two weeks.

Standard Forwarding Service

■ Standard mail forwarding will automatically send your mail to a specified address (general delivery addresses included) at no extra charge.

■ Each piece of mail is sent individually, versus the Premium Forwarding service, which sends a single bundle of mail each week on Wednesdays.

■ Does not include magazines, periodicals or junk mail.

Hold Mail

■ You can have your mail held at your home post office from 3 to 30 days and retrieve it when you return.

Paying Bills

■ There are several companies (many online) that will handle paying your bills or forwarding your mail while you are away. Probably the best known is St. Brendan's Isle, which services more than 3,000 cruisers from its offices in Green Cove Springs, FL.

■ If you aren't already doing it and your bank offers it, consider participating in online banking. You can set it up so many of your bills are automatically paid out of your checking account each month.

■ If you have a company that does not work with your bank's online bill pay service, see if they will take a credit card number and have them bill that every month.

■ Many companies will take credit card numbers over the phone for payment.

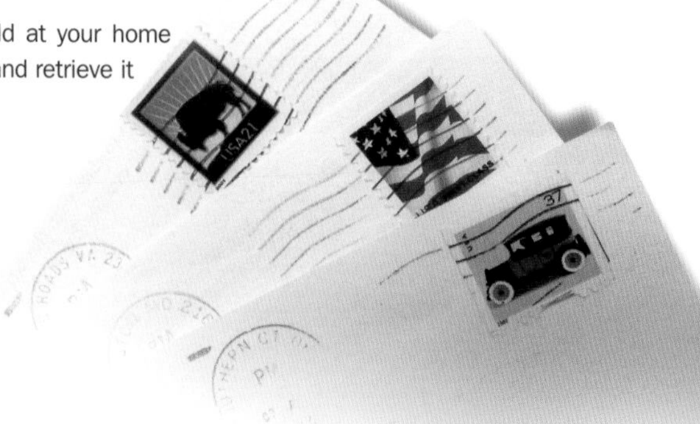

Charts and Publications

Charts are must-have for any passage on the Intracoastal Waterway (ICW) or the coastal waters covered in this guide. Charts are a two-dimensional picture of your boating reality—shorelines, channels, aids to navigation and hazards. Even in an age of electronic chart plotters, most mariners agree that paper charts have value and should be carried as a back-up. ICW charts incorporate an extremely helpful feature, a magenta line that traces the Waterway's path; some call it "The Magenta Highway."

The Internet Age

With widespread availability of the Internet, most all of the publications you'll need are available for download from the government in Adobe Portable Document File (PDF) format free of charge. While this is handy, keep in mind that the electronic versions are mainly for reference and planning purposes, as they are not practical for use at the helm while under way.

Once you download them, Coast Pilots and Light Lists can be printed, but since each edition weighs in at about 350-plus pages, they are best viewed online. If you think you'll be accessing one of these volumes frequently, buy the bound version from your chart agent.

NOAA's entire chart catalog is now available for viewing online. Since you can't print these charts, they are best used for planning and reference purposes. Many cruisers hop on their laptops the evening before their next departure and use these online charts to plan out the following day's travel, since they are up-to-date the moment you view them.

Find Web links for various publication download sites at the bottom of this page.

NOAA Charts

For most northern waters, you'll primarily use harbor and small-craft charts. Small craft charts are the small, folded strip charts that cover the ICW-centric portion of the coast. Harbor charts, as the name suggests, cover smaller waterways and ports.

NOAA Charts are updated and printed by the government on regular schedules—normally every one to two years. (Each new printing is called an edition.)

Third-party companies often reproduce NOAA charts into book/chart kit form. Many veteran ICW cruisers use these, as they have all the charts laid out in page order, which means you don't have to wrestle with large folded charts at the helm. Keep in mind that even the latest versions of these charts need to be updated with the Local Notice to Mariners to be timely and accurate.

Changes to the charts between printings are published in the U.S. Coast Guard Local Notice to Mariners, which is available exclusively online at www.navcen.uscg.gov/lnm.

A disadvantage of printed NOAA Charts is that the version on the shelf at your local store may be a year old or more. For the sake of accuracy, check back through the Local Notice to Mariners and note any corrections, especially for shoal-prone areas.

NOAA's complete chart catalog is also available for viewing as a planning or reference tool online at www.nauticalcharts.noaa.gov/mcd/OnLineViewer.html. Even if you have electronic charts on board, you should always carry a spare set of paper charts as back up. Electronics can and do fail. What's more, electronic viewing is limited by the size of the display screen, whereas a paper chart spread over a table is still the best way to understand "the big picture."

Print-on-Demand Charts

Print-on-Demand charts are printed directly by the chart agent at the time you purchase the chart. The charts are the ultimate in accuracy, as they are corrected with the Local Notice to Mariners on a weekly basis.

Print-on-demand charts are water-resistant, and there are two versions with useful information in the margins, including tide tables, emergency numbers, frequencies, rules of the road, etc. One version is for recreational boaters and one for professionals.

Print-on-Demand charts are available through various retailers, including Bluewater Books and Charts and West Marine.

Local Notice to Mariners

Each week, the U.S. Coast Guard publishes corrections, urgent bulletins and updates in the Local Notice to Mariners. One example of this is the removal or addition of a navigational mark. Serious boaters will pencil such changes directly on the charts as they are announced. Local Notice to Mariners are now available exclusively online at www.navcen.uscg.gov/lnm.

cont'd.

Local Notice to Mariners: www.navcen.uscg.gov/lnm/default.htm
NOAA Online Chart Viewer: www.nauticalcharts.noaa.gov/mcd/OnLineViewer.html
Light Lists: www.navcen.uscg.gov/pubs/LightLists/LightLists.htm
Coast Pilots: www.nauticalcharts.noaa.gov/nsd/cpdownload.htm
NOAA Tide and Tidal Current Tables: http://tidesandcurrents.noaa.gov

Government Publications

Light Lists

Light Lists provide thorough information (location, characteristics, etc.) on aids to navigation such as buoys, lights, fog signals, day beacons, radio beacons, RACONS and LORAN-C stations. For the Northern region, use Volume I, St. Croix River, ME, to Shrewsbury River, NJ, and Volume II, Shrewsbury River, NJ, to Little River, SC.

Light Lists can now be downloaded in PDF format free of charge from the U.S. Coast Guard by visiting this Web address: www.navcen.uscg.gov/pubs/LightLists/LightLists.htm.

Alternatively, you can order or purchase bound copies of Coast Pilots from your chart agent.

Coast Pilots

The U.S. Coast Pilot is a series of nine books providing navigational data to supplement NOS charts. Subjects include navigation regulations, outstanding landmarks, channel and anchorage peculiarities, dangers, weather, ice, routes, pilotage and port facilities. For the areas covered in the Northern edition of WATERWAY GUIDE, use Coast Pilots 1, 2 and 3.

Coast Pilots can also be downloaded free of charge from NOAA by visiting www.nauticalcharts.noaa.gov/nsd/cpdownload.htm, but you can purchase Coast Pilots from your chart agent if a bound copy is more convenient for your use.

Tides and Currents

Tide Tables give predicted heights of high and low water for every day in the year for many important harbors. They also provide correction figures for many other locations.

Tidal Current Tables include daily predictions for the times of slack water, the times and velocities of maximum flood and ebb currents for a number of waterways, and data enabling the navigator to calculate predictions for other areas.

Tide tables and tidal current tables are no longer published by NOS; several private publishers print them now and many chart agents carry them.

Additionally, tide and tidal current tables are now available for viewing online at http://tidesandcurrents.noaa.gov.

Distance Tables

Distances: Delaware Bay & River

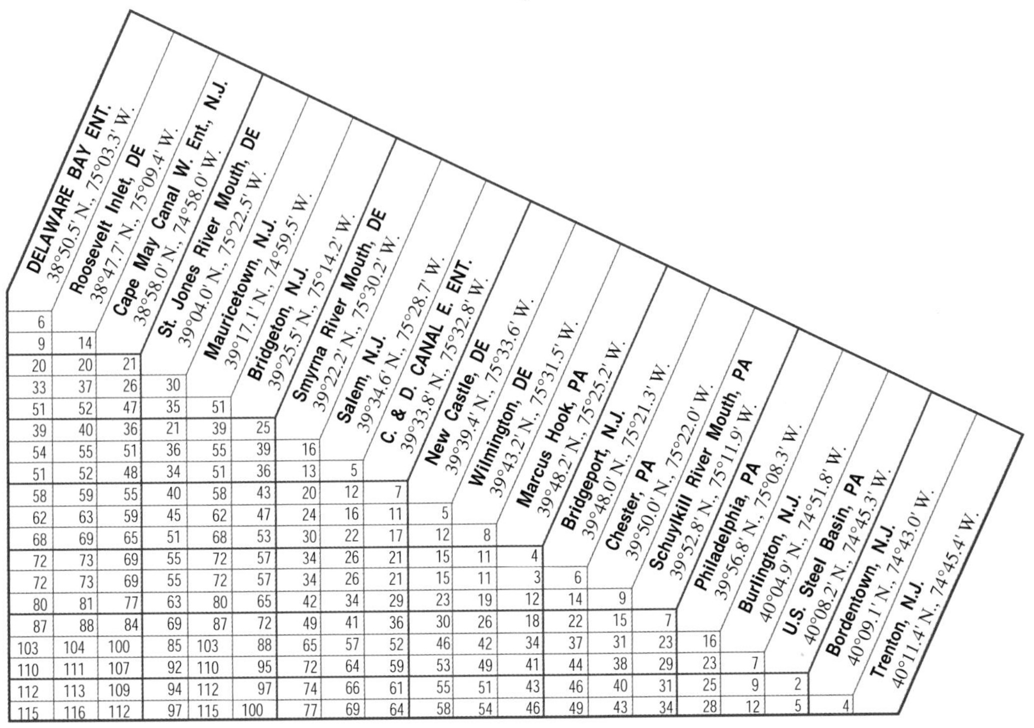

	Delaware Bay Ent.	Roosevelt Inlet	Cape May Canal W. Ent.	St. Jones River Mouth	Mauricetown	Bridgeton	Smyrna River Mouth	Salem	C. & D. Canal E. Ent.	New Castle	Wilmington	Marcus Hook	Bridgeport	Chester	Schuylkill River Mouth	Philadelphia	Burlington	U.S. Steel Basin	Bordentown
DELAWARE BAY ENT. 38°50.5' N., 75°03.3' W.																			
Roosevelt Inlet, DE 38°47.7' N., 75°09.4' W.	6																		
Cape May Canal W. Ent., N.J. 38°58.0' N., 74°58.0' W.	9	14																	
St. Jones River Mouth, DE 39°04.0' N., 75°22.5' W.	20	20	21																
Mauricetown, N.J. 39°17.1' N., 74°59.5' W.	33	37	26	30															
Bridgeton, N.J. 39°25.5' N., 75°14.2' W.	51	52	47	35	51														
Smyrna River Mouth, DE 39°22.2' N., 75°30.2' W.	39	40	36	21	39	25													
Salem, N.J. 39°34.6' N., 75°28.7' W.	54	55	51	36	55	39	16												
C. & D. CANAL E. ENT. 39°33.8' N., 75°32.8' W.	51	52	48	34	51	36	13	5											
New Castle, DE 39°39.4' N., 75°33.6' W.	58	59	55	40	58	43	20	12	7										
Wilmington, DE 39°43.2' N., 75°31.5' W.	62	63	59	45	62	47	24	16	11	5									
Marcus Hook, PA 39°48.2' N., 75°25.2' W.	68	69	65	51	68	53	30	22	17	12	8								
Bridgeport, N.J. 39°48.0' N., 75°21.3' W.	72	73	69	55	72	57	34	26	21	15	11	4							
Chester, PA 39°50.0' N., 75°22.0' W.	72	73	69	55	72	57	34	26	21	15	11	3	6						
Schuylkill River Mouth, PA 39°52.8' N., 75°11.9' W.	80	81	77	63	80	65	42	34	29	23	19	12	14	9					
Philadelphia, PA 39°56.8' N., 75°08.3' W.	87	88	84	69	87	72	49	41	36	30	26	18	22	15	7				
Burlington, N.J. 40°04.9' N., 74°51.8' W.	103	104	100	85	103	88	65	57	52	46	42	34	37	31	23	16			
U.S. Steel Basin, PA 40°08.2' N., 74°45.3' W.	110	111	107	92	110	95	72	64	59	53	49	41	44	38	29	23	7		
Bordentown, N.J. 40°09.1' N., 74°43.0' W.	112	113	109	94	112	97	74	66	61	55	51	43	46	40	31	25	9	2	
Trenton, N.J. 40°11.4' N., 74°45.4' W.	115	116	112	97	115	100	77	69	64	58	54	46	49	43	34	28	12	5	4

NAUTICAL MILES

Manasquan Inlet, NJ, to C&D Canal

	New York	Shark River Inlet	Manasquan Inlet	Bay Head	Mantoloking	Toms River	Seaside Park	Forked River	Barnegat Inlet	Beach Haven	Atlantic City	Mays Landing	Ocean City	Sea Isle City	Avalon	Stone Harbor	Wildwood	Cape May Harbor	Cape May Canal W. Ent.
NEW YORK, N.Y., (Battery)* 40°42.0' N., 74°01.0' W.																			
Shark River Inlet* 40°11.2' N., 74°00.5' W.	34																		
Manasquan Inlet* 40°06.1' N., 74°01.9' W.	40	6																	
Bay Head 40°03.8' N., 74°03.1' W.	44	9	4																
Mantoloking 40°02.2' N., 74°03.4' W.	46	11	6	2															
Toms River (town) 39°56.9' N., 74°11.8' W.	58	23	18	14	12														
Seaside Park 39°55.3' N., 74°05.0' W.	54	20	14	10	9	7													
Forked River (town) 39°50.1' N., 74°11.7' W.	63	29	23	19	17	15	10												
Barnegat Inlet 39°46.0' N., 74°06.3' W.	66	32	26	22	20	18	13	8											
Beach Haven 39°34.0' N., 74°14.8' W.	79	45	39	35	33	31	26	21	20										
Atlantic City 39°22.6' N., 74°24.9' W.	97	62	57	53	51	49	44	39	38	18									
Mays Landing 39°26.9' N., 74°43.4' W.	124	90	84	80	79	77	71	66	65	45	30								
Ocean City 39°17.3' N., 74°34.4' W.	108	74	68	64	63	60	55	50	49	29	13	18							
Sea Isle City 39°09.4' N., 74°42.0' W.	119	85	79	76	74	72	66	61	60	40	25	29	11						
Avalon 39°06.6' N., 74°44.0' W.	123	89	83	79	77	75	70	65	64	44	28	33	15	4					
Stone Harbor 39°03.4' N., 74°46.0' W.	128	94	88	85	83	81	75	70	69	49	34	38	20	9	5				
Wildwood 39°00.5' N., 74°49.8' W.	133	99	93	89	88	86	80	75	74	54	39	43	25	14	10	5			
Cape May Harbor 38°57.1' N., 74°52.6' W.	138	103	98	94	92	90	85	80	79	59	43	47	30	18	15	9	5		
Cape May Canal W. Ent. 38°58.0' N., 74°58.0' W.	142	108	102	98	96	94	89	84	83	63	47	52	34	23	19	14	9	4	
C. & D. CANAL E. ENT., DE 39°33.8' N., 75°32.8' W.	190	156	150	146	144	142	137	132	131	111	95	100	82	71	67	62	57	52	48

NAUTICAL MILES

Hudson River, NY, to Troy Lock

	NEW YORK (Battery) 40°42.0' N., 74°01.0' W.	Yonkers 40°56.1' N., 73°54.3' W.	Tarrytown 41°04.7' N., 73°52.2' W.	Nyack 41°05.4' N., 73°54.9' W.	Ossining 41°09.6' N., 73°52.3' W.	Haverstraw 41°11.8' N., 73°57.5' W.	Peekskill 41°17.3' N., 73°56.0' W.	West Point 41°23.1' N., 73°57.3' W.	Newburgh 41°30.1' N., 74°00.3' W.	Poughkeepsie 41°42.3' N., 73°56.5' W.	Hyde Park 41°47.3' N., 73°56.9' W.	Kingston 41°55.1' N., 73°59.0' W.	Saugerties 42°04.4' N., 73°56.7' W.	Catskill 42°13.0' N., 73°52.1' W.	Hudson 42°15.3' N., 73°48.1' W.	Athens 42°15.6' N., 73°48.5' W.	Coxsackie 42°21.0' N., 73°47.6' W.	Coeymans 42°28.5' N., 73°47.4' W.	Albany 42°37.9' N., 73°45.3' W.	Rensselaer 42°37.9' N., 73°45.1' W.	Troy 42°43.7' N., 73°41.8' W.	Watervliet 42°43.7' N., 73°41.9' W.
Yonkers	16																					
Tarrytown	24	9																				
Nyack	25	10	2																			
Ossining	29	14	6	6																		
Haverstraw	33	18	9	10	5																	
Peekskill	38	23	15	15	11	6																
West Point	45	29	21	22	17	13	8															
Newburgh	53	37	29	29	25	21	15	8														
Poughkeepsie	66	50	42	43	38	34	29	21	13													
Hyde Park	71	55	47	48	43	39	34	26	18	5												
Kingston	80	64	56	57	52	48	43	35	27	14	9											
Saugerties	89	74	66	66	62	58	52	45	37	24	19	12										
Catskill	99	83	75	75	71	67	61	54	46	33	28	21	11									
Hudson	102	86	78	78	74	70	64	57	49	36	31	24	14	5								
Athens	102	86	78	78	74	70	64	57	49	36	31	24	14	5	1							
Coxsackie	108	93	85	85	80	76	71	63	55	42	37	30	21	11	7	6						
Coeymans	115	100	92	92	88	84	78	70	62	49	44	38	28	19	14	14	7					
Albany	126	110	102	102	98	94	88	81	73	60	55	48	38	29	24	24	18	10				
Rensselaer	126	110	102	102	98	94	88	81	73	60	55	48	38	29	24	24	18	10	0			
Troy	132	116	108	108	104	100	94	87	79	66	61	54	44	35	30	30	24	16	6	6		
Watervliet	132	116	108	108	104	100	94	87	79	66	61	54	44	35	30	30	24	16	6	6	0	
Troy Lock 42°45.1' N., 73°41.1' W.	134	118	110	110	106	102	96	89	81	68	63	56	46	37	32	32	26	18	8	8	2	2

NAUTICAL MILES

Greenport, NY, to Manasquan Inlet, NJ

	Greenport 41°06.0' N., 72°21.5' W.	Sag Harbor 41°00.2' N., 72°17.7' W.	Riverhead 40°55.0' N., 72°39.4' W.	Shinnecock Canal, N. End 40°53.9' N., 72°30.3' W.	Shinnecock Inlet 40°50.3' N., 72°28.6' W.	Westhampton Beach 40°48.2' N., 72°38.4' W.	Moriches Inlet 40°45.8' N., 72°45.3' W.	Bellport 40°45.1' N., 72°56.0' W.	Patchogue 40°45.5' N., 73°01.2' W.	Bay Shore 40°42.8' N., 73°14.2' W.	Fire Island Inlet 40°37.8' N., 73°18.6' W.	Babylon 40°41.2' N., 73°18.9' W.	Amityville 40°39.6' N., 73°24.8' W.	Jones Beach 40°36.2' N., 73°30.8' W.	Jones Inlet 40°34.4' N., 73°34.9' W.	Freeport 40°37.6' N., 73°34.9' W.	Long Beach 40°35.7' N., 73°39.4' W.	East Rockaway Inlet 40°34.9' N., 73°45.4' W.	Rockaway Point* 40°32.4' N., 73°56.5' W.	NEW YORK (Battery)* 40°42.0' N., 74°01.0' W.
Sag Harbor	11																			
Riverhead	21	22																		
Shinnecock Canal, N. End	16	17	8																	
Shinnecock Inlet	21	22	13	5																
Westhampton Beach	28	29	20	12	9															
Moriches Inlet	34	35	26	18	15	7														
Bellport	42	43	34	26	23	15	11													
Patchogue	48	49	40	32	29	21	17	6												
Bay Shore	57	58	49	41	39	30	27	16	13											
Fire Island Inlet	62	63	54	46	44	35	32	21	18	9										
Babylon	61	62	53	45	42	34	30	19	17	5	8									
Amityville	66	67	58	50	47	39	35	24	22	10	12	6								
Jones Beach	72	73	64	56	54	45	42	31	28	17	16	13	7							
Jones Inlet	76	77	68	60	58	49	45	35	32	21	20	17	11	4						
Freeport	77	78	69	61	58	49	46	35	32	21	21	18	12	4	4					
Long Beach	80	81	72	64	61	53	49	38	36	24	24	21	15	8	5	6				
East Rockaway Inlet	85	86	77	69	66	58	54	44	41	29	29	26	20	13	10	11	5			
Rockaway Point*	94	95	86	78	75	67	63	53	50	38	38	35	29	22	19	20	14	9		
NEW YORK (Battery)*	107	108	99	91	88	80	76	66	63	51	51	48	42	35	32	33	27	22	13	
Manasquan Inlet, N.J.* 40°06.1' N., 74°01.9' W.	116	117	108	100	97	89	85	75	72	60	60	57	51	44	41	42	36	31	27	40

NAUTICAL MILES

Cape Cod, MA, to Newark, NJ

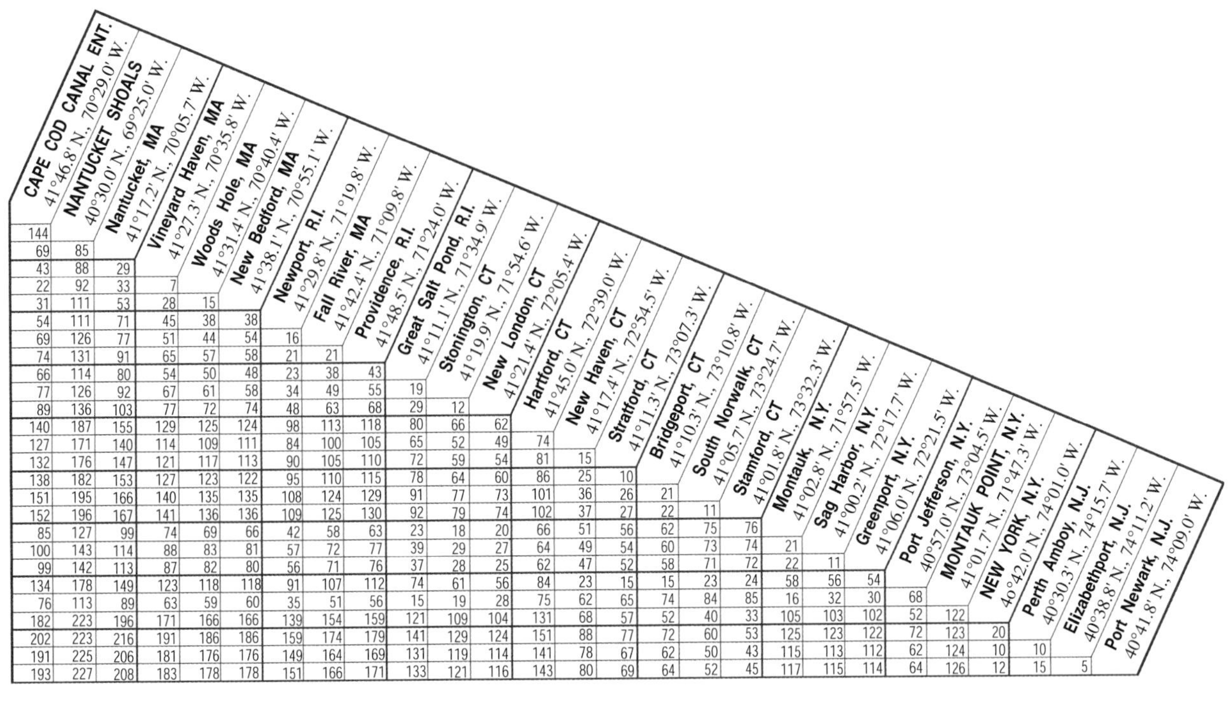

	CAPE COD CANAL ENT. 41°46.8' N., 70°29.0' W.	NANTUCKET SHOALS 40°30.0' N., 69°25.0' W.	Nantucket, MA 41°17.2' N., 70°05.7' W.	Vineyard Haven, MA 41°27.3' N., 70°35.8' W.	Woods Hole, MA 41°31.4' N., 70°40.4' W.	New Bedford, MA 41°38.1' N., 70°55.1' W.	Newport, R.I. 41°29.8' N., 71°19.8' W.	Fall River, MA 41°42.4' N., 71°09.8' W.	Providence, R.I. 41°48.5' N., 71°24.0' W.	Great Salt Pond, R.I. 41°11.1' N., 71°34.9' W.	Stonington, CT 41°19.9' N., 71°54.6' W.	New London, CT 41°21.4' N., 72°05.4' W.	Hartford, CT 41°45.0' N., 72°39.0' W.	New Haven, CT 41°17.4' N., 72°54.5' W.	Stratford, CT 41°11.3' N., 73°07.3' W.	Bridgeport, CT 41°10.3' N., 73°10.8' W.	South Norwalk, CT 41°05.7' N., 73°24.7' W.	Stamford, CT 41°01.8' N., 73°32.3' W.	Montauk, N.Y. 41°02.8' N., 71°57.5' W.	Sag Harbor, N.Y. 41°00.2' N., 72°17.7' W.	Greenport, N.Y. 41°06.0' N., 72°21.5' W.	Port Jefferson, N.Y. 40°57.0' N., 73°04.5' W.	MONTAUK POINT, N.Y. 41°01.7' N., 71°47.3' W.	NEW YORK, N.Y. 40°42.0' N., 74°01.0' W.	Perth Amboy, N.J. 40°30.3' N., 74°15.7' W.	Elizabethport, N.J. 40°38.8' N., 74°11.2' W.
NANTUCKET SHOALS	144																									
Nantucket, MA	69	85																								
Vineyard Haven, MA	43	88	29																							
Woods Hole, MA	22	92	33	7																						
New Bedford, MA	31	111	53	28	15																					
Newport, R.I.	54	111	71	45	38	38																				
Fall River, MA	69	126	77	51	44	54	16																			
Providence, R.I.	74	131	91	65	57	58	21	21																		
Great Salt Pond, R.I.	66	114	80	54	50	48	23	38	43																	
Stonington, CT	77	126	92	67	61	58	34	49	55	19																
New London, CT	89	136	103	77	72	74	48	63	68	29	12															
Hartford, CT	140	187	155	129	125	124	98	113	118	80	66	62														
New Haven, CT	127	171	140	114	109	111	84	100	105	65	52	49	74													
Stratford, CT	132	176	147	121	117	113	90	105	110	72	59	54	81	15												
Bridgeport, CT	138	182	153	127	123	122	95	110	115	78	64	60	86	25	10											
South Norwalk, CT	151	195	166	140	135	135	108	124	129	91	77	73	101	36	26	21										
Stamford, CT	152	196	167	141	136	136	109	125	130	92	79	74	102	37	27	22	11									
Montauk, N.Y.	85	127	99	74	69	66	42	58	63	23	18	20	66	51	56	62	75	76								
Sag Harbor, N.Y.	100	143	114	88	83	81	57	72	77	39	29	27	64	49	54	60	73	74	21							
Greenport, N.Y.	99	142	113	87	82	80	56	71	76	37	28	25	62	47	52	58	71	72	22	11						
Port Jefferson, N.Y.	134	178	149	123	118	118	91	107	112	74	61	56	84	23	15	15	23	24	58	56	54					
MONTAUK POINT, N.Y.	76	113	89	63	59	60	35	51	56	15	19	28	75	62	65	74	84	85	16	32	30	68				
NEW YORK, N.Y.	182	223	196	171	166	166	139	154	159	121	109	104	131	68	57	52	40	33	105	103	102	52	122			
Perth Amboy, N.J.	202	223	216	191	186	186	159	174	179	141	129	124	151	88	77	72	60	53	125	123	122	72	123	20		
Elizabethport, N.J.	191	225	206	181	176	176	149	164	169	131	119	114	141	78	67	62	50	43	115	113	112	62	124	10	10	
Port Newark, N.J. 40°41.8' N., 74°09.0' W.	193	227	208	183	178	178	151	166	171	133	121	116	143	80	69	64	52	45	117	115	114	64	126	12	15	5

NAUTICAL MILES

Calais, ME, to Cape Cod, MA

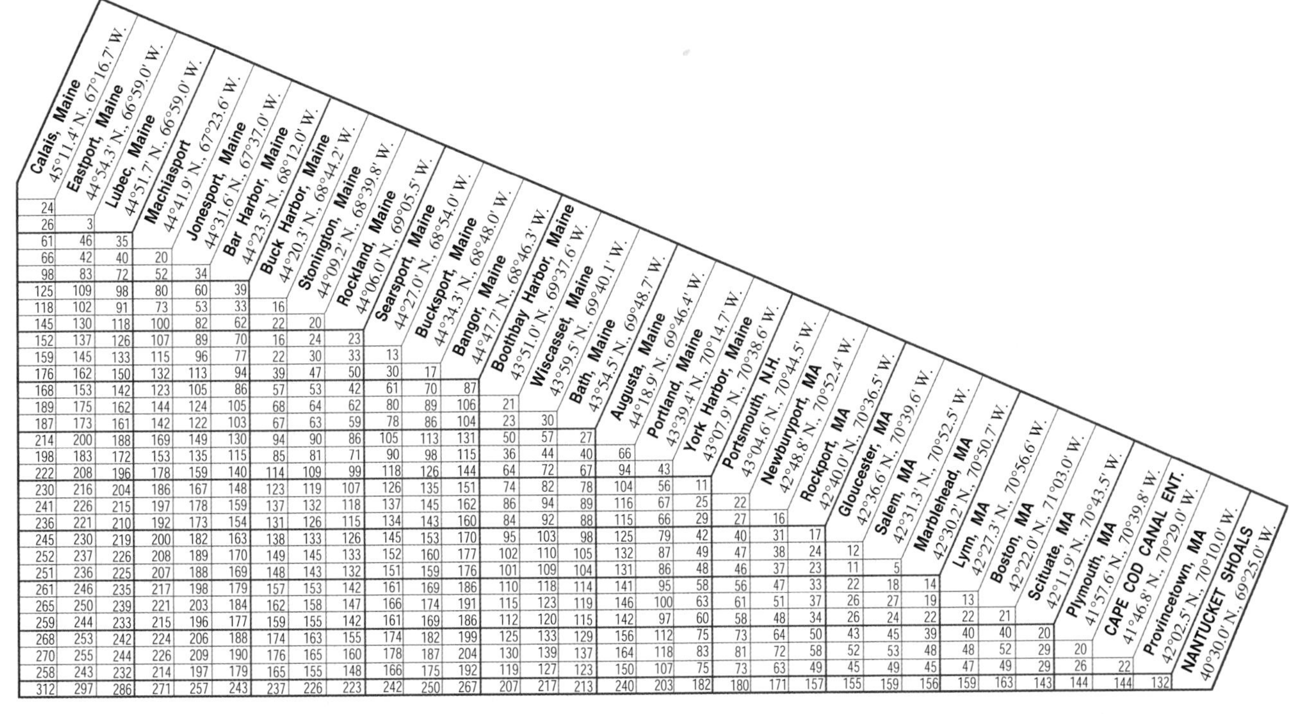

	Calais, Maine 45°11.4' N., 67°16.7' W.	Eastport, Maine 44°54.3' N., 66°59.0' W.	Lubec, Maine 44°51.7' N., 66°59.0' W.	Machiasport 44°41.9' N., 67°23.6' W.	Jonesport, Maine 44°31.6' N., 67°37.0' W.	Bar Harbor, Maine 44°23.5' N., 68°12.0' W.	Buck Harbor, Maine 44°20.3' N., 68°44.2' W.	Stonington, Maine 44°09.2' N., 68°39.8' W.	Rockland, Maine 44°06.0' N., 69°05.5' W.	Searsport, Maine 44°27.0' N., 68°54.0' W.	Bucksport, Maine 44°34.3' N., 68°48.0' W.	Bangor, Maine 44°47.7' N., 68°46.3' W.	Boothbay Harbor, Maine 43°51.0' N., 69°37.6' W.	Wiscasset, Maine 43°59.5' N., 69°40.1' W.	Bath, Maine 43°54.5' N., 69°48.7' W.	Augusta, Maine 44°18.9' N., 69°46.4' W.	Portland, Maine 43°39.4' N., 70°14.7' W.	York Harbor, Maine 43°07.9' N., 70°38.6' W.	Portsmouth, N.H. 43°04.6' N., 70°44.5' W.	Newburyport, MA 42°48.8' N., 70°52.4' W.	Rockport, MA 42°40.0' N., 70°36.5' W.	Gloucester, MA 42°36.6' N., 70°39.6' W.	Salem, MA 42°31.3' N., 70°52.5' W.	Marblehead, MA 42°30.2' N., 70°50.7' W.	Lynn, MA 42°27.3' N., 70°56.6' W.	Boston, MA 42°22.0' N., 71°03.0' W.	Scituate, MA 42°11.9' N., 70°43.5' W.	Plymouth, MA 41°57.6' N., 70°39.8' W.	CAPE COD CANAL ENT. 41°46.8' N., 70°29.0' W.	Provincetown, MA 42°02.5' N., 70°10.0' W.
Eastport, Maine	24																													
Lubec, Maine	26	3																												
Machiasport	61	46	35																											
Jonesport, Maine	66	42	40	20																										
Bar Harbor, Maine	98	83	72	52	34																									
Buck Harbor, Maine	125	109	98	80	60	39																								
Stonington, Maine	118	102	91	73	53	33	16																							
Rockland, Maine	145	130	118	100	82	62	22	20																						
Searsport, Maine	152	137	126	107	89	70	16	24	23																					
Bucksport, Maine	159	145	133	115	96	77	22	30	33	13																				
Bangor, Maine	176	162	150	132	113	94	39	47	50	30	17																			
Boothbay Harbor, Maine	168	153	142	123	105	86	57	53	42	61	70	87																		
Wiscasset, Maine	189	175	162	144	124	105	68	64	62	80	89	106	21																	
Bath, Maine	187	173	161	142	122	103	67	63	59	78	86	104	23	30																
Augusta, Maine	214	200	188	169	149	130	94	90	86	105	113	131	50	57	27															
Portland, Maine	198	183	172	153	135	115	85	81	71	90	98	115	36	44	40	66														
York Harbor, Maine	222	208	196	178	159	140	114	109	99	118	126	144	64	72	67	94	43													
Portsmouth, N.H.	230	216	204	186	167	148	123	119	107	126	135	151	74	82	78	104	56	11												
Newburyport, MA	241	226	215	197	178	159	137	132	118	137	145	162	86	94	89	116	67	25	22											
Rockport, MA	236	221	210	192	173	154	131	126	115	134	143	160	84	92	88	115	66	29	27	16										
Gloucester, MA	245	230	219	200	182	163	138	133	126	145	153	170	95	103	98	125	79	42	40	31	17									
Salem, MA	252	237	226	208	189	170	149	145	133	152	160	177	102	110	105	132	87	49	47	38	24	12								
Marblehead, MA	251	236	225	207	188	169	148	143	132	151	159	176	101	109	104	131	86	48	46	37	23	11	5							
Lynn, MA	261	246	235	217	198	179	157	153	142	161	169	186	110	118	114	141	95	58	56	47	33	22	18	14						
Boston, MA	265	250	239	221	203	184	162	158	147	166	174	191	115	123	119	146	100	63	61	51	37	26	27	19	13					
Scituate, MA	259	244	233	215	196	177	159	155	142	161	169	186	112	120	115	142	97	60	58	48	34	26	24	22	22	21				
Plymouth, MA	268	253	242	224	206	188	174	163	155	174	182	199	125	133	129	156	112	75	73	64	50	43	45	39	40	40	20			
CAPE COD CANAL ENT.	270	255	244	226	209	190	176	165	160	178	187	204	130	139	137	164	118	83	81	72	58	52	53	48	48	52	29	20		
Provincetown, MA	258	243	232	214	197	179	165	155	148	166	175	192	119	127	123	150	107	75	73	63	49	45	49	45	47	49	29	26	22	
NANTUCKET SHOALS 40°30.0' N., 69°25.0' W.	312	297	286	271	257	243	237	226	223	242	250	267	207	217	213	240	203	182	180	171	157	155	159	156	159	163	143	144	144	132

NAUTICAL MILES

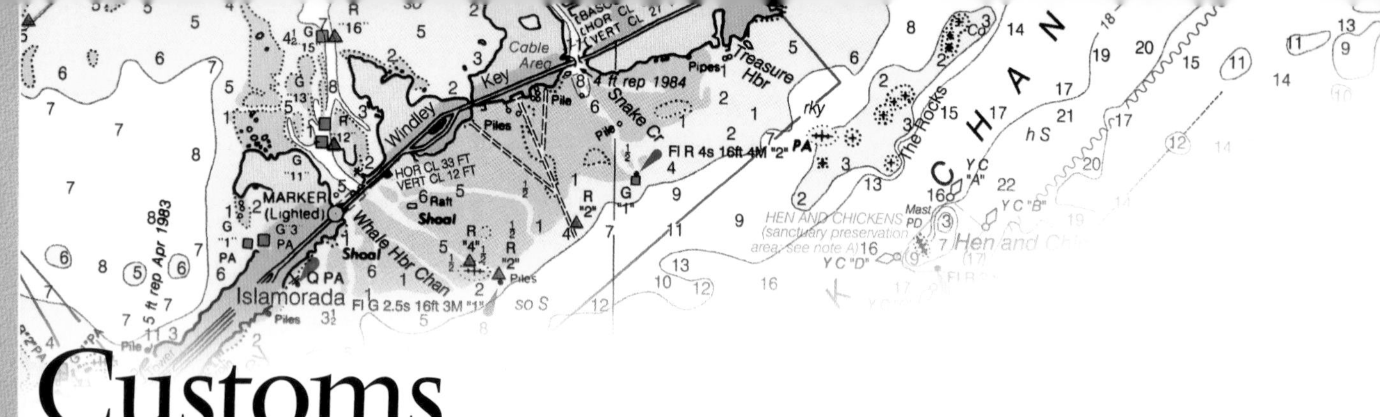

Customs

If you often go to Canada directly from the United States on a private pleasure boat, and would like to clear Customs and Immigration faster, you may be interested in the CANPASS Private Boats program.

To qualify, you have to be a citizen or permanent resident of Canada or the United States, pass a strict security check and pay $40 Canadian annually.

First, call the **Canada Border Services Agency (CBSA) toll free at 888-226-7277** within four hours of the time you will arrive in Canada. You will tell the CCRA when and where you will arrive, and give certain information about everyone on board. Everyone with you has to be a member of the program.

Next, you declare any goods anyone on board has bought. Any duty or tax they owe is charged to their Visa or MasterCard.

For an application, get a copy of the CANPASS Private Boats pamphlet at your local customs office or from CBSA.

■ How to Report if You Do Not Have a CANPASS Permit

1. Upon arrival into Canada, proceed to a designated telephone reporting station. (Call 204-983-3500 or visit www.cbsa.gc.ca for a list of reporting stations on your intended route.)

2. Contact CBSA by calling 888-226-7277.

3. Provide the following information: full name, date of birth and citizenship for each person on board. For travelers who are not returning residents, provide the purpose and length of stay in Canada or for returning residents, provide length of absence, passport and visa details, if applicable.

4. Declare all personal goods being imported, including firearms and weapons. If duties and taxes are payable, provide customs with your Visa or MasterCard number and expiration date.

5. The Customs officer will advise you whether you are free to leave the area and enter Canada, or if you have to wait for a Customs and/or Immigration officer to complete documents or conduct an examination.

6. At the conclusion of the Customs process, you will receive a report number for your records, as proof of your reporting.

■ Telephone Reporting Stations are Located in The Following Places:

Ontario: Fort Erie, Hamilton, Mississauga, Toronto, Kingston, Ottawa. *Quebec*: Quebec, Montreal, Lacolle. *New Brunswick*: Campobello, Deer Island, St. Andrews, Grand Manan, Saint John. *Nova Scotia*: Yarmouth, Shelburne, Lunenburg, Halifax, Canso, Port Hawkesbury, Sydney.

■ **Firearms:** Canada has strict rules about any small arms aboard. Absolutely no handguns or pistols are permitted. Period. You must leave handguns in a U.S. port until your return to the United States or mail them through U.S. mail to another port of entry for pick up there. Smuggling your handgun into Canada risks severe fines and confiscation.

As of Jan. 1, 2001, visitors who do not have a Canadian Possession and Acquisition License (PAL) will need to report their firearms at their point of entry. If you applied at least 60 days before your trip to Canada and you have not received your PAL, you can complete a Non-Resident Firearm Declaration (form JUS 909 E/F), and pay $50 Canadian. However, you are entitled to a $50 refund once you receive your PAL. You should request the Instruction Sheet Non-Resident Firearm Declaration Refund form from the Customs officer at your entry point. You must send the requested information to the Department of Justice after your PAL arrives.

Once confirmed, the JUS 909 E/F declaration will act as a temporary license and registration certificate while in Canada, and it is valid for 60 days.

Visitors may renew their temporary license anytime during a 12-month period without paying an additional fee. Unlicensed non-residents who plan to borrow a firearm in Canada must obtain a Temporary Borrowing License. Visitors will only be able to purchase ammunition with a Canadian firearms license, a confirmed firearms declaration form or a Temporary Borrowing License.

Temporary Firearms Borrower's license forms and further information on firearms laws are available at the Canadian Firearms Centre (see contact information at the end of this section). The Borrower's form must be completed before arrival into Canada and the cost of the license is $30 Canadian.

Firearm owners visiting Canada will be subject to the same safe storage and transportation regulations as Canadian firearm owners.

■ **Returning to the United States:** American yachts must be cleared by three U.S. agencies: Customs, Department of Agriculture (for plant pests) and Immigration (for citizenship). As a convenience to mariners, one boarding inspector effects clearance for all three agencies.

Returning yachts should fly the yellow quarantine flag and proceed to a public dock or marina at a point close to the border. Any boat that is anchored or tied up in U.S. waters is considered to have entered the United States. Immediately upon entry, the master must report arrival to authorities by calling the 24-hour communication center at 800-973-2867 or by contacting a local Customs office. The report should include the name of the boat, its nationality, its registration or documentation number, name of the master, names of the people on board, place of docking, arrival time and User Fee Decal. No one other than the person reporting arrival is permitted to leave the boat, and no articles may be taken ashore nor visitors allowed on board until clearance is effected. Violations incur a stinging penalty of $5,000.

If the Customs officer to whom you report requires an inspection, a boarding inspector will visit your boat. However, you may be cleared over the telephone if you have already purchased a User Fee Decal, in which case you will be given a release number, to serve as evidence of compliance with clearance regulations. Be sure to keep a log of all calls made to a Customs office.

■ **User Fee Decal:** A user fee decal costing $27.50 is available from the U.S. Customs Service at your port of entry. New customers may obtain an annual user fee decal by contacting:

U.S. Customs Service
Decal Program Administrator
P.O. Box 382030
Pittsburgh, PA 15250-8030
Tel: 317-298-1245
www.cbp.gov/xp/cgov/travel

This numbered decal must be affixed near the vessel's main boarding area. The number should be recorded, and it will be requested when a vessel reports to Customs after reentering U.S. waters. Boats smaller than 30 feet are not required to purchase a decal.

■ **Currency:** If you are carrying more than $10,000 in currency, traveler's checks or other negotiable instruments, you must report that information to Customs. Complete Form 4790 at any Customs office. Note that this regulation applies whether you are entering or leaving U.S. waters.

Note that, at the current exchange rate between the United States and Canada (as of this writing), $1 U.S. equals $1.08801 Canadian. Canadian mariners entering the United States should be aware that some mariners have had difficulty getting American boatyards to accept Canadian checks. Be prepared with U.S. dollars or credit cards.

■ **U.S. Ports of Entry:** This is a list of some U.S. ports of entry for the waters covered in this book. New York: Buffalo, Rochester, Oswego, Cape Vincent, Clayton, Alexandria Bay, Ogdensburg, Massena. Vermont: St. Albans, Burlington. Maine: Eastport, Lubec, Jonesport, Bar Harbor, Rockland, Belfast, Portland.

■ **Canadian Vessels:** At the first U.S. port of arrival, the master must immediately report and make formal entry as previously described in "Returning to the U.S." A cruising license will be issued, which will allow the vessel to cruise U.S. waters without making formal entry in every port. However, the master of a Canadian vessel must still call in to each subsequent port of entry visited (not every harbor), regardless of the cruising license. Each port of entry covers a specific geographic area, and the master should request a list from the first port visited. Failure to report may incur a $1,000 penalty.

■ **Canadian Competency of Operators of Pleasure Craft Regulations:** The Competency of Operators of Pleasure Craft Regulations require operators of pleasure craft fitted with a motor and used for recreational purposes to have proof of competency on board at all times. These requirements are being phased in over 10 years.

■ **Operator* Competency Requirements****
Date proof of competency required:
All operators born after April 1, 1983: Sept. 15, 1999.

■ All operators of craft under 4 meters long: Sept. 15, 2002.

■ All operators: Sept. 15, 2009.

■ For more information, call 800-267-6687 from within Canada, or 613-991-1313 from outside Canada.

*Applies to non-residents operating their pleasure craft in Canadian waters after 45 consecutive days. Operator card or equivalent issued to a non-resident by their state or country will be considered as proof of competency.

**These requirements apply in areas outside the Northwest and Nunavut Territories at this time.

SKIPPER'S HANDBOOK

Contact the following offices for more information:

U.S. Customs & Border Protection:
www.cbp.gov

U.S. Citizenship and Immigration Service:
www.uscis.gov

Canada Border Services Agency:
www.closa.gc.ca

Citizenship and Immigration Canada:
www.ci.gc.ca,
888-242-2100

Canadian Firearms Centre:
Ottawa, ON K1A OR2 Canada
Tel 800-731-4000
Fax: 613-825-0297
www.cfc-cafc.gc.ca

Canadian Coast Guard:
www.ccg-gcc.gc.ca

Customs & Border Protection - New York:
One Penn Plaza, 11th Floor
New York, NY 10119
Tel: 646-733-3100 Fax: 646-733-3245

Customs & Border Protection - Port of Boston:
Mason Street, Boston, MA 02108
Tel: 617-565-6200 Fax: 617-565-6277

Customs & Border Protection - Buffalo Field Office:
4455 Genesee St., Buffalo, NY 14221
Tel: 716-626-0400

CANPASS Processing Centre - Ontario:
4551 Zimmerman Ave.
Niagara Falls, ON L2E 6T1
Tel: 888-226-7277, 905-371-1477

CANPASS Processing Centre
St. John, NB
506-636-5064
www.cfc-cafc.gc.ca

Cape May to Barnegat Bay

CHARTS 12304, 12316, 12317, 12318, 12323, 12324

NEW JERSEY ICW —MILE 114 TO MILE 26

Because all of the New Jersey Intracoastal Waterway (ICW) from Cape May, NJ, to Manasquan Inlet is subject to rapid change, channels deepen and shoals form without warning. In general, cruising boaters report an easy passage for the entire length of the New Jersey ICW with depths ranging anywhere from 4.5 to 6 feet on the route. Depths of 4 feet (and sometimes less) do exist, however, so cruisers should always seek local knowledge to get the latest on current channel conditions. Low fixed vertical bridge clearances (35 feet in places) unfortunately make the inside route impractical for many cruising sailboats.

There are a total of 160 lighted aids to navigation between Cape May and Manasquan Inlet, all of which are removed each fall to avoid damage from ice during winter months. Boaters traveling in early or late fall should not assume that all charted aids to navigation will be present. Coast Guard Group Cape May (609-898-6995) attempts to service and reestablish all aids to navigation by Memorial Day each spring.

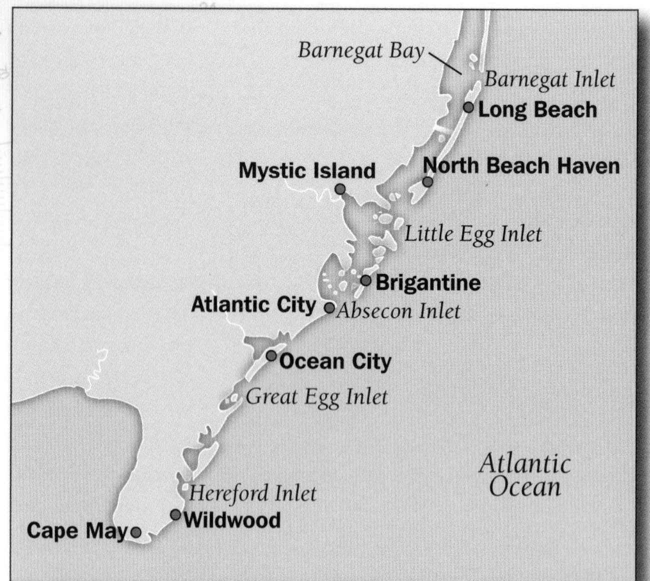

Cape May—Mile 114

The Cape May Inlet is a safe, all-weather entrance from the Atlantic Ocean into Cape May Harbor at the southern terminus of the New Jersey ICW (Mile 114). The well-protected harbor makes it a popular layover for skippers waiting out bad weather before heading north along the New Jersey coast, or those headed to the Delaware Bay or the C&D Canal farther north.

Cape May is reputed to be "the nation's oldest seashore resort." That heritage dates from at least 1812, peaking architecturally in the late 19th century. The entire town has been proclaimed a National Historic Landmark.

Cape May has claim to the largest collection of Victorian period houses in the country. Small gingerbread cottages nestle beside these grand showpieces—all preserved and restored, many tastefully pressed into commercial service. Graceful wrap-around porches and steeply peaked, lovingly rebuilt dormers adorn many houses within walking distance of the western harbor's marine facilities. The Cape May beaches are legendary, with sand dunes still nearly pristine and many beaches uncrowded. The harbor itself is a secure storm anchorage surrounded by restaurants, shops and marine facilities to support almost any need.

NAVIGATION: Use Charts 12304, 12214, 12316 and 12317. Use Atlantic City tide tables. For high tide, add 33 minutes; for low tide, add 19 minutes. Approaching Cape May Inlet from either the New Jersey ICW or the Atlantic Ocean, your landmark is a charted 641-foot LORAN tower, which is located on the east side of the inlet. Topped by a flashing red light, the tower is nearly four times the height of the 165-foot-tall Cape May Lighthouse (flashing white every 15 seconds) at the southwestern tip of the cape. One of the safest and best-marked inlets on the East Coast, Cape May Inlet is deep and visibly protected by substantial rock jetties on either side.

Entering Cape May Harbor is easy from every approach: from Delaware Bay through the jettied entrance to Cape May Canal; from the New Jersey ICW to the north; or through Cape May Inlet to the east. Ebb tides run east, both in the canal and in the inlet. NOAA Chart 12316 will be helpful in sorting out the buoys and depths for all three approaches.

Cape May Inlet is extremely busy at all times and you can expect to meet every type of vessel at every speed imaginable. The inlet is also popular with the fishing crowd and the mouth is often congested with small recreational fishing boats. The commercial fishing fleet generally has their outriggers extended while traversing the inlet, making them very beamy. The outriggers are not lighted and can be very difficult to see in poor light.

During the peak travel season when the weather and tide turn favorable, you can expect an armada of yachts to pour out of Cape May Harbor in both directions to take advantage of an opportunity for a smooth passage. On the other hand, it is also not uncommon to see yachts, even high-powered ones, return to Cape May after taking a pounding from the elements at work in both Delaware Bay and the Atlantic Ocean. Any attempt to challenge the opposition of both wind and tide along the axis of the bay is not recommended.

Northbound Offshore: The trip from Cape May to Atlantic City or beyond is very dependent on wind and waves. A departure from Cape May in a westerly or northwesterly wind can be made easier by staying within one to three miles from the beach. If, on the other hand, the winds are from the south or southwest, you can enjoy a less stressful trip farther offshore. A series of harbor entrance buoys can serve as waypoints as you cruise north. This offshore passage is advisable, as it will help you avoid shifting sandbars that may exist closer to shore. When transiting close to shore, a sharp watch should be kept for small-boat traffic.

Dockage: Cape May has many large, accommodating marinas. They all have transient slips, but it is a good idea to call ahead for availability. Near the west end of Cape May Harbor, adjacent to the Cape May Canal entrance, both Utsch's Marina (immediately west of the canal entrance) and Canyon Club Resort Marina (just east of the canal entrance) are full-service facilities that can accommodate deep-draft vessels on approach and at berth. Utsch's offers transients water, electricity and cable TV. Utsch's also has a courtesy dinghy dock available for those anchored out.

The Canyon Club Resort Marina has avenue-like docks, canopied by hundreds of outriggers, extending from the hulls of sportfishing boats dedicated to searching offshore canyons. There is usually ample transient space on floating cement docks that are accessible to the canal inlet and fuel dock. There is also a large in-ground pool in a well-landscaped setting, coin-operated laundry facilities, a convenient snack bar that serves breakfast (early) and lunch, a large repair shop and a ship's store with basic marine supplies.

Deep-draft vessels can be accommodated at South Jersey Marina, with its 7- to 12-foot dockside depths at low tide. The marina has a new bulkhead and a spacious deck for its customers, rebuilt docks and a pump-out station. Situated on Cape Island Creek, South Jersey Marina is reached by a straight-ahead course into the creek between green daybeacon "1" and red daybeacon "2" (instead of turning to starboard toward Cape May Canal at flashing red "12"). South Jersey Marina lies just beyond the commercial dock and the highly visible Lobster House restaurant. Turning room is at a premium here, but there is plenty of depth, and the marina's staffers skillfully maneuver large craft into position to match various skippers' plans for time and tide. Access to the fuel dock is easy, and the marina's restroom and shower complex is spotless.

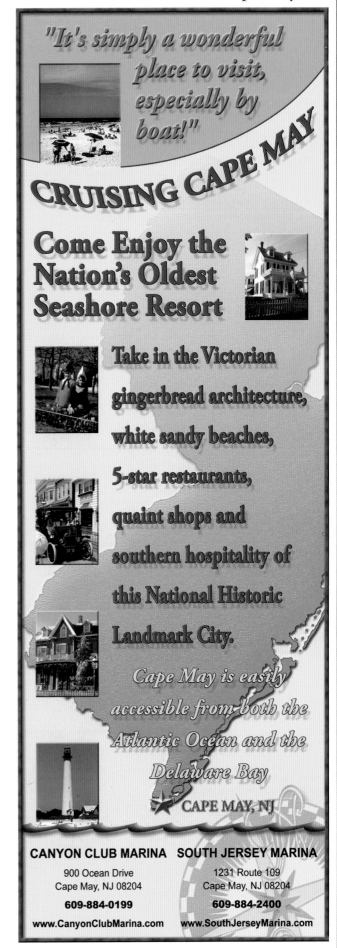

Additional slips may be available at the Corinthian Yacht Club on the south side of the harbor west of the

Cape May, NJ

CAPE MAY		Largest Vessel Accommodated	VHF Channel Monitored	Transient Berths / Total Berths	Approach / Dockside Depth (reported)	Floating Docks	Gas / Diesel	Groceries, Ice, Marine Supplies, Snacks	Repairs: Hull, Engine, Propeller	Lift (tonnage), Crane, Rail	1=110V, 2=220V, B=Both, Max Amps	Laundry, Pool, Showers	Pump-Out Station	Nearby: Grocery Store, Motel, Restaurant
		Dockage					Supplies		Services					
1. The Lobster House Restaurant 114	**609-884-8296**				**8/12**			**I**						**R**
2. South Jersey Marina 114 (Internet Access) (WiFi)	**609-884-2400**	**160**	**16/09**	**25/70**	**10/10**	**F**	**GD**	**IMS**	**HEP**	**L**	**B/100**	**LS**	**P**	**GMR**
3. Cape May Marine 114.5	609-884-0262	70	16	10/210	10/10	F	GD	IMS	HEP	L77	B/50	S	P	GMR
4. Roseman's Boat Yard 114.5	609-884-3370	60		/20	4/11	F	GD	I	H		B/50		P	GMR
5. Miss Chris Marina 114.5	609-884-3351	100	16	2/13	12/8	F	GD	IS			B/50		P	GMR
6. Utsch's Marina 114 (WiFi)	**609-884-2051**	**80**	**16/09**	**40/350**	**10/6**	**F**	**GD**	**GIMS**	**HEP**	**L35**	**B/50**	**LS**	**P**	**GMR**
7. Canyon Club Resort Marina 114 (Internet Access) (WiFi)	**609-884-0199**	**125**	**16/09**	**40/260**	**10/6**	**F**	**GD**	**IMS**	**HEP**	**L80**	**B/100**	**LPS**	**P**	**GMR**
8. Corinthian Yacht Club of Cape May 113.5	609-884-8000	50		3/	6/6	F					1/30	S		
9. Harbor View Marina 113	609-884-0808	50	16	20/200	7/20	F	GD	IMS	HP	L	1/30	S	P	R
10. Bree-Zee-Lee Yacht Basin 112.8	609-884-4849	40		5/500	4/5	F	GD	IM	HEP	L35	1/30	S		
11. Hinch Marina 112.5	609-884-7289	33		10/100	10/5	F	G	IMS		L	1/20	S	P	R
12. Two Mile Landing Marina 112.5	570-620-7719	135	16	15/64	17/6	F		I			B/50	LS	P	

Corresponding chart(s) not to be used for navigation. (icon) Internet Access (WiFi icon) Wireless Internet Access

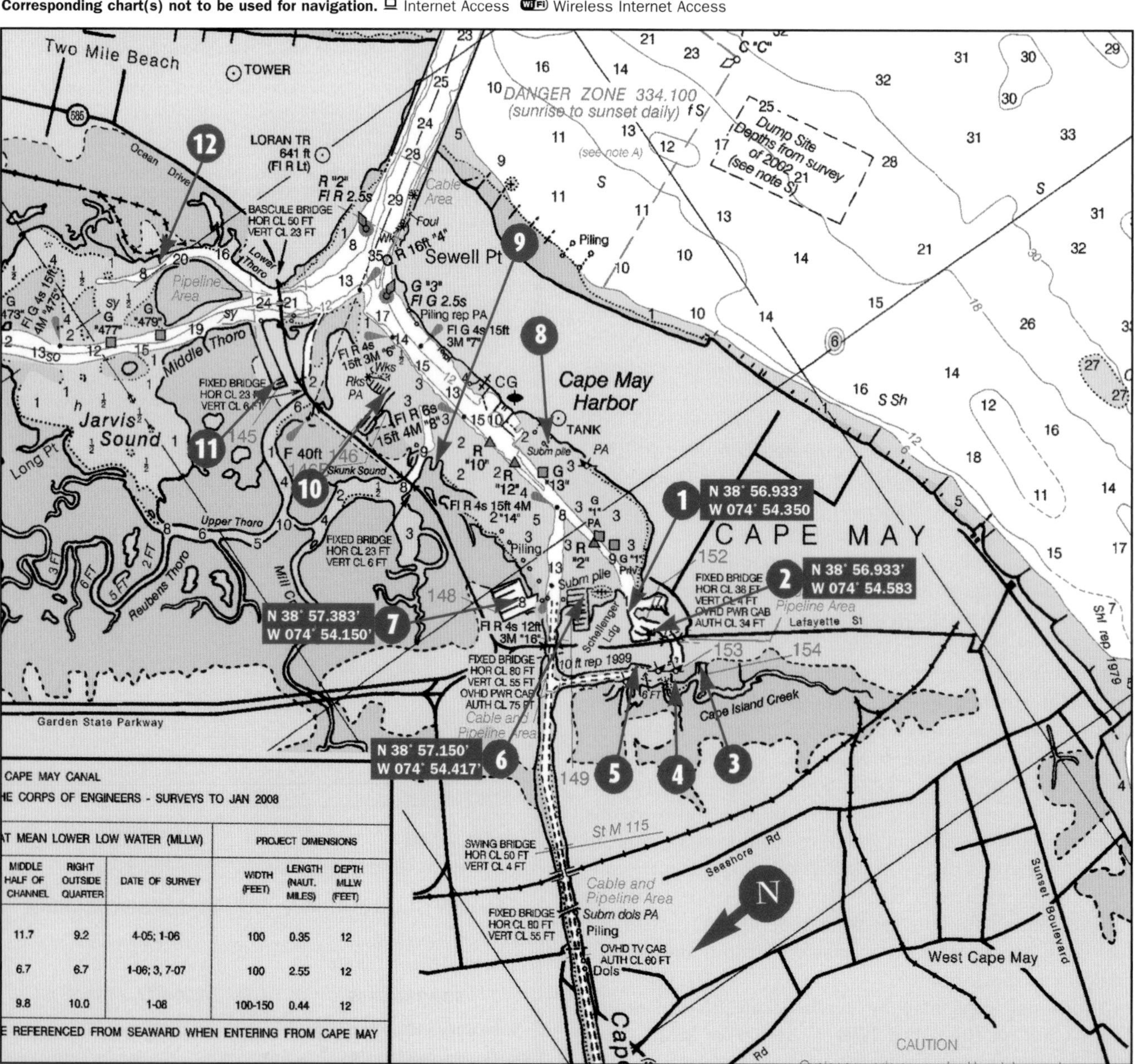

Coast Guard station. These are very popular with sailors and fill up quickly during the New Jersey ICW's heavily traveled seasons.

Harbor View Marina, directly across from Coast Guard Station Cape May, offers a deepwater fuel dock (both gasoline and diesel) and transient slips (7-foot access depth at mean low water) for boats up to 35 feet. The marina has recently doubled its total number of slips and has a ship's store and pump-out station available for its customers. The turn north from the channel into Harbor View Marina and Restaurant and Bree-Zee-Lee Yacht Basin should be made just after flashing green "7," adjacent to the Coast Guard's northernmost docks; head toward the middle entrance of the sea wall and then cruise adjacent to the wall to the westernmost entrance toward the fuel docks.

Other deep-draft slips are likely to be open at Two Mile Landing Marina on Lower Thorofare, immediately north of the bascule bridge (23-foot closed vertical clearance, monitoring VHF Channel 13 and opening on signal), east of the inner entrance of Cape May Inlet. There is plenty of water at the marina docks (at least 20 feet at mean low water), but maximum currents on Lower Thorofare can reach 3 to 4 knots during full flow. Other than at slack water, it is advisable to call ahead for assistance with lines and to approach dockside against the current. Still, the docks are of the modern, floating variety, the service is friendly and the restrooms/showers are large, airy and clean. No fuels or repair services are on the premises, but there are two restaurants here, one a casual crab-and-mallet affair, the other high-volume with tablecloths. A bar has been built right on the docks.

Anchorage: Though marina slips are usually available, even during the peak of fall migration, all bets are off during Cape May's frequent fishing tournaments. Fortunately, considerable anchorage space is available along the south side of the harbor, both east and west of the U.S. Coast Guard Station. West of the Coast Guard station, outside of (or even in) the mooring field, there should be ample space for relatively shallow-draft vessels in 5- to 10-foot depths at low tide. Deeper-draft boats typically anchor in front of the Coast Guard facility and to the east while awaiting favorable weather and tide to push on. Anchorage depths in this location, between the buoyed channel and the shore, range from 6 to 16 feet; holding is good in thick mud.

When the anchorage is crowded, particularly during the passage of cold fronts during fall and spring, two anchors may well be advisable (also a tolerance for early-morning Coast Guard reveilles and cadence calls as new recruits go through their paces at the base). No launch service is available, but it is a relatively short dinghy ride to marine facilities and restaurants to the west.

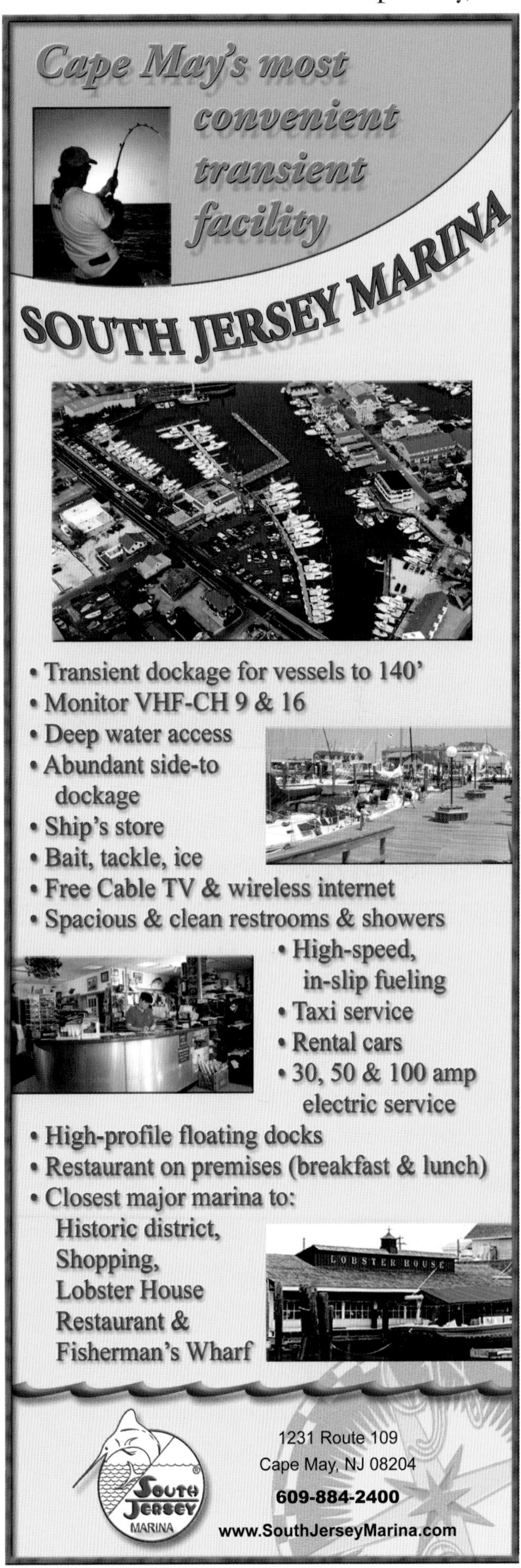

GOIN' ASHORE: CAPE MAY, NJ

As a summer tourist destination for nearly two centuries, Cape May takes pains to accommodate the varied tastes of its visitors. Multiple annual, monthly and weekly events in summer

A southwest view over Cape May Harbor. (Not to be used for navigation.) WATERWAY GUIDE PHOTOGRAPHY

Cruising with Skipper Bob and Waterway Guide... the Perfect Combination!

Excerpt from Skipper Bob's "The Great Circle Route" on Cape May, NJ

The village of Cape May itself is well worth a visit. Dating back to the early 1800s, the entire town has been declared a national historic district because of the large number of Victorian buildings. You can either stay at a marina there and walk ashore, or anchor in the harbor basin and dinghy ashore. I do not recommend anchoring overnight in the harbor basin, since it is rough due to the large number of wakes.

The 115 mile long New Jersey Intracoastal Waterway begins at Cape May and ends a mile 0 at Manasquan. The anchoring basin at mile 113 is across from the US Coast Guard Station. As soon as you proceed north under the bridge on the north side of the harbor, you will encounter few, if any cruisers; although you will see a fair number of local fishermen. The small open fishing boats are the worst problem, since they persist in fishing in the channel. Often you will encounter them anchored in the channel between the red and green markers. When you approach and ask them to move, they get downright indignant. "Why can't you go around?" They know the water is only deep in the channel. That is why they fish there. However, they do not seem to be able to take that next step in logic. "Big boats have to stay in the channel or run aground!"

The channel markers along the entire waterway were moved, replaced, and renumbered a number of years ago. If you have new charts, this should not be a problem. However, if you are using an older set of charts, be prepared to update your charts as you go along. Just remember to follow the green and red day marks in numerical order and you will not have a problem. ■

Historic home in Cape May, NJ

season—everything from major fishing tournaments and an annual hawk census to music festivals and local theatrical productions—dot the calendar. Yet the main attraction may be the Victorian town itself with its quaint houses and interesting shops, its pedestrian mall and seaside vistas from the boardwalk, not to mention its dozens of eager-to-please restaurants. Cape May is also known for its many fine bed and breakfast inns.

It is a little less than two miles from the Cape Island Creek-area marinas (an easy bike ride along Lafayette Road) to the Cape May Boardwalk to gawk at the large Victorian houses on the west side of the road. A trip down Washington Street from the marinas leads to the walking mall. If the walk to town seems too lengthy, there are taxis on call, and the local shuttle serves all the marinas. Rental bikes are available at several locations as another alternative.

Local aficionados will quickly recommend a number of restaurants that should meet almost any dining taste or mood. The Lobster House (at Fisherman's Wharf, 609-884-8296), a restaurant, raw bar, fish retailer and bakery, is hugely popular for its heaping seafood platters. The atmosphere is salty-casual, the pace is brisk and it is an easy walk from the major marinas. Fresco's (412 Bank St., 609-884-0366) is Northern Italian gourmet, while 410 Bank Street (same address, 609-884-2127) is a bit of New Orleans French Quarter. Washington Inn (801 Washington St., 609-884-5697) receives repeated kudos for its extraordinary wine cellar and fine selection of entrees to match.

Also close to the harbor, Lucky Bones Backwater Grille (1200 Route 109, 609-884-2663) is a casual restaurant created by the former Pelican Club family. In the same proximity, Copper Fish (1246 Route 109 South, 609-898-0354) has established a fine reputation, proclaiming a South Beach contemporary atmosphere with a steak and seafood focus.

The Oyster Bay Steak and Seafood Restaurant (609-884-2111) on Lafayette Street serves dinner on Friday and Saturday and has especially great desserts. If you are looking for ocean-view dining, try Martini Beach (609-884-1925) on Beach Avenue Friday through Sunday or Peter Shield's Inn & Restaurant (609-884-9090), also on Beach Avenue, serving dinner nightly starting at 5:30 p.m.

Cape May is still an active commercial fishing center, a rendezvous point for sport fishermen and a stopover for cruising boats. The offshore waters here are constantly probed by fishermen for catches ranging from tuna to marlin and, nearer to shore, lobsters are a common harvest. You will see commercial craft in Cape May Harbor rafted up between offshore voyages. Recently, Cape May has become a center for offshore whale-watching and porpoise-watching excursions. The big tuna and marlin fishing tournaments have moved to Cape May from Atlantic City.

In bad weather or during any layover, you can go crabbing in Cape May Harbor and fishing behind Cape May Inlet. If the weather is northwesterly, it is usually safe enough to fish a mile offshore in the Atlantic Ocean or, if northeasterly, off the entrance buoy to the canal on the Delaware Bay side. If the weather is southeasterly, you should stay put and wait it out by going ashore and doing some sightseeing.

LOBSTER HOUSE

(609) 884-8296

Fisherman's Wharf | Cape May, NJ 08204
Exit No. 0 Garden State Parkway

Cocktails • Luncheons • Dinners

UTSCH'S SINCE

COMPLETE MARINE FACILITIES

Located in Cape May Harbor on the south side of the Cape May Canal is a 300 slip, family owned and operated marina, nestled next to the world famous *Lobster House Restaurant* and *The Schooner America.*

From left to right, Ernest Utsch,III, Ernest Utsch, Jr. and Charles Utsch

When cruising north or south stop in and visit with the Utsch Family. Ernie, Jr., the founder–or one of his two sons, Ernie III or Charles–will greet you at their new gas and fuel dock. New 60-foot slips, high-speed diesel pumps, 30 and 50 AMP service, and nice high floating docks are available. We are open seven days a week in season to care for your needs and help you enjoy your stay in ***Historic Cape May***–a National Seashore Landmark.

Walk into town to see the Victorian architecture. Or, visit next door, (only 60 seconds walk) to the ***Lobster House Restaurant*** and the ***Schooner American Cocktail Lounge***. ***The Coffee Shop and Raw Bar*** are close by, and don't forget the Commerical Fishing Fleet.

We can also obtain car rentals, groceries, laundromat, bus service and bike rentals. Make your experience the ***Family Experience***, and visit with us. After being here five decades we still know how to say thank you... and still charge reasonable prices.

UTSCH'S MARINA
(609) 884-2051

www.capemayharbor.com

MARINA

1951

PRICES:

No Overtime "EVER", $90/Hr. Labor Rate, $2.50/Ft. Hauling with Haulouts & Wheel changes on Weekends

HOW DO WE DO IT?

Long ago Utsch's realized the need for equipment & reinvestment. That is why we own our own Dredge, Crane, Backhoe, Bulldozer, 3 Forklifts & 2 Travelifts. When others are in Florida in the winter–we maintain our marina.

SERVICE AND REPAIRS:

- Wireless Internet Access
- 2 Travelifts for hauling your powerboat or sailboat more efficiently: 35 Ton Open End Lift, 25 Ton Open End Lift
- Propeller and Hull Repairs
- Standing inventory of over 150 propellers (both new and used)
- Winter Storage Available
- Marine Store (and we mean starters, alternators, manifolds, risers, etc.)
- Picnic Tables & Barbeque Area
- New Deluxe Tile Showers & Restrooms
- Transient Slips Available
- Space Provided for Dinghies
- 5 ft. Water at Low Tide
- Brokerage on All Types of Boats
- Cable TV
- Laundry / Light Groceries
- Tackle Shop
- Engine Franchises:

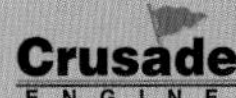

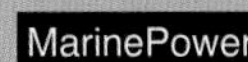

P.C.M.

WHERE WE ARE:

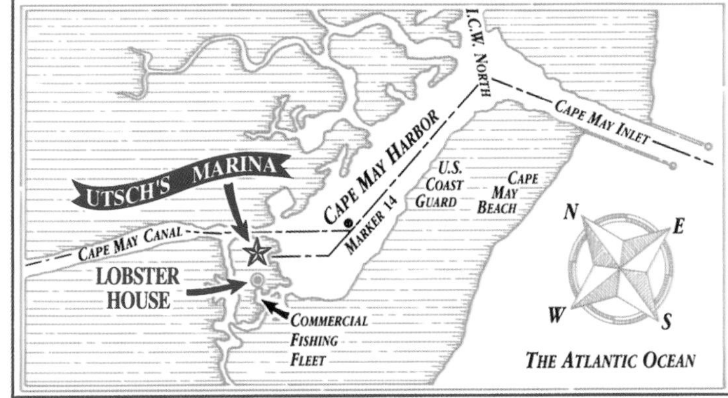

LOCATED BETWEEN CANAL AND SCHELLENGER'S LANDING

(609) 884-2051 www.capemayharbor.com

WE MONITOR CHANNEL 16 VHF

Discounts Available for Volume Fuel Purchases

We Love Sailboats!

Looking north-northwest into Cape May Inlet. (Not to be used for navigation.) WATERWAY GUIDE PHOTOGRAPHY

A taxi ride out to Cape May Point from the harbor brings you to the terminus of an important Indian trail. From here, the Indians took off to hunt whales in Delaware Bay. The point is also important to ornithologists, as Delaware Bay is a natural barrier for birds migrating the East Coast Flyway. During the fall migration, land and sea birds funnel down the long cape and wait at the point until winds are favorable for crossing the bay. Before or after the long open-water crossing, some 360 species of birds stop and rest here. The New Jersey Audubon Society's Cape May Bird Observatory at Cape May Point (at the tip of the peninsula) provides bird-watching platforms and lectures, and the restored Cape May Lighthouse can be climbed for a small fee. The view from the top of the lighthouse includes the Atlantic Ocean, Delaware Bay and the tip of the Cape. On a clear day, Cape Henlopen, DE, is visible across the bay. Cape May Point park is located four miles from the harbor and is easily reached by bicycle or taxi.

Cape May is a good spot to rendezvous with guests and crew members. You can get express buses to Philadelphia and New York, and the local airport is served by scheduled airlines and charter planes.

ADDITIONAL RESOURCES:

- Cape May County Department of Tourism, **www.thejerseycape.net**
- Chamber of Commerce of Greater Cape May, 609-884-5508, **www.capemaychamber.com**

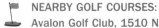

NEARBY GOLF COURSES:
Avalon Golf Club, 1510 N. Route Nine,
Cape May Court House, NJ 08210, 609-465-4653,
1-800-MID-IRON, **www.avalongolfclub.com**

NEARBY MEDICAL FACILITIES:
Cape Urgent Care: 900 Route 109
Cape May, NJ 08204 609-884-4357

Cape Regional Medical Center:
2 Stone Harbor Blvd.,
Cape May Court House, NJ 02810 609-463-2000

CAPE MAY TO STONE HARBOR

NAVIGATION: Use Chart 12316. Heading north up the New Jersey ICW, inside route, you will pass the Coast Guard installation to starboard, then Sewell Point, where the Cape May (Cold Spring) Inlet channel branches off to starboard and the New Jersey ICW heads to port.

The New Jersey ICW route between Cape May and Stone Harbor is protected, but boats drawing more than 4 feet will have to pay strict attention to the state of the tide. Between Cape May and Atlantic City (Mile 65), the controlling vertical clearance on the Waterway is 35 feet.

Wildwood

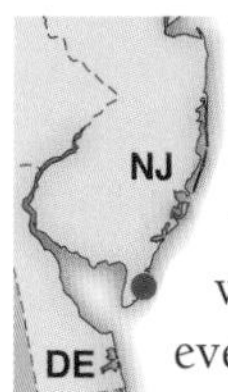

The New Jersey ICW route is easily followed to Wildwood, a beachfront resort town with a variety of attractions, including a beach boardwalk and several amusement parks. Visit www.wildwoodsnj.com for a monthly calendar of events. The Wetlands Institute is located near the Rio Grande Bridge in Stone Harbor and sponsors the two-day Wings 'n Water Festival every September. This festival is a "celebration of the coast" where maritime and wildlife artwork of internationally acclaimed painters, carvers, sculptors and photographers are present during the exhibition of their work. Check their Web site, www.wetlandsinstitute.org, for detailed event information at the institute.

NAVIGATION: Use Chart 12316. Use Atlantic City tide tables. For high tide, add 57 minutes; for low tide, add 1 hour 11 minutes. Shoaling was reported in July 2008 at green daybeacon "469," and green daybeacon "469A" was later added to further mark the shoal here. Shoaling has also been reported between green daybeacon "429" and red nun buoy "416", but the current (June 2008, Edition 34) chart shows 8- to 10-foot depths throughout. You will want to travel through this area with caution in case conditions have changed.

The North Wildwood Road Bascule Bridge at Mile 108 has been replaced with a fixed high-rise bridge with a 55-foot vertical clearance. The channel is shoaling on the south side of the channel from red daybeacon "452" to the bridge. Keep a sharp eye on the depth sounder when making the turn after clearing the bridge, even though the chart shows 5- to 7-foot depths in this area.

The Ocean Drive Bridge, between Stone Harbor and Nummy Island at Mile 104 (15-foot closed vertical clearance), leads to Hereford Inlet and requires four hour's notice for an opening at night (between 10 p.m. and 6 a.m.) during the season. During the off-season, Oct. 15 to May 15, it requires 24 hour's notice. Otherwise, it opens on signal. Do not attempt to travel from this bridge to the Atlantic Ocean through Hereford Inlet. Only skippers with the shallowest-draft vessels and current local knowledge (due to constantly shifting shoals) should attempt this passage. North of Wildwood, the New Jersey ICW heads away from Hereford Inlet, and shoaling can be expected at either end of Nummy Island.

Dockage: Schooner Island Marina, located on the Wildwood side of the Rio Grande Bridge (25-foot closed vertical clearance) near Ephraim Island, offers fuel and floating docks with water and electrical hookups at each slip. At last report, approach depths were 12 feet, with 8 feet at dockside.

Urie's Waterfront Restaurant and the Boathouse Restaurant and Marina Deck are close by and also have a few transient berths, but call ahead before heading in.

The Wildwood boardwalk is five blocks from the marinas and there are beautiful, wide, white sandy beaches a little farther on. With over two miles of arcade games, carousels, water parks and restaurants, Wildwood is a great family destination. There is a tram service that runs along the boardwalk from sunrise to sunset during the summer. The Doo Wop Trolley Tour is conducted in an old-fashioned trolley that runs all year through different routes around town.

Two blocks east of the marinas is a shopping area. Wildwood is known for its seafood restaurants and there is no shortage of them.

Anchorage: Wildwood has a good anchorage at Sunset Lake (Mile 110) that carries 5-foot depths at the entrance and holds deeper water inside. The current chart (June 2008, Edition 34) shows a shoal (3-foot depth) spot between flashing red "6" and flashing green "5." While heavily used, the anchorage affords privacy and easy access to nearby ocean beaches. Be aware that state markers in this area are removed in the winter.

Empty beach and boardwalk in Wildwood, NJ, against warm blue sky.

©IstockPhoto/fullvalue

Wildwood to Sea Isle City, NJ

WILDWOOD TO SEA ISLE CITY		Dockage					Supplies		Services					
		Largest Vessel Accommodated	VHF Channel Monitored	Transient Berths / Total Berths	Approach / Dockside Depth (reported)	Floating Docks	Gas / Diesel	Groceries, Ice, Marine Supplies, Snacks	Repairs: Hull, Engine, Propeller	Lift (tonnage), Crane, Rail	1=110V, 2=220V, B=Both, Max Amps	Laundry, Pool, Showers	Pump-Out Station	Nearby: Grocery Store, Motel, Restaurant
1. B & E Marine, A Virtual Boat Corp. 108.5	609-522-6440	35		5/60	5/5	F	G	IM	HEP	L25	1/30		P	GMR
2. Urie's Waterfront Restaurant 109	609-522-4189	65		10/10	10/6	F								GMR
3. Boathouse Restaurant & Marina Deck 109	609-729-5301	35		6/6	10/4	F					1/30			MR
4. Schooner Island Marina 109	609-729-8900	110	16/09	/300	12/8	F	GD	IMS	HEP	L60	B/50	LPS	P	GMR
5. Harry's Starcrest Marina	609-522-4132	25		/14	6/6	F	GD							GMR
6. Lighthouse Pointe Marina 109.5	609-729-2229	40	16/10	15/160	12/7	F		I			B/50	LS	P	GMR
7. Pier 47 Marina 109.5	609-729-4774	40		2/150	7/7	F	G	IMS	HEP	L10	B/50		P	GMR
8. Grassy Sound Marina 105.5	609-846-1400	30			16/6		G	IMS			1/50		P	MR
9. Stone Harbor Marina 102.5	609-368-1141	50	09	/186	4/4	F	GD	I	E	L	B/50	LS	P	GMR
10. Smugglers Cove 102	609-368-1700	60	68		6/6	F	GD	IMS			1/30			GMR
11. Camp Marine Services 101	609-368-1777	45		2/30	4/8	F			HEP	L30,C1			P	GMR
12. Avalon Pointe Marina Inc. 97	609-967-4100	100	16/09	8/100	10/10	F	GD	IMS	HEP	L70,C	B/50	S	P	GMR
13. Avalon Anchorage Marina 97	609-967-3592	38		/36	10/8	F	GD	IMS	HEP		1/30			R
14. Commodore Bay Marina 96.5	609-967-4448	88	16/72	10/110	6/10	F	GD	GI			B/50	LS		GMR
15. Minmar Marine & Boat Sales 93.5	609-263-2201	40	16/68	0/115	5/4	F	G	IMS	HEP	L30	1/30	S	P	GMR

Corresponding chart(s) not to be used for navigation. Internet Access   Wireless Internet Access

Stone Harbor

The New Jersey ICW route runs behind the barrier beach of this popular resort area. Stone Harbor has its own bird sanctuary, the only heron rookery located within a city. Both herons and egrets nest here, and bird-watchers come in late summer and early fall to watch these and other species that stop off during their migrations. There are many good seafood restaurants and beachfront activities. For current information about Stone Harbor, visit www.stone-harbor.nj.us or www.stoneharborbeach.com.

NAVIGATION: Use Chart 12316. Use Atlantic City tide tables. For high tide, add 1 hour 1 minute; for low tide, add 1 hour 12 minutes. The depths at Stone Harbor are generally good, and cruising boat amenities are more than adequate. The bascule bridge (Stone Harbor Boulevard, 10-foot closed vertical clearance, Mile 102) has restricted openings on weekends and holidays from Memorial Day to Labor Day. During this period the span opens every 20 minutes starting on the hour, between 6 a.m. and 6 p.m. The bridge periodically undergoes repairs and can be very slow, so use caution as you pass. Bridges in this area monitor VHF Channel 13.

■ GULL ISLAND THOROFARE TO OCEAN CITY, NJ

The New Jersey ICW route swings away from the barrier beach through Gull Island Thorofare (beginning at Mile 101), and then crosses Great Sound and wiggles its way through Ingram Thorofare.

NAVIGATION: Use Chart 12316. A fixed bridge (35-foot fixed vertical clearance) crosses the channel at Mile 98. The current (June 2008, Edition 34) chart shows shoaling just north of the bridge on the starboard side and again on port before the Townsends Inlet bridge immediately after red nun buoy "374." After passing Townsends Inlet, the route runs through twists and turns before crossing Ludlam Bay.

Shoal Spots: At this writing, the current chart (June 2008, Edition 34) shows several shoal areas along Ludlam Thorofare. Use special caution in this area. Great Sound and Ludlam Bay are extremely shallow outside the narrow channel (especially from flashing green "349" to quick flashing red "346") and some shoaling has been reported at the junction of Ben Hands Thorofare and Main Channel in the Devils Island Passage; use caution in these areas.

Inlets: Hereford, Townsends and Corson inlets are all given to shoaling. Hereford Inlet and Corson Inlet are unbuoyed and filled with breakers. They should not be used under any circumstances. In fact, at low tide, a sandbar known locally as "Champagne Island" has formed across Hereford Inlet.

To enter Townsends Inlet from the ocean, head southwest from the sea buoy, although you might have difficulty seeing the flashing red "4A" buoy from the sea. The channel is marked by red-and-white mid-channel markers and runs as close as 100 yards off Avalon Beach in some places. Best water can be found to the seaward side of the markers, which are uncharted, as they are changed frequently. The local Coast Guard station is only manned from spring until early fall, so transit this area carefully. A swift current often runs in the inlet, at the inlet bridge and in the ICW beyond.

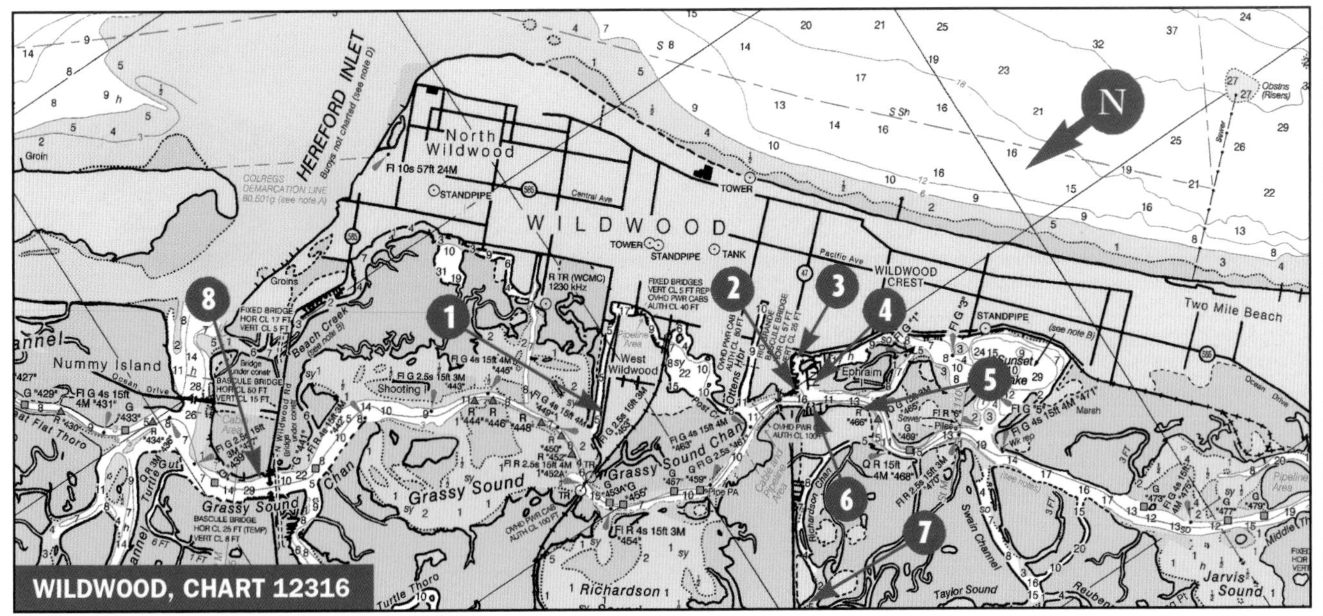

WILDWOOD, CHART 12316

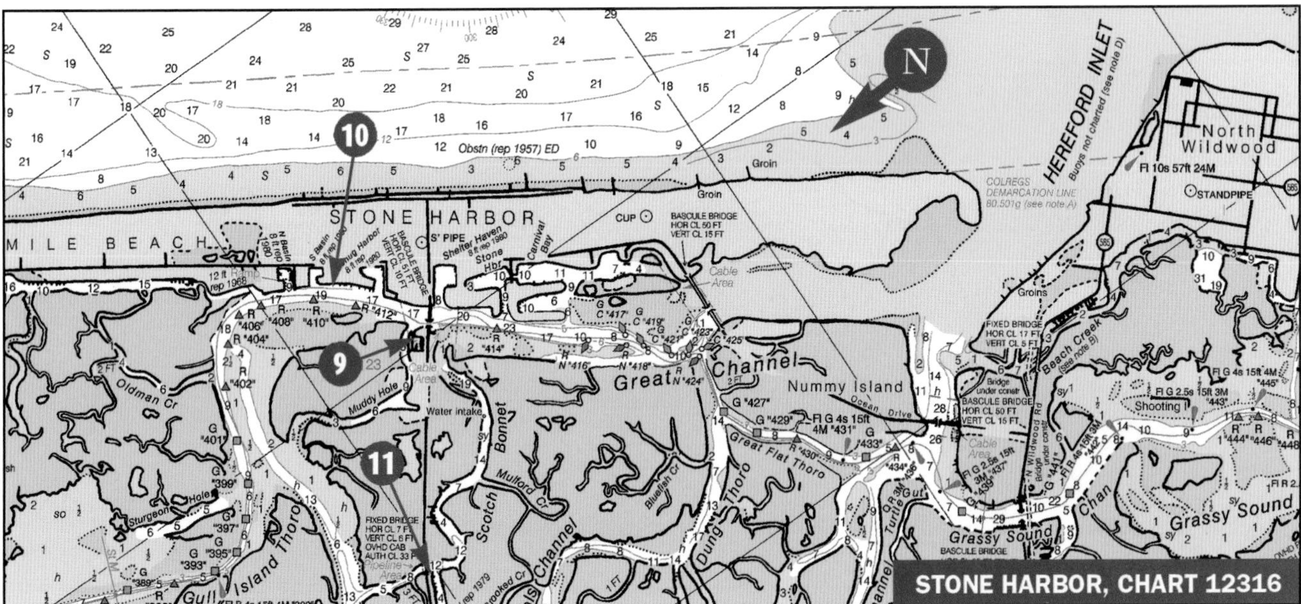

STONE HARBOR, CHART 12316

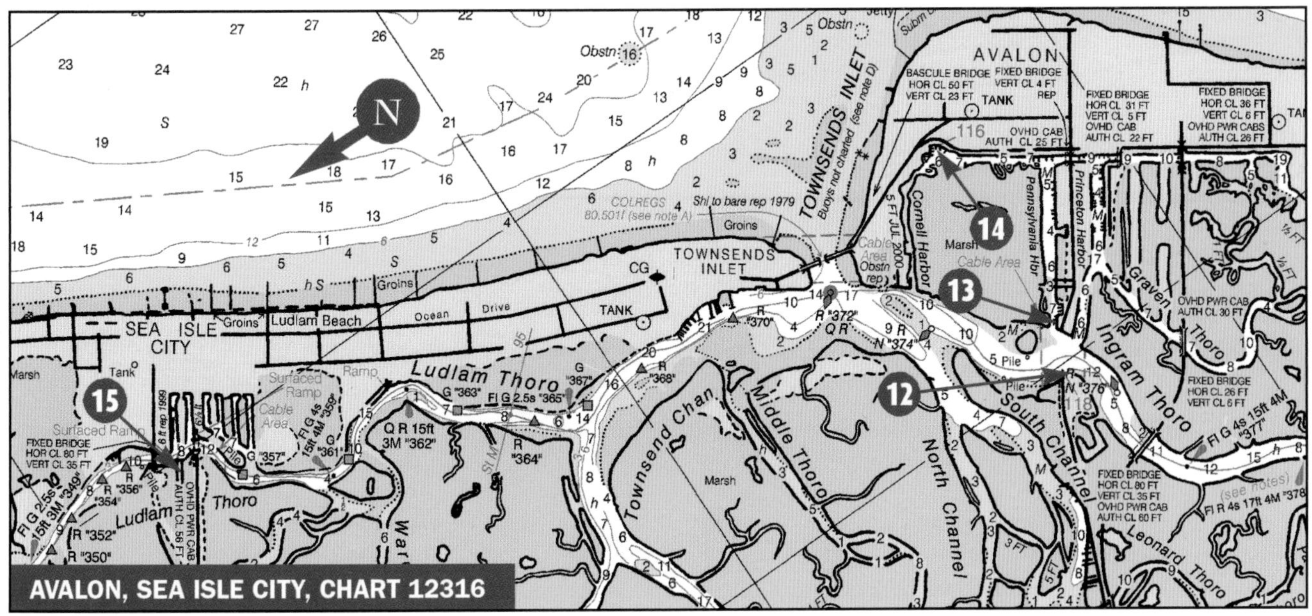

AVALON, SEA ISLE CITY, CHART 12316

CHAPTER 1

CAPE MAY TO BARNEGAT BAY

Great Egg Harbor, Ocean City Area, NJ

GREAT EGG HARBOR, OCEAN CITY AREA		Largest Vessel Accommodated	VHF Channel Monitored	Transient Berths / Total Berths	Approach / Dockside Depth (reported)	Floating Docks	Gas / Diesel	Groceries, Ice, Marine Supplies, Snacks	Repairs: Hull, Engine, Propeller	Lift (tonnage), Crane, Rail	1=110V, 2=220V, B=Both, Max Amps	Laundry, Pool, Showers	Pump-Out Station	Nearby: Grocery Store, Motel, Restaurant
		Dockage					Supplies		Services					
1. Thompson Marine & Engine	609-927-2415	50	16/68	/6	7/7		G	M	HEP	L40	1/30		P	
2. Bay Club Marina-Ocean City 79.5	609-398-4100	50		5/36	12/5	F					B/50			GMR
3. Somers Point Marina 1NW of 79	609-927-5900	30	16/68	/75	18/4	F		IMS	HEP	L6		S	P	GMR
4. Graef Boat Yard 1NW of 79	609-927-2205	50		/60	6/6	F		IM	HEP	L40	B/50			GMR
5. Harbor Cove Marina 1NW of 79	609-927-9600	30		/70	4/4	F		IMS	HEP	L35				MR
6. Seaview Harbor Marina 76	609-823-2626	125	10	25/300	10/7	F	GD	IMS			B/50	LPS	P	R
7. Captain Andy's Fishing Center 74.5	609-822-0916	60	16/68	/11	20/20		GD	IMS					P	GR
8. Sea Village Marina 2NW of 76	609-641-2699	42		1/75	5/3	F			HEP		1/50	LPS	P	M
9. All Seasons Marina 84.5	609-390-1850	50	16	/475	8/4.5	F	GD	IMS	HEP	L35	B/50	LS	P	GMR

Corresponding chart(s) not to be used for navigation. Internet Access WiFi Wireless Internet Access

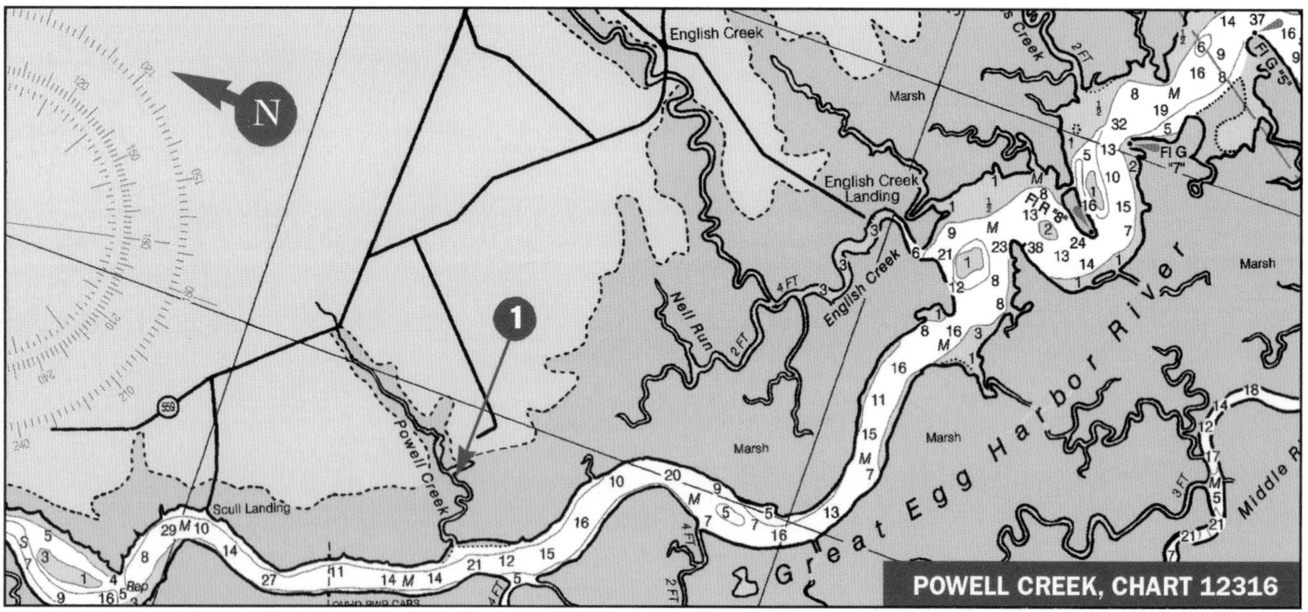

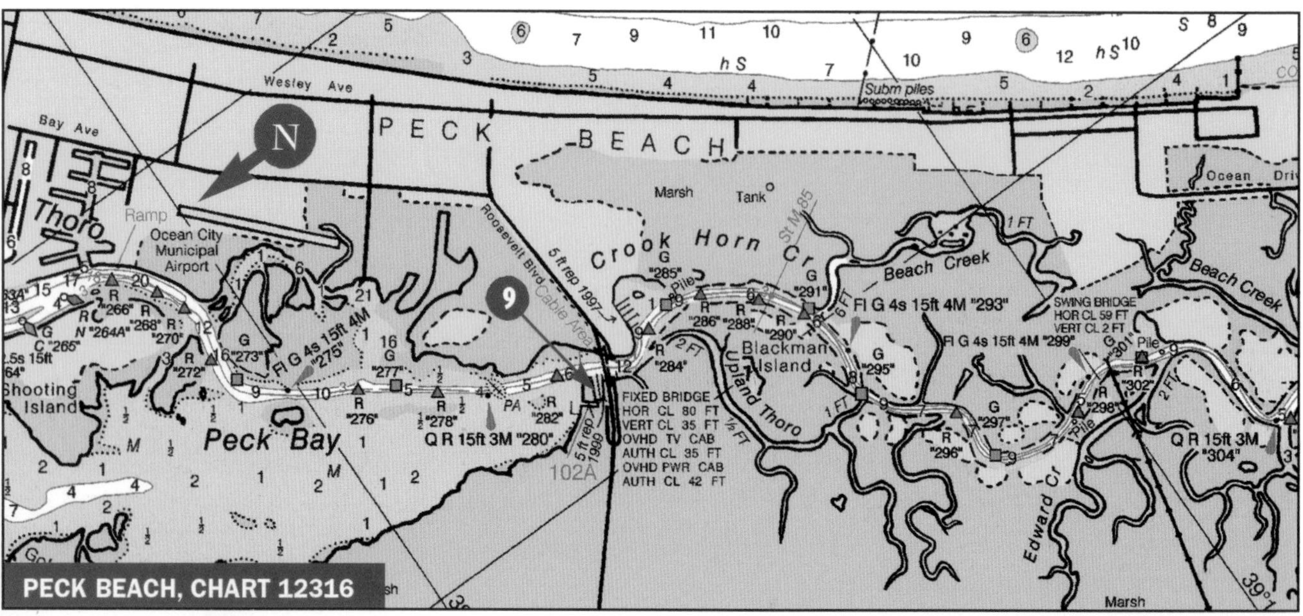

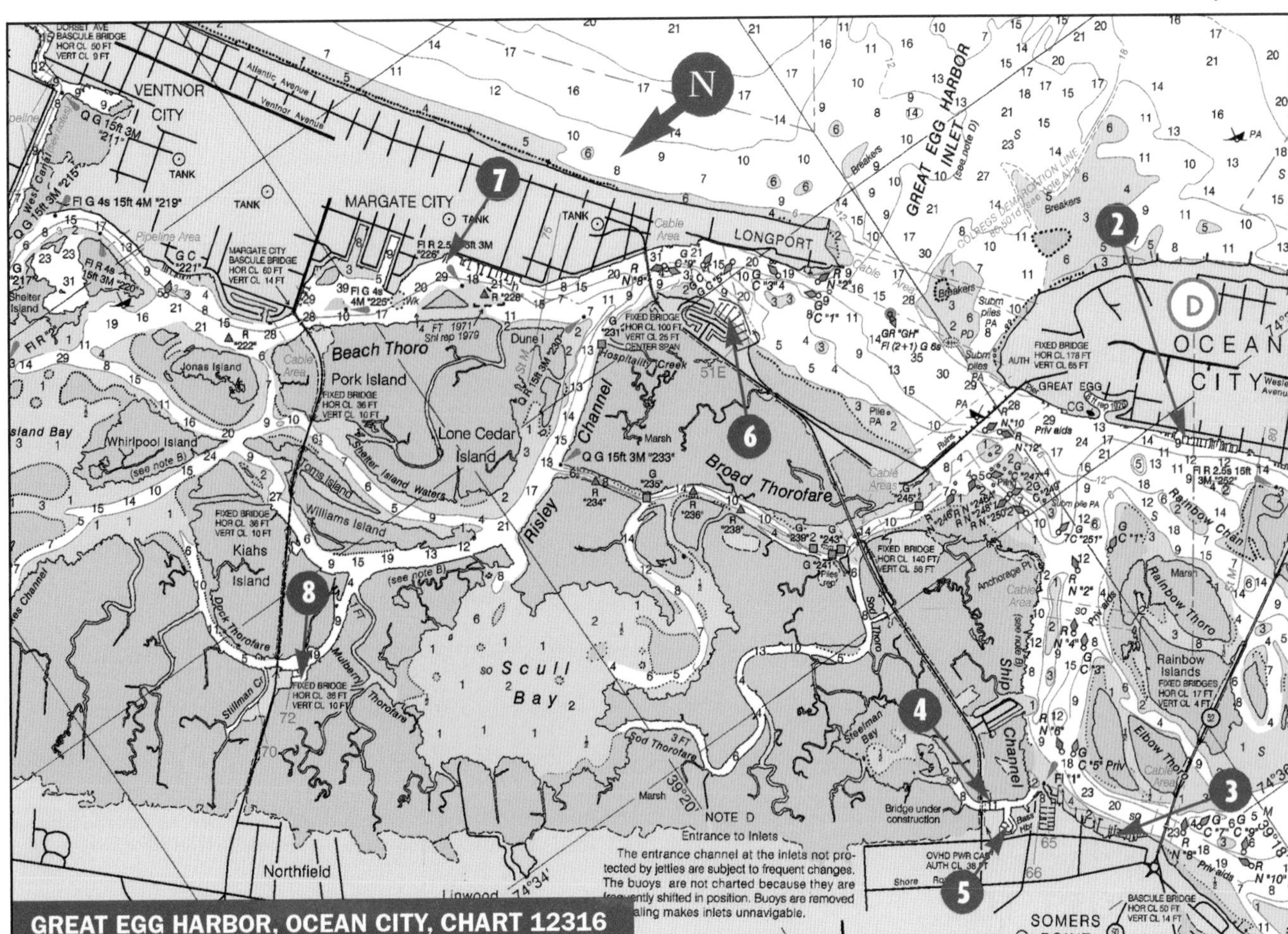

GREAT EGG HARBOR, OCEAN CITY, CHART 12316

Dockage: Avalon Pointe Marina (near red nun buoy "376") is a full-service facility, welcomes transients and offers fuel, floating docks, 25- to 75-ton lifts and all repairs.

Commodore Bay Marina, located in a quiet protected lagoon off Cornell Harbor at red nun buoy "374," south of the Townsends Inlet Bridge, has deepwater slips for boats up to 85 feet with full amenities. Several marinas are located just north of the 35-foot fixed vertical clearance bridge at Mile 85, which spans the lower end of Peck Bay at Crook Horn Creek. Call ahead to make reservations at any of these marinas on summer weekends, as docks can be especially crowded.

Ocean City—Mile 90

The resort town of Ocean City is set between the Atlantic Ocean, Great Egg Harbor Inlet and Great Egg Harbor Bay, with elegant homes and a splendid beach. Docks run side-by-side along the New Jersey ICW route, on the city waterfront and also across the harbor off the New Jersey ICW in Somers Point.

Ocean City is a good takeoff point for one of the New Jersey ICW's most attractive side cruises. The route runs along an unspoiled wilderness river, unknown even to many resident mariners. Meandering west from Great Egg Harbor Bay, Great Egg Harbor River is safe and well-marked, with deep cedar-stained waters and marshy pine-lined banks that offer a glimpse of the unspoiled New Jersey of old.

NAVIGATION: Use Chart 12316. Use Atlantic City tide tables. For high tide, add 1 hour; for low tide, add 1 hour 37 minutes. The Ninth Street Bascule Bridge (14-foot closed vertical clearance) has restricted openings on weekends and holidays between Memorial Day and Labor Day. During these times, the bridge opens on the hour and half-hour from 11 a.m. to 5 p.m. At all other times the bridge opens on signal.

A shoaling problem exists ahead of the Broad Thorofare Channel before you reach the Great Egg Harbor Inlet Bascule Bridge. DANGER SHOALING AHEAD signs have been posted on the markers. Check the latest edition of NOAA Chart 12316 and keep a close watch on the depth sounder in this area. Continual shoaling to 1-foot depths has been reported between quick flashing red "262" and red daybeacon "266" since July 2008 (note the long shoal on the chart).

Dockage: Heading northwest after clearing the Ninth Street Bascule Bridge along Ship Channel, numerous marinas are located at picturesque Somers Point. However, finding a transient slip may be difficult. Just before and just after Risley Channel, you might try Seaview Harbor Marina or Captain Andy's Fishing Center, but call ahead to inquire about availability first. See our marina listing tables for more details.

A northwest view into Absecon Inlet with Atlantic City visible to the left. (Not to be used for navigation.) WATERWAY GUIDE PHOTOGRAPHY

LONGPORT TO ATLANTIC CITY

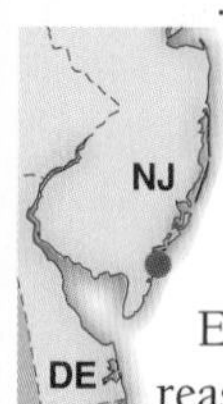

In pleasant weather, most skippers prefer to run outside from Ocean City to its companion resort, Atlantic City. It is only eight statute miles between sea buoys, and Ocean City's Great Egg Harbor Inlet is generally safe for passage in reasonable weather.

NAVIGATION: Use Chart 12316. Depths in Great Egg Harbor Inlet shift frequently and buoys are moved accordingly, so reliable local information is a must if you plan to try the inlet.

When entering Great Egg Harbor Inlet from the ocean, locating the first entrance buoy west of the sea buoy might be difficult, especially in heavy seas. The best approach is from the ocean side of the Great Egg buoy to red-and-white Morse (A) buoy "GE." Breakers might be prevalent because of frequent shoaling near red-and-white Morse (A) buoy "GE." Once this buoy has been sighted, stay close to the red-and-white center-channel entrance buoys—they are easy to spot. The Great Egg Harbor Inlet Bridge (56-foot charted fixed vertical clearance, charted at 65 feet) crosses the southwestern end of the inlet at Ocean City.

Inside Passage

Protected from gales and free of the small-boat fishing fleets, this is the route to take in heavy weather.

NAVIGATION: Use Chart 12316. Easterly winds in the summer raise tides for better channel depths, but spring and fall northwesterlies blow the water out to sea, making the New Jersey ICW channel even shallower. Make the passage only on a rising tide, and try to get local advice, as depths as shallow as 4 feet have been reported in some spots. Overhead controlling vertical clearance is set by the 35-foot fixed bridge at Mile 69. Note: A number of lighted daybeacons and special ice-proof markers have been installed along the northern sections of the New Jersey ICW; they may not coincide with the numbers on your chart.

North of Ocean City, the channel swings away from Great Egg Harbor Inlet, runs along Broad Thorofare, makes a right-angle turn into Risley Channel, and then takes a turn to port of about 120 degrees on Beach Thorofare past the resort of Margate City. At Mile 68.9 on Beach Thorofare is an Amtrak railroad swing bridge with a 5-foot closed vertical clearance. Plans are underway to remove the bridge tender and have the bridge operated remotely from Amtrak's Philadelphia dispatcher's office. Part of this proposal includes extending the bridge's wintertime non-operational periods into April. A high, arching fixed bridge (56-foot vertical clearance) crosses Broad Thorofare, just north of Ocean City and Great Egg Harbor Inlet at Mile 78. The remains of the old bascule bridge are now a fishing pier.

An alternate route runs across Great Egg Harbor Inlet (beginning at Mile 79) and joins the ICW again at Mile 75 at Longport. But to use this route, you must be able to clear a 25-foot fixed bridge at Mile 75.5. Be aware that after passing green and red buoy "GH," red markers will be to starboard until rejoining the New Jersey ICW beyond the fixed 25-foot vertical clearance bridge. Currents are very strong as you cross the inlet, so do not try this route in easterly winds.

The channel between Margate and Ventnor is generally deep and clear, but mind the strong currents that flow in this area between Great Egg Harbor and Absecon inlets. The Margate City bascule opens on signal.

Dockage: Facilities along the New Jersey ICW route to Atlantic City can be found at Longport, Margate City and Ventnor City. If you stop in Margate City, check out Lucy the Elephant, a local landmark with a colorful past. The 65-foot-high structure was built in 1881 as a tavern and inn. Today, the huge belly of the elephant houses a museum of local memorabilia.

Atlantic City—Mile 65

Long renowned for its classic boardwalk, wide sandy beaches, imposing piers and beachfront hotels, Atlantic City is now famous as a gambling colossus. The town is less well known for its all-weather inlet from the Atlantic Ocean and its secure harbor along a considerable and relatively uninterrupted stretch of New Jersey coastline.

The lights of Atlantic City are visible for 20 miles north or south on an offshore approach. Pay attention to the position of the entrance buoys if approaching in the dark, as they can be obscured in the background lighting of the casinos. This lighted backdrop, and others along the New Jersey shoreline, proved to be particularly hazardous to commercial shipping during World War II. German U-Boats would lay offshore at night and fire torpedoes at freighter traffic, which was conveniently—and fatally—silhouetted against the bright shoreline.

NAVIGATION: Use Chart 12316. Use Atlantic City tide tables. Atlantic City is easily approached from either the New Jersey ICW or the Atlantic Ocean, via Absecon Inlet. From the south, the ICW channel leaves Inside Thorofare and enters Beach Thorofare to swing in a wide semicircle behind the city. To reach most of the local marinas, repair yards and other marine facilities, you must head toward the ocean, under the fixed highway bridge (60-foot vertical clearance). Thereafter, enter Clam Creek in front of the U.S. Coast Guard station. Favor the ocean side of the channel as you make your way through the entrance, especially rounding red nun buoy "2," which marks a 5-foot (or less) shoal.

The ocean approach through Absecon Inlet is easy, though it can be a rollicking ride when a southerly wind is up. Hundreds of boats make the passage daily in all but the worst conditions. Enter from the sea buoy two miles offshore and honor the approach buoys to stay clear of the bar reaching toward the ocean along the northerly side of the channel. Channel depths are well-maintained to provide easy access to all but the largest commercial vessels. Follow the seaward buoy line into the very wide channel. Flashing green "7" has been removed from the end of the breakwater on the south entrance. There are also several permanent additions and a number of aids have been moved temporarily. As with all inlets, the buoys and markers can be moved often to reflect changing conditions; an up-to-date chart and Local Notice to Mariners (www.navcen.uscg.gov/lnm) are a must when entering any of the inlets along the New Jersey coast.

Dockage: Cruisers arriving in Atlantic City have several marina choices. The largest is the Senator Frank Farley State Marina (also known as the Trump or State Marina), situated on the west side of Clam Creek Basin, adjacent to the Trump Hotel Casino. This is a full-service marina with many transient slips. Reservations are a good idea, as the marina is often busy.

Other marinas and haul-out facilities are situated on the easterly side of Clam Creek Basin. Historic Gardner's Basin, the city marina, is located at the entrance to Gardner Basin, the first of three blind inlets leading east from Clam Creek Basin. The marina may have transient slips available with depths of up to 6 feet. Engines Inc., also located in Gardner Basin, offers a range of repair and refit services by its factory-trained mechanics. The city's dinghy dock is located here for those anchored out.

Kammerman's Atlantic City Marina, at the entrance to the second inlet from Clam Creek Basin, across from the Coast Guard station, offers transient slips with depths of up to 5.5 feet at mean low water. Kammerman's has the

Atlantic City, Mullica River, NJ

ATLANTIC CITY, MULLICA RIVER		Largest Vessel Accommodated	VHF Channel Monitored	Transient Berths / Total Berths	Approach / Dockside Depth (reported)	Floating Docks	Gas / Diesel	Groceries, Ice, Marine Supplies, Snacks	Repairs: Hull, Engine, Propeller	Lift (tonnage), Crane, Rail	1=110V, 2=220V, B=Both, Max Amps	Laundry, Pool, Showers	Pump-Out Station	Nearby: Grocery Store, Motel, Restaurant
		Dockage					Supplies		Services					
1. Senator Frank S. Farley State Marina 1S of 65 (Internet Access)	800-876-4386	300	/65	150/640	12/8	F	GD	GIMS			B/100	LPS	P	GMR
2. Gilchrist Restaurant 1S of 65	609-345-8278	65		3/3	20/35	F								R
3. Kammerman's Atlantic City Marina 1S of 65 (Wireless Internet Access)	**609-348-8418**	**150**	**16**	**8/15**	**9/9**	**F**	**GD**	**IMS**	**P**		**1/50**	**LS**	**P**	**GMR**
4. A. C. Wescoat Co. 1S of 65 (Internet Access)	609-345-1974	60			10/7	F		I	HP	L60,C	1/50			R
5. Engines Inc. 1S of 65	800-348-0083								E					
6. Historic Gardner's Basin 1S of 65 (Internet Access)	609-348-2880	50	09	10/45	12/6	F		I			B/30		P	MR
7. Nacote Creek Marina	609-652-9070	50		2/46	10/5	F	G	IM	HEP	L20	1/30		P	GMR
8. Viking Yachting Center	609-296-2388	52	16/72	14/248	10/10	F	GD	I	HEP	L60	B/30	PS	P	GMR
9. Chestnut Neck Boat Yard	609-652-1119	25		/42	30/35	F	GD	IMS	HEP	L25	1/30		P	GMR
10. Great Bay Marina	609-296-2392	43		2/139	4/4.5	F	GD	IMS	HEP	L20	1/30	S	P	

Corresponding chart(s) not to be used for navigation. Internet Access · Wireless Internet Access

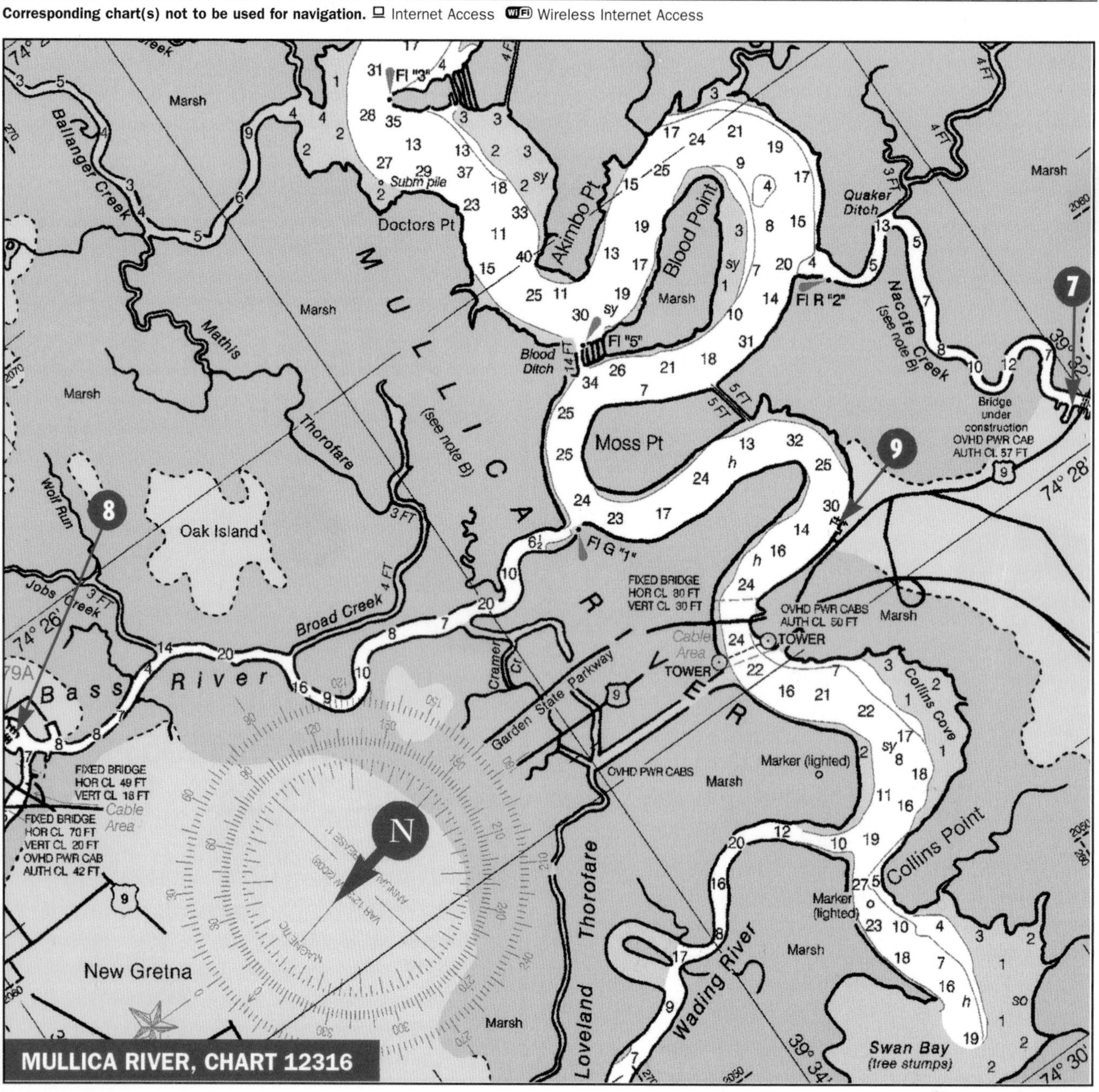

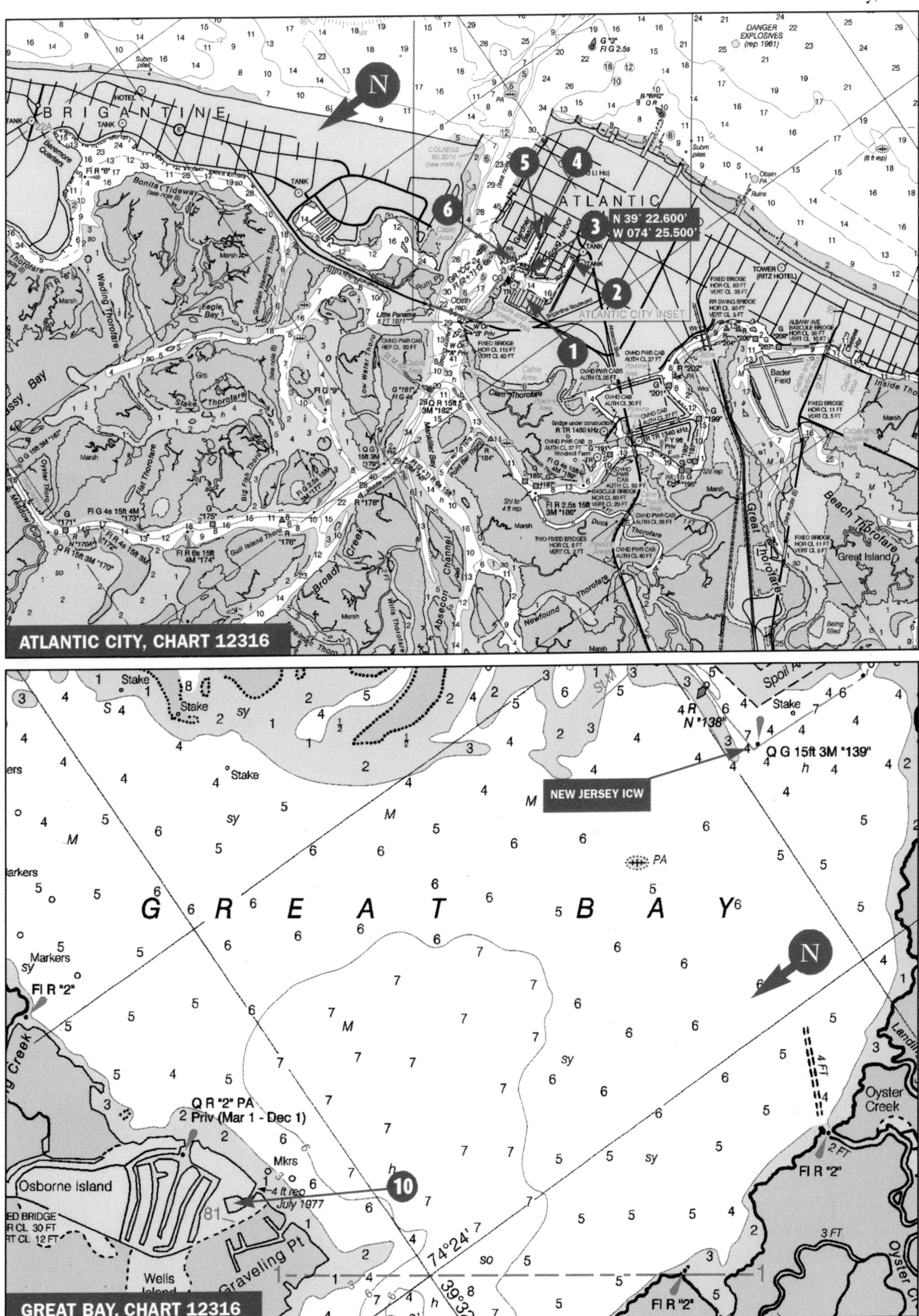
BRIGANTINE
ATLANTIC
N 39° 22.600'
W 074° 25.500'
ATLANTIC CITY INSET
Great Island
NEW JERSEY ICW
Q G 15ft 3M "139"
GREAT BAY
Fl R "2"
Q R "2" PA
Priv (Mar 1 - Dec 1)
Osborne Island
Oyster Creek
Graveling Pt
4 ft rep
July 1977
ATLANTIC CITY, CHART 12316
GREAT BAY, CHART 12316

largest fuel dock in the city (with 10-foot approach depths) and can arrange for repairs and other marine services with local subcontractors. It has restrooms and showers available to patrons, and the Atlantic City Boardwalk is just a short cab ride away.

Anchorage: The Coast Guard no longer permits anchoring in Clam Creek Basin. However, there is a substantial anchorage area south of the highway bridge in 8 to 22 feet of water with good holding. Take care to honor red nun buoy "2" at the mouth to Clam Creek Basin and green can buoy "13," as there is a shoal to the west of the line joining them. Proceed north of green can buoy "13" before turning into the anchorage. Expect challenging currents and a 5-foot tidal range in calculating appropriate scope. From there it will be a dinghy ride of about a half a mile to the basin, where a dinghy landing is available at the city marina in Gardner Basin.

GOIN' ASHORE: **ATLANTIC CITY, NJ**

One of the best cruising destinations on the New Jersey coast is Atlantic City. Whether you are planning a several-day stop or you need a place to get out of the weather, look no farther than this robust port that provides excellent shelter, full-service shoreside facilities, family recreation, great transportation, access to golf, a vast array of restaurants, boardwalk entertainment and beautiful views.

Atlantic City has been a tourist magnet since 1854, when Philadelphia speculators opened its railroad terminal. The boardwalk, built in 1870, was the first of its kind in the world. Today's boardwalk, which has been rebuilt over the years, stretches from Absecon Inlet southwest along four miles of spectacular beach. The beaches are lifeguard-patrolled from the inlet to the southern end. The boardwalk section, opposite the large casinos, has rides, restaurants and games of many types for the entire family.

During the Prohibition era and the Great Depression of the 1930s, the city became well known as a fast-paced party town, where contraband liquor, illegal gambling and other illicit activities were tolerated with a wink and a nod. But even the economics of spice and vice could not stem the city's post-World War II decline, as what was once trendy became tawdry. To counteract this decline, the city's fathers took the bold step of legalizing gambling in 1976, reestablishing the town as something of a "Las Vegas East." Today mammoth casino-hotel palaces dominate the city's economics as well as its blazing skyline, the latter having become the East Coast's most impressive all-night beacon for offshore cruisers.

For those wishing to try their hands at various wheels of fortune, the casinos are there to tempt and oblige. For others, the boardwalk can still provide hours of people-watching. Beyond the boardwalk, walks on the hard-packed sand and a dip in the cooling surf are ever available in the summer. Most will want to sample the city's excellent restaurant selection. There are dozens to choose from, but several receive consistent recommendations from locals in the boating community. Angelo's Fairmount Tavern (2300 Fairmount Ave., 609-344-2439) is family-owned and homey, serving stick-to-your-ribs Italian specialties for more than 70 years. Try the lobster ravioli with lobster sauce or the mussels fra diavlo. The tavern sells its homemade wine by the gallon. The Knife and Fork Inn (Atlantic & Pacific Aves., 609-344-1133), one of Atlantic City's four-star restaurants, has set a benchmark for fine dining since 1912 and Dock's Oyster House (2405 Atlantic Ave., 609-345-0092), with its sensational raw bar, serves excellent seafood and has been run by the same family since 1897.

The Harborview Restaurant (609-441-2000), offering waterfront dining inside the Trump Marina Resort is also highly regarded and convenient to the marina.

Atlantic City is an excellent place to pick up or let off guests. Train service to New York has been reestablished. There is frequent bus service to major cities (Philadelphia, New York, Newark), and scheduled helicopters can take you to and from midtown Manhattan. Limousine service to the Philadelphia airport is available, and Atlantic City has a commuter airport right on the ICW where you can pull the boat up and pick up or drop off your crew. It is believed to be the oldest municipally owned airport in the world; in fact, the word "airport" was coined here.

There is always a convention or some kind of contest going on here, too. The Miss America pageant and the Baby Parade both began in Atlantic City. Some of the best-equipped sportfishermen on the coast converge on the city for fishing tournaments, and the sight of the fleet roaring abreast out the inlet is impressive.

Mariners should be aware that some areas of Atlantic City are deemed unsafe. Visitors should not walk indiscriminately along the dock areas. The north side of Clam Creek, with marinas, hotels and a Coast Guard station, is well-patrolled and yacht facilities are fenced and guarded, but it is unwise to walk through the surrounding neighborhoods after dark. Instead, take a cab to any restaurants or businesses outside the boardwalk/casino area.

ADDITIONAL RESOURCES:

- Atlantic City Convention and Visitors Authority, **www.atlanticcitynj.com**

NEARBY GOLF COURSES:
Atlantic City Country Club, 1 Leo Fraser Drive, Northfield, NJ 08225, 609-236-4401, **www.accountryclub.com**

NEARBY MEDICAL FACILITIES:
Atlantic City Medical Center, 1925 Pacific Ave., Atlantic City, NJ 08401, 609-344-4081, **www.atlanticare.org**

ABSECON INLET TO BARNEGAT BAY

NAVIGATION: Use Chart 12316. The New Jersey ICW shoals easily in the stretch between Absecon Inlet and Great Bay; sometimes birds stroll on the sandbars building out into the channel. Many daybeacons along this route have been replaced by buoys, which may not be indicated on the chart. If you draw more than 4 feet, be sure to go through on a rising tide (half tide or better).

At Mile 64, a seven-mile alternate route for shoal-draft boats parallels the barrier beach at Brigantine, then rejoins the ICW at Mile 60. Brigantine offers some services, but controlling depths for this route are only 3 feet.

From just past Shad Island through Main Marsh Thorofare, the New Jersey ICW runs through the middle of the Brigantine National Wildlife Refuge. Do not wander away from the magenta line on your chart; shoals are close on both sides. The best way to observe the amazing variety of bird life in the refuge is by small boat or dinghy to explore the creeks and passages away from the ICW. The fall migrations are spectacular, but it can be extremely buggy in this area during the summer months.

Great Bay

NAVIGATION: Use Chart 12316. The stretch from Mile 59 at green daybeacon "157" to Mile 56 at flashing green "141," which leads into Great Bay, is subject to shoaling and must be traversed with great care. Shoaling to less than 3-foot depths has been reported in this area.

Stick dead on course when crossing Great Bay, which is extremely shallow. The bottom builds up every spring from the continuous sweep of inlet waters, so you should try to run this area on a rising tide. Although the channel is dredged nearly every year, this stretch will always suffer from shifting sands and uncertain depths.

At the northwest corner of Great Bay, the deep, winding Mullica River snakes its way west into the Pine Barrens. Three miles up the Mullica River, 14-foot-deep Blood Ditch Cut bypasses a nearly 2.5-mile-long loop in the river. Just beyond is the entrance to the deep Bass River, which leads north and is navigable to the town of New Gretna, home of the Viking Yacht Company, as well as numerous marinas and marine services. It is also a good hurricane hole.

Stay in mid-channel when passing to the west of Tow Island (Mile 53). Despite constant dredging, this area has a continuous shoaling problem. Underpowered auxiliaries with deep drafts should transit this area on a rising tide.

After rounding quick flashing red buoy "120" to port, watch very carefully for the next pair of daybeacons and favor the port side, due to possible shoaling from Tuckers Island to starboard. Prudence must prevail where the New Jersey ICW route crosses the twin inlets, Beach Haven and Little Egg, between Mile 55 and Mile 50. The ocean swells carry inside to break on shoal spots, but with care you can make the crossing in all but the worst weather conditions.

Prepare in advance to sort out the confusion of inlet and side-channel markers near Mile 50. The buoyed Marshelder Channel, which leads into Little Egg Harbor, can easily be mistaken for the New Jersey ICW. Check the buoy numbers before committing to a course. The magenta line denoting the New Jersey ICW leads directly across a shoal area. Depths here at dead low tide can be

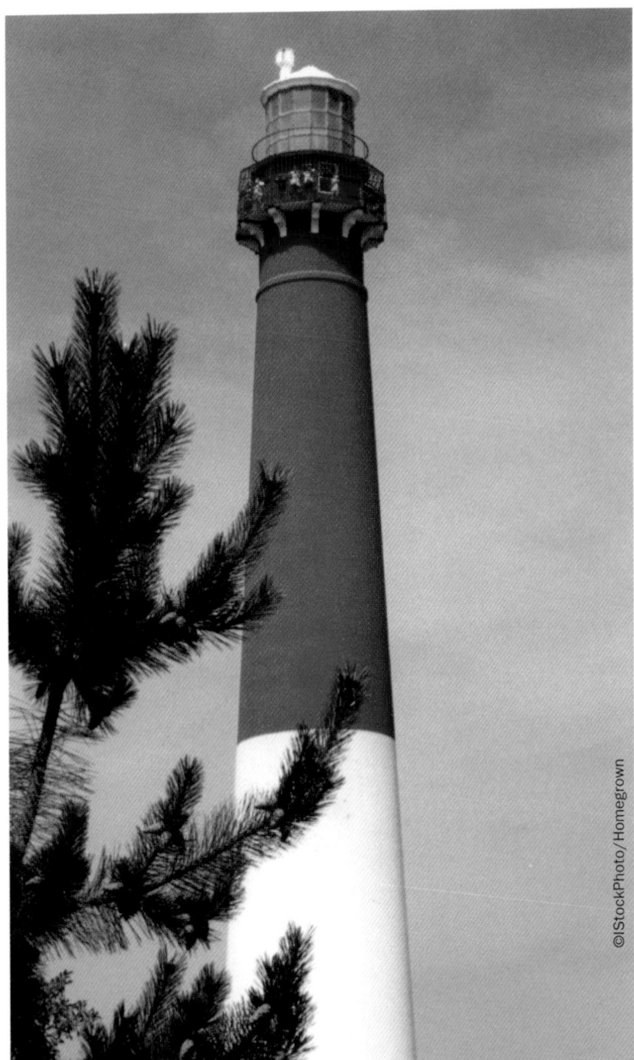

Barnegat Lighthouse (affectionately referred to as "Old Barney" by the locals) in Barnegat, NJ, standing 165-feet above sea level, is the second tallest lighthouse in the United States.

3 to 4 feet. Buoy numbering will generally conform to an up-to-date chart, but location might be quite different, as the Coast Guard is constantly moving buoys to keep up with the changing conditions.

Anchorage: Storm waves and day-to-day currents along shore and through the inlets make and unmake anchorages, and those you knew at one time should be approached carefully before trying them again. Shoal-draft boats will find good holding and shelter from southerly and westerly winds in Great Bay, a useful settled weather anchorage.

The old Coast Guard station in Shooting Thorofare (charted as "cupola") is now the Marine Science Center of Rutgers University's Center for Coastal and Environmental Studies. Skippers seeking a safe refuge when weather is rough around the inlets have often used this basin as a storm haven, but note that the sill to the basin has built up. Low-tide depths are minimal, so it is best to go in at high tide. There are usually good depths north of Hatfield Point in Newmans Thorofare, but be aware of submerged pilings between Hatfield Point and Fish Island.

Beach Haven to Surf City, NJ

BEACH HAVEN TO SURF CITY		Largest Vessel Accommodated	VHF Channel Monitored	Transient Berths / Total Berths	Approach / Dockside Depth (reported)	Floating Docks	Gas / Diesel	Groceries, Ice, Marine Supplies, Snacks	Repairs: Hull, Engine, Propeller	Lift (tonnage), Crane, Rail	1=110V, 2=220V, B=Both, Max Amps	Laundry, Pool, Showers	Pump-Out Station	Nearby: Grocery Store, Motel, Restaurant
		Dockage					Supplies		Services					
1. Tuckerton Marine	609-296-1820	40	16	5/60	5/8	F	GD	IM	HE		B/50	S	P	MR
2. Sheltered Cove Marina	609-296-9400	50	09	20/250	5/8	F	GD	IM	HEP	C	1/50	S	P	GR
3. Little Egg Harbor Yacht Club 45.5	609-492-2529	40			8/4						1/30	S		R
4. Beach Haven Yacht Club Marina 45.5 (WiFi)	**609-492-9101**	**80**	**16**	**10/60**	**8/8**		**GD**	**IS**			**B/50**	**LS**	**P**	**GMR**
5. Morrison's Beach Haven Marina 45.4	609-492-2150	60	68	4/130	5/5	F	GD	IM	EP	L30	B/50	S	P	GMR
6. Shelter Harbor Marina 48.8	609-492-8645	40	16	2/206	7/7	F					B/50	LPS	P	GMR
7. Eastern Marine 44.6	609-492-1118	42	16	4/35	8/4	F		IM	HEP	L35	B/30	S	P	GMR
8. Escape Harbor Marina 44	609-492-9108	40		/70	4/4					L4	1/30	LS		GMR
9. Southwick's Marina 44	609-492-5191	30	09	/90	3/5		G	IM	HEP	L6,C	1/20	S	P	GMR
10. Hagler's Marina 40	609-494-4509	30		10/70	3/4	F	G	IM	HEP			S		GMR
11. Hochstrasser's Marina 2NE of 40	609-494-5340	30		3/65	17/10		G	M	HEP	C	1/20			GMR

Corresponding chart(s) not to be used for navigation. Internet Access (WiFi) Wireless Internet Access

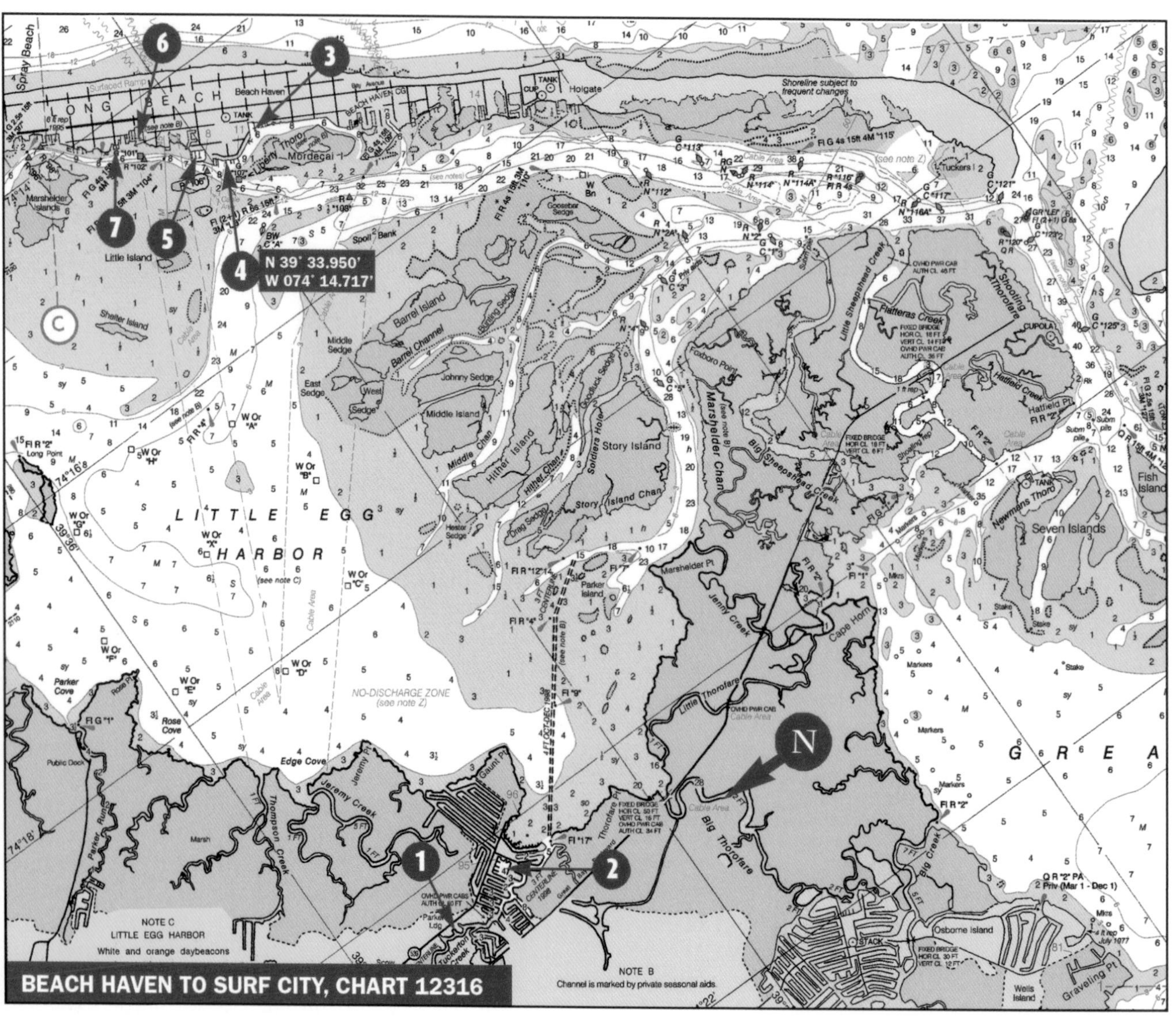

BEACH HAVEN TO SURF CITY, CHART 12316

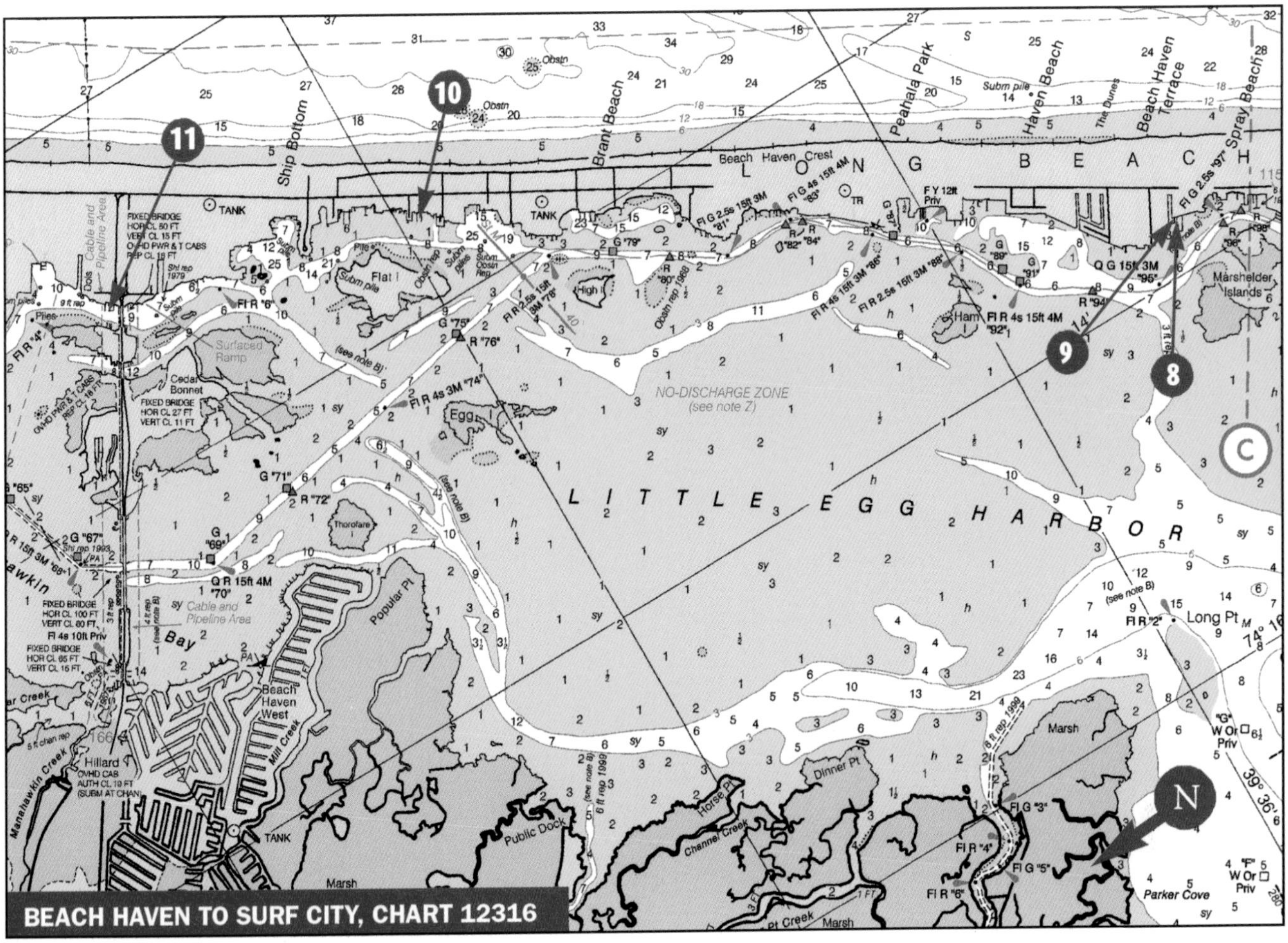

BEACH HAVEN TO SURF CITY, CHART 12316

Beach Haven Inlet, Little Egg Inlet

NAVIGATION: Use Charts 12316 and 12324. Use Sandy Hook tide tables. For high tide, add 16 minutes; for low tide, add 18 minutes. North of the twin inlets, the Waterway route passes behind aptly named Long Beach Island. At about Mile 40, at flashing red "78," a channel branches off to starboard from the New Jersey ICW. Boats with less than 15 feet overhead clearance prefer to leave the New Jersey ICW here and follow this channel along Long Beach Island, rejoining the New Jersey ICW at quick flashing red "62." On the beachside there is a cove with charted depths of 12 to 25 feet with room for four to six cruising boats.

Little Egg Inlet is well-marked with center-channel buoys (vertical red and white stripes) with sequential letters that start with "A" at the ocean end of this two-mile-long channel, and end at its junction with the ICW. The buoys here are uncharted. When progressing from one buoy to the next, scan for dogleg turns in the channel, which can easily be missed. These turns can position your vessel broadside or stern to breaking seas in unsettled weather. An easterly or southeasterly wind against a falling tide can produce serious wave action, which can obscure the buoys and create difficult steering conditions.

Beach Haven Area

NAVIGATION: Use Charts 12316 and 12324. Use Sandy Hook tide tables. For high tide, add 1 hour 18 minutes; for low tide, add 1 hour 23 minutes. North of the twin inlets, the New Jersey ICW route passes behind aptly named Long Beach Island. At about Mile 46, a channel heads off to starboard across Little Egg Harbor toward the village of Tuckerton. Leave flashing red "LB" to starboard and keep a watch for black and white can buoy "A," which marks a shoal to port. Another channel leads to the village from Mile 50, which is somewhat better marked. The nation's first Customs house was built at Tuckerton, and one is still there today.

You can bypass Little Egg Harbor by sticking to the New Jersey ICW channel running close along Long Beach. Beach Haven, Spray Beach, Ship Bottom and Surf City are

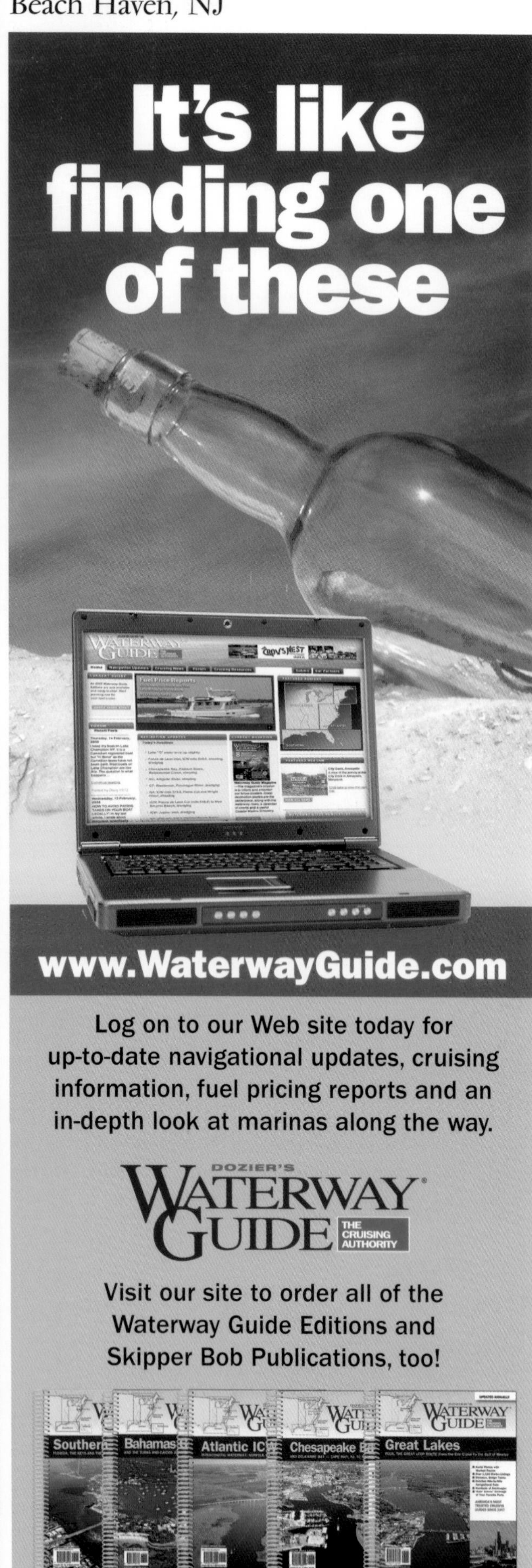

a few of the communities you pass in this section, all with marinas and hundreds of boats.

Boat traffic from this point north on the New Jersey ICW is heavy even during midweek. If you can, avoid traveling this stretch on weekends or holidays. The channel is extremely narrow in the vicinity of the bridge at Mile 37 (60-foot fixed vertical clearance), and depths outside it are only 1 or 2 feet. Be sure to keep on station. When the wind is westerly, the tide flowing across the channel can cause a boat to drift toward the edge.

Dockage: The Beach Haven Yacht Club Marina area offers a good combination of facilities, shopping, restaurants and entertainment. A berth almost anywhere along the shore has sea breezes and is close to public beaches. All public beaches along the New Jersey shore require a beach tag from Memorial Day to Labor Day, which can usually be purchased at the entrance to the beach.

Other dockage options include Morrison's Beach Haven Marina (red daybeacon "106") with floating docks and 5-foot depths alongside, a ship's store, repairs and a fuel dock, and Beach Haven Yacht Club Marina (green daybeacon "107"), a Shell marina with 8-foot depths, restroom and laundry facilities, cable television and convenience to Beach Haven's restaurants and shops. Eastern Marine is a BoatU.S. marina on Long Beach Island, adjacent to the New Jersey ICW.

Cruising Options

The narrow New Jersey ICW channel then crosses the flats of Manahawkin Bay before it enters broad, open Barnegat Bay at Mile 30. The bay provides miles of scenic cruising opportunities, making it one of the most popular boating areas on the East Coast. Barnegat Bay is a very busy body of water with constant marine traffic. Stay in the channel and keep a careful watch at all times. ■

WATERWAY GUIDE is always open to your observations from the helm. E-mail your comments on any navigation information in the guide to: editor@waterwayguide.com.

WATERWAY GUIDE advertising sponsors play a vital role in bringing you the most trusted and well-respected cruising guide in the country. Without our advertising sponsors, we simply couldn't produce the top-notch publication now resting in your hands. Next time you stop in for a peaceful night's rest, let them know where you found them—WATERWAY GUIDE, The Cruising Authority.

BRIDGE RESTRICTIONS FOR THE NJ ICW FROM CAPE MAY TO MANASQUAN

The upper portion of the passage behind Atlantic City presents no problems other than possible bridge delays and low speed limits (be sure to observe them). Theoretically, bridge openings are staggered to allow boats to make the entire passage without delay, but it doesn't always work that way, especially at peak auto traffic hours: 8 a.m. and 5 p.m. The official schedules are:

■ Cape May Canal Railroad Bridge across Cape May Canal, mile 115.1, at Cape May — Draw is maintained in open position and will close only for crossing of trains and maintenance. Train service generally operates as follows:

1) June through August-daily train service starting at 10 a.m. and ending at 7:30 p.m.; September through November, weekend service only, 10 a.m. and ending at 7:30 p.m.; December through March there is no train service, bridge is unmanned. When vessel is approaching draw in open position, vessel shall give opening signal. If no acknowledgement is received within 30 seconds, vessel may proceed with caution through open draw.

■ Two-Mile Bridge across Middle Thorofare in Wildwood Crest, mile 112.2 — Draw shall open on signal

■ Stone Harbor Boulevard Bridge across Great Channel at Stone Harbor, mile 102.0 — Draw shall open on signal except: from Memorial Day through Labor Day from 6 a.m. to 6 p.m. on Saturdays, Sundays and federal holidays, on the hour, 20 minutes after the hour, and 20 minutes before the hour. From October through March from 10 p.m. to 6 a.m. the draw will open if at least 8 hours notice is given.

■ Route 52 Ninth Street Bridge across Beach Thorofare at Ocean City, mile 80.4 — shall open on signal except: from Memorial Day through Labor Day from 8 a.m. to 8 p.m. the draw will open on the hour and on the half hour.

■ Dorset Avenue Bridge across Inside Thorofare at Ventnor City, mile 72.1 — shall open on signal except: from June 1 through Sept. 30, from 9:15 a.m. to 9:15 p.m. the draw will only open at 15 minutes and 45 minutes after the hour.

■ US 40-322 Albany Avenue Bridge across Inside Thorofare in Atlantic City, mile 70.0 — shall open on signal except:

1) year-round from 11 p.m. to 7 a.m. and from Nov. 1 through March 31 from 3 p.m. to 11 p.m., the draw will only open if at least 4 hours notice is given

2) from June 1 through Sept. 30 from 9 a.m. to 4 p.m. and from 6 p.m. to 9 p.m. the draw will only open on the hour and the half hour (from 4 p.m. to 6 p.m. the draw need not open)

■ Route 30 Bridge across Beach Thorofare at Atlantic City, mile 67.2 — shall open on signal except: year-round from 11 p.m. to 7 a.m. and from Nov. 1 through March 31 from 3 p.m. to 11 p.m. the draw need only open if at least four hours notice is given.

■ AMTRAK Automated Railroad Swing Bridge across Beach Thorofare in Atlantic City, mile 68.9 — shall operate as follows:

1) open on signal from 11 p.m. to 6 a.m., from 20 minutes to 30 minutes after each hour and remain open for all waiting vessels

2) opening of the draw span may be delayed for 10 minutes or if train is moving toward the bridge and has crossed the home signal for the bridge before the signal requesting opening of the bridge is given, train may continue across the bridge

3) When bridge is not tended locally and is operated from a remote location, closed circuit TV cameras shall be operated and maintained at the bridge site to enable the remotely located bridge controller to view both river traffic and the bridge

4) Radiotelephone Channel 13 (156.65 MHz) VHF-FM, will be maintained to facilitate communication in both remote and local control locations.

5) When draw is opening and closing, or in closed position, yellow flashing lights located on ends of center piers shall be displayed continuously until bridge is returned to fully open position.

■ S37 Bridge across Barnegat Bay at Seaside Heights, mile 14.1 — shall open on signal except:

1) from Dec. 1 through March 31 from 11 p.m. to 8:00 a.m. the draw need not open

2) from April 1 through Nov. 30 from 11 p.m. to 8 a.m. the draw need only open if at least 4 hours notice is given

3) from Memorial Day through Labor Day from 8 a.m. to 8 p.m. the draw will open on the hour and on the half hour.

■ County Route 528 Bridge across Barnegat Bay at Mantoloking, mile 6.3 — shall open on signal except: from Memorial Day through Labor Day on Saturdays, Sundays, and Federal holidays from 9:00 a.m. to 6:00 p.m. the draw will only open on the hour, 20 minutes after the hour, and 40 minutes after the hour.

■ Route 35 Bridge across the Manasquan River at Brielle, mile 1.1 — shall open on signal except:

1) from May 15 through Sept. 30 the draw need only open 15 minutes before the hour and 15 minutes after the hour on Saturdays, Sundays and Federal holidays from 8 a.m. to 10 p.m. and on Mondays to Thursdays from 4 p.m. to 7 p.m. and on Fridays from 12 p.m. to 7 p.m.

2) year-round from 11 p.m. to 8 a.m. the draw need only open if at least four hours notice Is given.

Barnegat Bay to Manasquan

CHARTS 12323, 12324

NEW JERSEY ICW —MILE 26 TO MILE ZERO

Barnegat Bay, popular with both powerboaters and sailors, is a designated national estuary with lovely scenery, superb beaches, plenty of shoreside attractions and inviting sailing conditions. When cruising this magnificent body of water, you will find a number of resorts preserving either the grand socialite splendor of an earlier day or a more modest and casual flavor. Piney rivers make excellent hurricane holes, and ancient New Jersey water traditions survive in many of the mainland villages.

The entire length of the New Jersey Intracoastal Waterway in Barnegat Bay is safe and sheltered with little more than a stiff chop during strong winds. Additionally, Barnegat Bay is a No Discharge Zone, meaning any and all on-board sewage must be stored in a holding tank and pumped out ashore. Even treatment devices such as a LectraSan may not be used.

In the spring and early summer, whenever a front of warm, humid air moves up from the south, be prepared for dense advection fogs when transiting the New Jersey ICW along the bay. North of Toms River, Barnegat Bay is shoal, but well-marked. Make certain to follow the markers with the familiar yellow logo of the ICW as you transit the bay. Do not be misled by side-channel markers and entrances to rivers that do not show the yellow logo of the ICW.

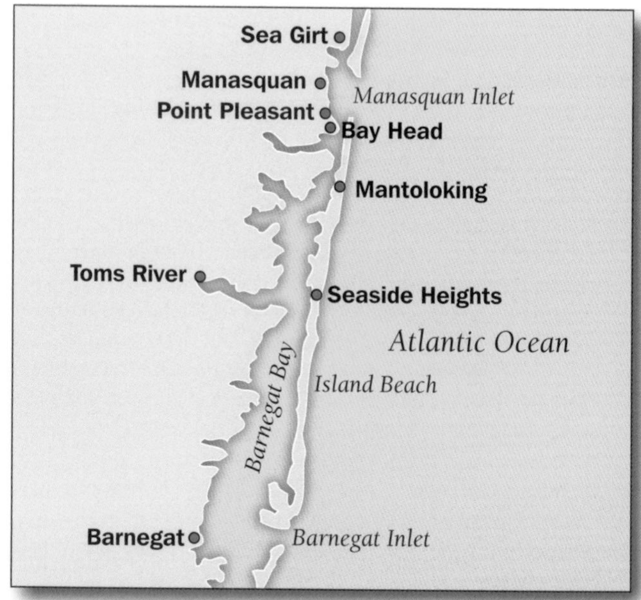

The southern portion of the Bay ranges from 8 to 10 feet deep in the channel, and dependable winds help make it one of the coast's most popular sailing centers. The diurnal wind pattern in this part of Barnegat Bay is for the sea breeze to begin at about 11 a.m., increasing by mid-afternoon to a velocity usually greater than that predicted. A windless day on Barnegat Bay is rare.

A good rule to remember when cruising Barnegat Bay is that the deepest water is to the west near the mainland,

Barnegat Lighthouse provides an excellent landmark for Barnegat Inlet. (Not to be used for navigation.) WATERWAY GUIDE PHOTOGRAPHY

and the shallowest on the east next to the barrier island. Keep a sharp lookout for the many crab trap buoys and eel trap buoys often scattered throughout the bay.

Mile 26

NAVIGATION: Use Chart 12324. When heading for Barnegat Inlet from the New Jersey ICW, note that flashing white fixed Morse (A) "BI," mounted on a dolphin (a cluster of pilings), marks the junction of the New Jersey ICW and Oyster Creek Channel, which is the preferred route to Barnegat Light and Barnegat Inlet.

Although the channel is reported to be maintained to 6-foot depths, it is subject to continual shifting and shoaling. Buoys are not charted because they are frequently moved to mark the best water. Double Creek Channel, which leads to the inlet from the southwest, is closed periodically due to shoaling. Check its status with locals before attempting to enter.

Barnegat Light

At the northern tip of Long Beach Island, next to Barnegat Inlet, is Barnegat Lighthouse, in the town of Barnegat Light. The light itself, at 165 feet high, is the second tallest lighthouse in the United States. The familiar red and white tower was commissioned into service in 1859 and served faithfully until 1944 when it was decommissioned. The light was relit on Jan. 1, 2009 and now flashes a white light every 10 seconds. A private group maintains the lighthouse.

NAVIGATION: Use Chart 12324. Three channels branch off at the uncharted green and red junction buoy next to the lighthouse. To the north is the channel leading out of Barnegat Inlet. To the west is Oyster Creek Channel, which leads to the New Jersey ICW on the west side of Barnegat Bay. The channel to the south enters the harbor at Barnegat Light, where marinas offer fuel, repairs, haul-out and transient berths. Barnegat Light is a large recreational and commercial fishing harbor.

Barnegat Inlet

NJ

DE

With fair weather and seas, the town of Barnegat Light can be a fine overnight stop for those traveling the coastline. Because it is about halfway between New York City and Cape May, a boat capable of 6-knot speeds can make the trip down the entire New Jersey coast in two daytime hops. (The three-day alternative for slower boats consists of overnight stops at Manasquan and Atlantic City.)

Barnegat Inlet has always been one to approach with caution. It can be especially rough in the case of an outgoing tide that is opposed by a strong easterly wind, as is the case with many of the New Jersey inlets. Because of the constantly shifting shoals across the entrance, it is advisable to seek local knowledge before entering this inlet. An inquiry on VHF Channel 16 will usually bring a response of good local knowledge of the inlet conditions. Call for advice and also trust your own prudence and judgment.

The Barnegat Light Coast Guard Station warns, "If you see waves breaking outside the inlet, do not proceed. If you have to (return through the inlet), you had better be wearing life jackets." Under these conditions, it would be wise to detour to Manasquan Inlet when heading north, or to Absecon (Atlantic City) Inlet if southbound.

NAVIGATION: Use Chart 12324. Use Sandy Hook tide tables. For high tide, add 1 hour 18 minutes; for low tide, add 1 hour 23 minutes. The south jetty of Barnegat Inlet is marked with a 37-foot-high tower made of black steel, which is eight feet in diameter and topped with a green light. Look for the triangular green "7" daybeacon portion during daylight hours.

Although the inlet channel between the jetties has been straightened, widened and deepened, potentially dangerous shoals have developed just outside the mouth of Barnegat Inlet, and experts say the shoaling on the ocean side of the inlet will always be a problem. These hazards are most treacherous with a strong northeast wind and an outgoing tide, which can build 6- to 8-foot breaking seas capable of dropping you on the bottom in the troughs. These are extreme conditions, not the normal occurrence, but prudence suggests you be aware of the possibility and, if this condition exists, consider an alternative entrance into the bay.

Dredges work on Barnegat Inlet three times a year, for a month at a time. During these periods, transiting the narrow passage past the dredge equipment can be difficult.

West of the lighthouse, Oyster Creek Channel joins Barnegat Inlet with Barnegat Bay. Buoys on this channel are uncharted and moved frequently, and the passage at night should never be attempted by the newcomer. Even in daylight, sharp doglegs of nearly 90 degrees can be easily overlooked and wide scans for the next set of buoys are mandatory, since missing a set will probably put you aground. Boats with a draft of 5 feet or more should only attempt to transit the Oyster Creek Channel on a rising tide. In June 2009, the channel was reported to have depths of 6 feet or more at mid-tide. However, shoals do shift and caution is advised.

Flashing red-and-white Morse (A) light "BI" marks the junction of Oyster Creek Channel and the New Jersey ICW on Barnegat Bay. This aid to navigation has a white light, which flashes Morse (A) (one short, one long). If heading north to Forked River or other destinations, do not cut this buoy. Leave it to starboard before turning north. There is extensive shoaling off of Sedge Islands inside the buoy.

Dockage: South of the inlet entrance at Barnegat Harbor are three marinas. The best chances for a transient slip are: The Marina at Barnegat Light, which can accommodate smaller cruisers (under 26 feet) and the occasional large vessel, if a regular slip holder is away. They have recently invested in new bulkheads and floating docks. Water depth on approach and at dockside is reportedly 8 feet; or Lighthouse Marina, where large vessels can be accommodated. Approach depths and at

Barnegat Bay, NJ

WARETOWN AREA, BARNEGAT INLET		Largest Vessel Accommodated	VHF Channel Monitored	Transient Berths / Total Berths	Approach / Dockside Depth (reported)	Floating Docks	Gas / Diesel	Groceries, Ice, Marine Supplies, Snacks	Repairs: Hull, Engine, Propeller	Lift (tonnage), Crane, Rail	1=110V, 2=220V, B=Both, Max Amps	Laundry, Pool, Showers	Pump-Out Station	Nearby: Grocery Store, Motel, Restaurant
		Dockage					Supplies		Services					
1. Andy's Barnegat Boat Basin 28	609-698-8581	34		15/15	6/6			IM	P		1/15			GR
2. Mariner's Marina 28	609-698-1222	40		5/200	6/6			M	HEP	L25	1/30	S	P	GMR
3. The Point at Key Harbor Marina, LLC 28	609-693-9355	70	16	40/265	6/6		GD	GIM	HP		B/50	LPS	P	R
4. Long Key Marina 26	609-693-9444	45	16	6/155	6/6	F	GD	IMS	EP	L15	B/30	LPS	P	GMR
5. Spencer's Bayside Marina 26 (Internet Access) (WiFi)	609-693-0100	55	16	2/26	5/6	F		IMS	E	L30	B/100	LS	P	GMR
6. Holiday Harbor Marina 26	**609-693-2217**	**65**		**4/230**	**5.5/6**		**GD**	**IMS**	**HEP**	**L50**	**B/50**	**LPS**	**P**	**GMR**
7. Rick's Marina 23.5	609-693-2134	50	09	10/77	10/10			IM	HEP	L30	B/50	S	P	GMR
8. Tide's End Marina 23.5	609-693-9423	44		2/35	10/6		G	IM	HEP	L35	B/50	S	P	GMR
9. Grant Boat Works 23.5	609-971-1075	55		7/50	10/10			M	HEP	L25,R	1/30	S		MR
10. Forked River State Marina 23.5	609-693-5045	50	16	4/125	6/6						1/30	LS	P	GMR
11. Wilbert's Marina 23.5 (WiFi)	609-693-2145	65	16	1/17	8/6		GD	GIMS			B/50	LPS	P	GMR
12. Silver Cloud Harbor Marina 23.5 (WiFi)	609-693-2145	65	16	10/80	8/6		GD	IM	HEP	L50	B/50	LPS	P	GMR
13. The Marina at Tall Oaks 23.5 (WiFi)	609-693-2145	65	16	10/100	8/6		GD	GIM	HEP	L50	B/50	LPS	P	GMR
14. Ted & Sons Forked River Marina 23.5	609-693-2185	40			6/6			M	HP	L	1/30	S		GMR
15. Townsend's Marina 23.5	609-693-6100	50		5/100	6/6	F		IM	HEP	L25	B/30	S	P	GMR
16. Captain's Inn 23.5	609-693-3351	70		30/45	7/6			IS			1/30	S		GMR
17. Southwinds Harbour Marina 23.5 (Internet Access) (WiFi)	609-693-6288	60	17	5/180	8/6		GD	GIMS	HEP	L25	1/50	LPS	P	GMR
18. Lighthouse Marina 26	609-494-2305	70	16	4/55	7/8		GD	GIM		L35	1/30	S	P	GMR
19. The Marina at Barnegat Light 26	609-494-6611	80		1/80	8/8			GIS	HEP		B/50			R

Corresponding chart(s) not to be used for navigation. Internet Access WiFi Wireless Internet Access

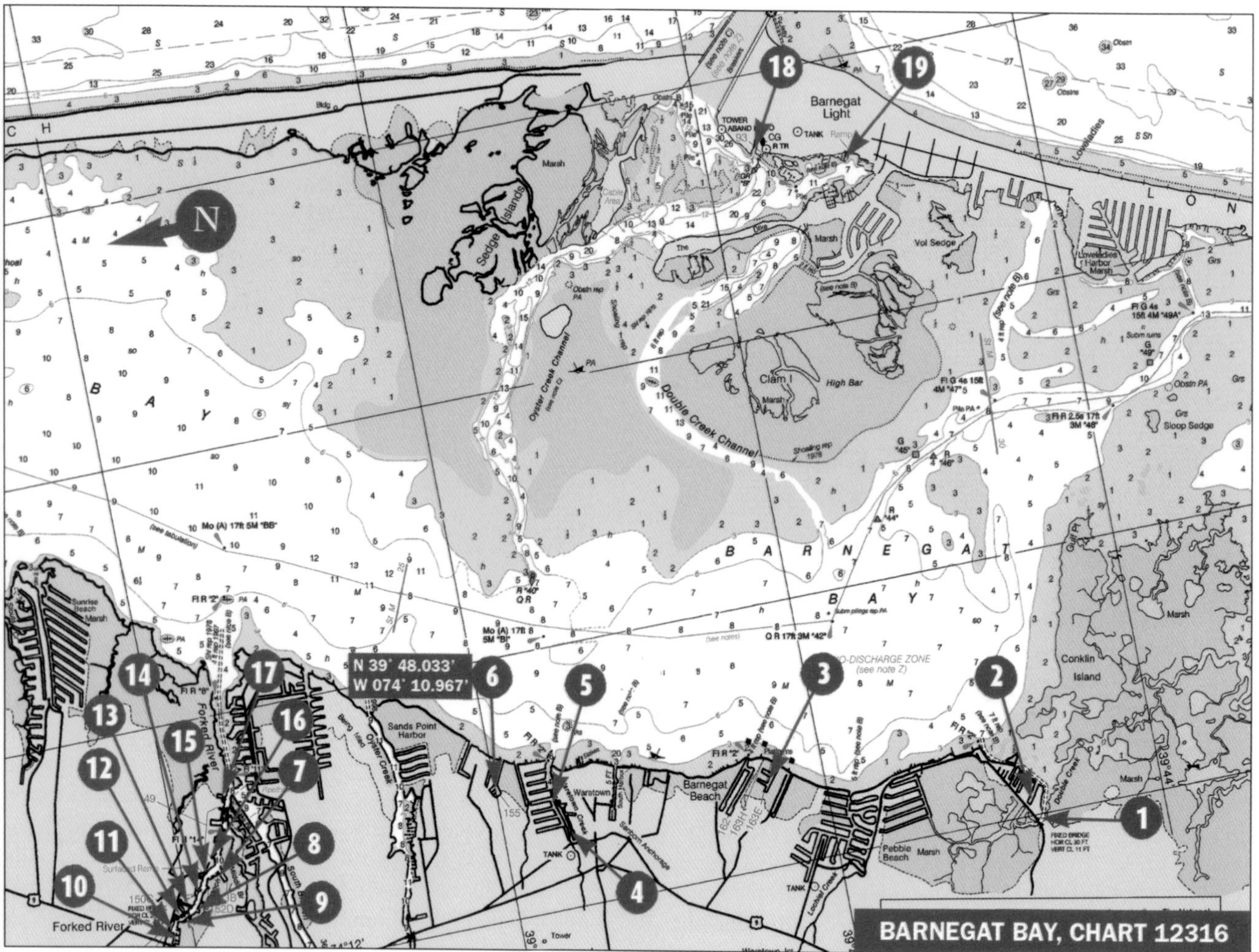

dockside are reportedly 7 feet. There are nearby groceries and restaurants. Call ahead to ensure availability.

Anchorage: In addition to its marinas, Barnegat Harbor has an excellent anchorage, known locally as Meyer's Hole, which is located just south of the harbor's intersection with Oyster Creek Channel. Aids to navigation in this area are privately maintained and frequently moved due to shifting shoals, but the channel leading to Barnegat Harbor is generally well-marked. Eleven-to 15-foot depths are available once inside. Be sure to anchor well away from the channel because of large commercial fishing boats berthed at the end of the harbor. A popular restaurant is located ashore about a block from the Coast Guard station.

Island Beach State Park

Island Beach State Park, a 10-mile-long strip of pristine barrier island, lies on the east side of the New Jersey ICW between Mile 25 and Mile 15. To this day, it is preserved in a natural condition.

Anchorage: At New Jersey ICW Mile 22, about 200 yards after passing flashing white Morse (A) "BB," you may see boats anchored to the east beside Island Beach State Park close to shore in an area known as Tices Shoal. You can anchor here (in hard sand), and then dinghy to shore to explore. There is a small sandy beach on the bay side and a walking path through the rolling dunes to the ocean beach about a quarter mile across the barrier island. This is a popular spot for local boaters on summer weekends. Boats drawing less than 5 feet can go directly east from the New Jersey ICW channel and find protection from northeast, east and southeast winds, and from wakes of boats traveling the New Jersey ICW.

Another good anchoring spot is along the mainland shore, north of Forked River. Anchor close to shore, next to the wetlands, in 5- to 6-foot depths with protection from winds in the western semicircle. You are farther from the wakes of boats using the Forked River channel here.

At the south end of Barnegat Bay, just off the mainland town of Barnegat Beach, anchor just north of Conklin Island for protection from the prevailing south and southwest winds. Quiet and protected overnight anchorage can also be found nearly anywhere along the shores of Toms River.

On the Mainland

On the west side of Barnegat Bay, across from the town of Barnegat Light, well-marked channels lead into Waretown and Barnegat Beach, with marine services available at both.

Dockage: In Waretown, Holiday Harbor Marina offers protected transient slips (for vessels up to 50 feet), fuel, repairs and pump-out. Spencer's Bayside Marina can accommodate vessels up to 75 feet and offers fuel, laundry, pool and shore power. There are also large, full-service marinas located in Double Creek (not to be confused with Double Creek Channel) in the mainland town of Barnegat, southwest of Mile 28 and quick flashing red "42." Use the marked channel entrance next to the condominiums. The marinas are just past the public dock and the two-story gazebo.

Forked River—Mile 24

At Mile 24 on the New Jersey ICW channel, the three branches of Forked (two syllables) River run back into the mainland. The two south forks are residential. Flashing red "2" marks the entrance to the river just west of Morse (A) marker "BB."

Dockage: The North Branch has all the facilities of interest to the cruiser: 11 boatyards and marinas, restaurants and, at the head of navigation, a state marina with a complimentary pump-out station. Near the state marina are grocery stores, restaurants, drugstores, churches and bus service to New York and Atlantic City. The Captain's Inn, halfway up the North Branch, has transient slips (white pilings) that are seldom filled. After dining, cruisers can stay in these slips overnight for a modest fee.

Although it can be somewhat buggy and hot on breathless summer nights, Forked River is one of the best hurricane holes on the coast. It has proven nearly impervious to even the worst blows. Stay in the channel when navigating the river, as shoaling is present on both sides.

Anchorage: Right at the mouth of Forked River, the charted 4-foot-deep bight on the south side of the channel, commonly called Sissy Cove, is popular for swimming and overnight anchoring.

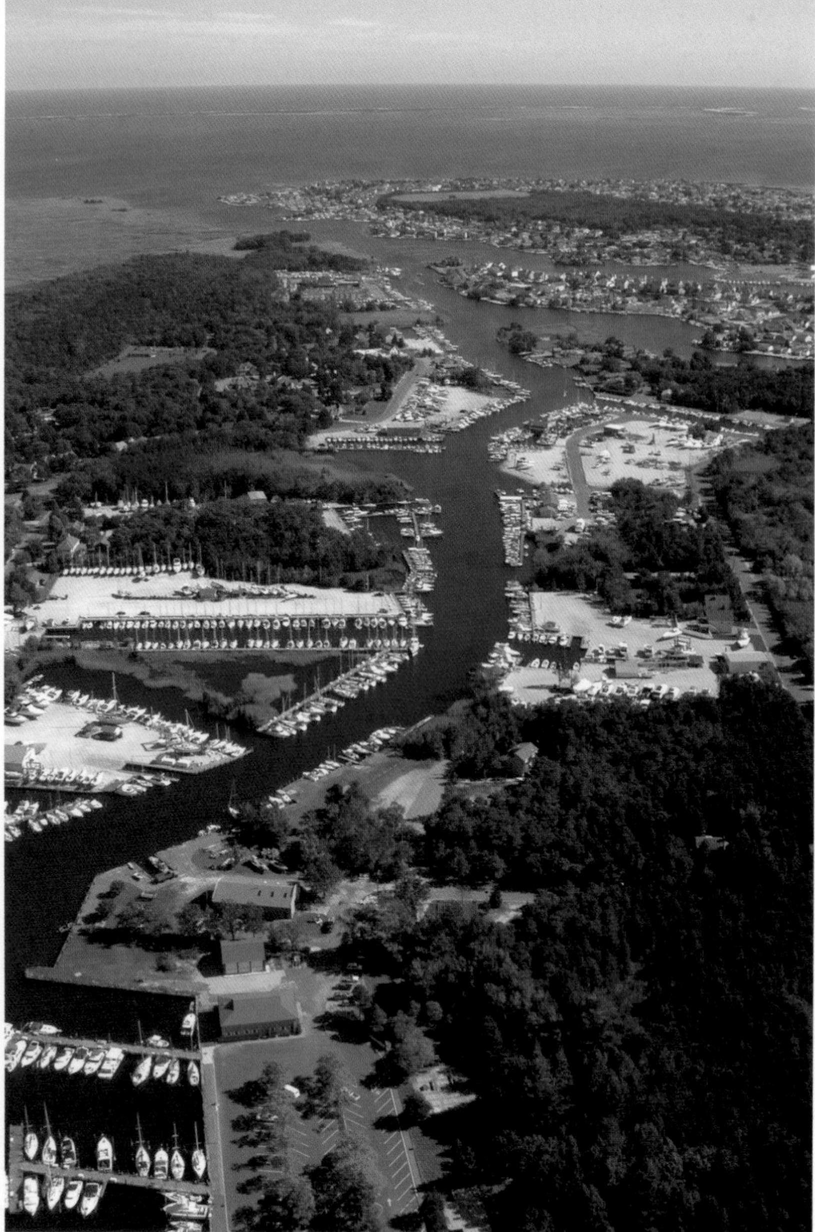

An eastern view over Forked River. (Not to be used for navigation.)
WATERWAY GUIDE PHOTOGRAPHY

Cedar Creek—Mile 20

North of Forked River, the west side of Barnegat Bay shows the hand of the dredge and the developer, and most of the channels lead to residential subdivisions. Cedar Creek retains the down-Jersey pine-and-cedar look, and it has emerged as a sailing center, worth a visit. Here you will find gas, supplies and overnight accommodations. Pay close attention to channel markers; shoaling is present on both sides of the channel.

Toms River—Mile 15

This picturesque stream, lined with houses and high banks, opens to the west, and a number of its attractive coves provide excellent anchorages. There are delightful possibilities for exploring and several marinas that accept transients (a few of which are complete resorts with swimming pools, nearby restaurants and shore accommodations).

The city of Toms River, a historic port dating to 1624, is located at the head of the river. Facilities and shore transportation can be found here. Toms River Yacht Club, founded in 1871, is among the oldest in the country. Some of the old captains' houses still line the street, and the town is working to preserve its maritime history. The Toms River Seaport Society has acquired several historic boats and other artifacts for its waterfront display, and there is an annual wooden boat festival held here, usually during July; call the Society at 732-349-9209 for dates and activities.

NAVIGATION: Use Chart 12324. Use Sandy Hook tide tables. For high tide, add 4 hours 2 minutes; for low tide, add 4 hours 29 minutes. When entering Toms River, stand off of Goodluck Point, as there is shoaling. There is also shoaling off of Long Point, so do not cut inside of flashing red "2."

Dockage: There are two large marinas that offer transient dockage in the town of Tom's River: Lighthouse Point Marina and Yacht Club and Cedar Cove Marina. Amenities at Lighthouse Point Marina include a pool, snack bar and a pump-out station. The marina only has about three slips available for transients, so call ahead for availability. Cedar Cove Marina has haul-out services (50-ton Travelift) and slips available for transients with drafts of 5 feet or less.

Mile 15 to Mile 6

Heading north from Toms River, heed all marks because there is shoaling on both sides of the New Jersey ICW, especially just beyond the two bridges at about Mile 14 that cross from the mainland to the resort town of Seaside Heights on the barrier beach.

NAVIGATION: Use Chart 12324. Be careful as you approach the bridges from the south. The channel is well-marked, but outside the magenta line are charted submerged objects and light pilings leveled by winter ice. Until picked up when new pilings are set out (usually in June), they constitute a hazard. After passing under the bridges, stay to the west side of the channel as you approach quick flashing green "29" to avoid shoaling that has been reported east of the channel.

The northernmost of the twin bridges is fixed, with a 60-foot vertical clearance. The state Route 37 Highway

Laurel Harbor, Cedar Creek, NJ

LAUREL HARBOR, CEDAR CREEK		Largest Vessel Accommodated	VHF Channel Monitored	Transient Berths / Total Berths	Approach / Dockside Depth (reported)	Floating Docks	Gas / Diesel	Groceries, Ice, Marine Supplies, Snacks	Repairs: Hull, Engine, Propeller	Lift (tonnage), Crane, Rail	1=110V, 2=220V, B=Both, Max Amps	Laundry, Pool, Showers	Pump-Out Station	Nearby: Grocery Store, Motel, Restaurant
		Dockage					Supplies		Services					
1. Laurel Harbor Marina 20.5	609-693-6112	40		0/150	4/4		G	IM	HP	L25	1/30	S	P	GMR
2. Cedar Creek Sailing Center/Marina 20.5 (WiFi)	732-269-1351	44	78	2/64	6/6			IM	HEP	L50,C	1/30	LS	P	GMR
3. Lanoka Harbor Marina 20 (Internet)	609-693-2674	50		15/200	5/6		GD	IM	HEP	L35	1/50	S	P	
4. Ocean Beach Marina Central 20	609-242-2200	40	68	/106	5/5		G	IM	HEP	L50	1/50	S	P	
5. Trixie's Landing 19.5	732-269-5838	20		/70	2/2	F	G	IMS	E			S		

Corresponding chart(s) not to be used for navigation. (Internet) Internet Access (WiFi) Wireless Internet Access

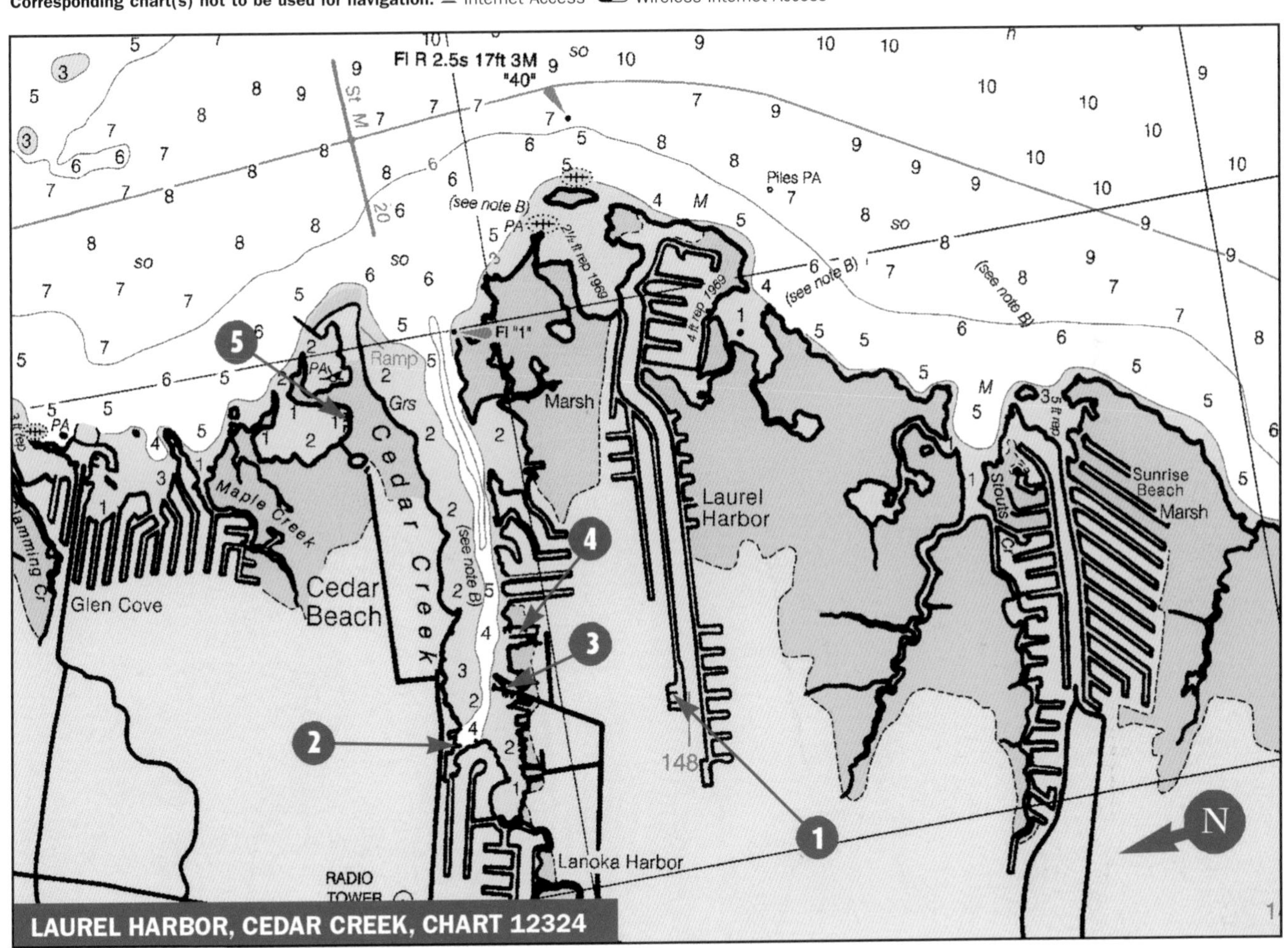

LAUREL HARBOR, CEDAR CREEK, CHART 12324

bascule bridge (30-foot closed vertical clearance) opens on the hour and half-hour from 8 a.m. to 8 p.m. from Memorial Day through Labor Day. From April through November, a four-hour advance notice is required from 11 p.m. to 8 a.m. The bridge opens on demand at all other times. Just north of the bridges, you must again pay close attention to the daybeacons because shallow flats crowd in on both sides and sandbars often move into the edges of the channel. Through the rest of this section, deep water is to the west, with shallow flats to the east.

Dockage: The towns of Seaside Heights, Lavallette and Normandy Beach string along the east side of the New Jersey ICW route and all have marinas—some welcome cruising craft—and can be reached through marked channels across the flats. At Seaside Heights, a mile-long amusement park is worth a stop, especially if you have young ones aboard. Marinas and a public dock are nearby.

Anchorage: There are communities on Kettle Creek and Silver Bay on the west side of Barnegat Bay near Mile 10. The latter is a prime anchorage, but is often crowded during the summer. Drop the hook anywhere along the south shore; just go far enough off the bank to catch the southerly breeze in order to be free of insects.

Toms River Area, NJ

TOMS RIVER AREA		Largest Vessel Accommodated	VHF Channel Monitored	Transient Berths / Total Berths	Approach / Dockside Depth (reported)	Floating Docks	Gas / Diesel	Groceries, Ice, Marine Supplies, Snacks	Repairs: Hull, Engine, Propeller	Lift (tonnage), Crane, Rail	1=110V, 2=220V, B=Both, Max Amps	Laundry, Pool, Showers	Pump-Out Station	Nearby: Grocery Store, Motel, Restaurant
		Dockage					Supplies		Services					
1. Ocean Gate Yacht Basin 15	732-269-2565	50		5/185	6/6		GD	IM	HEP	L38	B/50	S	P	GMR
2. Lighthouse Point Marina 15	732-341-1105	55		3/252	6/5			IMS	HEP	L25	B/50	LPS	P	GMR
3. Riverbank Marina 15	732-244-2106	45		/205	6/6	F	GD	IMS	HEP	L20	1/30	LPS	P	GMR
4. Tom's River Yacht Club (Members Only) 15	732-929-9809													
5. Island Heights Yacht Club 15	732-929-9813													
6. Nelson Marine Basin and Sailing Center 15	732-270-0022	40	79	1/100	5/6			M	HP	L	1/50	LPS	P	GMR
7. Dillon's Creek Marina 15 🖳	732-270-8541	45	72	2/210	5/5			IMS	HEP	L25,C	1/30	LS	P	GMR
8. Cozy Cove Marina 15	732-929-1171	35		2/85	6/6		G	IM	P	L15	1/15	S	P	GR
9. Pier One Marina, Restaurant & Motel 14	732-270-0914	80	09	17/65	7/7			IMS			B/50	S	P	GMR
10. Hobby Lobby Marine 12.5	732-929-1711	32		/75	5/3	F		IM			B/50	S		
11. Seaside Park Yacht Club 15.5	732-793-9611	50		1/41								S		MR
12. Lavallette Yacht Club 12	732-793-8747 (summer only)													
13. Ocean Beach Marina 11	732-793-7460	45		15/280	5/7		G	IM	HEP	L	B/50	S	P	R
14. Cedar Cove Marina 15 🖳	732-349-6600	62	77	/70	5/4				HEP	L50,C	1/50	S		GMR

Corresponding chart(s) not to be used for navigation. 🖳 Internet Access WiFi Wireless Internet Access

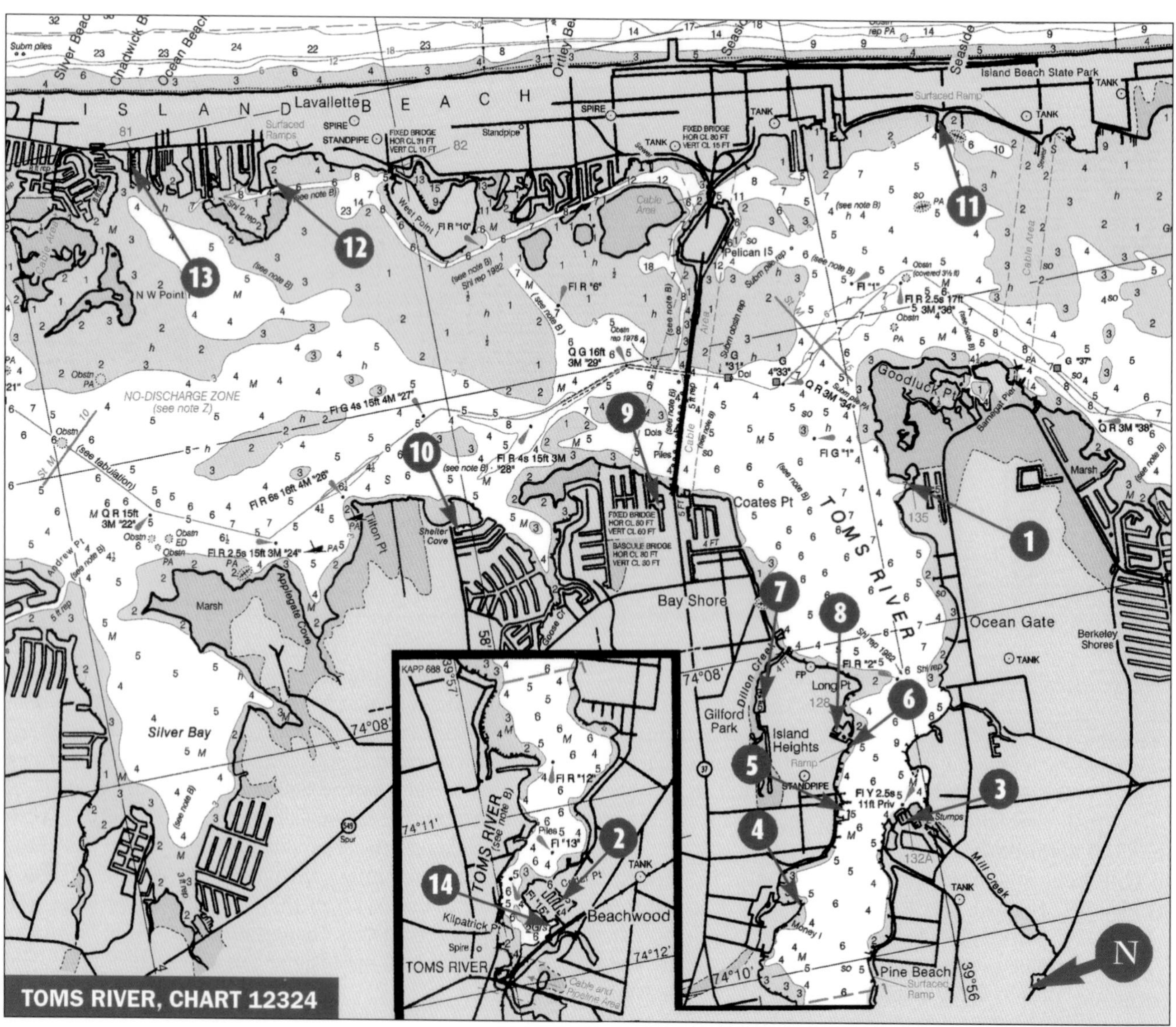

TOMS RIVER, CHART 12324

Toms River, NJ. (Not to be used for navigation.) WATERWAY GUIDE PHOTOGRAPHY

Mantoloking

NAVIGATION: Use Chart 12324. Use Sandy Hook tide tables. For high tide, add 4 hours 28 minutes; for low tide, add 4 hours 39 minutes. At Mantoloking, the New Jersey ICW is crossed by a new bascule bridge (30-foot closed vertical clearance) and leaves Barnegat Bay as it swings east to run close inside of the barrier beach. Between Memorial Day and Labor Day, the Mantoloking bascule bridge opens on the hour, 20 minutes after the hour and 20 minutes before the hour between 9 a.m. and 6 p.m. on weekends and holidays, and otherwise on signal.

Dockage: On the New Jersey ICW, in the Mantoloking area, yacht amenities are located on both the mainland and the beach. Most marinas will accommodate cruising yachts, and several offer a full range of services, restaurants and shore accommodations. Hinckley Yacht Services is a full-service marina open year-round and offers dockage, fuel and pump-out and can handle all types of repairs, upgrades and restorations. The cruiser-friendly marina, conveniently located just south of the bascule bridge at Mile 7, reports 8-foot approach depths.

Metedeconk River

Off the New Jersey ICW, west along the Metedeconk River, marinas and docks line the shore all the way to Bricktown. The river is navigable to Route 70, off the chart, and channels are privately maintained.

The Metedeconk River offers a calm, pleasant side trip past pine-lined shores with summer homes nestled beneath the trees. The entire river makes a fine anchorage, although seaweed can be a bother at times. A fall cruise on the Metedeconk River is especially enjoyable. The sun glows red in the evening against dark pines, ducks fly overhead, the water-skiers are gone and the docks are usually not crowded.

BAY HEAD TO MANASQUAN, NJ

The lovely seaside village of Bay Head marks the northern entrance to (or exit from) Barnegat Bay. Bay Head, often called "A Country Village by the Sea," has been a popular vacation spot since Victorian times and still treasures its culture and heritage; it is a great place to take a break and explore for a few days. Visit www.bayhead.org for details. Clustered around the southern end of Point Pleasant Canal are some of the boatyards that made New Jersey famous as a boatbuilding center. Many of these yards have consolidated and, while still building custom boats, now offer transient slips and complete marina services.

Bay Head, NJ

NAVIGATION: Use Chart 12324. Transiting this area through Bay Head to the Point Pleasant Canal, be aware that the New Jersey ICW runs through the complex of marinas and boatyards with rigid speed regulations, and the entire area is actively policed.

You must pass under a bascule bridge (30-foot closed vertical clearance) at Mile 5 prior to reaching Bay Head. Between Memorial Day and Labor Day, the Mantoloking Bascule Bridge opens on the hour, 20 minutes after the hour and 20 minutes before the hour between 9 a.m. and 6 p.m. on weekends and holidays, and otherwise on signal.

On the west side of Barnegat Bay, opposite Bay Head, the Metedeconk River and Beaverdam Creek are separated by long, narrow Wardells Neck. The river and the creek are entered from the northwest side of Herring Island. Only boats drawing less than 4 feet should attempt to enter from the southwest side of Herring Island, as water depths are reported between 2 feet and 3 feet at mean low water.

Dockage: This boating area is extremely popular. Yacht clubs and marinas abound, with a concentration along Beaverdam Creek west of Bay Head. The well-known Johnson Brothers Boatworks at the mouth of the Point Pleasant Canal offers friendly service to transients and provides all sorts of amenities, including a swimming pool, a large marine store and complete repairs. The boat shop continues to build its custom boats here. The Metedeconk River Yacht Club is located near the south side of the river just off the bay, and the Bay Head Yacht Club is located on the east side of the bay in Bay Head. Both are private and may offer reciprocal privileges to other yacht club members, but no dockage.

Point Pleasant Canal

The only way out of the bay on the northeast end is to transit the Point Pleasant Canal to the Manasquan Inlet via the Manasquan River. The two-mile-long canal connects Bay Head with the Manasquan River. Two lift bridges cross the canal, and cruisers should consider each before beginning a trip through the canal. The Bridge Avenue Bridge is first with a 30-foot closed vertical clearance (65-foot open vertical clearance), and the Route 88 Bridge is second with a 31-foot closed vertical clearance (65-foot open vertical clearance).

Before entering the canal, make detailed checks with the bridge tender at the Route 88 bridge regarding the condition of the current (contact the tender on VHF Channel 13 and refer to a specific bridge). If you are without adequate power, the trip can be challenging because of the great difference between the 4-foot tidal range at Manasquan Inlet and that of less than a foot at the Barnegat Bay end of the canal. Try to plan your transit through the canal to coincide with slack water.

Take extra care on the weekends and holidays when canal traffic is heaviest. In the vicinity of the bridge piers, quarters are tight and there is virtually no room to maneuver or turn around as you approach the bridges. The canal is lined on both sides with bulkheads. If wind and current are with you, allow plenty of space and time to do any required maneuvering. Do not follow another boat too closely, particularly around the bridges, and allow adequate time for the bridges to open completely before moving through the opening.

NAVIGATION: Use Chart 12324. An adequately powered auxiliary should be able to transit Point Pleasant Canal with no problem at any time when weather conditions are favorable. Underpowered sailboats (those able to make no more than 4 or 5 knots at full throttle) should limit themselves to an hour either side of slack water. If you must go through with the current during heavy traffic times, be aware that not all of the vessels going through the canal will be able to give way if you experience problems.

Tidal current tables provide the times of slack water for the Point Pleasant Canal. Predicted slack water is two to three hours after high or low tides in the Atlantic Ocean. This time can vary greatly, depending on the direction, strength and duration of the wind. Because of these variables, estimating time of slack water is a challenge. The safest time to make the passage is slack high water, when current is at a minimum. (Slack low water averages 0.2 knot faster.)

The three highway bridges in this area are the southernmost bridge across the canal (referred to as the Bridge Avenue Bridge), the northernmost bridge across the canal (called the Route 88 Bridge) and the Manasquan River Highway Bridge (referred to as the Route 35 Bridge). The Route 35 bascule bridge (30-foot closed vertical clearance) across the Manasquan River has restricted opening hours on weekends and holidays between May 15 and Sept. 30, when it opens 15 and 45 minutes past the hour from 8 a.m. to 10 p.m. and on demand during the night. The Route 88 Bridge and the Bridge Avenue Bridge open promptly on signal. A rail bridge is usually open except when trains are scheduled.

Point Pleasant, Brielle

The towns of Point Pleasant and Brielle face each other across the Manasquan River at Mile Zero on the New Jersey ICW, and the resort towns of Point Pleasant Beach and Manasquan face each other at the Manasquan Inlet. The Manasquan Inlet is said to be one of the widest and safest inlets on the New Jersey coast. The waters in this area form one of the busiest ports on the New Jersey ICW, with hundreds of berths, restaurants, chandleries, marinas, boatbuilders, repair yards and boat sales offices. Droves of charter captains are ready to take you deep-sea fishing; reservations are a must, especially on summer weekends.

The beach at Point Pleasant, splendid and clean, is privately owned—you must pay a fee. The boardwalk at Point Pleasant, with the usual arcades, rides and bars, terminates at the mouth of Manasquan Inlet. The Mantoloking and Bay Head beaches to the south of Point Pleasant Beach are also private and reserved for residents only.

Dockage: Marine provisions and groceries are just a short car ride from the Brielle waterfront, which offers dockage for transients. Brielle Yacht Club, just before the

Looking into Manasquan Inlet. (Not to be used for navigation.) WATERWAY GUIDE PHOTOGRAPHY

railroad bridge and Brielle Marine Basin, the first marina just beyond the railroad bridge (if traveling upriver), also offers dockage for transients and fuel, with significant lift capacity, full repair capabilities and a fully stocked marine store on-site. Among the machine shops and iron works at the Brielle waterfront is a competent diesel repair machine shop, founded in the 1940s.

Another option for dockage is to continue south through the Point Pleasant Canal to the Bay Head and Metedeconk River area, where you will find many receptive marinas.

Note: The Manasquan River and the Shark River are No-Discharge Zones. Overboard discharge of sewage (even treated by a device like a LectraSan) is strictly prohibited.

MANASQUAN INLET

Manasquan Inlet is normally easy to transit, thanks to its well-maintained jetties and depths. Wind against tide, however, can be a little rough.

NAVIGATION: Use Chart 12324. Use Sandy Hook tide tables. For high tide, subtract 12 minutes; for low tide, subtract 24 minutes. Channel depths in the Manasquan Inlet were last reported at 11 feet as far as the Route 35 bascule bridge, and then 5 feet to the Point Pleasant Canal and 7 feet in the river beyond. The channel between the Point Pleasant Canal and flashing red "6" is extremely narrow, with very shallow conditions on both sides. Make sure that the current does not sweep you out of the channel.

If you must enter the inlet under adverse conditions and your boat is fast, synchronize your speed with the speed of the seas and ride through on the back of a wave, keeping well aft of the crest. In a slow boat, throttle way down so that the waves will pass under your boat. If you are cruising in a moderate-sized sailboat and the wind is against the tide, turning around after committing to either enter or exit the inlet will probably not be an option. Be prepared for a bit of discomfort and very slow progress if you attempt to exit the inlet in a westerly wind against an incoming tide.

Slow down in the inlet: An incredible amount of commercial, charter and recreational boat traffic goes in and out of Manasquan Inlet. Exercise caution, and be sure to control your speed and wake in the inlet and the river; you are responsible for any damage done by your wake. The Coast Guard monitors inlet traffic closely and enforces safe boating practices.

The railroad bridge, about a mile from Manasquan Inlet, has a 3-foot closed vertical clearance; the Route 35 Highway bascule bridge has a 30-foot closed vertical clearance. The railroad bridge is normally open and is only closed as trains approach. The horizontal clearance through the railroad bridge is only 48 feet; use caution. The Route 35 Highway Bridge opens at 15 and 45 minutes

Mantoloking, Manasquan, NJ

MANTOLOKING, MANASQUAN		Largest Vessel Accommodated	VHF Channel Monitored	Transient Berths / Total Berths	Approach / Dockside Depth (reported)	Floating Docks	Gas / Diesel	Groceries, Ice, Marine Supplies, Snacks	Repairs: Hull, Engine, Propeller	Lift (tonnage), Crane, Rail	1=110V, 2=220V, B=Both, Max Amps	Laundry, Pool, Showers	Pump-Out Station	Nearby: Grocery Store, Motel, Restaurant
		Dockage					Supplies		Services					
1. Sunset Marina 10	609-361-1400	50	67	5/100	4/4		G	IMS	E	L25	1/30	S	P	GMR
2. Baywood Marina 8	732-477-3322	40		6/200	4/4	F	G	IM	HEP	L10	1/30	LPS	P	
3. Mantoloking Yacht Club 6	732-892-6281				4/4						1/60			
4. David Beaton & Sons 6	732-477-0259	42		/65	4/4			M	HEP	L15	1/15		P	GMR
5. Hinckley Yacht Services 6 🖳	732-477-6700	70	16	15/110	8/7		GD	IMS	HEP	L70	B/50	LS	P	MR
6. Mermaid's Cove Marina	732-477-3252	50	16	3/45	6/4	F		IMS	HEP	C/15	B/50	LS		GMR
7. Metedeconk Marina	732-477-9445	65		25/270	6/6	F				LC	1/50	S		GMR
8. Brennan Boat Company & Marina	732-840-1100	52	16	/73	4/4			I	HEP	L25	1/30	S	P	GMR
9. Jersey Shore Marina	732-840-9530	50		5/200	4/5		G	IM	HP	L20	1/30	PS	P	MR
10. Green Cove Marina	732-840-9090	50		/235	5/3		G	IM	HEP	L20,C	1/30	PS	P	GMR
11. Wehrlen Bros. Marina	732-899-3505	57		/200	5/4				HEP	L	1/30	PS	P	MR
12. Mentor Marine	732-295-4036	85	09	5/105	6/7	F		GIM	HP	L	B/50	S		GR
13. Cassidy's Marina	732-477-1111	30		5/100	6/4					L	B/50	S		GMR
14. Comstock Boat Works	732-899-2500	50	09	10/60	6/5	F	GD	IMS	HEP	L40	B/50	S	P	GMR
15. Arnold's Yacht Basin	732-892-3000	45		/193	6/5	F		S	HEP	L50	B/50	S	P	
16. Forsberg's Boat Works	732-892-4246	45		/60	4/4				HEP	L20	1/30	S		GMR
17. Metedeconk River Yacht Club	732-477-9781	36		1/64	4/4									
18. Dale's Marina, Sanzari Companies 4.5 🖳	732-892-1569	60		/70	7/7		GD	IMS			B/30	LS		G
19. Johnson Brothers Boat Works 1 🖳	732-892-9000	75	16/9	3/68	6/6			GIMS	HEP	L40,R	B/50	LPS	P	GMR

Corresponding chart(s) not to be used for navigation. 🖳 Internet Access (WiFi) Wireless Internet Access

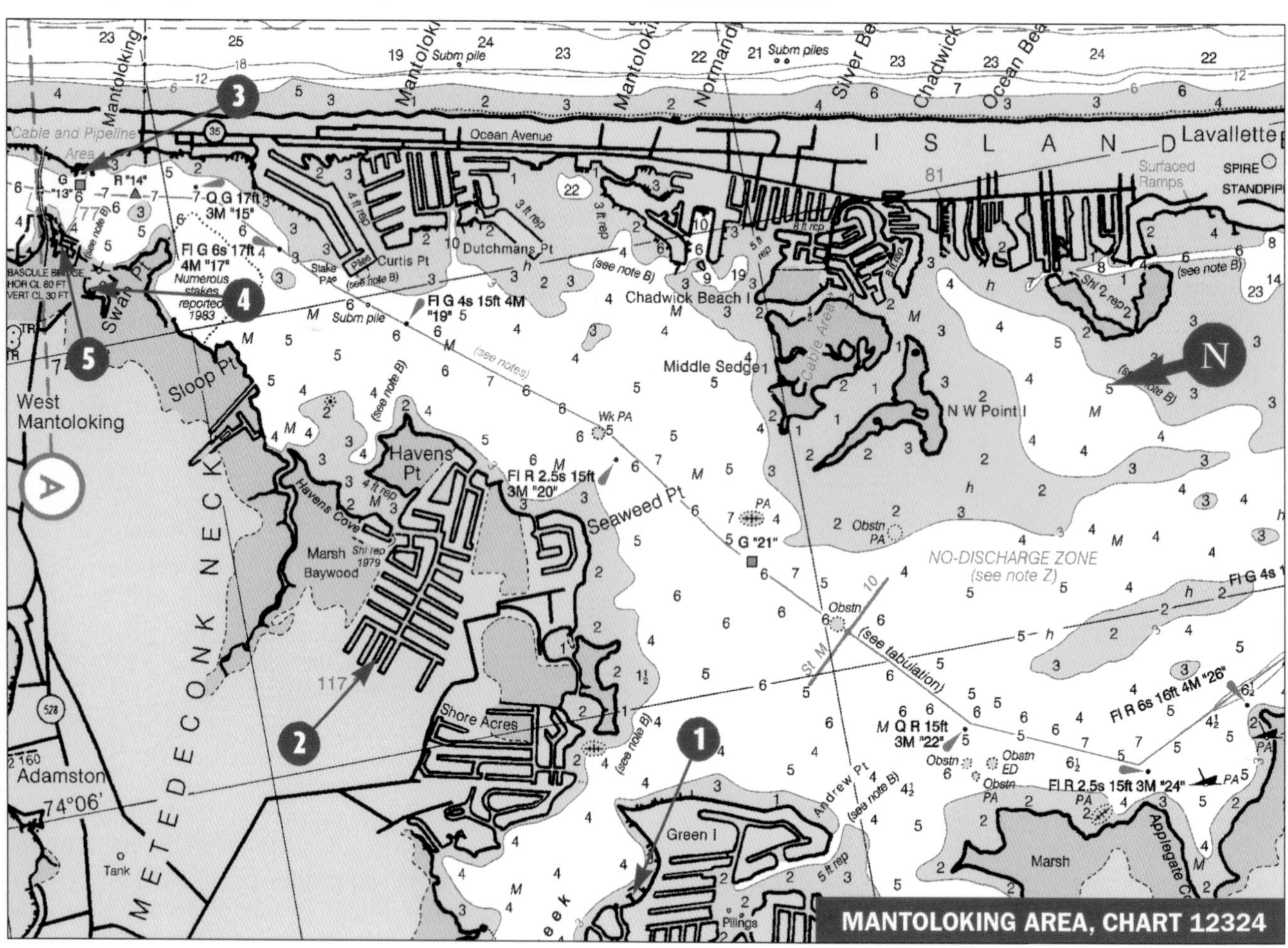

MANTOLOKING AREA, CHART 12324

Mantoloking, Manasquan, NJ

MANTOLOKING, MANASQUAN, CONT'D.		Largest Vessel Accommodated	VHF Channel Monitored	Transient Berths / Total Berths	Approach / Dockside Depth (reported)	Floating Docks	Gas / Diesel	Groceries, Ice, Marine Supplies, Snacks	Repairs: Hull, Engine, Propeller	Lift (tonnage), Crane, Rail	1=110V, 2=220V, B=Both, Max Amps	Laundry, Pool, Showers	Pump-Out Station	Nearby: Grocery Store, Motel, Restaurant
		Dockage					Supplies		Services					
20. Carver Boat Sales 4	732-892-0328	45		/16	4/6				HEP	L30	1/30			
21. Brielle Yacht Club & Sandbar Restaurant 1	732-528-6250	85		10/128	8/6		GD	IS			B/50	S		GMR
22. Brielle Marine Basin 1	732-528-6200	100	16/09	5/80	15/10		GD	IM	HEP	L70	B/50	S	P	R
23. Marine Max Mid-Atlantic Marina 2.5	732-840-2100	65		/220	6/4	F			HEP	L20	B/50	LS	P	MR
24. Peterson's Riviera Inn & Marina 2.5	732-840-0088	26			5/3			I			1/30			R
25. Crystal Point Yacht Club 2.5	732-892-2300	75	16	0/197	8/8	F	GD	IMS			B/50	PS	P	MR
26. Clark's Landing Marina, Bar & Grill 1.5	732-899-5559	60	05	5/182	5/6		GD	GIMS	HP	L	B/50	S	P	GMR
27. Garden State Yacht Sales & Marina .4	732-892-4222	70	16/09	6/70	6/6	F		GIMS	HEP	L50	B/50	S	P	GMR
28. Jack Baker's Lobster Shanty & Wharfside	732-892-9100	50	09		5/7									R

Corresponding chart(s) not to be used for navigation. Internet Access · Wireless Internet Access

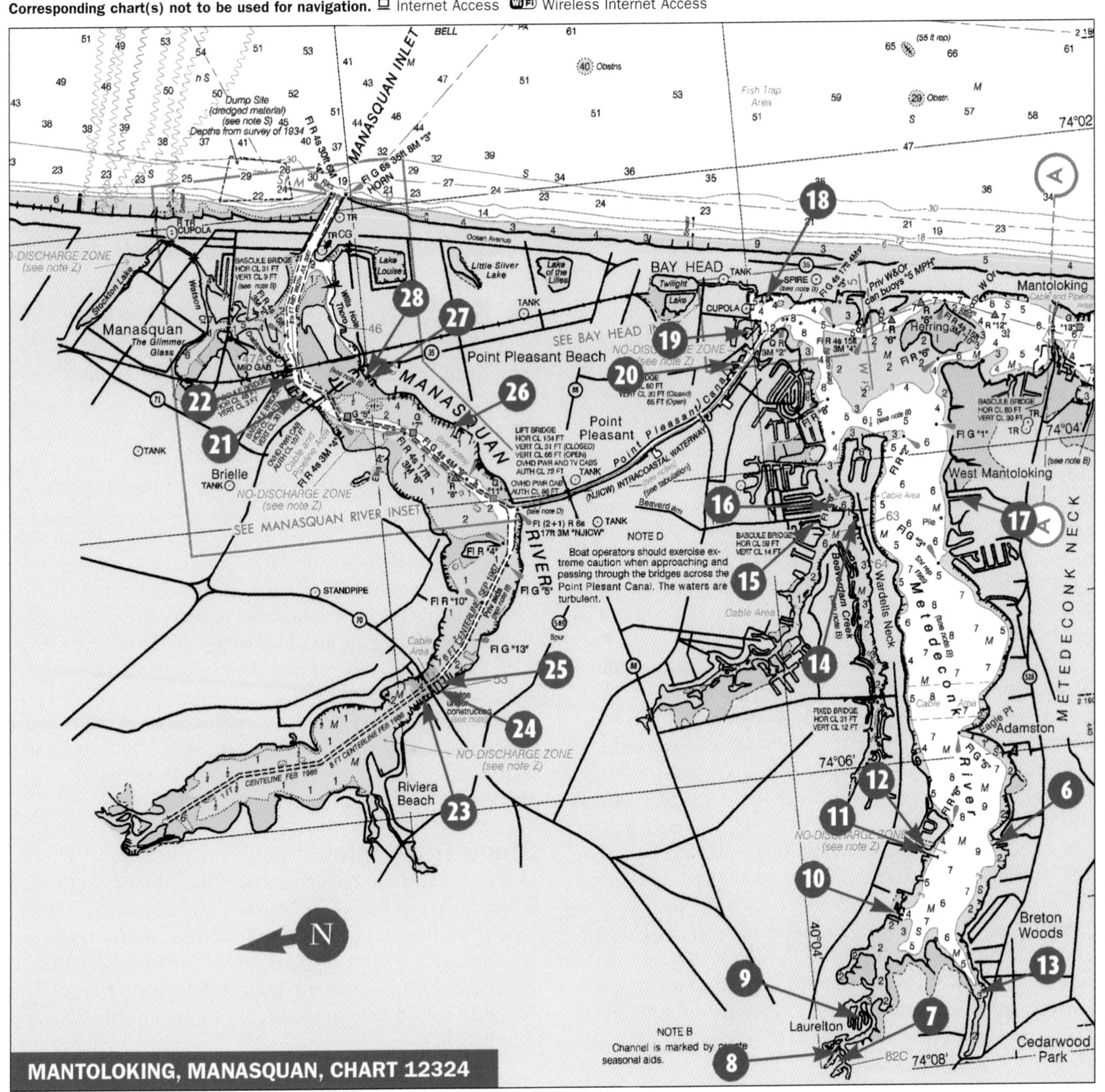

MANTOLOKING, MANASQUAN, CHART 12324

Looking west over Shark River. (Not to be used for navigation.) WATERWAY GUIDE PHOTOGRAPHY

past the hour on summer weekends and holidays from 8 a.m. to 10 p.m., and on signal at during the night hours.

The current at the railroad bridge is almost as strong as in the Point Pleasant Canal, and traffic can be extremely heavy, particularly on weekends after the bridge has been closed for a spell. Choose your time carefully for going through the railroad bridge.

Dockage: Most of the marinas are clustered around the railroad bridge and the Route 35 Highway Bridge about a mile from Manasquan Inlet. Farther up the river, the Crystal Point Yacht Club can accommodate vessels up to 100 feet and has easy offshore access, fuel, pump-out, a pool and motel rooms.

Anchorage: Manasquan anchorages are severely limited because space is lacking and heavy traffic creates considerable wake. Anchoring near the Manasquan Inlet Coast Guard station is no longer allowed because of shoaling.

For those who do not mind a little rock and roll, there is an anchorage along the north shore of the Manasquan River beyond Crystal Point Yacht Club, but most boaters feel more secure tied to a dock in this extremely busy harbor with its swift currents. Several good restaurants along the Manasquan River provide guest dockage.

Warning: If you intend to travel between Manasquan and Atlantic City via the New Jersey ICW (the inside route), Chart 12324 must be Edition 25 (Edition 33 is current) or newer, and Chart 12316 must be Edition 24 (Edition 34 is current) or newer. Navigation by older charts is virtually impossible.

SHARK RIVER

After exiting the Manasquan Inlet, Shark River Inlet is five miles north. There is no inside route. Don't rely on the landmarks named on the chart for fixing your position on the trip north or south. Multi-story buildings, which obscure the charted landmarks, are all along the shore.

NAVIGATION: Use Chart 12324. Use Sandy Hook tide tables. For high tide, subtract 13 minutes; for low tide, subtract 9 minutes. Just north of Manasquan Inlet, the charted danger area is an onshore military firing range. Red flags on the beach mean that firing is underway or scheduled shortly and that you should stay outside the privately maintained charted buoys.

Anchorage: It is possible to anchor in the north channel of Shark River, just before the fixed bridge. Be sure to stay out of the main channel, but do not get too close to the shallows near the shore.

Shark River Inlet

You can count on the Shark River Inlet for a storm haven along the stretch of coast between Manasquan and Sandy Hook. Twelve feet deep and considered safe for those not familiar with the area (Shark River Inlet was dredged in April 2009), it is also a worthwhile cruising stop. You will find ample accommodations, a busy charter fleet and fine beaches.

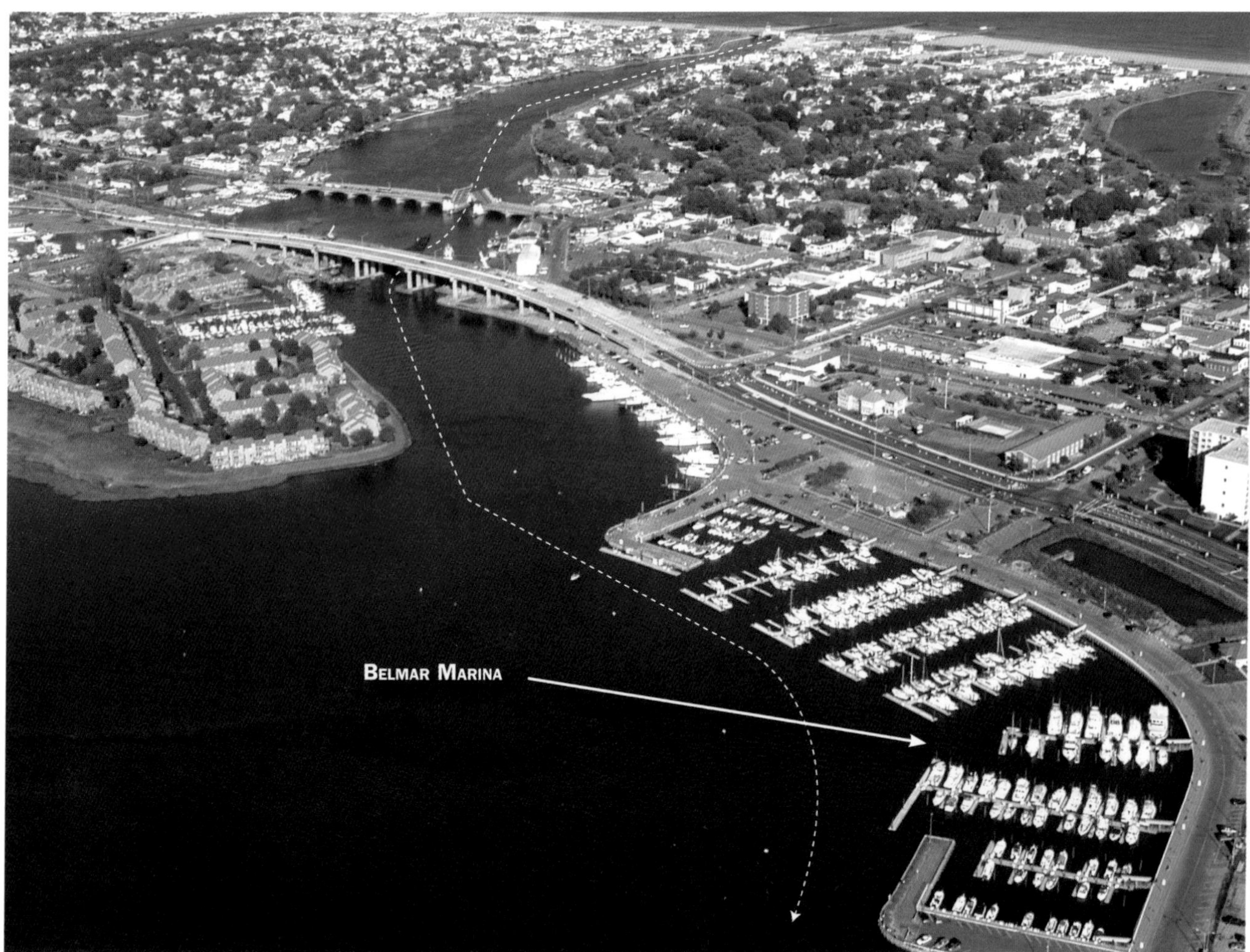

Looking northeast over Shark River. (Not to be used for navigation.) WATERWAY GUIDE PHOTOGRAPHY

NAVIGATION: Use Chart 12324. A bascule bridge (15-foot closed vertical clearance) that opens on the hour and the half-hour crosses Shark River Inlet near its opening to the ocean. On an incoming tide, do not enter the channel between the breakwaters until you are sure the bridge is going to open; maneuvering room is very limited, and a strong flood tide can sweep you down onto it quickly. Fishing party boats wait outside in all conditions until it opens.

Even in benign conditions, do not commit to passage until the span rises. Bridge tenders, aware of the hazard, are quick to open, but heavy auto traffic sometimes causes delays, especially on summer weekends.

Charted depth at the main docks in the Belmar Basin is 7 feet. Three bridges cross the south channel of the Shark River: the state Route 71 bascule bridge (13-foot closed vertical clearance); the railroad bascule bridge (8-foot closed vertical clearance); and the state Route 35 Bridge (50-foot fixed vertical clearance). The two bascule bridges have restricted openings from May 15 to Sept. 30; on weekends and holidays they open on the hour and half-hour only from 9 a.m. to 9 p.m. Weekday openings are on signal except between 4 p.m. and 7 p.m., when they open on the hour and half-hour.

Dockage: An outstanding facility, Belmar Marina lies on the south side of Shark River Island, less than one nautical mile from the Atlantic Ocean. Belmar Marina offers a vast array of amenities, including transient dockage, gas and diesel fuel, shore power, pump-out service, an on-site restaurant and 24-hour security. Local plans call for an exciting redevelopment project in the Belmar Marina area, Seaport Village, including an expanded riverwalk. Fine-dining, café-style restaurants and water tram service are all part of the marina area.

A.P.'s Inlet Marina offers floating docks, gas and diesel fuel, groceries and a pump-out station.

SHARK RIVER, NJ TO SANDY HOOK, NJ

The Atlantic Ocean is the only navigable route to Sandy Hook, 17 miles north of the Shark River Inlet. There is no inside route.

NAVIGATION: Use Chart 12324. Except in heavy weather, you can stay fairly close to shore (keeping far enough off

Shark River, NJ

SHARK RIVER		Largest Vessel Accommodated	VHF Channel Monitored	Transient Berths / Total Berths	Approach / Dockside Depth (reported)	Floating Docks	Gas / Diesel	Groceries, Ice, Marine Supplies, Snacks	Repairs: Hull, Engine, Propeller	Lift (tonnage), Crane, Rail	1=110V, 2=220V, B=Both, Max Amps	Laundry, Pool, Showers	Pump-Out Station	Nearby: Grocery Store, Motel, Restaurant
		Dockage					Supplies		Services					
1. A.P.'s Inlet Marina	732-681-3303	40		/24	14/6	F	GD	GIMS	HEP	LC	1/30			GMR
2. Belmar Marina	**732-681-2266**	**100**	**16**	**70/294**	**12/7**	**F**	**GD**	**GIMS**			**B/50**	**LS**	**P**	**GMR**
3. Total Marina at Seaview Inc.	732-775-7842	45	65	/150	12/5	F	GD	I	HP		1/30	S	P	GMR
4. Shark River Hills Marina	732-775-7400	45		10/180	6/4			IM	HEP	L15	1/30	S		GR
5. Bry's Marine	732-775-7364	40		1/20	4/8	F		IM	HEP	L25	1/30			GMR
6. Shark River Yacht Club Inc.	732-502-0094	65		6/166	6/6	F		IM	HEP	L25	B50	LS	P	GMR

Corresponding chart(s) not to be used for navigation. Internet Access Wireless Internet Access

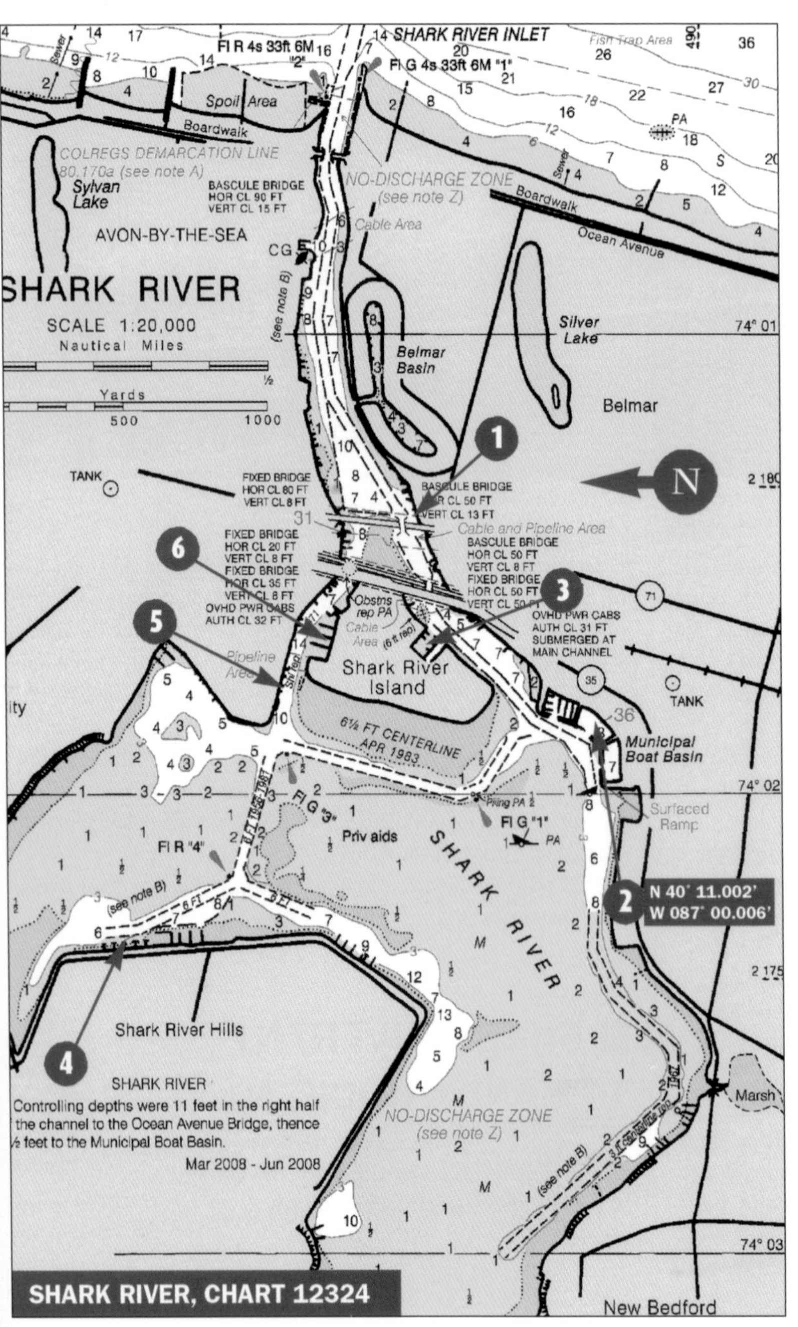

SHARK RIVER, CHART 12324

to clear rocks along the beach). In spring 2008, heavy shoaling was reported in False Hook Channel and NOAA charts 12324, 12327 and 12401 reflect these reports. It is best to use Sandy Hook Channel until dredging has taken place in False Hook Channel. The current close to the hook is quite strong at maximum flood and ebb, east on the ebb and west on the flood.

In heavy easterly weather, the preferred passage to follow is the main Sandy Hook Channel, which is well offshore. Ambrose Light Tower is eastward and clearly visible. Its flashing strobe light is so intense it can be mistaken for lightning.

Seas break on the long bar eastward from the point on Sandy Hook (note the 4-foot-deep lump). This bar sets up the famed "Sandy Hook rip," whose turbulent, tide-tumbled waters produce some of the best fishing (striped bass and bluefish) found anywhere on the Atlantic coast.

Cruising Options

Why not head north to Sandy Hook and enjoy some of that famous fishing? Coverage follows in the upcoming chapter. ■

The Perfect Stop On Your Next East Coast Cruise

Belmar

Whether you would like to stay for vacation or simply spend a safe and comfortable night on the way to your destination, **Belmar Marina is the perfect choice.**

Our beautiful, recently renovated marina, less than one nautical mile from the Atlantic Ocean, offers seasonal and transient dockage for vessels up to 120 feet. The federal channel and Shark River Inlet offers a 12 feet mean low water approach to the marina. Minimum draft at the new cement floating docks is 7 feet at mean low water.

Walk to fine casual dining and pubs, shopping, antique and art galleries and recreational activities. New Jersey Transit rail line servicing New York City to Bay Head, NJ is one block from the marina. Our beautiful white sand beach is less than one mile due east from the marina.

There's fun to be had virtually every day of the year in Belmar. In addition to the beach and boardwalk, great fishing and friendly people, Belmar offers numerous activities such as free concerts, Friendship Cup Sailing Regatta, Fall Festival, Seafood Festival, St. Patrick's Day Parade and many other events!

Marina Amenities:

- 70 New Transient Docks
- Diesel, Gas, Ice & Water
- 50 amp & 30 amp Electrical Service
- Clean Bathroom/Shower/Laundry Facilities
- State-of-the-Art 24 hr. Security
- Children's Beach, Playground, Tennis Courts
- Fishing Pier & Deep Sea Charters
- Pump Out Facilities
- Deli/Restaurant On-Site
- Bait & Tackle Shop
- Garbage & Recyclable Disposal
- Barbecue & Picnic Facilities
- Haul Out & Repair Facilities in Harbor
- Two Full Service Supermarkets are a short drive away.

For More Information Call

732.681.2266 or Radio Channel 16

www.belmar.com

Belmar Harbor:

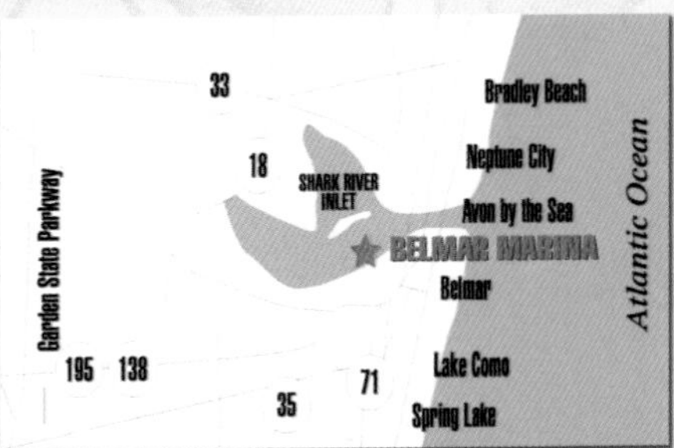

Belmar Marina is located 35 miles south of New York Harbor and 50 miles north of Atlantic City. It is easily accessible from Routes 195, 35, 18 and The Garden State Parkway. Mariners, set your waypoint to 40° 11.002′ N; 74° 0.0056′ W.

Sandy Hook Bay, Twin Rivers

CHARTS 12323, 12324, 12325, 12326, 12327, 12401, 12402

Sandy Hook Bay to the southeast, Raritan Bay to the west and Lower Bay (sometimes called Lower New York Harbor) to the north, the largest of the three, are charted as separate bays but, in reality, they are enclosed sections of a single body of water.

Sandy Hook, NJ, is part of the National Gateway Recreation Area, which includes ocean and bay beaches, nature trails, Fort Hancock (a former military base) and Sandy Hook Lighthouse, the oldest working lighthouse in the country (now a National Historic Landmark). The active Sandy Hook Coast Guard complex dominates the narrow peninsula inside the northern tip of the hook. From there the sandy dunes stretch several miles south before rejoining the mainland in Sea Bright, New Jersey.

If you have access to a car or bike, be sure to stop at Spermaceti Cove Visitors Center near the entrance to Sandy Hook State Park (about 3.5 nautical miles south-southeast of Sandy Hook Point Light) to pick up maps and brochures for a self-guided tour. Sandy Hook is a protected wildlife preserve and many areas of the dunes are closed to foot traffic to protect several species of birds. There are many different types of beaches on Sandy Hook, including those where clothing is optional (a two-mile-long portion of Gunnison Beach is the largest on the East Coast), and all are lifeguard-protected. When entering Sandy Hook by car, there is a per-vehicle charge from Memorial Day to Labor Day. Note that a vigorously enforced security zone exists in the vicinity of Naval Weapons Station Earle, about 1.25 nautical miles southwest of Sandy Hook Point Light in Sandy Hook Bay. The area is patrolled by the marine police and you will be stopped if you venture too close to the pier.

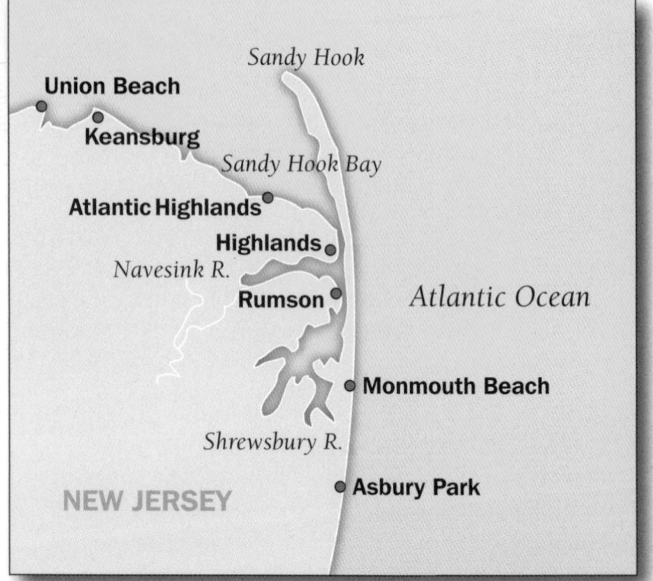

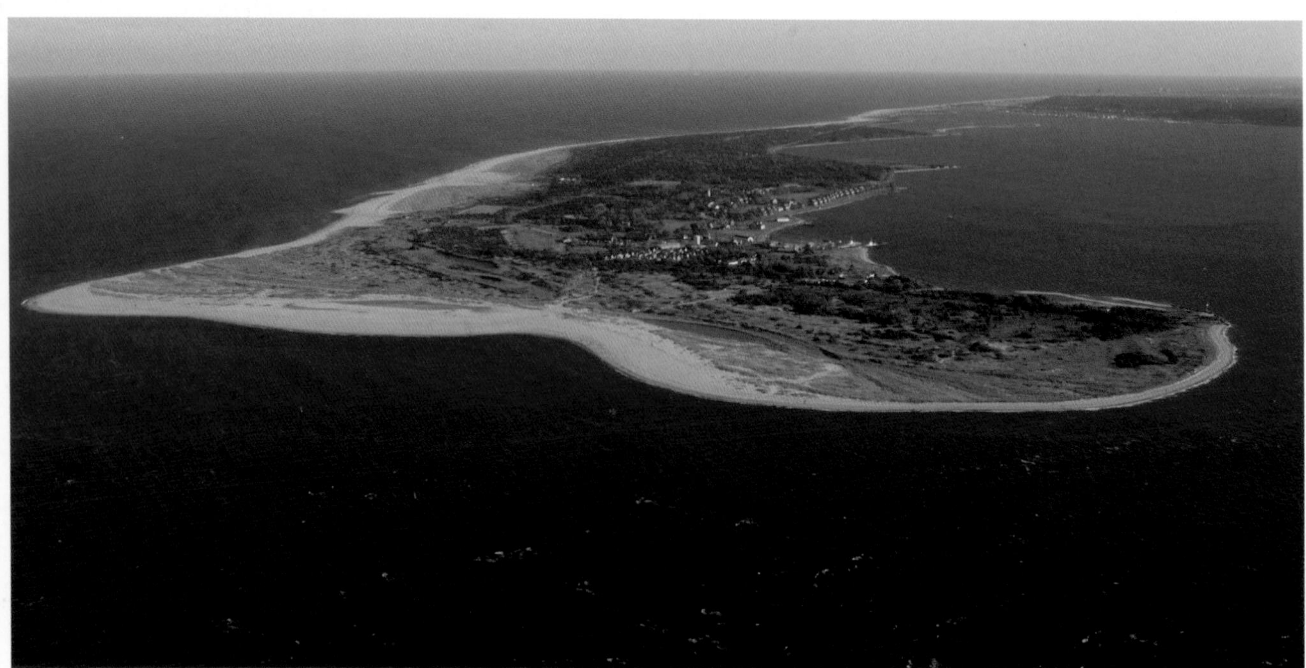

Looking south over Sandy Hook. (Not to be used for navigation.) WATERWAY GUIDE PHOTOGRAPHY

Sandy Hook Bay, NJ

SANDY HOOK BAY		Largest Vessel Accommodated	VHF Channel Monitored	Transient Berths / Total Berths	Approach / Dockside Depth (reported)	Floating Docks	Gas / Diesel	Groceries, Ice, Marine Supplies, Snacks	Repairs: Hull, Engine, Propeller	Lift (tonnage), Crane, Rail	1=110V, 2=220V, B=Both, Max Amps	Laundry, Pool, Showers	Pump-Out Station	Nearby: Grocery Store, Motel, Restaurant
		Dockage					Supplies		Services					
1. Leonardo State Marina	732-291-1333	45	16	/176	3/3	F	GD	GIMS			1/30	S	P	GMR
2. Atlantic Highlands Yacht Club	732-291-3232	130	09		10/10	F	GD	I			B/50	S	P	GR
3. Atlantic Highlands Municipal Harbor 💻	732-291-1670	150	09	8/480	8/7		GD	I		L50	B/100	S	P	GR

Corresponding chart(s) not to be used for navigation. 💻 Internet Access (WiFi) Wireless Internet Access

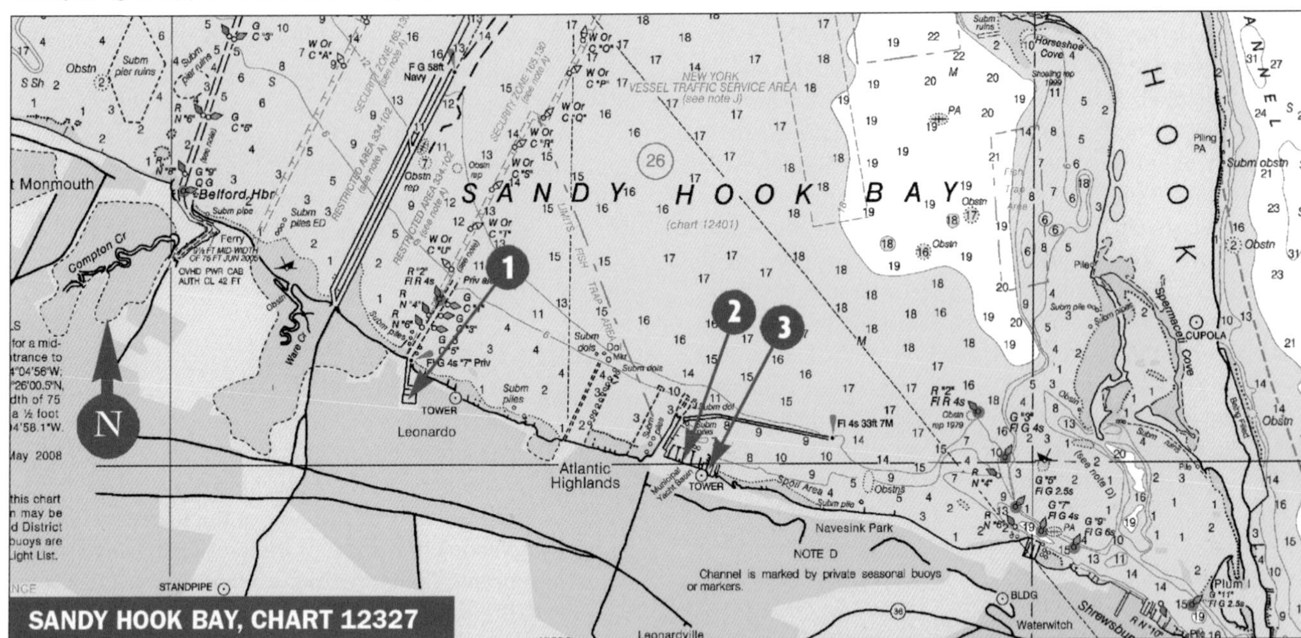

Looking north at Sandy Hook Bay, with Atlantic Highlands to the west. (Not to be used for navigation.)

Sandy Hook Bay

NAVIGATION: Use Chart 12327. Sandy Hook Bay is easily approached by well-buoyed thoroughfares—Sandy Hook Channel from the Atlantic Ocean, Chapel Hill Channel from New York Harbor and Raritan Bay East Reach from Raritan Bay—though multiple navigational aids on the intersecting channels and side channels can be confusing, especially in poor light. Recent revisions of NOAA Charts 12324, 12327 and 12401 indicate shoaling in the northern portion of False Hook Channel, which is located just west of False Hook.

If approaching Sandy Hook from the Atlantic Ocean, follow the Sandy Hook Channel around the hook into Sandy Hook Bay or, if continuing north into New York Harbor, deviate from the Sandy Hook Channel through the Swash Channel, and then join the Chapel Hill Channel at red and green nun buoy "CH." This route allows smaller vessels to avoid traveling in the Ambrose Channel, which usually has a significant amount of large ship traffic.

The Swash Channel is simple to navigate by following a course from Sandy Hook Channel (starting at the lighted front and back range markers for the eastbound channel), and then leaving the 54-foot-high flashing white (2) Romer Shoal Horn to starboard. If heading into Sandy Hook Bay, inside the tip of the "hook," green can buoys mark the shallows near shore; otherwise, depths at mean low water of 15 to 20 feet prevail on the route south to Atlantic Highlands. Keep a sharp lookout for the fish weirs (stakes) in this area, particularly when visibility is poor. They are rarely lighted and hard to see, even in daylight.

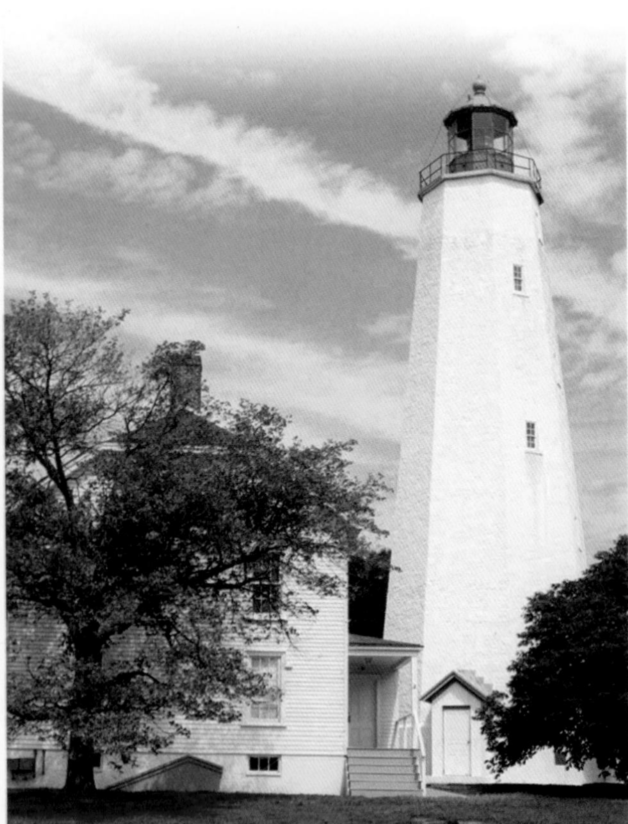

The lighthouse at Sandy Hook. (NOAA.)

Anchorage: In settled weather or during an east wind, there is decent anchorage off the charted Coast Guard station behind Sandy Hook with 20-foot depths at low tide. About two nautical miles south of the Sandy Hook northern tip, is the pretty and always-popular anchorage at Horseshoe Cove, where you will find deep water fairly close to shore. Unfortunately, severe winter storms over the past decade have submerged the once-visible sand spit that had protected the cove. The bar is now about 3 feet below the surface of the water, thereby removing the once protective nature of this anchorage.

In settled weather, there is plenty of room to anchor west of the bar with good holding (sand) in about 20 feet of water. Ashore, drums for garbage and recyclables are near the footbridge at the north end of Horseshoe Cove. You can dinghy ashore and explore ruins of World War II bunkers north of the cove or walk the boardwalk into the marshes to view the protected species of birds. You can walk to the beach on the island's eastern shore from here as well.

Atlantic Highlands, NJ

South of Sandy Hook, the very hospitable, shoreside village of Atlantic Highlands is an excellent storm haven and a great place to stop for a couple of days. It has everything one might want or need in the way of dockage, anchorage, provisions, transportation, municipal showers and restaurants, and presents a charming town within walking distance. If you have to wait for weather before continuing north, east or south, this is a perfect port for it. During severe storms from the north, however, incoming waves build to considerable heights over the long fetch across the bay from the New York side, some of them even making their way over the town's substantial breakwater.

NAVIGATION: Use Chart 12327. Use Sandy Hook tide tables. For high tide, subtract 10 minutes; for low tide, subtract 10 minutes. The protected harbor of Atlantic Highlands is situated three miles south of green can buoy "1," which marks the western end of Sandy Hook Point. The harbor's three-quarter-mile-long breakwater is marked by a 33-foot-high flashing white light at its eastern end. Both the light and the breakwater's end are sometimes difficult to spot from a distance, so set a waypoint or compass course for an efficient passage across Sandy Hook Bay. The breakwater's light beam was recently replaced with one of a higher intensity, however, so it may be easier to spot than previously reported. Commercial vessels also regularly enter the harbor at the western end of the breakwater, but this is not recommended without local knowledge.

Dockage: This area provides a great alternative to New York City dockage, with the SeaStreak high-speed ferry running several times daily to Manhattan and back

Atlantic Highlands, NJ. (Not to be used for navigation.) WATERWAY GUIDE PHOTOGRAPHY

from the Atlantic Highlands harbor. You can stay here and still enjoy the sights of New York City.

Atlantic Highlands Municipal Harbor has at least 480 berths that can handle vessels with drafts of up to 9 feet and lengths of up to 140 feet. Transient slips are usually available, but make advance reservations if you plan a weekend stay. An extensive fuel dock offers both gasoline and diesel fuel and a pump-out station. Restrooms are beneath the prominent, second-story harbormaster's office, you can purchase ice at a small shed out back and the municipal shower complex is a short walk to the west. Anchored-out visitors are required to pay for access to the town's shower complex.

Sailboats can usually rent a mooring from the Atlantic Highlands Yacht Club for a facilities fee, which includes access to the clubhouse, use of the municipal shower facilities and launch service (9 a.m. to 11 p.m. weekends; noon to 10 p.m. weekdays; call "Atlantic Highlands Launch" on VHF Channel 09). Powerboats will have to make arrangements for a slip at the Atlantic Highlands Municipal Harbor or anchor out. Dumpsters are conveniently located near the foot of virtually every dock.

Anchorage: There is usually plenty of anchorage room just inside the eastern end of the Atlantic Highlands breakwater and outside the mooring field or on the south side of the eastern end of the mooring field along the shore. Depths are 8 to 10 feet. This area is quite a distance to shoreside facilities, but there are ample dinghy landings: a dock immediately to the east of the harbormaster's office and floats at the head of each aisle past the fuel dock. Unlimited Atlantic Highlands launch service is extended to anchored boats for a daily fee of $25, which includes use of the municipal shower facilities.

GOIN' ASHORE:
ATLANTIC HIGHLANDS, NJ

This stable and unpretentious bayside village is a bedroom community for downtown New York City (with rapid water commuter services) and a friendly tourist town, reaching out to weekend vacationers and water-seekers. The recreational side of town clusters along the harbor with its multiple piers, sportfishing fleet and numerous restaurants. Its more traditional, commercial side stretches for about a mile along First Avenue, perpendicular to the harbor. A commuter boat service (SeaStreak) operates from Atlantic Highlands and the Highlands to Pier 11 near the South Street Seaport Museum and East 34th Street in Manhattan. During the week, several boats make the trip to New York in the morning and offer several return trips in the afternoon and evening until 11:15 p.m. The run takes about 45 minutes. The SeaStreak fast ferry to New York City is found at the west end of the Atlantic Highlands harbor, known as Pier One, and at Connors in the Highlands. Daily schedules are available online at www.seastreak.com.

Within easy walking distance of any dinghy landing, you will encounter the town's well-maintained tennis courts (near the municipal shower complex) and a band shell with concerts on Sundays during the summer.

Located south on First Avenue are the Skipper Shop (with charts, basic marine supplies and engine and prop repair services), Atlantic Coin Laundry, the Bank on the Green (with 24-hour ATM), Atlantic Highlands Cinemas' five theaters (nightly show times at about 7 p.m., 82 First Ave.) and First Avenue Playhouse (summer stock productions, 123 First Ave.). Foodtown, a small but complete supermarket, is about an eight-block hike out First Avenue at the junction of Bayshore Plaza Highway. The A&P is still farther on (Highway 36 and Valley Drive), but it is a relatively short trip by cab. Or, rent a car and drive over to Sandy Hook State Park for a day on the beautiful white beaches. Between Memorial Day and Labor Day there is a charge for each car entering Sandy Hook State Park.

Restaurants on or within short walking distance of the harbor are numerous and competitive, relying on satisfied customers for repeat business. Shore Casino (off Pier Four) is gigantic, where former first lady Barbara Bush reportedly had "the best chicken ever." Atlantic Bagel Company (74 First Ave.) serves breakfast and lunch only, and is very casual and inexpensive. Harborside Grill (lunch and dinner, 40 First Ave.) serves a varied menu, American style. Memphis Pig Out (67 First Ave.) has great ribs and moderate prices. Copper Canyon, on First Avenue, has fast become famous for its margaritas and Mexican food. Bel Vesuvio, also on First Avenue, is well-known for good Italian food and pizza. If it's hot dogs you crave, try Jersey Joe's Italian Hot Dogs.

ADDITIONAL RESOURCES:

- New Jersey Shore Guide, **www.shore-guide.com**

NEARBY GOLF COURSES:
Monmouth County Park System Golf Courses, 805 Newman Springs Road #1, Lincroft, NJ 07738, 732-842-4000, **www.monmouthcountyparks.com**

NEARBY MEDICAL FACILITIES:
Riverview Medical Center, 1 Riverview Plaza, Red Bank, NJ 07701, 732-741-2700, **www.meridianhealth.com**

Twin Lights

Twin Lights is situated 200 feet above sea level in Highlands, NJ. It overlooks the Shrewsbury River, Sandy Hook, Raritan Bay, New York skyline and the Atlantic Ocean. The Twin Lights were built in 1862 and dedicated by President Lincoln. They are the latest in a long line of lighthouses built on this promontory, one of the highest points of land on the Atlantic coast. The first light here was erected by New York merchants in 1765. A light has shone steadily here ever since, and today a state-maintained occulting white light can be seen from the north tower during the boating season. The Twin Lights now house a state-run nautical museum displaying marine artifacts and the original building of the old Life Saving Service. The museum is a short car ride from Atlantic Highlands Harbor.

RARITAN BAY

West of Atlantic Highlands, a number of harbors along the South Shore of Raritan Bay and on the North Shore of Lower Bay (Great Kills Harbor) provide protection for cruising mariners.

Leonardo

NAVIGATION: Use Chart 12327. The area around the huge Navy piers, just west of Leonardo, may undergo periodic dredging in an effort to maintain Weapons Station Earle. Surrounding the Navy Pier, the chart shows a restricted area that must be observed. The pier is used for loading and off-loading explosives. In May 1950, an explosion on the docks killed 31 workers and shattered doors and windows for miles around.

Due to increased security concerns, pleasure boaters should stay well clear of this and other military installations; expect to see security patrols on the water. Fines of $500 are given for the first offense. Any boater who finds it impossible to stay clear should immediately contact the U.S. Coast Guard by VHF radio or some other means. See the "Port Security" page located in the Skipper's Handbook section of this book for more information.

Raritan Bay and River, NJ

RARITAN BAY AND RIVER		Largest Vessel Accommodated	VHF Channel Monitored	Transient Berths / Total Berths	Approach / Dockside Depth (reported)	Floating Docks	Gas / Diesel	Groceries, Ice, Marine Supplies, Snacks	Repairs: Hull, Engine, Propeller	Lift (tonnage), Crane, Rail	1=110V, 2=220V, B=Both, Max Amps	Laundry, Pool, Showers	Pump-Out Station	Nearby: Grocery Store, Motel, Restaurant
		Dockage					Supplies		Services					
1. Morgan Marina	732-721-2290	40		5/285	15/10	F	G	IMS	HEP	L25,C	1/30	S	P	GMR
2. Lockwood Boat Works □ WiFi	**732-721-1605**	**50**	**72**	**6/178**	**5/5**	**F**	**GD**	**M**	**HEP**	**L35**	**1/30**	**LS**	**P**	**GMR**
3. Zuback's Marine	732-727-3953	42	68	3/35	14/10	F		MS	HEP	LCR	1/35			GMR
4. Vikings Marina □ WiFi	732-566-5961	35		2/175	6/6	F	G	IM	HEP	L20	1/30	S	P	GMR
5. Keyport Marine Basin	732-264-9421	32		6/275	6/5	F	G	GIMS	EP	L	1/30	S	P	GMR
6. Seaboard Marine □ WiFi	732-264-8910	32		/42	5/5	F		IM	HEP	L12	1/15	S		GMR
7. Lentze Marina Inc.	732-787-2139	53	16	5/125	7/7	F		GIMS	HEP	L12	1/50	LS	P	GMR

Corresponding chart(s) not to be used for navigation. □ Internet Access WiFi Wireless Internet Access

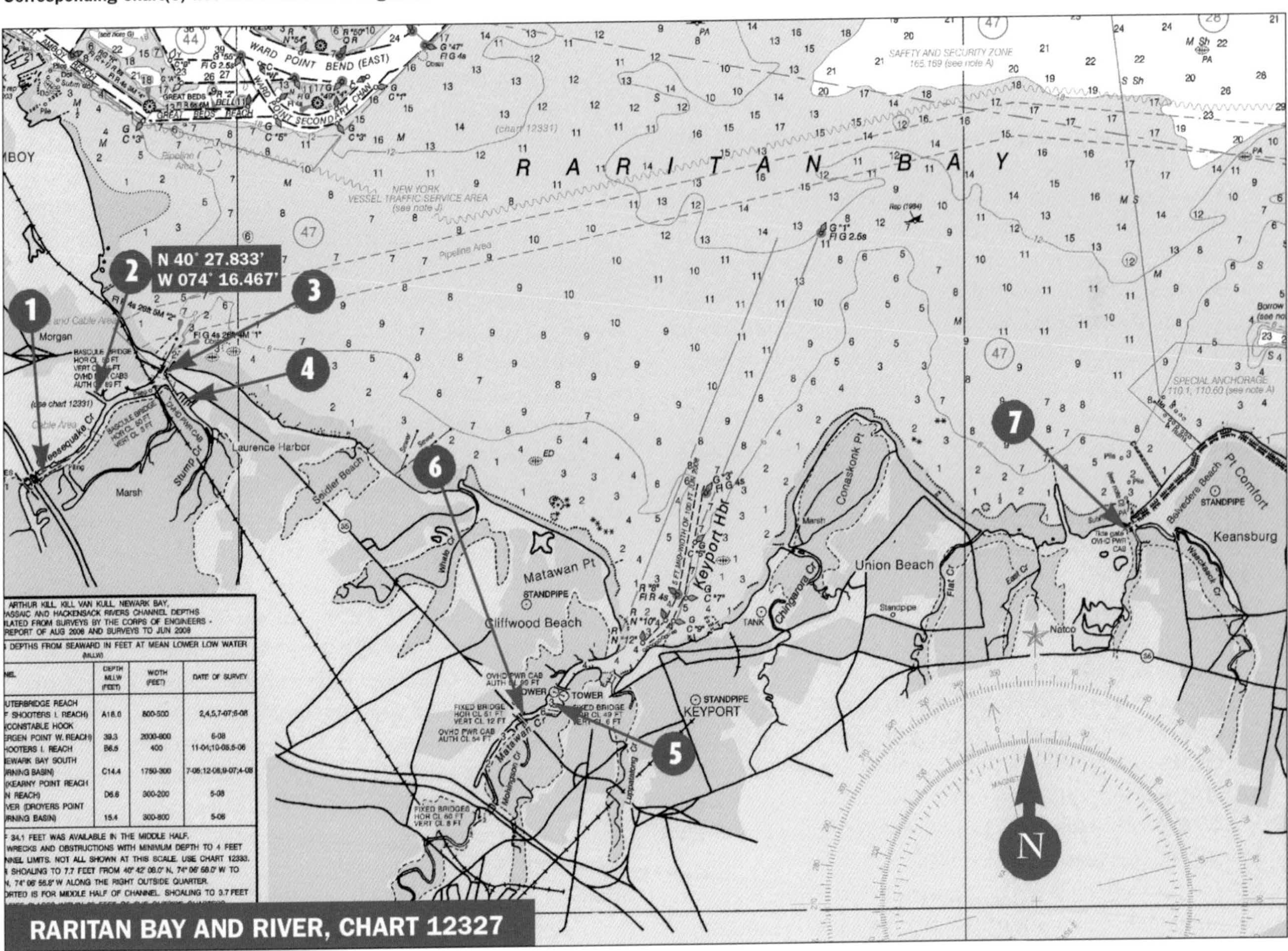

RARITAN BAY AND RIVER, CHART 12327

Dockage: Leonardo has an almost landlocked harbor that can get hot in summer. A 5-foot-deep channel leads to a basin with 7-foot depths. A state marina has some slips for transients, but maneuvering room is very tight here, and no anchoring space is available.

Belford Harbor, Keansburg, Keyport, and Morgan

NAVIGATION: Use Chart 12327. Belford Harbor is the first harbor west after the Leonardo pier. It has a well-marked entrance into Compton Creek between red and green can buoys and is very busy with commercial fishing traffic. There is an excellent seafood market in Belford where the local fishing fleet unloads daily. The market is located on the harbor.

West of Belford Harbor and Port Monmouth is the town of Keansburg and its facilities on Waackaack Creek, which are protected by tidal gates. There are no channel markers on entry and there is shoaling across the entrance. A better bet is to continue west to Keyport Harbor, which is easily entered through a well-marked, deepwater channel into Matawan Creek. Use Sandy Hook tide tables. For

AN ALTERNATE ROUTE

When there is a gale blowing from the southeast and an outgoing tide is causing an uncomfortable high, short chop south of The Narrows—and either Sandy Hook or New York Harbor is your destination—a trip through Kill Van Kull around the northwest side of Staten Island is a good alternative. The channel is well-marked and depths are excellent. Shoreline beautification and recreational projects have proliferated along these waters, making this trip a far cry from what it was just a decade ago. There is an excellent restaurant on the Kill in a marina directly across from Perth Amboy where slips are available while dining. Perth Amboy has two waterside restaurants of note, Seabra's Armory and The Barge. Both restaurants are next to the Perth Amboy Municipal Marina.

West of New York Harbor are a myriad of kills, rivers, streams and bays that are seldom on the itinerary of recreational boaters ("kill" comes from the Dutch and means channel, stream, creek or river). Long avoided because of their industrial atmosphere, these waters have gone through a remarkable metamorphosis. If you've traveled the normal route through New York Harbor more than once and are looking for something different, or if there's a gale blowing out of the southeast and a trip through the Narrows to Sandy Hook does not seem inviting, think about using the protected waters to the west of Staten Island as a new route.

The Kill Van Kull, to the north, and Arthur Kill, to the north and west, join to separate Staten Island from New Jersey. In the 1600s, New York and New Jersey each claimed Staten Island as its own. They agreed to settle the dispute with a sailboat race. New York's Capt. Charles Billip and his sloop Bently won the race. Staten Island became part of New York State, and eventually part of the New York City borough of Richmond. Billip was rewarded with lands and a manor house at Tottenville on Staten Island, where the Tottenville Ferry (no longer in existence) used to run to Perth Amboy, NJ. The historic Tottenville Ferry Terminal can be seen at the foot of Smith Street on the Arthur Kill.

NAVIGATION: Use Chart 12327 (Edition 100 was current at publication). When heading west from New York Harbor, Kill Van Kull branches off to the west of New York Harbor at red and green flashing red "KV" and leads to the industrial waterways of New Jersey. These waterways are the major channels for bulk, containerized and petroleum cargo in the Port of New York, so expect to share the traffic lanes with large ships, barges and tugboats that are constrained by the channel and unable to stop or turn easily. Shipping traffic in this area monitors VHF Channel 13.

The Kill Van Kull connects New York Harbor with Newark Bay and Arthur Kill. When heading west on Kill Van Kull from New York Harbor, Bayonne, New Jersey, is to the north and Staten Island to the south. Immed-iately after passing under the Bayonne Bridge and entering the southern end of Newark Bay, you will see North of Shooters Island Reach. At this point, bear left into Arthur Kill. Newark Bay South Reach, the route of container ships bound for Port Elizabeth and Port Newark, branches to the right. There is dredging underway in the Bayonne vicinity. This work is expected to continue, and boaters should be alert to the possible presence of work vessels. The Arthur Kill leads west and then south around Staten Island in a well-marked, protected channel. Just to the south of the intersection of Newark Bay South Reach and North of Shooters Island Reach is Shooters Island, a wildlife sanctuary. Mariners Harbor is located behind Shooters Island and has a full-service boatyard and marine store.

As you enter Kill Van Kull from New York Harbor, you are going inland and buoys are "red-right-returning" as would be expected, but when you head under the Goethals Bridge (leading to Bayway on the New Jersey side and Gulfport on the Staten Island side), you are heading out to sea and the buoys are suddenly reversed (red to port and green to starboard). In addition, the actual velocities and directions of tidal currents in Arthur Kill may deviate significantly from those shown in tidal current tables. There is a lift bridge (down is 31 feet and up is 135 feet) just north of the Goethals Bridge that is usually in the up position.

South of the Goethals Bridge, just before the Rahway River, is Pralls Island, a bird sanctuary that sports an ever-increasing population of gulls and herons.

Dockage: On the Staten Island shore, just below the Outerbridge Crossing in Perth Amboy, NJ, are small marinas offering some dockage and restaurants. On the New Jersey shore in Perth Amboy are The Perth Amboy Municipal Marina, Seabra's Armory restaurant (a brick building near the municipal marina), the Barge seafood restaurant, a launching ramp and the Raritan Yacht Club, which has guest moorings for reciprocal yacht clubs. Launch service is available for yacht club moorings from 7 a.m. to 11 p.m. daily. Both the yacht club and the municipal marina monitor Channel 09. Just south of the yacht club, on the southeastern tip of Perth Amboy where Arthur Kill joins Raritan Bay, a town park with a brick boardwalk wraps around the point.

Near the south end of Arthur Kill, expensive homes line the shoreline on Staten Island and Perth Amboy and South Amboy on the New Jersey side. Once in Raritan Bay, the New Jersey Highlands and Sandy Hook are easily seen to the east on a clear day. Keep in the channel when rounding Ward Point at the southerly tip of Staten Island.

high tide, subtract 1 minute; for low tide, add 7 minutes. There is shoaling on both sides of the channel on entry, so be sure to stay in the channel. Farther west on Raritan Bay is Cheesequake (also known as Morgan) Creek at Morgan, entered through jetties, though the east jetty might be submerged at high water. Use Sandy Hook tide tables. For high tide, add 12 minutes; for low tide, add 13 minutes. Flashing green "1" and flashing red "2" mark the entrance.

The Route 35 highway bascule bridge (25-foot closed vertical clearance) and the railroad bridge (3-foot closed vertical clearance) have restricted hours: From April 1 to Nov. 30, from 7 a.m. to 7 p.m., the draws open on the hour (on signal). The railroad bridge is usually open but closes on weekends three minutes before each hour for trains. When leaving Cheesequake (Morgan) Creek, make sure to be inside of the railroad bridge before it closes or stand the chance of missing the hourly opening of the bascule bridge. Both bridges crossing Cheesequake (Morgan) Creek monitor VHF Channel 13.

Dockage: The most complete facilities for boaters are found in Keyport Harbor and Cheesequake (Morgan) Creek. Within Keyport Harbor are a couple of marinas that may have transient slips and the Keyport Yacht Club, which has guest moorings for transient sailboats. There are also a few restaurants and the town is on the harbor.

After entering Morgan Creek, inside of the bridges, follow it a short way up to Lockwood Boat Works, a full-service marina with a few transient slips and a large marine store. They also do full repairs. It is best to call ahead to ensure availability. There are no channel markers inside Cheesequake (Morgan) Creek. Favor the west side to avoid mud flats and transit on a rising tide. There are three other marinas in the creek offering varying degrees of service.

Raritan River—Perth Amboy, South Amboy

NAVIGATION: Use Charts 12332 and 12327. For South Amboy, use Sandy Hook tide tables. For high tide, subtract 4 minutes; for low tide, add 8 minutes. The Raritan River (Chart 12332) flows at swift speed into Raritan Bay between Perth Amboy and South Amboy. It is navigable 11 miles to New Brunswick, through a crooked but well-marked channel, and carries a fair amount of industrial traffic and flotsam through the salt marshes. Depths diminish to about 4 feet in its upper reaches. Note that no fuel is available on the Raritan River, so plan accordingly.

The railroad bascule bridge (8-foot closed vertical clearance) between Perth Amboy and South Amboy carries heavy commuter traffic. It does not open from 6 a.m to 8:10 a.m. and from 5:15 p.m. to 6:35 p.m. on weekdays. The new fixed Victory Bridge, just beyond the railroad bascule, has a vertical clearance of 110 feet. The fixed bridges carrying vehicle traffic farther up are Route 9 and the Garden State Parkway.

About six miles up, the South River curves off to port, with shallow depths and limited facilities, past a 45-foot fixed vertical clearance bridge. Beyond the bridge, you come to New Brunswick, the head of navigation for the river and the home of Rutgers University and Johnson & Johnson pharmaceuticals. Here you can see the remains of the entrance to the Delaware and Raritan Canal, closed in 1933, which once linked New Brunswick to Trenton on the Delaware River. Recreational boaters rarely transit the Raritan River from Perth Amboy because facilities are limited.

The town of Perth Amboy is located at the intersection of the Raritan River, Arthur Kill and Raritan Bay. Pay attention to all channel markers in this area to avoid shipping traffic, as the ships must remain in the channels. There is plenty of water for pleasure craft outside of the channels except off of Ward Point at the tip of Staten Island, where it is not advisable to cut inside the red aids to navigation.

Dockage: Perth Amboy has a friendly yacht club (Raritan Yacht Club), and you will find supplies only a short walk up the street, in nearby Perth Amboy. A Supremo grocery is a short walk up Smith Street and a West Marine is several blocks farther on Market Street. The North Jersey Coast train station is a half mile from the harbor.

The yacht club offers guest moorings to reciprocal yacht club members. Just north of the yacht club is the Perth Amboy municipal marina, with occasional transient slips and a few town moorings. An old naval building on the harbor has been converted from a drill hall to a three-story restaurant, Seabra's Armory. The food is Portuguese and there is an outdoor deck for dining on Arthur Kill. The Barge, another well-known New Jersey seafood restaurant is directly across from Seabra's Armory. There is no fuel available in Perth Amboy. The nearest gas and diesel can be found at Lockwood Boat Works in Morgan Creek.

Great Kills Harbor (North Shore, Lower Bay)

Due east from Perth Amboy or due north from Sandy Hook is Great Kills Harbor. This is a harbor of refuge and provides an easy entrance to secure shelter, provisions and full-service marinas.

A more detailed account of Great Kills Harbor is provided in the "New York Bay, Hudson River" chapter of this Guide.

■ TWIN RIVERS—NAVESINK AND SHREWSBURY RIVERS

Inside of Sandy Hook and south beyond the Highlands Route 36 bascule bridge (35-foot closed vertical clearance), the Navesink and Shrewsbury rivers lace the northeastern corner of New Jersey with well-protected cruising waters. The rivers pass high, green banks, marshy islands and attractive residential areas. Yacht clubs, marinas

Navesink River, Shrewsbury River, NJ

NAVESINK RIVER, SHREWSBURY RIVER		Dockage					Supplies		Services					
		Largest Vessel Accommodated	VHF Channel Monitored	Transient Berths / [illegible]al Berths	Approach / Dockside Depth (reported)	Floating Docks	Gas / Diesel	Groceries, Ice, Marine Supplies, Snacks	Repairs: Hull, Engine, Propeller	Lift (tonnage), Crane, Rail	1=110V, 2=220V, B=Both, Max Amps	Laundry, Pool, Showers	Pump-Out Station	Nearby: Grocery Store, Motel, Restaurant
1. Captain's Cove Marina	732-872-1177			2/85	15/6			GI			1/30	LS		GMR
2. Marina on the Bay (Internet)	732-872-9300	120		6/148	12/10	F		IM	HEP	L35	1/30	S		GMR
3. Gateway Marina	732-291-4440x10	34	69	/32	10/8	F		IMS	EP	L	B/30	S		GMR
4. Bahrs Landing (WiFi)	732-872-1245	95	65	10/30	18/12	F	GD	I			B/50			GMR
5. Oceanic Marina	732-842-1194	50		1/110	6/5	F		IMS	HEP	L20	1/30	S	P	GR
6. Fair Haven Yacht Works (WiFi)	732-747-3010	65	09	1/80	6/6	F		IM	HEP	L15,C9	B/50	S	P	GMR
7. Irwin Marine (Internet) (WiFi)	732-741-0003	80	09	10/153	8/6	F		IM	HEP	L25	B/50	PS	P	GM
8. Molly Pitcher Inn/Marina (WiFi)	**732-747-2500**	**65**	**09**	**5/73**	**6/6**	**F**		**I**			**1/50**	**PS**	**P**	**GMR**
9. Oyster Point Hotel/Marina (Internet) (WiFi)	**732-530-8200**	**60**	**09**	**2/26**	**5/4**	**F**		**I**			**1/50**	**S**		**GMR**
10. Carriage House Marina (WiFi)	732-741-8113	50		6/37	10/10			GI	HEP	L25,C6	1/30	S	P	GMR
11. Surfside Marina	732-842-0844	30		1/52	6/4			M	EP	L	1/30	S		GMR
12. Navesink Marina	732-842-3700	60	16/72	/115	15/8	F	GD	IS	HEP	L	B/50	LS	P	GMR
13. Atlantis Yacht Club	732-222-9693	75	69	4/55	6/6						B/50	LPS	P	GMR
14. Channel Club Marina (WiFi)	732-222-7717	70	09	5/150	8/6		GD	IMS	HEP	L60	B/50	PS	P	GR
15. Patten Point Yacht Club (Internet)	732-229-2882	50		5/70	4/4						1/30	LPS	P	R
16. Pleasure Bay Yacht Basin	732-222-8563	42		/66	5/4			IM	HEP	L12	1/30	LS		
17. Oceanport Landing	732-229-4466	55		2/85	6/5	F		MS	HEP	L30	1/30	S	P	R

Corresponding chart(s) not to be used for navigation. (Internet) Internet Access (WiFi) Wireless Internet Access

and boatyards, waterfront restaurants with docks, scenic anchorages and old, established communities line the shores. In many places, the Atlantic Ocean is only a short walk away across the barrier strip.

NAVIGATION: Use Charts 12327 and 12324. Between Atlantic Highlands and Sandy Hook, at the town of Highlands, pick up flashing red buoy "2" marking the shared entrance of the Shrewsbury and Navesink rivers, which is charted as Shrewsbury River. The low intensity light can be lost among shore lights at night, so a daylight approach is recommended. Obtain the latest information on depths before heading in; navigation on ebb tides can be tricky.

Both the Navesink and Shrewsbury rivers have been designated as No-Discharge Zones (overboard discharge of raw or treated sewage is prohibited).

Soon after entering the Shrewsbury River, you pass a bascule bridge (35-foot closed vertical clearance) between Highlands and Seabright Beach. The draw opens on signal except on Saturdays, Sundays and holidays, from Memorial Day through Labor Day when it opens on the hour and half-hour from 7 a.m. to 8 p.m. The current runs swiftly here; watch out for turbulence under the bridge at full current.

A commuter boat service (SeaStreak) operates from Connors in Highlands, NJ, to Pier 11 next to the South Street Seaport Museum and East 34th Street in Manhattan, close to midtown shopping. During the week, several boats cruise to New York City in the morning and offer several return trips in the afternoon and evening until 11:15 p.m. The run takes about 45 minutes. The SeaStreak fast ferry to New York City is found at the west end of the Atlantic

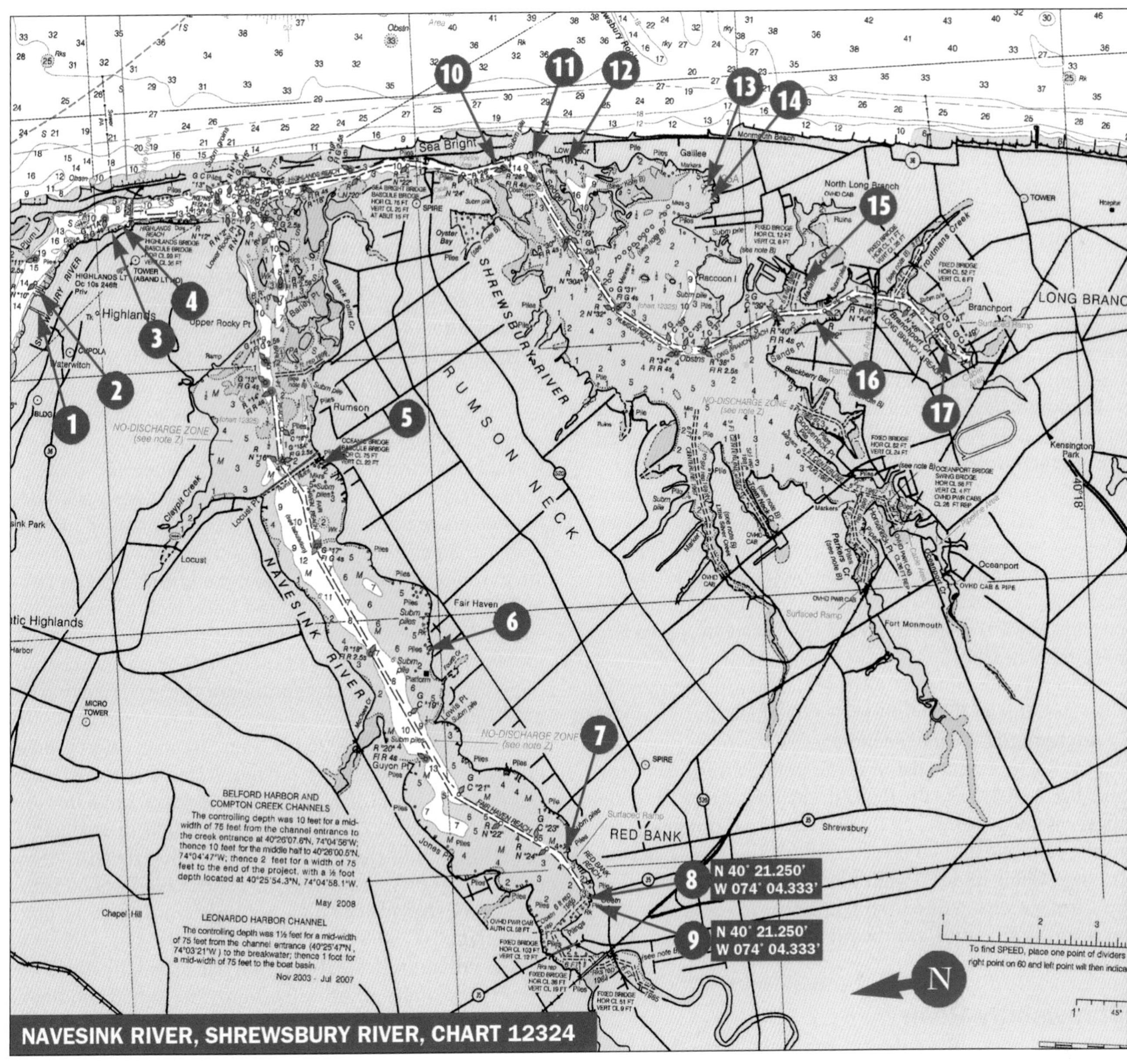

NAVESINK RIVER, SHREWSBURY RIVER, CHART 12324

Highlands harbor, known as Pier One, and at Connors in the Highlands. Daily schedules are available online at www.seastreak.com.

All sorts of marinas line this one-mile-plus stretch to the mouth of the Navesink River, which bears off westward to the town of Red Bank, NJ. Whether you take the Navesink or stay on the Shrewsbury River, be careful of three (charted) orange-striped white can buoys that mark a submerged rock wall extending northeasterly from the south side of the mouth of the Navesink River. Stick to the channel, even if you see a local boat head over the line. Note that the flashing red-and-green buoy "NS" marking the Shrewsbury/Navesink River junction appears to be all red until you are close aboard. This makes sorting out the proper channels confusing. Once the mid-channel marker is positively identified, the approach becomes straightforward.

Navesink River

The historic harborfront town of Red Bank, NJ, is at the head of navigation on the Navesink River. It is named for the color of its riverbanks. In the 1800s, Red Bank was a thriving shipping center and popular Victorian resort. Though it is still a commercial center, it retains its rural beauty and Victorian charm. Summer attractions in Red Bank include the Red Bank Jazz and Blues Festival (held the first weekend in June) and New Jersey's largest fireworks display on Fourth of July weekend. Red Bank offers many restaurants, full-service marinas, shopping and a main-line train station all within walking distance of any dockage or anchorage.

NAVIGATION: Use Chart 12324. Use Sandy Hook tide tables. For high tide, add 1 hour 17 minutes; for low tide, add 1 hour 57 minutes. Transiting the Navesink River requires local knowledge and close attention to depths. There are rocky ledges to the north and shoals on both sides of the narrow channel. The area between the junction of the Twin Rivers and the Locust Point bascule bridge is very tricky. At the opening to the Navesink River, pass between red and green junction buoy "NS" and red nun buoy "2," and then continue to follow the curving channel past red nun buoys "4" and "6," watching for shoaling in the vicinity of red nun buoy "6."

About a mile upriver from the mouth of the Navesink River, Barley Point Reach passes between sandbars that are bare at low tide. Controlling depth is only 2.5 feet; be sure to stay in mid-channel well past the Locust Point (Oceanic) bascule bridge (22-foot closed vertical clearance). From there on, you can find good anchorages under the bluffs with good holding.

Dockage: Boating amenities are along the south shore of the river, just below the Locust Point Bridge at Oceanic, and a mile farther up at Fair Haven.

The historic Molly Pitcher Inn overlooks the Navesink River at Red Bank, offering both fine dining and dockage. This is a state-of-the-art marina with all amenities, including wireless Internet service. The big yacht work business here has been family-run since 1884. Buses and trains provide quick transportation to New York City, and a large hospital is nearby.

Oyster Point Hotel is nearby and may have transient slips available at their full-service hotel facility.

Anchorage: A fine anchorage lies a mile upriver at Upper Rocky Point. Just past the point, turn to starboard and head back east up the old channel of the Navesink River. Make the turn well to the west of red nun buoy "10" to clear the shoal, then favor the north shore. You can stop in deep water under a high bluff. A small island protects you from wakes without stopping the breeze. If you plan to swim, trail a line overboard. The current is strong at maximum flood and ebb.

Shrewsbury River

The route goes on southward from its junction with the Navesink River, passing low and marshy shores with the channel cutting through shoal water on either side. Ashore on Rumson Neck, between the two rivers, the countryside still maintains a somewhat rural appearance.

NAVIGATION: Use Chart 12325. The Sea Bright bascule bridge (15-foot closed vertical clearance) connecting Rumson and Sea Bright has restricted openings. On weekends and holidays, from May 15 to Sept. 30, it opens only on the hour and half-hour between 9 a.m. and 7 p.m. It will not open for a sailboat unless the boat is under auxiliary power. Strong currents and congestion on the approach channel to the bridge make this an area for caution, requiring a firm grip on the helm.

South of Sea Bright, the route forks. The main channel branches west along Long Branch Reach and the narrow paths crook through shoals. A well-buoyed side route (which is privately marked) leads southward to Galilee, and then swings northwest to rejoin the main channel west of Sedge Island. Numerous lighted markers on the side route to Galilee and west of Long Branch Reach have been replaced with unlit buoys, although the most recent charts do not reflect this change. This triangular side passage was created as a turnaround channel for big steam-powered boats.

The rest of the Shrewsbury is shallow, but there are several creeks to explore. The fixed bridge over Parkers Creek has a 24-foot vertical clearance, while the swing bridge over Oceanport Creek (4-foot closed vertical clearance) has rush hour closings weekdays from May 15 to Sept. 15.

Dockage: North on the Shrewsbury River in the Highlands area, before the Shrewsbury intersects with the Navesink, Marina on the Bay offers transient dockage, repairs, shore power, numerous restaurants and other amenities.

In the vicinity of Galilee, the residential shore is sealed from the Atlantic Ocean by a massive sea wall. Numerous marinas and boatyards can be found here.

Boats that can clear the 25-foot fixed vertical clearance bridge across Pleasure Bay can cruise right to Long Branch, where a small park and bulkhead, known to few skippers and seldom used, make it possible to tie up. As in days past, when Long Branch was the queen resort of the New Jersey shore, swimming in the area remains the great summer attraction here.

In the 1870s, President Grant escaped the summer heat of the nation's capital here. Here, too, Diamond Jim Brady and Lillian Russell sipped champagne and savored the local oysters. Though much of that era is gone, including the oysters, some relics remain. Many new restaurants and high-end malls have popped up in Long Branch and it is once again becoming an in place to visit.

The commuter railroad to Bay Head is still called the New York and Long Branch, and the once fashionable Jockey Club, with its gambling casino and race track, is now lush Monmouth Park, where thoroughbreds race (June to August) within a mile of your mooring in Pleasure Bay.

Cruising Options

Ahead lies New York Harbor, one of the world's busiest and most exciting ports. From there, you can transit the East River to explore Long Island Sound and continue north to the U.S./Canada line. ■

Waterway Guide is always open to your observations from the helm. E-mail your comments on any navigation information in the guide to: editor@waterwayguide.com.

Introduction

New York Waters

At Sandy Hook, the skipper can set a course in any direction and head for a wide choice of destinations. To the south on the ocean side lie the beaches and inlets of the New Jersey coast or, to the south on the inside of Sandy Hook, await the popular harbors of Atlantic Highlands and the Shrewsbury and Navesink rivers. To the west across Raritan Bay are Arthur Kill and the town of Perth Amboy. To the north lies New York Harbor, offering a choice of the Hudson River, the East River to Long Island Sound or the Kill Van Kull, an alternate route around Staten Island. To the east Long Island, Rockaway Inlet and the entrance to the inside passage along the South Shore.

North through The Narrows into New York Harbor is the great city of New York, with its five boroughs, 8.2 million people and one of the world's finest natural harbors. Many superlatives apply to New York City, and it is not lacking in boating amenities. While there are a few possibilities in Manhattan, most of the marinas are found on the New Jersey side of the harbor in Jersey City and Hoboken. Ferries make the trip on a regular basis back and forth to Manhattan. These large, full-service marinas are close to provisioning, transportation and waterfront events.

Directly alongside the skyscrapers of Manhattan heading east, lies the magnificent East River, twisting its way past the South Street Seaport, the beautiful east-side buildings with penthouse gardens and Gracie Mansion, New York's mayoral home. The East River leads to that favorite cruising Mecca, Long Island Sound. If planned right, the trip through the East River can be extremely enjoyable.

Heading north from Manhattan, cruisers head up the Hudson River to connect with the Erie Canal and Lake Erie or the Champlain Canal and Lake Champlain. (Waterway Guide's Great Lakes edition contains details on these routes.)

Crossing New York Harbor

New York Harbor is one of the world's busiest. Ships and barges are always on the move in and out of the harbor, anchoring and docking at piers along the Hudson River, the East River and heading to ports in New Jersey. Tankers, freighters of all flags, cruise ships, naval vessels, a myriad of tugs and tows and recreational boat traffic—along with continual ferry service to and from Staten Island, New Jersey ports on the Hudson and through The Narrows to ports south—demand the full attention of even the most experienced skippers. Always give big ships the right-of-way; they have limited maneuvering room.

During periods of heightened alert by the Department of Homeland Security, recreational vessels might be required to check in with the Coast Guard before entering New York waters at www.uscgnewyork.com. More information regarding harbor restrictions can be found in the "Port Security Procedures" portion in the Skipper's Handbook section located in the front this guide. Warning: Carrying handguns without a permit aboard in New York waters is illegal.

CT NY

NAVIGATION: Use Chart 12327. The passage through New York waters demands strict observance of the "Rules of the Road" and careful planning to take advantage of the currents, which are extremely important to a smooth and timely passage. Strong currents, both predictable tidal flow and unpredictable eddies, must be considered. The current in New York Harbor can run up to 3.5 knots. It is best to plan your trip to have the current with you and not against you. When looking up tides for New York Harbor, base your reference on the Battery (i.e. low water or high water).

Watch for debris moving just below the surface in the current. Because of the waterways converging on the Harbor, debris is often carried in and out from many areas. Powerboats should slow down to reduce the chance of hitting such objects. Uncertain winds generally require that sailboats use their auxiliary engines when transiting the Harbor, definitely in the East River. All vessels should monitor VHF Channel 16 and stay alert to traffic that might be just around the corner. Shipping in the New York waters monitors VHF Channel 13.

New York Harbor waters are deep and well-marked. In fog or rain follow the main channel buoys closely, but you can also run just outside of the channel itself, in plenty of water, and still stay clear of big-ship traffic. Compass or

GPS courses might be needed to sort out one buoy from another. At night, take the extra time to be certain of the lights. An optional passage to reach the East River from the Verrazano Narrows Bridge is to hug the Brooklyn (east) shore of Upper Bay, stay east of Bay Ridge Flats through the Bay Ridge Channel and then travel east of Governor's Island through the Buttermilk Channel. This route avoids the large vessels, Staten Island ferries and the strong currents that can be found in Upper Bay.

Currents in The Narrows build up to 2.5 knots on the ebb and up to 2 knots during the flood. Skippers heading up the East River to Long Island Sound might want to base the times of their passage on Hell Gate currents. The strongest currents in New York Harbor (up to 5 knots) are found here at the northeastern end of Manhattan.

Passage through Hell Gate should be timed to carry a fair current; a visible "slack water" is rare. Skip to the "East River to Long Island Sound" chapter if you are turning east into Long Island Sound.

Hudson River

Cruising the lower Hudson River is generally straightforward. Aids to navigation are plentiful, mid-channel depths range from 15 to 175 feet and, north of Manhattan, marinas and hospitable yacht clubs are numerous. Overnight berths should be selected for maximum protection from the river's natural chop and the wake from passing recreational and commercial traffic. On the upper river, creeks (both natural and dredged) can make for good protected layover spots.

NAVIGATION: Use Charts 12327, 12341, 12343, 12347 and 12348. The route upriver is easily navigated for 91 miles to Kingston, but extensive middle grounds and steep-to shoals must be given a wide berth after this point. In the lower Hudson River, rocky shoals are common off the channel, and departure from the marked route must be made with caution and local knowledge. Above Kingston, the bottom is mostly sandy with some mud and grass but few rocks.

Hazards are few, consisting mainly of debris, both floating and submerged and, in spring, fish traps are present. In the Albany/Troy area, as in New York Harbor, drifting debris calls for an endless watch, particularly at tide change and during spring run-off.

Tidal water extends to Troy, where the mean tidal range varies from 3 to 5 feet, and currents can be strong (2 knots at The Battery with an average of 1.5 knots as far north as Albany). When you are northbound, you will be going away from the tidal current change and can hold a fair current longer than you will when southbound. Check tide tables before leaving.

South Shore

From Coney Island, and then north and east for 110 miles to Montauk Point, is Long Island's Atlantic Coast—the wind-swept South Shore of Long Island. Long barrier beaches run between most of the island's mainland and the Atlantic Ocean. Good depths are found a short distance offshore for most of the outside run, but the boater should know that there is considerable distance between inlets that are safe to enter, especially in poor conditions. If you plan an outside run, make certain to prepare your vessel accordingly. It is best to transit the outside in fair weather.

Inside the barrier islands of the South Shore are shallow bays, islands, marshes and canals that connect waterside communities. Dredged channels run from bay to bay, making a protected inside route that is part of the Intracoastal Waterway (ICW) system.

The Inside Route

The South Shore's inside route runs about 75 miles from East Rockaway Inlet to Shinnecock Canal, where you can cross to Great Peconic Bay and the fine Long Island "Fishtail" cruising waters that lead to Long Island Sound.

The main channels of the inside route are well-marked, but the project depth for dredged channels is 5 feet, and the battle against shoaling is constant. At the western end, depths tend to be more stable but, as the route passes east, shoal spots increase and boats with more than a 3-foot draft must monitor the depth sounder continuously.

Many of the bridges that cross the channels have restricted openings and limited hours of operation. The controlling vertical clearance on the inside passage is low, but you can take alternate channels that avoid the lower fixed bridges.

Suffolk County maintains do-it-yourself ginpoles for unstepping masts prior to transiting Shinnecock Canal, which is crossed by several low fixed bridges.

The Outside Run

If you are in a hurry and have the skill and proper equipment, you can run the coast offshore—a pleasant trip in good weather. In bad weather, however, the outside passage is unforgiving. Of the six inlets here, five are not to be trusted; most are changeable, shoal-prone and should be avoided unless you have local knowledge. You can try to follow a local boat into one of these inlets; otherwise, you have no choice but to make the long trek around Montauk Point. Before committing yourself to this route, make certain you will have favorable conditions and that you and your boat are well prepared for bad weather. ■

New York Bay/ Hudson River Distances

Nautical Miles (approximate) from Sandy Hook

LOCATION	MILE
NEW YORK BAY	
Sandy Hook Channel Light "15"	0
Ambrose	8.6
Rockaway Point	5.2
Great Kills Harbor, Crookes Point	6.5
Coney Island, Norton Point	6.0
Verrazano Narrows Bridge	7.8
The Battery	14.0
HUDSON RIVER	
George Washington Bridge	24
Harlem River	26
Tarrytown	39
Grassy Point	49
EAST RIVER	
Brooklyn Bridge	14.5
Hell Gate, Hallets Point	20
Whitestone Bridge	25
Throgs Neck Bridge	26
Execution Rocks	31

South Shore Distances

This table gives mileage along the South Shore of Long Island. All distances are measured in approximate nautical miles.

LOCATION	BETWEEN POINTS	CUMULATIVE
VIA ATLANTIC OCEAN		
Coney Island, Norton Point	0	0
Rockaway Point	4	4
East Rockaway Inlet	8.9	13
Jones Inlet	8.3	21
Fire Island Inlet	12.6	34
Moriches Inlet	27	61
Shinnecock Inlet	13.5	74
Montauk Point	31	105
Block Island, Southwest Point	15	120
VIA INLAND WATERWAY		
East Rockaway Inlet	0	0
East Rockaway*	7	
Point Lookout	9	9
Jones Inlet	1	10
Freeport*	4	
Jones Beach	4	14
Amityville*	11	
Fire Island	12	26
Bay Shore	9	35
Patchogue	13	48
Moriches Inlet	17	65
Westhampton Beach	7	72
Shinnecock Inlet	9	81
Shinnecock Canal	3	84

*Off-Waterway distance from main channel port

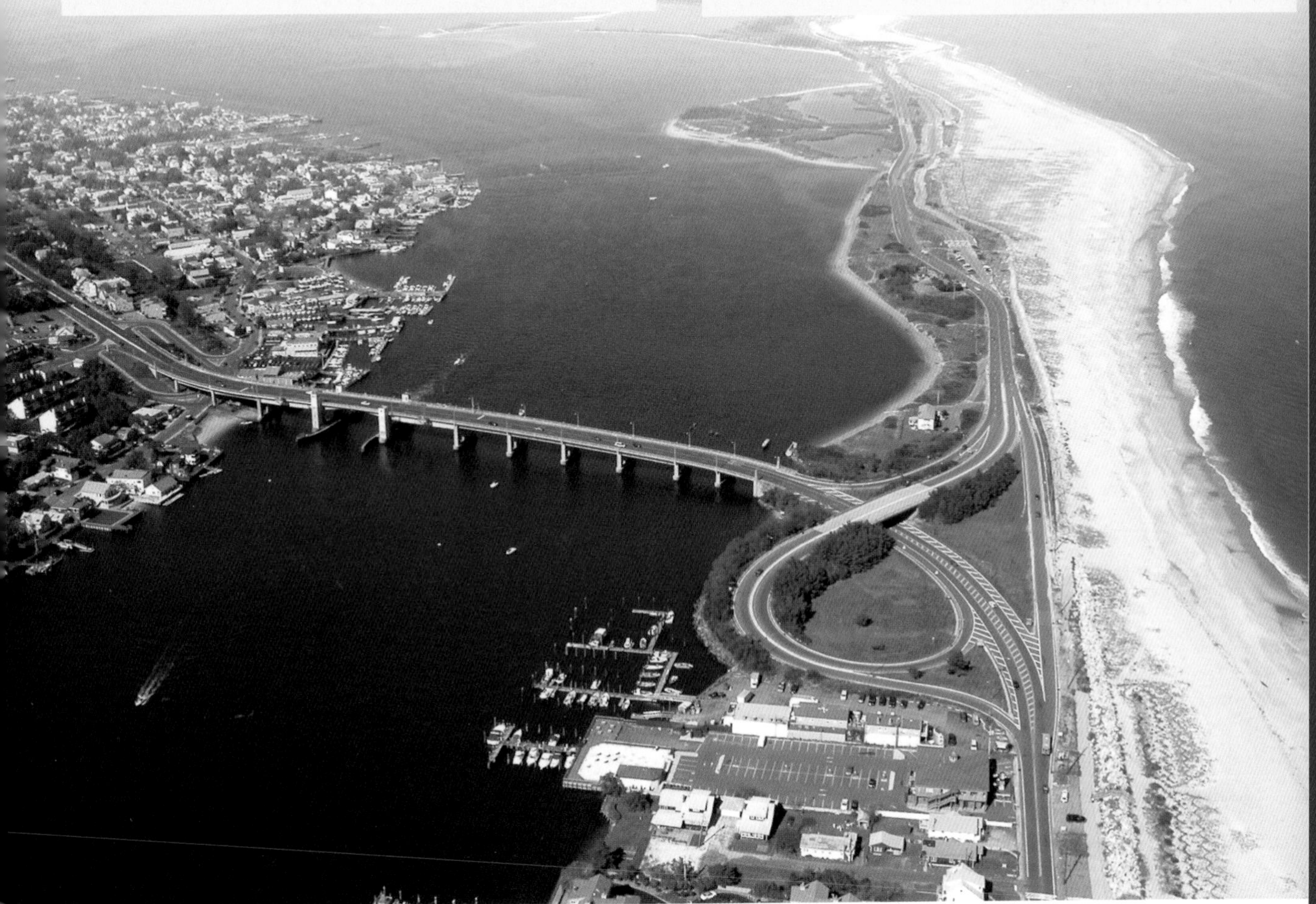

Looking north over Sandy Hook, NJ. (Not to be used for navigation.) F.J. Duffy/Granard Associates

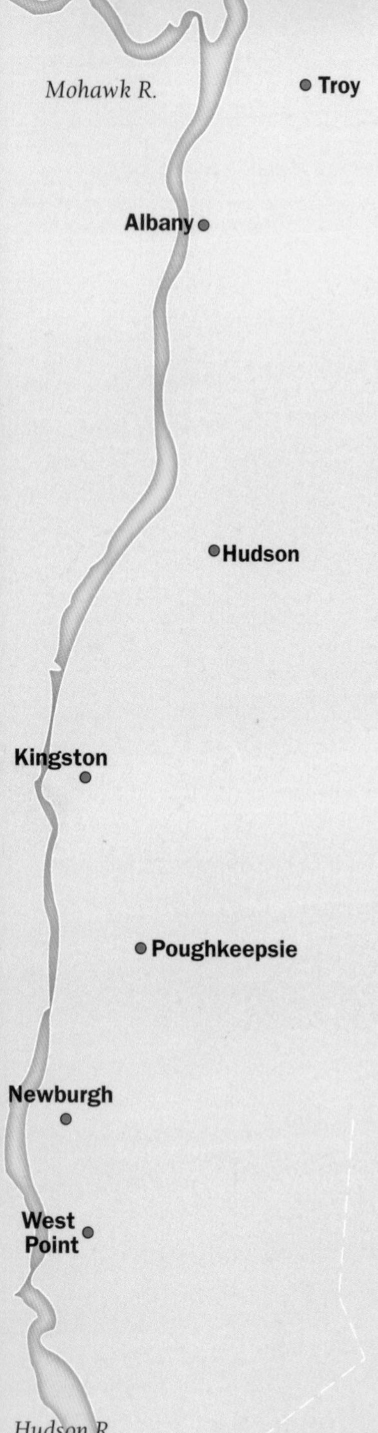

Section Contents

New York Bay, Hudson River	96
East River to Long Island Sound	126
South Shore — Western End	132
South Shore — Eastern End	142

WWW.WATERWAYGUIDE.COM

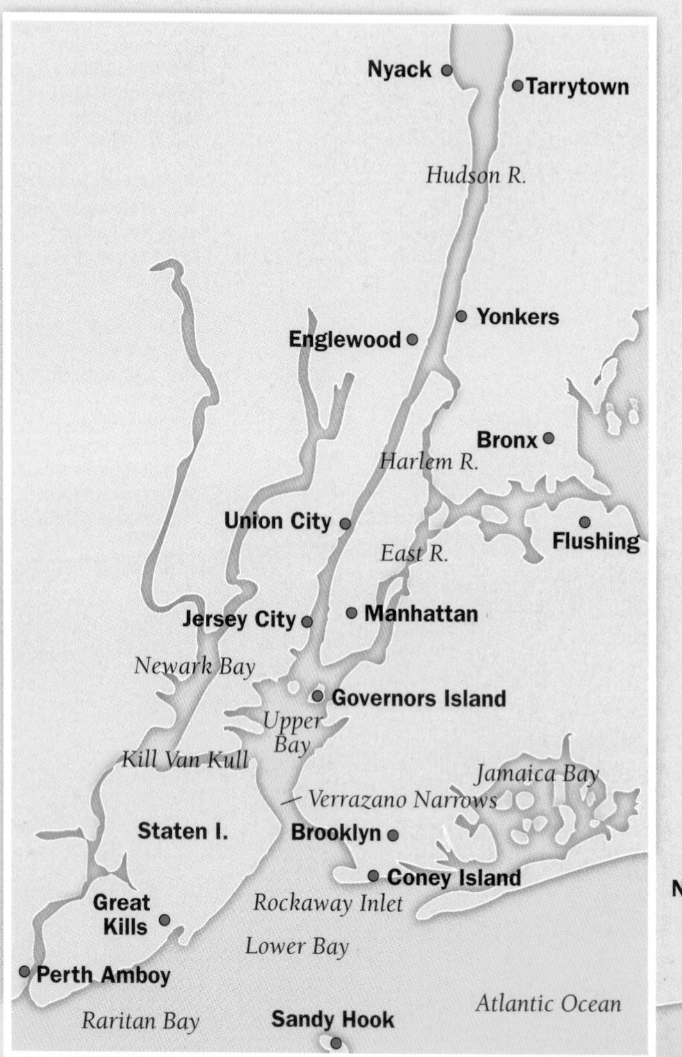

Planning

- Tide Tables 521
- GPS Waypoints 532

New York Bay, Hudson River

CHARTS 12326, 12327, 12333, 12334, 12335, 12339, 12341, 12342, 12343, 12345, 12346, 12347, 12348, 12363

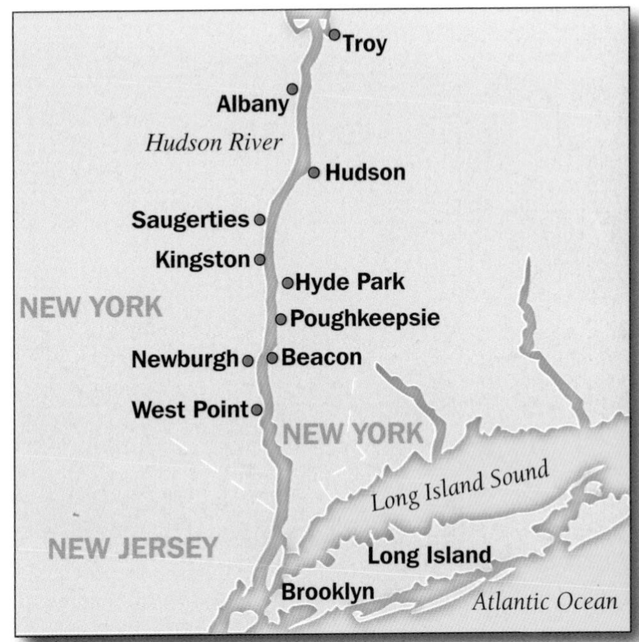

SANDY HOOK, NJ, TO THE NARROWS

NAVIGATION: Use Chart 12327. The run from Sandy Hook across Lower Bay to The Narrows into New York Harbor is eight miles, almost due north. On this course, pass west of Romer Shoal Light (the shoal itself is about two miles along), to avoid the breaking seas across a shallow spot southeast of the light, and two miles farther on, leave West Bank Light to port. Maintain a course well east of Swinburne and Hoffman islands, which lie due west of Coney Island's Norton Point. Do not attempt to explore these small islets lying off the Staten Island shore by boat. The water around them is too shallow.

Currents in the Lower Bay run up to 2 knots, so timing your transit of this area with a favorable current can shorten cruising time. Depths are good almost everywhere.

If visibility is poor, it is advisable to run GPS or compass courses. Channels are almost too well marked and the profusion of buoys, lights and lighthouses can be overwhelming at times.

You can also run outside the main shipping lanes where there is usually plenty of water. Stay close enough to follow the buoys, but off-channel enough to stay clear of big ships. All commercial traffic monitors VHF Channel 13 in New York waters. It is advisable to hail approaching vessels to agree on a passing strategy. The tugboat captains and pilots will respond and usually appreciate a call from even the smallest pleasure boat. There is great security in knowing exactly where a 1,000-foot-long car carrier is headed and that the captain acknowledges your existence.

Storm ports include Great Kills Harbor, a harbor of refuge, to the west on the south shore of Staten Island; Jamaica Bay; and Sheepshead Bay, just north of Coney Island. All are covered in detail in this chapter. The southern shore of Lower New York Bay is treated in the previous chapter, "Sandy Hook Bay, Twin Rivers."

Alternate Route

NAVIGATION: Use Chart 12327. For, St. George, Staten Island, use New York (The Battery) tide tables. For high tide, subtract 17 minutes; for low tide, subtract 15 minutes. When there are strong east or southeasterly winds, the trip from Sandy Hook across the unprotected bay to the entrance of New York Harbor at The Narrows can be rough and sometimes hazardous for small craft. When winds meet an opposing tidal current, it can be even worse, with the waters developing a high, short sea, which is especially pronounced as you approach The Narrows. During these conditions, for safety and comfort, consider the alternate, protected route via Arthur Kill to the west of Staten Island. Although the trip is twice as long, it is well-marked and there are no bridge delays. (This alternate route is covered in more detail in the previous chapter, "Sandy Hook Bay, Twin Rivers.")

STORM HAVENS, NY

Great Kills Harbor

Use Sandy Hook tide tables. For high tide, add 6 minutes; for low tide, add 21 minutes. Great Kills Harbor, the first storm haven on the northward route through Lower Bay before reaching The Narrows, is a harbor of refuge and a charming place to visit. Located on the east side of Staten Island, about seven miles northwest of Sandy Hook and 12 miles south of The Battery (Manhattan), it is almost completely landlocked. The entry into Great Kills Harbor is an easy one with a well-marked channel leading from

Great Kills Harbor, NY

GREAT KILLS HARBOR		Largest Vessel Accommodated	VHF Channel Monitored	Transient Berths / Total Berths	Approach / Dockside Depth (reported)	Floating Docks	Gas / Diesel	Groceries, Ice, Marine Supplies, Snacks	Repairs: Hull, Engine, Propeller	Lift (tonnage), Crane, Rail	1=110V, 2=220V, B=Both, Max Amps	Laundry, Pool, Showers	Pump-Out Station	Nearby: Grocery Store, Motel, Restaurant
		Dockage					Supplies		Services					
1. Mansion Marina	718-984-6611			20/230	12/5	F	GD	IS	HEP	L	B/50	S		GR
2. Nichols Great Kill Park Marine	718-351-8476	65		10/350	12/15	F		IMS		L35	1/30	S	P	

Corresponding chart(s) not to be used for navigation. Internet Access Wireless Internet Access

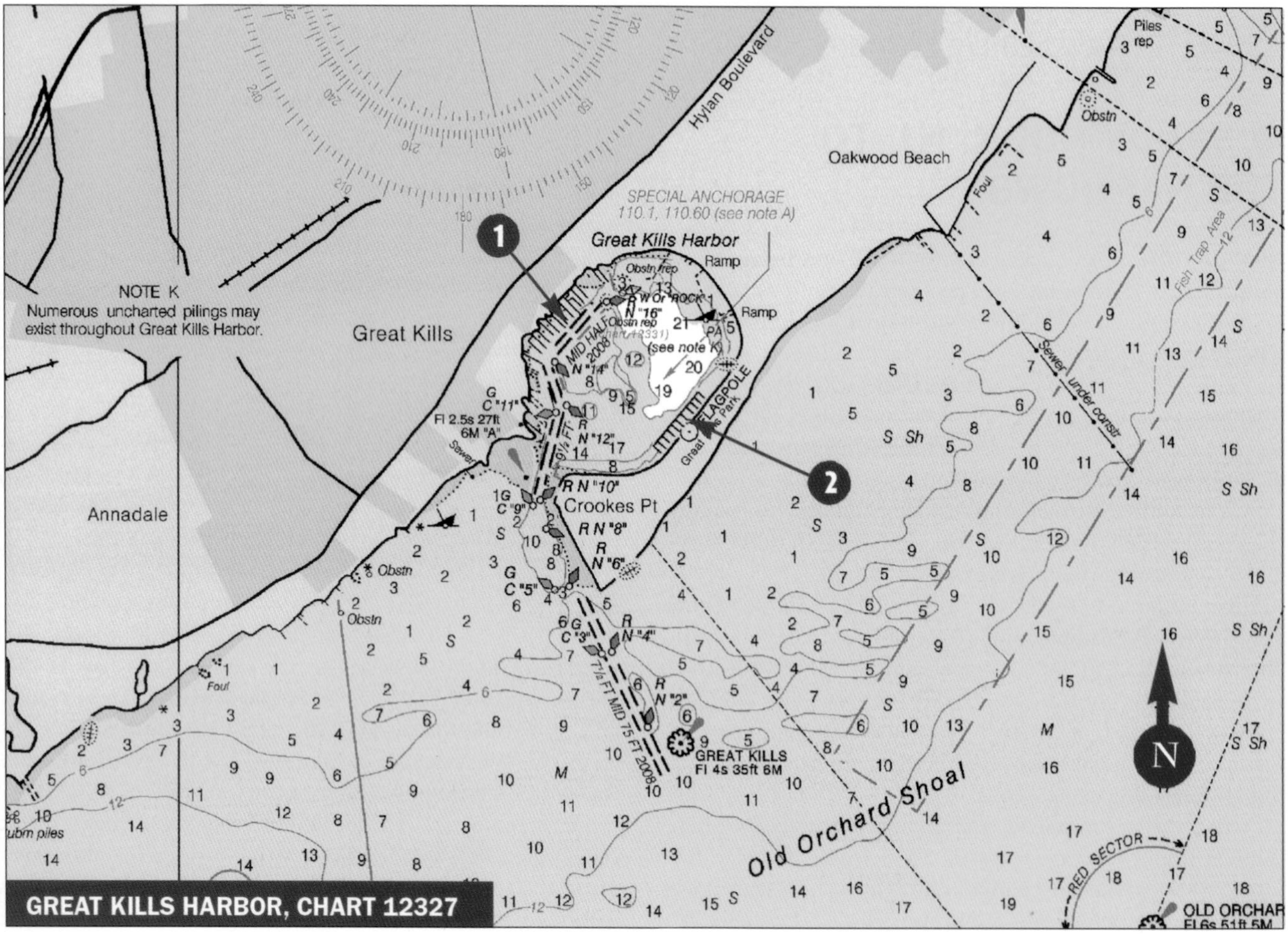

GREAT KILLS HARBOR, CHART 12327

the Lower Bay past Crookes Point into the harbor. A forward range is available to assist in keeping you on course through the inshore shoals.

Great Kills Harbor makes a good layover port for boats heading north or south, and the entrance can be run in almost any weather. Keep well to the east side when entering the basin to avoid shoaling to the west and, when in the harbor, be careful of the shallow area in the middle of the mooring field. Although this harbor is crowded with moorings, you can always find room to anchor between the northern boundary of the moorings and the shore.

Dockage: The Richmond County Yacht Club controls the majority of the moorings in the basin and can usually offer space to those from other yacht clubs. A small service fee includes use of the launch and shoreside facilities, including showers and a bar and grill. Nichols Great Kills Park Marine is a state-run 350-slip marina offering good transient accommodations; it also has pump-out service. Atlantis Marina and Yacht Club may be able to offer a slip, but call first, as they do not keep permanent slips available for transients. Mansion Marina, with a gas dock, may be able to offer a spot for the dinghy for a small fee.

GOIN' ASHORE: **GREAT KILLS AND STATEN ISLAND, NY**

The Great Kills basin is a very secure and ideal spot to plan your visit to New York City. It is blessed with excellent, efficient public transportation to the "City," with both express buses and the Staten Island Ferry leading to the New York City subway system. Great Kills, or "river," as the Dutch word implies, was

once a small port used for fishing and oystering. In the mid-1950s, the north entrance to the harbor was joined to Plum Island to form the basin and provide access to what became the Great Kills Park, with beaches, a snack bar, a bathhouse and hiking and jogging trails. Today there are three excellent restaurants along the west side of the basin.

Staten Island, home to about 500,000 residents, became part of New York state instead of New Jersey as the result of a sailing race. Both states laid claim to their stake, but New York's Capt. Charles Billip and his sloop Bently won the race, and Staten Island became part of New York state, and eventually the borough of Richmond. Billip was rewarded with lands and a manor house at Tottenville on Staten Island. "The Island" was later the site of North America's first Peace Conference and the first headquarters of the Republican Party.

The Snug Harbor Cultural Center, a former home for retired merchant seamen, has been converted to a large museum. Fort Wadsworth, the oldest continually fortified post in America, is located at The Narrows, adjacent to the Verrazano Narrows Bridge. Staten Island can provide for just about any kind of provisioning, medical emergency or boat repairs you might need. Pick up a mooring from the friendly Richmond County Yacht Club for $25 a night, on the western end of the harbor, or if you prefer a slip, Nichols Marina on the eastern end of the harbor does offer transient dockage. Contact the yacht club on VHF Channel 09. There is also extensive space for anchoring, if you prefer. From the yacht club, public transportation, restaurants, shops and other facilities are a short walk on Hylan Boulevard. Or, if you like, the yacht club has a super restaurant that is open on weekends through September.

ADDITIONAL RESOURCES:

- Everything Staten Island, **www.silive.com**
- Staten Island Ferry, **www.siferry.com**

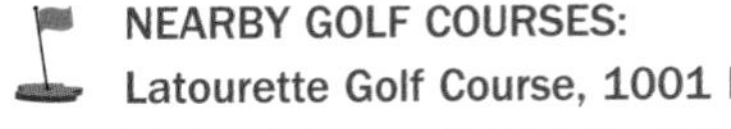

NEARBY GOLF COURSES:
Latourette Golf Course, 1001 Richmond Hill Road
Staten Island, NY 10306, 718-351-1889

NEARBY MEDICAL FACILITIES:
Staten Island University Hospital, 475 Seaview Ave.,
Staten Island, NY 10305, 718-226-9000,
www.siuh.edu

Rockaway Inlet

Use Sandy Hook tide tables. For high tide, subtract 7 minutes; for low tide, subtract 14 minutes. Jettied Rockaway Inlet, southeast of Coney Island, is wide, easy to enter, protected from north and east weather and makes an excellent port in a storm. Its only drawback is that it is a virtual dead end. Boats bound farther east on Long Island and wishing to take the inside route on the New York ICW must bypass Rockaway Inlet and head nine miles east along the coast for East Rockaway Inlet (covered in the "South Shore—Western End" chapter).

Inside Rockaway Inlet, Sheepshead Bay is to port as you enter, Dead Horse Bay is farther along and to port and Jamaica Bay is dead ahead. All three offer protection from the weather and interesting sightseeing. Because many of the harbors in this area accommodate a large number of local boats, it is often difficult to find a guest mooring or dockage. Anchoring is possible in Dead Horse Bay.

Sheepshead Bay

Long, narrow, colorful and crowded with recreational and commercial craft, Sheepshead Bay offers the closest dockage to Coney Island. Although little is available for transients, there are bait and fuel barges, and some of the yacht clubs can accommodate cruising boats on occasion.

Dockage: On the west side of Barren Island, Dead Horse Bay is a big, deep, protected bight featuring Gateway Marina, which is part of the Gateway National Recreation Area. Gateway Marina offers transient dockage, dry storage and full-service repairs, along with 24-hour security, a picnic area, shore power, pump-out service and a ship's store. The Sheepshead Bay Yacht Club monitors VHF Channel 68 and will welcome transients with launch service, a bar, swimming pool and other amenities. You can sometimes purchase fresh seafood from the fishing boats. Good seafood restaurants stand side by side across from the wharves.

Anchorage: There is an interesting pool with 20- to 24-foot depths just east of flashing red buoy "12," which is surrounded by shallower water. Shoal-draft vessels should be able to anchor in this spot by approaching from the north side of flashing red buoy "12." Proceed carefully and keep a close watch on the depth sounder.

To the east of Sheepshead Bay is Gerritsen Inlet, offering a few marinas for transients beyond the Shore Parkway Bridge (35-foot fixed vertical clearance). Dead Horse Bay also offers an anchorage.

Jamaica Bay

Jamaica Bay, seven miles long and 3.5 miles wide, is homeport to thousands of boats. It is protected from the Atlantic Ocean by barrier beaches, dotted with marshy islands and shallows and has well-marked channels with 10-foot depths throughout. Once a favored hunting area, much of the bay is now included in the Jamaica Bay and Breezy Point units of the Gateway National Recreation Area. Jamaica Bay is surrounded by noisy John F. Kennedy International Airport, city parks, Floyd Bennett Field, the Jamaica Bay Wildlife Sanctuary, Rockaway Beach and Jacob Riis Beach.

NAVIGATION: Use Chart 12350. Heading east from Rockaway Inlet, the channel passes under the Gil Hodges Memorial Lift Bridge (55-foot closed vertical clearance, 152-foot open vertical clearance), and then branches north and east. The bridge monitors VHF channels 13 and 16. It opens on signal between 8 a.m. and 4 p.m., Monday through Friday, but eight hour's notice is required at all other times.

The eastern channel runs along Rockaway Beach. A charted measured mile parallels a steel bulkhead along the south shore of the channel, south-southwest of Nova Scotia Bar. To make a circuit of Jamaica Bay (two fixed bridges at

Coney Island, Sheepshead Bay, NY

CONEY ISLAND, SHEEPSHEAD BAY		Largest Vessel Accommodated	VHF Channel Monitored	Transient Berths / Total Berths	Approach / Dockside Depth (reported)	Floating Docks	Gas / Diesel	Groceries, Ice, Marine Supplies, Snacks	Repairs: Hull, Engine, Propeller	Lift (tonnage), Crane, Rail	1=110V, 2=220V, B=Both, Max Amps	Laundry, Pool, Showers	Pump-Out Station	Nearby: Grocery Store, Motel, Restaurant
		Dockage					Supplies		Services					
1. Gateway Marina	718-252-8761	200	16	20/500	15/25	F		GIMS	HEP	L35	B/50	S	P	GMR
2. Sheepshead Bay Yacht Club 🖳	718-891-0991	50	68		45/15	F		IS			1/30	PS		GMR
3. Port Sheepshead Marina 🖳 (WiFi)	718-332-4030	50		3/15	15/10	F		S	HEP	C	1/30	LS		GMR
4. Marine Basin Marina	718-372-5700	75	69	25/200	7/20	F	GD	IMS	HEP	C	B/50	S		GMR
5. Brooklyn Marine	718-434-1616	60			40/20		GD	M	HEP					R
6. All Seasons Marine	718-253-5434	50	16	20/150	50/45	F	G	IM	HEP	L35	B/50	LS		GMR

Corresponding chart(s) not to be used for navigation. 🖳 Internet Access (WiFi) Wireless Internet Access

the northern end of Jamaica Bay limit the complete circuit to vessels having no more than 26 feet of vertical clearance), follow the channel through the Cross Bay Memorial Bridge (52-foot fixed vertical clearance) and the railroad swing bridge (26-foot closed vertical clearance) along the beach. This route dead-ends seven miles later in Thurston Basin beyond the airport, after passing Sommerville Basin, Norton Basin and Motts Basin. Retrace your course to Broad Channel, just east of the swing bridge, and then run north through Winhole Channel between the marshy islands to Grassy Bay. At Howard Beach, just west beyond a fixed bridge (26-foot vertical clearance), submerged pilings line both sides of the channel. Leaving Howard Beach toward the west, you must pass under the Cross Bay Boulevard Bridges (26-foot fixed vertical clearances). After passing Canarsie Beach are Paerdegat Basin (with a 29-foot fixed vertical clearance bridge across the entrance) and East Mill Basin, with a bascule bridge (34-foot closed vertical clearance). Both have deep entrance channels and offer transient facilities.

The Shore Parkway Bascule Bridge (34-foot closed vertical clearance) at Mill Basin monitors VHF Channels 13 and 16 and opens on signal. On summer Sundays and holidays, it is closed from noon to 9 p.m., but from two hours before to one hour after high tide, it will open on signal. You are asked to refrain from requesting openings during commuter times Monday through Friday, from 7 to 9 a.m. and from 4 to 6 p.m.

Coney Island

Use Sandy Hook tide tables. For high tide, subtract 4 minutes; for low tide, subtract 17 minutes. The tip of the Brooklyn mainland offers an interesting side trip with great sightseeing but no dockage. The world-famous Coney Island beaches have teemed with sunbathers for a century, and, on a hot summer day, it is sometimes hard to find the sand. Behind the beach are the boardwalk, an amusement area and scores of apartments.

Gravesend Bay

Use Sandy Hook tide tables. For high tide, subtract 1 minute; for low tide, add 3 minutes. Gravesend Bay is another of the storm harbors available to the cruiser heading north (and the one most directly on course from Sandy Hook to the Narrows). It is located about seven miles north of Sandy Hook on the Brooklyn shore, north of Coney Island's western tip just before the Verrazano Narrows Bridge. The bay is protected from every direction but the west, and marinas with floating docks can be found along the left channel and within Coney Island Creek.

Dockage: Marine Basin Marina offers floating docks for vessels up to 100 feet, repairs, gas, diesel, laundry and restrooms. Trains into Manhattan are within walking distance.

Anchorage: Though there are wrecks farther up, anchoring is safe near the mouth of Coney Island Creek, located about eight miles from The Battery at the tip of Lower Manhattan.

THE NARROWS TO THE BATTERY

The Verrazano Narrows Bridge, eighth among the world's largest suspension bridges, is located about eight miles north of Sandy Hook, NJ. It links Staten Island to Brooklyn and serves as the dividing line between Upper Bay and Lower Bay. Fort Wadsworth on Staten Island and Fort Hamilton in Brooklyn, both still standing, once guarded this mile-wide keyhole to New York Harbor.

Beyond the Verrazano Narrows Bridge on the Staten Island side is a quarantine station where ships anchor for clearance. The usual course into and out of the Upper Bay (New York Harbor) is either in the center of the channel or along the Brooklyn shore. Big freight terminals with ships loading and discharging are in the slips of Staten Island and Bayonne to the west, and Brooklyn to the east.

The Staten Island ferries run almost continuously between Staten Island and terminals on the east side of The Battery in Lower Manhattan. The Staten Island Ferries, large orange vessels, and a host of other ferries and sightseeing boats, create a busy marine traffic situation. Be

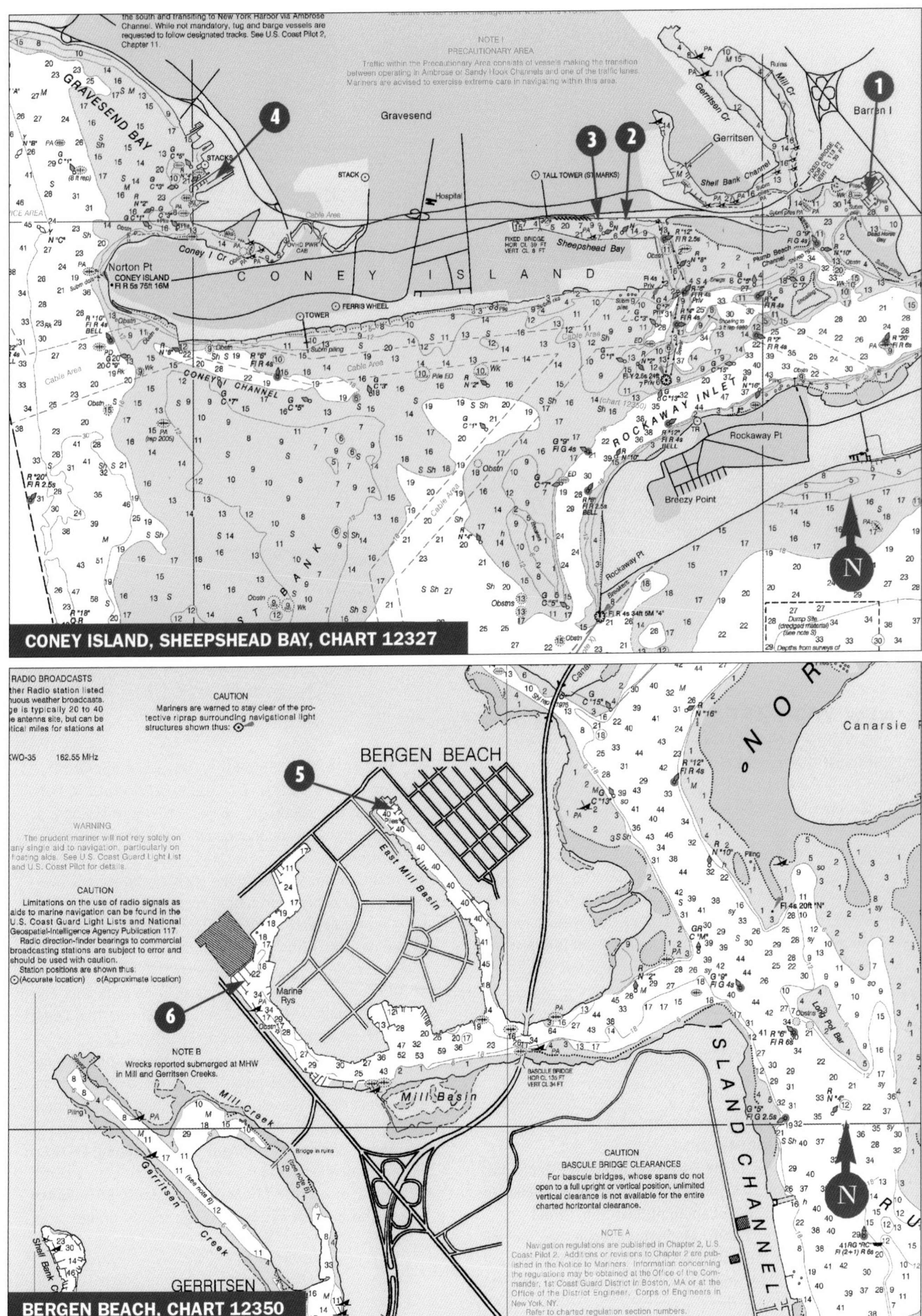
CONEY ISLAND, SHEEPSHEAD BAY, CHART 12327
the south and transiting to New York Harbor via Ambrose Channel. While not mandatory, tug and barge vessels are requested to follow designated tracks. See U.S. Coast Pilot 2, Chapter 11.
NOTE I
PRECAUTIONARY AREA
Traffic within the Precautionary Area consists of vessels making the transition between operating in Ambrose or Sandy Hook Channels and one of the traffic lanes. Mariners are advised to exercise extreme care in navigating within this area.
GRAVESEND BAY
Gravesend
STACK
TALL TOWER (ST MARKS)
Hospital
Gerritsen
Gerritsen Cr
Mill Cr
Barren I
Shell Bank Channel
Norton Pt
CONEY ISLAND
Fl R 5s 75ft 16M
Coney I Cr
CONEY ISLAND
Sheepshead Bay
FIXED BRIDGE HOR CL 39 FT VERT CL 8 FT
FERRIS WHEEL
TOWER
CONEY I CHANNEL
Cable Area
ROCKAWAY INLET
Rockaway Pt
Breezy Point
Plumb Beach Channel
Dead Horse Bay
Dump Site (dredged material) (see note S)
Depths from surveys of
BERGEN BEACH, CHART 12350
RADIO BROADCASTS
CAUTION
Mariners are warned to stay clear of the protective riprap surrounding navigational light structures shown thus:
BERGEN BEACH
WARNING
The prudent mariner will not rely solely on any single aid to navigation, particularly on floating aids. See U.S. Coast Guard Light List and U.S. Coast Pilot for details.
CAUTION
Limitations on the use of radio signals as aids to marine navigation can be found in the U.S. Coast Guard Light Lists and National Geospatial-Intelligence Agency Publication 117.
Radio direction-finder bearings to commercial broadcasting stations are subject to error and should be used with caution.
Station positions are shown thus:
(Accurate location) (Approximate location)
East Mill Basin
Marine Rys
Mill Basin
NOTE B
Wrecks reported submerged at MHW in Mill and Gerritsen Creeks.
Mill Creek
Gerritsen Creek
Shell Bank Cr
GERRITSEN
BASCULE BRIDGE HOR CL 135 FT VERT CL 34 FT
Canarsie
ISLAND CHANNEL
CAUTION
BASCULE BRIDGE CLEARANCES
For bascule bridges, whose spans do not open to a full upright or vertical position, unlimited vertical clearance is not available for the entire charted horizontal clearance.
NOTE A
Navigation regulations are published in Chapter 2, U.S. Coast Pilot 2. Additions or revisions to Chapter 2 are published in the Notice to Mariners. Information concerning the regulations may be obtained at the Office of the Commander, 1st Coast Guard District in Boston, MA or at the Office of the District Engineer, Corps of Engineers in New York, NY.
Refer to charted regulation section numbers.

Verrazano Narrows, looking northeast from Staten Island toward Brooklyn. (Not to be used for navigation.) F.J. Duffy/Granard Associates

NEW YORK AREA SECURITY ZONES

The Coast Guard reports that the following security zones apply to all vessels:

■ Upper New York Bay, around Liberty Island and Ellis Island: No vessels are allowed within 150 yards of either island.

■ Indian Point Nuclear Power Station on the Hudson River: No vessel is permitted within a 300-yard radius of 41°16'12.4"N, 073°57'16.2"W. Any vessel on the Hudson River in the vicinity of Indian Point is subject to random Coast Guard boarding.

■ Check for updated security advisories in New York Harbor and the East River at www.uscgnewyork.com., www.homeport.uscg.mil or by calling 718-354-4037. Report suspicious activities at 800-424-8802, National Response Center.

Additional security zones exist at the following locations:

■ United Nations: In the East River along the Manhattan shoreline from 125 yards offshore at the Queensboro Bridge to 175 yards offshore at East 35th Street.

■ Around Piers 84-96, Manhattan, bound by the following points: the northeast corner of Pier 96 where it intersects the seawall, thence to approximate position 40°46'23.1"N, 073°59'59.0"W, thence to approximate position 40°45'55.3"N, 074°00'20.2"W (NAD 1983), thence to the southeast corner of Pier 84 where it intersects the seawall, thence along the shoreline to the point of origin.

■ Within 25 yards of all bridge piers or abutments, overhead power cables and tunnel ventilators in the greater New York area and along the Hudson River.

■ Within 100 yards of all anchored or moored Coast Guard vessels.

■ Additional restricted areas exist in Newark Bay and around New York City. For details, consult the Coast Guard Local Notice to Mariners for District 1.

■ Roosevelt Island Bridge openings: When special security zones are put into place around the United Nations in the East River, vessels must go through the east channel of Roosevelt Island and under the Roosevelt Island Lift Bridge. Vessels requiring a bridge opening (40-foot closed vertical clearance) should call the tender at 646-772-9551 or on VHF Channel 13, at least 15 minutes before you plan on passing through the lift bridge.

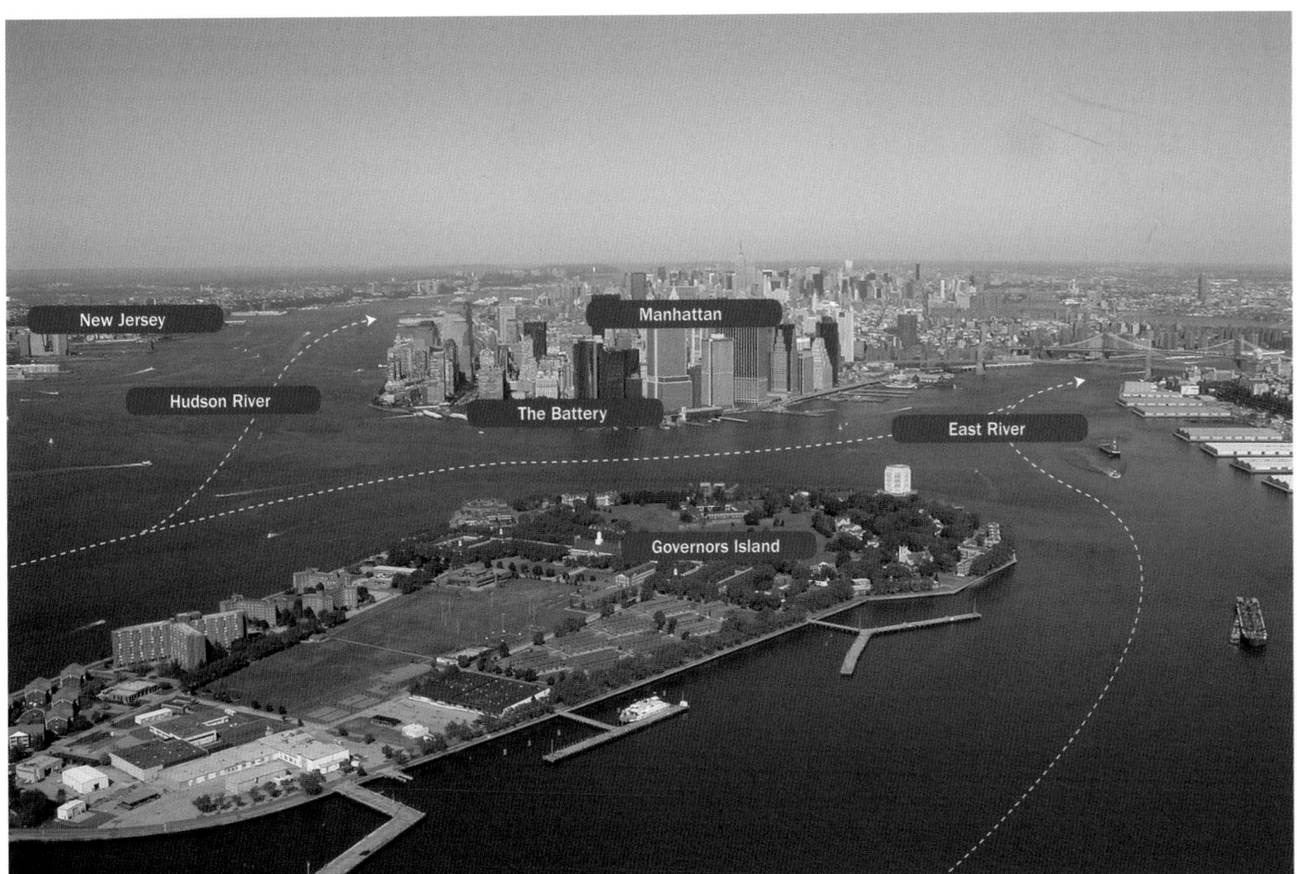

New York Harbor, looking north over Governors Island at The Battery and the tip of Manhattan, with the Hudson River to the west and the East River to the east. (Not to be used for navigation.) F.J. Duffy/Granard Associates

certain of your course if you cross the bow of one of these vessels, especially when taking into account the effect of currents on your progress.

Security has tightened substantially in New York Harbor and one can expect restrictions around prominent features, ferry terminals, ferries themselves and any military facilities. It is best to check with the Coast Guard if you have any doubts. Enforcement is quick and effective.

As you pass by the northern tip of Staten Island, the whole panorama of New York City is spread before you. On the New Jersey side is a condominium complex, Port Liberté, reminiscent of French canals and countryside. A well-marked channel leads into the canals and to a waterfront restaurant, The Pointe. Ahead, rising ever higher, are the densely packed skyscrapers of the Lower Manhattan financial district. To port is the Statue of Liberty—serene, lovely, 300 feet tall and facing southeast from her pedestal on Liberty Island. While it was possible to run fairly close to the copper-green landmark, you now must stay at least 150 yards from either Liberty or Ellis islands. No dockage exists on either island for recreational vessels. Ferry service runs to Liberty Island from The Battery and from Liberty State Park in Jersey City.

Ellis Island, through which millions of immigrants entered the United States and a new life, lies just north of the Statue of Liberty. From a distance, its Moorish towers and minarets still have the look of a fairy-tale castle. The entire island is a popular tourist magnet, and new facilities have been put in place to help visitors trace their lineage.

Across the harbor, a half-mile south of The Battery, is Governors Island, formerly the headquarters of the Coast Guard's Third District. Coast Guard operations specifically for New York Harbor are now headquartered in Bayonne, NJ, and Staten Island. The Atlantic Area Command previously based here now operates out of Portsmouth, VA.

Buttermilk Channel connects Upper New York Harbor with the East River between the east side of Governors Island and Brooklyn. Currents run hard in this channel, but it is less exposed to harbor chop and ferry traffic.

The Battery

At The Battery, the skyscrapers of Manhattan crowd right down to the water's edge. Battery Park is located around the point of Lower Manhattan where there are docks for sightseeing boats and slips for the Staten Island ferries and the smaller Governors Island and commuter ferries.

NAVIGATION: Use Chart 12327. At The Battery, the waters form a crossroads, each leading to spectacular cruising grounds. The route to Lake Champlain, the Erie Canal, the Great Lakes and Canada runs up the Hudson River (covered in the following pages), and the course to Long Island Sound, Cape Cod and New England begins with the East River (covered in the "East River to Long Island Sound" chapter).

THE BATTERY TO GEORGE WASHINGTON BRIDGE, UP THE HUDSON RIVER

One of the most thrilling passages for East Coast cruisers is the transit of New York Harbor and entry into the mighty Hudson River, known as the "Rhine of America."

New York Harbor

You will cruise through one of the world's busiest ports, passing within a few hundred yards of the Statue of Liberty, the spectacular Moorish architecture of Ellis Island, and the world-famous Battery, whose name is derived from a battery of 92 guns placed there by the British in 1693 to ward off attacks by the French. The renovated 1884 Fireboat Station adjacent to Battery Park displays a clock, built by Seth Thomas, which sounds the time with ship's bells.

Heading up the Hudson River, you will leave to starboard the old commercial and cruise ship wharves, which are slowly being demolished and rebuilt. World-famous private and charter yachts are sometimes seen moored here. Surfside 3 Marina at Chelsea Piers is part of a complex that includes Olympic-quality sports training facilities and Silver Screen Studios, Manhattan's largest center for film and television production. This 30-acre development between 17th and 23rd streets is housed in authentic pier buildings and also includes restaurants, a golf driving range, a 1.2-mile-long esplanade and a landscaped park, all overlooking the river. The marina monitors VHF Channel 68. Next comes the *Intrepid* Museum at Pier 86, where the aircraft carrier *Intrepid* houses the museum.

Dockage: Eight major marinas are situated on the Hudson River between The Battery and George Washington Bridge. On the Manhattan side of the river, North Cove Marina occupies a prime location in the heart of the financial district. The marina offers deepwater floating docks to visiting yachts.

About a mile north, at the Chelsea Piers, Surfside 3 Marina is part of an ambitious 30-acre sports multiplex, which includes an Olympic-sized swimming pool and gym, golf center and driving range, indoor ice skating rink, rock climbing center and batting practice area, with skating and rollerblading paths to The Battery. There are no fuel or pump-out facilities at the marina, but there are restrooms and showers available, with electrical, cable TV and telephone hookups at each berth. Dockhands are available to help you to your floating-dock slip, and concierge service is available. 79th Street Boat Basin, the New York City Municipal Marina, offers easy access to both uptown and downtown locations, as it is within easy walking distance of the 79th Street and Broadway subway station (not to mention world-famous Zabar's Deli at 80th Street). In addition to a limited number of transient berths, the marina has rental moorings, a dinghy dock, pump-out station and 24-hour security for its patrons.

On the New Jersey side of the Hudson River, Liberty Landing Marina dominates the southerly side of Morris Canal. Showers, an open-air canteen and other amenities are located at the decommissioned light ship, Winter Station, which serves as the marina office. All fuels, laundry facilities and a pump-out station are available. Be aware that, even though the fuel docks are floating, there are pilings that extend outward from the dock edge.

Ferry and water taxi service to Manhattan are immediately next door and offer expanded nighttime service during the summer months to New York and back, and the new light-rail line, located several blocks away, permits passenger service through Liberty Park and along the New Jersey shoreline to Bayonne, Hoboken and north. From the historic CRRNJ Railroad Terminal in the park, less than a block away, Circle Line offers multiple boat tours daily to both the Statue of Liberty National Monument and Ellis Island.

Liberty Harbor Marina, across from the World Trade Center site and northwest of the Statue of Liberty, offers dockage, fuel, repairs and 60-ton lift capacity.

Also located in Jersey City, Newport Marina amenities include a 500-foot-long wave attenuator protecting its entire basin, on-site PATH train service (minutes to Manhattan) and modern restrooms, shower and laundry facilities.

The Narrows to Tarrytown, NY

THE NARROWS TO TARRYTOWN		Dockage					Supplies		Services					
		Largest Vessel Accommodated	VHF Channel Monitored	Transient Berths / Total Berths	Approach / Dockside Depth (reported)	Floating Docks	Gas / Diesel	Groceries, Ice, Marine Supplies, Snacks	Repairs: Hull, Engine, Propeller	Lift (tonnage), Crane, Rail	1=110V, 2=220V, B=Both, Max Amps	Laundry, Pool, Showers	Pump-Out Station	Nearby: Grocery Store, Motel, Restaurant
1. Liberty Landing Marina	201-985-8000	200	72	60/560	22/12	F	GD	IMS	HEP	L60,C	B/100	LS	P	GMR
2. Liberty Harbor Marina & Dry Dock Inc.	201-386-7500	60	68	12/140	20/18	F	GD	IM	HEP	L60	B/50	LS	P	GMR
3. North Cove Marina	212-786-1200	180	69	20/50	25/18	F		I			B/100		P	GMR
4. Newport Marina	**201-626-5550**	**200**	**16/72**	**30/160**	**10/11**	**F**		**GIMS**			**B/100**	**LS**	**P**	**GMR**
5. Surfside 3 at Chelsea Piers	212-336-7873	200	68	20/75	50/8	F		IMS			B/50	S		GMR
6. Lincoln Harbor Yacht Club	**201-319-5100**	**220**	**74**	**50/250**	**27/12**	**F**	**D**	**IMS**	**P**		**B/100**	**LS**	**P**	**GMR**
7. Port Imperial Marina	201-902-8787	200	16/88	20/120	5/5	F	GD	IMS			B/100	LS	P	GMR
8. 79th Street Boat Basin	**212-496-2105**	**140**	**16/09**	**5/200**	**20/3**	**F**					**B/100**	**LS**	**P**	**GMR**
9. Edgewater Marina	201-944-BOAT	60	16/09	4/93	20/6	F	GD	GIS	HP	L	B/50	LS		GMR
10. Von Dohn Brothers	201-943-3424	35		4/44	8/8	F	GD	GIM	HP	L	B/30			GMR
11. Englewood Boat Basin	201-894-9510	50		/130	4/3		GD	MS	HEP	L50	1/50		P	
12. Alpine Boat Basin	201-768-1360	45		1/125	4/3		G	IS			1/30	S		

Corresponding chart(s) not to be used for navigation. Internet Access Wireless Internet Access

In addition to quiet transient dockage courtesy of a 700-foot wave suppression system, Lincoln Harbor Yacht Club offers concierge service, a guest lounge and mini workout center, with shopping and restaurants within walking distance.

Port Imperial Marina in Weehawken features great city views, concierge service, boat repairs, a golf center and a fine restaurant called Arthur's. Manhattan is just a four-minute ferry ride away.

Anchorage: Anchoring in New York Harbor is only allowed in designated anchorages. Note that these anchorages are designed for large ships and are located in the middle of the harbor; use of these areas requires permission from the Coast Guard. Anchoring behind Liberty and Ellis islands is no longer permitted.

Cruising boats often anchor just north of the 79th Street Boat Basin. But this area is wide open to the river's surge, and holding is poor. There is a charge to use the basin's dinghy dock, so a mooring (if available) may be a better alternative. The 79th Street subway station and the famous Zabar's Deli, at 80th and Broadway, are nearby.

HUDSON RIVER

Cruising the lower Hudson River is generally straightforward. Aids to navigation are plentiful, mid-channel depths range from 15 to 175 feet and, north of Manhattan, marinas and hospitable yacht clubs are numerous. Almost every town has some accommodation for cruising mariners. Overnight berths should be selected for maximum protection from the river's natural chop and the wake of passing traffic. Most marinas have breakwaters or barrier bulkheads. Charts might not accurately show some privately maintained markers. Some markers have been discontinued, while others might not have been replaced after winter ice. It should also be noted that many commercial marinas list or advertise themselves as clubs and are perfectly acceptable stopovers; they are not limited to yacht club members, nor do they observe reciprocity privileges.

On the upper river, creeks (both natural and dredged) make protected layovers. However, note the following:

Charts: Use Charts 12341, 12342, 12343, 12345, 12346, 12347 and 12348. Be sure to purchase these Hudson River charts, which cover the Hudson River from Days Point to Troy, NY, before making your trip. Only a limited number of marinas carry marine supplies, and even fewer carry charts of the river. One marina that often carries them is Liberty Landing (201-985-8000). Call them before you leave New York Harbor and begin heading upriver if you haven't obtained a Hudson River chart. There is fuel and a small chandlery on the north side of the Morris Canal.

Tidal Currents: Tidal water extends to Troy; the mean tidal range varies from 3 to 5 feet, and currents can be strong (2 knots at The Battery with an average of 1.5 knots as far north as Albany). When you are northbound, heading away from the tidal current change, you will hold a fair current longer than when southbound. For this passage, skippers should have a copy of the latest tide and tidal current tables aboard.

Docking: In the tidal portion of the Hudson, select your marina slip with great care. You will want to avoid slips that are in the cross current, as getting out of the slip at departure time will be difficult. You will also want to ensure that the marina is equipped with proper fendering to minimize damage to your boat.

Weather: The wind usually blows up or down the Hudson River, but near shore it tends to sweep toward the banks. Watch for summer squalls with sudden winds of up to 30 knots. Your only warning might be black clouds along the high west-bank bluffs. Get to the weather side of the river whenever you see indications of rough conditions ahead.

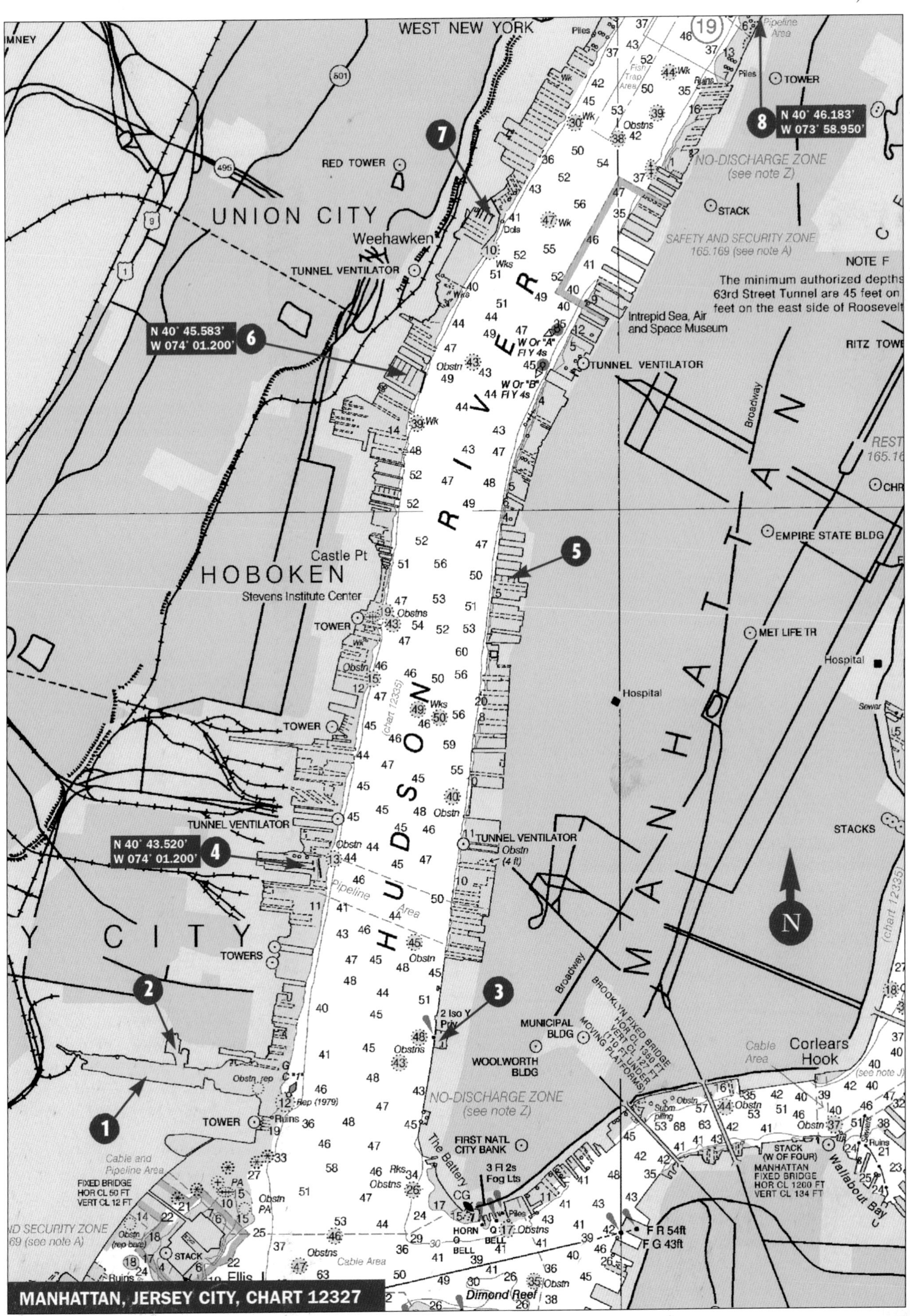
WEST NEW YORK
UNION CITY
Weehawken
HOBOKEN
Castle Pt
Stevens Institute Center
CITY
HUDSON RIVER
MANHATTAN
RED TOWER
TUNNEL VENTILATOR
TOWER
TOWERS
N 40° 46.183'
W 073° 58.950'
N 40° 45.583'
W 074° 01.200'
N 40° 43.520'
W 074° 01.200'
NO-DISCHARGE ZONE
(see note Z)
SAFETY AND SECURITY ZONE
165.169 (see note A)
NOTE F
The minimum authorized depths
63rd Street Tunnel are 45 feet on
feet on the east side of Roosevelt
Intrepid Sea, Air
and Space Museum
STACK
RITZ TOWE
Broadway
EMPIRE STATE BLDG
MET LIFE TR
Hospital
STACKS
MUNICIPAL
BLDG
WOOLWORTH
BLDG
BROOKLYN FIXED BRIDGE
HOR CL 1380 FT
VERT CL 127 FT
(10 FT UNDER
MOVING PLATFORMS)
Corlears
Hook
Cable
Area
FIRST NATL
CITY BANK
The Battery
3 Fl 2s
Fog Lts
MANHATTAN
FIXED BRIDGE
HOR CL 1200 FT
VERT CL 134 FT
Wallabout Bay
Cable and
Pipeline Area
FIXED BRIDGE
HOR CL 50 FT
VERT CL 12 FT
Pipeline
Area
Cable Area
Dimond Reef
F R 54ft
F G 43ft
N
MANHATTAN, JERSEY CITY, CHART 12327

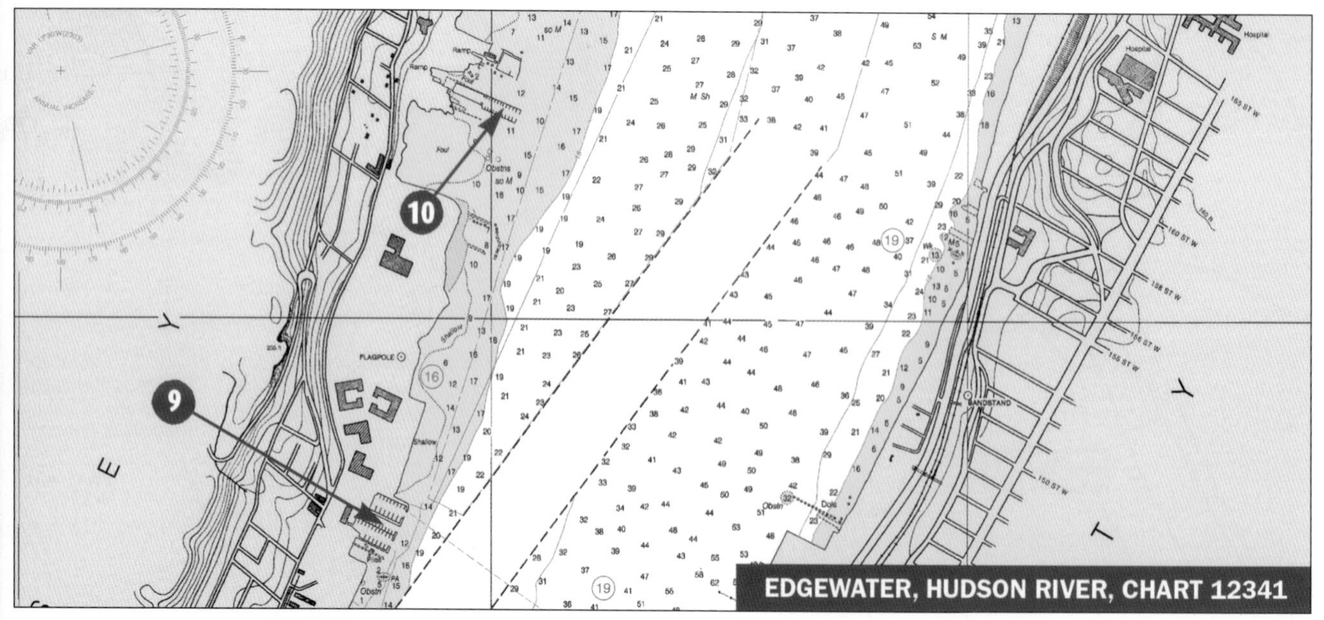

EDGEWATER, HUDSON RIVER, CHART 12341

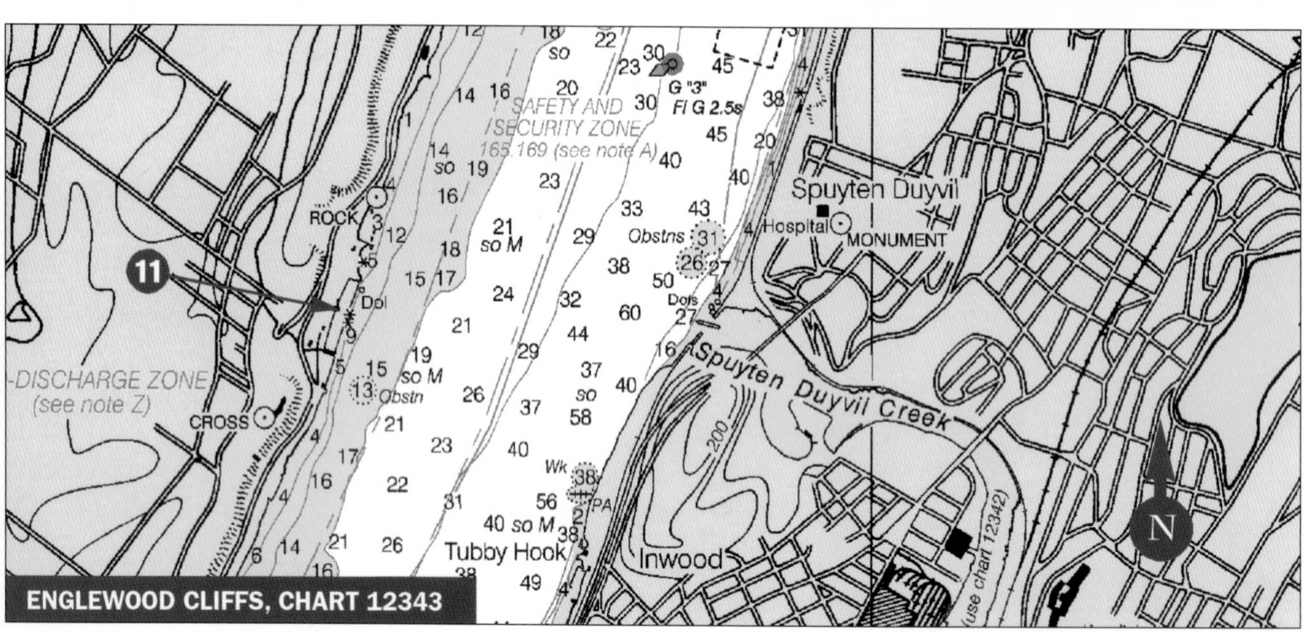

ENGLEWOOD CLIFFS, CHART 12343

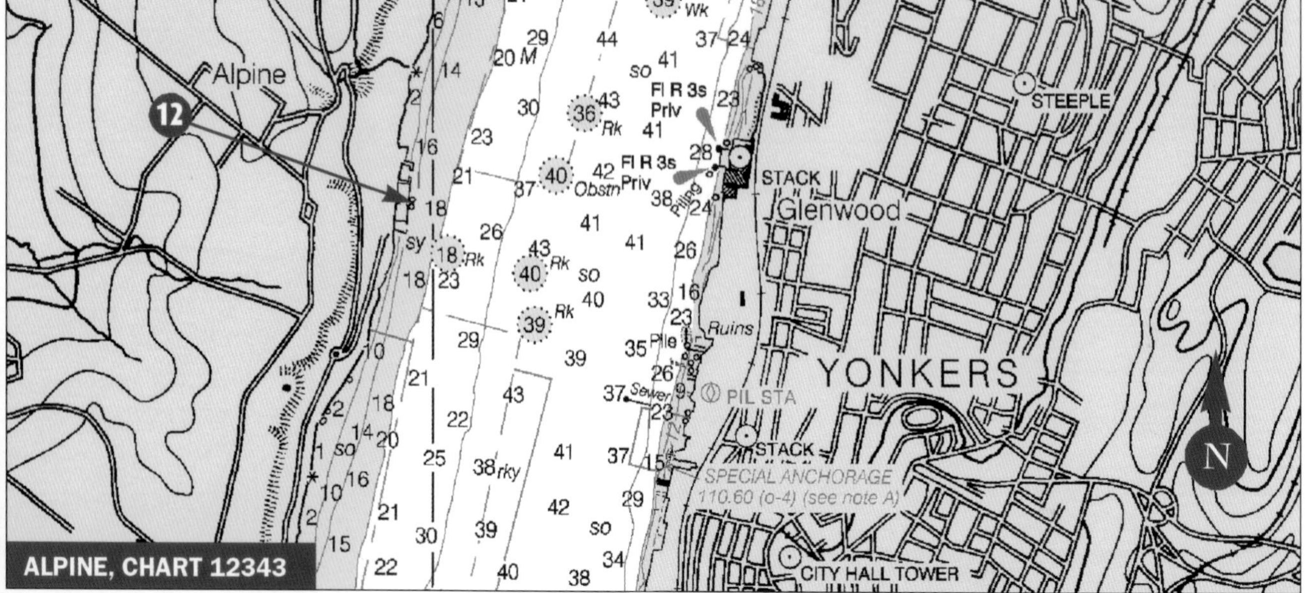

ALPINE, CHART 12343

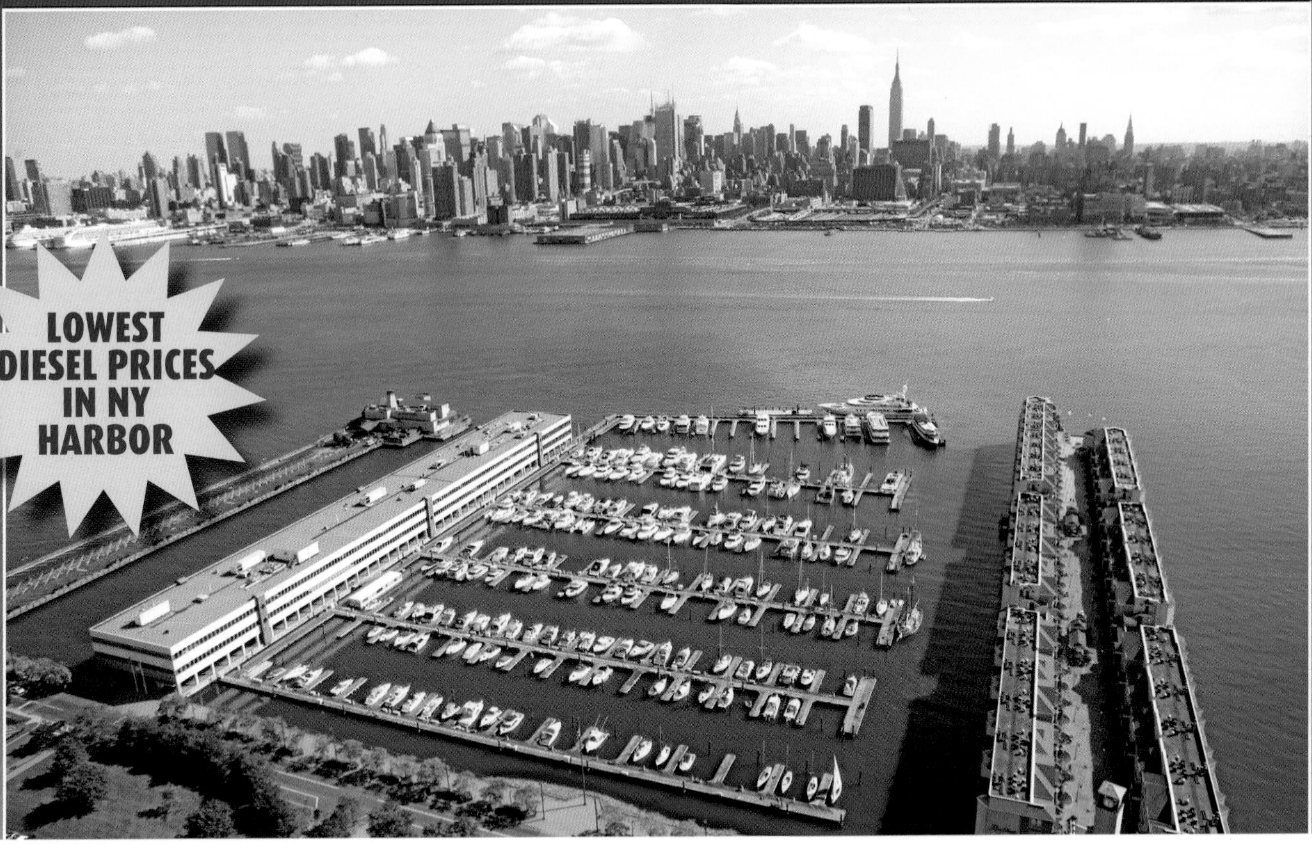

Hazards: Navigation is straightforward for the 91 miles to Kingston but, thereafter, extensive middle grounds and steep-to shoals must be given a wide berth. Be very cautious outside the lighted buoyed channel. In the lower river (Haverstraw to Kingston), rocky shoals are common off the channel and departure from the marked route must be taken with caution and local knowledge. Rocks pose little hazard above Kingston, but the mud and sand off-channel can be quite shoal, and grounding is a real danger.

Hazards are few, consisting mainly of debris, both floating and submerged, and fish traps in the spring. The latter, flagged, lighted and set out for the shad run, are concentrated in the 25 to 30 statute miles below Stony Point. In the New York City and Albany/Troy areas, drifting debris calls for a continuous vigil, particularly at tidal changes and in the spring, when runoff can carry sizable trees downriver.

Commercial traffic (heavy at times with barge activity) should be given full right-of-way, especially in poor visibility. Communicate, if you need to, on VHF Channel 13.

Hudson River Valley

The entire Hudson River Valley is in transition. Before World War II, these towns prospered as shipping and manufacturing centers. Kingston made brick and textiles and directed traffic in and out of the Delaware and Hudson Canal; Saugerties was famous for its fine paper; and Poughkeepsie was known for its beer. Most industries closed because goods could be produced abroad at much lower labor costs. Then IBM came to the Hudson Valley, employing 24,000 at its microprocessor plants in East Fishkill, Kingston and Poughkeepsie by 1991. Unfortunately, downsizing has cut approximately 14,000 of these jobs.

Former Gov. George Pataki (who enjoys fishing for striped bass on the Hudson) was successful in bringing some industry back to the communities along the Hudson River, and an active public/private tourism effort has enjoyed significant achievements promoting the lures of the Hudson Valley. Many of the riverside towns are being transformed from industrial centers to New York City suburbs.

■ GEORGE WASHINGTON BRIDGE TO TAPPAN ZEE BRIDGE

The George Washington Bridge opened in 1931 during the Great Depression. It was not until 30 years later that the lower, second deck (fondly known as the "Martha Washington Bridge") was added. Spuyten Duyvil (pronounced "spite-en die-vil") is the northern part of the Harlem River, the route followed by the famous Circle Line cruise boats during their scenic circumnavigation of the island of Manhattan.

Palisades

The aura of the New York metropolis quickly dissipates beyond the George Washington Bridge; the tall backdrop contrasts sharply with the 300- to 500-foot Palisades. Composed of columnar basalt, this striking series of cliffs is named for its visual similarity to old wooden barrier fortifications. If the wind is right, you can find a number of suitable anchorages close to shore at the base of the cliffs.

Warning: If you anchor here, prepare to be rolled during the night by some large wakes from an occasional tugboat. You might want to consider lashing gear down securely before retiring for the evening.

Yonkers, Hastings-on-Hudson, Dobbs Ferry and Irvington have no transient facilities, and the marinas are small local operations. Shallows and the ruins of old piers also make parts of this shore difficult to approach closely. The aforementioned three above Yonkers, though, are pleasant small villages. Irvington, too, has Lyndhurst, a beautiful former estate that now has outdoor classical concerts.

Dockage: On the west bank, the Alpine Boat Basin is exactly four nautical miles upriver from Spuyten Duyvil. The Alpine Basin is part of Palisades Interstate Park. If you want a night in quiet surroundings, head in here. There are showers, snack machines and shore power. The looming Palisades make going anywhere difficult, though a mile of switchback roads will take you to the town of Alpine.

Opposite Hastings-on-Hudson is the New Jersey-New York border. From this point to its headwaters in the Adirondack Mountains, the Hudson River flows entirely within New York State.

Piermont

Piermont Pier, the prominent mile-long point just north of the state border, was the terminus of the Erie Railroad tracks until 1850. During that era, this spot was a major rail and ship cargo transfer point. Pete Seeger's *Clearwater*, the Hudson River's famous replica of a North River sloop, may frequently be seen at the end of the pier. Although anchorage for protection from south winds can be found on the north side of the point, you should use caution in your approach—the shoaling is abrupt.

Piermont is a delightful waterfront village with a marina, waterfront restaurants and an upscale shopping plaza. Unfortunately, the shallow approach is not marked and requires a bit of local knowledge.

■ TAPPAN ZEE BRIDGE TO BEAR MOUNTAIN BRIDGE

The Tappan Zee Bridge carries the New York State Thruway, an important interstate highway linking New York City to Albany and Buffalo.

Tappan Zee to Ossining, NY

TAPPAN ZEE TO OSSINING		Largest Vessel Accommodated	VHF Channel Monitored	Transient Berths / Total Berths	Approach / Dockside Depth (reported)	Floating Docks	Gas / Diesel	Groceries, Ice, Marine Supplies, Snacks	Repairs: Hull, Engine, Propeller	Lift (tonnage), Crane, Rail	1=110V, 2=220V, B=Both, Max Amps	Laundry, Pool, Showers	Pump-Out Station	Nearby: Grocery Store, Motel, Restaurant
		Dockage					Supplies		Services					
1. Tarrytown Marina	914-631-1300	70	16/09	10/190	8/8	F	GD	IM	P	L	1/50	LS	P	GMR
2. Washington Irving Boat Club	914-332-0517	32	09	3/100	6/3	F		I			B	S		R
3. The Julius Petersen Boat Yard	845-358-2100	115	16/09	4/20	13/10	F		IM	HEP	L60,C	B/50	S	P	GMR
4. Westerly Marina	914-941-2203	100	68	10/180	8/6	F	GD	IM	HEP	L35	B/50	S	P	R
5. Shattemuc Yacht Club	914-941-8777	36	16	6/103	6/6	F	G	I		L	1/30	PS		MR

Corresponding chart(s) not to be used for navigation. ☐ Internet Access WiFi Wireless Internet Access

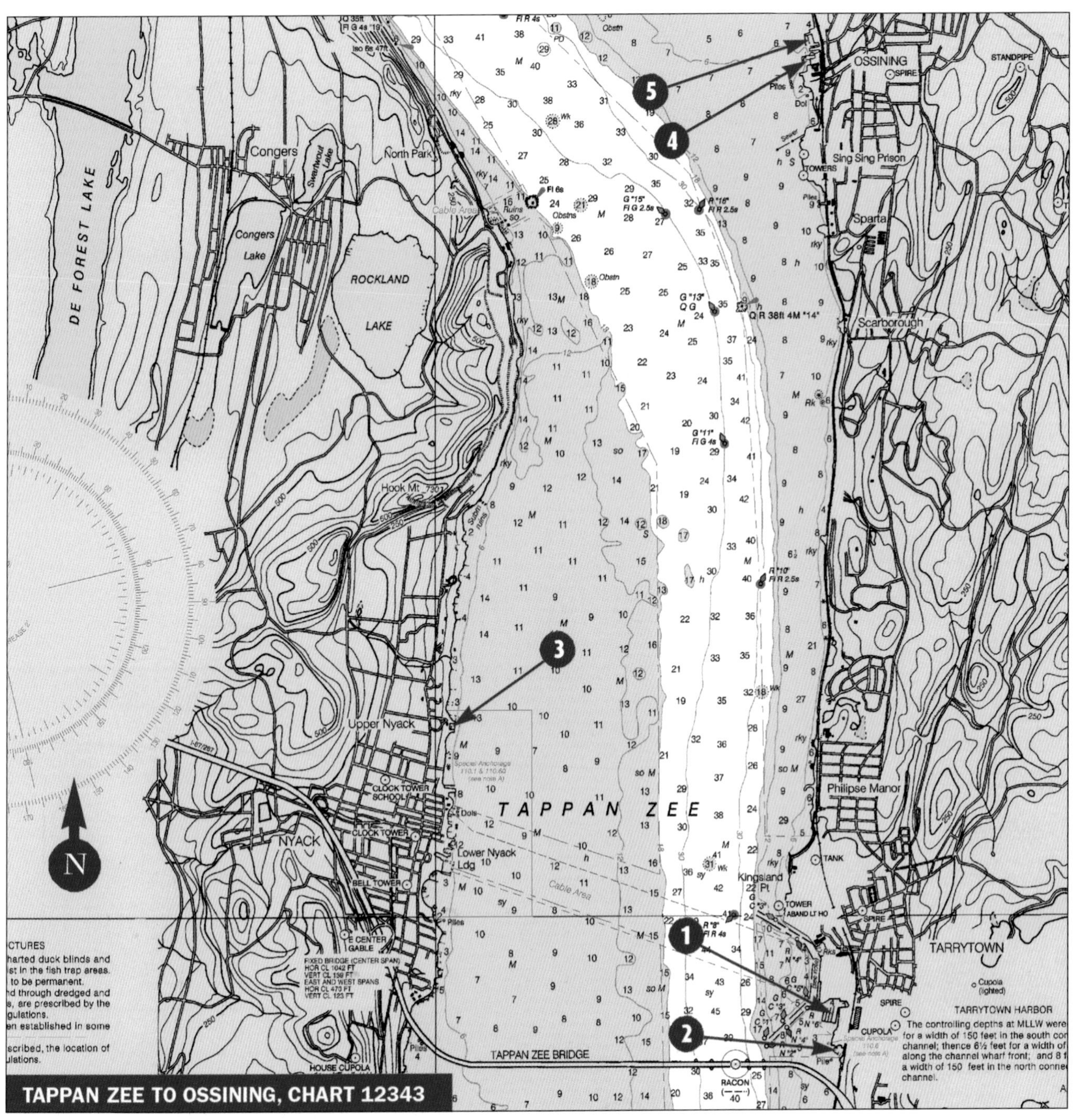

TAPPAN ZEE TO OSSINING, CHART 12343

Haverstraw Bay to Peekskill, NY

HAVERSTRAW BAY TO PEEKSKILL		Largest Vessel Accommodated	VHF Channel Monitored	Transient Berths / Total Berths	Approach / Dockside-Depth (reported)	Floating Docks	Gas / Diesel	Groceries, Ice, Marine Supplies, Snacks	Repairs: Hull, Engine, Propeller	Lift (tonnage), Crane, Rail	1=110V, 2=220V, B=Both, Max Amps	Pump-Out Station	Laundry, Pool, Showers	Nearby: Grocery Store, Motel, Restaurant
		Dockage					Supplies		Services					
1. Haverstraw Marina (Internet Access)	845-429-2001	150	16/09	75/1000	26/8	F	GD	GIMS	HEP	L35	B/50	LPS	P	GMR
2. Samalot Marine (Internet Access) (Wireless Internet Access)	845-429-0404							GIMS	HEP	C				
3. Penny Bridge Marine	845-786-5100	40		/120	5/4	F		IM	HEP	L35	1/30	S	P	
4. Minisceongo Yacht Club	845-429-9698	50	09	5/125	6/10	F	GD	I		L	1/30	LS	P	MR
5. Patsy's Bay Marina (Internet Access)	845-786-5270	50	12	15/200	5/6	F		IMS	HEP	L30	1/50	LPS		R
6. Stony Point Bay Marina & Yacht Club	845-786-3700	45	16/09	5/240	4/4	F		IS	HEP	L	B/50	LPS	P	GMR
7. Seaweed Yacht Club	845-786-8731	40			8/8			I			1/30	S	P	GMR
8. Cortland Yacht Club	914-739-3011	51		6/175	3/3	F		IS		LC	1/30	PS	P	GR
9. Viking Boatyard	914-739-5090	45	09	6/250	4.5/4.5	F		IMS		L	1/30	S		GR
10. Peekskill Yacht Club	914-737-9515	48	09	2/85	5/5			I		L25	1/30	S		GMR
11. Charles Point Marina	914-736-6942	40		10/80	5/3	F		IM	HEP	L25	1/30	S	P	GR
12. HALF MOON BAY MARINA (Internet Access) (Wireless Internet Access)	**914-271-5400**	**120**	**09**	**50/173**	**10/10**	**F**		**GIMS**			**B/50**	**LPS**	**P**	**GMR**

Corresponding chart(s) not to be used for navigation. (Internet Access symbol) Internet Access (WiFi symbol) Wireless Internet Access

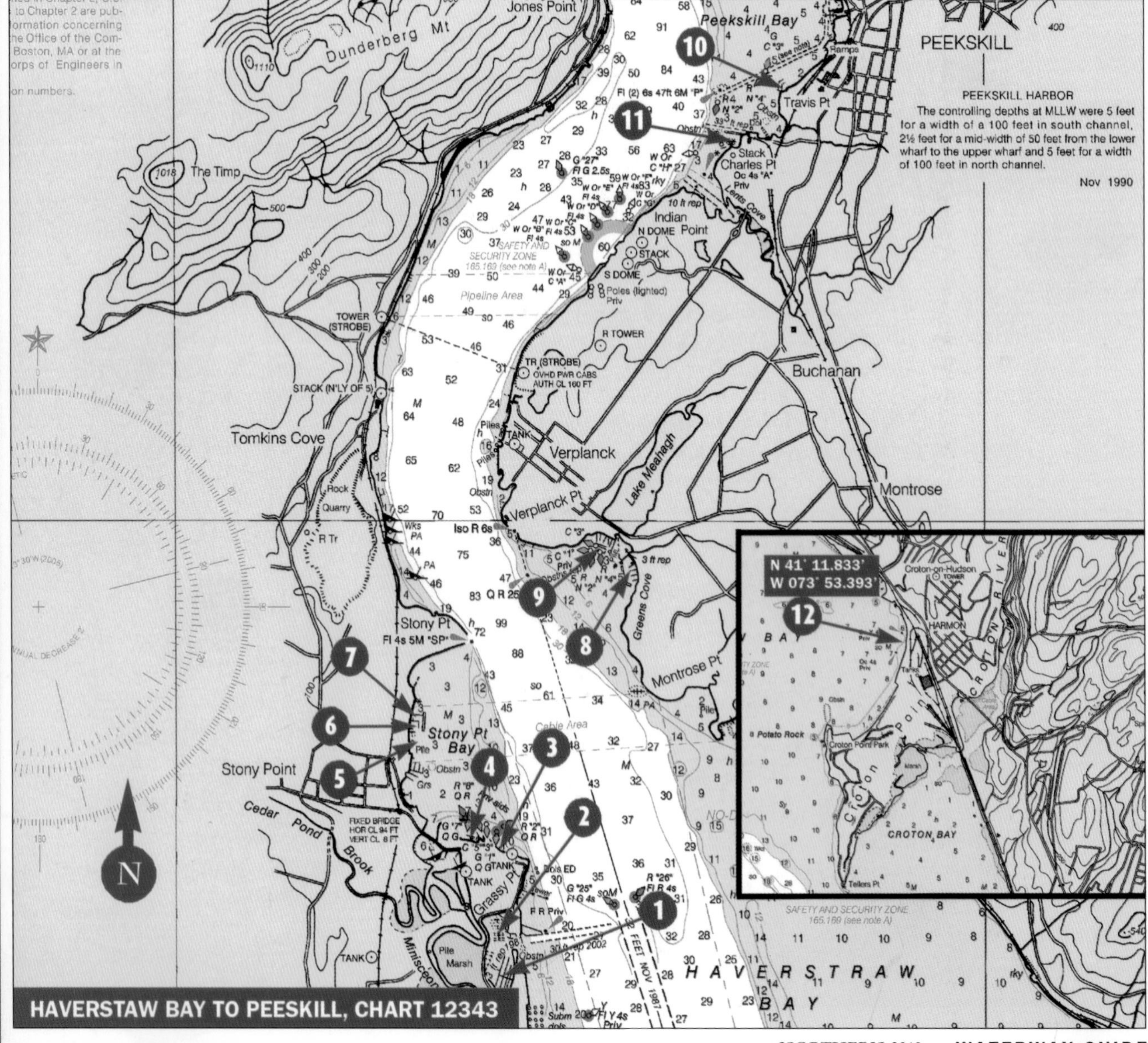

HAVERSTAW BAY TO PEESKILL, CHART 12343

Tarrytown (Sleepy Hollow)

Use New York (The Battery) tide tables. For high tide, add 1 hour 49 minutes; for low tide, add 1 hour 57 minutes. Just north of the bridge on the east bank is Tarrytown. According to Washington Irving, the author of "The Legend of Sleepy Hollow," the name derives from Dutch farm wives' complaining references to their husbands tarrying too long at the village tavern there. Following a referendum, however, nostalgic voters changed the town's name back to Sleepy Hollow. Tarrytown (or Sleepy Hollow) offers easy access and good provisioning. In recent years, the quaint, pretty main street has emerged as a minor nightlife center. The restored music hall is a centerpiece to this activity. This area is about a 20-minute uphill walk from the water.

Dockage: Its two marinas are next to one another, and the channel is well-marked. The southernmost is the Washington Irving Boat Club with docks that accommodate smaller boats. Just to the north is the larger Tarrytown Marina. Both facilities have good restaurants (the one at Tarrytown Marina is a bit more sophisticated) with outdoor dining on the river. If you want to dock and dine, your tie-up is complimentary. The Tarrytown Marina has more services geared toward transient boats. While you can obtain gas at either marina, only Tarrytown Marina has diesel. The Tarrytown Marina also has showers, a laundry and a marine supply store. A supermarket is a short walk away. Simply cross over the railroad via the bridge and turn north for about a block.

Upper Nyack

Dockage: Across the river at Upper Nyack is Julius Petersen Boatyard, identifiable by its large white buildings. On your chart, it is right next to the words "Upper Nyack." One of the Hudson River's two 60-ton lifts is here, as well as a 15-ton crane. Julius Petersen Boatyard is a traditional repair yard with a large technical staff able to quickly perform any level of boat repair. The large ship's store offers a broad selection of boating parts, supplies and electronics. Julius Petersen Boatyard has transient dockage, moorings and a wide variety of amenities. Groceries and one of the nation's largest malls are only a short cab ride away.

Just south of Julius Petersen Boatyard are the Hook Mountain Yacht Club (845-358-9874) and the Nyack Boat Club (845-358-9724), both offering reciprocal privileges to other yacht clubs. The Hook Mountain Yacht Club is quiet, with moorings available for transients from other clubs. The much larger Nyack Boat Club, the area's sailing center, has an extensive mooring field and maintains a few guest moorings. Launch service (VHF Channel 68) and a snack bar are available on weekends.

Nyack's center of town is about a mile away. This vibrant small town, known as the "Gem of the Hudson," is a center for the arts. In addition to its grand Victorian homes and many antiques shops, it offers a number of fine restaurants and a thriving nightlife.

Ossining (Sing Sing)

Ossining, on the eastern bank, was originally named Sing Sing, the same as the famous, sprawling hillside prison located here. At the turn of the century, a boycott of prison-made goods led the town to change its name to Ossining, allowing buyers to distinguish goods made at the prison from goods made in the town itself.

Dockage: On the river's east side, Half Moon Bay Marina in Croton-on-Hudson has protected transient slips with 10 foot depths, fuel, pump-out, wireless internet, pool, showers and laundry.

On the river's west side, to the north of and across the river from Croton Point, is the Haverstraw Marina complex. A wide selection of marine supplies can be found both here and at Samalot Marine.

Anchorage: Croton Point juts out into the river just north of Ossining, and except in west to north winds, it is one of the best anchorages on the river—certainly the best between here and New York City. Do not shortcut the point when going in, or you will find out that a shoal really does exist here.

Haverstraw Bay and Stony Point

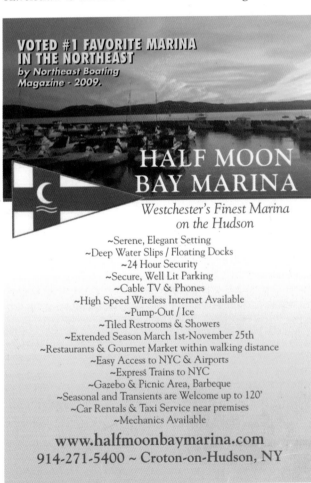

Use New York (The Battery) tide tables. For high tide, add 2 hours 15 minutes; for low tide, add 2 hours 42 minutes. Haverstraw Bay, northwest of Croton Point, is the widest part of the Hudson River—three miles across. The town of Haverstraw is nestled between the cliffs of High Tor to the west and the Hudson River. It was here in 1780 that turncoat Benedict Arnold schemed with British Major John Andre to betray and surrender West Point, a plot that was aborted with Andre's capture. The tree from which Andre was hanged still stands in the town square of Tappan, downriver, and the stagecoach inn where he was held prisoner still serves meals to wayfarers. Appropriately, it is called the 1776 House. This entire area was once the site of scores of brick factories. Cruising boats often use the north side of Stony Point as an overnight anchorage in south to west winds.

Around the bend of the river on the east side is the Indian Point Nuclear Power Plant. No docking is allowed here. A mile beyond is the city of Peekskill, named for Jan Peek, a Dutch trader who settled here in 1665. The channel is shallow and cruising amenities are limited.

Dockage: Haverstraw Marina, located south of Grassy Point, offers a variety of amenities for the cruising mariner.

Peekskill

The National Maritime Historical Society (914-737-7878) is located next to the Charles Point Marina in Peekskill. The maritime art gallery and an extensive information center of maritime history are open daily, including weekends. The channel to the marina is marked, but limited to vessels with no more than 5-foot drafts. Limited transient dockage is available here.

Dunderberg Mountain

Across the Hudson River is densely forested Dunderberg Mountain, the 1,000-foot-tall legendary dwelling of the Dutch goblin held responsible for summer storms. The mountain marks the southern limit of the Highland section of the river. For the next 10 miles, the river cuts through the Appalachian mountain chain, and is one of the most beautiful stretches of river scenery in the United States.

Bear Mountain

A mile or two north of Dunderberg Mountain is Bear Mountain, the site of the huge Bear Mountain State Park. To explore this striking mountainside park, you may anchor either in the bight between Iona Island and the tour-boat dock or, in most weather, north of the dock and before the Bear Mountain Bridge.

The dinghy dock is behind the tour-boat dock. Walk through the tunnel that passes under the railroad tracks, and then follow the macadam path up the mountain. The view of the river below, with your boat at anchor, makes a great photo. The path leads past an immense public swimming pool nestled in a mountain gully. Farther on is a trail way museum and a zoo, home of a fine collection of Hudson Valley animals and birds, including bobcats, black bears, foxes, owls and pheasants. Beyond is a mountain lake with scores of rental boats. Finally, you will arrive at a wonderful old hotel, complete with a restaurant and bar.

All but the tour-boat dock is hidden from view by the dense mountain foliage, so most boaters cruising this way are unaware of the park's existence. Now that you know about it, do not pass it by. It does crowd up with busloads of city folk picnicking on weekends, though.

It is here that you and your crew may first encounter the white swans, known as mute swans (an introduced species), often seen paddling leisurely around the river's coves as far north as Catskill. Keeping a count of the number you have spotted can be a challenging pastime, particularly for the younger members of the crew.

An image of the great Haverstraw landslide of 1906, largely caused by clay harvesting for the brick industry. Courtesy Haverstraw Brick Museum.

HAVERSTRAW BRICK-MAKING

Jacob Van Dyke began hand-making bricks in Haverstraw, NY, in 1771, taking advantage of the rich Hudson River clay deposits left behind by the glaciers during the Ice Age. More than 100 years later, there were over 40 brickyards along the Hudson River, many of them concentrated in Haverstraw.

While bricks from Haverstraw were helping build New York City, the brick industry was pushing closer and closer to the Haverstraw community. Decades of clay removal undermined the town banks, and, on Jan. 8, 1906, there was a landslide that resulted in 19 deaths and a massive loss of homes. Clay deposit depletion, the Great Depression and the introduction of new building materials caused the brick making industry to die out. In 1941, the Rockland County Brick Company, the last manufacturer standing, closed its doors for good.

Ashore in Haverstraw, the Haverstraw Brick Museum chronicles this industry and makes an interesting visit for boaters (www.haverstrawbrickmuseum.org).

The narrow section of the river between Iona Island and the eastern shore is known as The Race. The swiftest current on the Hudson River runs here. The island was the site of a navy arsenal from 1900 until after World War II, and some fences and buildings still remain.

Starting as early as March, the Hudson River, and the upcoming stretch particularly, is one of the most prolific striped bass fisheries on the East Coast.

■ BEAR MOUNTAIN BRIDGE TO NEWBURGH AND BEACON BRIDGE

The Bear Mountain Bridge, at the time of its completion in 1924, was the world's largest suspension bridge. In addition to carrying highway traffic, it also serves as the Hudson River crossing of the famous Maine-to-Georgia Appalachian Trail.

During the Revolutionary War, the Americans stretched a huge chain across the Hudson River just north of the Bear Mountain Bridge site to prevent British warships from passing. Unfortunately, the British seized the chain (sending it to Gibraltar to protect their own harbor), and then sailed up the river and burned the town of Kingston.

West Point

West Point, the United States Military Academy, which opened in 1802, is well worth the effort to visit from the water. If you would like to visit the Academy, first call the West Point harbormaster on VHF Channel 16 and ask if there is space at the Academy dock or if visitors are permitted during periods of heightened security. If no space is available, ask about using one of the mooring buoys. If there is still no space available, go across the river to the Garrison Yacht Club and Marina. From here, if you have a seaworthy dinghy with a motor, dinghy back across the river to the Academy. Be forewarned, however, that the Academy is a long and expensive cab ride from Garrison.

In addition to providing boaters with access to West Point, the town of Garrison has a small grocery store (at the marina in the dockmaster's building) and a busy train station.

The narrow section of the river just north of the Academy, designated as World's End, is the deepest section of the entire river. During the Revolutionary War, the Americans stretched another chain across the river here, but not in time to prevent the British from attacking the upriver town of Kingston.

Foundry Cove, Cold Spring

Foundry Cove is too shallow for most boats to use as an anchorage. Foundries cast cannon and shot here during the Civil War. Here, too, the first American iron warship—a revenue cutter—was built in the 1850s.

Dockage: Just beyond is the village of Cold Spring, with a riverfront green, a marina with a swimming pool, restaurant and, during the summer, village-sponsored water fiestas. Dockage at the marina is limited to boats of 30 feet or less. The Cold Spring Boat Club can be reached at 845-265-2465. Note that the transient docks here are open to river wakes.

Storm King Mountain

Storm King Mountain, a spectacular 1,355-foot-tall peak, rises above the western shore at the northern end of the Hudson's Highland section. The scenic highway that girds it was completed in 1940.

Dockage: Just north of Storm King Mountain, on the west side of the river, are the Cornwall Yacht Club (845-534-8835) and Panco Marine Fueling at Cornwall Landing (800-477-4OIL), which welcome transient boats. Storm King Mountain to the south and a waterfront park to the north make this a particularly scenic stop. Note, with the exception of the dock and moorings at West Point, Cornwall Yacht Club, approximately five miles away, is the nearest west bank dockage to the Academy. If an Academy visit is on your list, ask about the availability of a rental car. There is an Enterprise Rent-A-Car office in nearby Newburgh (800-736-8222).

Pollepel (Bannerman's) Island

Pollepel Island, widely known as Bannerman's Island, is four miles north on the eastern shore. Between 1900 and 1918, Frank Bannerman, a munitions dealer, built a replica of a medieval castle here as a summer resort and storehouse. In 1967, the state obtained the property, and tours were conducted until the castle burned in 1969. Today, because of the deteriorating condition of the building, landing on the island is no longer permitted.

Anchorage: You can find an interesting anchorage behind the island by heading close into shore at Breakneck Point and then carefully following the 7- to 10-foot channel northward toward the island. In this vicinity, the Catskill Aqueduct was completed in 1919. Passing hundreds of feet beneath the Hudson River, the aqueduct provides 500 million gallons of water each day for metropolitan New York City.

Newburgh and Beacon

Four miles north of Pollepel are the twin cities of Newburgh and Beacon. Despite being situated more than 60 miles inland, Newburgh was a 19th-century seaport and the home of whaling ships. George Washington's 1782-83 headquarters, the Hasbrough House, still stands here and is open to the public. Substantial waterfront development has sprung up in Newburgh during the last several years, mostly to accommodate local small craft. The Yacht Club (with its popular restaurant) continues to be a good stop for transient vessels.

Dockage: Front Street Marina offers dockage to transients and accommodates boats up to 70 feet. Front Street Marina can arrange for bulk delivery of diesel with prior notice.

West Point to Kingston, NY

WEST POINT TO KINGSTON		Largest Vessel Accommodated	VHF Channel Monitored	Transient Berths / Total Berths	Approach / Dockside Depth (reported)	Floating Docks	Gas / Diesel	Groceries, Ice, Marine Supplies, Snacks	Repairs: Hull, Engine, Propeller	Lift (tonnage), Crane, Rail	1=110V, 2=220V, B=Both, Max Amps	Laundry, Pool, Showers	Pump-Out Station	Nearby: Grocery Store, Motel, Restaurant
		Dockage					Supplies		Services					
1. Cornwall Yacht Club	845-534-8835	50	16	10/107	10/3	F	G	IS		L25	B/50	S	P	GMR
2. White's Hudson River Marina	845-297-8520	40		2/300	20/20	F	GD	IM	HEP	L25	1/30	S	P	
3. New Hamburg Yacht Club	845-298-1707	42		7/86	25/60			GIM			1/20			
4. West Shore Marina	845-236-3251	85	16/09	6/200	12/12	F	GD	IM	HEP	L25	B/50	S		GMR
5. Hyde Park Marina/Brass Anchor Restaurant	845-473-8283	200	16	20/150	40/7	F	G	IM	HEP	R	1/30	S		GMR
6. Poughkeepsie Yacht Club	845-889-4742	60		2/90	60/22	F		I		L25	1/30	S		
7. Hudson River Maritime Museum	845-338-0071	215			30/14	F					B/50	S		GR
8. Mariner's Harbor	845-340-8051			DINING										R
9. Kingston Municipal Marina (WiFi)	845-331-6940	200	16/71	42/85	11/8	F					B/50	S	P	GMR
10. Hideaway Marina (Internet)	845-331-4565	55	16/09	4/100	7/7	F		IMS	P	L35	1/30	LS	P	GMR
11. Jeff's Yacht Haven	845-331-9248	65	16	6/30	20/12	F		IM	HEP	L35,C,R	1/50	LS	P	MR
12. Rondout Yacht Basin (Internet) (WiFi)	845-331-7061	140	16/09	30/200	12/12	F	GD	IMS	HEP	L45	B/50	LPS	P	GMR
13. Lou's Boat Basin	845-331-4670	42	79	/50	11/10		GD	IM			1/30			GR
14. Certified Marine Service (Internet)	845-339-3060	45	16/09	5/110	15/12	F	G	IMS	HEP	L25,C10	B/50	S	P	GMR
15. Front Street Marina	845-661-4914	200	16/68	30/142	45/70	F		IMS			B/50	S	P	GMR
16. Torches Marina	845-568-0100	100		15/50	30/30	F					B/50			R

Corresponding chart(s) not to be used for navigation. (Internet) Internet Access (WiFi) Wireless Internet Access

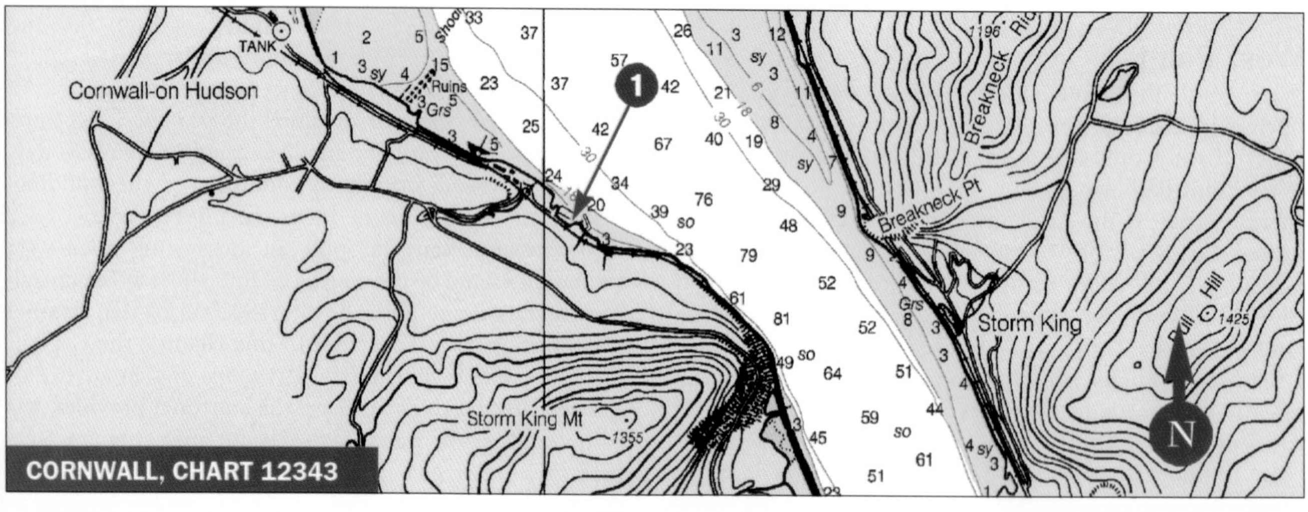

CORNWALL, CHART 12343

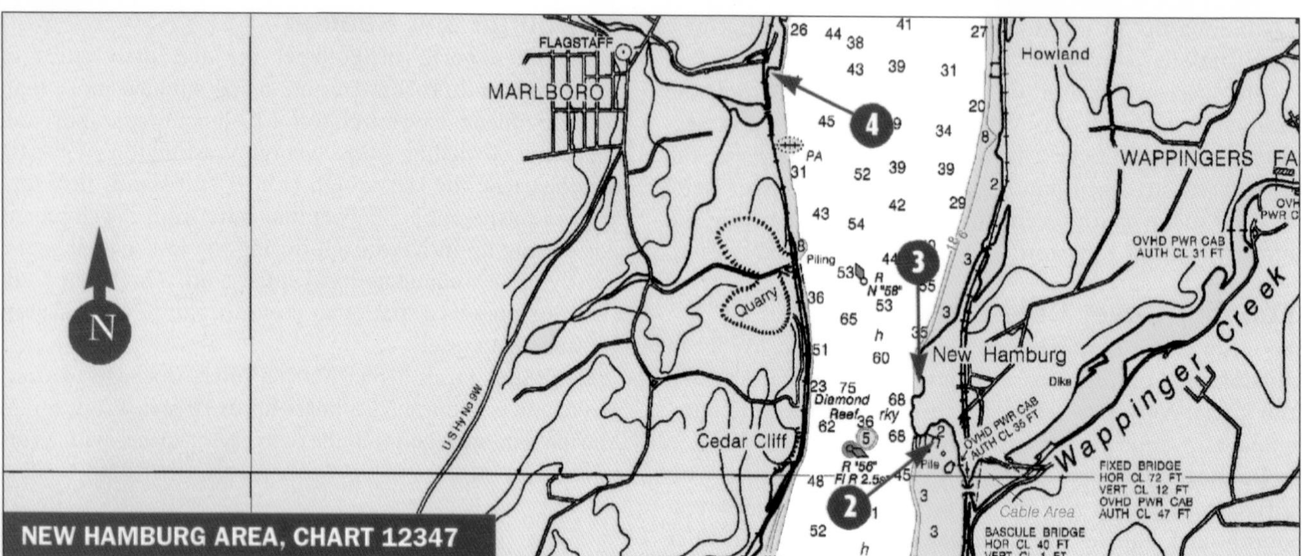

NEW HAMBURG AREA, CHART 12347

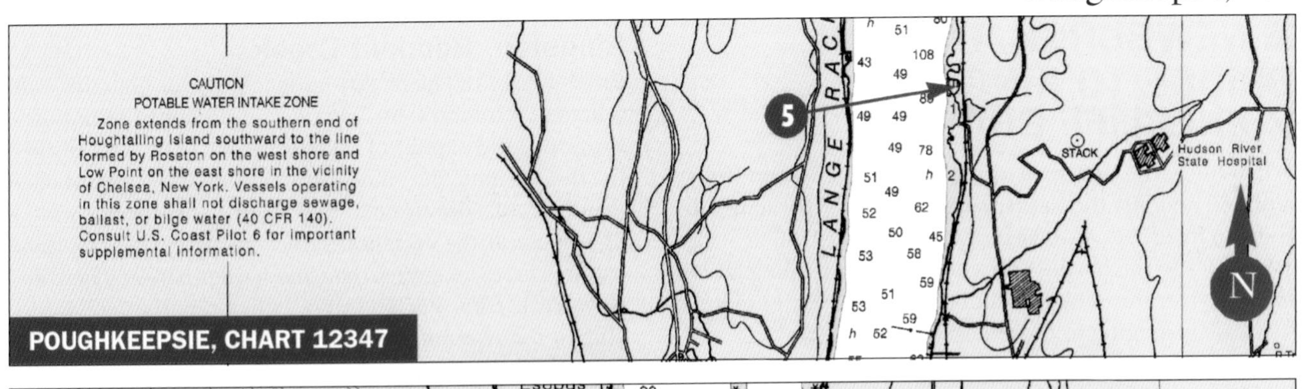

CAUTION
POTABLE WATER INTAKE ZONE
Zone extends from the southern end of Houghtalling Island southward to the line formed by Roseton on the west shore and Low Point on the east shore in the vicinity of Chelsea, New York. Vessels operating in this zone shall not discharge sewage, ballast, or bilge water (40 CFR 140). Consult U.S. Coast Pilot 6 for important supplemental information.
LANGE RACE
STACK
Hudson River State Hospital
5
N

POUGHKEEPSIE, CHART 12347

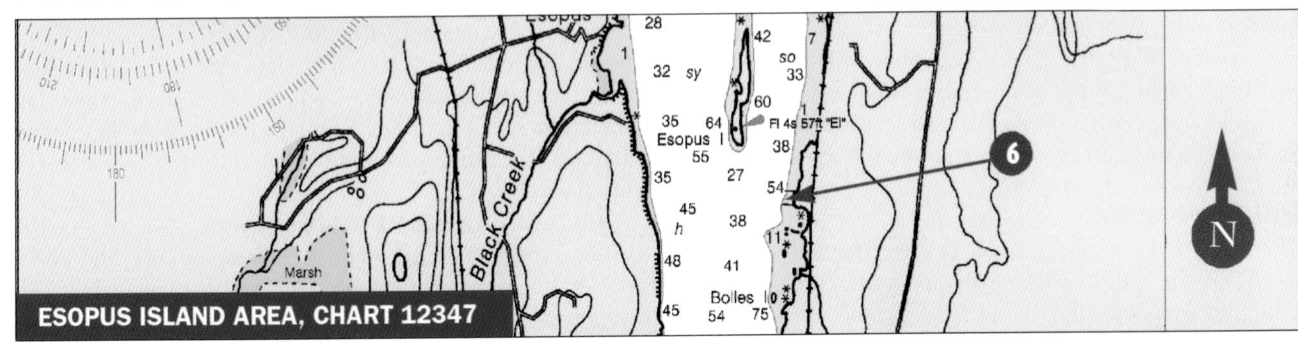

ESOPUS ISLAND AREA, CHART 12347

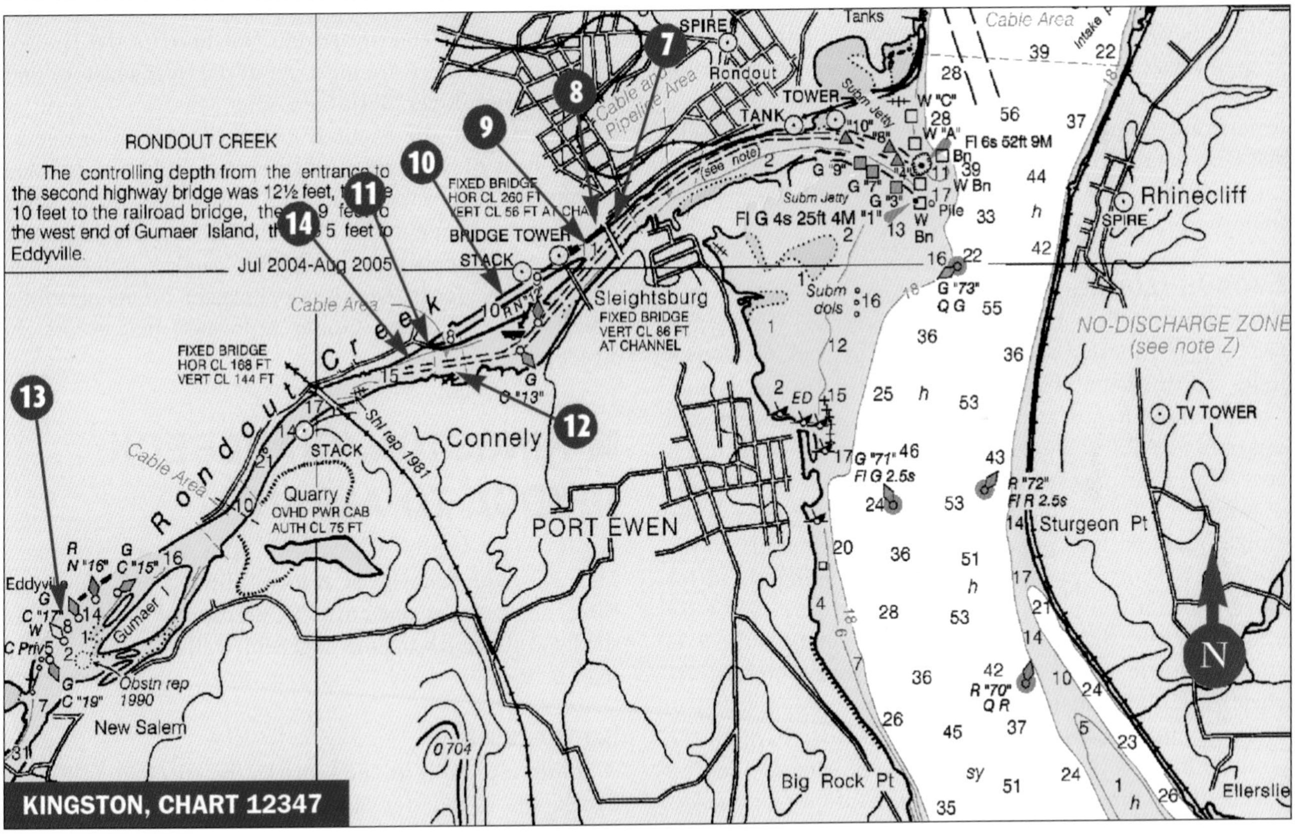

RONDOUT CREEK

The controlling depth from the entrance to the second highway bridge was 12½ feet, then 10 feet to the railroad bridge, then 9 feet to the west end of Gumaer Island, then 5 feet to Eddyville.

Jul 2004-Aug 2005

KINGSTON, CHART 12347

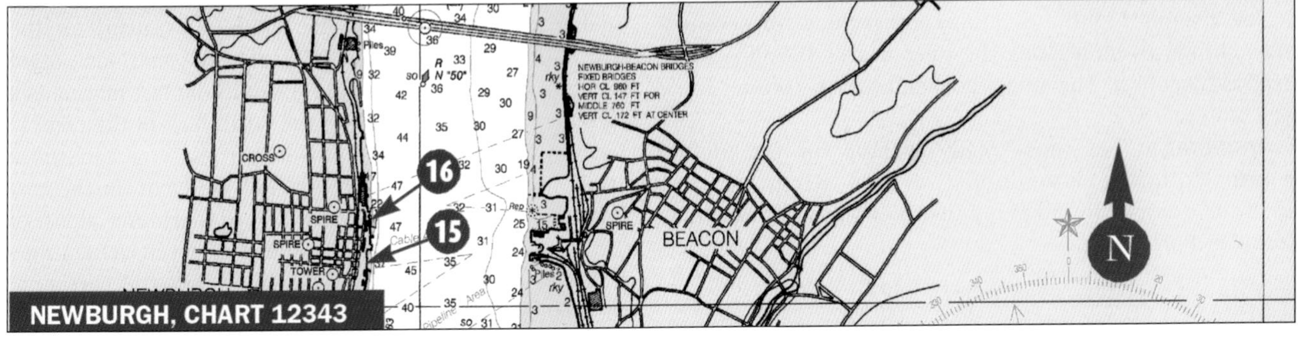

NEWBURGH, CHART 12343

■ NEWBURGH/BEACON BRIDGE TO KINGSTON/ RHINECLIFF BRIDGE

When built, the first span of the Newburgh/Beacon Bridge replaced not only the last remaining ferry service across the Hudson River, but also the oldest ferry in the United States. Two miles to the north of Newburgh and extending far out into the river from the east shore is a great array of moored sailboats belonging to the Chelsea Yacht Club.

The marina and the yacht club at New Hamburg are both convenient to grocery stores for provisioning. Across the river at Marlboro are a West Shore Marina and the Marlboro Yacht Club, both a hefty walk from a supermarket and a mall. There are no cruising facilities or protected anchorages between Marlboro and Poughkeepsie.

Poughkeepsie

The Mid-Hudson Suspension Bridge, opened in 1930, is one of the oldest bridges spanning the Hudson River. Poughkeepsie was the temporary capital of New York in 1777 and is home to Vassar College, one of the so-called "Seven Sisters," which is now co-ed. Although Poughkeepsie was once an active river port, its east bank has no marinas. On the west bank is Mariners Harbor, a waterfront restaurant that might provide overnight dockage. The massive Conrail railroad bridge has been in place for more than 100 years and once made Poughkeepsie an important railroad center.

Esopus Island, Port Ewen

Dockage: Skippers note—the Poughkeepsie Yacht Club (PYC) is not located at Poughkeepsie. Instead, it is seven miles north of the city, just southeast of Esopus Island. This friendly, handsome club welcomes all transient vessels and houses a lounge and a laundry. Floating dock space and moorings are available.

A mile farther north on the same side of the river is the Norrie Yacht Basin, a popular Hudson River marina on the grounds of Norrie State Park. Consider calling ahead for reservations if you plan to spend the night here (914-889-4200), but note that neither facility sells fuel. Both the PYC and the Norrie Yacht Basin are a short drive from historic Hyde Park, the former home of Franklin D. Roosevelt. The house is open for tours. Also located in Hyde Park on the Hudson River is the Culinary Institute of America; several excellent restaurants are located on the campus, and reservations are required well in advance, so plan accordingly.

The Esopus Lighthouse, the southernmost of several old lighthouses built along the river, marks the shoals of Esopus Meadows. This one, knocked askew by winter ice, was built in 1872.

Anchorage: For those ready to stop for the night before exploring Roundout Creek in Kingston, an anchorage can be found along the river's west shore, just south of Port Ewen.

Kingston, Rondout Creek

Use New York (The Battery) tide tables. For high tide, add 5 hours 20 minutes; for low tide, add 5 hours 34 minutes. Kingston, the capital of New York in 1777, was burned to the ground by the British after their ships had managed to slip up the river. Rondout Creek, with a lighthouse at the entrance, serves as the city's harbor and features more amenities than any harbor between here and New York City. For NOAA weather reports, pay special attention to warnings for Ulster & Dutches counties.

Dockage: Four transient marinas are located past the bridge on Kingston's Rondout Creek. Rondout Yacht Basin and Jeff's Yacht Haven are located on the left fork of the creek. Hideaway Marina and the City Docks are along the right fork. Rondout Yacht Basin has a well-stocked general store and pool, and Hideaway has an extensive marine store.

On the north side of Rondout Creek, just west of the bridge (56-foot fixed vertical clearance) are the town docks, where both water and electricity are available. The dockmaster can be found in the small octagonal building at dockside. Just a few steps from the docks is the Hudson River Maritime Center Museum. Nowhere on the Hudson River can travelers learn more about the river's history than at the Hudson River Maritime Center Museum. In addition to the museum, the restored historical waterfront district has an array of boutiques, craft stores and three restaurants within 500 feet of the docks. No longer does major shopping require a long uphill hike. On Fridays, Saturdays and Sundays, an inexpensive trolley bus makes regular stops near the city docks. See the dockmaster for its schedule. The Kingston Visitors Center is located just across the street from the docks.

■ KINGSTON/RHINEBECK BRIDGE TO ALBANY

The Kingston/Rhinebeck Bridge, three miles north of Kingston, was completed in 1957. Be aware that well-marked shoals to the north require large ship traffic to crisscross the river here.

Saugerties

A lighthouse, built in 1869, marks the entrance to Esopus Creek, the harbor for Saugerties. The name "Saugerties" is derived from the Dutch word for "sawmills." Although smaller than Kingston to the south, or Catskill to the north, this harbor is the home of three marinas, all of which provide transient space. Beyond the last marina is a cozy deepwater anchorage in the north fork of the creek.

Upon heading north from Saugerties, you can see a lovely old estate at the top of a hillside lawn on the east bank opposite daybeacon "95." This is Clermont, oldest of the Hudson River estates and home of seven generations of Livingstons, including Chancellor Robert Livingston, negotiator of the Louisiana Purchase and co-inventor with

Saugerties, NY

SAUGERTIES		Largest Vessel Accommodated	VHF Channel Monitored	Transient Berths / Total Berths	Approach / Dockside Depth (reported)	Floating Docks	Gas / Diesel	Groceries, Ice, Marine Supplies, Snacks	Repairs: Hull, Engine, Propeller	Lift (tonnage), Crane, Rail	1=110V, 2=220V, B=Both, Max Amps	Laundry, Pool, Showers	Pump-Out Station	Nearby: Grocery Store, Motel, Restaurant
		Dockage						Supplies		Services				
1. Saugerties Marina	845-246-7533	60		3/35	15/15	F	GD	IMS	HEP		1/30	S		GMR
2. Lynch's Marina	845-247-0995	50		4/50	12/12			IM			1/30	S		GMR

Corresponding chart(s) not to be used for navigation. Internet Access Wireless Internet Access

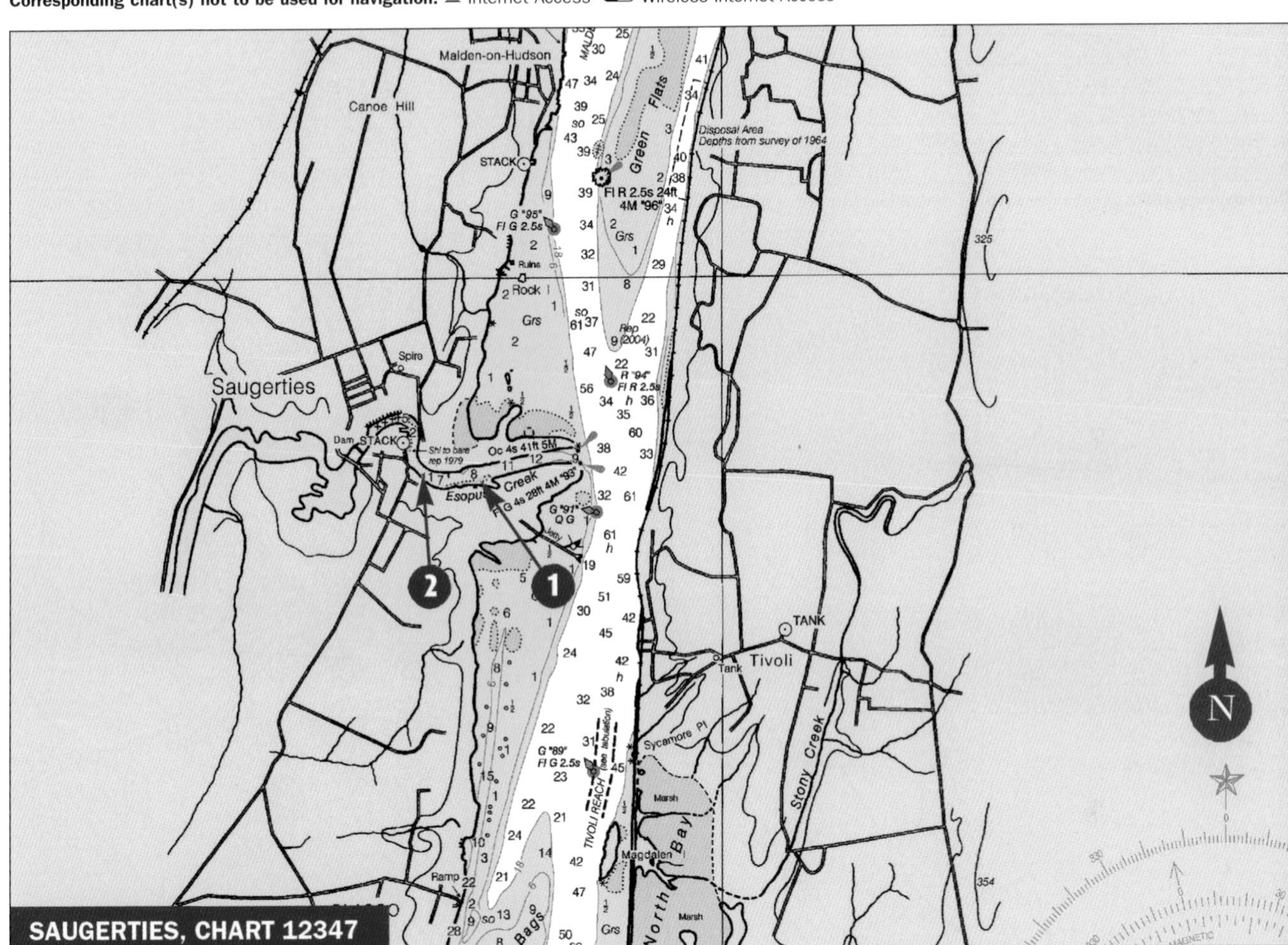

SAUGERTIES, CHART 12347

Fulton of the first practical steamboat. The British burned the original building, as they did the city of Kingston, in 1777. It is now a state historic site, open from May to October.

Catskill

Dockage: Catskill is a particularly busy harbor, so it is advisable to call ahead for reservations on weekends. There are three marinas in Catskill: Catskill Marina, Hop-O-Nose and Riverview Marine Services. Catskill Marina is nestled in a park-like setting close to town. Amenities include a restaurant, heated swimming pool and extensive restroom and shower facilities. Hop-O-Nose and Riverview Marine Services both have mast-stepping capabilities. Riverview Marine Services offers transient dockage, gas and diesel fuel and a pump-out station. Hop-O-Nose also has a popular on-premises restaurant. Mariner's Point Restaurant and Skippy's Raw Bar, both accessible by water, are located at the entrance to the harbor.

Immediately north of Catskill is the Rip Van Winkle Bridge, opened in 1935. While still south of the bridge, cast your gaze toward the top of Church Hill (marked on the chart), and you will see the outline of Olana, the spectacular 19th-century building that was home to Frederic Church, one of the best known of the Hudson River School artists.

Middle Ground Flats

The main ship channel passes east of Middle Ground Flats, but recreational craft frequently use the shorter route to the west, which has less current. The lighthouse at the junction of these two routes is built on a shoal—the scene of a fiery wreck in 1845, which killed 50 of 300 passengers

Catskill to Coeymans, NY

CATSKILL TO COEYMANS		Largest Vessel Accommodated	VHF Channel Monitored	Transient Berths / Total Berths	Approach / Dockside Depth (reported)	Floating Docks	Gas / Diesel	Groceries, Ice, Marine Supplies, Snacks	Repairs: Hull, Engine, Propeller	Lift (tonnage), Crane, Rail	1=110V, 2=220V, B=Both, Max Amps	Laundry, Pool, Showers	Pump-Out Station	Nearby: Grocery Store, Motel, Restaurant
		Dockage					Supplies		Services					
1. Riverview Marine Services Inc.	518-943-5311	75	16/68	6/24	10/8	F	GD	IMS	HEP	L20,C	1/30	LS	P	GMR
2. Catskill Marina	**518-943-4170**	**150**	**16/09**	**15/100**	**10/15**	**F**	**GD**	**I**			**B/100**	**LPS**	**P**	**GR**
3. Hop-O-Nose Marina	518-943-4640	120		30/70	10/15	F	GD	IM	HEP	L45	B/50	LPS	P	GR
4. Catskill Yacht Club	518-943-6459	40	16	3/40	20/10	F		I			1/30	S	P	GR
5. Hudson Power Boat Assoc.	518-828-9023	36	16/09	4/60	30/10	F	G	IS			1/30	S	P	R
6. Athens on the Hudson	518-945-1624	100		40/150	28/20	F		IS	HEP		1/50			R
7. Coxsackie Yacht Club	518-731-9819								Members Only					
8. Shady Harbor Marina & Water's Edge Rest.	518-756-8001	85	16	10/110	15/12	F	GD	IMS	HEP	L25,C	B/50	LPS	P	GMR
9. Coeymans Landing Marina	518-756-6111	60	16/09	8/85	8/10	F	GD	IMS	HEP	L38	1/50	LS	P	GMR

Corresponding chart(s) not to be used for navigation. Internet Access, WiFi Wireless Internet Access

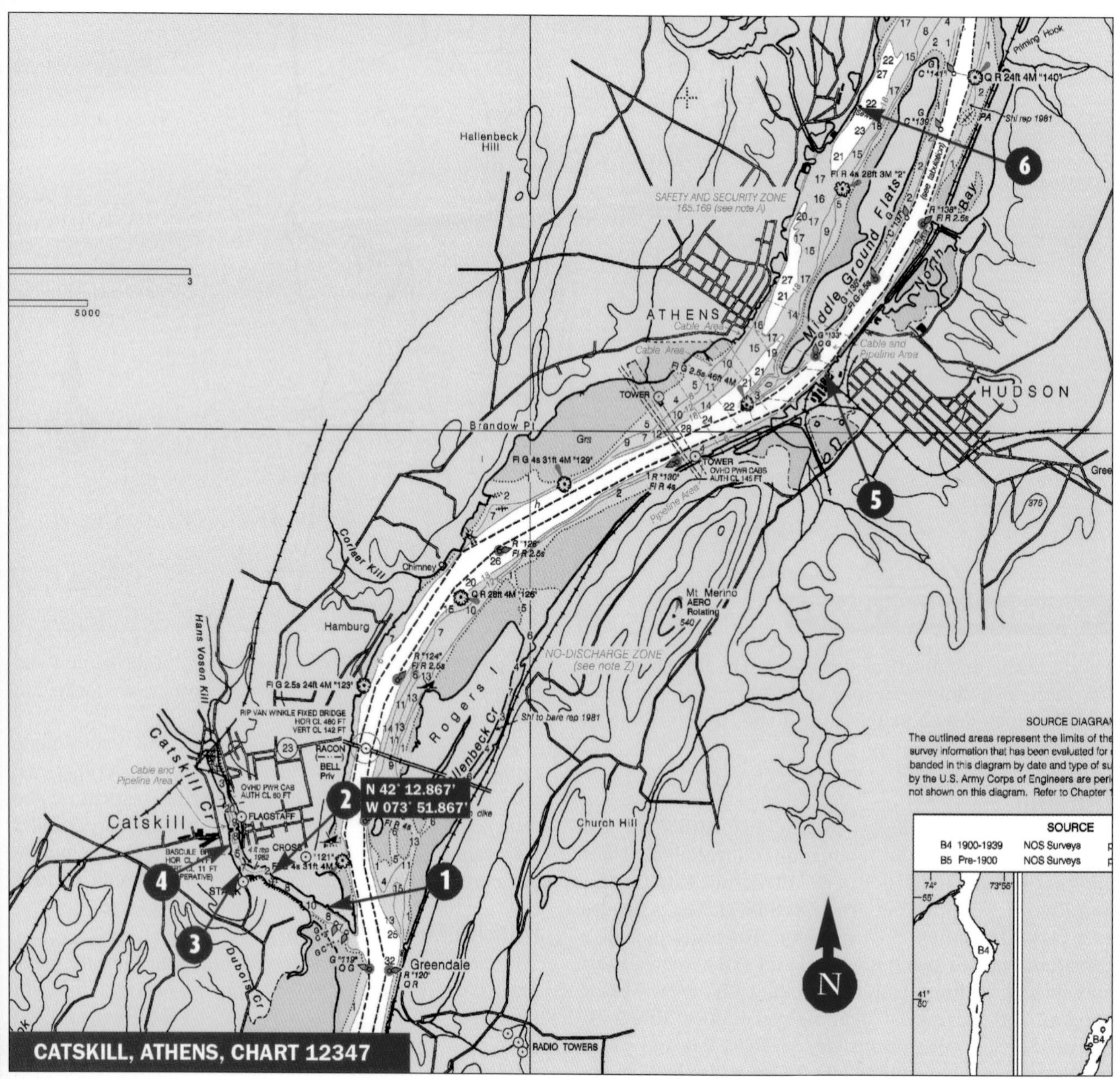

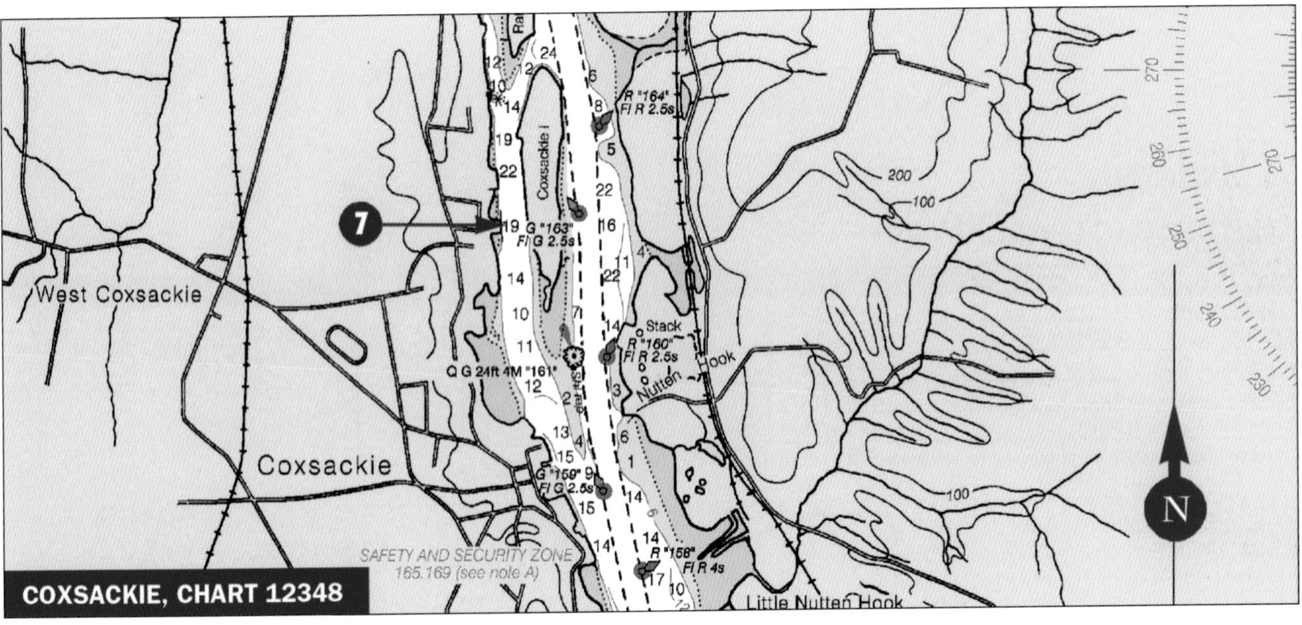

on the steamboat Swallow. The northwest side of Middle Ground Flats can be used as an anchorage, but take special care to stay well out of the way of passing vessels. From here, you can visit the town of Athens by dinghy.

Dockage: Just north of Athens on the west side of Middle Ground Flats is Athens on the Hudson Marina, with transient slips, repairs and an on-site restaurant.

Anchorage: You will find a better anchorage, although with a more difficult approach, behind Stockport Middle Ground above marker "150." The entrance is narrower than it appears on the chart, and the sides shoal abruptly. A depth sounder is essential here. Just north of the town of Coxsackie (pronounced "Cook-sacky") is another protected anchorage, located between Coxsackie Island and

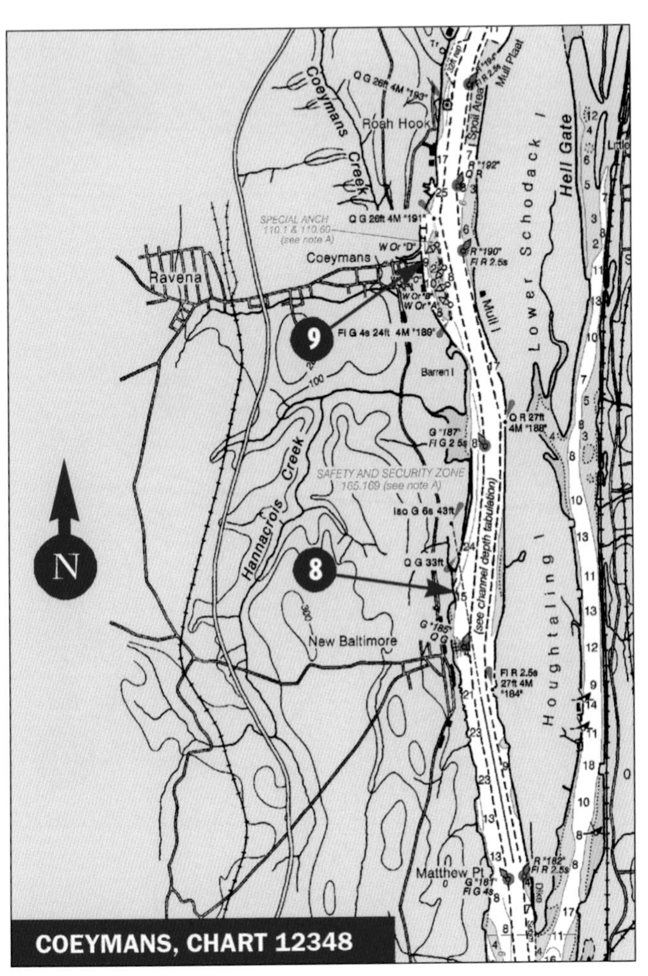

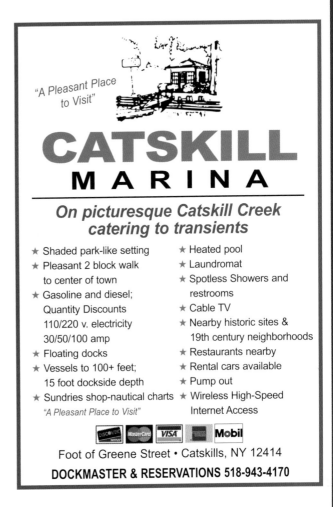

Castleton, Albany, Troy, NY

CASTLETON, ALBANY, TROY		Largest Vessel Accommodated	VHF Channel Monitored	Transient Berths / Total Berths	Approach / Dockside Depth (reported)	Floating Docks	Gas / Diesel	Groceries, Ice, Marine Supplies, Snacks	Repairs: Hull, Engine, Propeller	Lift (tonnage), Crane, Rail	1=110V, 2=220V, B=Both, Max Amps	Laundry, Pool, Showers	Pump-Out Station	Nearby: Grocery Store, Motel, Restaurant
		Dockage					Supplies		Services					
1. Castleton Boat Club	518-732-7077	80	16/09	5/55	12/8	F	GD	I			B/50	S	P	GR
2. Albany Yacht Club (Internet Access) (Wireless Internet Access)	518-445-9587	150	16/68	/80	25/18	F	GD	I			B/200	S	P	GMR
3. Troy Dock (Internet Access) (Wireless Internet Access)	518-272-6291	200	16/13	25/	21/21	F	GD	IM		C20	B/100	LS	P	GMR
4. Capital District Marina	518-237-3442	YARD SERVICE							HEP					
5. Van Schaick Island Marina	518-237-2681	80	16/13	6/100	15/12	F		IM	HEP	L35	B/50		P	GR

Corresponding chart(s) not to be used for navigation. Internet Access Wireless Internet Access

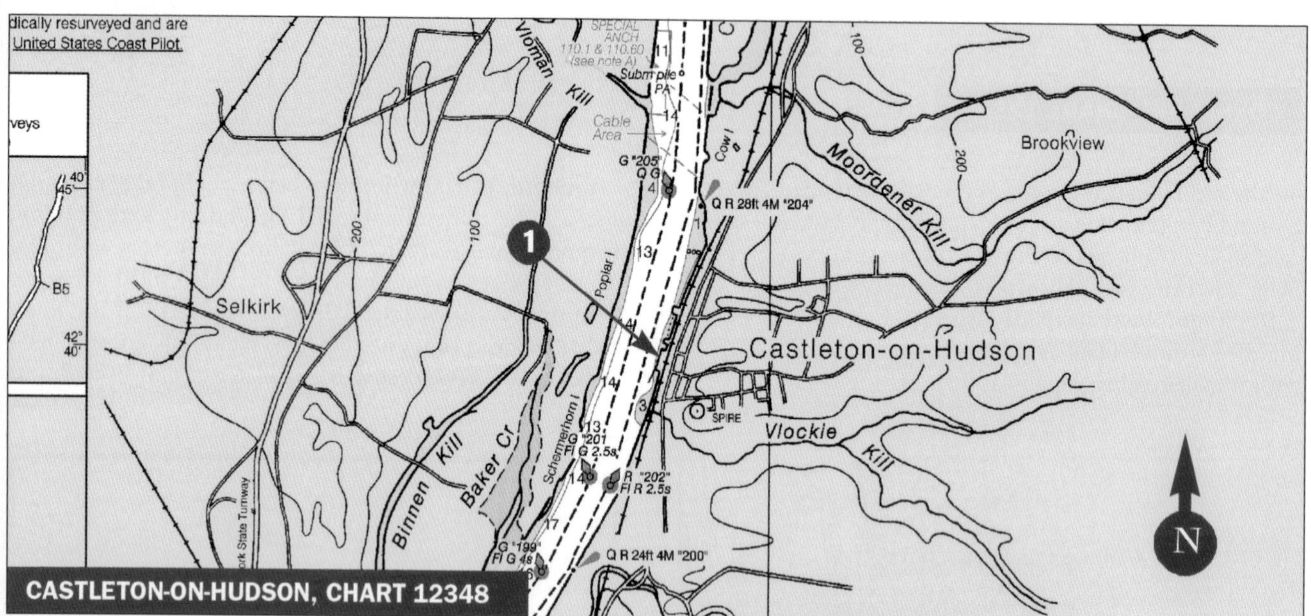

CASTLETON-ON-HUDSON, CHART 12348

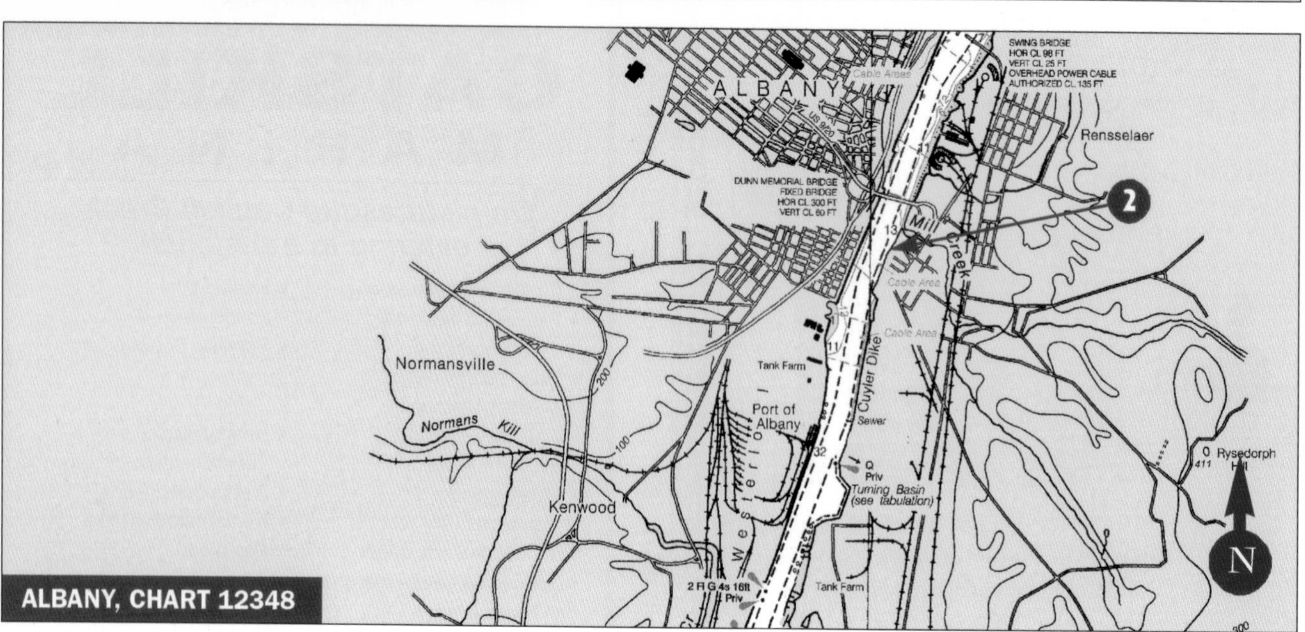

ALBANY, CHART 12348

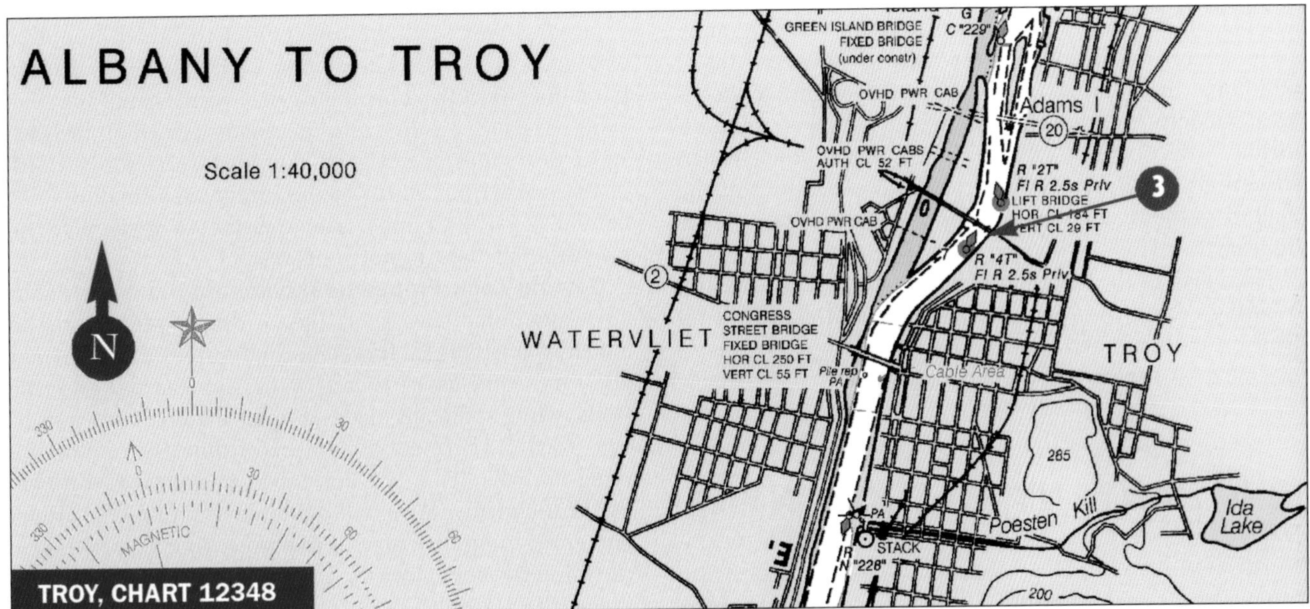

TROY, CHART 12348

the west bank of the river. Caution: It is reported that the bar at the south end of the island extends significantly farther to the south than the chart indicates.

Although the anchorage marked by white buoys just north of marker "170" is for big-ship use, recreational craft can find many attractive spots on the east side of Houghtaling Island.

New Baltimore

Dockage: Shady Harbor Marina, located at New Baltimore, is the first full-service marina past Catskill. It is open seven days a week, year-round, and transients are entitled to enjoy the swimming pool. The Boat House Restaurant, a popular waterfront dining spot with complimentary dockage, is located on the marina grounds.

Coeymans

Dockage: In Coeymans, transient space can be found at both Coeymans Landing Marina, with its lively Muddy Rudder Café, and Ravena-Coeyman's Yacht Club. Before leaving the river channel to head for these facilities, however, be sure to locate the position of the very long and very low north-south silt control dike. It is frequently underwater with only a few warning signs visible.

Castleton-on-Hudson

Use Albany tide tables. For high tide, subtract 17 minutes; for low tide, subtract 29 minutes.

Dockage: Castleton-on-Hudson is located just north of the highway and railroad bridges. The Castleton Boat Club offers a large crane for do-it-yourself mast-stepping. The club's rental moorings, located across the river, include use of club facilities (showers, restrooms, bar).

Sailors note: The only opportunity to get your mast unstepped north of here is at the Troy Town Dock and Marina.

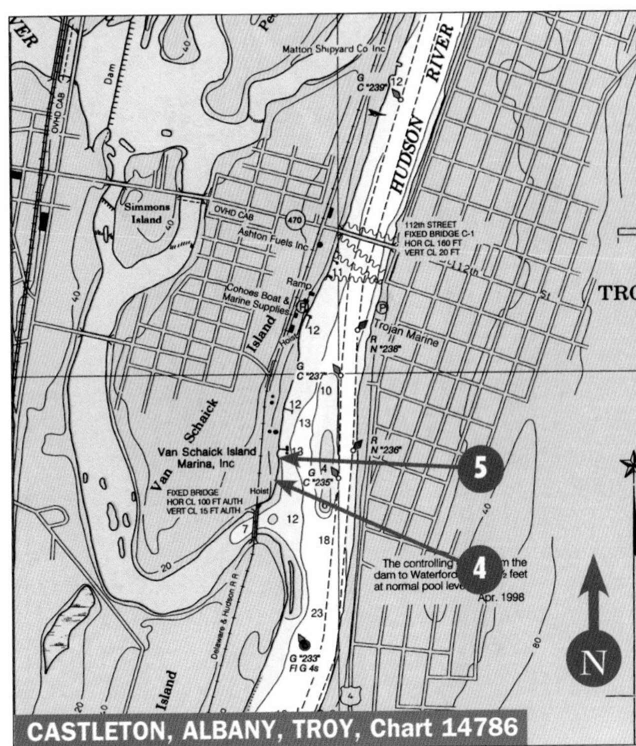

CASTLETON, ALBANY, TROY, Chart 14786

Albany

Use Albany tide tables. Six miles to the north, you will emerge from the serenity of the upper Hudson River into the sometimes-hectic activity of seagoing ships unloading their cargoes of imported automobiles, bananas, fuel and molasses at the Port of Albany. In 1851, 15,000 Erie Canal boats and 500 sailing ships cleared this port. Albany, the capital of New York, has a 4- to 5-foot tide, even though it is 144 miles from the ocean.

On the east bank, just before the 60-foot fixed bridge, is the Albany Yacht Club, which offers a warm welcome to all mariners. It is a fine base from which to visit the impressive Nelson A. Rockefeller Empire State Plaza, more often referred to as the South Mall. Built in the 1960s, this complex is a magnificent showplace of modern granite architecture. In addition to the state government office buildings, the complex is home to one of the country's great modern museums and an acoustically superb auditorium. Affectionately called "The Egg," this bowl-shaped structure can be seen amid the 10 other buildings of the mall from the river. A tour of this complex will be a highlight of your Hudson River cruise.

Just north of the bridge is a huge, restored 19th-century building, once the headquarters of the Delaware and Hudson Railroad, and now the headquarters of the mammoth New York State University system.

■ ALBANY, NY TO TROY, NY

North of Albany, on the west side of the river past the Interstate 90 and Menands bridges, is the Waterveliet Arsenal. Arms for U.S. military forces have been manufactured here since the arsenal's establishment in 1813.

In 1609, a longboat from Henry Hudson's ship, *Half Moon,* explored as far north as the present city of Troy, found the head of navigation and determined that, indeed, this was not the way to the Orient.

Troy

Use Albany tide tables. For high tide, add 8 minutes; for low tide, add 10 minutes. Troy is the home of Rensselaer Polytechnic Institute, an outstanding science and engineering college, and Emma Willard School, the first women's college in the United States. Both are visible from the water. In 1825, a Troy woman invented the detachable collar, making the city a famed collar- and shirt-manufacturing center. The Cluett-Peabody plant on River Street produced Arrow shirts. "Uncle Sam" Wilson, a local meat packer during the War of 1812, stamped beef for the army with his initials: "U.S. Beef." Later, a caricature of Sam Wilson came to personify the United States. His grave is in Troy's Oakwood Cemetery.

Dockage: Downtown Troy has a marina with several hundred feet of modern floating docks. Overnight transient docking and two-hour complimentary docking are both available here, and its convenient location makes this marina a fine supply stop. Be sure to call ahead if you are planning to have your mast unstepped here. This is the last place to have your mast unstepped if you intend on moving farther north through the locks. This is the last place to have your mast unstepped if you intend on moving farther north through the locks.

Troy Lock (Lock 1)

Lock 1, also referred to as the Federal Lock or the Troy Lock, is 153 miles from The Battery in New York City. The lock has a 16-foot lift and opens on request. This lock is the first of a long series that can take you to Buffalo on Lake Erie, Oswego on Lake Ontario or Whitehall on Lake Champlain.

Leaving Troy Lock, you next enter the quiet, non-tidal waters of the Lower Champlain Canal. Anchoring room is on the western shore between Green Island and Van Schaick Island. A full-service marina is located on the west shore just south of Bridge "C1." On the east shore, north of the marina but south of the bridge, is a floating dock behind a Price Chopper supermarket—a great place to provision for the trip north or west.

General Lock Procedures: Locks vary in many different ways. Some have short lifts or drops, while some lift a boat as much as 40 feet. The condition of the locks may also vary. Some have concrete walls, some have sheet metal walls, while some are made of other materials and can be very rough. There are a number of different options for tying up, whether it be via a tube or ones thrown to you by the locktender. You will definitely want to have proper fendering equipment aboard to protect your boat, While in the minority, some locks are very rough and can do severe damage to your boat.

Cruising Options

From here, the cruising yachtsman has several choices:

- Continue north up the Champlain Canal and cruise Lake Champlain.
- Head west on the Erie Canal to Buffalo and cruise Lake Erie.
- Head west on the Erie Canal and Oswego Canal to Oswego and cruise Lake Ontario.
- Follow option three, but instead of returning to Troy via the same route, cross Lake Ontario and return to Troy via the St. Lawrence and Richelieu rivers, Lake Champlain and the Champlain Canal—the route often referred to as the "Triangle Loop."
- For detailed information on these routes, reference Waterway Guide's Great Lakes edition. Our next chapter returns the cruiser to New York City and the East River, which connects the city's harbor to the major cruising grounds of Long Island Sound. ■

Waterway Guide is always open to your observations from the helm. E-mail your comments on any navigation information in the guide to: editor@waterwayguide.com.

Waterway Guide advertising sponsors play a vital role in bringing you the most trusted and well-respected cruising guide in the country. Without our advertising sponsors, we simply couldn't produce the top-notch publication now resting in your hands. Next time you stop in for a peaceful night's rest, let them know where you found them—Waterway Guide, The Cruising Authority.

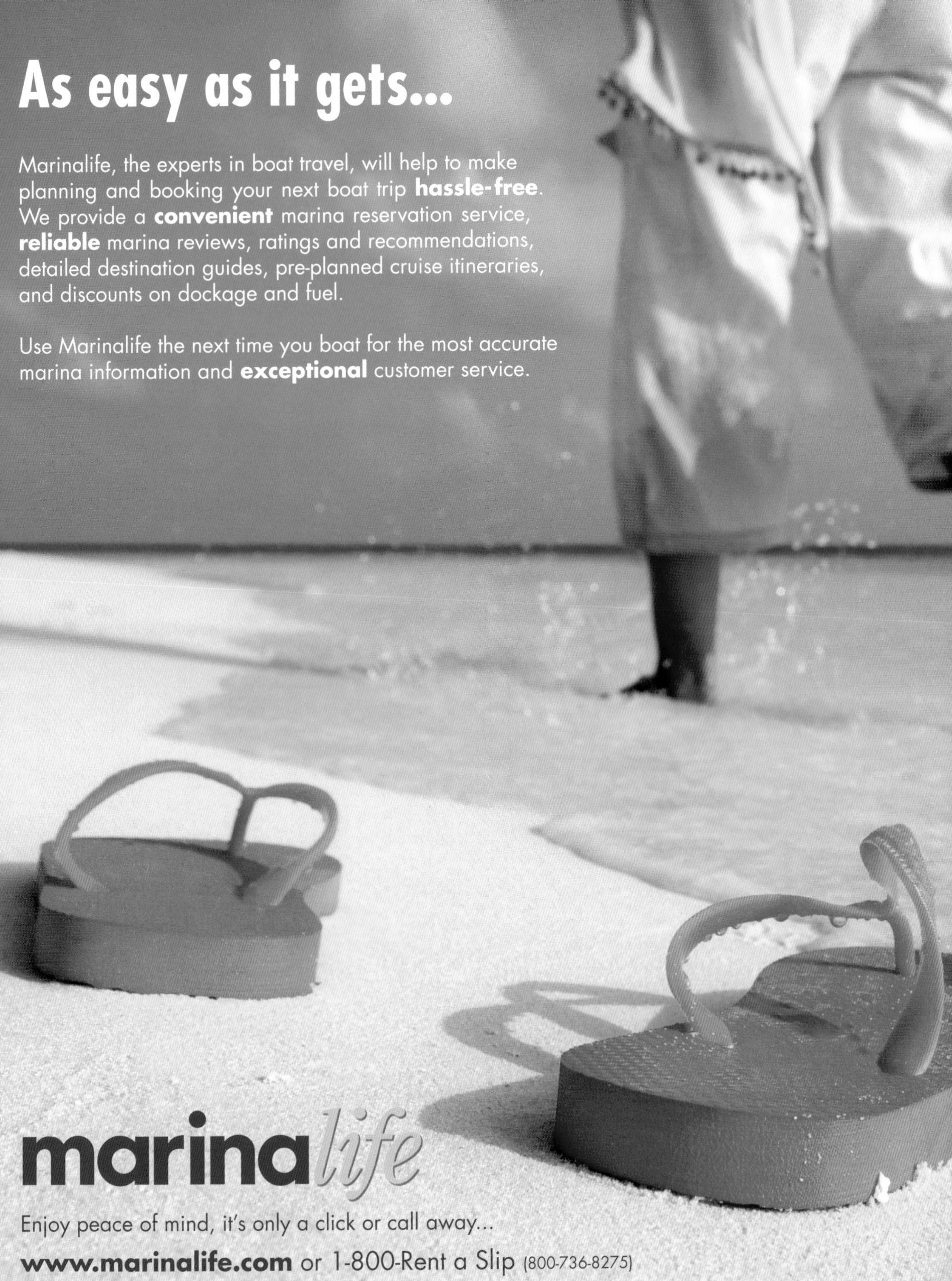

As easy as it gets...
Marinalife, the experts in boat travel, will help to make planning and booking your next boat trip hassle-free. We provide a convenient marina reservation service, reliable marina reviews, ratings and recommendations, detailed destination guides, pre-planned cruise itineraries, and discounts on dockage and fuel.
Use Marinalife the next time you boat for the most accurate marina information and exceptional customer service.
marinalife
Enjoy peace of mind, it's only a click or call away...
www.marinalife.com or 1-800-Rent a Slip (800-736-8275)

East River to Long Island Sound

CHARTS 12334, 12335, 12338, 12339, 12342, 12363, 12364-SC, 12366

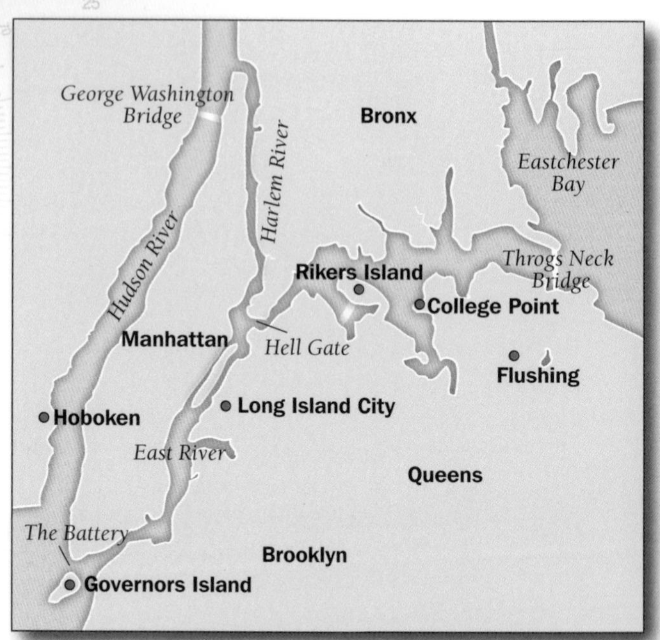

The 14-nautical-mile-long East River separates the boroughs of Manhattan and the Bronx from Brooklyn and Queens. It passes under eight high-level bridges, which are set against the spectacular backdrop of the Manhattan skyline. Running from The Battery to Long Island Sound, local lore holds that the East River is one of only two rivers in the world with two mouths and no source. (The other is the Harlem River, at the north end of Manhattan, also described in this chapter.)

NAVIGATION: Use Charts 12327, 12339, 12342 and 12366. This passage is suited to large ships; it is deep, well-marked and easy to follow. Recreational boats can follow the main channel or, in a couple cases, take shortcuts without danger. The key is to time the current correctly, which means consulting tide and tidal current charts, either on paper or in electronic form, because opposing current will seriously hinder your progress. In the vicinity of Hell Gate, the current can be dangerous for smaller boats. With velocities of more than 4 knots in this section, the current ebbs west and floods east (exactly opposite to the pattern on Long Island Sound). For instructions on how to time a passage through the challenging waters in the East River, turn to the explainer headlined "Transiting the East River" found in this section.

In its lower reaches, the cruise up the East River is dominated by big commercial ships heading to and from the docks on the Brooklyn shore. These ships maneuver awkwardly, hook up with tugs and are troubled by the strong current; you must stay out of their way.

The Staten Island and Governors Island ferries can be particularly troublesome because they cross the river frequently and at high speeds. Cross their wakes just after one or both have crossed the channel. Do not cut close to a docked ferry. If its powerful propellers are not throwing a monstrous wash into the channel, the ferry might be about to leave its slip and enter the channel with remarkable speed. In either case, you do not want to be nearby. There are also many small high-speed ferries and the well-known Circle Line tourist boats to negotiate. The safest course of action is to be aware of all traffic; these commercial vessels are working on a schedule.

The towers of Lower Manhattan rise to the west, and Wall Street runs right down to the water below Pier 15. A luxury condo-marina is perched at Battery Park City. North Cove Yacht Harbor was previously used by the Coast Guard and EMS following 9/11, but is now available to boaters. The magnificent Brooklyn Bridge, built in 1883 (127-foot fixed vertical clearance, or 110 feet if the construction platforms are suspended underneath), and the Promenade on the Brooklyn side complete the scene.

Security in the East River: There are significant security regulations in effect on the river that are continually updated and changed by the Department of Homeland Security and the U.S. Coast Guard. As of 2006, boaters were once again allowed west of Roosevelt Island, but skippers should always be alert to security changes and check online at http://homeport.uscg.mil before transiting the East River. While transiting the East River and other waters of New York City, note that the marine division of the New York Police Department monitors VHF Channel 16 and is available for assistance in an emergency. Study the Homeland Security portion of the Skipper's Handbook section found in the front of this Guide for more information.

Dockage: For years there has been talk of marina development at Fulton Landing, at the base of the Brooklyn Bridge, or on the Manhattan side of the East River. Dockage of any kind is only for the very adventurous. Large boats have secured a pier head here and there, but crumbling bulkheads, submerged pilings and fierce current discourage most boaters from touching shore in Lower Manhattan.

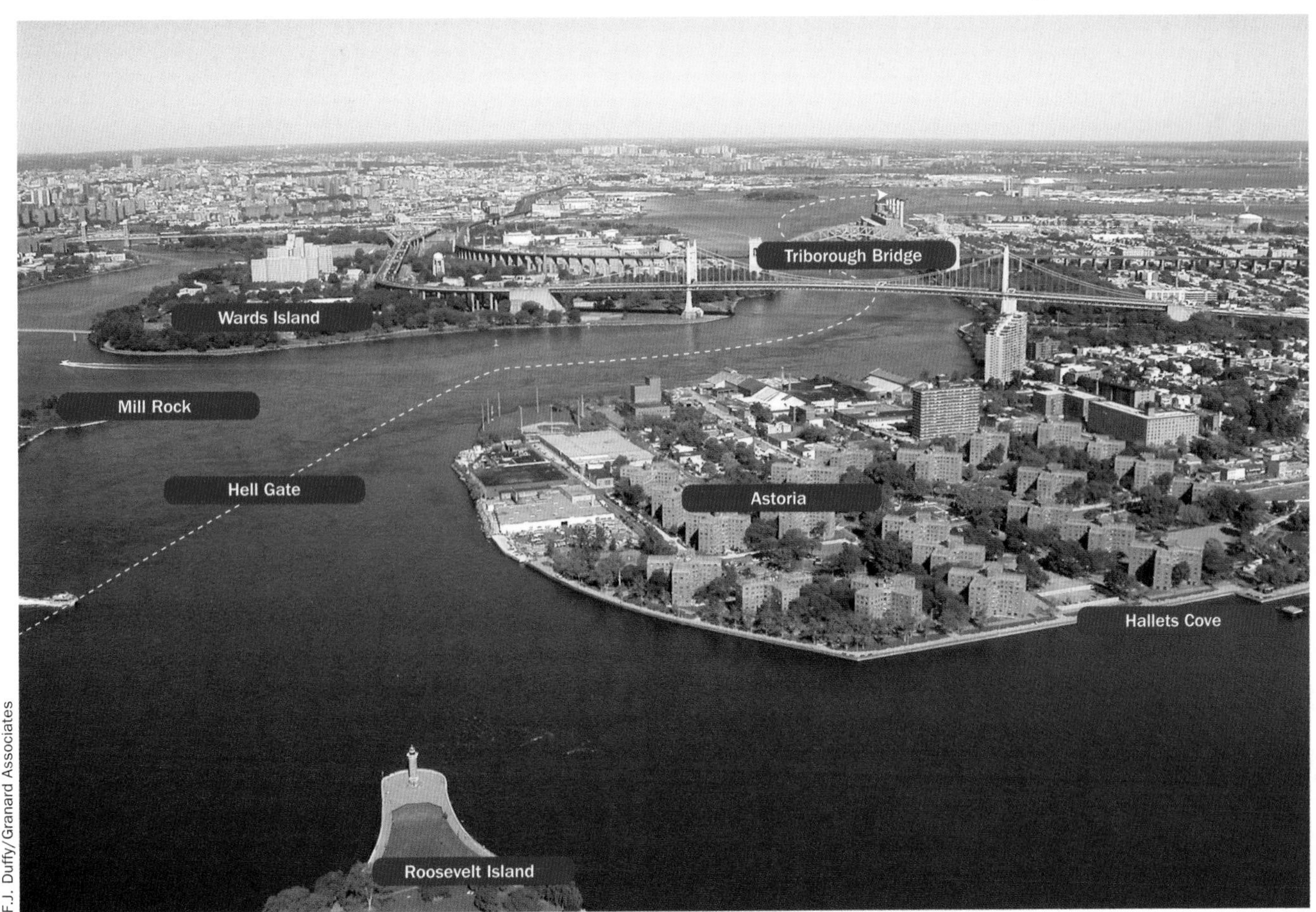

Looking northeast up the East River toward Hell Gate. (Not to be used for navigation.)

GOIN' ASHORE: **SOUTH STREET SEAPORT MUSEUM**

At Piers 16 and 17, on the lower east side of Manhattan, historic sailing ships lie at the same docks as ships have for over a century. Throughout the 18th and 19th centuries, the South Street Seaport district was New York City's center of commerce, culture and financial power. Known as the "Street of Ships," clipper ships docked along the East River to load and unload cargoes from all corners of the world. All of that changed when steamships arrived on the scene, with their deeper drafts requiring use of the Hudson River instead. The South Street Seaport Museum's 11-block complex includes a fleet of 19th-century clipper ships, four galleries, a working re-creation of a 19th-century print shop, a boatbuilding shop, a maritime craft center, museum shops, a library and numerous shops and restaurants. Two exhibits worth noting are: "Monarchs of the Sea," showcasing the impressive Der Scutt collection of ocean liner models and memorabilia, recently purchased by the museum, and "Harbor Voices and Images 9.11.01," which details the largely untold story of the maritime response to the events of Sept. 11, 2001, including the safe evacuation—by water—of more than a million people from Lower Manhattan. New exhibits include retrospectives on the history of the Fulton Fish Market, which has moved to a location in the Bronx, and family history cruises on the schooner Pioneer. With more than 100 shops and restaurants, the Seaport is open daily, Monday through Friday 10 a.m. to 9 p.m. and Saturday and Sunday 11 a.m. to 8 p.m. Check the South Street Web site for updated information on exhibits and performances on the piers.

ADDITIONAL RESOURCES:

- South Street Seaport, 212-748-8600, **www.southstseaport.org**

NEARBY GOLF COURSES:Lawrence Village Golf, Causeway and Rock Halls Roads, Lawrence, NY 11559, 516-239-1685

NEARBY MEDICAL FACILITIES: Beth Israel Medical Center, First Avenue and 16th Street, New York, NY 10003, 212-420-2000

Roosevelt Island

NAVIGATION: Use Charts 12327, 12339, 12342 and 12366. Roosevelt Island splits the East River at the United Nations, about five miles above The Battery. Boats can take either channel east or west of the island, except during security alerts when recreational vessels must keep to the east of Roosevelt Island.

The western channel is larger, with more spectacular views and fewer shoaling edges. A lift bridge (40-foot closed vertical clearance, 99-foot open vertical clearance) crosses the eastern channel. If you require a bridge opening, contact the tender on VHF Channel 13 or call (646-776-9551) at least 15 minutes prior to your requested opening. If you have to travel the eastern channel for security reasons, stay closer to the shore of Roosevelt Island; shoals extend from the Long Island side of the channel. The Queensboro Bridge (131-foot vertical clearance) crosses the East River about halfway up the length of Roosevelt Island, roughly opposite New York Hospital and Cornell Medical Center. The tramway passes overhead, marking Bloomingdale's to the west.

Dockage: Opposite Brooklyn's Newtown Creek (really more of an alley than a creek) is a small but popular marina that offers dockage and access to midtown Manhattan.

Harlem River

Although recreational boats do not heavily travel it, the Harlem River flows between the East River and the Hudson River eight miles away at the north end of Manhattan. (See Chart 12342 for Harlem River coverage.) Pay close attention to currents; the south-running (flood) current in the Harlem River coincides with the east-running current in Hell Gate.

Bridges: Fifteen bridges cross the Harlem River. A vessel needing less than 24 feet of vertical clearance will only require one bridge to be opened—the Spuyten Duyvil Railroad Swing Bridge (5-foot closed vertical clearance) where the Harlem River meets the Hudson River. The bridge tender can be hailed on VHF Channel 13. Current around this bridge's abutments can be very strong. In a favorable current, do not approach the bridge until it is open or you can be swept sideways into the abutments. Vessels needing more than 24 feet of vertical clearance must call the New York City Department of Transportation at 212-371-7836. Calls must be made at least four hours before passage, the bridges will only be opened after 10 a.m., and you must clear the last bridge by 5 p.m. A Department of Transportation crew will travel from bridge to bridge, opening them in succession.

The Metro-North Railroad Bridge (about three-quarters of a nautical mile from Randalls Island) is controlled by yet another entity (Conrail). Call the chief dispatcher's office (212-340-2050) to request an opening.

At Wards Island, you go under a graceful, arching, green pedestrian lift bridge (55-foot closed vertical clearance), one of the highest and longest footbridges anywhere. This end of the Harlem River is commercial, with junkyards, railroad switching yards and sprawling housing projects.

As you approach the Hudson River, the scenery improves. A series of small boathouses appear. These are the headquarters of rowing and sculling clubs founded more than a century ago when wealthy New Yorkers maintained country homes here. Columbia University's athletic field and crew house come up to port, followed by residential Inwood Park and Riverdale.

HELL GATE, NY, TO LONG ISLAND SOUND, NY

NAVIGATION: Use Charts 12339 and 12366. Use New York (The Battery) tide tables. For high tide, add 2 hours 58 minutes; for low tide, add 3 hours 45 minutes. Stay south and east of Mill Rock, and round Hallets Point with its 33-foot-high green flashing light. This is Hell Gate proper, and the flow of water will indeed be spectacular if you arrive at maximum current. These eddies and standing waves are not dangerous, except perhaps to small, open boats, but they deserve respect and a firm hand on the helm, as even large boats can be shoved around.

The only real danger is meeting a large commercial vessel or tug with barge and getting in the way. Avoid this by using VHF Channel 13 and keeping your eyes open ahead and astern.

Do not worry if your depth sounder jumps erratically; the bottom ranges from 34 feet to 107 feet to 59 feet in a few hundred yards, making whirlpools on the surface. Pass under the high-level Triborough Bridge (138-foot fixed vertical clearance) and a railroad bridge almost as high (134-foot fixed vertical clearance), and leave Wards and Randalls islands with Sunken Meadows Park, a Revolutionary War battlefield, to port. At Lawrence Point, you have passed safely through Hell Gate.

The main ship channel goes north, outside North Brother Island, but yachts pass easily through the shorter, more direct channel (minimum depth 25 feet) between it and South Brother Island. Just stay clear of off-channel shoals, rocks and ledges, and observe the buoys, keeping green markers to starboard, red to port. Channels leading south from here have their own buoy systems; do not confuse their daybeacons with those on the East River's west-east route to Long Island Sound.

In 1904, North Brother Island was the scene of the worst maritime tragedy in New York history. The excursion steamer *General Slocum* exploded and caught fire with more than 1,200 people aboard. The skipper ran the ship aground on North Brother Island, which served as a quarantine facility at the time. Due to the ferocity of the fire, the currents of the river and the inability of many people to swim, more than 1,000 people died.

Flushing Bay

Use New York (The Battery) tide tables. For high tide, add 17 minutes; for low tide, add 16 minutes. Just east of Rikers Island (the famous prison and an inhospitable place for those without official business), Flushing Bay offers good protection, a deep (14.5 feet) well-marked channel and, for those drawing 5 feet or less, ample anchorage room. Several marinas and two yacht clubs are situated just inside College Point. Prevailing mean low water depths of 4 to 5 feet, however, will discourage vessels with deeper keels.

Flushing Bay, Westchester Creek, NY

FLUSHING BAY, WESTCHESTER CREEK		Largest Vessel Accommodated	VHF Channel Monitored	Transient Berths / Total Berths	Approach / Dockside Depth (reported)	Floating Docks	Gas / Diesel	Groceries, Ice, Marine Supplies, Snacks	Repairs: Hull, Engine, Propeller	Lift (tonnage), Crane, Rail	1=110V, 2=220V, B=Both, Max Amps	Laundry, Pool, Showers	Pump-Out Station	Nearby: Grocery Store, Motel, Restaurant
		Dockage					Supplies		Services					
1. New York Skyports Marina	212-686-4548	130		3/20	15/9	F					1/50			GR
2. Arrow Yacht Club	718-359-9229	33	18		5/4	F			PRIVATE CLUB					GR
3. World's Fair Marina	**718-478-0480**	**200**	**71**	**20/300**	**14/10**	**F**	**GD**	**IMS**	**HEP**	**L50,C**	**B/100**	**S**	**P**	**GMR**
4. Metro Marine	718-823-0300	50		/40	15/5	F		IM		L	1/30	S	P	GR

Corresponding chart(s) not to be used for navigation. Internet Access Wireless Internet Access

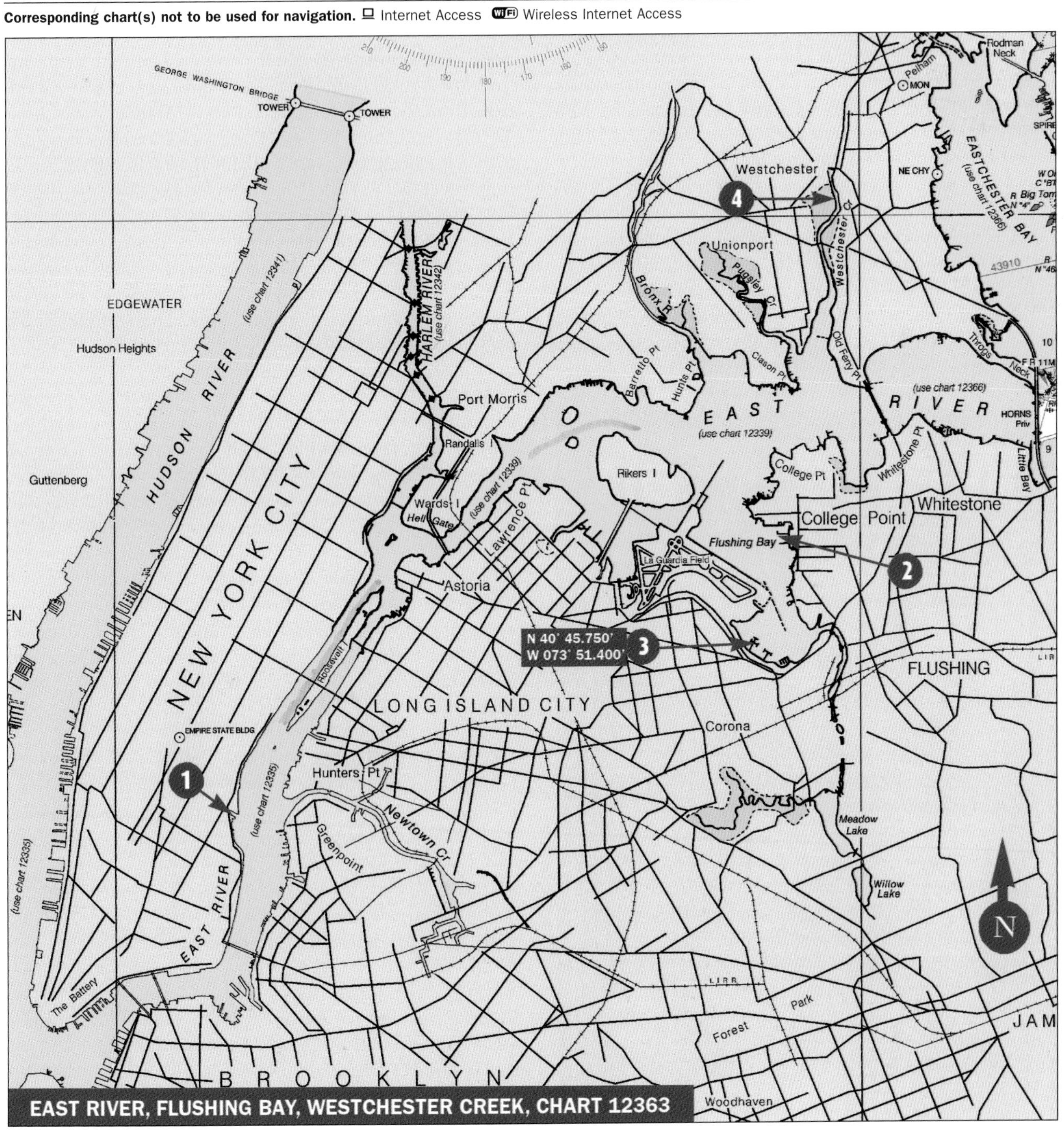

EAST RIVER, FLUSHING BAY, WESTCHESTER CREEK, CHART 12363

Flushing Bay, NY

Dockage: At the south end of the Flushing Bay channel, the World's Fair Marina complex can accommodate boats drawing up to 12 feet either at or just behind its ample fuel dock (immediately to the right at the end of the channel). Boats drawing 4 feet or less will find newer and more accommodating slips at the marina's extensive docks about a half mile farther to the right. There is locked-gate security here, restrooms/showers and a large waterfront restaurant. For reservations and docking instructions, call the marina on VHF Channel 71.

Almost two miles long, Flushing Bay is adjacent to LaGuardia Airport, along its western shoreline. (Note: You must not travel within 100 yards of any shore adjacent to the airport.) On the south are the 1939 New York World's Fair grounds (now a huge park) and Shea Stadium, home of the Mets (about a 15-minute walk). Though Flushing Bay may be short on charm—the New York Sanitation Department operates a refuse barge depot here, for example—it is an excellent base from which to visit the city or to change crews arriving or departing from New York's two major airports. The proximity of LaGuardia Airport on the west side of Flushing Bay will make itself immediately evident to boat-borne visitors, and John F. Kennedy International Airport (also in the borough of Queens) is not far. A subway stop is nearby for an inexpensive and inevitably colorful transit to Manhattan. Closer to hand, the Flushing shopping district is about a $6 cab ride away (the marina will call one for you), where a full range of shopping and restaurant possibilities is available within a few blocks.

When headed south, Flushing Bay is also a good place to wait out the slack tide, just before the southerly flow at Hell Gate, to facilitate an easy passage through the river.

Across the East River from College Point is the mouth of the commercial Bronx River, with Clason Point separating it from the mouth of Westchester Creek. The latter has a dredged and marked channel, with sales and repair available at the mouth and small-craft service upstream. From Old Ferry Point, the high-level Whitestone Bridge (135-foot fixed vertical clearance) crosses overhead. The long sweep of the Throgs Neck Bridge (138-foot fixed vertical clearance), generally accepted as the demarcation line between the East River and Long Island Sound, runs from the peninsula to just above Willets Point. Both Throgs Neck and Willets Point are strategic locations where fortifications were built in the early 19th century to protect New York City from attack. Granite-walled Fort Totten is at Willets Point. Fort Schuyler on Throgs Neck now houses the New York State Maritime Academy. The academy's school ship, a converted Navy transport usually berthed nearby when not underway, is where cadets learn merchant service skills. The shoreline now begins to look less urban, and Long Island Sound begins to appear to the northeast and east.

Anchorage: Close by the Throgs Neck Bridge are two overnight anchorages that afford protection from all but north and northeast winds. Both are convenient for those boats emerging from the East River too late in the day to get farther into Long Island Sound, and for boats that need to be in an early morning.position to catch the tidal current down the East River. The first is Little Neck Bay on the southeast side of the bridge. The second is along the northeast shore of Throgs Neck itself—between the neck and the bridge. (Sailboats should find at least 50 to 55 feet of vertical clearance under the sixth arch out from shore.) The charted depths of both areas are quite accurate.

Cruising Options

Long Island Sound awaits exploration. One of the most popular cruising grounds on the East Coast, the Sound has much to offer both sail and powerboaters. ■

WATERWAY GUIDE is always open to your observations from the helm. E-mail your comments on any navigation information in the guide to: editor@waterwayguide.com.

WATERWAY GUIDE advertising sponsors play a vital role in bringing you the most trusted and well-respected cruising guide in the country. Without our advertising sponsors, we simply couldn't produce the top-notch publication now resting in your hands. Next time you stop in for a peaceful night's rest, let them know where you found them—WATERWAY GUIDE, The Cruising Authority.

TRANSITING THE EAST RIVER

NAVIGATION: Use Charts 12327, 12334, 12335, 12339, 12342 and 12366. The passage through the East River is suited for large vessels: it is deep, well marked and easy to follow. Recreational boats can follow the main channel or, in two cases, take a shortcut if desired. One short cut is between North and South Brother islands near Rikers Island and the other, for vessels that are able to maneuver in the swift current and wish to transit under the 36th Avenue Lift Bridge (40 feet of vertical clearance in the down position), is through the east side of Roosevelt Island. Some care must be given to avoid following navigational aids that mark some of the small rivers that empty into the East River instead of the East River markers themselves.

The key to transiting the East River, either eastward or westward, is to time the currents correctly by consulting tide and tidal current charts, either on paper or electronically. Opposing currents in the river can reach over 5 knots and will seriously hinder your progress if the transit is not timed. Wind-driven chop, heavy traffic and inconsistent depths can further exacerbate these contrary currents. No wonder the name for the mid-point of the East River morphed over the centuries to become Hell Gate.

Proper timing for moving eastward or westward is based on getting through Hell Gate, which is about mid-point of the 14-mile-long East River between the Battery on the southwestern tip of Manhattan and the Throgs Neck Bridge on the eastern end of the river at the entrance into Long Island Sound. The East River current is the exact opposite of Long Island Sound current: East River current ebbs west and floods east, while Long Island Sound current ebbs east and floods west. The divide between these two systems is near the Throgs Neck Bridge.

A recreational boat heading upriver, eastward toward Long Island Sound can catch a good ride with the current if the boat arrives at The Battery at the tip of Manhattan two hours after low water there. This should result in the boat catching the flood up the East River and once into Long Island Sound catching the ebb eastward.

The object of the westward passage through the East River is to arrive at Hell Gate no less than two hours but up to three hours after high water at The Battery. The westward-bound recreational boat heading down the East River toward The Battery should try to pass under the Throgs Neck Bridge at or slightly before high tide at the bridge. By arriving at the Throgs Neck Bridge at this time, mariners can time their passage under the bridge to hit the current as it begins to ebb westward.

Smaller (and slower) vessels may wish to arrive at the Battery an hour after low tide when traveling eastward and up to an hour before high tide at the Throgs Neck Bridge when traveling westward. The relatively modest adverse current at the eastern end of the East River at that time should result in a slower but more subdued ride through Hell Gate.

This information needed to transit the East River is often incorporated in electronic charting software as tide and tidal current tables. Traditionally, mariners have relied on the Eldridge Tide and Pilot Book, which we have referred to for the hypothetical passage below. Using the September 19, 2008 tide tables and tidal current charts:

The ebb starts at The Race at 2:50 p.m. A mariner traveling westward on Long Island Sound wishing to transit the East River to The Battery will want to make sure that they are catching the flood from The Race (in Long Island Sound) and get to the Throgs Neck Bridge before 2:50 p.m.

High water at Kings Point (just east of the Throgs Neck Bridge) is 2:22 p.m. (Eldridge page 108).

Southwest ebb begins at Hell Gate at 1:27 p.m. (Eldridge Page 114).

High water at The Battery is 11:27 a.m. (Eldridge Page 126).

Current turns, becoming favorable for westbound travel at Hell Gate at 1:27 p.m. (Tidal Current Chart, Eldridge Page 129).

Conclusion: Using the example, the mariner will want to arrive at the Throgs Neck Bridge by 1:27 p.m. (at the earliest) when the ebb starts at Hell Gate. How the mariner times a passage after 1:27 p.m. should depend on boat speed through the water and how much help from the current the mariner wishes to have.

As you can see, westward travel requires more planning than eastward travel because the currents differ along the length of the river. The current on the lower portion of the East River, as it passes by Roosevelt Island, is generally stronger than at the upper end of the East River.

For example, four hours after high water at The Battery, the current at Rikers Island (east of Hell Gate) averages about 1.6 knots, while current on the favored western channel by Roosevelt Island (west of Hell Gate) averages about 5.2 knots. That's why it is so important to reach Hell Gate about three hours after high water at The Battery. By doing so, you can carry a fair current all the way to Sandy Hook if you wish to continue beyond the New York area.

By carefully planning one's passage through Hell Gate, the trip through the spectacular East River past the United Nations building, South Street Seaport and under the Queensboro, Williamsburg, Manhattan and Brooklyn bridges will most certainly be enjoyable. Lore has it the "Hell Gate" is a corruption of the Dutch "Hellegat," meaning "bright passage."

South Shore—Western End

CHARTS 12326, 12352

The windswept South Shore of Long Island stretches 115 miles from Coney Island to Montauk Point. The area is known for having thousands of boats, tens of thousands of people and great fishing. One can spend hours or days exploring the bays and coves of the South Shore, but only in a small shallow-draft boat. Fishing, clamming and oystering can take up idle hours at anchor. Hundreds of marinas and restaurants line the inside route and, if you have a shallow-draft vessel, you can take advantage of their amenities.

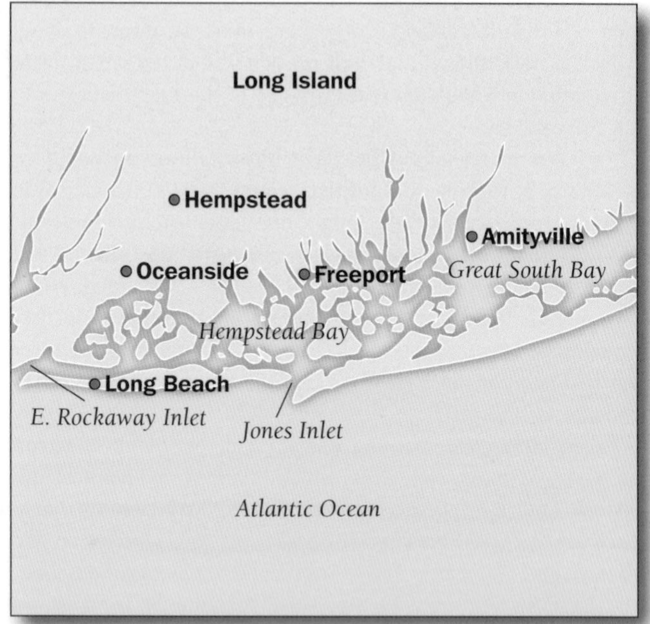

A long set of barrier islands runs between most of the island's mainland and the Atlantic Ocean. Inside the barrier islands are shallow bays, islands, marshes and canals connecting numerous waterside communities. Dredged channels run from bay to bay, making a protected route similar to an inland waterway passage.

Scores of bedroom communities line the shore; many were created artificially by depositing dredge spoil on thousands of acres of wetlands. Farther east, the scenery becomes more rural, but summer resorts dot both main-

Looking northeast over East Rockaway Inlet. (Not to be used for navigation.) WATERWAY GUIDE PHOTOGRAPHY

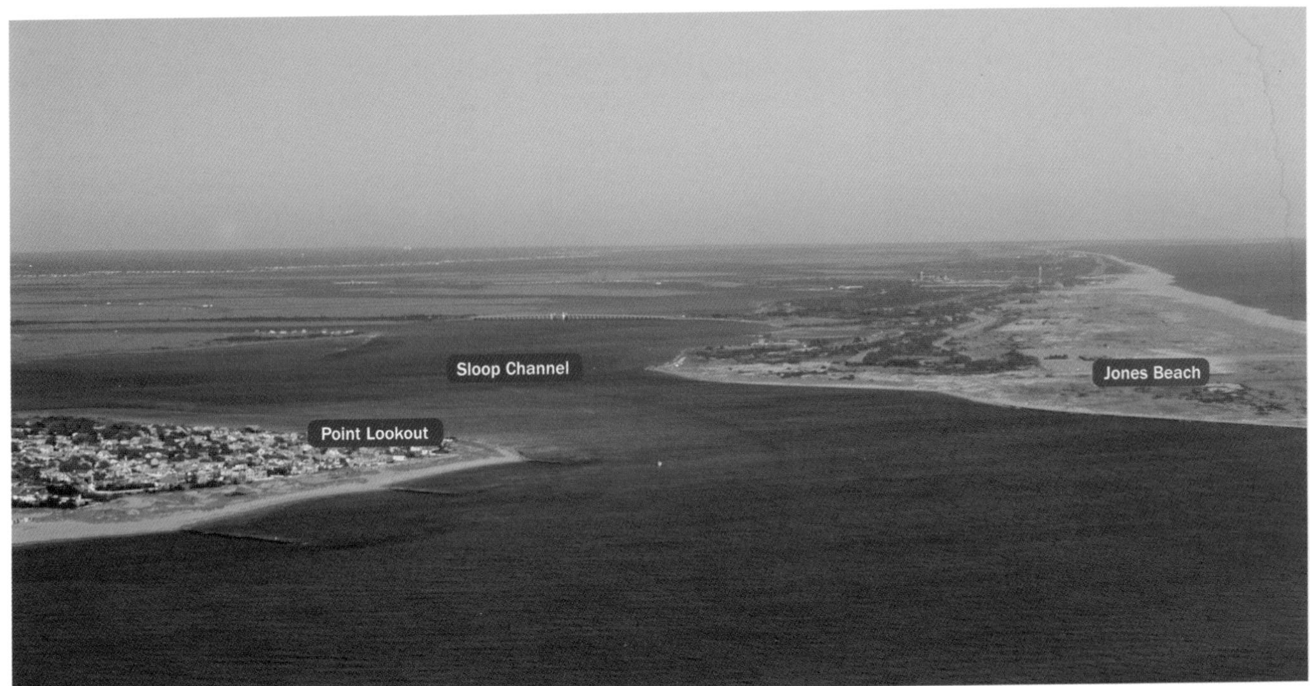

Looking northeast over Jones Inlet. (Not to be used for navigation.) WATERWAY GUIDE PHOTOGRAPHY

land and barrier beaches. The all-season metropolitan area creeps farther and farther east every year. Buses or trains to New York are readily available from almost any South Shore community. The South Shore of Long Island, like the shores of Long Island Sound, was settled in the early to mid-1600s. Colonial houses still stand, overlooking acres of newer developments.

Along the inside waters and along the ocean are broad strands of beach with fine white sand. Those beaches closest to New York are dense with swimmers and sunbathers in the summer months, while the more remote stretches are all but deserted. Eight state parks, some with beaches and most with boat basins, offer at least daytime use.

THE OUTSIDE RUN

If you are in a hurry, you can run this coast offshore. It is a pleasant trip in good weather if you have the skill and the proper boat. In bad weather, however, the outside passage is unpleasant and potentially hazardous. Thirty-foot depths are only a mile from shore except around Fire Island Inlet. Unfortunately, of the six inlets along the South Shore, only one, East Rockaway Inlet, is reliable for safe passage. Most are shoal-prone, continually shifting, and should be avoided except in cases of desperation. It is wise to call ahead for local knowledge, even in good weather.

Rockaway Inlet

The first inlet, five miles northeast of Sandy Hook, is Rockaway Inlet. It enters into Jamaica Bay but does not connect with the inside waterways. Jamaica Bay is basically a dead-end with no other inlets aside from the Rockaway Inlet used to enter it.

East Rockaway Inlet

NAVIGATION: Use Charts 12350 and 12352. Use Sandy Hook tide tables. For high tide, subtract 7 minutes; for low tide, subtract 14 minutes. Next, and preferable because it is wide and easy to navigate, is East Rockaway Inlet (known locally as Debs Inlet), which is 10 miles from Coney Island and 13 miles from Sandy Hook. The U.S. Army Corps of Engineers tries to maintain 12-foot depths here, but as with all inlets, use caution and good common sense. In good weather, you will find the inlet easy to enter. A flashing white (every four seconds) 33-foot-high tower marks the inlet's eastern jetty extending from Silver Point, and shoaling to 3- to 4-foot depths builds out from the jetty toward the west. If approaching from the east or south, give the jetty a wide berth on all sides. Keep East Rockaway Inlet in mind if the weather begins to deteriorate. Once inside, you can cruise comfortably while seas build outside. If conditions improve, you can head back out at the next opportunity—Jones Inlet. East Rockaway Inlet is the first inlet where you can enter if you choose to cruise the New York portion of the Intracoastal Waterway (ICW).

Jones Inlet

NAVIGATION: Use Chart 12352. Use Sandy Hook tide tables. For high tide, subtract 20 minutes; for low tide, subtract 25 minutes. Almost nine miles farther east, Jones Inlet is dredged periodically when bottom conditions warrant it. It is well-marked, but the buoys are uncharted and frequently must be moved. The inlet has been holding at 9 feet, but the current chart calls for cautious navigation. The western bar should be avoided. A VHF radio request for local knowledge is always a prudent move to avoid shoal areas that might have developed since the last buoy relocation.

East Rockaway Channel, Barnums Channel, NY

EAST ROCKAWAY CHANNEL, BARNUMS CHANNEL		Largest Vessel Accommodated	VHF Channel Monitored	Transient Berths / Total Berths	Approach / Dockside Depth (reported)	Floating Docks	Gas / Diesel	Groceries, Ice, Marine Supplies, Snacks	Repairs: Hull, Engine, Propeller	Lift (tonnage), Crane, Rail	1=110V, 2=220V, B=Both, Max Amps	Laundry, Pool, Showers	Pump-Out Station	Nearby: Grocery Store, Motel, Restaurant
		Dockage					Supplies		Services					
1. Davison's Metro Power Center	516-593-8100	60		/40	6/6	F		M	HEP	L75	B/50			GMR
2. Crow's Nest Marina	516-766-2020	50		6/120	15/12	F		IS	HEP	L40	1/30	S	P	GMR
3. Saltaire Marina	516-593-3321	25		/125	10/10	F								GMR
4. All Island Marine	516-764-3300	50	68	5/225	8/6	F	GD	GIMS	HEP	L35	1/30			R
5. Empire Point Marina	516-889-1067	50	09	4/110	15/8	F	G	IMS	HEP	L55	B/50		P	GMR

Corresponding chart(s) not to be used for navigation. Internet Access Wireless Internet Access

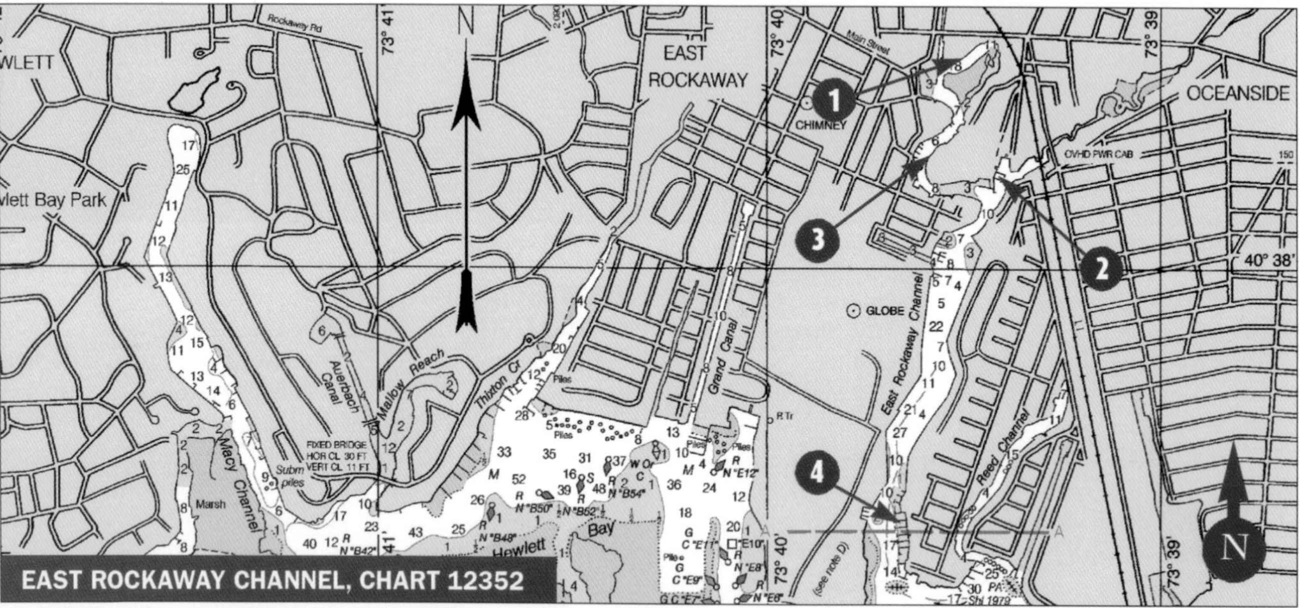

EAST ROCKAWAY CHANNEL, CHART 12352

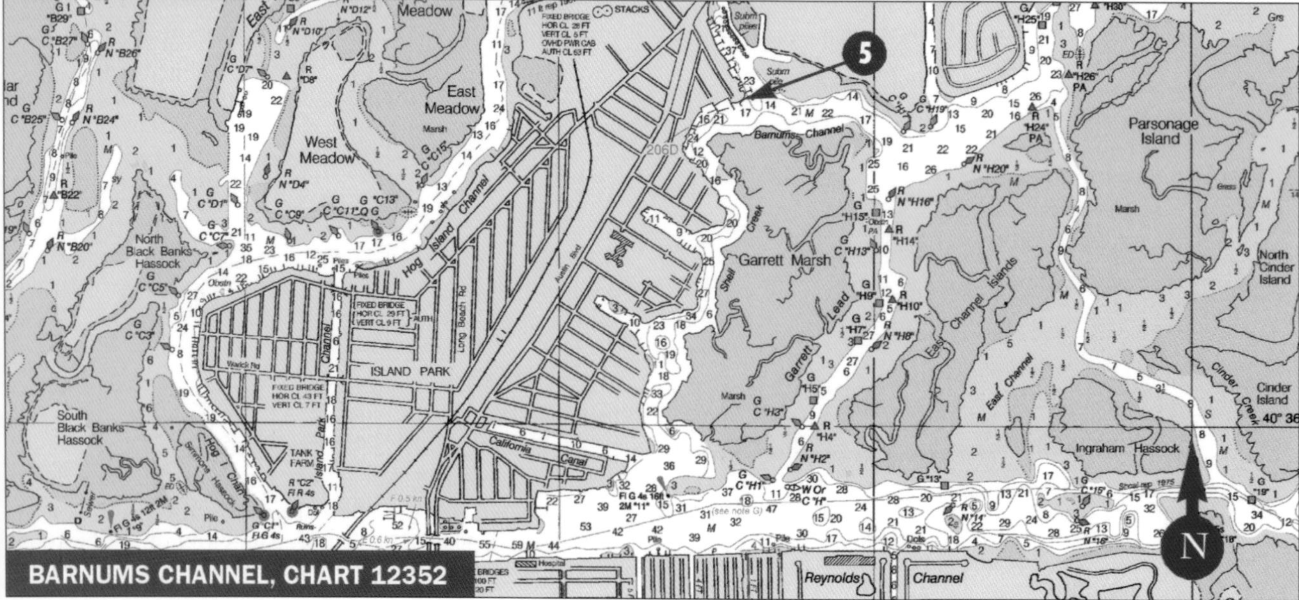

BARNUMS CHANNEL, CHART 12352

Fire Island Inlet

NAVIGATION: Use Chart 12352. Fire Island is about 13 miles beyond Jones Inlet. Its buoy system is excellent, but not charted because of the continuously shifting shoals. The Corps of Engineers does acknowledge that conditions remain unstable. The entrance is difficult without local knowledge, even in good weather, and is unsafe to enter when wind and tide oppose. In heavy weather, breakers bar the entrance. Do not attempt entry in poor visibility.

Once inside the inlet, depths improve along the southern edge of the channel. Upon entering, watch for quick flashing red buoy "10" and a series of green navigational aids, which will guide you toward the Robert Moses Bridge (65-foot fixed vertical clearance). The local Coast Guard (Station Fire Island) will give information to those unfamiliar with the area. In fair weather, you can use Fire Island Inlet to get to the open waters of Great South Bay while avoiding the tediously slow and crowded channel inside from Jones Inlet.

Moriches Inlet

NAVIGATION: Use Chart 12352. For Moriches Inlet, use Sandy Hook tide tables. For high tide, subtract 57 minutes; for low tide, subtract 1 hour 9 minutes. The last two inlets, both comparatively new, were broken through by storms in the 1930s. Moriches Inlet, 28 miles past Fire Island Inlet, is not buoyed, is subject to rapid shoaling and should not be attempted by strangers. Though usually closed to navigation, Moriches Inlet was "reopened" by severe wave action and erosion when a December 1992 storm swept up the East Coast with 90-mph winds. Although the current chart shows decent depths through the inlet, shoaling is continuous. Check with Coast Guard Station Moriches Inlet for current conditions. Inside the inlet, the channel with the best depths is found to the east along the shore of the barrier island.

Shinnecock Inlet

NAVIGATION: Use Chart 12352. Use Sandy Hook tide tables. For high tide, subtract 39 minutes; for low tide, subtract 1 hour 4 minutes. Shinnecock Inlet, 14 miles east beyond Moriches, had held the same 10-foot depths and channel position since 1968, but recent dredging has deepened the channel to 27 feet. If you are forced in for shelter, however, go carefully and slightly favor the west side of the channel. Enter the inlet between the flashing green tower ("1A") on the west jetty and the flashing red tower ("2A") on the east jetty. Shinnecock Light will appear to port as you enter, flashing red every 15 seconds. Many small fishing boats use the inlet, so be on the lookout during your approach.

THE INLAND WATERWAY

The inside route from East Rockaway Inlet runs about 75 miles through four big bays to Shinnecock Canal, where you can cross through to Great Peconic Bay and the north fork of Long Island.

The well-marked main channels of the inside route cut through marshes and across bars; pay close attention to the daybeacons. Call ahead for local knowledge on conditions and depths if you want to follow the privately maintained bush stake daybeacons into side channels.

Project depth for dredged channels is 5 feet, but the battle against shoaling is constant. At the western end, depths tend to be more stable, but shoal spots increase as the route progresses east. Boats with more than a 3-foot draft must check unfamiliar waters carefully before entering.

Bridges, many of which have restricted openings and limited hours of operation, often cross the channels. The controlling vertical clearance is 14 feet, but alternate channels can be used to avoid the low fixed bridges. Suffolk County maintains do-it-yourself gin poles for unstepping masts prior to transiting the Shinnecock Canal (covered in the next chapter, "South Shore—Eastern End"), which is crossed by several low fixed bridges.

Reynolds Channel

NAVIGATION: Use Chart 12352. This is the west-east route inside from East Rockaway Inlet for the eight miles to Jones Inlet. It is well-buoyed, with 7-foot minimum depths, but shoals border the channel at its eastern end. Currents run strong near all five bridges that cross the route and at the western end of the channel near Jones Inlet.

For the first three miles, the quarter-mile-wide Reynolds Channel is all that separates the Long Island mainland—with its major towns of Far Rockaway and Lawrence—from the barrier beach with Atlantic Beach and Long Beach. At Long Beach, the channel doglegs northeast into Hempstead Bay, a wide area dotted with massive islands and marshes. Strung along the barrier strip are the seaside resorts of Long Beach, Lido Beach and Point Lookout.

Dockage: On Reynolds Channel itself are private docks and waterfront cottages and, except for a few full-service marinas off-channel on the mainland, most of the boat facilities are fuel and fishing stations until you reach the state marina, offering free berths, near Jones Inlet.

Anchorage: It is inadvisable to anchor along Reynolds Channel due to the crowded conditions and the off-channel shallow water throughout this stretch.

Hog Island Channel

NAVIGATION: Use Chart 12352. The towns of Woodmere, Woodsburgh, East Rockaway and Oceanside are on the mainland side and are reached via several marked passages twisting through the marshes and islands north of Reynolds Channel. For a boat of more than 30 feet, Hog Island Channel is the only entrance. You enter it about four nautical miles east of East Rockaway Inlet by turning between two flashing lights to port. Flashing green buoy "C1" is located off the tip of Simmons Hassock, and flashing red buoy "C2" is on the tip of Island Park, a double island lying between Simmons Hassock on one side and Garrett Marsh on the other. Stay well clear of a series of green cans in Hog Island Channel; the better depths are to starboard.

Dockage: Three-quarters of a mile up Hog Island Channel, East Rockaway Channel branches off to port and on both sides of the latter are extensive full-service marinas offering all repairs. Hotels, restaurants and amenities are within easy reach of the waterfront.

Jones Inlet, Point Lookout & Short Beach, NY

POINT LOOKOUT & SHORT BEACH		Largest Vessel Accommodated	VHF Channel Monitored	Transient Berths / Total Berths	Approach / Dockside Depth (reported)	Floating Docks	Groceries, Ice, Marine Supplies, Snacks	Gas / Diesel	Repairs: Hull, Engine, Propeller	Lift (tonnage), Crane, Rail	1=110V, 2=220V, B=Both, Max Amps	Laundry, Pool, Showers	Pump-Out Station	Nearby: Grocery Store, Motel, Restaurant
		Dockage					Supplies				Services			
1. Hempstead Town Marina East	516-897-4128	70		/190	10/5	F					B/30	S	P	GR
2. Hempstead Town Marina West	516-897-4127	40		3/215	8/6	F					1/30	S		GR

Corresponding chart(s) not to be used for navigation. Internet Access Wireless Internet Access

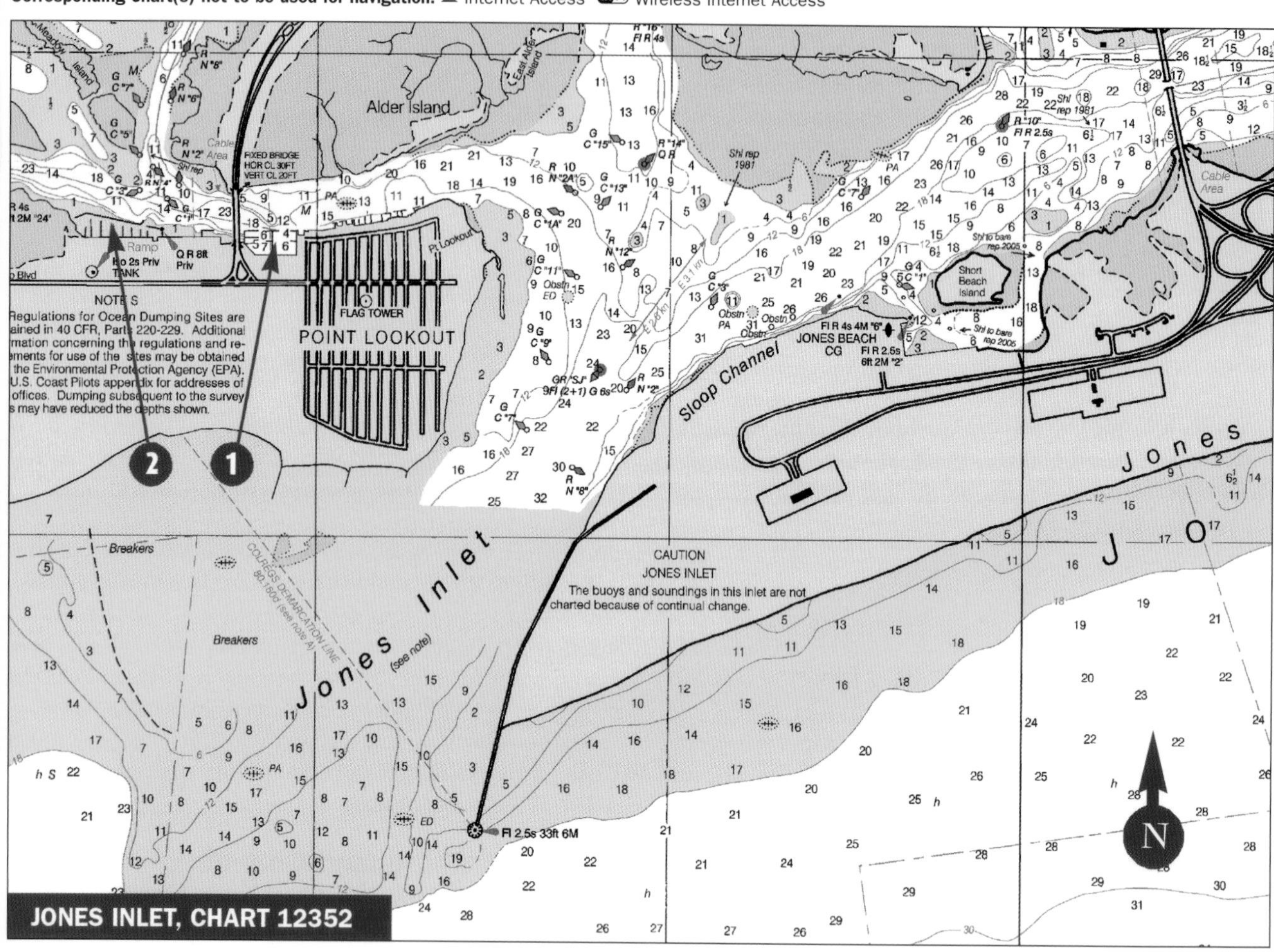

JONES INLET, CHART 12352

To Jones Inlet

NAVIGATION: Use Chart 12352. Just past the junction of Hog Island Channel and Reynolds Channel are three bridges joining Island Park to Long Beach: a railroad bascule bridge (14-foot closed vertical clearance) and twin highway bascules (20-foot closed vertical clearances).

About a third of a mile east of the highway bridges, on the south side of Reynolds Channel, is a dock of the Long Beach Hospital, marked by a square white sign with a red cross. Here boaters can obtain emergency medical attention.

Just west of Jones Inlet, Reynolds Channel goes under a 20-foot fixed vertical clearance bridge between Alder Island and Point Lookout. Enormous town marinas are on both sides of the bridge. The western one, near an oceanfront park where the swimming is good, welcomes transients. Their ability to serve transients is sometimes limited, so plan ahead and reserve a slip (516-897-4127).

The marinas have recently continued upgrading with new sections of floats. The town has purchased a parcel of land adjacent to the East Marina, where they plan to build a nature center. If you can pass under the bridge, you can continue to follow Reynolds Channel, cross Jones Inlet, with its strong currents, and enter Sloop Channel between Short and Jones beaches and the islands and marshes to the north.

If you cannot pass under the bridge, turn north a quarter mile west of it into Sea Dog Creek, which curves around Alder Island. Make a wide swing around green can buoy "3" entering the creek, as shoaling has been reported near

Baldwin & Freeport, NY

BALDWIN & FREEPORT		Largest Vessel Accommodated	VHF Channel Monitored	Transient Berths / Total Berths	Approach / Dockside Depth (reported)	Floating Docks	Gas / Diesel	Groceries, Ice, Marine Supplies, Snacks	Repairs: Hull, Engine, Propeller	Lift (tonnage), Crane, Rail	1=110V, 2=220V, B=Both, Max Amps	Laundry, Pool, Showers	Pump-Out Station	Nearby: Grocery Store, Motel, Restaurant
		Dockage					Supplies		Services					
1. The Mooring	516-766-0080	27		/60	4/4	F		M	HEP		1/30			G
2. Schooner Restaurant	516-378-7575	65		8/8	13/8	F								GR
3. Outboard Service of Al Grovers	516-379-7212	26		/125	20/8	F		M	HEP	L	1/15			GR
4. Fred Chall Marine	516-546-8960	50						M	HEP		1/30			GMR
5. Guy Lombardo Marina	516-378-3417	60	16/68	12/252	7/5	F	GD	I			B/50	S	P	GMR
6. Travelers Marine Engine Co.	516-868-1193	36		/14	4/3	F			HEP	L	B/50			GMR
7. Mako Marine 🖳	516-378-7331	90	10	5/50	10/12	F	GD	GIMS	HEP	L60	B/50	S		GMR
8. Yachtsmen's Cove	516-546-6026	70		15/160	10/6	F	D		HP	L60	B/50			MR
9. Ocean Marine	516-378-0105	70		2/105	12/12	F		GIMS	HEP	L70	1/50	S	P	GMR
10. Al Grover's High & Dry Marina	516-546-8880	40		5/300	6/6	F		M	HEP	L	B/50			GMR

Corresponding chart(s) not to be used for navigation. 🖳 Internet Access (WiFi) Wireless Internet Access

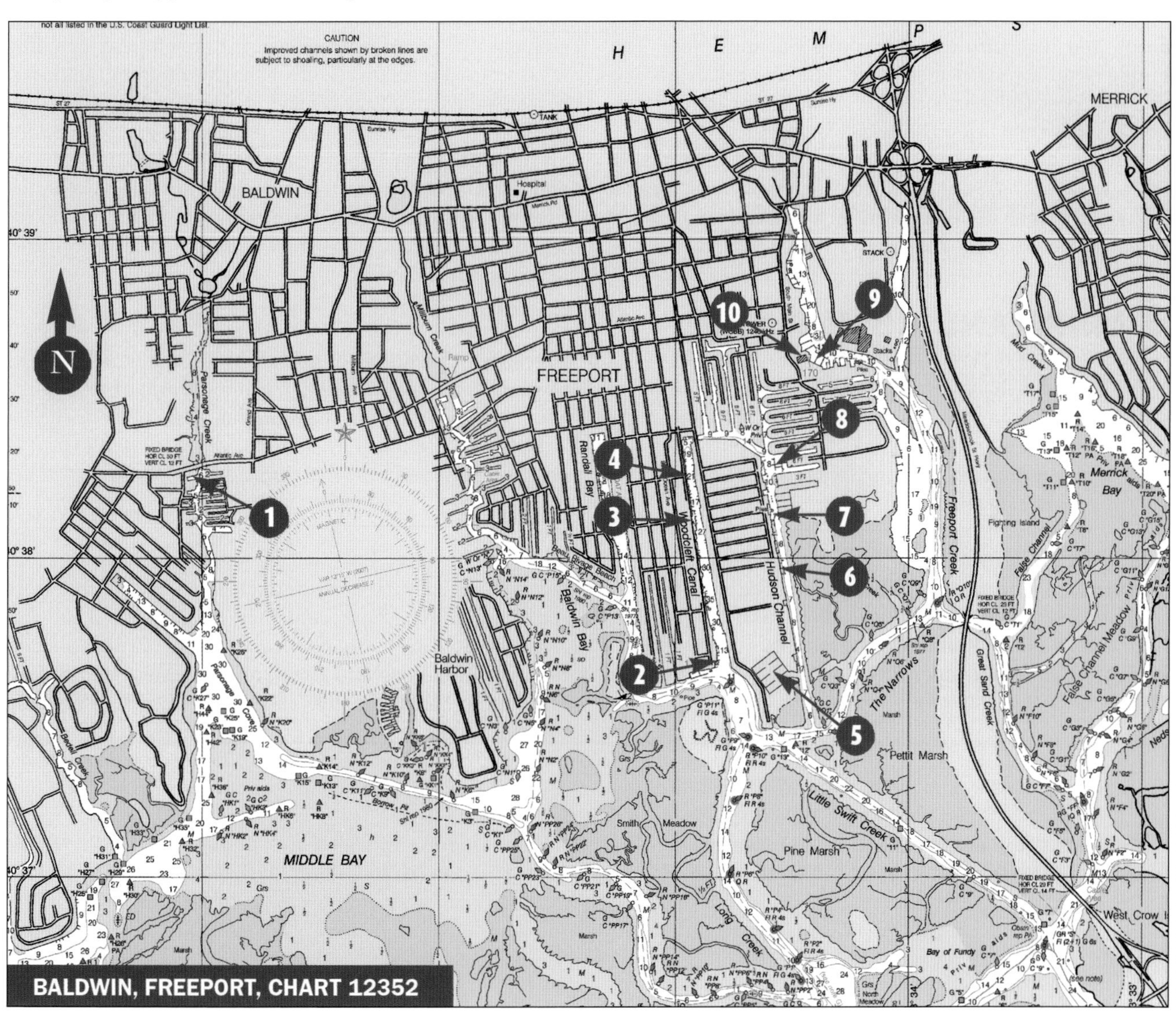

BALDWIN, FREEPORT, CHART 12352

East Bay, S. Oyster Bay, NY

MERRICK TO AMITYVILLE		Largest Vessel Accommodated	VHF Channel Monitored	Transient Berths / Total Berths	Approach / Dockside Depth (reported)	Floating Docks	Gas / Diesel	Groceries, Ice, Marine Supplies, Snacks	Repairs: Hull, Engine, Propeller	Lift (tonnage), Crane, Rail	1=110V, 2=220V, B=Both, Max Amps	Laundry, Pool, Showers	Pump-Out Station	Nearby: Grocery Store, Motel, Restaurant
		Dockage					Supplies		Services					
1. Blue Water Yacht Club	516-623-5757	45	18	5/260	5/5	F	G	IS	HEP	L	B/30	PS	P	R
2. Whaleneck Marina	516-378-8025	40		/150	5/9	F	G	S	HEP	L40	1/50	S		R
3. Ocean Outboard	516-378-6400	50		/26	15/10	F		IM	HEP	L	B/50	S		R
4. Wantagh Park Marina	516-571-7460	45		6/200	6/6	F					1/30	PS	P	GMR
5. Treasure Island Marina	516-221-7156	40		/400	8/6	F		M	HEP	L14	1/30	S	P	R
6. Gus Marine	516-541-1469	30		1/15	20/12	F	G	IM	EP					GMR
7. Delmarine	631-598-2946	50		3/40	4/6			M	HEP	L20	1/30		P	R

Corresponding chart(s) not to be used for navigation. Internet Access Wireless Internet Access

the buoy. In a little more than a mile, turn south on Long Creek, go through the highway bascule bridge connecting Meadow and Alder islands (21-foot closed vertical clearance), and then turn east into Sloop Channel. Note: The bridge is on a restricted schedule. Mooring platforms with flashing lights and telephones to call the tender for information are above and below the bascule bridge.

You can also cross Long Creek and, about a mile farther on, turn south on Swift Creek, but here you must clear a 20-foot fixed vertical clearance bridge to get to Sloop Channel and continue east along the waterway.

MAINLAND COMMUNITIES

North of Jones Inlet, a string of interesting communities stretches east from Baldwin through Freeport, the main yachting center for the area, and then to Amityville and the beginning of Great South Bay. Interlocking secondary channels (some natural, some dredged and most well-marked) twist under bridges, through marshes, sand flats and tiny islands, past man-made canals and fingers of reclaimed land. Depths must be watched carefully, as many channels are shoal or have silted in. But with local information on prevailing depths, one may enjoy several days of leisurely cruising in the maze of canals, sloughs and waterways in this area.

Baldwin

To get to Baldwin Bay and the Baldwin area, follow Sea Dog and Long creeks. Some marinas for transients are located on Milburn Creek at the head of Baldwin Bay. Others are available on Parsonage Cove, but they are generally not set up for transients. You can reach them by leaving Long Creek just north of Sea Dog Creek, and then heading westward on Scow Creek across Middle Bay.

Freeport

A major boating and fishing center with many services and repair yards, Freeport has several waterfronts, all crowded with local and commercial boats. Woodcleft Canal is reported to be 12 feet deep and busy, Hudson Channel is very straight and Freeport Creek is winding.

The mile of waterfront along Woodcleft Canal has the ambience of a seafaring village. All amenities, including local seafood restaurants, are a short walk from the docks. Most establishments will take care of cruising craft when possible. In season, the docks, restaurants and yacht clubs are crowded with fishermen, recreational boaters, diners and sightseers. To learn more about this area, visit the Freeport Historical Society museum at 350 S. Main St., where you will find a fascinating display of Freeport artifacts and information.

Freeport is reached via Long Creek, which has a town marina at the entrance to Hudson Channel, or by Swift Creek, which cuts through Pine and Petit marshes. The town, a short bus or taxi ride from the waterfront, is the shopping center for the surrounding area.

Dockage: Jones Inlet Marina was reportedly not in operation at press time (September 2009).

Merrick

Merrick is a busy little village laced with canals. From Sloop Channel, turn north into Haunts Creek across from Jones Beach State Park, and then head to the northwest along Broad Creek Channel to East Bay. Cruising facilities are located on Mud Creek at the western end of East Bay, and in Merrick Creek, east of Mud Creek. If entering Merrick Creek, note that green can buoy "G23" marks a large shoal area with depths of 3 feet or less. At Nicks Point in East Bay, a large marina and waterside restaurant overlook the harbor.

Anchorage: The wide part of East Bay between Whale Neck Point and White Point, with depths of 10 to 12 feet, is one of the few anchorage opportunities in this area. Try to avoid anchoring in the obvious routes leading to and from the creeks.

Bellmore, Wantagh and Seaford

NAVIGATION: Use Chart 12352. The approach to this area is either west or east of Jones Beach Causeway, which crosses Island Creek on a fixed bridge (12-foot vertical

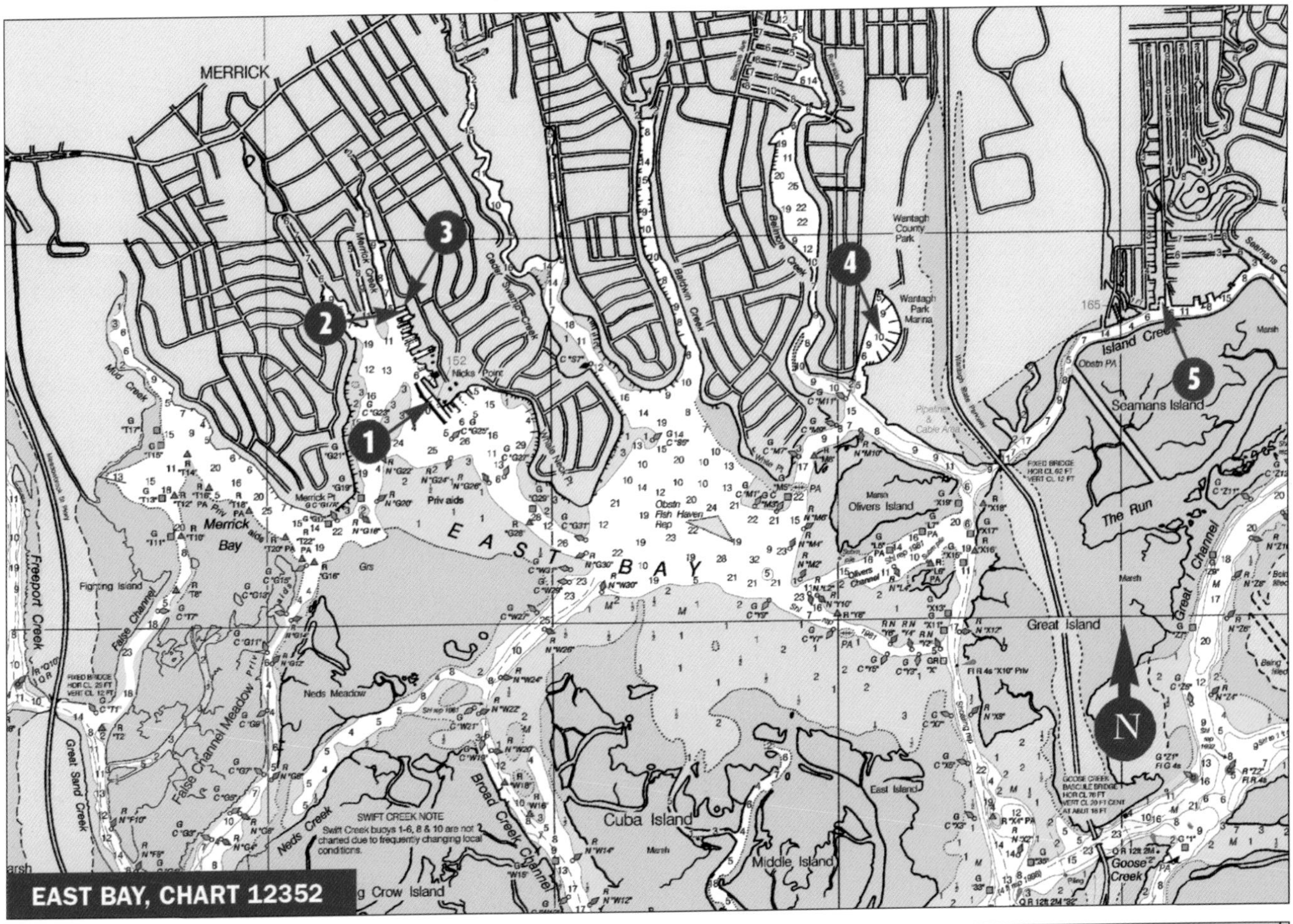
MERRICK
Merrick Creek
Wantagh County Park
Wantagh Park Marina
Island Creek
Seamans Island
Seamans Creek
Nicks Point
Merrick Pt
Merrick Bay
Fighting Island
Freeport Creek
False Channel
False Channel Meadow
Neds Meadow
Neds Creek
Great Sand Creek
EAST BAY
Olivers Island
Olivers Channel
Obstn Fish Haven Rep
Great Island
The Run
Great Channel
Cuba Island
Middle Island
East Island
Broad Creek Channel
Goose Creek
SWIFT CREEK NOTE
Swift Creek buoys 1-6, 8 & 10 are not charted due to frequently changing local conditions.
Crow Island

EAST BAY, CHART 12352

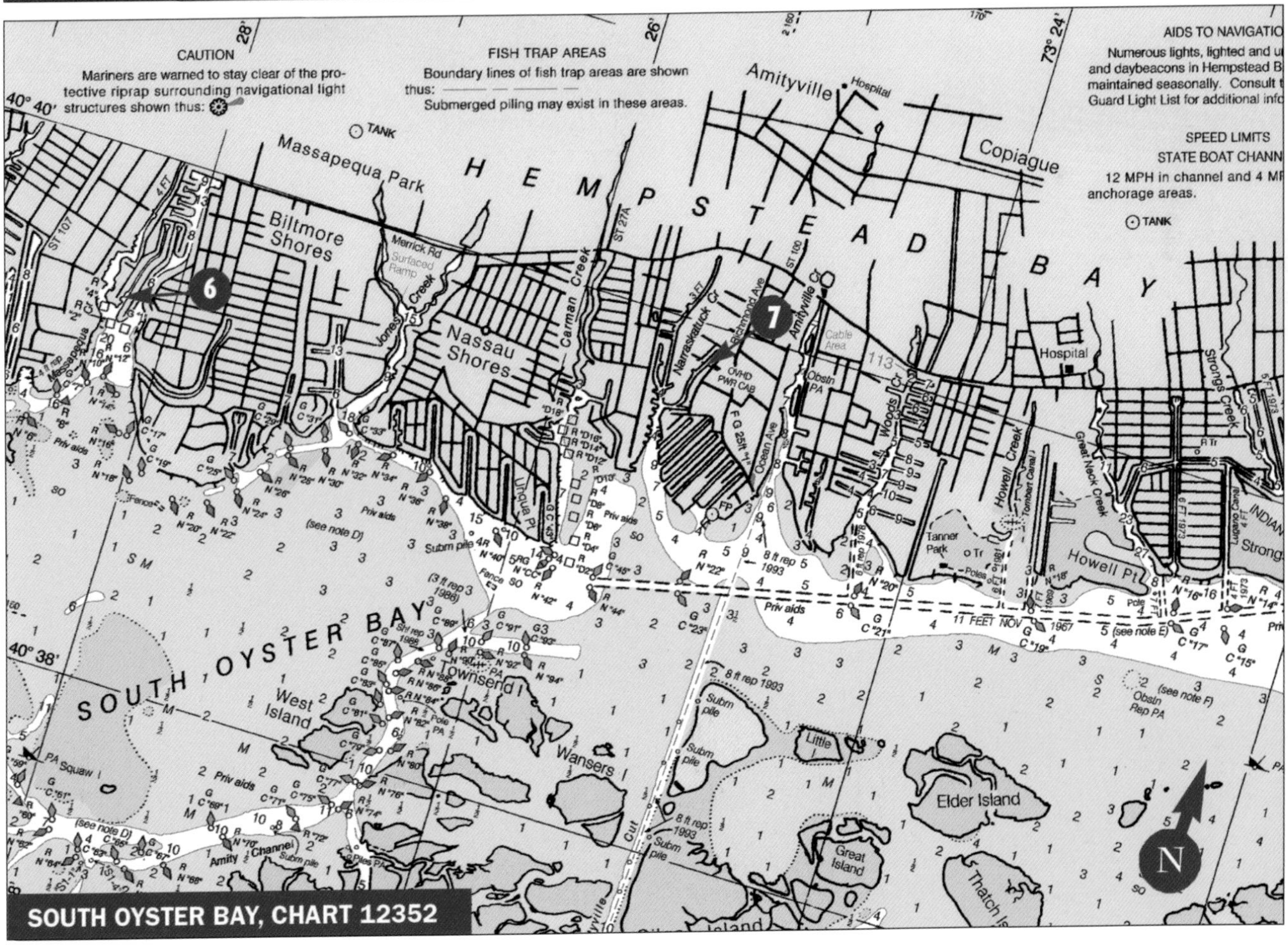
CAUTION
Mariners are warned to stay clear of the protective riprap surrounding navigational light structures shown thus:
FISH TRAP AREAS
Boundary lines of fish trap areas are shown thus:
Submerged piling may exist in these areas.
AIDS TO NAVIGATIO
Numerous lights, lighted and u
and daybeacons in Hempstead B
maintained seasonally. Consult t
Guard Light List for additional info
SPEED LIMITS
STATE BOAT CHANN
12 MPH in channel and 4 MP
anchorage areas.
Amityville
Copiague
Massapequa Park
HEMPSTEAD BAY
Biltmore Shores
Nassau Shores
Jones Creek
Carman Creek
Narrasketuck Cr
Amityville Cr
Woods Cr
Howell Creek
Great Neck Creek
Strongs Creek
Tanner Park
Howell Pt
SOUTH OYSTER BAY
West Island
Townsend I
Wansers I
Little I
Elder Island
Great Island
Thatch Is
Squaw I
Amity Channel
11 FEET NOV 1987

SOUTH OYSTER BAY, CHART 12352

clearance). To the south, the causeway crosses the Goose Creek Bascule Bridge (20-foot closed vertical clearance) from Great to Green Island. Channels of varying depths connect the three towns and each can be approached via marked routes from the inland waterway.

Dockage: In these densely populated communities, facilities tend to be occupied by local boats. Most, however, make every effort to accommodate transients. For cruisers, Seaford is the most important of the three communities. Its marinas, which are liberally sprinkled along Island Creek, Seamans Creek and Seaford Creek, offer many services. Wantagh Park, on Flat Creek near the Wantagh Bridge, has a well-marked entry channel. In addition to the marina, the park includes baseball fields, basketball courts, a swimming pool and tennis courts. You must pay a fee to dock and use the pool and tennis courts. The marina has limited space for transients, so call ahead (516-571-7460).

Massapequa, Biltmore Shores and Nassau Shores can be reached via privately marked and maintained channels from Seaford. These towns offer some services, but few are geared toward cruising boats. The area is crowded with private docks and attractive houses. Scores of canals are interconnected and are variously marked, but do not trust any unless they are charted and you have obtained local knowledge. These communities can also be reached from Amityville.

GOIN' ASHORE:
JONES BEACH, NY

World-famous Jones Beach State Park is comprised of 2,500 acres of the cleanest, finest ocean beaches anywhere, and miles of well-guarded swimming areas can absorb astonishing throngs of people without seeming overcrowded. Beginning at Jones Inlet and extending east along the barrier beach for about five miles, Jones Beach has a broad two-mile-long boardwalk, refreshment stands, restaurants, a huge swimming pool, abundant fishing, attractive anchorages and a well-run state marina. A 200-foot-high red brick tower, visible for 25 miles when floodlighted at night, serves as a striking landmark. From June through August, the Jones Beach Amphitheater (888-706-7600) or www.jonesbeach.com has music events every night. For the tree-hugger in you, there are nature walks available at the Theodore Roosevelt Nature Center.

ADDITIONAL RESOURCES:

- Jones Beach Events, **www.jonesbeachevents.com**

NEARBY GOLF COURSES:
Lido Golf Club, 255 Lido Blvd.,
Lido Beach, NY 11561, 516-889-8181,
www.lidogolf.com

NEARBY MEDICAL FACILITIES:
Lakeside Memorial Hospital, 156 West Ave.,
Brockport, NY 14420, 585-395-6095

Early morning sun on Jones Beach, NY.

Jones Inlet

Fishermen and local mariners regularly use Jones Inlet, but it should not to be attempted by newcomers to the area without local knowledge. Call Coast Guard Station Jones Beach on VHF Channel 16 for advice. The Long Island State Park Commission operates a marina at Short Beach just east of the inlet. The marina is always crowded, especially on weekends. Be careful when you dock; the water is shoal here. Nearby is a bird sanctuary where, in early summer, you can see terns, gulls, skimmers and sandpipers nesting in the marshes.

The Route East

NAVIGATION: Use Chart 12352. Once past the inlet, go through the Meadow-brook State Parkway Bascule Bridge (21-foot closed vertical clearance) and into Sloop Channel. Abeam of the mammoth water tower, the channel veers northeast under the Wantagh State Parkway Bridge (15-foot fixed vertical clearance) and around a marshy area. Boats that need more vertical clearance should swing north around Green Island, through Goose Creek Bascule Bridge (20-foot closed vertical clearance), southeast down Stone Creek, and then back to Sloop Channel. The Long Island State Park Commission operates state park area bridges, and a shortage of tenders makes for uncertain openings. Give advance notice if you need service. When turning back south down Stone Creek, give the northeastern point of Green Island a wide berth; shoals extend from this point. As you turn south, leave green daybeacon "1" to port and follow the channel. Use caution as you proceed; recent reports noted shoals encroaching from both Green and South Line islands.

State Boat Channel

NAVIGATION: Use Chart 12352. Running the length of Jones Beach (and its sister beaches beyond) to Fire Island Inlet is narrow, well-maintained State Boat Channel, with a speed limit of 12 mph. The channel is marked like a street with white-capped black poles; arrows point inward to indicate deeper water. It is usually swarming with fishermen anchored in mid-channel. To the north are marsh-bordered islets with circuitous channels leading through them to mainland communities.

South of the State Boat Channel is Jones Beach, followed by a string of county and town beaches and summer colonies. Tobay Beach has a landlocked anchorage at Tobay Heading. Gilgo Beach presents one of the South Shore's most attractive anchorages at Gilgo Heading. This sheltered bight almost always catches an ocean breeze across the narrow spit of land. Gilgo Beach also has a state park as nice as Jones Beach and rarely as crowded. Next is Cedar Beach, with its own basin, and Oak Beach, then the channel enters Great South Bay, with Captree Island, Fire Island Inlet and Fire Island.

Great South Bay

NAVIGATION: Use Chart 12352. Twenty-five miles long and five miles at its widest point near the western end, Great South Bay is the largest of the South Shore bays. It begins with a narrow channel through the shoals off Amityville on the mainland, and widens out to provide much of the shore's deepest water and prime sailing grounds. Mid-bay depths run from 7 to 10 feet, with some holes even deeper, but with shallower spots as well.

A number of creeks reach up from Great South Bay to Amityville itself, about two miles inland. Along the creeks are marinas and boatyards, most of which are for residents. A town wharf is on the bay, but it dries at low water. The area has several yacht clubs and a town beach for swimming.

This route affords the opportunity to drop anchor and dinghy to shallows where you can jump out and gather clams in abundance. Great South Bay also can be a rewarding for weakfish, drifting strips of squid for some of the tastiest fresh seafood along the coast.

Cruising Options

Keep heading west and you will enjoy the delightful towns and "Hamptons" of eastern Long Island. They have much to offer. ■

Waterway Guide is always open to your observations from the helm. E-mail your comments on any navigation information in the guide to: editor@waterwayguide.com.

Waterway Guide advertising sponsors play a vital role in bringing you the most trusted and well-respected cruising guide in the country. Without our advertising sponsors, we simply couldn't produce the top-notch publication now resting in your hands. Next time you stop in for a peaceful night's rest, let them know where you found them—Waterway Guide, The Cruising Authority.

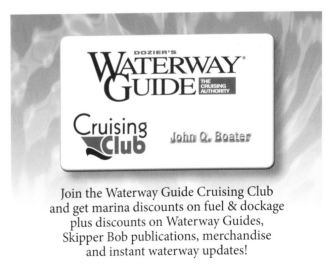

South Shore—Eastern End

CHARTS 12352, 12353

As you travel along the north side of Great South Bay, you may find it difficult to discern where the town of Copiague (pronounced "co-paig") ends and neighboring Lindenhurst begins. They appear to be one continuous community along the 11-foot-deep channel running east of Amityville. Both towns have marinas, boatyards, charter boats and commercial fishing fleets.

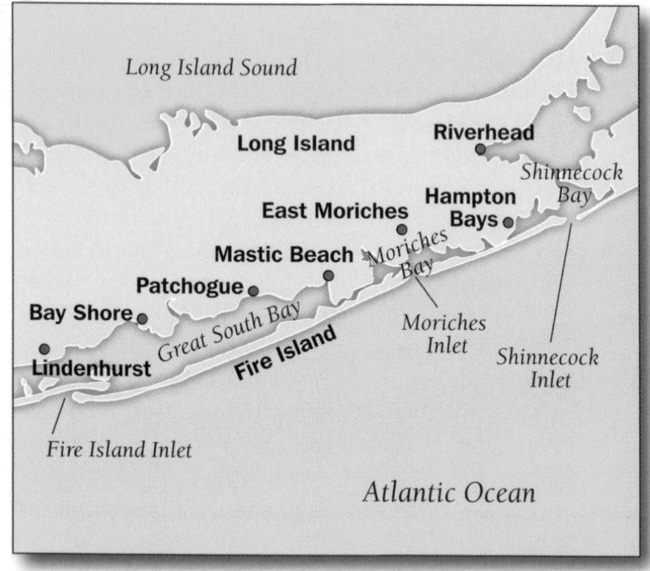

Lindenhurst

Lindenhurst is the fourth largest incorporated village in the state of New York and dates to a treaty signed with American Indians in 1657. Later settled by German immigrants, today it is a pleasant village and home to around 27,000 people. If you have a chance to go ashore here, take a walk around Feller's Pond, a shaded, relaxing spot.

Dockage: There are several full-service marinas in Lindenhurst with many amenities. Marine supplies can be bought in town, not far from the docks. Fox Creek Channel, a two-mile-long, 5-foot-deep, marked passage, joins Lindenhurst to the State Channel farther south.

Babylon

The next mainland town to the east is Babylon, with many marinas along its creeks, including a municipal dock, which is a long walk from the center of town. This pier offers water, electricity and restrooms. Nearby is Belmont Lake State Park, with hiking trails, picnic tables, playing fields, a lake with boat rentals and bridle paths.

NAVIGATION: Use Sandy Hook tide tables. For high tide, add 2 hours 11 minutes; for low tide, add 2 hours 41 minutes. The 6-foot-deep Oak Island Channel connects the waterfront with the State Channel east of Grass and Oak islands. Carefully observe the marked channel as you pass between Grass Island and the small-unnamed island to the east. Across Great South Bay from Babylon and connected by the Robert Moses Causeway (60-foot fixed vertical clearance) is Captree Island, a 300-acre state park devoted almost exclusively to fishing, with a bird sanctuary at the eastern end. Fishing piers, fuel and bait stations, along with charter and head boats for fishing, are located within the park. Channels lead to Captree State Park from east and west of the Robert Moses Causeway, linking it to the mainland. The State Channel cuts just south of it through a set of bascule bridges with 29-foot closed vertical clearances.

Dockage: Frank & Dick's Bait, Tackle, Food & Fuel, under new ownership, is on Seganus Thatch, just west of Captree Island, right on the channel. All South Shore waters are teeming with fish, and both sport and commercial fishing are prevalent here.

Fire Island

NAVIGATION: Use Chart 12352. For Fire Island Lighthouse, use Sandy Hook tide tables. For high tide, add 46 minutes; for low tide, add 1 hour 22 minutes. For Fire Island Inlet, Democrat Point, use Sandy Hook tide tables. For high tide, subtract 39 minutes; for low tide, subtract 27 minutes.

Fire Island Inlet is the only pass between the Atlantic Ocean and Great South Bay, but it should not be attempted without local knowledge. The U.S. Army Corps of Engineers dredges here periodically, but also indicates that conditions will not be dependable until an extensive stabilization program is begun. Periodically, powerful storms have played havoc with the shifting shoals and submerged buoys. Fishing around the inlet is excellent, and fishermen often crowd the approaches in any kind of weather. About two miles in from the mouth, the Robert Moses Bridge (65-foot fixed vertical clearance) crosses the inlet.

Copiague to Babylon, NY

COPIAGUE TO BABYLON		Largest Vessel Accommodated	VHF Channel Monitored	Transient Berths / Total Berths	Approach / Dockside Depth (reported)	Floating Docks	Gas / Diesel	Groceries, Ice, Marine Supplies, Snacks	Repairs: Hull, Engine, Propeller	Lift (tonnage), Crane, Rail	1=110V, 2=220V, B=Both, Max Amps	Laundry, Pool, Showers	Pump-Out Station	Nearby: Grocery Store, Motel, Restaurant
		Dockage					Supplies		Services					
1. Amity Harbor Marine	631-842-1280	45		2/76	7/7	F	G	MS	HEP	L	1/30	S		GR
2. Hidden Harbor Marina	631-842-0277	40			10/5				HEP	L10	1/30			GMR
3. La Sala Boat Yard	631-842-3222	45	16/09	2/58	10/5			M	HP	L25,C	B/50	LS	P	GMR
4. Surfside 3 Marina	631-957-5900	60	69	20/400	10/5	F	GD	GIM	HP	L	B/100	PS	P	R
5. Karl Tank Shipyard	631-957-5050	48		/15	10/8			GIMS	HEP	LI5	1/30			GMR
6. Anchorage Yacht Club Condominium (WiFi)	631-226-2760	60	16	/520	4/4	F	G	GIS	HEP	L40	B/30	PS	P	GMR
7. Islander Boat Center	631-669-3990	40		/100	6/6			M	HEP	L35,C	1/15			R
8. Long Island Yacht Club (Internet)	631-669-3270	52	72	/80	5/4						1/50	PS		GMR
9. Outboard Barn (Internet)	631-669-6060	30		12/20	12/15			M	HEP	L30	B/30	S		R
10. Suffolk Marine Center	631-669-0907	55		/41	7/5			M	HEP	L35	1/30			GR

Corresponding chart(s) not to be used for navigation. Internet Access WiFi Wireless Internet Access

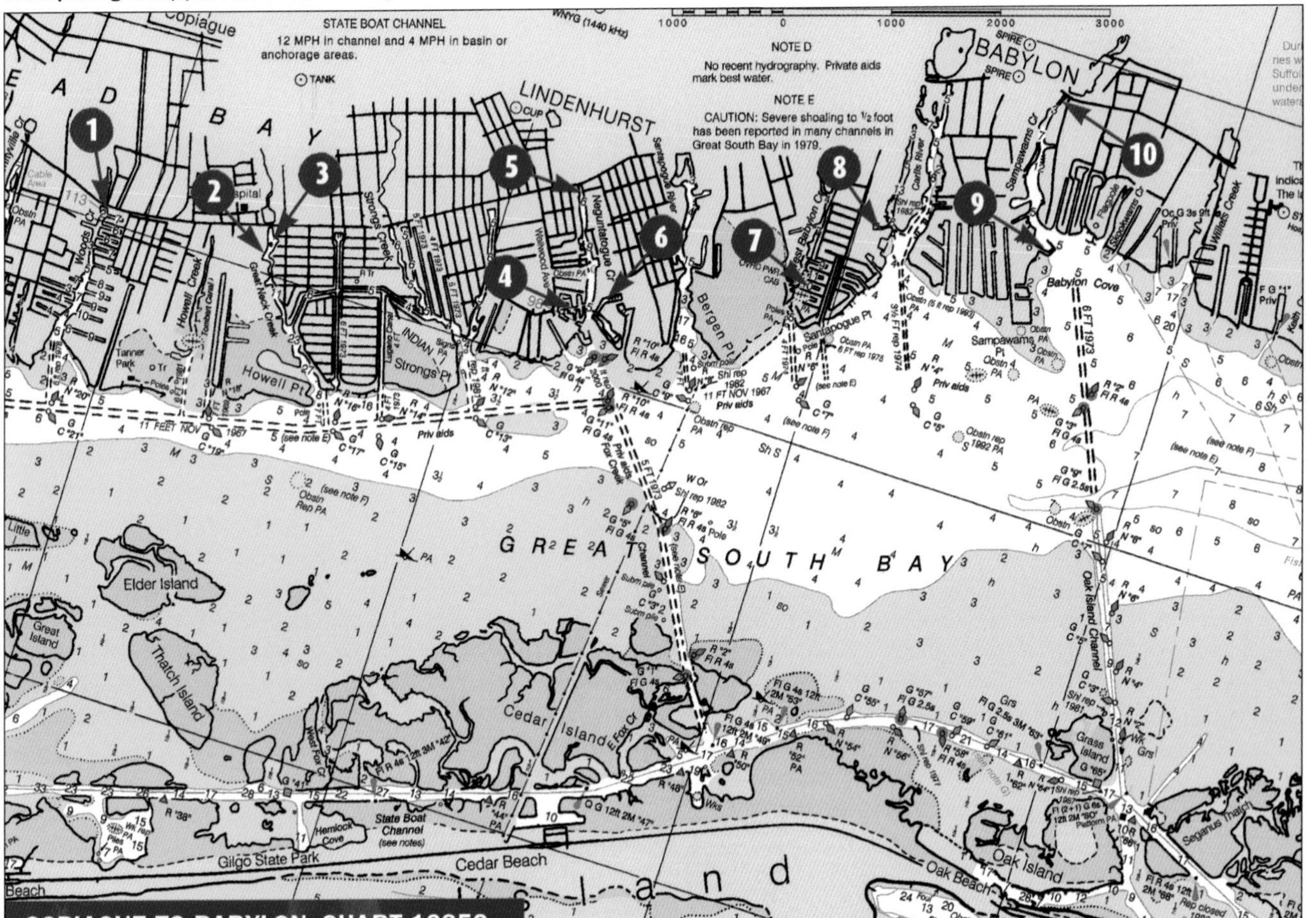

COPIAGUE TO BABYLON, CHART 12352

Dockage: The western end of Fire Island is given over to Robert Moses State Park, with day-use-only slips for boats up to 45 feet, carrying up to 6-foot drafts. East of the old Fire Island Light are the seaside towns of Saltaire, Fair Harbor, Ocean Beach, Point o' Woods, Sailors Haven, Cherry Grove, Davis Park and Watch Hill. Saltaire and Point o' Woods each have a yacht club. Sailors Haven and Watch Hill have National Seashore marinas that limit your stay to seven days. Amenities include picnic areas, nature trails and a visitor's center with exhibits. Davis Park has a town marina for residents only.

Anchorage: There are numerous spots to anchor in 10- to 23-foot depths between Fire Island and Captree Island, either east or west of the Robert Moses Causeway. Pay attention to your chart and stay clear of the main channel. Watch especially for the shoal area (marked with

Oak Island to Fire Island, NY

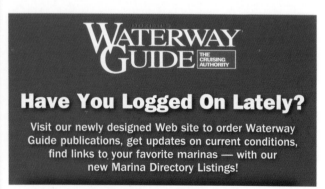

OAK ISLAND TO FIRE ISLAND		Largest Vessel Accommodated	VHF Channel Monitored	Transient Berths / Total Berths	Approach / Dockside Depth (reported)	Floating Docks	Gas / Diesel	Groceries, Ice, Marine Supplies, Snacks	Repairs: Hull, Engine, Propeller	Lift (tonnage), Crane, Rail	1=110V, 2=220V, B=Both, Max Amps	Laundry, Pool, Showers	Pump-Out Station	Nearby: Grocery Store, Motel, Restaurant
		Dockage					**Supplies**		**Services**					
1. Frank & Dick's Bait, Tackle, Food & Fuel	631-587-8442		71		8/8		GD	GIMS						GMR
2. Captree State Park Marina	631-669-0449	75			6/6		GD	IS						R
3. Robert Moses State Park Boat Basin	631-669-0470	43		/39	5/5							S	P	R
4. Sea View Marina	631-583-9380	58		30/53	7/7			GIM			B/50	S		R
5. Flynn's Marina & Restaurant	631-583-5000	50		36/50	9/9			GIMS			1/50			GMR
6. Sailor's Haven Marina	631-597-6171	65	09	46/46	8/8			IMS			1/50	S	P	MR
7. Fire Island Pines Marina 💻	631-597-9581	65	09	30/55	4/6			GI			B/50			MR
8. Davis Park Marina	631-597-6830	50		256/256	8/6			GIS			1/30	S	P	R
9. Watch Hill National Seashore Marina	631-597-3109	50	09	180/200	6/4			GIS			1/30	S	P	R

Corresponding chart(s) not to be used for navigation. 💻 Internet Access (WiFi) Wireless Internet Access

An eastern view into Fire Island inlet. (Not to be used for navigation.) WATERWAY GUIDE PHOTOGRAPHY

flashing red buoy "18") east of the bridge near the Fire Island shore. Note also the cable area east of the bridge; no anchoring is permitted here.

GOIN' ASHORE: **FIRE ISLAND, NY**

Much local lore surrounds the name of the island. It might have gotten its name from a tax clerk's error in copying the original name of "Five Islands." Another theory is that the name came from the fires built on the beaches to warn ships of shoals. Islanders might also have built fires here to lure the unwary onto the shoals to be looted. The name "Fire Island" might also have derived from the fires built by whalers to render blubber into oil.

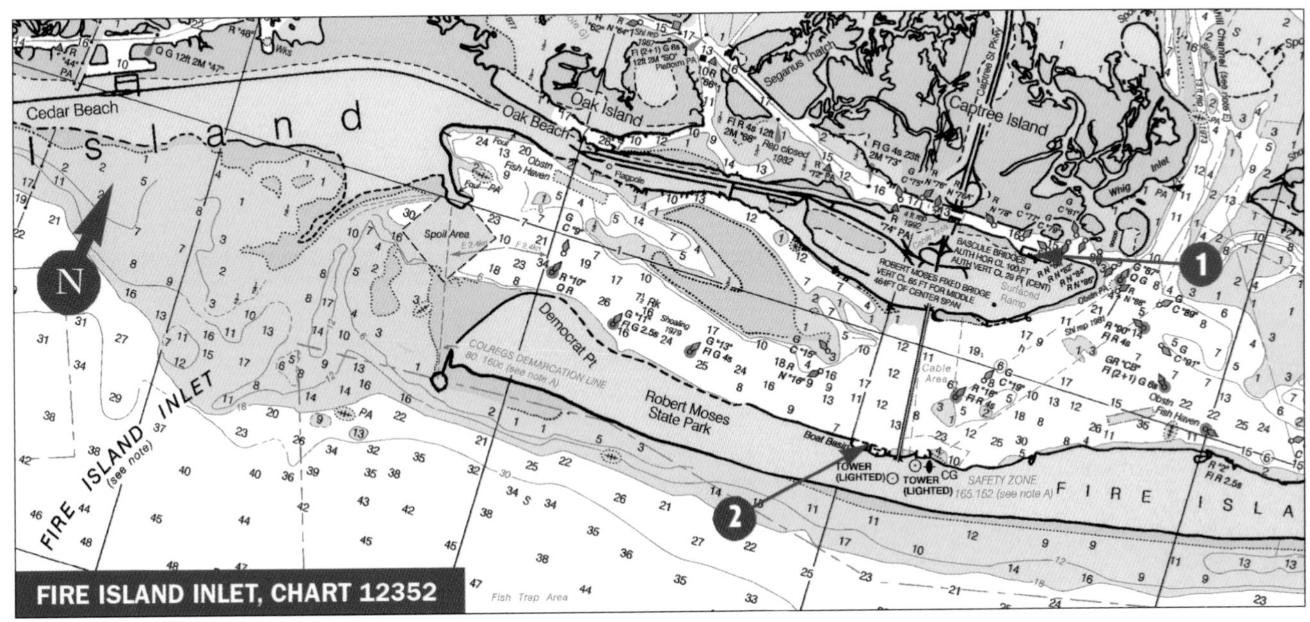

FIRE ISLAND INLET, CHART 12352

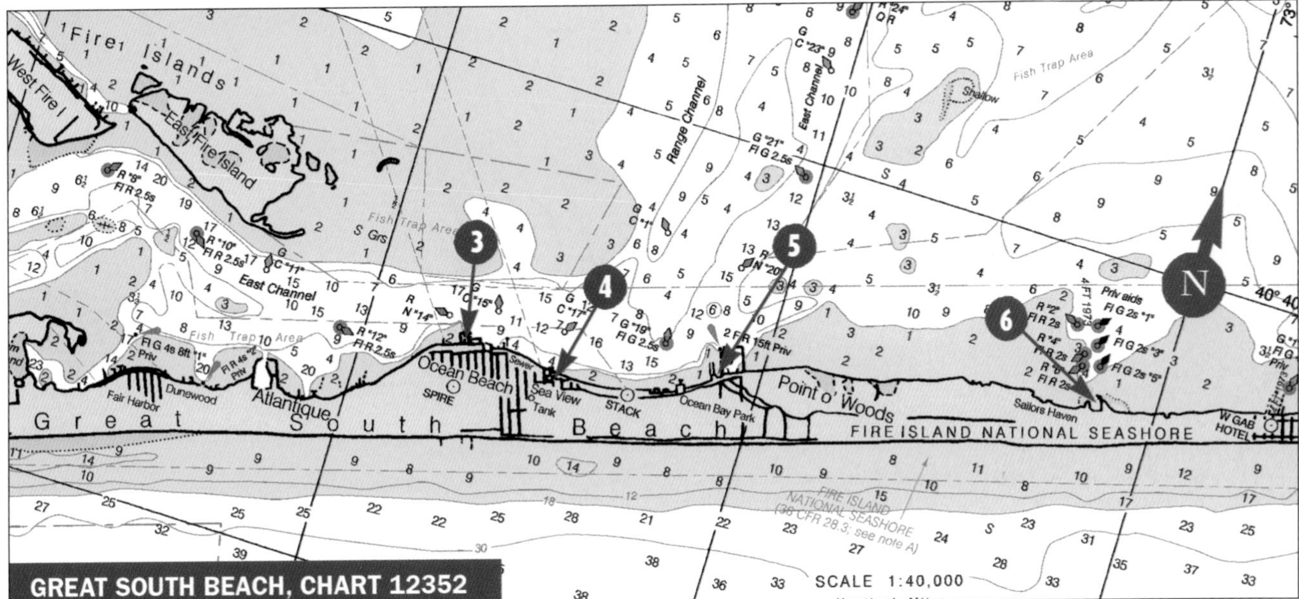

GREAT SOUTH BEACH, CHART 12352

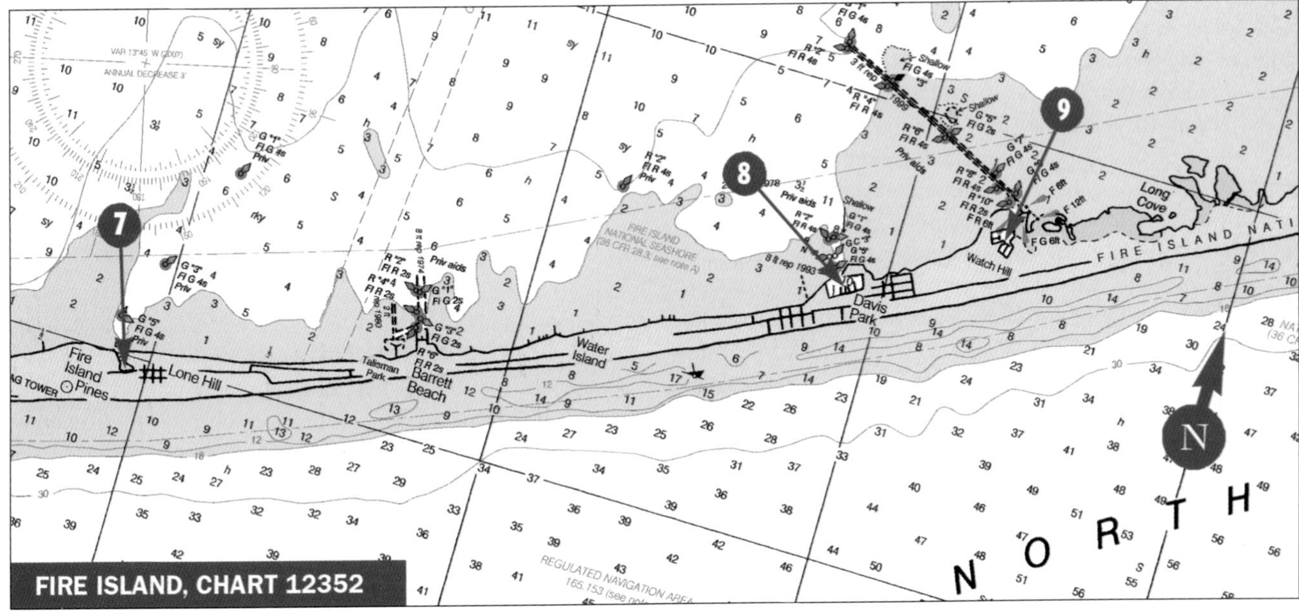

FIRE ISLAND, CHART 12352

Bay Shore to Islip, NY

BAY SHORE TO ISLIP		Largest Vessel Accommodated	VHF Channel Monitored	Transient Berths / Total Berths	Approach / Dockside Depth (reported)	Floating Docks	Gas / Diesel	Groceries, Ice, Marine Supplies, Snacks	Repairs: Hull, Engine, Propeller	Lift (tonnage), Crane, Rail	1=110V, 2=220V, B=Both, Max Amps	Laundry, Pool, Showers	Pump-Out Station	Nearby: Grocery Store, Motel, Restaurant
		Dockage					Supplies		Services					
1. Bay Shore Yacht Club	631-665-9518	50			6/6									
2. Burnett's Marina	631-665-9050	36	68	/150	5/5	F		I			1/30	S		GR
3. Seaborn Marina	631-665-0037	60		1/80	6/7		GD	M	HEP	L75	B/50			
4. Long Island Yacht Sales	631-665-5144	42		2/65	6/6			GIM	HEP	LC	1/30	S		GMR

Corresponding chart(s) not to be used for navigation. Internet Access Wireless Internet Access

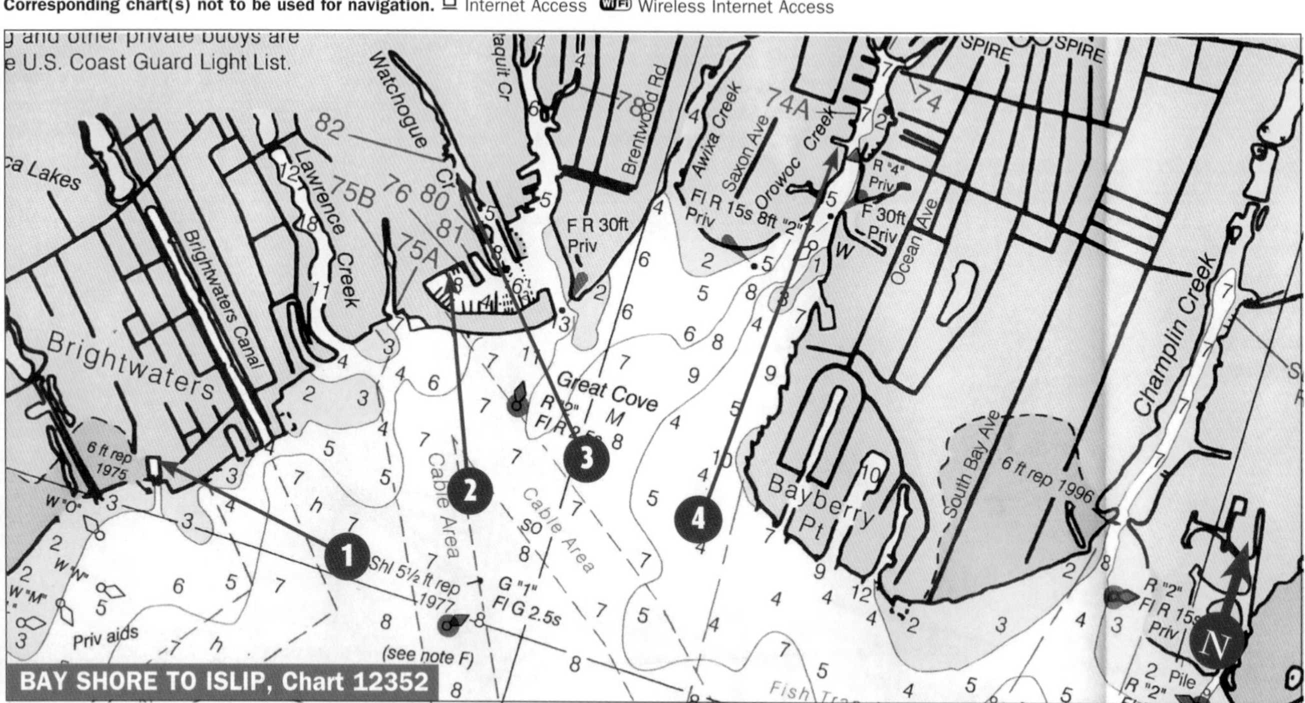

BAY SHORE TO ISLIP, Chart 12352

Fire Island has everything you might want when you think of destination beaches: restaurants, easy transportation, supplies and serenity. The restaurants are too numerous to mention, but Web sites abound with all the information you might need to plan your stay. The marinas on Fire Island do limit the stay of transients to seven days but there are plenty of good anchorages.

The island, 32 miles long and connected to the mainland by a series of marked channels through the sand flats and shoals of Great South Bay, was at one time a refuge for artists and writers. Now it boasts many summer communities, yacht clubs, hotels, restaurants, two state parks and the Fire Island National Seashore. Even so, long stretches of natural beach are alive with nothing but birds, wildlife and the occasional surf fisherman.

The National Seashore includes a campground, protected beaches, nature trails, two marinas, a historic lighthouse and Sunken Forest (a holly tree woodland with dark paths winding through it). Fire Island has many marinas, hotels, restaurants, nature areas, the Fire Island lighthouse, shops and rental homes. Several ferries make regular runs to and from the mainland.

ADDITIONAL RESOURCES:

- Fire Island Beaches, **www.fireislandbeaches.com**

NEARBY GOLF COURSES:
Bergen Point Golf Club, 69 Bergen Ave., West Babylon, NY 11704, 631-661-8282

NEARBY MEDICAL FACILITIES:
Brookhaven Memorial Hospital Medical Center, 101 Hospital Road, East Patchogue, NY 11772, 631-654-7100, **www.brookhavenhospital.org**

East on the Mainland

On the mainland, the big, bustling town of Bay Shore is the shopping and trading center for the surrounding area. It has all the necessary components of a good port of call: ample yacht services, good repair installations, a town pier, a yacht club, waterfront restaurants and hotels and a well-stocked shopping center within walking range of the harbor.

Oakdale to Sayville, NY

OAKDALE TO SAYVILLE		Largest Vessel Accommodated	VHF Channel Monitored	Transient Berths / Total Berths	Approach / Dockside Depth (reported)	Floating Docks	Gas / Diesel	Groceries, Ice, Marine Supplies, Snacks	Repairs: Hull, Engine, Propeller	Lift (tonnage), Crane, Rail	1=110V, 2=220V, B=Both, Max Amps	Laundry, Pool, Showers	Pump-Out Station	Nearby: Grocery Store, Motel, Restaurant
		Dockage					Supplies		Services					
1. Marina at Vanderbilt's Wharf	631-567-1231	46			5/4			IM	HP		1/30			R
2. The Riverview Restaurant	631-589-2761	85	16		6/6									R
3. Oakdale Yacht Service	631-589-1087	70	16/11	10/300	4/4		GD	IMS	HEP	L50	1/50	LPS	P	MR
4. Nicoll's Point Marina	631-589-8282	48		/64	5/3.5			IMS	HEP	L6	1/30			R
5. Snapper Inn Waterfront Restaurant	631-589-0248	50		40/60	4/4						B/50		P	R
6. Long Island Maritime Museum	631-854-4974	40		2/16	5/2						1/30			R
7. West Sayville Boat Basin	631-589-4141	50		5/100	6/6	F	G	M	HP	L	1/30	S	P	R
8. Land's End Motel & Marina	631-589-2040	42		3/38	5/5			I			1/30	P		GMR
9. Doug Westin's Boat Shop	631-589-1526	43	10	3/48	5/4		GD	IM	HEP	L12,C	B/30			GMR
10. Blue Point Marina	631-363-2000	40		/140	6/5		G	IM	HEP	L	1/30			R

Corresponding chart(s) not to be used for navigation. Internet Access Wireless Internet Access

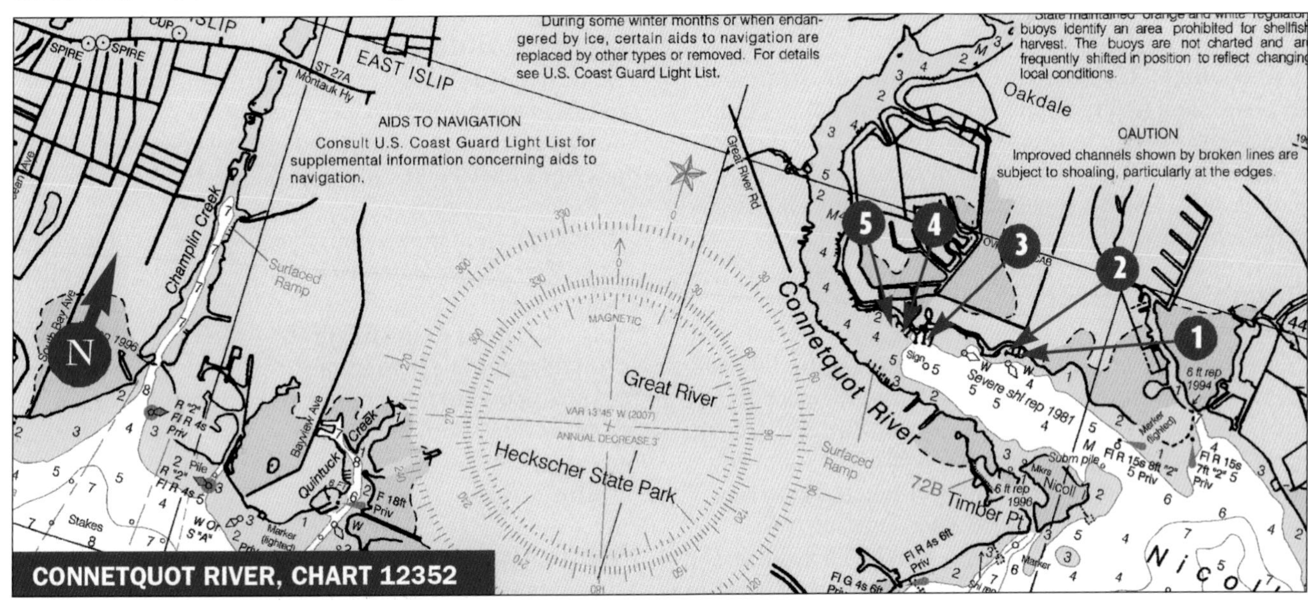

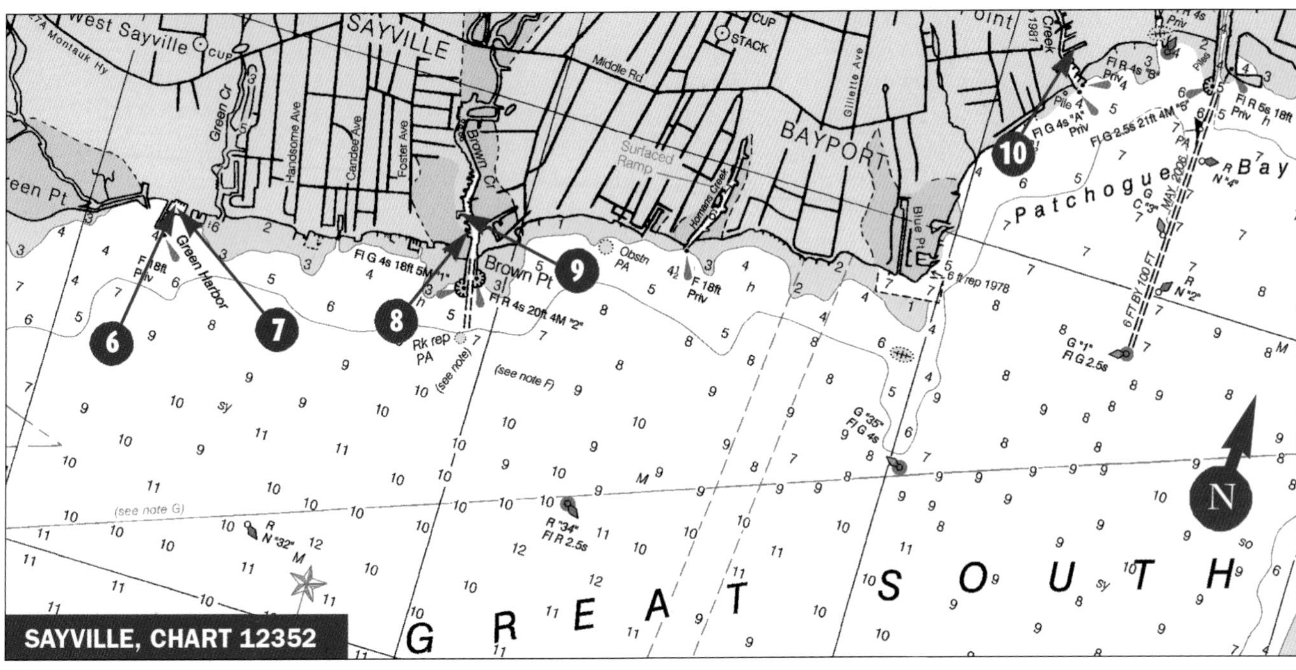

Connetquot River, NY

Bay Shore's artificial canals are lined with handsome homes and two main boating areas, Watchogue Creek and Penataquit Creek, where marinas are plentiful. While not all can handle transient boats, most will try. Located on Great Cove, Bay Shore's harbor and its creeks are well-protected. The marinas offer everything from charts to electronic repair, and activity is constant, with ferries running to Fire Island, fishermen coming and going, diners tying up to restaurants and sightseers walking along shore.

Half a mile east of the entrance to Bay Shore Harbor on Great Cove is Orowoc Creek. On the big jutting peninsula that ends at Nicoll Point is enormous Heckscher State Park with its bay beach, picnic, games and play areas, bridle paths and hiking trails. With a state-operated launching ramp in a small, protected harbor, this is an ideal place of refuge and a lovely anchorage, but overnight parking and docking are prohibited. The entry to the creek is marked by flashing red "2." There is an unmarked shoal on the eastern side of the creek, so be sure to stay close to flashing red "2."

Anchorage: The shoreline in this area of Great South Bay has many inviting opportunities to anchor, including Great Cove. Watch for boat traffic routes out of the creek to avoid wakes of numerous small boats launched at the park facility. Also note that this area has many underwater cable crossings.

Connetquot River

NAVIGATION: Use Chart 12352. Use Sandy Hook tide tables. For high tide, add 3 hours 19 minutes; for low tide, add 3 hours 32 minutes. Around Nicoll and Timber points, the Connetquot River empties into Nicoll Bay. A charming, secluded river with lovely wooded banks, the Connetquot River offers good anchorage, but not much in the way of depths. Favor the eastern shore when entering.

Known only to locals and Waterway Guide readers, the Connetquot River is one of the most abundant sea-run trout fisheries on earth. The state-run Connetquot River Preserve hatches some 28,000 brown, brook and rainbow trout per year, and they swim downriver to the Great South Bay to return in the spring as fish far too big for the little river from whence they came.

If you are a fly fisher, call ahead and reserve a morning or afternoon beat for a nominal fee (631-581-1005). If you do not want to leave your boat, drift around the river's mouth casting spoons and feathers. Be prepared for a sizable response.

This area is now the widest part of Great South Bay. Depths hold better, mid-bay shoals are fewer, and sailing is deservedly popular. Fleets of centerboard sailing craft gather in various harbors, beginning with Bay Shore.

Dockage: Two waterside restaurants encourage overnight docking for dinner guests. For the curious cruiser, the surrounding creeks in and around the former Vanderbilt estate (now a residential area and college campus) provide gunkholing opportunities for shallow drafts and dinghies. You will find full marine services at Oakdale. A marked channel connecting the inland route that parallels Fire Island with the route through Great South Bay runs across the bay south of Nicoll Point.

Sayville

A residential town with tree-lined streets and well-kept houses, Sayville has two waterfronts: Green Harbor in West Sayville, with a boatyard and marina, and Brown Creek, locally known as Browns River. The latter, the main boating center, is easy to enter between the jetties at Brown Point.

No longer do buoys direct you into Browns River, but a yellow tent marks the restaurant on the point, and the blue-and-white ferry boats shuttling in and out of the river can be easily followed. The dock-lined creek has slips for a ferry to Fire Island, a town pier for residents only, major repair yards serving the Great South Bay fishing fleets and many other marinas. Some of these marinas have pools, restaurants and shore accommodations for transients.

Bayport, Blue Point

The next towns to the east, Bayport and Blue Point, are typical eastern Long Island communities of the South Shore. Bayport has a yacht club and residents-only town dock, and Blue Point's town dock and town marina also are for residents only.

Dockage: A marina with limited facilities at Blue Point, Tabat Marine, accommodates transients and also offers repair facilities. Recent reports have indicated 4-foot approach depths to this facility.

Anchorage: The harbor off the yacht club in Blue Point provides good holding ground and is well-protected from all but a rare southeasterly. In this secluded anchorage, only the surge of the Patchogue ferries, a few miles east, disturbs the calm.

Patchogue

The shopping and industrial town for much of eastern Long Island, Patchogue is host to the Great South Bay sailing regatta on the last weekend in August every year. The town's waterfront takes care of hundreds of boats each season.

Deep Patchogue River, the main boating center, is entered between breakwaters from Patchogue Bay, a bight of Great South Bay. Marinas here range from fishing stations to complete repair operations.

East Patchogue

NAVIGATION: Use Chart 12352. As the Great South Bay comes to an end, so do its broad open reaches of relatively deep water. From here eastward, the inland route continues mainly along channels dredged out of the shoals. Project depth for the route is 6 feet, but expect shoaling, and check locally for current conditions.

Dockage: Lying between Swan River and Mud Creek is East Patchogue. Swan Creek has a yacht club and a friendly restaurant that encourages diners to stay as overnight dock guests. In Mud Creek, Sunset Harbor Marina offers full marine repair services and fuel as well as recreational facilities. A Dockside Grill and Tiki Bar complete the package.

Bellport Bay

NAVIGATION: Use Chart 12352. Howells Point, on the mainland about three miles east of Patchogue, marks the start of Bellport Bay. The villages of Bellport and Brookhaven are on its north shore, offering a scattering of marinas. The bay does become increasingly shallow here, though.

The course then doglegs into a dredged channel where markers must be observed and, at Smith Point, Bellport Bay appears. Here a bascule bridge (18-foot closed vertical) connects mainland Shirley with eastern Fire Island.

The shoal-bordered channel continues about three miles through Narrow Bay, which is only a few hundred feet wide, past Mastic Beach into the western approach to Moriches Bay.

Dockage: The restored Bellport Town Dock, which lies between Howells Point and Beaverdam Creek, provides ample room for visitors to tie up on the outside. The town, just a mile walk up a tree-shaded street, has all the charm of a New England village and boasts a chic pub and a couple of fine restaurants.

Brookhaven

Dockage: There is a full-service marina in Beaverdam Creek with 7-foot reported approach depths.

Anchorage: A delightful anchorage just north of the Bellport Town Dock is secluded and protected. Boats carrying a draft greater than 5 feet, however, should approach cautiously and check the state of tide before anchoring.

Moriches Bay

NAVIGATION: Use Chart 12352. For Moriches Inlet, use Sandy Hook tide tables. For high tide, subtract 57 minutes; for low tide, subtract 1 hour 9 minutes. Moriches Bay is about eight miles long, with central depths of 3 to 6 feet, sizable shoals in its southern reaches, many coves, and creeks that tend to shoal despite dredging. The towns of Moriches, East Moriches and Center Moriches rim the bay. The bay's shifting shoals change so rapidly that mariners often find it difficult to maneuver without running aground. Navigate cautiously and keep an eye on the depth sounder. Tree stakes will guide you through the deepest sections of the bay. Yachts are advised to leave the stakes to port going east. These makeshift markers follow a zigzag pattern north to Harts Cove, east to Seatuck Cove and south to the marked channel. They are an enormous boon to cruising boats that would otherwise need to call the Coast Guard or local marinas to get information on the shoaling.

Marinas are located on most of the creeks, but they are almost exclusively for local boats. Exceptions include Tuthill and Harts coves in East Moriches and East Branch, just in from Seatuck Cove at Speonk. The Corps of Engineers cautions that shoals of 1 to 5 feet have been reported in the vicinity of Tuthill Point, and 3 to 6 feet in Moriches Bay.

Blue Point, Patchogue to East Moriches, NY

BLUE POINT, PATCHOGUE TO EAST MORICHES		Largest Vessel Accommodated	VHF Channel Monitored	Transient Berths / Total Berths	Approach / Dockside Depth (reported)	Floating Docks	Gas / Diesel	Groceries, Ice, Marine Supplies, Snacks	Repairs: Hull, Engine, Propeller	Lift (tonnage), Crane, Rail	1=110V, 2=220V, B=Both, Max Amps	Laundry, Pool, Showers	Pump-Out Station	Nearby: Grocery Store, Motel, Restaurant
		Dockage					Supplies		Services					
1. Tabat Marine	631-363-6060	45		6/90	4/4		G	IM	HP		1			
2. Island View Marina	631-447-1234	45		/26	10/5		GD	IS		L			P	GMR
3. Sun-Dek Marina	631-207-1953	50	68	6/50	10/6		G	S			B/50			R
4. Frank M. Weeks Yacht Yard	631-475-1675	55		4/70	8/8			M	HEP	L60	1/30	S		GR
5. White Water Marine Service	631-475-5000	30			5/5	F		M	EP		1/30			MR
6. Dickson's Marine	631-475-1445		16/09		5/4		GD	IMS	HEP					
7. Sunset Harbor Marina	**631-289-3800**	**60**		**/413**	**6/6**		**GD**	**IMS**	**HEP**	**L30**	**B/50**	**PS**	**P**	**MR**
8. Leeward Cove South	631-654-3106	50		/260	5/5	F		IM	HEP	L25	1/30	S	P	R
9. Beaver Dam Marina	888-610-BOAT	65	16/68	10/100	10/7			M	HP	L	B/30	S		GMR
10. Silly Lily Fishing Station	631-878-0247	26	71	5/40	3/3	F	G	IMS	HEP					GR
11. Windswept Marina	631-878-2100	40	68	10/140	4/4	F	G	IMS	HP	L	1/30	S	P	GMR
12. Remsenburg Marina	631-325-1677	45		5/125	4/6	F	GD	IM	HEP	L25	1/30		P	G

Corresponding chart(s) not to be used for navigation. Internet Access Wireless Internet Access

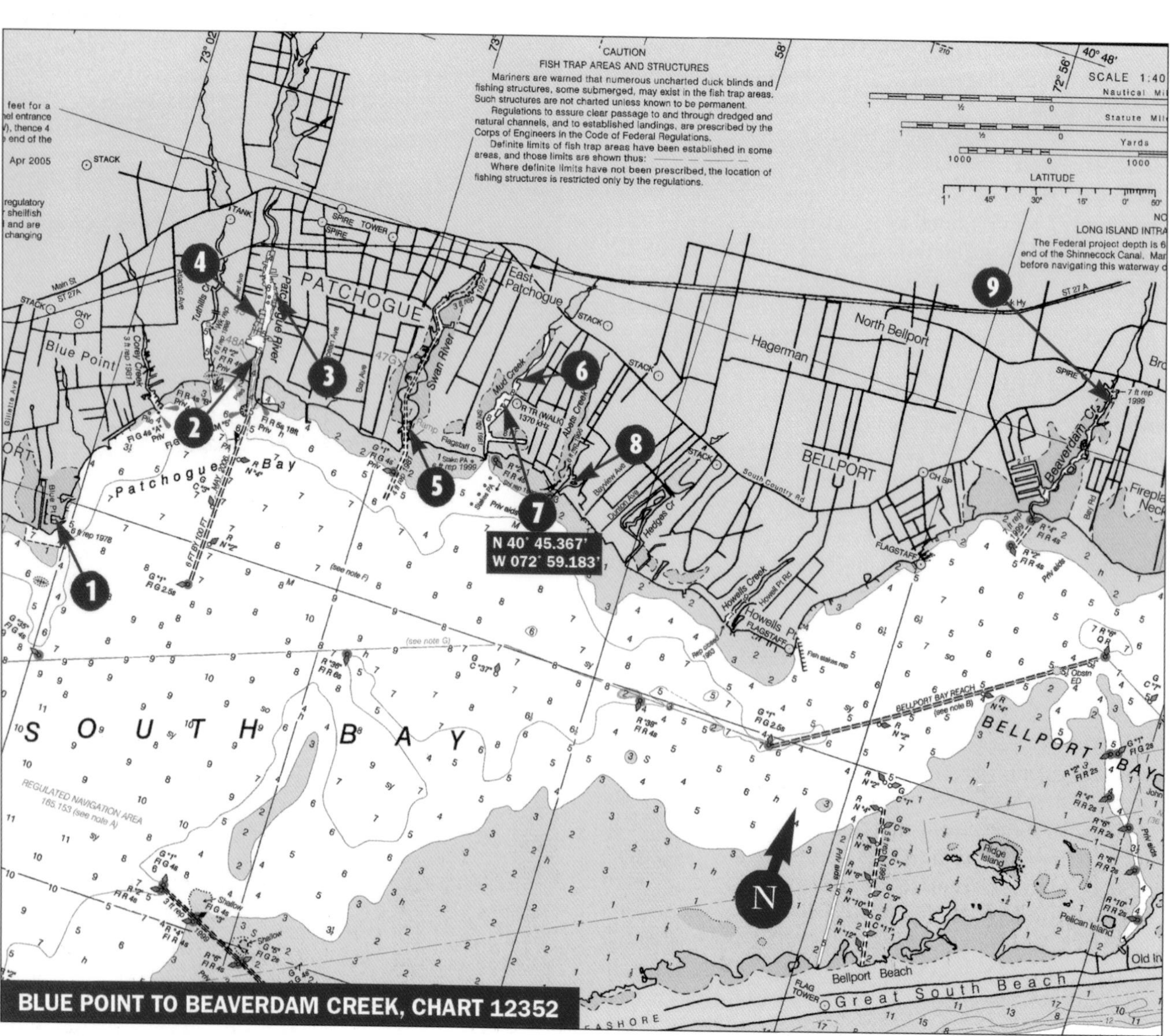

BLUE POINT TO BEAVERDAM CREEK, CHART 12352

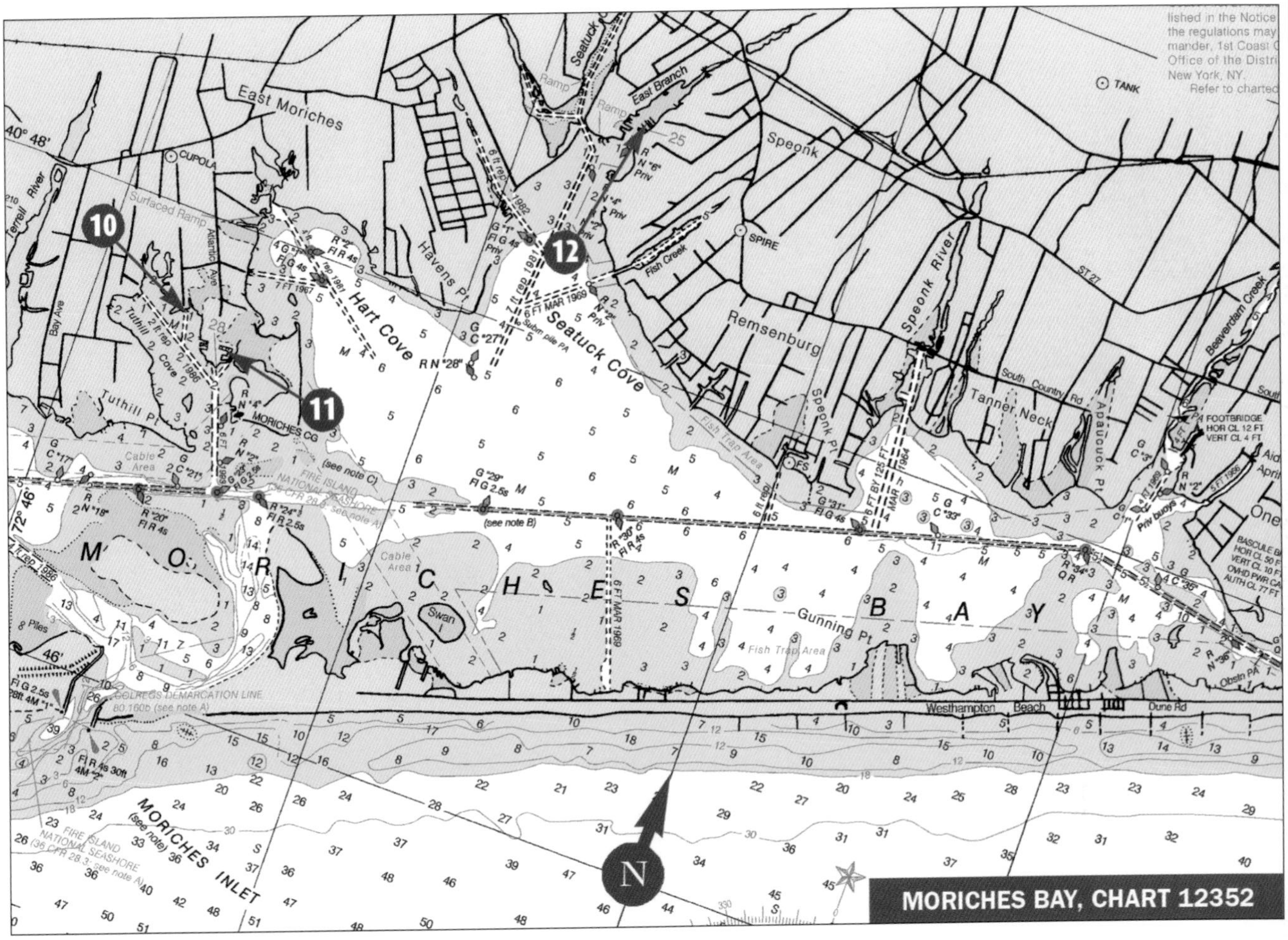

MORICHES BAY, CHART 12352

Moriches Bay

Use Only With Local Knowledge

Moriches Inlet. (Not to be used for navigation.) WATERWAY GUIDE PHOTOGRAPHY

Looking north over Patchogue River. (Not to be used for navigation.) WATERWAY GUIDE PHOTOGRAPHY

A WORTHWHILE DETOUR THROUGH "OLD CUT"

NAVIGATION: An interesting route east from Great Gunn is through a small channel known locally as "Old Cut." On the chart, there is a narrow unmarked channel through the shallows running 10 degrees (true) from Great Gunn. It intersects another channel, this one dredged but not buoyed. This channel leads you into the relatively deep water just inside Moriches Inlet. These are unstable channels, so slow and easy is the way.

From the inner mouth of Moriches Inlet, a curving channel leads back to the State Channel in Moriches Bay. Hug the southern and eastern banks of this channel until you are dead east (true) of the unnamed island inside the inlet. Then you can move to center channel. That unnamed island has become a home to the growing seal population of the South Shore bays. You'll see them basking on the beach, but they will take to the safety of the water if a boat comes too close.

To do some basking of your own, beach the boat along that curving channel (there is a steep drop-off). It is a quick walk to the ocean beach. But do not swim in the channel; fast-moving boats hug the shore.

Erratic Moriches Inlet has privately maintained lights at the seaward end, but it is not buoyed because of the inlet's rapidly changing, dangerous conditions. Though local boats and fishermen use it, the Coast Guard considers it unsafe. Officially, it is closed to navigation. Go east to Shinnecock Inlet (15 miles) or west to Fire Island Inlet (27 miles) for safer passages to the ocean.

Moriches Inlet remains the most untamed of the five South Shore inlets. The area around the inlet, too, is somewhat wild. To the east is a section of Westhampton Beach that the ocean is intent on reclaiming. To the west is the undeveloped eastern tip of Fire Island.

Near this eastern tip, there is a little-known park accessible only by foot or boat. Great Gunn Beach is a town-run park about three-quarters of a mile west of the inlet. Because eastern Fire Island is a national seashore, it is nearly undeveloped, and Great Gunn Beach fits these surroundings. Docks, restrooms and a narrow boardwalk to the beach are all the facilities here. At night, Great Gunn is nothing but the sweep of stars, the ocean and the inlet.

Dockage: On weekend days, Great Gunn attracts a small crowd of boats. Non-residents are charged for dockage, and you can stay overnight (the restrooms are locked at about 5 p.m.). It is also easy to anchor just off the docks and wade in—just allow for the tide. Great Gunn Beach is unmarked on the chart, but you will see the buoyed

Westhampton Beach and Inlet, NY

WESTHAMPTON BEACH, INLET	Phone	Largest Vessel Accommodated	VHF Channel Monitored	Transient Berths / Total Berths	Approach / Dockside Depth (reported)	Floating Docks	Gas / Diesel	Groceries, Ice, Marine Supplies, Snacks	Repairs: Hull, Engine, Propeller	Lift (tonnage), Crane, Rail	1=110V, 2=220V, B=Both, Max Amps	Laundry, Pool, Showers	Pump-Out Station	Nearby: Grocery Store, Motel, Restaurant
		Dockage					Supplies		Services					
1. Westhampton Bath and Tennis Hotel and Marina	631-288-2500	50	09	6/74	9/7			I			B/50	LPS	P	GMR
2. Surfside 3 West Hampton	631-288-2400	38	79	/30	3/3	F	G	IM	HEP	L10	1/30			GMR
3. Westhampton Beach Municipal Yacht Basin	631-288-9496	50	68	12/125	4/4							S	P	GMR

Corresponding chart(s) not to be used for navigation. Internet Access Wireless Internet Access

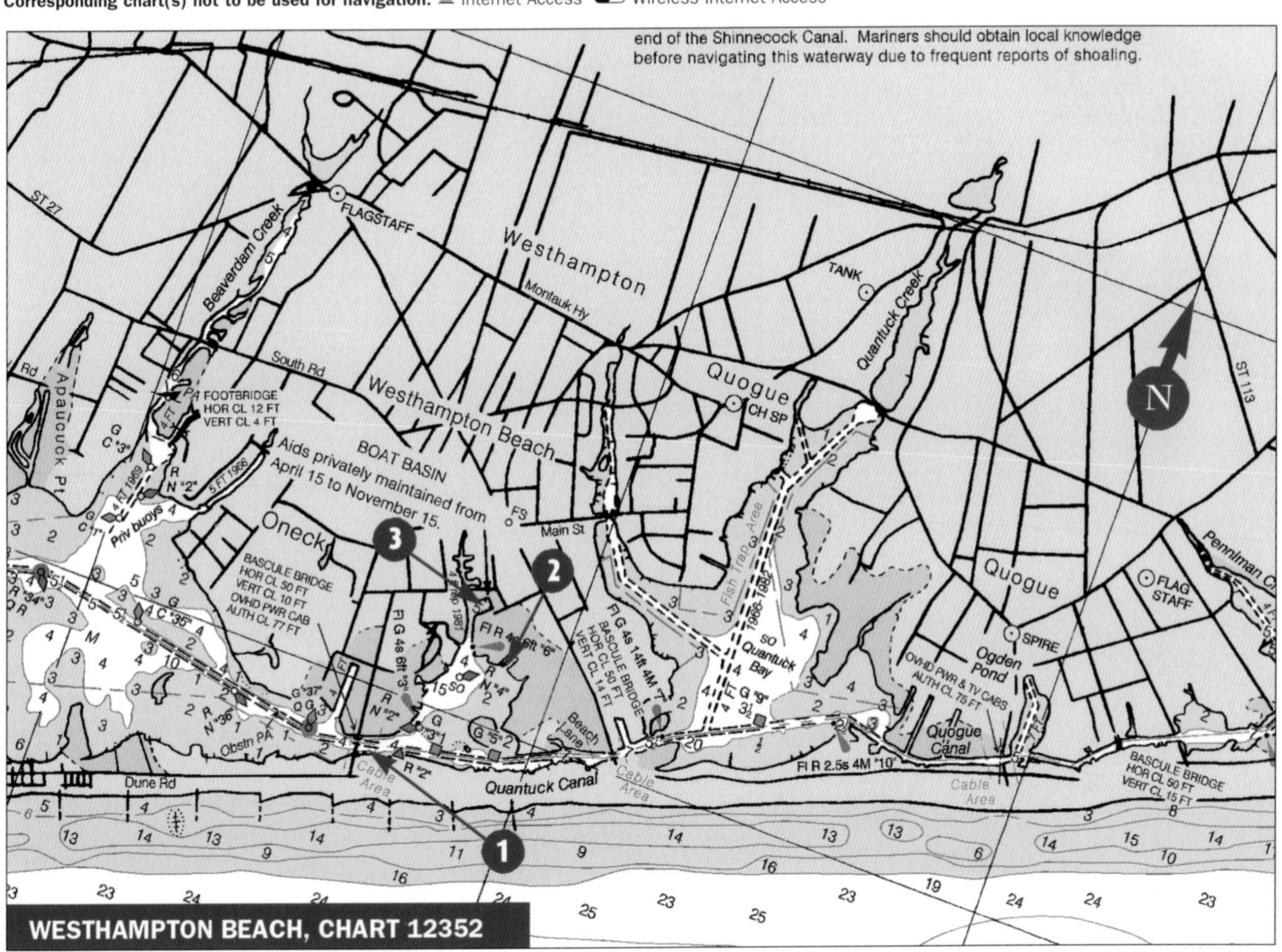

channel to it through the shallows of Moriches Bay. The channel ends exactly one nautical mile west of Moriches Inlet on Fire Island. There is more room to anchor east of the channel than west. Tuthill Cove, somewhat northwest of that curving channel, is recognizable by the Group Moriches Coast Guard station at its mouth. Just up-channel from Group Moriches is a small marina, Silly Lily Fishing Station, with transient dockage and fuel, but depths of only 3 feet.

As Moriches Bay opens up, the state channel passes Hart Cove and Seatuck Cove. Both have local marinas with some supplies and services. Seatuck Creek leads right to the pretty, small village of Eastport, which has the feel of old Long Island. The main street (Montauk Highway) is lined with old buildings snoozing in the sun. They house eateries, a deli, a couple of antiques dealers and a store specializing in stained glass.

South of Remsenburg is a spot on the barrier beach that was called Pike's Inlet for less than a year, while it existed. During the Halloween 1992 nor'easter, the ocean overran this narrow strip, and subsequent storms enlarged the breach until it was several hundred feet wide. Then the Corps of Engineers put a metal wall across it and poured sand into the breach to seal it.

Westhampton Beach

NAVIGATION: Use Chart 12352. South of Speonk Point, a large shoal extends north from Gunning Point and may encroach on the channel. About four miles east of Moriches

East Quogue, Shinnecock Bay, Inlet and Canal, NY

SHINNECOCK BAY, INLET, CANAL		Largest Vessel Accommodated	VHF Channel Monitored	Transient Berths / Total Berths	Approach / Dockside Depth (reported)	Floating Docks	Gas / Diesel	Groceries, Ice, Marine Supplies, Snacks	Repairs: Hull, Engine, Propeller	Lift (tonnage), Crane, Rail	1=110V, 2=220V, B=Both, Max Amps	Laundry, Pool, Showers	Pump-Out Station	Nearby: Grocery Store, Motel, Restaurant
		Dockage					Supplies		Services					
1. Aldrich Boatyard	631-653-5300	40		/65	6/6	F			HEP	L35				R
2. Hampton Shipyard	631-653-6777	65		/18	6/6				HP	LR	B/50			R
3. Spellman's Marine	631-728-9200	36		5/80	5/5			M	HEP	L35	B/50	S		GMR
4. Hampton Boat Works	631-728-1114	50		4/30	6/5	F			HP	L	1/30	S		M
5. Ponquoge Marina	631-728-2264	40		2/60	3.5/6	F			HEP	L30	1/30	S		GMR
6. Before the Bridge Restaurant	631-728-9111	24		17/	6/10						1/30			R
7. Innspot on the Bay	631-728-1200			8/10	3/3	F		I			1/30	LS		MR
8. Oakland's Restaurant & Marina	631-728-6900	60	68	10/42	5/6		GD	IS			B/50	S	P	GMR
9. Sherry & Joe Cores Best Boat Works	631-283-7359	38	68	3/44	4/4	F	G	IM	HEP	L12	1/30	S	P	MR
10. The Lobster Inn	631-283-1525			RESTAURANT	4/4									R
11. Colonial Shores Resort & Marina	631-728-0011	23		10/28	6/4	F		I				LPS		GMR
12. Jackson's Marina	631-728-4220	70	68	5/200	8/6	F	GD	IMS	HEP	L75	B/50	S	P	GMR
13. Shinnecock Canal Marina	631-852-8291	47		26/62	8/6	F					1/30	S	P	GMR
14. Hampton Watercraft & Marine	631-728-8200	60		/100	12/8		GD	IMS	HEP	L		S		MR
15. Modern Yachts	631-728-2266	60		/70	10/6		GD	IMS	HEP	L40,C	B/50	PS	P	GMR
16. Indian Cove Restaurant & Marina	631-728-5366	55			6/6		GD	I			1/30	S		R
17. Mariner's Cove Marine	631-728-0286	52		6/182	9/5	F		IMS	HP	R	1/30	S	P	GMR

Corresponding chart(s) not to be used for navigation. Internet Access Wireless Internet Access

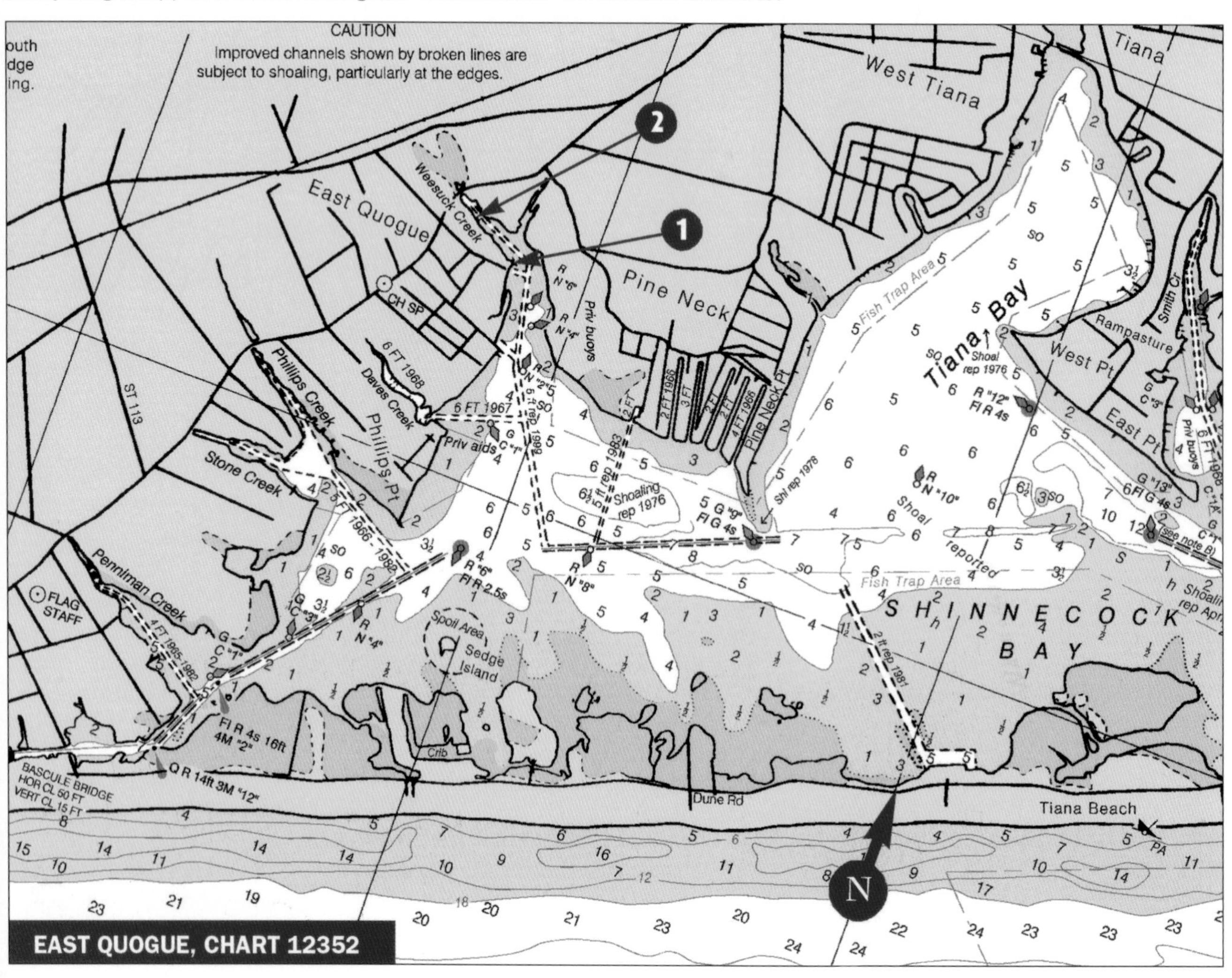

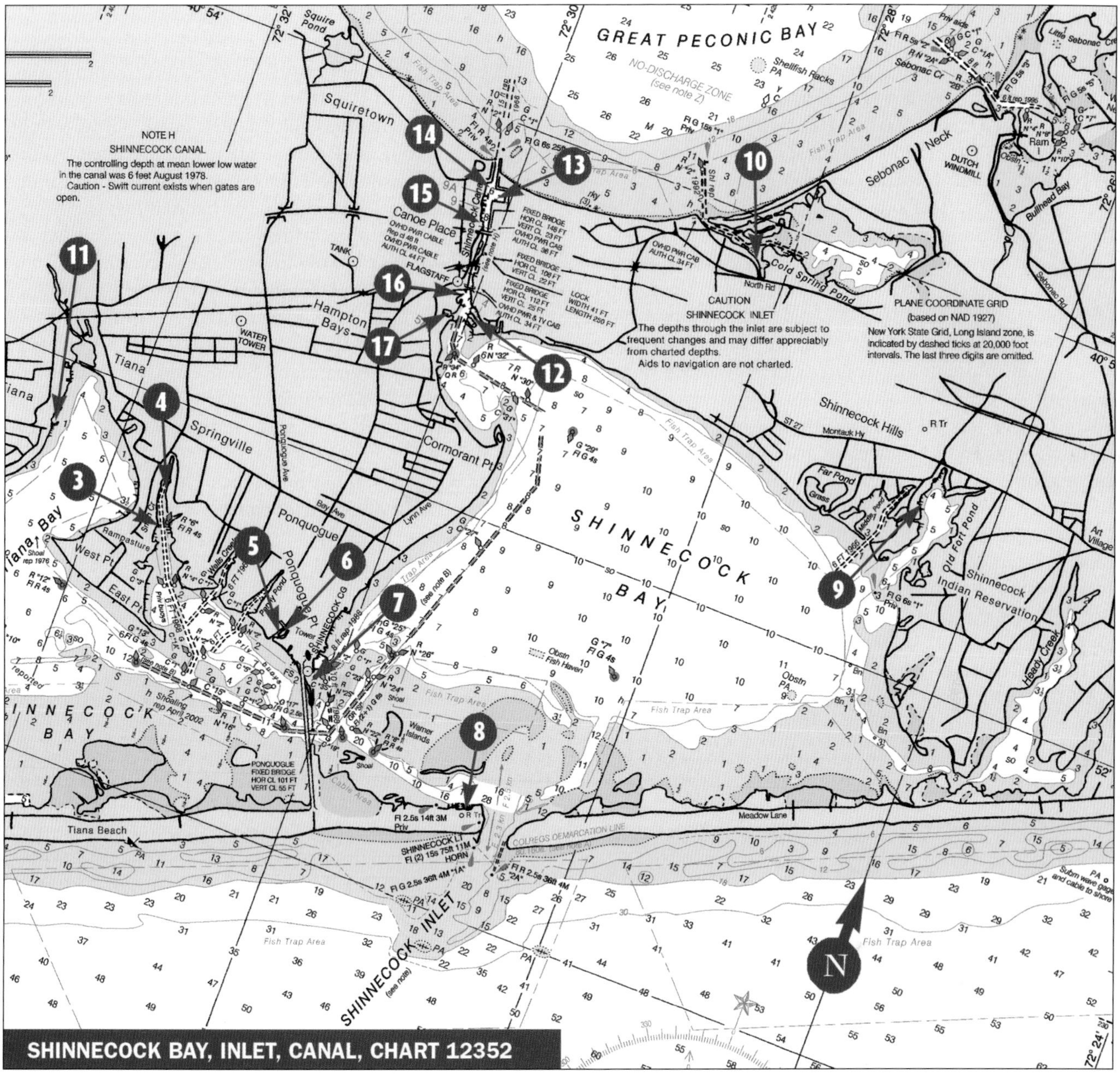

GREAT PECONIC BAY
NO-DISCHARGE ZONE (see note Z)
Shellfish Racks PA
Squiretown
Squire Pond
NOTE H
SHINNECOCK CANAL
The controlling depth at mean lower low water in the canal was 6 feet August 1978.
Caution - Swift current exists when gates are open.
Canoe Place
TANK
FLAGSTAFF
Hampton Bays
WATER TOWER
FIXED BRIDGE HOR CL 148 FT VERT CL 23 FT
OVHD PWR CAB AUTH CL 36 FT
FIXED BRIDGE HOR CL 106 FT VERT CL 22 FT
FIXED BRIDGE HOR CL 112 FT VERT CL 25 FT
OVHD PWR & TV CAB AUTH CL 34 FT
LOCK WIDTH 41 FT LENGTH 250 FT
OVHD PWR CAB AUTH CL 34 FT
Sebonac Neck
DUTCH WINDMILL
Cold Spring Pond
North Rd
CAUTION
SHINNECOCK INLET
The depths through the inlet are subject to frequent changes and may differ appreciably from charted depths.
Aids to navigation are not charted.
PLANE COORDINATE GRID
(based on NAD 1927)
New York State Grid, Long Island zone, is indicated by dashed ticks at 20,000 foot intervals. The last three digits are omitted.
Bullhead Bay
Little Sebonac Cr
Sebonac Cr
Ram I
Shinnecock Hills
Montauk Hy
ST 27
Far Pond
Tiana
Springville
Ponquogue
Ponquogue Pt
Cormorant Pt
Bay Ave
Lynn Ave
Tiana Bay
Rampasture
West Pt
East Pt
SHINNECOCK BAY
Fish Trap Area
Cable Area
Warner Islands
Obstn Fish Haven
Shinnecock Indian Reservation
Old Fort Pond
Heady Creek
Art Village
PONQUOGUE FIXED BRIDGE HOR CL 101 FT VERT CL 55 FT
Shoaling rep April 2002
Tiana Beach
Meadow Lane
COLREGS DEMARCATION LINE
SHINNECOCK LT
Fl (2) 15s 75ft 11M HORN
Fl 2.5s 14ft 3M Priv
SHINNECOCK INLET
Subm wave gage and cable to shore
N
3
4
5
6
7
8
9
10
11
12
13
14
15
16
17

SHINNECOCK BAY, INLET, CANAL, CHART 12352

Great Peconic Bay
Shinnecock Canal
Shinnecock Bay

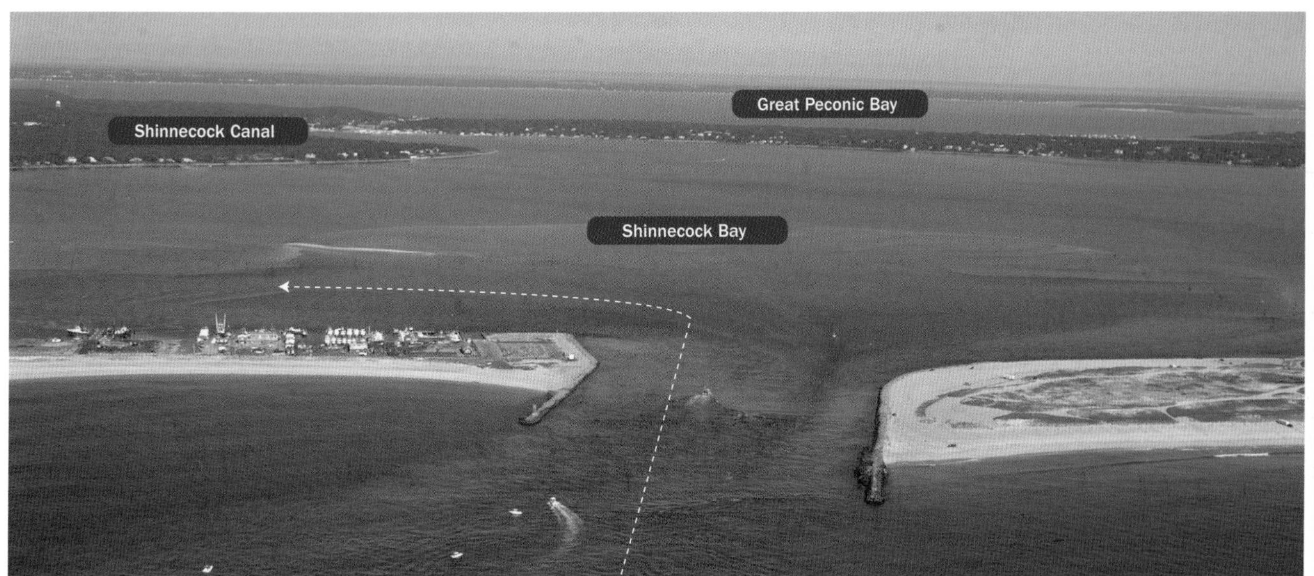

Looking north over Shinnecock Bay and inlet. (Not to be used for navigation.) WATERWAY GUIDE PHOTOGRAPHY

Inlet, transient accommodations are available along both sides of the channel at Westhampton Beach. In this area the channel angles into Quantuck Canal, with two bascule bridges just a mile apart. Shoaling has been reported at flashing red buoy "34," so use caution here. The first bridge has a 10-foot closed vertical clearance; the second a 14-foot closed vertical clearance. Just north of this area on the mainland side is Westhampton, one of Long Island's most popular summer colonies.

The channel leaves Quantuck Canal for a straight dredged course across Quantuck Bay, and then enters Quogue (rhymes with "fog") Canal. A little more than a mile long, it bends as shoals push out from the village of Quogue, an old summer resort with big homes but few marinas. A bascule bridge (15-foot closed vertical clearance) is near the western end of the canal. From May 1 through Sept. 30, the Quantuck and Quogue Canal bridges open on signal between 8 a.m. and 10 p.m. Just beyond the bridge, Quogue Canal enters Shinnecock Bay.

Dockage: Westhampton Bath and Tennis Hotel and Marina offers transient dockage with luxurious amenities including an Olympic-sized pool, a health club, tennis, an ocean beach and fine dining.

Shinnecock Bay and Inlet

NAVIGATION: Use Chart 12352. Use Sandy Hook tide tables. For high tide, subtract 39 minutes; for low tide, subtract 1 hour 4 minutes. Shinnecock Bay, last of the important South Shore bays, is a pivotal point for cruising boats. The inland passage along Long Island's South Shore ends here and, to the north, Shinnecock Canal gives direct access to Great Peconic Bay, the Long Island Fishtail area and the island's north shore. About seven miles long and closed off north and east by the Long Island mainland, the bay is divided by long, sandy Ponquogue Point, which joins the mainland via a 55-foot fixed vertical clearance bridge.

Shinnecock Bay starts unremarkably enough at the eastern end of narrow Quogue Canal where the channel turns hard to port. It follows a relatively straight course through 1- and 2-foot shoals past a series of private, dredged creeks (Penniman, Stone and Phillips) with attractive shores but no public marinas. Just off Phillips Point, the channel crooks to starboard, and transient boats have a choice of marinas.

Tiana Bay, an arm of Shinnecock Bay, lies east of Pine Neck (with its shallow finger canals). The bay is open and has fairly stable 5-foot depths instead of the bars, marshes and dredged cuts of most of the South Shore's eastern portion. According to local reports, shoals extend from Pine Neck Point nearly to the channel.

From Tiana Bay, the route passes the long finger of East Point, headland of Smith Creek, with shoals all about. Stick to the buoys. The narrow channel forks beyond the Ponquogue Fixed Bridge (55-foot vertical clearance) at Ponquogue Point, where the Shinnecock Coast Guard station is located. The starboard branch runs southeast toward Shinnecock Inlet, the port branch northeast to Shinnecock Canal. Both branches go through bars and marshes. The starboard channel toward Shinnecock Inlet passes between two of the three glorified mud flats that are called the Warner Islands. The smallest, westernmost of the islands has been locally renamed Seal Island. This has become another seal population center of the south bays.

Shinnecock Inlet, created by the great hurricane of 1938, was very unstable until 1968. Then it settled down and kept its position with 10-foot depths until a large federal project dredged the inlet to 27 feet and added to the stone breakwaters. Coast Guard Group Moriches reports that there is still some surf over the outer bar, but the worst is gone for now. Obtaining local knowledge is prudent until it is known if Shinnecock Inlet will stabilize. Marinas inside along the barrier strip cater to sportfishermen, and there are two restaurants.

Northeast of Shinnecock Inlet is Shinnecock Bay's larger section, an open expanse with 7- to 10-foot depths. You have to run about a half mile through shoals and then the bay opens out.

Beyond are the rest of the Hamptons: Southampton, East Hampton and Bridgehampton. Shinnecock Bay is convenient for visiting them. The Hamptons retain much of their Colonial charm, with trendy shops, gourmet restaurants, pleasant parks and beaches, which continue to draw the rich and famous as visitors and seasonal residents. No trip to the area would be complete without an excursion to any or all of them.

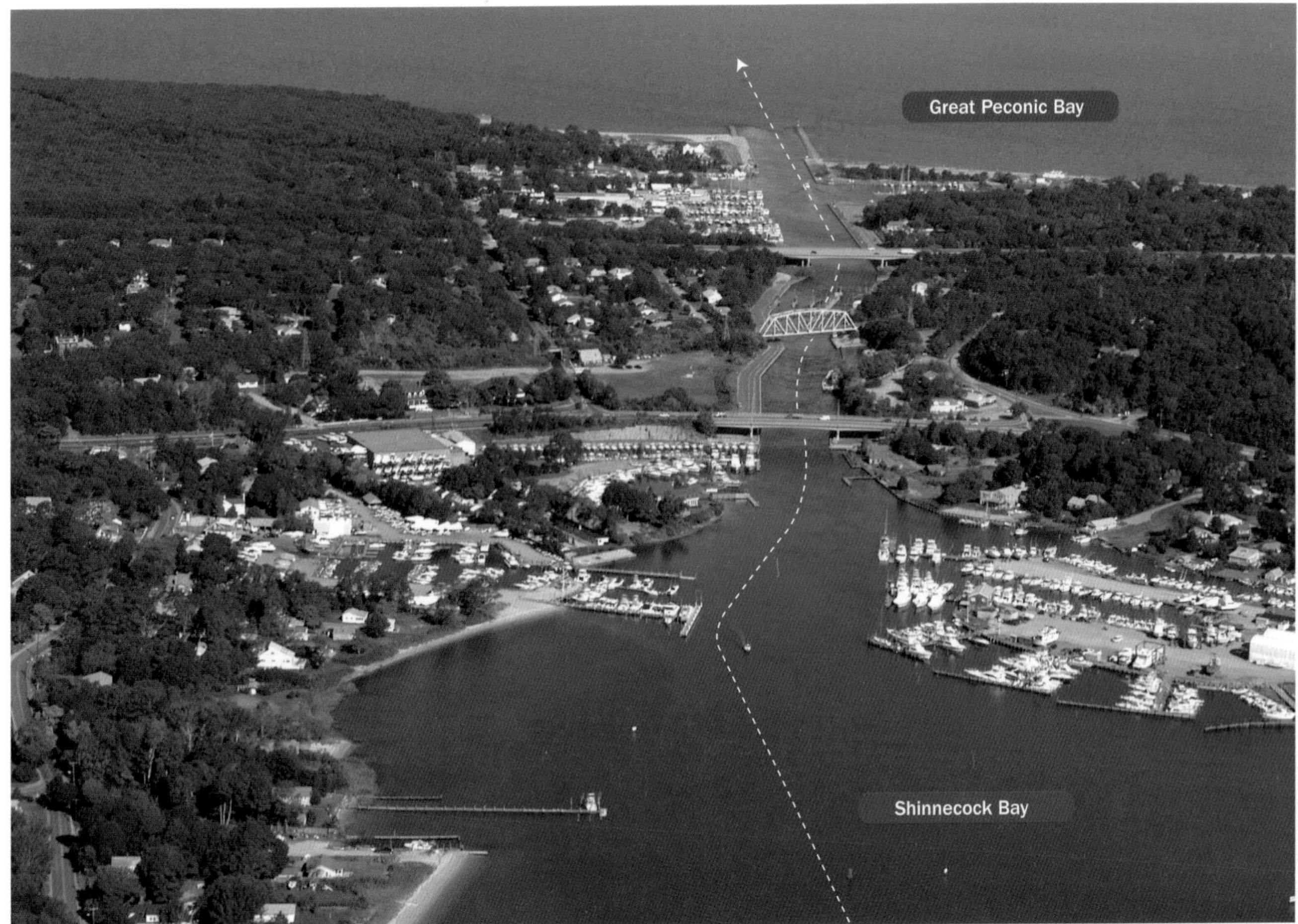

Looking north through the Shinnecock Canal. (Not to be used for navigation.) WATERWAY GUIDE PHOTOGRAPHY

Shinnecock Canal

In the northern corner of Shinnecock Bay, above Cormorant Point, is Shinnecock Canal, gateway to the Peconic Bays and Long Island's north shore. West of the canal is the lively community of Hampton Bays, with motels and good restaurants.

The part of the town along the canal was called Canoe Place until the end of the First World War, perpetuating the legend that a Montauk Indian chief dug the first canal to eliminate a canoe portage. It is still charted as Canoe Place.

NAVIGATION: Use Chart 12352. The mile-long canal is wide and deep for the steady passage of boats in both directions. Bridges and cables limit overhead clearance to 22 feet. But for sailboats, the county maintains free, unattended, do-it-yourself ginpoles for unstepping and restepping masts at each end of the canal.

About midway is a 250-foot-long lock, 41 feet wide, with 12 feet over the sills. The tide running southward opens the lock and parallel 27-foot tidal gates. Southbound boats usually use the tidal gates. Larger boats, however, are put through the lock whenever possible. Traffic lights control passage through the lock.

The passage is usually simple, if you take the current into account. When the gates are open, letting water from Peconic Bay run into Shinnecock Bay, the current can be as swift as 6 knots. Northbound boats, if underpowered, can have a hard time and should negotiate the canal at slack water.

Dockage: The banks of the canal are lined with marinas, boatyards and fishing stations, one after another, except near the lock. You can get about anything you need or want, from bait and dockage to repairs and food. Modern Yachts offers full-service repairs, fuel and transient dockage with cable television and a heated pool.

Cruising Options

At the northern end, you pass between the jetties into Great Peconic Bay and its satellite bays. (See the chapter titled "The Fishtail.") This is an easy run from South Shore to north, avoiding the long open passage around Montauk Point to Block Island Sound. ■

Planning

- Tide Tables 521
- GPS Waypoints 532

Section Contents

City Island to Port Chester	162
Greenwich to Bridgeport	174
Stratford to Westbrook	189
The Connecticut River	204
Niantic to Watch Hill	220
Little Neck Bay to Cold Spring Harbor	240
Huntington Bay to Plum Gut	253
The Fishtail	266

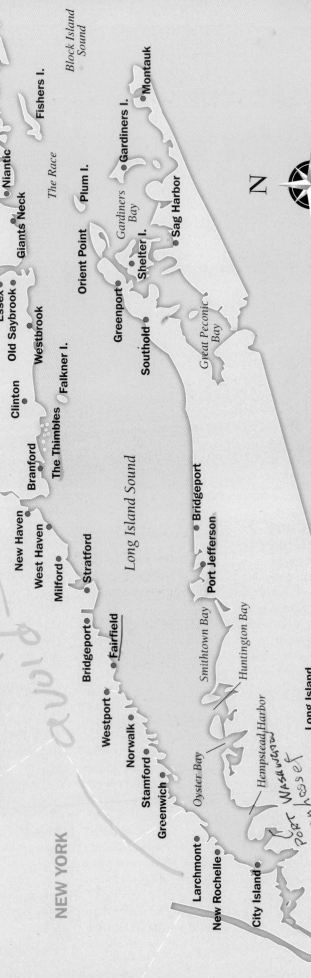

CONNECTICUT
NEW YORK
Thames R.
Westerly
Mystic
Stonington
Connecticut R.
New London
Niantic
Essex
Old Saybrook
Giants Neck
Clinton
New Haven
Branford
Westbrook
West Haven
The Thimbles
Falkner I.
Fishers I.
The Race
Milford
Block Island Sound
Orient Point
Plum I.
Bridgeport
Stratford
Westport
Fairfield
Greenport
Gardiners Bay
Gardiners I.
Norwalk
Long Island Sound
Shelter I.
Southold
Montauk
Stamford
Greenwich
Sag Harbor
Larchmont
Oyster Bay
Bridgeport
Smithtown Bay
Great Peconic Bay
New Rochelle
Port Jefferson
Huntington Bay
City Island
Hempstead Harbor
N
Long Island
Atlantic Ocean

Long Island Sound

Long Island Sound, a popular inland sea, lies between New York City and Block Island, RI. It is 90 nautical miles long, up to 20 miles wide and narrower at both ends. The Sound, as it is commonly known, is a major commercial artery, an important fishing and lobstering ground and one of the great cruising areas in the United States.

On weekends, Long Island Sound is covered with an armada of sailboats producing a spectacular sight. Yacht clubs throughout the Sound hold organized regattas for one-design and handicapped sailboats on a regular basis. When cruising the Sound under sail or power it is best to detour around and avoid plowing through the fleets to avoid interfering with the races.

Many mariners whose home port is on Long Island Sound never leave it, although they cruise all season long, year after year. Crisscrossing between Connecticut's rocky shore and Long Island's sandy beaches, they cruise the summer away—anchoring in isolated coves, visiting luxurious marina-cities, racing under sail, fishing, taking long side trips up navigable rivers and exploring big bays.

Cruising Characteristics

The weather here is generally hospitable, with infrequent fog and predictable summer thunderstorms. Thunderstorms, of course, bring their strong, gusty winds. The occasional northeaster, often lasting as long as three days, delivers winds, steep seas, low temperatures and torrents of rain. One shore or the other generally offers a lee, but a nasty chop with short seas is more usual. Continuous weather reports are broadcast on VHF-FM WX-1 from New York City and New London, CT. Most commercial radio stations broadcast boating forecasts during the season.

Winds pick up in early afternoon and get progressively stronger as the day wears on. Most powerboats wanting to make time get an early-morning start, or they travel at night when winds tend to die, using the chain of lights that defines a clear path down the center of Long Island Sound. Sailboats make the best time under sail during the breezy afternoons, or they can use auxiliary power to run the usually-placid night waters.

When under way at night, stay well clear of areas where there might be lobster pots, oyster beds and fish traps—all are, at best, difficult to spot. In addition, keep a sharp lookout for tugs with tows that often run the Sound at night. The tows are often very long lines and can be difficult to spot. It is also not advisable to attempt to enter a strange harbor after dark.

Tides and Currents

At the western end of Long Island Sound, an 8- to 10-foot rise and fall is to be expected; mean tidal range is about 7.5 feet. The tidal range drops to less than 3 feet as you travel east.

New York Tourism

Long Island Sound

Currents, not to be taken lightly, are strongest at the narrow western and eastern ends of Long Island Sound, reaching maximum velocity—up to 4 knots—at The Race and Plum Gut to the east. They taper off to half a knot in mid-sound but run hard around points and shoals. In general, the flood sets westerly and the ebb sets easterly. Riding a fair current can improve your cruising time substantially and make the trip more comfortable.

Aids to Navigation

Markers on Long Island Sound are frequent, with many lighthouses, both mid-channel and ashore, offering easy-to-locate reference points. Most rocks and reefs are well-charted and marked. Even in moderate fog—most prevalent at the Sound's eastern end during July and August—navigation is not too difficult. Heavy fog, which might greet the mariner several mornings a year throughout the Sound, can be thick enough to be dangerous even to experienced mariners. The Sound has an excellent overlapping system of fog signals, and it is well-charted. Compass and GPS courses along with accurate log keeping, however, are absolutely necessary in these conditions. Make sure to account for current in all courses.

The Direct Route East

NAVIGATION: For the hurried transient boater trying to make time through Long Island Sound, the navigation is straightforward. From the Throgs Neck Bridge at the Sound's western entrance, a GPS or compass course will lead you roughly northeast past the Sound's first important aid to navigation, Stepping Stones Light (pass on the north side), near City Island. Execution Rocks Lighthouse, which appears next, can be left on either hand. At Execution Rocks, the course changes to almost due east (magnetic), straight down the Sound to the midpoint of Stratford Shoal Lighthouse, about 30 nautical miles away. The course remains due east through the widest part of the Sound, almost 20 nautical miles across.

On the south side of Long Island Sound, called the North Shore of Long Island, the mariner will find large natural harbors with ample facilities and room to anchor. Hempstead Harbor, Oyster Bay and Huntington Harbor offer complete cruising grounds for small boats, which never have to leave the mouth of the harbor.

On the Connecticut shore, frequent small harbors cover the coast, along with numerous islands, rock outcroppings and river entrances. Marinas are ample, but are normally crowded with local boats. Advance reservations are necessary for dockside space. Many harbors are dominated by large elaborate yacht clubs, such as Larchmont, Indian Harbor in Greenwich and Pequot in Southport. Docking at these clubs will require reciprocal privileges from the skipper's home club. ■

North Shore Distances

Nautical Miles (approximate)

LOCATION	BETWEEN POINTS	CUMULATIVE
Throgs Neck Bridge	0	
City Island	3	3
New Rochelle	5	8
Mamaroneck	4	12
Greenwich	8	20
Stamford	6	26
South Norwalk	11	37
Stratford	6	43
New Haven	15	58
Guilford	17	75
Connecticut River:		
Saybrook	17	92
Essex	8	100
New London	14	114
Fishers Island	5	119
Mystic	5	124

South Shore Distances

Nautical Miles (approximate)

LOCATION	BETWEEN POINTS	CUMULATIVE
Throgs Neck Bridge	0	
Little Neck Bay	1	1
Manhasset Bay	4	5
Port Washington	2	7
Hempstead Harbor	6	13
Glen Cove	1	14
Oyster Bay Harbor	11	25
Huntington Bay	6	31
Huntington Harbor	2	33
Northport Harbor	4	37
Stony Brook	14	51
Port Jefferson	8	59
Mount Sinai	5	64
Mattituck	22	86
Orient Point	18	104
Montauk Point	24	128
Block Island	13	141

Cross-Sound Distances

The table below is a selection of major cruising stops on Long Island Sound and the distances between them. It is not a complete list of ports and is intended solely as a guide to cruise planning. All distances have been figured along the most direct course consistent with safe, normal navigation. All figures are approximate. Actual mileage will depend on variations of course, speed, boat, weather, currents and other cruising conditions.

FROM	MILES TO:	NAUTICAL	STATUTE
CITY ISLAND (off Belden Pt.)	Stamford	17	19
	Stratford	40	46
	Clinton	64	73
	Saybrook Point	79	91
	New London	85	98
	Mystic	89	102
	Oyster Bay Harbor	17	19
	Huntington Bay	20	23
	Port Jefferson	33	38
	Mattituck Inlet	54	62
	Orient Point	75	86
STAMFORD (East Branch, past hurricane barrier)	City Island	17	19
	Stratford	27	31
	Clinton	54	62
	Saybrook Point	56	64
	New London	75	86
	Mystic	73	84
	Oyster Bay Harbor	9	10
	Huntington Bay	10	11
	Port Jefferson	24	28
	Mattituck Inlet	45	52
	Orient Point	61	70
STRATFORD (2 miles up from outer breakwater light)	City Island	40	46
	Stamford	27	31
	Clinton	31	36
	Saybrook Point	39	45
	New London	53	61
	Mystic	57	66
	Oyster Bay Harbor	30	34
	Huntington Bay	25	28
	Port Jefferson	15	17
	Mattituck Inlet	28	32
	Orient Point	42	48
CLINTON (Cedar Island)	City Island	64	73
	Stamford	54	62
	Stratford	31	36
	Saybrook Point	11	13
	New London	25	29
	Mystic	30	34
	Oyster Bay Harbor	51	59
	Huntington Bay	47	54
	Port Jefferson	32	37
	Mattituck Inlet	15	17
SAYBROOK POINT	City Island	79	91
	Stamford	56	64
	Stratford	39	45
	Clinton	11	13
	New London	17	19
	Mystic	20	23
	Oyster Bay Harbor	61	70
	Huntington Bay	56	64
	Port Jefferson	40	46
	Mattituck Inlet	20	23
	Orient Point	9	10
NEW LONDON (abeam of Shaw Cove)	City Island	85	98
	Stamford	75	86
	Stratford	53	61
	Clinton	25	29
	Saybrook Point	17	19
	Mystic	12	14
	Oyster Bay Harbor	74	85
	Huntington Bay	70	81
	Port Jefferson	59	68
	Mattituck Inlet	34	39
	Orient Point	15	17
MYSTIC (abeam of Shaw Cove)	City Island	89	102
	Stamford	73	84
	Stratford	57	66
	Clinton	30	34
	Saybrook Point	20	23
	New London	12	14
	Oyster Bay Harbor	78	90
	Huntington Bay	75	86
	Port Jefferson	58	67
	Mattituck Inlet	35	40
	Orient Point	16	18
OYSTER BAY HARBOR (off Plum Point)	City Island	17	19
	Stamford	9	10
	Stratford	30	34
	Clinton	51	59
	Saybrook Point	61	70
	New London	74	85
	Mystic	78	90
	Huntington Bay	9	10
	Port Jefferson	25	29
	Mattituck Inlet	48	55
	Orient Point	64	73
HUNTINGTON BAY (Lloyd Harbor Light)	City Island	20	23
	Stamford	10	11
	Stratford	25	29
	Clinton	47	54
	Saybrook Point	56	64
	New London	70	80
	Mystic	75	86
	Oyster Bay Harbor	9	10
	Port Jefferson	20	23
	Mattituck Inlet	41	47
	Orient Point	58	67
PORT JEFFERSON (2 miles in from jetty light)	City Island	33	38
	Stamford	24	28
	Stratford	15	17
	Clinton	32	37
	Saybrook Point	40	46
	New London	59	68
	Mystic	58	67
	Oyster Bay Harbor	25	29
	Huntington Bay	20	23
	Mattituck Inlet	27	31
	Orient Point	44	51
MATTITUCK INLET (Mattituck Creek)	City Island	54	62
	Stamford	45	52
	Stratford	28	32
	Clinton	15	17
	Saybrook Point	20	23
	New London	34	39
	Mystic	35	40
	Oyster Bay Harbor	48	55
	Huntington Bay	41	47
	Port Jefferson	27	31
	Orient Point	20	23
ORIENT POINT (abeam of light)	City Island	75	86
	Stamford	61	70
	Stratford	42	48
	Clinton	15	17
	Saybrook Point	9	10
	New London	15	17
	Mystic	16	18
	Oyster Bay Harbor	64	73
	Huntington Bay	58	67
	Port Jefferson	44	51
	Mattituck Inlet	20	23

City Island to Port Chester

CHARTS 12363, 12364, 12366, 12367

NEW YORK, CONNECTICUT SHORE

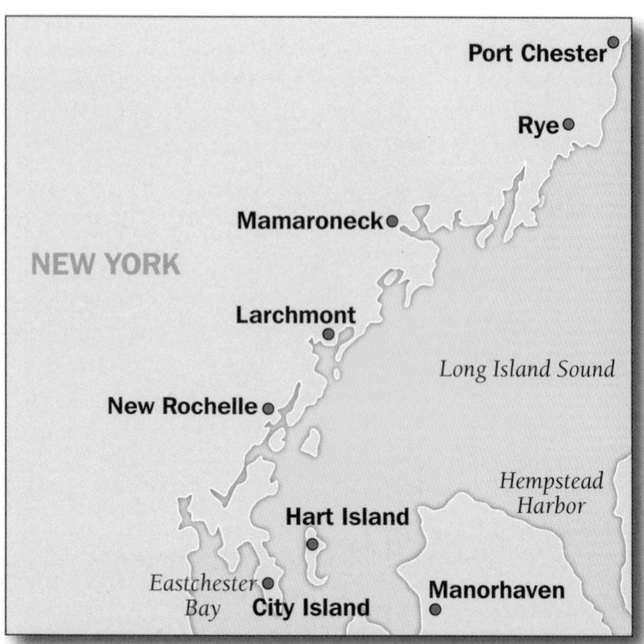

The Throgs Neck Bridge (138-foot fixed vertical clearance) marks the entrance to Long Island Sound on exiting the East River. After crossing under the Throgs Neck Bridge, turn sharply to the north around flashing red bell buoy "48," off the point of Throgs Neck, where the western end of Long Island Sound begins. Stepping Stones, a brownstone house perched on a stone foundation is located to the northeast, and is the first of Long Island Sound's charming and distinctive lighthouses. The "stepping stones" (jagged rocks, dry at low water) project southeast toward the Long Island shore of Long Island Sound and are marked by an occulting green (four seconds) light. Leave Stepping Stones to starboard and continue north.

Eastchester Bay, to the northwest, has a few shoals and rocks, all of which are well-marked. Along the western side of the bay is an almost landlocked cove with excellent protection where many yachts have ridden out storms without damage. The cove is at the entrance to Long Island Sound just inside Locust Point. To reach the cove, run northwest along Throgs Neck, under the north span of Throgs Neck Bridge (123-foot fixed vertical clearance), to the narrow entry, which has 5-foot depths. On the eastern side of Eastchester Bay lies a large moored fleet, and transient

Looking west over the Throgs Neck Bridge with New York City visible on the distant horizon.
(Not to be used for navigation.) WATERWAY GUIDE PHOTOGRPHY

moorings may be available from the several hospitable yacht clubs on the City Island shoreline north of the rock known as Big Tom, marked by red nun buoy "4."

City Island

In the 17th century, American Indians and early settlers knew the island as Great Minneford. It was renamed City Island when a group of developers bought up tracts on the island in the 18th century, planning to develop the place as a rival to New York City for world trade. The hoped-for trade hub did not materialize, but a major yachting center did.

Today this remarkable boating complex contains the first great concentration of yachts on the trip out of the East River to Long Island Sound. Part of New York City's Bronx borough, City Island is devoted to boating services: yacht clubs, marinas, shipyards, sailmakers, electrical and electronics technicians, engine mechanics and marine supply houses. Almost a self-contained community, it is connected to the mainland by a fixed single bridge (12-foot vertical clearance) on the northwest side of the island. City Island's "nautical village" character has been preserved over the years, although some marine businesses have given way to condominiums. Some of the best area boatyards are located on City Island and boaters travel great distances to have work completed on their vessels here.

NAVIGATION: Use Chart 12364. City Island can serve as a great stopover to refuel and/or time your transit through the East River and Hell Gate, or to serve as a stop before cruising east through Long Island Sound. Only a few instructions are necessary to approach City Island from Long Island Sound. Most shoals and rocks are buoyed and charted, but do not get too close to the dock-lined, rock-strewn shores. Even local mariners sometimes go astray on the large, menacing rock called Big Tom, west of the island's southern tip.

The clearly marked rock is the center of a triangle created by flashing red buoy "2" to the south, red nun buoy "4" to the west and white and orange can buoy "BT" to the east. Boats staying outside the marked triangle will have no problem, but periodically someone attempts a shortcut or becomes confused by the welter of small fishing vessels obscuring the buoys, and Big Tom claims another victim.

Approaching from the east, access to the eastern side of City Island may be had around Hart Island in either direction, though most skippers will find the route around the southern end more straightforward, especially in poor visibility. The northern passage around Hart Island is generally well-marked, though it has its share of obstructions, and many boats will be unable to circumnavigate City Island because of the restricted clearance (12-foot vertical clearance) of the fixed bridge connecting the north end of the island to the mainland at Rodman Neck. If attempting passage north of Hart Island, watch carefully for Pea Island, East Nonations and Middle Reef, which are all south of Davids Island and not marked.

Dockage: Yacht clubs, boatyards and marinas ring City Island, and a number of them offer accommodations to transient cruisers. On the west side of the island, Stuyvesant Yacht Club has mooring space for members of other clubs for a modest facilities fee. This will include 24-hour launch service ("Stuyvesant Launch" on VHF Channel 72) and use of the club's restaurant, restrooms and showers.

On the east side, Consolidated Yachts Inc. is a long-established, full-service yard with a 60-ton Travelift and a complete range of repair capabilities.

Immediately up-island, South Minneford Yacht Club offers floating slips (finger piers on either side) and clubhouse amenities (ample restrooms and showers) to cruising visitors. Next door, the Minneford Marina has substantial capacity to accommodate visiting boaters on its well-protected floating docks. Repairs can be arranged and a 40-ton lift is on-site. North Minneford Yacht Club and Boat Max make Minneford Marina their home.

Anchorage: You can usually find room to anchor with acceptable depths and holding on either side of City Island with the caveat that both are exposed to the weather and wakes of passing craft. The best protection is at the island's northeastern tip where Hart Island (with a tall radio transmission tower) gives shelter from the north, and two small rocky outcroppings give partial protection from southerly winds across the Sound. On still nights, with no wind to stabilize the boat, you might experience some uncomfortable wallowing. Another anchorage, protected from all

Looking north/northwest over City Island. (Not to be used for navigation.) WATERWAY GUIDE PHOTOGRAPHY

directions but the south, can be found off the northwest corner of City Island, between the bridge and the northerly end of the mooring field.

Anchoring is prohibited north of City Island off of Orchard Beach, which has been carved out of the rocky shore and filled with imported sand for beach goers.

GOIN' ASHORE: **CITY ISLAND, NY**

City Island has been a yacht-building and fitting-out port for almost a century. The greatest yards of their era—Nevins, Minneford, Consolidated and others—turned out legendary sailboats, such as *Bolero* and *Brilliant,* and renowned America's Cup defenders, including *Constitution* and *Intrepid.* After World War II, the local marine industry shifted its attention from custom luxury sailing yachts to lower-end fiberglass recreational boats. Today the island is a major weekend tourist and recreation destination with an overwhelmingly nautical flavor. Summer traffic—on both highway and sea channel—is intense.

Most critical provisioning, marine service establishments and restaurants are within walking distance of the mid-island docks on either side of City Island. Along the length of City Island Avenue, you will find multiple delis, antique shops, museums, galleries, a City Island IGA grocery (385 City Island Ave., 718-885-0881), a coin-operated laundry, pharmacy and a Sunoco station (410 City Island Ave., 718-885-9875), which sells diesel fuel and gasoline. Of particular note for nautical sightseers is Trader John Nautical Antiques (239 City Island Ave., 718-885-1658), well known for its marine "junk" and hard-to-find equipment, and the recently expanded and revitalized City Island Historical Museum (190 Fordham St., 718-885-0008) chronicling the island's colorful maritime and ship-building traditions, including a collection of watercolors of maritime themes and a library of maritime-related books.

Restaurants abound on City Island, with most of them available along the main street in the village. Those that receive particularly high marks from discerning locals include: City Island Lobster House Restaurant for waterfront dining (691 Bridge St., 718-885-1459); the Harbor House (565 City Island Ave., 718-885-1373); the Crab Shanty One (361 City Island Ave., 718-885-1810); Lobster Box (34 City Island Ave., 718-885-1952), a long-time favorite for seafood, with dockage available through North Minneford Yacht Club; Portofino (555 City Island Ave., 718-885-1220) for excellent Northern Italian selections; and Artie's Steak & Seafood (394 City island Ave., 718-885-9885), upscale and consistently first-rate.

ADDITIONAL RESOURCES:

- City Island Chamber of Commerce, **www.cityislandchamber.org**

NEARBY GOLF COURSES:
Pelham Split Rock Golf Courses,
870 Shore Road, Bronx, NY 10464, 718-885-1258

NEARBY MEDICAL FACILITIES:
Medical Group of City Island
340 City Island Ave., Bronx, NY 10464, 718-885-0333

City Island to New Rochelle, NY

CITY ISLAND TO NEW ROCHELLE		Largest Vessel Accommodated	VHF Channel Monitored	Transient Berths / Total Berths	Approach / Dockside Depth (reported)	Floating Docks	Gas / Diesel	Groceries, Ice, Marine Supplies, Snacks	Repairs: Hull, Engine, Propeller	Lift (tonnage), Crane, Rail	1=110V, 2=220V, B=Both, Max Amps	Laundry, Pool, Showers	Pump-Out Station	Nearby: Grocery Store, Motel, Restaurant
		Dockage					Supplies		Services					
1. Consolidated Yachts Inc.	718-885-1900	150		6/75	14/14	F		IM	HEP	L,C	B/50	S		GMR
2. Boat Max at Minneford Marina (Internet Access)	718-885-2000	110	77	40/164	17/10	F		IM	HEP	L40	B/50	S		GMR
3. Minneford Marina (WiFi)	**718-885-2000**	**110**	**77**	**12/164**	**17/10**	**F**		**IM**	**HEP**	**L40**	**B/50**	**S**		**GMR**
4. South Minneford Yacht Club (Internet Access)	718-885-3113	57	69	20/120	14/10	F		GIM	HP	L80	B/50	LS		GMR
5. New York Sailing Center & Yacht Club	718-885-0335								H			S		GMR
6. City Island Yacht Sales	718-885-2300	55	09	3/70	12/8	F	GD	IM	HEP	L30	1/50		P	GMR
7. Stelter Marine Sales	718-885-1300	28		/40	4/4	F		M	HEP		1/30			GR
8. Harlem Yacht Club	718-885-3078	70	72	15/115	8/4	F		I				S		GR
9. Stuyvesant Yacht Club	718-885-9840	40	72		7/6	F		I		L		S		GMR
10. City Island Yacht Club	718-885-2487		72		9/6	F					1/20	S		R
11. New Rochelle Municipal Marina (WiFi)	**914-235-6930**	**50**	**16/09**	**2/325**	**10/10**	**F**	**GD**	**IMS**	**HEP**	**L25**	**B/100**	**LS**	**P**	**GMR**
12. Polychron Marina	914-632-4088	35		/85	5/3	F		I		C	1/30			GR
13. G&R Marine Repair Service	914-632-4020								HEP	L25				
14. Castaways Yacht Club	**914-636-8444**	**75**		**2/100**	**14/7**	**F**	**GD**	**IS**	**HEP**	**L50**	**B/50**	**LPS**		**GMR**
15. Imperial Yacht Club Inc.	914-636-1122	65		/100	14/7	F	GD		HEP	L	B/50	LPS		GMR
16. Wright Island Marina	914-235-8013	65		10/150	11/9	F	GD	I	HP	L50	B/50	LPS	P	GMR
17. Huguenot Yacht Club	914-636-6300	65	73	5/60	16/8			I	P	LC	B/50	LPS		GMR
18. West Harbor Yacht Service	914-636-1524	60		2/30	8/6	F		IM	HEP	L15,C1	1/30	LS		GMR
19. New York Athletic Club	914-738-2700	70			7/7	F			CALL AHEAD					R

Corresponding chart(s) not to be used for navigation. (Internet Access icon) Internet Access (WiFi icon) Wireless Internet Access

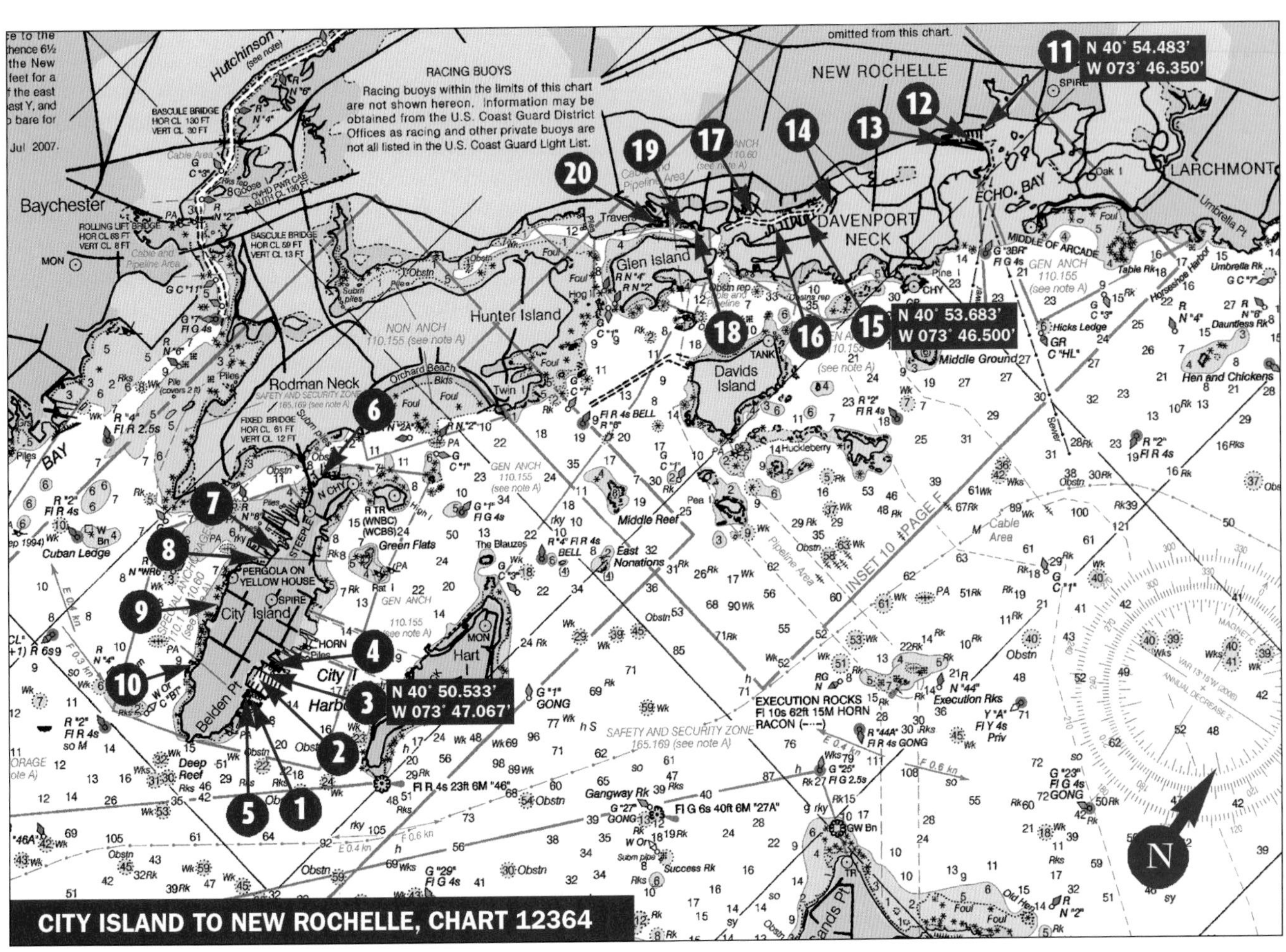

Looking northeast over Glen Island/Davenport Neck. (Not to be used for navigation.) WATERWAY GUIDE PHOTOGRAPHY

New Rochelle

The first city on the Westchester shore is New Rochelle, NY, with two yacht harbors, New Rochelle Harbor and Echo Bay (formerly known as Upper Harbor and Lower Harbor respectively), and one of western Long Island Sound's major landmarks: a tall, angular building topped with a square knob. Towering over the countryside like an enormous capped bottle, it is recognizable from well out on Long Island Sound. Both of New Rochelle's harbors are confined, but busy, and interesting for their constant activity. They are crowded with clubs, parks, marinas and moorings for thousands of widely assorted craft. New Rochelle Harbor is an excellent hurricane hole.

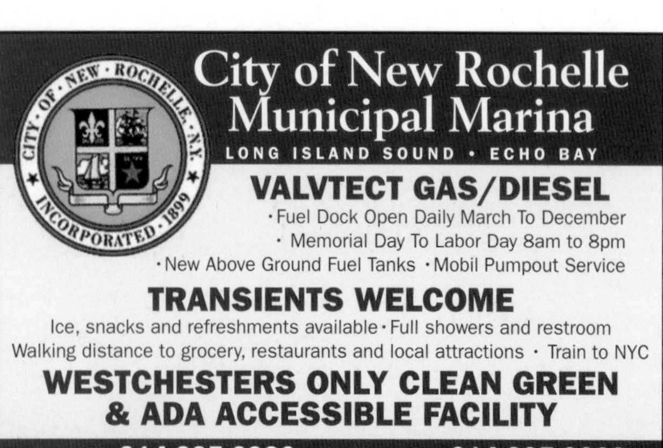

NAVIGATION: Use Chart 12364. Use Kings Point tide tables. For high tide, subtract 16 minutes; for low tide, subtract 18 minutes. The entry to New Rochelle from Long Island Sound is booby-trapped with obstructions and can be confusing to newcomers. Those without local knowledge should arrive before dark. The eastbound cruiser goes in either west (the shorter and more direct route) or east of Hart Island, which has 23-foot-high flashing red light "46" off its southern tip.

Approach to New Rochelle's three entries should be made with the chart close at hand. The westernmost approach to New Rochelle's Lower Harbor is the least used and requires local knowledge.

New Rochelle Harbor

NAVIGATION: Use Chart 12364. A normally well-maintained channel serves New Rochelle Harbor. Controlling depth is 8 feet as far as the head of the harbor, where shoals tend to develop.

If you enter from Long Island Sound northeast between Davenport Neck and Davids Island, pay close attention to the chart inset (page F on the small-craft chart) through these rock-strewn waters. Exit from New Rochelle to Long Island Sound by way of Huckleberry Island. An inside channel past Pine Island requires local knowledge.

A second entrance to New Rochelle Harbor that is more convenient for those coming from the Throgs Neck area is via a channel to the west of Davids Island

Looking northwest over New Rochelle. (Not to be used for navigation.) WATERWAY GUIDE PHOTOGRAPHY

and east of Goose Island. Pass between Corning Rock (green can buoy "9") and Aunt Phebe Rock (flashing red "10").

Dockage: New Rochelle's main eastern branch, inside Davenport Neck, is crowded and narrow, but protected, with plenty of marinas. Although some are restricted to local craft, several welcome transients and offer swimming pools and tennis courts. Castaways Yacht Club is a full-service facility and a Sunseeker Yachts distributor.

Wright Island Marina offers overnight slips, dockage for diners at its waterfront restaurant/bar, fuel, repairs, laundry, cable television and a swimming pool.

Located in well-sheltered waters at Davenport Neck is Imperial Yacht Club, only five minutes from New Rochelle proper. Imperial Yacht Club has all fuels, a lift, hull and propeller repairs, restrooms, showers and a pool. The facility is also only minutes away from motels, restaurants and grocery facilities.

G&R Marine Repair Service works on all marine engines and is an authorized Crusader, Onan, Westerbeke and Kohler dealer. Marinas on the north shore of the harbor are about a half-mile's walk to an assortment of stores on Shore Road, including a supermarket.

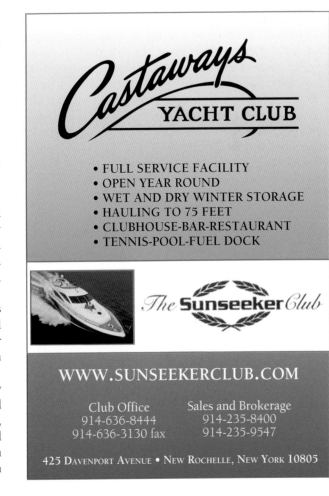

The southern branch of New Rochelle Harbor, below Neptune Island and its bascule bridge (13-foot closed vertical clearance), is cluttered with permanent moorings, so there is no room to anchor. Huguenot and Glen Island yacht clubs and the New York Athletic Club maintain extensive docks and handsome shore installations on

Neptune Island and on Travers Island, with guest slips and moorings available. In a storm situation, anchor west of the New York Athletic Club's main clubhouse in the Olympic Rowing Lagoon.

Anchorage: There is no anchorage available right in New Rochelle Harbor, but you do have two options. The first and preferred anchorage is in 14 feet of water just outside the harbor between the large white abandoned casino building on Glen Island's northeast corner and to the northwest of Goose Island. This anchorage is protected from all but north to northeast winds. Turn west into the anchorage after passing north of green can buoy "9," taking care to stay clear of the rocky shoal on the northeast corner of Goose Island. The second option is to stay south of Glen Island and turn into the anchorage lying to the southwest of red nun buoy "6."

Echo Bay (New Rochelle)

NAVIGATION: Use Chart 12364. Crowded Echo Bay is northeast of New Rochelle Harbor. It has an outer harbor open to the southwest and an inner harbor protected from all directions.

North of Huckleberry Island is the approach to Echo Bay, between Middle Ground (marked by green can buoy "1M") and 6-foot-deep Hicks Ledge (marked by green and red can buoy "HL"). During the summer, a private green light, on a prominent flagstaff on the point midway between Beaufort Point and Duck Point, is on a range with the Bailey Rock green flashing light to lead you between Hicks Ledge and Middle Ground into Echo Bay.

Once in Echo Bay, pass between red nun buoy "6" to starboard and green can buoy "5" to port at Duck Point, and then proceed to Beaufort Point, where you will leave red nun buoys "8" and "10" to starboard. Turn to port around Beaufort Point; there are 2-foot depths outside the channel. There are beaches near Duck Point, and around Beaufort Point is the narrow, sheltered and slip-lined inner harbor of Echo Bay.

Dockage: There are both a private marina and a large municipal marina that almost always have slips for transients. Fuel, laundry, pump-out service and showers are available at the New Rochelle Municipal Marina. They also feature wireless Internet.

Anchorage: On hot evenings, a cool, breezy (though exposed) anchorage usually can be found farther offshore off Huckleberry Island's northern shore, between flashing red buoy "2" and a log house on the shore. A better anchorage can be found in Echo Bay just south of the line between flashing green buoy "3BR" and green can buoy "5." Holding is good and well-protected from everything but the northeast to southeast.

GOIN' ASHORE:

NEW ROCHELLE, NY

New Rochelle was first settled in 1689 by Huguenots escaping religious persecution in France. Their landing site was the present day Hudson Park. Later, New Rochelle was the home of American Revolution philosopher Thomas Paine. His famous quotation, "These are the times that try men's souls," came from his book "Common Sense," which played a significant role in the lead-up to the Revolution. In the 1930s and '40s, New Rochelle was an active summer colony for New York actors. The song "Forty Five Minutes From Broadway," from George M. Cohen's play "Yankee Doodle Dandy," was a reference to New Rochelle. Eddie Foy Park is named after the actor.

The former Glen Island Casino, which sits prominently on the main channel into New Rochelle Harbor, was famous nationwide in the 1930s and early 1940s. Glen Miller debuted here, as did Doris Day. Live radio broadcasts from Glen Island introduced the rest of the country to the music of the Dorseys, Charlie Barnet and Ozzie Nelson. The imposition of gasoline and tire rationing in World War II, however, cut patronage, and the casino never regained its former glory. Despite its height above the water, the building's lower level was severely damaged by the nor'easters of 1992 and 1993.

It is about a 10-minute walk along Pelham Road from the marinas on New Rochelle Harbor and Echo Bay to a number of restaurants (New Rochelle has over 75 restaurants), Pelham Laundry (733 Pelham Road, 914-636-3881) and a grocery, Met Foods (430 Pelham Road, 914-636-0720). There are also restaurants overlooking both New Rochelle Harbor and Echo Bay. Sounds from Dudley's Parkview Restaurant (94 Hudson Park Rd., 914-235-4445) on Echo Bay can be heard until the wee hours of the morning. There are too many to name all but a few of the local favorites: Agostinos Italian Ristorante (969 Main St., 914-235-6019); Blue Ribbon West Indian Restaurant (6 Rochelle Place, 914-654-0470); Avenue Deli Café (74 North Ave., 914-632-5624); and Alfredo's Pizza Café (23 Division St., 914-235-2828). Post Marine (65 River St., 914-235-9800) and the post office are located in town about 1.5 miles inland. For taxi service, call Blue Bird Taxi at 914-632-0909.

ADDITIONAL RESOURCES:

- City of New Rochelle, **www.newrochelleny.com**

NEARBY GOLF COURSES:
Pelham Split Rock Golf Courses,
870 Shore Road, Bronx, NY 10464, 718-885-1258

NEARBY MEDICAL FACILITIES:
Sound Shore Medical Center,
16 Guion Place, New Rochelle, NY 10801,
914-632-5000, **www.ssmc.org**

Larchmont Harbor

CT NY

NAVIGATION: Use Chart 12364. Larchmont Harbor is protected from the east by a stone breakwater but open to the south and southwest. To enter, pass either side of Hen and Chickens Ledge. If you pass to the north, stay below Umbrella Rock, which is marked by green can buoy "7." You can also go between the breakwater's 26-foot-tall flashing red light "2" and the string of marked rocks and reefs to the west. Do not approach the launch dock—a marked reef lies in

Larchmont, Mamaroneck, NY

LARCHMONT TO MAMARONECK		Largest Vessel Accommodated	VHF Channel Monitored	Transient Berths / Total Berths	Approach / Dockside Depth (reported)	Floating Docks	Gas / Diesel	Groceries, Ice, Marine Supplies, Snacks	Repairs: Hull, Engine, Propeller	Lift (tonnage), Crane, Rail	1=110V, 2=220V, B=Both, Max Amps	Laundry, Pool, Showers	Pump-Out Station	Nearby: Grocery Store, Motel, Restaurant
		Dockage					Supplies		Services					
1. Larchmont Yacht Club	914-834-2440		72	10/270	12/7	F	GD	I		L		PS	P	G
2. McMichael Yacht Yard	914-698-4957	50	71	/15	10/10	F			HEP	C15	1/30			R
3. Derecktor Shipyards	914-698-5020	150		5/	12/12	F		M	HEP	L110,C1	B/100			GMR
4. Brewer Post Road Boat Yard ☐ WiFi	**914-698-0295**	**65**	**19**	**2/50**	**10/9**	**F**	**GD**	**IM**	**HEP**	**L50,C**	**B/50**	**S**		**GR**
5. Harbor Island Municipal Marina	914-777-7744	50	16	2/400	6/6	F		M			1/		P	GMR
6. Nichols Yacht Yard Inc.	914-698-6065	90		/165	10/10	F		M	HEP	L50	1/50	S	P	MR
7. McMichael Rushmore Yard	914-381-2100	40	71	/50	10/5	F			EP	C15	1/30			MR
8. Mamaroneck Beach and Yacht Club	914-698-1130	100	10	10/60	6/7	F				C	B/50	PS		MR

Corresponding chart(s) not to be used for navigation. ☐Internet Access WiFi Wireless Internet Access

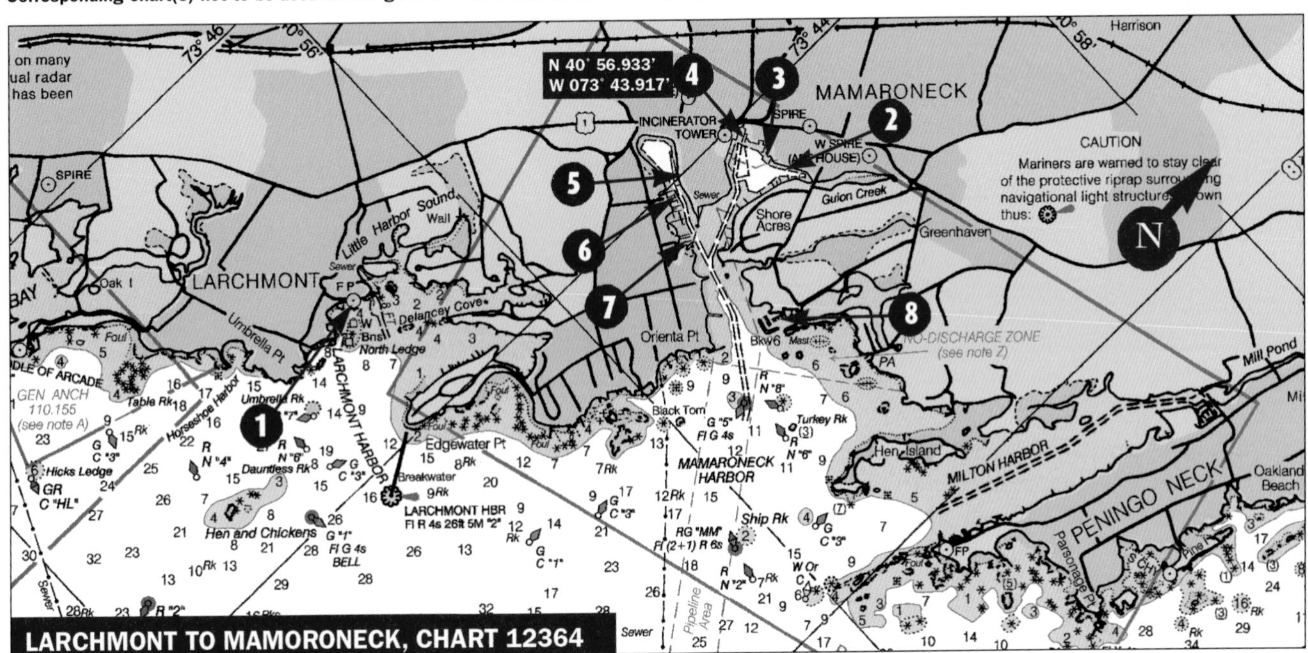

LARCHMONT TO MAMORONECK, CHART 12364

front of it. Skirt the shoals along Satans Toe inside the breakwater; keep clear of North Ledge also, which is bare at half tide, and has unmarked rocks in the center. East of Larchmont, the shore along Satans Toe and Delancey Point is rocky and shoal. Handsome estates, overlooking Long Island Sound, line the shore.

Dockage: Larchmont Harbor is a small cove with a big yacht club and ample yachting history. The yacht club is headquarters for Larchmont Race Week in mid-July, drawing hundreds of competing sailboats. One of Long Island Sound's oldest clubs, Larchmont welcomes accredited members of other yacht clubs for overnight stays or for meals on its big porch overlooking the fleet. The harbor is typically crowded, but guest moorings are usually available. Launches monitor VHF Channel 72. If you are lucky, you will get to ride in one of two 1927 Nevins wooden launches.

Anchorage: Anchorage is scarce in Larchmont. Some alternatives would be to pick up a guest mooring, move farther west to the Glen Island area or east to either Mamaroneck or Milton Harbor. On a calm night, you can also try anchoring either west of Hen and Chickens Ledge, near Horseshoe Harbor, or on the edge of the mooring field behind the breakwater. Both anchorages are exposed from the southeast through the west.

GOIN' ASHORE: LARCHMONT, NY

Larchmont took its name from the majestic trees that line the shady, meandering roads along the small harbor. The stately homes, with their very broad porches, complement a walk through the neighborhood. Manor Park, on the bay, is a short walk from the Larchmont Yacht Club and a lovely destination when the need to get some exercise becomes apparent. If you are visiting from another yacht club and are able to obtain a guest mooring at Larchmont Yacht Club, you will need a jacket to dine in the yacht club dining room.

John Richbell originally purchased the land from the chieftains Wappaquewam and Manhatahan and started a trading business with the West Indies. By 1872 Larchmont

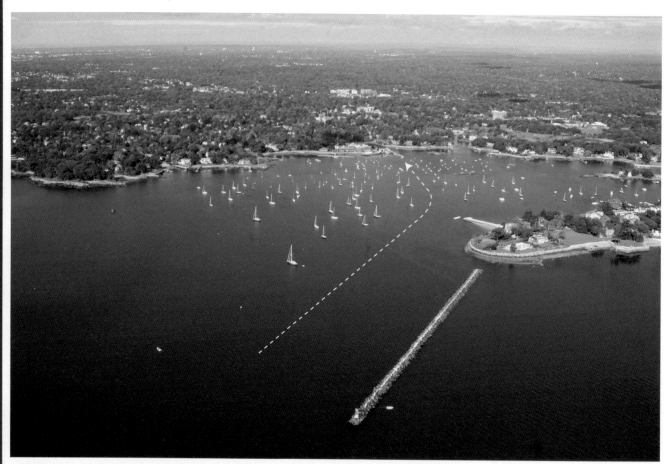

Looking northwest over Larchmont Harbor. (Not to be used for navigation.) WATERWAY GUIDE PHOTOGRAPHY

had become a summer resort and land could be purchased for $3,000 per acre. The land was then divided into lots for homes. Larchmont Yacht Club was established in 1880 by the many people spending the summer away from New York.

The town of Larchmont stretches along the Boston Post Road and is a good walk from the yacht club. The usual bank, antiques stores, galleries, a hardware store, a pharmacy and grocery stores are available in the downtown area.

Larchmont is one square mile with many good restaurants, several of which are within walking distance from the harbor, including: Larchmont Tavern (104 Chatsworth Ave., 914-834-9821); (914-834-9821); Chat 19, an American Grill with live music (19 Chatsworth Ave., 914-833-8871); Hunan Larchmont for Chinese (1961 Palmer Ave., 914-833-0400); Ristorante La Sala, fine Italian cuisine (2047 Boston Post Road, 914-833-7900); Bellizzi Italian Restaurant for Southern Italian and Pizza in a family setting (1272 Boston Post Road, 914-833-5800); Encore Bistro Francais Bistro Café (22 Chatsworth Ave., 914-833-1661) and Kearns Larchmont Deli (135 Chatsworth Ave., 914-834-1022).

The town is lovely to walk around and during the summer months there are concerts and art festivals in the park. The Concerts-in-the-Park series runs from mid July, every Thursday during the month of July night at 7:15 p.m. in Flint Park. The town offers several wine and spirits stores, with an excellent selection of wines. For taxi service, call 914-834-4000.

ADDITIONAL RESOURCES:

- Village of Larchmont, **www.villageoflarchmont.org**

NEARBY GOLF COURSES:

Saxon Woods Golf Course, 315 Old Mamaroneck Road, Scarsdale, NY 10583, 914-231-3461

NEARBY MEDICAL FACILITIES:

Sound Shore Medical Center of Westchester, 16 Guion Place, New Rochelle, NY 10801, 914-632-5000, **www.ssmc.org**

Mamaroneck Harbor

NAVIGATION: Use Chart 12364. Make your entrance from Long Island Sound at "42nd Street"—flashing red bell buoy "42." Head northwest about one mile for flashing green buoy "5" at Outer Steamboat Rock, leaving Ship Rock's flashing (red) red-over-green buoy "MM" to starboard. Round Outer Steamboat Rock in the center of the outer harbor for the narrow channel to the inner harbors. The 4-mph speed limit is strictly enforced. At the junction buoy, channels lead to either side of Harbor Island. The Mamaroneck Harbor flashing (red) red-over-green buoy "MM" was reported extinguished on several occasions over the years. Boaters should report deficient or inoperative aids to navigation to the closest Coast Guard station.

Looking northwest over Mamaroneck Harbor. (Not to be used for navigation.) WATERWAY GUIDE PHOTOGRAPHY

Dockage: Mamaroneck is a most hospitable harbor for transient boaters. The village's busy main street ends at the harbor, so services and entertainment are only a short walk away. Mamaroneck also has courtesy and guest docks for transients.

In addition to the outer harbor, there are two inner basins—West Basin and East Basin. At the end of the East Basin, close to the center of town, is a long floating dock adjacent to a launching ramp. Brief tie-ups are allowed here, when ramp conditions permit, for a walk into town. The old-fashioned Brewers True Value Hardware Store (161 E. Boston Post Road, 914-698-3232) stocks an incredible variety of goods.

The West Basin is home to Harbor Island Municipal Marina. Transients can be accommodated at the floating dock just offshore from the marina. Space is on a first-come, first-served basis. The harbormaster monitors VHF Channel 16 and is located in the large building east of the float.

Brewer Post Road Boat Yard and the other private marinas welcome transients on a space-available basis.

Anchorage: Although somewhat exposed, it is possible to anchor in the outer harbor in 8- to 10-foot depths northeast of Outer Steamboat Rock, avoiding Turkey Rock and the unnamed rock marked by red nun buoy "8."

Milton Harbor

NAVIGATION: Use Chart 12364. The "42nd Street" buoy (flashing red "42") is also the entrance marker for Milton Harbor in Rye, NY. Just east of Ship Rock, (marked by flashing red (2+1), red-over-green buoy "MM"), head north-northeast between green can buoy "5" and red nun buoy "6," marking the start of the harbor channel. According to NOAA Chart 12364, the channel has a 4-foot centerline depth. Leave West Rock and Scotch Caps, a line of reefs, well to starboard. The harbor is exposed to the southwest.

Dockage: The town-run marina is usually full, but will try to accommodate transients. Stores are within a short walk. American Yacht Club, located on the point, welcomes members of affiliated yacht clubs and may have guest moorings available.

Anchorage: There are still places to anchor in Milton Harbor, but watch your swing and the depth (tidal range here is about 7 feet). You can dinghy to the town marina if you anchor out, but there may be a time limit on how long you can stay tied up.

Port Chester/Byram River

East of Manursing Island, with its wildlife preserve, beach clubs and estates, lies Port Chester Harbor, which is enclosed by the towns of Rye and Port Chester. Supplies are a cab ride away from the harbor, but a short walk from the Byram River, which feeds into the harbor.

Rye and Port Chester, NY

RYE AND PORT CHESTER		Largest Vessel Accommodated	VHF Channel Monitored	Transient Berths / Total Berths	Approach / Dockside Depth (reported)	Floating Docks	Gas / Diesel	Groceries, Ice, Marine Supplies, Snacks	Repairs: Hull, Engine, Propeller	Lift (tonnage), Crane, Rail	1=110V, 2=220V, B=Both, Max Amps	Laundry, Pool, Showers	Pump-Out Station	Nearby: Grocery Store, Motel, Restaurant
		Dockage					Supplies		Services					
1. Shongut Marine	914-736-1707	38		1/22	6/10	F			HP		1/30			GR
2. Tide Mill Yacht Basin	914-967-2995	70	68	2/55	7/8	F	GD	M	HEP	L35	B/50	S		
3. Rudy's Tackle Barn	203-531-5928	27			12/3			IM						R

Corresponding chart(s) not to be used for navigation. Internet Access Wireless Internet Access

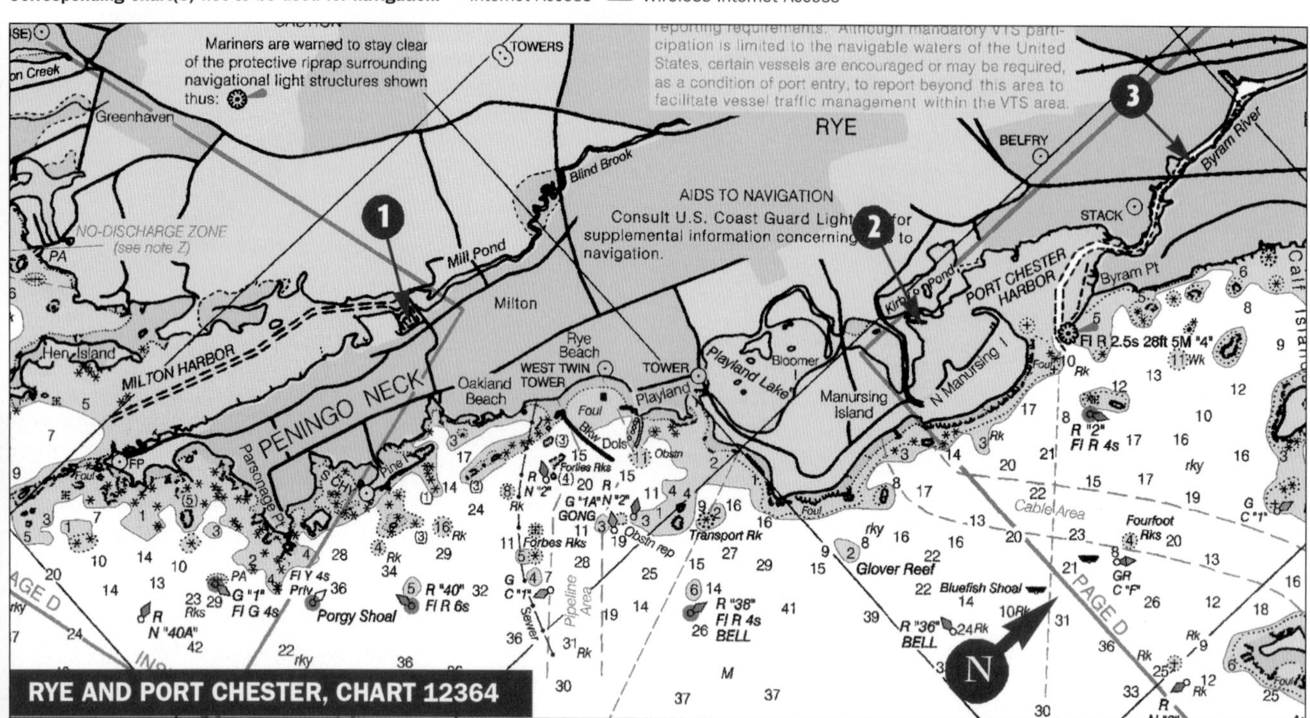

RYE AND PORT CHESTER, CHART 12364

Looking northwest over Port Chester. (Not to be used for navigation.) WATERWAY GUIDE PHOTOGRAPHY

This quiet harbor is lined with handsome homes, and some anchorage can be found in deep water south of the flashing green light.

NAVIGATION: Use Chart 12364. Do not cut the buoys marking Manursing Island Reef (green can buoy "3") and Great Captain Rocks (flashing red buoy "2") just outside the breakwater. Farther out in the harbor, watch out for two large barge moorings near the Fourfoot Rocks green-over-red can buoy "F." One is an easy-to-spot large white cylinder. The other is a dark-colored sphere, low in the water and hard to see, with colored lines streaming from it. It is about midway between the white mooring and the Fourfoot Rocks buoy. The buoy and the moorings are unlit, so approach after sunset is not advised.

Dockage: To port heading upriver, a privately marked channel leads to a small marina with an 18th-century building that has been photographed and painted countless times. The marina will take transients if there is space, but a cab ride is necessary to reach any facilities.

To starboard, outside the mouth of the Byram River, lies the Port Chester Yacht Club. This small hospitable club has guest moorings, but there is usually nobody around except on weekends. A restaurant just inside the river mouth will usually allow complimentary overnight dockage if you have dinner there. Again, supplies are a cab ride away.

Byram River is a surprise. The lower river is tree-lined and scenic, but as you round the bend under the highway bridge (60-foot fixed vertical clearance), the river suddenly becomes an industrial creek, with barges, bulkheads and small marinas hugging the banks.

Downtown Port Chester has been revitalized after losing much of its industrial base in the 1970s and '80s. The downtown area now boasts Restaurant Row and many retailers including Costco (1 Westchester Avenue, 914-935-3108), Bed Bath and Beyond (25 Waterfront Place, 914-937-9098), Marshall's (20 Waterfront Place, 914-690-9380) and a Super Stop and Shop grocery with pharmacy (25 Waterfront Place, 914-937-7318). Byram, CT, is on the right bank, also with some stores. The small marinas will take transients if they can.

Cruising Options

Ahead lies the entire Connecticut shore of Long Island, some 80 miles of exquisite yachting, snug harbors, beautiful scenery and extensive marine facilities. ■

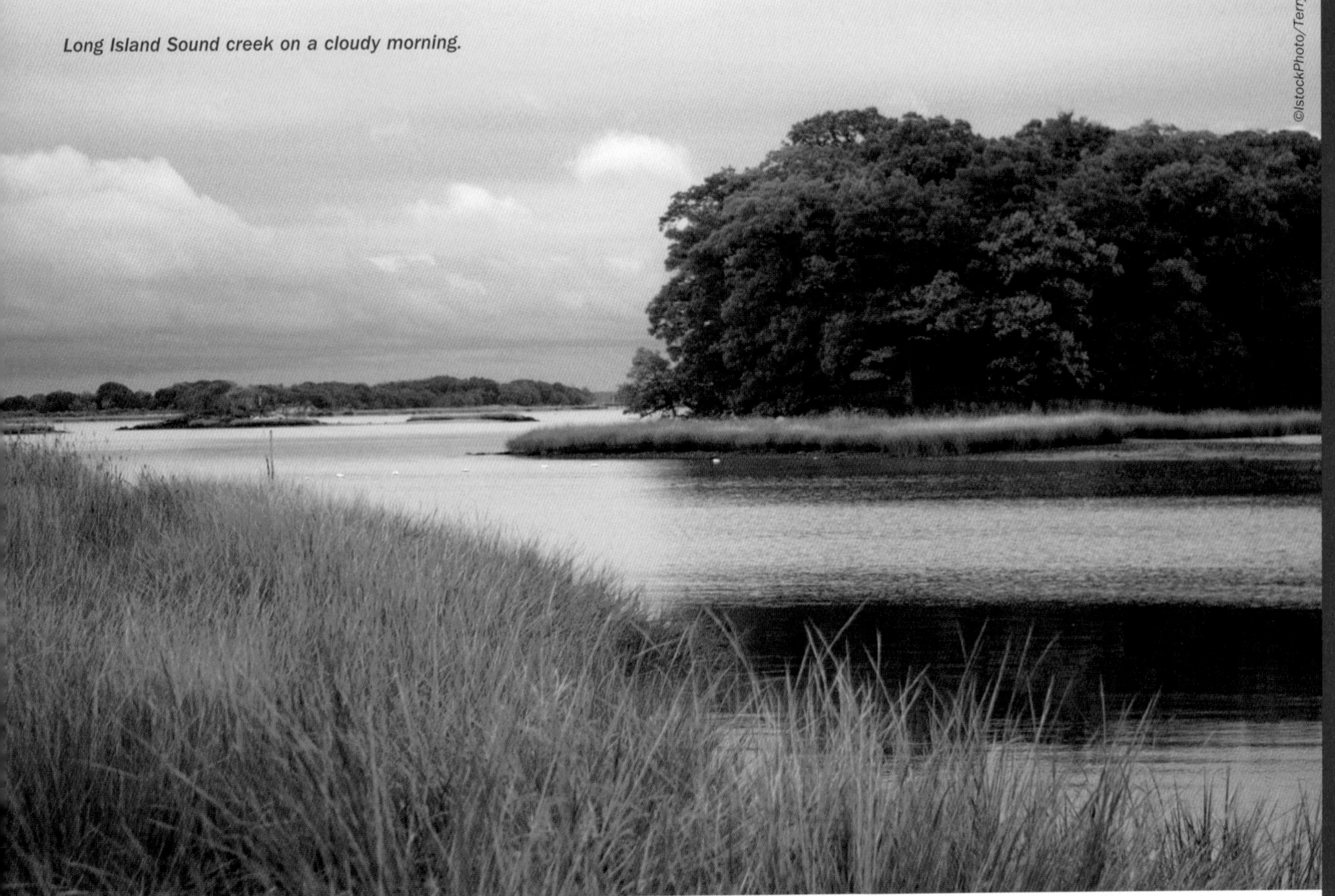

Long Island Sound creek on a cloudy morning.

©IstockPhoto/TerryJ

Greenwich to Bridgeport

CHARTS 12363, 12364, 12367, 12368, 12369

■ CONNECTICUT SHORE

The 80 miles of Connecticut shore begins at Port Chester, NY, on the eastern bank of the Byram River. Connecticut offers snug harbors, industrial ports, summer resorts, many beautiful offshore islands and some amazing boating facilities. Harbors here are close together, with varying accommodations for cruising boats. Some are equipped with marinas, shore diversions and services; others offer anchorages in remote surroundings. The major harbors are well-buoyed and easy to enter, but all require caution and close attention to the chart, as the Connecticut shores abound with rocks and ledges.

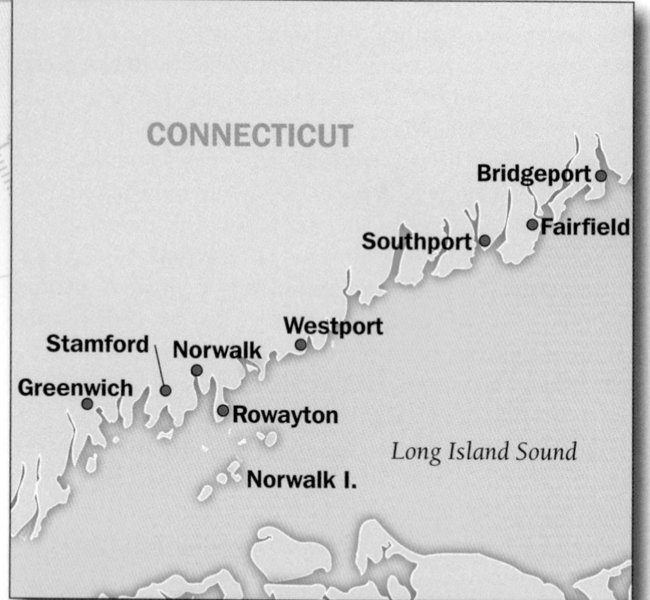

Greenwich

The first harbor in Connecticut is Greenwich, an excellent layover port, offering all the amenities characteristic of a gilt-edged East Coast yachting center. Main Street is a short walk from the harbor. There are many shops offering everything from designer clothes to stationery and excellent restaurants ranging from cafes, bistros and delis to gourmet continental. Some large and famous sailing yachts and an impressive row of waterfront estates complete the picture of Greenwich, including the much-photographed retreat of Boss Tweed, who sparked the New York movement to this area. New York City politicos were enticed to wear nautical finery and embrace the new and rapidly growing sport of yachting on the protected waters in front of this retreat. The Greenwich Marine Police (203-622-8044) are helpful but will charge a fee for a non-emergency tow. Indian Harbor Yacht Club, in Greenwich Harbor, established in 1889, is one of the oldest and most famous on Long Island Sound.

Byram Harbor, Calf Islands

This westernmost of the Greenwich harbors offers many moorings, a pretty park and beach and a municipal boat club, but has few amenities for the transient mariner.

Dockage: The Byram Marina has 100 moorings for vessels up to 36 feet carrying up to 7-foot drafts. The dockmaster can be reached at 203-532-9019 from 10 a.m. to 5:30 p.m. Many of these moorings are assigned to seasonal users, but transients are welcome. All four Greenwich marinas operate from April 15 to Nov. 15.

Anchorage: There are two fine anchorages in the vicinity of the Calf Islands, one on either side of the reef that connects them. Base your selection on the forecasted direction of the wind and waves, and do not forget the 6- to 7-foot tidal range when choosing your spot.

The northern Calf Island is privately owned, but reportedly you can beach the dinghy on the east shore and go ashore for a swim. Stay in this area only and remove all trash when you depart. Southern Calf Island is owned by the Greenwich YMCA (203-869-3381). A small dock with a landing float is on the north side of the island where you can drop off passengers; beach the dinghy on the small beach nearby. Big boats cannot get close to the island. The YMCA charges a landing fee to use the trails.

Captain Islands

Less than two miles offshore are the three Captain Islands, marking the southern edge of Captain Harbor. Great Captain, a half-mile long, has a popular beach, a couple of semi-protected anchorages and an early 19th-century stone lighthouse. Stay clear of a diamond-shaped marker over a sunken wreck 40 feet off the beach. The Greenwich Ferry, serving Great Captain and Little Captain islands, is only for Greenwich residents. Wee Captain, the last of the three islands, is private. A measured-mile course (60-240 degrees true) with charted shore ranges runs from the tip of Great Captain to the tip of Little Captain, but recent reports indicate that the markers are obscured by trees.

Greenwich Harbor

NAVIGATION: Use Chart 12364. Enter Greenwich Harbor from Long Island Sound via Captain Harbor. Newcomers to this area should use the eastern approach, through water comparatively free of rocks and shoals. Honor both the

Looking northwest over Greenwich. (Not to be used for navigation.) WATERWAY GUIDE PHOTOGRAPHY

flashing gong (green buoy "1") and can (green can buoy "1A") marking Hen and Chickens. The yacht club is to starboard when entering the harbor, with its fleet at moorings to the south.

Dockage: Greenwich Harbor, close to downtown Greenwich and the railroad station, is dominated by the Indian Harbor Yacht Club (203-869-2484), which offers transient moorings to members and reciprocal yacht clubs only. If you are a guest at Indian Harbor Yacht Club, you will need a jacket to dine in the dining room. Fuel, bait, fine dining and overnight accommodations are available ashore, but you must go farther past the club for these services. Delamar Hotel, at the head of the harbor, has alongside space for transients. Several popular restaurants are close to the upper, eastern side of the harbor.

GOIN' ASHORE: GREENWICH, CT

On Bluff Island, off Greenwich Point, are mooring holes claimed to have been cut by the Norsemen around 1100. They inserted poles into the holes to which they tied their boats. This allowed them to make a hasty departure if the natives became unfriendly. Verrazano, an Italian explorer working for the French Crown, was the first European to visit these waters in 1534.

Greenwich has a rich and diverse history. When the Puritans wanted to settle in this area in 1640, they bought the land from the American Indians for 25 coats. During the American Revolution, Greenwich was a garrison town with the British and Americans taking turns occupying the town. The seven-year war took a dreadful toll on the area, destroying many homes, crops and lives. In 1848, with the arrival of the railroad, the Irish came to work on the tracks and many stayed. After the Civil War, Greenwich became a resort for those wishing to escape the heat of Manhattan, and people such as the Gimbels and Rockefellers amassed huge tracts of land to build estates for which the area later became famous.

The Bruce Museum (203-869-0376, 1 Museum Drive, open Tuesday through Saturday, 10 a.m. to 5 p.m. and Sunday 1 p.m. to 5 p.m.) charges a small entry fee but is free every Tuesday. The museum is a family arts and science museum housed in a Victorian manor. The Natural History section, with exhibits that visitors can touch, brings to life the area's natural development. The museum has several other sections devoted to art, especially the decorative arts.

Greenwich is considered by many to be the dining capital of Connecticut, with restaurants such as Jean-Louis (203-622-8450, 61 Lewis St.), which is listed on the top ten romantic restaurants list in the United States by Forbes Traveler and is known for its fine classic French dining. You can also can also order beautiful dinners to go off the regular menu. The Boxcar Cantina (203-661-4774, 44 Old Field Point Road) is good for southwest, Mexican, American and American Indian food

Greenwich to Stamford, CT

GREENWICH TO STAMFORD		Largest Vessel Accommodated	VHF Channel Monitored	Transient Berths / Total Berths	Approach / Dockside Depth (reported)	Floating Docks	Gas / Diesel	Groceries, Ice, Marine Supplies, Snacks	Repairs: Hull, Engine, Propeller	Lift (tonnage), Crane, Rail	1=110V, 2=220V, B=Both, Max Amps	Laundry, Pool, Showers	Pump-Out Station	Nearby: Grocery Store, Motel, Restaurant
		Dockage					Supplies		Services					
1. DELEMAR Greenwich Harbor	203-661-9800	150	09/78	10/15	9/8	F					B/100			GMR
2. Palmer Point Marina and Ship's Store	203-661-1243	55	16/68	2/140	6/6		GD	IMS	HEP	L35	B/50	S	P	GMR
3. Beacon Point Marine	203-661-4033	70		10/300	12/2	F	GD	IM	HEP	LC	B/50	LPS	P	GMR
4. Stamford Landing Marina	203-965-0065	50	09	/130	17/9	F		I			B/50	LS	P	GMR
5. MacDonald Yacht Rigging	203-323-5431						YACHT RIGGING							
6. Maritech Marine Electronics	203-323-2900						MARINE ELECTRONICS REPAIRS							
7. Brewer Yacht Haven Marina (Internet Access, WiFi)	**203-359-4500**	**150**	**09**	**100/650**	**10/8**	**F**	**GD**	**IM**	**HEP**	**L60**	**B/100**	**LS**		**GMR**
8. Harbor Park Marina/Dockhouse Deli	203-324-3331	100	09	20/75	12/12	F	GD	GI			B/100	S	P	GMR
9. Harbor House Marina	**203-977-8772**	**80**	**68**	**/100**	**12/8**	**F**		**I**			**B/50**	**LS**		**GMR**

Corresponding chart(s) not to be used for navigation. Internet Access WiFi Wireless Internet Access

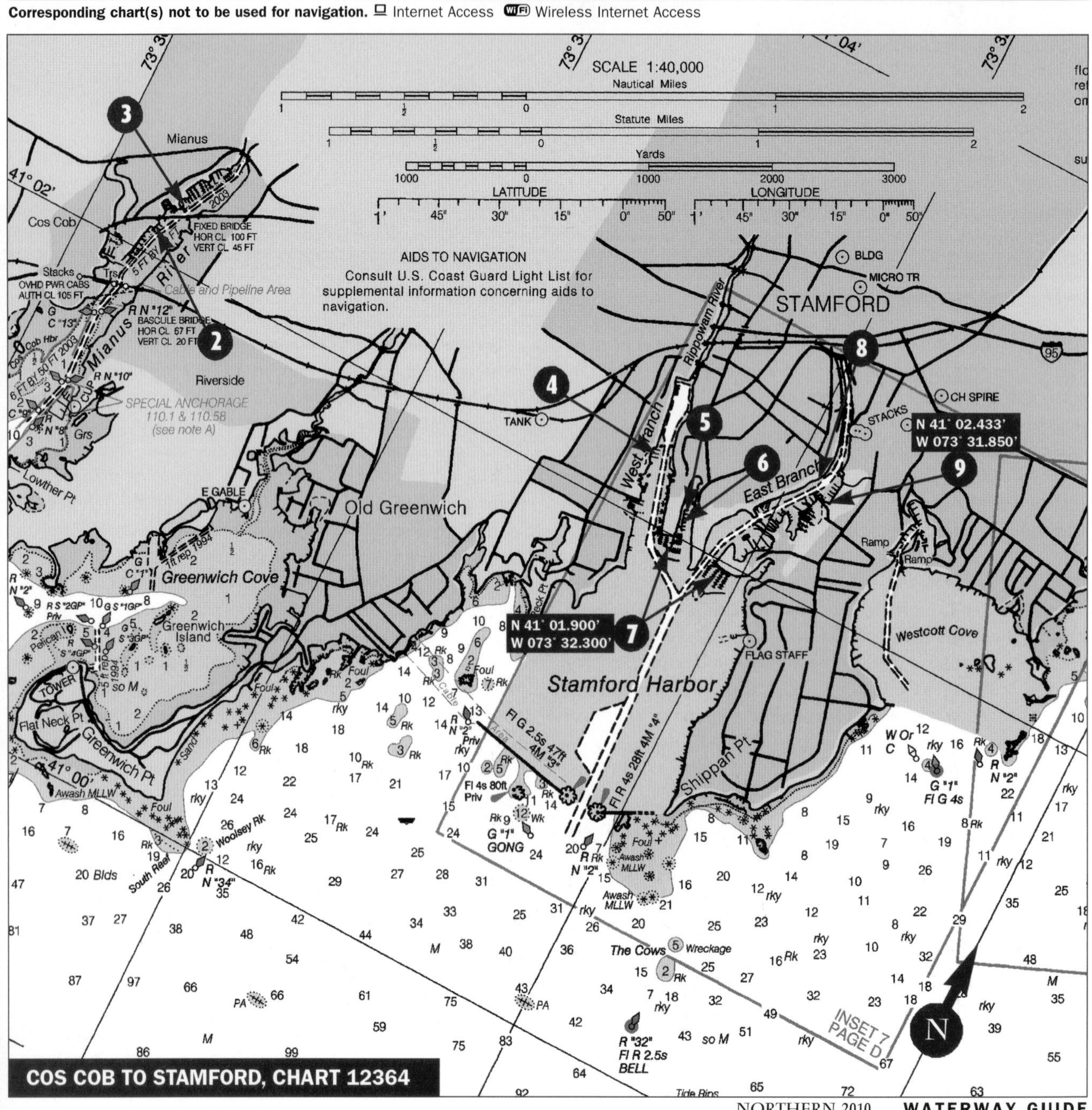

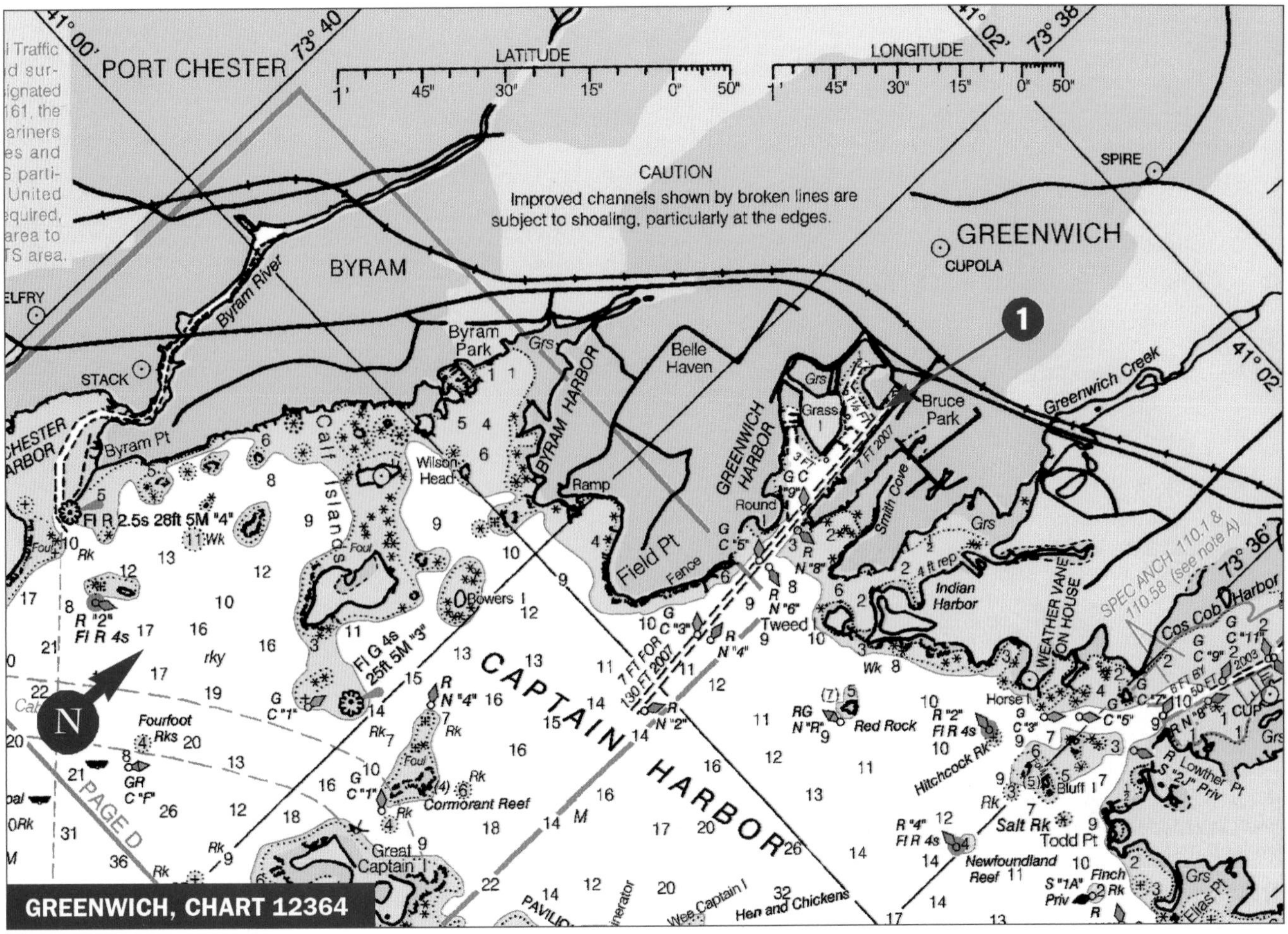

GREENWICH, CHART 12364

and serves a great margarita. The Elm Street Oyster House (203-629-5795, 11 W. Elm St.) is another local favorite.

Shopping in downtown Greenwich offers the opportunity to experience many of New York's finest boutiques without having to visit the "City." More than 100 boutiques line the downtown streets, and a number of wine stores, galleries and antiques stores are interspersed throughout. If provisions are needed, take a taxi to the local Stop & Shop. For taxi service, call Greenwich Taxi (203-869-6000). A short walk from the harbor, train service to New York is frequent and readily available.

ADDITIONAL RESOURCES:

- Town of Greenwich, **www.greenwichct.org**

NEARBY GOLF COURSES:
Griffith E. Harris Golf Course, 1300 King St., Greenwich, CT 06831, 203-531-7261

NEARBY MEDICAL FACILITIES:
Greenwich Hospital, 5 Perryridge Road, Greenwich, CT 06830, 203-863-3000, **www.greenhosp.org**

Indian Harbor

This small cove just east of Greenwich Harbor has no facilities, many mud flats, a few boats at moorings and room to anchor clear of the shoals—only shoal-draft boats need apply. The channel, westward of Tweed Island, follows the west bank. Work your way in slowly and carefully pick a spot.

Cos Cob Harbor

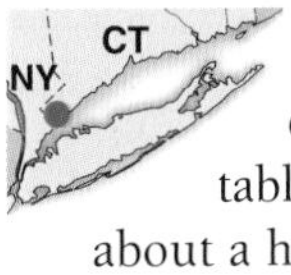

Cos Cob Harbor, which is actually the entrance to the Mianus River, is the best-equipped harbor in Greenwich. The hospitable Riverside Yacht Club is on the eastern shore about a half mile inside. The view from the club's dining porch is as good as the food served there. There is also a 300-slip municipal marina with room for boats up to 22 feet, and a few slips available for 26-foot-long vessels.

Looking north over Stamford Harbor. (Not to be used for navigation.) WATERWAY GUIDE PHOTOGRAPHY

NAVIGATION: Use Chart 12364. Use Bridgeport tide tables. For high tide, add 5 minutes; for low tide, add 11 minutes. Coming in from Long Island Sound between Flat Neck Point and the Captain Islands, leave Newfoundland Reef's flashing red buoy "4" to starboard, and Red Rock (with its red-over-green nun buoy "R") to port. A sharp turn to starboard around Hitchcock Rock's flashing red buoy "2" leads to the dredged, marked entrance.

Keep strictly to the center of the channel to get the most depth. Six-foot depths supposedly exist as far as the yacht club, but between it and the railroad bascule bridge (20-foot closed vertical clearance) depths diminish to less than 5 feet. Farther beyond the bridge you will find only 4.5-foot depths. At low tide, careful piloting is required in this upper stretch south of the fixed bridge (45-foot vertical clearance).

Dockage: Marinas begin to appear upriver from the railroad bridge and continue beyond the highway bridge. They offer extensive services and accommodate transients. The village of Cos Cob is within a long walk of the waterfront. The Delmar on Greenwich Harbor is one of the best luxury hotels in the world. The hotel is home to L'Escale (203-661-4600, 500 Steamboat Road), an excellent Mediterranean restaurant. The hotel monitors channel 71 for dockage reservations.

Greenwich Cove

Although Greenwich Cove is the largest and most attractive of the coves in the Greenwich area, it is also chock full of moored boats that leave precious little space for anchoring. Most of the remaining area is too shoal for all but the shallowest-draft boats.

Dockage: There are two municipal marinas in this area of Greenwich. Grass Island has 150 slips and offers free tie up space during the daytime, but charges for overnight stays. Grass Island also has mooring space for about 75 boats up to 36 feet with 5-foot drafts; call the dockmaster at 203-618-9695.

Greenwich Point Marina has 250 moorings for vessels up to 36 feet and up to a 7-foot draft; call 203-698-7792 Thursday through Monday to arrange for mooring rental.

Stamford Harbor

NAVIGATION: Use Chart 12364. Use Bridgeport tide tables. For high tide, add 3 minutes; for low tide, add 8 minutes. Stamford has one of Long Island Sound's easiest entrances, with a lighted range for night entry, and two well-marked and lighted breakwaters at the entrance. From offshore, the city's tall stacks and high-rise buildings are easy to spot. When approaching, keep to the west of The Cows (marked by flashing red bell buoy "32") and of Shippan Point. Follow the chart carefully as you proceed; many rocks lie between these points.

The large outer harbor can kick up a chop in strong winds, but reasonable anchorage can be found just behind the western breakwater. Proceed north, tight to red marker "2" on the west end of the breakwater, and tuck in tight behind the breakwater in about 10 feet of water. West of the channel is a large mooring buoy used by barges, along with a number of yacht club moorings. To the east, off the main channel, is the stately Stamford Yacht Club (203-323-3161, 97 Ocean Drive West), which sponsors the famous Labor Day Weekend Vineyard Race. It welcomes members of recognized clubs. Beyond the club, the channel forks into the East and West branches.

Dockage (East Branch): East Branch offers several marinas and a yacht basin, all tucked safely inside the hurricane barrier. The channel into the harbor is straightforward, offers 10- to 11-foot depths and carries all the way through to Stamford. Follow the right-hand channel to Brewer Yacht Haven East, which can be recognized from the breakwater by the large brick buildings that surround it.

Farther up the East Branch to starboard is the Harbor House Marina which offers transient slips with 8-foot dockside depths and laundry and shower facilities.

Though the town marina is for local boats only, you can tie up long enough for loading and unloading. Be aware, though, that the security gates at each dock allow you to leave with no key, but require keys to get back in. Beyond the charted hurricane barrier are two repair yards, one of them is Harbour Square Marina and Dock House Deli (203-324-3331, 860 Canal St.) with transient dockage, a deli and gourmet catering.

Dockage (West Branch): West Branch is deeper and wider, and has one of the most elaborate sales and service centers on the East Coast, Brewer Yacht Haven West. Do not enter the marina at the southern end; continue up West Branch about 500 yards to the gas dock. Radio ahead, and the dock attendants will stand by to help you dock at the finger piers, if needed. Brewer Yacht Haven West offers just about every service, including access to dining facilities at Ponus Yacht Club (203-323-7157), sail repair and a 60-ton lift.

GOIN' ASHORE: STAMFORD, CT

Stamford was settled in 1640 and named by its original settlers for the English town. The yachting facilities in Stamford are extensive and shore diversions are numerous, making this an ideal yachting destination for long or short layovers.

Stamford has three harbors: Stamford Harbor, with a large outer harbor and two protected inner branches, and Westcott Cove and Cove Harbor to the east (around Shippan Point). Breakwaters protect Stamford Harbor, with two branches at its head: East Branch and West Branch. The 80-foot-tall lighthouse on Harbor Ledge, next to the west breakwater, can be seen far out into Long Island Sound. The entrance through the breakwater is a quarter mile east of the lighthouse. To the east of Shippan Point are Westcott Cove and Cove Harbor, both unprotected from the south. The latter, with a difficult entry requiring local knowledge, is devoted entirely to local boats.

Stamford, while a typical northeastern city with high-rise offices and apartments dotting the skyline, is also a great port to visit and an excellent spot to dock and catch a train into New York City. The Stamford Train Station (203-363-5781, Washington Boulevard and S. State St.), a long walk or short cab ride from the waterfront, has frequent trains to New York City and other points along the coast. Downtown Stamford has excellent shopping, movie theaters and more than 40 restaurants. It is a hike from the marinas, so a taxi (Stamford Yellow Cab, 203-967-3633) would probably be in order. If you are staying at the Stamford Yacht Club, a jacket is required for dining in the restaurant.

Stamford's downtown area is lively, with the Stamford Center for the Arts (203-358-2305, 61 Atlantic St.) and the Palace Theater (203-325-4466, 61 Atlantic St.) both offering live performances. Diverse restaurants abound, including Mitchell's Fish Market (203-323-3474, 230 Tressor Blvd.), Bennett's Steak and Fish (203-978-7995, 24 Spring St.), Napa & Co. (203-353-3319, 75 Broad St.) and the Sierra Grille (203-329-7151, 1022 High Ridge Road). The upscale Stamford Town Center Mall (203-324-0935, 100 Grayrock Road) has more than 100 shops and restaurants.

ADDITIONAL RESOURCES:

- City of Stamford, **www.ci.stamford.ct.us** or **www.connecticutstamford.com**

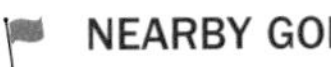

NEARBY GOLF COURSES:
E. Gaynor Brennan Municipal Golf Course,
451 Stillwater Road, Stamford, CT 06902,
203-324-4185

NEARBY MEDICAL FACILITIES:
Stamford Health System,
30 Shelburne Road, Stamford, CT 06904,
203-276-7000, **www.stamhealth.org**

Westcott Cove

NAVIGATION: Use Chart 12364. Enter around Shippan Point, east of Stamford Harbor, and leave flashing green buoy "1" to port on approach. A residents-only beach is located at the cove's head, and a small landlocked inner lagoon offers good depths and total protection. Though the lagoon is crowded and confined, and the outer cove is open to the south, this harbor is pleasant and easy to enter if you stay to mid-channel. A neo-Spanish building with a red tile roof makes a good landmark.

Darien, Rowayton

The whole area between Stamford and Fivemile River comprises Darien. The Gut (better known as Darien Harbor), Goodwives River and the town of Noroton lie within the western section of this area; Fivemile River is to the east. The entrances to both rivers require local knowledge, and there is only one marina in Fivemile River that can accommodate transients.

NAVIGATION: Use Chart 12364. The entrance to Fivemile River can be seen only from the south, but it is easy to enter. The channel, dredged through shoals on both sides, starts at flashing green buoy "3" a mile north of Greens Ledge Light. Watch for lobsterpot buoys.

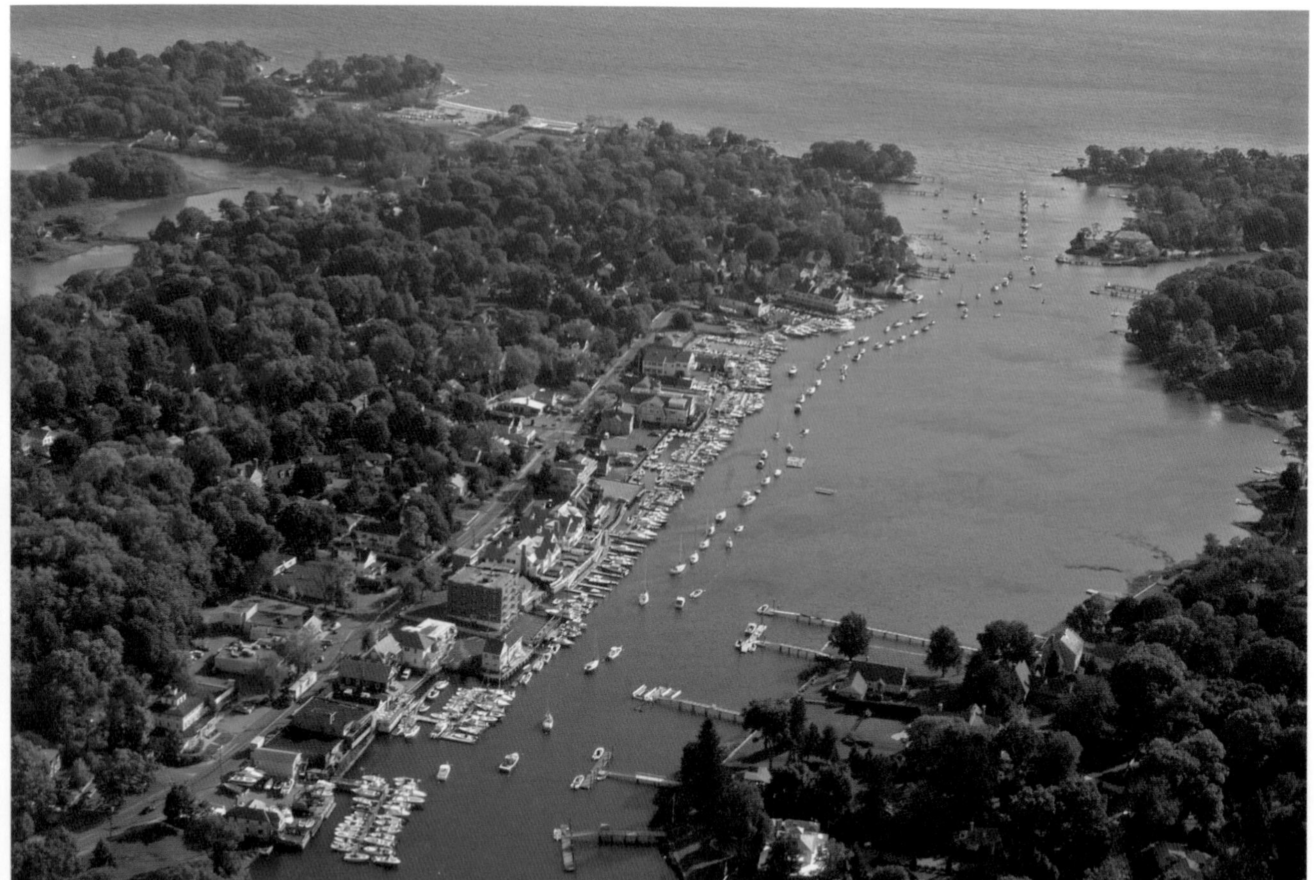

Looking south over Fivemile River. (Not to be used for navigation.) WATERWAY GUIDE PHOTOGRAPHY

Fivemile River is actually only one mile long. It is narrow but protected, with good depths throughout. On the western bank, Darien is lined with houses, while the village of Rowayton is nestled on the east side. Moorings are everywhere, and a few boatyards offer services, supplies and sometimes a place to tie up. There is no place to anchor; just finding room to turn around can be a problem. The best advice is to go to the end and turn around carefully in 6-foot depths. Along Rowayton's waterfront you will find a post office and stores. You can buy local steamers and lobsters, as well as most marine supplies here.

Anchorage: Just west of the mouth of Fivemile River is a great spot for anchoring in any breeze except from the east. Depths are around 10 to 15 feet with good holding. Cruisers have reported a quiet night at anchor here within 100 yards of shore while northwest winds are gusting up to 30 knots. To reach this spot, proceed on a course of 355 degrees magnetic from Greens Ledge Light, pass green can "1" to port, and then proceed into the unnamed cove between Contentment and Butlers Islands.

Norwalk

Norwalk, nicknamed "Oyster Town," is a cruising favorite, especially for mariners zigzagging Long Island Sound and crossing over from Huntington Bay on the Long Island shore. Norwalk's four primary maritime areas offer anything you are likely to want: good protection, marinas, repairs, yacht clubs, restaurants, beaches and good anchorage. The scenery includes hundreds of local boats, bow-to-stern weekend traffic amid the oyster stakes and crowds of people fishing, swimming, picnicking and clamming.

The westernmost Norwalk harbor is Wilson Cove, just past Noroton Point from Fivemile River. Although many yachts moor here permanently, it can be rough even in a moderate southwesterly wind.

The six-mile chain of Norwalk Islands, protecting Norwalk Harbor itself, is made up of 16 islands. They were used during the Revolutionary War by Continental whaleboat crews who ran out into Long Island Sound to harass the British ships, and then retreated to the shelter of the islands' rocks.

NAVIGATION: Use Chart 12364. Use Bridgeport tide tables. For high tide, add 9 minutes; for low tide, add 15 minutes. The entrance to Norwalk Harbor and Norwalk River, through Sheffield Island Harbor, north of the Norwalk Islands, is easy. The high-intensity softball field lights can be seen from as far away as Bridgeport throughout the boating season. Another landmark is a 350-foot-tall orange-and-white power plant stack on Manresa Island, on the western side of the harbor mouth. Go west around Greens Ledge and give the reef west of Sheffield Island (known as Smith Island to people here) a good berth. Follow the well-marked Sheffield Island Harbor channel past Manresa Island into Norwalk Harbor. Watch for barge traffic coming out of the power plant basin.

As you go upstream, the river changes, flowing through marshes filled with waterfowl. It is worth exploring, but

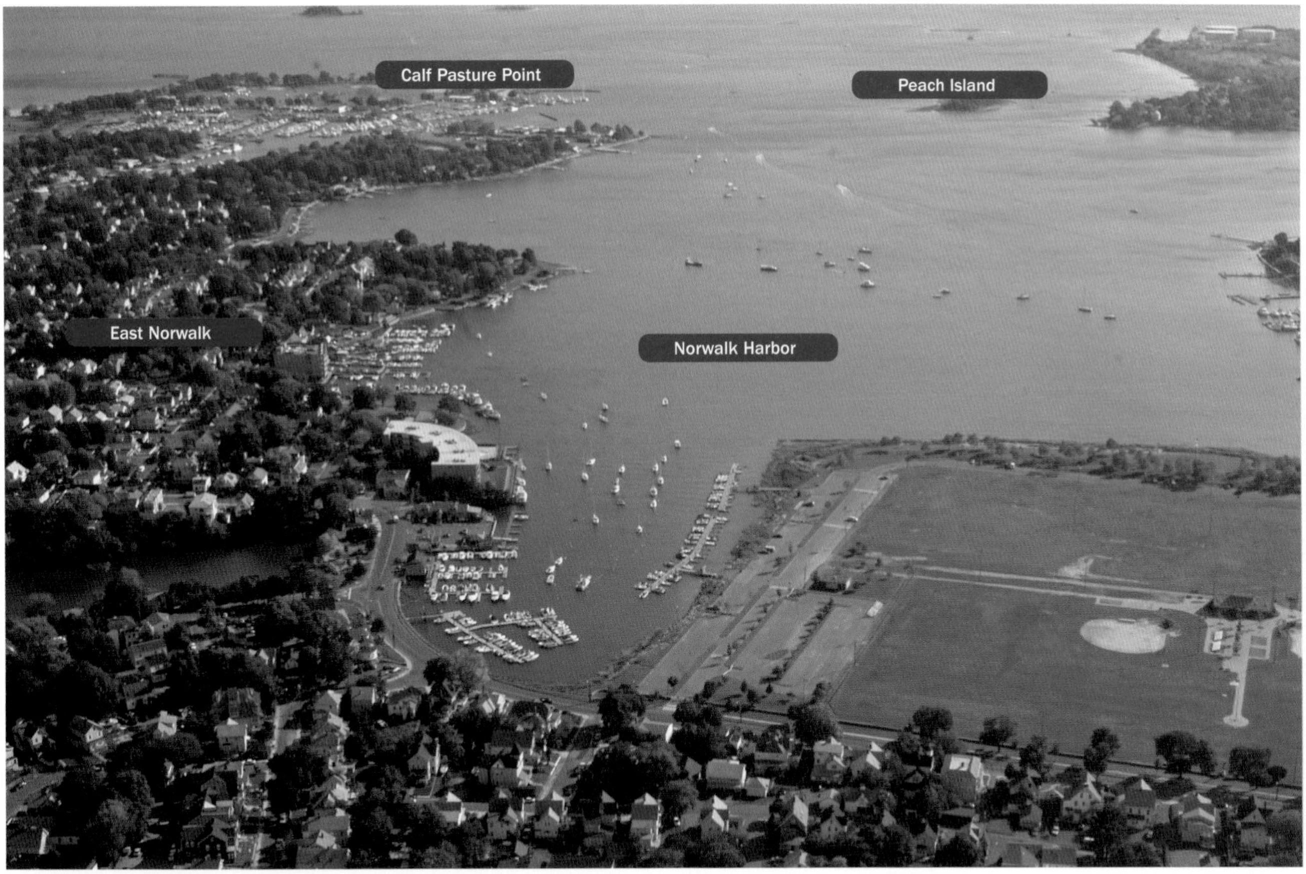

Calf Pasture Point
Peach Island
East Norwalk
Norwalk Harbor

Looking south over Norwalk Harbor. (Not to be used for navigation.)

Rowayton to Norwalk, CT

ROWAYTON TO NORWALK		Largest Vessel Accommodated	VHF Channel Monitored	Transient Berths / Total Berths	Approach / Dockside Depth (reported)	Floating Docks	Gas / Diesel	Groceries, Ice, Marine Supplies, Snacks	Repairs: Hull, Engine, Propeller	Lift (tonnage), Crane, Rail	1=110V, 2=220V, B=Both, Max Amps	Laundry, Pool, Showers	Pump-Out Station	Nearby: Grocery Store, Motel, Restaurant
		Dockage					Supplies		Services					
1. Boatworks, Inc.	203-866-9295	45	68	5/80	7/7			IM	HP	C25	1/30		P	GR
2. Wilson Cove Marina	203-866-7020	50	78	/80	6/6	F		I	HP	LC	1/30	S		
3. Wilson Cove Yacht Club	203-853-0922	50	78		6/6			I	HP	LC		S		
4. Norwalk Yacht Club	203-866-0941	50	78	6/130	7/7			I						
5. Rowayton Yacht Club	203-854-0807	30	68		10/2			I				S		R
6. Total Marine	203-838-3210	80		10/60	15/9	F			HEP	L7,C	B	S		R
7. Rex Marine Center	203-866-5555	50		5/60	12/6	F		IM	HEP	L30	1/50	S	P	R
8. Norwest Marine	203-853-2822	48	69	/65	12/8	F	GD	IM	HEP	L	1/50			GR
9. Oyster Bend Marina	203-853-1600	60		6/72	12/8	F		IMS			B/50	S		MR
10. David S. Dunavan Visitors Dock	203-849-8823	60	16/09	20/20	12/8	F							P	GR
11. Norwalk Cove Marina Inc. (WiFi)	**203-838-2326**	**170**	**09/72**	**5/400**	**10/7**	**F**	**GD**	**IMS**	**HEP**	**L160,C**	**B/100**	**LS**	**P**	**GMR**
12. Sprite Island Yacht Club	203-866-7803	33	12	/8	8/8	F	PRIVATE CLUB							R

Corresponding chart(s) not to be used for navigation. Internet Access (WiFi) Wireless Internet Access

do so in the dinghy; the channel winds through shallow flats. Several bridges are closed during rush hours. The first bridge you will encounter is a bascule bridge with an 8-foot closed vertical clearance. Farther upstream is a swing bridge with a 16-foot closed vertical clearance. Although there are more bridges farther up the Norwalk River, you can call any of their bridge tenders on VHF Channel 13.

Eastbound mariners depart Norwalk Harbor through Cockenoe Harbor. The buoyed channel (green to starboard) threads through islands and shoals to 61-foot Peck Ledge Lighthouse. Keep the lighthouse to starboard and then turn sharply southeast, staying off Cockenoe Island's southern and eastern shoals, to reach open water. After passing Peck's Ledge, be sure to alter course to starboard, and then pass red nun "4" to port; this marks Channel Rock buoy.

Dockage: A large, full-service marina, Norwalk Cove Marina offers transient dockage, gas and diesel fuel, marine supplies and a pump-out station. The marina has four lifts and a complete repair facility.

Anchorage: Many popular spots to drop the hook are available in the lee of the islands—in particular, the large area east of Chimon Island. Enter from the north, and proceed slowly over the 6-foot bar to anchor in 10-foot depths just east of Chimon Rocks. The western shore of Cockenoe Island is also a popular anchorage. You can go ashore to swim, hike or camp; on weekends, it seems like everyone does.

GOIN' ASHORE: **NORWALK, CT**

The Norwalk Visitors Dock (VHF Channel 09, 203-829-8892, Buschbaum Boulevard, Veterans Park) is an ideal first stop for visiting boaters. Located on the east side of the river and just south of the first bascule bridge, the long floating docks are part of a large boat-ramp facility. This is an ideal location to stay, but if you want an overnight spot at the docks, reservations are suggested, especially on weekends. Stores are right across the street and a short walk over the bridge puts the visitor in the center of SoNo, South Norwalk's sophisticated nightlife and tourism district, fully renovated in the late 1970s and anchored by the Maritime Center.

Maritime Aquarium at Norwalk (203-852-0700, 10 N. Water St.) is devoted to the preservation of Long Island Sound. The aquarium features more than 1,000 marine animals native to Long Island Sound and its watershed. Tanks portray successive levels of life in Long Island Sound, from shallow tidal areas filled with oysters, sea horses, lobster and small fish to the 110,000-gallon open tank with sharks, bluefish, striped bass and rays. Harbor seals cavort in a special indoor/outdoor tank and are fed at 11:45 a.m., 1:45 p.m. and 3:45 p.m. daily. There are also two rambunctious river otters in a woodland shoreline habitat. The Maritime Aquarium also houses an IMAX theatre with a rotating slate of movies. For more information, visit their Web site at www.maritimeaquarium.org. The aquarium is open daily from 10 a.m. to 5 p.m., and during July and August hours are extended to 6 p.m.

Calf Pasture Point, on the east side of Norwalk Harbor, was once an Indian grazing ground, then a Colonial settlement. It was burned out in 1779 when a fleet of British vessels landed on the point. Today it is bordered to the east by a mile-long crescent beach and to the west by the full-service Norwalk Cove Marina, home of the annual Norwalk International Boat Show. Hobie Cat, Widgeon and windsurfer rentals and lessons can be found on the public beach adjacent to the marina.

Up the busy Norwalk Channel another mile is a municipal dock, launching ramp and two marinas, which primarily serve local boaters.

SoNo, the historic waterfront neighborhood of South Norwalk, features turn-of-the-century architecture and a quaint gas-lit shopping and restaurant district. Also in the neighbor-

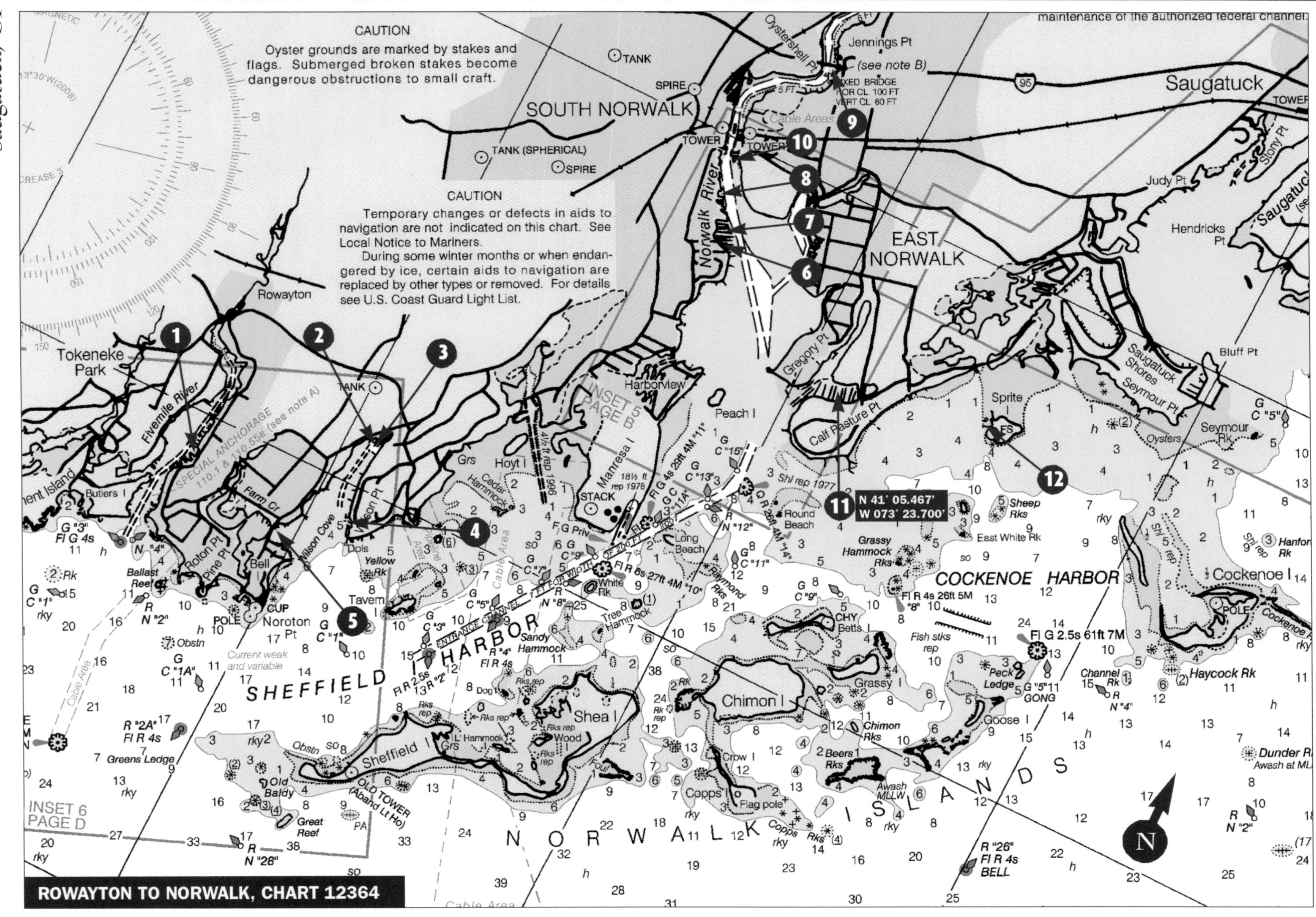
CAUTION
Oyster grounds are marked by stakes and flags. Submerged broken stakes become dangerous obstructions to small craft.
CAUTION
Temporary changes or defects in aids to navigation are not indicated on this chart. See Local Notice to Mariners.
During some winter months or when endangered by ice, certain aids to navigation are replaced by other types or removed. For details see U.S. Coast Guard Light List.
maintenance of the authorized federal channel.
SOUTH NORWALK
EAST NORWALK
Saugatuck
Rowayton
Tokeneke Park
Fivemile River
Norwalk River
SPECIAL ANCHORAGE 110.1 & 110.55a (see note A)
FIXED BRIDGE HOR CL 100 FT VERT CL 60 FT
(see note B)
INSET 5 PAGE B
INSET 6 PAGE D
N 41° 05.467'
W 073° 23.700'
SHEFFIELD I HARBOR
COCKENOE HARBOR
NORWALK ISLANDS
ROWAYTON TO NORWALK, CHART 12364

hood are coffee shops, restaurants, theaters and art galleries. The area's many art studios inspired the popular SoNo Arts Celebration, which is held the first weekend in August every year featuring a parade of giant puppets and the creations of over 150 fine artists and craftsmen surrounded by an atmosphere of music and dance. The neighborhood's working maritime heritage lives on at Tallmadge Brothers, the largest oyster producer in the state of Connecticut. The company has over 22,000 acres of oyster beds and has been in business in Norwalk for over 130 years. The Norwalk Seaport Association (203-838-9444, 132 Water St., www.seaport.org), located atop Tallmadge Brothers, offers tours of the operation. The Seaport Association's annual Oyster Festival, held the weekend after Labor Day, helps fund restoration of Sheffield Island's historic lighthouse and many other non-profit organizations. Westport Star Cab Company, 203-227-5157, can provide transportation from the marinas (a two-minute ride).

ADDITIONAL RESOURCES:

- City of Norwalk, **www.norwalkct.org** or **www.norwalkconnecticut.com**

NEARBY GOLF COURSES:
Oak Hills Park Golf Course, 165 Fillow St., Norwalk, CT 06850, 203-838-101

NEARBY MEDICAL FACILITIES:
Norwalk Hospital, Maple Street, Norwalk, CT 06856, 203-852-2000, **www.norwalkhosp.org**

Saugatuck River, Westport

The Saugatuck River, which leads to Westport, is interesting to explore, with attractive houses, restaurants, shops, yacht clubs, a public recreational complex and a summer theater.

NAVIGATION: Use Chart 12364. Entrance to the Saugatuck River from Long Island Sound should be made east of flashing green buoy "1" marking Georges Rock. Head northwest on either side of flashing green buoy "3" to the entrance to the marked channel in the river, between Cedar Point and Seymour Rock. The town yacht basin is in the enclosed area to starboard, just behind Compo Beach. Moving farther in, follow the well-marked channel carefully as it winds up and around Bluff Point, hugging the western shore, with depths outside the markers as shallow as 1 foot.

Dockage: The town-operated yacht basin at the river's mouth is jammed with local boats at fore-and-aft moorings. The yacht clubs, all hospitable, are crowded and might be unable to take care of visiting boats. Boaters who are unable to access Westport may want to proceed to Norwalk and use ground transportation to visit Westport. Reportedly, some private restaurant docks will let you tie up while you dine.

Farther up the Saugatuck River (through a somewhat challenging channel with 3- to 5-foot depths in places) is The Mooring Restaurant (203-227-0757, 299 Riverside Ave.), on the west bank, about one-third of a nautical mile above three (one bascule, one fixed, one swing) bridges. It reserves two slips for visiting boats. An outdoor patio overlooks the Saugatuck River. The restaurant, a friendly place with moderate prices, occupies an old mill building that was moved from its original site in the 1970s.

Anchorage: Anchorages in the vicinity of the town are extremely limited, swing room is minimal and the channel winds tortuously. Because of one shallow spot downriver, this area is best not approached near dead-low water. The 7-foot tidal range, though, will give you good water most of the time. Another option for anchoring is to lie just offshore in the lee of Cockenoe Island, dinghy to the municipal marina and taxi into town.

GOIN' ASHORE: **WESTPORT, CT**

In 1777, the British fleet arrived at the mouth of the Saugatuck River, intending to burn Danbury, where American munitions were stored. Benedict Arnold rallied the local militia against the British and a stand was made at Campo Beach, a native word meaning "a bear fishing." The British withdrew, and today there is a statue honoring the militiamen, complete with musket, powder horn and tunic, not far from Campo Beach. Twin cannons, which blasted 42-pound balls, also mark the event at Campo Beach Park.

F. Scott Fitzgerald and wife Zelda honeymooned on Campo Beach in the 1920s. This was also the home of Charles and Ann Morrow Lindbergh. Today the rich and famous live side by side with the descendants of the original Yankee farmers. Westport is a town of many beautifully-maintained buildings that appear on the National Historic Register.

Westport offers a large number of very good restaurants catering to every taste and price level. Some of the local favorites include Southport Brewing Company (203-256-2337, 2600 Post Road), Pane Vino (203-255-1153, 1431 Post Road), Bobby Q's (203-454-7800, 42 Main St.), Blue Lemon (203-226-2647, 7 Sconset Square) and the River House Tavern (203-226-5532, 299 Riverside Ave.). For taxi service call Westport Star Taxi (203-227-5157).

ADDITIONAL RESOURCES:

- Town of Westport, **www.ci.westport.ct.us**

NEARBY GOLF COURSES:
Longshore Club Park Golf Course, 260 Compo Road S., Westport, CT 06880, 203-222-7535

NEARBY MEDICAL FACILITIES:
Westport Family Health Clinic, 728 Post Road E., Westport, CT 06880, 203-291-3800

Saugatuck River and Westport, CT

SAUGATUCK RIVER AND WESTPORT		Largest Vessel Accommodated	VHF Channel Monitored	Transient Berths / Total Berths	Approach / Dockside Depth (reported)	Floating Docks	Gas / Diesel	Groceries, Ice, Marine Supplies, Snacks	Repairs: Hull, Engine, Propeller	Lift (tonnage), Crane, Rail	1=110V, 2=220V, B=Both, Max Amps	Laundry, Pool, Showers	Pump-Out Station	Nearby: Grocery Store, Motel, Restaurant
		Dockage					Supplies		Services					
1. Cedar Point Yacht Club	203-226-7411	50	/78	5/90	10/10	F		IS		C1	1/30	S		GMR
2. Compo Yacht Basin	203-227-9136	53	16/11	6/470	10/10	F	G	IS			1/30		P	R

Corresponding chart(s) not to be used for navigation. ☐ Internet Access WiFi Wireless Internet Access

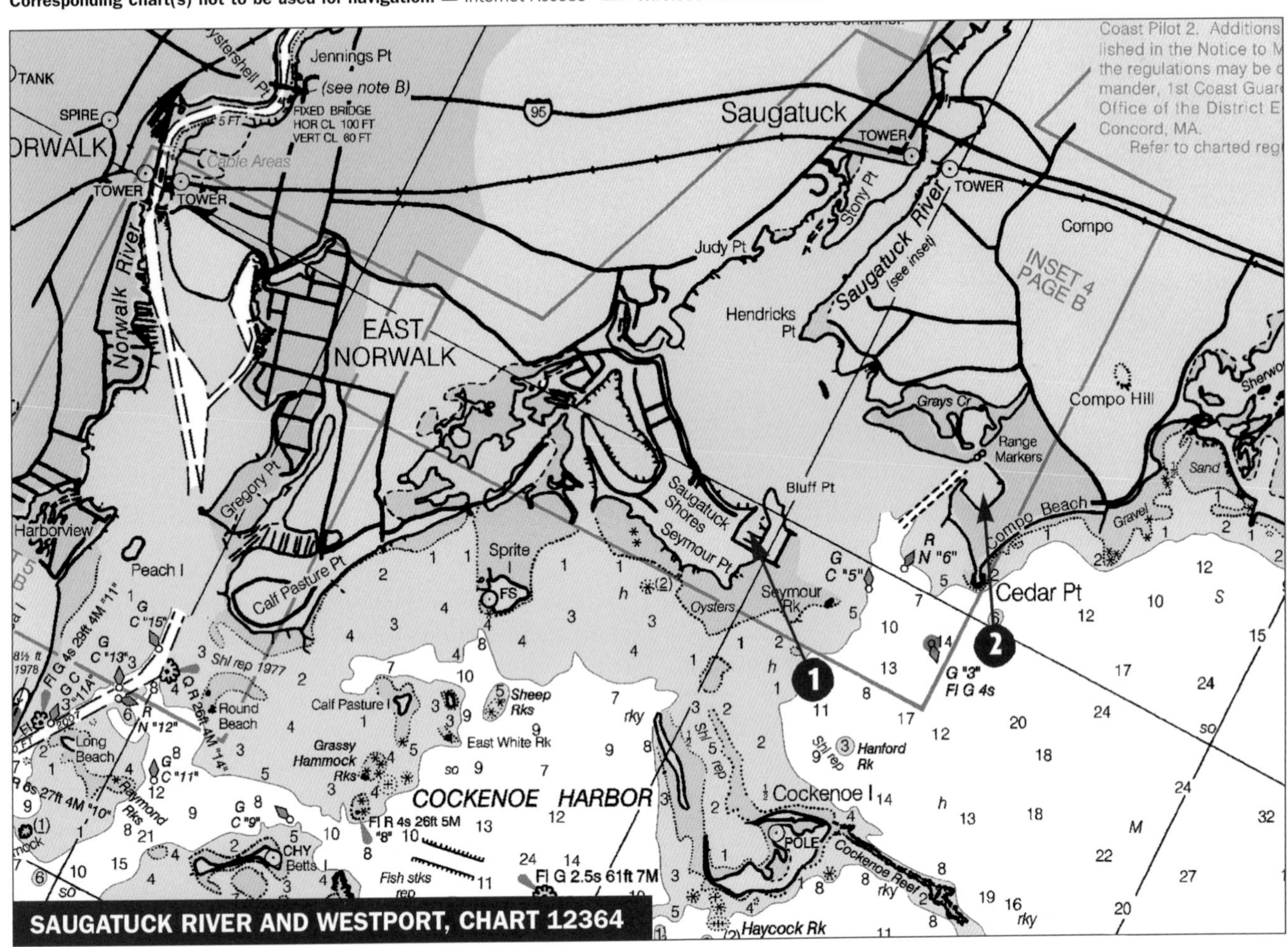

SAUGATUCK RIVER AND WESTPORT, CHART 12364

■ SOUTHPORT, CT TO BRIDGEPORT, CT

NAVIGATION: Use Chart 12364. Southport is a Colonial town, with a tiny crowded harbor and a narrow dredged channel through shoals (some with only .5 feet of water). Enter the harbor west of Sasco Hill Beach on the chart. Watch for a shallow spot (5.5 feet) between the breakwater and the outer buoy. It is a difficult harbor to keep dredged, but you can use it with no problem if you go slowly and cautiously. Once inside the harbor, do not go beyond the moorings to reach the open water beyond the yacht club; the water is very shallow.

Heading from Southport toward Black Rock Harbor, give the end of Penfield Reef a wide berth to keep clear of the numerous smaller rocks and Black Rock itself. Be sure that the flashing light you see is at the end of the reef, and then head for flashing red gong buoy "2" marking the Bridgeport Harbor entrance about 1.5 miles away. Do not make your turn for Black Rock Harbor until you are midway between those markers, following a course of about 330 degrees magnetic.

Dockage: Pequot Yacht Club in Southport (203-292-9116, 669 Harbor Road) may have a guest mooring available, with gas, diesel, ice, water and modest restroom and shower facilities. The club does not monitor any VHF channels. The town dock, located to port as the channel widens, allows complimentary 30-minute tie-ups.

Ashore, there are few commercial establishments amid the stately homes and lush gardens. It is about a block from

Looking northeast over Cedar Creek. (Not to be used for navigation.) WATERWAY GUIDE PHOTOGRAPHY

the yacht club to the village's few stores and restaurants. Driftwood Coffee Shop (203-255-1975, 325 Pequot Ave.) is a favorite for breakfast and lunch, and the Spic and Span Market & Deli (203-259-1688, 329 Pequot Ave.) offers ready-made entrees, sandwiches and limited grocery items, including Angus beef and free-range chicken. The only choice for dinner is The Horseshoe Restaurant (203-255-8624, 355 Pequot Ave.) located across from the post office.

Black Rock Harbor

Black Rock Harbor, almost two miles west of Bridgeport, is that industrial city's main harbor for recreational boats. It has a deep, well-marked channel, is easy to enter and has ample transient facilities. The harbor is sheltered to the east by Fayerweather Island, part of Bridgeport's big Seaside Park, with an abandoned lighthouse at the tip.

Dockage: Two marinas located on Cedar Creek can accommodate transients. Captain's Cove offers dockage with all utilities at its main marina and less expensive, no-frills dockage at a second facility, with ferry service linking the two. Captain's Cove is home to charter fishing boats, the tall ship *HMS Rose*, and an extensive collection of nautical memorabilia. Upstairs above the restaurant and dance floor is a model of the *Titanic*. Next door, Cedar Marina offers transient dockage with water, power, cable TV and phone lines.

Guest moorings may be available from the two yacht clubs in the harbor—Black Rock Yacht Club (203-335-0587, 80 Grovers Ave.) and Fayerweather Yacht Club (203-576-6796, 51 Brewster St.). Both may respond on VHF Channel 16. There is virtually no space to anchor in the inner harbor. There is a friendly, upbeat bar located in the Fayerweather Yacht Club.

Black Rock is a pleasant neighborhood of west Bridgeport. Fairfield Avenue, a 10-minute walk from the marinas, has interesting restaurants and shops, including Arizona Flats (203-334-8300, 3001 Fairfield Ave.) for southwestern food, Black Rock Castle (203-336-3990, 2895 Fairfield, Ave.) for an Irish pub atmosphere and Taco Loco (203-335-8228, 3170 Fairfield Ave.) for Mexican. Caution is advised when continuing east beyond these businesses. Boaters also may want to consider a harbor tour or a visit to the *Nantucket* lightship, a floating lighthouse dedicated to preserving America's maritime heritage.

Bridgeport

NAVIGATION: Use Chart 12364. Use Bridgeport tide tables. This industrial city, about 50 miles from New York City, is easy to spot. Its tall stacks, factories, oil tanks and power plants are all visible from Long Island Sound. The large tankers, ferries and freighters traveling its big, well-marked channel are equally evident. Bridgeport Harbor, the city's second harbor after Black Rock Harbor, is a working harbor and the arrival port for two weekly

Black Rock Harbor and Bridgeport, CT

BLACK ROCK HARBOR, BRIDGEPORT		Largest Vessel Accommodated	VHF Channel Monitored	Transient Berths / Total Berths	Approach / Dockside Depth (reported)	Floating Docks	Gas / Diesel	Groceries, Ice, Marine Supplies, Snacks	Repairs: Hull, Engine, Propeller	Lift (tonnage), Crane, Rail	1=110V, 2=220V, B=Both, Max Amps	Laundry, Pool, Showers	Pump-Out Station	Nearby: Grocery Store, Motel, Restaurant
		Dockage					Supplies		Services					
1. Fayerweather Yacht Club	203-576-6796	50	14		7/5	F	G	I			1/15	S	P	GR
2. Fayerweather Boat Yard	203-334-4403	45	REPAIR SERVICE					M	HEP	LC				R
3. Captain's Cove Seaport	203-335-1433	200	18	30/400	18/13	F	GD	IM	HP	LC	B/50	LS	P	GR
4. Cedar Marina Inc.	203-335-6262	60		/175	20/7	F		I	HEP	L	1/30	S	P	R
5. Derecktor Shipyards 🖳	203-336-0108	400			22/18	F		I	HEP	L600, C100	B/200			GMR
6. Pequonnock Yacht Club Inc.	203-334-5708	50	16/09	10/198	6/5	F	GD	IM			1/50	S		MR
7. Lou's Boat Basin LLC	203-336-9809	42		2/30	30/6	F		IMS			1/30			GMR
8. Miamogue Yacht Club	203-334-9882	50		/173	15/8	F	G	IS			B/50		P	R
9. East End Yacht Club	203-366-3330	40		/200	10/10	F	G	I			1/30	S		MR

Corresponding chart(s) not to be used for navigation. 🖳 Internet Access (WiFi) Wireless Internet Access

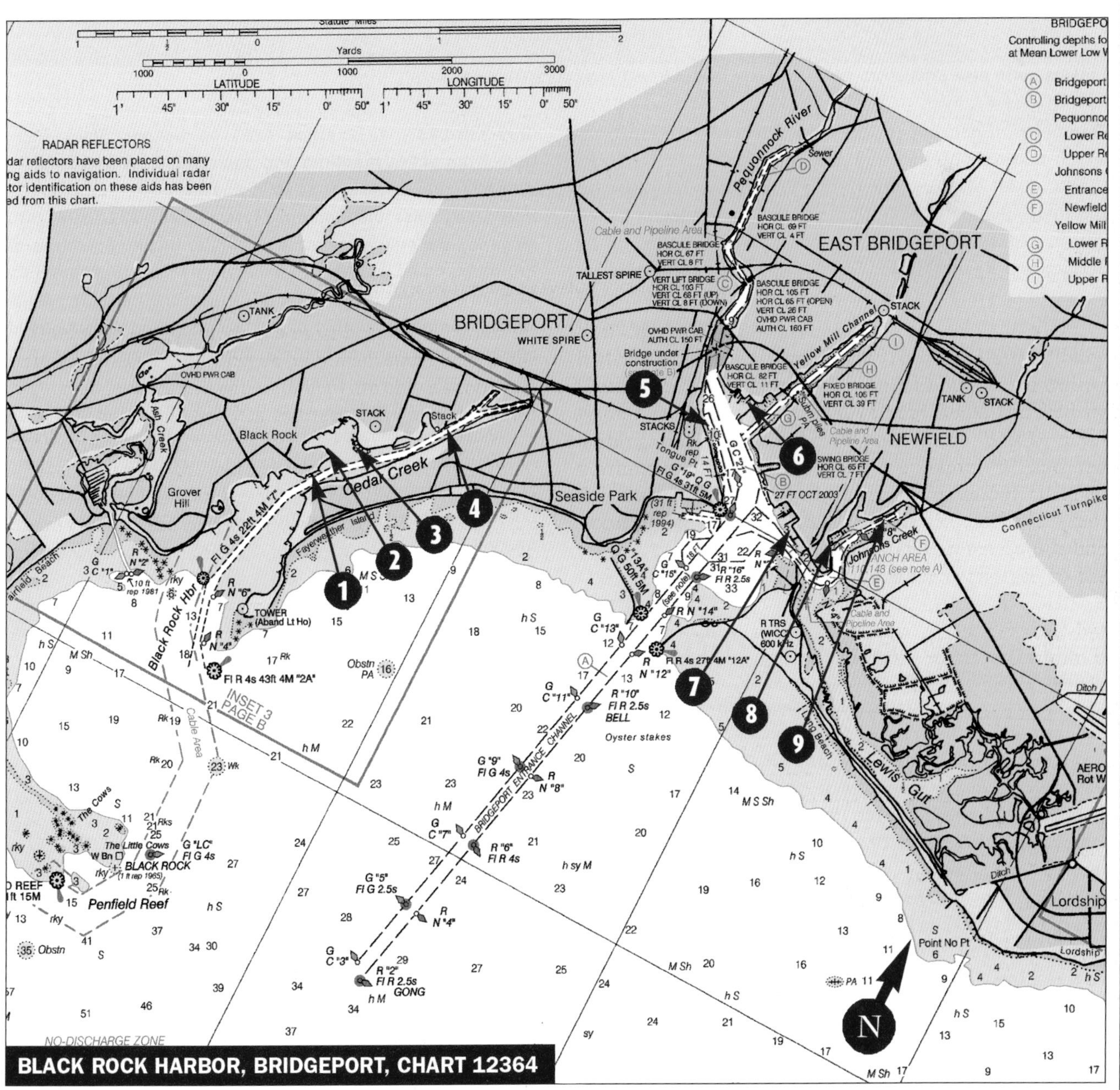

Looking north over Bridgeport. (Not to be used for navigation.) WATERWAY GUIDE PHOTOGRAPHY

shipments of bananas for the New England market. It has a well-marked entrance and deep water.

Dockage: Marinas able to handle cruising boats are on the main channel, above the entrance to Johnsons Creek (the first marked channel to starboard). Hitchcock's Marine Service and Ryan's Marine Services can both accommodate larger vessels and can handle most service needs. Dolphin's Cove Restaurant, (203-335-3301, 421 Seaview Ave.) at Yellow Mill Channel, offers free overnight dockage with dinner. All of Bridgeport's marinas are located adjacent to serious industrial areas. While security is good at the marinas, the surrounding areas are not conducive to wandering about. The Bridgeport-to-Port Jefferson ferry service transports passengers and vehicles across Long Island Sound six times daily. Contact ferries on VHF Channel 13 if you anticipate a close encounter. Be prepared to give way, as the ferries require room to turn and maneuver.

GOIN' ASHORE: BRIDGEPORT, CT

Bridgeport is built on the Pequannock River, meaning "cleared field," which refers to the fields cleared by the American Indians north of Black Rock Harbor. In 1637 the Pequot tribe fled when chased by the colonists. The bloody defeat of the Pequot came in a swamp in what is now known as Fairfield.

The first bridge across the Pequannock was financed by a lottery and, in 1800, the city, now having a bridge and a port, thus became known by the name of Bridgeport. Shortly afterwards P.T. Barnum, founder of the "Greatest Show on Earth," was drawn to the area because of its rapid growth. Bridgeport's harbors, plus the termination of the railway, clinched its position as a manufacturing town.

Bridgeport has a number of decent restaurants and evening entertainment opportunities that are best reached by taxi from the harbor. Not to be missed Is Captain's Cove Seaport (203-335-1433, 1 Bostwick Ave.) on Historic Black Rock Harbor, an active maritime and amusement center complete with restaurants, shops, exhibits and galleries. Admission Is free. Don't miss the Barnum Museum (203-331-1104, 820 Main St.), the only museum dedicated to the life and times of P.T. Barnum and Bridgeport's industrial heritage. Built in 1893, Barnum's last great architectural project, the museum's highlights include a miniature circus, period clown costumes and personal mementos of Barnum, Tom Thumb and Jenny Lind. The museum is open Tuesday through Saturday from 10 a.m. to 4:30 p.m. and Sunday 12 p.m. to 4:30 p.m. year-round.

Connecticut's Beardsley Zoo (203-394-6565, 1875 Noble Ave.) has a distinctive collection of animals native to North and South America. Intimate in size and very family oriented, Beardsley is open from 9 a.m. to 4 p.m. year-round, except for major holidays.

ADDITIONAL RESOURCES:

- City of Bridgeport, **www.ci.bridgeport.ct.us**

NEARBY GOLF COURSES:
Short Beach Golf Course, 1 Dorne Drive,
Stratford, CT 06615, 203-381-2070

NEARBY MEDICAL FACILITIES:
Bridgeport Hospital, 267 Grant St.,
Bridgeport, CT 06610, 203-384-3000,
www.bridgeporthospital.org

Cruising Options

The 30-mile-long stretch of coastline between Bridgeport and Westbrook features outstanding architectural relics, tiny offshore islands, tidal rivers and snug coves. Covered in the next chapter are Stratford, New Haven, Branford, the scenic Thimble Islands, Guilford and Westbrook. ■

Stratford to Westbrook

CHARTS 12354, 12363, 12364, 12369, 12370, 12371, 12372, 12373, 12374, 12375

■ CONNECTICUT SHORE

Stratford

NAVIGATION: Use Chart 12364. For Stratford, use Bridgeport tide tables. For high tide, add 23 minutes; for low tide, add 23 minutes. To reach Stratford on the Housatonic River, approach the river (about five miles north of Stratford Shoal Lighthouse and opposite Port Jefferson on the Long Island Shore) through open obstruction-free water. Tall chimneys at Devon, about a mile upriver from Stratford, are a good offshore landmark for the entrance between Milford Point's long lighted breakwater (its inner end submerges at three-quarter-high tide) and projecting Stratford Point. Stratford Point has shoals on all sides, an early 19th-century lighthouse and well-staked oyster beds to the east. The English settled this historic city, named for Shakespeare's Stratford-on-Avon, in 1639.

Currents in the Housatonic River's narrow channel run swiftly, so try to hit it at flood tide when entering. Mean tidal range at Stratford is 5.5 feet; less as you move upriver. The flood sets to the west and can push you toward the flats along the channel if you get caught off guard.

Dockage: Brewer Stratford Marina is located just across the channel (west) from Nells Island and offers all services.

Anchorage: At Nells Island, in the bend across from Stratford, the Housatonic River opens into better country with good water in the yacht club and marina area. Anchoring in the river is not recommended, due to the swift current. If absolutely necessary, anchor off the northern tip of Nells Island. Consider setting two anchors, as a single anchor might break out during the current change.

If you go ashore by dinghy, an outboard is a must. A second option is to anchor on the west side of the river just north of the highway and railway bridges, where the current is not as strong.

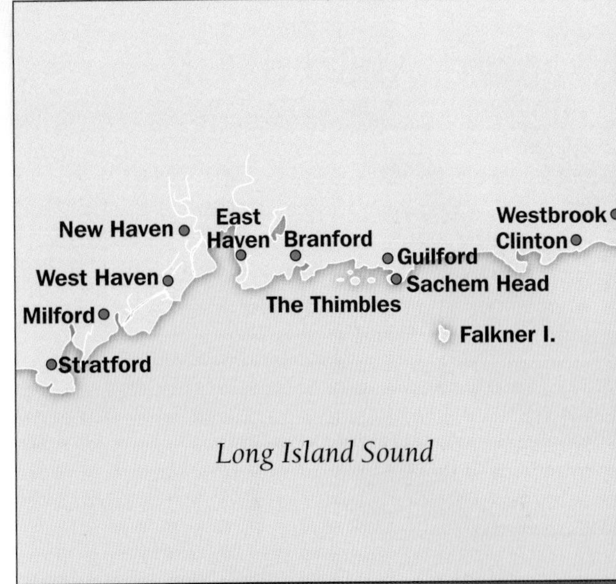

GOIN' ASHORE: **STRATFORD, CT**

Stratford is rich in both history and beauty. Shipbuilding was an important industry along the Housatonic River dating back to the 1700s. In the 1800s, large schooners were built here—most notably the 280-ton *Helen Mar*.

The Great Meadows Salt Marsh, on the east side of the river, is one of the largest unditched marshes in New England. The water is excellent and the river and marsh teem with fish and birdlife.

Stratford has been the home of the Sikorsky Helicopter Company for many years and provided a strong base to the Stratford economy. In 1939, Igor Sikorsky flew the first helicopter at his Stratford manufacturing plant and, to this day, the company manufactures helicopters for both the military and civilian markets. The local airport was named in Sikorsky's honor.

Provisioning is good in Stratford, with several malls occupied by Wal-Mart (150 Barnum Ave. Cutoff, 203-502-7631), Staples (955 Ferry Blvd., 203-375-1884), Home Depot (350 Barnum Ave. Cutoff, 203-386-9815) and Shaw's Supermarket (250 Barnum Ave. Cutoff, 203-378-4296). Dining out offers the Outriggers Restaurant at Brewer Stratford Marina (203-377-8815) overlooking the Housatonic River and the marsh. Pootatuck Yacht Club, next door (100 Housatonic Ave., 203-375-1000), has a public dining room, which is open for dinner Thursday through Sunday from 5 p.m. to 10 p.m. and for brunch Saturday and Sunday starting at 10:30 a.m. A short walk farther into town brings you to Knapps Landing Restaurant (520 Sniffens Lane, 203-378-5999). Brewer Stratford Marina has a reasonable supply of marine materials and a West Marine is located about three miles east on U.S. Route 1.

ADDITIONAL RESOURCES:

■ Town of Stratford, **www.townofstratford.com**

NEARBY GOLF COURSES:
Short Beach Golf Course, 1 Dorne Drive, Stratford, CT 06615, 203-381-2070

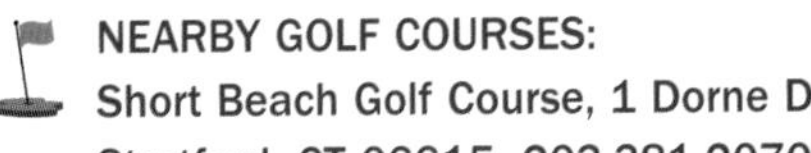

NEARBY MEDICAL FACILITIES:
Covenant Family Medicine, 2103 Main St., Stratford, CT 06615, 203-377-3666

Stratford, Milford, CT

STRATFORD, MILFORD		Largest Vessel Accommodated	VHF Channel Monitored	Transient Berths / Total Berths	Approach / Dockside Depth (reported)	Floating Docks	Gas / Diesel	Groceries, Ice, Marine Supplies, Snacks	Repairs: Hull, Engine, Propeller	Lift (tonnage), Crane, Rail	1=110V, 2=220V, B=Both, Max Amps	Laundry, Pool, Showers	Pump-Out Station	Nearby: Grocery Store, Motel, Restaurant
		Dockage					Supplies		Services					
1. Brown's Boat Works	203-377-9303	45		/80	/6			I	HEP		1/50	S		MR
2. Brewer Stratford Marina (Wireless Internet Access)	**203-377-4477**	**90**	**09**	**10/200**	**15/12**	**F**	**GD**	**IM**	**HEP**	**L35,C**	**B/50**	**LPS**	**P**	**GMR**
3. Pootatuck Yacht Club	203-377-9068	70		/66					PRIVATE CLUB					
4. Flagship Marina	203-874-1783	35		/100	10/6	F		M	P		1/30	S		MR
5. Marina at the Dock	203-378-9300	85	09		13/12	F		GIS	HP	L50	B/50	LS	P	GR
6. Milford Landing (Internet Access, Wireless Internet Access)	203-874-1610	65	09	40/40	9/7	F		I			B/50	LS	P	MR
7. Milford Boat Works (Internet Access, Wireless Internet Access)	203-877-1475	50	68	20/200	9/8	F	GD	IM	HE	L35,C	1/30	LS	P	GMR
8. Port Milford Marina	203-877-7802	60	09		8/8			IM	HEP	L	1/30	S		GMR
9. Milford Yacht Club (Wireless Internet Access)	203-783-0065	75	68	10/80	10/7	F		IS		L2	1/50	PS		GMR
10. Spencer's Marina	203-874-4173	36	09	1/13	7/6	F	G	IM	HEP		1/50	S		GMR

Corresponding chart(s) not to be used for navigation. Internet Access, Wireless Internet Access

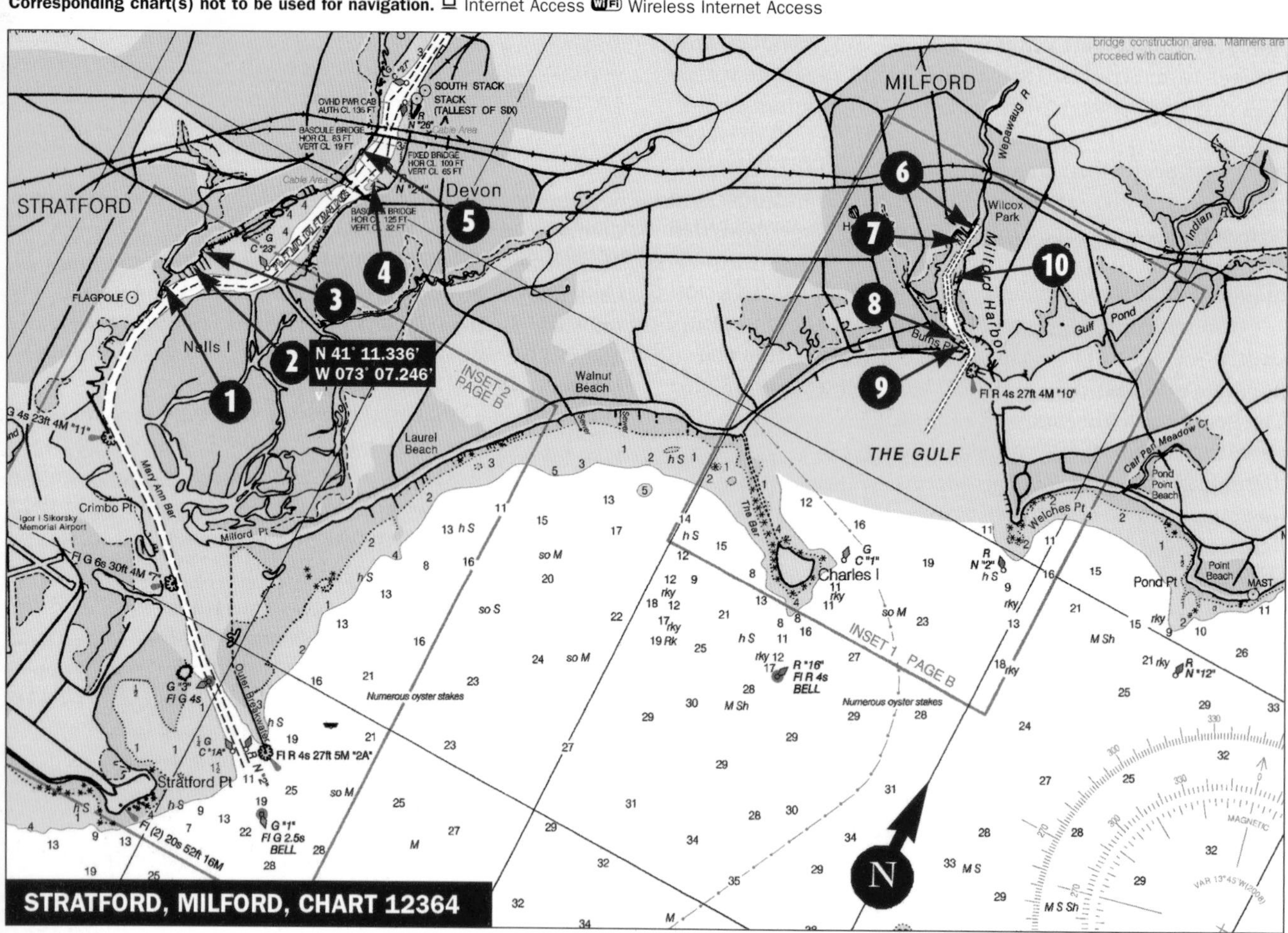

Devon

NAVIGATION: Use Chart 12364. Upriver, the Housatonic is scenic, with green hills coming right down to the water. About two miles north of Stratford, on the east bank, is Devon, actually a small business section of Milford. You must negotiate a bascule bridge (32-foot closed vertical clearance) at Devon. The bridge tender can be reached on VHF Channel 13, call sign KXJ-695, or by phone at 203-579-6203. Do not expect it to open during rush hours, 7 a.m. to 9 a.m., and 4 p.m. to 5:45 p.m., or at night, 9 p.m. to 5 a.m. If you wish to cruise above Devon, call the railroad bridge (19-foot closed vertical clearance) at 212-340-2050; it opens by appointment only. The river carries only 4-foot depths, but is navigable and marked for eight miles to Shelton. It is a pretty side trip for shallow-draft boats.

Dockage: Beyond the bascule bridge, but before the railroad bridge, is the modern Marina at the Dock, featuring all amenities including a picnic area.

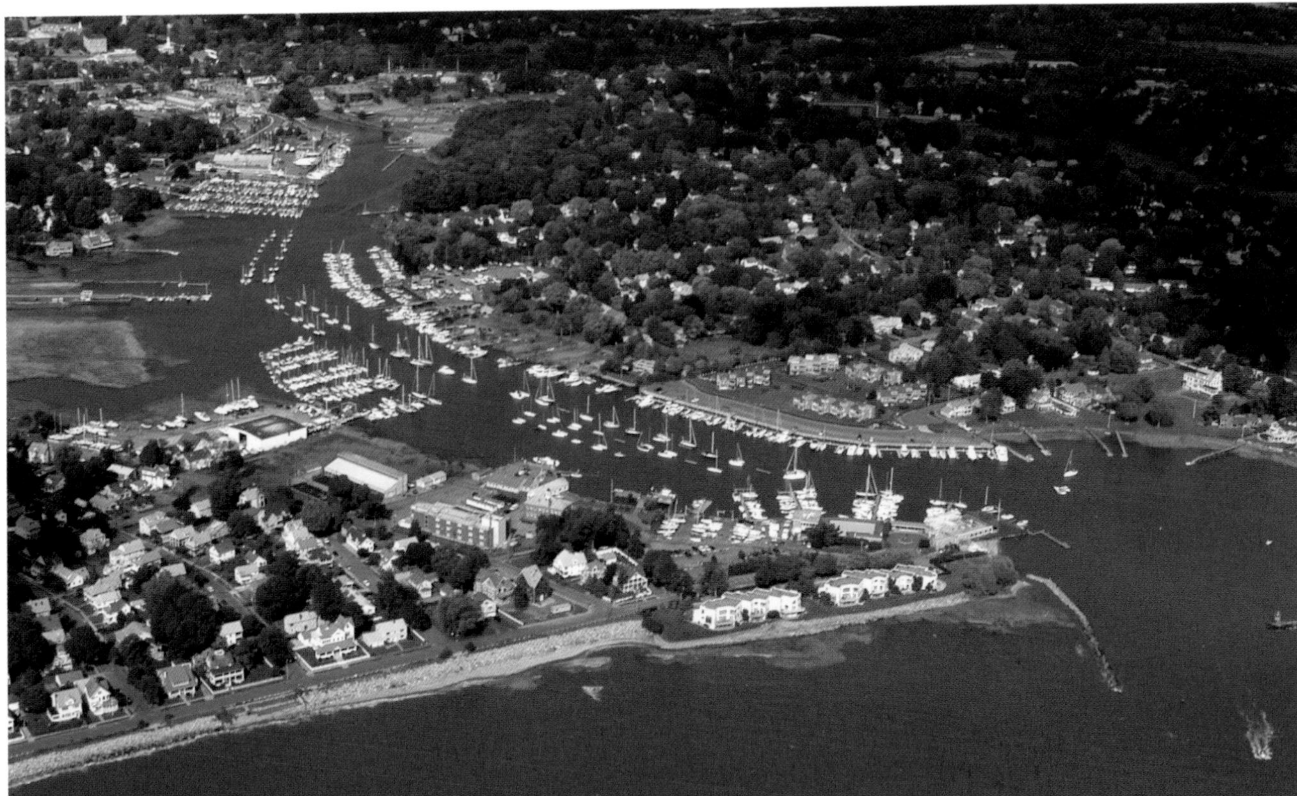

Looking north over Milford Harbor. (Not to be used for navigation.) WATERWAY GUIDE PHOTOGRAPHY

Milford Harbor

Approximately four miles east of Stratford is the attractive summer resort and yachting center of Milford, located at the mouth of the Wepawaug River. It has an easy-to-enter, well-protected but crowded harbor with good marinas that cater to transient mariners. Captain Kidd and other pirates roamed these waters, and buried treasure is rumored to be lost here. The Milford Historical Society (34 High St., 203-874-2664) is housed in three historic homes. Part of their display includes a wonderful collection of American Indian artifacts.

In the mooring-cluttered harbor, a seemingly endless flotilla of small sailing craft is constantly on the move. At the head of the harbor is Milford Landing, a municipal marina for transients. Located next to a pretty public park, it offers tennis courts and a short walkway to town. Other dockage and repair options are available, including the lively Milford Yacht Club, which will berth any cruising boat (although club privileges are reserved for members of reciprocating yacht clubs).

NAVIGATION: Use Chart 12364. Use Bridgeport tide tables. For high tide, subtract 8 minutes; for low tide, subtract 10 minutes. Entry is through The Gulf, past low, rocky, partly wooded Charles Island, keeping green can buoy "1" to port. The channel into Milford is well-marked and it is best to stay inside the buoys; the water is very shallow on both sides as you approach the harbor. The U.S. Army Corps of Engineers tries to maintain 8- to 10-foot depths throughout the channel, but the most current NOAA chart shows 5-foot depths. Slowly work your way in to determine if 8-foot depths exist in the enlarged anchorage area west of the channel. Many of the marinas also strive to maintain 8-foot depths at their facilities.

Anchorage: Inside The Gulf behind Charles Island, you can anchor in 10 to 12 feet of water. It is protected from all directions but the east, and holding is good. A narrow isthmus, which disappears at high tide, connects the island with the mainland. Go right up to the north side of the island for best protection. On still nights with nothing to hold your bow to the wind, you might wallow in the slight surge from Long Island Sound.

New Haven

New Haven, Connecticut's second largest city, is situated almost 70 miles northeast of New York City. While it is a commercial port and the home of Yale University, New Haven is one of Long Island Sound's most important harbors of refuge for commercial shipping. The harbor is industrial and busy. Yet there are two marinas here, out of the hubbub of the inner harbor, that do cater to visiting yachts. Others planning to take advantage of New Haven's attractions may want to leave their boats in Milford or Branford, opting for public transportation to the city.

NAVIGATION: Use Charts 12372 and 12371. For New Haven Harbor, use Bridgeport tide tables. For high tide, subtract 1 minute; for low tide, subtract 6 minutes. The two-mile-wide harbor is protected in part by breakwaters, and its channel is deep, well-marked and able to handle virtually any vessel. The West River channel, to port from

New Haven, CT

NEW HAVEN		Largest Vessel Accommodated	VHF Channel Monitored	Transient Berths / Total Berths	Approach / Dockside Depth (reported)	Floating Docks	Gas / Diesel	Groceries, Ice, Marine Supplies, Snacks	Repairs: Hull, Engine, Propeller	Lift (tonnage), Crane, Rail	1=110V, 2=220V, B=Both, Max Amps	Laundry, Pool, Showers	Pump-Out Station	Nearby: Grocery Store, Motel, Restaurant
		Dockage					Supplies		Services					
1. New Haven Yacht Club	203-469-9608	45	68	1/	8/2	F						S		G
2. West Cove Marine	203-933-3000	45		10/120	10/8	F	G	I		L	1/50	PS	P	GMR
3. City Point Yacht Club	203-789-9301	40	09		7/6	F	RECIPROCAL PRIVILEGES				1/30	S		GMR
4. Oyster Point Marina	203-624-5895	100	09	6/124	11/7	F	GD	GIM	HP		B/50	LS		MR

Corresponding chart(s) not to be used for navigation. Internet Access Wireless Internet Access

the ship channel after entry, is also well-marked, though narrower, and deep enough to accommodate almost any recreational vessel. Outside the channels, however (with the exception of Morris Cove), the harbor is shoal and not navigable. The inner harbor ("New Haven Reach") has no facilities for cruising yachts.

Dockage: About a half mile into the West River channel, Oyster Point Marina has transient slips to accommodate boats with drafts of up to 7 feet. The marina offers both fuel and boat repairs. West Cove Marina is located about a half mile farther upriver (on the westerly side in West Haven), past the stationary highway bridge (23-foot fixed vertical clearance). The marina has dock space for visiting yachts, complemented by a heated pool, cook-out facilities, a clubhouse with a laundry room, showers and restrooms, a fish-cleaning station and a friendly and comfortable atmosphere. You can buy gasoline and ice, and there is a bait and tackle shop nearby. A convenience store, drugstore, fast-food restaurants and a well-regarded Italian restaurant are all within walking distance. Taxicabs are on call for trips to New Haven.

Anchorage: Just inside the breakwater and to starboard, Morris Cove provides good holding and an easy route in and out of the Sound. However, recreational craft may find the cove to be less than adequately protected and open to unwelcome surges and currents.

GOIN' ASHORE: NEW HAVEN, CT

Only a short cab or bus ride away, New Haven has all the attractions of a major American city in a small package. For sightseeing, a stroll among Yale University's classic gargoyled halls and ivy walls, juxtaposed modern architecture, the "tables down at Morey's," windowless secret societies and spacious college walks is, alone, worth the trip to town. Yale's Beinecke Rare Book Library (121 Wall St., 203-432-2977) is one of the best of its kind in the world. You can see an original copy of the Gutenberg Bible here. Other nearby book collections are extraordinary as well. The Peabody Museum of Natural History (170 Whitney Ave., 203-432-5050, Monday through Saturday, 10 a.m. to 5 p.m., Sunday, 12:00 p.m. to 5 p.m.) is one of the oldest and largest history museums in the country. The dinosaur collection there is a treat for kids of any age. Connecticut Children's Museum (22 Wall St., 203-562-5437, call for hours) is dedicated specifically to kids seven years of age and younger. The Eli Whitney Museum (915 Whitney Ave., 203-777-1833, call for hours) has restored Whitney's gun factory, where mass production originated. There are numerous programs and workshops on the principles behind machinery and technology.

The city is also a booming center for the arts, with legions of galleries, studios, repertory companies and theaters. The Shubert Theatre (247 College St., 203-624-1825) was the debut venue for such plays as "Oklahoma," "My Fair Lady" and "The King and I." The Long Wharf Theater (222 Sargent Drive, 203-787-4282) and the Yale Repertory Company (York and Chapel streets, 203-432-1234, October through May) are two of the more famous theater companies, where major stage and film stars have gotten their starts. Summer visitors can enjoy Jazz in the Parks, Friday Flicks and a huge Fourth of July celebration. Visit www.visitnewhaven.com for all schedules and events.

Possibilities for shopping and restaurants are numerous; inquire locally on the best spots. A train station and bus terminal will require a taxi from the harbor.

ADDITIONAL RESOURCES:

- New Haven Online, **www.cityofnewhaven.com** or **www.visitnewhaven.com**

NEARBY GOLF COURSES:
Alling Memorial Golf Club, 35 Eastern St., New Haven, CT 06513, 203-946-8014, **www.allingmemorialgolfclub.com**

NEARBY MEDICAL FACILITIES:
Yale-New Haven Hospital, 20 York St., New Haven, CT 06510, 203-688-4242

Branford

Branford is the best port of refuge and easiest harbor entry in the almost 20 miles stretching between New Haven and Clinton. It is a charming community with many fine old restored homes dating from Colonial days, when it was an important salt works (meat for Revolutionary War troops was preserved in Branford salt), a Yankee trading center

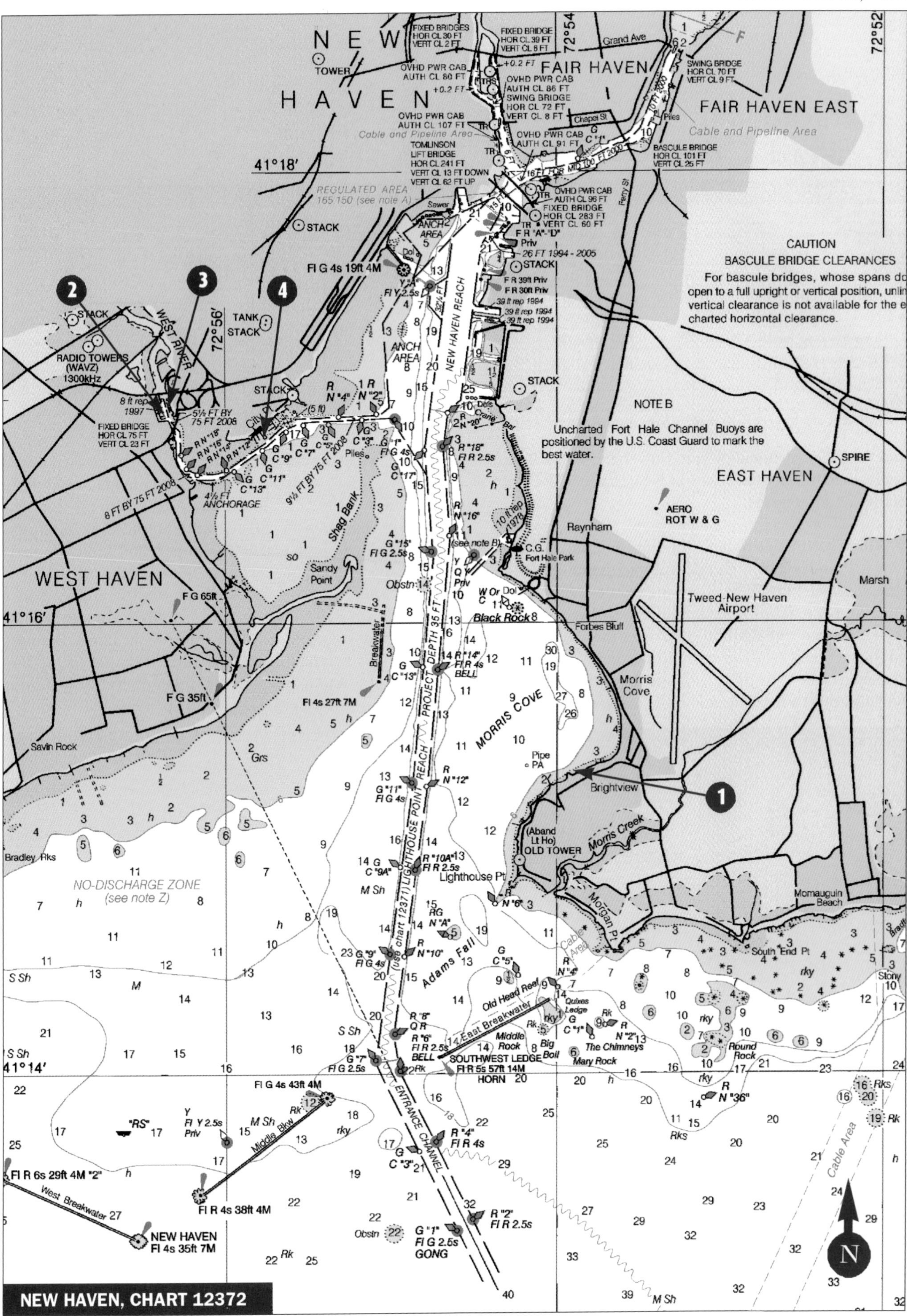
NEW HAVEN
FAIR HAVEN
FAIR HAVEN EAST
WEST HAVEN
EAST HAVEN
CAUTION
BASCULE BRIDGE CLEARANCES
NOTE B
Uncharted Fort Hale Channel Buoys are positioned by the U.S. Coast Guard to mark the best water.
Tweed-New Haven Airport
NEW HAVEN REACH
LIGHTHOUSE POINT REACH
ENTRANCE CHANNEL
MORRIS COVE
Lighthouse Pt
Black Rock
Sandy Point
Shag Bank
Savin Rock
Bradley Rks
NO-DISCHARGE ZONE (see note Z)
SOUTHWEST LEDGE
NEW HAVEN CHART 12372

Branford and Guilford, CT

BRANFORD, GUILFORD		Largest Vessel Accommodated	VHF Channel Monitored	Transient Berths / Total Berths	Approach / Dockside Depth (reported)	Floating Docks	Gas / Diesel	Groceries, Ice, Marine Supplies, Snacks	Repairs: Hull, Engine, Propeller	Lift (tonnage), Crane, Rail	1=110V, 2=220V, B=Both, Max Amps	Laundry, Pool, Showers	Pump-Out Station	Nearby: Grocery Store, Motel, Restaurant
		Dockage					Supplies		Services					
1. Branford Yacht Club	203-488-9798	60		/210	10/10	F	GD	I			1/50	S	P	GR
2. Brewer Bruce and Johnson's Marina-West (WiFi)	**203-488-5613**	**50**	**66/09**	**10/350**	**12/11**	**F**	**GD**	**GIMS**	**HEP**	**L30**	**B/50**	**S**	**P**	**GMR**
3. Goodsell Point Marina	203-488-5292	45		2/175	8/8	F			HP	L25,C			P	GMR
4. Dutch Wharf Boat Yard and Marina Inc.	203-488-9000	65		1/75	10/10	F		M	HEP		B/50	S		R
5. Indian Neck Yacht Club	203-488-9276	40		/90	8/8		G	I			1/30	S		
6. Branford Landing Marina	203-483-6544	65		3/30	8/8	F		IMS	HEP	L50,C	1/30	S		GR
7. Brewer Bruce and Johnson's Marina (WiFi)	**203-488-8329**	**70**	**09**	**35/500**	**7/7**	**F**		**IM**	**HEP**	**L50**	**B/50**	**LPS**	**P**	**GMR**
8. Guilford Boat Yards Inc.	203-453-5031	30		2/8	1/6	F		M	HEP	L10	1/15			GMR
9. Brown's Boat Yard (Internet Access)	203-453-6283	40	16	2/40	6/5	F	GD	M	HEP	L25	1/30			G
10. Guilford Yacht Club	203-415-3427	100	71	5/158	6/8	F		I			1/50	PS	P	GR

Corresponding chart(s) not to be used for navigation. Internet Access (WiFi) Wireless Internet Access

and the original home of Yale University. Today Branford is more of a residential annex to New Haven and a town of many condominiums.

NAVIGATION: Use Chart 12372. For Branford, use Bridgeport tide tables. For high tide, subtract 5 minutes; for low tide, subtract 13 minutes. Entering Branford from Long Island Sound requires threading a series of rocks guarding the entrance to the Branford River, but they are well-charted, buoyed and relatively easy to make out, offering little challenge when visibility is good. Eastbound boats turn northward between Cow and Calf (marked by flashing red bell buoy "34") to port and Five Foot Rock (marked by red nun buoy "32") to starboard. Pass west of Blyn Rock's flashing red buoy "2" and Bird Rock's red nun buoy "4." The buoyed channel leads between Big Mermaid (a high rock, marked by flashing green "7") to port and Little Mermaid rock (marked by red nun buoy "6") to starboard on entry.

Dockage: Visiting cruisers can almost always find a berth on the Branford River. Just behind the Branford Town Dock (immediately to port on entering the river), Branford Yacht Club maintains an excellent facility that can accommodate visiting yachtsmen from other clubs (reciprocating privileges) at its deepwater (10-foot depths at mean low

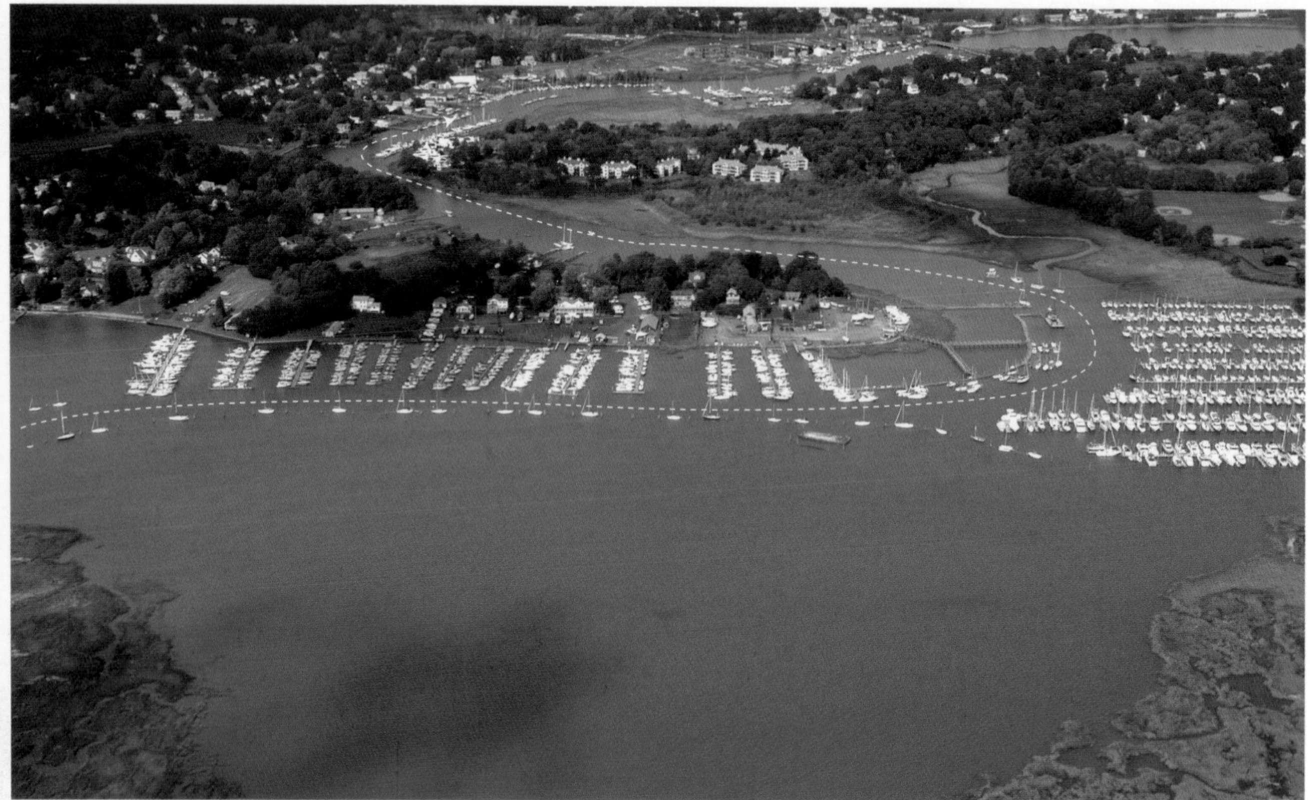

Looking north over Branford. (Not to be used for navigation.) WATERWAY GUIDE PHOTOGRAPHY

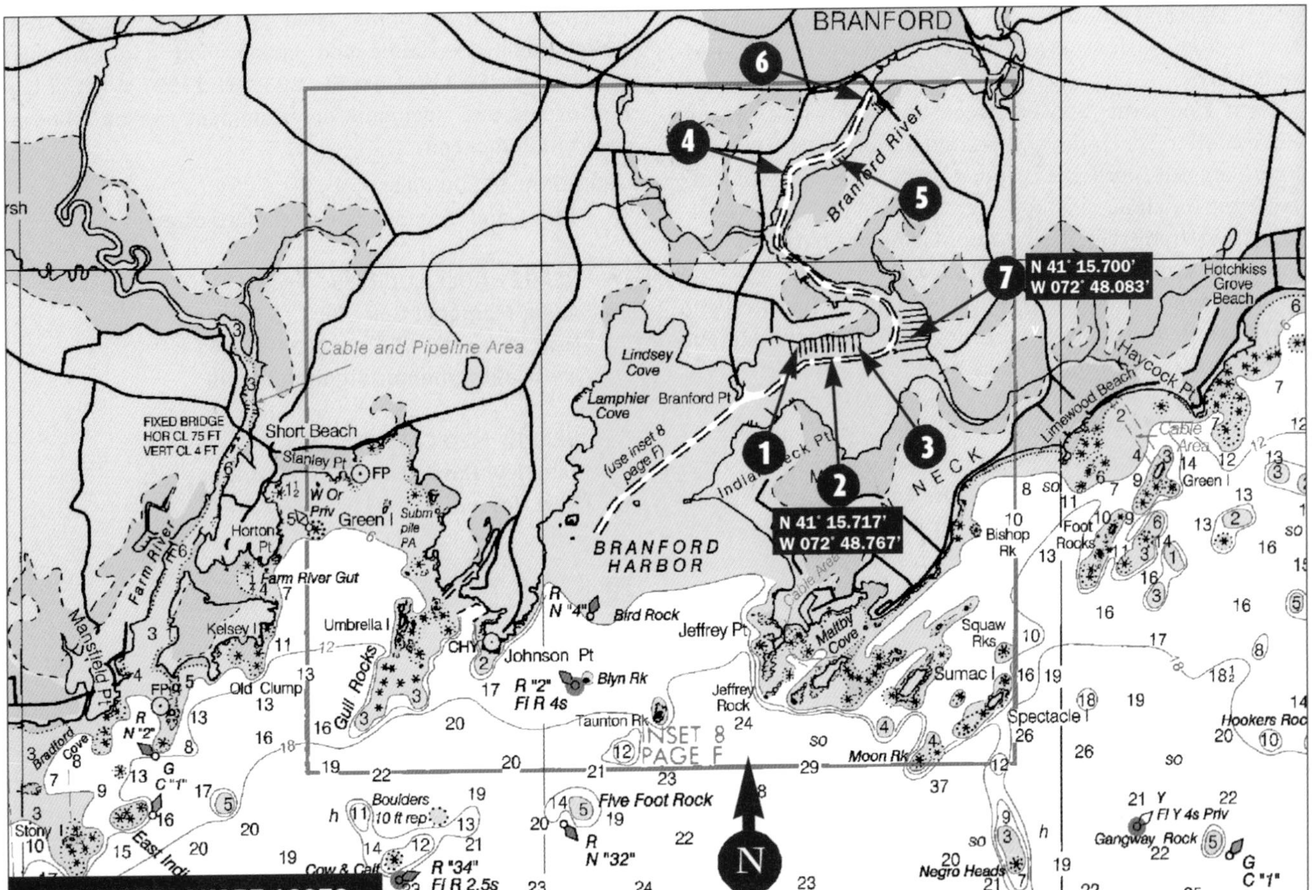
BRANFORD
Branford River
N 41° 15.700'
W 072° 48.083'
N 41° 15.717'
W 072° 48.767'
Hotchkiss Grove Beach
Haycock Pt
Limewood Beach
Cable Area
Cable and Pipeline Area
Lindsey Cove
Lamphier Cove
Branford Pt
(use inset 8 page F)
Indian Neck Pt
NECK
FIXED BRIDGE
HOR CL 75 FT
VERT CL 4 FT
Short Beach
Stanley Pt
FP
W Or Priv
Green I
Subm pile PA
Horton Pt
Farm River
Farm River Gut
Kelsey I
Mansfield Pt
Umbrella I
Gull Rocks
CHY
Johnson Pt
R N "4"
Bird Rock
R "2" Fl R 4s
Blyn Rk
Jeffrey Pt
Jeffrey Rock
Taunton Rk
BRANFORD HARBOR
Maltby Cove
Bishop Rk
Squaw Rks
Sumac I
Spectacle I
Moon Rk
Foot Rocks
Green I
Hookers Rock
Old Clump
Bradford Cove
R N "2"
G C "1"
Stony I
East Indian
Boulders 10 ft rep
Cow & Calf
R "34" Fl R 2.5s BELL
Five Foot Rock
R N "32"
INSET 8 PAGE F
Negro Heads
21 Y Fl Y 4s Priv
Gangway Rock
G C "1"

BRANFORD, CHART 12372

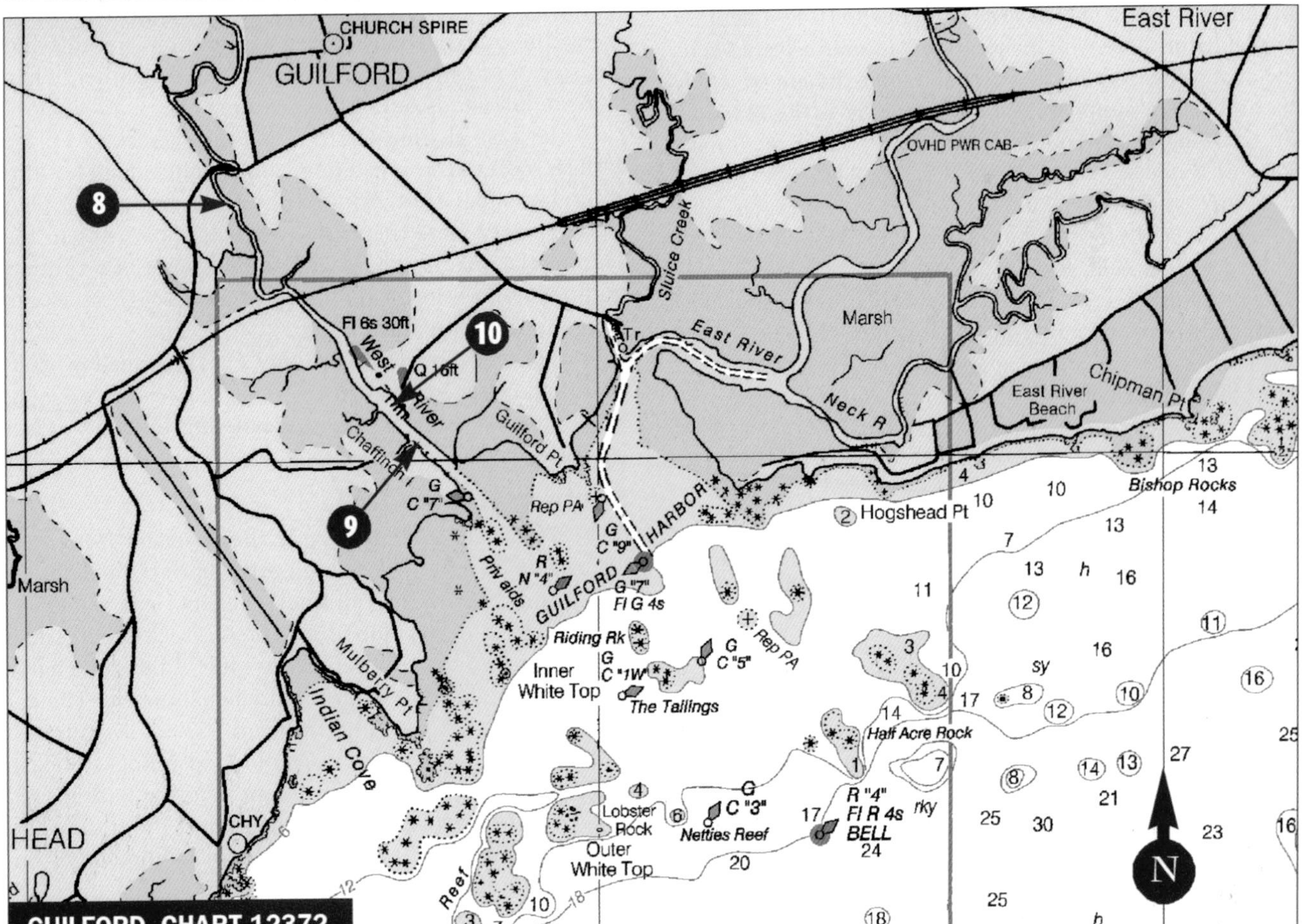
CHURCH SPIRE
GUILFORD
East River
OVHD PWR CAB
Sluice Creek
Marsh
East River
Neck R
Chipman Pt
East River Beach
Fl 6s 30ft
West River
Q 16ft
Chaffinch
Guilford Pt
Tr
G C "7"
Rep PA
G C "9"
R N "4"
Priv aids
GUILFORD HARBOR
G "7" Fl G 4s
Riding Rk
G C "1W"
Inner White Top
The Tailings
G C "5"
Rep PA
Hogshead Pt
Bishop Rocks
Half Acre Rock
Mulberry Pt
Indian Cove
Marsh
CHY
HEAD
Lobster Rock
Outer White Top
G C "3"
Netties Reef
R "4" Fl R 4s BELL
rky
Reef

GUILFORD, CHART 12372

water) slips and moorings. Gasoline, diesel fuel, ice, pump-out, restrooms, showers and clubhouse amenities are available here.

Next door, the Brewer Bruce and Johnson's Marina - West offers deep-draft slips and moorings to visitors. Fuels, engine, hull and prop repairs and pump-out are available on-site.

Farther along, Goodsell Point Marina has both slips and moorings available in depths of at least 8 feet.

Just beyond Goodsell Point Marina, around the bend in the river and on the opposite side, Brewer Bruce and Johnson Marina ordinarily has numerous slips (on newly rebuilt concrete or composite-decking docks with 30- to 50-amp electrical service and cable TV), accommodating vessels with drafts of up to 8 feet. Transient moorings also are available. A full range of repairs and services are available here, supported by a parts department and marine supply store. A coin-operated laundry, restrooms/showers and a pump-out station are also on-site, as is Sam's Dockside Restaurant (197 Montowese St., 203-488-3007). Cruisers who are tired of the summer heat will enjoy a dip in the marina's swimming pool.

Farther upriver, Dutch Wharf Boat Yard and Marina may have slips available for transients (call ahead), though the yard's reputation has been built upon its fine wooden boat restorations and repairs rather than resort-style amenities. The Harbor Street Market restaurant (312 Harbor St., 203-483-1612) is within walking distance.

Near the end of the Branford River's dredged channel, Branford Landing may have a transient slip (6-foot depths) available for those who make a reservation in advance. Fuels and repair services are available here, as are showers, ice and marine supplies. The Calypso River Grill (50 Maple St., 203-481-1211) and Branford River Lobster retail market (50 Maple St., 203-627-5173) are on-site.

Nearby Indian Neck Yacht Club rents deepwater slips to visitors and offers moorings (without launch service). Showers, fuel and ice are available at the clubhouse. The Branford River, like many Connecticut tributaries, has strong currents. Be aware of the direction and strength of the current when docking at any of the marinas listed. Call for docking assistance if the current is running strong.

GOIN' ASHORE: BRANFORD, CT

The village center of Branford is a significant hike—more than two miles—from any of the marinas. Though there are period houses to view and a number of quaint shops, there is little in the village center to hold the interest of skippers and crew bent on serious reprovisioning. The shopping mall with a Stop & Shop, drugstore and discount liquor store is another three miles farther on U.S. Route 1.

Locally recommended restaurants include: Lenny's Indian Head Inn (205 S. Montowese St., 203-488-1500), rustic, very popular and closest to the marinas, with transportation provided; La Luna Ristorante, (168 Main St., 203-483-9995), Italian and in town; Darbar India, (1070 Main St., 203-481-8994), highly recommended Indian food and Southport Brewing Co. (850 W. Main St., 203-481-2739). A list of current events and additional entertainment can be found at www.branfordct.com.

ADDITIONAL RESOURCES:

- Town of Branford, **www.branford-ct.gov**

NEARBY GOLF COURSES:
Alling Memorial Golf Club, 35 Eastern St.,
New Haven, CT 06513, 203-946-8014,
www.allingmemorialgolfclub.com

NEARBY MEDICAL FACILITIES:
Yale-New Haven Hospital, 20 York St.,
New Haven, CT 06510, 203-688-4242

EAST OF BRANFORD

For the next eight miles east of Branford, the intervening shore is wild, marshy and dotted with summer communities and granite quarries. It is rocky, challenging for those unfamiliar with the area and should be approached with caution and careful study of the chart. All of the harbors here are packed with local boats, require local knowledge and have no room or amenities for transients.

First of these harbors is tiny, crowded Pine Orchard, a summer community with fine homes, lots of rocks and a yacht club unexpectedly large and ambitious for a harbor this size. You can anchor outside in good weather, when there are no winds out of the east or south.

To the east of Pine Orchard is Stony Creek, a village with an oyster fleet, lobstermen and a public dock for dinghies and small craft. You will find gas, ice, a snack bar and a grocery store there. An excursion boat runs to the Thimble Islands from here and carries on a two-century tradition of passenger and freight service. Sightseers can go on hourly tours.

Anchorage: Just beyond Stony Creek, a shallow-draft boat can anchor in Joshua Cove as long as care is taken to avoid unmarked Leetes Rocks on entering, and no weather is expected out of the south.

Sachem Head

NAVIGATION: Use Chart 12372. For Sachem Head, use Bridgeport tide tables. For high tide, subtract 11 minutes; for low tide, subtract 15 minutes. Sachem Head is the harbor just west of Guilford. It is pretty, rock-lined, small and dominated by a friendly yacht club of the same name located immediately to starboard when entering. The approach is relatively straightforward. Using flashing red bell buoy "22" as a guide to avoid Goose Rocks Shoals, progress can be made in good depths to the flashing red light (every three seconds) at the end of the breakwater at the entrance to the harbor, which is maintained by Sachem Yacht Club from June to September.

Looking southeast over Clinton Harbor. (Not to be used for navigation.) WATERWAY GUIDE PHOTOGRAPHY

Inside there is little room to anchor, but there may well be a vacant guest mooring in 5 to 10 feet of water (call ahead to the yacht club on VHF Channel 09 for availability). On a quiet summer evening, it is a pleasant stop, though there are no amenities except a pay phone at the clubhouse. Wide open to the prevailing southwesterlies, however, this is no place to be when the wind is up. Club members complain of caroming boats, wrenched loose from their moorings here at least once a season by significant waves blown in from the long fetch across Long Island Sound.

The Thimble Islands and Stony Creek

Just west of Sachem Head, off the Connecticut shore between Branford and Guilford, are the Thimbles, the largest group of islands on Long Island Sound. These clumps of rock form a narrow alley of deep water down the middle. Serving as the shore side to The Thimbles, Stony Creek is a busy spot occupied by a plethora of small boats, ferries and fishermen. There are several dinghy docks available. Activity starts early and carries well into the evening.

Anchorage: With the exception of the harbor in Stony Creek, anchorages are everywhere, and even on crowded summer weekends, you can usually find protection and deep water. The favorite anchorages are anywhere on the line between green can buoy "1" (between High and Pot islands) and green can buoy "11" (near East Crib Island), to the northwest, in 10 to 20 feet of water.

Another anchorage is found east of Pot Island, which is approached from the east by leaving red nun buoy "2CR" to starboard. While exposed to westerly and southwesterly winds, the area to the north of West Crib Island is a good option. Take particular care to observe the underwater cable areas servicing the many islands. A water taxi service is available for those not wishing to use the dinghy. Proceed cautiously—swimmers are usually diving off the cliffs or paddling between boats. At the height of the season, a small barge might be anchored north of Pot Island selling hot dogs and cold drinks. No services or facilities are available on the islands.

GOIN' ASHORE:

THE THIMBLE ISLANDS AND STONY CREEK, CT

The Thimble Islands consist of 25 inhabited islands and hundreds of pink granite rock formations that scatter into Long Island Sound off the unique coastal village of Stony Creek. This cluster of islands very much resembles the endless islands off the coast of Maine. The Islands and Stony Creek have comprised a popular summer community since the days of Captain Kidd, who used to hide his ships among the rocky cliffs within High Island. President Taft was well known for vacationing in the Islands.

The Thimble Islands were created more than 10,000 years ago when glacial action exposed ancient granite bedrock. As the glacier moved, it picked up loose soil and stone and pried loose blocks of granite, leaving the Islands after the glacier melted.

Although the Thimbles are private, the Outer Island is run by the Stewart B. McKinney Association in cooperation with the U.S. Fish and Wildlife Service. Access to the island is limited, but during the summer on the weekends (weather permitting) a docent is usually available. Check online at www.friendsofouterisland.org for the summer schedule.

Stony Creek is well worth a dinghy ride. There is a small dock for tie-ups, and a trip to Stony Creek Market (178 Thimble Island Road, 203-488-0145) for a hearty breakfast on the porch will not disappoint. There is a small public beach and you will see many tourists who have come for a Thimble Island Cruise on the Sea Mist. Sea kayaking is a very popular activity in and around Stony Creek and the Thimbles. Check out the Branford Chamber of Commerce Web site for kayak rental information.

ADDITIONAL RESOURCES:

- Town of Branford, **www.branford-ct.gov** or **www.branfordct.com**

NEARBY GOLF COURSES:
Guilford Lakes Golf Course,
200 N. Madison Road,
Guilford, CT 06437, 203-453-8214

NEARBY MEDICAL FACILITIES:
Yale-New Haven Hospital, 20 York St.,
New Haven, CT 06510, 203-688-4242, **www.ynhh.org**

Guilford

The village of Guilford provides a glimpse of New England architectural history at its best. Many of the structures dating back to the 17th century have survived, and a walk through the charming harborside area is memorable. The shopping area and services are also available within a short walk of the harbor.

NAVIGATION: Use Charts 12372 and 12373. Use Bridgeport tide tables. For high tide, subtract 11 minutes; for low tide, subtract 21 minutes. Guilford is located between the West and East rivers about three miles north of rock-lined and uninhabited Falkner Island. Though the entrance to West River is buoyed, it is rather shallow.

The East River entry is easier, though it will require sharp attention and good visibility for the newcomer. The entrance channel into the East River has anywhere from 3.5 to 8 feet of water in the main channel, the shallowest part being in the approach to Guilford Point, especially between green can buoy "9" and red nun buoy "10." Upriver, the National Audubon Society maintains a 150-acre reserve, protecting the tidal estuary and providing a panorama of scenic views.

Dockage: About a mile inland of the entrance, Brown's Boat Yard, on the west side of the West River, is primarily a working yard, offering numerous marine services with a new 25-ton lift to facilitate haul-outs. In a pinch, a transient slip might be arranged on the yard's floating docks along the river.

Transients will find ample space at Guilford Yacht Club's well-staffed marina, a short distance farther upriver on the east side. The club's yacht basin has been dredged to 8-foot depths under modern, floating docks. Overnight dockage comes with dockside water and electricity, access to the club's heated pool, restrooms, showers and a clubhouse. The village of Guilford, where supplies can be found, is about a half mile away and a pleasant walk (or easily-obtained ride) from the clubhouse.

GOIN' ASHORE:
GUILFORD, CT

In addition to an intriguing mixture of old and new architectural styles (a restored 18th-century shop next to a 1990s bungalow, for example), Guilford's "Classic Connecticut" town green, a short walk from the harbor, is ringed with useful village amenities for cruising skippers and crew.

Guilford Food Center (77 Whitfield St., 203-453-4849) has a comprehensive line of basic groceries and a good selection of meats and produce. Cilantro Specialty Foods (85 Whitfield St., 203-458-2555) has just that, along with an excellent selection of coffees. Also on the green are Page True Value Hardware (9 Boston St., 203-453-5267), Guilford Savings Bank (1 Park St., 203-453-6759 with a 24-hour ATM) and Breakwater Books (81 Whitfield St., 203-453-4141), along with various boutiques and galleries. Sunday concerts on the green are anticipated events. The Guilford Rotary puts on a Lobsterfest in mid-June each year.

For history buffs, Guilford boasts five historic house museums and all of them are very good examples of 17th, 18th- and 19th-century architecture. The Henry Whitfield State Museum (248 Old Whitfield St., 203-453-2457) remains the oldest stone house in New England and contains many artifacts of 17th-century Guilford and the Puritan life of the period.

The well-established Stonehouse Restaurant (506 Old Whitfield St., 203-458-3700) also receives high praise for its varied menu and excellent service. Maritime Grill (2548 Boston Post Road, 203-453-0774) is another favorite. Larger stores and the usual mix of fast-food restaurants will be found some blocks north on U.S. Route 1.

ADDITIONAL RESOURCES:

- Guilford Chamber of Commerce, **www.guilfordct.com**

NEARBY GOLF COURSES:
Guilford Lakes Golf Course, 200 N. Madison Road,
Guilford, CT 06437, 203-453-8214

NEARBY MEDICAL FACILITIES:
Yale University Health Services, 17 Hillhouse Ave.,
New Haven, CT 06511, 203-432-0123

Clinton and Westbrook, CT

CLINTON, WESTBROOK		Largest Vessel Accommodated	VHF Channel Monitored	Transient Berths / Total Berths	Approach / Dockside Depth (reported)	Floating Docks	Gas / Diesel	Groceries, Ice, Marine Supplies, Snacks	Repairs: Hull, Engine, Propeller	Lift (tonnage), Crane, Rail	1=110V, 2=220V, B=Both, Max Amps	Laundry, Pool, Showers	Pump-Out Station	Nearby: Grocery Store, Motel, Restaurant
		Dockage					Supplies		Services					
1. **Cedar Island Marina** 🖳 WiFi	**860-669-8681**	**120**	**09**	**70/400**	**6.5/8**	**F**	**GD**	**GIMS**	**HEP**	**L35,C22**	**B/100**	**LPS**	**P**	**GMR**
2. Harborside Marina	860-669-1705	180		/10	20/9	F			HEP		B/50			GMR
3. Port Clinton Marina	860-669-4563	50	09	10/110	9/9	F	GD	M	HP	L	B/50	S		GMR
4. Marshview Marina LLC	860-399-1111	30	69	2/38	4/4	F		IM	HEP	L3	1/30			GMR
5. **Brewer Pilots Point Marina North** 🖳 WiFi	**860-399-5128**	**60**	**09**	**/250**	**10/6**	**F**		**I**	**HEP**	**L35**	**B/50**	**PS**	**P**	**GMR**
6. **Brewer Pilots Point Marina South** 🖳 WiFi	**860-399-7906**	**120**	**09**	**10/500**	**10/8**	**F**	**GD**	**IMS**	**HEP**	**L**	**B/50**	**PS**	**P**	**GMR**
7. Harry's Marine Repair	860-399-6165	40		3/76	8/8	F	G	IM	EP	L10,C	1/30	S	P	R
8. **Brewer Pilots Point Marina East** 🖳 WiFi	**860-399-6421**	**50**	**09**	**/80**	**10/6**	**F**			**HEP**	**L**	**B/50**	**S**	**P**	**GMR**
9. Custom Navigation Systems	860-399-5511	MARINE NAVIGATION & ELECTRONICS												
10. Pier 76 Marina 🖳	860-399-7122	25		80/260	6/3	F		IM	EP					R

Corresponding chart(s) not to be used for navigation. 🖳 Internet Access WiFi Wireless Internet Access

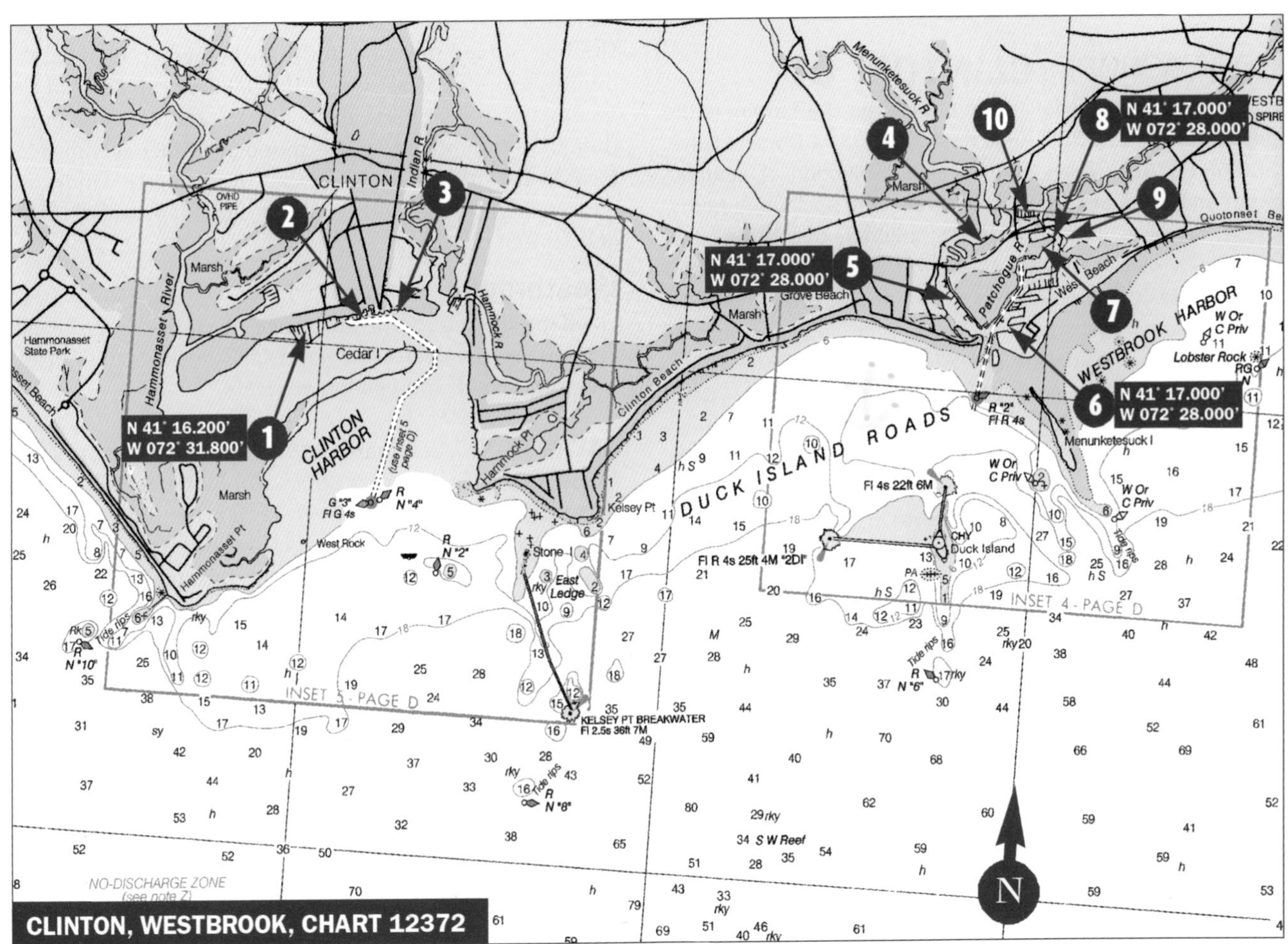

CLINTON, WESTBROOK, CHART 12372

Clinton

Clinton Harbor is a "must stop" on most any boater's itinerary when transiting Long Island Sound from either direction. It is located in a perfect location, a good day's run, for mariners transiting to or from ports east such as Block Island, Newport or Mystic. This harbor has just about everything: ease of entry, excellent protection, accommodating marinas, eye-appealing views of sea and strand and good sightseeing, dining and reprovisioning. Marinas are the way to go, as there is no adequate anchorage here.

NAVIGATION: Use Chart 12372. The approach is unencumbered south and west of Kelsey Point Breakwater, aside from a marked 5-foot shoal (red nun buoy "2") at the shore end of the rock jetty. Swift currents run in the channel here on both tides, and it is wise to pay attention to possible sideslip and an almost certain grounding on the shallow banks on both sides of the channel.

Dockage: Two Clinton marinas cater to transient boaters. They appear to starboard on the channel immediately after rounding Cedar Island, which is to the west. The somewhat rustic Port Clinton Marina is first, with about 10 transient berths (fore and aft on floating docks) in good depths.

Cedar Island Marina operates a full-service facility with deep water, floating docks, pump-out, electrical hookups, a large heated pool, a play area for children (and even a children's activities director), spacious shower, laundry facilities and repair services. Gasoline and diesel fuel are available at the marina's easy-access fuel dock. The marina also has its own biology staff that conduct continuing ecological research projects in the area. A local shuttle bus makes frequent stops at the marina to transport visitors to Clinton's premium outlets, abundant antiques stores and a local winery.

GOIN' ASHORE: **CLINTON, CT**

A few steps from Cedar Island Marina, on the harbor, is the popular Ernie & Rocky's Aqua Restaurant (34 Riverside Drive, 860-664-3788), which offers a good selection of seafood, meat and salad dishes, Italian entrees and acclaimed homemade desserts. If traveling with children, this is an ideal restaurant near your vessel. Also on the waterfront, BB&G Lobster (fresh lobsters daily and seafood at retail) has a local following of many years standing. Other facilities, such as Clinton Grain & Hardware (27 W. Main St., 860-669-8255), the post office (2 W. Main St., 860-669-4155), Liberty Bank (8 E. Main St., 860-669-5773, with ATM), a CVS pharmacy (14 E. Main St., 203-245-3165) and Chip's Pub III (24 W. Main St., 860-669-8463) a local favorite for casual dining, are a little more than a half mile north in "downtown Clinton" on U.S. Route 1. Additional reprovisioning possibilities are 1.5 miles north on U.S. Route 1, at the Stop & Shop Supermarket (Boston Post Road, 860-669-2228). There is a West Marine store (860-664-4060) in town at 266 E. Main St.

The town of Clinton is a gem, displaying a wide variety of 19th-century housing styles. Of particular interest is the Stanton House (ancient store, inn and fascinating museum, 63 E. Main St., 860-669-2132). With a substantial sampling of its original stock of goods and records from Colonial store days, it represents a unique portrait in time. French nobleman and soldier the Marquis de Lafayette lodged here in Revolutionary days. Also worth a look is the renovated gold-leaf schooner weathervane on the period-piece town hall, from the 1930s. The Capt. Dibbell House Bed and Breakfast (21 Commerce St., 860-669-1646) has excellent accommodations in a restored early 19th-century setting. If you are in the mood for hiking, Peters Memorial Woods is nearby and has many beautiful hiking trails.

ADDITIONAL RESOURCES:

- **Clinton Chamber of Commerce, www.clintonct.com**

NEARBY GOLF COURSES:
Guilford Lakes Golf Course, 200 N. Madison Road, Guilford, CT 06437, 203-453-8214

NEARBY MEDICAL FACILITIES:
Yale-New Haven Hospital, 6 Woodland Rd., Madison, CT, 203-245-3205

Duck Island

Anchorage: Two lengthy breakwaters extend north and west from Duck Island to create Duck Island Roads (with no supplies and only a beach landing). Added protection is afforded by a third breakwater to the west, reaching seaward from Stone Island off Kelsey Point.

A favored anchorage is found just inside the northern arm off Duck Island in 7- to 14-foot depths at low tide. Holding is good throughout the anchorage, though depths diminish to 4 to 5 feet inside the lights at each end of the breakwaters. Swimming is good here, and it is a popular, though not unduly crowded, spot on summer evenings for local boats and distance cruisers. In northerly winds, anchoring is good right off Grove Beach with a sandy bottom and 10-foot depths.

Westbrook

Good protection and a full range of amenities are available just to the north of Duck Island in the waters of the Menunketesuck and Patchogue rivers.

NAVIGATION: Use Charts 12372 and 12374. For Westbrook, use Bridgeport tide tables. For high tide, subtract 24 minutes; for low tide, subtract 32 minutes. Enter through a dredged channel marked by flashing red buoy "2," which must be left to starboard. The can and nun buoys marking this passage must be carefully observed; otherwise, grounding is a near certainty. Note that green can buoy "5" is situated approximately 25 yards south of the navigable channel to the Menunketesuck River, so a sharp left turn at green can buoy "5" will provide unfortunate results.

In addition, the Menunketesuck River has shoaled along its western side; deeper water is found along the dock faces located to the east. The Patchogue River bears slightly to the right from the dredged channel and offers a 7-foot-deep, 125-foot-wide alternative to the Menunketesuck. Both rivers are busy passageways and, unfortunately, no anchoring is permitted in either river.

Dockage: The eastern side of the Patchogue River is almost wholly taken over by Brewer Pilots Point Marina (north, south and east), which is one of the largest (more than 800 slips) and best-equipped facilities on Long Island Sound. It offers a large pool and changing rooms, multiple shower and restroom buildings, tennis and volleyball courts, a modern clubhouse with indoor/outdoor cooking facilities and a TV room, boating supplies and a

Looking north over the Patchogue River. (Not to be used for navigation.) WATERWAY GUIDE PHOTOGRAPHY

well-stocked parts department, which will match marine-discount prices. Brewer Pilots Point Marina is also known for superior workmanship; vessels travel from afar to have their boats cared for here.

Berths on Pilots Point's floating docks are usually available, but on holidays and mid-summer weekends, advance reservations are recommended. Brewer's R Dock was recently reconfigured to accommodate more boats in the 50-foot range. These larger slips are in high demand, so call ahead (860-399-7906). Much of the America's Cup 12-meter work used to take place here, and the yard is one of the few yards in the country that produces lead keels weighing upwards of 40,000 pounds for high-tech race circuit contenders.

Today, though, most of Pilots Point's biggest sheds are given over to work on world-class racer/cruisers and premier charter vessels. Virtually any repair can be completed here. A courtesy van service is available for local shopping trips. If you run out of docking options, one of the smaller marinas at the head of the harbor may have transient slips, as well.

GOIN' ASHORE: **WESTBROOK, CT**

What began as a farming community and later a shipbuilding center during the American Revolution, is today one of the best stopover ports for cruising boaters on Long Island Sound.

David Bushnell invented the submarine here in 1776. The wood and steel *American Turtle* was a hand-powered, one-man submarine that submerged when its ballast tanks were filled with water. Used in the unsuccessful attempt to attach a torpedo to the belly of the 64-gun British Man-o-War *Eagle* in New York Harbor during the Revolution, the submersible was the forerunner to the modern-day submarine. The Military Historians Museum, located on the green in Westbrook, displays a large selection of American military uniforms.

From the harbor of Westbrook, you can access many services; several are within easy walking distance of the marinas along Boston Post Road (U.S. Route 1). Immediately west of the bridge over the Patchogue River, Bill's Seafood (548 Boston Post Road, 860-399-7224) has a rustic atmosphere, riverside tables and decent live jazz on weekends to complement fresh-fried catch in a basket and a favorite brew.

Just beyond, Humphrey's Grill and Bar (5 Sycamore Way, 203-481-7735) serves a variety of chicken wing concoctions, stacked-high sandwiches of all sorts and a full menu of grilled items. Farther west, Lenny & Joe's Fish Tale (86 Boston Post Road, 860-669-0767) is popular for its complete line of seafood possibilities. A half mile farther toward Clinton, the Westbrook Lobster Co. (346 E. Main St., 860-664-9464, open daily, 11 a.m. to 8 p.m.) specializes in fresh and frozen fish at retail, fresh-baked breads, smoked fish and a Clambake in a Can just add water and cook on you own stove or grill.

East of the river bridge, near the entrance to Brewer Pilots Point Marina's east and south yards, Custom Navigation Systems (633 Boston Post Rd., 860-399-5511) is where the marinas turn for expert assistance with marine electronic needs and repairs; and Sobstad (404 Boston Post Road, 860-399-8899) makes custom sails in its large loft. Water's Edge Inn and Resort (1525 Boston Post Road, 860-399-5901) serves gourmet dishes in an elegant setting, along with a superb view about a mile-and-a-half farther east. Many more restaurants and stores can be found in Old Saybrook, about four miles east of the Westbrook marinas.

Located just west of Westbrook and visible as you enter, Duck Island is the resident summer home for gulls, cormorants, ducks, snowy egrets, glossy ibises and great blue, green and black-crowned night herons. If you are a nature lover, stay alert for this beautiful bird life.

ADDITIONAL RESOURCES:

■ Town of Westbrook, **www.westbrookct.us**

NEARBY GOLF COURSES:
Fox Hopyard Golf Club, 1 Hopyard Road, East Haddam, CT 06423, 860-434-6644, **www.golfthefox.com**

NEARBY MEDICAL FACILITIES:
Middlesex Medical Center, 260 Westbrook Road, Essex, CT 06426, 860-358-3851

Long Sand Shoal

NAVIGATION: Use Chart 12372. Two miles southeast of Duck Island Roads is the beginning of Long Sand Shoal. Well-buoyed and charted, it extends from there about six miles east to the entrance of the Connecticut River. Boats heading for the Connecticut River from Duck Island Roads should go north of the shoal. For others, the choice depends on the current, which runs about 2 knots and is generally stronger south of the shoal.

If you are riding a fair current heading up Long Island Sound, stay to the south and get the extra lift. If you are bucking the current, stay to the north where it is weaker and be sure to keep south of the charted rocks off Cornfield Point on the Connecticut coast. Be especially conscious of Hen and Chickens, which are rocks just west of Cornfield Point. While well-charted and well-marked, it is easy to go astray in poor visibility.

Cruising Options

Now that you are so close, don't miss the opportunity to cruise up the Connecticut River, one of the most beautiful rivers on the Connecticut coast. You will find peaceful anchorages, lush scenery, extensive facilities and interesting stops. The following chapter offers more details. ■

The Connecticut River

CHARTS 12372, 12375, 12377, 12378

The magnificent Connecticut River, flowing southward for 400 miles into Long Island Sound, is the largest and longest river in New England and is the only major river in Connecticut with no city at its mouth. Even though a shoal at the river's entrance prevented the entry of commercial ships, it was a path of trade and communication for the American Indians and settlers from Europe. The Indians called it Quonehtacut or "Long Tidal Water."

First-time visitors are surprised to "discover" the unspoiled natural beauty of the lower river, much of it seemingly unchanged since the days of the Colonial traders and boatbuilders. The Connecticut River's busy entrance quickly gives way to pastoral undulations—lined by quiet marshes and occasional intriguing coves and creeks. Protected and secluded anchorages are accessible via a number of inlets and off-channel backwaters. But don't be fooled by this tranquil beauty; not far into the river are marinas, restaurants, anchorages, waterside activities, Saybrook and Essex, CT.

Situated a couple of miles or so above the bascule railroad bridge (closed vertical clearance 19 feet) and the Route 95 fixed bridge (vertical clearance 81 feet), Essex is a favorite for many cruising families because of its fun-filled harbor with the village one block away. Full-service marinas, a friendly yacht club, quaint shops and restaurants offer everything for the cruising family. A short distance farther, on the east side of the river, is Hamburg Cove, a favorite anchorage of many Long Island Sound cruisers. The cove has an easy entrance and plenty of deep water inside. It does get crowded on weekends during the summer months, so get there early for a good spot.

Along most of the river there is ready access to first-rate marinas, restaurants and sightseeing opportunities: live-theater presentations, a steam train and scenic railway, a medieval castle, festivals, museums and galleries.

NAVIGATION: Use Charts 12372, 12375, 12377. The river is well-marked, wide, deep and easy-to-run, but currents can sometimes run swiftly near the mouth. Farther upstream, the channel narrows and bears a more vigilant watch. Large commercial vessels (tug-propelled barges and sightseeing boats) use the Connecticut River and need extra maneuvering room, particularly when currents are at their peak. (Contact these vessels on VHF Channel 13 to ascertain their intentions.) Keep in mind that vessels going with the current have right-of-way, unless other vessels are encumbered by draft or other circumstances. About 10 miles upstream, near the town of Deep River, the salt water of the estuary changes to fresh river water.

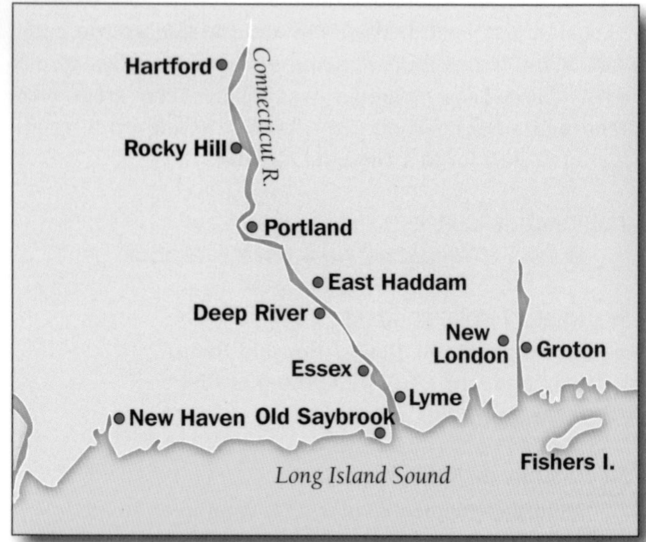

The entry into the Connecticut River is distinguished by two handsome lighthouses—one on the western breakwater, the other one inside on Lynde Point. Built around 1800, Lynde Point Lighthouse, abutting a gabled house, is white, tapering and many-sided, with long windows climbing the south side. Be sure to head for the southernmost, less-visible lighthouse, marking the entrance around the breakwater.

Entry between the breakwaters is easy, but if wind and tide are opposing, conditions can be a bit choppy. Allow for the current's set at all times, and stay clear of off-channel shoals inside the eastern breakwater. Do not attempt to cross the open water east of the breakwaters. As with any inlet, keep a sharp lookout for other vessels.

Note: There have been several No-Wake Zones established on the Connecticut River that are strictly enforced by Connecticut Marine Police.

Anchorage: In northerly or light winds, the area outside of Saybrook in Long Island Sound itself, just west of the breakwater and close in to the beach, is a popular swimming and picnicking anchorage for local boats. Never anchor here in strong southerly or southwesterly winds; it is a dangerous lee shore. Heavy fog can develop here, even when the weather is clear in Saybrook. Just inside of the Connecticut River on the western side is South Cove, which is not navigable and has very shallow water. A little farther north on the west side is North Cove. This is a small cove with deep water in the very tight channel. However, you can find a spot to anchor near the end, close to shore. There are limited facilities here, but it is good for a quick in-and-out trip off the Sound.

Saybrook Point, CT

SAYBROOK POINT		Largest Vessel Accommodated	VHF Channel Monitored	Transient Berths / Total Berths	Approach / Dockside Depth (reported)	Floating Docks	Gas / Diesel	Groceries, Ice, Marine Supplies, Snacks	Repairs: Hull, Engine, Propeller	Lift (tonnage), Crane, Rail	1=110V, 2=220V, B=Both, Max Amps	Laundry, Pool, Showers	Pump-Out Station	Nearby: Grocery Store, Motel, Restaurant
		Dockage					Supplies		Services					
1. Harbor One Marina (Internet Access) (Wireless Internet Access)	860-388-9208	150	09	/86	20/8		GD	IM	HP		B/200	LPS		GMR
2. Saybrook Point Inn & Marina (Internet Access) (Wireless Internet Access)	860-395-3080	200	09	35/120	20/12	F	GD	IM	HP		B/200	LPS	P	GMR
3. North Cove Yacht Club	860-388-9132		78	Moorings										

Corresponding chart(s) not to be used for navigation. Internet Access Wireless Internet Access

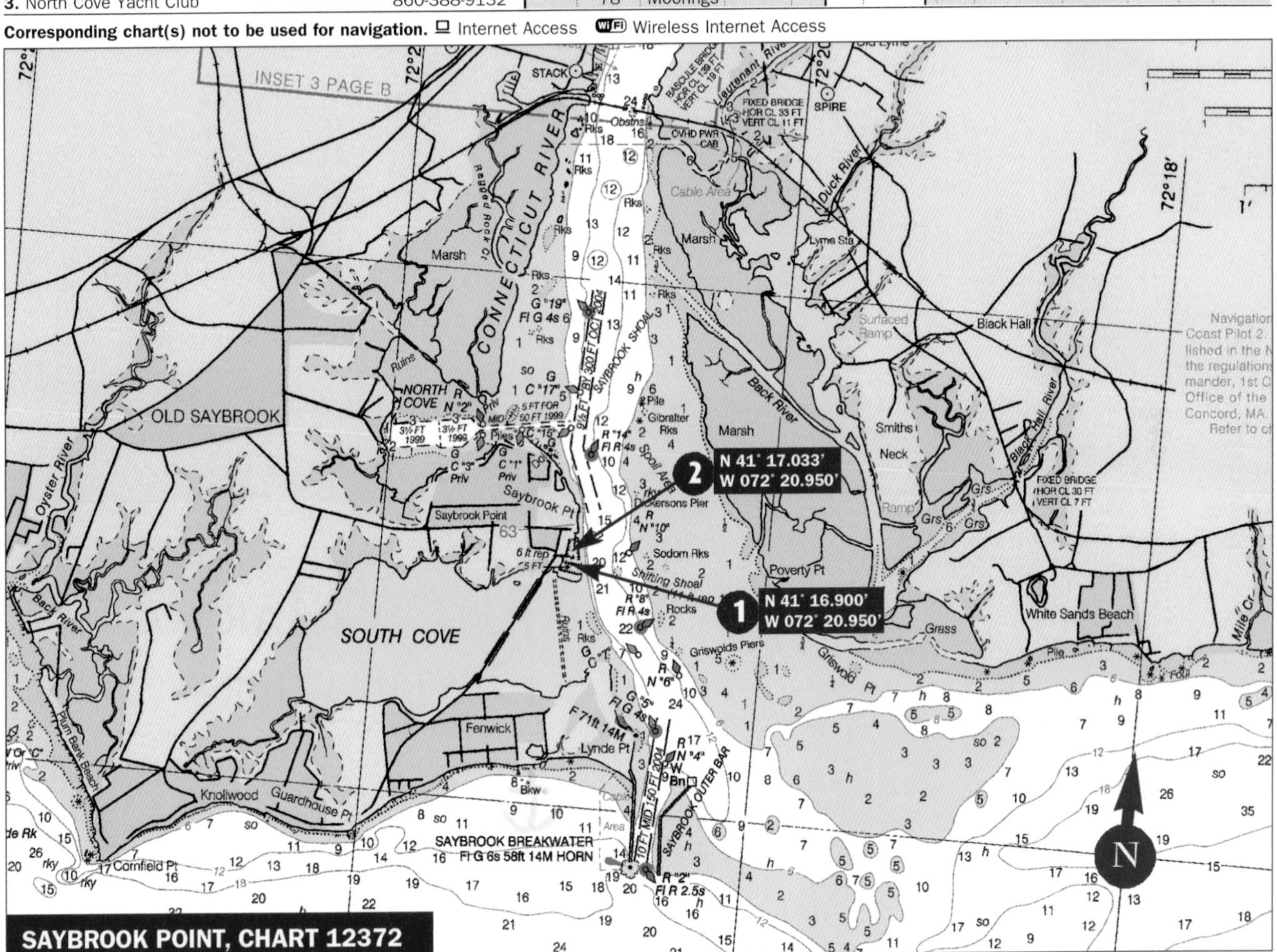

Saybrook Point, Old Saybrook

NAVIGATION: Use Chart 12375. For Saybrook Point, use New London tide tables. For high tide, add 1 hour and 11 minutes; for low tide, add 53 minutes. Do not deviate from the Saybrook Outter Bar Channel to attempt to pass over the Saybrook Bar on the east side of the river as the ruins of the old shad fishing piers remain here. Less than a mile inside the entrance to the Connecticut River is Saybrook Point, located on the west bank.

Dockage: Saybrook Point is home to Harbor One Marina and the Saybrook Point Inn Marina and Spa. Both of these marinas are very busy, and reservations are advisable, but each facility will usually fit you in. Contact the Harbormaster at the town of Old Saybrook for availability of their guest moorings. North Cove Yacht Club (VHF Channel 78) offers launch service, restrooms and showers for a small fee.

Harbor One Marina, the first marina on entering the Connecticut River, has 24-hour dock service and a small gourmet-style restaurant on the premises, is near bus and train depots and is within walking distance to other restaurants.

Saybrook Point Inn Marina and Spa, Connecticut's first Clean Marina, has complete modern spa facilities, including a fitness center with an indoor/outdoor pool and exercise room, which are all available to its cruising visitors. You will find decked docks with creatively carved pilings featuring local wildlife, moped rental, complimentary bicycles, courtesy shuttle to the amenities of the village of

Looking north over the Saybrook Breakwater. (Not to be used for navigation.) WATERWAY GUIDE PHOTOGRAPHY

Old Saybrook to Essex, CT

OLD SAYBROOK TO ESSEX		Largest Vessel Accommodated	VHF Channel Monitored	Transient Berths / Total Berths	Approach / Dockside Depth (reported)	Floating Docks	Gas / Diesel	Groceries, Ice, Marine Supplies, Snacks	Repairs: Hull, Engine, Propeller	Lift (tonnage), Crane, Rail	1=110V, 2=220V, B=Both, Max Amps	Laundry, Pool, Showers	Pump-Out Station	Nearby: Grocery Store, Motel, Restaurant
		Dockage					Supplies		Services					
1. Ragged Rock Marina	860-388-1049	45	09	10/230	5/6	F		IMS			1/30	LS	P	MR
2. Between the Bridges South	860-388-3614	100	09	/100	/6	F		I	HEP	L25	B/50	S		MR
3. Between the Bridges North	860-388-1431	120	09	6/300	14/7	F	GD	IMS	HEP	L60	B/50	PS		GMR
4. Oak Leaf Marina Inc.	**860-388-9817**	**100**	**09**	**10/100**	**24/18**	**F**		**IM**	**HEP**	**L35,C**	**B/100**	**LS**		**GMR**
5. Brewer Ferry Point Marina WiFi	**860-388-3260**	**55**	**09**	**4/146**	**8/5**	**F**	**G**	**IM**	**HEP**	**LC**	**B/50**	**LPS**	**P**	**GMR**
6. Offshore East Marina	860-388-4532	40		2/30	8/8	F		IM	HP	LCR	1/30	S		MR
7. Island Cove Marina	860-388-0029	40	09	/10	7/7	F		I				S		MR
8. Old Lyme Marina Inc.	860-434-1272	60	09	10/34	15/20			IM	HP	L	B/50	S		GMR
9. Old Lyme Dock Co.	860-434-2267	200	09	3/21	13/13	F	GD	I	P		B/100	S		GMR
10. Brewer Dauntless Marina (formerly the Chandlery) Internet WiFi	**860-767-8267**	**125**	**68**	**2/40**	**12/10**	**F**	**GD**	**IMS**			**B/50**	**LS**	**P**	**GMR**
11. Essex Yacht Club	860-767-8121	100	68	4/43	12/9	F		I			B/50	S		GR
12. Brewer Dauntless Shipyard & Marina Internet WiFi	**860-767-2483**	**115**	**09**	**15/110**	**10/12**	**F**		**GIMS**	**HEP**	**L35,C15**	**B/50**	**LPS**	**P**	**GMR**
13. Essex Boat Works Inc.	860-767-8276	80	09	5/30	10/10			M	HEP	L50	B/50			GMR
14. Essex Island Marina Internet WiFi	860-767-1267	150	09	70/130	9/9	F	GD	GIS	EP	L30	B/100	LPS		GMR

Corresponding chart(s) not to be used for navigation. Internet Access WiFi Wireless Internet Access

Old Saybrook, an excellent waterfront restaurant and free pump-out service. Fort Saybrook Monument Park (860-395-3123) is adjacent to Saybrook Point Marina where a boulder marks the site where Yale University stood from 1707 to 1716.

GOIN' ASHORE:

OLD SAYBROOK, CT

A little more than a mile away, the village of Old Saybrook has grocery and spirits stores, a hardware store, North Cove Outfitters (860-388-6585, 75 Main St.) (for outdoor goods and fishing tackle), clothing and specialty shops and a large mall with a supermarket and the usual chain stores. The local Super Stop & Shop grocery store (860-388-0850, 665 Boston Post Road at Old Saybrook Shopping Center) is open until midnight Monday thru Saturday and until 9 p.m. on Sunday for late-night provisioning excursions. A local farmers market operates every Saturday and Wednesday during the season. Taxi service is provided by Essex Taxi (860-767-7433).

You will find restaurants here to suit every taste and budget. Jack's Restaurant (860-388-3231, 26 Bridge St. at Harbor One Marina), is open daily and serves breakfast and lunch. An excellent waterfront restaurant, Terra Mar Grill (860-388-1111, 2 Bridge St.), graces the premises at Saybrook Point Marina, and serves freshly prepared meals al fresco on the terrace during the summer. Next door, to the north, the Dock and Dine Restaurant (860-388-4665, 146 College Ave.) has offered wonderful seafood for two generations. An on-site dock provides ample room for tie-up on the riverside. Penny Lane Pub (860-388-9646, 150 Main St.) provides an eclectic British setting for cuisine that consistently receives good reviews. East of the Post Road (U.S. Route 1), the Cuckoo's Nest (860-399-9060, 1712 Boston Post Road) has zesty Mexican and Cajun specials. Vinnie's Saybrook Fish House (860-388-4836, 99 Essex Road) is straightforward, unadorned and repeatedly written up as the "best seafood restaurant" in the state. Pizza Works (860-388-2218, 455 Boston Post Road) serves what the name suggests and has one of the most elaborate model train displays anywhere. Home-style cooking can be found at Pat's Kountry Kitchen (860-388-4784, 70 Mill Rock Road East) where they

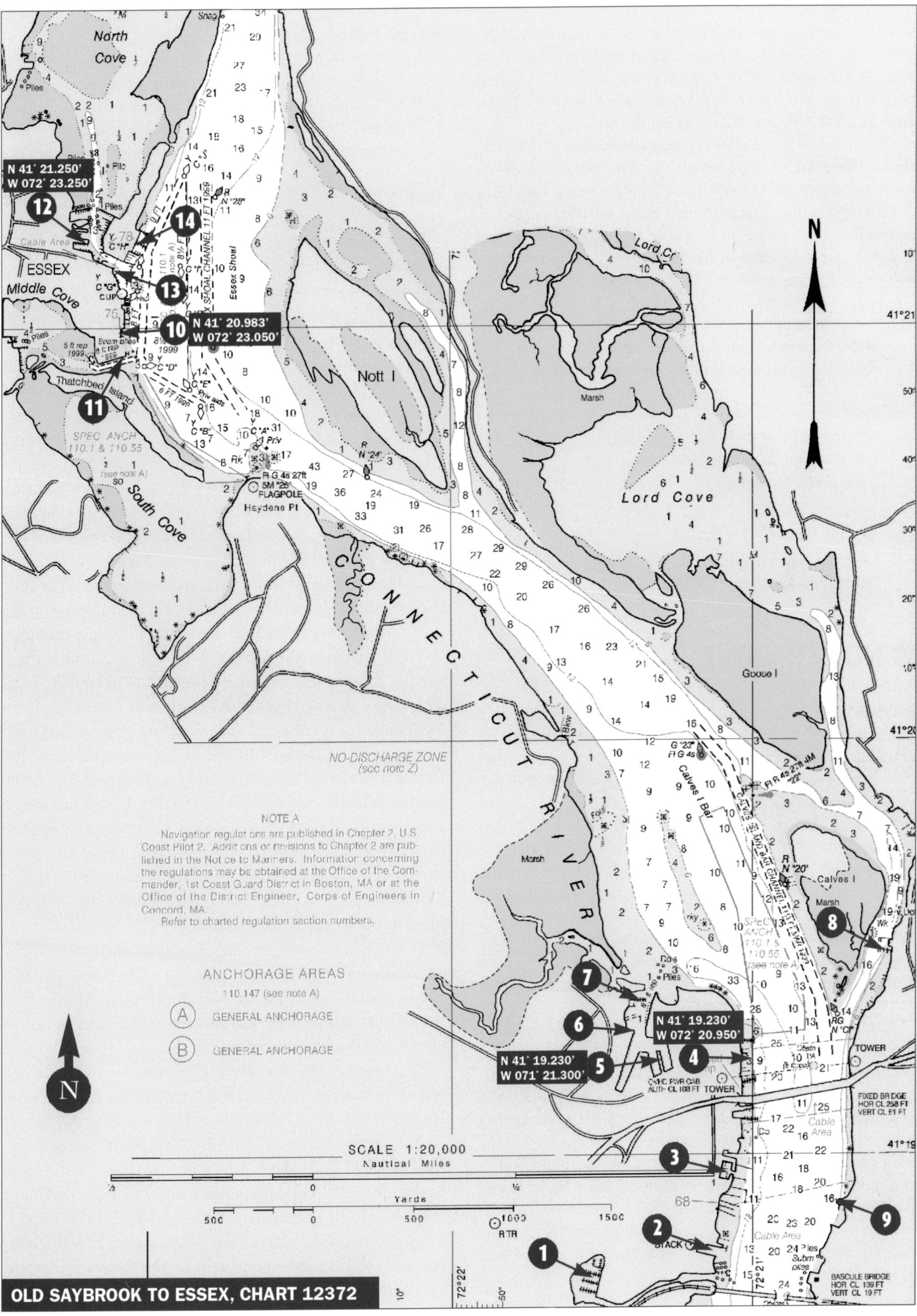

North Cove
Essex Shoal
ESSEX
Middle Cove
Thatchbed Island
SPEC ANCH 110.1 & 110.55
South Cove
Haydens Pt
FLAGPOLE
Nott I
Lord Cove
Lord Cr
Marsh
Goose I
Calves I
Calves I Bar
CONNECTICUT RIVER
NO-DISCHARGE ZONE (see note Z)
N 41° 21.250' W 072° 23.250'
N 41° 20.983' W 072° 23.050'
N 41° 19.230' W 072° 20.950'
N 41° 19.230' W 071° 21.300'
NOTE A
Navigation regulations are published in Chapter 2, U.S. Coast Pilot 2. Additions or revisions to Chapter 2 are published in the Notice to Mariners. Information concerning the regulations may be obtained at the Office of the Commander, 1st Coast Guard District in Boston, MA or at the Office of the District Engineer, Corps of Engineers in Concord, MA.
Refer to charted regulation section numbers.
ANCHORAGE AREAS
110.147 (see note A)
A GENERAL ANCHORAGE
B GENERAL ANCHORAGE
SCALE 1:20,000
Nautical Miles
Yards
FIXED BRIDGE HOR CL 258 FT VERT CL 81 FT
BASCULE BRIDGE HOR CL 139 FT VERT CL 19 FT
TOWER
STACK
Cable Area
OLD SAYBROOK TO ESSEX, CHART 12372

serve their famous clam hash. Liv's Oyster Bar (806-395-5577, 166 Main St.), Jack's Saybrook Steak (860-395-1230, 286 Main St.), Zang's Food of Asia (860-388-3999, 455 Boston Post Road, by the Train Station) and Aspen Restaurant & Bar (860-395-5888, 2 Main St.) round out the list.

Old Saybrook is one of the earliest settlements in Connecticut—walking tours of the town are not to be missed. Katharine Hepburn maintained her home here for many years. Labor Day 2009 heralded the grand opening of Katharine Hepburn Cultural Arts Center (The Kate) at 300 Main St. For recreation, there is a mini-golf park right on the water-front near the marinas and a public indoor tennis facility is close by.

ADDITIONAL RESOURCES:

- Old Saybrook Chamber of Commerce, **www.oldsaybrookct.com** or **www.oldsaybrook.com**

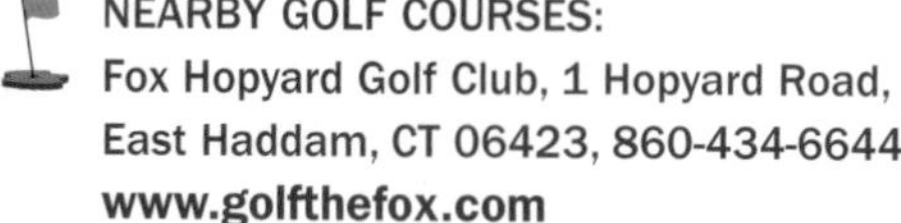

NEARBY GOLF COURSES:
Fox Hopyard Golf Club, 1 Hopyard Road, East Haddam, CT 06423, 860-434-6644, **www.golfthefox.com**

NEARBY MEDICAL FACILITIES:
Lawrence & Memorial Hospital, 633 Middlesex Turnpike, Old Saybrook, CT 06475, 860-388-5881

NORTH COVE

NAVIGATION: Use Charts 12372 and 12375. Immediately around the corner from Saybrook Point is North Cove. The entrance is straightforward with a channel marked by a series of green can buoys. The entrance has a charted depth of 5 feet shallowing to 3.5 feet once in the cove. In poor visibility leave flashing red buoy "14" to starboard, and then look to port for green can buoy "15" leading the way in.

Dockage: A bit farther north, in the shadow of the Inter-state 95 (I-95) Bridge (81-foot fixed vertical clearance), Oak Leaf Marina may have transient dock space available, even for 100-foot-plus boats, in water that accommodates even the deepest keels. This is primarily a working yard, with marine supplies and a variety of repair services available.

Anchorage: The protection is good in North Cove, and more than 100 permanent moorings have been placed here. If enough of the boats are away cruising, as they frequently are, transient boaters might be able to find anchoring room within the dredged area, or might also try borrowing a mooring. This is an excellent, well-protected anchorage with good holding. Its quick entrance off the Sound makes it a good choice when time is tight or the weather turns bad. Dredging of North Cove to 6-foot depths was scheduled to begin in September 2009. Call an area marina for more information or check the navigation updates section at www.waterwayguide.com.

Ferry Point, Old Lyme

NAVIGATION: Use Charts 12372 and 12375. Almost two miles north of Saybrook Point, the Old Lyme drawbridge, a railroad bascule bridge (19-foot closed vertical clearance, monitors VHF Channel 13), is usually open. This bridge carries the busy Amtrak line, and will close and lock whenever a train approaches. The good news is that there is rarely a lengthy closing.

Dockage: From here, marinas and boatyards are located on both sides of the Connecticut River. Located just off the Connecticut River, three miles north of Long Island Sound, Brewer Ferry Point Marina is an extremely secure hurricane hole. The marina features floating and fixed docks equipped with power, water, wireless Internet access and cable TV. The marina offers the personal service of a small yard with the highly trained staff and amenities of a first-rate Brewer Yard. Dock personnel monitor VHF Channel 09 and are available daily during the summer to assist you with gas, ice, pump-out and all your boating needs. A picnic area and grills, plus a play-scape and pool give families a variety of fun to choose from. Brewer Yacht Sales now has an office on-site and offers Edgewater Boats.

Old Lyme Dock Co. is located on the eastern side between the railroad bridge and the high-level Baldwin Bridge to the north, which carries I-95 (81-foot fixed vertical clearance). You will recognize the marina by its yellow main building, the big Texaco sign and an oversized American flag. Transients are welcomed here with a large, easy-access fuel dock and slip space for visitors. Call ahead for reservations.

Just north of the I-95 Bridge on the eastern side of the Connecticut River, nestled behind Calves Island, Old Lyme Marina, a family-run, full-service facility, has 65 moorings, usually with eight to 10 available for transients, and 26 slips, with six or more available for transients. Enter this sheltered and beautiful spot only from the south, leaving red-over-green buoy "CI" and the ledge it marks a respectful distance to port.

The northern route, around flashing red "22," is rocky at the entrance, shallower than the chart indicates, and masks obstacles lurking in the bottom mud. Marine personnel discourage even shallow-draft runabouts from this area. Call ahead to check for availability.

Two blocks away is a shopping center. Turn right at the top of the marina driveway, and then take the first left onto Huntley Street, which leads directly to the shopping center on U.S. Route 1. You will find an A&P grocery store (860-434-1433, 90 Halls Road), several banks, a liquor store and a post office. A second plaza has a large, well-stocked hardware store, Annie's Kitchen (860-434-9837, 9 Halls Road) for light gourmet meals, sandwiches and baked goods (packed to go or served on-site) and the Hideaway Restaurant and Pub (860-434-3335, Old Lyme Shopping Center)

About a half-mile east on U.S. Route 1, turning left at the light on Route 1-A, is the famous Old Lyme Inn Grill (860-434-2600, 85 Lyme St.), which offers elegant dining in a wonderfully peaceful atmosphere with three fireplaces and a 100-year-old oak bar. A block farther away on Route 1-A, the Bee and Thistle Inn (860-434-1667, 100 Lyme St.) has been voted by Connecticut Magazine readers as the most romantic dining spot in the state (although the Old Lyme Inn might be a close second).

Art enthusiasts will enjoy a visit to the Florence Griswold Museum (860-434-5542, 96 Lyme St.), known as the home of American Impressionism where the talented artists lived and painted. The Lyme Academy of Fine Arts (860-434-5232, 84 Lyme St.), one of the few accredited fine arts schools in the country, and Lyme Art Association (860-434-7802) both display rotating exhibits of contemporary art work.

Essex

NAVIGATION: Use Chart 12375. Use New London tide tables. For high tide, add 1 hour 39 minutes; for low tide, add 1 hour 38 minutes. North of Old Lyme, the well-marked main river channel skirts the western shore of Calves Island and its marshy bar, and then winds gently for several miles to Essex, about five miles north of Saybrook Point. There are no markers for slightly more than two miles, but the river is wide and deep. Watch for red nun buoy "24" to avoid the shoal water off Nott Island, just downstream from Essex. This charming town, long a favorite cruising destination, is compact and its attractions are easily accessible by foot from the marinas and town dock at the western edge of the Connecticut River. First settled in 1648, Essex rapidly established itself as a Colonial boatbuilding center. Over the centuries, hundreds of boats have been built here, including the first American Man-o-War ship. Though the lofting sheds are gone, enough flavor of the town's maritime past remains to make it a magnet for visitors touring by land and water.

Dockage: On the Connecticut River proper, Brewer Dauntless Marina (formerly The Chandlery at Essex) has 33 easy-access slips on modern floating docks and more than 50 moorings. Most evenings, several slips, a fair number of moorings, and the 150' fixed dock will be open to incoming transients. Ashore, you will have access to modern restroom, shower, and coin-operated laundry facilities. Services and the facilities at Brewer Dauntless Shipyard (a short walk) are available to Marina customers. Launch service is available from 8 a.m. to 8 p.m., Monday through Friday, and 8 a.m. to 11 p.m. on weekends. In the past, the staff has been willing to transport transients to the nearest propane refill station, which is about a mile away; ask at the Dock office for details. Several other marine related businesses are located on the premises, including Boatique (a supplier of unique boating needs) as well as Essex Corinthian Yacht Club.

Immediately south, Essex Yacht Club usually has 10 to 12 moorings available to transients with launch service (8 a.m. to 9 p.m. daily) for a facilities fee. The clubhouse has a panoramic view of the river from its spacious second-story deck, matched by superb lounge, shower and restroom facilities below. Visitors have access to the club dining room—lunch is served daily from 11 a.m. to 2 p.m.

Somewhat better protection from the Connecticut River wash is found north of the prominent Essex town dock at the entrance to North Cove. Brewer Dauntless Shipyard and Marina offers deepwater floating slips, modern restroom/shower and laundry facilities and access to the marina pool. An extensive parts department, major repair services and a 35-ton lift are available at the yard.

Anchorage: Anchorage is no longer a good prospect at Essex, because of the strong reversing tides and the crowding of the mooring field outside the channel. Many boaters do sidle up to Nott Island to drop a hook off the east side of the main channel, though only for swimming or a lunch stop. Currents are quite strong here, but the holding is excellent in firm mud.

GOIN' ASHORE: **ESSEX, CT**

Essex is a small, lively New England town with lovely Colonial- and Federal-style homes, sedate clapboard shops, galleries featuring local artists, many of whom are marine artists, and several very good restaurants lining Main Street. This is the street to go to when in Essex. You will find an excellent deli, gift shops, upscale boutiques, the post office (prominently situated on Main Street), an old-fashioned barbershop (behind the post office) and three banks with 24-hour ATMs. Village Provision Company (860-767-2341, 6 Main St.) has a good supply of groceries, dairy products, veggies, household items, rental bicycles and videos. That's The Spirit Shoppe (11 Main St., 860-767-8979) has one of the most extensive wine selections in eastern Connecticut and will deliver. A FedEx drop box is located just north of Griswold Corners.

The Essex Library (33 West Ave., uphill from the town square at the head of Main Street, 860-767-1560) is open Tuesday through Thursday from 10 a.m. to 8 p.m., Monday and Friday from 10 a.m. to 5 p.m., Saturday from 10 a.m. to 1 p.m. and Sunday from 1 p.m. to 5 p.m. for free Internet access and book-lending services. Summer hours may vary. Cruisers interested in visiting nearby villages and towns while using Essex as a base can call Essex Taxi (860-767-7433).

One of the best-known restaurants in Essex having operated continuously since 1776 and one on every cruiser's itinerary is The Griswold Inn (36 Main St., 860-767-1776). It has long been the restaurant of choice for Connecticut Yankees seeking traditional American fare in a classic setting at moderate prices. "The Griz," as locals know it, is an institution of museum quality, housing a large private collection of Currier and Ives maritime prints, antique firearms and nautical oil paintings. having operated continuously since 1776. Sunday brunch at The Griz is renowned in this part of the state, and sailors share a fondness for sea chantey night (Mondays) at the inn's cavernous bar. Nearby, Essex Coffee & Tea Co. (860-767-7804, 51 Main St.) opens daily at 7 a.m., serving special coffee blends and delicate pastries.

The Black Seal Seafood Grille (15-C Main St., 860-767-0233) is a good choice for more casual dining and offers full dinners as well as sandwiches and pub fare.

As a reminder of the town's nautical and commercial past, the Connecticut River Museum (860-767-8269, 67 Main St.), on the Steamboat Dock at the foot of Main Street, maintains a rich collection of memorabilia. Exhibits rotate on the first floor gallery; permanent collections are stored upstairs. Another throwback to an earlier age, the Connecticut Valley Railroad Co. (860-767-0103 about a mile and a half to the west at 1 Railroad Ave.) makes a fascinating collection of old steam locomotives and passenger and freight cars available to visitors. Daily steam train rides are available to travel up river to Chester and an optional riverboat tour is available. Two-hour dinner excursions are available on weekends.

ADDITIONAL RESOURCES:

- Essex Online, **www.essexct.gov** or **www.essexct.com**

NEARBY GOLF COURSES:
Fox Hopyard Golf Club, 1 Hopyard Road, East Haddam, CT 06423, 860-434-6644, **www.golfthefox.com**

NEARBY MEDICAL FACILITIES:
Middlesex Hospital-Shoreline Medical Center, 260 Westbrook Road, Essex, CT 06426, 860-358-3700

NORTH COVE TO SELDEN CREEK, CT

North of Essex, along the Connecticut River's prettiest stretch, marshy bars of spartina grass gradually fade as steep cliffs appear, sprouting trees from rugged outcroppings along the eastern shore. Cattle can be seen grazing on wall-lined fields, and moored boats dot the coves.

Hamburg Cove

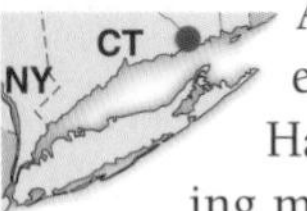

About a mile upriver from Essex, on the eastern (starboard heading upriver) side, Hamburg Cove is a favorite spot among cruising mariners. It is almost round and landlocked, offering total protection and magnificent natural surroundings. Crowded on weekends and frequently hot during the summer, the cove is deep almost to its green banks.

NAVIGATION: Use Chart 12372. The narrow entrance east of Brockway Island (with 8-foot depths) is marked, but the privately maintained buoys must be followed exactly. Do not cut any of the buoys. Fifty-foot boats can be seen far up the creek in the town of Hamburg, but the channel is narrow and challenging, with little turning room or dock space in the inner harbor.

Dockage: From Hamburg Cove, it is a short dinghy ride to the inner harbor, where a dinghy dock is available at both Cove Landing Marina and the Hamburg Cove Yacht Club. The Cove Landing Marina has a 35-ton lift and generally specializes in the restoration and overhaul of wooden boats, but virtually any repair can be arranged here. The marina also has restrooms and showers, pump-out and a small ship's store. Both block and cube ices are available here. Just up the driveway to the left, you will find H.L. Reynolds (860-434-2494, 254 Hamburg Road), an old-fashioned general store selling basic provisions (canned and packaged goods, cold cuts, bread, beer and soft drinks). The current proprietor, Jane DeWolf, carries on in the tradition of her great-grandfather, her grandfather, her mother and her father, but she has added some new touches. Jane is a miniature-dollhouse collector and has turned part of the store into a display, much of it for sale. (Included among the miniatures is a replica of the H.L. Reynolds store itself as it might have looked at the turn of the century.) The walls are festooned with local town memorabilia, and a supply of used paperback books and an eclectic tag-sale room are in the back of the store.

Anchorage: Hamburg Cove is congested with private moorings, with little room to anchor properly. The local practice is to pick up a vacant mooring and be prepared to move if the owner returns. Better yet, take one of Cove Landing Marina's marked orange rental moorings (first-come, first-served). Anchorage is still possible west of Brockway Island, but enter and leave only from the south—the north side is shoal.

Selden Creek

NAVIGATION: Use Chart 12377. Beyond Brockway Island, just past Brockway Landing on the eastern shore, is the unmarked entrance to primitive Selden Creek, an excellent gunkhole where American boats hid from British raiders during the Revolutionary War. The narrow creek, with a marsh-bordered entrance and no aids to navigation, lies amid cliffs and high hills. Large boats have little room to move around. Depths, however, run from 8 to 13 feet in the lower reaches and 3 to 4 feet in the upper, where the creek runs into Selden Cove, with its shallow channel, back to the Connecticut River. A visit to Selden Creek makes a marvelous trip in the dinghy. Watch out for tree stumps as you go. Locals say that shallow-draft boats can make it back to the river via the back channel, but do not take that as gospel.

DEEP RIVER TO HARTFORD, CT

At Deep River tidal waters from Long Island Sound cease to influence the freshwater's drain from the north. Here the channel briefly divides around Eustasia Island. There are good depths to either side, though the main channel is marked to the east. If you venture into the western channel, keep an eye on the depth sounder around Eustasia Island in the area of Chester Creek Bar. The best depths are found near the eastern shore of the river.

Dockage: For convenient dockage or ready access to the special anchorage at the north end of Chester Creek Bar, take the fork west of Eustasia Island (leave flashing green "35" on the rock pile just south of the island to starboard). The floating docks of Brewer's Deep River Marina visibly line the banks to port. The marina's long facing dock with gasoline and diesel makes fueling and pump-out (free) a simple matter. Transient dock space is never a problem in this protected and tranquil setting, and from here it is a relatively easy dinghy ride to Selden Neck State Park for excellent hiking, exploration of Selden Creek backwaters or a trip to Gillette Castle. The marina has spotless restrooms/showers, a pool, extensive picnic and grill areas, laundry facilities, a lift and full-time mechanical and repair staff. There are plenty of parking spaces for crew changes. The amenities of a modern village are less than a mile away.

Anchorage: Good anchorage is at hand in 5- to 10-foot depths north of Eustasia Island on the west side of the river.

Deep River

Deep River is the home of the annual Fife and Drum Muster (third Saturday in July), which vividly recalls the area's Revolutionary War tradition. The town is a good place to reprovision, dine and take care of a few chores while enjoying the river's attractions immediately to the east. Eight-tenths of a mile's walk from the marina, the single traffic light signals your arrival "downtown." The Family Laundry (860-526-1016, 168 Main St.) is immediately across the street. A block and a half to the left are an Adam's Super Food Store (860-526-2807, 193 Main St.), West Marine Express (860-526-2236, 183 Main St.), Community Pharmacy (860-526-5379, 197 Main St.), and Shore Discount Liquors (860-526-5197, 211 Main St.). You can find a good meal at a reasonable price in a casual setting at Ivory Restaurant & Pub (860-526-2528, 1 Kirtland St.) just north of the traffic light. Those who want shoreside sleeping accommodations should try Riverwind Inn (860-526-2014, 209 Main St.).

Dockage: North of the intersection of the Connecticut River and Pratt Creek is Brewer Deep River Marina, a full-service facility with all fuels, pump-out, restrooms/showers and repair services. This marina is known for impeccable floating docks equipped with electric, cable, telephone and water, all set within a serene wildlife environment. Docking and maneuvering are made simple by the attentive dock staff, always available by radio. Brewer Deep River Marina offers outside storage, a 25-ton Travelift and a 20-ton hydraulic trailer. The staff maintains a regular winter work schedule and is available to take care of almost every maintenance need, including mechanical, electrical, finish work, carpentry and rigging.

Deep River is home to Pratt Cove and Selden Neck State Park, which both offer an opportunity for viewing tremendous wildlife. If you have a kayak, this is the perfect place to use it, or row your dinghy across to the surrounding marshland and wonderful creeks. Please be sensitive to these preserved areas. Deep River offers a shuttle (for a minimal charge) to explore Chester, Essex and Old Saybrook. Ask about pick-up times at the marina.

Half a mile beyond the north end of Eustasia Island, Chester Marina South (860-526-9076) formerly Connecticut River Marina is now part of Chester Marina in the creek and has cut a narrow channel into its family-run "working man's marina." Small boats and do-it-yourself projects are the norm here, but the marina can accommodate boats with 6-foot drafts and lengths of up to 40 feet.

Chester Creek, immediately to the north (also on the west side of the river) is home to two more marinas and the private Pattaconk Yacht Club (860-526-5626). Boats drawing up to 5 feet can find accommodations here. Chester Marina (860-526-2227), just inside the mouth of the creek, offers slips with electric hookups for boats up to 40 feet, with a pool and a ship's store. A short distance farther down the creek, Hays Haven Marina has 230 slips with floating docks, electrical hookups and 5-foot depths; there always seems to be room for visiting yachts. Gas, diesel, ice and boat supplies are available, and the village of Chester is less than a mile away.

About a half-mile above the Chester-Hadlyme ferry landing (beneath Fort Hill), Chisholm Marina has a deep channel cut into the west bank, which leads into its secure boat basin handling boats drawing 6 feet and up to 65 feet long. The marina's fuel dock (gas and diesel) is immediately accessible at the river's edge. Various classic wooden river yachts and blue water cruisers, including a number of liveaboards, are berthed in this immaculate yard. Still, there is almost always room for visitors. This is a family-operated, full-service facility with a 35-ton lift able to hoist boats with up to a 17-foot beam. From Chisholm's pristine, park-like setting, it is about a mile (left at the main road) to a small shopping center where you will find the Liberty Bank (860-526-6000, 151 Main St.) with ATM. The village of Chester is another mile and a half away.

Almost within hailing distance of any of the Chester marinas (12 miles above the river's mouth), Gillette Castle (860-434-2494, 67 River Road), open 10 a.m. to 5 p.m., Memorial Day through Columbus Day), is an almost irresistible attraction. Built by a highly successful (and largely eccentric) Shakespearean stage actor, William Gillette, this unique "home" adds commanding river views to the extraordinary experience of a tour. An example of Gillette's eccentricity: Of the 47 interior doors in the castle, none are identical. It is best to leave your boat on the Chester side of the river, and then take either your dinghy or the ferry across. There is a small landing available near the ferry slip for dinghy tie-up.

GOIN' ASHORE: CHESTER, CT

One of Connecticut's most picturesque villages, Chester has been restored beyond its original 19th-century charm. An opportunity to view the housing stock in this village—from early Colonial and Victorian to modern—makes this a "must stop" on a trip up the Connecticut River. Village amenities are adequate; within a block are two banks (one with an ATM), the post office,

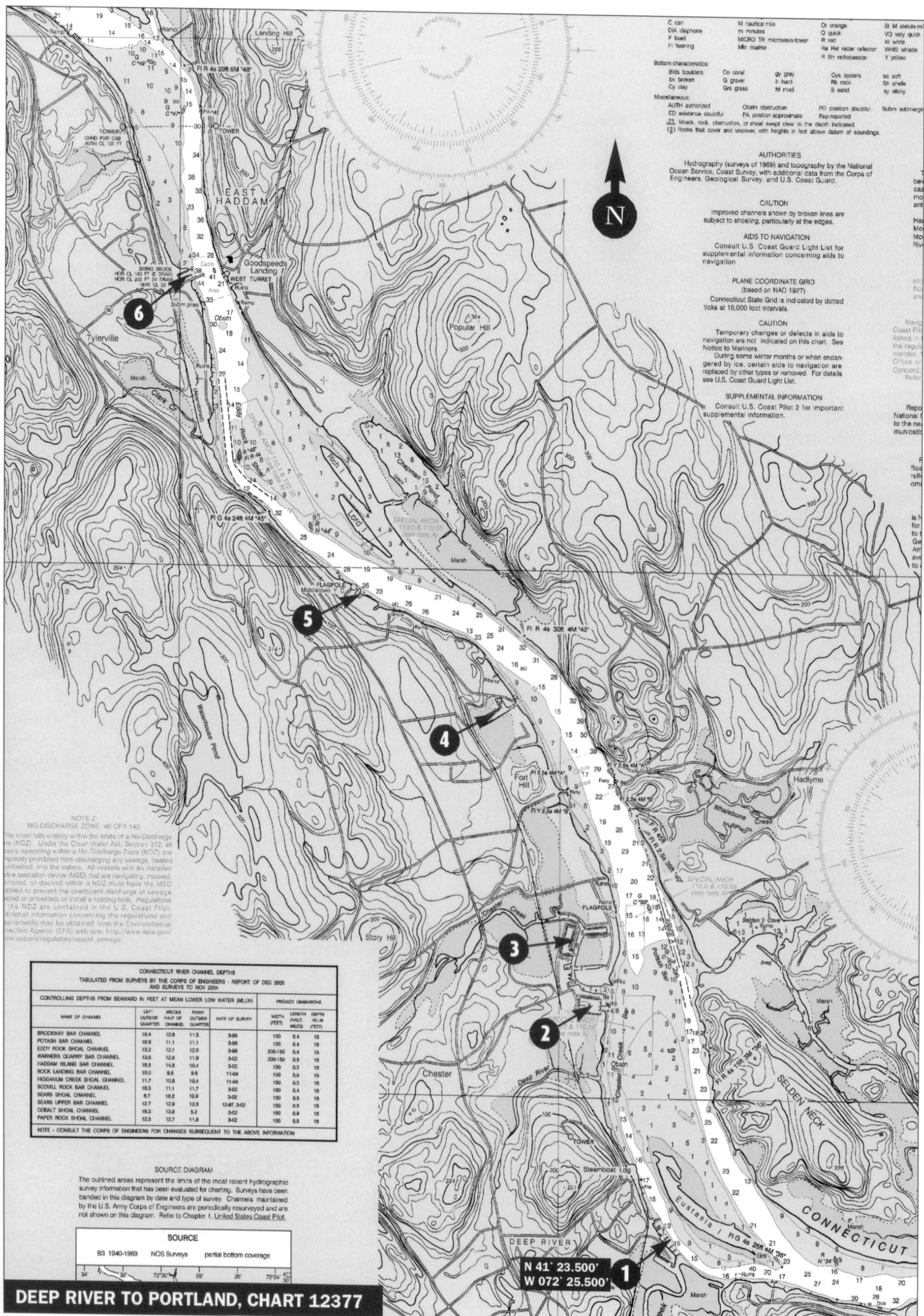

CONNECTICUT RIVER CHANNEL DEPTHS
TABULATED FROM SURVEYS BY THE CORPS OF ENGINEERS - REPORT OF DEC 2005 AND SURVEYS TO NOV 2004

CONTROLLING DEPTHS FROM SEAWARD IN FEET AT MEAN LOWER LOW WATER (MLLW)					PROJECT DIMENSIONS		
NAME OF CHANNEL	LEFT OUTSIDE QUARTER	MIDDLE HALF OF CHANNEL	RIGHT OUTSIDE QUARTER	DATE OF SURVEY	WIDTH (FEET)	LENGTH (NAUT. MILES)	DEPTH MLLW (FEET)
BROCKWAY BAR CHANNEL	10.4	10.8	11.5	3-99	150	0.4	15
POTASH BAR CHANNEL	10.9	11.1	11.1	3-99	150	0.4	15
EDDY ROCK SHOAL CHANNEL	13.2	12.1	12.0	3-99	200-150	0.4	15
WARNERS QUARRY BAR CHANNEL	13.6	12.6	11.9	3-02	200-150	0.5	15
HADDAM ISLAND BAR CHANNEL	16.5	14.5	10.4	3-02	150	0.3	15
ROCK LANDING BAR CHANNEL	10.0	9.6	9.6	11-04	150	0.5	15
HIGGANUM CREEK SHOAL CHANNEL	11.7	10.8	10.4	11-04	150	0.3	15
SCOVILL ROCK BAR CHANNEL	10.3	11.1	11.7	3-02	150	0.4	15
SEARS SHOAL CHANNEL	6.7	10.2	10.9	3-02	150	0.5	15
SEARS UPPER BAR CHANNEL	12.7	12.9	13.5	12-97, 3-02	150	0.5	15
COBALT SHOAL CHANNEL	16.3	13.8	5.2	3-02	150	0.9	15
PAPER ROCK SHOAL CHANNEL	12.5	12.7	11.9	3-02	150	0.5	15

NOTE - CONSULT THE CORPS OF ENGINEERS FOR CHANGES SUBSEQUENT TO THE ABOVE INFORMATION

SOURCE DIAGRAM

The outlined areas represent the limits of the most recent hydrographic survey information that has been evaluated for charting. Surveys have been banded in this diagram by date and type of survey. Channels maintained by the U.S. Army Corps of Engineers are periodically resurveyed and are not shown on this diagram. Refer to Chapter 1, United States Coast Pilot.

SOURCE
B3 1940-1969 NOS Surveys partial bottom coverage

DEEP RIVER TO PORTLAND, CHART 12377

Deep River to Portland, CT

DEEP RIVER TO PORTLAND		Largest Vessel Accommodated	VHF Channel Monitored	Transient Berths / Total Berths	Approach / Dockside Depth (reported)	Floating Docks	Gas / Diesel	Groceries, Ice, Marine Supplies, Snacks	Repairs: Hull, Engine, Propeller	Lift (tonnage), Crane, Rail	1=110V, 2=220V, B=Both, Max Amps	Laundry, Pool, Showers	Pump-Out Station	Nearby: Grocery Store, Motel, Restaurant
		Dockage					Supplies		Services					
1. Brewer Deep River Marina (WiFi)	**860-526-5560**	**50**	**09**	**20/250**	**15/15**	**F**	**GD**	**IM**	**HEP**	**L25**	**B/50**	**PS**	**P**	**GMR**
2. Hays Haven Marina Inc.	860-526-9366	48		4/220	6/6	F	GD	IS	P	L	B/50	S	P	GR
3. Chisholm Marina	860-526-5147	40	09	6/130	8/6	F	G	IMS	HEP	L35,C	1/50	S	P	GMR
4. Middlesex Yacht Club	860-526-5634	50			10/9			I			1/30	PS		
5. Andrew's Marina at Harper's Landing (Internet) (WiFi)	860-345-2286	55	68	3/76	6/6	F	G	IM	E		1/50	S	P	GMR
6. Damar, Ltd./Midway Marina	860-345-4330	45	13	5/80	12/7	F		MS	HEP	L10,C	1/30	S	P	R
7. Cobalt Marine	860-267-2093	50		1/18	6/10	F		M	HP		1/30			
8. Portland Boat Works Inc.	860-342-1085	60		/45	10/10		G	IM	HP		1/30	S		GMR
9. Yankee Boatyard and Marina	860-342-4735	50	68	6/80	20/10	F	GD	IMS	HEP	L20,C	1/50	S	P	GMR
10. Portland Riverside Marina	860-342-1911	40		10/70	20/15	F	GD	IMS	HP	L	1/30	S		GMR
11. Middletown - Harbor Park	860-250-1534				16/10	F	G							
12. Petzold's Marine Center	860-342-1196	63	09	6/25	15/10	F	G	M	HP	L55	1/30			
13. Wethersfield Cove Yacht Club	860-563-8780	45		4/17	4/15	F	G	M			1/30			GR

Corresponding chart(s) not to be used for navigation. Internet Access · WiFi Wireless Internet Access

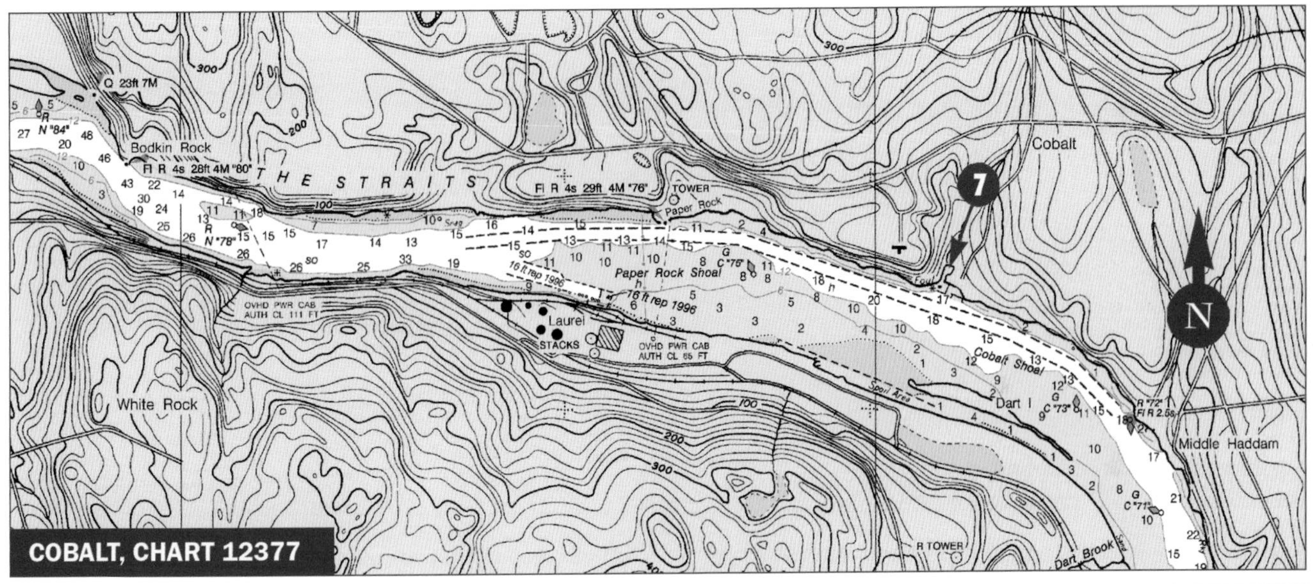

COBALT, CHART 12377

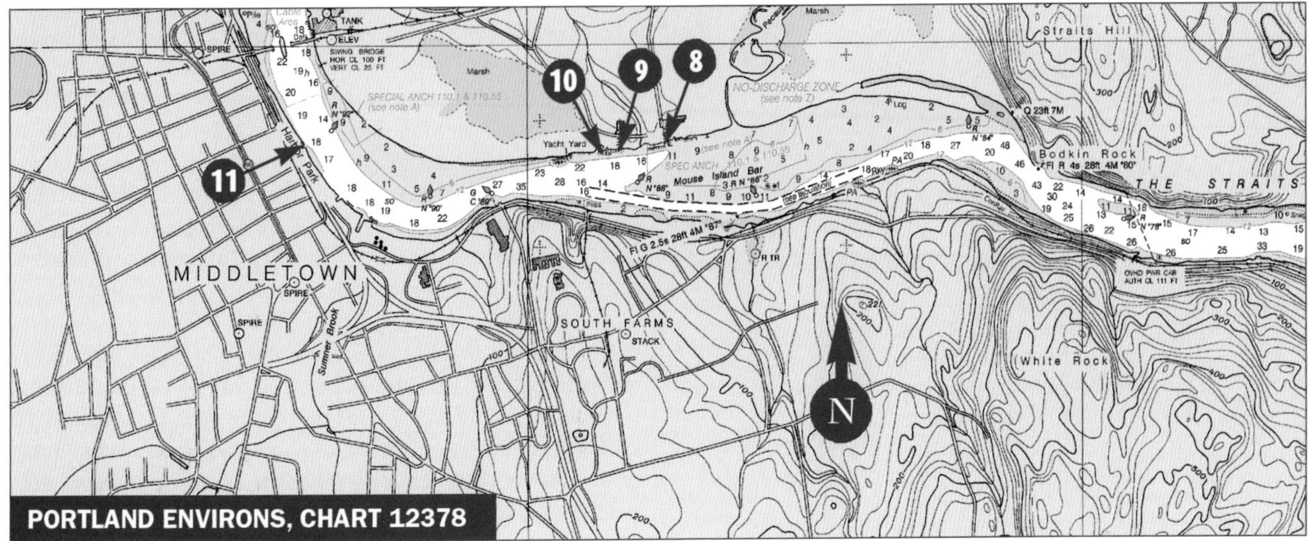

PORTLAND ENVIRONS, CHART 12378

CONTINUED ON THE FOLLOWING PAGE

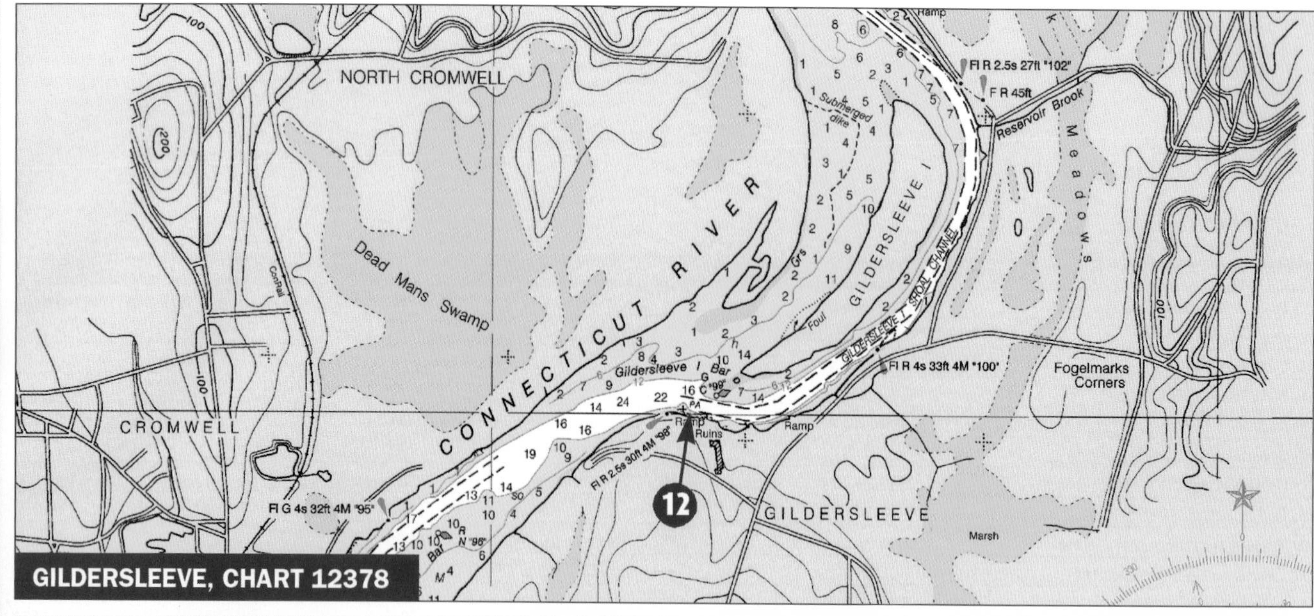

GILDERSLEEVE, CHART 12378

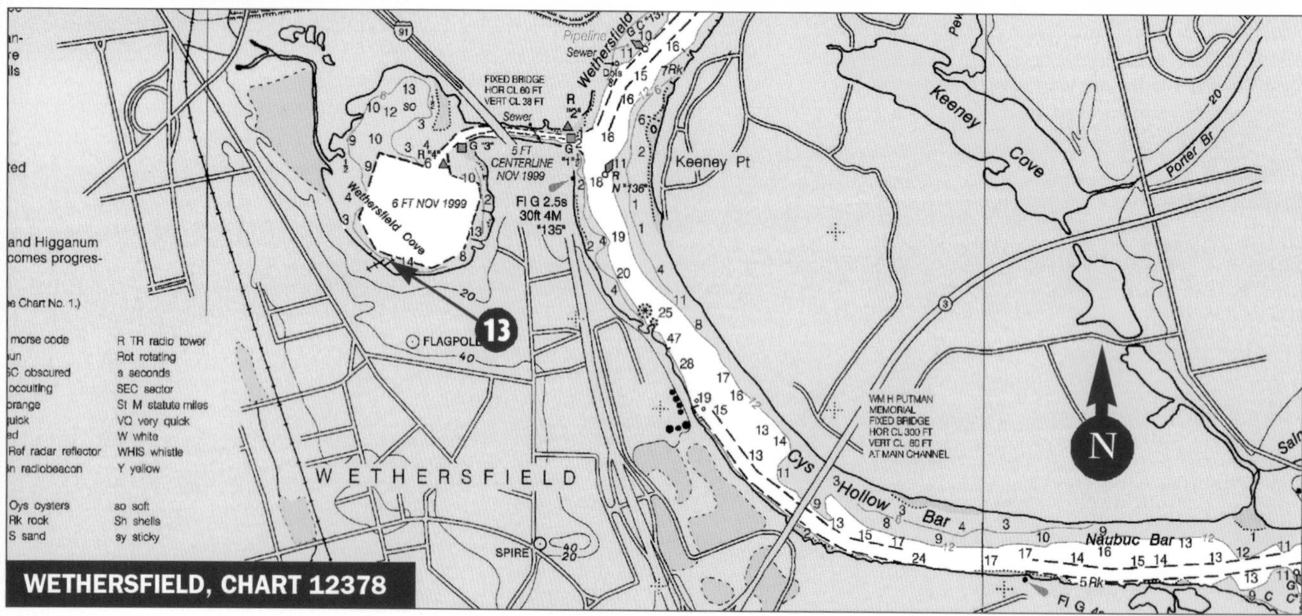

WETHERSFIELD, CHART 12378

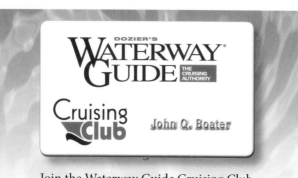

a FedEx drop box, a package store, a couple of antiques shops, scattered galleries featuring original works of local artists. The village of Chester is also home to the Goodspeed-at-Chester/ The Norma Terris Theatre (860-873-8668, 33 N. Main St.), an offshoot of the Goodspeed Opera House of East Haddam located in an old kintting needle factory.. But here the stage is for new plays and experimental theater. Call for reservations and schedules. Also of note is The Meeting House Players (860-526-4516) which perform at Chester Meeting House (860-526-0015, 4 Liberty St.) and the Chester Fairgrounds (860-526-5947, 11 Kirkland Terrace). Schedules of events can be found at www.chesterct.com.

Restaurants in Chester are notable and folks from other towns often dine here. Restaurant Du Village (860-526-5301, 59 Main St., dinners only, Tuesday through Sunday) has just 12 tables in the romantic setting of a simple but exquisite French provincial inn. Advance reservations are a must. Fiddlers Seafood Restaurant (860-526-3210, 4 Water St., closed Mondays) serves such specialties as mesquite-grilled shrimp. Next to Fiddlers is The Wheatmarket, (860-526-9347, 4 Water St.) which sells fresh daily deli luncheon specials and gourmet items to take back to the boat. On Main Street, Mad Hatter Bakery and Cafe (860-526-2156, 23 Main St.) offers hearth-baked breads and light lunches, and The Pattaconk 1850 Bar & Grill (860-526-8143, 33 Main St.) has an old-fashioned taproom in front and a dining room with light fare at reasonable prices in the back. Don't miss the array of galleries in Chester, including the Leif Nilsson Spring Street Studio and Gallery (860-526-2077, One Spring St.)., Chester is also home for the Chester Sunday Market, a farmers market held on Main St. from May through early October 9 a. m. to 1 p.m., and the Lobster Festival held the second Saturday in September.

ADDITIONAL RESOURCES:

- Town of Chester, **www.chesterct.org**

NEARBY GOLF COURSES:
Fox Hopyard Golf Club, 1 Hopyard Road,
East Haddam, CT 06423, 860-434-6644,
www.golfthefox.com

NEARBY MEDICAL FACILITIES:
Chesterfields Health Care Center, 132 Main St.,
Chester, CT 06412, 860-526-5363

East Haddam

Three miles above Chester, the 80-year-old swing bridge unmistakably locates the village of East Haddam. The town is best known for the Goodspeed Opera House, (860-873-8668, 6 Main St.) where three lively, full-production Broadway musicals are revived annually. It is open from April through December, and tickets may be difficult to get on short notice during the summer months, but the management says it is well worth a try, particularly on weeknights.

NAVIGATION: Use Chart 12377. For Haddam, use New London tide tables. For high tide, add 2 hours 48 minutes; for low tide, add 3 hours 8 minutes. East Haddam's swing bridge (22-foot closed vertical clearance) opens on request on the half-hour (contact the tender on VHF Channel 13) from Memorial Day to Oct. 31. Just up from East Haddam is the entrance to the narrow Salmon River. The river carries good depths for about a mile up into Salmon Cove, and then shoals considerably. Give Cones Point a wide berth, follow the deep water on the west side of Grass Island, and then turn east and north. The cove is a quiet overnight spot for boats with moderate drafts.

Dockage: The Goodspeed Opera House maintains a 120-foot deepwater dock (no other facilities) just south of the bridge for its waterborne visitors (860-873-8664 for dock reservations). North of the bridge on the west side of the river, Andrew's Marina almost always has a few slips available for transients, including easy-access floating docks with plenty of water. These are connected with power and water, and visitors have access to the marina's restroom and shower facilities. Basic boating supplies, gasoline (only) and ice are also available here.

Anchorage: Those preferring to anchor will find plenty of space south of the Goodspeed dock and east of the channel, in 7 to 11 feet of water. Be aware, however, of the Goodspeed Airport runway, and give it some serious thought before anchoring off the runway's end.

GOIN' ASHORE: **EAST HADDAM, CT**

Basic shoreside amenities are within easy walking distance on either side of the river. Bank of America has a branch office nearby with an ATM (800-432-1000, 40 Main St.). Dinner at the Victorian-styled Gelston House (860-873-1411, 8 Main St.) can be a special treat, or you might want to enjoy the reasonably-priced luncheon specials and unbeatable river panorama. (It is possible to arrange courtesy daytime dockage when making a lunch reservation.) Across the street, La Vita Gustosa (860-873-8999, 9 Main St.) serves traditional Italian Trattoria-style cuisine. A walk of less than a mile, west of the river, will take you to another bank, a liquor store, a general store with basic groceries and deli items and a couple of pizza parlors. This is also the home of the Gillette Castle (860-434-2494, 67 River Road), (open 10 a.m. to 5 p.m., Memorial Day through Columbus Day, built by William Gillette best known for his role as Sherlock Holmes. The castle, which stands approximately 200 feet above sea level, with imposing granite walls, 4 to 5 feet thick, and 24 oddly shaped rooms is a great place to explore. The Chester-Hadlyme Ferry (860-443-3856) crosses the Connecticut River from East Haddam to Chester from 7 a.m. to 6:45 p.m. daily and 10:30 a.m. to 5 p.m. on Saturday and Sunday. The cost is $3 per car and $1 per bicyclist or pedestrian.

ADDITIONAL RESOURCES:

- Town of East Haddam, **www.easthaddam.org**

NEARBY GOLF COURSES:
Fox Hopyard Golf Club, 1 Hopyard Road,
East Haddam, CT 06423, 860-434-6644,
www.golfthefox.com

NEARBY MEDICAL FACILITIES:
Lawrence & Memorial Hospital,
339 Flanders Road East
Old Lyme, CT 06371, 860-739-6437

Middletown

The home of Wesleyan University, Middletown is located past Middle Haddam and through the scenic Straits. On weekends you can visit the Submarine Library and Museum (860-346-0388, 440 Washington St.), which has the most complete submarine library anywhere, featuring clippings of all submarines since 1900. Complimentary dockage is available while you enjoy the view when dining at Harbor Park Restaurant (860-347-9999, 80 Harbor Drive).

Hartford, CT

NAVIGATION: Use Chart 12378. Be wary of gravel around Mouse Island Bar. Although it is well-marked with buoys and a range, inattentiveness causes problems. It has been reported that a good number of boats kiss the bottom there, especially downriver.

Portland

Across the river from Middletown is Portland, once an important quarrying and shipbuilding port. Dockage and repairs are available on the waterfront. The old quarries, flooded and inactive now, produced much of the sandstone for New York City's famous brownstone houses, and dinosaur tracks were often found on the quarried slabs.

Dockage: There are three marinas in a row on the east bank across from Portland. As the river curves to the north, a large restaurant on the west bank offers dockage and waterside dining. Sunday brunch is very popular and crowded.

There are few marine facilities above Portland. The stretch above the bridge to Gildersleeves Island is uneventful if you don't try to pass to the west of the island, where there is a submerged dike. Just below Gildersleeves Island, on the east bank, is Petzold's Marina. If you do not stop here, keep in mind that the next available stop is Wethersfield Cove. The annual River Raft Race from Guildersleeve Island to Portland Riverside Marina features homemade rafts competing in various fun and unusual divisions for prizes in late July or early August.

Rocky Hill to Wethersfield Cove

From Portland, the Connecticut River starts to meander in broad loops that are reminiscent of the Mississippi River. Though there are quite a few ranges, mostly for downriver craft, to guide you through the curves and the bars, pay close attention to steerage and the depth sounder here.

Rocky Hill is a quiet village with a small marina, a snack bar, a ferry landing, a launch ramp and a courtesy dock, all grouped closely on the west bank. Pull into the courtesy dock, have a hot dog and watch the Rocky Hill Ferry, the oldest continuously operating river-crossing ferry in the country.

NAVIGATION: Use Chart 12378. At Rocky Hill, the river curves hard to starboard and Two Piers Bar is ahead. The bar has an upriver range (most are downriver), fixed red over flashing red (2.5 seconds). Coming upriver out of Two Piers Bar, the river starts a broad loop to port, where Glastonbury Bar is located. Because the lower channel is not buoyed, the best bet is to hug the outer bank and watch the depth sounder. The upper channel is buoyed, but still tricky. The shallows extend in a curve within the buoys, so if you were to try a straight shot from inner buoy to inner buoy (especially between green cans "123" and "121"), you might go aground. Locals also say that the Glastonbury Bar is a problem for downriver boats. They tend to take too wide a turn and ground on the outer curve.

After Glastonbury Bar, the river takes a tighter loop to starboard, and Press Barn Bar is ahead. It is not a bad one, and the downriver range is probably not critical for recreational craft. The next loop, to port, is not bad either and, as the river straightens out, the William H. Putman Memorial Bridge (80-foot fixed vertical clearance) and the Cys Hollow Bar are ahead. Stay to the "southwestern third" of the river for about one-quarter nautical mile on either side of the bridge. The only hazard left, midway between the bridge and Wethersfield Cove, is an unmarked rock off the west bank, almost blocked by an unmarked point.

Wethersfield Cove

Wethersfield Cove offers the most comfortable layover near Hartford (about four more miles upstream) for boats that can clear a 38-foot fixed vertical clearance bridge. The yacht club's channel is privately marked, but enter slowly; there is 6 feet of water in the basin, but there is shoaling at the entrance.

Dockage: Hospitable Wethersfield Cove Yacht Club will allow you to use a mooring, or dock space may sometimes be available, with power, water and gas. This is a small, quiet club, where everything closes down by 9 p.m. Even though the yacht club sits in a residential neighborhood, a main street is only a one-block walk to a four-lane road where you will find a variety of stores and restaurants.

GOIN' ASHORE: **HARTFORD, CT**

To visit Hartford, it is best to dock at Wethersfield Cove and proceed into the city by taxi. (For taxi service, call either Airport Express Livery & Taxi 860-836-8294 or Yellow Cab 860-666-6666.) Hartford has virtually no place to tie up and anchorage, while possible, is difficult in the narrow areas outside the main channel. Depths are in the 6-foot range but can change due to fluctuating river levels. If you decide to anchor out and dinghy ashore, be sure to lock your dinghy. The riverfront has been undergoing a restoration, Riverfront Recapture, featuring the addition of several hotels, a convention center and many new restaurants.

The Dutch established a trading fort at the Hartford location in 1633, but it was the Puritans, led by the Rev. Thomas Hooker, who established the first colony in 1635. In 1662, Hartford became the capital of Connecticut. At the beginning of the 19th century, men would meet at the docks and make agreements to share the risks and profits on the cargo ships going forth to trade overseas. This was the beginning of Hartford's reputation as "Insurance City." Later in the century, Hartford became the center of the abolitionist movement and the tobacco industry. It was also the home of the Colt Firearms Factory, which manufactured the Colt Revolver, known as "the fastest gun in the west."

Today, the majority of Hartford attractions are cultural and historical. There are also the usual commercial and entertainment activities found in any large city. The Wadsworth Atheneum Museum of Art (860-278-2670, 600 Main St.), which opened in 1842, spans 5,000 years of history and includes

Greek bronzes, American furniture and a contemporary mixed media installation. Hartford was once home to American legend Samuel Clemens and his home, the Mark Twain House & Museum (860-247-0998, 351 Farmington Ave.), has been restored. In 1874, the Gothic Revival home cost him $40,000. Its oddities include a window over the fireplace that allowed Twain to watch snowflakes and flames at the same time. In this house. Hours are Monday through Saturday, 9:30 a.m. to 5:30 p.m. and Sunday 12 p.m. to 5:30 p.m. Twain wrote some of his greatest works, including "The Adventures of Tom Sawyer," "The Adventures of Huckleberry Finn" and "A Connecticut Yankee in King Arthur's Court." The Twain House can only be seen on guided tours (860-493-6411). You can also take a riverboat cruise from this lovely city.

A good lunch spot in the vicinity of Trinity College is Timothy's Restaurant at 243 Zion St. (860-728-9822); it is said to serve the cheapest, best and most plentiful home cooking in Hartford. Mozzicato De Pasquale's Bakery and Pastry Shop (860-296-0426, at 329 Franklin Ave.) is just the place to dawdle over a cappuccino and pastry or perhaps a cup of gelato.

ADDITIONAL RESOURCES:

- Hartford Image Project, **www.hartford.gov** or **www.hartford.about.com**

NEARBY GOLF COURSES:
Goodwin Golf Course, 1192 Maple Ave.,
Hartford, CT 06115, 860-956-3601

NEARBY MEDICAL FACILITIES:
Hartford Hospital, 80 Seymour St.,
Hartford, CT 06102, 860-545-5000,
www.harthosp.org

Above Hartford

NAVIGATION: Use Chart 12378. Above Hartford, the Connecticut River is unimproved, navigable only for boats with less than 3-foot drafts and 8-foot vertical clearances. The channel shifts constantly, with bars and other obstructions; local knowledge is necessary. Ten miles above Hartford, near Windsor Locks, shallows can make the river impassable at certain times of year. A few miles above Windsor Locks, in Suffield, the ruins of a dam end all normal navigation (locals tell of small jet boats making it through here).

Above the Holyoke, MA, dam, a long stretch of the Connecticut River is used by boaters who must trailer their boats into or out of the water. It is reported that 30 to 40 miles of the river are navigable above the dam.

Cruising Options

To continue exploration of the Connecticut coast, head east toward Niantic from the mouth of the Connecticut River, on to Mystic and, eventually, Watch Hill in Rhode Island. Each port has its own personality and each has much to offer cruising families. ■

WATERWAY GUIDE is always open to your observations from the helm. E-mail your comments on any navigation information in the guide to: editor@waterwayguide.com.

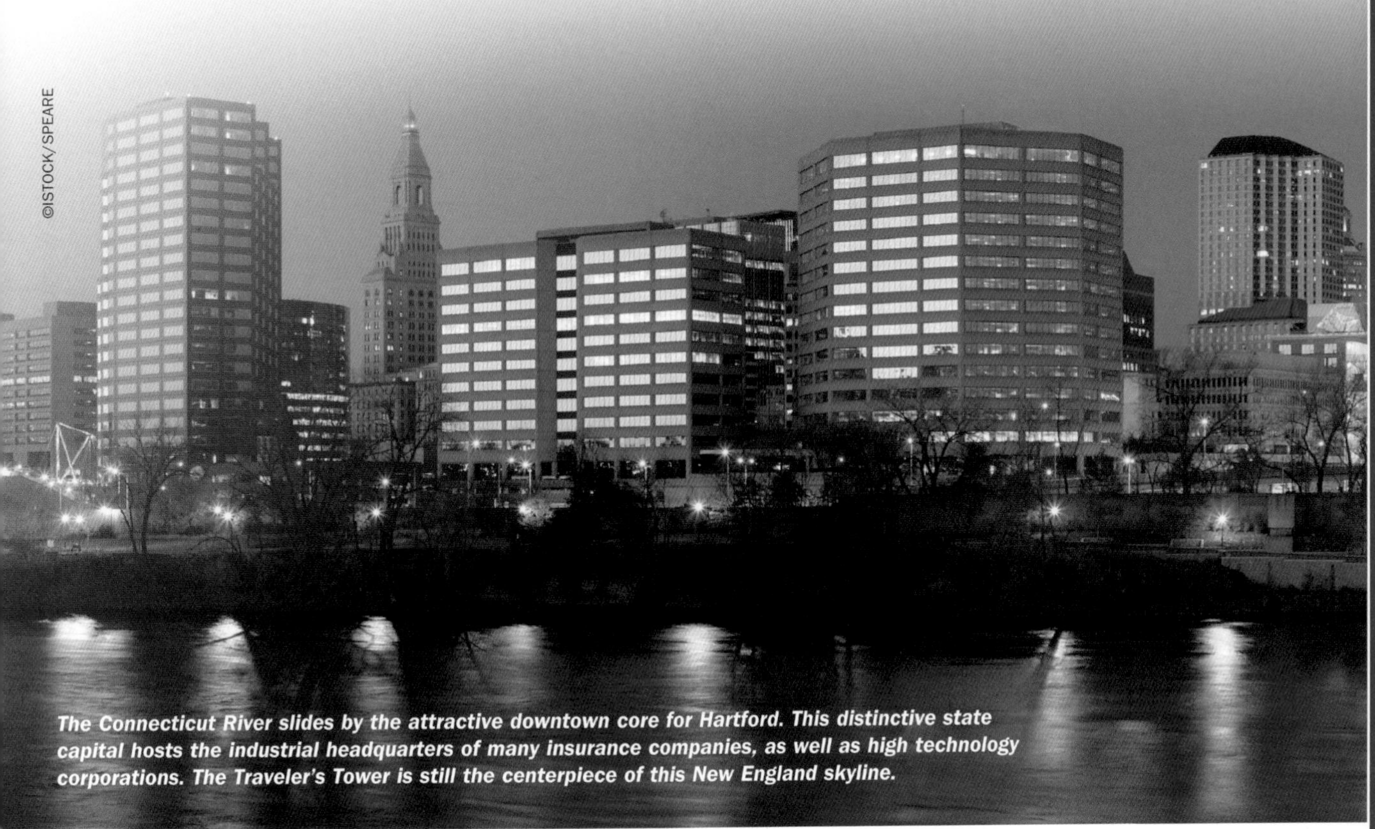

The Connecticut River slides by the attractive downtown core for Hartford. This distinctive state capital hosts the industrial headquarters of many insurance companies, as well as high technology corporations. The Traveler's Tower is still the centerpiece of this New England skyline.

Niantic to Watch Hill

CHARTS 13205, 13211, 13212, 13213, 13214, 13215, 12354, 12358, 12372, 12373, 12374, 12375

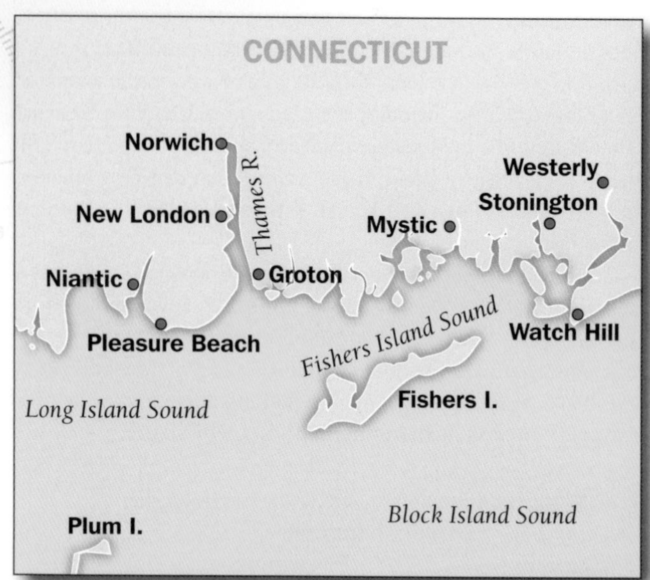

■ CONNECTICUT, RHODE ISLAND SHORE

NAVIGATION: Use Charts 12372 and 13211. Six miles east of the Connecticut River is big and open Niantic Bay, with Black Point on the western headland and a prominent power plant on the eastern shore, noted on the chart simply as "STACK 389 ft."

The only hazard along the way is the well-marked and well-charted Hatchett Reef. The only shelter between the Connecticut River and Niantic Bay is in the Giants Neck area in the lee of Long Rock and Griswold Island. If you enter, do so with caution; the rocks in this area are charted but numerous.

You will find better protection in the Niantic River, located at the northern end of the bay, which is accessible through a well-marked, narrow (50-foot-wide) dogleg channel, leading through an Amtrak railroad bridge (11-foot closed vertical clearance) and the Route 156 Highway Bridge (32-foot closed vertical clearance) beyond. It is best to enter the river at slack water or against the current to maintain control while negotiating the bridge passages and turns in the channel beyond.

Departing Niantic Bay, eastbound mariners should give a wide berth to flashing red bell buoy "6" to avoid the shoals in the vicinity of White and Little rocks. South of Bartlett Reef (clearly marked by a 35-foot-high lattice tower with two international orange diamonds on its face) strong currents funneling through The Race (farther south) begin to make themselves evident on either tide.

Currents south of Bartlett Reef are the strongest in Long Island Sound, and the waters are also the deepest (more than 300 feet in spots). Opposing winds and current can create sloppy conditions here. In a southwest breeze, an eastbound cruiser can stay in the lee of Twotree Island and Bartlett Reef by running the Twotree Island Channel to Goshen Point. Reefs and rocks are adequately marked, but be aware of your location at all times because visibility can drop suddenly on the Sound and currents can set you far from your intended course. If entering New London Harbor, leave green can buoys "3," "5" and "7" to port.

This is also submarine territory. These partially submerged vessels can be seen slicing the surface with their "sails," often startlingly close to shore. Don't be surprised if one breaks the surface near you. Be on the lookout, as well, for frequent ferry crossings in this area, as it bisects a major route between Orient Point and New London.

Niantic

Niantic is a harbor of refuge and a commodious layover for cruisers in search of rest and provisions. Ample dock space and quiet anchorages are within walking distance, and boat repairs, marine services, reprovisioning and restaurants are nearby.

NAVIGATION: Use Charts 12372 and 13211. Use New London tide tables. For high tide, add 52 minutes; for low tide, add 57 minutes. Two closely spaced bridges cross the curving entrance channel of the Niantic River. With little maneuvering room and tidal currents approaching 4 knots on either tide, full attention is recommended on this passage.

The first bridge, a railroad bascule (11-foot closed vertical clearance), opens on signal as long as oncoming trains are not within range. It is best to contact the bridge tender on VHF Channel 13 before you approach. The second is the Niantic River Bridge carrying Route 156 (32-foot closed vertical clearance at mean low water), which is closed to accommodate rush-hour traffic between 7 a.m. and 8 a.m., and then again between 4 p.m. and 5 p.m. For boats with high vertical clearance requirements, approach only when your signal is acknowledged; it is best to coordinate your passage with the tenders of both bridges via VHF. Contact the highway bridge tender on VHF Channels 13 or 16. It is advisable to make this passage during slack water on either tide. The beauty of the Niantic River and the amenities available make this transit well worth the modest effort required. Current charts refer to all

Niantic, CT

NIANTIC		Largest Vessel Accommodated	VHF Channel Monitored	Transient Berths / Total Berths	Approach / Dockside Depth (reported)	Floating Docks	Gas / Diesel	Groceries, Ice, Marine Supplies, Snacks	Repairs: Hull, Engine, Propeller	Lift (tonnage), Crane, Rail	1=110V, 2=220V, B=Both, Max Amps	Laundry, Pool, Showers	Pump-Out Station	Nearby: Grocery Store, Motel, Restaurant
		Dockage					Supplies		Services					
1. Boat's Inc. (Internet Access) (Wireless Internet Access)	860-739-6251	36	71	10/186	8/6	F	GD	IM	HEP		1/30	PS	P	GMR
2. Harbor Hill Marina (Internet Access) (Wireless Internet Access)	860-739-0331	50		2/70	8/6	F					1/30	S	P	GMR
3. Port Niantic	860-739-2155	58	09	2/81	8/6	F		I	HEP	L30	B/50	S	P	GMR
4. Three Bells Marina	860-739-6264	48	09	2/150	6/7	F	GD	IMS	HP	L	1/20	PS	P	GMR

Corresponding chart(s) not to be used for navigation. Internet Access Wireless Internet Access

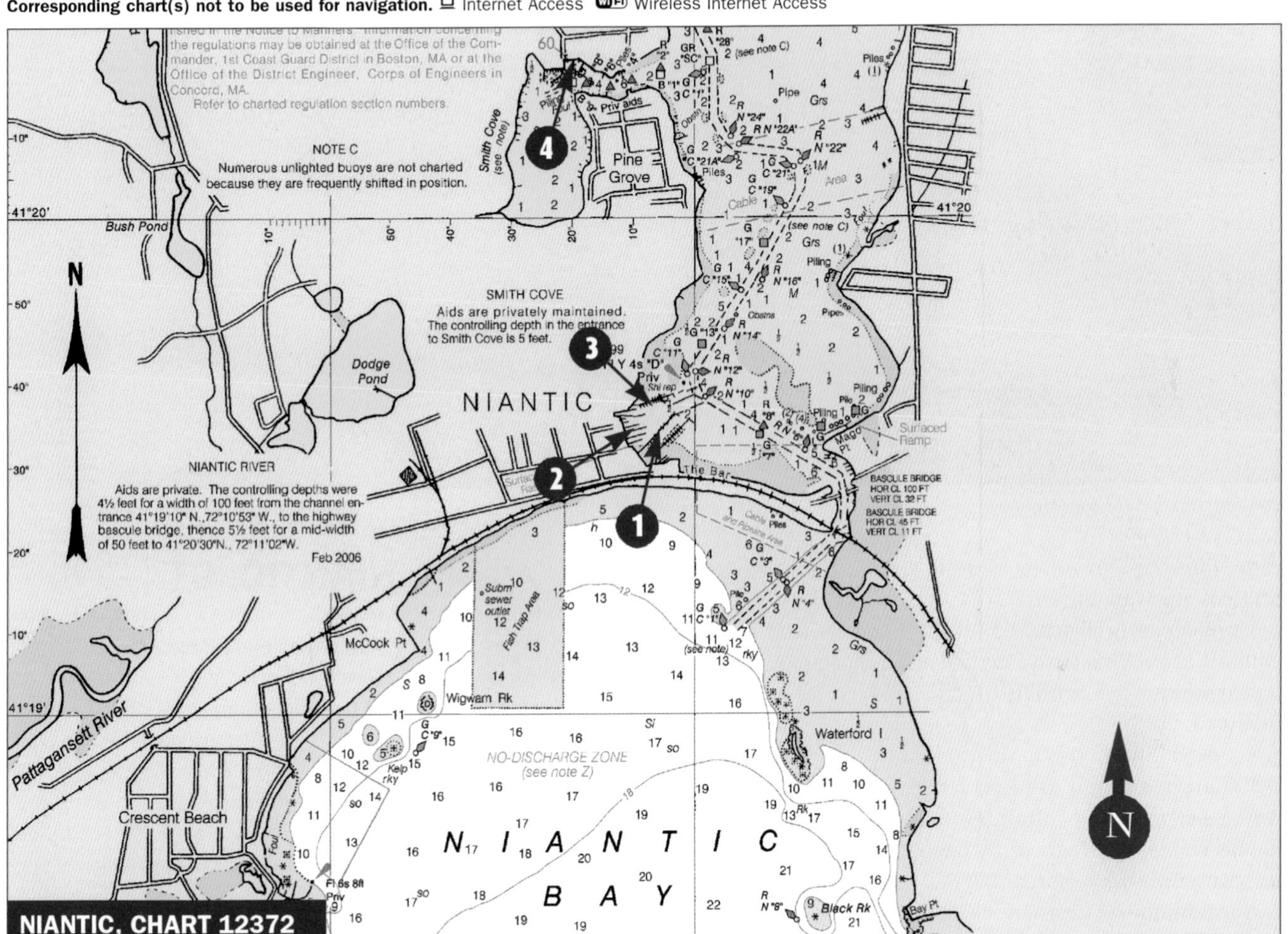

the regulations may be obtained at the Office of the Commander, 1st Coast Guard District in Boston, MA or at the Office of the District Engineer, Corps of Engineers in Concord, MA.
Refer to charted regulation section numbers.
NOTE C
Numerous unlighted buoys are not charted because they are frequently shifted in position.
Smith Cove (see note)
Pine Grove
Bush Pond
SMITH COVE
Aids are privately maintained. The controlling depth in the entrance to Smith Cove is 5 feet.
Dodge Pond
NIANTIC
NIANTIC RIVER
Aids are private. The controlling depths were 4½ feet for a width of 100 feet from the channel entrance 41°19'10" N.,72°10'53" W., to the highway bascule bridge, thence 5½ feet for a mid-width of 50 feet to 41°20'30"N., 72°11'02"W.
Feb 2006
The Bar
BASCULE BRIDGE HOR CL 100 FT VERT CL 32 FT
BASCULE BRIDGE HOR CL 45 FT VERT CL 11 FT
Surfaced Ramp
McCook Pt
Wigwam Rk
Fish Trap Area
Subm sewer outlet
NO-DISCHARGE ZONE (see note Z)
Pattagansett River
Crescent Beach
Waterford I
Black Rk
Bay Pt
N I A N T I C
B A Y
N

NIANTIC, CHART 12372

Niantic River markers as "private aids" because they are frequently moved. The channel is only 4 to 5 feet deep at mean low water, with knee-deep water just outside the channel. Past the bridges, the channel is well-marked and easy to negotiate, but the numerical sequence of the buoys and daybeacons must be strictly noted. At the end of the first dogleg above the bridges, it is possible for boats drawing 6 feet or less to approach the dock ends and fuel docks of the marinas on the western shore, but even this may be challenging because of the substantial shoals located just beyond the dredged areas surrounding the docks. The center of the village of Niantic is a two-block walk from the western shore waterfront.

Dockage: At the first channel bend to starboard inside the river bridges, Boats Inc. offers some of the largest and most complete marina facilities in the harbor. Though mainly a small-boat facility, there is room on the seaward docks for 30 transients. You will find showers with lockers, a substantial ship's store, custom canvas and fabrication shops, extensive repair shops, a bait-and-tackle shop and even a liquor store on the premises.

Harbor Hill Marina and Bed and Breakfast, next to Boats Inc., can usually accommodate a few transients at floating docks with 6-foot depths. The daily dockage rate includes water, electricity and cable TV, modern restrooms, showers and a continental breakfast at the inn.

For those anchored out, there is a dinghy dock, or you can call for a launch ride for the price of a tip to the driver. Port Niantic, immediately to the north, may also have va-

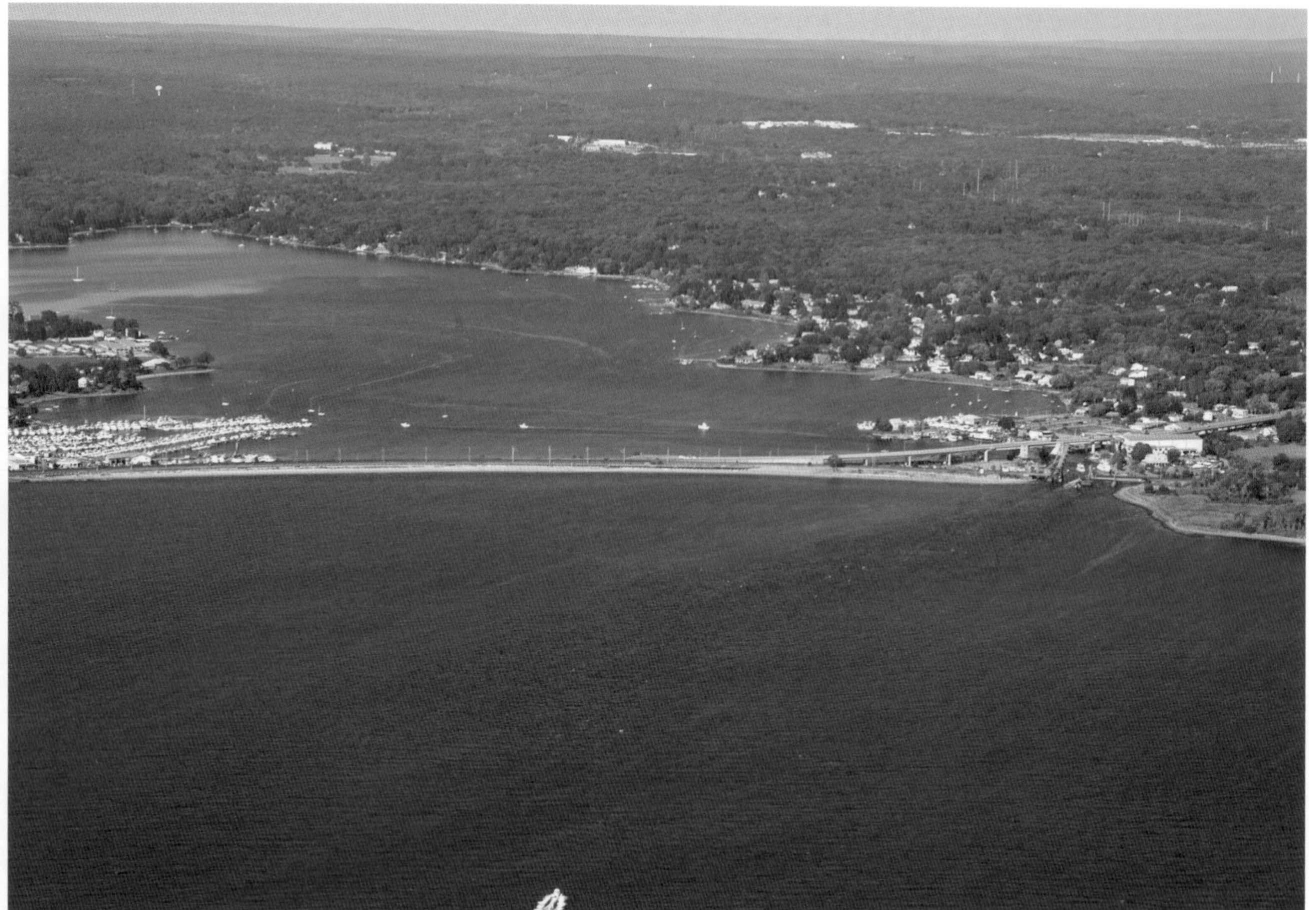

Looking north over Niantic. (Not to be used for navigation.) WATERWAY GUIDE PHOTOGRAPHY

cant transient slips at its floating docks. Fuel and repair services are available here.

Upriver, the well-marked, deep channel winds past the community of Pine Grove to the entrance of pretty and protected Smith Cove, with its friendly, full-service marina and boatyard.

To enter Smith Cove, turn left into the marked channel at green and red daybeacon "SC." The town-dredged, 5-foot-deep channel (mean low water, 2.5-foot tidal range) is reasonably well-marked by daybeacons and naked poles for two-tenths of a mile to Bayreuther Boat Yard. The yard can accommodate transient boats with drafts of up to 4 feet, and a couple of spaces on floats can handle keels of up to 6 feet. Boaters at the slips or floats here, as well as those anchored out, can refuel (both gas and diesel) and also utilize the ample dinghy dock, repair and fabrication shops, pool, showers and snack bar. The village is about a mile and a half away, but a ride to town can usually be arranged.

Anchorage: Farther upriver, the Niantic Bay widens, becomes deeper yet, and provides some lovely anchorages with good holding and attractive surroundings. The scenery and quiet atmosphere are reminiscent more of a New England freshwater lake than those of a surfside recreational community.

GOIN' ASHORE: **NIANTIC, CT**

One of the wonderful advantages of staying in Niantic is its proximity to Mystic Seaport, Mystic Aquarium, Foxwoods Casino, the Mohegan Sun Casino and New London. Niantic is centrally located, two hours from Boston and two hours from New York. The shops in Niantic are clustered around the intersection of Route 156, just west of the highway bridge over the entry channel and little more than a block away from the marinas nearest to the harbor entrance. There are two supermarkets, Adams Super Food Store (58 Pennsylvania Ave., 860-739-8136) and the large Colonial Market IGA (243 Main St., 860-739-5431), as well as a post office (58 Pennsylvania Ave., #2, 860-739-8211), CVS Pharmacy (58 Pennsylvania Ave., 860-691-0381), Citizens Bank (with 24-hour ATM, 43 Pennsylvania Ave., 860-739-1300), Niantic Cinemas (with inexpensive first-run movies, 279 Main St., 860-739-6929), Main Street Laundromat (258 Main St., 860-739-2768) and Village Wine and Spirits (241 Main St., 860-739-8870).

NEARBY GOLF COURSES:
Cedar Ridge Golf Course, 34 Drabik Road,
East Lyme, CT 06333, 860-691-4568,
www.cedarridgegolf.com

NEARBY MEDICAL FACILITIES:
Lawrence & Memorial Hospital, 365 Montauk Ave.,
New London, CT 06320, 860-442-0711

New London and Groton

New London is located on the western side of the Thames River, with its smaller sister port of Groton on the eastern side. Having emerged as a thriving whaling port, rivaling even New Bedford, MA, during the 19th century, New London is the largest and busiest commercial port in eastern Connecticut. It is also an important harbor of refuge, home to major U.S. Navy and Coast Guard facilities and, in recent times, a leading recreational yachting center with excellent marinas, convenient reprovisioning and reliable restaurants.

NAVIGATION: Use Charts 12372, 13212 and 13213. Use New London tide tables. The New London/Groton Harbor is located a short distance up the busy, heavily traveled Thames River. Except for water traffic, the harbor entrance is uncomplicated and well-buoyed. Two distinctive lighthouses stand at the entrance: one a two-story, mansard-roofed and red-brick building that stands on the bare footprint of a harbor rock; the second, a classic tower off Osprey Beach.

Entry from the south is clearly marked. Pick flashing green buoy "1" and flashing red buoy "2" and then follow the channel between the lighthouses into the Thames River. If entering from the east, through Pine Island Channel, be aware of the many rocks in this area. While the channel is marked, don't stray to port on entry.

Most recreational boating facilities are on the New London side of the Thames River, south of the bridges in Green Harbor and Shaw Cove. The Groton side of the river is heavily industrialized, dominated by General Dynamics' Electric Boat Plant, which has built a substantial part of the U.S. Navy's underwater submarine fleet. Despite security zones around the plant and submarines awaiting completion or repairs, it is still possible to cruise slowly past an extraordinary collection of undersea warships, including the Sea Wolf and Los Angeles-class attack subs, possibly even a Trident-class "boomer" (Inter-Continental Ballistic Missile) submarine. Note: In addition to the Navy's rigorous monitoring of security zones around its ships and facilities, the U.S. Coast Guard is strict in enforcing a 6-mph speed limit within 200 feet of all docks and piers in the harbor.

Three bridges, a railroad bascule (30-foot closed vertical clearance) and twin, fixed highway spans (135-foot fixed vertical clearances) cross the Thames River a little more than three miles north of the harbor lights. Boats requiring a clearance of over 30 feet should alert the railroad bridge tender on VHF Channel 13. Keep in mind that railroad bridges are locked down well in advance of oncoming trains on this coastal Amtrak route. Similarly, be sure to consider the maneuverability requirements of large commercial vessels in this active port and shipping lane.

Dockage: Excellent yachting facilities, nautical services and supplies are located in two adjacent bights on the New London side of the Thames River. Green Harbor, approximately one mile inside the harbor entrance, features two marinas, both offering transient slips and services. Thamesport Marina has slips available at deepwater fixed docks, and showers, refueling, repairs and an on-site restaurant are also available. Next door, Burr's Marina has slips, which are rented daily during the summer months, with 9-foot depths, electrical service, cable TV and water. Moorings and launch service are also available for transients. Burr's has a pool, restrooms, showers, laundry facilities and repair services. Schooners Restaurant (250 Pequot Ave., 860-437-3801) is on-site. From Green's Harbor, it is about three miles to downtown New London.

Shaw Cove, just a mile north of Green Harbor, is totally protected and offers dockage at Crocker's Boatyard, where cruisers will find deepwater floating slips (up to 170 feet) with water and electricity. Crocker's is a full-service yard with a 75-ton lift and substantial repair capabilities. The yard's accommodations include showers, laundry, restrooms, supplies and an in-ground swimming pool.

Restaurants, including The Tavern (345 Bank St., 860-442-4844), Jasmine Thai Restaurant (470 Bank St., 860-442-9991), Steak Out Restaurant (385 Bank St., 860-442-5282) and the Hot Rod Café (357 Bank St., 860-447-2320) are within convenient walking distance. A short distance farther north, the New London Waterfront Park has four different piers offering a variety of daytime and overnight transient dockage possibilities. Call 860-442-2489 for information. This location is at the foot of the town of New London. From here walk straight up the hill into town.

GOIN' ASHORE: **NEW LONDON, CT**

New London is a thriving seaport overflowing with spirit and excitement. A waterfront boardwalk from Shaw Cove allows visitors to amble north into town to sample the scores of restaurants, including Bangkok City Thai Cuisine (123 State St., 860-442-6970), a local favorite for tasty entrees in a homey atmosphere; Tony D's (92 Huntington St., 860-443-9900), a favorite for Italian; Zavala Authentic Mexican (2 State St., 860-437-1891); Captain Scotts Lobster Dock (80 Hamilton St., 860-439-1741) and Illiano Trattoria (929 Bank St., 860-447-9390) for continental, Italian and pizza.

Many interesting shops, galleries and boutiques are thriving in town. During the summer and fall seasons, from 9:30 a.m. to 2 p.m. every Tuesday and Friday, there is a farmer's market, offering fresh produce, flowers and cheese on Eugene O'Neill and Pearl streets. Whale Row features restored 19th-century houses that are open to the public, and the recently renovated 1888-vintage train station is not only interesting to look at, it also offers convenient Amtrak rail transportation to Boston and New York City. Ocean Beach Park (six miles south of downtown), offers a mile of sandy beach, amusements and a boardwalk. Civil War-era Fort Trumbull is now open as a state park. Or, dock your boat in New London and hop aboard the New London to Block Island Ferry and spend the night on Block Island. Bike rentals are available in Old Town on Block Island when you arrive. Check the schedule at www.goblockisland.com.

ADDITIONAL RESOURCES:

- City of New London, **www.ci.new-london.ct.us**

New London and Groton, CT

NEW LONDON AND GROTON		Largest Vessel Accommodated	VHF Channel Monitored	Transient Berths / Total Berths	Approach / Dockside Depth (reported)	Floating Docks	Gas / Diesel	Groceries, Ice, Marine Supplies, Snacks	Repairs: Hull, Engine, Propeller	Lift (tonnage), Crane, Rail	1=110V, 2=220V, B=Both, Max Amps	Laundry, Pool, Showers	Pump-Out Station	Nearby: Grocery Store, Motel, Restaurant
		Dockage					Supplies		Services					
1. Thamesport Marina	800-882-1151	150	09/68	15/118	20/15		GD	IMS	HP		1/50		P	GMR
2. Burr's Marina	860-443-8457	110	09	25/136	12/9		GD	IMS	HEP	L20	B/50	LPS	P	GMR
3. Crocker's Boatyard Inc.	860-443-6304	150	09	5/230	12/12	F	GD	IMS	HEP	L70	B/50	LPS	P	GMR
4. New London Waterfront Park	860-447-5201	295	09	35/35	15/15	F						LS		GMR
5. Thames Harbor Inn and Marina	860-445-8111	100		12/22	50/50	F		GI				L		
6. Pine Island Marina	860-445-9729	52	68	10/110	7/5	F		IMS	HEP	LC	1/30	LS	P	
7. Shennecossett Yacht Club	860-445-9854	50	09/68	/240	7/6		GD	I		L	B/30	S	P	GMR
8. Gales Ferry Marina	860-464-2146	40	12	5/70	6/5	F	GD	IM		L35	1/30	LS		GMR
9. The Marina at American Wharf	860-886-6363	170	68	100/200	30/10	F	GD	I			B/100	LPS	P	GMR

Corresponding chart(s) not to be used for navigation. Internet Access Wireless Internet Access

NEARBY GOLF COURSES:
Norwich Golf Course, New London Turnpike, New London, CT 06320, 860-889-6973

NEARBY MEDICAL FACILITIES:
Lawrence & Memorial Hospital, 365 Montauk Ave., New London, CT 06320, 860-442-0711

GOIN' ASHORE: **GROTON, CT**

In 1868 the eastern edge of Groton became a navy yard and in World War I it was officially commissioned as a submarine base. A visit to Groton should include a visit to the U.S. Navy Submarine Force Museum, home of the *USS Nautilus*, the world's first nuclear submarine and now a National Historic Landmark. The museum traces the development of submarines from David Bushnell's Revolutionary War *American Turtle* (with a full-scale model) to the most advanced boats of today's underwater navies. The museum features an interactive style that appeals to all ages. Located at One Crystal Lake Road, adjacent to the Navy Submarine Base, it is open during the summer from May 1 to Oct. 31, Wednesday to Monday, from 9 a.m. to 5 p.m., and Tuesday from 1 p.m. to 5 p.m. (winter hours vary). Admission is free (800-343-0079).

Revolutionary War buffs may want to visit Fort Griswold, the site of the 1781 massacre of American defenders by British troops led by Benedict Arnold. Today the site includes ramparts, battlements and buildings dating from the Revolution as well as a 134-foot granite monument to the defenders. Visit the museum located in the state park for the full story of the battle; call for the opening hours. Admission is free (860-445-1729).

Groton has several shopping centers, but they are only accessible from the marinas with transportation. Cove Mall is a good choice for reprovisioning. The Fisherman Restaurant (860-536-1717) at 937 Groton Long Point Road is very popular for its views and classic American seafood dishes. Paul's Pasta Shop (223 Thames St., 860-445-5276) specializes in homemade pastas and sauces. Angelo's Pizzeria (90 Plaza Ct., 860-445-1400) features gourmet brick-oven pizza and full Italian dinners.

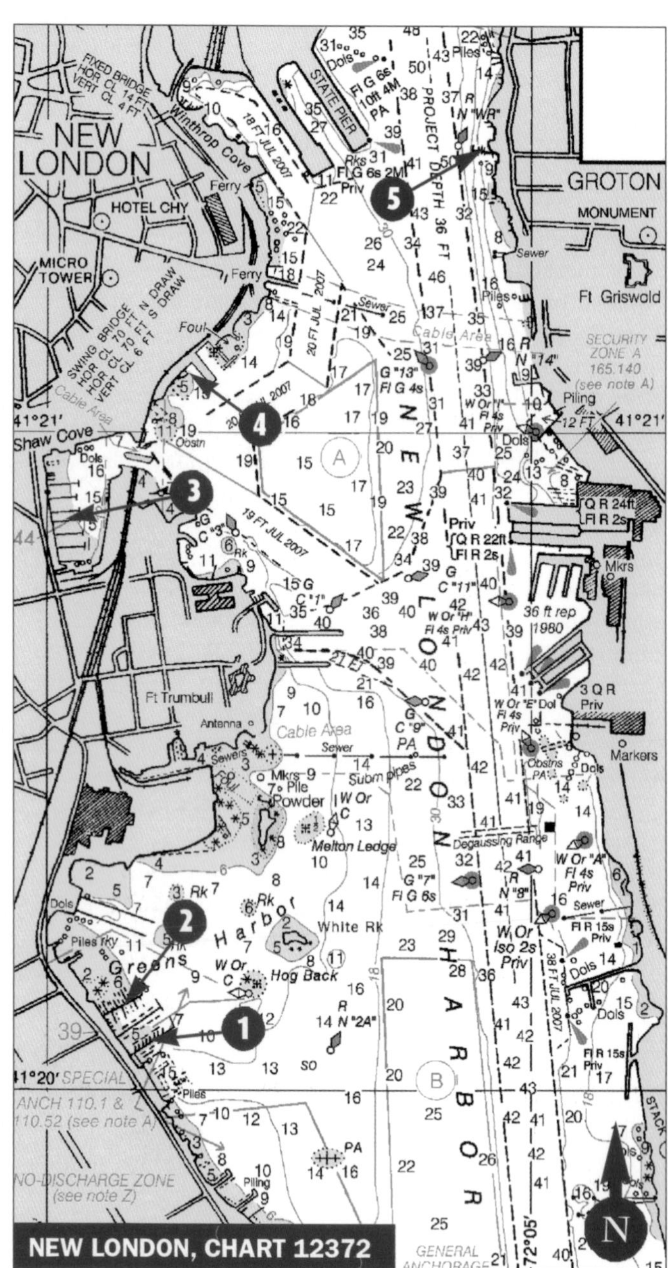

NEW LONDON, CHART 12372

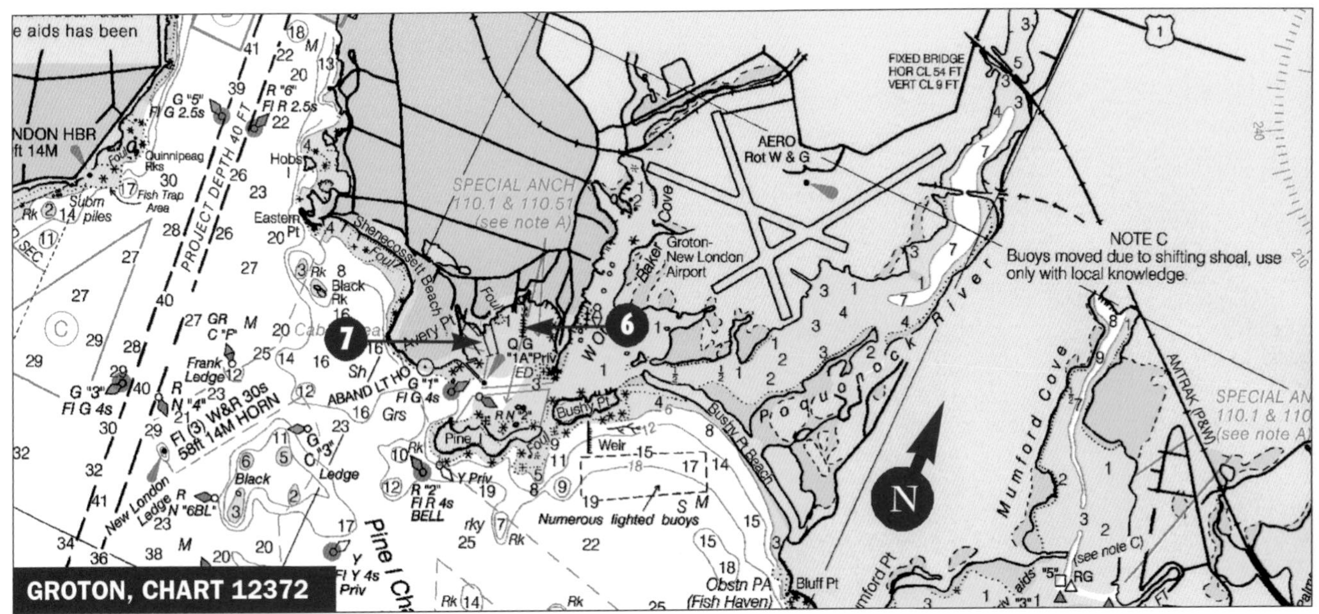

GROTON, CHART 12372

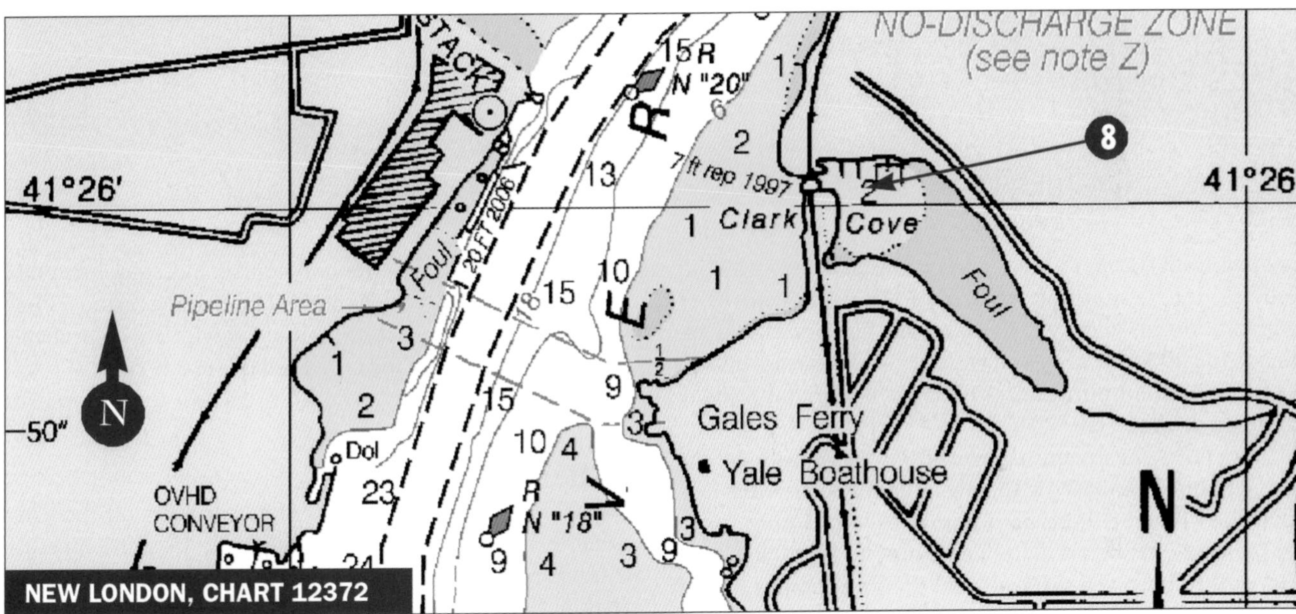

NEW LONDON, CHART 12372

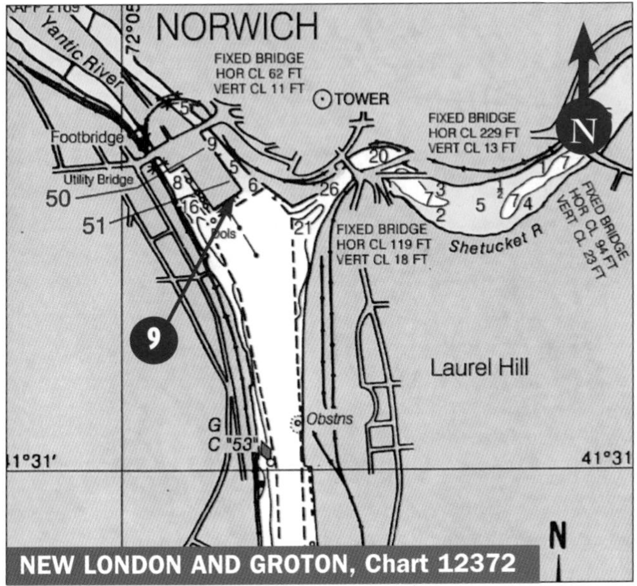

NEW LONDON AND GROTON, Chart 12372

ADDITIONAL RESOURCES:

- Town of Groton, **www.town.groton.ct.us** or **www.grotonconnecticut.com**

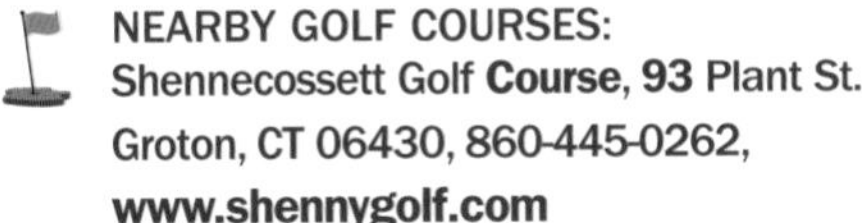

NEARBY GOLF COURSES:

Shennecossett Golf Course, 93 Plant St., Groton, CT 06430, 860-445-0262, **www.shennygolf.com**

NEARBY MEDICAL FACILITIES:

Lawrence & Memorial Hospital, 365 Montauk Ave., New London, CT 06320, 860-442-0711

New London and Groton to Norwich

Beyond the Thames River bridges, the U.S. Coast Guard Academy (31 Mohegan Ave., 860-444-8444) dominates the bluff along the river, with its Georgian brick buildings and white clock tower. The Academy visitors center

Looking northeast over New London. (Not to be used for navigation.) WATERWAY GUIDE PHOTOGRAPHY

is open from 9 a.m. to 5 p.m. daily. The public can attend movies, tours, sporting events and the occasional band concert, but no docks are available for visitors. If you are lucky, the 295-foot square-rigger, *Eagle*, America's ambassador, will be in port. She is open to visitors on Sunday afternoons in the fall.

Two miles upstream along the Groton shore is the Navy Submarine Base, with row after row of submarines stretched out for more than a mile. About a mile north of the base, just below Gales Ferry, are the Yale (blue) and Harvard (crimson) boathouses and training quarters for the annual spring rowing regatta, the nation's oldest intercollegiate sporting event. During Race Week, New London is like Louisville during Kentucky Derby week. Boats come in from all over the northeast, and anyone expecting accommodations should make reservations well in advance. Special trains are scheduled, the shores are full of spectators and the river is full of boats.

Norwich, about 11 miles upriver from New London, is at the head of the Thames River. The trip upriver is pleasant, passing the U.S. Coast Guard Academy, the Groton New London Submarine Base and Mohegan Sun Casino. The river traffic is light and the channel is well-marked. There are several dikes above Easter Point, most notably Mohegan Dike near the Mohegan Pequot Bridge, which submerges at half tide. Norwich has many new restaurants and shops in the downtown area, as well as art galleries and theaters.

Dockage: The city pier at Chelsea Landing allows 24-hour free dockage for transients. The 200-slip Marina at American Wharf offers all amenities including a waterfront restaurant, swimming pool, miniature golf course and complimentary shuttles to both Foxwoods and Mohegan Sun casinos. Fuel, laundry facilities and free pump-out service are all available on-site. The Marina can accommodate vessels up to 200 feet in length. This popular spot also plays host to fireworks for Independence Day.

Fishers Island

Six-mile-long Fishers Island is only two miles off the Connecticut shore, but belongs to New York. Its shore- line has several small harbors, suitable for anchoring, but only West Harbor has facilities for cruising boats. It is peaceful and well-protected if you want to escape the weather or heavy fog often found in the Watch Hill passage. According to the 2000 census, the island hosts a year-round population of 389 people; there are very limited amenities ashore.

NAVIGATION: Use Charts 12372 and 13214. For Fishers Island, use New London tide tables. For high tide, subtract 4 minutes; for low tide, subtract 4 minutes. The best approach to West Harbor from the west is south of North Dumpling Lighthouse, between flashing red bell buoy "2" off the tip of Fishers Island and the green can buoy "3" marking South Dumpling. Follow the red lighted buoys along the shore to the West Harbor entrance channel. Note that the rebuilt North Dumpling Lighthouse is now a private home.

Other Fishers Island harbors offer good gunkholing. The westernmost of these is Silver Eel Cove, where the New London ferry docks. Visiting boats are not welcome, because maneuvering room for the ferry is limited.

Fishers Island, NY

FISHERS ISLAND		Largest Vessel Accommodated	VHF Channel Monitored	Transient Berths / Total Berths	Approach / Dockside Depth (reported)	Floating Docks	Gas / Diesel	Groceries, Ice, Marine Supplies, Snacks	Repairs: Hull, Engine, Propeller	Lift (tonnage), Crane, Rail	1=110V, 2=220V, B=Both, Max Amps	Laundry, Pool, Showers	Pump-Out Station	Nearby: Grocery Store, Motel, Restaurant
		Dockage					Supplies		Services					
1. Fishers Island Yacht Club Marina	631-788-7036	130	09	15/50	9/8			IS			B/50	S		GMR
2. Fishers Island Mobil	631-788-7311						GD	I						
3. Pirates Cove Marine Inc.	631-788-7528	40	09	/15	10/6	F		M	HEP	L20, C15	1/30			GR

Corresponding chart(s) not to be used for navigation. Internet Access Wireless Internet Access

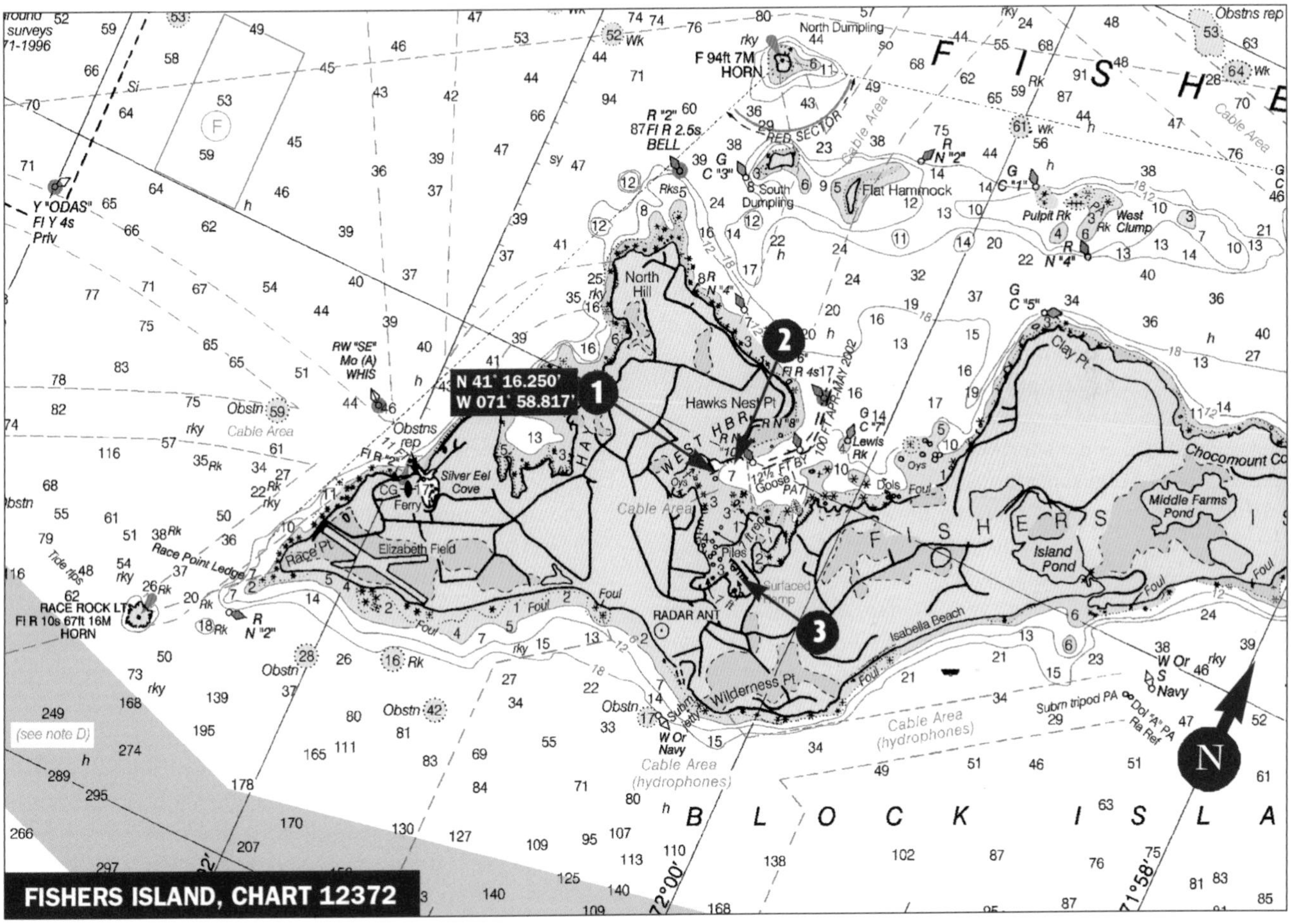

FISHERS ISLAND, CHART 12372

The next harbor east is Hay Harbor, which should not be entered without local knowledge. It is shoal, rocky and crowded with sailing dinghies. Farther east, in Chocomount Cove between Clay Point and Brooks Point, you can anchor in peace if the wind is moderate and blowing out of the south.

Farthest east is East Harbor, with a private club and golf course nearby. The harbor has excellent holding, although it is open to the northwest and exposed to wakes from vessels traveling along Long Island Sound. You can take the dinghy ashore for a round of golf or a pleasant walk along the country roads, but no services are available. West Harbor is the best place on the island to find facilities and services.

Dockage: Fishers Island Yacht Club Marina offers dockage, launch service, ice and water. Farther up the harbor, past Goose Island via a private channel with good depths, a small shipyard sits in a well-protected cove. Though busy with local clientele and without transient dockage, it sells lobsters and corn in season.

Anchorage: Well-protected except in northerly and northeasterly winds, West Harbor will accommodate a good number of boats at anchor, and the holding ground is good. Anchorage is available in the northeastern part of the harbor, with a scenic view of the sunset. No anchoring is permitted in the inner harbor.

GOIN' ASHORE:
FISHERS ISLAND, NY

In 1664, the Duke of York gave the island to New York under a land grant, but the Winthrops were allowed to remain on the island with their small farms. Later in 1863, Robert Fox purchased the island for $55,000 and restored farming here. During the Prohibition-era 1920s, rum-running was prevalent. Also in the 1920s, a summer colony was planned and the farmland was turned into estates with large homes, many of which can be seen from the waterside.

Fishers Island is very private to this day and the whole eastern end of the island is gated. The western end offers some interesting strolls and a short walk into the small village, where the Henry L. Ferguson Museum (631-788-7239) traces the history of Fishers Island from the time of the American Indians to present day. The findings from a number of archeological digs are also on display here.

In the village there are very limited amenities. Pequot Inn has a restaurant that offers snacks and light fare, plus an interesting selection of international beers; call ahead for dinner reservations (246 Montauk Ave., 631-788-7246). Entertainment is offered Thursday through Saturday. Also in the village, Toppers (631-788-7833) has ice cream, the Pickett Fence (631-788-7299) offers gifts and the News Café (Equestrian Ave., 631-788-7123) serves light breakfasts and lunches.

For bird-watchers, Great Gull Island, just off West Harbor, has the largest nesting populations of common and roseate terns on the East Coast.

ADDITIONAL RESOURCES:

- Fishers Island, **www.fishersisland.net**

NEARBY GOLF COURSES:
Shennecossett Municipal Golf, 284 Plant St.
Groton, CT 06430, 860-445-0262,
www.shennygolf.com

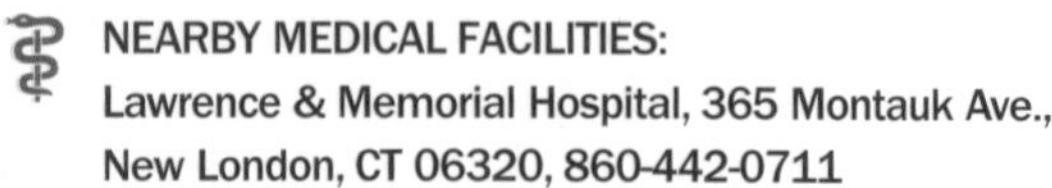

NEARBY MEDICAL FACILITIES:
Lawrence & Memorial Hospital, 365 Montauk Ave.,
New London, CT 06320, 860-442-0711

Mystic River

NAVIGATION: Use Charts 12372 and 13214. Enter Mystic River south of Groton Long Point, leaving both of its red obstruction buoys at the point to port. From red nun buoy "22," marking Groton Long Point, take a course of 066 degrees magnetic to Whale Rock, leaving it to starboard and Mouse Island to port. Just beyond, the Mystic River approach channel begins its winding, well-marked path through reefs. Take time to sort out the buoys, and make sure not to skip any markers. They are all numbered, and the channel poses little problem for the focused skipper. Inside the harbor, the channel curves, zigzags and loops among shoals and flats in a generally northerly direction. Continue to follow the numbered buoys consecutively; they do not follow a straight-line course, and it is easy to miss some.

Noank

The quaint seafaring village of Noank, dating back to the 1820s, all but fills the small peninsula guarding the entrance to the Mystic River. Except for the three major marinas within easy walking distance, Noank is quiet and noncommercial, a place for pensive walks with classic seascape vistas. Noank also makes a great stop for those running the Sound and looking for a quick overnight mooring.

NAVIGATION: Use Charts 12372 and 13214. Use New London tide tables. For high tide, subtract 22 minutes; for low tide, subtract 8 minutes. A brief detour from the entrance to the river (minding the aids to navigation to the west of Mouse Island) leads past the protective uncharted breakwater into Noank's West Cove. Be sure to give Mouse Island's sloping western rock ledges ample room to starboard while staying within the green daybeacons to port. The channel is periodically dredged, but you should expect no more than 6-foot depths (some of it hard ledge) at low water.

On the easterly side of the Noank peninsula, from Noank Light, the Mystic River channel runs offshore of Morgan Point with its dormered lighthouse, then follows the Noank shore closely, hugging its projecting piers. The easterly side of the channel tends to shoal, so give the nuns a fair berth to starboard as you pass. Stay aware of current and wind affecting your course, so as not to be set outside the channel.

Dockage: Spicer's Noank Marina in West Cove is usually filled to capacity with seasonal rentals; sometimes there may be transient dock space available while local tenants are off cruising. Spicer's ample floating docks provide ready access to electrical and telephone hookups and water. Spicer's is a full-service operation (major lift and repair capabilities) that also takes pride in the size and cleanliness of its restrooms and showers. There is an on-premises chandlery and, within the immediate vicinity, a sail loft and bait and tackle shop. Spicer's also maintains a large mooring field on both sides of the breakwater. There is usually a transient tie-up available here, including launch service from Spicer's (9 a.m. or 10 a.m. to 6 p.m. or 7 p.m. during the season, call "Spicer's Launch" on VHF Channel 68).

On the Mystic River side of the peninsula, inside Morgan Point just past red nun buoy "8," the Noank Shipyard welcomes transient vessels of almost any description and draft on its docks and moorings (with launch service). In addition to dockage, the yard has an easy-access, 350-foot fuel dock, 70-ton lift and a complete set of specialty repair and fabrication shops on-site. Noank Village Boatyard is about three-quarters of a mile farther north on the Mystic River channel. The yard is now greatly expanded and able to accommodate boats of up to 90 feet on its 500 feet of face dock along the river with 30- and 50-amp electrical service available at each slip. A rental mooring may be open here as well, and two pump-out stations are available to customers. The yard has virtually any marine repair capability, with a 35-ton Travelift for haul-outs. At the same time its owners lay claim to the best and cleanest shower/restroom facilities on the river with a welcoming attitude toward visitors. A loaner car is usually available for trips to town, and there is a free hook-up for Internet users at the yard office.

Anchorage: In West Cove there may be an anchorage spot or two left outside the increasingly filled mooring field, though this area is relatively shallow (6 to 7 feet at low water) and quite exposed to winds and wakes from the south. Similarly, the "Special Anchorage" areas charted east of the Noank peninsula will support drafts of no more than 5 feet at low water, and they, too, are all but completely filled with local mooring floats. A better bet, at least for a fair-weather anchorage, is located just east of Ram Island in depths of 9 to 11 feet with good holding in firm mud. This is not the place, however, to wait out the passage of a front; it is wide open to the northeast. The island is private and the owners do not welcome uninvited guests, yet it is a scenic spot to drop a day hook or enjoy a quiet summer evening's layover.

GOIN' ASHORE: NOANK, CT

Though the village is small and a throwback to a simpler time, it is a surprisingly good place to stop for basic boat provisioning, a good meal out and, given three major yards in the immediate vicinity, virtually any boat part or service needed. At the village center, Universal Food Store (17 Pearl St., 860-536-3767) has all the basics, plus freshly prepared pizza and calzones to go. Mystic River Baking Co. (15 Pearl St., 860-536-0182) for truly fresh and delicious baked goods and specialty desserts) and the Universal Package Store Noank (17 Pearl St., 860-536-0122) are next door. Carson's Variety Store (43 Main St., 860-536-0059) prepares legendary sandwiches and has an old-fashioned soda fountain—in addition to Ice Cold Ice (or so the sign says). For the younger set, the town maintains a popular playground next to Carson's. For an excellent seafood lunch or dinner, try the rustic and weathered Seahorse Restaurant (65 Marsh Road, on West Cove next to Spicer's, 860-536-1670). The baked bluefish there in season is as good as it gets and the price is right. Abbott's Lobster in the Rough (117 Pearl St., south of the village center, 860-536-7719) has long had the largest lobster pound in southern New England and some of the most devoted customers for this type of dining. Abbott's also maintains six deepwater slips just off the channel where you can tie up for a spell and order only steps from your boat or dinghy. About a mile east of West Cove, The Fisherman (937 Groton Long Point Road, 860-536-1717) has great views of the surrounding saltwater marsh.

NEARBY GOLF COURSES:
Birch Plain Golf Course, 119 High Rock Road
Groton, CT 06340, 860-445-9918

NEARBY MEDICAL FACILITIES:
Lawrence & Memorial Hospital, 404 Thames St.,
Groton, CT 06340, 860-445-0494

Mason Island to Mystic

Though connected to Mystic Village by a serviceable bridge, Mason Island has long held itself somewhat apart from the mainland, largely retaining its rural-residential character. Still, there are excellent marinas and marine services, easily accessed from the river, dotting the island's northern perimeter. Over the Masons Island Causeway, in Mystic proper, the village fairly hums with the bustle of tourists, summer traffic on U.S. Route 1 and amenities to match. Mystic Seaport Museum (75 Greenmanville Rd., 860-572-5315) is located north of the bascule bridge (4-foot closed vertical clearance) on U.S. Route 1.

NAVIGATION: Use Charts 12372 and 13214. For Mystic Village, use New London tide tables. For high tide, subtract 22 minutes; for low tide, subtract 8 minutes. As the

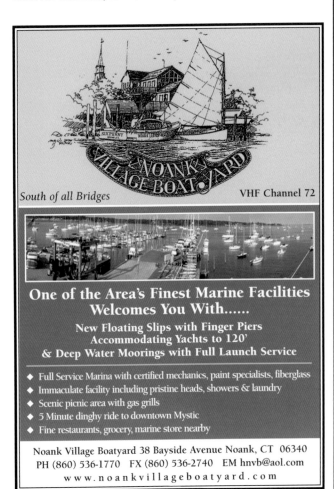

Mystic River, CT

MYSTIC RIVER		Largest Vessel Accommodated	VHF Channel Monitored	Transient Berths / Total Berths	Approach / Dockside Depth (reported)	Floating Docks	Gas / Diesel	Groceries, Ice, Marine Supplies, Snacks	Repairs: Hull, Engine, Propeller	Lift (tonnage), Crane, Rail	1=110V, 2=220V, B=Both, Max Amps	Laundry, Pool, Showers	Pump-Out Station	Nearby: Grocery Store, Motel, Restaurant
		Dockage					Supplies		Services					
1. Spicer's Noank Marina	860-536-4978	52	68	20/444	7/7	F		IM	HEP	L38,C	B/50	LS	P	GR
2. Noank Shipyard (Internet Access) (Wireless Internet Access)	860-536-9651	300	09	/158	14/12	F	GD	IMS	HEP	L70	B/50	LS	P	GR
3. NOANK VILLAGE BOATYARD (Internet Access)	**860-536-1770**	**120**	**72**	**15/150**	**10/8**	**F**		**IS**	**HEP**	**L35**	**B/50**	**LS**	**P**	**GMR**
4. MYSTIC SHIPYARD (Internet Access)	**860-536-6588**	**160**	**09/68**	**25/160**	**15/12**			**I**	**HEP**	**L50,C**	**1/50**	**LPS**	**P**	**GMR**
5. Fort Rachel Marine Service	860-536-6647	60	09	6/115	8/8	F		GIM	HE	L35	1/50	S		GMR
6. Mystic Downtown Marina	860-572-5942	60	08	5/28	10/8	F		I			1/30	LS	P	GMR
7. Steamboat Inn	860-536-8300													
8. MYSTIC SEAPORT MUSEUM AND DOCKS	**860-572-5391**	**200**	**09/68**	**40/40**	**12/11**			**I**			**B/50**	**LS**		**GMR**
9. Seaport Marine (Wireless Internet Access)	860-536-9681	130		10/85	12/12			M	HP	L	B/100	S		GMR
10. Gwenmor Marina Inc.	860-536-0281	48	13	4/110	6/6	F		IMS	HP	L35	1/30	S		GMR
11. BREWER YACHT YARD AT MYSTIC (Wireless Internet Access)	**860-536-2293**	**75**	**09**	**5/232**	**15/11**	**F**	**GD**	**IM**	**HEP**	**L35**	**B/50**	**LPS**	**P**	**GMR**
12. Mason's Island Marina	860-536-2608	43	09	6/100	4.5/8	F		IMS	HEP	L25,C	1/30	S		GMR
13. Mystic River Marina (Internet Access)	860-536-3123	150	09	25/165	14/14		GD	IMS	HEP	L35	B/100	LPS	P	GMR

Corresponding chart(s) not to be used for navigation. (Internet Access icon) Internet Access (Wireless Internet Access icon) Wireless Internet Access

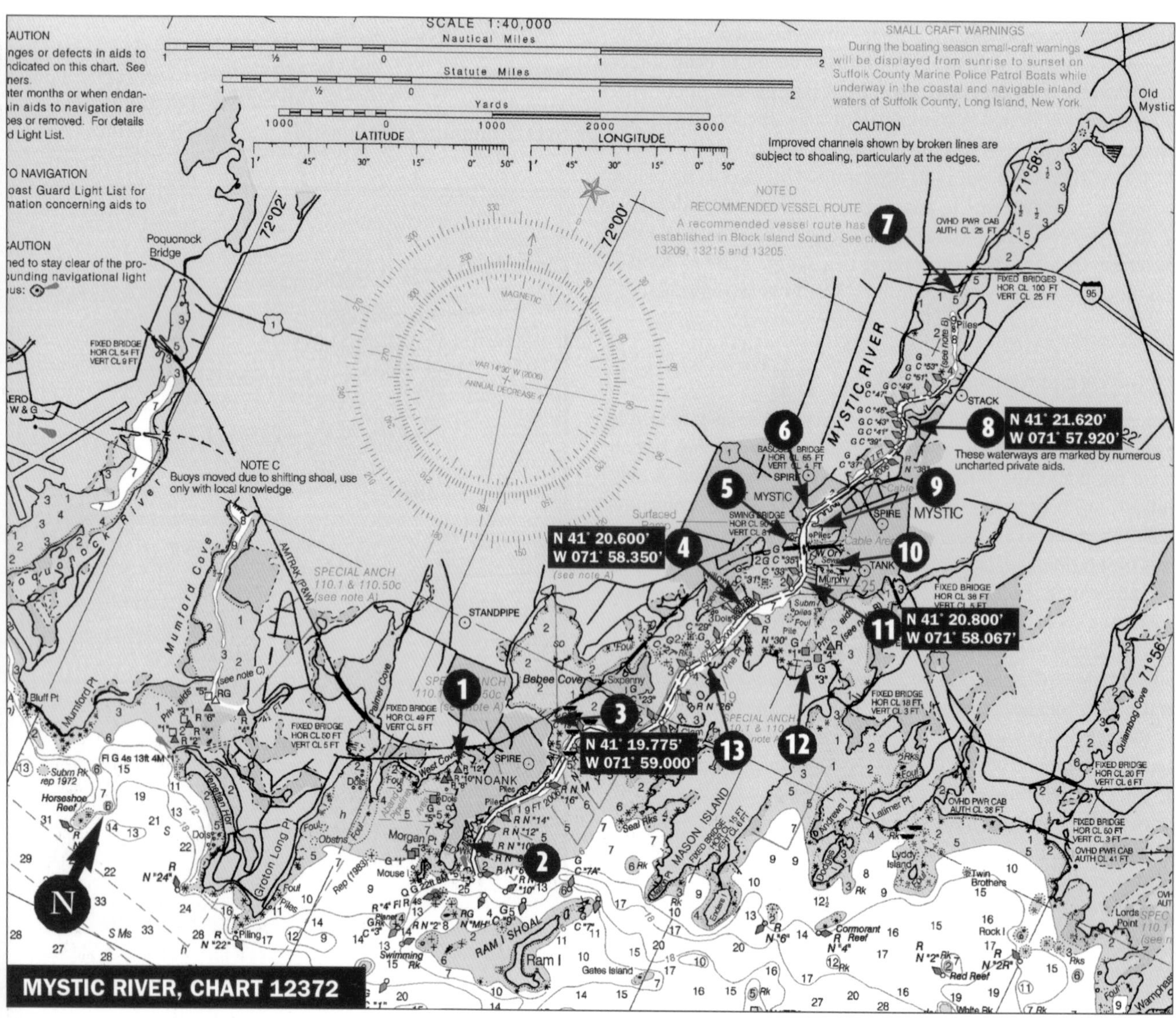

Joseph Melanson of www.skypic.com

Looking north over Mystic. (Not to be used for navigation.)

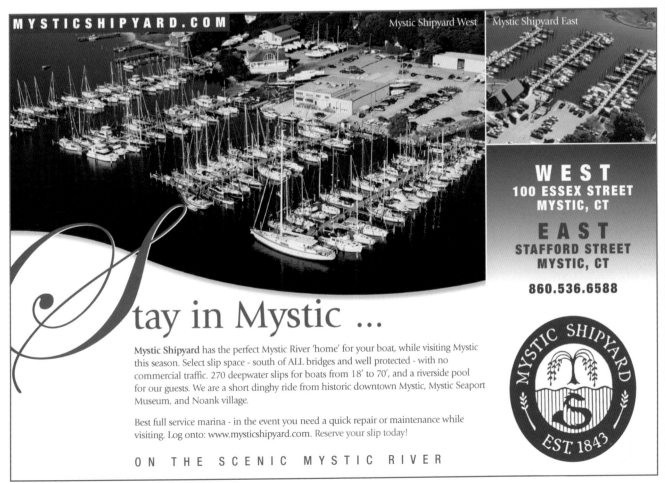

Noank shoreline falls away to the west, the Mystic River channel continues north to the buoys that are easiest to miss (and you do not want to). After observing these buoys, turn sharply to starboard for the next pair off Mason Island at Ram Point, where the channel runs on a straight, well-marked course for about a mile and a half to Willow Point. There the channel doglegs right for a distance of just over half a mile to Murphy Point, where it curves sharply to port (toward the northwest) to the Amtrak railroad swing bridge. Before attempting passage through the railroad bridge, call the tender on VHF Channel 13 for the next scheduled closing. The wait for a closed bridge can be considerable, but the scenery is pleasant, the current moderate and there is room to maneuver. The channel curves to starboard beyond the railroad bridge, and the river narrows as it deepens. Docks and small marine facilities line the banks.

Dockage: After tracking the western shore of Mason Island north, Mystic River Marina appears along the channel, just south of Pine Point. This full-service facility has all fuels, a pump-out station, a marine store, a pool, a restaurant and a complete range of repair services. On the western side of the river, at Willow Point, Mystic Shipyard extends a welcome to transient boaters with docks able to handle virtually any size recreational vessel with repair, rigging and mechanical services to match. There is a pool here as well.

Farther north, at Murphy Point on the easterly side of the river, Brewer Yacht Yard at Mystic has extensive floating docks in a protected cove, a large swimming pool, customer lounge, clean restrooms and showers, all served by a helpful staff. Full-time mechanics are on duty to handle virtually any repair requirement. Given its proximity to Mystic Village, this is a popular place in season; reservations are highly recommended. North of the railroad bridge, off the starboard side of the channel, Seaport Marine Inc. is the full-service yacht yard closest to downtown Mystic. All village amenities are within easy walking distance, and the yard has a 60-ton lift available to accommodate repairs.

Anchorage: Those with determination, skill and drafts of under 6 feet may still find anchorage possibilities along the southwest shore of Masons Island, but swing room will be in short supply as the growing number of local moorings has crowded out most of the available space clear of the channel.

GOIN' ASHORE:
MYSTIC VILLAGE, CT

Within reasonable walking distance from most of the Mystic River marinas, the village is picturesque, compact and quite busy in season. This is a prime summer weekend destination for many Connecticut residents and tourists from around the country and beyond. Much enhanced by the early-American-styled Mystic Seaport Museum, immediately north of the bridge, the village's quaint shops and dining spots are strung out along Main Street (U.S. Route 1) on either side of the unique bascule bridge at the hub of activity. West of the bridge, boutiques, galleries, restaurants and gift shops with a marine theme crowd both sides of the street. Bank Square Books (53 W. Main St., 860-536-3795) offers generous selections in many categories, and there are several banks (with ATMs) around as well. Mystic Army & Navy Store (37 W. Main St., 860-536-1877) sells actual military surplus along with the ersatz variety. Mystic Pizza (56 W. Main St., 860-536-3700) is famous for the motion picture by that name.

Along East Main Street (east of the bridge), S&P Oyster Co. (1 Holmes St. at the bridge, 860-536-2674) is popular for its moderately priced fare and great river view. Across the street, Bravo Bravo Restaurant (20 E. Main St., 860-536-3228) is justly acclaimed for its creative pastas. About a block east of the bridge, you will find the post office. Full reprovisioning possibilities will require transportation two miles farther east at the A&P (179 Stonington Road, 860-536-5813). There are also small markets within a short walk of the marinas. Also on the easterly side of town, Flood Tide Restaurant (3 Williams Ave., 860-536-8140) draws repeat business because of its interesting entrees (amaretto rainbow trout and lamb Florentine, for example) and moderate prices.

Though the village is itself a magnet for summer tourists, no first-time visit here could be complete without a tour of the Mystic Seaport Museum, just a few block's walk to the north. Still farther north (about two miles along Route 27), Mystic Aquarium and Institute for Exploration (55 Coogan Blvd., 860-572-5955, daily 9 a.m. to 5 p.m.) is the single most-visited attraction in the state of Connecticut. Its exhibits and demonstrations are captivating for children of all ages.

ADDITIONAL RESOURCES:

- Mystic, **www.mystic.org**

NEARBY GOLF COURSES:
Pequot Golf Club, 127 Wheeler Road #A,
Stonington, CT 06378, 860-535-1898

NEARBY MEDICAL FACILITIES:
Lawrence & Memorial Hospital, 14 Clara Drive,
Mystic, CT 06355, 860-245-0565

Mystic Seaport Museum

Mystic Seaport, a simulated historical port at work, is a window open to America's maritime history. Some of the popular exhibits include working renovated ships and the preservation shipyard, where vessels are constructed or reconstructed using traditional methods of the 18th century.

NAVIGATION: Use Charts 12372 and 13214. The Mystic River's narrow section ends at a one-of-a-kind bascule bridge (vertical clearance 8 feet), which opens at 40 minutes past the hour, between 7:40 a.m. and 6:40 p.m. during the summer months and on signal at other times. Contact the tender on VHF Channel 13 for an opening advisory even beyond the peak summer season. Note: Boats moving with the tide have the right-of-way when the bridge opens. Beyond the bascule bridge (at U.S. Route 1), the Mystic River opens up to embrace the classic harbor of another century. Stick with the channel marked by a series of

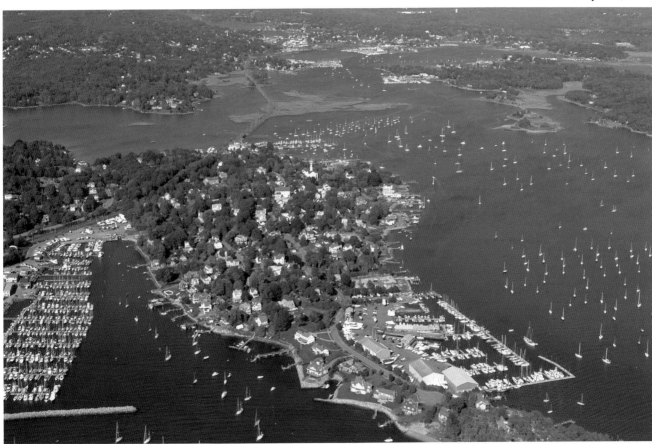

Looking northeast over Mystic Harbor. (Not to be used for navigation.) WATERWAY GUIDE PHOTOGRAPHY

green cans, however. Outside the channel, the "harbor" is quite shallow and unsuitable for either navigation or anchorage.

Dockage: The Mystic Seaport docks can accommodate between 40 and 45 boats per night, more when clubs and groups are prepared to raft up. Still, holiday weekends and special events such as the Sea Music Festival and the Antique and Classic Boat Rendezvous draw that kind of crowd, usually taking up all possible dock spaces. Since no moorings are available and anchorage is impossible outside the Seaport's relatively narrow channel, boaters intending to visit should call ahead for reservations. Reduced dockage rates are available for Mystic Seaport Museum members, including museum admission for all aboard. Modern shoreside facilities are found amid the restored sheds and boathouses. The wharves have freshwater spigots, 110-volt power and free pump-out service. Ice can be purchased from the dock attendant. After the visitor's gates have closed, a slip at Mystic Seaport offers a special treat, the chance to roam this unique village among the ghosts of ancient tars and the sights and smells of seafaring in another time.

Anchorage: The Mystic Harbor Management Commission has placed four seasonal buoys outlining the perimeter of a shallow transient anchorage area east of the Mystic Shipyard in Mystic Harbor. The fairway to the boatyards to the east is south of this anchorage, which is north of Masons Island. The buoys are white with the letter "A" in a circle and the word "Transient" in black

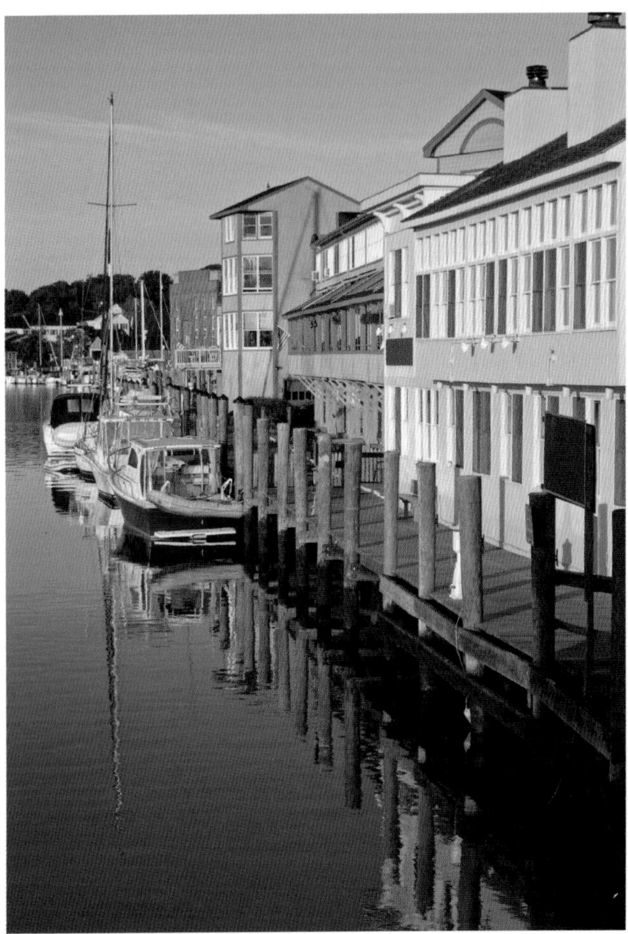

Mystic, CT. ©IstockPhoto/DenisTangneyJr

letters. The southeast area has a depth of 3 feet at mean low water and tapers to 5 feet toward the northwest. A second shallow transient anchorage area with limited space is upriver north of the federal channel. A sign at the northern end of the Mystic Seaport Museum refers to the last federal marker and requests that the channel beyond not be obstructed. The time limit for anchoring for all transients is seven days. Both anchorages are No-Discharge Zones.

GOIN' ASHORE:
MYSTIC SEAPORT MUSEUM

Visitors wander here along the quays and cobbled harbor lanes, stopping at ancient shops, houses and churches while boarding classic wooden boats—all now restored to pristine condition. Climb aboard the only remaining wooden whaler, the *Charles W. Morgan*, the last of the dory-laden Grand Banks fishing schooners, the *L. A. Dutton*, and the opulent but sleek (and still fast) sloop *Brilliant*. Chat up the players in period costume who are steeped in their characters' lives, trades and viewpoints. Other attractions include one of the finest nautical libraries in existence, a planetarium, masthead carvers, classic boat and model builders, chantey singers, hoop rollers, courses and lectures on all manner of nautical subjects and a kaleidoscope of priceless maritime treasures on display. Not to be missed is a river tour on the Sabino, the nation's last coal-fired steamer. For general museum information and hours, call 860-572-0711. Mystic Seaport has its own extensive snack bar (The Galley Restaurant on the Village Green), an excellent bakery and an extraordinary nautical gift and bookstore. The Maritime Gallery (with original art, models and prints for sale) is a major exhibit in its own right. At the northern entrance to the museum, the Seaman's Inne Restaurant & Pub (105 Greenmanville Road, 860-572-5303) offers traditional American fare in an authentic Colonial setting suited to the most cultivated tastes.

ADDITIONAL RESOURCES:

- Mystic Seaport Museum, **www.mysticseaport.org** or **www.mystic.org**

NEARBY GOLF COURSES:
Pequot Golf Club, 127 Wheeler Road #A, Stonington, CT 06378, 860-535-1898

NEARBY MEDICAL FACILITIES:
Lawrence & Memorial Hospital, 14 Clara Drive, Mystic, CT 06355, 860-245-0565

Stonington

Connecticut's easternmost cruising port, Stonington lays claim (with some justice) to having the most beautiful harbor on the East Coast. This village peninsula, called the Borough, is home to Connecticut's only remaining fishing fleet.

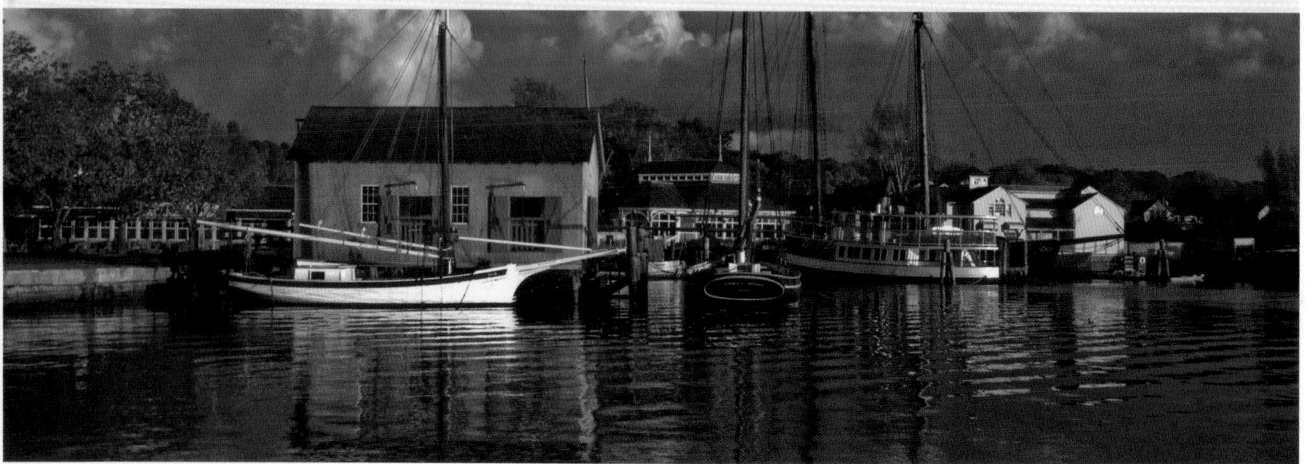

Stonington, CT, and Watch Hill, RI

STONINGTON AND WATCH HILL		Largest Vessel Accommodated	VHF Channel Monitored	Transient Berths / Total Berths	Approach / Dockside Depth (reported)	Floating Docks	Gas / Diesel	Groceries, Ice, Marine Supplies, Snacks	Repairs: Hull, Engine, Propeller	Lift (tonnage), Crane, Rail	1=110V, 2=220V, B=Both, Max Amps	Laundry, Pool, Showers	Pump-Out Station	Nearby: Grocery Store, Motel, Restaurant
		Dockage					Supplies		Services					
1. Dodson Boatyard	860-535-1507	120	78A	20/45	7/7	F	GD	IMS	HEP	L55,C15	B/50	LS	P	GMR
2. Stonington Harbor Yacht Club (WiFi)	860-535-0112		78		9/	F		I			1/30	S	P	GMR
3. Watch Hill Docks	401-348-4005	110	09	3/20	6/8			I			B/50		P	MR

Corresponding chart(s) not to be used for navigation. Internet Access (WiFi) Wireless Internet Access

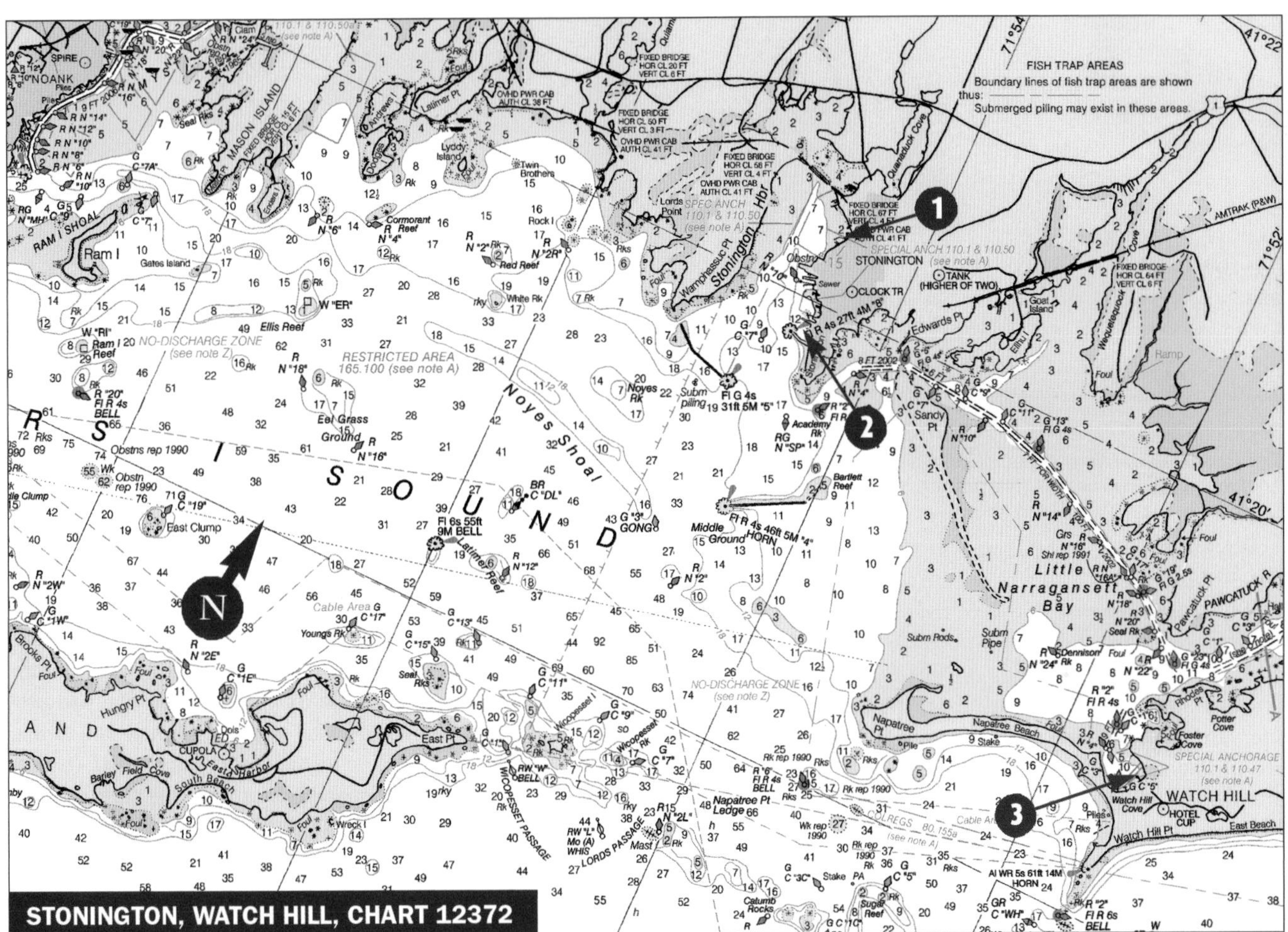

STONINGTON, WATCH HILL, CHART 12372

NAVIGATION: Use Charts 12372 and 13214. Stonington is most directly approached from Mystic Harbor via the well-buoyed passage north of Ram Island, south of Mason Point and Enders Island. Continuing eastward, passage should be between the white "ER" beacon marking Ellis Reef to starboard, and red nun buoys "6" and "4" to port. Skippers of deep-draft vessels should favor the nun buoys to avoid the rock at 5-foot depths just north of Ellis Reef. Also watch for the charted but unmarked White Rock, a 5-foot-deep spot south of red nun buoy "2," which marks Red Reef. A course favoring the red nun buoys should leave you well clear of White Rock. Take care in this area, which, like the rest of Fishers Island Sound, is well known for its bottom-jarring shoals. Daybeacons with the warning Rock are to be taken at their word.

The approach to Stonington Harbor, and to the Little Narragansett Bay channel leading to Watch Hill, is straightforward and plainly marked by the widely spaced green-and-red four-second flashing lights situated on towers atop the ends of the two breakwaters protecting the harbor. The horn sounding from 46-foot red flashing "4" to starboard can be heard from a considerable distance. The breaker arm to port restricts visibility of outbound vessels from this approach, making a wide rounding of the green beacon and allowance for ample reaction time advisable in this relatively busy channel. Shallow-draft boats may also make entrance at the shore side of the breaker just to the south of Wamphassuc Point; there are submerged rocks at the point, however, and the passage is narrow, best left to those with local knowledge.

Looking south over Stonington Harbor. (Not to be used for navigation.) WATERWAY GUIDE PHOTOGRAPHY

Dockage: Dodson Boatyard, at the head of the harbor, has 400 feet of linear dock space for visitors, though most will likely be directed to one of the yard's numerous rental moorings. Dodson's has extended dock space to include 640 feet of floating working docks. The latter include unlimited launch service to and from the dock and access to the yard's newly renovated and individualized shower/restroom facilities. The all-service yard offers both gasoline and diesel fuel and complete repair and fabrication services. Priority attention is accorded transients during the summer season with a 50-ton lift for haul-outs. Dodson's has a well-stocked chandlery and parts department, quick turnaround on propane fills, coin-operated laundry machines surrounded by an impressive trade-and-take book collection and ample parking across the road.

Anchorage: Unfortunately there is little anchorage available behind Stonington's inner breakwater (westerly side of the channel) in 9 to 15 feet of water at low tide, as moorings have gradually filled in this traditional place of refuge from the rough chop of Long Island Sound. During all but the calmest weather, rollers sneaking around the edges of the breakwaters can turn an evening here into "a moving experience." For launch service throughout the harbor (for a fee), call "Dodson Boatyard Launch" (VHF Channel 78) for a pick-up. Pump-out service is also available (free of charge) with a call to "Westerly Pump-out Boat" on VHF Channel 09. (Ask at Dodson's about the pump-out boat's scheduled availability in Stonington.)

GOIN' ASHORE:
STONINGTON BOROUGH, CT

An easy couple of blocks south of the Dodson Yard on Water Street, Stonington Borough boasts the third largest collection of historic houses and sites in Connecticut, many dating from the mid-18th century. Some of the architectural highlights include the former homes of notable patriots, shipwrights and shipmasters (among them the first American captain to circumnavigate the globe, and the first American to sight Antarctica), the Stonington Lighthouse (a first for the federal government in 1823) and the cannons that beat back an attempted British invasion during the War of 1812.

Many upscale shops and services dot the narrow Colonial streets. Additional stops on Water Street include Noah's Restaurant (113 Water St., 860-535-3925), with items such as "Noah's Best Worst," char-grilled salmon with cucumber-dill sauce, and Tuscan crab cakes; Tom's Newstand (133 Water St., 860-535-1276), with the New York Times and other out-of-state newspapers and business publications; and the Stonington Village Food Market (522 Stonington Rd., 860-535-1559) offering delivery of dry and baked goods, meats, deli items and limited fresh produce to your boat on request. If you don't find what you need here, it is more than two miles to the nearest grocery. Across the street from the Village Market, the intimate Water Street Cafe (142 Water St., 860-535-2122), where reservations are a must, serves moderately priced lunch and dinner entrees such as "roasted duck breast with peanut noodles and sesame vinaigrette."

Another pleasure of visiting Stonington is the Farmer's Market (4 High St., 860-535-2236), located on the green overlooking the harbor, on Saturday mornings. Browse the stands offering fresh produce, breads and other baked goods, flowers and more.

Stonington has increasingly become a Mecca for antiquing, drawing patrons to more than a dozen high-end shops here. In addition, you will find the Village Coiffure (117 Water St., 860-535-2727) and the old-style Village Barber Shop (107 Water St., 860-535-2241). Unique fabrics, designed in Stonington, may be found at the Hungry Palette (105 Water St., 860-535-2021). Young sailors will appreciate the village children's park located one block south of the Water Street shops.

Farther south on Water Street, the sign for Skipper's Dock (66 Water St., 860-535-0111), directs you out to the substantial pier (with parking) to the casual over-water restaurant at dock's end. Here a commanding view of the outer harbor's remaining commercial fleet and the inner harbor's sailboat flotilla will only enhance the excellent seafood selections on the restaurant menu, served in a friendly and familiar atmosphere. Waterborne diners are encouraged to tie up at its 500-foot dock and may lie alongside overnight for a nominal fee. (No water, electricity or other amenities are available, however.)

Closer to the mooring area are the post office (20 Broad St., 860-535-0454), an extensive free library (20 High St., 860-535-0658) and a bookstore called The Book Mart (17 High St., 860-535-0401). Brooks Pharmacy (37 Broad St., 860-599-4030) is about three blocks from the Dodson Yard.

ADDITIONAL RESOURCES:

- Borough of Stonington, **www.borough.stonington.ct.us**

NEARBY GOLF COURSES:
Pequot Golf Club, 127 Wheeler Road #A, Stonington, CT 06378, 860-535-1898

NEARBY MEDICAL FACILITIES:
Lawrence & Memorial Hospital, 14 Clara Drive, Mystic, CT 06355, 860-245-0565

Watch Hill

Just over the Connecticut/Rhode Island state line, at the Pawcatuck River, is the quaint village of Watch Hill, RI, featuring long-established seaside estates, an attractive and relatively uncrowded town beach, two sprawling clapboard-sided inns, numerous shops and boutiques oriented to the summer tourist trade and the friendly Watch Hill Yacht Club. The harbor is large, protected and swim-friendly.

NAVIGATION: Use Charts 12372 and 13214. For Watch Hill Point, use Newport tide tables. For high tide, add 41 minutes; for low tide, add 1 hour 16 minutes. After clearing the breakwaters protecting Stonington Harbor, the entrance to Little Narragansett Bay is marked by a red-over-green nun buoy marked "SP," located several hundred yards off Stonington Point. From there, hold a tight course to flashing red buoy "2," which marks Academy Rock (6 feet deep at low water). Then keep a sharp watch to stay within the nuns and cans marking the narrow channel, which has silted in spots to depths of 6 feet or less at low tide.

Take particular care in rounding Sandy Point and honoring flashing green buoy "5," where the water runs swiftly and deep, despite how narrow the channel appears. Many local boaters find the northern shore of Sandy Point appropriately named and an appealing stop for lunch or swimming; occasionally you will find one of them encroaching on the channel between flashing green buoy "5" and green can buoy "9." It is unsafe to cut across the bay to starboard before coming abeam flashing green buoy "23." The entry into Watch Hill is well-marked and well-charted.

Watch Hill Cove should be entered only via the marked 100-foot-wide channel, which carries 6.5 feet at mean low water. The cove is small, attractive and noncommercial, with many local boats, including classic wooden tenders and motor cruisers, as well as Herreshoff and other notable sailing designs.

Note that Little Narragansett Bay, like the rest of Rhode Island waters, is a No-Discharge Zone (prohibiting the discharge of any sewage, even if it has been treated). Here the prohibition is easily honored with a call to "Westerly Pump-Out Boat" on VHF Channel 09.

Dockage: Immediately shoreside on entering Watch Hill Cove, attractive Watch Hill Yacht Club (monitoring VHF Channel 10) maintains five rental moorings, available on a first-come, first-served basis, including launch service and use of the club's facilities and showers. Immediately to port of the yacht club on approach, Watch Hill Docks has eight slips for transients with ample depths, and a free dinghy dock for those anchored out. This is a popular spot on summer weekends; call in advance for a reservation.

Anchorage: Just west of Watch Hill is a sheltered body of water protected to the south by Napatree Beach and Point. This anchorage, with 7- to 9-foot depths, is extremely popular with locals as well as cruising boats, both power and sail. Holding is good and rafting is popular. It is not at all unusual to see 200 or more boats anchored here over a sunny summer weekend. Swimming is good in the bay, or for a more bracing dip, the easterly end of Long Island Sound (relatively open to the Atlantic Ocean) is but a short walk over the dunes. Dinghies land or anchor by the dozens on the bay side of Napatree Beach, for an easy trek to the surf or to the amenities of Watch Hill ashore to the east. To the west, about a mile's pleasant beach walk to Napatree Point, are the still-visible remains of Fort Mansfield, a pre-World War I shore battery destroyed by the hurricane of 1938.

GOIN' ASHORE: WATCH HILL, RI

Many of the houses and hotels in Watch Hill were destroyed by a hurricane in 1938. Long-time summer residents preserve the past of their village in their automobiles, shops and restaurants and in their period homes and mansions. In parking lots along the waterfront, you are likely to spot an early-model Ford, Nash or even a Hudson Silver Hornet. The Book & Tackle

Pawcatuck River, CT

PAWCATUCK RIVER		Largest Vessel Accommodated	VHF Channel Monitored	Transient Berths / Total Berths	Approach / Dockside Depth (reported)	Floating Docks	Gas / Diesel	Groceries, Ice, Marine Supplies, Snacks	Repairs: Hull, Engine, Propeller	Lift (tonnage), Crane, Rail	1=110V, 2=220V, B=Both, Max Amps	Laundry, Pool, Showers	Pump-Out Station	Nearby: Grocery Store, Motel, Restaurant
		Dockage					Supplies		Services					
1. Watch Hill Boat Yard	401-348-8148	50	09	2/81	5/5	F		I	EP	C	1/30	S		GMR
2. Avondale Boat Yard	401-348-8187	75	09	5/96	10/8	F	GD	IM	HEP	CR	B/50	S	P	
3. Greenhaven Marina	860-599-1049	32		4/65	9/6	F		IMS			1/30			
4. Frank Hall Boat Yard	401-348-8005	46	09/18	/106	6/6	F		IM	HEP	L25	B/50	S	P	R
5. Westerly Yacht Club	401-596-7556	35		2/18	12/		G				1/30	LS	P	
6. Pier 65 Marina	401-596-6350	60	09	2/22	8/7	F		M	HP	L30	1/30	S		GMR
7. Norwest Marine Inc.	860-599-2442	55	68	/140	7/8	F	G	IMS	EP	L35	B/50	LS	P	R
8. Connors and O'Brien Marina	860-599-5567	27		/75	5/8			M	HP		1/30			MR
9. Viking Marina	401-348-8148	45		/50	6/6	F			HEP	L15	1/30	S		GR

Corresponding chart(s) not to be used for navigation. Internet Access Wireless Internet Access

Shop (122 Bay St., 401-596-0051) is old and eclectic, featuring scads of dusty books, a few recent paperbacks and postal cards from the 1960s and earlier, but no tackle. The row shops along Bay Street have modernized their stocks in recent years (more designer clothing, tourist trinkets and trendy gifts), but the inns and restaurants cling to their traditional offerings and ambience.

Excellent dining can be found at Olympia Tea Room with its 1940s-style booths (74 Bay St., 401-348-8211). There you are encouraged to fashion your own appetizers to taste with smoked bluefish pate, bruschetta, black olives, red peppers and anchovies, followed by something on the order of fresh native littleneck clams and sweet sausage over linguini in a light marinara sauce. Another wonderful restaurant can be found in the northeast corner of the Watch Hill Cove at the Watch Hill Inn, where you can enjoy a light lunch or indulge in a full dinner at the Seaside Cafe (38 Bay St., 401-348-6333), offering a panoramic view of the harbor. On the Atlantic side, over the "hill," you can see the vast yellow and white structure (visible for miles from sea) of the Ocean House (1 Bluff Ave., 401-315-5599), a great spot for a cool drink, a spectacular view of Block Island on a clear day or a meal in a grand Victorian setting. Café Expresso II (98 Bay St., 401-348-3103) and Bay Street Deli (112 Bay St., 401-596-6606) are available for lighter fare. There is no supermarket nearby. The Coast Guard has turned over the 61-foot lighthouse on Watch Hill to a private group that is restoring it and adding a museum. Already restored is the classic carousel at the water's edge, doing a whirligig business with the younger set, complete with all the brass rings they

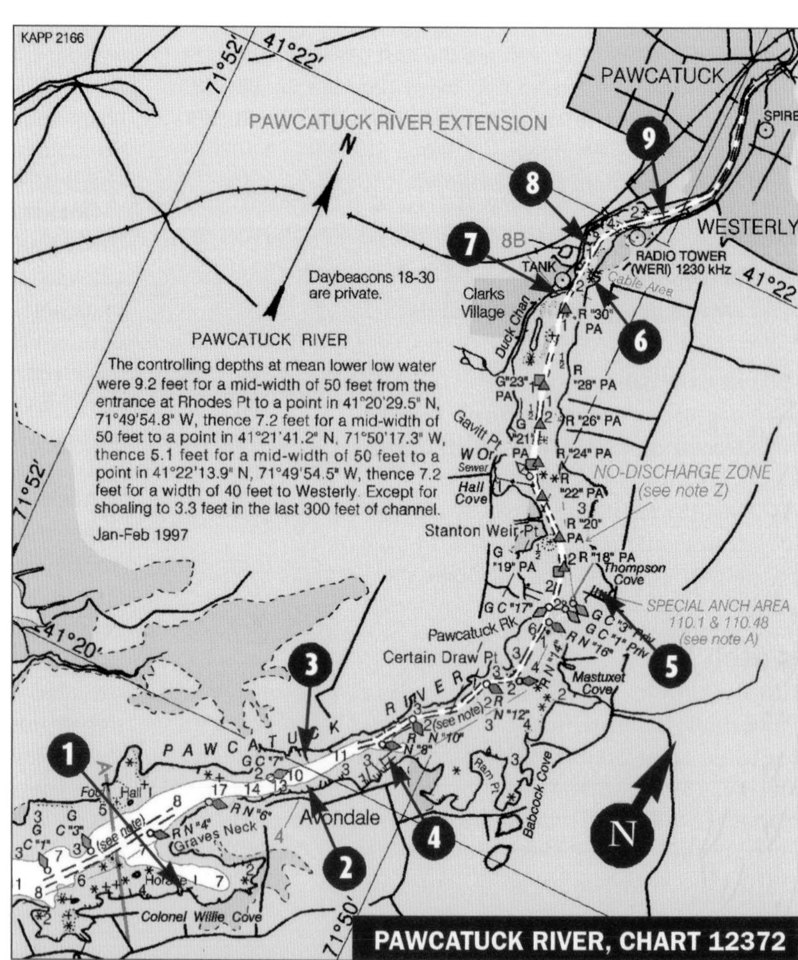

can nab. The summer season is filled with activities such as big screen movies on the beach, car shows, art exhibits, etc.

ADDITIONAL RESOURCES:

■ Visit Watch Hill, **www.visitwatchhill.com** or **www.watchhillinn.com**

NEARBY GOLF COURSES:
Elmridge Golf Course, 229 Elmridge Road, Pawcatuck, CT 06379, 860-599-2248, **www.elmridgegolf.com**

NEARBY MEDICAL FACILITIES:
Lawrence & Memorial Hospital, 37 S. Broad St., Pawcatuck, CT 06379, 860-599-5477

Watch Hill to Westerly

From Watch Hill, the well-buoyed Pawcatuck River wends its way northward through the towns of Avondale and Westerly to Pawcatuck. Depths outside the narrow channel do not encourage attempts to anchor, and marinas upriver cater primarily to the local boating community.

Dockage: Frank Hall Boat Yard in Avondale, the largest of the lot, may have a vacant slip to rent, as might the nearby Lotteryville Marina. You will want to call ahead for availability, however, and for current information on approach depths.

Heading Eastward

NAVIGATION: Use Charts 12372 and 13205. There is no exit from the southern side of Little Narragansett Bay. You must retrace your path north of Sandy Point, and then head south to the Napatree Point Ledge flashing red bell buoy "6." Head east past Watch Hill Point, with its photogenic lighthouse, and go through Watch Hill Passage. This extremely narrow course has a swift current; if you must transit in fog or high winds, pay close attention to all markers and travel slowly. Watch Hill Passage, while well-marked and usually easy to follow when visibility is good, is often loaded with lobster traps, but it is the only route a newcomer should use. Be sure to keep a sharp lookout. Wicopesset, Catumb and Sugar Reef passages are best left to local boats whose skippers know them.

Cruising Options

Zigzagging back across Long Island Sound brings the cruising skipper once again to Long Island's beautiful north shore. The marinas and sights at Manhasset Bay, Hempstead Harbor, Oyster Bay and Cold Spring Harbor offer everything a cruising family would ever want in the way of comfort and cruising amenities. ■

Waterway Guide is always open to your observations from the helm. E-mail your comments on any navigation information in the guide to: editor@waterwayguide.com.

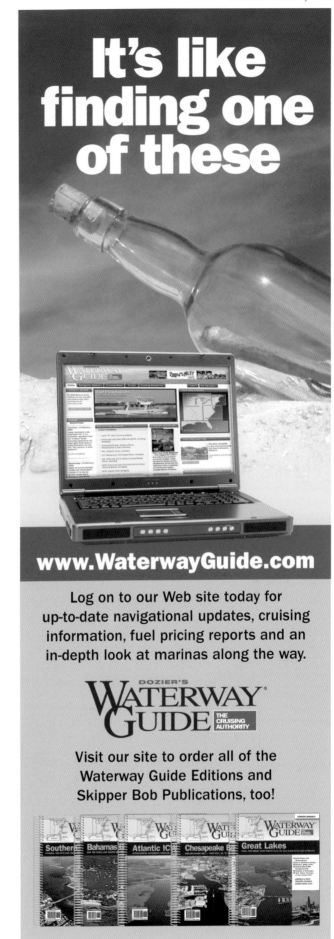

Little Neck Bay to Cold Spring Harbor

CHARTS 12363, 12364, 12365, 12366, 12367

LONG ISLAND NORTH SHORE

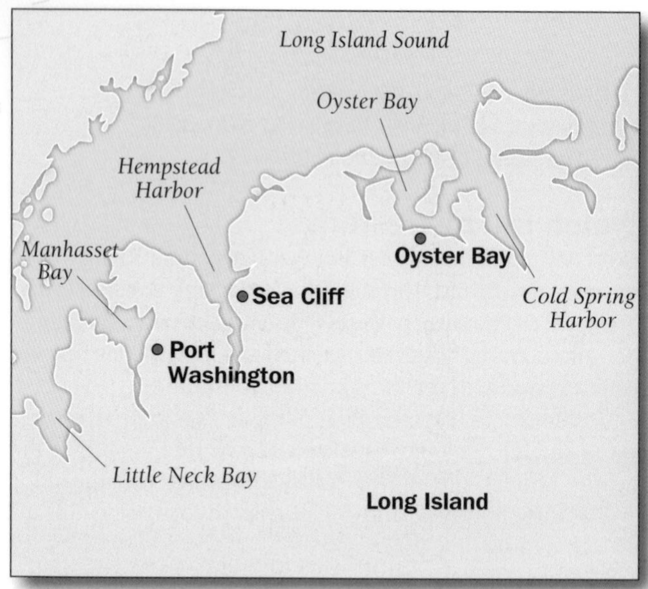

The North Shore of Long Island, sometimes called the "South Shore" of Long Island Sound, is a cruiser's paradise. It is easy to navigate, well-marked and well-charted with few obstructions, generally deep water, many recreational boats, extensive facilities and deepwater anchorages and convenient land transportation.

The bays at the western end of the Long Island shore, each with multiple harbors, are deep and protected and offer complete facilities. The bays are easy to enter and crowded with marinas, yacht clubs, restaurants and shore activities. The rise and fall of the tide on portions of the North Shore is substantial (6 to 8 feet), so some marinas have floating docks. At the western end of Long Island Sound, the waterway is narrow, making it easy to crisscross back and forth between Long Island and Connecticut harbors. The eastern end of the Long Island shore is quite different—mostly unbroken beach, high bluffs (sandy or rocky), sparsely settled, with only two substantial harbors in almost 60 miles.

The North Shore of Long Island begins in New York City (borough of Queens) just past Throgs Neck. Here at Willets Point, Fort Totten's century-old stone walls stand at the southern side of the dividing line between Long Island Sound and the East River.

Little Neck Bay

Little Neck Bay is the first harbor on the Long Island shore after you leave the East River. It is a large-mouthed bay where the shores are thickly settled, but it features some of the best anchorages in the crowded New York City area.

NAVIGATION: Use Chart 12364. The straightforward entrance is between Willets Point on the west and Kings Point on the east. Marked by a 220-foot-high flagpole, the 65-acre campus of the U.S. Merchant Maritime Academy (516-773-5000, 300 Steamboat Road, Kings Point, NY) was once the estate of Walter P. Chrysler, the automobile manufacturer, who used to commute to New York City by boat. The mansion's interior is now divided into small offices, but the grounds are open to the public on weekend afternoons and during Saturday morning reviews. The Academy has quite a sailing fleet, too. The American Merchant Marine Museum (516-466-9696) is located in Barstow House on the campus is the home of the National Maritime Hall of Fame. William Barstow invented the electric meter, by which electric usage is measured for billing, and was also responsible for lighting the Brooklyn Bridge.

On the eastern shore, at Udalls Mill Pond just south of the charted dam, is the Saddle Rock Grist Mill (516-571-7900), a 16th-century water mill that still operates, depending on the tides. Now owned by Nassau County, it is open to the public on summer weekends. You can bring the dinghy over to take a closer look, but you cannot land here; the property is privately owned.

Anchorage: Little Neck Bay has 6-foot depths down the middle with shallows along the banks and in the southeastern corner. Many boats are moored here, but there are several good places to anchor unless the wind is out of the north. The cove halfway down the eastern shore has a quiet southwest corner despite a nearby well-traveled highway. Transient facilities are limited.

East of Little Neck Bay

NAVIGATION: Use Chart 12364. You can pass north of Stepping Stones Lighthouse, keeping it to starboard, or cruise along the shore. For the shore route, keep about midway between red nun buoys "4" and "2" on the southern edge of Stepping Stones reef and the shoreline. It is much easier and safer, however, to pass Stepping Stones shoal to starboard on its northwest end.

Manhasset Bay

Manhasset Bay is one of the most popular and most complete harbors on the North Shore. It has deep water throughout, good holding and is easy to enter day or night. It is an ideal stopover whether transiting east or west on Long Island Sound. The marinas offer complete facilities, the yacht clubs are friendly and offer guest moorings to other yacht club members, the shopping, provisioning and restaurants are well within reach of the marinas and repair yards are numerous.

The bay's diversions are so complete that some boats dock here in the spring and stay through the summer. Manhasset Bay is surrounded by the towns of Sands Point, Manorhaven, Port Washington, Plandome, Great Neck and Kings Point. Manhasset is slightly inland, and New York City is about 40 miles away by highway or railroad. The bay is 7 to 17 feet deep for most of its 3.5-mile length. It offers protection against most winds and a snug harbor for numerous vessels.

NAVIGATION: Use Charts 12364, 12366, and 12363. For Manhasset Bay, use Kings Point tide tables. For high tide, subtract 12 minutes; for low tide, subtract 12 minutes. The wide, unobstructed entrance to Manhasset Bay is between Hewlett Point and Barker Point. Do not cut either point coming in; both have rocks just offshore. About a mile inside, the crooked finger of Plum Point, which extends out from the eastern shore almost halfway across the bay, is marked by flashing green buoy "1." Plum Point protects the inner harbor. A sizable and strictly enforced No-Wake Zone begins at the point. The inner harbor is also a No-Discharge Zone; discharge of raw or treated sewage is prohibited here.

Manorhaven

Manorhaven, with a population of around 6,000, is the largest boating community in the state of New York. Six marinas and two yacht clubs here provide 1,300 slips and 300 moorings.

Dockage: Brewer Capri West and East marinas are located just inside the protective arm of Plum Point. Formerly separate facilities, the two are now combined under Brewer management to provide a complete range of integrated marine services. Available are 335 wide and modern floating slips to accommodate virtually any recreational vessel, with golf carts to assist loading and unloading, large service and parts departments, four Travelifts topping out at 75 tons (available seven days a week), easy-access fuel docks, two pump-out stations and a small but attractive pool. In between Capri's two main piers, the friendly and colorful North Shore Yacht Club (monitoring VHF Channel 78) maintains a small pier of its own, along with 10 to 15 moorings open to transients. These are available to visitors for a modest facilities fee, which includes launch service and access to the club's restrooms and showers.

Farther into Manhasset Bay, closer to the amenities of Port Washington, and tucked behind the protective hook of Toms Point, another cluster of docks and marine services welcomes visitors while also tending to the needs of hundreds of local boats. Tom's Point Marina, just inside the point, is family-run and eager to please, with 130 slips (10 or so available to transients), accommodating boats up to 36 feet. A Quantum Sails, LIS is on the premises.

Next door, Manhasset Bay Marina welcomes transients with 285 floating slips, each complete with power, cable TV and telephone hook-ups. Modern, clean restrooms and showers are at the foot of the dock complex. Twenty-five moorings with launch service are offered, as are the marina's full-service and repair capabilities and 75-ton lift capacity.

Port Washington

Port Washington is the second largest boating center in Manhasset Bay. It is the largest town on the bay, with dozens of restaurants (several of them within walking distance of the docks), a huge variety of stores and services of all kinds.

Dockage: North Hempstead Town Dock (directly across from Toms Point), complete with a dinghy dock, is available for pump-outs and water. The town offers complimentary pump-out service to boats on the hook or at moorings via its pump-out barge (hail on VHF Channel 09).

The nearby Brewer Capri at Inspiration Wharf is a small, full-service marine facility offering slips with immediate access to town. "Yacht Club Row" (Knickerbocker Yacht Club, Manhasset Bay Yacht Club, and Port Washington Yacht Club) stretches out along this section of the bay, supporting competitive racing programs and a parade of social events. Members of clubs with reciprocal rights can almost surely find moorings with launch service or dockage, along with access to excellent club amenities included in the price of a facilities fee.

The town of Port Washington operates a number of town moorings, which are available for free for two nights. The Port Washington Water Taxi, 516-767-1691, monitoring VHF Channel 09, operates the mooring balls on behalf of the town. A round-trip fare from a mooring ball or anchorage is $8 per person.

Anchorage: There are three popular anchorages in Manhasset Bay. The first is in the southeast corner near Leeds Pond, used on weekends for raft-ups and swimming. In the southern end of the bay, Plandome is the most protected area to drop the hook. Plum Point Cove, at the entrance of the harbor behind Plum Point, also provides a well-protected anchorage area, convenient to Plum Point Beach, which can be used for swimming, water skiing and dinghy landings. The beach is only accessible by water and can only be used to the high tide mark. All these anchorages provide views of the beautiful waterfront estates that surround Manhasset Bay.

Manhasset Bay, NY

MANHASSET BAY		Largest Vessel Accommodated	VHF Channel Monitored	Transient Berths / Total Berths	Approach / Dockside Depth (reported)	Floating Docks	Gas / Diesel	Groceries, Ice, Marine Supplies, Snacks	Repairs: Hull, Engine, Propeller	Lift (tonnage), Crane, Rail	1=110V, 2=220V, B=Both, Max Amps	Laundry, Pool, Showers	Pump-Out Station	Nearby: Grocery Store, Motel, Restaurant
		Dockage					Supplies		Services					
1. Brewer Capri Marina West Internet Access, Wireless Internet Access	**516-883-7800**	**150**	**09/71**	**20/220**	**7/7**	**F**	**GD**	**IMS**	**HEP**	**L30**	**B/100**	**LPS**	**P**	**GMR**
2. North Shore Yacht Club	516-883-9823	65	78	10/100	15/5	F		I				S		GR
3. Brewer Capri Marina East Internet Access, Wireless Internet Access	**516-883-7800**	**150**	**09/71**	**20/115**	**7/7**	**F**		**IMS**	**HEP**	**L75**	**B/100**	**LPS**	**P**	**GMR**
4. Tom's Point Marina	516-883-6630	45	68	10/130	5/5	F			HEP	LC	B/30	LS		GR
5. Quantum Sails Long Island Sound	516-944-5660	SAILMAKER			8/6									
6. Manhasset Bay Marina/La Motta's Rest. Internet Access, Wireless Internet Access	516-883-8411	110	09	/285	8/6	F	GD	IM	HE	L75	B/50	LS	P	GR
7. Gulfway Marine Service	516-767-0113	30			12/12			GIM	HEP					R
8. North Hempstead Town Dock	516-767-4622	100	09/16	5/	12/6	F		GIM	HEP					R
9. Louie's Oyster Bar & Grille	516-883-4242	65	68	/10	5/4	F		I			1			R
10. Brewer Capri Marina at Inspiration Wharf Wireless Internet Access	**516-883-7800**	**80**	**09/71**	**0/30**	**8/8**	**F**		**IMS**	**HP**	**LC**	**B/50**		**P**	**GMR**
11. Knickerbocker Yacht Club Wireless Internet Access	516-883-7655	50	69	/12	9/6	F		I			1/30	PS		GMR
12. Manhasset Bay Yacht Club	516-767-2150	100	68	20/240	7/6	F		IS			1/30	PS		GMR
13. Port Washington Yacht Club	516-767-9749	100	74	20/240	7/6	F		IS			1/30	PS		GMR

Corresponding chart(s) not to be used for navigation. Internet Access WiFi Wireless Internet Access

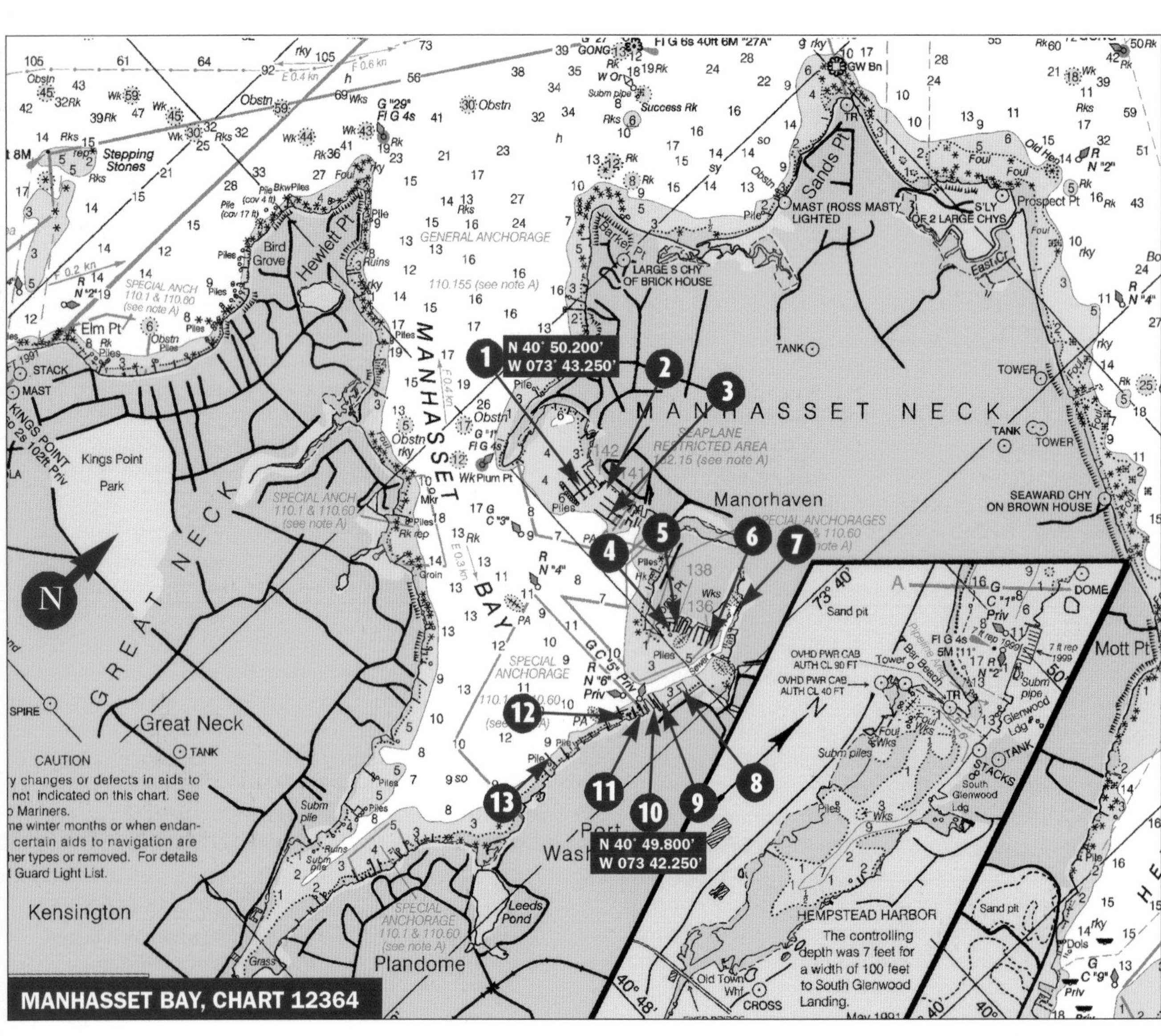

Looking east over Manhasset Bay toward Port Washington. (Not to be used for navigation.)

GOIN' ASHORE:
MANHASSET BAY, NY

Manorhaven and Port Washington both provide access to the shoreside of Manhasset Bay. Part of the village complex is residential Plandome, with the Science Museum of Long Island (1526 Plandome Road, 516-627-9400) gracing the shores of Leeds Pond.

In 1898, the Long Island Railroad established a station in Port Washington; the 17-mile-long route to Penn Station in New York City is still in operation. In 1937, Pan American Airlines started flying-boat service from Manhasset Bay to Bermuda and expanded that service to the first transatlantic passenger crossings. The service, however, was short-lived due to World War II.

The Port Washington town dock is a place to leave the dinghy while you stroll though town and also the location of a small Farmer's Market, which operates every Saturday morning, specializing in organic produce. The John Sousa Bandstand in Sunset Park, adjacent to the town dock, is the location of concerts throughout the summer. Facilities in Port Washington stretch along the three major streets: Shore Road, Main Street and Port Washington Boulevard. Main Street provides a snapshot of the idyllic small-village lifestyle, with trees, wild flowers, benches and a wide variety of shops lining the thoroughfare, including small boutiques, art galleries, antiques shops, jewelry stores, banks, restaurants and hardware stores. A large modern library is several blocks up from the waterfront. The Long Island Railroad station (516-822-5477) on Main Street between Haven Avenue. and South Bayles Avenue. provides frequent service to downtown New York. Port Washington Boulevard will take you to more shops, such as Dolphin's Book Shop (516-767-2650, 941 Port Washington Blvd.) and Baskin Robbins (516-883-1870, 923 Port Washington Blvd.). Shore Road leads to several malls (less than a 10-minute walk from the town dock), where you can reprovision at Stop & Shop (516-767-6914, 66 Shore Road) or King Kullen (516-883-9733, 3 Shore Road). West Marine (516-944-1729, 16 Sound View Marketplace on Shore Road) and Soundview Cinema (516-944-3900, 7-9 Sound View Marketplace) a six-theater cinema are located in the same mall as King Kullen. Across the street you will find Bottles Wine & Spirits (516-883-1634, 63 Shore Road) a new wine and liquor store and a laundry, Waters Edge French Dry Cleaners (516-767-3562, 118 Shore Road).

Port Washington is an excellent stop for dining ashore. Bagel shops, pizzerias, delicatessens, cafes and a Starbucks are all located on Main Street. Finn MacCool's (205 Main St., 516-944-3439), Main 415 Steak and Lobster House (415 Main St., 516-767-6246) and Ayhan's Shish Kebab (286 Main St., 516-883-1515) are local favorites. The following three fine restaurants are attached to marinas: DiMaggio's Seafood and Grill (516-944-5900) at Brewer's Capri East; Louie's Oyster Bar and Grill (516-883-4245), between the town dock and

Brewer's Capri Inspiration; and LaMotta's Waterside Restaurant (516-944-7900) at the Manhasset Bay Marina. Farther away in Manhasset is the upscale Americana Manhasset Mall (516-627-2277, 2060 Northern Blvd.), known as the "Miracle Mile" and its 50 international boutiques and shops. For taxi service, call Deluxe Transportation Service 516-883-1900.

ADDITIONAL RESOURCES:

- Port Washington Guide, **www.pwguide.com**

NEARBY GOLF COURSES:
Harbor Links Golf Course, One Fairway Drive,
Port Washington, NY 11050, 516-767-4816

NEARBY MEDICAL FACILITIES:
St. Francis Hospital - Roslyn,
100 Port Washington Blvd.,
Roslyn, NY 11576, 516-562-6000

Manhasset Bay to Sands Point

NAVIGATION: Use Charts 12364, 12366 and 12363. Boats eastbound from Manhasset Bay should round Barker Point, going on either side of Gangway Rock. Local boats often cut inside the white and orange can buoy marking Success Rock, but it is not advisable unless you know the area. Run between the lighted buoys off Sands Point to starboard and Execution Rocks to port. The grouping of the lighthouse and small buildings at Execution Rocks constitutes a major landmark and the most important aid to navigation in western Long Island Sound. Leave plenty of room around the ledge at Execution Rocks. The name is derived from a local belief that, during the Revolutionary War, British soldiers chained American patriots to the rocks at low tide and let them drown when the tide rose.

Anchorage: One of Long Island Sound's best beaches (unnamed on the chart, but known locally as Half Moon Beach) is the stretch of shore between Barker Point and Sands Point. Boats anchor in the bight just off the beach with excellent holding.

Hempstead Harbor

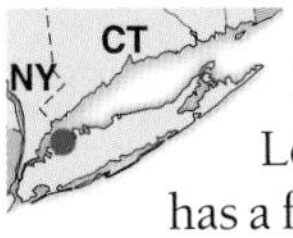

NAVIGATION: Use Charts 12364, 12366 and 12363. Hempstead Harbor, southeast across Long Island Sound from Mamaroneck and Rye, has a four-mile-wide entrance between Prospect and Matinecock points. The harbor is open to the northwest. Cruisers have noted that a night on a mooring or anchor, even behind the breakwater, would be safe but very uncomfortable in a northwest or westerly wind. Exiting the harbor against wind and waves from these directions can be a long motor, especially in a sailboat with light auxiliary power. It narrows gradually for 4.5 miles.

Glen Cove and Sea Cliff

The breakwater makes a protected anchorage that was often used by J.P. Morgan's Corsair and other vessels of the great steam-yacht period. The New York Yacht Club's Station Ten, now at Harbour Court in Newport, RI, was once

Glen Cove Marina
Glen Cove Creek/Hempstead Harbor

76 Shore Road • Glen Cove, NY 11542
P 516-759-3129 • F 516-759-3306
gcmvmg@aol.com

The marina is located on Glen Cove Creek on the eastern side of Hempstead Harbor. Head south into Hempstead Harbor and turn east at the yellow buoys, into Glen Cove Creek. Marina is the second one you come to on your starboard side.

DOCKAGE RATE: $3.00 foot
CREDIT CARDS: MC/Visa/AMEX
HOURS: 8am-5pm
TRANSIENT/TOTAL SLIPS: 5/300
VHF MONITOR/WORKING: 9
DEPTH MLW: Channel 15'
TIDE RANGE: 8'
LOA MAX: 60'
DOCKS: Floating
ELECTRIC: 30amp/100, 50amp/220
FUEL: Gas and Diesel
PUMP-OUT: No
HEADS/SHOWERS: Yes
LAUNDRY: No
POOL/GRILLS: No
INTERNET/WIFI: No
CABLE: No
PET FRIENDLY: Yes
SHIP'S STORE: No
MEETING FACILITIES: No
REPAIRS: Yes
LIFT/TONS: 50 Travelift
STORAGE: Yes
YACHT BROKERAGE: Yes
RESTAURANT: On site
GROCERIES: 2 miles
NEAREST TOWN: Glen Cove

Whether your destination is Glen Cove or you just need a place to pull in, Glen Cove Marina offers a safe, protected harbor not far from New York City. We are a full service 300 slip marina able to accommodate boats from 16' to 60'. With a 50 ton Travelift hauling is never a problem. And if you're looking for a quick bite to eat, or a complete dinner, our on site restaurant is ready to serve your dining needs.

Hempstead Harbor, Glen Cove, NY

HEMPSTEAD HARBOR, GLEN COVE		Largest Vessel Accommodated	VHF Channel Monitored	Transient Berths / Total Berths	Approach / Dockside Depth (reported)	Floating Docks	Gas / Diesel	Groceries, Ice, Marine Supplies, Snacks	Repairs: Hull, Engine, Propeller	Lift (tonnage), Crane, Rail	1=110V, 2=220V, B=Both, Max Amps	Laundry, Pool, Showers	Pump-Out Station	Nearby: Grocery Store, Motel, Restaurant
		Dockage					Supplies		Services					
1. Hempstead Harbour Yacht Club	516-671-0600	50	72		8/6							S		
2. **Glen Cove Marina**	**516-759-3129**	60	09	5/300	15/6	F	GD	IM	HEP	L50,C	B/50	S		GMR
3. **Brewer Yacht Yard at Glen Cove** (WiFi)	**516-671-5563**	75	09	10/300	8/8	F	GD	IM	HEP	L60,C	B/50	LPS	P	GR

Corresponding chart(s) not to be used for navigation. ☐ Internet Access (WiFi) Wireless Internet Access

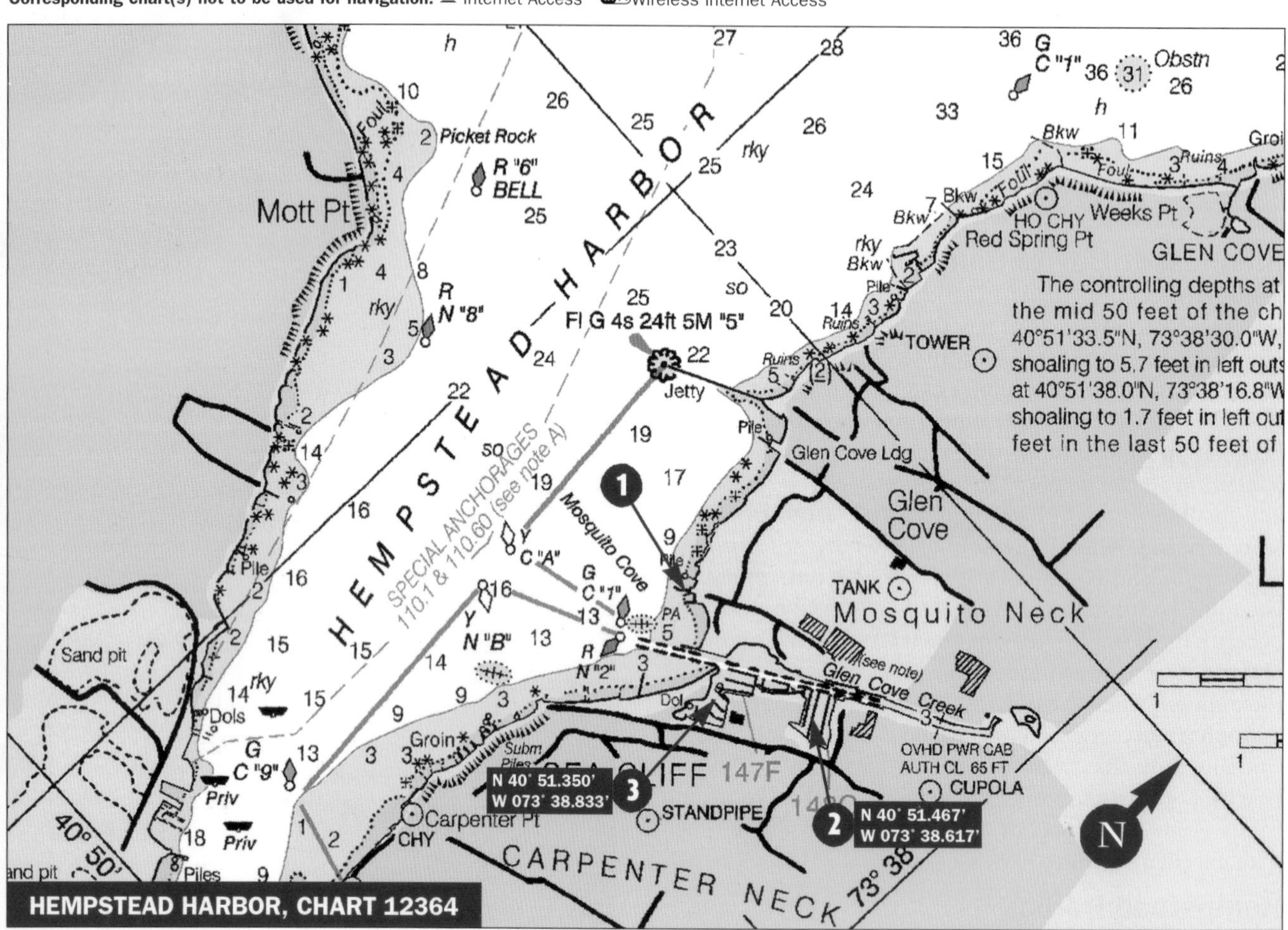

HEMPSTEAD HARBOR, CHART 12364

located here. Morgan Memorial Park overlooks the breakwater from a cliff. The park has picnic tables, flower gardens, paths, beaches and a panoramic view of Long Island Sound.

Below the breakwater is Mosquito Cove (from "musceta," the Indian word for "grassy flats," as Glen Cove was called until 1834). The cove, home to the hospitable Hempstead Harbour Yacht Club, may serve as a landing spot for those who set a hook in the ample anchorage areas beyond the mooring fields lining the east side of the harbor inside the breakwater. Transient vessels are often able to secure an overnight mooring here. Here, too, is the entrance to Glen Cove Creek, the deepest, best-protected, most active yachting port in Hempstead Harbor.

NAVIGATION: Use Chart 12364. Glen Cove Creek would be almost imperceptible on first-time arrival but for yellow can buoy "A" and yellow nun buoy "B" marking the outer channel. When you are centered between the two buoys, face the creek to the west and green entrance can buoy "1" and red nun buoy "2" will show the way to the narrow channel between the bulkheads. At low tide, in particular, deeper-draft boats should favor the right side of the channel on entry, closer to the collapsing bulkhead to starboard. There should be 6.5-foot depths here at mean low water and substantially more otherwise, given the 8-foot tidal range.

Dockage: Brewer Yacht Yard at Glen Cove is immediately to starboard (hard right) beyond the bulkheads, offering modern floating docks, enthusiastic service, easily accessed floating fuel docks and professional workmanship.

Just beyond, Glen Cove Yacht Services has ample room for transients (depths to 6.5 feet), all fuels, a 60-ton lift and one of the most helpful and well-stocked chandleries on Long Island Sound.

Still farther along, Glen Cove Marina also has transient slip space, fuel, repair and other services. If planning a stop in Glen Cove, try to plan ahead and make advance reservations.

Just north of the creek is the 62-acre Garvies Point Museum and Preserve (50 Barry Drive, 516-571-8010), which documents the life and culture of Long Island Indians. The grounds include nature trails and an abundance of wildlife. To reach Garvies Point from the north shore of Glen Cove Creek, you can walk along the shore past the yacht club to the steps leading up the bluff. From the south side you can walk about a mile and a half around the head of the creek, or dinghy over.

Reprovisioning at Glen Cove must be done about two miles north of the cruising facilities at the Stop & Shop Supermarket (177 Forest Ave., 516-759-1440), or at the Rising Tide Natural Market (42 Forest Ave., 516-676-7895). Fleet Bank (111 Forest Ave., 800-841-4000) and CVS (65 Forest St., 516-676-2298) can be found nearby and about a mile south up the steep hill, there is another grocery store, the Sea Cliff Market (347 Glen Cove Ave., 516-674-8663), in the Village of Sea Cliff. The area has many very good restaurants. In Glen Cove, Henry's Luncheonette (242 Glen Cove Road, 516-676-3344), across from City Hall, serves home cooked meal and desserts. Dine on the waterfront at the Warf at Steamboat Landing (76 Shore Road, 516-759-3921) or enjoy Italian cuisine at Stangos Restaurant (19 Grove St., 516-671-2389). Times Square (242 Glen Cove Road, 516-676-3344) replaces the former La Teranova Ristorante. Customize a savory salad at Sweet Tomatoes (170 Forest Ave., 516-671-4481) or stop next door for Chinese takeout at China King (170 Forest Ave., 561-676-8181). In the quaint Victorian setting of Sea Cliff, K.C. Gallagher's (325 Sea Cliff Ave., 516-656-0996) sets the standard for American and continental fare.

East from Hempstead Harbor

The route around Matinecock Point, past Oak Neck and Rocky Point on Centre Island, follows what was once the most elegant stretch of Long Island. The shore, lined with handsome estates, is also lined with rocks and requires careful navigation. Behind Oak Neck Point on the low-lying shore is the village of Bayville, a resort community with pretty cottages and fine public beaches replete with the requisite hot-dog stands, ice cream parlors and cocktail lounges, as well as amenities for cruising boats.

Oyster Bay

Oyster Bay, located east of Hempstead Harbor and south of Stamford, CT, is one of the least crowded, most attractive and unspoiled harbors on Long Island Sound. It is home to the famous yacht club, Seawanhaka Corinthian, which commands the entrance to Oyster Bay Harbor. The Sagamore Yacht Club is also in Oyster Bay.

The handsome sailing fleet here chooses two excellent harbors as homeports: Oyster Bay Harbor and Cold Spring Harbor. Deep, protected anchorages abound throughout both harbors. Several marinas cater to transients, and the bay contains one of Long Island Sound's best gunkholes, the Sand Hole at Lloyds Neck, located at the bay's eastern entrance.

Oyster Bay Harbor is a long horseshoe with Centre Island (not really an island) in the middle. The harbor offers fine beaches, beautiful estates, a well-kept oyster fleet and a choice of generous, sheltered anchorages.

NAVIGATION: Use Charts 12364 and 12365. For Oyster Bay Harbor, use Bridgeport tide tables. For high tide, add 7 minutes; for low tide, add 13 minutes. To enter Oyster Bay from the west off Long Island Sound, round green bell buoy "17," north of Centre Island Reef, and stay clear of the rocks off hilly Rocky Point. The preferred course is southeast across the bay, leaving Cold Spring Light, where current runs strong, to starboard. Boats drawing under 7 feet frequently cut through the light's red sector, running west about halfway between Cold Spring Light and red nun buoy "4" off Plum Point. Inside, the inner bay shoots off in several directions: southeast to Cold Spring Harbor, and southwest to make the four-mile U-turn around Centre Island through Oyster Bay Harbor, and around into West Harbor.

Dockage: Oyster Bay Marine Center may have a slip available for cruising visitors (by advance reservation only), and can usually offer a mooring with launch service included, 7 a.m. to 11 p.m., or until 1 a.m. on weekends. The yard has a full range of marine services available, though it is best known for its sailboat rigging and fiberglass composite work. Both diesel fuel and gasoline are available on the T-dock. To approach these facilities, take the branch of the marked channel leading toward the large fuel tanks. The branch channel then makes a hard right just before shore, leading past the fuel dock. Ashore, the marina has a shower/restroom building and a marine supply store. From here it is an easy walk to the town's superb park and playground, the Long Island Railroad's Oyster Bay station and amenities of the village. The town docks next to the marina offer no space to transients.

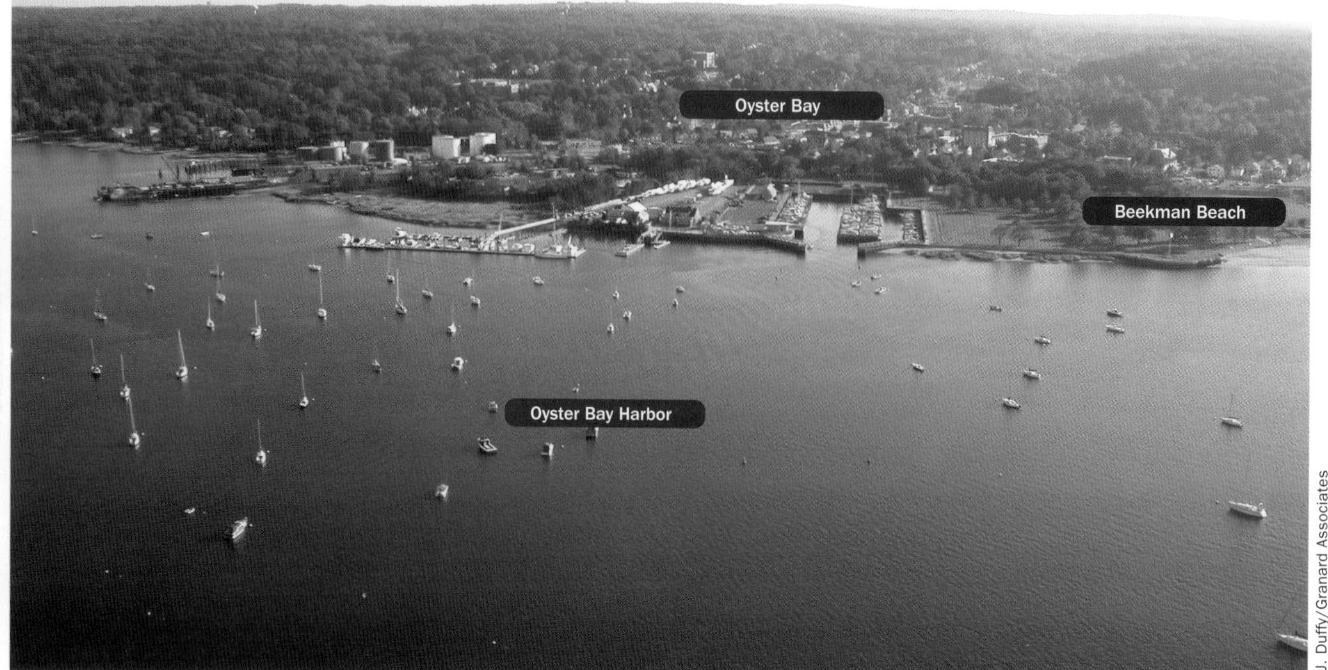

Looking south over Oyster Bay. (Not to be used for navigation.)

Anchorage: South of Centre Island, protection and pleasant surroundings can be found in the big cove between the town of Oyster Bay and the high wooded bluffs of Cove Neck, two miles long and a mile wide. It has little current, holding is good and it never seems to be crowded, though there might be a club raft-up or two during summer months. A great variety of waterfowl can be seen in the marshes at the head of the cove, especially during the seasonal migrations. Another peaceful anchorage area is along the southwest shore of Mill Neck on Mill Neck Creek. This is also a great place to hunker down in a blow. A popular anchorage with good holding in 6 to 8 feet of water is in West Harbor, adjacent to the northwest of Centre Island. It is a wide open body of water with good depth and protection all around with few moorings and lots of beaches.

Although the bight south of Plum Point is a designated anchorage, only the yacht club fleet—all on moorings—uses it. Because of the strong current, the depth and the scoured bottom, anchoring is not recommended. For best security, try to arrange for a guest mooring.

OYSTER BAY

The Town of Oyster Bay, comprised of 18 small hamlet communities, cuts across the western neck of New York's Long Island. Although the town touches the Atlantic Ocean on the southern shore, the heart of the town is centered around the picturesque Oyster Bay Harbor on Long Island's protected northern shore. Collectively, the 18 hamlets boast over 600 acres of parklands and pristine beaches weaving along both the north and south shores. Oyster Bay Harbor is the termination point of the Oyster Bay Branch of the Long Island Railroad (http://www.mta.info/lirr/), making it a convenient spot to tie up and head into New York City for a day trip.

The town enjoys a rich history, with the name "Oyster Bay" being first recorded in 1639. Originally inhabited by Native Americans, Long Island was included in the famous purchase of New York by the Dutch. In the following years, Oyster Bay changed hands among Dutch, British, and New Englanders, with somewhat fluid boundaries. The town remained an agricultural backwater until its most famous resident, Theodore Roosevelt, brought the town into the spotlight by making his home, Sagamore Hill, the summer White house.

Today, Oyster Bay is a prosperous and picturesque suburb, retaining vestiges of rural charm while offering all of the modern amenities. With the easy train ride from New York City, city dwellers and tourists alike are lured to Oyster Bay each year for its festivals, beaches, and parks. Tie up in Oyster Bay during the warmer months and you will find a host of events and activities at your fingertips. July and August bring people from all over Long Island and New England for the free "Music Under the Stars" concert series, featuring a variety of top musical acts playing at one of Oyster Bay's parks or beaches on a rotating, almost nightly, schedule (www.oysterbaytown.com). For the golfers among you, Oyster Bay has a nationally ranked public golf course and driving range with reasonable green fees (www.oysterbaytown.com), open mid-March through mid-December. For more information call 516-677-5961. October brings the Oyster Festival, billed as the biggest waterfront festival on the eastern seaboard, with music, games, crafts and, of course, delicious seafood (http://www.theoysterfestival.org).

Oak Neck, Oyster Bay and Cold Spring, NY

OAK NECK, OYSTER BAY, COLD SPRING HARBOR		Largest Vessel Accommodated	VHF Channel Monitored	Transient Berths / Total Berths	Approach / Dockside Depth (reported)	Floating Docks	Gas / Diesel	Groceries, Ice, Marine Supplies, Snacks	Repairs: Hull, Engine, Propeller	Lift (tonnage), Crane, Rail	1=110V, 2=220V, B=Both, Max Amps	Laundry, Pool, Showers	Pump-Out Station	Nearby: Grocery Store, Motel, Restaurant
		Dockage					Supplies		Services					
1. Bridge Marina	516-628-8688	42		3/52	7/7	F		IM	HEP	R	1/30			GMR
2. Oyster Bay Marine Center	**516-922-6331**	**160**	**71**	**4/32**	**13/13**	**F**	**GD**	**IM**	**HP**	**C**	**B/50**	**S**	**P**	**GMR**
3. Sagamore Yacht Club	516-922-0555	40	78		10/7							S		GR
4. H&M Powles Marina	631-367-7670	31	10	MOORINGS	20/4	F	GD	IMS	EP				P	GMR
5. Whalers Cove Yacht Club	631-367-9822	44	09	/50	15/25	F		I			1/30			GR

Corresponding chart(s) not to be used for navigation. Internet Access Wireless Internet Access

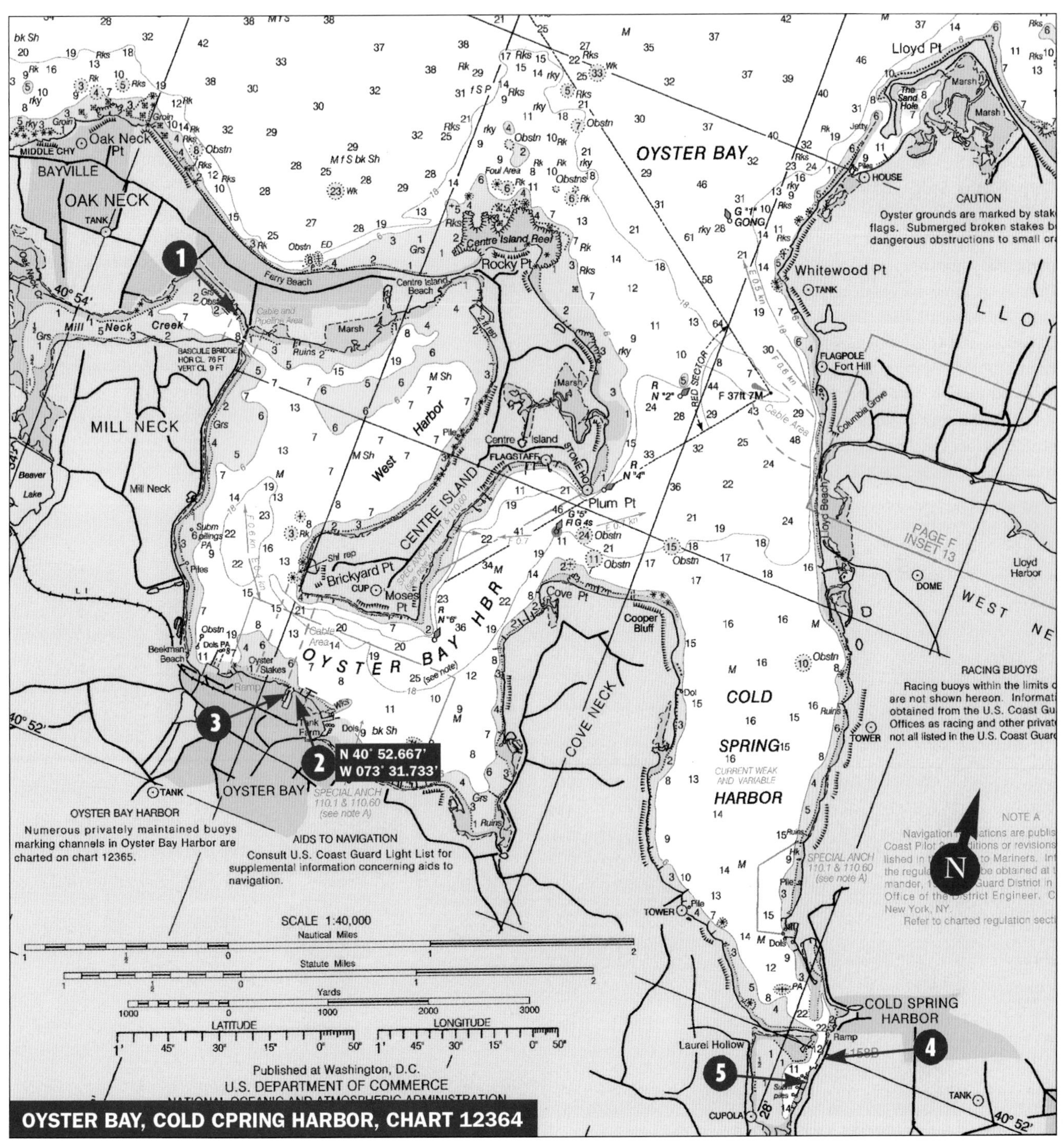

OYSTER BAY, COLD CPRING HARBOR, CHART 12364

GOIN' ASHORE: **OYSTER BAY, NY**

The seaside village of Oyster Bay referred to as the "Gold Coast," provided the glamorous setting for Fitzgerald's The Great Gatsby (about a five-minute walk from the docks) combines a pleasant mix of commercial services, restaurants and well-shaded houses. Raynham Hall Museum (516-922-6808, 20 W. Main St.), situated in the center of the village, was built in 1740 and served as both British headquarters for the Queen's Rangers during the American Revolutionary War and home to members of the Culper Spy Ring. It was also the home of Robert Townsend, Gen. George Washington's famous spy who brought to light Benedict Arnold's plot to turn West Point over to the British. It is open Tuesday through Sunday, from 1 p.m. to 5 p.m. The museum boasts one of the few remaining British "Red Coats" from the American Revolutionary War.

Nearby, clustered around the intersection of South Street and West Main Street, is a laundry, Bay Cleaners (516-922-3269, 117 South St.), a Bank of America (516-922-5501, 157 South St.) and State Bank of Long Island (516-922-0200, 135 South St.) both with 24-hour ATM, a pharmacy, Snouder's Corner Drug Store (516-922-4300,108 South St.) and many restaurants.

Wild Honey Dining & Wine (1 E. Main St., 516-922-4690), once the summer executive office for President Theodore Roosevelt, now serves a sophisticated menu of upscale cuisine. Canterbury Ales Oyster Bar and Grill (46 Audrey Ave., 516-922-3614) is cozy, traditional and loaded with Roosevelt memorabilia. Oysters are the house specialty, served with creative American fare. The Homestead Restaurant (516-624-7410, 107 South St.) has something for every taste. Dine in the stately Roosevelt Room, in an airy greenhouse or al fresco. The menu is extensive. Cafe al Dente (2 Spring St., 516-922-2442) serves authentic and contemporary Italian cuisine in an attractive setting. Fiddleheads (516-922-2999, 62 South St. #B) serves up a contemporary menu and impressive desserts. For a special occasion worthy of a five-star restaurant, Mill River Inn (160 Mill River Road, 516-922-7768) serves fine continental cuisine in an intimate setting. Reservations are a must.

Roosevelt's family home, a Queen Anne-style house, is now preserved as Sagamore Hill National Historic Site. The National Park Service conducts tours each day seasonally (9 a.m. to 4 p.m. on the hour) of the Roosevelt home at Sagamore Hill Rd. off Cove Mill Road about three miles from the village. These tours are limited in size and often sell out early. The Roosevelt Museum at Old Orchard is open every day from 10 a.m. to 5 p.m. Admission to the building is free, and visitors can enjoy movies and exhibits at their leisure. Call 516-922-4788 for visitor information. Roosevelt's body is buried nearby in the small Young Hill Cemetery. Oyster Bay Taxi can be reached at 516-921-2141.

The more opulent, if less well known, Coe Hall and Planting Fields Arboretum State Historical Park (516-922-9210, 1395 Planting Fields Road) draws numerous visitors who are attracted to the estate's extraordinary arboretum and to the numerous musical events staged in this setting during the summer months. If it's gardens you like, visit the Planting Fields Arboretum, more than 400 acres of gardens, woodlands, and the spectacular greenhouses. In the summer, there are concerts on the lawn.

Fall cruisers may enjoy the annual Oyster Bay Oyster Festival in October, a gala weekend of outdoor events celebrating Teddy Roosevelt's birthday and the mollusk that gives the region its name. Each year, more than 50,000 oysters are served on the half shell.

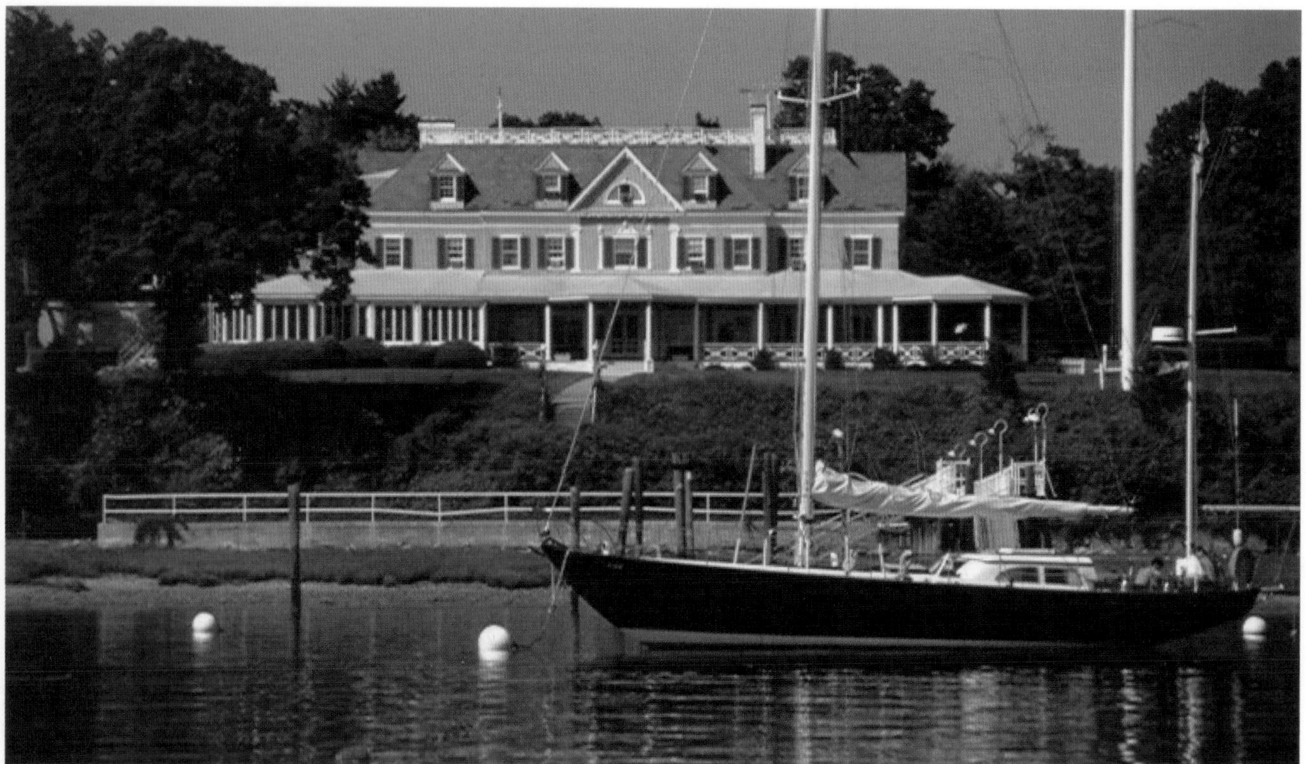

The seawanhaka Corinthian Yacht Club. Photo courtesy Douglas McCormick.

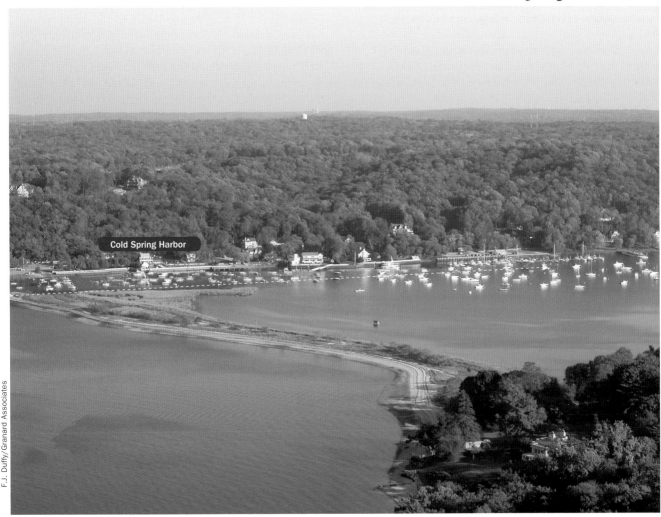

F.J. Duffy/Granard Associates

Looking east over the cozy anchorage of Cold Spring Harbor. (Not to be used for navigation.)

ADDITIONAL RESOURCES:

- Chamber Of Commerce, 70 E. Main St. Oyster Bay, NY 11771, 516-922-6464
- Town of Oyster Bay, **www.oysterbaytown.com**

NEARBY GOLF COURSES:
Oyster Bay Golf Course, One Southwoods Road, Woodbury, NY 11797, 516-677-5960

NEARBY MEDICAL FACILITIES:
Huntington Hospital, 270 Park Ave., Huntington, NY 11743, 631-351-2000
www.hunthosp.org

Mill Neck Creek

Feeding West Harbor off Oyster Bay from the west, Mill Neck Creek skirts the south shore of Oak Neck and secluded Bayville. Cruising or anchoring at this end of the bay, it is common to see the labor-intensive activities of Oyster Bay's colorful oyster fleet, working the bottom in the traditional manner. Though the village is small, shoreside attractions there include several well-recommended restaurants and a grocery store.

Dockage: It is an easy walk to the village from the Bridge Marina, just inside the drawbridge over Mill Neck Creek. The bridge tender can be contacted on VHF Channel 13, or by calling 516-571-8510 for an opening any day during the season from 7 a.m. to 5 p.m. The marina's floating docks are crowded with boats undergoing repairs, rendering transient space scarce and making an advance call for availability a necessity. There are shoreside restrooms but no showers or fuel. Besides boat services (including a ship's store), the popular attraction is the marina's Clam Bar, which sends out a courtesy launch to customers anchored, moored or tied up at the marina's courtesy float on call (air horn only, VHF is not monitored, 516-628-8688). The marina can be approached, even at low tide, with at least 9-foot depths and can accommodate boats of substantial size.

Cold Spring Harbor

Bordered by the 180-foot cliffs of Cooper Bluff, Cold Spring Harbor is an uncluttered bay almost three miles long and a mile wide. It has several unposted beaches where you can land without trespassing, wooded hills on the east and west sides and the village of Cold Spring Harbor in the southeast corner. Its wooded surroundings and steep shores make this harbor seem more like a beautiful northern inland lake than a piece of Long Island Sound.

Cold Spring Harbor, NY

Anchorage: Much of the village's anchorage area is now taken up with permanent moorings, though you may still be able to anchor with good depths, holding and wind protection (except from the northwest) north of Cold Spring Beach, a skinny stretch of shore with a bulbous tip that almost closes up the inner harbor. South of Cold Spring Beach, the harbor is filled with the local mooring field. Keep to the middle of the narrow, deep channel leading in. Inside are good depths along the eastern shore, which will take you to H & M Powles Marina. Powles may rent moorings for a day stop or overnight, including launch service (6:30 a.m. to 11 p.m.). Both gasoline and diesel fuel are available here with a controlling depth of 5 feet at mean low tide (9-foot tidal range). Other amenities are minimal (ice, refreshments, bait and tackle), but it is no more than a third-of-a-mile walk to town from the dock. 105 Harbor (105 Harbor Road, 631-367-3166), serving relatively expensive but well-prepared continental cuisine, is immediately across the street from the dock. Immediately south of the marina, Whalers Cove Yacht Club has a few slips for its members, but they are seldom available to others. Nearby, Cold Spring Harbor Beach Club (631-692-6546, 101 Shore Road) caters to families, so expect lots of children. The club offers rental moorings to transients.

GOIN' ASHORE:

COLD SPRING HARBOR, NY

Cold Spring Harbor was so named by settlers in 1653 because of the harbor's icy freshwater springs. From 1836 to 1860, it was one of Long Island's leading whaling ports, and later an active fishing village. There are many beaches in the area that are open to the public. As you stroll along the beaches and come upon a private section, law provides that you may walk along the wet sand portion of the beach below the high tide line.

The village of Cold Spring Harbor preserves the maritime history of Long Island in the Whaling Museum (631-367-3418, 301 Main St.), amid the cluster of 18th- and 19th-century houses overlooking the narrow harbor. A permanent exhibit, "Mark Well the Whale," displays a scrimshaw collection, a fully equipped whaleboat, ship models, whaling implements, figureheads and a diorama of Cold Spring Harbor in its whaling heyday (open Tuesday through Sunday, 11 a.m. to 5 p.m.). Cold Spring Harbor is also home to the Cold Spring Harbor Research Laboratory (516-367-8800, One Bungtown Rd.), an institution famous for its ground breaking research programs in neuroscience, cancer, genomics, plant biology and bioinformatics and the DNA Learning Center (516-367-5170), the world's first Biotechnology Museum offers exhibits and educational programs for all ages. Cold Springs Harbor Fish Hatchery & Aquarium (516-692-6768, 1660 Route 25A) raises a variety of species of trout to stock ponds and turtles are raised for release into the wild. The aquarium exhibits almost every freshwater species of fish, frogs, toads, turtles and snakes found in this area and provides educational programs for all ages.

Provisioning in Cold Spring Harbor can be completed at a fair-sized supermarket, Pete's Hometown Grocery (845-265-4172, 349 Main St.) and Gourmet Goddess (631-692-9646, 111 Main St.), which has just what the name implies, as well as tempting deli sandwiches and salads. By all accounts, the place to go for a special meal is Grasso's (134 Main St., 631-367-6060), where a full menu of traditional Italian dishes with live music is served and try Tillies Eatery (631-659-3631, 181 Main St., Suite G), a restaurant with lighter fare located across the street. 105 Harbor Restaurant (631-367-3166, 105 Harbor Road) serves up not only a beautiful view, but also various exotic dishes including frog legs, duck and rabbit. Bedlam Street Fish and Clam Company (631-692-5655, 55 Main St.) promises fresh seafood meals.

ADDITIONAL RESOURCES:

■ Cold Springs Area Chamber of Commerce, 845-265-3200, **www.coldspringschamber.com**

NEARBY GOLF COURSES:
Oyster Bay Golf Course, One Southwoods Road, Woodbury, NY 11797, 516-677-5980

NEARBY MEDICAL FACILITIES:
Huntington Hospital, 270 Park Ave., Huntington, NY 11743, 631-351-2000, **www.hunthosp.org**

The Sand Hole

The Sand Hole is one of the most popular gunkholes on Long Island Sound. It offers an easy anchorage when transiting the Sound in either direction. Surrounded by a state park, it is a hike to get to by land. But every boat on Long Island Sound heads there on summer weekends, so it can get crowded and noisy. The Sand Hole was originally dredged by the adjoining Marshall Field and Fairchild estates for yachts. There is but one house overlooking it, on long-established private land. The rest of the surrounding land is grassland, beach and some marshland. Many leave their boats to go to the beach or walk. Stay away from the house's guarded land, though.

NAVIGATION: Use Charts 12364 and 12365. To reach The Sand Hole, steer about 50 degrees magnetic from green gong buoy "1" at the mouth of Oyster Bay. You will see the jetty (except at high tide), but give it a wide berth before turning in. The Sand Hole has two basins, and the inner basin almost appears to be barred by shallow water. In fact, at low tide, depths are only about 4 feet. However, leading just off the spit that divides the basins is a deep, narrow channel leading to the inner basin.

Cruising Options

Continuing east along the north shore of Long Island, the mariner reaches the large basin that forms Huntington Bay. The following section covers this area all the way to Mattituck and the beginning of the "Fishtail." ■

Huntington Bay to Plum Gut

CHARTS 12354, 12358, 12362, 12363, 12364, 12365

■ LONG ISLAND NORTH SHORE

Sprawling inward from Long Island Sound, Huntington Bay is the largest of Long Island's basins and marks the beginning of Suffolk County (Nassau County is to the west). The wide entrance to Huntington Bay lies between two high, wooded headlands, each almost an island in itself, connected to the mainland by a narrow, sandy isthmus. To the west is private Lloyd Neck; to the east, the jutting headland of Eatons Neck, with its famous old lighthouse and Coast Guard station.

Huntington Bay narrows as it goes south, and then spreads out to the east, west and south into seven separate, sheltered inner harbors lined by the villages of Huntington, Centerport and Northport. Counterclockwise from the west, these are: Lloyd Harbor, Huntington Harbor, Northport Bay (an entity in itself, with its own towns, harbors and coves), Centerport Harbor, Northport Harbor, Duck Island Harbor and Price Bend. Eatons Neck Cove is just inside the mouth at the eastern entrance. Boating amenities are everywhere, along with crowded anchorages and isolated coves, good beaches and fine restaurants.

Lloyd Harbor

This westernmost harbor is shaped like a tulip, with the wide outer harbor forming the flower and long, narrow inner harbor making the stem. The outer harbor, almost a half-mile long, has a few boats at moorings, attractive houses hidden among the trees and a small summer camp, but no docks or marinas. It is cool, thickly wooded and very crowded on weekends.

NAVIGATION: Use Charts 12364 and 12365. Enter north of Huntington Harbor Lighthouse, a storybook graystone residence that tends to fade into the surroundings and can be difficult to spot from a distance. The narrow channel is clearly buoyed, with stakes and poles marking obstructions or shoal spots.

Extending westward, the inner harbor runs nearly a mile and a half toward Oyster Bay. It provides an interesting dinghy trip and is good for windsurfing, but it is too shallow for deep-keeled boats.

Rules for boating in Lloyd Harbor: Rafting is allowed, but you must maintain a safe distance from other boats.

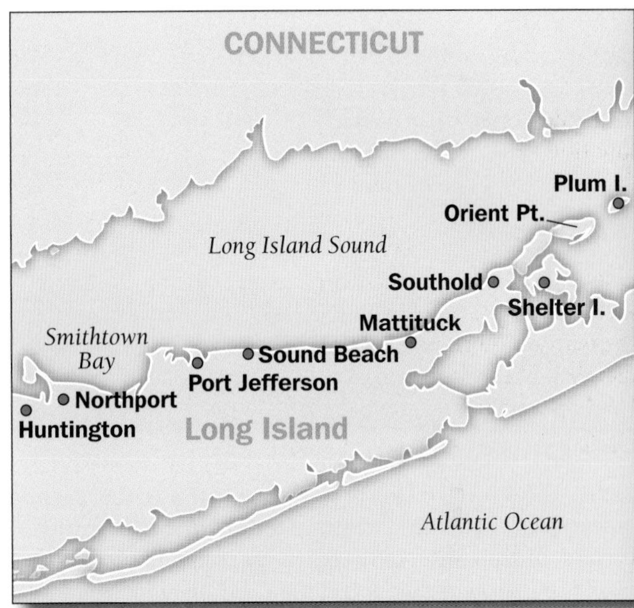

Anchorage: Anchoring is prohibited in the inner harbor. Several hundred feet west of Lloyd Harbor green can buoy "3" and red nun buoy "4" (not Huntington Harbor buoys), a floating sign states: Transient Anchorage South And East. Although this anchorage area provides good protection from the prevailing southwest winds, it is wide open to surge and wakes from the constant stream of boats that use the Huntington Harbor channel. The speed limit is 5 knots. Stay away from the buoyed water-skiing area.

Huntington Harbor

At the southwestern end of Huntington Bay, just around the lighthouse from Lloyd Harbor, a well-marked channel leads into Huntington Harbor. Although this is one of the best-protected harbors in Long Island Sound, it is also more tightly packed with boats than any eastern Long Island Sound harbor. Provisions and supplies are close at hand, and anything the cruising mariner is likely to require is also readily available. The waters are usually crowded with racing sailboats or cruisers, so proceed slowly through the fleet and be sure you do not pull a wake.

NAVIGATION: Use Charts 12364 and 12365. For Huntington Harbor, use Bridgeport tide tables. For high tide, subtract 1 minute; for low tide, add 7 minutes. The narrow but well-marked entrance runs between a boulder reef extending out from West Neck to starboard, and 1- and 2-foot shallows around Wincoma Point to port upon entry.

Looking south over Huntington Harbor. (Not to be used for navigation.)

Favor the West Neck shore and allow for the 2-knot current through the narrows. Dominating the entrance from a hill on the southern shore is baronial Coindre Hall (101 Browns Road, 631-854-4410), which is open to the public.

After rounding flashing green buoy "7," the channel swings east for about 1,000 yards before turning south into the harbor's lower end. Watch your wake as you navigate the channel; a 5 mph speed limit is strictly enforced.

Dockage: Well inside the protection of East Neck, left of the channel, the long-established Huntington Yacht Club welcomes visiting yachts to its 103-slip (floating dock) marina with access to the club's excellent modern amenities, including an Olympic-size swimming pool and an excellent restaurant. Water, power and cable TV are provided at every dock; gasoline and diesel are at the fuel dock. Or if you prefer, rent one of the club's 54 moorings (swift launch service included) for a modest facilities fee.

At the head of the harbor, Willis Marine Center also offers transient slips, moorings and fuel. Next door, West Shore Marina Marine has the largest dock complex in the harbor. In addition to modern floating docks, showers and restrooms, a ship's store, a coin-operated laundry, a swimming pool and picnic area, the marina has full repair capabilities and a 35-ton lift. Elsewhere in the harbor, two smaller marinas rent transient slips, and several independent concerns rent moorings with launch service to the village.

GOIN' ASHORE: **HUNTINGTON, NY**

The town of Huntington offers one of the most sophisticated arts communities in the area. Heckscher Museum (631-351-3250), on Prime Avenue, has a fine collection of paintings. The Cinema Arts Centre (423 Park Ave., 631-423-7611) is a showcase for unusual films. Several popular restaurants are within walking distance.

At the head of the harbor, Compass Rose Marine (15 Ill Dam Road, 631-673-4144) has a huge inventory of marine supplies and can order parts for rapid delivery. The center of the village is about a 15- to 20-minute walk from the marinas situated along the inner harbor, but complete reprovisioning is convenient at King Kullen supermarket (631-385-7365) at 50 New York Ave., just a few blocks away.

There are numerous good restaurants in Huntington. A few within walking distance to the harbor that receive strong recommendations from locals include Piccolo (215 Wall St., 631-424-5592) for well-served, excellent continental cuisine, and Bravo! Nader (9 Union Place, 631-351-1200), which is quaint, Italian and romantic. Pancho Villa's (311 New York Ave., 631-549-0022) has excellent Mexican food. The village has interesting shops and is well worth a walking tour.

Halesite, on the eastern side of the harbor, is the place where patriot Nathan Hale landed on his fatal mission. He is commemorated by an inscribed boulder, visible from the water, halfway between Huntington Harbor and Centerport Harbor.

ADDITIONAL RESOURCES:

- Town of Huntington, **http://town.huntington.ny.us**

NEARBY GOLF COURSES:

Crab Meadow Golf Course, 220 Waterside Road, Northport, NY 11768, 631-757-8800, **www.crabmeadow.com**

NEARBY MEDICAL FACILITIES:

Huntington Hospital, 270 Park Ave., Huntington, NY 11743, 631-351-2000, **www.hunthosp.org**

Huntington Harbor, NY

HUNTINGTON HARBOR		Largest Vessel Accommodated	VHF Channel Monitored	Transient Berths / Total Berths	Approach / Dockside Depth (reported)	Floating Docks	Gas / Diesel	Groceries, Ice, Marine Supplies, Snacks	Repairs: Hull, Engine, Propeller	Lift (tonnage), Crane, Rail	1=110V, 2=220V, B=Both, Max Amps	Laundry, Pool, Showers	Pump-Out Station	Nearby: Grocery Store, Motel, Restaurant
		Dockage					Supplies		Services					
1. Gold Star Battalion/Coneys Marine	631-421-3366	45	09		15/8	F		I	HEP	C	1/30	S	P	
2. Knutson Marine	631-549-7842	60	09	5/100	10/8	F		IMS	HEP	L35	B/50	LS		R
3. Huntington Yacht Club	631-427-4949	100	68	20/103	/12	F	GD	IS			B/100	PS	P	GMR
4. Compass Rose Marine Supply	631-673-4144	MARINE SUPPLIES						M						R
5. Knutson's Yacht Haven Marina	631-673-0700	100		4/38	12/12	F		M	HEP	L35	B/50	S		GR
6. Huntington Town Dock	631-351-3255				15/6									R
7. Coneys Marine	631-421-3366	55	09		15/12	F		GIMS	HEP	L	1/30	LS	P	GR
8. Willis Marine Center	631-421-3400	65	09	12/110	12/10	F	GD	GIM	HEP	L35,C	B/50	LS	P	GR
9. Mill Dam Marina	631-351-3255													
10. West Shore Marina	631-427-3444	110	09	30/308	15/15	F		IMS	HEP	30	B100	LPS	P	GR
11. Long Island Yacht Services	631-549-4687		10		8/8					L	1/30			

Corresponding chart(s) not to be used for navigation. Internet Access Wireless Internet Access

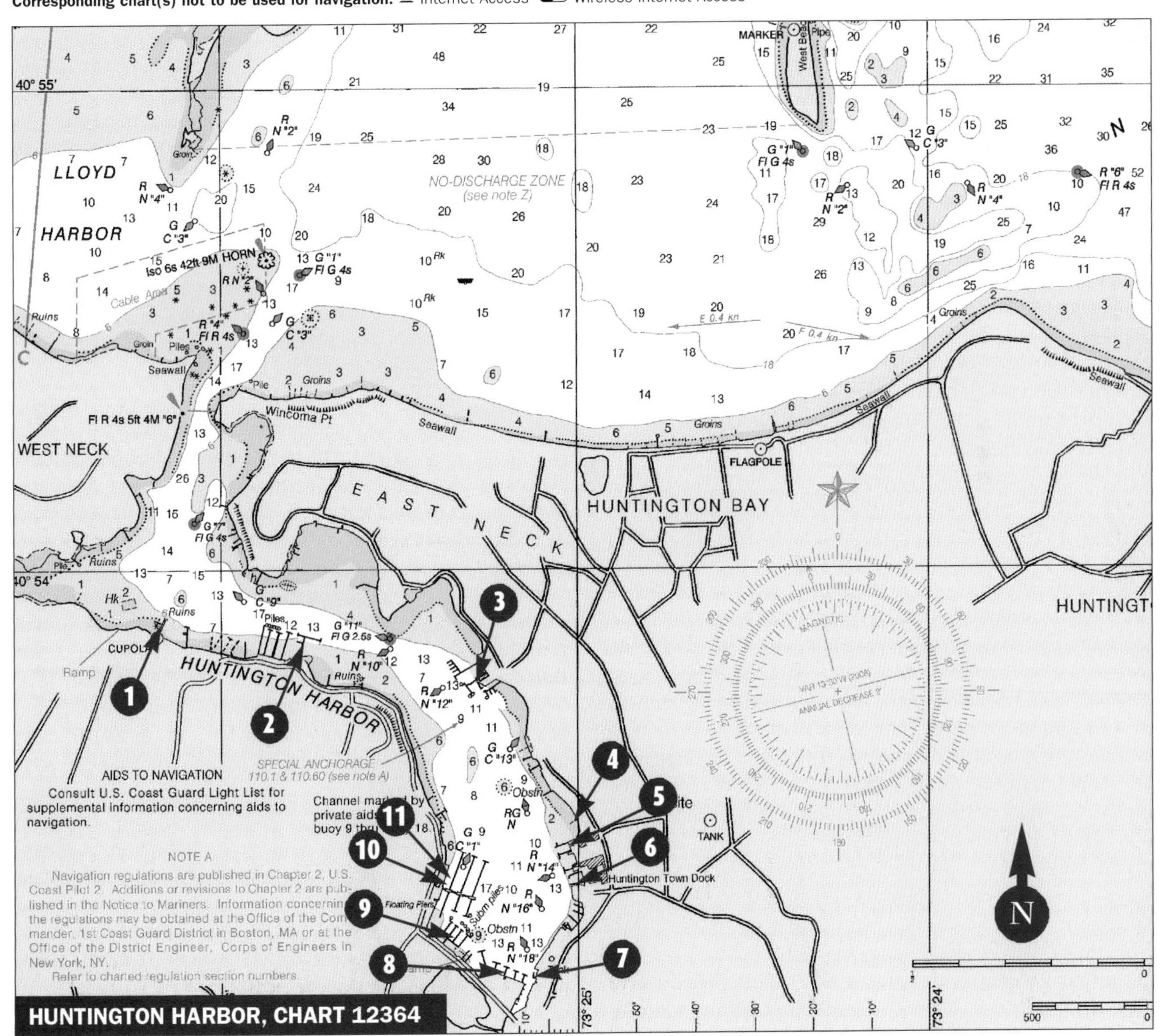

LLOYD HARBOR
WEST NECK
EAST NECK
HUNTINGTON BAY
HUNTINGTON HARBOR
NO-DISCHARGE ZONE (see note Z)
Wincoma Pt
FLAGPOLE
TANK
Huntington Town Dock
SPECIAL ANCHORAGE 110.1 & 110.60 (see note A)
Channel marked by private aids buoy 9 thru
AIDS TO NAVIGATION
Consult U.S. Coast Guard Light List for supplemental information concerning aids to navigation.
NOTE A
Navigation regulations are published in Chapter 2, U.S. Coast Pilot 2. Additions or revisions to Chapter 2 are published in the Notice to Mariners. Information concerning the regulations may be obtained at the Office of the Commander, 1st Coast Guard District in Boston, MA or at the Office of the District Engineer, Corps of Engineers in New York, NY.
Refer to charted regulation section numbers.
HUNTINGTON HARBOR, CHART 12364

Order Waterway Guides online at www.WaterwayGuide.com or call toll-free 800-233-3359

Northport Bay

The eastern arm of Huntington Bay is Northport Bay, a separate body of water with its own complex of harbors and coves, sandy beaches, a neat town on the harbor and a colorful resident shellfishing fleet.

NAVIGATION: Use Charts 12364 and 12365. For Northport Bay, use Bridgeport tide tables. For high tide, subtract 5 minutes; for low tide, add 4 minutes. The entrance channel begins at flashing green buoy "1" just off West Beach, a mile-long spit extending south from Eatons Neck. Do not cut this light too closely or go inside it; a sandbar comes out from the point. The well-marked channel lines up clearly to the east. Mind the navigational aids; a 2-knot current might put you on shoals and rocks. Be especially mindful of red nun buoy "4," which marks a 3-foot-deep spot in what seems like the middle of the bay.

Centerport Harbor—In Northport Bay

Going counterclockwise from the west around Northport Bay, the first harbor is Centerport Harbor on the southern shore, opposite Duck Island Harbor and separated from Northport Harbor to the east by Little Neck. Centerport Harbor is easily the quietest harbor in the area. It offers some services for shoal-draft boats and a restaurant ashore. You can explore the coves and marshes by dinghy.

Northport Harbor

Dockage: Just to port on entering the channel through the moorings, you will see the dock and modern clubhouse of the Northport Yacht Club. Except on summer weekends, when reservations are suggested, the club usually has enough moorings for transient members of other clubs, with launch service on call (at least 8 a.m. to 9 p.m. on weekdays, and later on weekends, launch monitors VHF Channel 71) and access to the club's dining room and bar, ample shower and changing rooms and a pool. Members and visitors may purchase gas and diesel fuel here as well. There is dockside pump-out and a pump-out boat (call on VHF Channel 09).

Farther up the harbor, Seymour's has a few slips and a dozen moorings for visitors. Launch service is available, but it is a relatively short pull to the dinghy landing just inside the town dock. All spaces at the dinghy dock are rented out to locals. There is a $200 fine for violations. Check with the on-site dockmaster about where to tie up your dinghy.

Just beyond Seymour's, the lengthy town dock (marked by a gazebo on its north end) offers free two-hour tie-ups, and possibly longer on less crowded weekdays (convenient for shopping in the village). After 8 p.m., an overnight fee is charged, but a portion of it is refunded if you leave by 11 p.m. This accommodates people who want to come in just for the evening. No water or electricity are available, and you will want to put out a fender board to stay off the pilings during the 7-foot tide change. Still farther up the harbor to port, boats drawing less than 5 feet can dock at Britannia Yacht and Racquet Club, a full-service marine facility and Texaco StarPort fuel stop with a ship's store, repairs, a health club, a pool and tennis courts. The approach channel is well-buoyed.

Anchorage: Anchorage in Northport Harbor is not possible, as the whole area is occupied with mooring balls. Anchorage is available just outside the harbor north and northwest of Bluff Point. Holding is good, but you are exposed to north and northwest winds. The dinghy ride to the nearest landing will require strong arms at the oars or, preferably, a motor.

GOIN' ASHORE: NORTHPORT, NY

After you enter Northport Harbor, when the yacht club is off your port bow, start scanning the west shore (there are no buoys to use as references). Directly across from the yacht club, you will see an aircraft hangar. A few hundred yards north of the hangar, a dark, slate-roofed building sits on the water's edge. This was the beach house for the Eagle's Nest, summer home of William K. Vanderbilt. The hangar housed his seaplanes.

The mansion sits near the beach house, overlooking the water from a distance. It is a "modest" 24-room affair, but it looks like a fairy-tale castle. The columns near the main entrance are from the ruins of Carthage. The oak-paneled organ room contains a $90,000 pipe organ. One of the bathtubs was carved from a solid block of black marble and sports gold fixtures.

Separate from the main house is a marine museum with approximately 16,000 specimens of marine life, presented in a setting of their natural habitat. The Vanderbilt mansion (180 Little Neck Road) and grounds are operated as a museum by Suffolk County. Although a visit will require a cab ride, it is a place you should not miss for a peek at the grandeur that was America's original Gold Coast. Hours vary with the seasons, but the house is generally open for tours Tuesday through Sunday; call 631-854-5555 for more information.

Ashore, Northport's charm is easily sampled via a pleasant walk along the waterfront and through the classic town park, with its children's playground, bandstand and dock-front benches offering relaxing views of this colorful harbor. Shopping is concentrated along Main Street, just across from the park. Here, you will find the Northport Village Gourmet Deli (40 Main St., 631-261-6662) with its large selection of salads, baked goods and domestic and imported beers. Across the street, the Northport Harbor Deli (631-261-6808) prepares hot and cold sandwiches to go. Within a couple of blocks, there is an old-fashioned Hardware Co. (90 Main St., 631-261-4449), Jones Drug Store (100 Main St., 631-261-7070), the Northport Tasting Room and Wine Cellar (70 Main St., 631-261-0642) and two banks, Chase Bank and ATM (54 Main St., 631-261-8400) and the First National Bank of Long Island (105 Main St., 631-261-0331). Readers will also enjoy a visit to The Dog-Eared Bookstore at 146 Main St. (631-262-0149).

Several of the many restaurants in Northport have been recommended by cruisers and are worthy of mention. On Main Street are Skipper's Pub (34 Main St., burgers, steaks, seafood and Sunday brunch, 631-261-3589), Bistro 44 (44 Main St., 631-262-9744), Caffe Portofino, (249 Main St., 631-262-7656) and The Ship's Inn (78 Main St., 631-261-3000).

ADDITIONAL RESOURCES:

- Village of Northport, **www.villageofnorthport.com**

Northport Harbor, NY

NORTHPORT HARBOR		Largest Vessel Accommodated	VHF Channel Monitored	Transient Berths / Total Berths	Approach / Dockside Depth (reported)	Floating Docks	Gas / Diesel	Groceries, Ice, Marine Supplies, Snacks	Repairs: Hull, Engine, Propeller	Lift (tonnage), Crane, Rail	1=110V, 2=220V, B=Both, Max Amps	Laundry, Pool, Showers	Pump-Out Station	Nearby: Grocery Store, Motel, Restaurant
		Dockage					Supplies		Services					
1. Northport Yacht Club	631-261-7633	50	71		7/4			I			1/15	S		R
2. Seymour's Boat Yard	631-261-6574	60	68	4/12	8/7	F	GD	I	HEP	L50	1/30		P	R
3. Centerport Yacht Club	631-697-8691	45	68	MOORINGS	8/6							PS		GMR
4. Northport Village Dock	631-261-7502	300			6/6						1/15			GR
5. Brittania Yachting Center	631-261-5600	73	09	15/310	5/9	F	GD	IMS	HEP	L55,C	B/100	PS	P	GMR

Corresponding chart(s) not to be used for navigation. Internet Access Wireless Internet Access

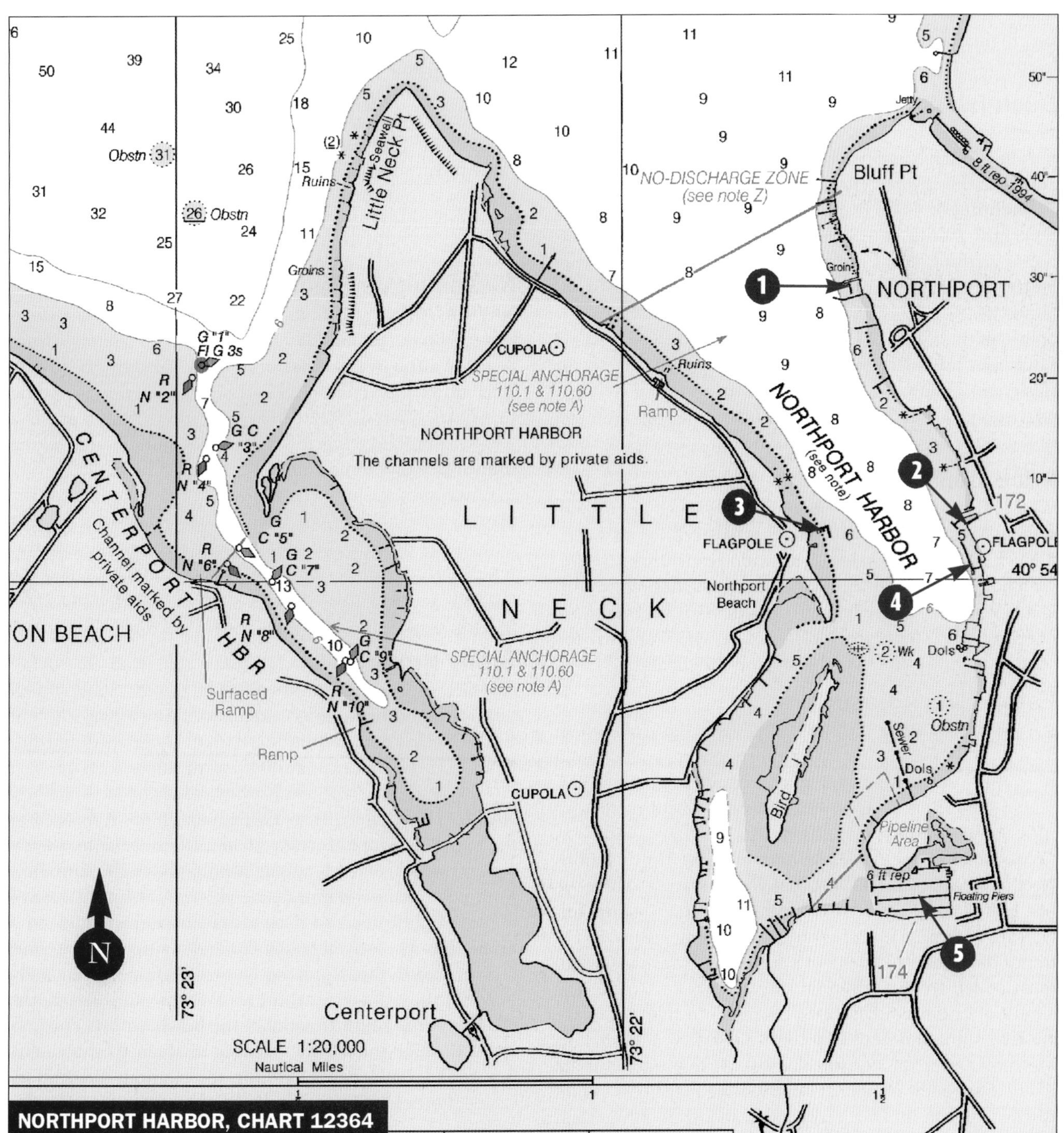

NORTHPORT HARBOR, CHART 12364

NEARBY GOLF COURSES:
Northport Golf Course, 79 Middleville Road, Northport, NY 11768, 631-261-8000

NEARBY MEDICAL FACILITIES:
Huntington Hospital, 270 Park Ave., Huntington, NY 11743, 631-351-2000

Asharoken Bight

Although large and open, the bight along Asharoken Beach has ample depth and good holding ground, while offering adequate protection and a breeze on otherwise airless nights. Rafting is not permitted in the town of Asharoken, which includes Eatons Neck Basin, Price Bend and Asharoken Bight. The "no rafting" law is strictly enforced by the local marine police.

Duck Island Harbor

West of Asharoken Beach, on the northern side of Northport Bay, Duck Island Harbor is an attractive gunkhole, secluded and well-protected, but without docks or supplies.

Anchorage: Good overnight anchorage is available just inside the mouth in 6-foot depths, but the rest of the harbor is shallow. Local ordinances forbid anchoring within 50 feet of the shore and require holding tanks or self-contained heads.

Best entry is west of Duck Island Bluff. (The Duck Island Bluff light no longer appears on the most recent chart for this area.) Follow the band of deep water around its western bend and anchor inside the mouth of the cove. You will find good water north of the entrance.

Price Bend

West of Duck Island Harbor is wishbone-shaped Price Bend, a popular anchorage with fine beaches, crowds of boats, picnickers and swimmers. It is wide open to the south, with holding ground that leaves much to be desired, so this is a better lunch or swimming spot than an overnight anchorage. When entering, do not cut corners or turn too soon. Just follow the buoys to stay off the shoals.

Eatons Neck Basin

Eatons Neck Basin is a terrific, convenient overnight spot for those transiting the Sound and not wishing to enter any of the larger harbors. This is strictly an anchorage, with no amenities; landing ashore is not permitted. Known locally as Coast Guard Cove, this tiny harbor at the tip of Eatons Neck is home of the local Coast Guard station. The cove has been exempted from the local ordinance against anchoring within 50 feet of shore. The flashing green "1" entrance buoy marks the end of a submerged breakwater and must be left to port. Even on summer weekends, there is almost always room here. Good depths run right up to the western shore but depths become shallower, and anchoring spots fewer, east of the channel. At low tide, you are likely to see a few clam boats arrive. Note that Coast Guard rescue craft can throw a heavy wake, and be doubly certain not to anchor in the channel or anywhere that might interfere with their operations.

Eatons Neck to Stony Brook

NAVIGATION: Use Charts 12364 and 12365. For Stony Brook, Eatons Neck Point, use Bridgeport tide tables. For high tide, add 2 minutes; for low tide, add 8 minutes. Heading east from Huntington Bay, give Eatons Neck Point a wide berth. Depths are as shallow as 4 feet for almost a mile to the northeast. The white stone lighthouse, one of the oldest and most significant on Long Island (established in 1792 on direct orders from George Washington), stands on the point 144 feet above water. At night, its light is powerful and easy to pick up, but by day the structure tends to disappear into the bluffs and is not easily visible from offshore.

Most cruising boats cut straight across the broad bight (about 10 miles wide) called Smithtown Bay by picking up green can buoy "13" off of Eatons Neck and running 100 degrees magnetic to green gong buoy "11A" off of Old Field Point (northwest of Port Jefferson) in favor of the more direct route along Long Island Sound. When you are bucking a foul current, however, the trip along the beach and bluff-lined shore is easier and faster, due to a weaker current velocity.

Nissequogue River

NAVIGATION: Use Charts 12364 and 12365. The Nissequogue River (Indian for "clay country") is a short stream near the attractive beaches of Sunken Meadow State Park. The entrance is reported to carry 8-foot depths, according to NOAA Chart 12364. Sunken Meadows State Park is a 520-acre property that offers beaches, hiking and biking trails, three nine-hole golf courses and a clubhouse.

Enter from flashing red buoy "2," and then tick off the charted navigational aids carefully as you head in. Rocks and shoals outside the dredged channel bare at low water. A marina with a restaurant welcomes boaters, and the river offers less crowded bathing beaches and exploration by dinghy.

Stony Brook

Another of Long Island's appealing towns, Stony Brook lies in the southeastern corner of Smithtown Bay, south of Crane Neck Point. While the harbor is crowded and difficult to enter, it is a rewarding port of call.

NAVIGATION: Use Charts 12364 and 12365. Approach to the harbor is over a bar (less than 2 feet deep at mean low water), which extends about a mile above the entrance. Minimum channel depth inside is 5 feet. Mean tidal range is more than 6 feet, so deeper-draft boats can enter on a rising tide. The privately marked and maintained entrance channel leads east from the charted flashing green buoy "1." Just short of going ashore on West Meadow Beach, the channel turns south to parallel the beach. Strong currents speed through the narrow opening between West Meadow Beach and Long Beach, calling for cautious navigation. Inside, Porpoise Channel leads southwest to Stony Brook.

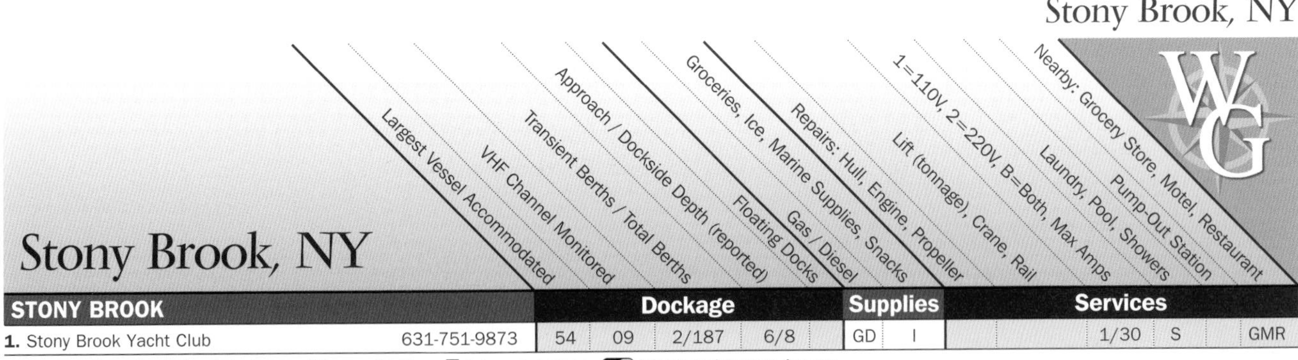

Stony Brook, NY

STONY BROOK		Largest Vessel Accommodated	VHF Channel Monitored	Transient Berths / Total Berths	Approach / Dockside Depth (reported)	Floating Docks	Gas / Diesel	Groceries, Ice, Marine Supplies, Snacks	Repairs: Hull, Engine, Propeller	Lift (tonnage), Crane, Rail	1=110V, 2=220V, B=Both, Max Amps	Laundry, Pool, Showers	Pump-Out Station	Nearby: Grocery Store, Motel, Restaurant
		Dockage					Supplies		Services					
1. Stony Brook Yacht Club	631-751-9873	54	09	2/187	6/8		GD	I			1/30	S		GMR

Corresponding chart(s) not to be used for navigation. Internet Access · Wireless Internet Access

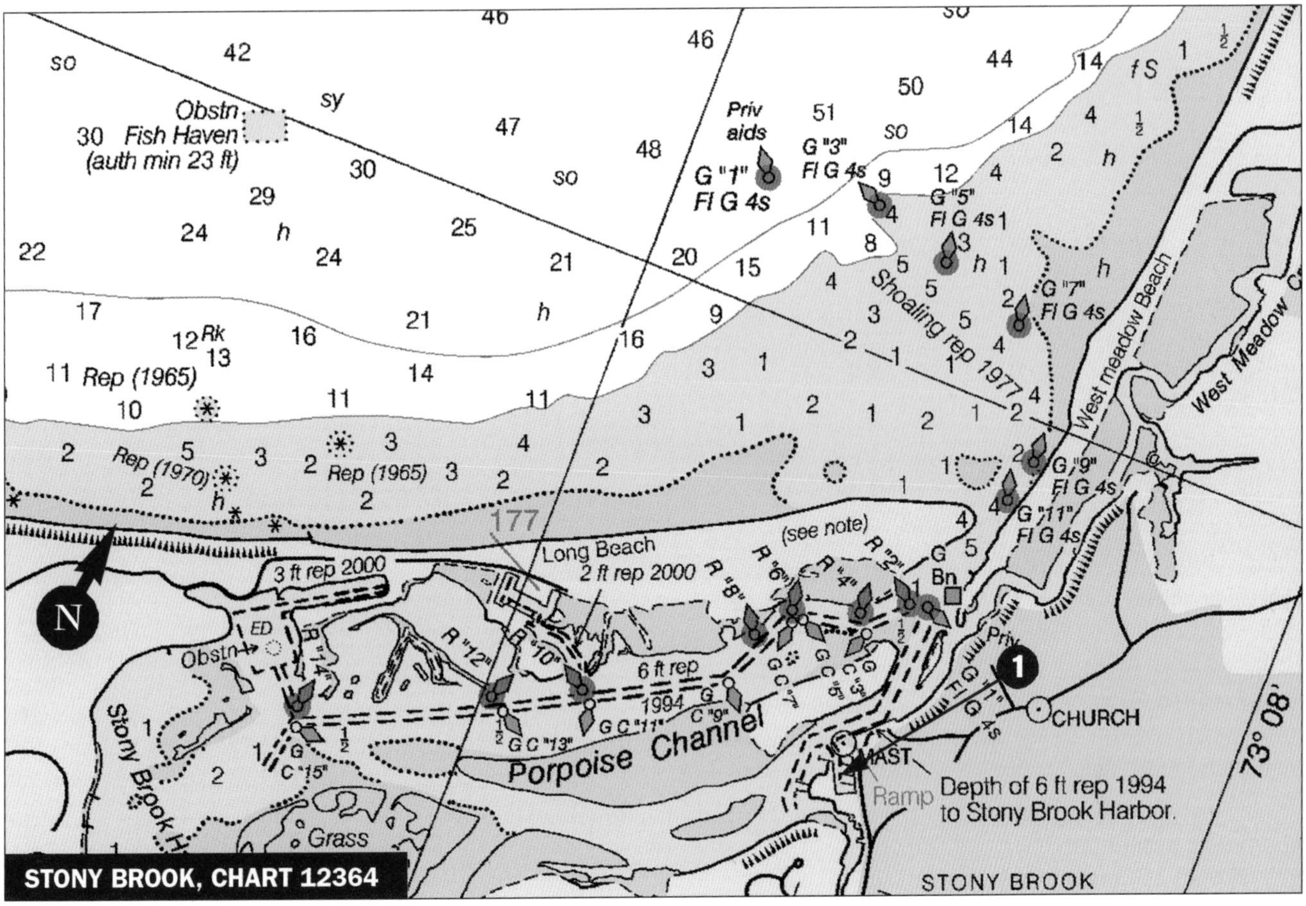

STONY BROOK, CHART 12364

Dockage: Stony Brook Yacht Club is private, but can occasionally offer a slip or mooring buoy. There is a strong current, so care must be taken when maneuvering. There is a small town dinghy dock available for three-hour tie-ups.

GOIN' ASHORE:
STONY BROOK, NY

The Stony Brook area dates back to Revolutionary times when George Washington traveled the Heritage Trail, now state Highway 25A. While the British Army reprovisioned from Stony Brook's grist mill, Washington's spy ring concurrently operated from the town.

In 1941, Ward Melville created Stony Brook Village Center, one of the first planned business centers, as part of his "living Williamsburg." The Colonial-style center now houses 35 quaint shops and restaurants. Don't miss the post office with its mechanical eagle atop the building that flaps its wings on the hour. The historic Stony Brook Grist Mill, c. 1751, where millers are still grinding grain, is on Harbor Road, a five-minute walk from the Village Center. The mill is open Wednesday through Sunday, June through August, for a $2 fee (631-751-2244 or 631-689-3238).

The State University at Stony Brook/Staller Center is a 17,000-student university on 1,100 acres. The five-theater Staller Center for the Arts features professional music, dance, film, theater and an art gallery. The Long Island Museum of American Art, History and Carriages (631-751-0066), comprised of three museums, featuring America's finest carriage collection, is on Main Street. It is open year-round, Wednesday to Saturday, from 10 a.m. to 5 p.m., and Sunday from noon to 5 p.m.

Stony Brook has some excellent restaurants, including the Mirabelle Restaurant at the Three Village Inn (150 Main St., 631-751-0555) opposite the Village Center; the Country House Restaurant (1175 Route 25A, 631-751-3332) adjacent

Looking northwest over Port Jefferson. (Not to be used for navigation.) WATERWAY GUIDE PHOTOGRAPHY

to the Carriage Museum and, in the Village Center, the Brook House (123 Main St., 631-751-4617), the Golden Pear Café (97 Main St., 631-751-7695) and the delightful Robinson's Tea Room, (also at 97 Main St., 631-751-1232) featuring a full English Tea.

ADDITIONAL RESOURCES:

■ State University of New York at Stony Brook, **www.sunysb.edu**

NEARBY GOLF COURSES:

Smithtown Landing Country Club, 495 Landing Ave. #1, Smithtown, NY 11787, 631-979-6534

NEARBY MEDICAL FACILITIES:

Stony Brook University Hospital, Nicolls Road and East Loop Intersection, Stony Brook, NY 11790 631-89-8333, **www.stonybrookhospital.com**

Port Jefferson

Port Jefferson is a deep, two-mile-long bay. If you are traveling east, it is the last real harbor until Mattituck, some 26 miles farther on. Port Jefferson is justly popular, protected, convenient to town—which is located on the harbor—and has boating amenities and beaches where you can swim and picnic. There are also excellent anchorages within the harbor, east and west of the entrance. A large fleet is on moorings, and plenty of sheltered anchorages are available. You can take the railroad to New York City, a ferry to Bridgeport, CT, or make convenient connections by air via MacArthur Airport at Islip.

NAVIGATION: Use Charts 12364 and 12362. Port Jefferson is best approached from the sea buoy (red-and-white Morse (A) whistle "PJ") about a mile northwest of the entrance to the harbor. Coming from Connecticut, the 100-foot-high bluff of Mount Misery Point offers a prominent landmark. Once inside the entrance buoys, head for the church spire in the center of town, situated between the large hospital to the east and the Port Jefferson powerhouse stacks to the west. The narrow cut between Mount Misery Point and the lighted end ("flashing red "2") of Old Field Beach can be crowded and, when wind and tide are opposed, quite turbulent. Currents average 2.5 knots on the flood, and 2 knots on the ebb. Otherwise there are few obstructions or dangers on the bay, save for the frequent and swift-traveling Port Jefferson-to-Bridgeport ferries. Be watchful and be prepared to give way to the ferries.

Port Jefferson Harbor

NAVIGATION: Use Charts 12364 and 12362. Stretching north from the head of the harbor, below the high-banked eastern shore, much of Port Jefferson's recreational fleet lies tethered at moorings. Here also are the transient rental moorings maintained by Setauket Yacht Club, which can be raised on VHF Channel 09, and Port Jefferson Launch on Channel 68. The well-marked harbor channel leads directly to a hub centering on the Town Marina, ferry dock and the unmistakable power station. Keep clear of this area to allow for the passage of commercial traffic, and also be aware of the car-carrying ferries, which back toward the power station on each return to Bridgeport.

Dockage and Moorings: Danford's Inn and Marina, just east of the ferry dock, offers the protection of its wooden sea barrier, floating docks with 10-foot depths, finger piers, a luxurious game room, exercise facilities and private shower rooms. If you anchor out, you can dinghy to Danford's dock, which has a 10-foot limit and is available for a small fee. Gasoline and diesel fuel are available at the marina's fuel dock at the west end of the wooden sea barrier. Danford's has traditionally offered specially priced packages for boaters who wish to abandon ship in favor of the inn's elegant rooms and dining facilities. Otherwise, dockage is available, with electricity, cable and phone service. Short tie-ups are available at hourly rates.

West of the ferry landing, Port Jefferson Town Marina may have transient space available on an hourly or daily basis. Depths at the Town Marina's stationary docks run to a maximum of 6 feet, though there may be space for deeper-footed vessels alongside the fuel dock. The town dock's manager and attendants monitor VHF Channel 09. Attendants are on duty (and run security checks) 24 hours daily. Free pump-outs are available at the courtesy dock.

Friendly Setauket ("see-talk'-it") Yacht Club has 20 designated transient moorings (yellow balls) in addition to vacant members' moorings available for rental, including launch service (9 a.m. to 11 p.m.) and use of the club's facilities. Showers and restrooms are downstairs in the clubhouse. The upstairs bar is open on Fridays. You can fill your water tanks at the club's dock, and there is ice at the boathouse.

The largest mooring operation in the harbor is run by Port Jefferson Launch, which rents its 40 moorings (bright red balls) and provides launch service to and from its location adjacent to the ferry dock. Hail "Port Jefferson Launch Service" on VHF Channel 68. The launch operates Sunday through Thursday, 8 a.m. to 10 p.m., and Fridays, Saturdays and holidays, 8 a.m. to midnight.

Anchorage: Just to the east of the entrance, Mount Misery Cove (the "Sand Pit" or "the Bluffs") is a popular anchorage. Though not shown on the chart, depths are ample (about 15 feet), and holding is good. Mount Misery Cove is now fully occupied by mooring balls, and room for anchorage is extremely limited.

To the west of the entrance, the cove behind Old Field Beach is also reputed to be a secure and quiet anchorage in depths ranging from 7 to 11 feet at mean low water.

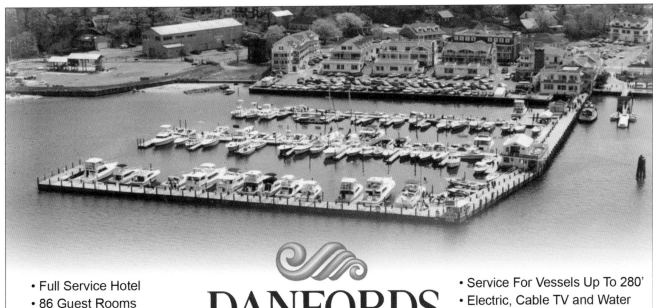

Port Jefferson, Mount Sinai, NY

PORT JEFFERSON, MOUNT SINAI		Largest Vessel Accommodated	VHF Channel Monitored	Transient Berths / Total Berths	Approach / Dockside Depth (reported)	Floating Docks	Gas / Diesel	Groceries, Ice, Marine Supplies, Snacks	Repairs: Hull, Engine, Propeller	Lift (tonnage), Crane, Rail	1=110V, 2=220V, B=Both, Max Amps	Laundry, Pool, Showers	Pump-Out Station	Nearby: Grocery Store, Motel, Restaurant
		Dockage					Supplies		Services					
1. Port Jefferson Town Marina (WiFi)	631-331-3567	50	09	/150	20/		GD	I			B/50	LS	P	MR
2. Danford's Marina and Inn (WiFi)	**631-928-5200**	**270**	**09**	**75/75**	**25/18**	**F**	**GD**	**I**			**B/50**	**LS**	**P**	**GMR**
3. Setauket Yacht Club Inc.	631-473-9650	60	68		12/5	F		I			1/15	S		GMR
4. Ralph's Fishing Station	631-473-6655	50	67	5/51	15/15	F	GD	IMS	EP	L	1/30			GR
5. Mt. Sinai Yacht Club	631-473-2993	45	09	10/99	17/12	F	GD	GIMS			1/50	S	P	R
6. Old Man's Boatyard	631-473-7330	50		5/65	12/12	F		M	HP	LC	1/30			

Corresponding chart(s) not to be used for navigation. Internet Access (WiFi) Wireless Internet Access

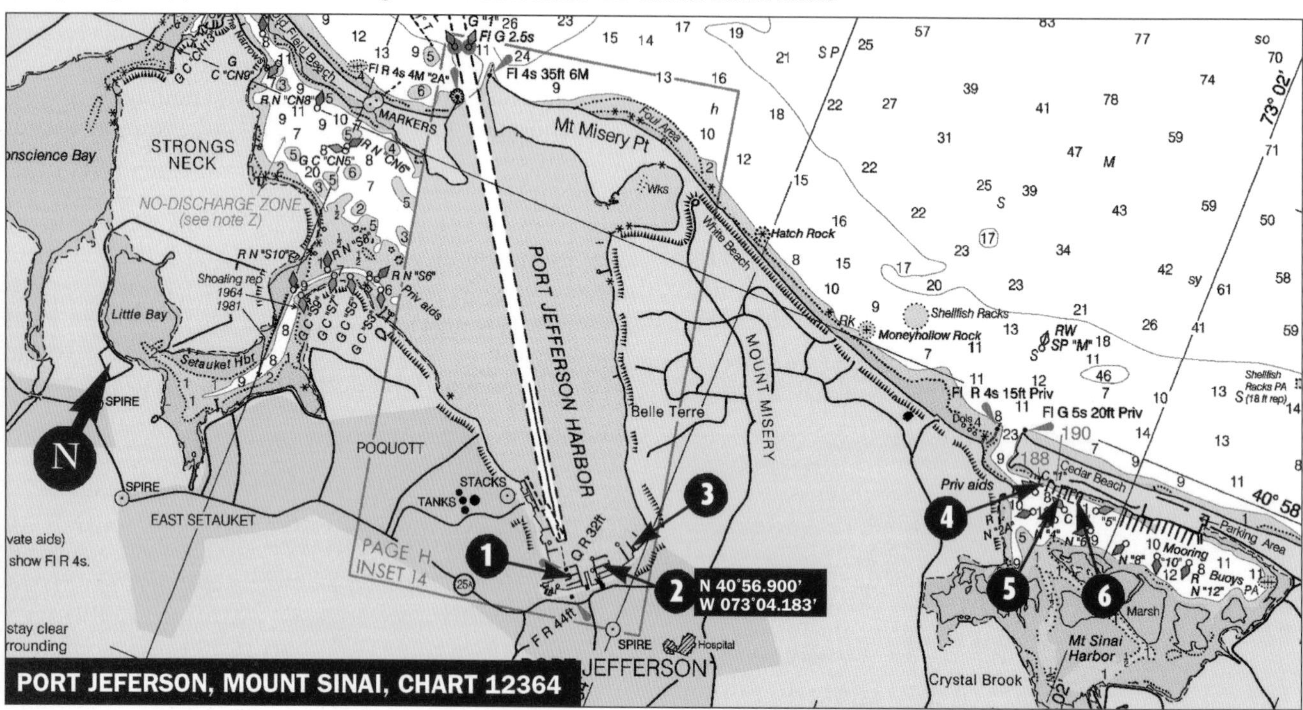

PORT JEFERSON, MOUNT SINAI, CHART 12364

However, several shallow spots (3- to 6-foot mounds) require deep-draft vessels to proceed with some care at less than half-tide. North of the mooring field, there is good holding and plenty of room for anchorage within a reasonable distance from shore. Launch service is offered by Port Jefferson Launch. Call "Port Jefferson Launch" on VHF Channel 68, or you can take your tender to the dinghy dock immediately east of Bayles Dock, which is inside the Danford's Marina sea barrier. A mooring is not recommended during a blow from the north, since the harbor's considerable fetch will permit a build-up of 2- to 3-foot seas.

GOIN' ASHORE:

PORT JEFFERSON, NY

Port Jefferson is a picturesque waterside village, much revived from its less attractive, industrial days. It had a long history as a shipbuilding village, and many remnants of this past are preserved here. The centerpiece of the Port Jefferson waterfront is the Village Center, which is part of a harborfront park. The former Bayles Shipyard building, east of Danford's Inn, has a 2,300-foot promenade. The town of Port Jefferson offers lots to do. The hilly streets in town leading to the harbor are bursting with museums, historic homes, shops, restaurants and varied architectural styles, such as Steamboat Gothic.

Most amenities are situated up and down Main and East Main streets, which run south from the waterfront. Moore's Gourmet Market (125 Main St., 631-928-1143) has a good selection of condiments, teas, coffees, spices, pates and cheeses, as well as gourmet take-out entrees for a special (though pricey) meal aboard.

Port Jefferson Village Grocery (328 Main St., 631-476-0107), a small but well-stocked grocery and deli, is located up the hill on Main Street, just past the theater.

Along East Main Street, on the rise a block above the harbor, you will find Tiger Lily Café (vegetarian and non-vegetarian selections, 156 E. Main St, 631-476-7080). The Good Times Book Shop (150 E. Main St., 631-928-2664) has an extensive, well-organized collection of used books, including substantial literature and history selections. The Port Jefferson Free Library (631-473-0022) is off East Main Street at 100 Thompson St. For those in search of a vintage bottle of wine, Pindars Wine Store is located on the harbor at 117 Main Street.

There are numerous restaurants in Port Jefferson, including The Steam Room (4 E. Broadway, 631-928-6690), located across from the ferry dock, which serves reasonably-priced fresh seafood and "ripple fries." Pasta Pasta (234 E. Main St., 631-331-5335) serves gourmet pizza, specialty pastas, chops and seafood specialties daily, for both lunch and dinner. For something different, Costa de Espana Restaurant (9 Trader's Cove, just east of Main Street, 631-331-5363) prepares excellent Spanish meals. The Wave Restaurant at Danford's Hotel and Marina, located on the harbor (631-928-5200), serves popular seafood dishes. It is often crowded when the ferries arrive from Bridgeport or on weekends. 25 East American Bistro (25 E. Broadway, also at Danford's Marina, 631-928-5200) has an excellent waterfront view, an extensive menu and good service.

ADDITIONAL RESOURCES:

- Village of Port Jefferson, **www.portjeff.com**

NEARBY GOLF COURSES:
Heatherwood Golf Club, 303 Arrowhead Lane, South Setauket, NY 11720, 631-473-9000

NEARBY MEDICAL FACILITIES:
St. Charles Hospital, 200 Belle Terre Road, Port Jefferson, NY 11777, 631-474-6000

Setauket

Located on the west side of Port Jefferson Harbor, the remote little 17th-century town of Setauket (settled by the Puritans) offers a fascinating side trip for dinghies or small, shoal-draft boats. The entrance to the Setauket harbor is suitable for a 5-foot draft, but the harbor is fully occupied with mooring balls and anchorage is non-existent. There is a good dinghy dock adjacent to the marina, which will also allow you to tie up. The village center is about a mile and a half away.

NAVIGATION: Use Chart 12364. A narrow, crooked, privately buoyed channel slices through Port Jefferson's western shore to meander its shallow way southward between Tinkers Point and the high, wooded bluff of Strongs Neck. Tidal rise and fall is almost 7 feet, but the channel and little harbor have a tendency to silt in. Mud flats are all around.

Dockage: Setauket has a small, private marina at the head of the inlet surrounded by well-kept, Colonial-style homes. The small village has a good-sized shopping center featuring Wild by Nature (198 Route 25A, 631-246-5500), a unique organic store, a number of boutiques and the Rolling Pin Bakery (1387 Route 25A, 631-689-2253), with its delightful baked goods and selection of breads. Any other sights and amenities are a walk of about a mile and a half to the village.

Mount Sinai

After leaving Port Jefferson, travel east for about three miles beyond high Mount Misery to Mount Sinai Harbor. Once an uncharted marshy gunkhole, inhabited mainly by ducks and mosquitoes, the harbor was eventually dredged and converted to a boat-packed, well-protected port, with good anchorages, a fine beach and pleasant surroundings.

Considering the immense number of boats moored here, it is surprising that relatively few moorings are available for transients to enjoy this beautiful spot. Mount Sinai is important to cruisers in search of gasoline or diesel fuel (easily accessible from Long Island Sound) and repairs.

NAVIGATION: Use Chart 12364. For Mount Sinai Harbor, use Bridgeport tide tables. For high tide, add 4 minutes; for low tide, add 18 minutes. Mount Sinai Harbor is clearly marked, first by an offshore red-and-white "M" buoy, then by the unnumbered flashing green light at the end of the east breakwater. The harbor entrance hooks to port on entry but is wide enough for comfortable ingress with at least 12-foot depths throughout the harbor's well-marked main channel. On entering the harbor, however, locals advise giving the sandy beach (easily visible to port inside the entry jetties) a wide berth when making the left turn into the harbor mooring area. The shoal extending from the beach into the channel is not marked.

Dockage: As you enter the harbor, the fuel dock and facilities of Ralph's Fishing Station and Marina are immediately evident to port. In addition to fuel service, the marina maintains six transient moorings, with launch service to the dock. Sometimes there is also transient space available on the docks, with access to the marina's restrooms and showers. Immediately past the marina, the friendly Mount Sinai Yacht Club has six moorings available to visitors for a modest facilities fee. Limited dock space may also be available for transients.

About a quarter mile east along the harbor channel, Old Man's Boatyard has the only full-service repair operation between Northport and Mattituck. Old Man's Boatyard may have a transient slip available if you call during a weekday (516-473-7330); they are closed on weekends.

GOIN' ASHORE: **MOUNT SINAI, NY**

Activity in Mount Sinai centers on the peninsula with a beautifully developed beach located on the Long Island side; the beach is dedicated to the residents of the Village of Brookhaven. The closest village to Mount Sinai is Port Jefferson and can be reached by taxi. Just off the peninsula on North Country Road is Miller Place Inn (195 N. Country Road, 631-928-7624), again a short taxi ride away. Ralph's is locally famous for its snack bar, which serves basket-to-go orders for breakfast, lunch and dinner. Life at the Mount Sinai Yacht Club centers on a large, congenial bar, which is open to the breeze via a wide door on good days, serving snacks, lunch and drinks to members and

Mattituck, NY

MATTITUCK		Largest Vessel Accommodated	VHF Channel Monitored	Transient Berths / Total Berths	Approach / Dockside Depth (reported)	Floating Docks	Gas / Diesel	Groceries, Ice, Marine Supplies, Snacks	Repairs: Hull, Engine, Propeller	Lift (tonnage), Crane, Rail	1=110V, 2=220V, B=Both, Max Amps	Laundry, Pool, Showers	Pump-Out Station	Nearby: Grocery Store, Motel, Restaurant
		Dockage					Supplies		Services					
1. Mattituck Inlet Marina and Shipyard Inc.	631-298-4480	90		10/65	/10	F	GD	M	HEP	L70	B/50	S		R
2. Matt-A-Mar Marina	631-298-4739	80	09/68	20/124	9/9	F	GD	IM	HEP	L50	B/50	PS		GMR
3. Strong's Marine LLC	631-298-4770	42	68	/100	4/4	F	G	IM	HEP	L	1/30	S	P	GMR

Corresponding chart(s) not to be used for navigation. Internet Access Wireless Internet Access

MATTITUCK, CHART 12354

guests alike. Members have personalized bar-money rocks to keep the wind in check; "visitor" rocks are also available. A variety of restaurants deliver to the clubhouse on call (menus at the bar).

Much of the extensive marsh area is set aside as a nature reserve and is an important nesting area for a number of birds. Ralph's Marina rents sturdy two-seat kayaks for explorations of the tidal estuary.

NEARBY GOLF COURSES:
Rolling Oaks Golf Course, 181 Route 25A, Rocky Point, NY 11778, 631-744-3200

NEARBY MEDICAL FACILITIES:
St. Charles Hospital, 200 Belle Terre Road, Port Jefferson, NY 11777, 631-474-6000

Mattituck

The 40 miles between Mount Sinai and Plum Gut can be long ones for slow boats, and Mattituck is the only stopover between the two areas. While Mattituck is a well-protected, quiet, relaxed village typical of eastern Long Island, it is usually thought of as an emergency port. The entry into Mattituck can be very challenging when the winds are out of the north and the water depth is difficult at low tide. The two-mile-long creek is winding at first, then straight, with sand, marshes, trees and many lovely houses along its banks. Once inside, however, it can feel airless on a hot day. Though it is totally protected, there is very little swing room at anchorage because of the many boats.

NAVIGATION: Use Charts 12358 and 12354. For Mattituck Inlet, use Bridgeport tide tables. For high tide, add 4 minutes; for low tide, subtract 4 minutes. It is difficult to see the entry to Mattituck Inlet from offshore, but the dredged and jettied 7-foot-deep channel creates a deep gap in the shoreline bluffs. The jetties at Mattituck have been extended, and the lengthened breakwater helps build up sand on the western side of the inlet, forming a good beach for swimming.

The best approach is to take a compass course due south from green gong buoy "3A," one mile north of the entrance, and then watch for flashing white "MI" at the end of the western jetty. The entrance channel is well-marked and carries 6-foot depths. If your draft is even close to 6 feet, enter on a rising tide.

A heavy sea can build up in the entrance in northerly winds blowing against an ebb current. Once inside the inlet and past the sharp turn to port, keep in mid-channel, but favor the outside edge when the creek turns to avoid shoaling on the inside of the bends. Tidal range is more than 5 feet, and currents run as much as 3 knots. Currents diminish as you travel up the creek, however, and depths might decrease somewhat. In the upper creek, observe the very small, privately maintained channel buoys, which can appear to be fishing floats. The turning basin and anchorage at the head of the creek have 7-foot depths.

Dockage: The area offers repair yards, waterside restaurants and marinas. One marina caters to small, open fishing boats and has a No Transients sign. Another large marina and shipyard offers hauling and repairs, but its slips are full of large, permanently docked boats. The Matt-A-Mar Marina at the head of the creek is the only marina catering to transients. They monitor VHF Channel 09.

Anchorage: The only anchorage available is all the way at the head of the inlet. The holding in the anchorage is not ideal, but the area is well-protected.

Great Peconic Bay is only a mile overland to the south. The North Fork of Long Island is less than three miles wide at this point.

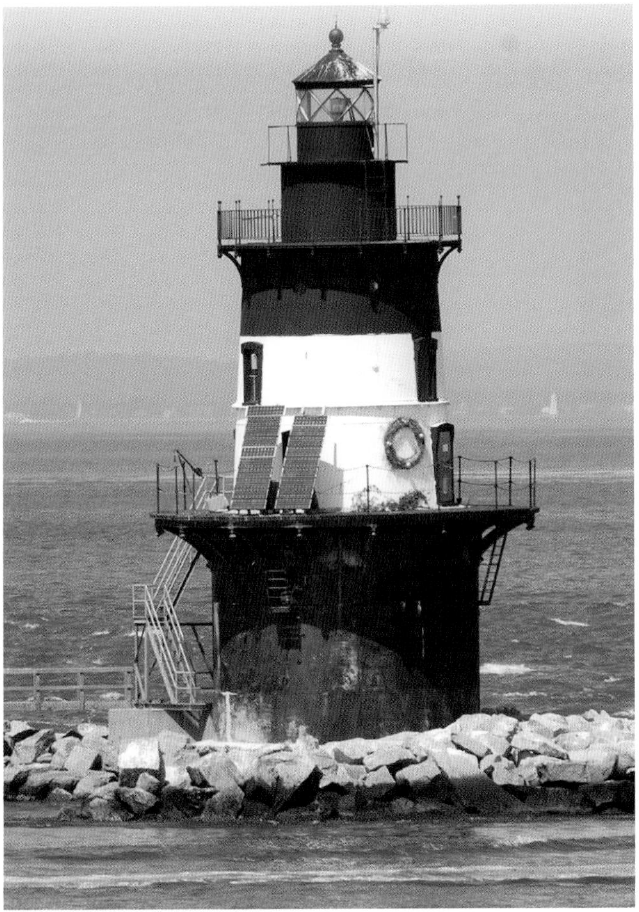

This photo was taken in the body of water known as "Plum Gut" on Long Island, New York, while on the ferry to New London from Orient Point. The lighthouse has the distinction of leaning to one side. ©IstockPhoto/NathalieCloix

GOIN' ASHORE: MATTITUCK, NY

In 1812 there was a tidal grist mill in Mattituck Inlet. The creek was dammed and the mill turned both night and day. The old mill can still be seen at the Old Mill Restaurant (5775 W. Mill Road, 631-298-8080) on your right not long after entering the inlet. By 1902, there was no market for the grist mill and so it was sold for $300 and later became a restaurant. With New York a convenient distance away, stories naturally abound of bootlegging here during Prohibition in the 1920s. The kitchen of the Old Mill had a drop door where fish carcasses where disposed of, and bags of "hooch" made an entry.

Today, kayaking is a popular activity in the protected waters of the Mattituck Inlet. Kayaks are available for rent at Matt-A-Mar Marina. The inlet is also home to many wading birds and has a large population of osprey nesting on many of the daybeacons. There are a couple of commercial fishing docks and they are willing to sell fresh fish when available.

Nearby on state Highway 25 is a Waldbaums Shopping Center that can cater to almost any need. The town is only a 10-minute walk from the town dinghy dock. (Call 631-298-9617 for Far East taxi service.) Love's Lane, especially, has a good number of small shops and boutiques. Restaurants convenient to the Mattituck harbor include the Red Door (13560 Main Road, 631-298-4800) and Village Pizza-Matituck (13550 Main Road, 631-298-8910). A Touch of Venice (2255 Wickham Ave., 631-298-5851) is located at Matt-A-Mar Marina and the Old Mill Inn lies about a mile out toward the mouth of the inlet. They both have dinghy docks and the Old Mill Inn (631-298-8080) can accommodate your boat for the duration of your meal. Some of the famous Long Island vineyards are in the area and most offer retail opportunities, tours and wine tasting.

ADDITIONAL RESOURCES:

- Mattituck Chamber of Commerce, **www.mattituckchamber.org** or **www.mattituckny.com**

NEARBY GOLF COURSES:

Cedars Golf Club, 305 Cases Lane, Cutchogue, NY 11935, 631-734-6363

NEARBY MEDICAL FACILITIES:

Central Suffolk Hospital, 1300 Roanoke Ave., Riverhead, NY 11901, 631-548-6000

Cruising Options

From Mattituck, the coast stretches on eastward, generally bluff, rocky, inhospitable and unbroken by harbors for almost 18 miles to Orient Point. The water is generally deep close inshore (the 10-fathom curve is less than a mile offshore at most points), and currents are strong. Landmarks include: the light high on Horton Point; tall water tanks at Greenport, on the far side of the Long Island land mass; and water tanks on Plum Island, way to the east, well past Orient. The 65-foot Orient Point Light, called the Teapot, marks Plum Gut and serves as the turning point into Gardiners Bay. ■

The Fishtail

CHARTS 12352, 12353, 12354, 12358, 13209, 13215

Some of the finest cruising grounds on the East Coast can be found within the Fishtail of Long Island. On the far eastern end of Long Island, the island splits into two flukes from a deep cleft beginning at the town of Riverhead. Known as the Fishtail, this area is comprised of deep bays, large islands and big jutting peninsulas that create miles of attractive cruising territory with good harbors and generally deep water. The northern fluke of the Fishtail runs about 30 miles, from Riverhead to Orient Point, and the southern fluke is some 40 miles long, stretching from Riverhead to Montauk Point.

Below Plum Gut inside of Orient Point is Gardiners Bay, separated from Block Island Sound and the open ocean by Gardiners Island. Gardiners Bay is the entrance to Shelter Island Sound, the Peconic Bays and an intriguing assortment of small bodies of water extending west to Riverhead. Big, irregularly-shaped Shelter Island sits in the middle and nearly joins the flukes of the Fishtail. About eight miles east of Riverhead on the south fork, Shinnecock Canal connects the south shore of Long Island with the New York inland waterway.

From Gardiners Bay through Little Peconic Bay, the water depths are a minimum of 20 feet in the main channels, and 10 feet or more through Great Peconic Bay. Project depths to the head of navigation at Riverhead are 6 feet. Currents run swiftly in narrow channels but normally do not exceed 2 knots. Marinas and anchorages are plentiful, and dredging has opened many once-inaccessible side creeks and small bays to deep-draft boats. (Depths reported are controlling levels at the time of writing, but dredged channels have a habit of silting in, so verify depths locally.)

In the following pages, Waterway Guide first covers the "outer flukes" of the Fishtail, including Shelter Island, traveling counterclockwise from Orient Point to Montauk. Then Waterway Guide covers the less-frequented waters of Little and Great Peconic bays, ending at the Shinnecock Canal.

Plum Gut

NAVIGATION: Use Chart 13209. Plum Gut, between Orient Point and Plum Island, is one of three exits from Long Island Sound and is the usual route to ports in Gardiners Bay, the Peconic Bays and Montauk Point. Boats bound for Block Island or other New England ports usually exit Long Island Sound via The Race. Plum Gut, a deep, narrow passage (less than three-quarters of a mile wide and one mile long), is a funnel through which the sea surges with tremendous force at maximum current. Normal velocities are 3.5 knots on the flood and more than 4 knots on the ebb, but currents can top 5 knots. Tiderips are the norm, and passage can be turbulent when wind and current oppose. Study the tide and current tables and plan your passage (whether east or west) when a fair current or slack water can be expected. Those with a love of fishing are advised to drop a trolling lure overboard at any opportunity; you are entering some of the richest striped bass and bluefish grounds on earth.

A sight worth noting when departing Long Island Sound via Plum Gut is the decaying pile of stones known locally as "The Ruins." Located just north of Gardiners Island, it was once connected to the island by a narrow spit of sand. A lighthouse was built there in 1854, but the islet was separated from Gardiners Island by a storm. The lighthouse fell into disuse and eventually disappeared. During the Spanish-American War, a fort was constructed on Gardiners Island (part of the chain of fortifications aimed at keeping the Spanish from attacking New York). It has been used as a bombing target, and has now fallen into ruins. The public is prohibited access to the area, because unexploded artillery shells pose a threat.

The North Fork

Plum Gut guides you into Gardiners Bay. About a mile in are three major docks. In the first slip, the New London ferries tie up between dolphins. Boats ferrying workers to the Plum Island Animal Disease Laboratory (closed to the public) use the second. The third is too shallow at low tide for deep-draft boats. To the southwest is Orient Beach State Park with good fishing and swimming. The water is deep almost to the beach, and this is a good fair-weather anchorage.

Orient Harbor

NAVIGATION: Use Charts 12358 and 13209. For Orient, use New London tide tables. For high tide, add 37 minutes; for low tide, add 36 minutes. Just north of Long Beach Point, Orient Harbor opens up to the southwest, with the village of Orient located on its northeastern shore. Do not cut between flashing red bell buoy "2" and the restored lighthouse at the west end of Long Beach, charted as "LT HO." Instead, follow the channel between flashing red bell buoy "2" and green can "3," keeping the area immediately southwest of the lighthouse at a respectful distance. This will prevent an encounter with the shoals that creep southward.

Dockage: Though Orient Harbor is open to prevailing southwesterly winds, many skippers make it their jumping-off point for Montauk or Block Island. In the fall, the harbor can be crowded with sportfishermen. Holding is good in 7- to 20-foot depths in front of the Orient Yacht Club. Transient dockage may be available from Orient Wharf Co. on the rough wooden bulkhead in front of the red clubhouse, but you will want to make sure your boat is well-fendered. An additional slip or two may be available inside the barrier wall (to the left of the clubhouse on approach) with at least 6-foot depths at mean low water. The floating dinghy dock is located just inside the yacht club slips, and there is a large trash receptacle on the main pier above.

Anchorage: During settled weather, good anchorage is found in 10- to 20-foot depths within easy reach of the shore's edge along the north side of Long Beach Point between the two picturesque, working fish weirs. Holding is secure in heavy mud in the relatively deep trough running perpendicular to the shore.

If you work your way east above the weir closest to the point, you will notice a decided drop-off from the 8- to 10-foot depths paralleling the shore. Hard-mud holding is excellent in the deeper trough, while a secure set in the surrounding shallower waters is typically thwarted by extensive areas of hard-packed stones. (You will encounter thousands upon thousands more of these on the stony beach.) Take care in navigating this area to avoid the additional floating nets that are sometimes stationed here. This is a relatively popular place on weekends, yet the feeling is remote, reminiscent more of Maine than Long Island.

GOIN' ASHORE: ORIENT, NY

Orient is an excellent place to recapture the all-but-lost joys and unhurried pace of what once typified small town America. Quaint, small houses date back to the 1700s, boasting tales of Indian raids and a visit from George Washington. Huge exotic trees and well-loved lawns and gardens adorn the tranquil streets. Turn left at the head of the yacht club wharf and walk a few blocks along Village Lane to reach Orient Country Store (930 Village Lane, 631-323-2580), selling sandwiches, beer, sodas, shaved-ice cones, newspapers, a few dry goods and block or cube ice (Monday through Saturday, 7:30 a.m. to 5:30 p.m.). The small (antique) post office (980 Village Lane, 631-323-9760) is nearby, and the Oysterponds Historical Society's compound (1555 Village Lane, 631-323-2480) is across the street, open Thursday, Saturday and Sunday, 2 p.m. to 5 p.m., May through September. Orient Beach State Park, located at the east end of North Country Road, offers 10 miles of beaches ideal for shelling, bird-watching and nature study. Call 631-323-2440 for more information and hours of operation. Walking and shelling along the north side of Long Beach Point is a special treat. There is no sand here. The "beach" is an expansive strand of colorful, smooth and rounded pebbles, intermixed with countless thousands of rosehips, yellow poppies and edible beach peas. The Cross Sound Ferry operates a vehicle/passenger ferry service between Orient Point and New London, Connecticut.

ADDITIONAL RESOURCES:

- **Long Island Guides, www.northforkguide.com**

NEARBY GOLF COURSES:
Islands End Golf and Country Club, Route 25, Greenport, NY 11944, 631-477-0777

NEARBY MEDICAL FACILITIES:
Eastern Long Island Hospital, 201 Manor Place, Greenport, NY 11944, 631-477-1000

Greenport

Greenport is the largest marine center on eastern Long Island and has become a recreational boater's haven and destination port.

During the 19th and early 20th centuries, more than 20 whaling ships berthed here. Greenport is still the annual site of a tall-ship rendezvous, but now they come for fun, not commerce, at the end of a regatta. Little of the port's commercial waterfront remains, most of it replaced by upscale condominiums and modern marinas.

NAVIGATION: Use Charts 12358 and 13209. Use New London tide tables. For high tide, add 1 hour 5 minutes; for low tide, add 49 minutes. Almost eight miles south-southwest of Orient Point, across the mile-wide pass north of Shelter Island, Greenport is easily reached via a deep, well-marked channel. Landmarks include a water tank, white church spire and, at night, a television tower with a fixed red light. A flashing red beacon at the south end of the breakwater off Youngs Point marks the harbor entrance.

Stirling Basin (known locally as Stirling Harbor) is the primary recreational boating center. The entrance is along the buoyed channel leading northwest from the outer harbor and roughly parallels the jetty. Favor the west shore on entry to avoid the shoal extending southwest of Youngs Point. West of the narrow cut upon entry into the nearly landlocked basin, you can see an abstract stone monument honoring sailors lost at sea. The red nun just farther west of the monument marks the channel's edge.

Dockage: Directly across the town's mooring field on entry, Brewer Yacht Yard at Greenport is popular with locals;

An aerial view of Greenport. (Not to be used for navigation.) WATERWAY GUIDE PHOTOGRAPHY

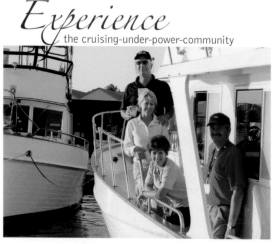

virtually all slips fill for the season. Call ahead to check transient slip availability. This is a full-service facility with quality repair service, a substantial parts department, modern shower and laundry facilities, an inviting pool and the attractive Salamander Cafe on the premises.

Immediately to the west is Brewer Stirling Harbor Shipyard & Marina, an even larger facility. The marina's excellent amenities make it a cruising destination for various boating clubs as well as individual cruisers. Still, there is usually space available, except for the busiest weekends. Brewer Stirling Harbor Marina is designed for boater privacy—slips cleverly organized for dockage in small clusters, screened by environmentally engineered plantings. There is a large pool and cabanas with restrooms and showers, barbecue areas and a full schedule of summer events, including trips to the local vineyards. You can expect a complimentary bag of ice daily, multiple washers and dryers to use, public phones, all fuels and extensive repair services. The marina provides courtesy car service to and from town, several miles distant by road from this side of the harbor.

Across the basin, to port on entry, Townsend Manor Inn Marina is a charming, comfortable and quiet transient marina with plenty of space. Expect all the amenities, including an extra-large pool, modern showers/restrooms, a well-regarded restaurant on the premises and an easy walk to town. At the head of the basin, Greenport Seafood Dock & Market (222 Atlantic Ave., 631-477-0055) has dockage for customers only, but this is the place for variety in fresh seafood and jumbo lobsters.

Outside Stirling Basin, at Greenport's harbor proper, there are additional tie-up possibilities at Claudio's Marina Restaurant and Clam Bar (111 Main St., 631-477-0627). This area is not so well-protected; you will want to rig fender boards for protection against wakes that bounce along unprotected bulkheads. The short-term dockage charge will be applied against your meal and drink tab at Claudio's Restaurant or on-dock Clam Bar (111 Main St., 631-477-1889). The town of Greenport maintains the Mitchell Park Marina on Front Street. They offer new restrooms and showers with complimentary wireless Internet at new floating docks that are protected by an extensive wave suppression system.

Moorings: Greenport's town moorings are immediately evident upon entering Stirling Basin. These are white lobster-style buoys with yellow pick-up toggles. The dinghy dock is located opposite the monument at the harbor entrance. From here, it is less than a 10-minute walk to Greenport's business district and primary commercial waterfront. From the dinghy dock, walk due west on Sterling Street to Carpenter Street, left on Carpenter for two blocks, right for one block on Capital Street to Main Street, then turn left for the brief walk to the center of the business district and waterfront.

Anchorage: You can anchor inside the jetty (allowing ample room for traffic in the marked channel to Stirling Basin), but this is a restless spot offering scant protection. Better anchorage is possible in Gull Pond, east of the breakwater. Two side creeks there offer possibilities for dinghy exploration.

GOIN' ASHORE: **GREENPORT, NY**

Shopping, boat restocking and dining are made easy in the village's clustered shops, a short walk away from the Main Street Wharf. Across Main Street from Claudio's famed restaurant (family-run since 1870 and well worth a visit for an elbow bend at Manuel Claudio's long and ornate antique bar), Preston's (102 Main St., 800-836-1165) has one of the most complete chandleries and nautical shops on all of Long Island Sound, as well as dockage for customers. A few doors away, White's Hardware (120 Main St., 631-477-0317) has a nautical orientation and a huge selection of specialty and working-marine items. The Book Scout (126 Main St., 631-477-8536) has an unusual collection of used books with concentrations in nautical, photography and art subjects, along with a large selection of LP jazz and blues records.

A couple of blocks farther along Main Street, the Cheese Emporium (208 Main St., 631-477-0023) offers cheeses, pates, specialty coffees, teas and other gourmet items. Claudio's Wines & Liquors (219 Main St., 631-477-1035) has what the name suggests. Also on Main Street, the Chase Bank has a 24-hour ATM out front. Half a block north of the Main Street Wharf, a left turn (west) on Front Street and a right on First Street quickly takes you to a large IGA grocery store (101 South St., 631-477-0101 at First Street). Across from the IGA, Triangle Sea Sales (36 South St., 631-477-1773) is something of a nautical museum store with everything from

Greenport, Southold and Shelter Island, NY

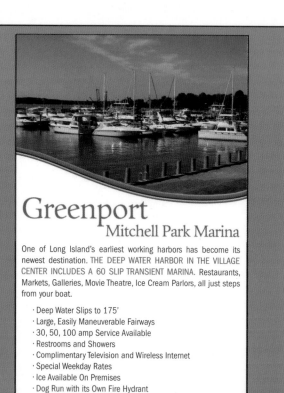

GREENPORT, SOUTHOLD, SHELTER ISLAND		Dockage					Supplies		Services					
		Largest Vessel Accommodated	VHF Channel Monitored	Transient Berths / Total Berths	Approach / Dockside Depth (reported)	Floating Docks	Gas / Diesel	Groceries, Ice, Marine Supplies, Snacks	Repairs: Hull, Engine, Propeller	Lift (tonnage), Crane, Rail	1=110V, 2=220V, B=Both, Max Amps	Laundry, Pool, Showers	Pump-Out Station	Nearby: Grocery Store, Motel, Restaurant
1. Orient by the Sea Restaurant & Marina	631-323-2424	50	09	10/90	6/10	F	GD	IM	E		B/100	S		R
2. Townsend Manor Marina	**631-477-2000**	**55**	**09**	**50/50**	**8/7**	**F**	**G**	**I**			**1/50**	**LPS**		**GMR**
3. Triangle Sea Sales	631-477-1773			MARINE PARTS										GMR
4. Brewer Stirling Harbor Marina 💻 WiFi	**631-477-0828**	**120**	**09**	**6/190**	**12/10**	**F**	**GD**	**I**	**HEP**	**L50**	**B/50**	**LPS**	**P**	**GMR**
5. Brewer Yacht Yard at Greenport 💻 WiFi	**631-477-9594**	**55**	**09**	**10/192**	**7/7**	**F**		**IM**	**HEP**	**L70**	**B/50**	**LPS**	**P**	**GMR**
6. Greenport Yacht and Ship Co.	631-477-2277	120		6/6	20/12				E		1/30			GMR
7. S.T. Preston and Son	631-477-1990	65		10/10	20/8			M						GMR
8. Claudio's Marina, Restaurant and Clam Bar WiFi	631-477-0355	200	16	35/35	45/15		GD	GIMS	HEP	LR	B/100	LS	P	GMR
9. Greenport Mitchell Park Marina WiFi	**631-477-2200**	**250**	**11**	**61/61**	**45/20**	**F**		**I**			**B/100**	**S**	**P**	**GMR**
10. Brick Cove Marina WiFi	631-477-0830	55	16	30/138	6/6	F		IMS	HEP	L30	B/50	LPS	P	R
11. Goldsmith's Boat Shop	631-765-1600	32	09/68	/109	3/5	F	G	M			1/30			R
12. Port of Egypt Marine	631-765-2445	35	68	/150	5/5	F	GD	IMS	HP	L25	1/30	LPS	P	GMR
13. The Pridwin Hotel	631-749-0476	50	04	5/10	5/						1/30	LPS		MR
14. Shelter Island Yacht Club	631-749-0888	75	71		10/7	F		I			1/15	S		GMR
15. Jack's Marine	631-749-0114	60	09	MOORINGS	10/8	F	GD	GIM					P	GMR
16. Dering Harbor Marina	631-749-0045	185	07/09	30/45	12/12	F	GD	GIMS			B/100	S	P	GMR
17. Coecles Harbor Marina and Boatyard	631-749-0700	60	09	25/40	6/6	F	GD	IM	HP	L	1/30	LPS	P	GMR
18. Ram's Head Inn	631-749-0811			MOORINGS	10/6									MR
19. The Island Boatyard and Marina	631-749-3333	60	09/68	35/77	6/6	F	GD	GIMS	HEP	L25	B/50	LPS	P	GMR

Corresponding chart(s) not to be used for navigation. 💻 Internet Access WiFi Wireless Internet Access

antique shroud lines, ship's telegraphs and old nets to modern nautical lamps and new lobster pots.

The post office (131 Front St., 631-477-1493) and Village Cinema Greenport (with four theaters showing first-run movies, 211 E. Front St., 631-477-8600) are farther west on Front Street. Turn toward the water on Third Street to reach the Shelter Island Ferry Terminal and the East End Seaport Marine Museum (in the old train station, 631-477-2100) open May through December, Friday through Sunday, 1 p.m. to 6 p.m.). Ferries run from Greenport to New London, CT; taxi service is available to Orient Point and train and bus service are available to most of Long Island and New York City. Cruisers with children, or childlike cruisers, cannot miss the 1920s carousel in Mitchell Park.

Many restaurants are available in Greenport, including the Chowder Pot Pub (104 Third St., 631-477-1345) for fresh seafood in a casual, neighborhood setting; the Hellenic Snack Bar & Restaurant (5145 Main Road, East Marion, 631-477-0138 9577) for Greek cuisine and indoor/outdoor dining; and The Loft (48 Front St., 631-477-3080). Townsend Manor Inn (714 Main St., 631-477-2000) is an upscale choice with a varied menu emphasizing seafood and an active bar. Salamander Bakery and General Store (414 First St., 631-477-3711) offers gourmet foods to go.

NEARBY GOLF COURSES:

Islands End Golf and Country Club, Route 25, Greenport, NY 11944, 631-477-0777

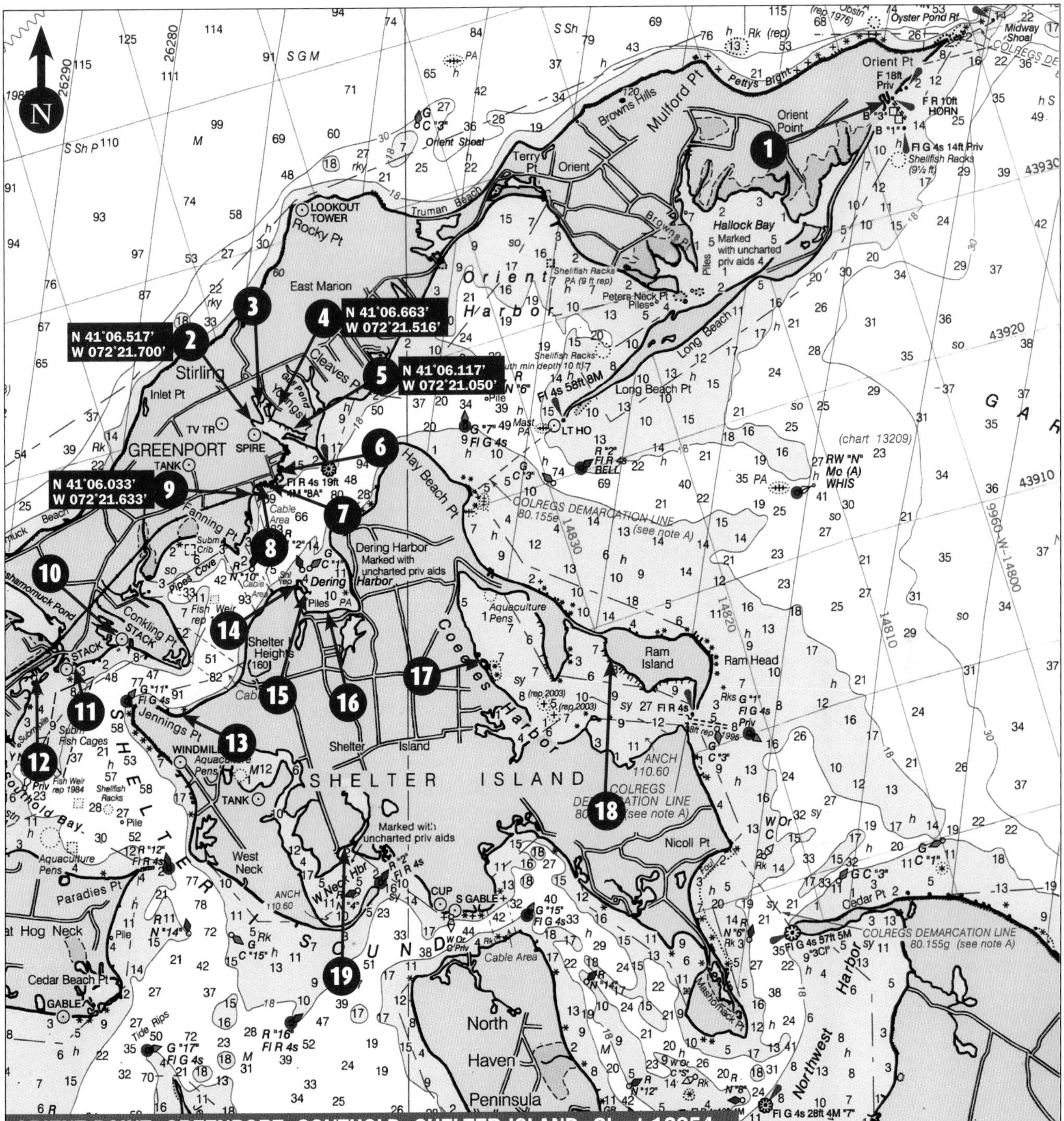

ORIENT POINT, GREENPORT, SOUTHOLD, SHELTER ISLAND, Chart 12354

NEARBY MEDICAL FACILITIES:
Eastern Long Island Hospital, 201 Manor Place, Greenport, NY 11944, 631-477-1000

Southold Bay

Directly west of Shelter Island, Southold Bay has a small harbor and an attractive village. Mill Creek is the entrance to Hashamomuck Pond and has a few marinas that welcome cruising boats. Southold itself is west of Mill Creek and is a pleasant place to visit in a shoal-draft craft.

Shelter Island

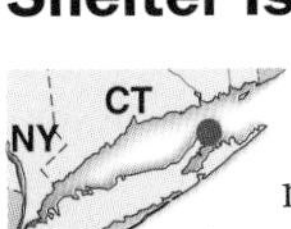

Known as the jewel of the Fishtail, Shelter Island becomes crowded during the summer months as the island's many harbors offer a selection of destinations that cater to every delight.

Take in the tranquil setting of Smith Cove and Majors Harbor or head into Dering Harbor, West Neck Harbor or Coecles Harbor and their numerous marinas.

Two ferries connect Shelter Island with the mainland. One goes to Greenport on the North Fork; the other goes to North Haven Peninsula and Sag Harbor on the South Fork. Shelter Island is an elegant summer enclave whose distinctive, diverse harbors and shady byroads cry out for exploration. About four miles long by five miles wide, with rolling, wooded terrain, sheltered beaches, attractive homes and serpentine roads, the island is entirely surrounded by well-marked channels. The shoreline has protected harbors on all sides, and you can circumnavigate the island in a few hours, with a lunch stop at either Smith Cove or Majors Harbor. Just watch for charted shoals close inshore, especially near Ram Head and Hay Beach Point.

Note: The town discourages the off-loading of trash on the island. Bottles, cans and paper must be separated for acceptance at each harbor's recycling center; otherwise, non-recyclable trash must be placed in Town of Shelter Island disposal bags available for purchase at each center.

Dering Harbor

Cruising counterclockwise from Greenport will bring you to Dering Harbor, where a mooring in the shadow of Shelter Island Heights offers a peaceful contrast to the bustle of Greenport, a mile north across the channel.

NAVIGATION: Use Charts 12358 and 13209. Entry is straightforward with 8- to 14-foot depths into the center of the harbor opening, favoring Dering Point to the northeast to avoid shoals extending from the south side of the entrance. The charted "Disposal Area" (long-ago-discarded oyster shells) presents no hazard to navigation.

Dockage: The Shelter Island Yacht Club makes its moorings available to members of clubs on the reciprocal list for a facilities fee, which covers launch service to its classic 19th-century facility and use of the club's dining room, bar and showers. There is also recycling pickup here. Piccozzi's Dering Harbor Marina at the head of the harbor has a limited number of rental moorings and dock space. Piccozzi's accepts recyclable trash in the official Shelter Island garbage disposal bags, rents bicycles, sells all fuels (including propane), and has a coin-operated laundry and game room. The town dock next to Piccozzi's permits a complimentary two-hour tie-up. During the summer, Dering Harbor is popular, so it is best to call ahead to reserve a mooring or slip now that anchorage space is so limited.

Anchorage: The mooring field occupies virtually all of the harbor's anchorage space, though a small boat might find a spot at the east end of the cove. Although Dering Harbor is open to the north, it is a good place for a secure mooring when the wind is up from any other direction.

West Neck Harbor

NAVIGATION: Use Charts 12358 and 13209. West Neck Harbor, a favorite among cruisers with local knowledge of the entrance, is scenic and well-protected with good holding in a muddy bottom. Across Shelter Island Sound from Gleason Point on the North Haven Peninsula, the entry between the bar at the end of Shell Beach and flashing red buoy "2" is daunting on review of the chart and appears challenging at first on-site observation. Yet the water is deep here, even at low tide, allowing reliable access to knowledgeable skippers of large boats with drafts of 5 feet and more. At low tide, the deep channel is located midway between the end of the Shell Beach bar and the nun; at high tide, favor flashing red buoy "2" slightly. Thereafter, your chart displays the correct path, hugging the contour at about 100 yards off the north side of Shell Beach with an eye to the depth sounder for chart-matching numbers. Avoid straying to starboard. It is best to pick a rising tide for a first attempt, but the serenity beyond is well worth a little anxiety at the entrance.

Dockage: The unobtrusive Island Boatyard offers transient slips, repairs, a dockside deli, tavern, showers and laundry machines, a game room, trash disposal, a pool and use of a van for access to restaurants and shopping. Simply follow the dredged, well-marked channel (6-foot depths at mean low water) to the fuel dock. The Island Café (63 S. Menantic Road, 631-749-3355, with a full range of entrees and a long dessert menu) and Shipwreck Bar are on the premises.

Anchorage: Non-residents are limited to a 48-hour stay, and they must anchor in the southern end of the harbor in the area designated by several anchoring buoys. There has been shoaling along the channel to West Neck Bay and, therefore, depths of somewhat less than those indicated on the chart can be expected.

Smith Cove and Majors Harbor

These two unspoiled coves on the southern shore of Shelter Island are pretty, quiet and easy to enter, with high green banks, good beaches, clean water, ample depths and good protection except in southerly winds. Smith Cove, the westernmost of the two, is also larger and deeper. It offers good anchorage close to a long stretch of undeveloped beach (open to the south) and is reported to have good fishing. The western end of the cove serves as the ferry landing to North Haven and Sag Harbor. With strong current and opposing wind, the passage from West Neck Harbor to Smith Cove can be bouncy.

Majors Harbor, to the southeast, is an attractive bight with no services and no landing available ashore. On entering, give Majors Point and its off-lying rocks a clear berth.

Coecles Harbor

The entrance to Coecles (pronounced "cockels") Harbor is located on the eastern shore of Shelter Island about six miles southwest of Orient Point. This large, tree-lined harbor offers an idyllic, Maine-like setting, excellent anchorage, a traditional full-service marina and a choice of well-regarded restaurants. It is also a delightful spot to find tiny yellow and orange coecles shells, which appear almost transparent in the sunlight.

NAVIGATION: Use Charts 12358 and 13209. Coecles Harbor is accessible through a privately marked channel just south of Ram Island. Best approach depths will be found at about 30 yards off flashing green buoy "1" and green can "3," which are followed by green can buoy "5" to port. Boats drawing 6 feet or more will want to wait for a rising tide (3-foot tidal range) before attempting an entry. Dredging has widened the opening between Reel Point (flashing red four-second light) and Sungic Point (green can buoy "5").

Dockage: Coecles Harbor Marina and Boatyard, at the west end of the harbor, may be easily reached on any tide by vessels with drafts less than 5 feet. The only significant shallow spot consists of a narrow 5-foot-deep mud "hump" extending southwest of red nun buoy "10" off Little Ram Island. Otherwise, the center harbor areas carry 6- to 8-foot depths with substantially better depths at high tide. The marina maintains 50 moorings with 7-foot depths at low tide, about half of which are available to visitors.

Anchorage: The designated anchorage in Coecles Harbor is just to port after entry and is clearly marked by orange and white markers. Be sure to turn to port well before reaching green can buoy "7" and the rocks that lie just beyond that buoy. This area is a designated No-Discharge Zone and, from May 15 to Sept. 15, anchorage is limited to a 48-hour stay, with a posted $250 fine and towing fees assessed against violators. This protects local shell fishing, which is available to anyone who secures a town permit. The rustic surroundings in the anchorage are a part of the Mashomack Nature Conservancy, which takes up one-fourth to one-third of the island. You can dinghy to the stone beach here, but signs warn against walking above the waterline to protect nesting terns and gulls. For a small fee, Coecles Harbor Marina offers use of its dinghy dock and facilities to those anchored out.

GOIN' ASHORE: SHELTER ISLAND, NY

Experience a little slice of small-town New England in the midst of Shelter Island's charm. The island can be circumnavigated by boat or dinghy and one can enjoy the many picturesque harbors, with their mix of classic working boats and beautiful yachts. Settled in 1638, Shelter Island came by its name either through a free translation of an Indian name meaning "island protected by islands," or because it was a shelter for persecuted Quakers.

The Havens House (16 S. Ferry Road, 631-749-0025), is where the island's history comes to life. The mainstay industries of Shelter Island are tourism, boatbuilding and fishing. At the Burns Road Landing is the beginning of the 12-station Coecles Harbor Marine Trail. You can rent kayaks from Shelter Island Kayak Tours (71 N. Cartwright Road, 631-749-1990) or head out by dinghy. Rent a bike from Coecles Harbor Marina (631-749-0700) and enjoy the Nature Conservancy's Mashomack Preserve (47 S. Ferry Road, 631-749-1001) and its many miles of interconnected trails. The preserve has 2,100 acres of natural habitat and hosts many events throughout the year. Four well-marked trails range from 1.5 to 11 miles long. The visitor's center has maps, programs and guided hikes available. It is open Wednesday to Monday from 9 a.m. to 5 p.m. (April through September). The nearby Vine Street Café (41 S. Ferry Road, 631-749-3210) features indoor and deck dining.

Along with a number of Hinckleys and other fine yachts maintained at Coecles Harbor Marina year-round, the 38-foot Shelter Island Runabout is built here. Conceived by singer/songwriter Billy Joel, this yacht combines modern construction techniques with classic styling to produce a distinctive yacht capable of quick commutes to New York City or daytrips to favorite destinations. The company welcomes visitors to tour the shops where the boats are built. At the ship's store, you can review the menus of local restaurants and arrange for courtesy transportation.

A dinghy trip to the docks or landing south of the narrow neck of land between Little Ram Island and Ram Island will put you within a block's walk of the Ram's Head Inn (108 Ram Island Drive, 631-749-0811), famous for superb and romantic dining in a formal setting.

Dering Harbor is the choice for shopping. George's IGA supermarket (75 N. Ferry Road, 631-749-0382) and The Island Food Center (184 N. Ferry Road, 631-749-3358) are adequate for provisioning. Ferry Road is the "downtown" of Shelter Island's commercial activity, where you will find Jack's True Value hardware store (188 N. Ferry Road, 631-749-0114) , Bliss' Department Store, and, farther down the road, Harbor Gallery (184 N. Ferry Road, 631-749-2694). The comfortable-looking Dory Restaurant (185 N. Ferry Road, 631-749-4300) specializes in home-cooked American fare and offers jazz on Thursdays and rock 'n' roll on Saturdays all summer long. For more upscale dining with seaside Victorian charm, try the Chequit Inn at 23 Grand Avenue (631-749-0018). Another highly recommended restaurant is Sweet Tomato (15 Grand Ave., 631-749-4114) for its Italian and Continental cuisine. The Capital One Bank (631-749-1300) has a convenient ATM at 29 West Neck Road.

In Dering Harbor bike rentals are available from Piccozzi's (631-749-0045) for exploring the Mashomack Preserve. For taxi service on Shelter Island, call 631-749-4252.

ADDITIONAL RESOURCES:

- Shelter Island, **www.shelter-island.org**

NEARBY GOLF COURSES:

Shelter Island Country Club, 26 Sunnyside Ave.,
Shelter Isle Hts, NY 11965, 631-749-0416

NEARBY MEDICAL FACILITIES:

Dr. Peter A. Kelt, 141 S. Ferry Road,
Shelter Island, NY 11964, 631-749-3149

Noyack Bay

East of North Haven Peninsula, this quiet bay has accommodations for shallower-draft boats, and a few stores and restaurants are within walking distance of the harbor. Noyack Bay is inexpensive in contrast to many surrounding areas. Just outside the bay, fishing is good in the rips off high, needle-sharp Jessup Neck. The neck itself is part of a nature preserve with paths and picnic tables.

Jessup Neck Basin, in the southwestern corner of the bay, is just barely navigable because of shallow depths. Boats do moor here, however, and it is quiet since the nature preserve almost surrounds it.

Dockage: Mill Creek, on the south shore, is a snug harbor with dockage and limited anchoring. The Inn at Mill

Creek (3253 Noyac Road, 631-725-1116), with its Oasis restaurant and fish market (631-725-7110), offers some slips (4-foot depths). The town dock has an enforced two-hour tie-up limit. It is no more than a quarter mile walk to the Noyac Deli (3348 Noyac Road, 631-899-3749), Noyack Liquors liquor store (3354 Noyac Road, 631 725-0330), Cappelletti Italian Grill (3284 Noyac Road, 631-725-7800) and Giordano's Ristorante Italiano (3360 Noyac Road, 631-725-4444). The marinas are also an easy walk to Trout Pond, which is excellent for freshwater swimming.

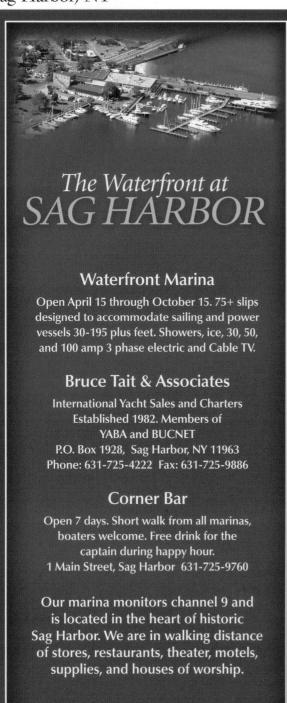

Sag Harbor

Sag Harbor is one of the major cruising ports on eastern Long Island. Two important harbors provide extensive services for most any need. The town is close to both harbors and is brimming with shops, Colonial houses, restaurants and monuments to Sag Harbor's history as a whaling port.

NAVIGATION: Use Charts 12358 and 13209. Use New London tide tables. For high tide, add 1 hour; for low tide, add 48 minutes. Sag Harbor is about 10 miles south of Plum Gut, 12 miles northeast of Shinnecock Canal and is easily approached from the east or west. A long breakwater extends most of the width of the harbor, but it is easy to enter the deep channel between the western end and North Haven. If you are approaching Sag Harbor from the east, to avoid a large rock field, do not cut any of the buoys. Make sure you pass very close to, or west of, green-and-red can "SH." Every year, a good number of boats pile up on the rocks, some with serious damage.

Heading east from Sag Harbor, stick to the well-marked channel, favor the Shelter Island side, and stay north of the numerous rocks marked by flashing green buoy "11." Sand Spit is a large shoal partly bare at half-tide north of the channel and marked by a small tower. To the north, Mashomack Point, a famous osprey rookery, is a popular spot for bird-watchers.

Dockage: Inside the Sag Harbor breakwater, you will find several possibilities for transient slips. The numerous town moorings are no longer available as transient rentals. At the eastern end of the harbor, Sag Harbor Yacht Yard is primarily a working yard, yet may have a rental slip available.

The Sag Harbor Yacht Club, immediately west (no club affiliation required), offers slips to transients; advance reservations are recommended, especially for peak weekends. The Yacht Club offers many amenities including a health club, a picnic area with gas grills, car rentals and flight services, bike rentals and catering services. Next door, the Waterfront at Sag Harbor offers transient dockage, clean showers and 100-amp shoreside power. Long or short-term tie-ups may also be possible at the village wharf. Call the harbormaster (7 Bay St.) on VHF Channel 09 or (631-725-2368) for availability and directions.

The completely protected inner harbor, Sag Harbor Cove, lies just beyond the fixed bridge (21-foot fixed ver-

Noyack and Sag Harbor, NY

NOYACK AND SAG HARBOR		Largest Vessel Accommodated	VHF Channel Monitored	Transient Berths / Total Berths	Approach / Dockside Depth (reported)	Floating Docks	Gas / Diesel	Groceries, Ice, Marine Supplies, Snacks	Repairs: Hull, Engine, Propeller	Lift (tonnage), Crane, Rail	1=110V, 2=220V, B=Both, Max Amps	Laundry, Pool, Showers	Pump-Out Station	Nearby: Grocery Store, Motel, Restaurant
		Dockage					Supplies		Services					
1. Mill Creek Marina	631-725-1351	45		5/145	4/4	F	G	I	HP	L25	1/15	S	P	GR
2. Hidden Cove Marina Inc.	631-725-3333	40	09	/56	6/6	F	G	GIMS	HP		1/15			GMR
3. Sag Harbor Yacht Yard	631-725-3838	65	10	/25	13/12	F		IM	HEP	L35	B/50	S	P	GMR
4. Sag Harbor Yacht Club (Internet Access, Wireless Internet Access)	**631-725-0567**	**250**	**09**		**11/11**		**GD**	**IM**			**B/200**	**S**	**P**	**GMR**
5. The Waterfront at Sag Harbor (Wireless Internet Access)	**631-725-3886**	**195**	**09**	**15/75**	**10/12**	**F**		**I**			**B/100**	**S**		**GMR**
6. Sag Harbor Cove East	631-725-1605	85	09	20/80	8/7	F		I			1/50	LS		MR
7. Village of Sag Harbor Dock	631-725-2368	200	09	25/311	10/10	F					1/50	S	P	GMR
8. Ship Ashore Marina	631-725-3755	45	09	/45	5/5	F	G		HEP	L30	1/30	S	P	GMR
9. Sag Harbor Cove West (Wireless Internet Access)	631-725-3939	80	09	6/84	8/8	F	GD	I			B/50	LS	P	GMR

Corresponding chart(s) not to be used for navigation. Internet Access, Wireless Internet Access

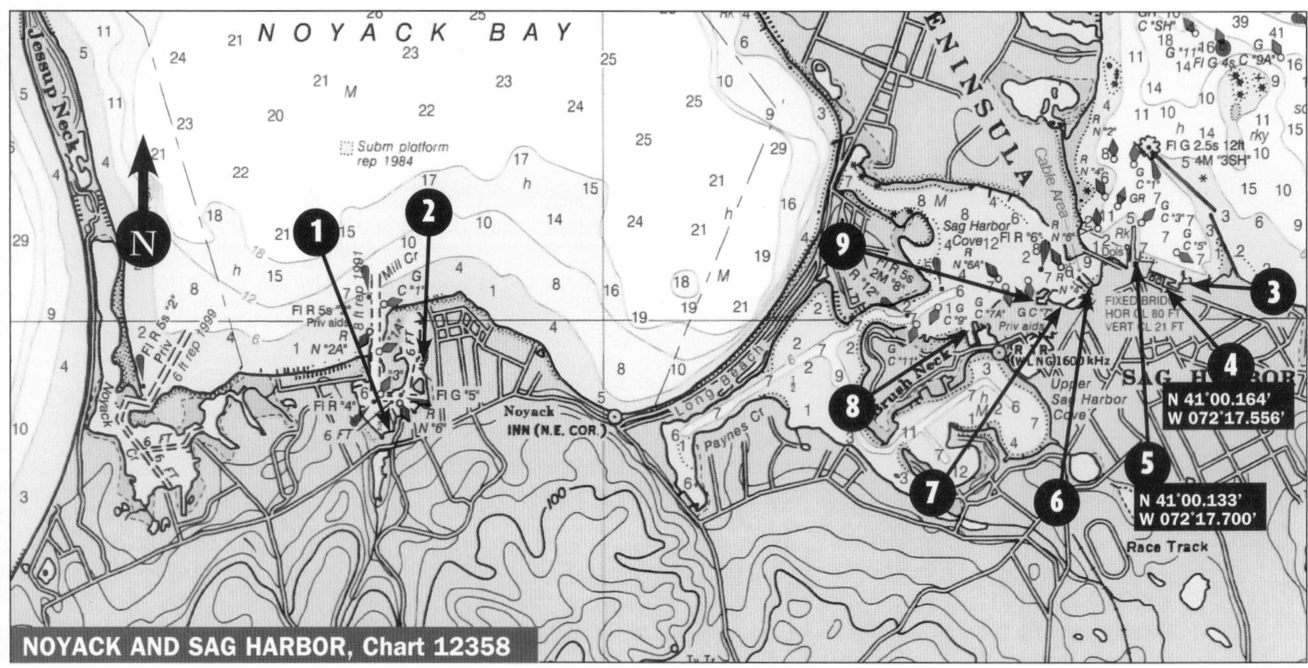

NOYACK AND SAG HARBOR, Chart 12358

tical clearance) to starboard of the entry channel. There is a $250 fine for sailing in the harbor if your boat has auxiliary power. Inside the cove, Sag Harbor Cove East and West marinas have various amenities and slip space for transients. Fuel is available at several of the marinas here. Overnight accommodations are directly across from the Sag Harbor Cove marinas.

Anchorage: In settled water, boats may be seen anchored in 10 to 15 feet of water outside the breakwater to the east, having threaded the shoals marked by flashing green buoy "11" and the green can "1" just west of the shoal's rocky outcrop. From here, you can dinghy into the town dinghy dock to visit the shopping and dining district.

Northwest Harbor, just south of Cedar Point, can make a fine anchorage on a summer's night. It offers peace and quiet, as long as the wind does not build out of the west. There are no amenities here, but the harbor affords a beautiful panorama across the water.

GOIN' ASHORE: SAG HARBOR, NY

Most of Sag Harbor is a National Historic Site. Its history centers heavily on its days as a whaling port, although it was inhabited well before Europeans settled here. In the mid-1800s, almost half the total population of Sag Harbor served on whaling ships. The Sag Harbor Whaling Museum (631-725-0770) at 200 Main St. in an 1845 Greek-revival mansion built for a whaling tycoon, displays exhibits and artifacts of whaling. When you arrive in Sag Harbor, check with the tourist information center, located in a windmill at the town dock, for complete details of local attractions.

One block from the docks in the harbor, along Main Street, you can find almost any type of reprovisioning, stores, shops and dining options. Within the restored-antique setting on Main Street, you can visit Schiavoni's IGA (48 Main St., 631-725-0366), with a wide selection of groceries, fresh meats, produce and deli specialties. Also on Main Street are Sag Harbor Liquor (52 Main St., 631-725-0054), the Sag Harbor Cinema (90

Looking southwest over Sag Harbor. (Not to be used for navigation.) WATERWAY GUIDE PHOTOGRAPHY

Main St., 631-725-0010) and Emporium Hardware. There are three bookstores along Main Street: Black Cat Books (78 Main St., 631-725-8654), Metaphysical Books and Tools (83 Main St., 631-725-9393) and Paradise Books (126 Main St., 631-725-1114). If you need Internet access, try the John Jermain town library, located at Main and Union streets. The post office (21 Long Island Ave., 631-725-8968), Sag Harbor Launderette (20 Main St., 631-725-5830), several banks with 24-hour ATMs and Provisions Natural Food Market and Café (7 Main St., 631-725-3636) are all within shouting distance of the waterfront. The Dock House (1 Long Wharf, 631-725-7555), on the town wharf just west of the outer harbor marinas, has the fresh catch at retail, a take-out raw bar and frozen seafood entrees. There's an ice cream parlor next door called Sag Harbor Ice Cream (Long Wharf, 631-725-5058) and another across the street, The Ice Cream Club (7 Main St., 631-725-2598).

Sag Harbor also has a wide assortment of restaurants, many within walking distance of the docks. Some of the restaurants in Sag Harbor include B. Smith's Restaurant (Long Wharf and Bay Street, 631-725-5858) for "eclectic cuisine" in a casual atmosphere with a great harbor view; Spinnaker's (63 Main Street, 631-725-9353) for lobster, seafood, pasta, steaks and vegetarian entrees; and Phao-Thai Kitchen (29 Main St., 631-725-0101). For old-fashioned elegance and award-winning cuisine in a memorable setting, try the historic American Hotel (49 Main Street, 631-725-3535). There's quite a bit going on in Sag Harbor at night along Main Street. The town swells with summer vacationers during the summer months and there is no lack of revelers. The wineries on the North Fork of Long Island have become numerous and have gained an outstanding reputation. Visit the Sag Harbor Chamber of Commerce for information and locations if a visit is in order.

ADDITIONAL RESOURCES:

■ Sag Harbor Village, **www.sagharborny.gov** or **www.sagharborchamber.com**

NEARBY GOLF COURSES:

Sag Harbor Golf Club, Golf Club Road, Sag Harbor, NY 11963, 631-725-2503

NEARBY MEDICAL FACILITIES:

Eastern Long Island Hospital, 201 Manor Place, Greenport, NY 11944, 631-477-1000

Three Mile Harbor

A big, heart-shaped body of protected water, with a pair of coves at its head, Three Mile Harbor is one of the most attractive cruising ports on the East Coast. The two-mile-long, scenic harbor has fine beaches, all manner of marine services, good anchorages and restaurants. It is the closest port to the summer resort of East Hampton (three miles from the head of the harbor, hence the name).

NAVIGATION: Use Chart 13209. For East Hampton, Three Mile Harbor entrance, use New London tide tables. For high tide, add 39 minutes; for low tide, add 19 minutes. Three Mile Harbor is 15 miles west of Montauk Point, eight

Looking north over Three Mile Harbor. (Not to be used for navigation.) WATERWAY GUIDE PHOTOGRAPHY

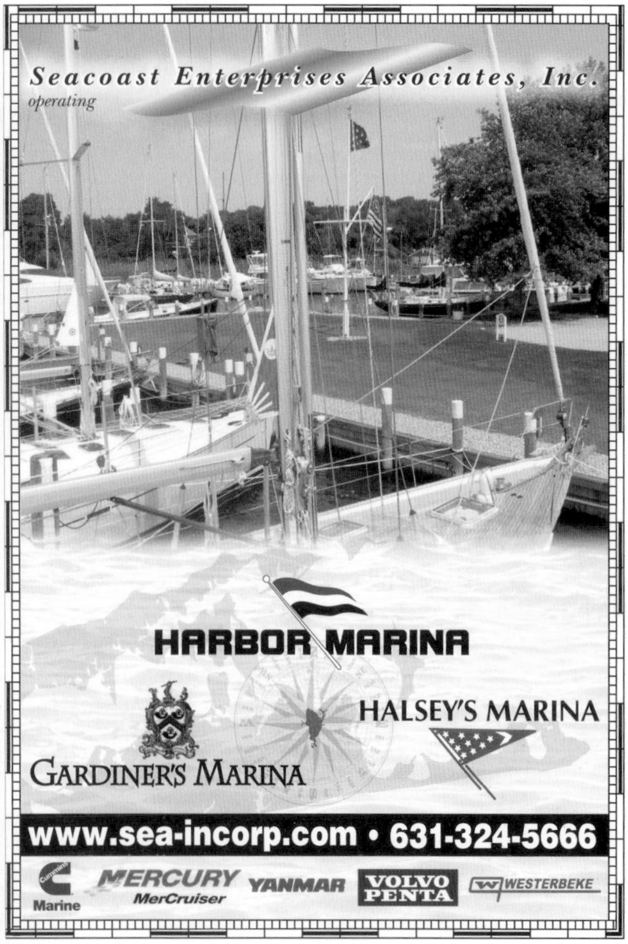

miles south of Plum Gut and six miles east of Sag Harbor. The narrow, shoal-edged entrance between Sammys Beach and Maidstone Park Beach is plainly announced by the red-and-white Morse (A) "TM" bell buoy and marked by green can "1" and red nun "2" at the beginning of the entrance channel. Note: Three Mile Harbor has been designated a No-Discharge Zone, making it illegal to dump even treated effluent into the harbor. Pump-out stations are located at Harbor Marina and East Hampton Point Marina.

Dockage: Docking and marine service opportunities are extensive along the eastern shore of Three Mile Harbor. Harbor Marina is first to port on entry; turn into the marina's channel immediately after the can buoy. Family owned and operated, Harbor Marina is a full-service yard, located in a quiet setting with its own private beach on Sedge Island. Access is easy to the marina's floating docks and fuel dock (depths of more than 6 feet at low water). Restrooms and showers are modern, and there is a well-stocked boating supply store with a parts department on the premises. Transients are welcome and space is usually available.

Above the marina store, Bostwick's Seafood Grill and Oyster Bar (631-324-1111) is popular with both Long Islanders and New York City weekenders for tasty presentations at moderate prices and wide-angle views of the harbor. At the municipal dock next door, you can buy fresh lobsters off the boat. About a mile farther along, Maidstone Harbor Marina usually has a few transient slips available in a quiet, well-protected setting.

Three Mile Harbor, NY

THREE MILE HARBOR		Largest Vessel Accommodated	VHF Channel Monitored	Transient Berths / Total Berths	Approach / Dockside Depth (reported)	Floating Docks	Gas / Diesel	Groceries, Ice, Marine Supplies, Snacks	Repairs: Hull, Engine, Propeller	Lift (tonnage), Crane, Rail	1=110V, 2=220V, B=Both, Max Amps	Laundry, Pool, Showers	Pump-Out Station	Nearby: Grocery Store, Motel, Restaurant
		Dockage					Supplies		Services					
1. Harbor Marina (Internet Access)	**631-324-5666**	**50**	**09**	**1/95**	**12/8**	**F**	**GD**	**GIMS**	**HEP**	**L15**	**1/50**	**S**	**P**	**GMR**
2. Maidstone Harbor Marina	631-324-2651	80			9/8			GIM			B/100	LPS	P	R
3. East Hampton Point Marina & Boatyard (Internet Access, Wireless Internet Access)	631-324-8400	89	09	10/55	8/7		GD	GIMS	HEP	L40,C	B/50	LPS	P	GMR
4. Shagwong Marina	631-324-4830	50	09	2/40	7/6	F		I			1/30	LPS	P	GMR
5. Halsey's Marina (Internet Access, Wireless Internet Access)	**631-324-5666**	**85**	**09**	**5/42**	**8/8**			**I**	**HEP**		**B/50**	**LS**		**GMR**
6. Gardiner's Marina (Internet Access, Wireless Internet Access)	**631-324-5666**	**100**	**09**	**6/45**	**9/6**	**F**		**I**	**HEP**		**B/50**	**LS**		**GMR**
7. East Hampton Town Dock	631-329-3078	36			8/6			GIM			1/15			R
8. 3 Mile Harbor Boatyard	**631-324-1320**	**60**		**/72**	**8/8**	**F**		**IM**	**HP**	**L40**	**B/50**			**R**
9. East Hampton Marina	631-324-4042	26			5/6		G	M	EP					R

Corresponding chart(s) not to be used for navigation. Internet Access — Wireless Internet Access

1 — N 41°01.803' W 072°11.323'

5 — N 41°00.316' W 072°10.883'

6 — N 41°00.114' W 072°10.922'

8 — N 40°58.000' W 072°11.000'

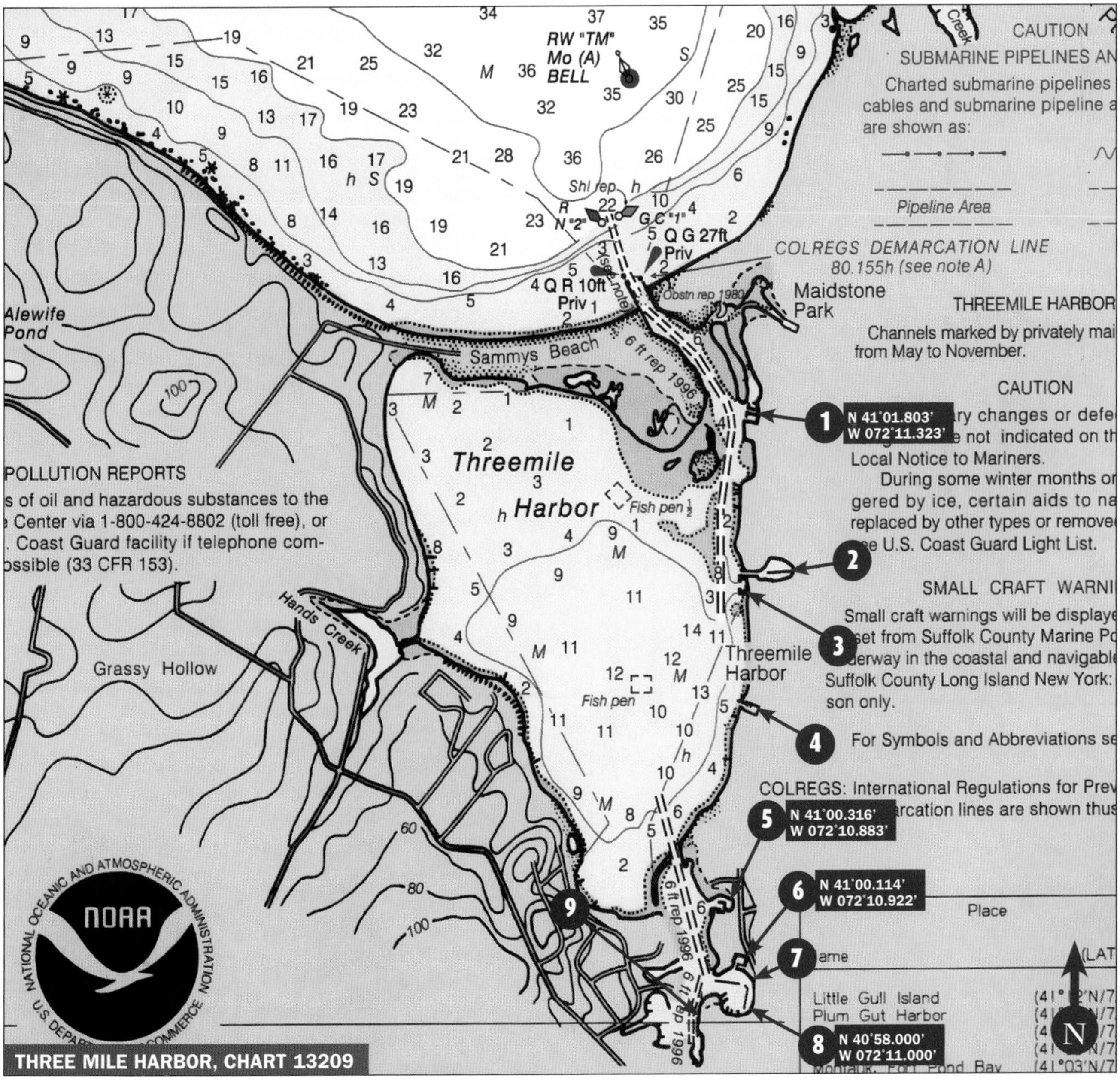

THREE MILE HARBOR, CHART 13209

East Hampton, NY

Next door to Maidstone Harbor Marina, East Hampton Point Marina and Boatyard operates a full-service boatyard (with a 40-ton lift) in a resort-style setting, which includes a tennis court, a pool, elegant changing rooms, showers and a laundry room; they also offer van service to town and the beaches. There are usually about a dozen slips (accommodating boats up to 95 feet) available to transients; call ahead for a reservation. East Hampton Point Marina also offers facilities passes for those anchored out or moored. These passes afford full use of the resort amenities, trash disposal and a place at the dinghy dock inside the protective barrier. The restaurant at East Hampton Point Restaurant (295 Three Mile Harbor Road, 631-329-2800) is housed in an attractive lighthouse-like structure, its centerpiece a classic, fully-rigged Olympic racing contender.

About a quarter mile farther south, the Shagwong Marina (now managed by East Hampton Point Marina) may have slips available in the marina's highly protective, man-made harbor surrounded by quiet, park-like grounds. Still farther south, first along the marked channel leading to the head of the harbor, Halsey's Marina has the presence of the small, highly exclusive yacht club it once was; there are usually a few vacant, well-protected slips available here. Amenities include excellent shower/restroom facilities, public phones, a laundry room, cable TV and broadband Internet access at most slips.

At the head of the harbor, Gardiner's Marina (now under the same ownership as Harbor Marina) has transient slips available in a protected, park-like setting.

Three Mile Harbor Boatyard (across the turning basin) has a long-standing reputation for excellent repair service, dockage and the most complete marine supply and parts store in the area. This location also provides the closest dockage to the Village of East Hampton (three miles distant).

Anchorage and Moorings: Inside the breakwater-protected entrance, the dredged channel runs between shores for a half mile before opening up to the vistas of a large and scenic harbor. The eastern shore is well-developed with marinas, boatyards, restaurants and fish docks. In contrast, the western side remains wild, rimmed with high green hills and dense forest along the shoreline, which occasionally parts to reveal the existence of a cloistered summer home. Marsh grass and sandy patches of beach are visible off to the north.

Although the number of private moorings has been increasing in the harbor recently, most of the south end of the harbor is still open for excellent anchorage options in 9- to 12-foot depths at low water. There is rarely a crowd, even on otherwise busy summer weekends.

On approaching the anchorage, be sure to honor the second red marker off (and fully past) the wood-barricaded docks of East Hampton Point Marina before turning to starboard. This will avoid a shallow but nearly invisible bar that extends along the west side of the channel. Holding is relatively good here in soft mud, but wave action can be significant when severe winds whip across the relatively modest protection of overgrown dunes to the north or south. The town's free pump-out service can be summoned on VHF Channel 73 ("Pump-out Boat").

For those desiring the security of a fixed mooring, the town has established six of them (marked "T") just inside the channel. Simply pick up a mooring pennant and await the harbormaster's launch (or pump-out boat) to collect the fee.

GOIN' ASHORE:
EAST HAMPTON, NY

Three miles from the head of Three Mile Harbor, the Village of East Hampton is surely Long Island's most precious and pricey summer retreat. A cab ride to town from the nearest marina costs about $10. (Call Midway Taxi 631-324-9111 or Lindy's Taxi 631-907-1111 for taxi service.) The Village of East Hampton, referred to as "America's Most Beautiful Village," is fairly unscathed by modern clutter; its trees, greens, windmills and the famous Town Pond are preserved as they were when the historic village was first settled by a group of farmers in 1648. Farming was the livelihood until the mid-1800s, when the town began to develop into a summer resort for the wealthy and art-oriented.

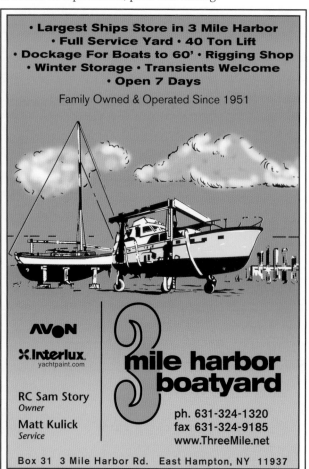

The Town Pond was once a watering hole for cattle but today it is an integral part of the East Hampton Historic District. Adjacent to the Town Pond is the South End Cemetery, which once formed the church yard for East Hampton's first meeting house. The cemetery contains tombstones dating back to the 17th century. The Village Green, or Common, originally stretched from Town Pond to Hook Mill Green and the track along its edge forms the Main Street of East Hampton today. The Hook Windmill was built by Nathaniel Doming IV in 1806. It incorporates the original main post of the 1736 Hook Mill. This picturesque mill, located at the north end of Main Street, is kept in working order by the Village of East Hampton. It is a marvel of wood technology and is open to the public for tours during the summer months for a small fee.

The Guild Hall (158 Main St., 631-324-0806) is an outstanding art museum and well-respected theatrical house. The building contains the famous John Drew Theater, three art galleries, the museum's art collection and gardens. It receives more than 80,000 visitors each year.

East Hampton has virtually anything you could possibly want: a grocery store, two pharmacies, a hardware store, a superb bookstore, numerous high-end kitchen and home-decor shops, multiple antiques shops and various banks. A distinguishing characteristic of East Hampton is its unique collection of boutiques, running from the individualistic to the bizarre, each seemingly in search of new plateaus in style. With over 80 dining establishments in East Hampton, diners may choose anything from a casual pub with al fresco dining to an elegant restaurant. A trip to East Hampton would not be complete without a visit to Dreesen's Market (33 Newtown Lane, 631-324-0465), home of Long Island's most famous doughnuts, where they sell In excess of 400,000 of the sweet treats per year. Their doughnut machine in the front window cranks out hot, fresh doughnuts before your eyes.

There are several restaurants around the harbor, while others will require a taxi. A few of the restaurants on Three Mile Harbor include: Michael's at Maidstone Park (28 Maidstone Park Road, 631-324-0725), offering an American menu; The Maidstone Market and Deli (514 Three Mile Harbor Road, 631-329-2830), open for long hours in the summer with homemade soups and fresh breads; Bostwicks Restaurant (423 Three Mile Road, 631-324-1111) and East Hampton Point Restaurant (295 Three Mile Harbor Road, 631-329-2800), for elegant dining.

ADDITIONAL RESOURCES:

- Hamptons Online, **www.hamptons.com** or **www.easthampton.com**

NEARBY GOLF COURSES:

Montauk Downs State Park, South Fairview Avenue, Montauk, NY 11954, 631-668-1100

NEARBY MEDICAL FACILITIES:

Southhampton Hospital, 240 Meeting House Lane, Southampton, NY 11968, 631-726-8200
www.southamptonhospital.org

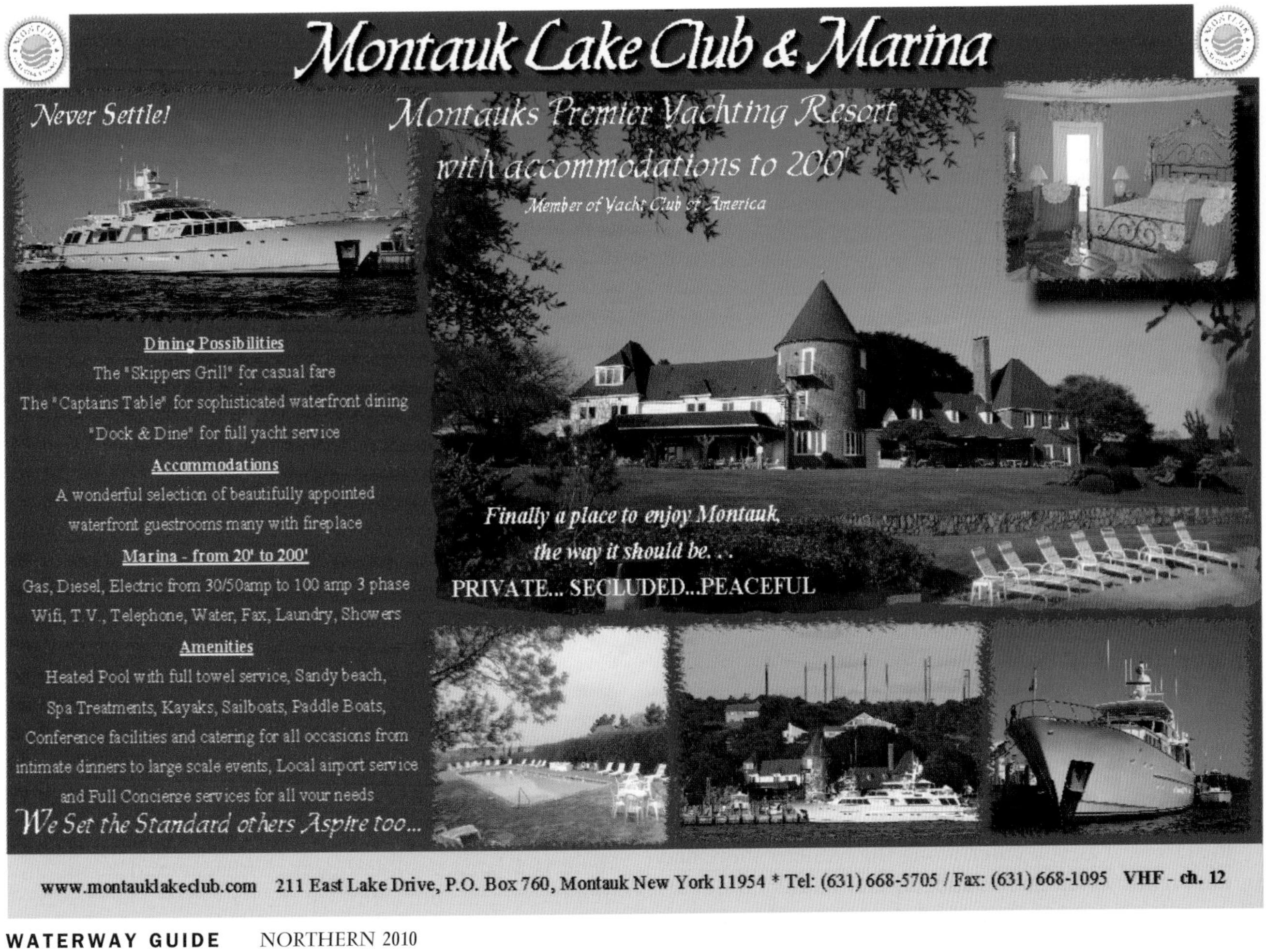

Route to Montauk

NAVIGATION: Use Chart 13209. For Montauk Harbor entrance, use New London tide tables. For high tide, subtract 24 minutes; for low tide, subtract 16 minutes. From Three Mile Harbor, the route curves around Hog Creek Point, southwest of Gardiners Island, past Acabonack Harbor, Napeague Harbor, Fort Pond Bay, Lake Montauk and on to Montauk Point itself. Harbors along the route tend to be shoal, wild and interesting, but safer for dinghy exploration (in good weather) than for anchorages. Dredged Acabonack Harbor silts in easily; Devon Yacht Club Basin, in the southwest corner of Napeague Bay, offers emergency shelter, but the yacht club does not welcome transients; dredged Napeague Harbor is protected but prone to shoaling.

Montauk

Until the mid-1920s, the eastern tip of Long Island was far better known for its cattle ranching and quiet freshwater fishing on Lake Wyandannee (now Lake Montauk) than for its present-day repute as a land's end tourist mecca and saltwater angler's paradise. Then in 1926, visionary developer Carl Graham Fisher blasted through the narrow spit separating the shallow lake from Long Island Sound, the beginning realization of grandiose plans to make Montauk the "Miami Beach of the North." Complete with an imposing "Manor House" hotel, Tudor mansions overlooking the lake and Fisher's "skyscraper" (still fully functional in the village), the idea was to transform the East End's windswept landscape into a polished summer yachting and fishing resort. Though the dream was stalled and interrupted by the Great Depression, storms and war, Fisher's fundamental concept has more than succeeded.

Montauk is famous for tuna, marlin, swordfish and shark fishing in its offshore waters, and for outstanding sportfishing and yachting facilities ashore. The surf around Montauk Point serves as one of the East Coast's premier striped bass fisheries, and the area has become a hotbed of saltwater fly-fishing.

Excellent marinas cater to sportfishermen and cruisers of all descriptions. The place buzzes with activity during the summer, yet it is easy to escape to a quiet spot with a near-empty seascape. The beaches are superb, both on the Block Island Sound side and Atlantic Ocean side. There is a dude ranch where you can hire horses to gallop the strands at either of two huge state parks; Montauk Downs has excellent golfing; the classic Montauk Lighthouse beckons; and the picturesque nearby village has all the necessary amenities.

NAVIGATION: Use Chart 13209. Enter Montauk Harbor, in the northern part of Lake Montauk, via a channel protected by lighted jetties. Favor the western jetty, allow for the 2.5-knot current, and keep clear of off-channel rocks inside the breakwaters. The current chart indicates 12-foot depths.

To starboard as you enter, along the western shore and in the bight west of Star Island, are Montauk's headquarters for charter, head and excursion boats to Block Island and Mystic Seaport. To port, the well-marked channel takes you to Lake Montauk and several opportunities for dockage and other facilities in less hectic surroundings.

From Montauk Point, east or south, you are in the open Atlantic Ocean, and your vessel should be prepared for open ocean and changes in the weather. Rips make up off the point near Endeavor Shoal. Unexpected fog also is something to be reckoned with. On Block Island Sound, the famous long swells can put you to sleep, but in a blow they can be challenging. Know your weather as thoroughly as possible before starting to or from Montauk.

Dockage: As you bear east of Star Island, past the large, red-roofed Coast Guard station, the 232-slip facility of the Montauk Yacht Club Resort & Marina comes immediately into view. The marina has recently been refurbished, with a new boardwalk, railings and piers. Yachting Magazine recently named this marina one of the top 10 yachting destinations in North America. Virtually every possible amenity is available, including indoor and outdoor pools, modern restrooms, showers and saunas, a fitness center and tennis courts. There is even a concierge to facilitate restaurant, horseback riding and golf reservations, or to make arrangements for guests who wish to stay ashore in the resort's rooms or villas. FedEx shipments are picked up at 1 p.m., and fax machines are continually available. Breezes Cafe (631-668-3100), at poolside, offers both inside and outside dining. Inside is a large, more formal restaurant, Gulf Coast Kitchen, with an expansive circular bar, Turtle Lounge in the base of the resort's lighthouse.

Dockage reservations are necessary at the marina on major weekends; otherwise, transient space is usually available. Across the channel from the resort, Gone Fishing Marina is a full-service operation with a 25-ton lift, complete repair facilities and tackle for sportfishing. From here, it is a significant ride by dinghy or car to either the inner harbor or village, but a restaurant and bar are on-site, and delightful Gin Beach (memorializing Prohibition days) is only a short walk to the north with water that is a little warmer than the ocean. This is the only beach with a roped off protected swim area. Lifeguards are on duty 10 a.m. to 5 p.m. daily during the summer season.

For those desiring a really quiet location on the lake, the choice will be Montauk Lake Club and Marina. Transient space is available at their floating docks, and both gas and diesel fuel are available. On-site, there is a pool, laundry and clean restrooms and showers.

Montauk Harbor (turn to starboard on entering the channel) is crowded and active. On the west side of Star Island, the Star Island Yacht Club & Marina is a "hardcore" fishing center—with virtually all boats sprouting outriggers next to their floating docks. Major fishing tournaments regularly run from here; services, equipment and baits for saltwater anglers are complete. A full-service repair and parts center can handle jobs up to the capacity of its 70-ton lift. For lay days or non-fishing crewmembers, there is a large pool and deck, barbecue and picnic area and the largest ship's store on the East End. The Star Deck

Montauk, NY

MONTAUK		Largest Vessel Accommodated	VHF Channel Monitored	Transient Berths / Total Berths	Approach / Dockside Depth (reported)	Floating Docks	Gas / Diesel	Groceries, Ice, Marine Supplies, Snacks	Repairs: Hull, Engine, Propeller	Lift (tonnage), Crane, Rail	1=110V, 2=220V, B=Both, Max Amps	Laundry, Pool, Showers	Pump-Out Station	Nearby: Grocery Store, Motel, Restaurant
		Dockage					Supplies		Services					
1. Uihlein Marina and Boat Rentals	631-668-3799	50	14	5/18	9/9	F	G	GIMS	HEP	L	1/30	S		MR
2. Montauk Marine Basin (WiFi)	631-668-5900/7500	100	19	75/200	7/8		GD	GIMS	HEP	L	B/50	LS		MR
3. Diamond Cove Marina	631-668-6592	50	19	18/80	6/6	F	GD	GIM	HP	L	B/50	S		GMR
4. Westlake Fishing Lodge and Marina	631-668-5600	55	19	15/99	5/3			IM	HEP		1/30	S		MR
5. Snug Harbor Marina	631-668-2860	50	09	25/80	6/6	F					1/30	LPS		MR
6. Star Island Yacht Club and Marina	**631-668-5052**	**140**	**09**	**75/150**	**10/6**	**F**	**GD**	**GIMS**	**HEP**	**L70**	**B/100**	**LPS**	**P**	**GMR**
7. Gone Fishing Marina	631-668-3232	50	19	30/150	6/6		GD	GIMS	HP	L	1/30	LS	P	GMR
8. Montauk Yacht Club Resort & Marina (WiFi)	**631-668-3100**	**200**	**09**	**124/232**	**7/12**			**GIMS**			**B/100**	**LPS**		**GMR**
9. Montauk Lake Club and Marina (Internet) (WiFi)	**631-668-5705**	**200**	**12**	**20/104**	**9/9**	**F**	**GD**	**IS**			**B/100**	**LPS**		**MR**

Corresponding chart(s) not to be used for navigation. ▭ Internet Access (WiFi) Wireless Internet Access

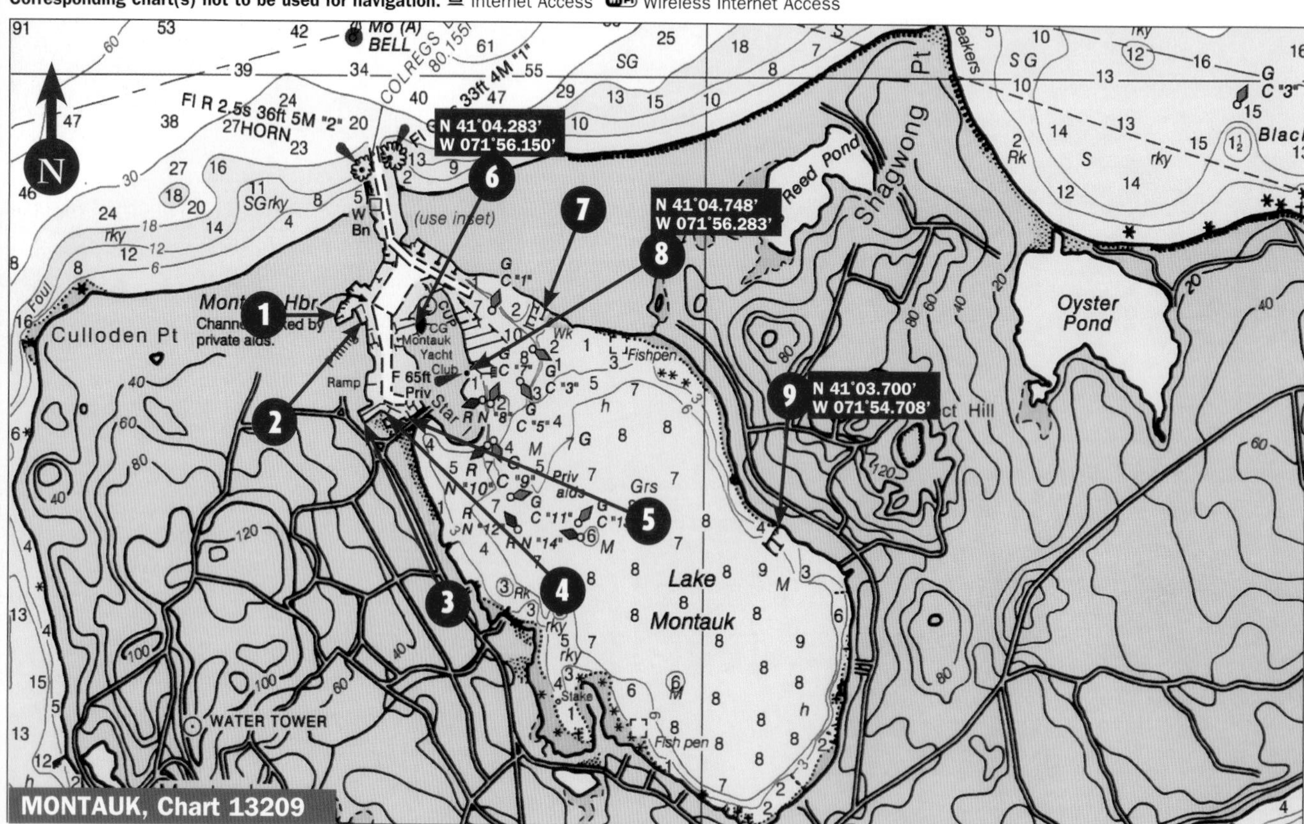

MONTAUK, Chart 13209

Grill on premises serves three meals a day, 8 a.m. to midnight.

Dockage on the west side of the inner harbor is within easy walking distance of urban-style amenities and the Gosman's Dock Complex (500 W. Lake Drive) of restaurants and shops. The first major facility is Montauk Marine Basin, a hard-working yard with lift capabilities of up to 80 tons, certified mechanics and an impressive range of engines and equipment, including a large inventory of marine supplies. Montauk Marine Basin has floating-dock slips with complete hook-ups for transients.

At the head of the harbor, Westlake Fishing Lodge & Marina usually has a few slips for transients in a laid-back but well-organized facility. The rustic Fish Tales Galley (631-668-4875) is oriented toward serious fishermen. Breakfast begins at 4 a.m.; box lunches to go are for the ordering; and dinners run to straightforward seafood, steaks and chops. Next door, Snug Harbor Marina has a good reputation with long-term cruisers and family fishing boats as a peaceful location with floating docks.

Anchorage: In the main channel east of Star Island, buoys must be followed carefully to clear the shoal (2- to 6-foot depths) extending southwest from the eastern shore. The channel to the southeast part of the lake is clearly outlined with town markers. There is also anchoring room, but holding ground is poor, so use ample scope when you

Looking southwest over Lake Montauk Inlet and Star Island. (Not to be used for navigation.) WATERWAY GUIDE PHOTOGRAPHY

drop the hook. If you do anchor in the lake, the local marinas usually do not mind accommodating your dinghy, and some provisions are available at most of them.

GOIN' ASHORE: **MONTAUK, NY**

Montauk is really two villages, one at the harbor within walking or dinghy distance of the marinas or boats anchored out; the second a couple of miles away on the Atlantic Ocean side. At the harbor, you will find the Suffolk County National Bank (631-668-4333, 15 W. Lake Drive, with ATM) and the Gosman's Dock Complex mini-mall (500 W. Lake Drive) with a fresh seafood market (631-668-5645), clam bar (631-668-2549), ice cream shop and casual clothing shop (631-668-3174). Gosman's Restaurant & Bar (631-668-5330) offers strictly-fresh, no-frills seafood and front-row seats for the daily boat parade. Nearby, Gaviola's Montauk Market (631-668-1031, W. Lake Drive and Wells Avenue) is a small but complete grocery with a deli, fresh meats and prepared sandwiches. The Dock at Montauk (west side of the harbor at Town Dock, 631-668-9778, 1 Town Road) serves seafood and chops in a friendly tavern atmosphere and is open for lunch, afternoon snacks and dinner. Dave's Grill (631-668-9190, 468 W. Lake Drive) on the waterfront, dinner only, open May through October, is the more upscale choice, with dining indoors or out. It is priced a bit higher and said to be worth it. West Lake Clam & Chowder House (631-668-6252, 382 W. Lake Drive) is known for its wonderful fresh seafood served in a variety of ways.

In "downtown" Montauk, complete reprovisioning and shopping can be combined with a trip to the ocean beach. Montauk's large IGA grocery store (631-668-4929, 654 Montauk Highway) is situated just a short distance from the dunes of Kirk Park's beach a few blocks west of the village center. Some of the marinas provide courtesy transportation to town; otherwise, Lindy's Taxi (631-668-4747/8888) and Montauk Taxi (631-668-2468) offer this service.

In the village are a couple of pharmacies, The Montauk Corner Store (631-668-6081, 710 Montauk Highway Suite C) and White's Drug & Department Store (631-668-2994, 95 Montauk Plaza), which carries an amazing collection of useful items, banks with ATMs, Suffolk County National Bank (631-668-5300, 746 Montauk Highway) and Bridgehampton National Bank (631-668-6400, 1A The Plazas), the post office (631-668-2218, S. Edison), Montauk Bake Shoppe (631-668-2439, 29 The Plaza) famous for the jelly croissant, a hardware store, Becker Home Center (631-668-2368, 775 Montauk Highway) with propane, but no natural gas. Barnacle Books (631-668-4599, 37A The Plazas) is a full-service bookstore open year round. Though there are several spirits shops in the village (none at the harbor), the best selection of wines is found at White's Liquor Store (631-668-2426, 711 Montauk Highway) offers free delivery.

Shagwong Restaurant (774 Main St., 631-668-3050) is said to be "well worth a special trip," both for its 1920s-style atmosphere (Tudor architecture from the Carl Fisher era, complete with pressed-tin ceilings) and for its sensational seafood. Also highly recommended is the Oyster Pond Restaurant and Bar (631-668-4200, 4 S. Elmwood Ave.), for traditional Italian specialties.

Montauk is only 17 nautical miles from Block Island, 14 from Plum Gut, 13 from Three Mile Harbor and 11 from The Race. Its landmark lighthouse, circa 1797, is one of the oldest and most important on the coast. Towering 168 feet over the water at Montauk Point, the light still serving as an active aid to navigation can be seen 19 miles at sea, flashing white every five seconds, and it has a radio beacon on 286 kHz. Its horn is one two-second blast, every 15 seconds. Tours can be arranged through the Montauk Point Lighthouse Museum (www.montauklighthouse.com, 631-668-2544, 2000 Montauk Highway) near the lighthouse. The area around Montauk Light is considered a haven for avid bird-watchers, especially during the off-season. The peninsula is a natural stopover during spring and fall migrations, and is the southerly wintering limit of some species.

In summer, a visit to Suffolk County's 1,200-acre Montauk Park on East Lake Drive will surprise sightseers who might not expect to find a lush forest with flowing freshwater streams within sight of the Atlantic Ocean. It is located on the last few sandy miles of beach near Montauk Point. Hickory trees (settlers used the oil from the hickory nuts to dose their rheumatism and light their lamps), blue beech and 22 species of ferns, including the rare rattlesnake fern, grow here. You might see harmless black snakes up to five feet long as you walk. Be sure to use insect repellent; there is a serious Lyme-disease tick problem throughout the Long Island woods.

Bring a blanket or beach chair to "Monday Night Concerts on the Green" featuring great music by local performers starting at 6 p.m. every Monday night in the summer. Enjoy the 1.5-hour beach/trail horseback rides through thousands of acres of parkland at Deep Hollow Ranch, (631-668-2744, three miles east of Montauk Village) the oldest cattle ranch in the country dating back to its 1658 origin.

ADDITIONAL RESOURCES:

- Long Island Guides, **www.montaukny guide.com** or **www.onmontauk.com** or **www.montauk-online.com**

NEARBY GOLF COURSES:

Montauk Downs State Park, 50 South Fairview Ave.
Montauk, NY 11954, 631-668-1100

NEARBY MEDICAL FACILITIES:

Southhampton Hospital, 240 Meeting House Lane,
Southampton, NY 11968, 631-726-8200
www.southamptonhospital.org

Montauk Medical Center, 699 Montauk Highway
Montauk, NY 11954 631-668-3705

■ PECONIC BAYS— NORTH SHORE

Little Peconic Bay, about five miles long, is full of interesting coves and bywaters (many dredged). It is southwest of the circumnavigation of Shelter Island and it is large, deep and usually airless in the summer.

Hog Neck Bay, with two pretty streams (Corey Creek and Richmond Creek), is located in the northwest corner of Little Peconic Bay. Both streams have good beaches, narrow-dredged channels and no services. Project depth is 7 feet, but both creeks are better for dinghies than big boats.

Needle-sharp Jessup Neck and Great Hog Neck mark the eastern edge of the Peconic Bays. Farther around Nassau Point is Cutchogue Harbor. Half a dozen gunkholes, good duck hunting, fine beaches and a charming town with one of the country's oldest houses characterizes this side bay. Cutchogue Harbor has Haywater Cove, Broadwater Cove, Mud Creek and East Creek. Some are dredged basins for local boats, but most are shoal. All offer interesting exploration by dinghy. A cove, unnamed on the chart but known locally as The Horseshoe, north of Nassau Point, offers a protected anchorage for vessels with 5-foot drafts.

Around the harbor are a number of marinas that will accommodate cruising boats. Wickham Creek, locally known as Boatmen's Harbor, is at the northwest side of the harbor and is closest to Cutchogue. Stay to mid-channel—shoals are to port.

In the bay's western corner, New Suffolk is the port for Cutchogue, a mile inland. The latter is named for the Corchaug Indian tribe. You can tour the Old House, a 17th-century English farm cottage with period furnishings and a National Historic Landmark. The village has a commercial fishing fleet, a restaurant, rowboat rentals and bait sales. Boating amenities are on Cutchogue Harbor and up Schoolhouse Creek (unnamed on the chart). Check depths locally. Braun's Seafood (631-734-6700, 30840 Main Road) in Cutchogue is the leading seafood dealer in the East End and will sell to retail customers. The entire region is famous for wineries and farm stands.

Jessup Neck

The waters around the sand spit of Jessup Neck, a wildlife preserve with picnic grounds, provide good fishing, especially for blues and weakfish. East of Jessup Neck's sharp points are Noyack Bay and Shelter Island. On the south shore of Noyack Bay is Mill Creek, a good harbor with an easy entrance (covered earlier). It offers not only snug anchorage, but also accommodations for cruising boats, with excellent dining ashore. Trout Pond, just inland, is a good spot for some freshwater swimming. Noyack Bay itself has a sandy beach where you can rent sailboards. This area extends a warm welcome to cruising mariners.

Robins Island

Dividing Little and Great Peconic bays is Robins Island, privately owned but at the center of a conservation controversy. The 435-acre island is home to rare animal and plant species, and Suffolk County hopes to be able to acquire and protect it. Landing on the island is forbidden.

Two marked channels go past Robins Island: North Race, more protected but spotted with shoals; and South Race, the preferred passage for deeper-draft boats. It is marked better, but subject to tide rips when current and wind oppose.

Deep Hole Creek, James Creek

Most of the interest in five-mile-wide Great Peconic Bay is on its south shore (covered in the next section). The north shore has extensive shoals broken by occasional dredged channels to such bywaters as Deep Hole and James creeks, both in Mattituck, just a mile from Mattituck Creek, which flows north to Long Island Sound. Both have beaches, amenities for local boats only and dredged 5-foot depths, which are subject to shoaling. Exercise caution when entering.

Flanders Bay

NAVIGATION: Use Chart 12358. Large, full of shoals and with a twisting channel, this westernmost arm of Great Peconic Bay is the last link in the Peconic chain. Enter between Miamogue and Red Cedar points; follow all aids to navigation carefully and keep a close eye on your depth sounder. The bay has nice creeks, some deep enough for larger boats, but most for dinghy navigation.

Flanders Bay is the gateway to the Peconic River and Riverhead. Its two best cruising ports are South Jamesport, just inside Miamogue Point, and Meetinghouse Creek at Aquebogue. Both have dredged entrances with marinas catering to transient boats, and both make good layover ports for visiting Riverhead.

Riverhead

Settled in 1690, Riverhead, the Suffolk County seat, has good shops, supply stores, restaurants and an inn, but few transient boat amenities. Much like the North Fork, this area is famous for farm stands and wineries. Riverhead has more than 20,000 acres involved in crops or vineyards, and local seasonal produce abounds in season.

NAVIGATION: Use Chart 12358. For Riverhead, South Jamesport, use New London tide tables. For high tide, add 2 hours 34 minutes; for low tide, add 2 hours 43 minutes. You can get to Riverhead via the Peconic River's narrow, marsh-bordered channel with 6-foot project depths. Buoys lead you to the head of navigation, two miles from Flanders Bay. A 25-foot fixed vertical clearance bridge crosses the Peconic River about a mile downstream of the village, so most sailboats cannot make it all the way.

GOIN' ASHORE: RIVERHEAD, NY

Riverhead is often referred to as the "Gateway to Long Island's East End." Historic Main Street offers fine restaurants, specialty retail shops, health food stores, art galleries, an old-style 1950s luncheonette and an offbeat coffee shop with live performances. Stop by the Information booth near the Riverhead riverfront dock and pick up a copy of the Downtown Reporter which provides information about local events.

The East End Arts & Humanities Council, (631-727-0900, 133 E. Main St.) long a regional center for classical music and fine arts, is located nearby. The Atlantis Marine World Aquarium (631-208-9200, 431 E. Main St.) provides a kid-friendly look at life under the surface of our waters. Scheduled events are available at www.atlantismarineworld.com or by phone.

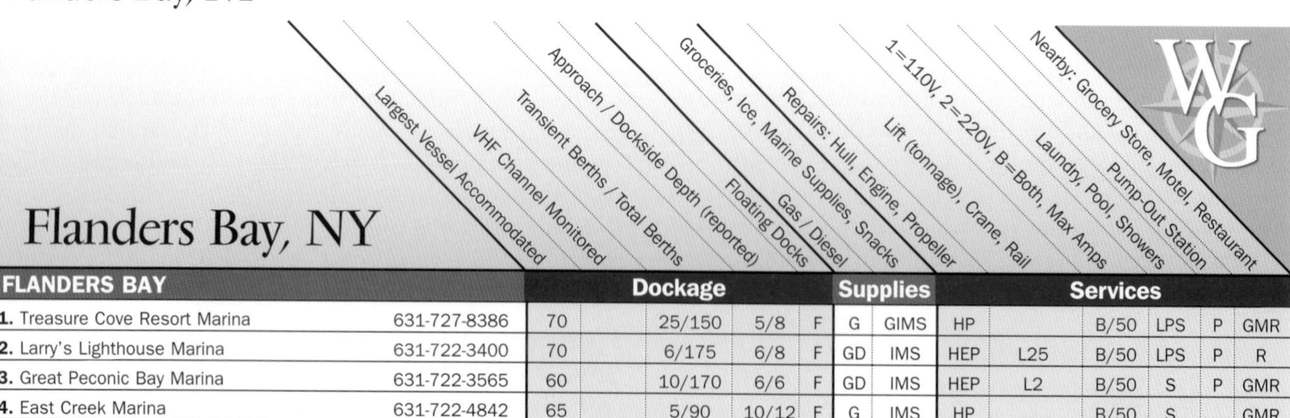

Flanders Bay, NY

FLANDERS BAY		Largest Vessel Accommodated	VHF Channel Monitored	Transient Berths / Total Berths	Approach / Dockside Depth (reported)	Floating Docks	Gas / Diesel	Groceries, Ice, Marine Supplies, Snacks	Repairs: Hull, Engine, Propeller	Lift (tonnage), Crane, Rail	1=110V, 2=220V, B=Both, Max Amps	Laundry, Pool, Showers	Pump-Out Station	Nearby: Grocery Store, Motel, Restaurant
		Dockage					Supplies		Services					
1. Treasure Cove Resort Marina	631-727-8386	70		25/150	5/8	F	G	GIMS	HP		B/50	LPS	P	GMR
2. Larry's Lighthouse Marina	631-722-3400	70		6/175	6/8	F	GD	IMS	HEP	L25	B/50	LPS	P	R
3. Great Peconic Bay Marina	631-722-3565	60		10/170	6/6	F	GD	IMS	HEP	L2	B/50	S	P	GMR
4. East Creek Marina	631-722-4842	65		5/90	10/12	F	G	IMS	HP		B/50	S		GMR

Corresponding chart(s) not to be used for navigation. Internet Access Wireless Internet Access

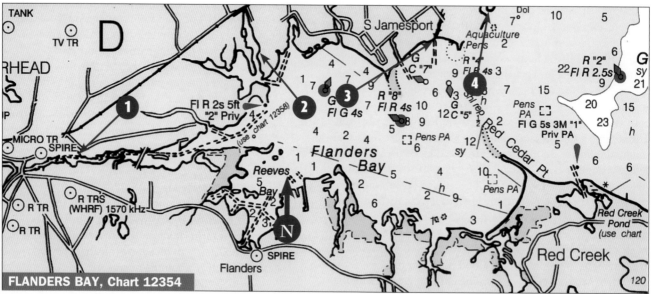

FLANDERS BAY, Chart 12354

The fully renovated Vail Levitt Music Hall (631-727-5782, 18 Peconic Ave.), an 1880s landmark, presents a packed schedule of entertainment events (www.wvail-leavitt.org) each month. The 20,000-square-foot Dinosaur Walk Museum (631-369-6556, 221 E. Main St.) has exotic animals and fauna on display. The Suffolk Theater (631-208-0003, 11 W. Main St.), totally restored to its 1933 Art Deco splendor, is now a popular performing arts center. The Riverhead Raceway (631-727-0010, 1785 Old country Road) is an excellent venue for small track NASCAR and other racing events. The Suffolk County Historical Museum (631-727-2881, 300 W. Main St.) offers exhibits of local history, a research library and educational programs. The town is also a convenient staging area for tours of area wineries. A taxi can be hired from East End (631-727-0400).

Digger O'Dell's (631-369-3200, 58 W. Main St.) is an Irish pub widely known for its prime rib. Hy Ting Restaurant (631-727-1557, 54 W. Main St.) is the place to go for Chinese food. Tweed's Restaurant and Buffalo Bar (631-208-3151, 17 E. Main St.) is located in the restored Victorian style, turn of the century, J. J. Sullivan Hotel featuring a magnificent mahogany bar from the 1893 Chicago World's fair. Local, farm raised bison from the owners herd is featured on the menu as well as fresh seafood and innovative specials. The head of a buffalo shot by Teddy Roosevelt presides over the bar area. If steak suits you, dine at the Rendezvous Restaurant (631-727-6880, 313 E. Main St.).

The Peconic River offers a splendid getaway for a quiet kayak or canoe paddle though the marshes. Treasure Cove Resort Marina (631-727-8386, 469 E. Main St.) rents bicycles, canoes, kayaks and paddle boats. The surrounding area abounds in wineries and most are available for tours and tasting. West Marine (631-727-2498, 1095 Old Country Road) is available for boating supplies. Just out of Riverhead is the Tangier Mall, (631-369-2732, 1770 W. Main St.) which bills itself as America's largest outlet center.

ADDITIONAL RESOURCES:

- Riverhead Chamber of Commerce, **www.riverheadchamber.com**

NEARBY GOLF COURSES:

Cherry Creek Golf Links, 900 Reeves Ave., Riverhead, NY 11901, 631-369-6500, **www.cherrycreeklinks.com**

NEARBY MEDICAL FACILITIES:

Central Suffolk Hospital, 1300 Roanoke Ave., Riverhead, NY 11901, 631-548-6080

Cutchogue Harbor, Peconic Bay, Shinnecock Canal, NY

CUTCH. HARBOR, PECONIC BAY, SHINN. CANAL		Largest Vessel Accommodated	VHF Channel Monitored	Transient Berths / Total Berths	Approach / Dockside Depth (reported)	Floating Docks	Gas / Diesel	Groceries, Ice, Marine Supplies, Snacks	Repairs: Hull, Engine, Propeller	Lift (tonnage), Crane, Rail	1=110V, 2=220V, B=Both, Max Amps	Laundry, Pool, Showers	Pump-Out Station	Nearby: Grocery Store, Motel, Restaurant
		Dockage					Supplies		Services					
1. New Suffolk Shipyard	631-734-6311	40	09	5/70	5/6	F	G	GM	HEP	L25,C	1/30	S	P	GMR
2. Cutchogue Harbor Marina Inc.	631-734-6993	50	09	2/110	6/9	F	GD	IMS	HEP	L30	B/50	LS	P	GMR
3. Peconic Marina	631-283-3799	30		5/100	4/5	F	GD	IMS	HEP		1/20	S		GR
4. Shinnecock Canal Marina	631-852-8291	50		15/62	8/6	F					1/30	S	P	GMR
5. Jackson's Marina	631-728-4220	70	68	5/200	8/6	F	GD	IMS	HEP	L75	B/50	S	P	GMR
6. Mariner's Cove Marine	631-728-0286	52		6/182	9/5	F		IMS	HP	R	1/30	S	P	GMR
7. Indian Cove Restaurant & Marina	631-728-5366	55			6/6		GD	I			1/30	S		R
8. Modern Yachts Inc.	631-728-2266	60		/70	10/6		GD	IMS	HP	C	B/50	PS	P	GMR
9. Hampton Watercraft & Marine	631-728-8200	60		/100	12/8		GD	IMS	HEP	L		S		MR

Corresponding chart(s) not to be used for navigation. Internet Access Wireless Internet Access

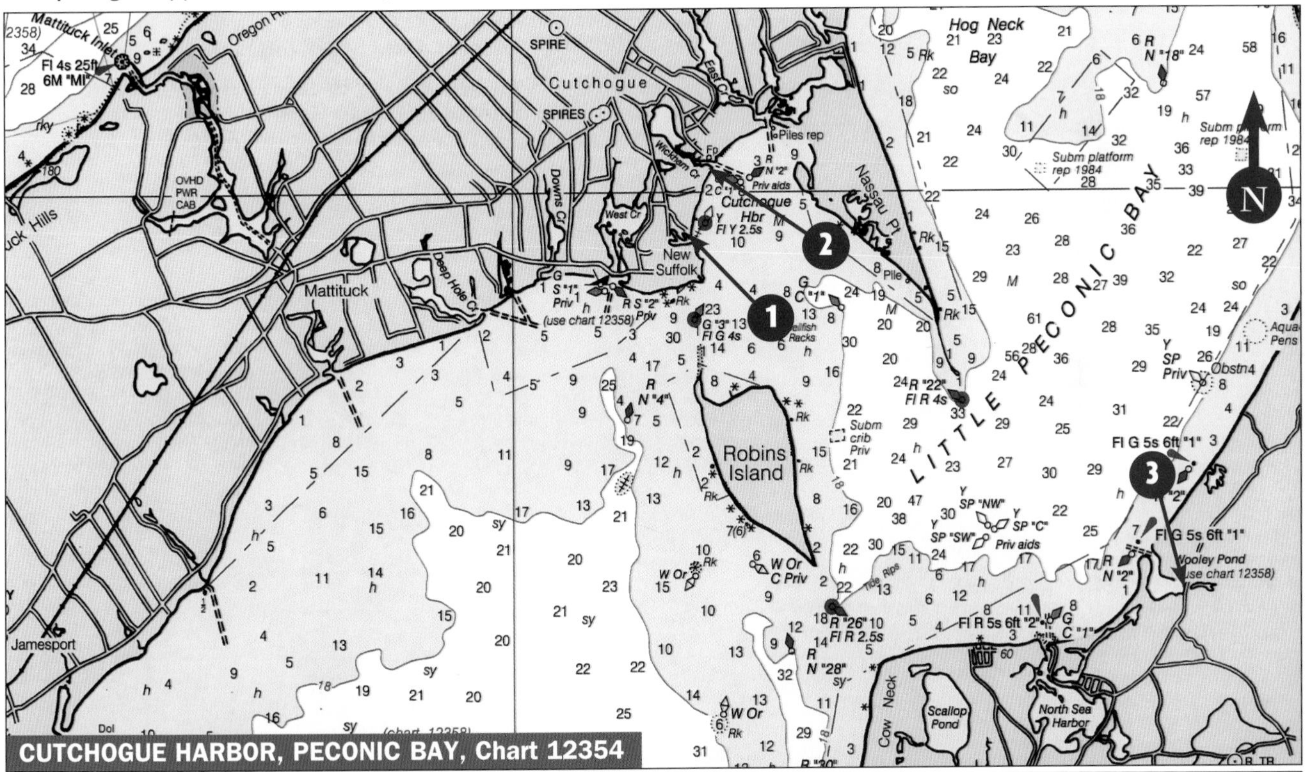

CUTCHOGUE HARBOR, PECONIC BAY, Chart 12354

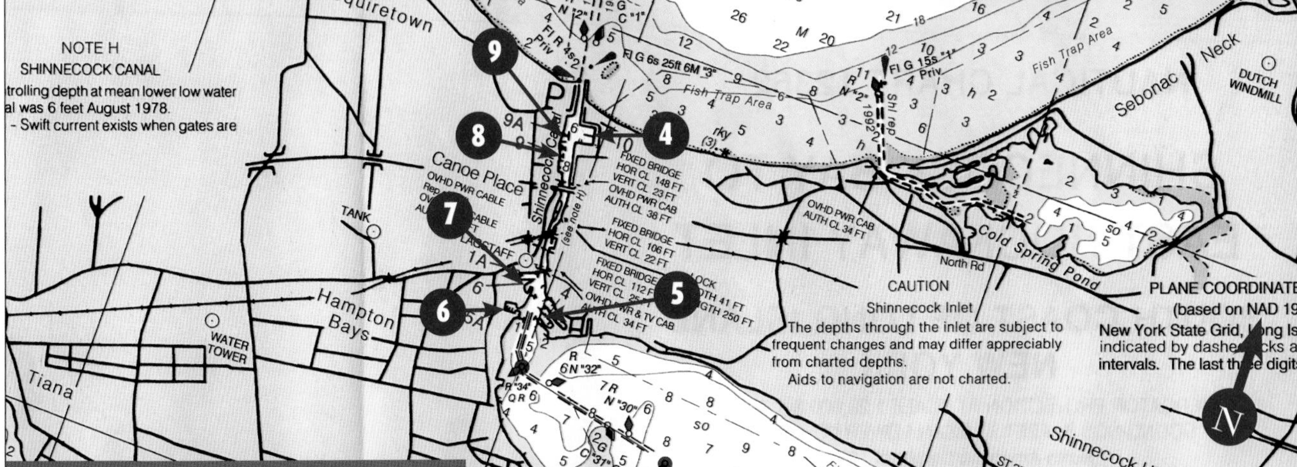

SHINNECOCK CANAL, Chart 12352

PECONIC BAYS—SOUTH SHORE

The Shinnecock Canal, North Sea Harbor, Sebonac Creek and three dredged gunkholes define the south shore of the Peconic Bays. WATERWAY GUIDE covers the canal last because it is a passage to another part of Long Island.

NAVIGATION: Use Chart 12358. The first gunkhole, Red Creek Pond, is reached via Red Creek, just east of Red Cedar Point beyond Flanders Bay. Red Creek's pond area is wild and unspoiled, and charted with 5-foot depths. The creek itself is narrow, locally marked and suitable only for shallow-draft boats. The next gunkhole, Cold Spring Pond, is one mile east of the Shinnecock Canal. The dredged channel goes only part way. In a small protrusion to the south, off the dredged channel, is the Lobster Box restaurant, which has docks and will sometimes allow an overnight stay.

Almost two miles farther up the coast is Sebonac Creek, Southampton's main yacht harbor. The dredged channel entrance is reported to have 5-foot depths. Inside are a town dock, a private yacht club, attractive coves and shallow Bullhead Bay next door.

Anchorage: Spacious North Sea Harbor has good anchorage but shallow depths. Conscience Point, well inside the harbor, is where the town's founders landed in 1640. Pick your anchorage carefully even if you see other boats nearby, because locals may be sitting in shallows or on mud at low tide. They may not care about leaving, but you most likely do.

Shinnecock Canal

NAVIGATION: Use Chart 12358. This easy-to-use canal runs between Peconic and Shinnecock bays, joining Long Island's northern and southern shores. A single jetty leads into the well-marked and lighted canal entrance from Great Peconic Bay, about eight miles east of Riverhead. Fixed bridges set controlling vertical clearance at 22 feet. The banks are lined with marinas, boatyards, restaurants and fishing stations. At each end of the canal is a do-it-yourself gin pole, which you can use to unstep or step your sailboat's mast at no charge.

Shinnecock Bay is described in the chapter on the South Shore of Long Island, "South Shore—Eastern End."

Cruising Options

From Montauk, boaters can head to any number of great cruising grounds, most notably nearby Block Island or the Elisabeth islands off the Massachusetts coast. ■

WATERWAY GUIDE is always open to your observations from the helm. E-mail your comments on any navigation information in the guide to: editor@waterwayguide.com.

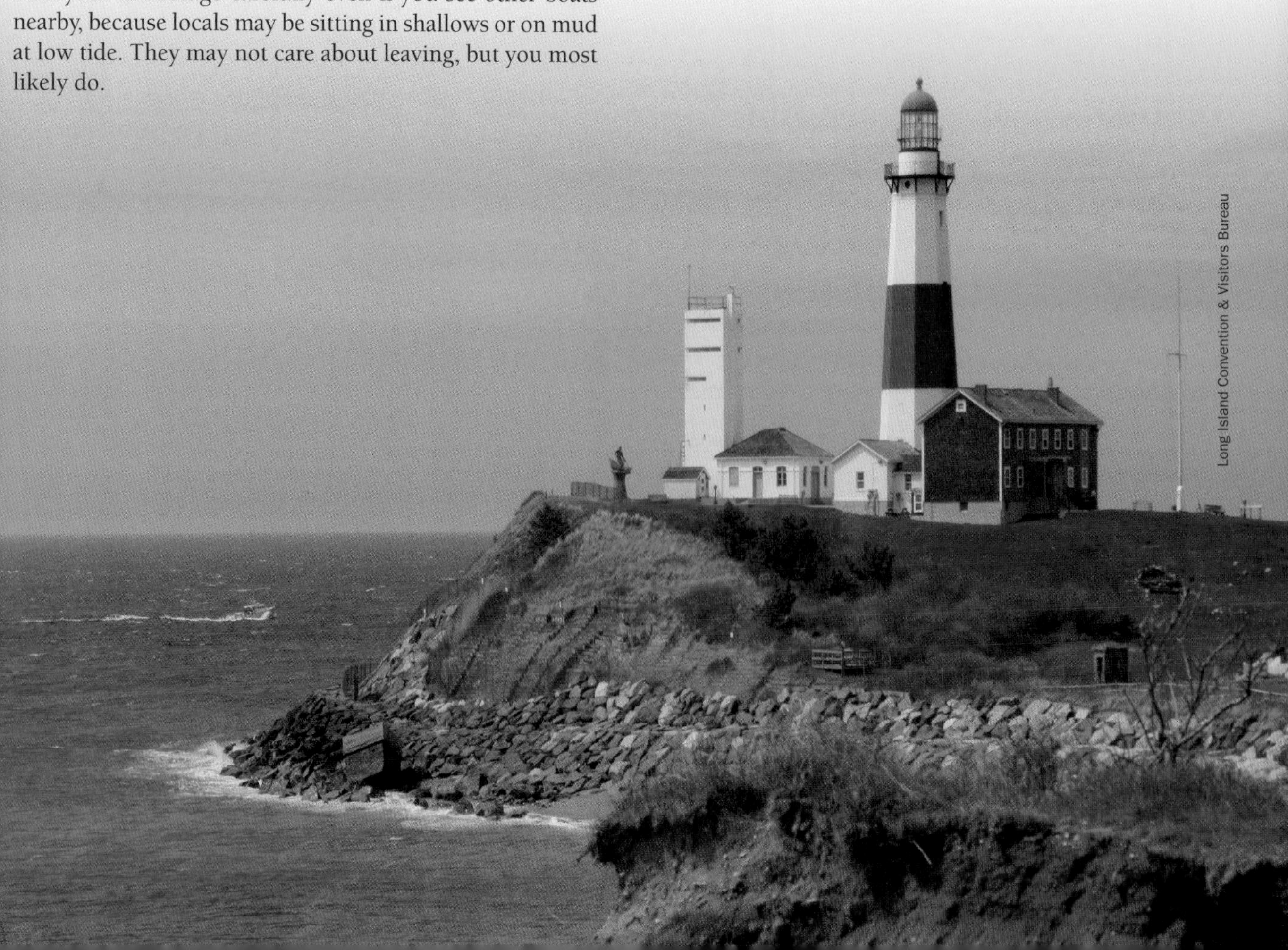

Long Island Convention & Visitors Bureau

Introduction

Block Island & Narragansett Bay

After exiting Long Island Sound through the current-washed Race, mariners enter the varied cruising grounds of southern New England—Block Island Sound, the Atlantic coast of Rhode Island and the justly famous waters of Narragansett Bay, including Newport.

After covering Block Island, WATERWAY GUIDE crosses Block Island Sound to Point Judith, cruises up both passages of Narragansett Bay, into the yachting mecca of Newport and on up to Providence and Mount Hope Bay. The Sakonnet River, the easternmost part of Narragansett Bay, is covered last in the "Narragansett Bay" section.

Although highly industrialized, Rhode Island is completely water-oriented. Narragansett Bay, cutting 25 miles inland, gives the state a very long shoreline, considering its diminutive size. Rhode Island's seafaring tradition dates back more than 300 years and survives all along the shores of Narragansett Bay. Fishermen still make a living from the sea, yachts from around the world converge on Newport and visiting mariners tie up at guest moorings maintained by the state, or at the many marinas in the maze of harbors here.

Rhode Island waters can be demanding. To reach Block Island in a small boat is to venture across an open ocean, out of sight of land on all but the clearest days. You should review your boat's safety and navigational gear and the crew's preparedness before you set out.

Cruising Characteristics

You can expect fog, with or without warning. Many days will have at least some, and you might be in and out of fog all day. It may be thick "Down East" fog, the sort rarely seen farther south and west. At this point on the coast, serious cruisers consider radar as a standard aid to navigation. From here to the north and east, fewer and fewer boats of more than 30 feet can be seen without their domed or discus-shaped radar antennas mounted on a mast or atop a stern pole or pilot house. At the least, boats in these waters should carry high-mounted radar reflectors to improve their visibility to others.

Seas may seem calm, but with a change of tide or wind, they might suddenly become choppy. You will encounter strong currents and big tidal ranges. Keep an eye out for lobster pots, rocks and ledges.

A watchful eye on the chart, the compass and the weather is always necessary. These waters are among the most beautiful on the East Coast, but under poor conditions, they can be dangerous indeed. Tugs with barges far astern, stealthy submarines operating at full speed and crisscrossing recreational boat traffic should keep the skipper and crew alert. ■

Photo: Rhode Island Economic Development Corporation

Section Contents

Block Island, Point Judith	293
Narragansett Bay	303

Pawtucket
Pawtuxent R.
Providence
Barrington
Somerset
Apponaug
Warren
Mount Hope Bay
Warwick
East Greenwich
Fall River
Bristol
Tiverton
Narragansett Bay
Quonset Pt.
MASSACHUSETTS
Wickford
Sakonnet River
Conanicut Island
RHODE ISLAND
Westport Pt.
Newport
Sakonnet
Brenton Pt.
Wakefield
Narragansett Pier
Westerly
Charlestown
Galilee
Jerusalem
Point Judith
Rhode Island Sound
Weekapaug
Block Island Sound

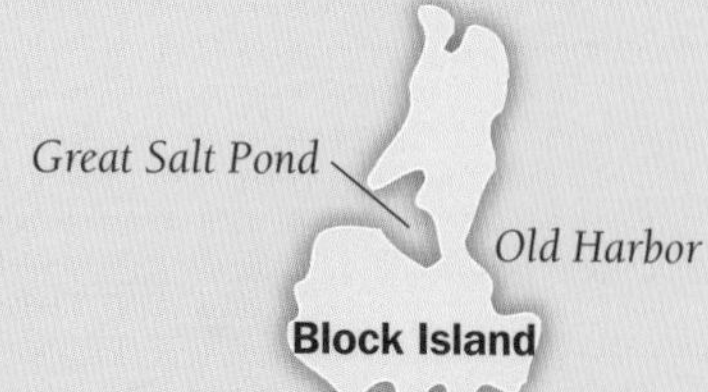

Atlantic Ocean

Planning

- Tide Tables 521
- GPS Waypoints 532

Block Island, Point Judith

CHARTS 13205, 13215, 13217, 13218, 13219

RHODE ISLAND WATERS

Lying alone in the long Atlantic Ocean swells, this stranded piece of frequently-fog-bound Rhode Island real estate is situated 12 miles south of the mainland. Just six miles long and three miles wide, Block Island has, nevertheless, become a favorite stop for well-traveled cruising mariners.

The pork chop-shaped island has a 20-mile-long shoreline, high clay bluffs and lonely beaches known mainly to gulls, seabirds and the occasional seal. Often called the "Bermuda of the North," Block Island's temperatures are often 10 degrees cooler than the mainland in summer and warmer in winter. It might be foggy, cool and damp during the early morning and evening, but sometimes when fog is heavy outside the breakwaters, the sun is shining on the island proper. A considerable wind often whistles over the island and creates problems for the anchored fleet in Great Salt Pond, while just beyond the breakwaters, calms prevail and sailboats that reduced sail area in expectation of a rough passage to the mainland find themselves wallowing without wind in the rolling swells from the southwest.

Passages to Block Island

Boats converge on Block Island from all directions: southeast from the Connecticut shore, about 25 miles via The Race; southeast 15 miles from Watch Hill Passage; southwest 26 miles from Newport; northeast from Montauk Harbor about 17 miles; and south from Point Judith, some 10 miles across Block Island Sound.

The long, lazy ground swells characteristic of Block Island Sound heave gently, even in good weather. Submarines operate throughout the area, appearing when least expected (especially interesting in the fog), and ferries, freighters, naval vessels and barge traffic crisscross the waters continuously.

While the odds are good for a trouble-free crossing, Block Island Sound should always be accorded proper respect. Easy swells can become steep seas in minutes, and fog is frequent—sometimes patchy, and often all-encompassing and unnerving with the volume of big-ship traffic. You might leave the mainland in sunshine, suddenly find yourself in miles of pea soup and then if your navigation is right, make your landfall in full sunshine. Current swirls out through The Race, which can significantly affect your navigation efforts.

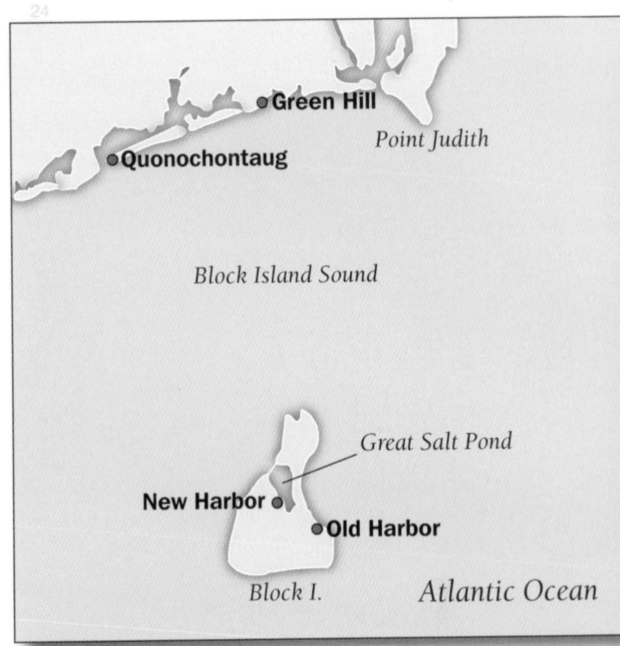

NAVIGATION: Use Charts 13215 and 13217. If you make your approach in clear weather, you will think at first that you are looking at two islands. Great Salt Pond almost bisects the island, and the shore on both sides of the pond is low. The land in between will appear as you get closer, though, with higher ground to the south. Do not cut flashing green "1BI" rounding the northern end of the island. That treacherous bar has caught many skippers who thought they were in deep water.

Many boats sail right up to shore on the southern and western sides of the island, but unmarked rocks are all around, and the prudent skipper will stay outside the proper marks. Currents run strong here, southeasterly on the ebb, westerly on the flood.

Great Salt Pond, New Harbor

Great Salt Pond, in the center of the island, is more than a mile long and almost as wide, with New Harbor stretched along its southeastern perimeter. The 11.5-foot-deep entry channel was cut through from Block Island Sound to the natural salt pond in 1895 after several earlier attempts had failed.

NAVIGATION: Use Chart 13217. The channel is well-marked and easy to enter, with red bell buoy "2" outside and directly in line with the channel and 49-foot-high flashing red "4" at the end of the entrance-protecting jetty to starboard on entry. The channel heads straight past the thinly-staffed Coast Guard station (also to starboard)

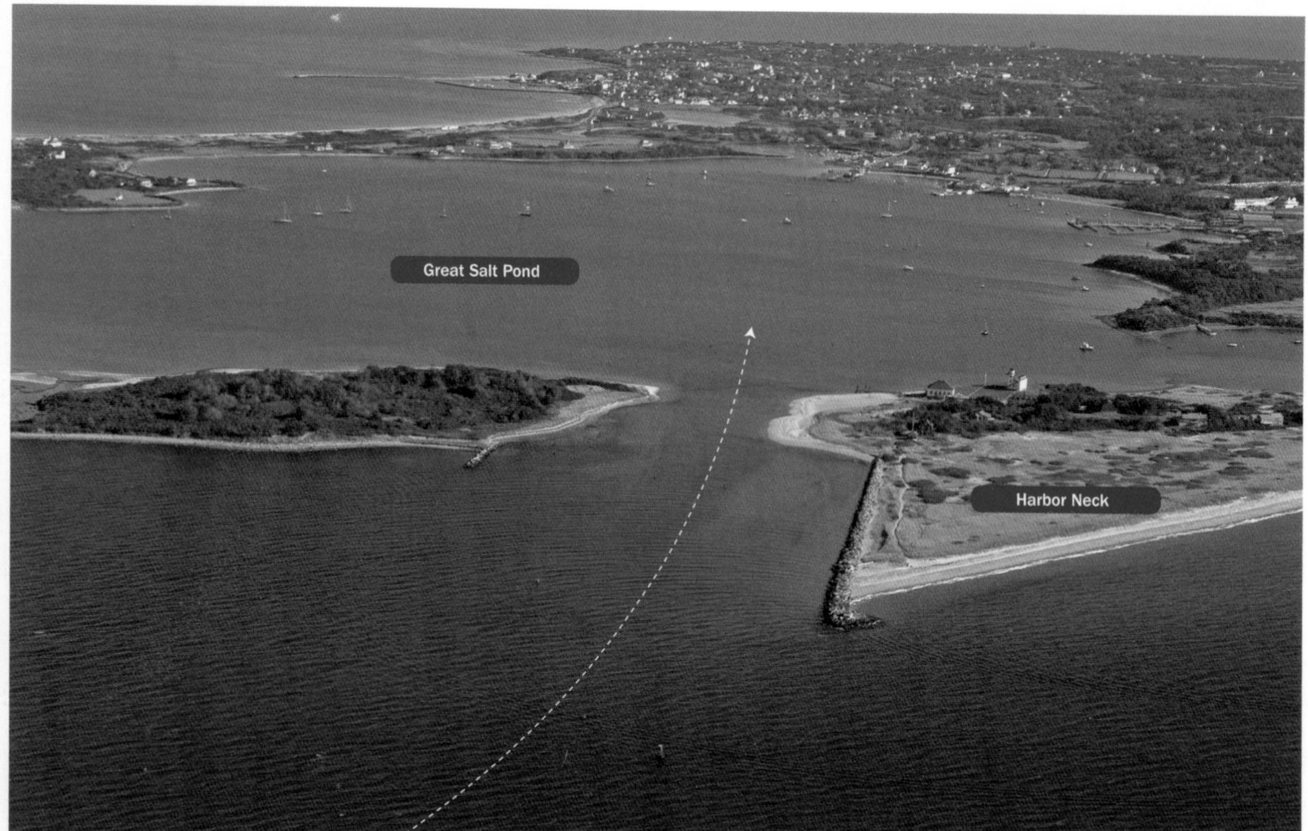

Looking southeast over Block Island and Great Salt Pond. (Not to be used for navigation.) WATERWAY GUIDE PHOTOGRAPHY

and into Great Salt Pond itself. Prevailing southwesterlies and local racing traditions encourage sailing vessels to enter under canvas, which causes no particular difficulty. Sailing traffic with a wide range of speed and maneuverability, depending on waterline lengths and reefing points, along with power cruisers at various levels of strength and determination, can make the short passage interesting and colorful. In Great Salt Pond, the water is deep almost to the banks, with few rocks or obstructions except at the southwestern corner.

New Harbor offers all the attributes of a cruising mecca: easy access, plenty of water, good marinas with repair capabilities, room to anchor (though holding is unreliable, particularly when numerous boats attempt to find secure holding in 35- to 50-foot depths on short scopes), excellent beaches and plenty to enjoy ashore.

Dockage: Four marinas line the southern shore of the pond. Champlin's Marina and Resort is first on entry and the largest in the harbor. In addition to all fuels, extensive dockage, a coin-operated laundry facility, pump-out and launch service to and from the mooring and anchorage fields ("Shortstop" on VHF Channel 68), Champlin's has the island's only movie theater, a hotel, a huge swimming pool (adjacent to an appealing private beach on the saltwater pond) and a variety of game courts. Hot showers and Champlin's pool are available only to paying patrons at its docks. There also are a basic-needs grocery, a pizza shop and a bevy of bikes for hire. Aldo's Bakery is situated here as well. This bakery makes early morning yacht calls via Boston Whaler (June through September), accompanied by stentorian salutations of "Andiamo" to announce their arrival.

Next door to the east, Block Island Boat Basin maintains extensive floating docks with a pump-out station for its customers. For boats moored or anchored out, Block Island Boat Basin has ice readily available at the dock house and a water tap at the wharf end of the launch/dinghy dock. Old Port Launch (VHF Channel 09) serves the harbor with two launches based here. Block Island Boat Basin's innermost dock, east of the marina's main wharf, is reserved for dinghies, with parking spaces for the launches and pump-out boats. Wireless Internet is available at Block Island Boat Basin's docks for a daily fee.

Payne's Dock (at the east end of the pond) and Smuggler's Cove of Block Island (still farther east, along the privately marked channel north of Payne's docks) are somewhat smaller, but both have transient dockage, fuels, restaurants and possibilities for lodging. The Mahogany Shoals Bar at the end of Payne's Dock is funky, unique and a local landmark. Finn's Seafood Restaurant (401-466-2473), at the foot of Payne's Dock on Water Street, is noted for its swordfish and well-prepared seafood dishes at moderate prices. The Samuel Peckham Inn (401-466-5000), a small waterfront resort, is well-known for its straightforward presentations of fresh seafood and steaks. Next door, the venerable B.I. Narragansett Inn (401-466-2626) offers breakfast, lunch and dinner by reservation. The Block Island base for the new high-speed ferry from Point Judith is located at the end of Payne's Dock.

Block Island, RI

BLOCK ISLAND		Largest Vessel Accommodated	VHF Channel Monitored	Transient Berths / Total Berths	Approach / Dockside Depth (reported)	Floating Docks	Gas / Diesel	Groceries, Ice, Marine Supplies, Snacks	Repairs: Hull, Engine, Propeller	Lift (tonnage), Crane, Rail	1=110V, 2=220V, B=Both, Max Amps	Laundry, Pool, Showers	Pump-Out Station	Nearby: Grocery Store, Motel, Restaurant
		Dockage					Supplies		Services					
1. Champlin's Marina, Hotel and Resort	401-466-7777	195	68	240/250	20/20	F	GD	GIMS	HEP		B/50	LPS	P	GMR
2. Block Island Boat Basin	401-466-2631	110	09	85/85	9/9	F		GIMS	E		B/50	S	P	GMR
3. Payne's Dock	401-466-5572	200		75/75	20/16		GD	GIS			B/50	S	P	GMR
4. Smuggler's Cove	401-466-7961	55	68	12/	6/10	F		I	P		1/30	S	P	MR
5. Aldo's Place	401-466-5871	50			4/5		GD							R
6. Block Island Harbormaster	401-466-3204			MOORINGS										

Corresponding chart(s) not to be used for navigation. Internet Access Wireless Internet Access

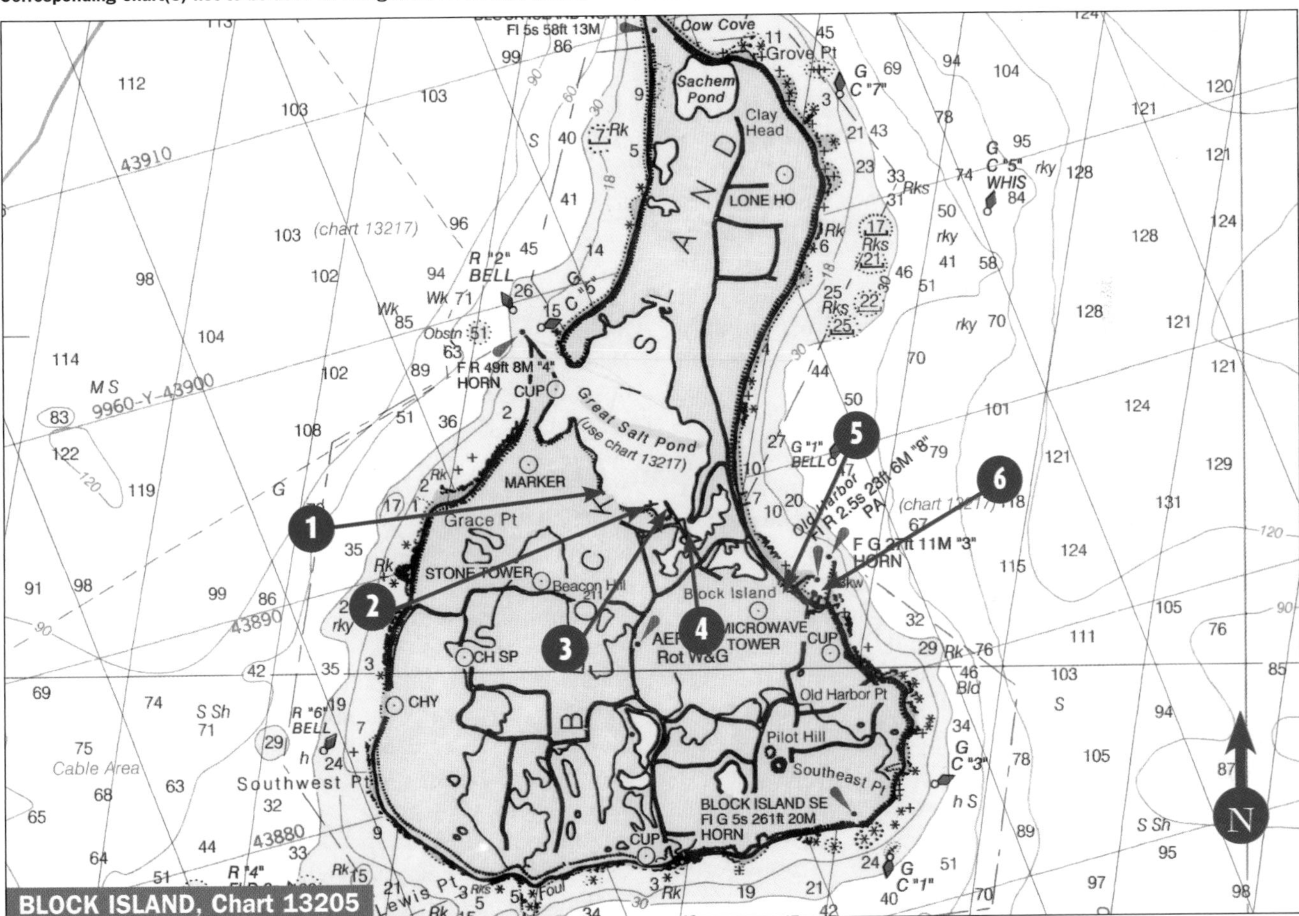

BLOCK ISLAND, Chart 13205

Block Island is often quite crowded on high-season weekends and holidays. As many as 2,000 boats encamp here over the Fourth of July, when a festive, carnival-like atmosphere overtakes the island, and its parade expands contemporary understandings of "patriotism." The day is topped by a bikini contest on the beach, impromptu boat horn symphonies and revelries far into the night. Over a normal summer weekend, the island easily accommodates some 1,200 to 1,300 boats, though latecomers should expect all moorings to be taken, many with rafts, and shallow-depth anchorage space long gone or quite crowded.

Moorings: The town's 100 moorings are a bright Granny Smith apple green and are located in the southwest corner of Great Salt Pond in front of the marinas. (All other moorings are private.) Early arrivals should simply pick up the pennant of an available green buoy. The harbormaster's launch will drop by to collect the fee. Rafting of up to two boats is permitted but not required. Skippers of larger boats (40-foot lengths or more) should contact the harbormaster on VHF Channel 12 for directions to an appropriate tie-up. The town has a number of heavier moorings for larger vessels.

Great Salt Pond is a No-Discharge Zone—even treated effluent cannot be discharged overboard. The town of

New Shoreham makes it easy to comply with this law by providing free pump-out service for any boat in the harbor. Simply call "Pump-out Boat" on VHF Channel 73. Although service is fast and efficient, on holiday weekends it is best to call early in the day to be put on the list.

With a trash permit, you can bring unseparated trash for disposal in the dumpsters located at the Block Island Boat Basin collection station. The Frederick Benson Town Beach pavilion, housing the town's showers, is reached via an easy (motorized) dinghy ride to the east side of the pond, where you can beach at the town's wooden walkway over the marsh grass, midway along this undeveloped stretch of the pond. From there it is a short trek across the road and dunes to the beach and south to the pavilion. Showers are available for a fee, as well as numerous private changing rooms. The surf is cool and refreshing on even the hottest day. Chairs, umbrellas and windscreens may be rented at the pavilion.

Anchorage: Unlike some other popular harbors, Great Salt Pond almost always has adequate room to anchor, although the open spaces were reduced somewhat as more areas were set aside for undisturbed shellfish beds. These areas (roughly the northwestern half of the harbor) are well-marked as NO ANCHORAGE zones. Town of New Shoreham ordinances also require yachts to stand clear of the marked channel area between the harbor entrance and the pier marked FERRY at the southeastern end of the harbor.

The anchoring area is expanded during July and August; the current Block Island Web site boasts anchorage space for 1,000 boats. The standard rule of anchoring at Block Island is to dig in deeply and keep an eye on the weather, particularly when rafted. Chain is especially appropriate here, and adequate scope is a must in depths of 20 to 50 feet with a grassy bottom. Launch service is available to boats anchored out. However, waiting times might be somewhat longer than for those on moorings. Call on VHF Channel 68. Dinghy dockage is also available at floats located at Champlin's Marina and Block Island Boat Basin. The cost of a rental mooring, as opposed to anchoring, is a good investment in this harbor, when safety and convenience are considered.

Block Island collects a 50-cent landing fee from every adult who arrives by private boat or ferry. In many cases, the fee is collected on the honor system, via collection boxes at every marina and town dock.

A useful single-page harbor guide is available from the patrol boat, at every marina and at the harbormaster's office in the town hall. To send for a copy in advance of your visit, send a self-addressed stamped envelope to: Harbormaster, Town of New Shoreham, Drawer 220, Block Island, RI 02807. The "Block Island Summer Times" is another useful free guide to local landmarks and events. Current events on the Island can be monitored at the Block Island Web site (www.blockisland.com).

Old Harbor

This small refuge, protected from the ocean by breakwaters, is on the island's eastern side and is not accessible from New Harbor.

NAVIGATION: Use Chart 13217. The straight entry is easy to navigate, except in strong easterlies when seas are heavy. You are aided in fog by jetty lights and a foghorn. A small inner harbor in the southeastern corner has a town dock and offers excellent protection from heavy weather, except from the north. Because there is heavy traffic from ferry boats and fishermen, recreational craft are prohibited from anchoring in the Inner Harbor, and anchoring anywhere in Old Harbor can be a problem.

Old Harbor is mainly used by commercial boats, fishermen and charter boats. Depths are good (about 10 to 15 feet). You can land your dinghy on the sandy beach of the outer harbor, and showers are available in the Old Harbor dockmaster's building. Ferries leave from here for Point Judith, RI, and New London, CT, about 11 times a day in peak season—early June through Labor Day—and less frequently in the off-season.

GOIN' ASHORE: OLD HARBOR, RI

Ashore at Old Harbor, the Victorian hotels and ramshackle buildings of the island's main settlement largely pre-date construction of the channel to Great Salt Pond. The overland hike of a little more than two miles is well worth the effort, even in inclement weather, though the preferred method of touring this scenic vacation spot is by bicycle. Moped rentals are available, though they are a leading source of noise, and are also frowned upon by local homeowners.

Several miles to the south and just across from Sachem Pond, Settler's Rock commemorates the landing of the 16 European families who purchased the island and first came ashore in 1661. For want of a natural harbor on the island, they swam ashore, as did their animals, which landed along the spot still called Cow Cove. The dormant lighthouse at Sandy Point was the fourth of its kind—its predecessors having either succumbed to the sea, or, in one case, placed in such a way as to cause, rather than prevent, shipwrecks.

At the other end of the island, Southeast Light (the Atlantic seaboard's brightest) is perched in stark relief atop Mohegan Bluffs, some 200 feet above the sea. In an extraordinary "house moving" operation in 1993, the massive 1873 brick structure was moved 360 feet on a zigzag escape route from the cliff's edge to save the lighthouse from the advancing peril of erosion. The Block Island Southeast Lighthouse Foundation is currently raising funds to restore the historic landmark and to open a museum in the lightkeeper's house. On a postcard-pretty day, a view of the lighthouse and its surrounding seascape is not to be missed. A lookout deck with wooden stairs descending to the beach is situated just past the lighthouse, with ample parking for cars and bicycles. The Mohegan Trail leading past the lighthouse turns westward toward Rodman's Hollow, a conservation area of subtle beauty. A map is a must for explorers and may be obtained from any of the numerous bike-rental shops.

The village at Old Harbor offers everything from trinkets for the day-trippers who come by ferry to trendy sportswear, imported goods and artful crafts. A large country store just across the street from the ferry landing holds an adequate supply for the basic larder and a reasonable collection of wine and spirits. Virtually all of the restaurants or hotels along Water Street offer al fresco dining with colorful views of the passing scene as well as of the water. The National Hotel appears to have the monopoly on old-fashioned rocking chairs, while the Harborside Inn has the best vantage point to review the comings and goings of ferry operations. On the waterside of Water Street, to the right and past the charter boat docks, Finn's Seafood Restaurant and Raw Bar has the fresh catch in wide variety, with a retail seafood store next door. Ballard's Inn is enormous, accommodating parties of 20 as easily and efficiently as couples. More fresh lobster is likely to be served here on an average day than anywhere else west of the Maine coast.

Farther up the hill to the south, several old inns provide, along with drink and hearty fare, magnificent seascapes from their porches. The Hotel Manisses is a particular favorite. Diners can choose between the canopied outdoor deck and a glassed garden terrace to sample fish and meats from the Manisses smokehouse, fresh seafood from the raw bar and vegetables picked directly from extensive gardens on the premises. The Gatsby Room is a more casual way to enjoy the cuisine of the Hotel Manisses. Eli's is another local favorite for seafood and other offerings; the portions here are very generous.

The post office, an excellent deli and a bookstore are located in the new Victorian-style building on High Street (on the heights above Ballards). South of Old Harbor on High Street, Block Island Health & General Store has "everything you'd expect to find in a mainland drugstore, except prescriptions." A long block west of Old Harbor (where Dodge Street becomes Ocean Avenue), Washington Trust Co. (the island's only bank) has an ATM. A few steps north of the bank, "The Deck" at McGovern's Yellow Kittens Tavern is an ideal place for a well-presented, low-budget lunch with an unsurpassed view of Crescent Beach.

Toward Great Salt Pond (west on Ocean Avenue), you'll find a large grocery store with basic groceries, including fresh meat and vegetables and current out-of-town newspapers. Farther toward New Harbor, the small Block Island Hardware is well-stocked with an eye toward boating requirements. Across from the power station, still farther west, the natural foods market offers organic produce (some locally grown), specialty nuts, grains, coffees and condiments. The Shoreline bills itself as the best-stocked Patagonia store in Rhode Island and offers great outdoor clothing for the entire family.

ADDITIONAL RESOURCES:

- Block Island Tourism Council, **www.blockislandinfo.com**

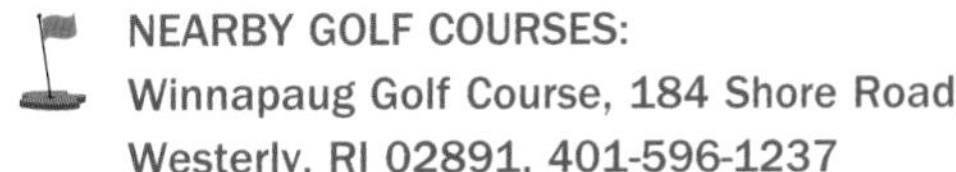

NEARBY GOLF COURSES:
Winnapaug Golf Course, 184 Shore Road, Westerly, RI 02891, 401-596-1237

NEARBY MEDICAL FACILITIES:
South County Hospital, 100 Kenyon Ave., Wakefield, RI 02879, 401-782-8000

Block Island to the Coast

NAVIGATION: Use Chart 13215. In planning a transit from Block Island to the Rhode Island mainland, keep in mind that you will encounter strong currents, lots of boat traffic, frequent fog and a significant shipping lane. Whether coming from the Salt Pond or around the north side of the island from Old Harbor, you should set your course from the vicinity of flashing green bell buoy "1BI." From that mark, it is only about 10 miles to the easternmost buoy of Point Judith.

Be alert for the strong currents flowing in or out of Long Island Sound and Narragansett Bay. This area can be quite choppy and confused, particularly when strong currents and winds are in opposition. If your destination from Block Island is Narragansett Bay, chart a course to Breton Reef, well east of Point Judith. Under all conditions, keep an eye on the mouth of Narragansett Bay for departing cruise ships and other large commercial traffic. If a close encounter is expected, contact the ship on VHF Channel 13. Outbound ships might be headed east into the Atlantic Ocean, up Buzzards Bay, or west into Long Island Sound.

Point Judith, Harbor of Refuge

West of Point Judith, the Rhode Island shore to Watch Hill is 18 miles of beach, with occasional rocky projections and a few "inlets" navigable only by very small boats, and mainly at high tide. For the mariner, this section of coast between Watch Hill and Point Judith has little to offer. Perhaps on a calm day you can anchor off the beach for a dinghy ride ashore to swim. This stretch of coast can be very long indeed if the current is foul. East of Point Judith are the cruising grounds of Narragansett Bay.

Completed just after the turn of the century, the Point Judith Harbor of Refuge, a V-shaped sea barrier more than a mile long, provides one of the few easy-access shelters in a long stretch of deceptively difficult water. Additional granite sea arms stretching from the mainland complete a protective shield with marked openings to the east and west. Passage through either opening is easy in good visibility.

NAVIGATION: Use Chart 13219. Take special care upon entering from the west, because the breakwater obscures outbound boats in the channel directly inside the wall. Point Judith is the home of one of the largest commer-

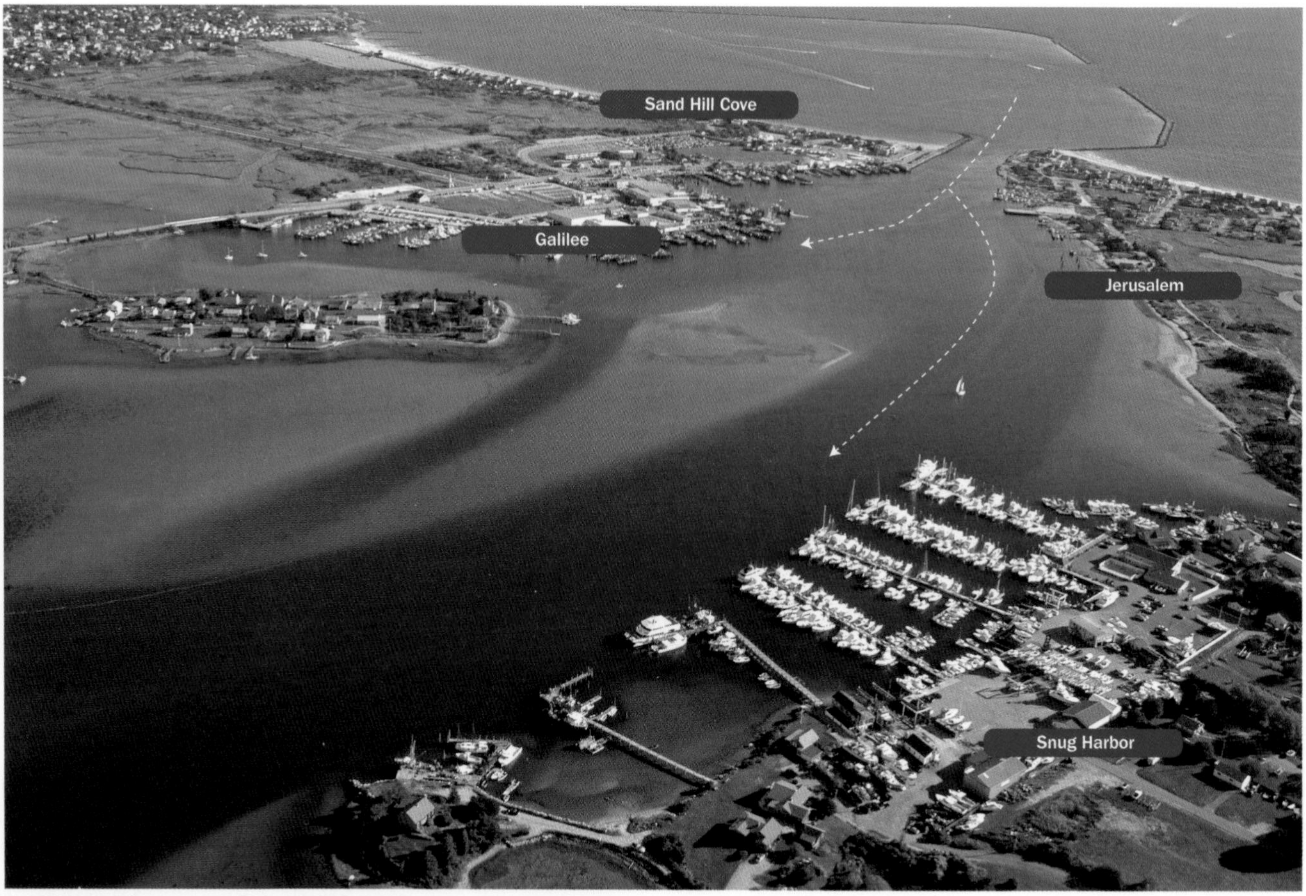

Looking southeast over Point Judith Pond. (Not to be used for navigation.) WATERWAY GUIDE PHOTOGRAPHY

cial fishing fleets on the North Atlantic seaboard and a major terminus for the fast-moving Block Island Ferry, so an approaching skipper who cuts close to the port side of the western opening of the refuge can get a considerable surprise.

If approaching from Narragansett Bay, give Point Judith the respectable sea room it deserves. A warning light has been at this location for nearly 200 years, and for good reason—swift currents, unexpectedly strong winds and submerged boulders mark the memory of countless ships lost in this area over the centuries. Be cautious also of the thicket of lobster pots and fish traps you'll find in the region east of the refuge.

The passage into the harbor at the eastern breakwaters west of Point Judith itself are first marked by flashing red buoy "2" followed by flashing green "3" on the west breakwater itself. The western entrance is marked on the northern breakwater by flashing green "3" and its southern neighbor, flashing red "2." Each entrance carries 18- to 30-foot depths.

Anchorage: The V-shaped breakwater that protects the Harbor of Refuge provides good anchorage when conditions are calm. Holding here is less than ideal, though, as heavy patches of kelp foul the bottom. In addition to double-checking for a secure set, choose a spot well within the "V," standing clear of vessels on course from the east entrance through the breakwater to the dredged channel (beginning at the west entrance) leading into Point Judith Pond.

Point Judith Pond, RI

POINT JUDITH POND		Largest Vessel Accommodated	VHF Channel Monitored	Transient Berths / Total Berths	Approach / Dockside Depth (reported)	Floating Docks	Gas / Diesel	Groceries, Ice, Marine Supplies, Snacks	Repairs: Hull, Engine, Propeller	Lift (tonnage), Crane, Rail	1=110V, 2=220V, B=Both, Max Amps	Laundry, Pool, Showers	Pump-Out Station	Nearby: Grocery Store, Motel, Restaurant
		Dockage					Supplies		Services					
1. Snug Harbor Marina Inc.	401-783-7766	70	66	1/11	6/6	F	GD	GIMS			B/50			GR
2. **Belle Vue Yachting Center** (Internet Access) (Wireless Internet Access)	**401-782-8899**	**110**	**09**	**4/75**	**10/10**	**F**	**GD**	**IM**			**1/50**	**LPS**	**P**	**GMR**
3. **Point Judith Marina** (Wireless Internet Access)	**401-789-7189**	**110**	**09**	**3/150**	**10/12**	**F**	**GD**	**IMS**	**HEP**	**L50**	**B/50**	**LPS**	**P**	**GR**

Corresponding chart(s) not to be used for navigation. Internet Access Wireless Internet Access

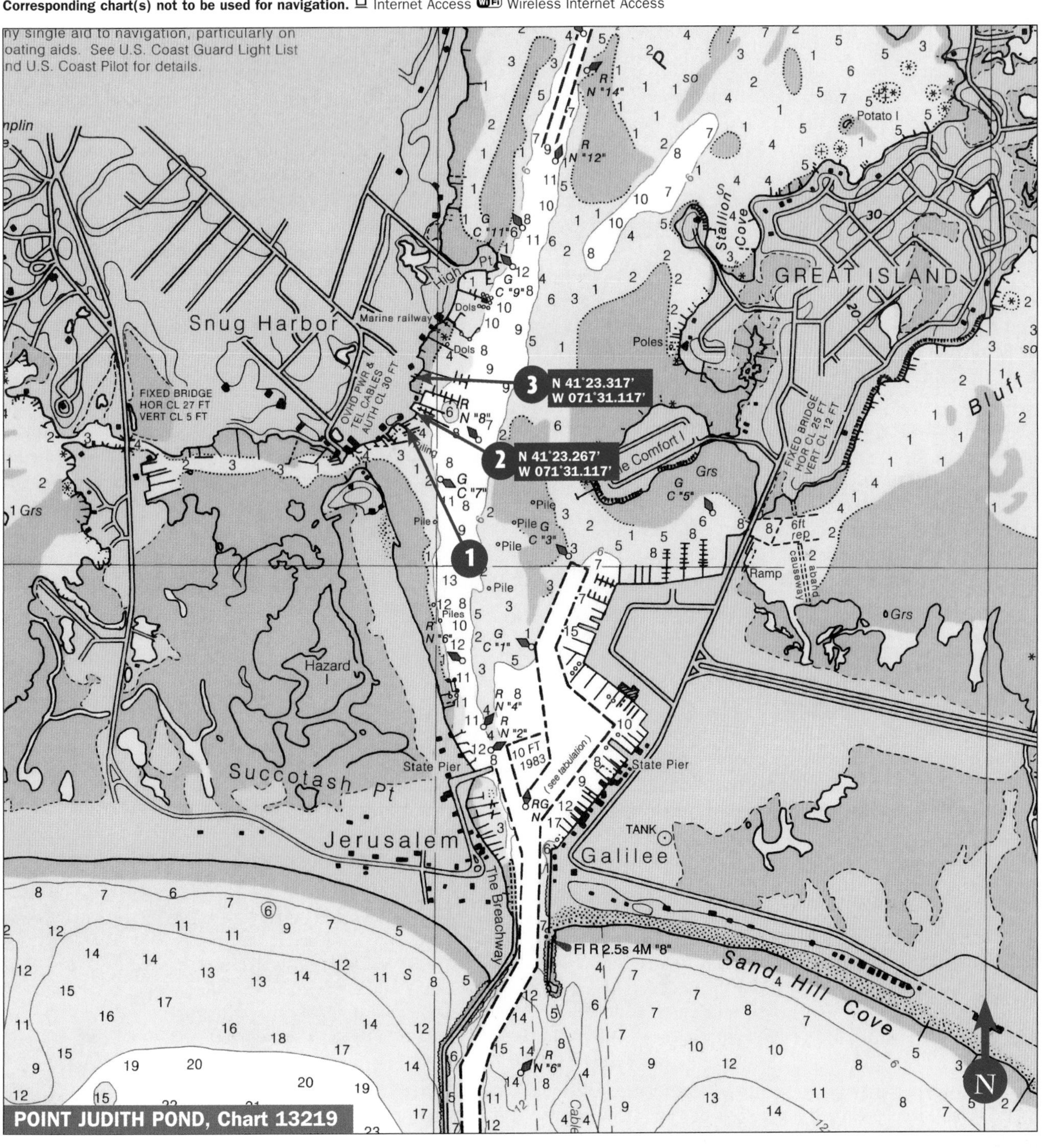

POINT JUDITH POND, Chart 13219

Point Judith Pond, RI

As a precaution against sudden wind shifts to the northwest during one of the frequent summer nighttime squalls in this area, avoid locations overly close to the breakwater. Some shoaling has occurred along the inside of the breakwater, and a substantial sandbar is developing in an area approximately 100 yards to the right (facing seaward) of the white flashing light located at the apex of the "V." When northerly winds interrupt the prevailing southwesterlies, it is best to anchor in the lee of Galilee, off the beach at Sand Hill Cove. Under these conditions, secure anchorage in sand and mud can be found in depths of 7 to 12 feet at mean low water. Whatever the location in the Harbor of Refuge, the surge attending Block Island Sound's characteristic ground swells seems to find its way through the breakwater. Moderate to heavy conditions outside will provide plenty of movement inside the harbor.

In September 2003, Hurricane Isabel missed the Rhode Island coast by many miles, but the storm surge and winds of 35 to 40 knots created unsafe conditions for any vessel. In the event of serious storm conditions, seek shelter farther inland in Narragansett Bay or its tributaries.

Point Judith Pond

You will find better protection and more interesting scenery in Point Judith Pond, called Salt Pond by the people here. Its shores and islands are lined with fishing villages, summer cottages and well-equipped marinas. Depths for 3.5 miles to the head of the pond are enough for boats with drafts of up to 6 feet, but get up-to-the-moment information, if possible. The channels, dredged out of shoal and marsh, can silt up quickly after a storm.

Note: The ninth edition of Chart 13219 has some incorrect buoy numbers in the channel. The 12th edition (October '01) was the most current NOAA edition of this chart available at publication save for print-on-demand (POD) charts. Online editions have been updated to April 2009.

Galilee and Jerusalem

NAVIGATION: Use Chart 13219. Enter the pond by running strong currents between the rock jetties at The Breachway, in the northwest corner of the Harbor of Refuge. Currents at full tidal flow make 3 to 4 knots through this narrow passage, where commercial and recreational traffic can be intense. Weaving, leaping and capsizing jet skiers contribute yet another dimension to the already turbulent waters, while fishermen and gawkers line the jetty to point and place their bets on which ones will survive. Sailing in or maneuvering underpowered boats against the tide here are bad ideas.

Once through The Breachway, the channel almost immediately divides at a prominent red and green bell buoy—Galilee to starboard with its big state piers, berthing the commercial fishing fleet and the Block Island Ferry, and Jerusalem to port, seemingly a village of cottages. Off the piers, a fair-sized area has been dredged, but the current remains strong here and larger vessels need all the room available.

There are no real provisions on the Galilee side for cruisers, although visiting boats may tie up at the state pier for as long as two hours. Those wishing a more extensive visit might do well to remain outside the pond, taking the dinghy in for shore activities or a swim.

Cruising facilities are also scarce—almost nonexistent—on the Jerusalem side, south of Snug Harbor. Visitors will do better to move farther north into the pond, and then take the run back by motorized dinghy for a visit to Jerusalem's excellent beach (outside and west of the Harbor of Refuge) or for a meal at Jerusalem's Capt. Jack's Restaurant.

GOIN' ASHORE: GALILEE, RI

Galilee may not be an ideal provisioning stop, but if you have a craving for fresh seafood, this is the place. Galilee's sea-oriented commerce is located along a single street paralleling Point Judith Pond. Handrigan Seafoods (next to the Coast Guard station, 401-789-6201) has that sweet smell of fresh fish and shellfish. ABC Lobster nearby has its namesake aplenty, fresh fish and prepared seafood to go. About a block north (just past the Galilee Marine Trade Center), Fish's Famous Foods offers a steaming single lobster with corn and potato; they have tanks of live, fresh lobsters and crabs. For sit-down service, George's of Galilee (on the edge of Salty Brine Beach, 250 Sand Hill Cove Road, 401-783-2306) is the standby—no frills, just mounds of savory delights from the sea and a selection of pastas. Across the street, Champlin's Fish Market (401-783-3152) is rustic and modestly priced, with mostly fried or steamed seafood, prepared to your order for pick-up at the service window. Eat at their picnic tables or take it back to the boat. (Champlin's even has a small dinghy dock just to starboard inside The Breachway to accommodate cruising patrons.) Top of the Dock Restaurant (294 Great Island Road, 401-789-7900) is more upscale but still casual and modestly priced. For restocking the larder, little else is available, though you can find a few basic items, a small deli and newspapers at the Galilee Grocery and Gourmet (401-783-5164, across from Top of the Dock). The Block Island Ferry terminal is here.

ADDITIONAL RESOURCES:

- **Galilee Business Directory, www.narragansettri.com/galilee**

NEARBY GOLF COURSES:
Winnapaug Golf Course, 184 Shore Road, Westerly, RI 02891, 401-596-1237

NEARBY MEDICAL FACILITIES:
South County Hospital, 100 Kenyon Ave., Wakefield, RI 02879, 401-782-8000

Snug Harbor

A marked channel, carrying at least 6-foot depths at low water, leads north on the west side of the pond to Snug Harbor, almost a mile above the entrance.

Wakefield, RI

WAKEFIELD		Largest Vessel Accommodated	VHF Channel Monitored	Transient Berths / Total Berths	Approach / Dockside Depth (reported)	Floating Docks	Gas / Diesel	Groceries, Ice, Marine Supplies, Snacks	Repairs: Hull, Engine, Propeller	Lift (tonnage), Crane, Rail	1=110V, 2=220V, B=Both, Max Amps	Laundry, Pool, Showers	Pump-Out Station	Nearby: Grocery Store, Motel, Restaurant
		Dockage					Supplies		Services					
1. Billington Cove Marina	401-783-1266	35	6	3/80	4/4	F	G	IMS	HEP	LCR	1/30	S		M
2. Silver Spring Marine 🖳	401-783-0783	40	7	12/85	5/5	F		IM	HP	L35	1/30	PS		GMR
3. Ram Point Marina	401-783-4535	60	09/66	2/150	6/6	F	GD	IMS	HEP	C	B/50	LS	P	MR
4. Marina Bay Docking	401-789-4050	50	09	2/65	6/5	F		I	E		B/30	S		R
5. Stone Cove Marina (WiFi)	401-783-8990	45	71	4/165	6/6	F	G	IMS	EP		1/30	S		GMR
6. Long Cove Marina	401-783-4902	24		3/45	6/4	F						S		GR

Corresponding chart(s) not to be used for navigation. 🖳 Internet Access (WiFi) Wireless Internet Access

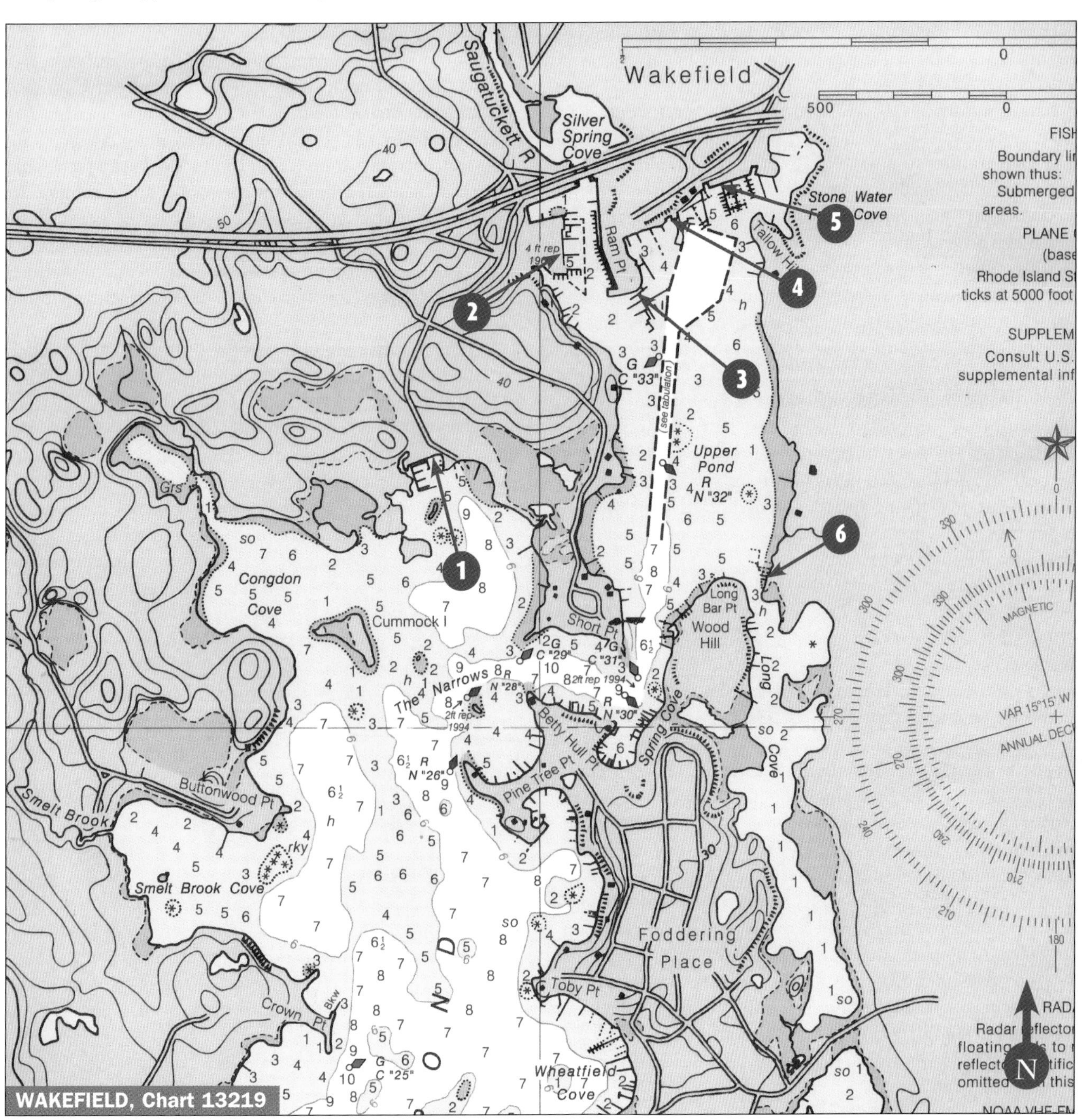

NAVIGATION: Use Chart 13219. Note that there has been significant shoaling reported between red nun buoy "6" (just north of the State Pier on the Jerusalem side) and green can buoy "7." Just past the large wooden piling north of red nun buoy "6," begin to trace the crescent of the shoreline at a distance of approximately 150 to 200 feet off the beach, gauged to leave green can buoy "7" about 100 feet off to port. You will notice deep-draft commercial vessels taking this course, where there are 8- to 10-foot depths.

Be cautious farther upstream and observe all channel markers. Boats drawing much over 5 feet may touch bottom (in soft mud) at low water, even in the center of the channel. Locals advise hugging the port side between green can buoys "17" and "19." After that point, depths increase to 9 feet at low water until reaching the 5- to 6-foot shoal preceding green can buoy "25," just north of the passage between Gardner Island and Beach Island. As with all such channels, try to make the passage on a rising tide if you have a deep-draft vessel.

At red nun buoy "28," just north of Pine Tree Point, the channel takes a sharp turn to starboard into The Narrows, and then another to port to head for the Upper Pond. Give the point a fair berth.

Dockage: Quiet Snug Harbor, on the western shore just north of The Breachway, offers easy-access dockage, marine facilities, fuel and casual restaurants. The first marina to port caters primarily to serious fishermen (five fishing tournaments take place here annually) but they usually have a few transient slips with up to 5-foot depths (restrooms, but no showers). Besides a well-stocked tackle shop and ship's store, the marina has its own snack bar and a small grocery with fresh seafood in season. It is best to call on VHF Channel 66 for exact directions before powering into the fuel dock. Shoaling extended north and east of green can buoy "7" at this writing and they advised to hold off the can to the east by at least 100 feet before circling north, and then west into the fuel dock.

Immediately to the north, the Belle Vue Yachting Center offers deepwater floating docks for transients. Electricity, phone and cable TV are available at every slip. Dockage includes access to the center's pool and clubhouse, showers and a coin-operated laundry. This marina has diesel fuel, pump-out and emergency repairs; advance reservations are recommended.

Just to the north, Point Judith Marina has slips for transients and an easy-access, alongside fuel dock. The marina's owner-managers take pride in having "found a mechanical niche to fill." There's a serious parts department for the most common diesel brands (factory authorized dealers for Cummins, Volvo, Yanmar, Ford Lehman and Westerbeke), and virtually any other repair is available here for boats up to 50 feet in length. The locally familiar fire-engine-red vessels of BoatU.S.-affiliated Safe Sea quick-response towing and rescue operation also are on call. From any of these locations in Snug Harbor, it is easy to arrange a rental car or call a taxi for reprovisioning in nearby Wakefield or for sightseeing inland.

Anchorage: Anchorage-intent cruisers should take the Gardner Island-Beach Island passage south (following the chart closely) to drop a hook northeast of Plato Island. Holding is excellent here in firm mud, but shoaling extends from the east tip of Plato Island, so check with a depth sounder to be sure you have adequate swinging room. Plato Island is inhabited; respect the owner's privacy. The adjacent islands are also private, yet you may explore with appropriate respect for their natural settings. From here on a summer's morning, you can watch the quahog fishermen muscle their clam rakes for hours, pulling this delicacy from the restored and now-clean pond waters. Good fishing has returned here as well; flounder, stripers and blues are all said to be susceptible to the right rig in season.

Wakefield

The Upper Pond at Wakefield is almost entirely filled with private moorings, making anchoring quite difficult, yet there is plenty of dock space at reasonable rates.

Dockage: At the head of the Upper Pond, Marina Bay Docking usually has several slips to accommodate boats up to 40 feet, carrying up to 6-foot drafts. Docks are somewhat rustic but adequate, showers are available and a center-harbor location all but guarantees a good breeze. South Shore Grille is at the head of the dock (with an ample dinghy dock). For an apparently out-of-the-way location, the food is exceptional, served with a casual, deck-side ambience and a serene water view.

To port on entry to the Upper Pond (immediately beyond the University of Rhode Island Sailing Center), Ram Point Marina is a full-service facility with ample space for transients, depths to 6 feet, an impressive ship's store and the customer-friendly attitude of a family business. There are floating docks, one transient mooring, picnic areas, a jogging trail, an outside stage for summer concerts, clean showers, a public phone, laundry machines and repair services.

Stone Cove Marina may have a few transient berths, accommodating up to 6-foot drafts. The marina has showers available for guests, plus a substantial fishing and boating supply store. Any of these marinas will respond to a call on VHF Channel 09.

Within a half mile as the crow flies (the interstate highway pattern makes it a difficult and longer walk) is a major shopping mall with a Super Stop & Shop, Ames, other stores and chain restaurants (walk under the U.S. Route 1 overpass, north one long block, then right about two-tenths of a mile to the plaza on the right).

Cruising Options

From Wakefield, the cruiser has only to voyage back south through Point Judith Pond and the Harbor of Refuge, and then head northeast around Point Judith Horn into Narragansett Bay and a string of inviting cruising stops, including Wickford, Jamestown, Bristol and Sakonnet Harbor. ■

Narragansett Bay

CHARTS 13218, 13219, 13221, 13223, 13224, 13225, 13226, 13227

■ RHODE ISLAND WATERS

Newport, though one of the East Coast's major yachting centers, is by no means the only attraction on Narragansett Bay. Named for Rhode Island's original inhabitants, the bay stretches 18 miles from the entrance to the mouth of the Providence River—with Providence, the state capital, seven miles upriver.

Rolling hills, green fields, woods and houses surround Narragansett Bay. It offers protected waters, well-marked waterways, sheltered coves and attractive ports of call. You can anchor anywhere you find a lee or a cove, and in many places you can go ashore for a swim, picnic or hike.

Modern marinas, excellent marine repairs, services, suppliers, pump-out stations, restaurants, shore transportation and accommodations are easy to locate throughout the bay. Yet the popularity of this "Jewel of Rhode Island" continues to outpace the availability of slip space and moorings. Those wanting the convenience of dockage or moorings should reserve them in advance.

NAVIGATION: Use Chart 13221. No longer identified by the once-imposing Brenton Reef Light tower, the entrance to the bay is marked by flashing red-and-white Morse (A) Narragansett Bay Entrance lighted whistle buoy "NB," also announcing itself with the familiar RACON B of its predecessor.

Both East and West passages of Narragansett Bay are deep and well-marked. These two entrances to the bay are split by Conanicut Island, marked at its point by Beavertail Point Light (64-foot-tall tower; flashing white every nine seconds; horn blast every 30 seconds in fog), preceded to seaward by green and red bell buoy "NR."

Beavertail Point Light is on the National Historic Register. The original stone base, uncovered during the hurricane of 1938, was constructed in 1749, making it the third oldest lighthouse in America. The present granite tower is just north of the original light. A ranger and naturalist are on duty to give tours of the state park in the summer. During any significant storm, such as a nor'easter, hundreds of people visit Beavertail to watch the waves and surf. Sadly, a fatality occurred during Hurricane Isabel in 2003 when one person was washed off the rocks.

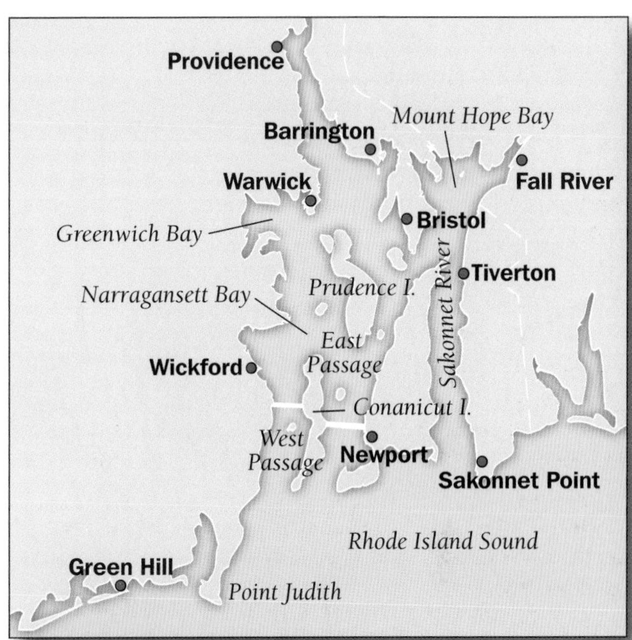

■ WEST PASSAGE

NAVIGATION: Use Chart 13221. About seven miles northeast of Point Judith, the entrance to West Passage lies between Whale Rock (flashing green gong buoy "3") and Beavertail Point. Unless seas are pounding in from the southern sector, the passage is normally calm.

Dutch Island Harbor

This protected cove, on the west side of Conanicut Island, 2.5 miles north of Beavertail Point, is easy to enter from either north or south. Dutch Island protects it on the west; only northerly winds can make it unpleasant. Turning and anchor room are ample with good holding in 9- to 17-foot depths. Scenic paths and abandoned forts make for good exploring on Dutch Island (part of the Rhode Island Park System).

Moorings: Guest moorings are available from Dutch Harbor Boat Yard (overnight, or for an afternoon stopover, including launch service from the mooring field or north anchorage; hail NOVA on VHF Channel 69). Hull and engine repairs are available, but fuel is not. For its guests, restrooms and showers are located in the office. A dumpster and a public phone are across the street. Dutch Harbor Boatyard has also added pump-out service at moorings or anchor—hail "Making Headway" on VHF Channel 69.

Another important service offered by Dutch Harbor Boatyard is wireless Internet; available for a daily fee. From this tranquil and protected location, the excellent

Wickford, RI

WICKFORD		Largest Vessel Accommodated	VHF Channel Monitored	Transient Berths / Total Berths	Approach / Dockside Depth (reported)	Floating Docks	Gas / Diesel	Groceries, Ice, Marine Supplies, Snacks	Repairs: Hull, Engine, Propeller	Lift (tonnage), Crane, Rail	1=110V, 2=220V, B=Both, Max Amps	Laundry, Pool, Showers	Pump-Out Station	Nearby: Grocery Store, Motel, Restaurant
		Dockage					Supplies		Services					
1. Wickford Yacht Club	401-294-9010	50	09		7/7			I						GMR
2 Pleasant Street Wharf Inc.	401-294-2791	35		2/42	13/10	F	GD	IM	EP	L15	1/30	S		GMR
3. Wickford Marina (Wireless Internet Access)	**401-294-8160**	**100**	**10**	**6/62**	**12/8**	**F**		**I**			**B/50**	**LS**	**P**	**GR**
4. Johnson's Boatyard	401-294-3700	40		/45	4/4	F		M	HEP	L15	1/20	S		
5. Wickford Shipyard Inc.	401-884-1725	60		6/135	9/9	F	GD	IM	HEP	L50,C	B/50	LPS		GMR
6. Brewer Wickford Cove Marina (Wireless Internet Access)	**401-884-7014**	**80**	**09**	**10/151**	**10/9**	**F**	**GD**	**IM**	**HEP**	**L80**	**B/50**	**LS**	**P**	**GMR**

Corresponding chart(s) not to be used for navigation. Internet Access · Wireless Internet Access

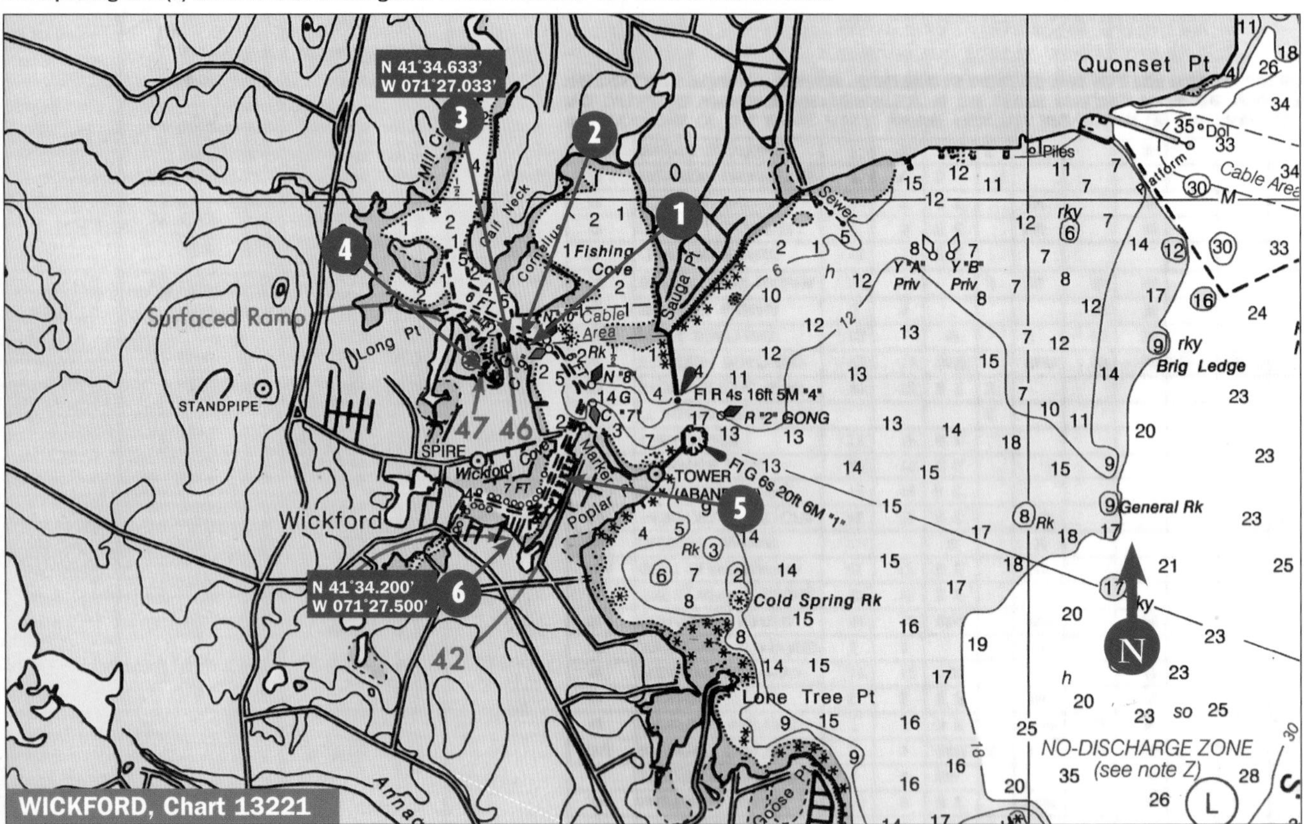

restaurants and amenities of Jamestown are an easy half-mile walk to the east. For a full description of the delights of Jamestown, see the "Goin' Ashore" section later in this chapter.

Anchorage: Uncomplicated anchorage in firm mud is located just outside the mooring field along the southeastern side of Dutch Island Harbor in 13- to 15-foot depths at low water or, particularly when there is a chance of a northerly, in the small bight at the northeastern side of the harbor. No launch service is available to boats anchored out. There is, however, an ample public dinghy dock next to the town pier (immediately south of the boatyard dock). You can offload your trash at the town-maintained dumpster just above the dinghy dock and use the do-it-yourself pump-out station at the town's easy-access, deep-draft dock, accommodating boats to about 40 feet.

Wickford

On the mainland shore of West Passage, Wickford is one of Narragansett Bay's most charming cruising destinations. Wickford's Main Street has one of the best and least pretentious collections of 18th- and early 19th-century buildings anywhere. There is nothing ersatz or "restored" about these structures; they are just old, lived in and well-maintained. Beyond a not-to-be-missed walking tour down Main Street to view these Colonial structures, the village offers an accommodating selection of marine service facilities, reprovisioning possibilities and shops.

MA
RI

NAVIGATION: Use Chart 13221. Use Newport Tide Tables. For hight tide, add 3 minutes; for low tide, subtract 6 minutes. Wickford's fine harbor (two harbors, really)

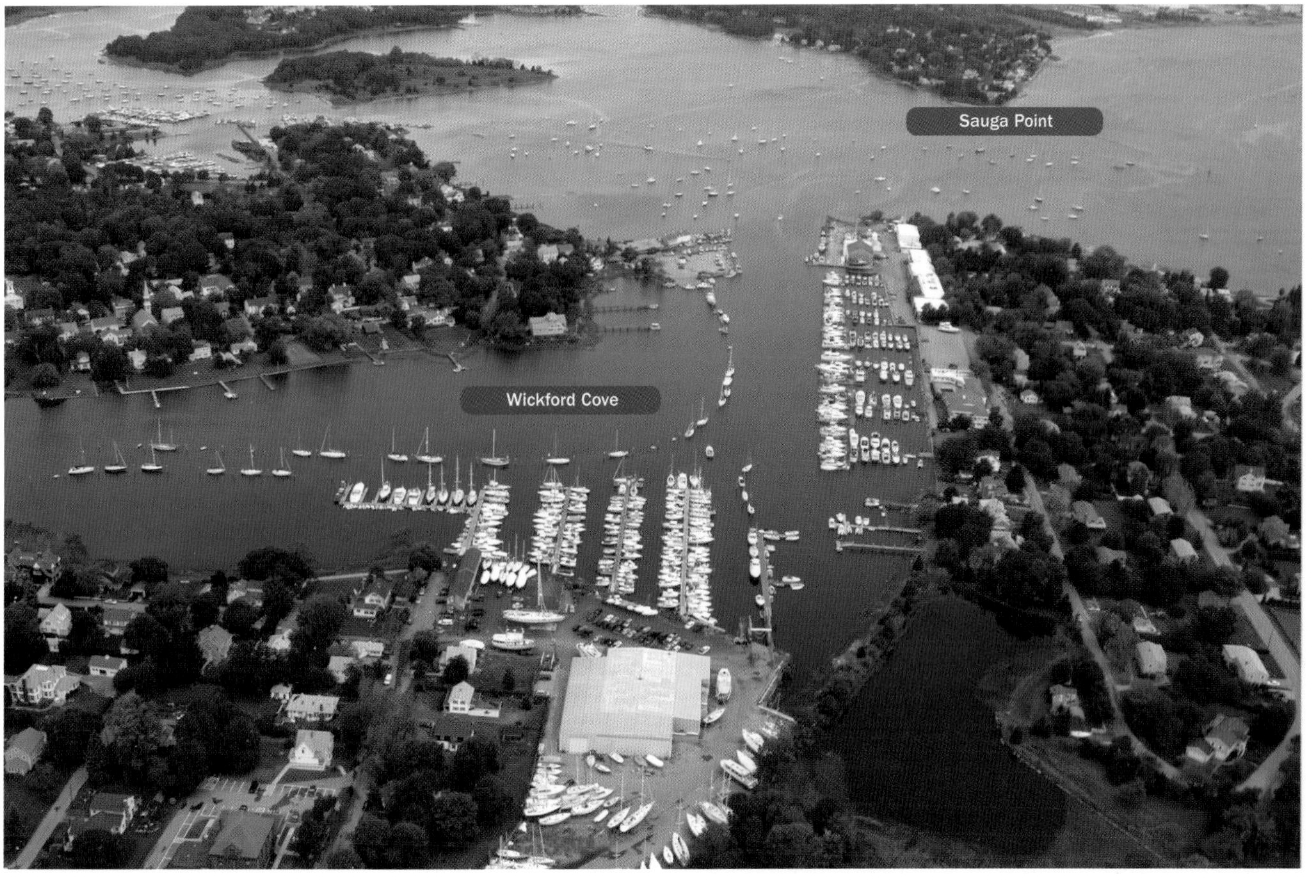

An aerial view of Wickford, RI. (Not to be used for navigation.) WATERWAY GUIDE PHOTOGRAPHY

is located three miles northwest of the double-spanned Jamestown-North Kingstown fixed bridge (135-foot fixed vertical clearance) connecting Conanicut Island to the mainland at North Kingstown.

Heading up the bay for Wickford, keep Fox Island to port and do not cut between it and Rome Point. While there is plenty of water in this area, there are also plenty of rocks. Wickford's outer harbor is easily entered due west of red gong buoy "2" between the well-marked, lighted ends (flashing green "1" and flashing red "4") of the jetties guarding the mooring field within. The channels and coves of Wickford Harbor (but not the full outer harbor) are dredged to a 7-foot minimum depth throughout. You can count on 8-foot depths in Wickford Cove, but take care to stay in the channel.

Dockage: For those wishing only a brief visit to the village, the Wickford Town Dock lies immediately parallel to Brown Street (the town's primary shopping row). The dock is substantial in size, carries 7-foot depths at mean low water, and permits a free two-hour tie-up that is immediately convenient for shopping and reprovisioning. Dinghies may be tied up just inside the town dock.

Many facilities for visiting boaters are in Wickford Cove, via the well-marked channel to port after entering the outer harbor. Wickford Shipyard, first on the left and immediately across from the town's commercial wharf, is a full-service operation with floating docks, gasoline and diesel fuel, lift and repair service, a marine store, a swimming pool, showers, restrooms and a coin-operated laundry.

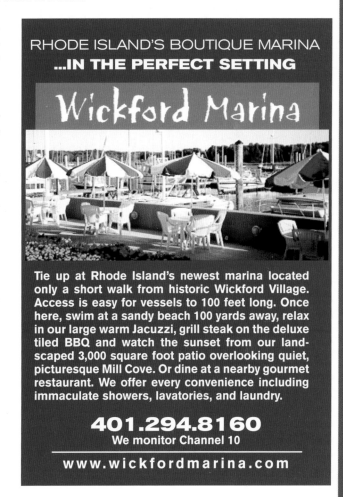

Wickford, RI

Brewer Wickford Cove Marina is next, with 155 slips, 44 moorings and 39 between-pilings moorings. Brewer is a full-service operation, offering diesel engine, outboard, hull and prop repairs, rigging refits and painting and fabrication services. Use of the marina's showers and laundry room is complimentary. Brewer's has added an e-mail address for making reservations for a slip: wcmdockmaster@byy.com. Mechanics and the yard's 50-ton lift are available on weekdays and Saturdays during the season.

Nantucket Ship Chandlery, located on the premises, has an interesting collection of nautical consignment items in addition to boat supplies at prices competitive with the largest discount suppliers. Safe Sea (BoatU.S.-affiliated) quick-response rescue and towing boats are also on call at Brewer's docks. This is the closest base for a walking or dinghy excursion to the village.

Additional marine facilities are on Mill Cove via the dredged, 7-foot-deep marked channel to starboard after entering the breakwater. The Wickford Yacht Club, immediately to port on arrival at the cove, typically has several moorings for visiting yachts. Next door, Pleasant Street Wharf may have transient dock space, in addition to fuel, restrooms, showers, ship's supplies and ice.

Immediately beyond the Rhode Island State wharf (also to port), Wickford Marina offers floating docks. Dockside depths accommodate drafts of 7 feet or more at low water. The marina's separate showers and restrooms are top of the line in quality. Its Jacuzzi overlooks Mill Cove's mooring field and unspoiled 60-acre estuary to the north. There is ample room to picnic here, and you are welcome to use the commercial-style gas-fired grill. From Mill Cove, it is a pleasant four-tenths of a mile to the center of Wickford's historic village. Wickford Marina offers a new concept in dining: Prepared frozen entrees shipped in from Angelo's Civita Farnese of Providence are available at the marina for a special onboard meal. Coffee and doughnuts are available gratis on summer weekends from 8 a.m. to 11 a.m.

Moorings: The town of North Kingstown provides two free moorings (bright orange, marked NK MOORING 24-HOUR USE) just inside the breakwater, to port on entry. Additional private moorings are usually open for a nightly rental on assignment by the harbormaster (call on VHF Channel 09). Brewer's Launch (also monitoring VHF Channel 09) provides on-call water taxi service (free, though a tip to the launch driver is much appreciated) throughout the harbor. Brewer Wickford Cove Marina maintains six heavy-duty, short-term rental moorings outside the breakwater, though this can be a restless spot when the wind picks up.

Anchorage: Beyond a tight spot or two just inside Wickford's protective entrance jetties, west of red gong buoy "2," little suitable anchorage space remains inside either harbor.

Because of the scarcity of anchorage room inside the breakwater, visiting skippers frequently take advantage of settled summer weather to anchor south of the abandoned tower (preceding the port-side jetty of the harbor entrance) off Wickford's town beach in 7- to 8-foot depths at low water. Holding is excellent on a sand-mud bottom and protection is good from prevailing winds, including a clocking wind to the northwest.

You will want both a chart and a rising tide to help you pick your way in past two shallow (2- and 3-foot-deep) spots on the open path to the best beachside anchorage. Additional anchorage room is increasingly favored by visiting yachts north of the harbor entrance, outside the small mooring field there. Holding is secure in 15- to 20-foot depths, but the fetch for prevailing southwesterly winds and front-driven northerlies is substantial. It can get rocky here in these conditions, even boisterous.

GOIN' ASHORE: **WICKFORD, RI**

From a berth in either cove, be prepared for about a half-mile trek to the commercial facilities along Brown Street, parallel to the inner harbor. It may be more convenient, particularly from a mooring or Wickford Cove dock, to take your dinghy or your boat for a short-term tie-up alongside the town dock (10-foot depths) at the head of Wickford Cove and immediately across the parking lot from Ryan's Market. Ryan's is an old-fashioned, small-scale supermarket with fresh vegetables and fruit, fresh-cut meats and fish and dry goods.

In a short walk along East Main and Brown streets, you will locate a large pharmacy and sundry store, Wickford Package Store (with a fairly extensive, if pricey, selection of wines), a new and used bookstore, Five Main (offering the talented renderings of local marine artists), several antiques shops, an antique consignment arcade and Wilson's clothing store. Champlin's Seafood of Wickford, selling the freshest catch, smoked fish and stuffed quahogs, retail and wholesale, is located on Gardiner's Wharf (land's end of East Main Street). You can land your dinghy at the town's floating dock, north of the commercial wharf. At the other end of town, at the junction of Brown Street and Route 102, Fleet Bank has an ATM. Across from the bank, Coastal Yacht Rigging has parts and solutions for rigging and mooring problems.

For an out-of-galley experience, Wickford is a village of diners: the Waterfront Grill (hearty, early-served breakfasts, great sandwiches at lunchtime and tables outside along the water); Wickford Diner (classic, dining car style, favored by many locals); Harborside Grill (plentiful, inexpensive breakfasts); and The Place in Wickford (Greek pizzas, calzones and sandwiches)—are all within steps of each other on Main Street. The Wickford Gourmet (on Main Street just off Brown Street) also serves light luncheons al fresco, but "gourmet" is clearly the correct word choice. Inside, a storehouse of edible treasures and specialties—dozens of exotic cheeses and pates, coffee varieties and roasts from all over the world, boutique oils, vinegars, hot sauces, pastas and spices—will add zest to anyone's food lockers.

The Seaport Tavern Restaurant (16 W. Main St., 401-294-5771) serves superb seafood (mussels, steamers, clams and calamari) selections and salads at lunchtime daily at tables overlooking the tidal pool, and a full dinner menu for intimate, inside dining in the evening. Away from the village, the Carriage Inn has been serving hungry visitors for more than

230 years. It will shuttle visiting mariners to and from their boats to sample the inn's casual dining in a Colonial atmosphere; call 401-294-2727 for reservations or take-out service. For those with access to a ride, the best value in the area for American fare in hearty portions is Gregg's Restaurant & Pub (4120 Quaker Lane/Route 2).

Visitors to Wickford in the summer season can enjoy Tuesday night concerts in the village center and extended shopping hours in all stores on the first Friday of each month.

Wickford's fine 18th-century buildings open to the public include: Smith's Castle, a Colonial great house, with an 18th-century herb and flower garden and doll collection; Old Narragansett Church, the oldest Episcopal church still standing north of Virginia; and the Fireman's Memorial. Every year in mid-July, the town hosts an extensive art festival, billed as the oldest open air art festival in the United States. In August, Wickford presents its International Quahog Festival. ("Gray Quahog" T-shirts are Wickford's answer to Martha's Vineyard's "Black Dog.")

ADDITIONAL RESOURCES:

■ Wickford Village Association,
www.wickfordvillage.org

NEARBY GOLF COURSES:
North Kingstown Municipal Golf Course,
North Kingstown, RI 02852, 401-294-0684,
www.northkingstown.org

NEARBY MEDICAL FACILITIES:
Kent County Memorial Hospital, 455 Toll Gate Road,
Warwick, RI 02886, 401-736-4288

Allen Harbor

Two and a half miles north of Wickford is Allen Harbor. Wickford Harbor and Allen Harbor, originally maintained by the Navy as part of the Sea Bee's training center, are now under the jurisdiction of the North Kingstown harbormaster. Well-protected Allen Harbor offers slips and 80 moorings. Moorings are more likely to be available than slips; contact the harbormaster on VHF Channel 16 or the marina at 401-294-1212. The town of North Kingston has established a pump-out station at Allen Harbor.

NAVIGATION: Use Chart 13221. The approach is somewhat tricky, so stay between the entrance buoys and aim straight for the harbor entrance. Keep an eye on the depth sounder; shoals are on either side. If you draw more than 5 feet, enter on a rising tide. Once inside, you will find depths of 10 to 11 feet. When you continue north, stay outside of green can buoy "3," marking Calf Pasture Point's outer limit.

Calf Pasture Point to Warwick Point

NAVIGATION: Use Chart 13221. In all but the clearest weather, follow at least a rough compass or specific GPS course for the entire section between Quonset Point and Warwick Point. This precaution will not only keep you clear of Calf Pasture Point but also of the buoyed rocks a mile east of Potowomut Neck. Shoal water extends well to the east of Sandy Point.

Greenwich Bay

Greenwich Bay is a three-mile-long arm of Narragansett Bay with three good harbors. Ashore are parks, beaches, shoreside amusements, transportation and boating amenities. Shoals and rocks are usually well-marked, although some buoy numbers may not match the chart.

NAVIGATION: Use Chart 13221. From the south, pass well east of buoyed (flashing green buoy "1") Round Rock off Potowomut Neck, and do not cut across the shoal east of Sandy Point. Follow the chart and buoys through the deep channel south of Warwick Point's lighthouse. Once inside, you have a choice of several good harbors. Clockwise from the southwestern corner, they are Greenwich, Apponaug and Warwick coves.

East Greenwich

The long, finger-like harbor for this town, Greenwich Cove, is fully protected from all but strong northeasters. It is also one of Narragansett Bay's most popular stops, boasting a fair mix of marine facilities and amenities along the western edge with a backdrop of unspoiled greenery on the eastern side.

NAVIGATION: Use Chart 13221. Though approach and entry to the cove are relatively easy, this is no place to cut buoys. Stay well north of green can buoy "5" (marking Sally Rock) in starting your path to green can buoy "7," leaving red nun buoy "6" well to port, but skirting the shoaling that extends north of Long Point. Having honored green can buoy "7" to port, you will see an extensive mooring field come into view. There still may be anchorage space available on the east side of the cove, but swing room is in increasingly short supply.

Dockage: Norton's Shipyard and Marina (immediately west of green can buoy "7") has 185 rental slips and 100 moorings served by the marina's launch, a ship's store and decades of experience in marine repairs. Norton's has added wireless Internet service and replaced 90 percent of their docks in recent years. The Maritime Restaurant serves modestly priced breakfasts and lunches.

Farther south, the East Greenwich Yacht Club is likely to have a guest mooring for visitors from other recognized clubs, with launch service to its docks and facilities. Farther along, Harborside Lobstermania is highly regarded for its named specialty as well as other seafood. It has dockage for its waterborne patrons. Next door, the Blue Parrot Cafe offers casual dining and cocktails al fresco, or in a more formal setting indoors. Another excellent restaurant choice is Twenty Water Street with both inside and outside dining possibilities, located at Milt's Marina. There is transient slip space here as well. East Greenwich Marina and Greenwich Cove Marina, still farther toward the head of the harbor, are both likely to have transient slips and moorings.

Greenwich to Warwick Cove, RI

GREENWICH TO WARWICK COVE		Largest Vessel Accommodated	VHF Channel Monitored	Transient Berths / Total Berths	Approach / Dockside Depth (reported)	Floating Docks	Gas / Diesel	Groceries, Ice, Marine Supplies, Snacks	Repairs: Hull, Engine, Propeller	Lift (tonnage), Crane, Rail	1=110V, 2=220V, B=Both, Max Amps	Laundry, Pool, Showers	Pump-Out Station	Nearby: Grocery Store, Motel, Restaurant
		Dockage					Supplies		Services					
1. Greenwich Cove Marina	401-885-6611	50			10/8						1/30			R
2. Harbourside Lobstermania	401-884-6363				10/8	F					1/30			R
3. Table 28 Restaurant	401-884-2002			RESTAURANT										R
4. Twenty Water Street Restaurant	401-885-3700	100		8/32	15/8						B/50			R
5. Milt's Marina @ TWS Restaurant	401-885-3700	100		8/22	15/8						B/50			R
6. East Greenwich Yacht Club	401-884-7700	75	09	/120	12/10	F	GD	I			B/50	LS		R
7. Norton's Shipyard & Marina Inc.	401-884-8828	300	09	40/185	8/10	F		IMS	HEP	L35,C	B/50	S		GMR
8. Brewer Yacht Yard at Cowesett	**401-884-0544**	**60**	**09**	**10/250**	**8/8**	**F**		**IM**	**HP**	**LC**	**B/50**	**PS**	**P**	**GMR**
9. Brewer Greenwich Bay Marina	**401-884-1810**	**300**	**09**	**100/510**	**12/12**	**F**	**GD**	**GIMS**	**HEP**	**L60**	**B/200**	**LPS**	**P**	**GMR**
10. Apponaug Harbor Marina	401-739-5005	50		2/348	8/5	F		GIM	HE	L35,C	1/30	S	P	GMR
11. Ponaug Marina	401-884-1976	42	14	2/130	5/4	F	G	I	HP		1/30		P	R
12. Angel's Marina	401-737-9805	40			6/6			I	P		1/15			R
13. Harbor Light Marina	401-737-6353	50	09	2/170	8/6		GD	I	HEP	L	B/50	LS	P	
14. Warwick Cove Marina	401-737-2446	44		/100	7/6	F	G	IMS			1/30	S	P	R
15. Brewer Greenwich Bay Marina North B	401-884-1810	80	09	20/380	10/7	F	GD	GIMS	HEP	L25,C	B/50	PS	P	GR
16. Brewer Greenwich Bay Marina North A	401-884-1810	80	09	10/190	10/7	F	GD	GIMS	HEP	L40	B/50	PS	P	GR
17. Wharf Marina Inc.	401-737-2233	50		3/85	6/6	F		M	HEP	R	1/30		P	GMR
18. Bay Marina Inc.	401-739-6435	50		/200	6/6	F		M	HEP	LC	1/30	S	P	GR

Corresponding chart(s) not to be used for navigation. Internet Access; WiFi Wireless Internet Access

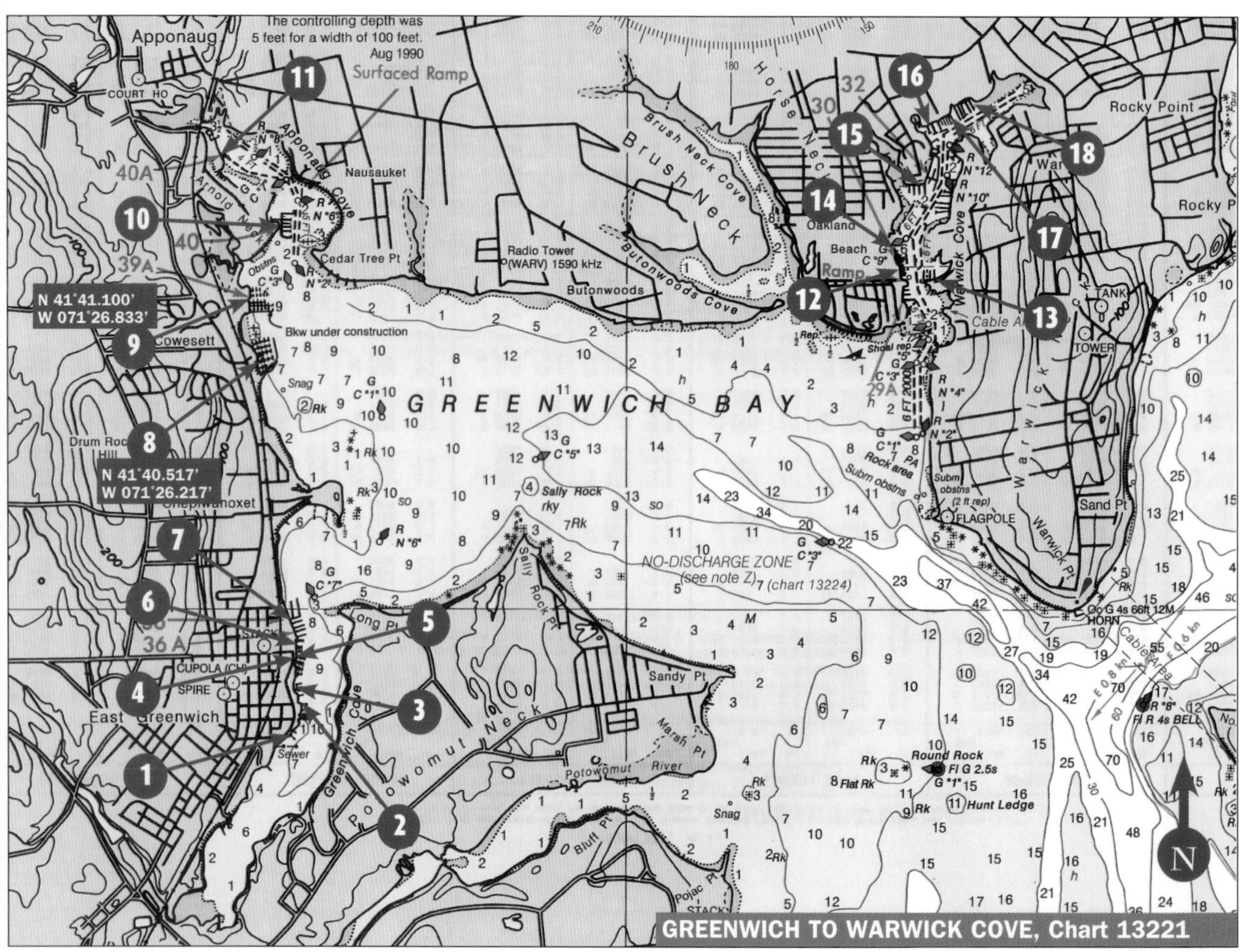

GREENWICH TO WARWICK COVE, Chart 13221

East Greenwich, (pronounced "green-witch") the village, is a short hike uphill and seems both literally and figuratively to be "on the other side of the tracks," lacking the charm of its waterfront. Still, the reprovisioning possibilities here are quite good. Under the railroad tracks on King Street, two blocks uphill to Post Road, and then six blocks south, Dave's Super Market is large and complete. Discount Liquors nearby is almost equally large. There is also a coin-operated laundry here.

Apponaug Cove

About a mile due north of Greenwich Cove is Apponaug Cove, with a direct, easy entrance between Arnold Neck to the west and Cedar Tree Point to the east.

NAVIGATION: Use Chart 13221. The well-buoyed, 5-foot-deep channel extends about a mile to a railroad bridge, with a bend to the west halfway up. Check locally for latest depths; the edges of the channel shoal up periodically. The U.S. Army Corps of Engineers reports that almost 5 feet of water is available except at the head of the channel, where it shoals to 3-foot depths.

Dockage: Protected from all but strong southerly winds, the cove and the area immediately adjacent have several substantial marinas and other services. Brewer Yacht Yard at Cowesett is the first to port after passing green can buoy "1" on approach. The yard is easily entered with 8- to 9-foot depths and is well-protected by bulkheads once inside. A deepwater transient berth is almost certain to be at your disposal here; with it come the amenities of the marina's showers and changing rooms, pool, repair facilities, fuels and the well-regarded Outrigger's Restaurant overlooking the docks from above.

The Brewer Yacht Yard at Cowesett and its sister facility of Brewer Greenwich Bay Marina have a combined total of 1,200 slips. Both marinas now offer wireless Internet at all slips and a complete complement of amenities. Brewer Yacht Yard at Cowesett also has 18 seasonal moorings available.

Immediately to the north, the Brewer Greenwich Bay Marina Club is a full-service facility with fuel and some repair services, as well as transient slips for deep-footed craft. Coastal Marine Supply and a Chart House Restaurant are located in the same compound. Just inside the cove to port, the Apponaug Harbor Marina is home to the Apponaug Yacht Club, popular with sailing visitors. Either a slip or mooring is usually available here, though you will have to go elsewhere for fuel or repair services. Town moorings are located well inside the harbor. Shores of the cove are attractive, the pleasant little town of Apponaug is near the harbor and within easy reach are shore accommodations, supplies and beaches.

Theodore Francis Green Airport (called Providence, though it is really in Warwick), Rhode Island's largest, is less than a 10-minute taxi trip away, making this an easy port to drop off or to pick up guests. The downside, of course, is that the departure and approach ends of the airport's main runway make marina visitors well aware that a busy airport is close at hand. Flights start departing at 6 a.m.

Warwick Cove

In the northeastern sector of the bay, busy Warwick Cove is loaded with fishing stations and marinas (some filled to capacity with local boats). This is another harbor convenient to the T.F. Green (Providence) Airport.

Looking northwest over Warwick Cove. (Not to be used for navigation.) WATERWAY GUIDE PHOTOGRAPHY

NAVIGATION: Use Chart 13221. Leaving Greenwich Bay, turn north between Warwick Point and Patience Island, a state park and estuarine sanctuary. At Conimicut Point, Narragansett Bay becomes the deep and well-marked Providence River (described later). When wind and tide oppose, you might experience an aggressive riptide in the narrow passage between Warwick Point and Patience Island.

Anchorage: The narrow, dredged entrance is well-marked around a shoal that is exposed at low water off the southeastern end of Horse Neck. Between here and the harbor head are moorings and an anchorage basin. Make contact with the harbormaster through Warwick Town Hall. He will direct you to a mooring or a spot to anchor for the night.

Dockage: Warwick Cove has a number of sizable marinas; all of which have a few transient slips available at any given time. Brewer Greenwich Bay Marina North has two yards and a total of 570 slips.

EAST PASSAGE

Of Narragansett Bay's two passages, cruisers generally favor East Passage. Less than two miles wide at most points, it runs deep to the north, between the bay's three large islands: Conanicut and Prudence on the west, and 12-mile-long Aquidneck Island on the east.

NAVIGATION: Use Chart 13221. Use Newport tide tables. When Newport-bound, enter the deep, well-buoyed passage between Beavertail Point and the 40-foot-tall Castle Hill Lighthouse, past magnificent waterfront establishments, including the Hammersmith estate. If entering from the east, honor quick flashing red whistle buoy "2" off Brenton Reef, and then look for red gong buoy "4" and red bell buoy "6." The pre-Civil War Fort Adams marks the entrance to Newport Harbor, where the water is deep right up to its banks.

Newport

Newport is often considered the center of yachting in the Northeast, and rightfully so. Just about every boat traveling the coast makes a stop at Newport. Big yachts in particular, both sail and power, lay over at one of several repair yards, putting in for crew changes, provisioning or refurbishing. Most important, yachts and tourists stop in Newport for the spectacle of the incredible collection of vessels from all over the world and the interesting people who travel on them. It is probably the most sophisticated yachting center on the coast, vying with Fort Lauderdale for the title of "Yachting Capital of the World." Fine varnish work, onboard catering, custom rigging services, new keel designs—Newport is where to find it.

NAVIGATION: Use Chart 13223. Use Newport tide tables.Newport Harbor is well-protected, yet wide at the mouth, easy to enter and deep throughout. The only cautionary advice for first-time skippers rounding 40-foot-tall flashing red "2" and red nun buoy "4" off the point north of Fort Adams is to be aware that large, unusual and otherwise distracting vessels ply these busy waters in profusion, often under full sail and occasionally at speeds that mock known safety limits. Take more than ordinary caution and concentrate on the navigational and tie-up tasks at hand.

GOIN' ASHORE:
NEWPORT, RI

Newport abounds in maxi-yachts, 70-knot powerboats, cruise ships, round-the-world racers and luxurious cruising palaces. These waters are a terminus for many of the world's great races, such as the Cruising Club of America's Newport-to-Bermuda Race on even years, and the OSTAR single-handed Race, as well as the Maxi Series, the Classic Yacht Regatta and, often enough, the Admiral's Cup trials, the New York Yacht Club Cruise and other special events.

The America's Cup trials and races dominated Newport for many decades, and the legacy of that event is evident everywhere. The main street along the waterfront is called America's Cup Avenue. At moorings around the harbor, you will see many 12-meter racers from the classic period of the America's Cup. These refurbished racers are used for day charters and occasional regattas.

Looking west-northwest over Newport. (Not to be used for navigation.) WATERWAY GUIDE PHOTOGRAPHY

Newport and Environs, RI

NEWPORT AND ENVIRONS		Largest Vessel Accommodated	VHF Channel Monitored	Transient Berths / Total Berths	Approach / Dockside Depth (reported)	Floating Docks	Gas / Diesel	Groceries, Ice, Marine Supplies, Snacks	Repairs: Hull, Engine, Propeller	Lift (tonnage), Crane, Rail	1=110V, 2=220V, B=Both, Max Amps	Laundry, Pool, Showers	Pump-Out Station	Nearby: Grocery Store, Motel, Restaurant
		Dockage					Supplies		Services					
1. Ida Lewis Yacht Club	401-846-1969	50	78A	2/18	12/8			I			1/50	S	P	GR
2. West Wind Marina LLC	401-849-4300	200	09	50/60	/13	F	D	I			B/100	LS	P	GMR
3. Casey's Marina 💻	401-848-5945	200	09	/14	16/14	F	D	I			B/100	S		GMR
4. Newport Marina 💻 WiFi	401-849-2293	150	09	15/45	15/10	F		I			B/100	LPS		GMR
5. Brown & Howard Marina, LLC	**401-846-5100**	**250**	**09**		**14/14**			**I**			**B/100**			**MR**
6. Newport Onshore Marina 💻 WiFi	401-849-0480	100	09	/8	12/5	F		I			B/100	LS		MR
7. Forty 1°North 💻 WiFi	401-846-8018	250	09	25/29	40/12	F		I			B/200	LS	P	GMR
8. Newport Yachting Center	800-653-3625	180	09	150/200	22/18	F	GD	IM			B/100	LPS	P	GMR
9. Oldport Marine Services 💻 WiFi	401-847-9109	70	68	MOORINGS				IM	HEP					MR
10. Bannister's Wharf 💻 WiFi	**401-846-4500**	**280**	**09**	**24/24**	**20/17**	**F**	**GD**	**GIMS**			**B/100**	**S**		**GMR**
11. Newport Harbor Hotel & Marina 💻 WiFi	**401-847-9000**	**150**	**09**	**65/65**	**17/8**	**F**		**I**			**B/100**	**LPS**	**P**	**GMR**
12. Newport Yacht Club	401-846-9410	140	78	10/64	20/15			IS			B/50	S	P	GMR
13. Newport Shipyard WiFi	401-846-6000	315	09	60/60	20/20	F	D	IS	HEP	L330,C	B/100	LS	P	GMR
14. Goat Island Marina 💻 WiFi	**401-849-5655**	**200**	**09**	**25/200**	**19/17**	**F**	**GD**	**GIS**	**E**		**B/100**	**LS**	**P**	**GMR**
15. Brenton Cove Moorings	401-849-2210	60	09	14/28	14/	F		S			B/50	S		GMR

Corresponding chart(s) not to be used for navigation. 💻 Internet Access WiFi Wireless Internet Access

Newport is usually crowded in the summer, both on the water and ashore. The visitors center, at the northeastern end of the harbor, can provide a complete guide to shore events, services and historic highlights. They are likely to recommend a tour of the Newport mansions, a visit to nearby Hammersmith Farm where JFK and Jackie had their wedding reception, and a romantically scenic Sunday brunch at the Inn at Castle Hill. Enrich your stay in Newport with any of these activities.

CENTER HARBOR: Step from the launch or dinghy and you will be greeted by the fullest possible array of shops and services. From the Black Pearl Restaurant, boasting one of the finest wine cellars in New England, to an active tattoo parlor, from trendy boutiques to a fudge factory and overabundant T-shirt stores, the possibilities for dining, shopping and browsing are nearly endless. Within a four-block walk, you will find several establishments worth visiting. The Clark Cooke House/The Candy Store (Bannister's Wharf, 401-849-2900) offers fine dining and a great view above—below are casual dining and grog for the crew at Bistro, and dancing till the wee hours at the Boom Boom Room. Next door to the Old Port Marine launch, the Mooring Restaurant (Sayre's Wharf in the former headquarters of the New York Yacht Club, 401-846-2260) is known for well-presented fresh seafood, moderate prices and a great view of the harbor. An easy walk east of the waterfront at the corner of Marlborough and Farewell streets, the White Horse Tavern (401-849-3600) is ancient, elegant and well worth the cost for superbly prepared traditional American chops and seafood. Or, if you would rather cook your own seafood, the

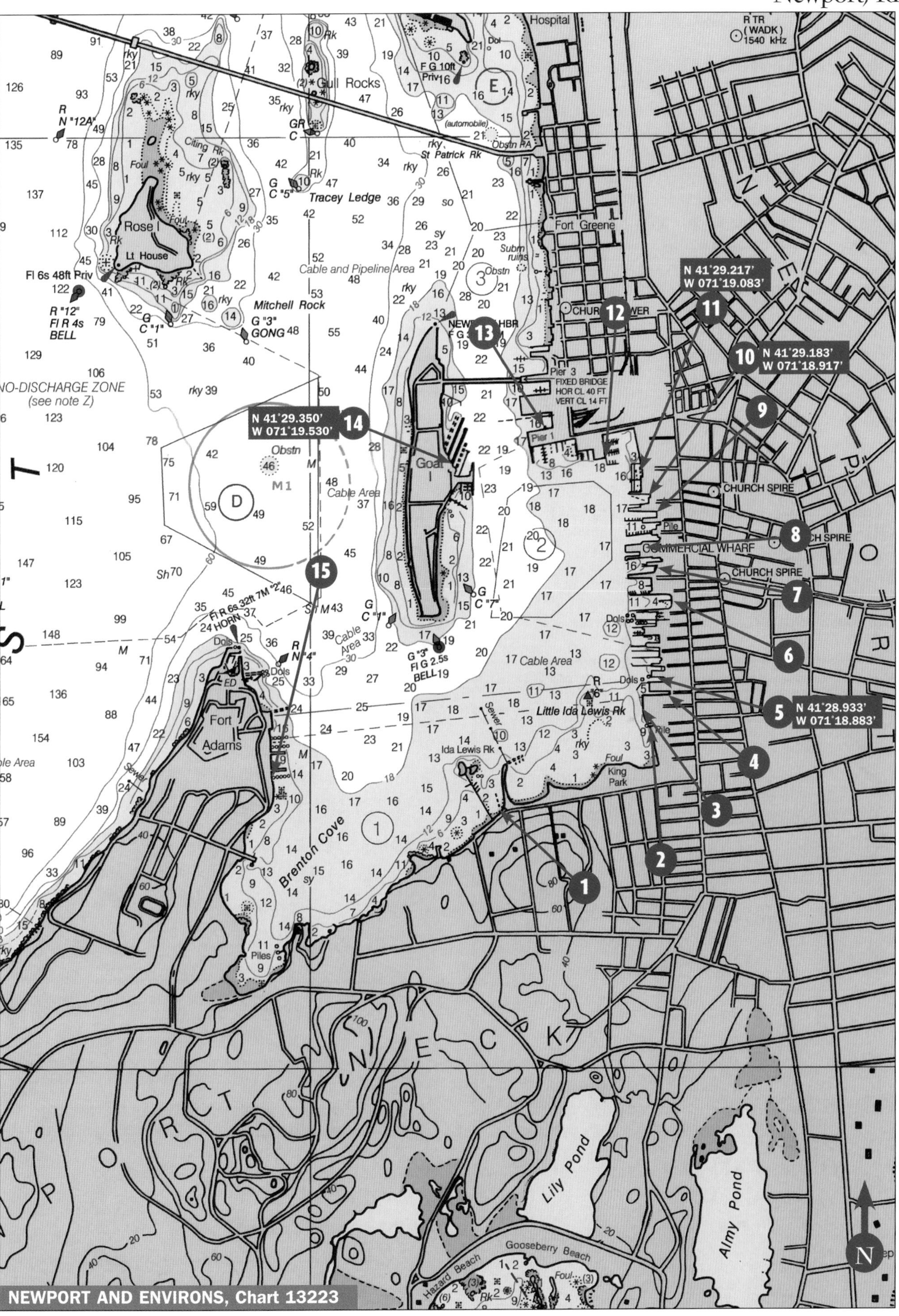

NEWPORT AND ENVIRONS, Chart 13223
N 41°29.217' W 071°19.083'
N 41°29.183' W 071°18.917'
N 41°29.350' W 071°19.530'
N 41°28.933' W 071°18.883'
Rose I
Lt House
Gull Rocks
Tracey Ledge
Mitchell Rock
Cable and Pipeline Area
NO-DISCHARGE ZONE (see note Z)
Fort Greene
Hospital
Goat I
Fort Adams
Brenton Cove
Little Ida Lewis Rk
Ida Lewis Rk
King Park
COMMERCIAL WHARF
CHURCH SPIRE
FIXED BRIDGE HOR CL 40 FT VERT CL 14 FT
Pier 3
Pier 1
Lily Pond
Almy Pond
Gooseberry Beach
Hazard Beach
St Patrick Rk
Citing Rk

very best can be purchased at the Aquidneck Lobster Co. on Bowen's Wharf.

Just down Thames Street from the center of town are a coin-operated laundry and a deli. Armchair Sailor (a few blocks farther south at Thames and Thomas streets) is a fine place to lose an afternoon browsing through an impressive selection of nautical books. Restocking the galley involves about a half-mile hike uphill from the harbor (two long blocks east of Thames Street to two shopping centers on either side of Bellevue Avenue, but each with a full-size grocery store, one an excellent hardware store, and a wine and spirits shop.

Two blocks north of Oldport Marine's launch dock is the Seaman's Church Institute, where you will find clean showers with soap and fresh towels for a small fee. The Institute also has coin-operated laundry machines and serves the most reasonably priced breakfasts and lunches in town, either at its always convivial counter or in the full-service dining room. This venerable institution has been looking out for the special needs of seafarers for generations and deserves the kind words and donations it receives from the yachting community.

Walking south on Thames Street from The Newport Yachting Center gives a visitor many dining and shopping choices. Salas Dining Room is the perennial favorite for feeding a crew on a budget with large portions of tasty Italian fare. Slightly upscale is Puerini's up the hill at 24 Memorial Blvd.; Café Zelda, 528 Thames St., serves a well-rounded menu and wonderful desserts. A complete listing of dining opportunities can be found at the dining directory page at www.gonewport.com.

BRENTON COVE: Next to Fort Adams State Park, the Museum of Yachting is the only museum dedicated solely to recreational boating; it's a must-see site for cruisers. Displays at the museum include classic yachts in the water and out, small craft, models, artwork, documents and trophies. Call 401-847-1018 for information.

ADDITIONAL RESOURCES:

- Newport County Convention and Visitors Bureau, **www.gonewport.com**

NEARBY GOLF COURSES:
Newport National Golf Club, 324 Mitchells Lane, Middletown, RI 02842, 401-848-9690, **www.newportnational.com**

NEARBY MEDICAL FACILITIES:
Newport Hospital, 11 Friendship St., Jamestown, RI 02835, 401-846-6400

Brenton Cove, Center Harbor, Goat Island

Tucked inside the protective arm dominated by Fort Adams, Brenton Cove is filled with private and rental moorings. You can rent a transient mooring from Brenton Cove Moorings, along with launch service. This spot is removed from the churn of activity in Center Harbor and, as such, it is a quiet place to review the ongoing spectacle, though you will spend more time waiting for, and riding, the launch.

Forget the prospect of serenity during mid-June of every even-numbered year, however, when the cove becomes a rendezvous center for the finest and best equipped ocean-racing yachts in the world, as their crews make last-moment preparations for the biennial Newport-to-Bermuda race. The shore of Brenton Cove is home to Harbor Court, the Newport base of the New York Yacht Club

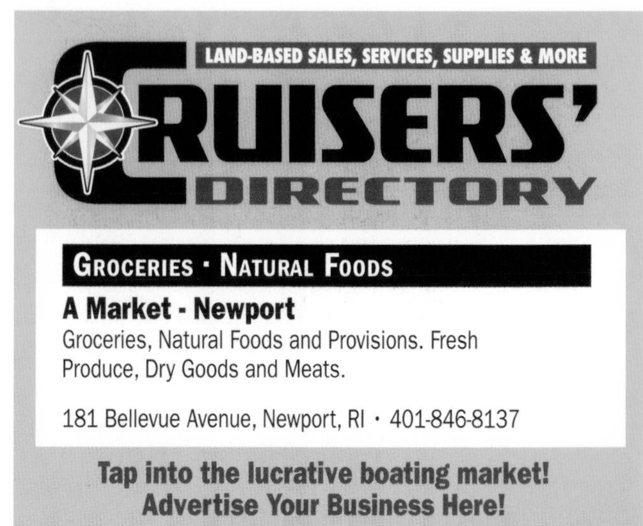

(NYYC). This impressive structure was previously the home of John Nicholas Brown of Brown University fame and was purchased and converted by the NYYC in the 1990s.

Dockage: Despite Newport's popularity, slips are usually available for visitors. Newport Yachting Center, home of the annual Newport Boat Show, is easy to spot on entering Center Harbor, marked by the high-rise TEXACO sign.

Bannister's Wharf is immediately to the north (identified by the big green sign and shingled office with floating docks stemming from its 240-foot-long main pier). The marina can accommodate vessels with drafts of up to 17 feet and lengths of up to 200-plus feet. You can take on fuel from the marina's classy, wooden-housed gasoline and diesel pumps, find clean shower and laundry facilities shoreside, and even rent a quaint, waterside room for overflow guests. There is also a pump-out service.

Farther north, Newport Harbor Hotel & Marina has 60 slips on floating docks available for transients. With dockage comes access to the Hotel & Marina's large, indoor pool, showers and saunas. Waverley's Restaurant is on-site.

Newport Yacht Club, on the north side of the basin, often has transient slips available on a reciprocal basis to members of other recognized clubs. The fee includes use of the club's facilities, including restrooms, showers and cocktail lounge, as well as access to what are reputed to be the "best ice cubes in town."

On the south end of Center Harbor, Brown and Howard Wharf Marina (just south of the large, brown-shingled condominium complex) has two long, fixed docks (especially suitable for large, well-fendered recreational craft), plus a sizable floating dock. There is ample parking here and a restaurant and classic pub on the premises.

West Wind Marina on Waites Wharf can accommodate vessels up to 177 feet, with 24-hour security, full electrical hookups, concierge service, restrooms, showers and laundry, and adjacent restaurants and bars.

Casey's Marina on Spring Wharf offers diesel fuel (call for low fuel cost), floating docks with 14-foot depths and pump-out, along with lift and repair services.

At the Newport end of the Goat Island Bridge is Newport Shipyard, which has undergone a recent refurbishing and management change. It boasts excellent facilities for large yachts but can accommodate cruisers of all sizes. The showers and laundry are first class, and the captain's TV room and lounge (equipped with Internet stations) are great. There is a wonderful small restaurant on shipyard premises for breakfast and lunch. The shipyard is convenient to all of downtown Newport, especially the Newport Transportation Center, where buses connect to local points as well as Boston, New York and beyond. Inside the Transportation Center is a well-staffed and complete visitors information desk. Newport has always been a town of festivals and continues to be a venue for large gatherings.

Across the harbor on Goat Island, Goat Island Marina is a full-service operation with fuel and repairs to serve yachts at its 200 slips. Transient slips are usually available and there is an adjacent luxury hotel. Among the Newport marinas, only Goat Island Marina operates on a first-come, first-served (no reservation) basis.

Anchorage: Just east of Brenton Cove, in the area fanning out north off the Ida Lewis Yacht Club (conspicuous on the rocky island of the same name and at the end of a long pier from shore), limited anchorage space remains available. Skippers are warned to stay to the inside of the cable area marked on the harbor chart. Cannons are fired for "colors" from the clubhouse lawn at 8 a.m. and sundown, alerting crews to raise and lower the standards of many nations throughout the harbor.

The holding here is good in mud, but you will need substantial swing room with the ebb and flood of the tide. Anchoring is no longer permitted in Brenton Cove proper, where moorings have triumphed fully in the battle for available space.

You can find additional anchorage, however, north of the causeway leading to Goat Island. Moorings also are proliferating in this area, so give special consideration to scope with respect both to depth and swinging circle in relation to those on shorter tethers.

Launch service is available from Oldport Marine Service, but be prepared to wait because it takes time for launches to circumnavigate the harbor and make frequent stops. Use the launches if you plan frequent trips ashore, as the large harbor, with its normal heavy traffic, can make conditions unsafe for small dinghies, especially at night.

Moorings: Commercially run mooring areas operate at three locations: Center Harbor in front of the wharves; Brenton Cove to the south; and north of the Goat Island Causeway. Oldport Marine Services (VHF Channel 68, horn signal or 401-847-9109) maintains a substantial field of moorings in Center Harbor and a reliable launch service. You will find water and garbage disposal at Oldport's dock on Sayre's Wharf. The launch also serves Brenton Cove (leaving from Sayre's Wharf), but only on the hour. Additional transient moorings (26 of them) may be rented from Brenton Cove Moorings (VHF Channel 09) at the extreme northeast corner of Center Harbor. Both single-ball, helix moorings and bow-to-stern tie-ups are available. Rental moorings also may be available from the Ida Lewis Yacht Club (VHF Channel 78A or 401-846-1969) in Brenton Cove or from the Newport Yacht Club (VHF Channel 09 or 401-846-9410) on the north side of the harbor. Otherwise, it is best to call the harbormaster (VHF Channel 09 or 401-848-6492) for advice. This is not the place to assume that a vacant mooring may simply be borrowed for the evening.

A mobile pump-out station services the entire harbor. Simply call "Pump-out Boat" on VHF Channel 09. The pump-out boat will also pick up your trash for a small fee.

Jamestown

Two miles across East Passage from Newport is the summer resort and residential town of Jamestown, on Conanicut Island. Jamestown has much to interest the cruising boater. There are several excellent restaurants and shops in an idyllic village setting, a full-service marina, transportation facilities and good places to walk or cycle amid vistas of crashing surf, sheer cliffs, rolling pastures and woodlands.

Dockage and Moorings: Conanicut Marine Services Inc. (VHF Channel 71 or 401-423-7157) operates the recreational waterfront at the village center, supervising 205 seasonal and transient moorings, 100 floating-dock slips and 1,200 feet of deep fixed-pier dockage. The launch service to the mooring field is fast, and the drivers are deserving of a gratuity for their careful and courteous work. Clean restrooms and showers are open 24 hours, all fuels are available (including propane and compressed natural gas) and kayaks can be rented. There is an extensive ship's store and chandlery at 20 Narragansett Ave., next to the Oyster Bar Restaurant. Wireless Internet is available for a daily or weekly fee.

A pump-out boat serves vessels on moorings or at the dock. The Jamestown-Newport ferry takes passengers and bicycles to Newport and back with stops at Fort Adams and Goat Island every 90 minutes (8:15 a.m. to 10 p.m. from Sunday through Thursday, and until 11:30 p.m. on Friday and Saturday; VHF Channels 16 and 71). Complete mechanical, carpentry and hull and rigging repair shops and a 200-ton railway are part of the complex. The bus stop for transportation to Kingstown and Newport is immediately north of the marina's parking lot.

On entering East Passage from Block Island Sound, Jamestown Boat Yard is the first yacht facility you will encounter, sheltered from prevailing southerlies by Bull Point at the southeastern tip of Conanicut Island. The yard maintains deep-draft floating docks and 70 moorings with immediate access to one of the oldest and most renowned yacht repair and refit yards in the country. Although there are no showers, and the village is a 20-minute walk away, tie-ups here are in high demand. From the docks and mooring field, the view across The Dumplings toward Newport is glorious, and nearby Fort Wetherill State Park is great for walks, picnics and exploration of the World War II fortifications.

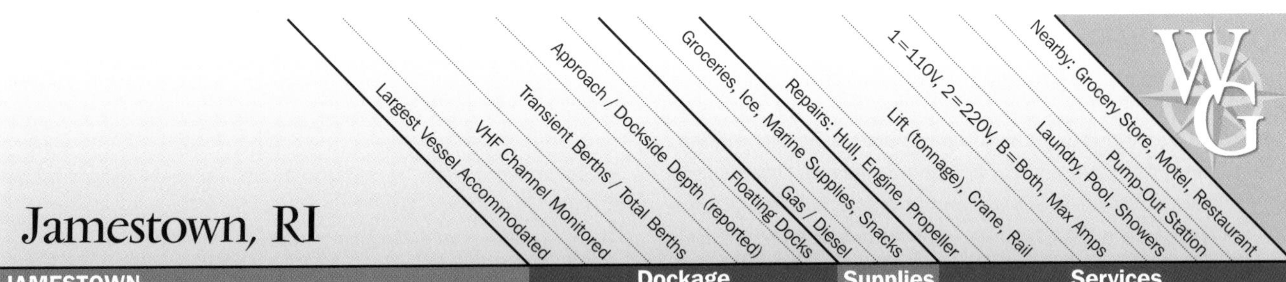

Jamestown, RI

JAMESTOWN		Largest Vessel Accommodated	VHF Channel Monitored	Transient Berths / Total Berths	Approach / Dockside Depth (reported)	Floating Docks	Gas / Diesel	Groceries, Ice, Marine Supplies, Snacks	Repairs: Hull, Engine, Propeller	Lift (tonnage), Crane, Rail	1=110V, 2=220V, B=Both, Max Amps	Laundry, Pool, Showers	Pump-Out Station	Nearby: Grocery Store, Motel, Restaurant
		Dockage					Supplies		Services					
1. Dutch Harbor Boat Yard	401-423-0630	55	69	MOORINGS	15/12			I	HEP	R		S	P	GMR
2. Jamestown Boat Yard	401-423-0600	70	72		12/7			IM	HEP	L35,C,R	/50	S		
3. Clark boat Yard & Marine Works	401-423-3625													
4. Conanicut Marine Services Inc. (Internet Access) (Wireless Internet Access)	401-423-7157	175	71	20/305	35/15	F	GD	GIMS	HEP	L30,C10,R	B/100	LS	P	GMR

Corresponding chart(s) not to be used for navigation. Internet Access Wireless Internet Access

JAMESTOWN, Chart 13221

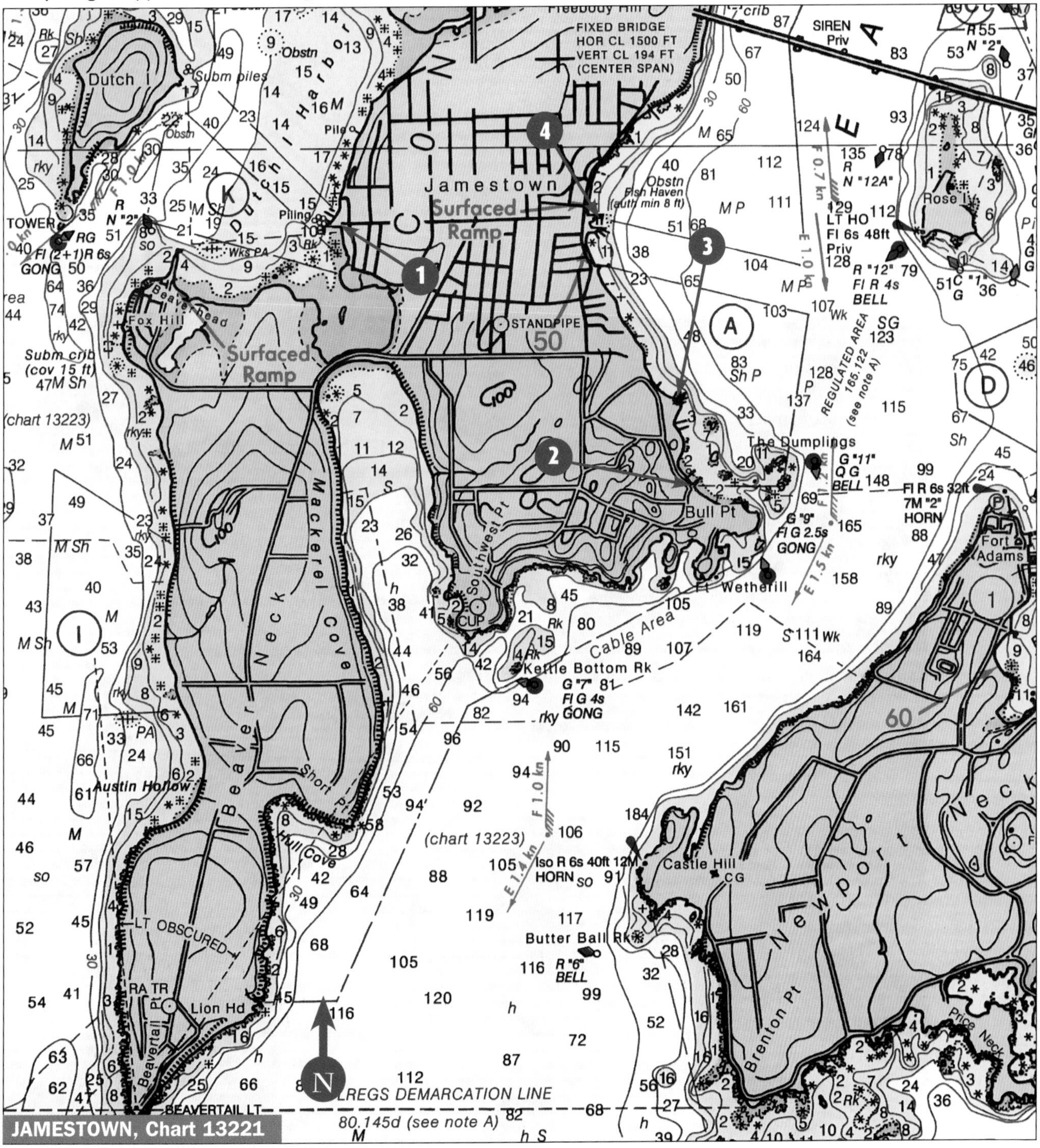

GOIN' ASHORE:
JAMESTOWN, RI

The small and attractive resort village begins at the marina, with a bakery, ice cream shop, deli and East Ferry Liquors next door to the Conanicut Building. The Conanicut Building houses the dockmaster's office; laundry, restroom and shower facilities; parking; the aforementioned Jamestown-Newport Ferry; and Watch Hill Yacht Sales. Across the street from the marina, within a three-block walk along the village's single business street (Narragansett Avenue, perpendicular to Conanicut Avenue, tracing the East Passage shore), you will find East Ferry Market and Deli for fresh coffee, pastries and food items, unusually well-stocked Jamestown Hardware, Bank of Newport and Fleet Bank (both with ATMs), House of Pizza, Del Nero Dry Cleaners & Laundry, Xtra Mart convenience store with ATM and Baker's Pharmacy.

The post office is at the top of the rise on Narragansett Avenue, where a right turn takes you to the town library (with Internet access) and a large, elaborate and turreted play-scape that will delight any youngsters aboard. A left turn here leads immediately to refurbished McQuade's Marketplace and its excellent stock of high-quality fruits, veggies, cheeses, meats, condiments and specialty items. Adjoining are a coin-operated laundry center and Ace's Pizza. Page's Liquor Store is across the street and "The Lush Group" is next door. In addition, the nearby Jamestown Museum has a permanent exhibit of the various historic Jamestown ferries that predated contemporary bridges to the mainland and Newport.

Most of the village's restaurants cluster on Narragansett Avenue about a half block west of the harbor. A few doors west, the casual Jamestown Oyster Bar and Grill (401-423-3380) is a friendly local hangout that attracts a crowd at and around the bar for reasonably priced fresh fish, superb chowder (all three varieties—Manhattan, Rhode Island and New England) and beers, wines and other potables.

Situated about three tenths of a mile north of the ferry wharf, the Bay Voyage Inn (150 Conanicus Ave., 401-423-2100) delivers one the most elegant dinner menus in the area and consistently receives Rhode Island Monthly's "Best Brunch Award" for a weekly Sunday spread that is pricey but phenomenal. Chopmist Charlie's is great for friendly atmosphere and fresh seafood.

ADDITIONAL RESOURCES:

- Jamestown-Conanicut Island Visitor Information, **www.jamestown-ri.info**

NEARBY GOLF COURSES:
Newport National Golf Club, 324 Mitchells Lane, Middletown, RI 02842, 401-848-9690, **www.newportnational.com**

NEARBY MEDICAL FACILITIES:
Newport Hospital, 11 Friendship St., Jamestown, RI 02835, 401-846-6400

NORTHWARD ON EAST PASSAGE

Seven miles north of Newport, on the east side of East Passage just above Dyer Island, is the village of Melville, a large, sophisticated yachting center.

Melville

Dockage: A large marine complex, now owned by Hinckley Yachts, introduces itself at water's edge with Little Harbor Marine, a marina and major boatyard with 100 protected deepwater slips and lift and repair capabilities for boats up to 130 feet in length. At winter hauling time, the high-end yacht display at this yard is better than a boat show. Hinckley has multiple operations here, with separate locations for design, custom boat, spar and systems construction and sales. The Hinckley (formerly Ted Hood) Marine Complex is also home to an array of top-flight specialty marine shops and fabricators, including Doyle Sails, Sobstad Sailmakers, The Rigging Company, Ocean Instruments, Electra Yacht, Cay Electronics, Life Raft & Survival Equipment Inc. and S&S Fabrics Products. A good casual restaurant is next door, as is a chandlery.

Within an easy walk you can reach a convenience store and liquor store, and West Marine's Aquidneck Island outlet is about a 10-minute drive away. There is ample parking, and you can easily arrange for a rental car at Little Harbor Marine.

The space formerly occupied by Alden Yachts is now home to Hunt Yachts, builders of the Surfhunter line of Raymond Hunt designs. For the cruiser, Hunt offers fuel, a full-service repair yard, storage and dockage for vessels up to 100 feet.

Potter Cove

Anchorage: Near the north end of Prudence Island, Potter Cove (not to be confused with another Potter Cove charted just north of the Newport Bridge on Conanicut Island) offers good shelter, but no amenities are available here. This natural basin is almost landlocked by the elbow of a curving sand spit. The entrance is well-buoyed, though it will not look that way on first approach from the north. You must locate and honor all three nun buoys ("2," "4" and "6"—all of them red) to starboard, lest you snare your keel on the shoals off Gull Point.

Inside, what was once a relatively extensive anchorage area has been taken over by a ragtag collection of mooring floats, dropped in by frequent visitors from local ports. On weekday evenings, many of their owners are likely to be elsewhere, and you are free to take one if you trust whatever may lie below holding it. Note that the cove runs shallow to the north, punctuated by miniscule Shell Island, which is just visible at low tide, and by a wreck marked by a Coast Guard buoy.

On busy summer weekends, a better bet may be to set a hook in 10 to 11 feet of water off the pebbled beach running to the southeast, taking a dinghy in for exploration

Melville, East Passage, RI

MELVILLE, EAST PASSAGE	Largest Vessel Accommodated	VHF Channel Monitored	Transient Berths / Total Berths	Approach / Dockside Depth (reported)	Floating Docks	Gas / Diesel	Groceries, Ice, Marine Supplies, Snacks	Repairs: Hull, Engine, Propeller	Lift (tonnage), Crane, Rail	1=110V, 2=220V, B=Both, Max Amps	Laundry, Pool, Showers	Pump-Out Station	Nearby: Grocery Store, Motel, Restaurant
	Dockage					Supplies		Services					
1. The Hinckley Company's Little Harbor Marine 🖳 401-683-7100	120	09	/100	20/15			IM	HEP	L180	B/50	LS	P	GMR
2. NE Boatworks at East Passage Yachting Ctr. 401-683-4000	112	09	20/380	15/15		GD	GIMS	HP	L	B/100	LS	P	GR
3. Hunt Yachts 401-324-4205	150	07	20/30	17/17	F	GD	IMS	HEP	L100, C30	B/100		P	GMR

Corresponding chart(s) not to be used for navigation. 🖳 Internet Access (WiFi) Wireless Internet Access

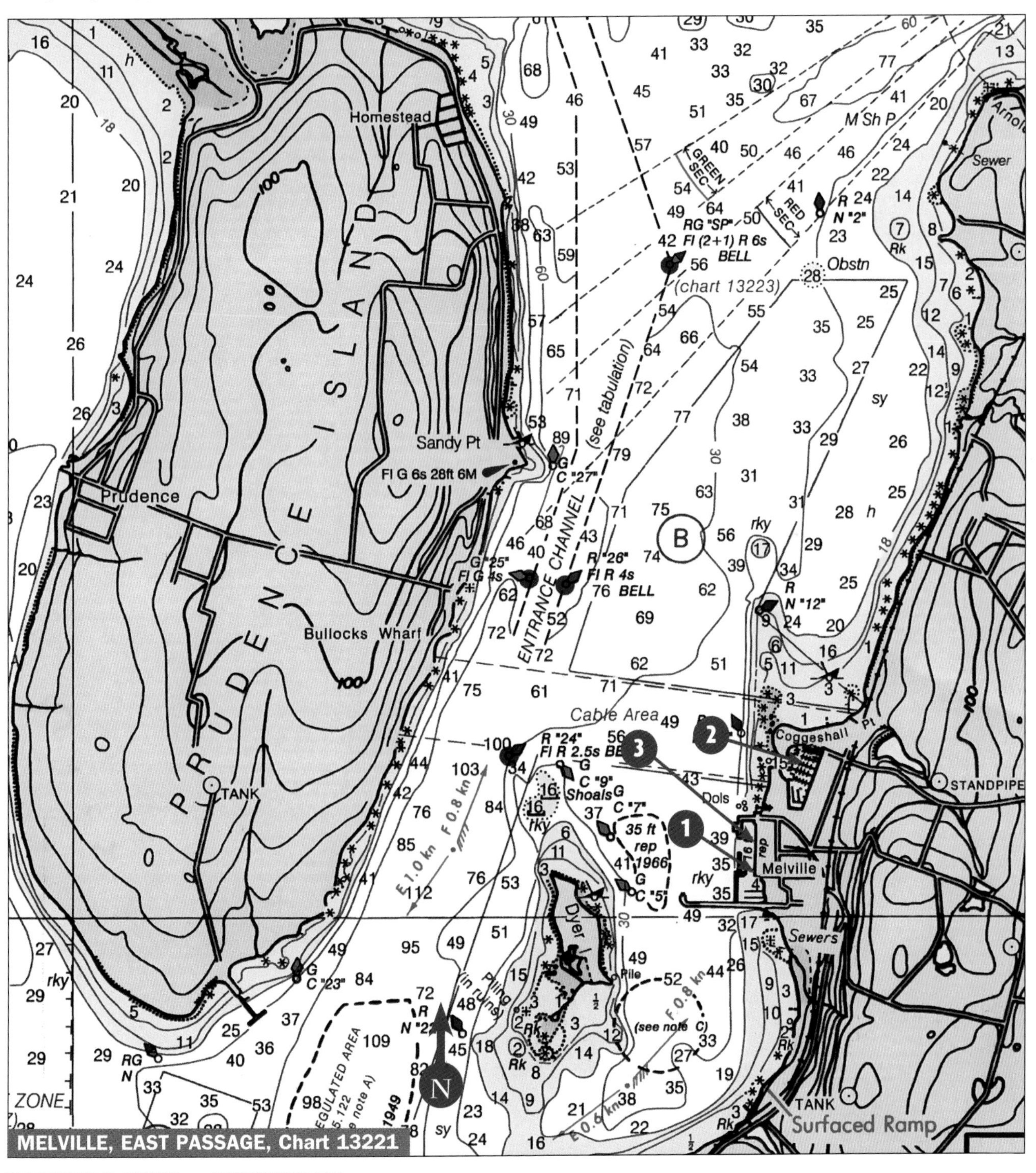

Bristol, Barrington, RI

BRISTOL, BARRINGTON		Largest Vessel Accommodated	VHF Channel Monitored	Transient Berths / Total Berths	Approach / Dockside Depth (reported)	Floating Docks	Gas / Diesel	Groceries, Ice, Marine Supplies, Snacks	Repairs: Hull, Engine, Propeller	Lift (tonnage), Crane, Rail	1=110V, 2=220V, B=Both, Max Amps	Laundry, Pool, Showers	Pump-Out Station	Nearby: Grocery Store, Motel, Restaurant
		Dockage					Supplies		Services					
1 Bristol Marine	401-253-2200	115	69	6/20	12/8	F		I	HEP	L50	B/50	S	P	GMR
2. Bristol Yacht Club	401-253-2922	45	68	MOORINGS	12/6			I				S		MR
3. Herreshoff Marine Museum/America's Cup Hall of Fame	**401-253-5000**	**200**	**68**	**8/12**	**16/7**	**F**		**S**			**B/100**	**S**		**GMR**
4. Stanley's Boat Yard Inc.	401-245-5090	50	16	3/161	10/5	F		I	HP	L	1/30	S	P	GR
5. Barrington Yacht Club	401-245-1181		68	MOORINGS	7/7	F	GD	GIMS			1/30	S	P	GR
6. Striper Marina Inc.	401-245-6121	45	65	4/110	8/6	F	G	IM	EP	R	1/30			GR

Corresponding chart(s) not to be used for navigation. Internet Access Wireless Internet Access

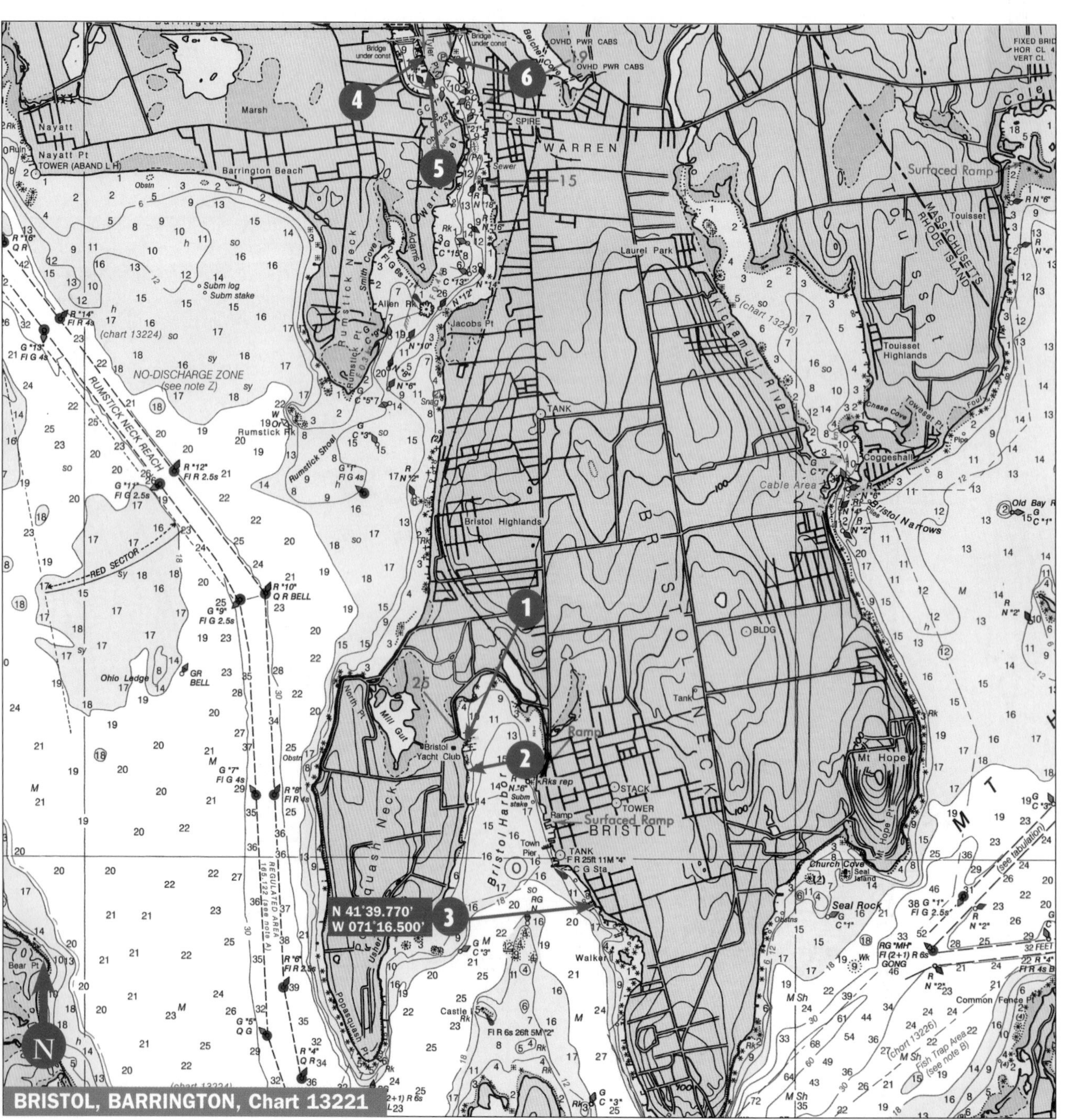

of the Narragansett Bay Estuarine Sanctuary surrounding the cove. Frequent swells from boat traffic in the channel beyond will find their way into this anchorage.

Knowledgeable locals argue that recent crowding of the area has not spoiled the natural beauty of the sanctuary or excellent clamming in the shallows.

Bristol

Cupped securely between the arms of Popasquash and Bristol necks, Bristol Harbor is one of Narragansett Bay's most important for recreational boating. The town invites visiting cruisers for reprovisioning and sightseeing, but its major claim to fame is its oldest-in-the-country Fourth of July parade. Here America's annual birthday celebration is never-ending; preparations seem to begin July 5 for the following year.

NAVIGATION: Use Chart 13221. Use Newport tide tables. For hight tide, add 13 minutes; for low tide, add 0 minutes. Bristol Harbor is two miles long and over a mile wide. It is big enough and generally deep enough to accommodate a large local fleet with anchorage room to spare. Although open to the south, it is protected to the north, east and west, and the well-marked channels on either side of Hog Island make for a painless entry. Nonetheless, take care to honor the channel buoys marking the shoal extending northward of Hog Island and the rocky ledge on the southeast of Popasquash Neck.

Dockage: The Herreshoff Marine Museum/America's Cup Hall of Fame has 8 dockside slips and approximately 20 morings available for transients. For museum information, admission and hours, call 401-253-5000. To port, as you approach the harbor's extensive mooring field (more than 500 moorings), you will spot Bristol Marine. This famous yard is now a full-service marina with both rental slips and moorings to complement its extensive repair and refit shops. Reservations for slips or moorings should be made at 401-253-2200. The yard has a 50-ton lift, capable of handling yachts to lengths of 70 feet. You can rent a kayak here, and there is launch service to the downtown waterfront. Farther into the harbor, also to port, Bristol Yacht Club rents moorings to visitors for a facilities fee, which includes launch service, access to the club's dinghy dock and use of the shower/restroom facilities in the clubhouse annex. From here it is a pleasant mile-long walk to town, though you can often find a ride. Ask the Bristol harbormaster about additional moorings; call on VHF Channel 09. The popular Herreshoff Museum also has rental moorings and offers an excellent location for visiting town. Call 401-253-5000 or hail on VHF Channel 68 for more information.

Anchorage: Ordinarily, you will find ample space to anchor outside the mooring field. When the prevailing southwesterlies stiffen up, the harbor can develop a noticeable chop, though in most other conditions it is pleasant and comfortable. It is a bit of a pull into town from the anchorage area, but a visit to this homey and interesting town is well worth the effort. You can tie up your dinghy just north of the old stone armory in front of Rockwell Park. Cruisers who are not visiting the town can anchor east of Hog Island, south of Bristol Harbor proper. Good holding can be found north of can "3" in 17- to 25-foot depths.

GOIN' ASHORE: BRISTOL, RI

Most of Bristol's commercial establishments are located on Hope Street, a block east of Thames Street, which runs along the harbor's edge. A drugstore, barbershop, Fleet Bank, two old-fashioned ice cream parlors, a liquor store and antiques stores are interspersed among grand old homes preserved from an earlier time. For those who go for seafood fresh, fried and straightforward, Quito's Shellfish Restaurant (401-253-4500) has a market atmosphere, modest prices and a water view. Fine dining, also with a heavy tilt toward the sea's produce, can be found at S.S. Dion on the harbor at the north end of town (401-253-2884). The Lobster Pot Restaurant, popular with locals and visiting boaters, is on the harbor south of the Herreshoff Museum. Roberto's in the 300 block of Hope Street offers a great Italian menu. A new player on the dining scene is Persimmon (31 State St., 401-254-7474), offering modern American cuisine using the freshest available ingredients.

Bristol is famous for the Herreshoff Manufacturing Co., located on the eastern bank, which built some of the largest and fastest yachts, including *Reliance* (over 200 feet long), and the J-boats *Rainbow* and *Yankee*. The facility is now a museum and no longer an active yard. The museum dock might have some

Herreshoff yachts visiting, though. Admission is free, though visiting hours are limited to specific times by days of the week, May through October. Recently, the museum has added the America's Cup Hall of Fame, including *Defiant*, one of the boats from the winning 1992 team. Call ahead (401-253-5000) for a current schedule.

Bristol is also famous as the home of the country's oldest and grandest Fourth of July celebration. On the day itself, the town is mobbed, thronging to an hours-long parade and collateral celebrations everywhere. The parade route is marked by a red, white and blue stripe down the center of the street. In view of the traffic jams, arrival by boat may well be the best way to visit this special event. At any time of year, Blithewold Gardens, on Ferry Road south of the Herreshoff Museum, is well worth a visit—open from 10 a.m. to 4 p.m. (401-253-2707). Blithewold features a 45-room mansion, 33 acres of gardens and an arboretum. For those who want to stretch their limbs on foot or by bicycle, the paved and well-marked East Bay Bike Path begins at Independence Park at the southeast end of the harbor, then winds its way 14 miles inland to Barrington and ultimately to East Providence.

ADDITIONAL RESOURCES:

- Discover Bristol, **www.discoverbristol.com**

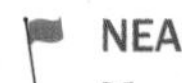

NEARBY GOLF COURSES:
Montaup Country Club, 500 Anthony Road, Portsmouth, RI 02871, 401-683-0955

NEARBY MEDICAL FACILITIES:
Charlton Memorial Hospital, 363 Highland Ave., Fall River, MA 02720, 508-679-3131

Warren, Barrington

NAVIGATION: Use Chart 13221. A narrow, winding channel angles and crooks its way north on Warren River, eastward of Rumstick Neck. The channel threads around and through shoals, but aids to navigation are ample here.

At Tyler Point, about two miles upstream, the Barrington River flows in from the northwest. Here, to the east, is the industrial boatbuilding town of Warren, homeport to a cruise liner that travels to New England, Canada, Florida and the Bahamas. To the west is Barrington, the main recreational boat center for the area.

Dockage: Barrington has a good harbor with strong currents, but protection from all winds. A yacht club welcomes members of other clubs with reciprocal privileges. Contact Barrington Yacht Club launch Noreaster on VHF Channel 68. Even though there is a large local fleet, marinas do welcome transients. The harbormaster in Barrington makes a real effort to assign moorings by making efficient use of the space available in this popular harbor.

PROVIDENCE RIVER

West of Warren, at Conimicut Point, Narragansett Bay becomes the deep and well-marked Providence River. The other point on the mile-wide mouth is Nayatt, on the eastern shore. A 58-foot-high rip-rap-lined lighthouse a half-mile off Conimicut Point leads traffic, mostly oceangoing and other commercial craft, into the river.

Bullock Cove

This popular, nearly landlocked cove on the eastern shore is the first harbor heading north on the Providence River.

NAVIGATION: Use Chart 13221. A well-marked channel from Bullock Point leads into the cove, beginning at flashing green buoy "1." At mean high water, expect 10-foot depths, but with a 6-foot tidal range, skippers of deep-draft boats will want to check the local tide table or call ahead to the marina before entering.

Dockage: Brewer Cove Haven Marina dominates the easterly shore with its floating dock complex. A full-service marina and boatyard, Brewer has water and 30- and 50-amp electrical service at each slip, modern shower/restroom facilities, a swimming pool, loaner bikes and courtesy transportation. This is a major repair center in its own right; Marine Metal Fabricators and Ken's Canvas also are on-site. The city of East Providence maintains about a dozen rental moorings in the relatively narrow harbor. Call the harbormaster on VHF Channel 09 for availability. There is a dinghy landing at the town dock.

Pawtuxet Cove

This narrow, dredged cove is a little farther upriver and on the western shore, behind Pawtuxet Neck. An anchorage basin is in a diked area south of the entrance (use Chart 13224). The village of Pawtuxet was founded in 1638 and is an interesting historic place to visit.

NAVIGATION: Use Chart 13221. Use tide tables for Newport. For high tide, add 6 minutes; for low tide, subtract 11 minutes. Enter Pawtuxet Cove from the main river channel through a straight cut lined by rocks and shoals. Private range lights help you through the opening between the point and the end of the dike. At the opening, turn north for the harbor and marinas, or turn south for the anchorage.

In recent years, the entrance channel had shoaled to less than 6 feet, but the Army Corps of Engineers has completed dredging the channel to an average depth of 6 to 8 feet. Check locally for latest depths in the channel.

Edgewood

A concentration of marinas stands between the northern end of Pawtuxet Neck and Fields Point, on the outskirts of the city of Providence on the river itself, but well off the main channel. Close by are shore accommodations and transportation, and to the west, less than a mile away, is Roger Williams Park, which includes a zoo with a monkey

Providence River, RI

PROVIDENCE RIVER		Largest Vessel Accommodated	VHF Channel Monitored	Transient Berths / Total Berths	Approach / Dockside Depth (reported)	Floating Docks	Gas / Diesel	Groceries, Ice, Marine Supplies, Snacks	Repairs: Hull, Engine, Propeller	Lift (tonnage), Crane, Rail	1=110V, 2=220V, B=Both, Max Amps	Laundry, Pool, Showers	Pump-Out Station	Nearby: Grocery Store, Motel, Restaurant
		Dockage					Supplies		Services					
1. Brewer Cove Haven Marina (Internet Access) (Wireless Internet Access)	**401-246-1600**	**90**	**09**	**10/260**	**9/10**	**F**	**GD**	**IM**	**HEP**	**L120**	**B/50**	**PS**	**P**	**GR**
2. Pawtuxet Cove Marina	401-941-2000	50		6/98	6/4	F		GI	HP	L25	1/30	LS	P	GMR
3. Rhode Island Yacht Club	401-941-3335	70	78	/77	8/6			I		L2	B/50	S	P	R
4. Edgewood Yacht Club (Internet Access)	401-781-9626	40	14	6/60	6/5	F		I			1/30	LS	P	
5. Port Edgewood (Wireless Internet Access)	401-941-2000	80		12/154	11/6	F	G	GIM	HEP		1/50	LS	P	R

Corresponding chart(s) not to be used for navigation. Internet Access Wireless Internet Access

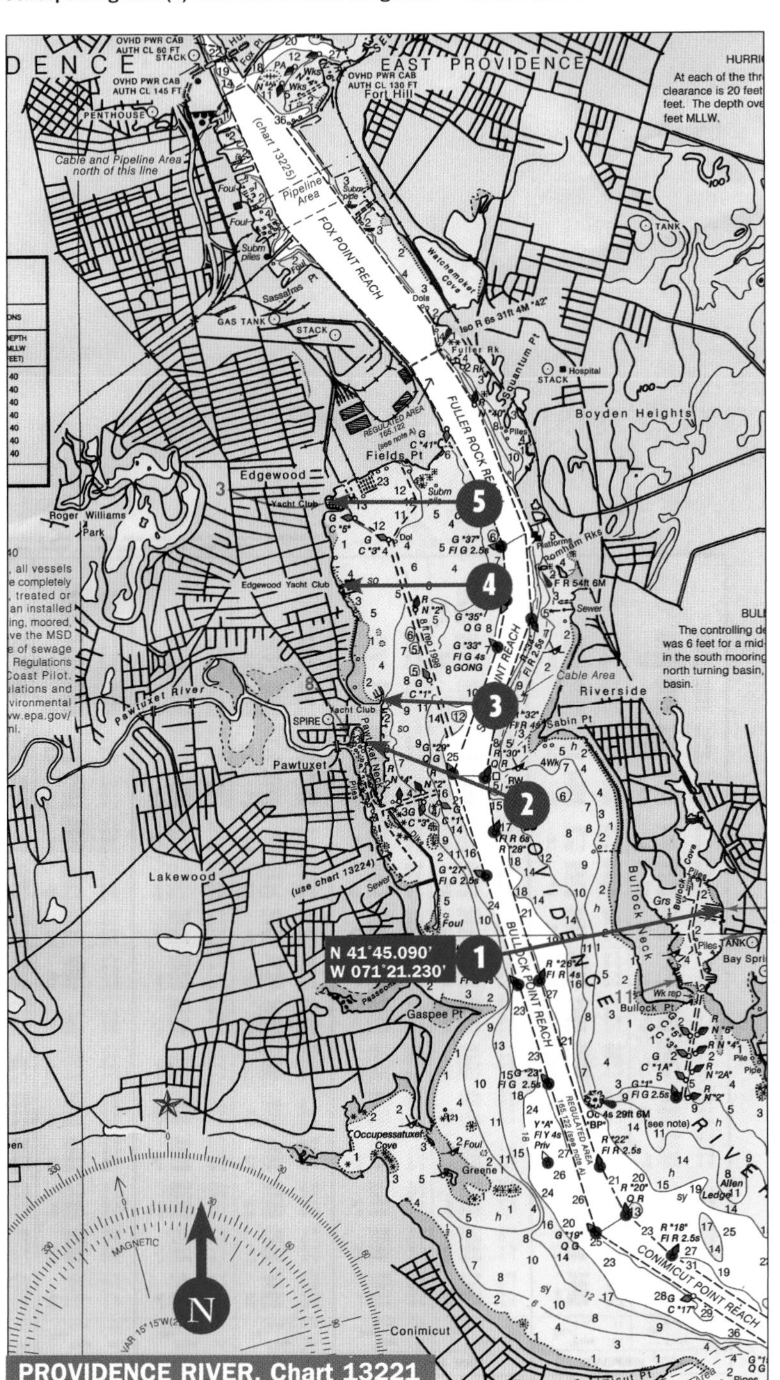

island and seal pools, a chain of small lakes, notable flower gardens, tennis courts, a museum of natural history, planetarium and popular outdoor theater.

Edgewood is as close to Providence as most boats get. Only a short ride from the center of town, it makes an ideal layover spot from which to visit the historic city. The river from here up is heavily commercial, and the waterborne traffic is fearsome. Some accommodations for recreational craft can be found at the repair yard in East Providence on the Seekonk River. (This is actually as far up the river as you can go; a hurricane barrier blocks further navigation on the Providence River.)

MOUNT HOPE BAY

The Rhode Island/Massachusetts border divides Mount Hope Bay. High Mount Hope itself is on Bristol Neck. It was once the stronghold of Indian chief King Phillip, the son of Massasoit and chief of the Wampanoag tribe who led a war against New England colonists in the 17th century. Even-higher Pocasset Hill is in North Tiverton on the eastern shore.

Mount Hope Bay is easy to reach from busier waters and it offers safe and scenic cruising. Its upper eastern shore is the waterfront for Fall River, a mill town with heavy commercial boat traffic plying well-marked channels.

Anchorage: Along the northern shore of Mount Hope Bay, coves at the entrance to each of three small rivers offer potential anchorages and opportunities for dinghy exploration beyond navigable depths. To the west, the Kickamuit River offers the best protection in a soft mud bottom with depths from 7 to 26 feet.

Take care on entry to thread the buoys precisely through aptly-named Bristol Narrows. In the event of an approaching storm, this is a

Mount Hope Bay, Taunton, RI

MOUNT HOPE BAY, TAUNTON		Largest Vessel Accommodated	VHF Channel Monitored	Transient Berths / Total Berths	Approach / Dockside Depth (reported)	Floating Docks	Gas / Diesel	Groceries, Ice, Marine Supplies, Snacks	Repairs: Hull, Engine, Propeller	Lift (tonnage), Crane, Rail	1=110V, 2=220V, B=Both, Max Amps	Laundry, Pool, Showers	Pump-Out Station	Nearby: Grocery Store, Motel, Restaurant
		Dockage					Supplies		Services					
1. Swansea Marina	508-672-8633	34			13/6		G							
2. Captain J.J. O'Connell Co.	508-672-6303	75		4/25	7/5	F	G	M	HEP	L60	B/50			
3. Somerset Marine Inc.	508-678-0040	80	16	6/110	6/6	F	G	I	HP		B/50	S		MR
4. Taunton Yacht Club	508-669-6007	40	68	2/40	5/8		G	I			1	S		GR
5. Shaw's Boat Yard Inc.	508-669-5714	60		2/50	7/6	F		IM	HEP	C	1/30	LS		GR

Corresponding chart(s) not to be used for navigation. Internet Access Wireless Internet Access

good choice for shelter, but arrive early—many local boats use Kickamuit as a hurricane hole.

In the center, Cole River empties into an unnamed cove between Touisset and Gardners Neck. During most summer weather, there is good anchorage along the western shore of the cove just north of the Rhode Island/ Massachusetts line in 9 to 12 feet of water. Swansea Marine on the east side of the cove is a full-service facility that may have a slip or mooring available. It is also possible to anchor off the marina, just beyond the mooring field in 9- to 11-foot depths. The Cole River itself, beyond the cove, is not navigable (despite the several deep-footed vessels that have somehow found the way to a protected berth beyond the breakwater). However, it is a good place to explore by dinghy. The best time to enter is at slack tide just before the ebb. Otherwise, an unfavorable current can present quite a challenge.

The Lee River to the east has no facilities, but it has no obstructions either and is closest to the marked channel to Fall River. In a pinch, you can drop a hook here in soft mud with 8 to 11 feet of water in the shadow of a massive electric plant.

Just above the bridge at Fall River, you can visit the famous battleship *Massachusetts,* star attraction of Battleship Cove. Besides "Big Mamie," you will see the submarine *Lionfish,* the destroyer *Joseph P. Kennedy Jr.*, the gunboat *Asheville* and P.T. Boat *796*. Next door, the Marine Museum at Fall River has many nautical history exhibits. Boating visitors can anchor in the cove and dinghy ashore.

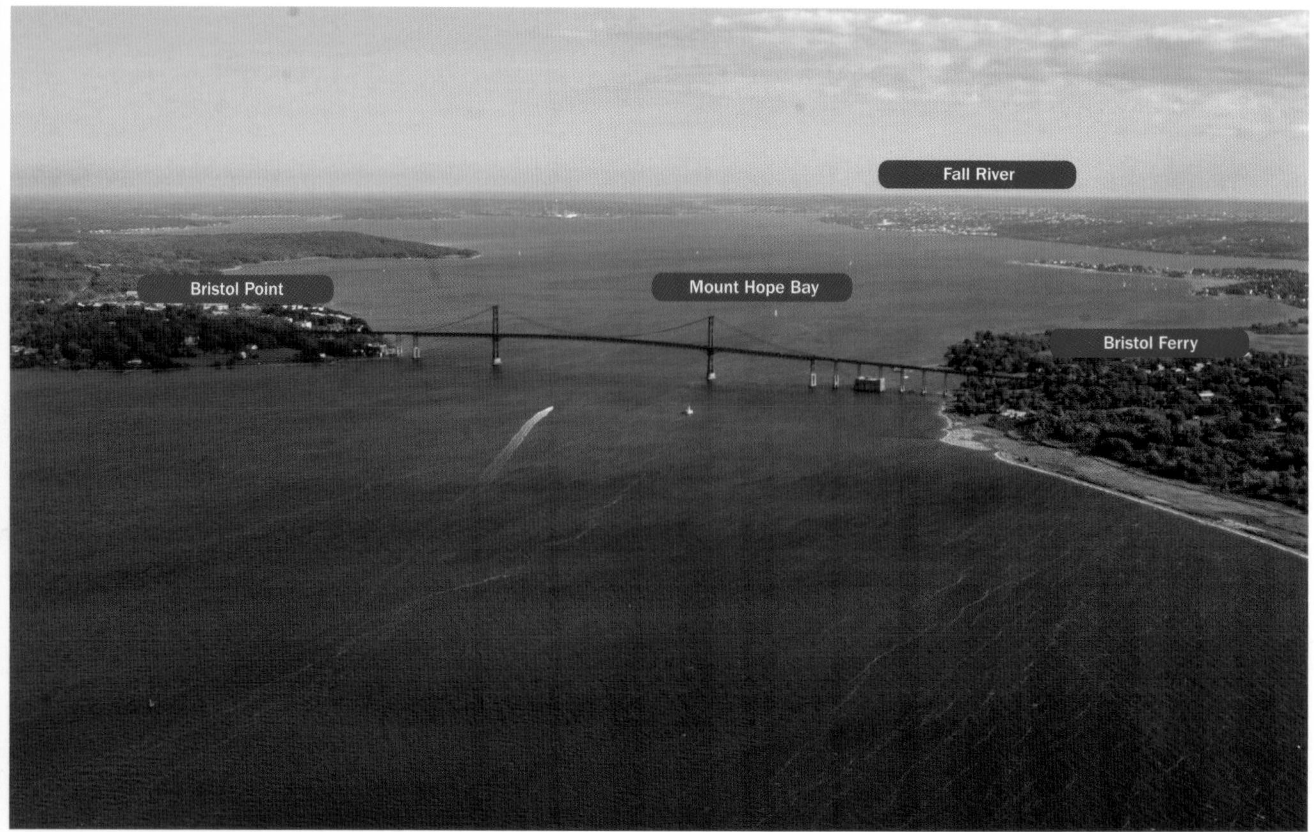

Looking over Mount Hope Bay. (Not to be used for navigation.) WATERWAY GUIDE PHOTOGRAPHY

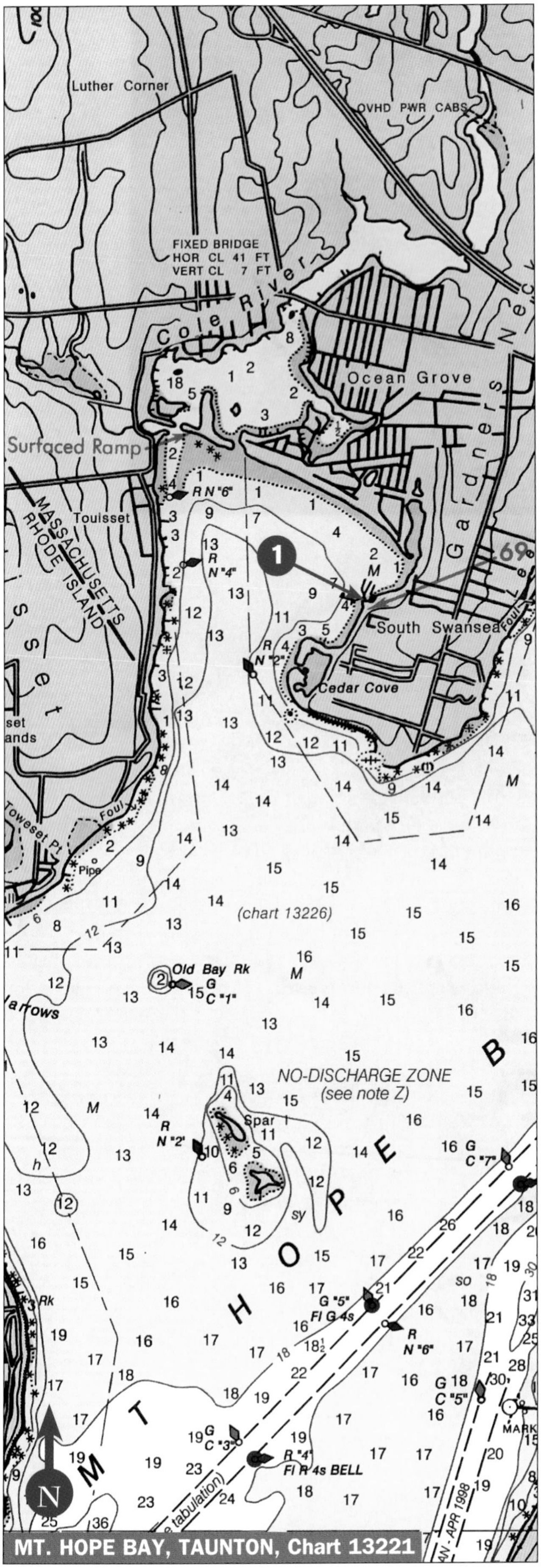

Luther Corner
OVHD PWR CABS
FIXED BRIDGE
HOR CL 41 FT
VERT CL 7 FT
Cole River
Ocean Grove
Gardners Neck
Surfaced Ramp
Touisset
MASSACHUSETTS
RHODE ISLAND
South Swansea
Cedar Cove
TowESet Pt
Pipe
(chart 13226)
Old Bay Rk
NO-DISCHARGE ZONE
(see note Z)
Spar
MT HOPE B
Fl G 4s
Fl R 4s BELL
MT. HOPE BAY, TAUNTON, Chart 13221

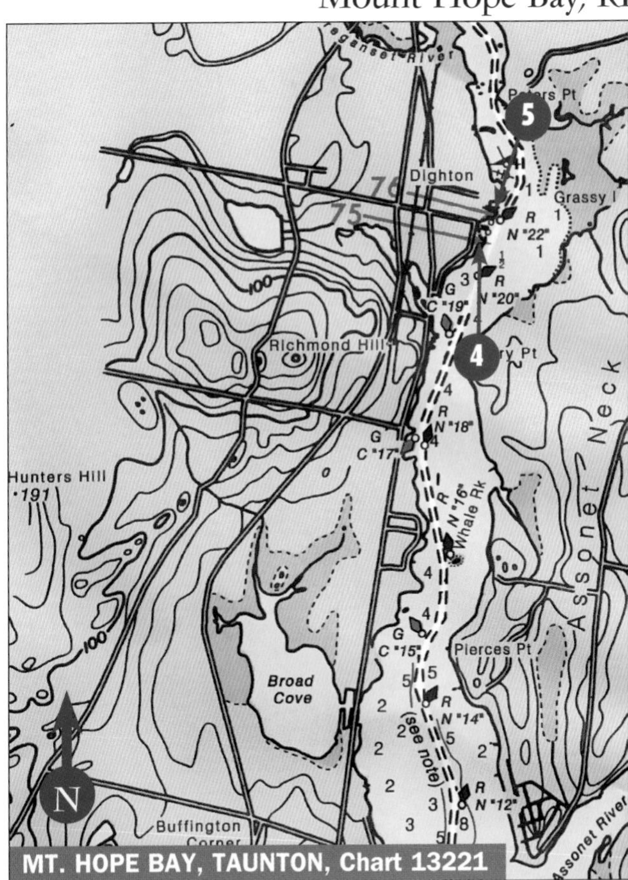

MT. HOPE BAY, TAUNTON, Chart 13221

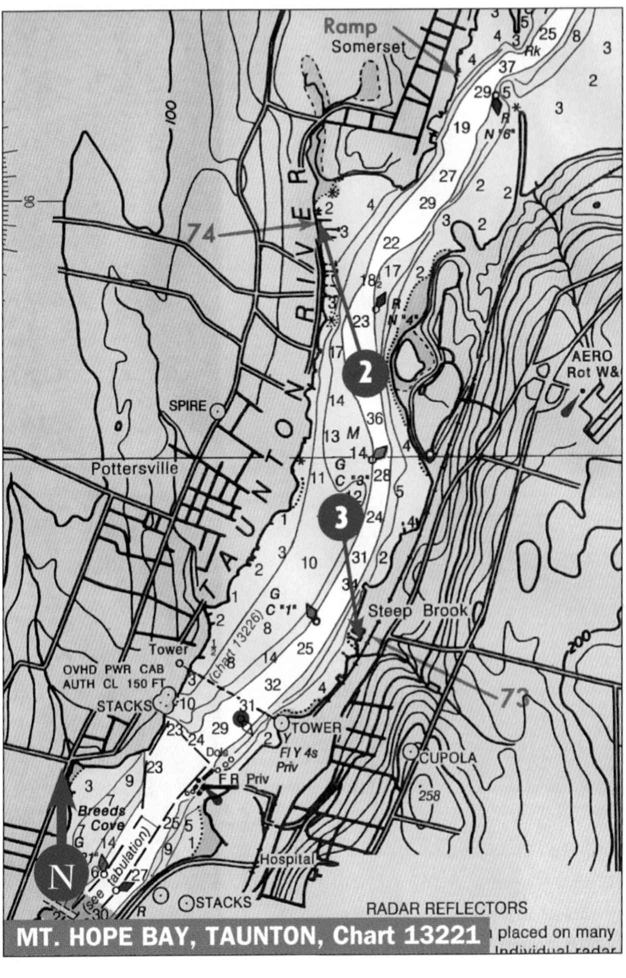

MT. HOPE BAY, TAUNTON, Chart 13221

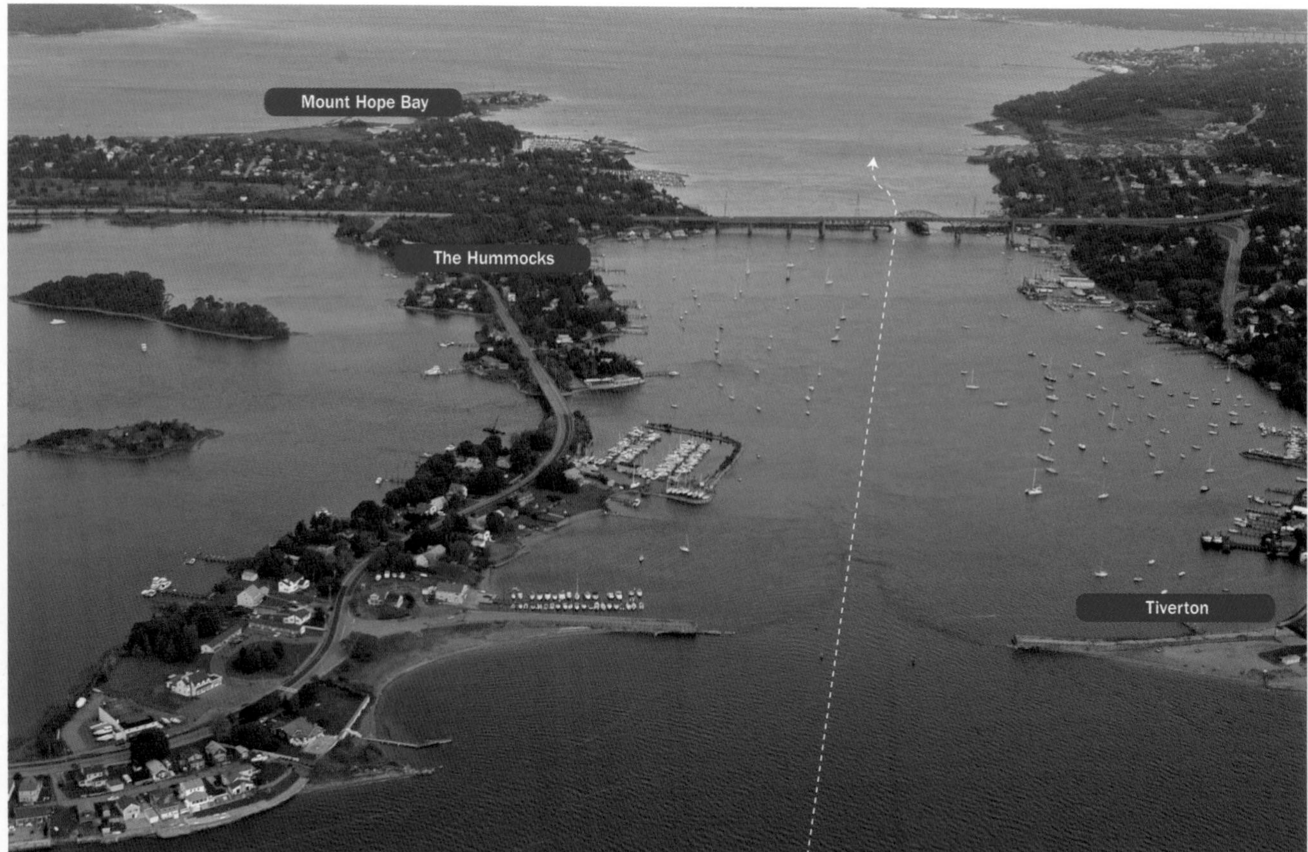

Looking north over the Sakonnet River. (Not to be used for navigation.) WATERWAY GUIDE PHOTOGRAPHY

On up the Taunton River, you go through a bascule bridge with a 27-foot-closed vertical clearance, past a boatyard at Steep Brook and a marina on the western shore.

■ SOUTH ON SAKONNET PASSAGE

The Sakonnet River, lying between Aquidneck Island and the mainland, is easternmost of the Narragansett country's north-south waterways. Many fishermen and recreational boats use the 13-mile-long river, named Saughkonet by the Indians for "black goose place." Its waters and anchorages seem dramatically under-utilized, particularly in comparison to the crowded waters of Newport, not far to the west. The route is deep, the main channel is close to midstream, and all shoals and obstructions are clearly marked. A scattering of towns and harbors offer recreational boat amenities. Tiverton is just south of Mount Hope Bay and north of small, wooded Gould Island, which sits dead center in the Sakonnet River.

NAVIGATION: Use Chart 13221. Use Newport tide tables. For high tide, subtract 9 minutes; for low tide, add 13 minutes. Enter the river from Mount Hope Bay by going eastward around Common Fence Point, Aquidneck's northernmost tip. Turning south, the river narrows into picturesque Tiverton Basin, the Sakonnet's most active boating center. About a half mile south of Common Fence Point, just south and west of green canbuoy "17," Brewer Sakonnet Marina has well-protected transient dockage and full-service facilities. A half mile farther south, the railroad swing bridge (12-foot closed vertical clearance) is usually open. Traveling south, leave the swing span to port; going north, leave it to starboard. The fixed bridge immediately beyond has a 65-foot vertical clearance. Be prepared for swift currents at the bridges except at slack water.

Tiverton

MA
RI

During the Revolutionary War, Tiverton gained acclaim for a particularly daring and successful raid on the British by one of its parishioners, Col. William Barton. (He led a raiding party to capture a British general.) Today only a tower remains of the historic Fort Barton, and there is little else around to attract tourists. For boaters, however, it is a protected and attractive spot with ample facilities on both sides of the river. Nevertheless, significant depths, swift currents and commercial traffic in the basin make anchoring unwise. In this area, it is far better to locate a mooring or a slip.

Dockage: On the eastern side, just south of the bridges, the Tiverton Yacht Club has a friendly welcome for visitors from other clubs, usually a vacant mooring available and sometimes even a slip at the club's dock. A small grocery store is located near the clubhouse. Just beyond, Standish Boatyard has deep-draft slips and moorings for visiting

Sakonnet River, RI

SAKONNET RIVER		Largest Vessel Accommodated	VHF Channel Monitored	Transient Berths / Total Berths	Approach / Dockside Depth (reported)	Floating Docks	Gas / Diesel	Groceries, Ice, Marine Supplies, Snacks	Repairs: Hull, Engine, Propeller	Lift (tonnage), Crane, Rail	1=110V, 2=220V, B=Both, Max Amps	Laundry, Pool, Showers	Pump-Out Station	Nearby: Grocery Store, Motel, Restaurant
		Dockage					Supplies		Services					
1. Brewer Sakonnet Marina (WiFi)	**401-683-3551**	**60**	**09**	**4/320**	**6/7**	**F**	**GD**	**I**	**HEP**	**L35,C**	**B/50**	**LPS**	**P**	**GMR**
2. Standish Boat Yard	401-624-4075	70	16	4/24	35/10	F	GD	IM	HEP	CR	B/30	S	P	GMR
3. Pirate Cove Marina	401-683-3030	70	09	25/76	25/7	F	GD	IM	HP	L	B/50	S	P	GMR
4. Sakonnet Point Marina	401-635-4753	60	06	3/31	3/8	F		I			1/30			R

Corresponding chart(s) not to be used for navigation. Internet Access (WiFi) Wireless Internet Access

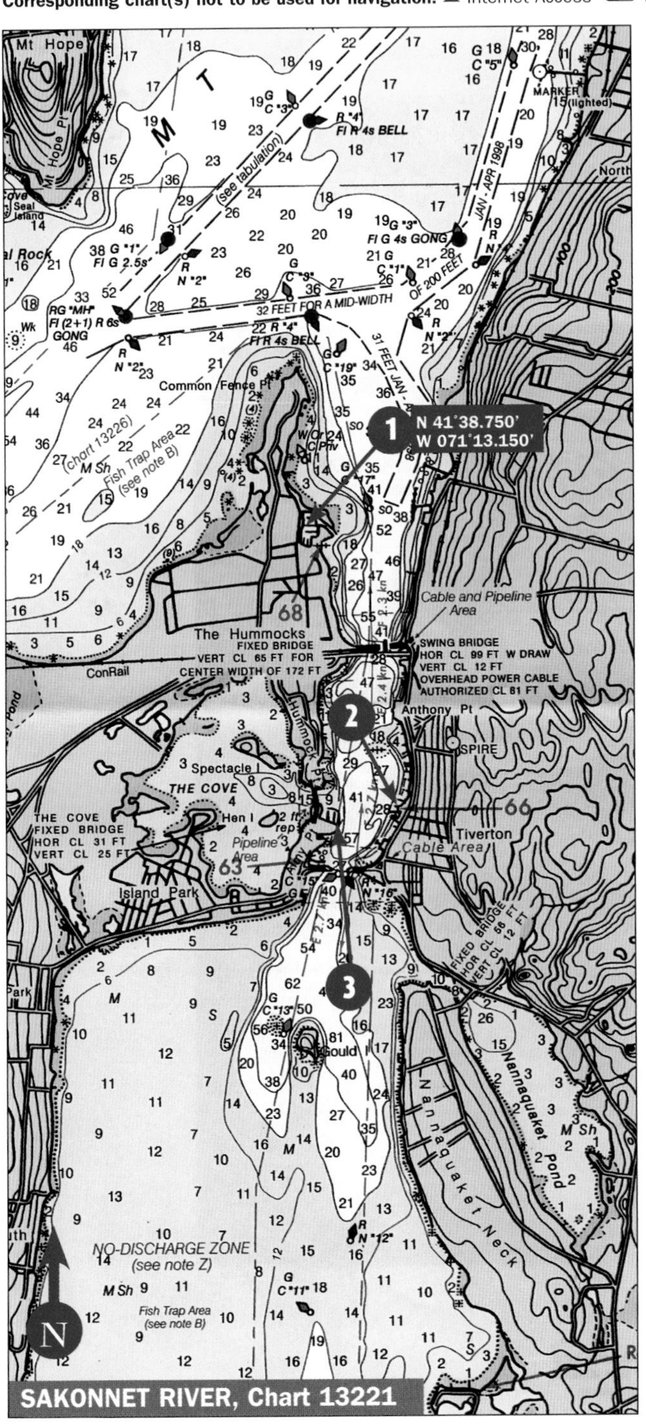

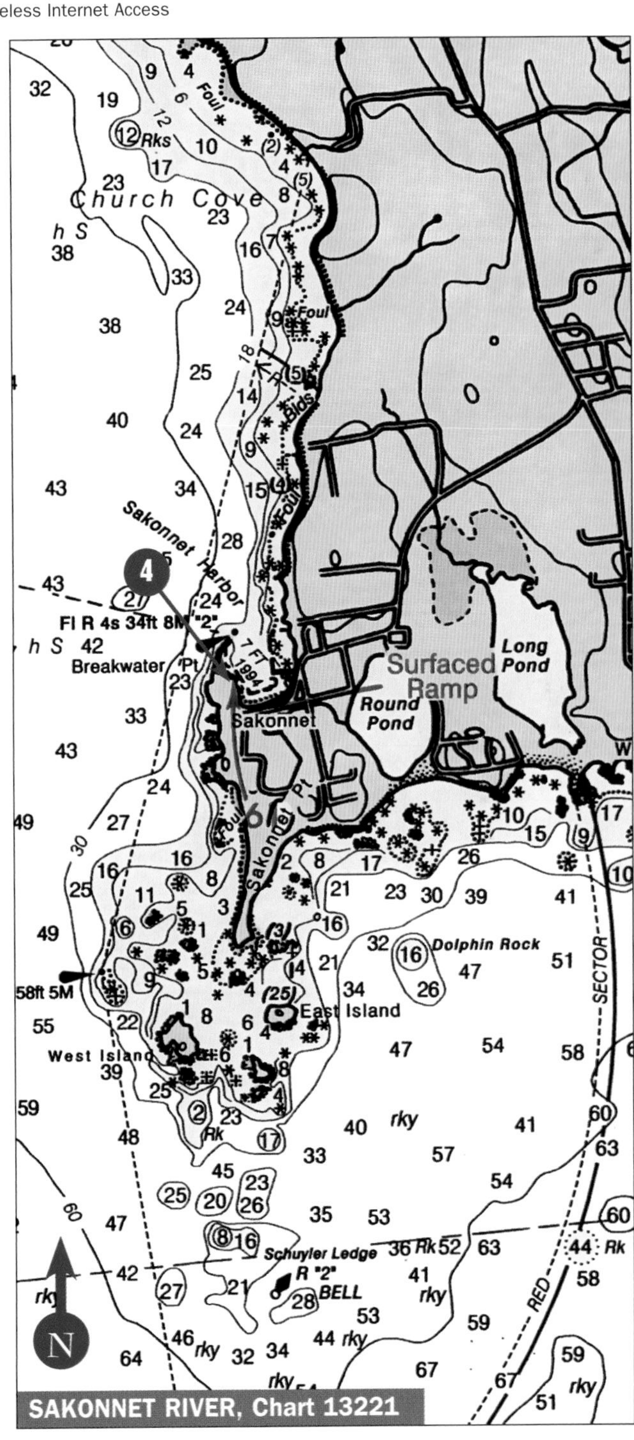

cruisers, marine supplies, all fuels and repair services. On the west (Portsmouth) side of the channel, Pirate Cove Marina also has a full-service facility to support the needs of transients who rent the marina's slips and moorings. Within easy walking distance, 15 Point Road has a reputation for excellent food and a superb river view.

Anchorage: For boats drawing 4 feet or less and having vertical clearance requirements of less than 25 feet, The Cove, just west of Tiverton Basin at Hummock Point, is a favorite gunkholing spot. Most cruisers, though, will have to reserve this spot for dinghy exploration. At the south end of the basin, the rustic remains of the 1810 stone bridge that linked Tiverton to Aquidneck for 150 years are still in evidence, restricting the flow of water in an already tight passage; expect swift currents here on either tide.

Fogland Harbor

Anchorage: About halfway down the river from Tiverton, seven miles north of the river's mouth, Fogland Point juts out from the eastern shore to create a big bight. It is easy to enter, roomy and wide open to the north, with good holding ground but no services. Plenty of water is at the mouth, but don't go too far in; depths tend to shoal. Below High Hill Point on the eastern side of the river is an unnamed cove, which has been known to serve as a good anchorage. Watch for the large spread of aquaculture floats, where oysters for Newport's best restaurants are grown.

Sachuest Cove

Anchorage: On the west side of the mouth of the Sakonnet River, behind Flint Point, is Sachuest Cove. Give plenty of room to unmarked rocks charted off Flint Point. The cove is open to the northeast, but its anchorage is seldom crowded and makes a welcome change from the Newport scene. You might experience a slight surge from the bay but it is usually comfortable for an overnight stay. No amenities are available. On the western shore, however, is 300-acre Norman Bird Sanctuary, with a museum, marked trails and a nice bathing beach, which offers excellent swimming with lifeguards on duty.

Sakonnet Harbor

On the eastern side of the Sakonnet River near its mouth, Sakonnet Harbor is well-protected from the south and east behind Sakonnet Point, and from the west by an 800-foot breakwater extending northward from Breakwater Point.

NAVIGATION: Use Chart 13221. Identify the entrance by four-second flashing red light "2" at the breakwater's end. The usable harbor is quite small, and it is unlikely you will locate a secure anchorage on the hard, kelp-strewn bottom. Local fishermen discourage access with a string of fish traps running parallel to the breakwater and across the harbor entrance at about 200 yards offshore during the summer months. After the first week of June, the best route of entry is that used by the fishing boats—upriver from the south, below the traps, standing off the breakwater at about 50 yards, then turning abruptly to starboard at the entrance. Before early June, however, the fish-trap line is strung at right angles from the breakwater, making the southern approach impossible. Barrels and high-standing radar reflectors at each end mark the traps; nevertheless, spotting them can be quite difficult in fog or when the wind is up. Additional traps, similarly marked, are to the southwest of red bell buoy "2A," near the center of the river.

It is easy to exit the river between Sakonnet and Sachuest points, but be alert for often-inconspicuous floating fish nets, traps, weirs and lobster pots. Stay close to the buoys. Rocks, reefs and islets surround the prominent abandoned lighthouse off Sakonnet Point. The same precautions apply when entering the river, though even in poor visibility, these impediments may be far less daunting than the boisterous seas that can squall up suddenly in Rhode Island Sound to the south.

Quite a few mariners on the trek between Cape Cod Canal or the Islands and Newport have been forced to take an unintended turn into the river when conditions in the sound deteriorated. Once inside, they have been amazed to find that the angry 10-foot waves, powered by 35- to 40-knot gusts outside, fall away almost immediately to placid waters and gentle breezes in the protection of the river's banks. The Sakonnet River is an excellent refuge to keep in mind when planning an outside passage south of Narragansett Bay.

Dockage: Once inside the harbor, you may be lucky enough to locate one of the state of Rhode Island's guest moorings. Sakonnet Point Marina may have transient slips available for boats up to 45 feet, but it is best to call ahead. There are no showers or amenities and no fuel. The local yacht club across the harbor welcomes cruising travelers. A nearby beach offers good swimming.

Sakonnet Harbor is the boating center for the resort area of Little Compton, three miles inland. The Rhode Island Red chicken was established at Little Compton, and that hardy bird has been honored by the Sakonnet Vineyard, about five miles from the harbor. The only solar-heated winery in the east, it produces about 10,000 cases of wine a year and has named one of its vintages "Rhode Island Red." Winery tours are Wednesdays through Sundays, and tastings are held each day, 10 a.m. to 6 p.m. Call 401-635-8486 for more information.

Cruising Options

From here, most boaters will elect to head over to Buzzards Bay and the popular islands of Martha's Vineyard, Nantucket or Cuttyhunk. But do not forget the less crowded and equally charming smaller ports along the Massachusetts mainland, covered in the next chapter. ■

Waterway Guide is always open to your observations from the helm. E-mail your comments on any navigation information in the guide to: editor@waterwayguide.com.

Waterway Guide advertising sponsors play a vital role in bringing you the most trusted and well-respected cruising guide in the country. Without our advertising sponsors, we simply couldn't produce the top-notch publication now resting in your hands. Next time you stop in for a peaceful night's rest, let them know where you found them—Waterway Guide, The Cruising Authority.

Introduction

Buzzards Bay & The Islands

The big, crooked arm of Cape Cod and its island neighbors represent some of the most famous and beloved summer communities in the United States. Much of the charm of the whole area—bound by Buzzards Bay on the west, Vineyard and Nantucket sounds on the south, the Atlantic Ocean on the east and Cape Cod Bay on the north—comes from the dominating influence of the Atlantic Ocean, always nearby in one form or another. Tiny, deep harbors, such as Falmouth or Oak Bluffs on Martha's Vineyard, all thick with boats, could not be more different from the big, sprawling harbors like Nantucket and Edgartown, or the little secluded hideaways, such as Katama Bay. The variety of nautical scenery is part and parcel of the area's charm.

Businesslike commercial harbors like New Bedford, with its huge fishing fleet, and Woods Hole, with its oceanographic fleet, contrast with the elegant yacht harbors of Quissett, with its local small-boat fleet, and Padanaram, across Buzzards Bay, with its traditional wooden-boat fleet.

Distances

This table lists both point-to-point and cumulative distances for Buzzards Bay, Cape Cod and the offshore islands. All measurements are given in approximate nautical miles.

LOCATION	BETWEEN POINTS	CUMULATIVE
BUZZARDS BAY—WESTERN SHORE		
Buzzards Bay Tower	0	0
Padanaram, breakwater	10	10
New Bedford, breakwaters	4	14
Marion, Bird Island	12	26
Cape Cod Canal, Hog I. Ch.	2	28
BUZZARDS BAY—EASTERN SHORE		
Cape Cod Canal	0	0
Phinneys Harbor	3	3
Pocasset Harbor	4	7
West Falmouth	5	12
Quissett Harbor	5	17
Woods Hole	3	20
Quicks Hole	9	29
Cuttyhunk Harbor	4	33
CAPE COD—SOUTH SHORE		
Woods Hole	0	0
Falmouth Inner Harbor	5	5
Waquoit Bay	4	9
West Bay/Osterville	10	19
Hyannis	8	27
Bass River	9	36
Wychmere Harbor	9	45
Stage Harbor, Chatham	5	50
FROM WOODS HOLE		
Woods Hole	0	0
Buzzards Bay Tower	18	18
Menemsha Bight	12	30
Vineyard Haven	14	44
Oak Bluffs	3	47
Edgartown	5	52
Nantucket breakwaters	21	73
Great Point	5	78

Dockage

Finding a dockside slip for an overnight stay around Cape Cod might prove difficult in the peak season during July and August. Skippers accustomed to tying up every night and plugging into shore power might have a tough time finding that kind of dockage. Large local boats, power and sail alike, usually ride to moorings, and slips are rare in many popular harbors. Make reservations where possible, but often marinas in this area will not take any advance reservations. The rule is generally first-come, first-served. You should call the marina of your choice on VHF radio as you come within range, or try calling them via cellular phone if you have one. If slips are not available, ask for a mooring of suitable size. If that fails, be prepared to anchor or, at worst, move on to the next harbor. To avoid end-of-day disappointment, plan to arrive early in the afternoon of the day you need accommodations, particularly in crowded harbors such as Hyannis and Nantucket.

Cruising Conditions

Cape Cod is full of good harbors, delightful gunkholes, clear water for swimming, good eating and sightseeing ashore. But the weather changes continually and deserves constant attention. Adverse conditions can be tough on inexperienced navigators. Study up on navigational skills if in doubt, and do not hesitate to stay comfortably tied up in port if weather conditions are not to your liking.

Warning

Laws in Massachusetts prohibit the carrying of handguns on vessels in state waters without a permit. Permits must be applied for in person. Jail sentences and stiff fines await offenders. For more information, contact the Massachusetts State Police at 617-566-4500. ■

Planning

- Tide Tables 521
- GPS Waypoints 532

Section Contents

Buzzards Bay	332
Cape Cod South Shore	352
The Islands	364

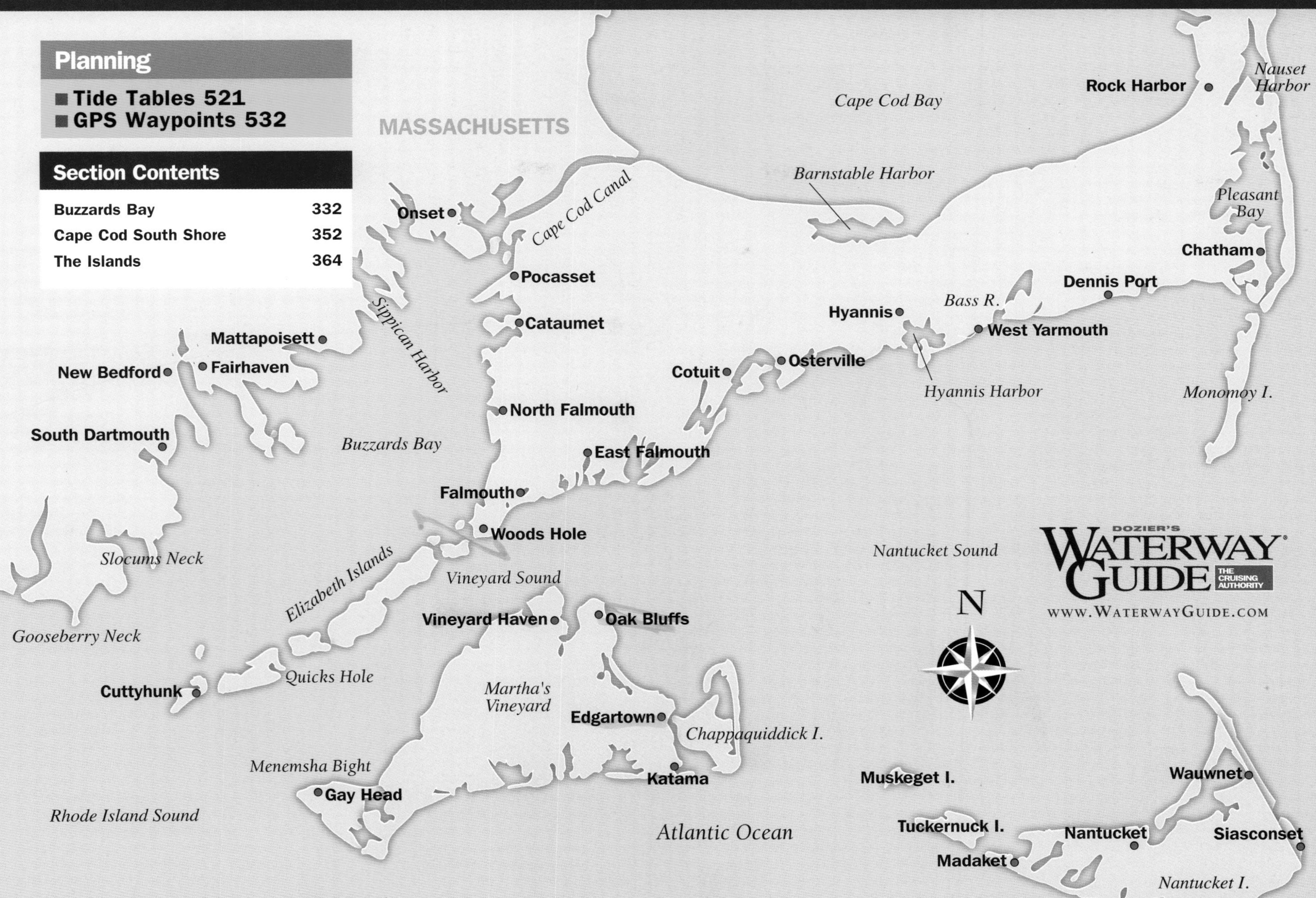

Buzzards Bay

CHARTS 13218, 13228, 13229, 13230, 13232, 13235, 13236

MASSACHUSETTS COAST

East of the border between Rhode Island and Massachusetts, Buzzards Bay begins an almost 30-mile northeasterly sweep to the Cape Cod Canal. Starting at its wide western entrance, almost five miles across from Hen and Chickens off Gooseberry Neck to Sow and Pigs Reef off Cuttyhunk, the Bay runs broad and open, bulging in the middle and narrowing at the top, at the western entrance to the Cape Cod Canal. The wise navigator will consult tide tables based on high and low tides at Boston to make cruising or anchoring decisions. The tidal current charts for Narragansett Bay to Nantucket Sound are also useful.

Prevailing southwesterly winds always seem to blow—15 to 20 knots is normal for any summer afternoon. They funnel up the narrowing bay to create short, steep seas. A 4- to 5-foot sea-state is not unusual, especially on an ebb tide, which opposes the southwesterly winds, creating the characteristic Buzzards Bay chop.

The fog on Buzzards Bay tends to burn off by late morning, but a haze might linger. Despite its reputation as a rough body of water, the bay provides fine sailing and snug harbors. Many sailors consider it the finest sailing area in New England, with reliable winds and many charming natural harbors on both shores.

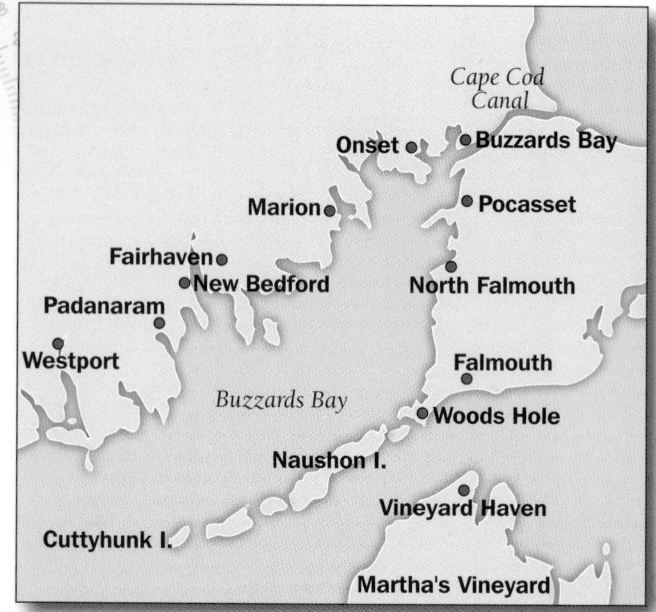

Westport

Less than three miles west of Gooseberry Neck, the one-time whaling center of Westport Point is now a recreational boating and commercial fishing port. Virtually landlocked behind the overlapping points of The Knubble, with its lighthouse on a granite mound, and Horseneck Point, Westport Harbor is well-protected in all but near-hurricane conditions. Despite the formidable approach shown on the chart, sailboats routinely traverse the relatively shallow entrance and flats-strewn channel to the amenities within. The low-lying but lush scenery is characteristic of what was once typical in southern New England harbors—low stone walls girding narrow fields leading to the sea, rushing streams, green marshes and sandy beaches, all prefacing the weathered-shingle houses and 19th-century commercial structures of a picturesque uphill village, crowded with active watermen and recreational boaters.

NAVIGATION: Use Chart 13228. Use Newport tide tables. For high tide, add 9 minutes; for low tide, add 33 minutes. The narrow entry at the mouth of the Westport River, between The Knubble and Horseneck Point, is visible only from close inshore. The shallow bar at the entrance (controlling depth of 6 feet at low water) is dynamic, and constricted currents from the estuary's two branches can reach 4 knots at full ebb. Those who know the area advise to not try the entrance during poor visibility or in a southerly blow.

From flashing white Morse (A) red and white bell buoy "WH" near Twomile Rock, head toward the 35-foot (flashing green every six seconds) beacon at the eastern tip of The Knubble, being sure to honor green daybeacon "3" marking Twomile Rock itself on approach. When the Dogfish Ledge buoy (green can buoy "5") is abeam to port, look for red nun buoy "6" off Halfmile Rock, and leave it to starboard. Pass red nun buoy "6" fairly close to be sure to avoid the charted but unmarked rock due south of The Knubble, which shows 2 feet at mean low tide. The opening into the harbor should now be visible. After rounding The Knubble, follow the channel markers carefully into Westport Harbor, along the northeast shore of Acoaxet and the Lions Tongue, into the snug cove about a mile west of the village of Westport Point. The Coast Guard remarked the entire channel in 2001; the current chart (13228, 11th Edition) may not reflect all of these changes, however, the on-line and print-on-demand charts were updated in September 2009.

When you leave Westport, stand well offshore and clear south of the cluster of ledges at Hen and Chickens and The Wildcat, the last marked by green can buoy "1" and

Looking north over Westport Harbor. (Not to be used for navigation.) WATERWAY GUIDE PHOTOGRAPHY

a prominent wreck marked by a slanting pipe that sticks 20 or more feet out of the water. The next harbor east of Slocums Neck is the unnamed divot leading to Little and Slocum rivers (between Barneys Joy and Mishaum points), which is too shoal for transit. The entrance bar is nearly bare at low tide and the channel is unmarked.

Dockage and Moorings: To starboard on entry into Westport Harbor, about one-third of a mile west of the village landing, F.L. Tripp & Sons usually has transient rental moorings available, but transient slips are no longer offered here. Tripp's is a family-run, full-service marina with restroom/shower facilities, coin-operated laundry machines, gasoline and diesel, marine supplies and complete repair services. Tripp's has been in business for more than 70 years and builds its own line of boats, the Tripp Anglers.

Rental moorings are marked with a small yellow float. Launch service is available from Memorial Day to Labor Day; hail the launch service on VHF Channel 09. There is a picnic area, a small but attractive beach at the west end of the docks (next to the floating dinghy landing) and ample automobile parking.

On the surf side of the access road to Tripp's, the town's parking lot shows the way to the sandy beach path across gorgeous, wind-swept dunes to unspoiled Horseneck Beach (popular with surfers because of its open-ocean frontage) and to the Cherry and Webb Conservation Area on Horseneck Point.

Next door to Tripp's yard, the Westport Yacht Club's unpretentious, weathered clubhouse matches the friendly attitude of its members. The club cannot offer dock space, but may have a mooring for visitors from other clubs. The club's Saturday and Sunday brunch is open to customers of Tripp's and to its own visitors.

Note: Westport Harbor and the east and west branches of the Westport River are No-Discharge Zones. Sealed heads, holding tanks and using a pump-out station (available at Tripp's) are required.

Anchorage: Cruisers recommend not anchoring overnight at Westport because the swift current scours the bottom and holding is poor. However, if you go up the East Branch of the Westport River, through the bascule bridge (21-foot closed vertical clearance), you will find good protection east of Great Island in 6-foot depths.

Watch for Sunk Rock, which is charted but unmarked, in the center of the channel upriver from the bridge. The privately-marked East Branch of the river makes a worthwhile dinghy trip.

On a rising tide, you can explore all the way to Hix Bridge, but note that this trip requires a shallow-draft boat. The shores are lovely, and rolling hills with summer cottages are sprinkled among the working farms whose fields stretch down to the water's edge. The islands in the river are privately owned; some have houses on them.

In a northerly breeze, there is shelter in the lee of Mishaum Point. Leave red nun buoy "2" to starboard and proceed cautiously toward the mouth of Little River. Anchor in 14- to 17-foot depths with a soft bottom. Do not go east of a line from red nun buoy "2" to the fixed bridge across the Little River, and watch for the charted 6-foot spot to the west of that line.

Westport, MA

WESTPORT		Largest Vessel Accommodated	VHF Channel Monitored	Transient Berths / Total Berths	Approach / Dockside Depth (reported)	Floating Docks	Gas / Diesel	Groceries, Ice, Marine Supplies, Snacks	Repairs: Hull, Engine, Propeller	Lift (tonnage), Crane, Rail	1=110V, 2=220V, B=Both, Max Amps	Laundry, Pool, Showers	Pump-Out Station	Nearby: Grocery Store, Motel, Restaurant
		Dockage					Supplies		Services					
1. F.L.Tripp & Sons Inc. (Internet Access)	508-636-4058	65	09	4/175	15/15		GD	IM	HEP	C15	1/50	LS	P	GMR
2. Westport Yacht Club	508-636-8885	60			8/12			I			1	S		
3. The Back Eddy Restaurant	508-636-6500		09	/10	11/7	F		I			1/50			R

Corresponding chart(s) not to be used for navigation. Internet Access Wireless Internet Access

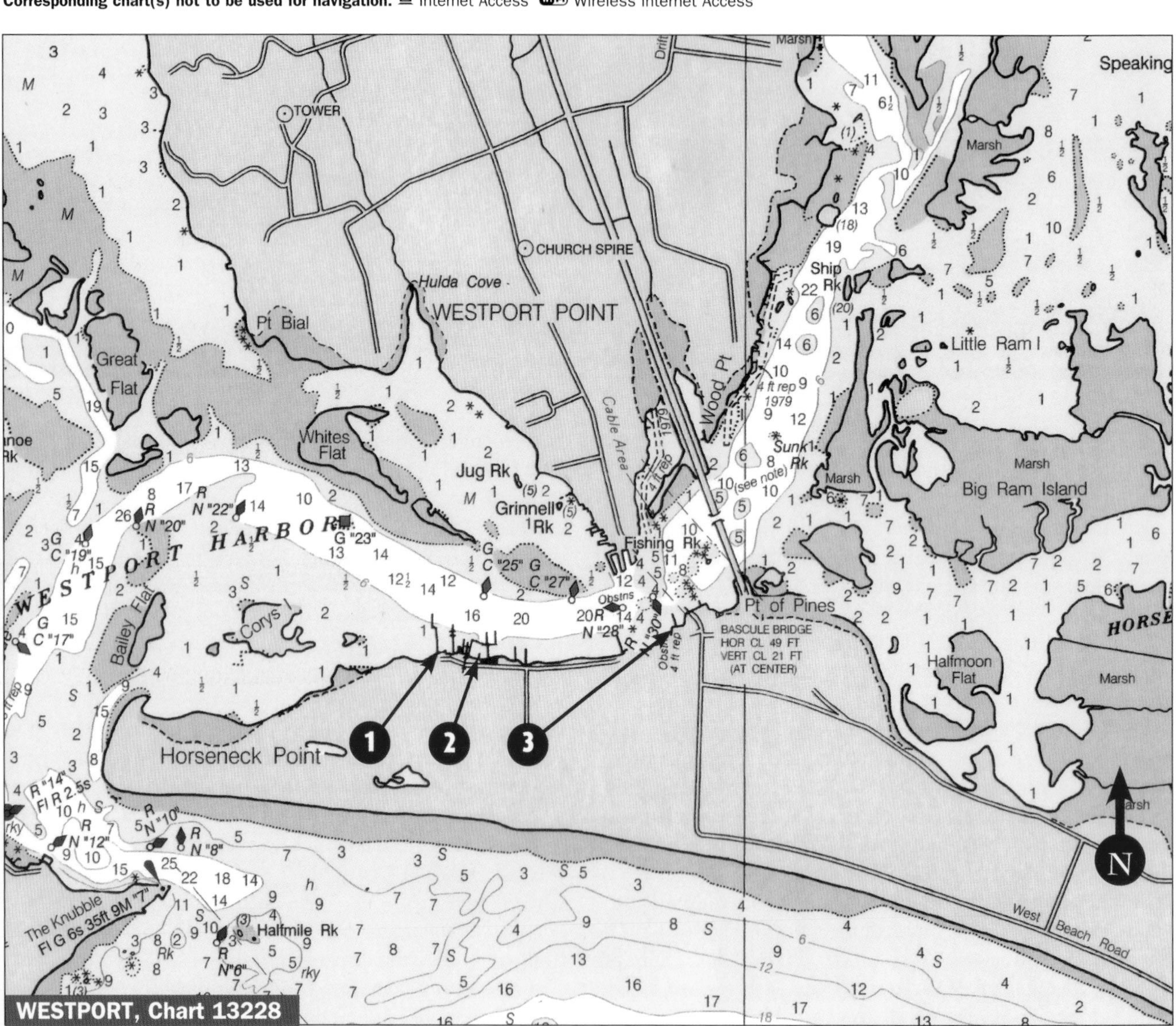

WESTPORT, Chart 13228

GOIN' ASHORE: WESTPORT, MA

The well-preserved 19th-century homes in this unspoiled fishing village are, alone, worth a launch or dinghy ride across the river, but there is more. At Lee's Wharf (on the town landing) the shack-like fish market (open 10 a.m. to 10 p.m. in season) is renowned for its fresh fish (cut to order), lobsters and clams. The Paquachuck Inn offers homey accommodations with a marvelous view for guests. A gentle uphill walk through the quiet village will take you to the post office and Westport Point Market (open 8 a.m. to 8 p.m. during the summer). The latter has basic food and sundry items, some fresh produce and cold cuts, the New York Times, Wall Street Journal and Boston Globe, cold beer and a decent wine selection. The market also carries gourmet, fresh-baked daily bread varieties. The central village of Westport is four to five miles north of Westport Point. There, a variety of restaurants, a pharmacy, a bank and a full-sized supermarket may make it worthwhile to call for a taxi. Also several miles from the harbor, the 100-acre

Westport Rivers Vineyard (417 Hixbridge Road) welcomes visitors to its award-winning winery for free 20-minute tours, wine tasting and review of the vineyard's art gallery (weekends, noon to 5 p.m.).

ADDITIONAL RESOURCES:

- Town of Westport, **www.westport-ma.com**

NEARBY GOLF COURSES:
Montaup Country Club, 500 Anthony Road,
Portsmouth, RI 02871, 401-683-0955

NEARBY MEDICAL FACILITIES:
Saint Anne's Hospital, 795 Middle St.,
Fall River, MA 02721, 508-675-5688

Padanaram (South Dartmouth)

Beyond Mishaum Point and north two miles beyond Round Hill Point, Apponagansett Bay forms an open harbor that has been famous to sailors for generations. Invariably known as Padanaram (pay-dan-air-am), despite its designation as "South Dartmouth" on the charts, this is the home of the large and active New Bedford Yacht Club and the Concordia yard, once builders of the graceful wooden yawl of the same name. This busy and colorful harbor is the mooring ground and point of departure for thousands of Buzzards Bay cruisers and racers. It is a favorite destination port for many others.

NAVIGATION: Use Chart 13229. The harbor approach is rock-strewn but straightforward once you are on course. Enter the passage north of Dumpling Rocks slowly until you sort out the buoys, referring to the appropriate chart. Honoring green gong buoy "7" and 52-foot flashing green "7" marking Dumpling Rocks, take a course of 031 degrees magnetic to flashing red (2+1) red-over-green buoy "AB," and then take a course of 331 degrees magnetic to avoid Ragged Rocks and Hussey Rocks on the western shore. Twenty-five-foot-tall flashing red "8" marks the entrance to Apponagansett Bay.

Dockage and Moorings: The red-roofed New Bedford Yacht Club (NBYC) and its vast mooring field dominate Padanaram and Apponagansett Bay. Indeed, most cruising visitors rent one of the club's guest moorings here. There are no reservations. Simply stand off red nun buoy "12" near the seawall and hail the NBYC launch on VHF Channel 68 for mooring directions. The facilities fee includes launch service and access to the club's spacious accommodations with a 19th-century flavor, excellent dining facilities and shower rooms. Though dock space is in very short supply, a slip may be available from time to time; call the dockmaster for availability. Gasoline, diesel fuel, trash disposal, public phones and a fax machine are also available. Still farther toward the head of the harbor, at the bridge, Davis & Tripp Inc. operates a large and active repair facility, with possible transient space, supplies, ice and all fuels. Cruisers have recently reported additional moorings on the west side of the channel with plenty of availability and great protection during a strong northeasterly blow.

Anchorage: You will find plenty of anchorage space beyond the mooring field, outside the harbor channel and southwest of red nun buoy "10." There is good holding here in 10- to 12-foot depths quite close to the west shore of the bay. This area, however, is exposed to the east and southeast. When the wind is up from this general direction, be prepared for a wet dinghy ride.

GOIN' ASHORE: **PADANARAM, MA**

This quaint, compact village is a good place to enjoy the nautical ambience, poke in the shops, dine and restock the lockers. Both the New Bedford Yacht Club and the Concordia Company front Elm Street, where you will quickly encounter the post office and a FedEx drop box in front of The Packet, an upscale gift shop and women's clothing store. The Village Market (a short block away on Bridge Street) stocks fresh meats and produce, general groceries, over-the-counter drugs and major newspapers. Padanaram Fine Wines and Spirits is next door. Immediately across Bridge Street, Cecily's sells prepared-to-order sandwiches and gourmet deli items, cheese and fresh breads (take out or eat on the premises). From here, within a radius of 50 yards, are galleries and gift shops, an old-fashioned barbershop and the Village Bookshop with a good selection of nautical books and some charts. Tasty breakfasts, specialty salads, sandwiches and great cookies can be found at Fieldstone's (302 Elm St.). For serious dining at a moderate price, locals suggest Warden's (7 Water St., just east of the bridge). Contact the Dartmouth Natural Resources Trust (508-991-2289) for a guide to walking trails around the village. Check for seasonal produce at Cornell Organic Farm (508-996-8048).

ADDITIONAL RESOURCES:

- Coastal Villages of Rhode Island and Massachusetts, **www.coastalvillages.com**

NEARBY GOLF COURSES:
Whaling City Golf Course, 561 Hathaway Road,
New Bedford, MA 02740, 508-966-9393

NEARBY MEDICAL FACILITIES:
St. Luke's Hospital, 101 Page St.,
New Bedford, MA 02740, 508-997-1515

New Bedford, Fairhaven

New Bedford Harbor, at the mouth of the Acushnet River, is busy, commercial, colorful and imbued with a historic seafaring flavor. Two towns line the harbor head and river—New Bedford on the west and Fairhaven to the east—connected by Route 6, which makes both accessible to the

Padanaram, New Bedford, Fairhaven, MA

PADANARAM, NEW BEDFORD, FAIRHAVEN		Largest Vessel Accommodated	VHF Channel Monitored	Transient Berths / Total Berths	Approach / Dockside Depth (reported)	Floating Docks	Gas / Diesel	Groceries, Ice, Marine Supplies, Snacks	Repairs: Hull, Engine, Propeller	Lift (tonnage), Crane, Rail	1=110V, 2=220V, B=Both, Max Amps	Laundry, Pool, Showers	Pump-Out Station	Nearby: Grocery Store, Motel, Restaurant
		Dockage					Supplies		Services					
1. New Bedford Yacht Club	508-997-0762	70	68	/100	10/9		GD	I		L30	1/30	S	P	GR
2. Concordia Company Inc.	508-999-1381	50	09	1/60	10/10	F		M	HE	L30,C10	B/30			GR
3. Davis & Tripp Inc.	508-993-9232	70	09	1/90	15/12	F		IM	HE	L60,C	B/50			GR
4. Fairhaven Shipyard Companies South Yard (Internet Access, Wireless Internet Access)	**508-999-1600**	**200**	**09**	**20/165**	**18/12**	**F**	**GD**	**IM**	**HEP**	**L330,C**	**B/100**	**LS**		**GMR**
5. Fairhaven Shipyard Companies North Yard (Internet Access, Wireless Internet Access)	**508-999-6266**	**200**	**16/09**	**/20**	**20/16**	**F**			**HEP**	**L150,R**	**B/50**		**P**	**GMR**
6. Sea Fuels Marine	508-992-2323	230	11		13/13	Fuel with 24 hour notice								
7. Pope's Island Marina	508-979-1456	150	09/74	10/188	10/10	F		IS			B/50	LS	P	GMR
8. Seaport Inn & Marina	508-997-1281	85		8/104	7.5/	F					B/50	LS	P	GMR

Corresponding chart(s) not to be used for navigation. Internet Access Wireless Internet Access

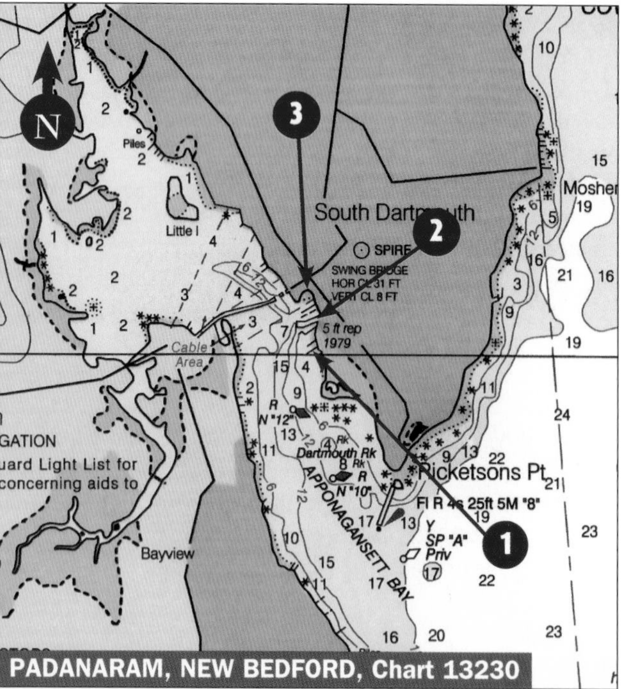

PADANARAM, NEW BEDFORD, Chart 13230

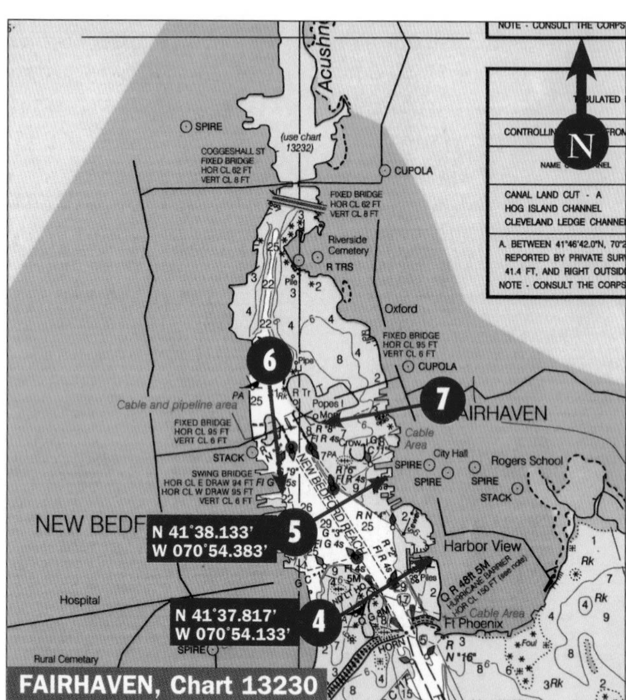

FAIRHAVEN, Chart 13230

area's major recreational boating center on Popes Island. Today the harbor is an active commercial and fishing port, still boasting a fleet of trawlers, draggers, scallopers and lobster boats. It also serves Cuttyhunk, Martha's Vineyard and Nantucket with scheduled ferries and commuter aircraft.

A massive stone hurricane barrier has made New Bedford/Fairhaven a snug harbor of refuge. The near mile-long barrier encloses the harbor except for a 150-foot channel passage. If a major storm threatens, gates are closed across the opening.

NAVIGATION: Use Chart 13229. Use Newport tide tables. For high tide, add 7 minutes; for low tide add 7 minutes. From the Buzzards Bay fairway buoy to the hurricane barrier—approximately eight miles—the Fort Phoenix Reach approach channel is clearly marked, and most obstructions are not of a nature to bother recreational craft. All but a couple of the odd-numbered, port-hand channel markers now carry flashing green lights. Current through the narrow barrier opening runs up to 2.5 knots, with a slight easterly set.

Dockage: Inside the harbor, Sea Fuels Marine operates a renovated fuel dock accomodating vessels up to 230 feet. Because of its central location and extensive floating docks, Popes Island Marina provides convenient dockage for most recreational boats entering the harbor. On entry, past the hurricane barrier, directly to starboard of New Bedford Reach (the harbor's buoyed channel) and north of Crow Island, the city of New Bedford has created a modern facility, which usually has deep-draft space for visitors. Dockside amenities include gleaming showers and restrooms, a coin-operated laundry, ice and public phones—but no fuels.

Most cruisers choose to take a cab rather than walk the considerable distance to town for sightseeing and repro-

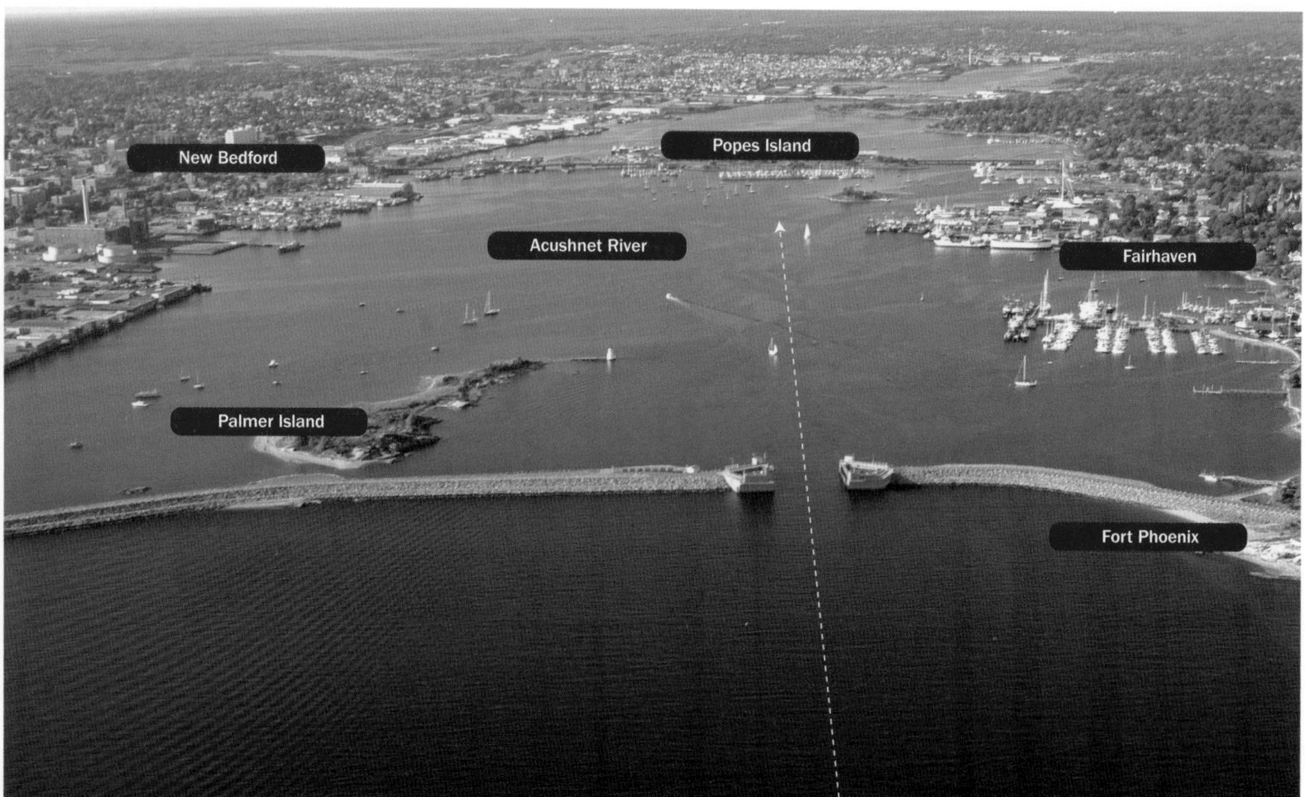

Looking north up the New Bedford Reach. (Not to be used for navigation.) WATERWAY GUIDE PHOTOGRAPHY

visioning. There are plenty of lighted parking spaces at the head of the docks for those meeting friends or changing crews. West Marine and Fairhaven Hardware have large stores immediately across Route 6 in front of the marina.

On the Fairhaven side of the harbor, south of Crow Island, two major boatyards offer repair and reconstruction service to recreational or commercial vessels of substantial size.

Fairhaven Shipyard South is first on entry to the harbor in a cluster of nautical support companies: Rigging Only, Ocean Options Inc. (Sea Frost and Grunert refrigeration), Sea Recovery (desalination systems) and Precision Propeller Service.

Fairhaven Shipyard North is next, immediately south of Crow Island, identifiable by its 160-ton lift and extensive sheds for marine work. Both of these working yards are likely to have transient space, though most visitors come with repairs or special equipment installations in mind.

GOIN' ASHORE: NEW BEDFORD, FAIRHAVEN, MA

New Bedford was once the hub of the American whaling industry, and it retains many a reminder of the days when its fleet was larger than all others combined. Thanks to history-minded citizens, much of the ancient character has been preserved in the New Bedford Heritage State Park, which includes most of the city. Within walking distance of the waterfront, visitors can view exceptional architectural examples of private cottages, homes and mansions built during the first half of the 19th century. The superb New Bedford Whaling Museum (18 Johnny Cake Hill, 508-997-0046, open all year) and the Seamen's Bethel Church (15 Johnny Cake Hill, 508-992-3295), with the pew once occupied by "Moby Dick" author Herman Melville, are easy to visit on foot. The Historic District is proud of the Zeiterion Theatre, built in 1923 and home to vaudeville shows.

Café Arpeggio (800 Purchase St.) in the Historic District of New Bedford is a great spot for gourmet coffee, sandwiches, soups, homemade ice cream and free Internet access.

Fairhaven, on the opposite side of the harbor, is an increasingly important base for repairs and supplies. Here you will find marine specialists for engines, machinery and fabrication, rigging, propellers, electronics, canvas and sails.

ADDITIONAL RESOURCES:

- City of New Bedford, **www.ci.new-bedford.ma.us**

NEARBY GOLF COURSES:
Whaling City Golf Course, 561 Hathaway Road, New Bedford, MA 02740, 508-966-9393

NEARBY MEDICAL FACILITIES:
St. Luke's Hospital, 101 Page St., New Bedford, MA 02740, 508-997-1515

Mattapoisett

Mattapoisett is beautiful and easy to enter. The village is postcard New England—clapboard, picturesque and historic. During the heyday of the whaling industry, some

Fairhaven, Mattapoisett, MA

FAIRHAVEN, MATTAPOISETT		Largest Vessel Accommodated	VHF Channel Monitored	Transient Berths / Total Berths	Approach / Dockside Depth (reported)	Floating Docks	Gas / Diesel	Groceries, Ice, Marine Supplies, Snacks	Repairs: Hull, Engine, Propeller	Lift (tonnage), Crane, Rail	1=110V, 2=220V, B=Both, Max Amps	Laundry, Pool, Showers	Pump-Out Station	Nearby: Grocery Store, Motel, Restaurant
		Dockage					Supplies		Services					
1. Earl's Marina & Comorant Marine	508-993-8600	45	18	3/115	4.5/4.5	F	GD	IMS	HEP	C	1/30	LS	P	R
2. Mattapoisett Boatyard Inc.	508-758-3812	50	68	2/6	12/6		GD	IMS	HE	L35,C	1/30	S	P	MR

Corresponding chart(s) not to be used for navigation. Internet Access Wireless Internet Access

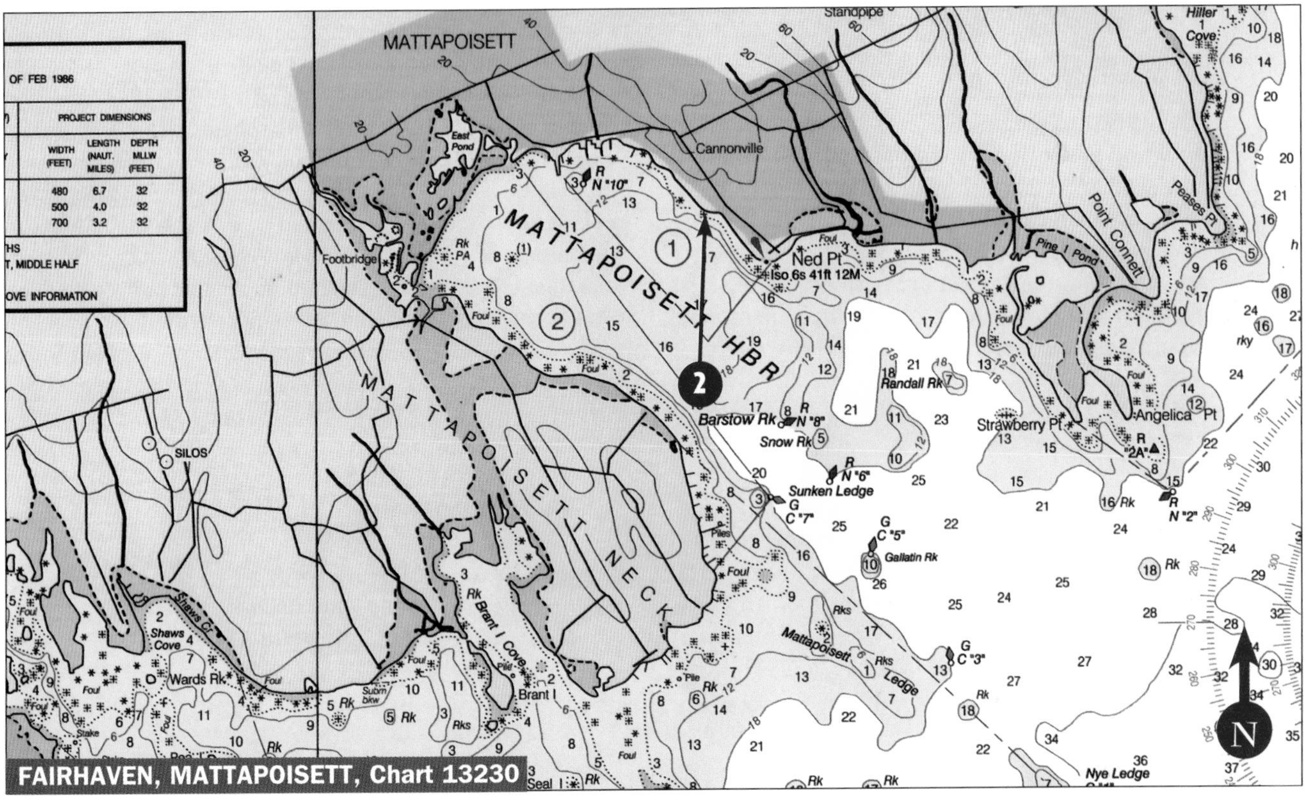

FAIRHAVEN, MATTAPOISETT, Chart 13230

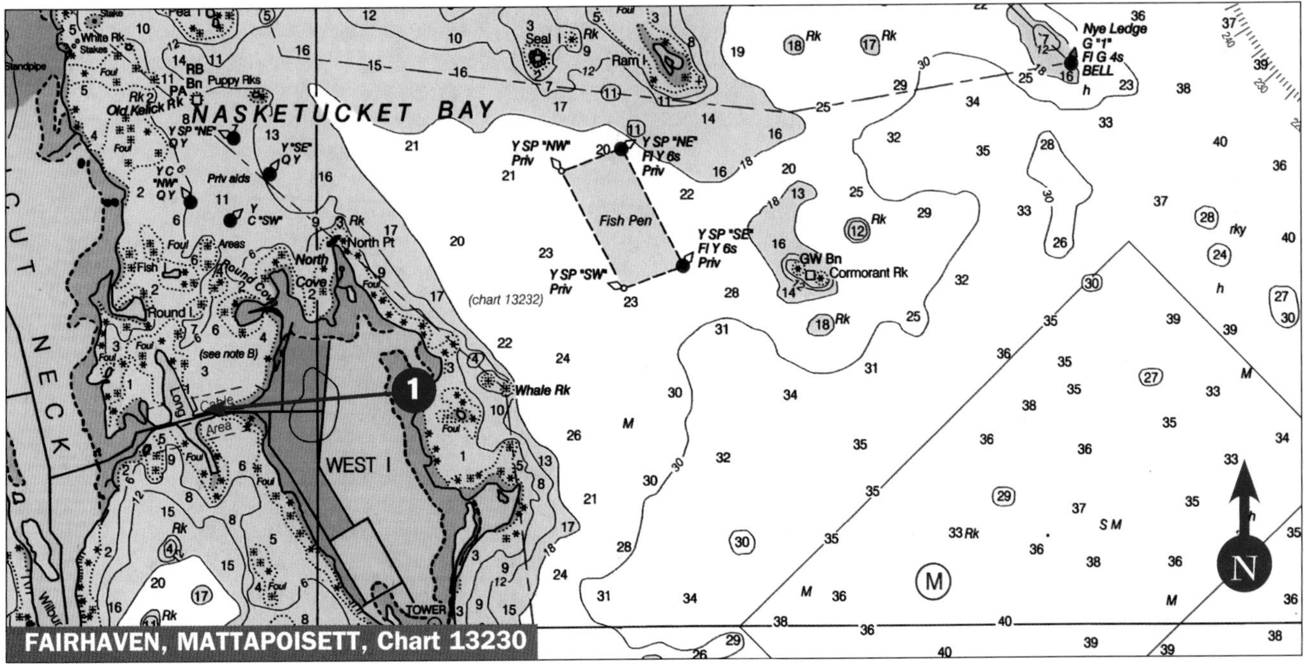

FAIRHAVEN, MATTAPOISETT, Chart 13230

of the finest whaling ships in the world were built here. Shipyard Park at the village center commemorates a time when some 400 men worked the yards, and the bowsprits of mighty vessels shrouded the roadways.

The harbor itself is an inverted "U" from the southeast, funneling in the prevailing southerlies—quite pleasant on a hot, light-air day, but a roiling experience when the wind pipes up across the diagonal-width fetch of Buzzards Bay. More than one crew has lost its breakfast here while waiting for the fog to lift above incoming 4- to 5-foot waves.

NAVIGATION: Use Chart 13229. Use Newport tide tables. for high tide, add 11 minutes; for low tide add 20 minutes. Although the approach is straightforward, numerous submerged obstructions lie outside of, at or near buoys marking the generous channel access. Snow Rock, for example, will find the bottom of a 5-foot-draft vessel straying beyond the channel marked by red nun buoys "6" and "8." It is best to remain carefully within the channel markers until well past red nun buoy "8."

Dockage and Moorings: Mattapoisett Boatyard (east side of the harbor and north of Ned Point) maintains transient moorings; the most obvious ones are painted international orange and anchored directly in front of the yard's landing. If those are occupied or you would rather be closer to the village, call the yard on VHF for directions. Helical-screw system anchors hold at least half of the yard's moorings; they handily survived Hurricane Bertha in 1996. The boatyard operates a launch service to and from town or its own dock (until 8 p.m. during the summer months), which is included in the mooring fee. This yard also provides fuel, ice, showers, a significant parts inventory, free pump-out and major repairs. There is also a self-service pump-out facility available at the town wharf, open 24 hours a day. Next door, the Mattapoisett Yacht Club has an active sailing program and is friendly to visitors (often offering hot coffee at the door) but it has few reciprocal privileges to offer.

At the head of the harbor, three substantial town piers provide space for transient tie-ups, but fender your vessel thoroughly against damage from the rough timbers and pilings.

Anchorage: There may be limited anchorage space near the town piers, south of red nun buoy "8," but avoid blocking the roundabout channel circling the harbor's center mooring area. You can find additional anchorage room southwest of the town piers in 8- to 12-foot depths at low tide and along the north side of the substantial bight in about 15-foot depths at low water just inside Ned Point. As in many New England harbors, there are more moorings and fewer anchorage areas each year. Plan accordingly and reserve ahead.

GOIN' ASHORE: MATTAPOISETT, MA

A quiet and beautiful walk in this quaint seaside village is free for the ambling. At the heart of the village, directly across from the town docks, the Kinsale Inn (formerly known as the Mattapoisett Inn, 13 Water St., 508-758-4922, reservations recommended) is located in the Joseph Meigs House (c. 1799) and serves hearty American dinners and casual, light lunches, including some delicious Irish specialties. On the harbor side of Water Street, the Shipyard Galley offers outstanding, fresh baked goods and soups, sandwiches and deli items. Close to a mile north of the harbor on Route 6 at Barst Street, Mattapoisett Chowder House (20 County Road, 508-758-4782) repays those who take the walk with serious chowders and seafood, served in a casual atmosphere at modest prices. Nearby are the Seaport Pharmacy (with current newspapers and magazines, one-day film processing, fax and copy service), Cerulli's Gourmet Foods and Cafe and a small grocery. The Mattapoisett Coin Laundry (drop-off and self-service) is on Pearl Street, just south of Route 6. An annual civic celebration is the Harbor Days Weekend, which is held the third weekend in July each year. The Mattapoisett Historical Museum (open daily year-round) gives an interesting overview of the area.

ADDITIONAL RESOURCES:

- Town of Mattapoisett, **www.mattapoisett.net**

NEARBY GOLF COURSES:
Acushnet River Valley Golf Course, 685 Main St., Acushnet, MA 02743, 508-998-7777

NEARBY MEDICAL FACILITIES:
St. Luke's Hospital, 101 Page St., New Bedford, MA 02740, 508-997-1515

Marion (Sippican Harbor)

Tranquil and easy to enter, Sippican Harbor is the route to the beautiful town of Marion, with its ancient trees shading narrow, cottage-lined streets. Protected moorings, marinas and shops offer all you are likely to need, making this a favorite layover port for cruising boats.

NAVIGATION: Use Chart 13229. Use Newport tide tables. For high tide, add 10 minutes; for low tied, add 12 minutes. Bird Island to the east, with its lighthouse, and Converse Point to the west, with a flagpole and large summer house, clearly mark the entry to Marion. Keep clear of the Converse Point rocks by honoring flashing green buoy "3" and green can buoy "5" to port, and then laying a course for red nun buoy "6." Simply follow the well-marked, 6-foot (or better, on most tides) channel to the harbor head. Though the channel is dredged periodically, it shoals quickly beyond the buoys, and turning room can be at a premium during the busy summer season.

Marion, Wareham, MA

MARION, WAREHAM		Largest Vessel Accommodated	VHF Channel Monitored	Transient Berths / Total Berths	Approach / Dockside Depth (reported)	Floating Docks	Gas / Diesel	Groceries, Ice, Marine Supplies, Snacks	Repairs: Hull, Engine, Propeller	Lift (tonnage), Crane, Rail	1=110V, 2=220V, B=Both, Max Amps	Laundry, Pool, Showers	Pump-Out Station	Nearby: Grocery Store, Motel, Restaurant
		Dockage					Supplies		Services					
1. Beverly Yacht Club	508-748-0540	50	68		/7			I				S		GR
2. Barden's Boat Yard Inc.	508-748-0250	55	68	7/90	5/8			IM	HEP	L,C		S	P	GR
3. Burr Bros. Boats Inc.	508-748-0541	65	68	2/34	6/6	F	GD	IM	HEP	L40,C	B	S	P	GR
4. Zecco Marina 💻	508-295-0022	55	16/9	10/120	8/6	F	GD	IMS	HEP	L35,CR	B/30	S	P	GMR
5. Cape Cod Shipbuilding Co.	508-295-3550	44			12/9	F			H	L	1/30			R

Corresponding chart(s) not to be used for navigation. 💻 Internet Access (WiFi) Wireless Internet Access

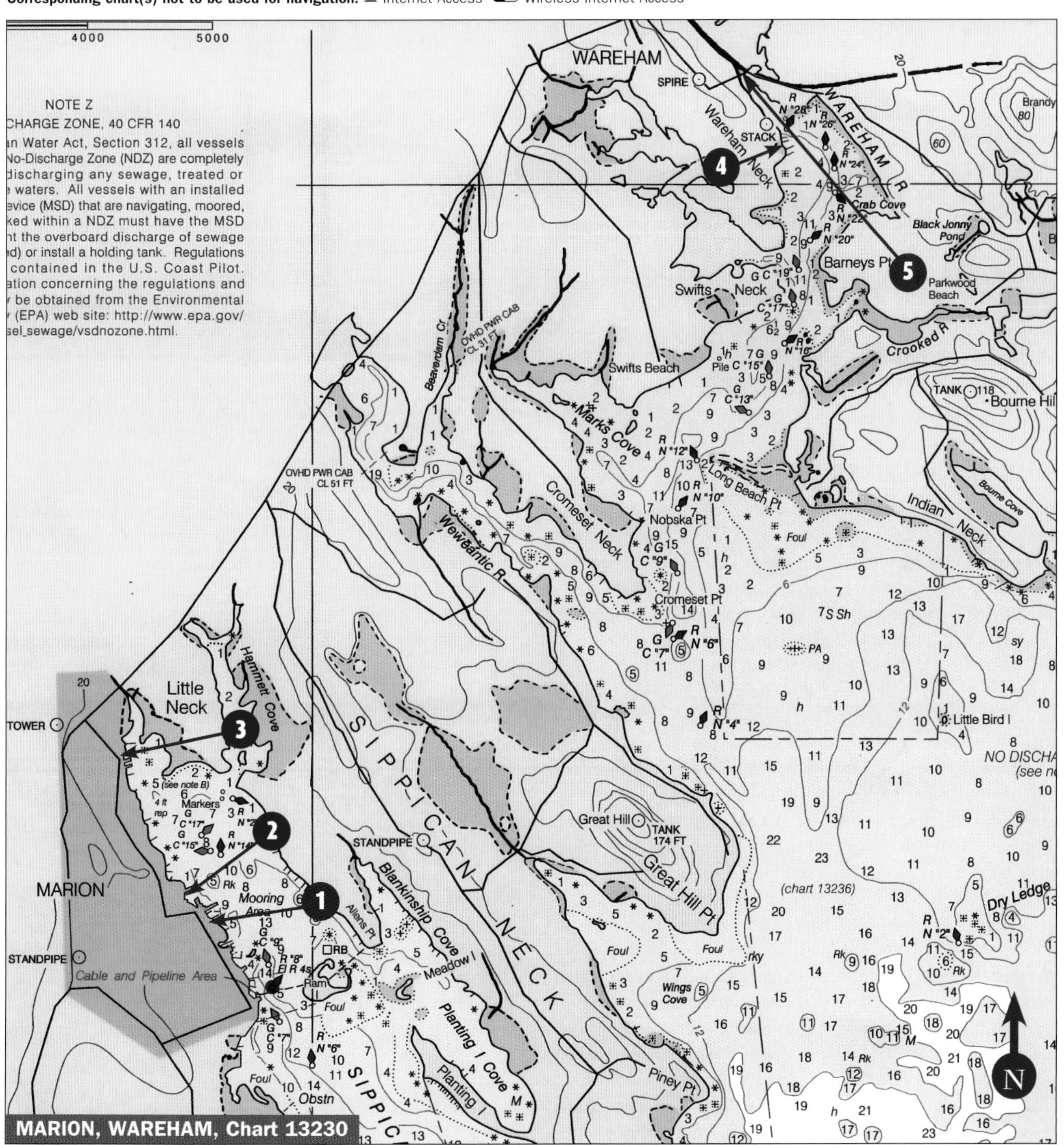

Dockage and Moorings: The distinguished Beverly Yacht Club becomes visible to port as you pass green can "9." Members of other recognized clubs may be able to secure a mooring there for a facilities fee. Barden's Boatyard, immediately beyond, a complete repair facility, rents moorings and operates a public launch service. There is a dinghy dock here, but no slips or fuels are available. Next door, the town landing has dock space to accommodate 20-minute tie-ups to take on drinking water or to use the town's free mobile pump-out service. Call the harbormaster on VHF Channel 09 or by phone (508-748-3535) for the pump-out service. Beneath the harbormaster's office, for a small charge, the town provides clean restrooms and showers and two large dumpsters on the side of the building next to the road.

At the head of the harbor, Burr Bros. Boats Inc. offers a complete range of marina and marine repair facilities in a pastoral setting. This family-run operation has a large ship's store, parts department, specialty repair, paint and composition shops, all fuels and a 40-ton lift. The well-marked entry channel carries 6-foot depths at mean low water (most tides are in the 4-foot range). The yard also offers transient moorings and slips at floating concrete docks.

Anchorage: Although there is no anchorage in Marion proper, boats can anchor in outer Sippican Harbor in settled weather. In years past, the New York Yacht Club Cruise has anchored 175 boats in the vicinity prior to a mass transit through the Cape Cod Canal.

GOIN' ASHORE: MARION, MA

This residential town, with its tidy and beautifully landscaped lawns, clapboard cottages, shops and notable houses, also has a natural history museum, a historic society, art center and the Tabor Academy, an independent secondary school, easily recognized by its extensive red roofs. Tabor Academy understandably includes sailing in its curriculum and maintains a fleet of launches, day sailors, rowing shells and the 92-foot schooner, *Tabor Boy.*

Founded in 1679, the town was first called Sippican, but was renamed Marion in the mid-19th century in honor of the Revolutionary War hero, General Francis Marion, the "Swamp Fox."

Virtually all shopping is within two blocks (to the left) of the town dock on Front Street. Marion General Store has basic provisions, cheeses, wine and beer, ice and baked goods made on the premises. In an accessible cluster of shops nearby are a spirits shop, bookstore, Hiller's Fuels (for propane refills), the post office and a gift shop. The Marion First Congregational Church just a block farther south is an American Greek Revival classic with a Christopher Wren-style steeple. Its bells toll by the hour. The Sippican Historical Society Museum (Main Street just east of Front Street, open summers by appointment) has quite a collection of local memorabilia, including the old post office, an early kitchen and a number of Gerard Curtis Delano's Indian paintings. Modern postal drop boxes, including an Express Mail box are out front.

Back toward the town dock, a few yards west on Cottage Street, Harriet's Restaurant (lunch and dinner, Tuesday through Sunday) serves dinner entrees such as red pepper fettuccini with scallops, porcini mushrooms, pancetta and grilled mushrooms. Behind Harriet's, the Cake Lady has an amazing repertoire of delectable desserts. Next door, Galloway's is a popular spot for ice cream. At the head of the harbor, near Burr Bros. Boats, the Wave Restaurant is noted by locals for "a good meal at a good price." The Frigate Steak House is located at 806 Mill St. and specializes in all cuts of prime beef as well as other entrees. The Marion Café (313 Wareham) is another good choice for lunch or dinner.

ADDITIONAL RESOURCES:

- Town of Marion, **www.townofmarion.org**

NEARBY GOLF COURSES:
Little Harbor Country Club, Little Harbor Road,
Wareham, MA 02571, 508-295-2617

NEARBY MEDICAL FACILITIES:
Tobey Hospital, 43 High St.,
Wareham, MA 02571, 508-295-0880

Wareham

Just about two miles up the Wareham River and five miles from Cleveland Ledge Channel is Wareham. Remote from the main route to the Cape Cod Canal, it nonetheless makes an attractive base for exploring. This resort territory offers good beaches, busy protected coves, crowded anchorages and wonderful scenery.

NAVIGATION: Use Chart 13229. The river channel is winding but well-marked, with a depth of 8 feet. Shallow water lies outside the channel on either side; watch buoys carefully to stay in deep water.

A popular anchorage is to starboard, beyond Long Beach Point; note that Long Beach Point might be completely submerged at high tide. Pass red nun buoy "12" close to starboard to avoid shoals extending from the northeast. Steer for green can buoy "13" immediately after rounding red nun buoy "12." Near Wareham, the river narrows and currents of up to 3 knots can be expected.

When a southwester meets a strong current flowing westward out of the canal, the head of Buzzards Bay can become rough with short, steep seas. The eastbound skipper should lay over at Marion under these circumstances. The westbound skipper, anticipating these conditions, can seek the shelter of Onset Harbor, 1.5 miles west of Hog Island Channel, to wait for more favorable weather.

Onset

Whatever the weather, Onset makes an attractive cruising stop and a good place to await favorable wind and tide for a trip across the bay or north through the Cape Cod Canal. This Victorian seaside village offers protection from most winds, attractive white sand beaches, accessible facilities and good anchorage.

NAVIGATION: Use Chart 13229. Use Newport tide tables. For high tide, add 41 minutes; for low tide, add 1 hour 25

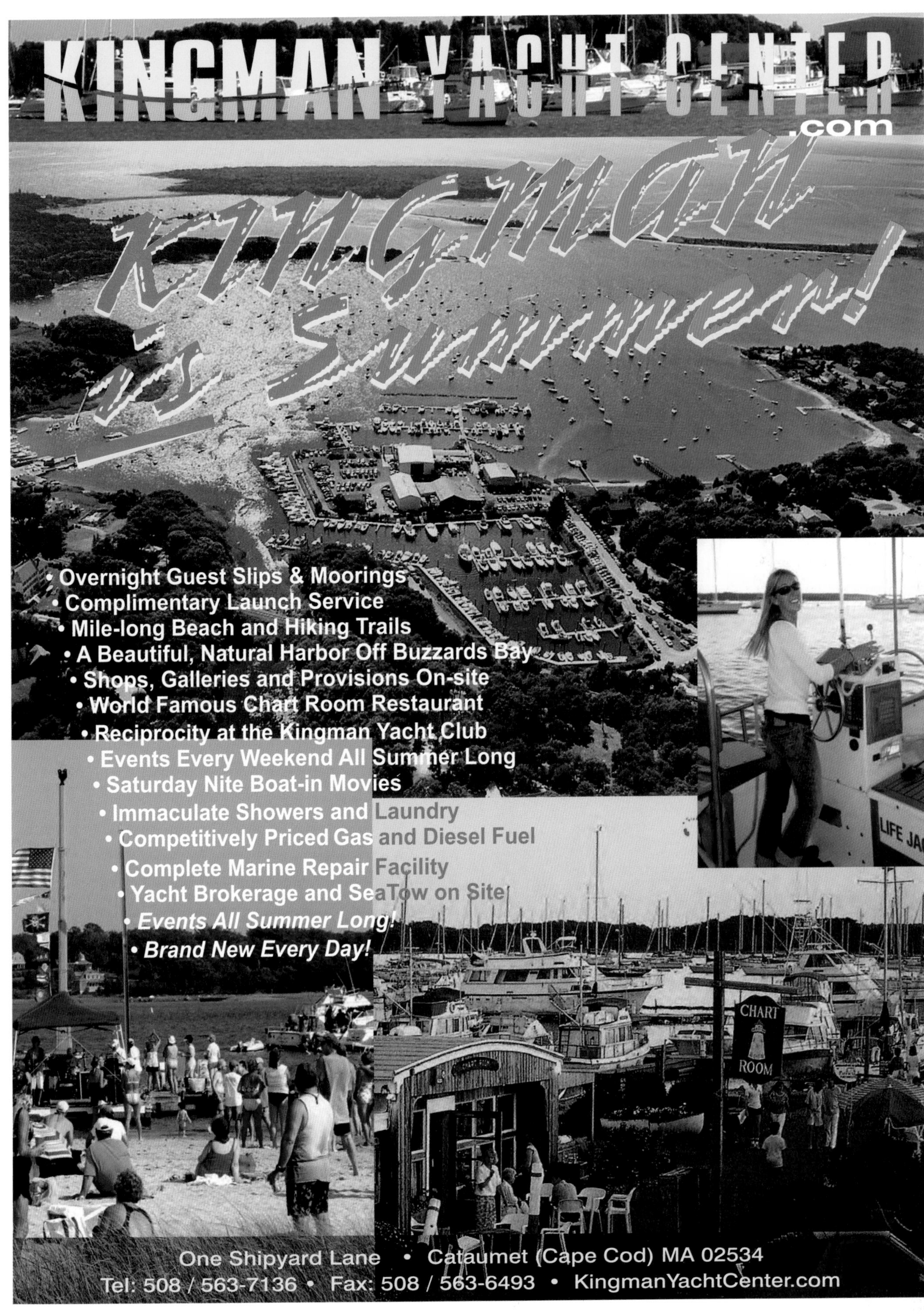
KINGMAN YACHT CENTER
.com
Kingman is Summer!
• Overnight Guest Slips & Moorings
• Complimentary Launch Service
• Mile-long Beach and Hiking Trails
• A Beautiful, Natural Harbor Off Buzzards Bay
• Shops, Galleries and Provisions On-site
• World Famous Chart Room Restaurant
• Reciprocity at the Kingman Yacht Club
• Events Every Weekend All Summer Long
• Saturday Nite Boat-in Movies
• Immaculate Showers and Laundry
• Competitively Priced Gas and Diesel Fuel
• Complete Marine Repair Facility
• Yacht Brokerage and SeaTow on Site
• Events All Summer Long!
• Brand New Every Day!
CHART ROOM
One Shipyard Lane • Cataumet (Cape Cod) MA 02534
Tel: 508 / 563-7136 • Fax: 508 / 563-6493 • KingmanYachtCenter.com

Onset to Megansett Harbor, MA

ONSET TO MEGANSETT HARBOR		Largest Vessel Accommodated	VHF Channel Monitored	Transient Berths / Total Berths	Approach / Dockside Depth (reported)	Floating Docks	Gas / Diesel	Groceries, Ice, Marine Supplies, Snacks	Repairs: Hull, Engine, Propeller	Lift (tonnage), Crane, Rail	1=110V, 2=220V, B=Both, Max Amps	Laundry, Pool, Showers	Pump-Out Station	Nearby: Grocery Store, Motel, Restaurant
		Dockage					Supplies		Services					
1. Point Independence Yacht Club	508-295-3972	70	09	15/65	8/7	F	GD	IS			1/50	LS	P	GMR
2. Onset Bay Marina	508-295-0338	150	09	10/110	8/8	F	GD	IMS	HEP	L65	B/50	LS	P	GMR
3. Taylor's Point Marina	508-759-2512	45	16/09	2/147	6/9	F	GD	IMS			B/50	LS	P	MR
4. Monument Beach Marina	508-759-3105	40	16/09	2/61	9/6		G	I			1/30	S		M
5. Kingman Yacht Center (Internet Access) (Wireless Internet Access)	**508-563-7136**	**100**	**71**	**240/240**	**8/10**	**F**	**GD**	**GIMS**	**HEP**	**L70**	**B/50**	**LS**	**P**	**GR**
6. Parker's Boatyard Inc.	508-563-9366	45	69	4/9	6/8	F	GD	IM	HEP	L35,C	1/30	S	P	GMR
7. Brewer Fiddler's Cove Marina (Internet Access) (Wireless Internet Access)	**508-564-6327**	**55**	**09**	**/133**	**7/9**	**F**	**GD**	**IM**	**HP**	**L**	**B/50**	**LS**	**P**	**GMR**

Corresponding chart(s) not to be used for navigation. Internet Access · WiFi Wireless Internet Access

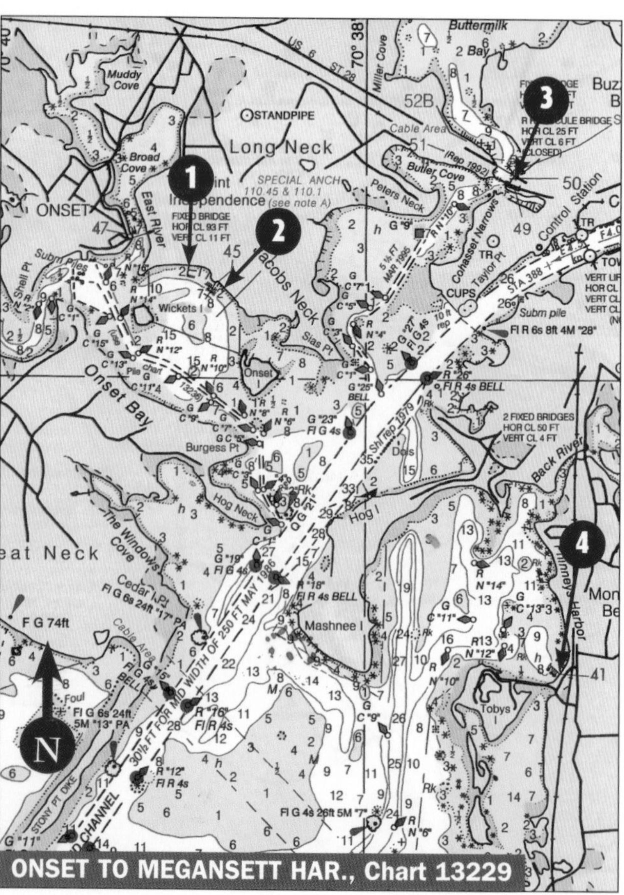

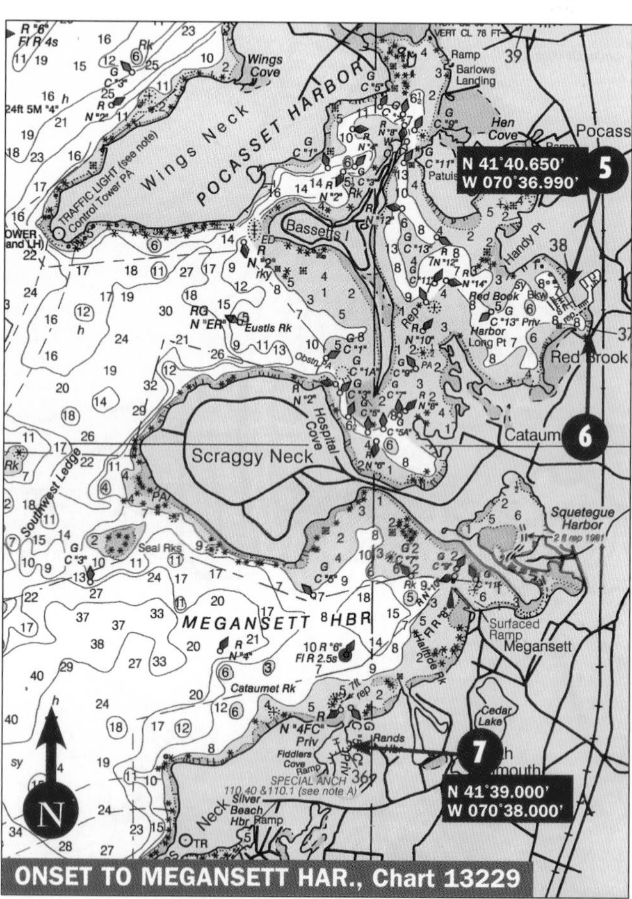

minutes. Examine the chart carefully so that the course is clearly fixed in your mind before making the sharp turn to Onset from Hog Island Channel. Buoys in this area have been renumbered repeatedly over the past decade; at last visit, the turning point for the channel leading to Onset Bay was just south of quick flashing green "21." Green can "1," immediately east of Hog Neck, begins the sequential marks of the Onset Channel. Allow for swift current, which may attempt to push your boat into a buoy or other obstruction. Beyond Burgess Point, the current diminishes. Be wary of possible shoaling on the starboard side between green can buoys "3" and "5."

Dockage and Moorings: Immediately to port across the bay, once you have passed red nun "10" on the Onset Channel, Onset Bay Marina maintains a large mooring field and substantial transient dockage with electricity and cable TV. The marina is a full-service repair facility with mechanics on call. There are two dinghy docks, and it is an easy run from here to excellent beaches and the town's dinghy landing (at the end of the marked channel, beyond East River) for access to shops and restaurants. Just west of the marina, the friendly Point Independence Yacht Club will rent slips to visiting boaters for a reasonable facilities-use fee. Though the club is oriented primarily to powerboats, its 8-foot depths dockside can accommodate almost any recreational vessel. Gasoline, diesel fuel and pump-outs are available. The small but attractive clubhouse is on a clean and protected beach, modern showers and restrooms are inside and it is within walking distance of restaurants, shops and churches.

Farther west, the town docks at Onset Pier provide six floating finger slips. The town also rents two transient moorings. Call ahead on VHF Channel 09 for availability. There are no public showers, though public restrooms are across the street, and dumpsters on the pier will accommodate your trash. The town's dinghy dock is crowded, but the resourceful will be able to tie up for an hour or so. Watch for inattentive sunbathers on your approach and check in with the harbormaster's office on the pier.

Anchorage: Holding is good between Wickets Island and Onset Island, outside the mooring field, in 8-foot depths at low water. For skippers of boats drawing 5 feet or less who are eager to make a quick morning getaway, there is also space with good holding in dense mud west of the Onset Channel between Hog Neck and Burgess Point. Be alert for swirling currents in this location.

GOIN' ASHORE: **ONSET, MA**

Onset Village, with its wide and beautiful public beach, is within walking distance, to the west of the marina and yacht club on Onset Avenue, just uphill from the town docks. The Onset Village Market combines a grocery and meat market with a substantial liquor store, and will provide return-trip transportation and/or grocery delivery for a small fee. Within a block are the post office, Onset Hardware Store, a bookstore with an extensive used book selection, a beauty salon, barber shop, ice cream store, laundry/dry cleaners and saltwater taffy shop. Close at hand are public tennis and basketball courts and a playground.

Locally recommended restaurants include Marc Anthony's for Italian-American food and Steve's Pier View for the "best breakfasts in town." The Blue Oyster Bistro and Grille on Onset Avenue and The Stonebridge Bistro on East Boulevard are the most recent additions to Onset's dining options. Cup of the Bay is a unique coffee shop located in a Victorian Home at 3 W. Central St. About a 30-minute walk east of the village, on the busy Cranberry Highway, Lindsay's Seafood Restaurant is touted as the best of the lobster and chowder houses along the strip. The restaurant will provide transportation on call. Onset has an almost unparalleled degree of public access to shore and beaches. The Onset Protective League assures that. The Onset Scenic Trail is a relaxing route for pedestrians, bicyclists and motorists.

ADDITIONAL RESOURCES:

■ Onset Bay Association, **www.onsetvillage.com**

NEARBY GOLF COURSES:

Bay Pointe Country Club, Onset Avenue, Onset, MA 02558, 508-759-8802

NEARBY MEDICAL FACILITIES:

Tobey Hospital, 43 High St., Wareham, MA 02571, 508-295-0880

Cape Cod Canal

Heavily traveled, well-marked and attractive, the Cape Cod Canal cuts across the neck of Cape Cod to points north and east, saving boats from the long and arduous trip through Nantucket Shoals and around Cape Cod to reach Boston or Maine.

The canal opened in 1914. It was 15 feet deep and 100 feet wide, and accidents were frequent. The modern-day version is the world's widest sea-level canal, with a channel width of 480 feet. Its average depth is now 32 feet.

Anyone who transits the Cape Cod Canal will likely recognize the campus of the Massachusetts Maritime Academy on Taylor Point. Its training ship, *T.S. Enterprise,* at 540 feet in length, dominates the west end of the canal. Both the academy and ship are available for tours at no charge. Call 508-830-5000 for more information.

NAVIGATION: Use Chart 13229. All vessels larger than 65 feet must contact the Marine Traffic Controller on VHF Channel 13 before entering the canal. The seven-mile-long land cut can be almost clear of fog when both Buzzards and Cape Cod bays are thick with it. Once inside the confines of the canal, the 10-mile trip from Cedar Point on Great Neck to Cape Cod Bay is scenic and well-protected from the weather. However, the reverse passage south of Cedar Point, headed into Buzzards Bay, can be brutal, particularly when the ebb tide bound for Buzzards Bay is fueled by a piping southwesterly wind. That combination can challenge even adequately powered boats and moderately strong stomachs.

Despite the width and depth of the canal, tidal range conflict between the Cape Cod Bay end (9 feet) and the Buzzards Bay side (4 feet) remains fierce, creating currents of about 3.5 knots on the eastward-setting flood and 4 to 6 knots on the ebb. Give careful attention to the tide and tidal current charts and make a very conservative estimate of the time you will need to pass both through the canal and beyond, in order to allow for the effects of a foul-setting tide. For example, an ebbing tide will considerably slow eastbound mariners to the east of the traffic light and control tower at the tip of Wings Neck. Westbound, an entrance into the canal from Cape Cod Bay at slack water prior to a flood tide will result in favorable current well down Buzzards Bay. For the eastbound cruiser, the current is not as concentrated in Cape Cod Bay after a transit of the canal.

Even though commercial traffic is heavy on the canal, you should have no difficulties if you pick tide and weather carefully, proceed cautiously and stick to the right side of the channel as if driving on a highway. The U.S. Army Corps of Engineers also cautions that the canal is a No-Wake Zone; boaters must observe a 10-mph speed limit, yet complete their transit within 2.5 hours.

This last requirement makes it particularly important to calculate your speed-versus-tide requirements with some care. All boats must be under power, as sailing through the canal is not permitted; neither are turning around, fishing or anchoring. Finally, as you transit the canal, monitor VHF Channel 13 for communications from the Corps of Engineers and be ready to alert them to emergency situations.

Two fixed highway bridges cross the canal, both with 135-foot fixed vertical clearances. The single railroad lift bridge crossing the canal is virtually always open except during the occasional passage of a train to or from Cape Cod. Closed vertical clearance is a mere 7 feet, so very few vessels will clear the bridge during a closure. If running with a strong, favorable current, look well ahead to assure passage under the bridge, as turning at the last minute may not be an option.

Important note: Cruisers may no longer anchor in the tiny Harbor of Refuge, a dredged pocket of deep water at the eastern (Cape Cod Bay) end of the canal, but dockage is usually available through the Sandwich Marina (see Dockage below). The charted commercial pilings opposite the entrance to the Harbor of Refuge are reserved for barge traffic, which might arrive at any time, and recreational boats are banned from using these pilings. Video monitors will pick you up immediately, and a Coast Guard boat will arrive quickly to ask you, in no uncertain terms, to move along.

Dockage: The Sandwich Marina accepts transients, but you should make arrangements in advance to rent slip space from the marina if you wish to lie over at the eastern end of the canal. Twenty-four slips are earmarked for transients and more are usually available. All slips are now modern floating docks and a new bathhouse was recently built. The easily-accessed fuel dock is open until 8 p.m. during boating season to facilitate cruisers who want to catch a favorable current without waiting overnight. Be sure to plan your transit of the canal, eastbound or westbound, with this limitation in mind. Overnight docking on the fuel dock is rarely an option. The marina offers fuel and an excellent restaurant just across the street. Shower facilities are available for slip holders and transients.

Anchorage: There is a good anchorage area at the western end of the canal, inside the pilings just below the Maritime Academy on Taylor Point. It is located on the east side of the channel, in 10 to 20 feet of water.

BUZZARDS BAY —EASTERN SHORE

The eastern shore of Buzzards Bay is generally high and handsome, with fine old trees and houses. Water is comparatively deep close to the banks, and the shore is indented by wide, open bays and protected harbors. Working south from the Cape Cod Canal, the first of the harbors is big, open and shoal-dotted Phinneys Harbor, with a marked entrance and the town of Monument Beach on its eastern shore. Mashnee Island forms its western boundary, Tobys Island its eastern one.

NAVIGATION: Use Chart 13229. To avoid the shoal area south of Mashnee Island, an east- or westbound boat in Hog Island Channel should use the markers abeam of Phinneys Harbor as a turning point. Estimate the midway point (shown on Chart 13229), and then turn directly toward the entrance to Phinneys Harbor. Sailors making short tacks should be wary of ledges close to the southern end of Mashnee Island. The route to an anchorage and small marina at Monument Beach is well-marked to the west, north of Tobys Island. Keep a mid-channel course to avoid rocks to the east and south of the channel.

Dockage and Moorings: Monument Beach Marina is located in a beautiful setting with a fine public beach to either side of its main pier. You can get mooring or dock space from the marina, which accommodates 8-foot drafts (mean low water) with water and 30-amp electric service alongside. The rental fee includes shower and restroom access, and a snack bar is open in season. Monument Beach is one of three marinas run by the town of Bourne. The others are Taylor Point Marina and Pocasset River Marina, which has 17 slips suitable for small craft only. From the marina, it is seven-tenths of a mile to the village of Monument Beach, where you will find a post office, ice cream parlor, movie rental shops and Perry's Boat Yard, with a complete line of fishing tackle and supplies and experienced advice to go with it.

Anchorage: The conspicuous rock pile off the eastern side of Mashnee Island serves as a guide to the deepwater gully that leads to a secure anchorage, protected from the north but open to the south. You can find additional anchorage on a hard bottom outside the mooring field off Monument Beach Marina. The most protected anchorage in the area lies in the northeastern corner of Phinneys Harbor, near the entrance to Back River, which is very shoal—do not venture upstream.

Pocasset

Depending on weather conditions, Pocasset has a number of refuges. One is open to the northwest; the others are nearly landlocked. They are all tucked below Wings Neck, with its abandoned lighthouse and canal traffic light, to the north. Almost an island, Scraggy Neck reaches out to the south. Three-pronged Bassetts Island subdivides the water.

NAVIGATION: Use Chart 13229. You can enter through either of two narrow, twisting, shoal-prone passages. The northern one inside Wings Neck is a little deeper and more popular but quite unmanageable when the tide ebbs against a southwester. The southern entrance, along Scraggy Neck, has good depths. Boats with 5-foot drafts can enter even at low water.

Anchorage: Around the western point of Bassetts Island, there is a secure anchorage in the sweeping bight along the northern side of the island. The charted wreck

Looking northeast over Red Brook Harbor. (Not to be used for navigation.) WATERWAY GUIDE PHOTOGRAPHY

off Bassett's western point reportedly no longer presents a threat to navigation.

Most of Bassetts Island is privately owned. However, the town owns the south end of the island and it is open to the public. In addition, Barlows Landing, on the mainland, north of the island's northern arm, permits dinghy tie-ups at the floating dock in front of the small pier next to the town beach. From this location, it is a half-mile walk up a gentle grade to the village. Hen Cove, strictly for shoal-draft boats, at the town of Pocasset, has a dock, a launching ramp and scattered rocks.

Barlows Landing Village

Little more than a wide spot at the crossing of two secondary roads, this hamlet less than half a mile from its namesake landing can, in a pinch, offer a few important commodities. Pocasset Hardware is here, as is a Cumberland Farms store, a barber shop, the Corner Cafe (breakfast, lunch and bakery goods) and Graziella's Italian Restaurant. About one-third of a mile farther east, you can do basic provisioning at Larry's Market, which is next to the post office.

Red Brook Harbor

Large, well-protected Red Brook Harbor, at the village of Cataumet, has ample boating amenities, good anchorage and pleasant surroundings.

Dockage: Kingman Yacht Center dominates the harbor on entry with its extensive dock complex and massive sheds. This is Cape Cod's largest full-service marina and boatyard, with 10-foot dockside depths, 235 guest slips and 130 moorings, showers and laundry, gifts and provisions, complete marine repairs and maintenance, and gas, diesel fuel and ice. The Chart Room Restaurant is on the premises, overlooking the docks. High-speed wireless Internet service is available throughout the dock areas and mooring fields.

Immediately south of Kingman Yacht Center, in a protected cove, Parker's Boat Yard runs a small, high-quality operation—a full-service yard with "a yacht club atmosphere." Parker's maintains an even larger mooring field and may have a few slips available at its floating docks. It is quite a hike for reprovisioning from this location, but a call to a taxi can provide the wheels. Red Brook Harbor Yacht Club operates on the grounds of Parker's Boatyard; information can be found at www.rbhyc.com.

Hospital Cove

NAVIGATION: Use Chart 13229. The final harbor in this big semicircle of harbors is Hospital Cove at Cataumet; you can reach it either from Red Brook Harbor or via the southern entrance around Scraggy Neck from Buzzards Bay. Handsome and scenic, the shores of this harbor are dotted with greenery and pleasant houses.

On exiting this circuit of harbors, give full respect to the buoys marking Southwest Ledge just to the west of Scraggy Neck. A charted rock, exposed at high water, is located just to the north of red nun buoy "10," which marks the northwestern side of the ledge. A forbidding area of rocks also lies just south of red nun buoy "2."

Anchorage: While the cove provides good holding in a relatively secluded spot, the gradual increase of moorings here has limited the anchorage to a comparatively small area near the channel. Make allowance for swing room, both in relation to the channel and to the moored boats toward land. There are no public landings and no marinas—just peace and quiet, except in strong northwesterly winds. Piping southwesterlies can also be quite noticeable here, because they blow across the narrow isthmus leading from Cataumet to Scraggy Neck, but fortunately the short fetch prevents significant wave action from building up.

Megansett Harbor

Wide open to the west, Megansett Harbor lies between Scraggy Neck and Nyes Neck. It has three well-protected inner harbors and a large bight, protected only from the north, in the outer harbor east of the bulge of Scraggy Neck.

Dockage: At North Falmouth, on the southern side of outer Megansett Harbor, southeast of Cataumet Rock (at red nun buoy "4"), the 9-foot-deep channel to Fiddlers Cove is dredged frequently and well-marked. Inside this virtual hurricane hole of protection is Brewer Fiddler's Cove Marina. A courteous staff tends to floating docks, and mechanics are on call seven days a week. Transient slips include water, electric, cable TV and pump-out. The accommodating clubhouse, with a full kitchen and private tiled showers, is open to all guests. Amenities include a pool table, television and Internet access. The facility includes a ship's store and laundry. For restaurants and other amenities you will need a taxi.

Anchorage: Inner Megansett Harbor, on the eastern shore, has a narrow, marked entry with a bar that shoots out from the breakwater. Beyond are a launching ramp, hospitable yacht club and town dock. At its eastern end, around a projecting point of land, is Squeteague Harbor, a cove with a shallow (less than 3-foot depths) and difficult entry, but good depths and anchorage once inside. There is very limited space to drop the hook, though; moorings take up most of the available space. It is well worth exploring, if only by dinghy or shoal-draft boat. South of Nye's Neck, you may find secure anchorage and protection from a northerly in Wild Harbor. The entry is marked by green "1" and red "4" and has adequate depth for most cruisers. Avoid this harbor if there is a prediction of wind shift to the prevailing southwest, as it is completely exposed.

West Falmouth Harbor

Roughly two miles south of Megansett Harbor, this harbor's entrance is narrow, and the channel is given to shoaling. The anchorage here is small and the town wharf, which is off the eastern shore, does not offer transient moorings. Nearby coves are great for gunkholing by dinghy. But for boats drawing as much as 3 feet, the amenities are limited. Charted rocks are submerged 4 to 6 feet in the harbor.

Quissett Harbor

The standout harbor for this area, about six miles south of West Falmouth, Quissett Harbor has generally deep water, high, wooded shores with handsome houses, good protection and easy entrance—but no provisions. The small peninsula enclosing the northern side of the harbor is now a nature preserve that is well worth a trip ashore for a walking tour.

NAVIGATION: Use Chart 13229. The entrance, between The Knob, a prominent hillock on the northern point, and Gansett Point, is well-marked. Follow the channel carefully to avoid the rocks beyond its confines. A course too much to starboard at red nun buoys "4," "6" or "8" will result in contact with a very hard bottom. The proliferation of local boats and boatyard moorings has all but eliminated swing room in both the inner and outer harbors. Dropping a hook in either location is discouraged.

Moorings: Quissett Harbor Boatyard usually has an open rental mooring. Simply attach to a vacant one and the yard's skiff will eventually appear in the evening to collect the fee. There is no launch service, but the pump-out boat (Woosh) will respond to a hoisted orange flag (the locally understood signal) or a request of the yard's launch driver or dockmaster. You will find a sizable dinghy landing, water, ice and "good advice" at the boatyard dock, though you should limit your tie-ups to 20 minutes for crew changes. A dumpster, limited parking and a public phone are located immediately shoreside, but there is no fuel. During the summer season a scheduled "trolley" stops here with service to Woods Hole and Falmouth; (800-526-8532).

■ WOODS HOLE

Woods Hole marks the difficult and sometimes-dangerous passage between Buzzards Bay and Vineyard Sound, at the southwestern tip of Cape Cod, and the appealing scientific and resort community of the same name. Woods Hole consists of three unique harbors: Great Harbor, wide, deep and open to the south; Eel Pond, a hurricane hole in the center of the village; and Little Harbor, given over to U.S. Coast Guard government and scientific operations.

Woods Hole Passage

MA
RI

NAVIGATION: Use Chart 13229. Tidal currents of 5 knots or more make Woods Hole a strait to be entered with respect if the current is running at its maximum. Even with your boat under control, the short distance is inevitably an interesting piloting experience. A less taxing approach is to plan for the passage at slack tide just as it is turning in your favor. Consult your tide tables and be sure to study a large-scale chart before you enter the passage.

Chart 13235 of Woods Hole is helpful, but not absolutely necessary if you have Chart 13229, showing the present buoys. Note that buoy numbers run from Vineyard

An aerial view of Woods Hole. (Not to be used for navigation.) WATERWAY GUIDE PHOTOGRAPHY

Sound to Buzzards Bay, so if you enter from the west, red nuns are kept to port. The current rarely drags under the oversized buoys, so laying a course is relatively simple. Keep in mind, however, that the current does not exactly follow the channel. At full flow, you may find yourself pushed off course and straining to correct in an underpowered vessel. Except at slack water, you will also encounter tidal swirls that require a firm hand at the helm to stay in mid-channel. Unless you have radar, avoid this passage when visibility is poor. The northern channel is the better choice for low-powered craft. It takes plenty of thrust to negotiate the sharp turn in Broadway, the southern channel.

If passing from Buzzards Bay to Vineyard Sound in a strong favorable current, be very aware of red nun buoy "2," which marks the edge of the shoals extending from Red Ledge. It is not unusual to see vessels pushed east toward these shoals. The exit from Woods Hole to Vineyard Sound is wide and clearly marked. Great Ledge lays almost dead center; it is well-marked and you can pass it on either side. The route west of Great Ledge, however, between flashing green buoy "1" and flashing red bell buoy "2" is less confined and easier to follow.

Dockage and Moorings: The most secure transient berth is at Woods Hole Marine in Eel Pond. Enter the pond through the channel (controlling depth 7 feet) leading under the ancient bascule bridge (5-foot closed vertical clearance) in the center of the village. The bridge will open on signal (VHF Channel 13 or horn) on the hour and half-hour. The marina's docks are immediately to port past the bridge, connected to Shuckers Raw Bar. A slip is usually available, but given the diminutive size of this facility and the limits to maneuverability in this pinched harbor, you should make a reservation and ask for specific directions. There may be transient moorings, with a dinghy landing at the restaurant. The facility has showers, restrooms and all fuels; pump-outs are free, and there is a mechanic on call. The staff will arrange tours of the local marine institutions, and a trolley bus leaves from out front for Falmouth every 30 minutes. Note: The marina closes its showers and launch service at 6 p.m. and reopens them at 8 p.m. To the west in Great Harbor, small but friendly Woods Hole Yacht Club may have a few services or a vacant mooring available to visitors from other clubs. This area is exposed to the south, however, with a considerable fetch for wave buildup.

Anchorage: Great Harbor has ample anchorage space, but because of the southern exposure here, a spot as far as draft will permit into the cove at the northwest corner of the harbor is best. This area is about a mile from the village center, but a motorized dinghy makes the ride under the bascule bridge (5-foot closed vertical clearance) to the Eel Pond dinghy landing reasonably convenient. The premier anchorage associated with Woods Hole is in Hadley's Harbor, covered in the chapter titled "The Islands."

West Falmouth, Woods Hole, MA

WEST FALMOUTH, WOODS HOLE		Largest Vessel Accommodated	VHF Channel Monitored	Transient Berths / Total Berths	Approach / Dockside Depth (reported)	Floating Docks	Gas / Diesel	Groceries, Ice, Marine Supplies, Snacks	Repairs: Hull, Engine, Propeller	Lift (tonnage), Crane, Rail	1=110V, 2=220V, B=Both, Max Amps	Laundry, Pool, Showers	Pump-Out Station	Nearby: Grocery Store, Motel, Restaurant
		Dockage					Supplies		Services					
1. West Falmouth Dock & Harbor	508-457-2550	30			4/5		LOADING & UNLOADING ONLY							
2. Quissett Harbor Boat Yard	508-548-0506	85		12/86	11/16	F		I	HEP	R			P	GMR
3. Woods Hole Yacht Club	508-548-9205	65			6/6							S		GMR
4. Woods Hole Marine	508-540-2402	50	09	1/26	7/15			GIMS			1/30	S		GMR

Corresponding chart(s) not to be used for navigation. Internet Access Wireless Internet Access

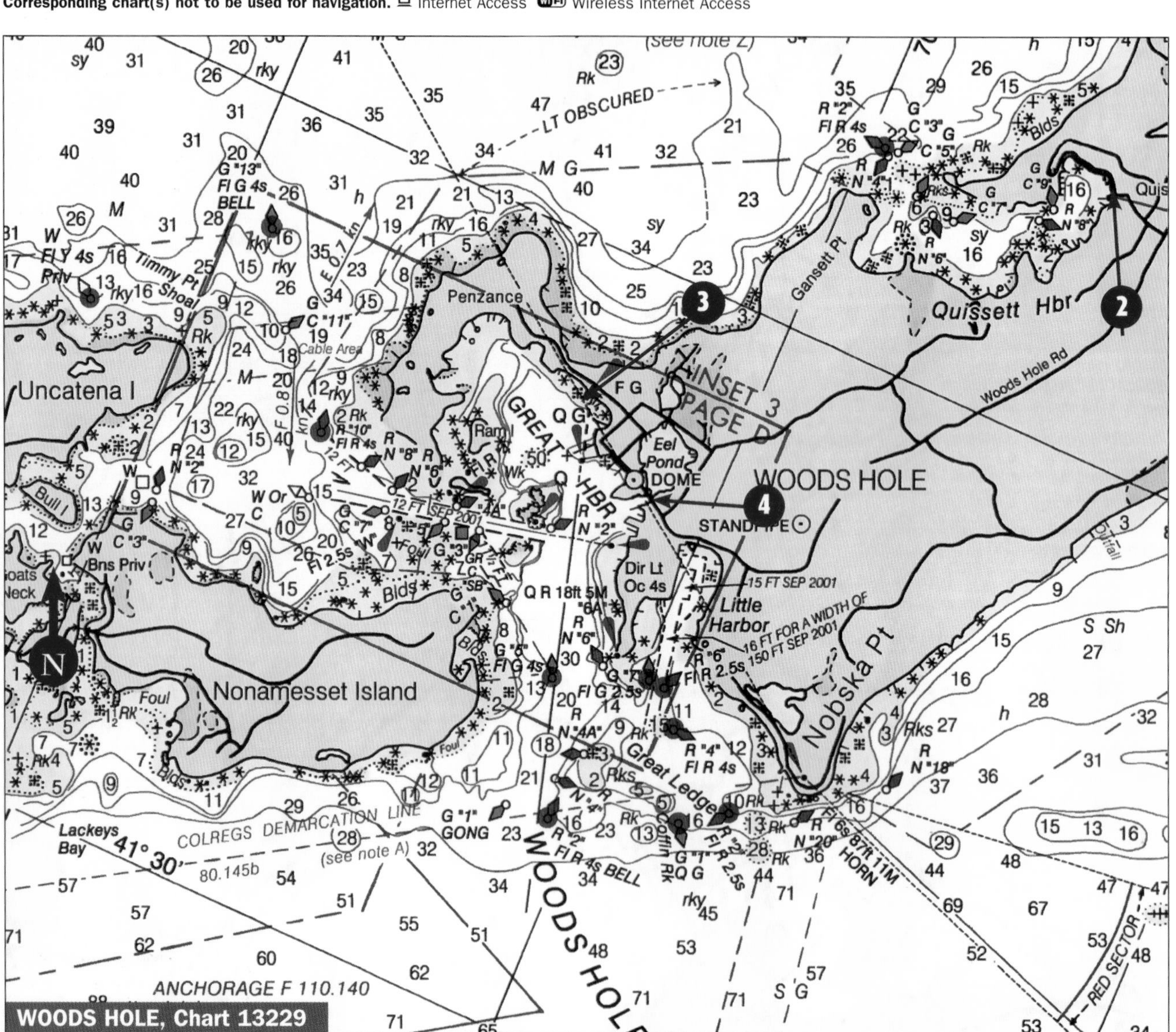

GOIN' ASHORE: **WOODS HOLE, MA**

This tiny village is home to some of the world's most renowned and important marine and oceanographic institutions, all within a short walk. The Aquarium of National Marine Fisheries Service (508-495-2000, at the west end of Water Street) is open daily during the summer, and Monday through Friday otherwise. Marine Biological Laboratory (508-289-7623, on Water Street just west of the marina) schedules three tours each afternoon during July and August; reservations are strongly recommended. The Exhibit Center of Woods Hole Oceanographic Institution (508-289-2663, 15 School St.) is open daily from Memorial Day to Labor Day and on a more limited schedule beyond those dates. The Woods Hole Historical Museum (508-548-7270, 573 Woods Hole Road) has a variety of nautical and local historical exhibits; it is open in the summer, Tuesday through Saturday. The

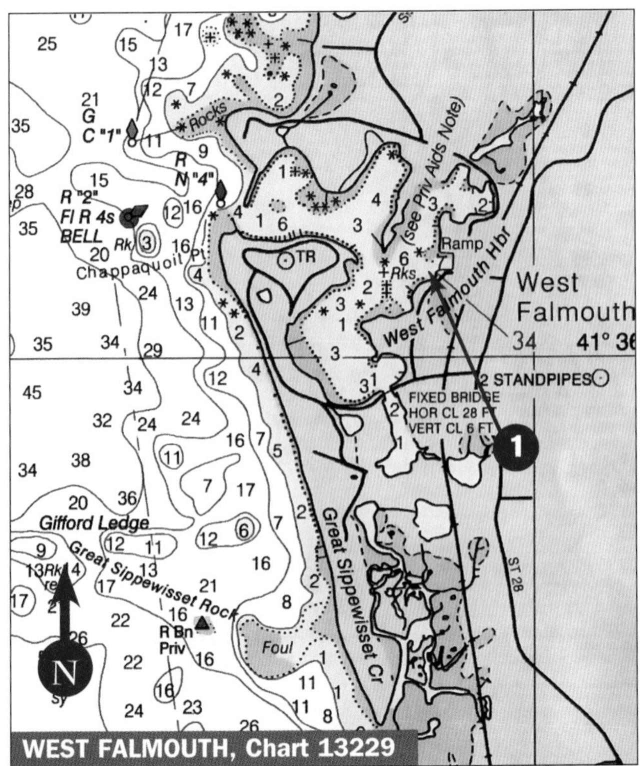

WEST FALMOUTH, Chart 13229

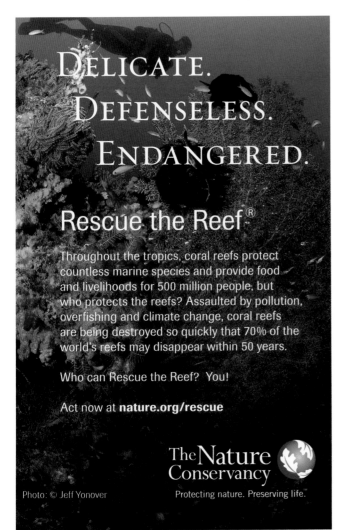

U.S. Geological Survey's Marine Geology and Hydrology Coast Division is also on-site, as are a sizable U.S. Coast Guard contingent and major public ferry terminals for trips to Martha's Vineyard and Nantucket. The private ferry for Naushon Island residents operates from here as well.

Most commercial establishments are on Water Street in front of Eel Pond. Food Buoy Market, around the corner from the marina, has a limited selection of fresh and frozen foods, canned goods, deli items and ice. Across the bridge at Luscombe Avenue, Woods Hole Pharmacy has the usual sundries and a selection of magazines and out-of-town newspapers. A package store is here as well. Beyond these basics and tourist-oriented trinket and T-shirt shops, much of the commercial space is devoted to casual-style restaurants. At Shuckers "World Famous" Raw Bar, directly on Eel Pond west of the bridge, lobster is the specialty, often served with Nobska Light Beer, brewed in Falmouth. The Landfall Restaurant nearby has fish, chips and sandwiches, with a view of the channel and pond, and The Fishmonger's, with a great view of Woods Hole Passage, is long on salads and seafood. Pie in The Sky on Water Street offers an assortment of homemade pastries, locally roasted organic coffee and free Internet access. Check the bulletin board at the Community Hall on Water Street for current events in town.

ADDITIONAL RESOURCES:

- Woods Hole Business Association, **www.woodshole.com**

NEARBY GOLF COURSES:
Falmouth Country Club, 630 Carriage Shop Road, East Falmouth, MA 02536, 508-548-3211, **www.falmouthcountryclub.com**

NEARBY MEDICAL FACILITIES:
Falmouth Hospital, 100 Terrace Heun Drive, Falmouth, MA 02540, 508-548-5300

Cruising Options

Coming up next is the southern shore of Cape Cod, long a popular summer resort for its good beaches and pleasing towns. As the old Patty Paige song said, "You're sure to fall in love with old Cape Cod." ■

WATERWAY GUIDE is always open to your observations from the helm. E-mail your comments on any navigation information in the guide to: editor@waterwayguide.com.

WATERWAY GUIDE advertising sponsors play a vital role in bringing you the most trusted and well-respected cruising guide in the country. Without our advertising sponsors, we simply couldn't produce the top-notch publication now resting in your hands. Next time you stop in for a peaceful night's rest, let them know where you found them—WATERWAY GUIDE, The Cruising Authority.

Cape Cod—South Shore

CHARTS 13229, 13235, 13237, 13244, 13246, 13248

■ MASSACHUSETTS WATERS

Along Cape Cod's south shore are lovely harbors with well-maintained depths and plenty of marinas, but quite a few are unable to accommodate transients. Almost all harbors have enough water for 3- to 4-foot draft boats, and some can take care of deeper-draft boats. Some have shoal entrances but deep water inside, so deep-draft boats can come in at half-tide or better. However, check ahead on depths or anchor out and come in by dinghy to find the best water. For generations this beach-lined shore, punctuated by mansions and cottages, has drawn a steady stream of vacationers, many of whom come by boat.

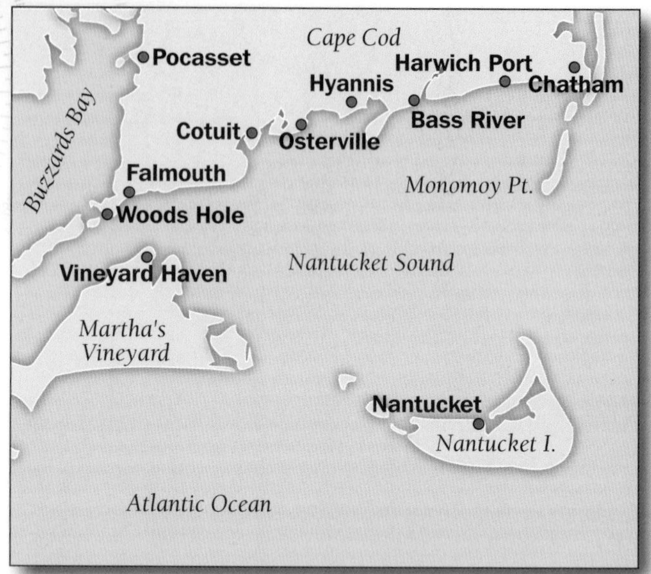

Falmouth, Green Pond

Falmouth is not only a good base for cruising the islands, it also has one of Cape Cod's best harbors, with at least 8-foot depths and every conceivable amenity. It is thoroughly protected and easy to enter.

NAVIGATION: Use Chart 13229. For Falmouth Heights, use Boston tide tables. For high tide, subtract 16 minutes; for low tide, subtract 9 minutes. Flashing red bell buoy "16," about a half mile offshore, marks the approach to the breakwater entrance. The entrance is straightforward, if narrow, with 6-foot depths (mean low water) that are relatively consistent in the channel and throughout the dredged harbor.

Past the entrance, the harbor broadens slightly, and both banks are lined with slips, boatyards and marine amenities. The center of the basin is filled with moorings, but you may not anchor here. The harbor rules require a sealed head (this is a No-Discharge Zone), and a pump-out station is at the town dock.

Dockage and Moorings: After you enter, Falmouth Marine is at mid-harbor to port, with 15 moorings (at least four for transients) and limited transient slip space. Shoreside, this establishment offers all fuels, water, showers, ice, repairs and marine supplies.

Next door, the Flying Bridge Restaurant has an easy-access fuel dock (at the MOBIL sign) and several small finger piers for restaurant patrons. Farther down, also to port, the Falmouth Town Marina has 75 berths perpendicular to the seawall, two moorings and space for transients. The harbormaster's headquarters has showers. You will find ample parking, making this spot a good place to change crews.

Across the harbor, both East Marine and MacDougalls' Cape Cod Marine Service Inc. have extensive marine amenities. MacDougalls' makes both moorings and slips available to transients and offers a large chandlery and retail supply store, as well as specialty shops for installations, custom fabrications, sail making and repairs. High-speed Internet access, phone and cable television hook-ups are available at the slips.

GOIN' ASHORE: **FALMOUTH, MA**

Although the town of Falmouth is located about a mile away, most of the essentials for provisioning and reviving water-weary crews are close to the marinas. The Windfall Market, West Marine and John's Liquor Store all are on the west side of Scranton Avenue, across from the Town Marina harbormaster's office. A self-service laundry is a five-minute walk north. Farther along, at the end of Scranton Avenue and to the right, a fair-sized mall boasts chain stores and fast-food restaurants. Nearer the mouth of the harbor on the west side, the Clam Shack provides seafood to order. The Harbor View Fish Market sells the day's fresh catch.

At the head of the harbor, on the eastern side, the Island Queen will take you to Oak Bluffs on Martha's Vineyard (passengers only). Band concerts on the western side of the marine park provide entertainment on Thursday evenings during the summer.

Falmouth Harbor, MA

FALMOUTH HARBOR		Largest Vessel Accommodated	VHF Channel Monitored	Transient Berths / Total Berths	Approach / Dockside Depth (reported)	Floating Docks	Gas / Diesel	Groceries, Ice, Marine Supplies, Snacks	Repairs: Hull, Engine, Propeller	Lift (tonnage), Crane, Rail	1=110V, 2=220V, B=Both, Max Amps	Laundry, Pool, Showers	Pump-Out Station	Nearby: Grocery Store, Motel, Restaurant
		Dockage					Supplies		Services					
1. Woods Hole Boat Sales	508-548-2626	65	78	/2	8/8		D	I			1/30			MR
2. Falmouth Marine & Yachting Center	508-548-4600	70	09	/23	10/12	F	GD	I	HEP	L70	B/50	S	P	GMR
3. Flying Bridge Restaurant	508-548-2700	40	RESTAURANT											R
4. Falmouth Town Marina	508-457-2550	200	16/09	20/75	9/6	F		I			B/100	S	P	GMR
5. Pier 37	508-540-0123	35	09		10/6	F	G	IM	HP					GMR
6. North Marine	508-457-7000	40			8/6	F	GD	IM	HEP	LCR				GMR
7. EM Falmouth, dba East Marine	508-540-3611	50	16/09	1/15	10/10		GD	I	HEP	L35	B/100	S		GMR
8. MacDougalls' Cape Cod Marine Service (WiFi)	**508-548-3146**	**120**	**16/09**	**10/95**	**10/10**	**F**	**GD**	**IMS**	**HEP**	**L75, C10**	**B/50**	**LS**	**P**	**GMR**

Corresponding chart(s) not to be used for navigation. Internet Access (WiFi) Wireless Internet Access

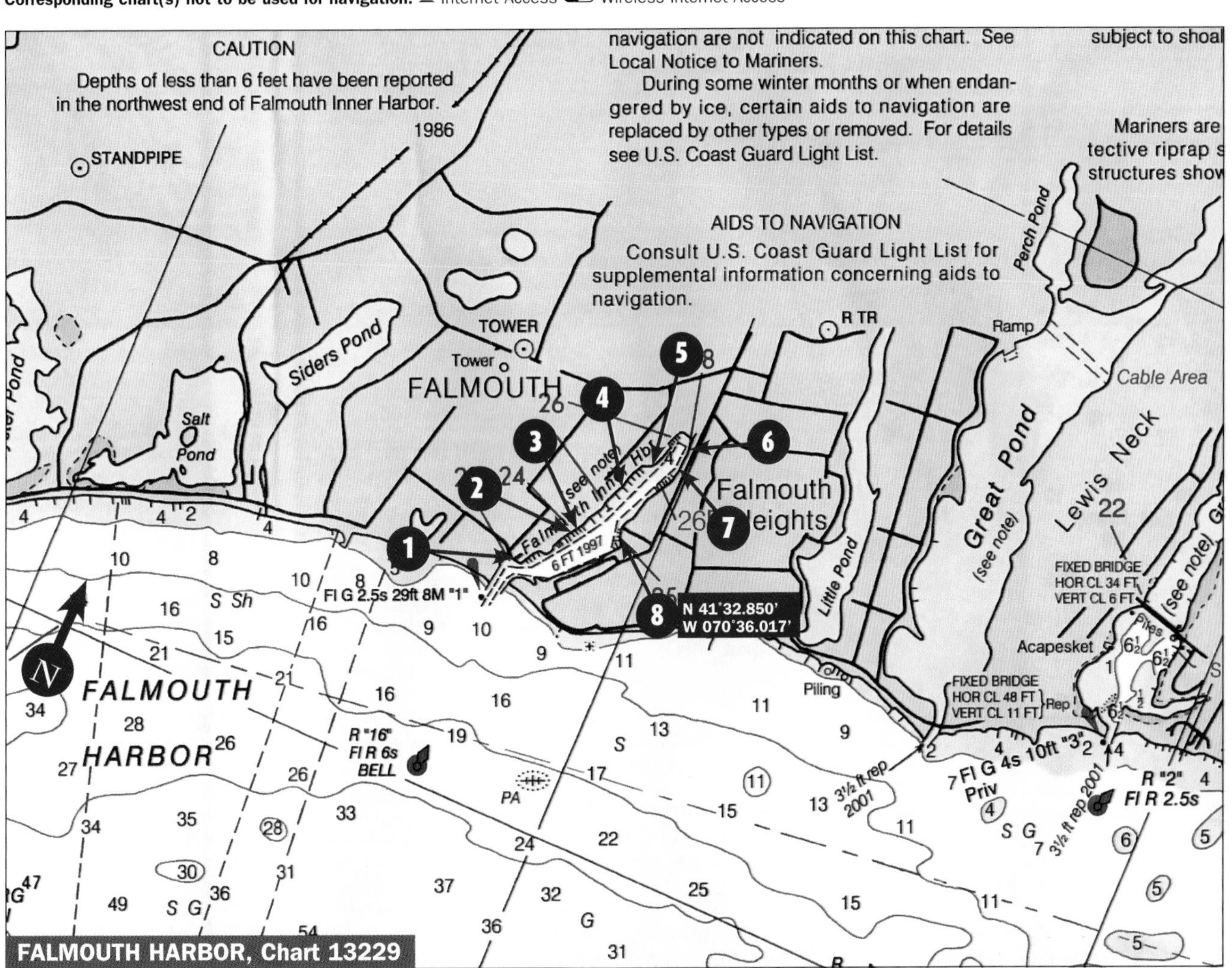

In town (turn left at the northern end of Scranton Avenue), the seasonal bustle of a seaside resort village awaits you. Houses built by ship owners and sea captains in the 18th and 19th centuries surround the traditional village green. Accommodations and dining possibilities are almost unlimited. You will find multiple galleries, a gourmet shop, pharmacy, photo shop, hardware store, bookstore, numerous gift and clothing stores and even the College Light Opera Company. Restaurant choices in Falmouth include The Coonamessett Inn, Firefly Woodfire Grill and Bar, and La Cucina Sul Mare Ristorante, which are all close to the harbor. Check in at Cape Cod Bagel or Betsy's Diner for breakfast or lunch. A must for chocolate lovers is Ben and Bill's Chocolate Emporium, a branch of the Edgartown, MA, institution.

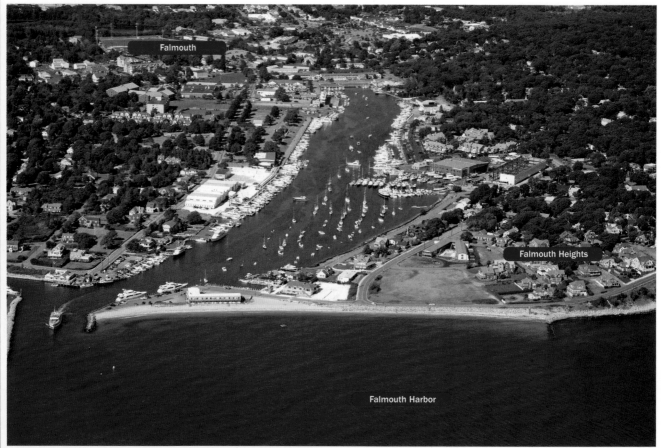

Looking north over Falmouth Inner Harbor. (Not to be used for navigation.) WATERWAY GUIDE PHOTOGRAPHY

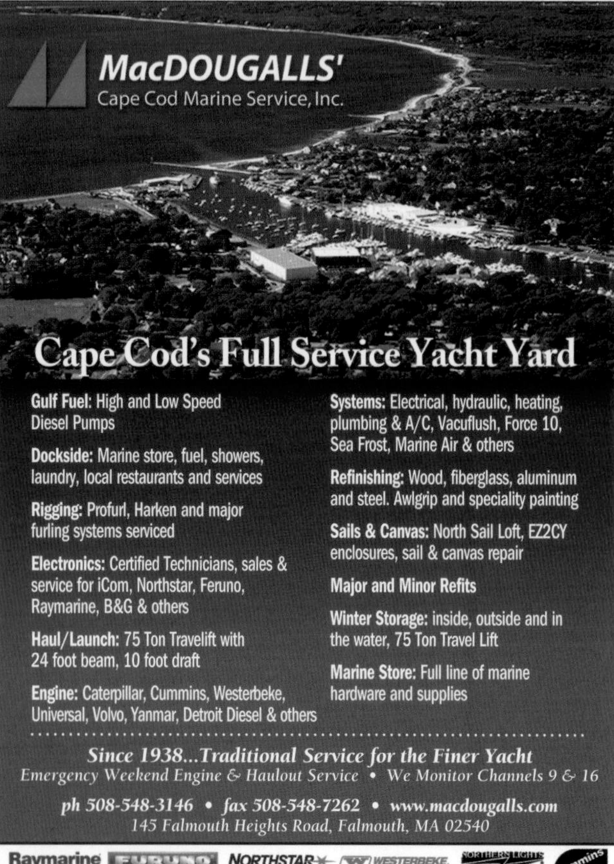

ADDITIONAL RESOURCES:

■ Falmouth Chamber of Commerce, **www.falmouthchamber.com**

NEARBY GOLF COURSES:
Falmouth Country Club, 630 Carriage Shop Road, East Falmouth, MA 02536, 508-548-3211, **www.falmouthcountryclub.com**

NEARBY MEDICAL FACILITIES:
Falmouth Hospital, 100 Terrace Heun Drive, Falmouth, MA 02540, 508-548-5300

Green Pond

Green Pond, two miles east, is almost two miles long. It is a quiet and peaceful little harbor with a narrow breakwatered entry and 6-foot depths. Green Pond has a boatyard, town dock and boats at moorings, but no anchoring is allowed in Green Pond. For a glimpse of the local scenery, take a dinghy trip above the bridge. To port, a bait shop sells fresh local lobsters and clams.

NAVIGATION: Use Chart 13229. A fixed bridge (6-foot vertical clearance) is about a quarter of a mile inside. Stay well clear of both corners at the southern end; there are extensive 1-foot shallows.

A northern view over Cotuit Bay. (Not to be used for navigation.) WATERWAY GUIDE PHOTOGRAPHY

Waquoit Bay

About three miles east of Green Pond is the narrow entrance to Waquoit Bay, home to hundreds of boats. Toward the head of the bay are permanent and transient moorings.

NAVIGATION: Use Chart 13229. The entrance between Washburn Island and Dead Neck (South Cape Beach) is well-marked. Controlling depth in Waquoit Bay is 4 feet, and you can leave the marked channel to make a side trip to the mouths of the Great and Little rivers. Approach the southwestern tip of Seconsett Island with caution; there are shoals extending from this point into Waquoit Bay.

Off the northernmost tip of Washburn Island is a channel marker for the Seapuit River. Head to the southwest on the river to Seapuit Point, then round the point and head north for Edwards Boat Yard, which offers most repairs and has picnic tables set out among flowers and shade trees. Slips or moorings for transients are scarce; call ahead before cruising into this area with the idea of staying overnight.

Returning to Nantucket Sound, you can try an alternate route. Head southwest down the Scapit and Childs rivers to Eel Pond and through the Menauhant jetties. Depths at the jetties can be as shallow as 2 feet, so go on a rising tide. Any aids to navigation are privately set and maintained; use caution.

Cotuit, Osterville

NAVIGATION: Use Chart 13229. For Cotuit Highlands, use Boston tide tables. For high tide, add 1 hour 17 minutes; for low tide, add 47 minutes. About eight miles farther east is Cotuit Anchorage. Here, between Popponesset Beach and Wianno Beach on Nantucket Sound, two buoyed channels lead inland to one of the most beautiful harbor complexes on the south shore. Westernmost is the 4-foot channel to Cotuit and Cotuit Bay. The 7-foot-deep eastern channel leads to West Bay and Osterville, one of Cape Cod's deeper, more reliable harbors.

Inside, via either passage, is a big, almost circular area with a well-buoyed, continuous waterway leading through three bays and a narrow river. Each offers coves and creeks for gunkholing, good beaches, fine anchorages, ample yacht amenities and charming towns. The complete landlocked circuit can be made without leaving sheltered water, although a boat drawing 5 feet or less has a better chance of a successful circuit of Osterville Island.

Cotuit Bay

For the eastbound mariner, Cotuit Bay is first. The town of Cotuit, whose old-line summer residents maintain the big houses and historic buildings there, is within walking distance of the town dock. The east side of Cotuit Bay is all Osterville Grand Island.

Green Pond to Osterville, MA

GREEN POND TO OSTERVILLE		Largest Vessel Accommodated	VHF Channel Monitored	Transient Berths / Total Berths	Approach / Dockside Depth (reported)	Floating Docks	Gas / Diesel	Groceries, Ice, Marine Supplies, Snacks	Repairs: Hull, Engine, Propeller	Lift (tonnage), Crane, Rail	1=110V, 2=220V, B=Both, Max Amps	Laundry, Pool, Showers	Pump-Out Station	Nearby: Grocery Store, Motel, Restaurant
		Dockage					Supplies		Services					
1. Green Pond Marine Inc.	508-457-9283	50	09	5/60	6/6		GD	IM	HP		B/50	S		MR
2. Edwards Boatyard Inc.	508-548-2216	45	16/09	1/36	4/4		GD	IM	HP	R	1/30	S	P	R
3. Cotuit Town Wharf	508-790-6245	50			5/5		G	G						
4. Crosby Yacht Yard Inc.	508-428-6958	90	09/72	10/125	6/5	F	GD	IMS	HEP	L70	B/50	S	P	GR
5. Nauticus Marina	508-428-4537	120	16/09	/5	7/8	F					B/100	S		GR
6. Oyster Harbors Marine	508-428-2017	100	79A	1/110	6/6	F	GD	IMS	HP	L	B/50	S	P	GMR
7. Corey Yacht Docks	**617-633-1151**	**80**	**09**	**4/4**	**8/9**						**B/100**	**S**		**GMR**

Corresponding chart(s) not to be used for navigation. Internet Access Wireless Internet Access

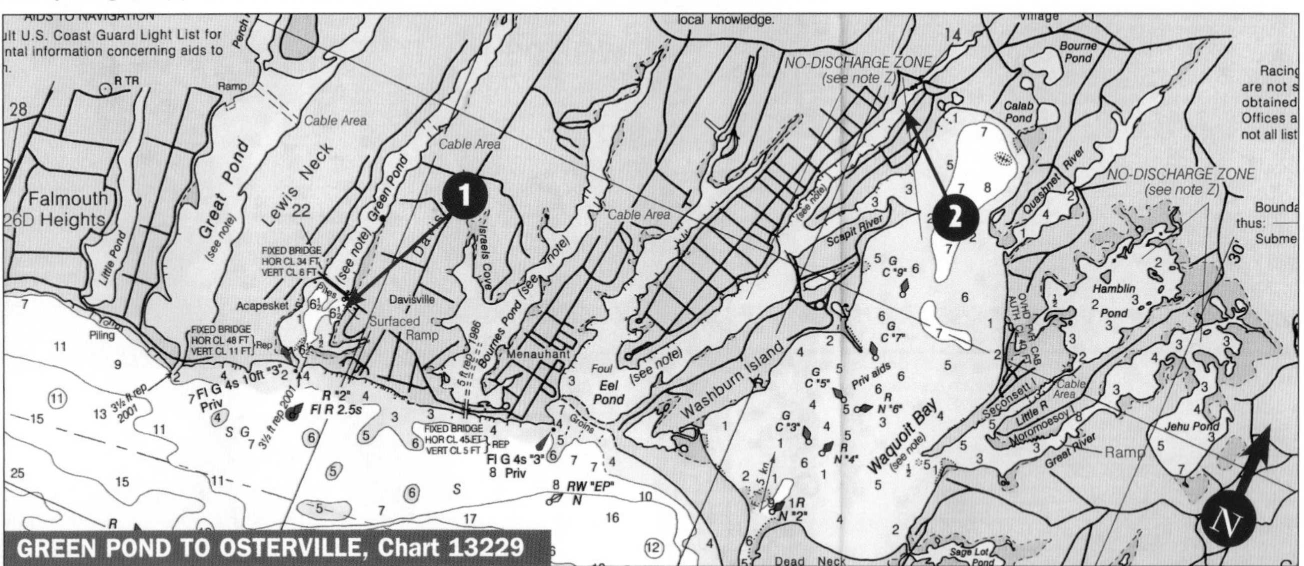

GREEN POND TO OSTERVILLE, Chart 13229

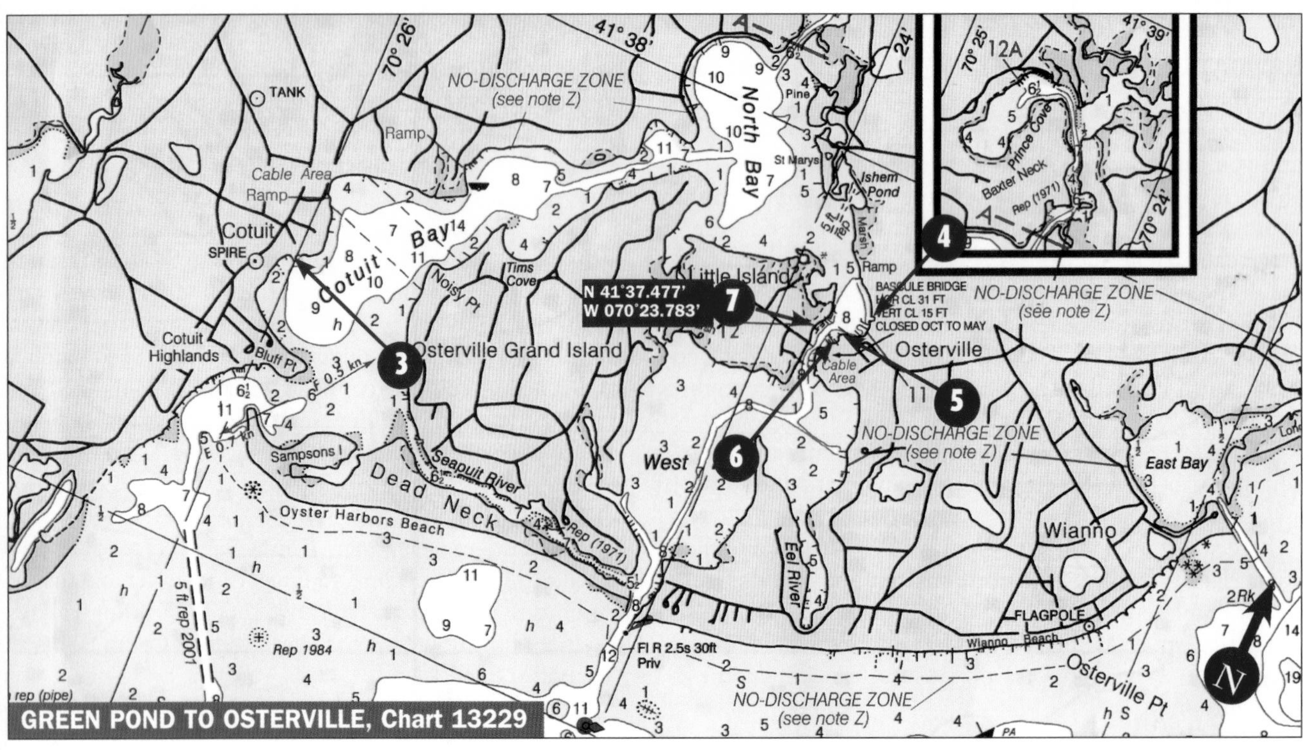

GREEN POND TO OSTERVILLE, Chart 13229

West Bay and Osterville. (Not to be used for navigation.) WATERWAY GUIDE PHOTOGRAPHY

NAVIGATION: Use Chart 13229. A long, dredged channel leads for more than a mile through 1- and 2-foot shoals that encroach closely on either side. The channel makes an S-curve around the pointing finger of Sampsons Island and then around Bluff Point. Stay well off the point.

The narrow channel lies close to the shore of Sampsons Island and is somewhat parallel to it until the small black buoy (the buoys marking the channel are privately maintained). Enter Cotuit on a rising tide.

Dockage and Moorings: On the west shore of Cotuit Bay, you can tie up at the town dock for a half-hour, or rent a mooring and dinghy ashore. A grocery store is right across the street, and restaurants and shops can be found at a nearby shopping mall. The trek to the mall is more than a mile, but it is a pleasant walk in good weather. The Cotuit Library offers Internet access and the Cotuit Center for the Arts usually has an exhibit of local art on display.

North Bay

North Bay is the connecting link to Cotuit Bay, and West Bay is the entry to delightful Prince Cove (shown as an extension on panel C of Chart 13229).

NAVIGATION: Use Chart 13229. From the naturally deep water (7 to 10 feet) at the northern end of Cotuit Bay, the buoyed passage leads across more shoals past Point Isabella into North Bay, where you will find one of the best anchorages around. According to local authorities, this channel is good for 5 feet. Prince Cove is best investigated by dinghy because it has a narrow, hard-to-negotiate entry.

West Bay, Osterville

Most of the West Bay activity is around the bridge. A yacht club with a large fleet and anchorage among the moorings is to the south, and the town landing is to the north.

Convenient to Osterville-proper, Corey Yacht Docks has transient space available with 9-foot dockside depths and modern restrooms and showers ashore.

Two big shipyards, with all services and supplies, build and repair boats. Crosby's Yacht Yard has been running since 1850 and offers docking and moorings, haul-out and repairs, showers and laundry and a seasonal restaurant, Keepers, which serves lunch and dinner from May to September. Call for reservations for dockage or a mooring. Osterville has grocery stores and laundry facilities, art, antiques and gift shops. A short walk from the marina area is Wimpy's, great for burgers, seafood, salads and excellent desserts. Nearby is Sweet Tomatoes for pizza or

The Osterville Cheese Shop for soups, salads and fresh sandwiches. Osterville Village provides a natural food store, a bank with ATM and a hardware store with limited marine supplies.

NAVIGATION: Use Chart 13229. From Nantucket Sound, the narrow dredged approach to West Bay is deep, well-marked and has a breakwater on both sides. Inside, it branches: the left fork leads to Cotuit Bay via Seapuit River, and the main 6-foot channel runs northward up West Bay, between shoals. This route angles eastward, then northward through the bascule bridge (15-foot closed vertical clearance), which connects Osterville on the east with Little Island and Osterville Grand Island to the west. Little Eel River, in the southeastern corner of West Bay, is worth a dinghy trip, but it shoals at the entrance.

Seapuit River

NAVIGATION: Use Chart 13229. The final link in the Cotuit-North-West bays circuit is Seapuit River, west of the entrance to West Bay from Nantucket Sound. From West Bay it leads between the dunes of Dead Neck (landing is prohibited) and the southern shore of Osterville Grand Island. The chart shows a shoal spot at the point where it enters Cotuit Bay, but local experts claim that the controlling depth is 4 feet.

Hyannis Port, Hyannis

Hyannis was settled by a handful of Puritans well over 400 years ago, and their surnames still figure prominently in the town's grand list. More recently, the town has been famous for the comings and goings of relative newcomers—to the "Kennedy compound" (easily identified on entering the inner harbor). One of the most popular areas on Cape Cod, Hyannis Harbor is deep and easy to enter, with summer traffic of all sorts—yachts under sail, commercial vessels, charter fishing and "head boats," Martha's Vineyard and Nantucket ferries and recreational boats of all kinds.

NAVIGATION: Use Chart 13229. For Hyannis Port, use Boston tide tables. For high tide, add 1 hour 3 minutes; for low tide, add 31 minutes. The most straightforward approach to Hyannis from the west is through the buoyed channel (respecting the buoys marking numerous rocks and ledges on approach from east or west). Following the lead of the red and white Morse (A) "HH" bell buoy, head north toward the Hyannis breakwater. Once inside, you can see the Kennedy compound, which faces the harbor and Nantucket Sound. From the breakwater east, the dredged (to 11-foot depths) and marked channel begins its long sweep through Lewis Bay toward Harbor Bluff. There, on approach, the channel angles sharply to port on a direct course to Hyannis' busy inner harbor, with its access to marine services and town amenities.

Dockage: On entering Lewis Bay, the Hyannis Yacht Club, west of the channel behind Dunbar Point, has both transient slips and moorings (with launch service) available for a facilities fee to members of other recognized clubs.

At the inner harbor and within the protection of Harbor Bluff, large and modern Hyannis Marina can accommodate vessels of almost any depth and length requirements, including megayachts to 200 feet. The marina is a gorgeous resort in a club-like setting and a full-capability service and repair yard. There are floating docks with water, power, cable and telephone lines at each slip, a harborside pool (with Trader Ed's Cabana Bar at poolside), a full-menu restaurant named Tugboat's, private showers and a discount ship's store. The marina also has wireless high-speed Internet access dockside, and offers a laundry, a game room and an Internet café.

Anchorage: Cruisers that prefer anchoring can find good holding in 7 to 9 feet of water northeast of crescent-shaped Egg Island in Lewis Bay. The remainder of Lewis Bay is suitable in settled weather, but open to the southwest.

GOIN' ASHORE: **HYANNIS, MA**

The largest community on Cape Cod, Hyannis over the past 30 years has reinvented itself as a cosmopolitan destination. For cruisers, the town's attractions are close at hand, just a country-mile away from the waterfront (guests in a hurry can use the Hyannis Marina courtesy vans). With more than 40 restaurants grouped so closely together, Main Street has become the restaurant capital of the Cod peninsula, offering a range of fare that includes fresh local seafood, Brazilian, Thai, Indian and Spanish tapas; there are also bistros, cafes and parlors serving homemade ice cream.

Hereabouts you will also find art galleries, boutiques, a carousel, bowling alley and a well-stocked hardware store.

Hyannis is rich in culture and things to do. Throughout summer, on Thursday evenings, the town hosts Main Street Festival, which incorporates a farmers market. During the warm months, the venerable Cape Cod Melody Tent (781-383-9860) frequently features headliners; past performers include Hootie and the Blowfish, Aretha Franklin, Lynyrd Skynyrd, John Hiatt, Tony Bennet, BB King, Crosby, Stills and Nash and the Moody Blues.

Another unique attraction is the Cape Cod Scenic Railroad (508-771-3800), which offers a dinner train to the Cape Cod Canal.

History buffs will enjoy a visit to the JFK Museum, showcasing the life of John F. Kennedy, with a focus on his time spent in the Hyannis area. At the harbor, the Cape Cod Maritime Museum is an easy stop on your walk to town. For a surf-and-turf look at the area, sign up for the amphibious Duck Boat Tour.

Main Street restaurant possibilities: Fazio's Trattoria offering country Italian (508-775-9400); Thai House with exotic cuisine in a quiet setting (508-862-1616); La Petite France Café serving French bread baguette sandwiches, pastries and platters to go (508-775-1067); Embargo, famous for fine dining, tapas and martinis (508-771-9700); and Harry's Blues Bar with Cajun and Creole specialties has live music nightly (508-778-4188).

At the West End of downtown, Misaki serves sushi (508-771-3771), while The Paddock, family-owned for 40 years, is a local favorite for seafood and steak (508-775-7677). The Roadhouse Cafe, South Street, combines fine dining

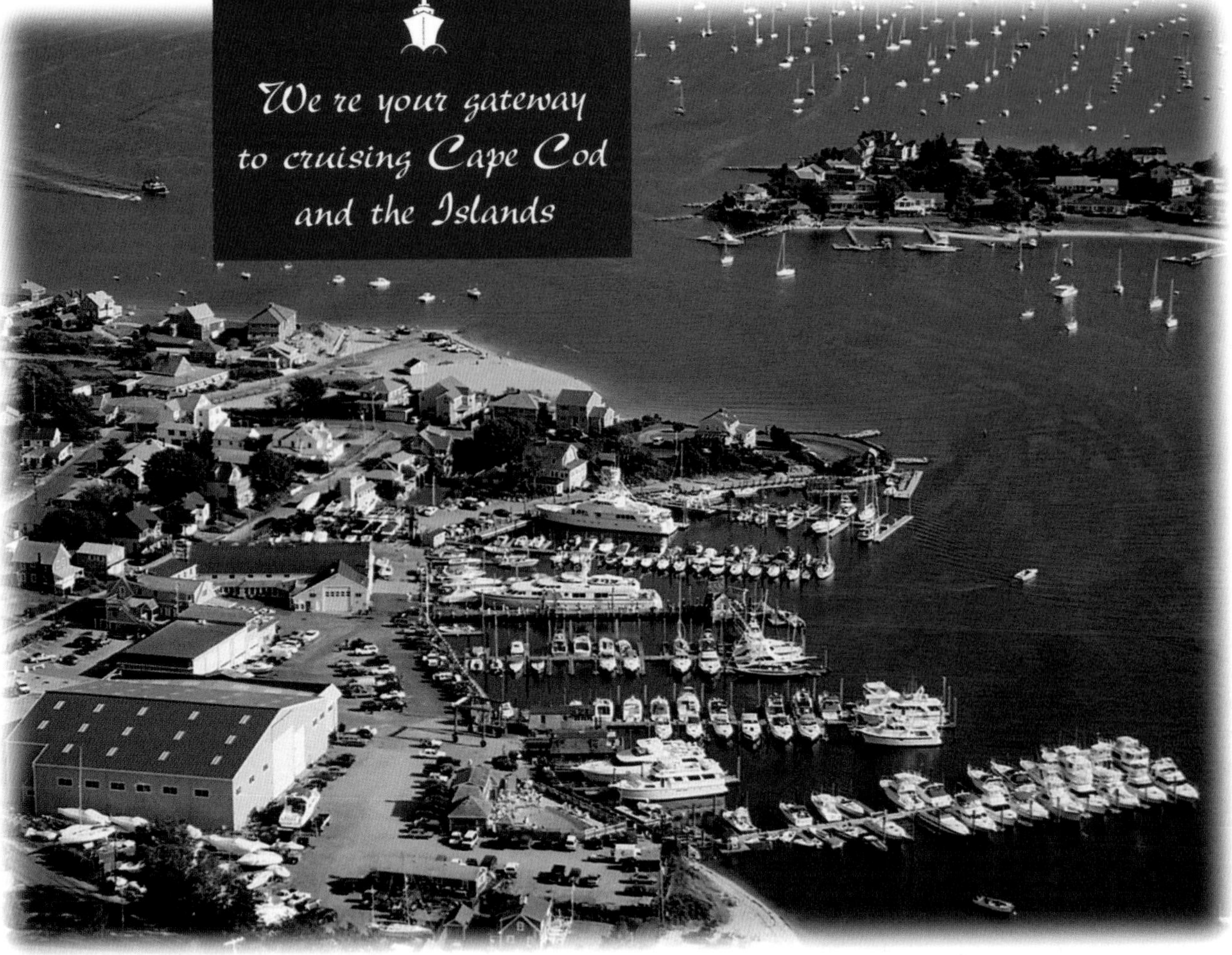

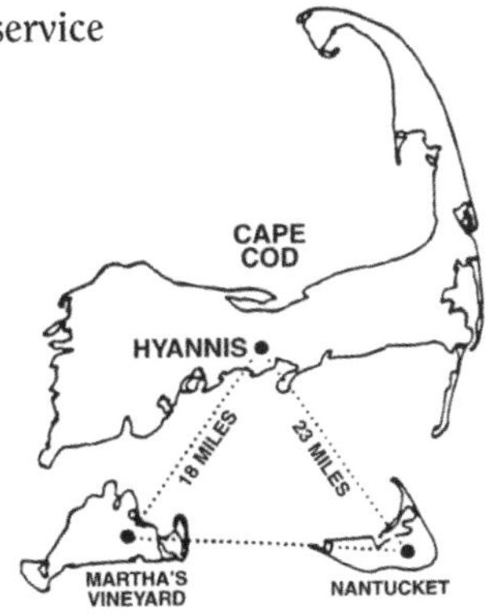

Hyannis, West Dennis, MA

HYANNIS, WEST DENNIS		Largest Vessel Accommodated	VHF Channel Monitored	Transient Berths / Total Berths	Approach / Dockside Depth (reported)	Floating Docks	Gas / Diesel	Groceries, Ice, Marine Supplies, Snacks	Repairs: Hull, Engine, Propeller	Lift (tonnage), Crane, Rail	1=110V, 2=220V, B=Both, Max Amps	Laundry, Pool, Showers	Pump-Out Station	Nearby: Grocery Store, Motel, Restaurant
		Dockage					Supplies		Services					
1. Hyannis Yacht Club	508-778-6100	140	09	/24	10/8			GIM			B/30	S		R
2. Bismore Park	508-790-6327	75	16/09	2/24	12/8						1/50		P	GMR
3. Hyannis Marina/Tugboats Restaurant 🖳	**508-790-4000**	**200**	**09/72**	**25/180**	**13/15**	**F**	**GD**	**GIMS**	**HEP**	**LC**	**B/100**	**LPS**	**P**	**GMR**
4. Ship Shops Inc. 🖳	508-398-2256	50	09/12	1/40	6/6		GD	IM		L	1/30			GMR
5. Bass River Marina 🖳 WiFi	508-394-8341	45	71	4/160	10/10		G	IM	HEP	LCR	B/50	S	P	GMR

Corresponding chart(s) not to be used for navigation. 🖳 Internet Access WiFi Wireless Internet Access

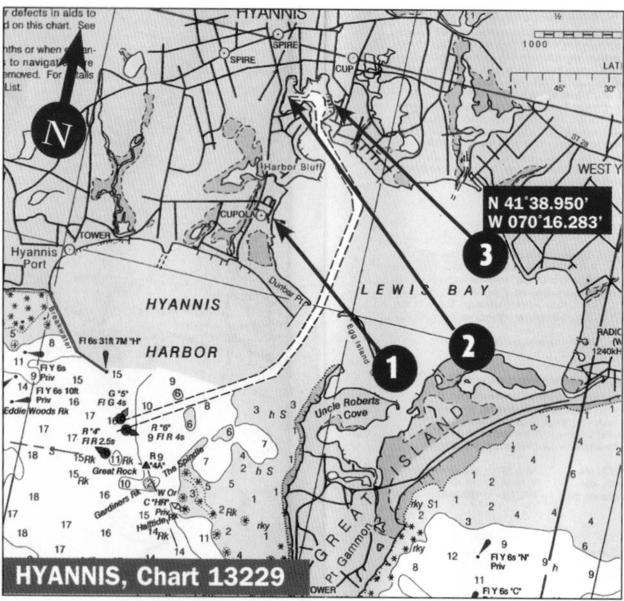

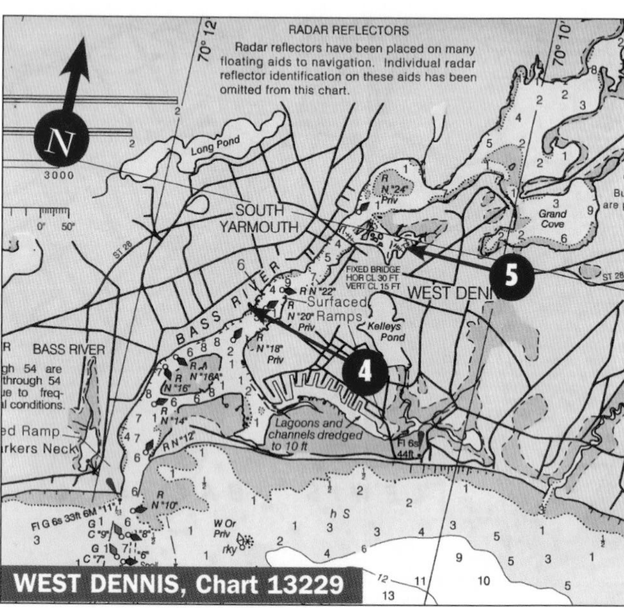

Looking south at Hyannis over the north shore of Lewis Bay. (Not to be used for navigation.) WATERWAY GUIDE PHOTOGRAPHY

and an award-winning wine collection with jazz on Monday and Tuesday nights (508-775-2386). Take your dinghy right up to Baxter's Boathouse, on Hyannis Harbor for great night life and fried seafood fresh from local waters (508-775-4490).

For a jolly time with other nautically inclined folks, Trader Ed's Cabana Pool Bar at the Hyannis Marina boasts a raw bar and live entertainment on weekends; the event tent is a popular venue for group rendezvous (508-790-8686). Tugboats, another eatery at the marina, lets you dine on fresh seafood dishes while enjoying a view of the harbor.

Beyond Main Street, Hyannis has all the amenities of a growing city, including shopping malls, supermarkets, fish markets, veterinarians, car rental agencies and the full range of specialty shops. Hyannis is also a transportation hub with regular bus service to Boston and a busy municipal airport with daily flights to New York and Boston. Boston's Logan International Airport is only about an hour and 15 minutes away by car.

ADDITIONAL RESOURCES:

- Main Street Hyannis: **www.hyannismainstreet.com**
- Bait and fish gear: **www.powderhornoutfitters.com**
- Hyannis Anglers Club: **www.hyannisanglersclub.com**
- Tidal information links: **www.boatma.com/tides**
- Hyannis Chamber of Commerce: **www.hyannis.com**

NEARBY GOLF COURSES:
Twin Brooks Golf Course, 35 Scudder Ave.,
Hyannis, MA 02601, 508-862-6980,
www.twinbrooksgolf.net

NEARBY MEDICAL FACILITIES:
Mid-Cape Medical Center (no appointment necessary),
489 Bearses Way, Hyannis, MA 02601,
(508) 771-4092

Cape Cod Hospital, 27 Park St.,
Hyannis, MA 02601, 508-771-1800,
www.capecodhealth.org

Parkers River

NAVIGATION: Use Chart 13229. An uncharted but privately marked channel, reportedly good for a 3-foot draft, cuts across Dogfish Bar to the mouth of Parkers River, less than three miles east of Point Gammon. Cottage owners in the area keep their small boats in the river.

Bass River

One of Cape Cod's prettiest rivers and a popular cruising area for small boats, the long, winding Bass River loops lazily inland toward the towns of Yartmouth and West Dennis.

NAVIGATION: Use Chart 13229. Flashing red bell buoy "2" marks the beginning of the approach into the Bass River. The approach to the jettied entrance, across Dogfish Bar, is narrow, and depths fluctuate from about 7 to 3.5 feet, depending on when it was last dredged and the amount of silting since. Enter only on a rising tide if your boat draws any more than 3 feet.

Dockage: Attractive houses, old windmills, several restaurants, hotels, motels, good-looking yachts and fine marinas are in both South Yarmouth and West Dennis. The Bass River Marina (limited to powerboats because of the 15-foot fixed vertical clearance bridge) offers slips, moorings, a restaurant and shopping mall.

Harwich Port

With three good harbors, fine beaches, good restaurants, full services and typical East Cape beauty, Harwich Port has a colorful 300-year history as a shipbuilding, whaling and cod-fishing center.

Allen Harbor

NAVIGATION: Use Chart 13229. Allen Harbor is so well-protected that the entrance is hard to find, and you will not see the harbor until the last turn of Doanes Creek. You enter past a breakwater and privately maintained markers to run up Doanes Creek, which has 4-foot depths.

Dockage: Small and full of boats, Allen Harbor has a town dock, a private yacht club and a full-service marina for powerboats. Allen Harbor is particularly popular with shoal-draft powerboats. It is a mile walk to Harwich Port's stores, restaurants and art gallery, and a half mile to the laundry.

Wychmere Harbor

NAVIGATION: Use Chart 13229. Depths in the harbor are 4 feet at mean low water. A breakwater protects the entrance, and the narrow pass to Wychmere Harbor has a 4-foot controlling depth.

Moorings: One of the most popular on the south shore, this round, nearly landlocked harbor is jammed with moorings. The crowded harbor no longer has dockage for transients, but if you ask at the town dock, someone might be able to point out a mooring or an available slip.

Saquatucket Harbor

This harbor shares a common entrance with Wychmere Harbor. Project depths are 6 feet, but the channel offers 4 feet. You will find 6-foot depths in the anchorage, but shoals are encroaching. To find out if a slip is available, call the town marina on VHF Channel 16 or 68.

Stage Harbor, Chatham

Large, protected, interesting Stage Harbor is the last port on the south side of Cape Cod and the logical take-off point for boats making the outside run around the hook to Provincetown. As much a fishing port as a yacht harbor, Stage Harbor has appealing creeks and coves, good boating amenities and anchorages.

NAVIGATION: Use Chart 13229. For Saquatucket Harbor, use Boston tide tables. For high tide, add 46 minutes; for low tide, add 16 minutes. When approaching Chatham

Harwich Port, MA

HARWICH PORT		Largest Vessel Accommodated	VHF Channel Monitored	Transient Berths / Total Berths	Approach / Dockside Depth (reported)	Floating Docks	Gas / Diesel	Groceries, Ice, Marine Supplies, Snacks	Repairs: Hull, Engine, Propeller	Lift (tonnage), Crane, Rail	1=110V, 2=220V, B=Both, Max Amps	Laundry, Pool, Showers	Pump-Out Station	Nearby: Grocery Store, Motel, Restaurant
		Dockage					Supplies		Services					
1. Allen Harbor Yacht Club	508-432-9774	55	09		6/4	F		I				S	P	
2. Allen Harbor Marine Service Inc.	508-432-0353	50		3/52	6/6	F	GD	IMS	HEP	L9	1/30		P	GMR
3. Saquatucket Municipal Marina	508-430-7532	55	68	10/195	6/8	F	GD	I			1/20	LS	P	GMR

Corresponding chart(s) not to be used for navigation. Internet Access WiFi Wireless Internet Access

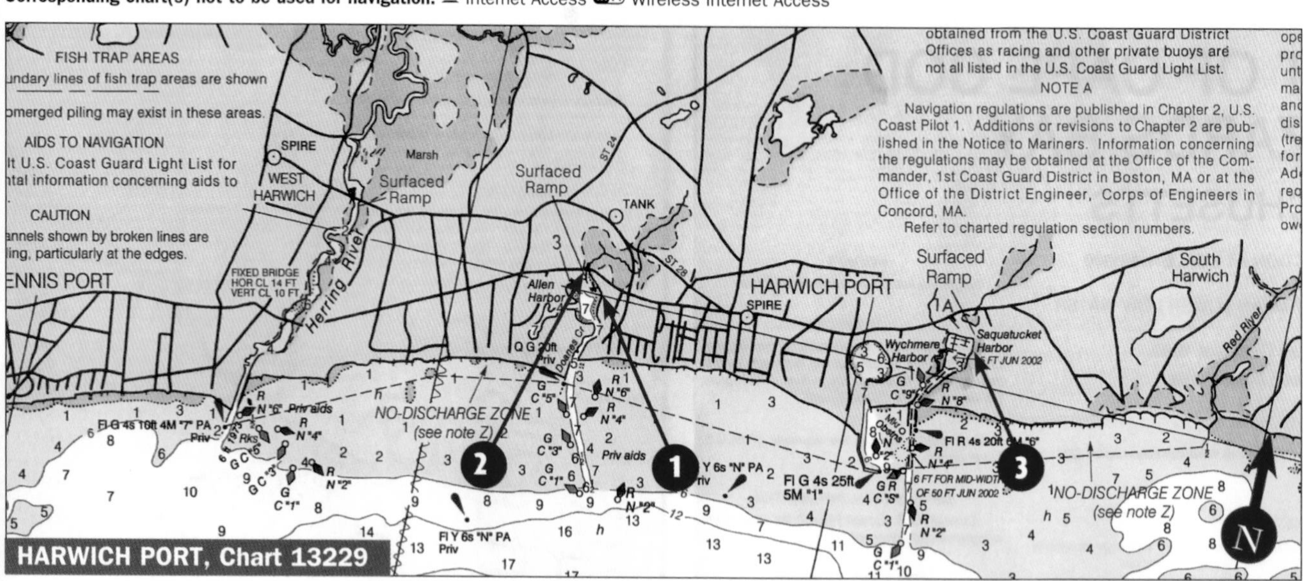

HARWICH PORT, Chart 13229

Roads, watch for fish weirs on the northwestern side and along the edge of shallows on the Martha's Vineyard side of Monomoy Island. The main channel from Chatham Roads into Stage Harbor is dredged frequently, but the U.S. Army Corps of Engineers advises that this is a very dynamic area, subject to constantly shifting shoals, and that boaters should seek local knowledge before using the channel.

You can reach Stage Harbor via a land cut through Harding Beach. To reach the inner harbor, follow the main channel buoys. A yacht club float is to port as you enter the harbor, followed by a commercial wharf and a repair yard with a small float.

The town of Chatham has installed a drawbridge (8-foot closed vertical clearance) at the entrance to the Mitchell River so that sailboats drawing 6 feet or less can now enter Mill Pond. Openings are regulated as follows: from May 1 to Oct. 31 from 8 a.m. to 4 p.m., one hour notice is required (call the Town of Chatham Police Department for an opening: 508-945-1213). The police indicate that there is not a great deal to attract boats above the bridge but a small repair yard and a few moorings; it is mostly occupied by local boats.

Very shoal-draft boats, aided by local knowledge, use the cut between Morris Island and Monomoy Island to reach Chatham Harbor. Otherwise, you must circumnavigate Monomoy Island to reach this shoaling passage inside the barrier beach. Even this route, however, calls for caution and local knowledge of the shoals. The route through Chatham Harbor to Pleasant Bay and farther on to the head of navigation at Orleans is an enjoyable dinghy trip.

Several years ago, a winter storm broke through the barrier of South Beach. This opening has widened dramatically, causing erosion damage to Town Beach. Inquire locally about further damage that may have been caused by subsequent storms.

Anchorage: You can anchor behind Harding Beach Point south/southeast of red nun "6" or just off the channel northeast of green can "7A." Otherwise, you can rent a mooring from either of the boatyards in Stage Harbor.

Cruising Options

No cruiser, or New England visitor for that matter, should miss the fabulous islands of Nantucket and Martha's Vineyard. Complete coverage follows in the next chapter. ■

WATERWAY GUIDE is always open to your observations from the helm. E-mail your comments on any navigation information in the guide to: editor@waterwayguide.com.

Chatham, MA

CHATHAM		Largest Vessel Accommodated	VHF Channel Monitored	Transient Berths / Total Berths	Approach / Dockside Depth (reported)	Floating Docks	Gas / Diesel	Groceries, Ice, Marine Supplies, Snacks	Repairs: Hull, Engine, Propeller	Lift (tonnage), Crane, Rail	1=110V, 2=220V, B=Both, Max Amps	Laundry, Pool, Showers	Pump-Out Station	Nearby: Grocery Store, Motel, Restaurant
		Dockage					Supplies		Services					
1. Stage Harbor Marine	508-945-1860	114	09	1/30	10/6	F	GD	IMS	HEP	C	1/30		P	GM
2. Oyster River Boat Yard	508-945-0736	34	16	MOORINGS	3/5	F	G	IM	HEP		1/30			MR
3. Outermost Harbor Marine	508-945-2030	36	80	/80	3/3	F	G	IMS	HP		30		P	GM
4. Peas Boat Works & Marine Railway	508-945-7800	50			7/7			M	HP		1/20			R
5. Ryders Cove Boat Yard	508-945-1064	30	09	MOORINGS	4/4		G	M	HE	L				

Corresponding chart(s) not to be used for navigation. Internet Access Wireless Internet Access

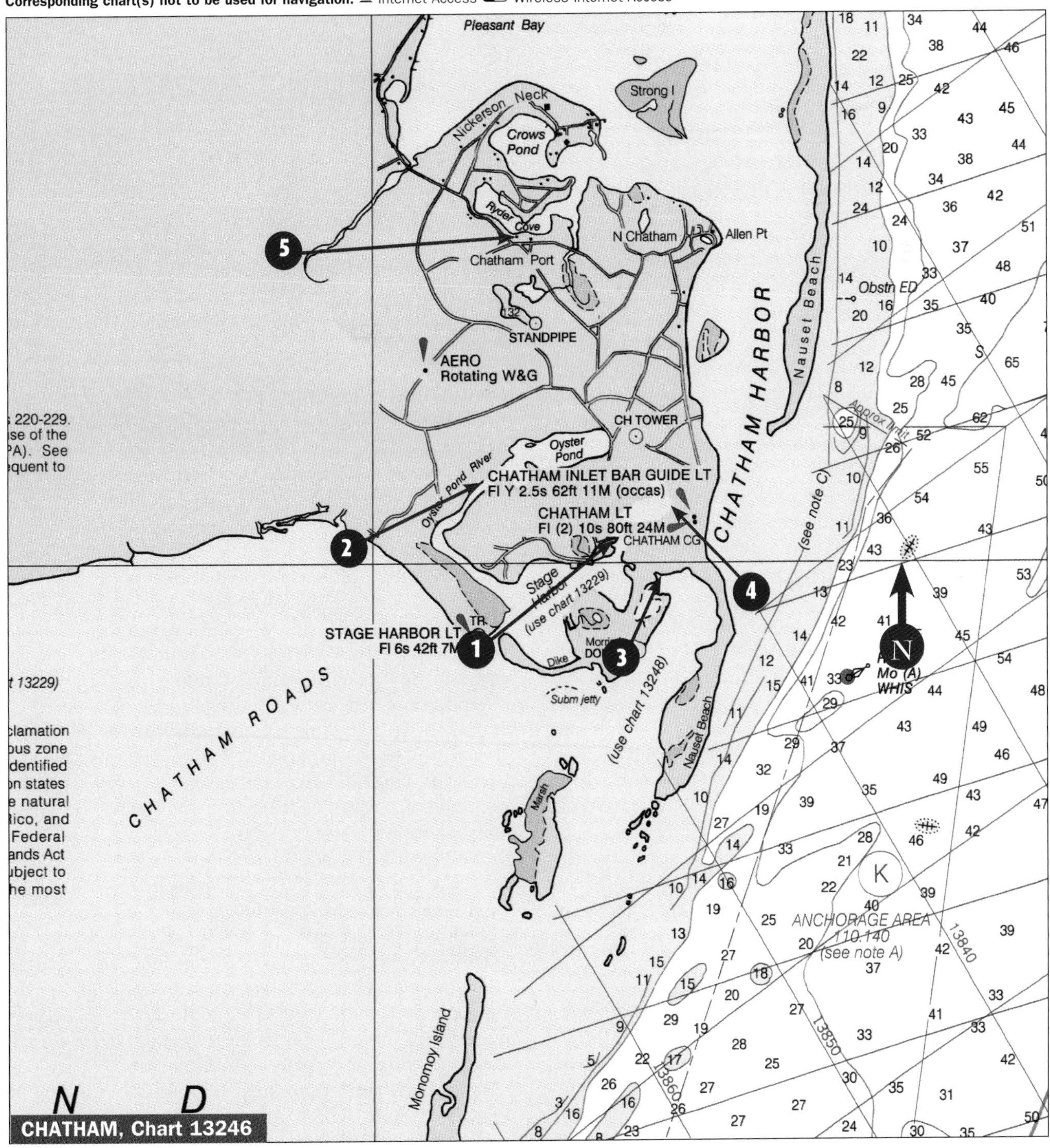

The Islands

CHARTS 13218, 13229, 13230, 13233, 13237, 13238, 13241, 13242, 13244

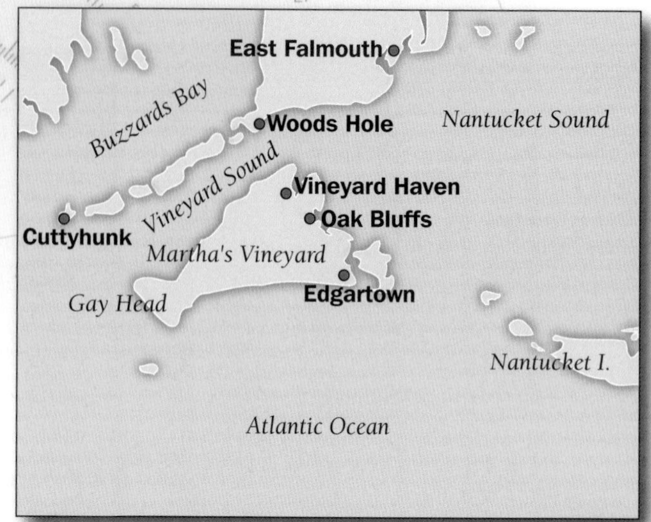

MASSACHUSETTS WATERS

The islands below Cape Cod are the favored cruising grounds for thousands of recreational boaters. Here you find true island diversity, ranging from the high-profile glamour of Martha's Vineyard to the solitude of Cuttyhunk Island. These islands have something to offer nearly everyone, no matter what they are seeking. Each season, the best-known harbors grow ever more congested, while lesser-known ports are being "discovered" by those who seek refuge from the crowds.

The Elizabeth Islands

Extending about 14 miles off the southwestern end of Cape Cod, the Elizabeth Islands form part of the northern shore of Vineyard Sound, separating it from Buzzards Bay. The islands are of varying sizes and are privately owned, with the exception of Cuttyhunk and Penikese. The latter is now a sanctuary for gulls and terns.

Mariners are permitted to land in certain areas if they observe the rules: leave dogs and guns (you must have a gun permit) aboard; build fires only below the high-water mark; keep to the trails; do not try any bushwhacking; and clean up after your visit.

Elizabeth Islands Passages

Between the islands are four passages from Buzzards Bay into Vineyard Sound: Canapitsit Channel; Quicks Hole; Robinsons Hole; and Woods Hole. Canapitsit Channel and Robinsons Hole can be used in calm weather with caution. Uncharted rocks and strong currents can make these areas unsafe for all but local mariners. Quicks Hole and Woods Hole are the safest, deepest and best-marked passages. When making a passage through Quicks Hole, consider a lunch or swim stop in an excellent anchorage on the southern side of the passage. There is good holding out of the channel and a sandy beach nearby.

Cuttyhunk

MA RI

Westernmost of the island chain is Cuttyhunk, named for the Indian word meaning "land's end." Cuttyhunk was discovered in 1602 by English explorer Bartholomew Gosnold, who proclaimed himself "ravished" by its beauty. Here, a primitive island atmosphere is within easy reach of South Shore and Cape Cod ports, offering a particularly attractive stopover en route to Martha's Vineyard and Nantucket.

NAVIGATION: Use Chart 13229. For Cuttyhunk, use Newport tide tables. For high tide, add 1 hour 20 minutes; for low tide, add 1 hour 15 minutes. The Middle Ground red-and-green buoy "MG" marks the entrance to Cuttyhunk from the west. Leave red nun buoy "2W" and red nun "4" well to starboard on approach to avoid Whale Rock, marked by a white-and-orange obstruction buoy, and Pease Ledge, southwest of red nun buoy "4." Red bell buoy "6" is posted to the northwest of the entrance to the inner harbor channel jetty, which is marked by a 25-foot-high tower with a six-second red flashing light ("8") to starboard, and green can buoy "9" to port on entry.

Depths reported on the Cuttyhunk Harbor inset of NOAA Chart 13229 may understate the actual depth (dredged to 10 feet in recent years). But if your keel and fear of shoaling run deep, phone or radio ahead to the harbormaster (VHF Channel 09, 508-990-7578). The approach from the east is marked by red-and-white Morse (A) bell buoy "CH." On entering the outer harbor from the east, leave red nun buoy "2E" affirmatively to starboard to avoid shoals that extend southward from Gull Island.

Dockage: Those desiring a slip at the town docks should call ahead to the town of Gosnold harbormaster (VHF Channel 09 or 508-990-7408, 6 a.m. to 9 p.m.). Although boats with drafts of up to 6 feet can be accommodated, maximum low-water depth at most of the town's 50 slips (non-floating docks with finger piers) is 4 feet.

Anchorage and Moorings: Just inside Cuttyhunk Pond, a dredged, square mooring area is clearly charted

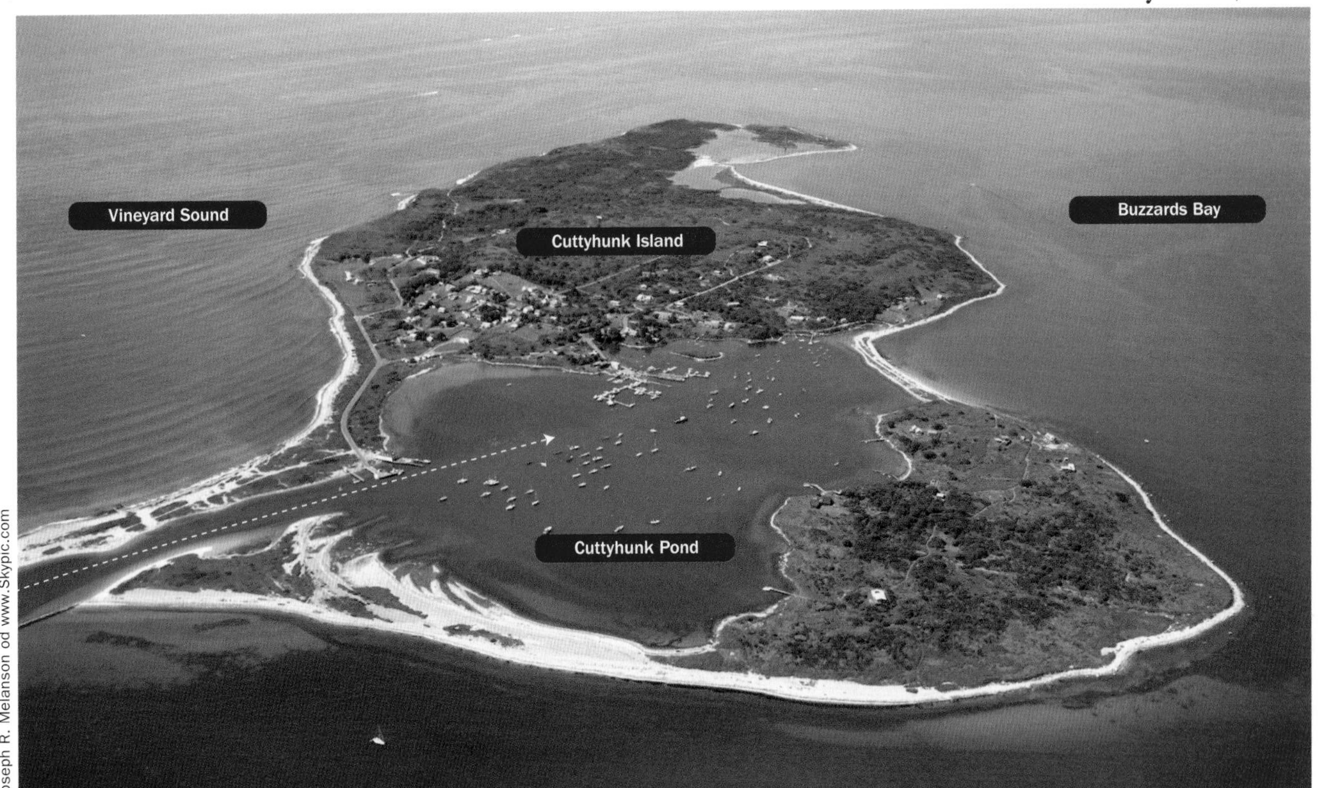

Looking southwest over Cuttyhunk Island and Cuttyhunk Pond. (Not to be used for navigation.)

and well-marked. Anchorage inside the white corner markers, north of the town moorings, may be possible for early arrivals, though a thin grass cover makes holding less than ideal. The area outside the white buoys has not been dredged, and it shallows rapidly. There is additional anchorage in the outer harbor, with potentially good holding in a hard sand-mud mix, and 12 to 17 feet of water at low tide. Patches of grass can frustrate a clean anchor set in this area, however. Considering Buzzards Bay's well-earned reputation for strong onshore afternoon winds, be certain you are firmly secured before going ashore or retiring below.

In the inner harbor, 46 closely spaced rental moorings (marked Town Of Gosnold) fill the dredged anchorage north of the town marina. They are available on a first-come, first-served basis, and you must supply your own line to secure your boat. Plan to have a bridle and chafing gear ready (as well an agile hand forward) to thread the eye of the unusual stand-up pennant on these moorings. A relatively short tether is advised in view of the limited swing room. (No more than two boats are permitted to raft.) The town launch will come by early in the evening to collect the mooring fee.

Private rental moorings are located in the outer harbor—north along the beach, offered by Jenkins, or south along the protective seawall, offered by Frog Pond Marine (508,992,7530, VHF Channel 72). In 2009, there were 30 moorings marked by orange balls and black stand-up pennants along the beach in 12 to 15 feet of water. Plan to use the dinghy from both inner and outer harbors; there is no launch service serving Cuttyhunk.

All the mooring fields are likely to be filled to capacity on summer weekends and holidays. Fortunately, there is still room to anchor northwest of Pease Ledge, between the ledge and Whale Rock. Several caveats are in order, however. There are several shallow spots in this area, making it advisable to consult the Cuttyhunk chart before dropping a hook. Even then, uncharted patches of grass may frustrate a good anchor set. Whether at anchor or moored, boats in the outer harbor will be exposed, uncomfortable and potentially at risk to a lee shore in a northerly blow.

GOIN' ASHORE: **CUTTYHUNK, MA**

Much of Cuttyhunk is privately owned, and cross-country bushwhacking is discouraged, as a matter of respect for both property rights and the Lyme-disease-carrying deer ticks found lurking in the underbrush. However, a walk along the roads around the inner harbor and along Vineyard Sound's beaches should not be missed. The paved road, leading west to its dead end at the island's highest point, is also a must for spectacular views of this eastward-running archipelago, its surrounding waters and the distinctive cliffs of Martha's Vineyard to the southeast.

At the foot of the rise, directly inland from the docks, The Corner Store has gifts, books and local art. Uphill and to the right, the rustic town hall makes Saturday night a movie night. The white-clapboard library (next to the still-operating, one-room schoolhouse) is open on limited hours, as is the nearby historical society building, which combines historical exhibits with displays of local art.

Cuttyhunk, Elizabeth Islands, MA

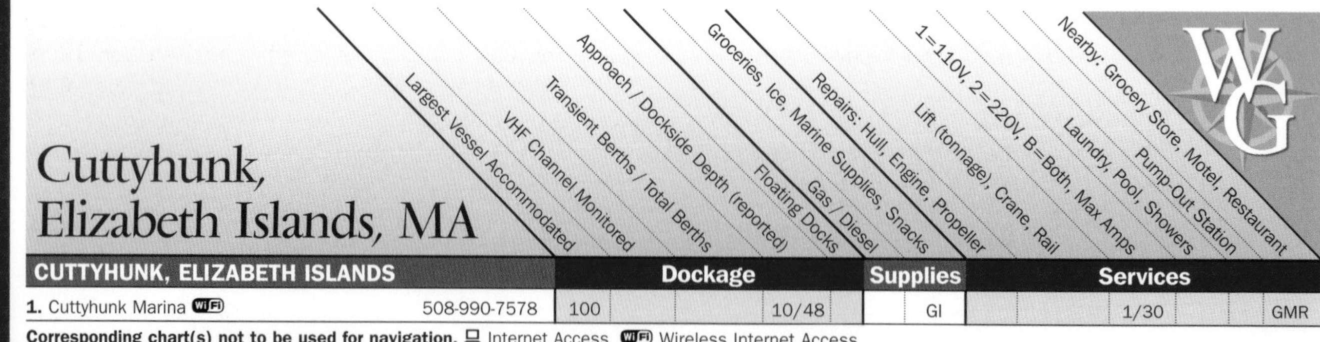

CUTTYHUNK, ELIZABETH ISLANDS		Largest Vessel Accommodated	VHF Channel Monitored	Transient Berths / Total Berths	Approach / Dockside Depth (reported)	Floating Docks	Gas / Diesel	Groceries, Ice, Marine Supplies, Snacks	Repairs: Hull, Engine, Propeller	Lift (tonnage), Crane, Rail	1=110V, 2=220V, B=Both, Max Amps	Laundry, Pool, Showers	Pump-Out Station	Nearby: Grocery Store, Motel, Restaurant
		Dockage					Supplies		Services					
1. Cuttyhunk Marina (WiFi)	508-990-7578	100			10/48			GI			1/30			GMR

Corresponding chart(s) not to be used for navigation. Internet Access (WiFi) Wireless Internet Access

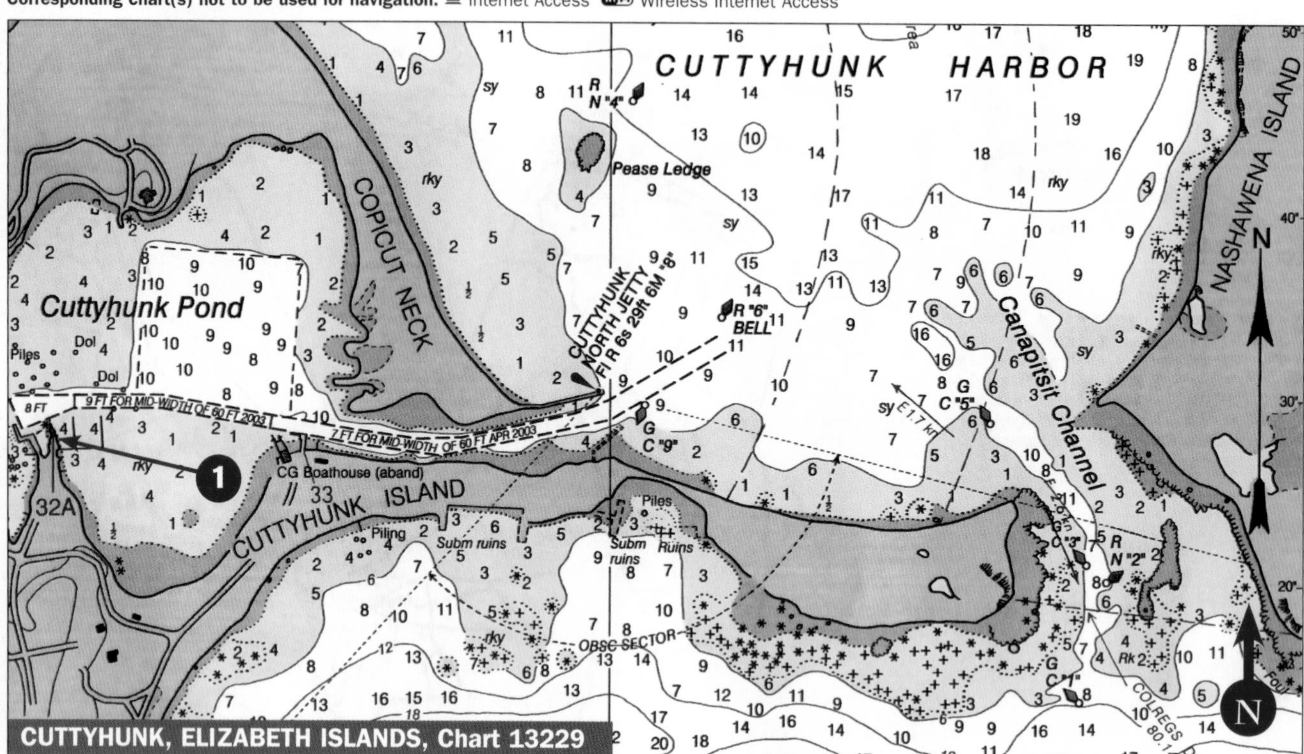

CUTTYHUNK, ELIZABETH ISLANDS, Chart 13229

Cuttyhunk's only food store, the Island Market, is also located up the rise from the docks, on the left. There you will find a limited supply of dry goods, deli items, freshly prepared sandwiches and salads to go, soft drinks and unusual local handicrafts on sale.

Not to be missed is a tour of the Cuttyhunk Fishing Club (founded in 1894). Opened to the public in 1998 after years of near dormancy as a private club, it is repainted but otherwise almost exactly as it was when William Howard Taft accompanied President Theodore Roosevelt for a fishing trip here. Breakfast on the porch (or inside) comes with breathtaking views of the Elizabeth Islands to the east and Martha's Vineyard to the southeast. The furnishings, fittings and ancient library create an aura of rustic comfort that seems to expect the return of Roosevelt, his cronies and their fishing stories at any moment. The club serves a memorable breakfast (7 a.m. to 11 a.m. daily) to the public, as well as to its inn guests. At Frog Pond Marine, Soprano's Pizza serves pizza, seafood, coffee and desserts from 5:30 p.m. to 8 p.m. (508-992-7530).

Most of the island's other amenities are found in the weathered shacks along Fisherman's Dock. The Harbor Raw Bar sells farm-fresh shellfish from the owner's local oyster and clam beds, along with stuffed quahogs, chowder and clam rolls. Boat delivery begins at 5:30 p.m.; call on VHF Channel 72. The Lobster Pound ("Old Squaw" on VHF Channel 66) often has fresh fish in addition to lobsters, and block and cube ice (2 p.m. to 6 p.m.). Also stop by Bart's Cart (somewhere on Broadway) for breakfast and lunch, Friday thru Tuesday.

Three public telephone booths are located next to the expanded dinghy landing (just landward of the town marina). Here, as well, are daily newspapers and Cuttyhunk's recycling center, accepting separated clear, green and brown glass, plastics, aluminum and other metals. Mixed trash can also be deposited here for a small fee. Public restrooms are next to the recycling trailers, but there are no shower facilities. Token-operated laundry machines may be found at Pete's Place, a short walk away. Bayside Air offers daily-chartered seaplane flights, landing next to the dinghy dock, to and from New Bedford, MA. Complimentary wireless Internet service is available as far as the outer harbor.

Cuttyhunk's fuel facility (both gasoline and diesel) is next to the abandoned red-roofed Coast Guard building. The fuel dock is also the Cuttyhunk home of *Alert II,* the island's dependable ferry to and from New Bedford, which is run by Cuttyhunk Boat Lines (508-992-1432).

ADDITIONAL RESOURCES:

- Cuttyhunk Island, **www.cuttyhunk.net**

NEARBY GOLF COURSES:
Falmouth Country Club, 630 Carriage Shop Road, East Falmouth, MA 02536, 508-548-3211, **www.falmouthcountryclub.com**

NEARBY MEDICAL FACILITIES:
Falmouth Hospital, 100 Ter Heun Drive, Falmouth, MA 02540, 508-548-5300

NAUSHON ISLAND

Anchorage: As you cruise the Vineyard Sound side of Naushon Island, you can anchor in Tarpaulin Cove when the weather permits. The cove has wooded shores and a fine beach, but it is open to the south and east. The best protection is in the southwestern corner, due north of the 78-foot-high lighthouse, in about 11 feet of water at low tide (about 150 to 200 yards south/southwest of green can buoy "1"). The scene ashore is reminiscent of 18th-century America—a classic seaside farmhouse with various outbuildings, rambling stone walls and deserted beaches. Tarpaulin Cove can easily accommodate 75 large boats without crowding.

On the Buzzards Bay side of Naushon Island, Kettle Cove makes a good daytime stop. It is open to the north, but on a fine day with a southwesterly breeze, you can drop the hook, have lunch and swim from the beach.

Hadley Harbor

Naushon Trust owns Naushon Island, and most of the land is clearly posted against trespassing, but cruising boats are welcome in peaceful Hadley Harbor, a totally protected natural refuge, easily accessible from Buzzards Bay.

NAVIGATION: Use Chart 13229. Enter through the narrow passage just off the northwestern corner of Nonamesset Island, then proceed to the east and south around the western end of Nonamesset Island, leaving the privately maintained daymark well to starboard. This marker identifies the edge of the shoals extending eastward from Uncatena Island, directly to the west. From here the channel narrows as it passes eastward of Bull Island, then widens as it turns to the west, then south, around Goats Neck.

Anchorage: The far end of the harbor is crowded with moorings, but excellent anchorage is available north of the private landing and boat houses, between Bull Island and Goats Neck. A number of moorings have been established in the inner harbor, available at no cost on a first-come, first-served basis. This has reduced the area available for anchoring.

Some shoals and rocks are located along the littoral, so skippers should feel their way cautiously and make anchoring allowances for shifting winds during the evening. Anchorage should be avoided in any place where the channel is constricted. The Naushon Ferry, bringing freight and passengers from Woods Hole, needs plenty of room to maneuver.

The harbor is so popular that those planning to stay overnight should arrive early in the afternoon. Keep a lookout for latecomers who might anchor indiscriminately. Public access is permitted on Bull Island, where picnic grounds are maintained by the Forbes family during the season. Just take your dinghy to the small landing on the southeast corner of the island. Dogs should be kept on leashes, and barbecue fires tended responsibly. Signs warn of ticks and danger of Lyme disease; be sure to apply your insect repellent liberally.

East of Hadley Harbor proper and north of Nonamesset Island is a large area suitable for anchorage in southwesterly breezes, but untenable in northerlies of 20 knots or more. Seas build in the long fetch down the Cape Cod shore and make this area uncomfortable and unsafe.

MARTHA'S VINEYARD

A distance of less than four miles divides Martha's Vineyard from the southern shore of Cape Cod. A relaxed summer resort, the Vineyard has four distinctively different harbors (Menemsha, Vineyard Haven, Oak Bluffs and Edgartown), high land, wooded bluffs, historic towns and handsome houses. The southern and western shores consist of rolling moor, ocean beach, salt marsh and the multicolored cliffs of Gay Head towering high above the sea. Colored veins of earth-hued clay (white, yellow, tan, sienna, rust, brown) make the cliffs a muted rainbow.

American Indians, who make and sell pottery fashioned from the colored clay run a small museum and snack bar at Gay Head, which has been officially renamed Aquinnah in honor of the original Indian inhabitants. Many long-time residents and visitors will still refer to Gay Head, but all road signs have been changed. Other gift and craft shops, as well as restaurants and snack shops, are worth a visit. You can walk to (Aquinnah) Gay Head Light for a magnificent view of the Elizabeth Islands. Unfortunately, Aquinnah is not easily accessible by boat. For a more complete tour, cruisers might be well advised to rent a car or obtain other transportation from several rental agencies south of the ferry terminal in Vineyard Haven.

Menemsha

Consciously quaint Menemsha, about three miles east of Aquinnah on the Vineyard Sound side, is a fishing port working at staying unspoiled. You can hike along vacant dunes, watch the long liners unload, kibitz with local artists and get a decently prepared meal or deli sandwich here. The Menemsha Basin is home port to lobster boats, trawlers, sportfishermen and charter and party boats. Shanties used by fishermen line the picturesque but crowded harbor head.

Martha's Vineyard, MA

MARTHA'S VINEYARD		Largest Vessel Accommodated	VHF Channel Monitored	Transient Berths / Total Berths	Approach / Dockside Depth (reported)	Floating Docks	Gas / Diesel	Groceries, Ice, Marine Supplies, Snacks	Repairs: Hull, Engine, Propeller	Lift (tonnage), Crane, Rail	1=110V, 2=220V, B=Both, Max Amps	Laundry, Pool, Showers	Pump-Out Station	Nearby: Grocery Store, Motel, Restaurant
		Dockage					Supplies		Services					
1. Menemsha Texaco Service	508-645-2641	120	09/88		11/11		GD	IMS						G
2. Menemsha Harbor	508-645-2846	70	09	30/100	12/12		GD	GI			B/50	S	P	GMR
3. Vineyard Haven Town Dock	508-696-4249	60	09	/15	7/7							S	P	GMR
4. The Black Dog Wharf	508-693-3854	125	72	25/35	10/10						B/50	LS		GMR
5. Vineyard Haven Marina	508-693-0720	200	09	52/52	12/12		GD	GIM			B/100	LPS	P	GMR
6. Tilsbury Wharf Company	508-693-9300	250		8/15	12/6		GD	I		L	B/100	S		GMR
7. Martha's Vineyard Shipyard	508-693-0400	50	09/73		12/10			IM	HEP	L35				GMR
8. Maciel Marina	508-693-4174	38	09	4/8	4/8	F	G	IM	HP		1/30	S	P	MR
9. Oak Bluffs Marina, Martha's Vineyard	508-693-4355	120	71	75/80	8/10			I			1/50	S	P	GMR
10. Dockside Marina	508-693-3392	60	09/71	8/8	12/7		GD				B/50	S	P	GMR
11. Edgartown Harbor	508-627-4746	60	74	3/3	20/25	F	GD	IMS	HP		B/50	S	P	GMR
12. Mad Max Marina	**508-627-7400**	**150**	**71**	**9/9**	**15/15**						**B/50**			**MR**
13. Edgartown Yacht Club	508-627-4361		72	LIMITED RECIPROCITY										GMR

Corresponding chart(s) not to be used for navigation. Internet Access Wireless Internet Access

For the fresh catch, try Poole's Fish Market or Larsen's Fish Market on the eastern side of the basin. About a quarter mile south of the commercial docks, the long-established Home Port Restaurant is said to be well worth the wait for a table. The Bite is a take-out or eat-in place that promises "the best fried clams" and a menu of fried-to-order seafood and chicken entrées. The Beachplum Inn and Restaurant (508-645-9454) is considered one of the finest dining experiences on Martha's Vineyard. Remember that many of the towns on The Vineyard are dry, so "bringing your own" is the rule when it comes to alcohol. This method is permitted at most restaurants.

Across the street from the Home Port, at the head of the inner harbor, a small grocery store has the basics as well as (on the right days) fresh island-grown produce. The Menemsha Post Office is also located there. Next door, The Galley offers lunch, ice cream and sodas. Menemsha Blues, a clothing company, started here and now has four stores on the island. Martha's Bike Rentals (800-559-0312) will deliver and pick up bikes anywhere on the island.

NAVIGATION: Use Chart 13233. Access to the harbor is straightforward; it can handle commercial drafts of up to 18 feet and the entrance is marked by the green bell buoy "1," which is located approximately 300 yards off the channel's mouth. A 25-foot-high tower with a green four-second flashing light ("3") indicates the end of the seawall to port; a stone jetty is prominent to starboard. The currents in this passage are straightforward and swift. It is best to pick a slack tide for entry.

Since the Coast Guard has ceased to maintain the inner channel to Menemsha Pond, all but dinghies and extremely shallow-draft boats are confined to the basin and the channel within about 200 yards from the entrance. Past red nun buoy "4," the channel is no longer dredged and shifts with the shoals and seasons. The area above is beautiful, however, and well worth exploration by small boat.

Dockage: Transients can be accommodated in Menemsha Basin at town slips along the western side, available on a first-come, first-served basis. Two heavy town moorings (and other moorings off the beach) are offered on the same basis, but you can expect to raft. Menemsha is a No-Discharge Zone with a $1,000 cash fine for violators (treated effluent included). A pump-out station is now available. Just contact the harbormaster (located in the small shed just to the east of the harbor entrance) on VHF Channel 16 or 508-645-2846.

Vineyard Haven

The island's chief port, Vineyard Haven has a busy harbor that serves as the primary ferry terminal and the foremost commercial and recreational marine center. The harbor is wide and open to the northeast, but a rock breakwater protects the inner harbor beach and recreational beach from all but the worst of the incoming swells. Beyond marine facilities ashore, Vineyard

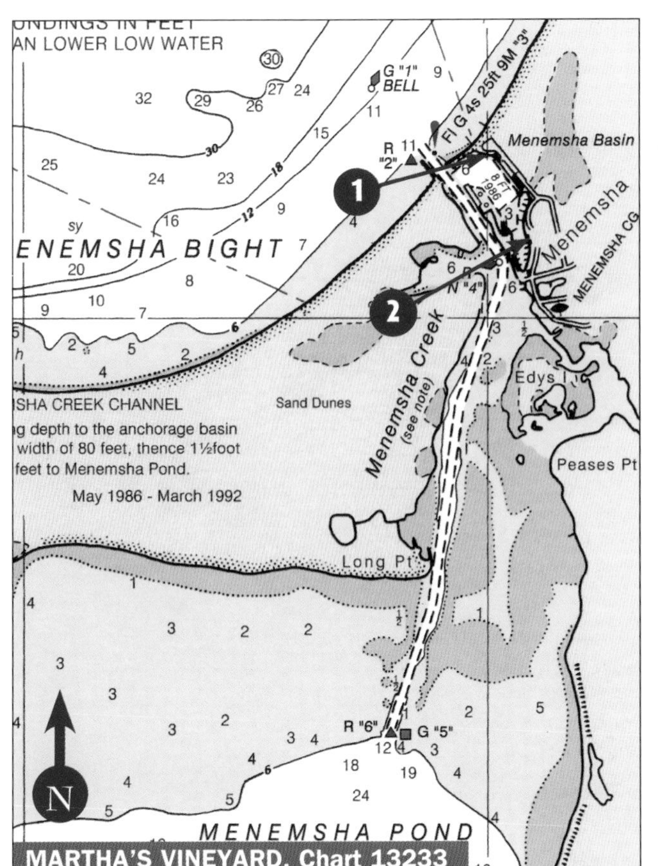

MARTHA'S VINEYARD, Chart 13233

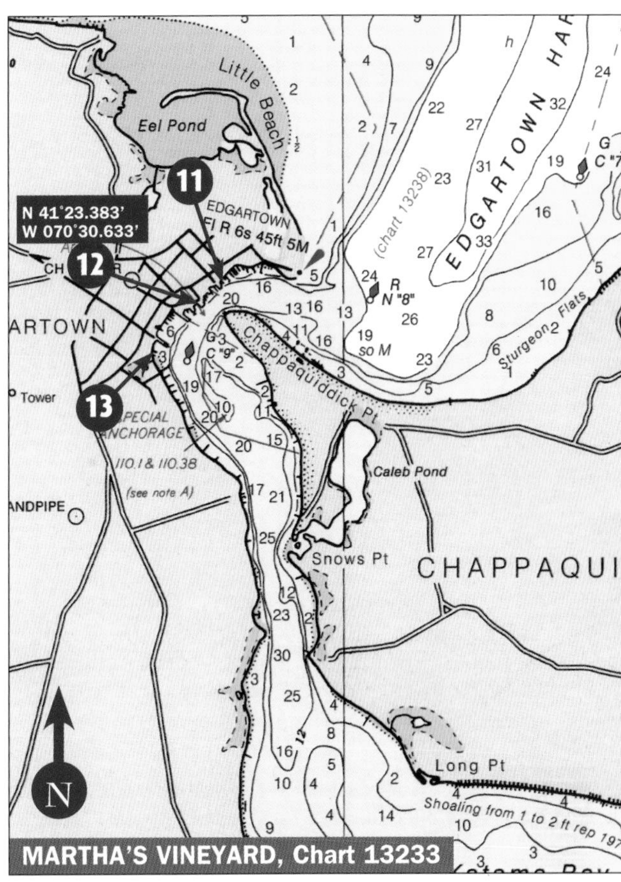

MARTHA'S VINEYARD, Chart 13233

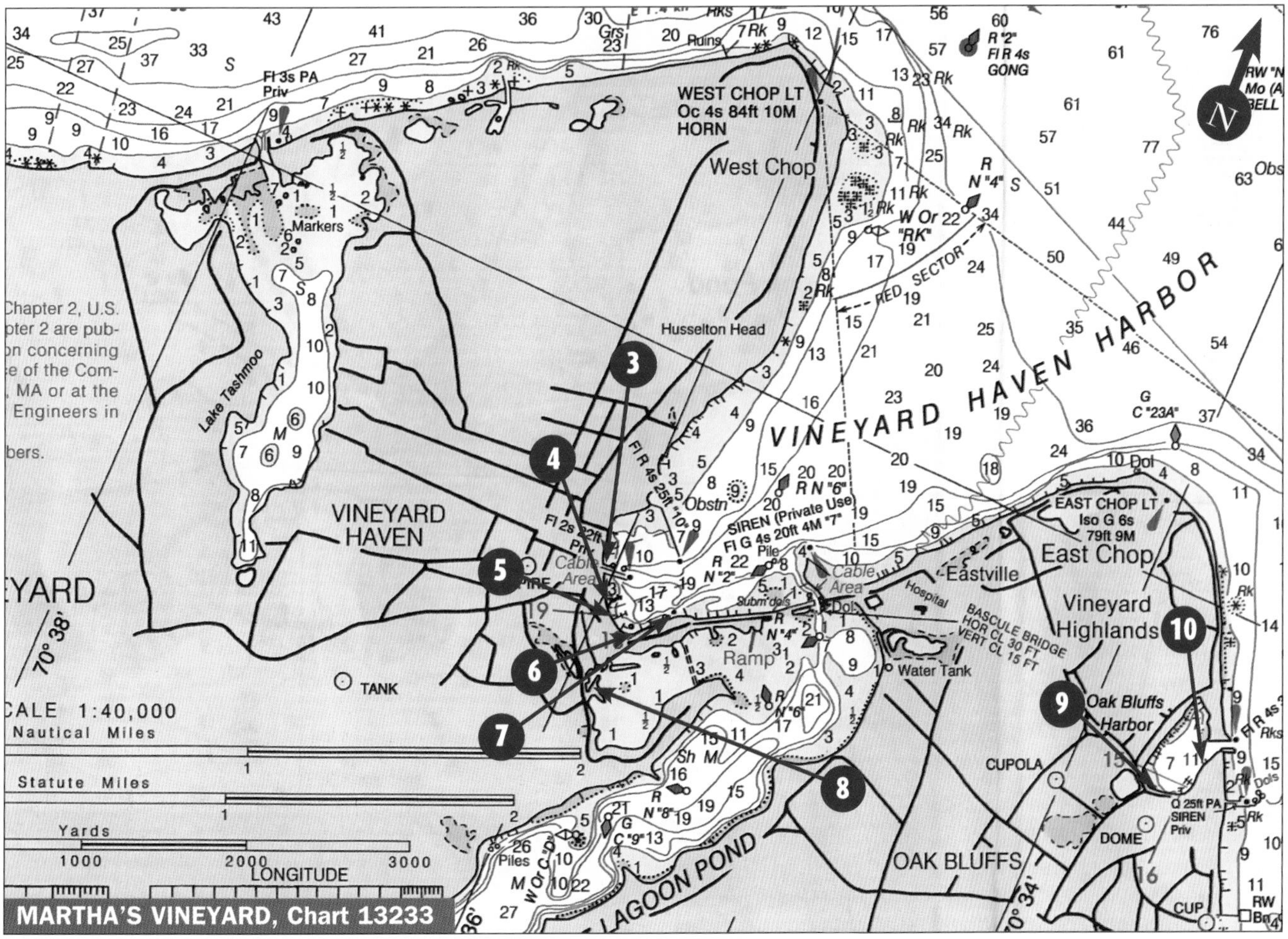

Fl 3s PA Priv
WEST CHOP LT
Oc 4s 84ft 10M
HORN
West Chop
R "2" Fl R 4s GONG
R N "4"
W Or "RK"
RED SECTOR
Markers
Lake Tashmoo
Husselton Head
VINEYARD HAVEN HARBOR
Chapter 2, U.S.
pter 2 are pub-
on concerning
e of the Com-
, MA or at the
Engineers in
bers.
VINEYARD HAVEN
Fl R 4s 25ft "10"
Fl 2s 22ft Priv
R N "6"
SIREN (Private Use)
Fl G 4s 20ft 4M "7"
G C "23A"
EAST CHOP LT
Iso G 6s 79ft 9M
East Chop
Eastville
Hospital
BASCULE BRIDGE
HOR CL 30 FT
VERT CL 15 FT
Vineyard Highlands
Oak Bluffs Harbor
Ramp
Water Tank
TANK
CUPOLA
Q 25ft PA SIREN Priv
DOME
OAK BLUFFS
LAGOON POND
SCALE 1:40,000
Nautical Miles
Statute Miles
Yards
1000 2000 3000
LONGITUDE
70° 38'
70° 34'

MARTHA'S VINEYARD, Chart 13233

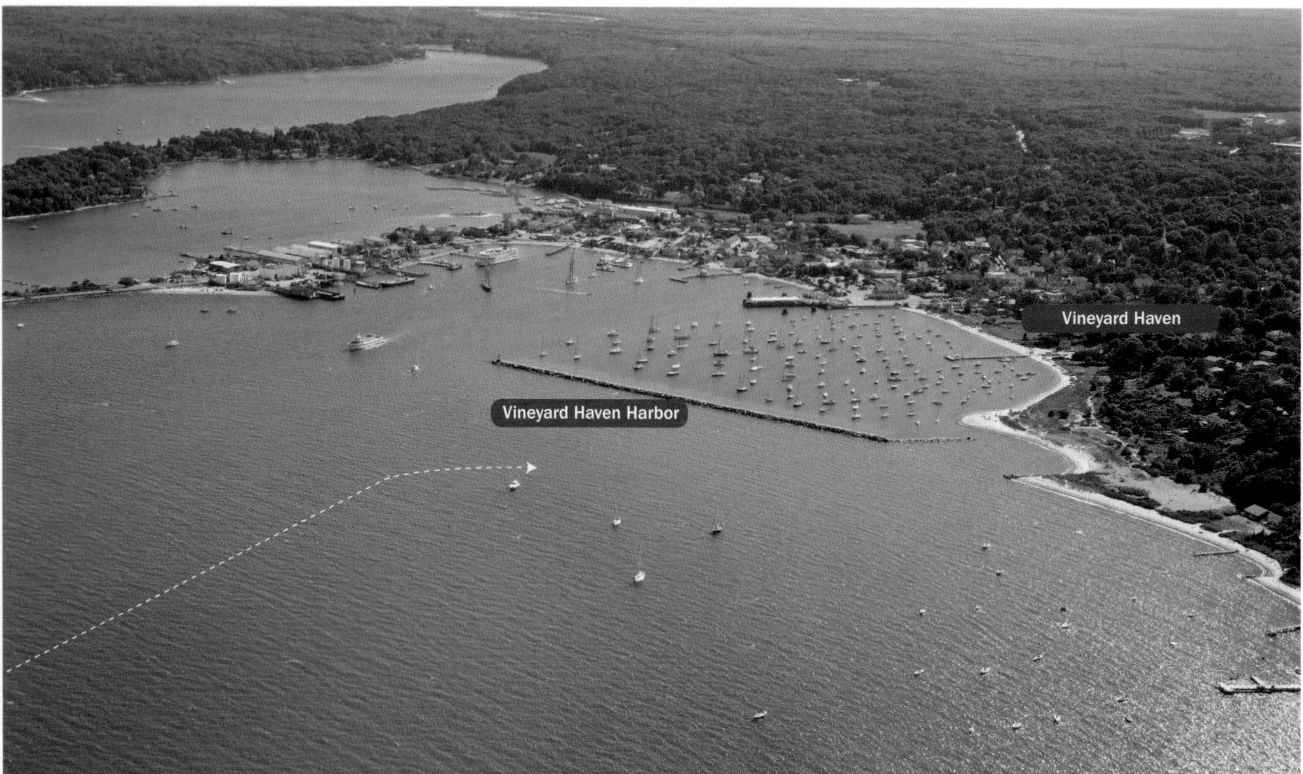

Looking southwest over Vineyard Haven and Vineyard Haven Harbor. (Not to be used for navigation.) WATERWAY GUIDE PHOTOGRAPHY

Haven has just about any recreational and reprovisioning opportunity you might want, set in the ambience of an old New England village.

NAVIGATION: Use Chart 13233. Enter between the lighthouses on the headlands of West Chop and East Chop. The harbor mouth is more than a mile wide at its outermost extremity, narrowing gradually upon approaching the inner harbor breakwater and the ferry wharf at harbor's head. Buoys on entry are gauged to deep-draft vessels. However, due respect must be paid the rocky ledges along the eastern shore of West Chop, beginning at Allegheny Rock (marked by green can "25") and west of red nun buoy "4."

Dockage: Vineyard Haven's municipal dock offers the most protected tie-ups (tucked behind the breakwater), whether hitched to the pier or tethered to a town mooring. Short-term tie-ups are possible in 8- to 10-foot depths alongside the municipal pier (10 a.m. to 4 p.m. at hourly rates), and an overnight stay may be arranged as well. Most will want to take advantage of one of the town's 150 rental moorings. Call the harbormaster (VHF Channel 09 or 508-696-4249) for availability and directions. A dinghy dock is available on the north side of the pier, and the harbormaster's office is just inland of the town beach.

Near the ferry docks, Coastwise Wharf Co. has dock space available for transients and rental moorings with launch service. Also at the head of the harbor, Tisbury Wharf Co. rents short-term space to vessels of virtually any size, with dockside depths to 11 feet and lengths of up to 200 feet. This yard also has major repair capabilities and a 50-ton lift for haul-outs. Martha's Vineyard Shipyard (its pier well to port after passing the breakwater) does not cater to visiting boaters' dockage needs. However, it does have major lift and repair capabilities.

Anchorage: Substantial anchorage room is still available outside the mooring field along the easterly side of West Chop, south of the rocky outcrop marked by a warning buoy and inside a line between red nun buoys "4" and "6." Holding is good here on a firm bottom in 8 to 20 feet of water, but the area is fully exposed to the northeast and to the wakes of frequently arriving and departing ferries. During the approach of Hurricane Isabel in 2003, the local authorities were advising that any transients would be asked to leave the mooring fields, both inside and outside the jetty. A visiting cruiser would be advised to seek shelter elsewhere or plan a haul-out at one of the boatyards in the event of an approaching major storm.

GOIN' ASHORE:
VINEYARD HAVEN, MA

Most of the shops in Vineyard Haven are clustered along Main Street, a walk of about 130 yards up the incline through Owen Park, at the head of Tisbury Municipal Pier. Left on Main Street from the town pier, you will find Bunch of Grapes Book Store, (open 9 a.m. to 9:30 p.m. daily); Bowl and Board, and its huge collection of wood-crafted items; and clothing shops, a jeweler, a kite store, Mad Martha's Ice Cream and a theater featuring first-run films.

Farther south on Main Street, the Health Club at Tisbury Inn offers showers (with a towel and the use of the hot tub and sauna; or complete use of the club's facilities, including pool and weight room; both for a fee). An A&P supermarket is just across from the Steamship Authority parking lot on Water Street, and Black Dog Cafe is south on the harbor side. Behind the A&P on a side street is a large True Value hardware store. At the end of Water Street, at the major (and difficult-to-cross) intersection with Lagoon Pond Road and Beach Road, the post office is located on the far corner, alongside a Cumberland Farms convenience store. Toward Oak Bluffs, on Beach Road, are bicycle, moped and car rental establishments. The Artcliff Diner is a special place for breakfast and lunch, favored by locals for its eclectic décor and ever-changing menu.

In addition to the usual tourist clam bars and snack shops, a couple of Vineyard Haven restaurants are particularly worthy of mention. Le Grenier French Restaurant (Upper Main Street, 508-693-4906) offers an elegant alternative to galley chow—quail with grapes, or rack of lamb with rosemary and currant sauce, for example. There is a French bakery on the premises. The Black Dog Tavern (Beach Street Extension at the end of Water Street, 508-693-9223) is famous throughout New England for its T-shirts and caps and for its robust, nautical atmosphere and hearty dishes to match. Coop de Ville (12 Circuit Ave., 508-693-3420) offers casual food, including eight varieties of wings. Louis' Tisbury Eatery (350 State Road, 508-693-3255) is the place to go for innovative pasta dishes and pizza. Tisbury is a dry town, so bring your own beer; the restaurants will chill it. Vineyard Haven is a wonderful place to walk. Ask at the harbormaster's office about a walking tour of the town.

ADDITIONAL RESOURCES:

- Martha's Vineyard Online, **www.mvol.com**

NEARBY GOLF COURSES:
Mink Meadows Golf Club, 320 Golf Club Road, Vineyard Haven, MA 02568, 508-693-0600

NEARBY MEDICAL FACILITIES:
Martha's Vineyard Hospital, 1 Hospital Road, Vineyard Haven, MA 02568, 508-693-0410

Lagoon Pond

One of the least known pleasures of Martha's Vineyard is the beautiful, ample and well-protected harbor of Lagoon Pond, just southeast of Vineyard Haven Harbor and securely nestled beneath the bluffs of East Chop.

Powerful blows from the northeast can easily be ridden out beneath the highest of Lagoon Pond's tan-and-white cliffs on the eastern shore.

NAVIGATION: Use Chart 13233. Maciel Marine maintains 16 clearly marked rental moorings along the western side of the pond and three more outside the pond entrance. The antique bascule bridge (15-foot closed vertical clearance) is no longer operated by Maciel Marine, but by a private individual. Call "Lagoon Drawbridge" or "Maciel Marine" on VHF Channel 16 to arrange an opening. The bridge opens on signal from Dec. 31 until May 5; otherwise, it is opened upon request according to the following schedule: from 8:15 a.m. until 8:45 a.m.; from 10:15 a.m. until 11 a.m.; from 1:15 p.m. until 1:45 p.m. (July through August only); from 3:15 p.m. until 4 p.m.; from 5 p.m. until 5:45 p.m.; and from 7:30 p.m. until 8 p.m. Reports of bridge problems in previous years warrant a call ahead for current status. Be aware that boaters in the pond may have difficulty getting out because of erratic bridge operation.

The pond is navigable (controlling depth 6.5 feet at mean low water) and well-marked throughout its one-and-three-quarter-mile length. However, do not mistake the Maciel channel markers leading to starboard on entry for the main channel buoys. Also pay attention to the white private buoy at Robbins Rock and leave it to starboard. Maciel Marine is located at the head of the shallow bay west of Cedar Neck. You will find ample dinghy docks, restrooms and trash disposal, along with hospitable marine services. It is essential that you call ahead; transient accommodations are rare during the season. Five Corners of Vineyard Haven is located several hundred yards to the north on Lagoon Pond Road. Both Vineyard Haven and Lagoon Pond are No-Discharge Zones. The free town pump-out boat (on call, VHF Channel 09) serves boats at marinas, on moorings or anchored out. An additional pump-out station is available at the Tisbury town wharf inside the breakwater.

Oak Bluffs

Just beyond the high bluffs of East Chop lies Oak Bluffs, known in the 19th century as the "Cottage City of America" when it attracted Methodists from all over the country for the Martha's Vineyard Camp Meeting. Here they came to pray, preach and repent in the spirit of religious fervor, annually setting up their tents in this seaside wilderness. Gradually, tiny houses replaced the tents, each with a small front porch, all gaily painted and festooned with gingerbread and scrollwork. In 1879, the main meeting tent, a one-ton affair, was replaced by the wood-and-wrought-iron Tabernacle—100 feet high, 130 feet across and seating more than 3,000—at the center of the village. More than 100 years later, the religious fervor has ebbed, but the radiating glow of hundreds of Japanese lanterns hanging on the Tabernacle continues annually on Illumination Night at the end of each season.

Today, Oak Bluffs is the Vineyard's resort harbor. It is crowded and hectic, but the scene is festive and there is much to enjoy. The blocks of gingerbread houses merit repeated walking tours; music fills the air at the Tabernacle at Trinity Park on most weekend evenings; the Flying Horses, America's oldest operating platform carousel (dating from 1876), operates just half a block east of the town harbor; and beautiful Ocean Park Gazebo is the center of an impressive fireworks display on Illumination Night.

NAVIGATION: Use Chart 13233. For Oak Bluffs, use Boston tide tables. For high tide, add 32 minutes; for low tide, subtract 12 minutes. Some skippers consequently pass up Oak Bluffs Harbor because it always looks full. Actually,

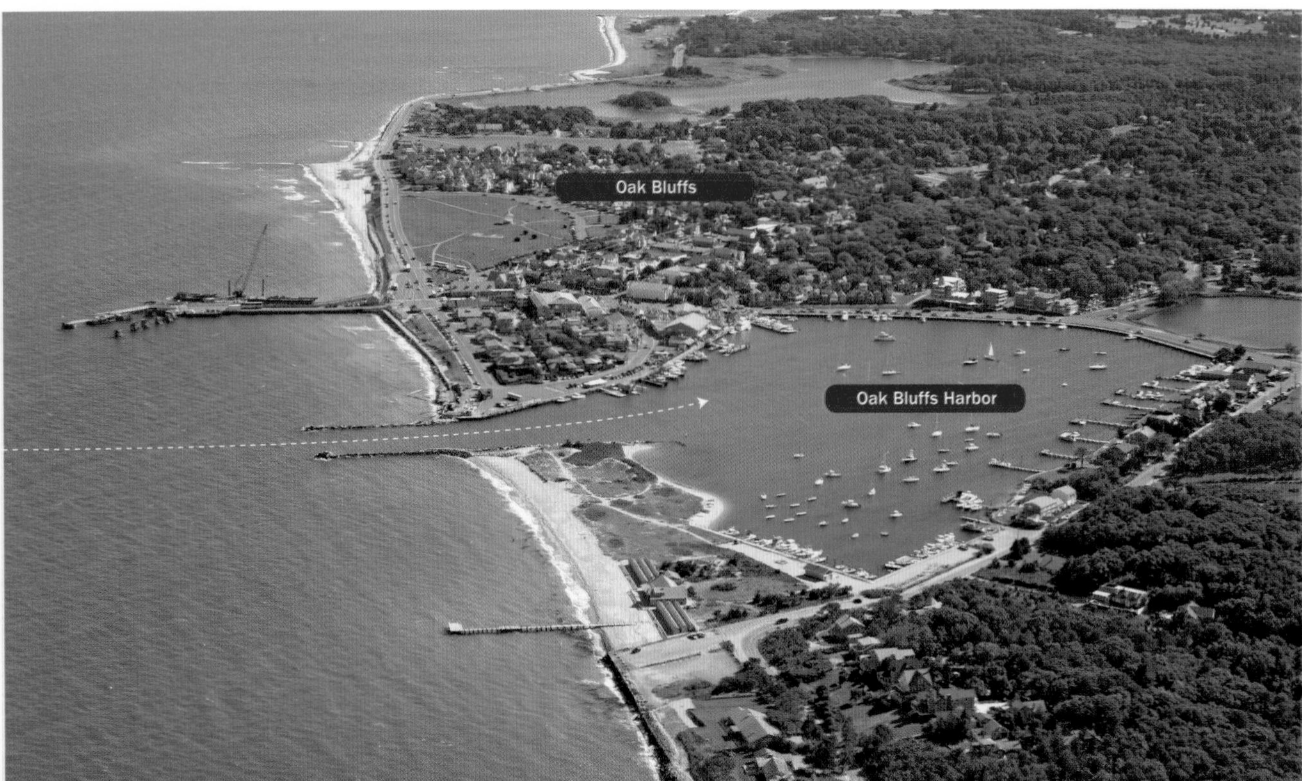

Looking south over Oak Bluffs and Oak Bluffs Harbor. (Not to be used for navigation.) WATERWAY GUIDE PHOTOGRAPHY

because of the careful organization of this harbor, far more mooring and slip space is available here than in either Vineyard Haven or Edgartown. The landlocked harbor has a dredged, breakwatered entry good for 7-foot depths at mean low water. Access is straightforward, marked by a red four-second flashing light atop a 30-foot-high tower at the end of the breakwater to starboard on entry. Be careful during the arrival or departure of the passenger ferry. Sharing space in the harbor channel with this vessel is not advisable.

Dockage and Moorings: The town maintains 50 heavyweight moorings, geared to a rafting ethos appropriate to a small and popular harbor. These unusual pear-shaped floats are marked TOWN OF OAK BLUFFS. You will need your own bridle line if yours is the first boat to attach to one of these moorings. On high-season weekends, expect to raft (up to four boats per mooring—sail with sail, power with power). On this basis, mooring space availability is not normally a problem except on peak summer weekends. Call the Oak Bluffs Marina, Martha's Vineyard, for directions on entry. Later the marina launch will collect the fee, or you can pay at the marina manager's office at harbor's edge. The town has reconstructed (and extended) finger piers along the south side of the harbor to accommodate sizable boats (up to 140 feet) and an additional 120 slips along the west wall for smaller vessels. To reserve a berth, write or call the Marina Manager well in advance of high season, P.O. Box 1327, Oak Bluffs, MA 02557; 508-693-4355; fax 508-693-7402. The Oak Bluffs Marina now provides launch service during the summer season. The Oak Bluffs launch will run from June 29 to Labor Day, from 8 a.m. to 10 p.m.; hail on VHF Channel 71. For cruisers with their own tenders, the dinghy dock can accommodate 100 dinghies. Fresh water is available here, and there are multiple public telephones, municipal restroom and shower facilities, and four trash dumpsters located conveniently around the harbor. This is a No-Discharge Zone; the discharge of effluent (even treated) is illegal.

Two Texaco fuel docks (same private management) are located just beyond the harbormaster's office, to port after entry. Note that it is not possible to take on water while refueling at either of these docks. The management explains that this unusual policy is meant to discourage sailboats from taking up dock space that can be more profitably used for pumping fuel into the larger tanks of power vessels. To replenish water tanks, you will need to contact the Oak Bluffs Marina manager who will direct you to an available town slip.

GOIN' ASHORE: OAK BLUFFS, MA

The Wesley, an authentically preserved Victorian hotel with 62 rooms, dominates the harbor skyline. Crews from boats at the docks or on moorings across the street can purchase showers there, including a towel, face cloth and soap. An arcade filled with tourist shops is on the eastern side of the harbor, and a fair-sized marine supply store and an Italian restaurant are in the area. Bags of ice are available at the fast-food stand at the harbor head, and bike and moped rentals seem to be everywhere. To the left from the harbor, two movie theaters offer nightly features. The Island Theater at the corner of Lake and Circuit avenues has a "bad weather" matinee policy, with 1 p.m. special showings accordingly.

Circuit Avenue (named for the circuit ridden by many of the campground preachers) is the main street for shopping. On the eastern side of Circuit Avenue, the Corner Store sells all manner of sundries, from sunblock to the" Sunday New York Times. Farther along, there is an excellent small supermarket with a good deli department; Vineyard Wine & Cheese Shop has an impressive stock at the island's best prices; long-established Phillips Hardware Store has a surprising collection of hard-to-locate items; and there is a hairstylist and DaRosa's office and art supplies store. About halfway down Circuit Avenue, to the left in a small walking mall, you will find the post office, a bank, and Martha's Vineyard Gourmet Cafe & Bakery. Through the mall and across Kennebec Avenue is Oak Bluffs Laundry.

Restaurants are causal and fast food and breakfast restaurants abound, catering to the ferry trade. Linda Jean's (25 Circuit Ave., 508-693-4093) has modest prices and is especially popular. Various pubs—Giordano's Restaurant and Clam Bar (107 Circuit Ave., 508-693-0184), The Ritz Café (4 Circuit Ave., 508-693-9851) and Offshore Ale Co. (Kennebec Ave, 508-693-2626) serve food and drink. Situated on State Road, John's Fish Market/Sandy's Fish and Chips (508-693-1220) offers fresh seafood and a menu of fresh fried-to-order specialties.

ADDITIONAL RESOURCES:

- Oak Bluffs Association, **www.oakbluffsmv.com**

NEARBY GOLF COURSES:
Mink Meadows Golf Club, 320 Golf Club Road, Vineyard Haven, MA 02568, 508-693-0600

NEARBY MEDICAL FACILITIES:
Martha's Vineyard Hospital, 1 Hospital Road, Vineyard Haven, MA 02568, 508-693-0410

Edgartown

An elegant town that takes itself and its yachting seriously, old Edgartown is beautiful, expensive and crowded in the summer. Many impressive yachts belonging to the rich and famous are moored here in season. Particularly striking are the classic wooden power vessels, kept in peak condition by ever-polishing, multi-member crews. Ashore, elegant antique houses—all meticulously restored—are everywhere. With the help of prevailing sea breezes, grand shade trees provide natural air conditioning, and flowers abound. Famous newscaster Walter Cronkite called Edgartown his home.

NAVIGATION: Use Chart 13233. For Edgartown, use Boston tide tables. For high tide, 57 minutes; for low tide, add 18 minutes. Entry to Edgartown Harbor is relatively simple. However, a line of nuns and buoys, announced on entering the channel at red bell buoy "2," must be observed, leaving them to starboard. They mark multiple rock outcroppings that extend northeast from Middle Flats off Edgartown's Little Beach. Although the inner harbor is deep and well-marked, currents of several knots, at the height of the tidal flow, and distractions from the usual stream of recreational traffic are compounded by frequent and rapid cross-channel transits by the Chappaquiddick ferry, *On Time,* between its Edgartown landing and Chappaquiddick Point. On entering the inner basin, do not cut off green can buoy "9," even though the mooring field beyond it gives the illusion of safe passage. The sandbar between the can and Chappaquiddick Point has snagged many a keel.

Dockage: Though moorings in Edgartown Harbor are numerous, actual dockage is in short supply. Mad Max Marina, located just beyond the town dock to starboard on entry, has deepwater transient slips available during the season, but the demand for them is great. Advance arrangements are suggested. Otherwise, the Edgartown harbormaster controls some 700 moorings in the harbor, about 100 of which are reserved for transients on a first-come, first-served basis. A new online reservation system (www.edgartownharbor.com) is available, but it is still advisable to arrive early in the day to secure your reserved mooring. Early arrivals should call on VHF Channel 09 for availability and directions. Launch service is available from Old Port Marine (VHF Channel 68, operating 8 a.m. to midnight). You can take in your trash on the launch (or in your dinghy) for disposal in the dumpster at dockside.

The town runs the fuel station at North Wharf, where there are also showers and restrooms. Fresh water may be taken on from the water barge just off North Wharf. Propane refills, however, will require a trip to the Vineyard Propane (508-693-5080) at Dukes County Airport, some distance inland.

Edgartown takes the problem of pollution seriously; boats are forbidden to discharge sewage of any kind (even treated) into harbor waters. A free pump-out station, operating 9 a.m. to 5 p.m., is stationed on Memorial Wharf (the one with the roof and walkway on top, next to the *On Time* ferry landing). In addition, the town pump-out boat is on call (VHF Channel 74) with free service to all those anchored out or on moorings.

Anchorage: Shortly before entering Edgartown's inner harbor, you will find ample anchorage space (increasingly popular with large charter vessels and schooners) off Sturgeon Flats on the northerly side of Chappaquiddick Island in 8- to 16-foot depths at low water. This area is exposed to the north, however, and likely will challenge your comfort levels in all but the calmest weather.

Inside the harbor, anchoring is no longer permitted in the crowded mooring field east of the harbor channel, but ample swing room and good holding usually await cruising visitors south of the mooring area along the Chappaquiddick shore; good holding always can be found in upper Katama Bay. Keep an eye on the harbor chart and your depth sounder, on approaching an appealing spot, particularly as you head south, farther into the bay.

Katama Bay is reasonably well-protected from all but strong southerly winds, and it continues to be a naturalist's delight. Ospreys, terns, whippoorwills and a variety of

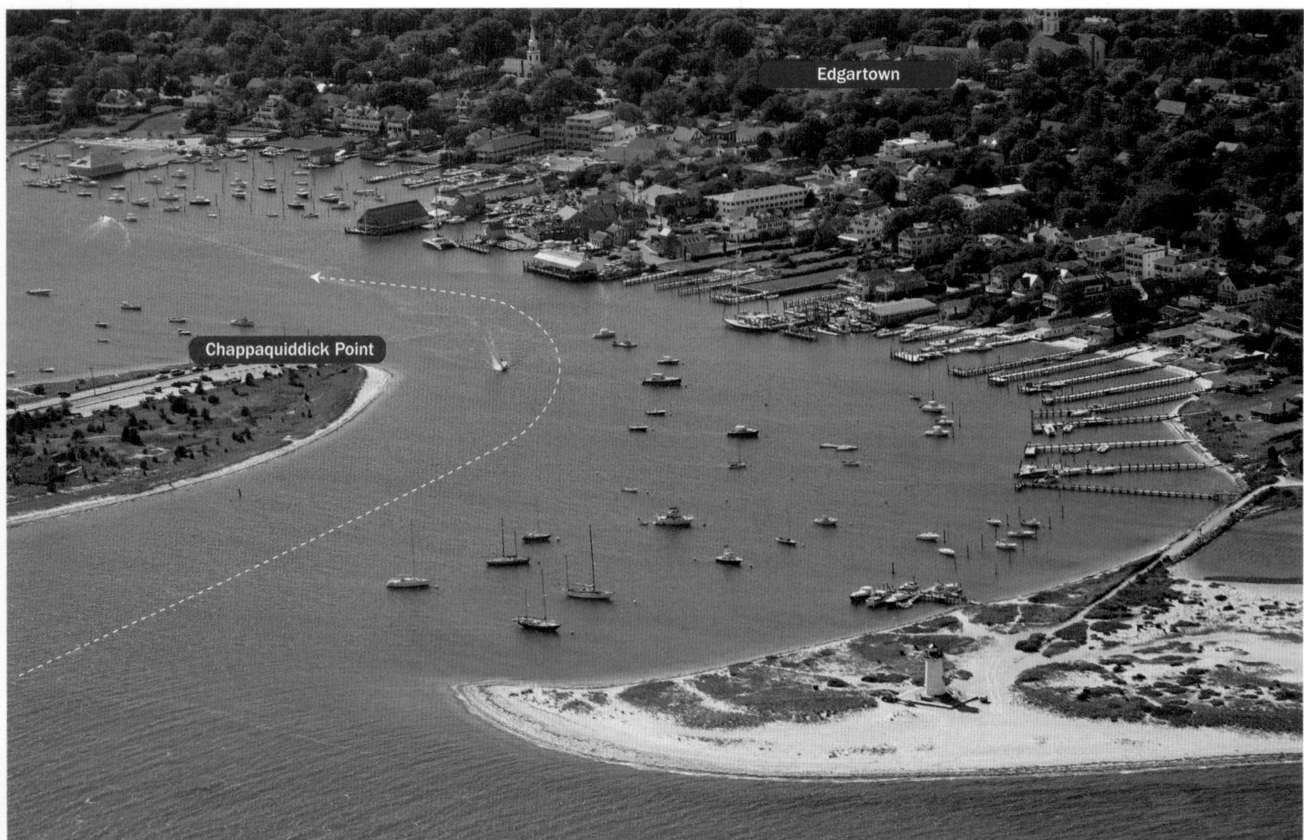

Looking southwest over Edgartown and Chappaquiddick Point. (Not to be used for navigation.) WATERWAY GUIDE PHOTOGRAPHY

gulls all seem to thrive here. Near-deserted South Beach, one of the most unspoiled and beautiful in the islands, is a relatively easy motorized dinghy ride from almost any spot in the bay. Check with the Edgartown harbormaster before anchoring anywhere in town waters.

An additional and exceptionally pleasant day anchorage can be found in Cape Poge Bay on Chappaquiddick. The narrow passage into the bay is marked by green can buoy "7," located about a thousand yards due west of the entry. Shoaling restricts the passage of deep-draft boats much beyond North Neck, and cautious skippers might choose to anchor before reaching the inner shallows preceding the 9- to 10-foot-deep center bay. The approximately 2-foot tidal range here should discourage boats of more than a 4-foot draft from attempting passage to the inner bay even on a rising tide. The town of Edgartown no longer permits overnight anchorage on Cape Poge Bay.

The town dinghy dock (located in front of the Navigator Restaurant, next to the Edgartown Yacht Club) is always overcrowded on mid-summer weekends. For this reason, the town has added an additional landing area at North Wharf.

GOIN' ASHORE: **EDGARTOWN, MA**

Lining the harbor, gracious homes of long-ago sea captains suggest unspoken tales of whale oil, mutinous crews and wooden ships lost in frigid seas while anxious wives paced the widow's walks above. Many of these restored houses along the tree-lined streets are now elegant shops with goods and services to match almost any desire. Within just a few blocks of the harbor you will encounter a near endless variety of nautical and sportswear and gift shops: Fligor's Department Store (east of Main Street on North Water Street); Martha's Vineyard National Bank (with ATM and major credit card services, corner of Main and North Water streets); The Paper Store for current newspapers and sundries; and Bickerton and Ripley bookstore for a large selection of beach novels and current releases. The building housing the U.S. Post Office (Church Street, just east of Main Street) doubles as the municipal transportation center. There you can catch a bus for South Beach (every 15 minutes between 10 a.m. and 6:30 p.m.). Frequently scheduled buses also depart for Oak Bluffs and Vineyard Haven, less frequently for Gay Head (Aquinnah). Clustered around the waterfront are interesting galleries, including one that specializes in marine models. Here also is the Chappaquiddick ferry landing (immediately east of the town wharf), where *On Time*—both of them—make short but frequent transits (7:30 a.m. to midnight).

Reprovisioning possibilities are limited in the immediate harbor area, though a couple of small, classy convenience stores do sell some of the basics, plus beer and wine. More complete grocery shopping requires a trip farther afield, most easily and cheaply on the town's colorful trolley, which stops nearest the harbor at the parking lot in front of Among the Flowers Café (North Water Street and Mayhew Lane). The trolley makes the several-miles transit to Mariner's Landing on Upper Main Street, allowing stops to accommodate your shopping needs along the way. En route you will notice a retail

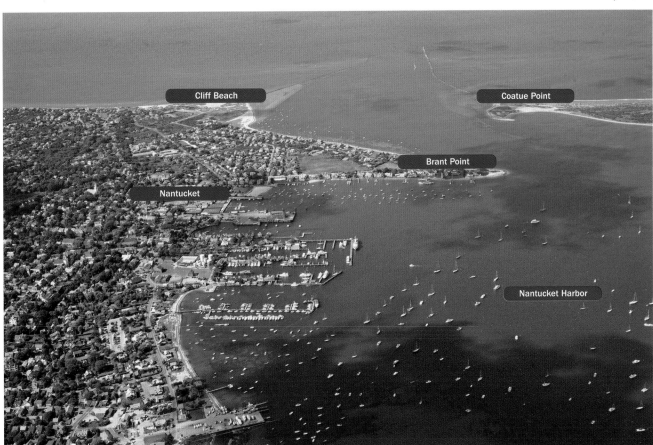

Looking north over Nantucket Harbor. (Not to be used for navigation.) WATERWAY GUIDE PHOTOGRAPHY

seafood shop, major supermarket, Shiretown Meat Market (just below the market) and a liquor store. Near the harbor, Edgartown Books (44 Main St.) has author signings all summer, taking advantage of the great number of writers who make their home on Martha's Vineyard. A short block away is Scoops, purveyor of excellent homemade ice cream, espresso and other coffee delights.

Edgartown offers an almost overwhelming variety of restaurants, ranging from open-air-casual to the most elegant. The Navigator Restaurant and Boathouse Bar at the foot of Main Street (in front of the town dinghy dock) is reliable for plentiful hors d'oeuvres, hearty New England fare, drinks and a bustling harbor view. The same may be said of the nearby Seafood Shanty (31 Dock St., 508-627-8622), with live music on weekends. David Ryan's (11 N. Water St., 508-627-4100) serves café-style downstairs and elegant entrees upstairs. For the ambience and cuisine of a creative Parisian-style bistro, there is Alchemy (71 Main St., 508-627-9999). By most accounts, L'Etoile at the Charlotte Inn (27 S. Summer St., 508-627-4151, by reservation nightly in season, 6:30 p.m. to 9:45 p.m.) is acclaimed as the island's finest for premier continental dining. Lure (25 Dunes Road) offers fine dining and complimentary water taxi service from Edgartown harbor; call 508-627-3663 for more information.

Martha's Vineyard offers some unique shore experiences. Late season visitors can wander the twisting turning courses of the cornfield mazes at the Farm Institute (508-627-7007). Naturalists will enjoy a guided kayak tour of the Felix Neck Wildlife Sanctuary (508-627-4850), and for fishermen, the Martha's Vineyard Striped Bass and Bluefish Derby is run in September and October of each year. The 2010 running will be the 65th year of this great event.

ADDITIONAL RESOURCES:

- Town of Edgartown, **www.edgartown-ma.us**

NEARBY GOLF COURSES:
Mink Meadows Golf Club, 320 Golf Club Road, Vineyard Haven, MA 02568, 508-693-0600

NEARBY MEDICAL FACILITIES:
Martha's Vineyard Hospital, 1 Hospital Road, Vineyard Haven, MA 02568, 508-693-0410

■ NANTUCKET

American Indians aptly named Nantucket—the word means, "land far at sea." Whaling dominates both the history and current mystique of this far-flung and naturally barren sea island. By 1700, islanders—Europeans and Indians alike—had already begun the serious pursuit of whales in long boats from the shore. Half a century later, Nantucket had become preeminent in the American whaling industry. Until the economic basis for whaling collapsed with the efficient recovery of petroleum in the late 19th century, whaling dominated almost every aspect of Nantucket life and was the sole basis of island wealth.

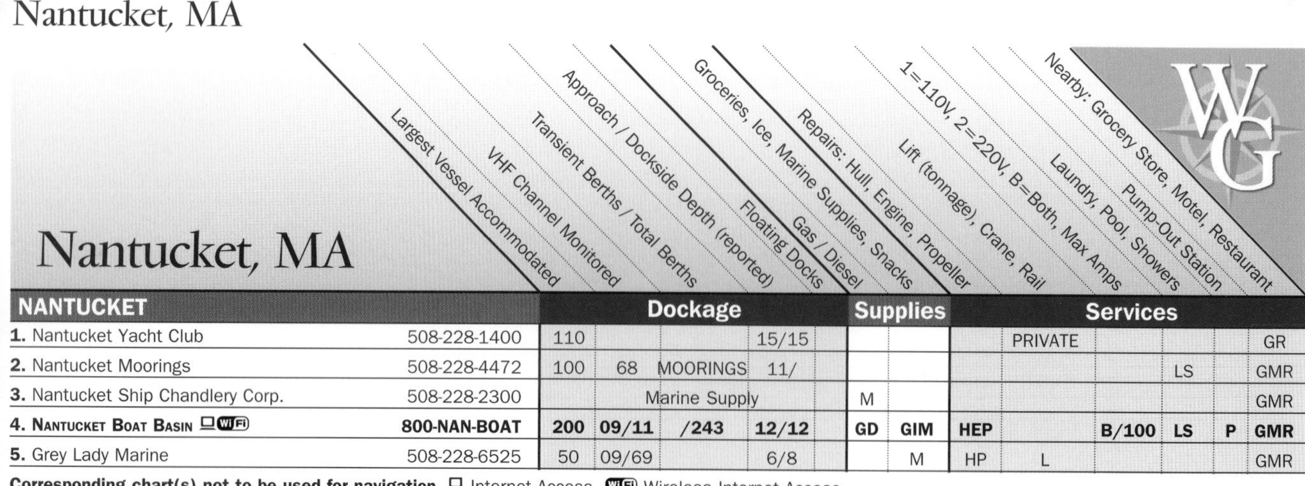

Nantucket, MA

NANTUCKET		Largest Vessel Accommodated	VHF Channel Monitored	Transient Berths / Total Berths	Approach / Dockside Depth (reported)	Floating Docks	Gas / Diesel	Groceries, Ice, Marine Supplies, Snacks	Repairs: Hull, Engine, Propeller	Lift (tonnage), Crane, Rail	1=110V, 2=220V, B=Both, Max Amps	Laundry, Pool, Showers	Pump-Out Station	Nearby: Grocery Store, Motel, Restaurant
		Dockage					Supplies		Services					
1. Nantucket Yacht Club	508-228-1400	110			15/15					PRIVATE				GR
2. Nantucket Moorings	508-228-4472	100	68	MOORINGS	11/							LS		GMR
3. Nantucket Ship Chandlery Corp.	508-228-2300			Marine Supply			M							GMR
4. Nantucket Boat Basin	**800-NAN-BOAT**	**200**	**09/11**	**/243**	**12/12**		**GD**	**GIM**	**HEP**		**B/100**	**LS**	**P**	**GMR**
5. Grey Lady Marine	508-228-6525	50	09/69		6/8			M	HP	L				GMR

Corresponding chart(s) not to be used for navigation. Internet Access Wireless Internet Access

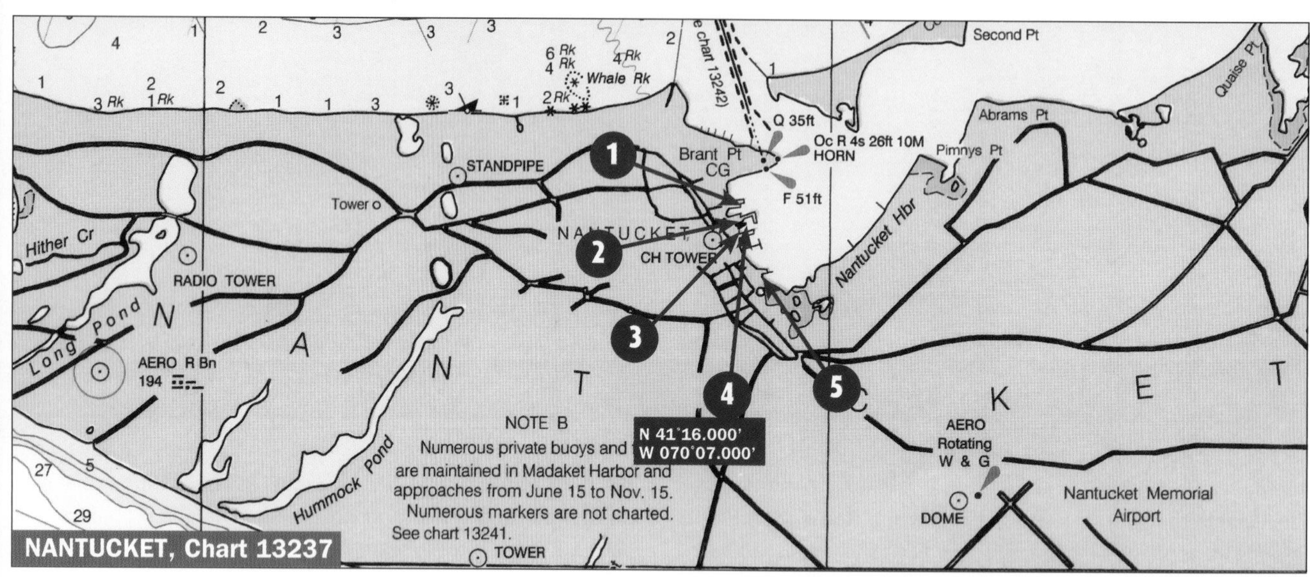

NANTUCKET, Chart 13237

Today, Nantucket's wealth is largely imported from the mainland via fashionable summer residents, itinerant yachtsmen and an army of tourists.

NAVIGATION: Use Chart 13241. For Nantucket, Great Point, use Boston tide tables. For high tide, add 43 minutes; for low tide, add 28 minutes. A passage to Nantucket crosses some 30 miles of open water, and may call for some navigation in fog. The journey to Nantucket from the west is between shoals: south of Horseshoe Shoal; north of Hawes, Norton and Cross Rip shoals; and then east of Tuckernuck Shoal. The closer to the shoals your course, the more noticeable the tidal rips will be.

Aids to navigation are widely spaced. Frequent dead reckoning and GPS fixes should be considered mandatory, as is a keen lookout (with radar if possible) for other recreational boats, fishing vessels and ferries that frequent these much-traveled waters. If, as sometimes happens, the sky is clear and the water sparkling, the island stands out in spectacular fashion, though its highest point is only 108 feet above sea level. The red-and-white bell buoy "NB" marks the entrance to the buoyed 1.5-mile channel leading to Brant Point. Semi-submerged breakwaters to either side reveal the danger of straying beyond the channel's confines. A navigational range (two towers: the first a quick-flashing light, and the second a constant light) will come into view directly down the center of the channel, situated just west of the Brant Point Lighthouse. Follow the channel buoys while rounding the lighthouse to starboard, with a watchful eye for ferryboats and other vessels that must also negotiate this relatively narrow passage. Once beyond Brant Point, the Nantucket Boat Basin becomes immediately evident ahead, and just to the south of the boat basin enclosure, the town pier usually has a raft of fishing vessels tied to its T-shaped end. To the east of the wide inner-harbor channel upon entry, a large mooring field also should be visible.

Dockage: Nantucket Boat Basin sets an industry standard for service at its transient marina. You will find 243 slips to accommodate boats from 30 to 280 feet (with some exceptions for smaller boats), as well as dockside electricity, water, fuels (including propane refills), ice, public phones and waste disposal—with individualized pump-out stations designed to reach virtually every slip. Ashore are restroom and shower facilities, a large 24-hour coin-operated laundry, rental cottages, rustic artists' studios along the wharves and even a park for "animal needs." The Boat Basin's concierge, whose headquarters is located on the fuel dock, will arrange restaurant reservations, sightseeing trips, car rentals, medical appointments and baby-sitting services. The Nantucket Boat Basin

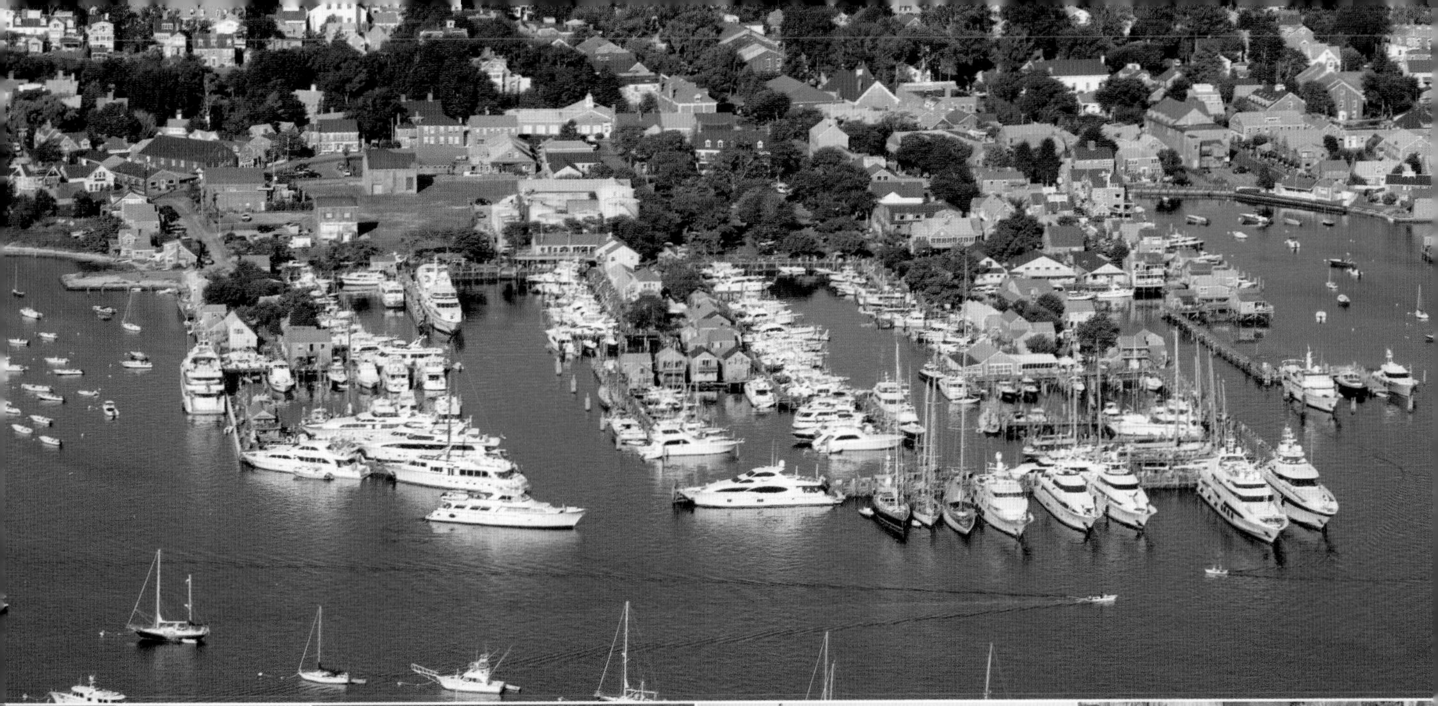

A world-class marina on a breathtaking island. What moor could one ask?

Nantucket Boat Basin caters to some of the world's most discerning travelers, welcoming them to the island of Nantucket. With its eclectic mix of shops, restaurants, and galleries set amidst miles of stunning coastal scenery, Nantucket is a rare blend of unique charm and natural beauty. And as a world-class marina just one block from downtown Nantucket, the Boat Basin offers a travel experience that's always perfection, from ship to shore.

240 SLIPS | COMPLETE AMENITIES | CONCIERGE SERVICE | AWARD-WINNING RESTAURANTS | LUXURY SPA ACCESS

800.NAN-BOAT   nantucketboatbasin.com   Open year round

NANTUCKET. UNFORGETTABLE STAYS.

Nantucket Island Resorts owns a unique collection of premier hotels, cottages, island residences, and a marina.

WHITE ELEPHANT • WHITE ELEPHANT HOTEL RESIDENCES • THE WAUWINET • JARED COFFIN HOUSE
THE COTTAGES & LOFTS • NANTUCKET BOAT BASIN

nantucketislandresorts.com

offers wireless Internet access (Wi-Fi) throughout their facility. The management recommends early reservations (before March) for this popular end-destination marina; many peak-season weekends are booked as much as a year in advance. There is not likely to be any other slip space available on the island.

Nantucket Moorings Inc. holds the exclusive town franchise for transient moorings, and maintains a field of 125 round white floats secured by heavy tackle. Expect to pay daily rates for these (without other services) that are among the highest in New England. Even at this premium, the popularity of this destination harbor is such that an advance reservation is highly recommended. For an extra fee, Harbor Launch (VHF Channel 68) will provide reliable service, (on a mooring or at anchor) and their dock ashore will dispose of your trash. On calm days, the town dock (south of the highly visible Nantucket Boat Basin fuel dock) is within relatively easy dinghy distance of the mooring field. One of these dinghy docks is found just inside the southern side of the town's T-shaped pier. Farther toward shore, a loading float will accommodate boats with up to 5-foot drafts at low tide. A second, larger dinghy float complex is on the north side of the pier closer to shore.

Water is available at the T-end of the town pier, where you will also find a free pump-out station. (Access to these facilities is often blocked by a raft of commercial fishing boats.) At the head of the dock, just behind the harbormaster's office, are restrooms, showers and a public phone. To the side of the harbormaster's office, on the right, recycling bins require separation of cans, aluminum, plastic and glass, and a dumpster is available for mixed trash. You can purchase bags of cube ice inside the office. The center of town is a pleasant two-block walk to the right from here.

The harbormaster requests that new arrivals check in with him as soon as they are secured, primarily to inform them of the harbor's clean waters policy and other restrictions. Nantucket is a federal No-Discharge Zone: no dumping of sewage—treated or untreated—is permitted; holding tanks must be used; and heads must be sealed. In addition to the town's pump-out station at the end of the town dock, Nantucket Boat Basin offers courtesy pump-out service at its fuel dock, immediately north of the municipal pier. And for boats on moorings or at anchor, the town operates a free pump-out boat: call "Head Hunter" on VHF Channel 09 or contact the harbormaster (also VHF Channel 09 or 508-228-7260) for pump-out hours and availability.

Anchorage: Anchorage space in the "General Anchorage" defined in NOAA Chart 13242 is almost completely filled with moorings. Some limited anchor room still remains due east of the Coast Guard station in 15 to 20 feet of water. Holding is excellent here in hard sand. However, this area is quite exposed and can be bouncy in all but the calmest weather (a seeming rarity in Nantucket). When the wind pipes up from the northwest, expect 3-foot waves or greater—chain (even in calm weather) is the preferred rode. Somewhat quieter ground may be found east of the extensive shoaling area in east center harbor (see NOAA Chart 13242). There you will find more sand (and some grass) in 7- to 12-foot depths at low water. Since the shoal is unmarked, nose your way in carefully to avoid grounding. Or if you do not mind a considerable dinghy ride to town, there is plenty of swing room and 7- to 19-foot depths in the second harbor bay to the east, beyond First Point. Holding is spotty (more grass), but the scenery is splendid. Wherever you anchor in Nantucket Harbor, the protection afforded by a nearby "landmass" seen on the chart is deceptive—low-lying dunes just do not block the wind. The fetch is considerable, particularly from the east and northwest, portending wet dinghy (even launch) rides and rock-and-roll evenings during all but the most settled weather.

GOIN' ASHORE: NANTUCKET, MA

Nantucket's cobblestone streets are bordered by the extraordinary Colonial, Georgian and Greek Revival houses of ship's captains and whaling merchants. Many of the buildings of the time are also still intact: the Pacific National Bank, built in 1818 with whaling money; the Pacific Club, circa 1772; and the Old Mill, built in 1746, with its still-operational, wind-driven wooden machinery. The Nantucket Whaling Museum (13 Broad St., call 508-228-1894 for hours and prices), operated by the Nantucket Historical Association, has a world-class collection of whaling artifacts, exhibits and tours, adding to an understanding of the lore and technique of this bygone era. A new addition is a fully reconstructed 46-foot-long sperm whale skeleton that is now on display at the museum. The Nantucket Life-Saving Museum (158 Polpis Road, 508-228-1885) offers a window on the danger and daring heroics of the whaling era, when you had to go to sea, but "did not have to come back."

In and around Nantucket's architectural and historical treasures, the village offers a surprising variety of goods and services. The Pacific National Bank, at the head of Main Street's cobblestone shopping district, offers full banking services and an ATM (inside only). Murray's Toggery, adjacent to the bank, provides traditional clothing for good value, including the authentic Nantucket Reds. Island Pursuits, at the east end of Main Street, offers nautical clothing and foul weather gear. Mitchell's Book Corner (corner of Main and Orange streets) is crowded with books, knowledgeable sales personnel and eager patrons. A number of shops sell classic Nantucket Lightship baskets, faithfully reproduced by local artisans with scrimshaw decorations of authentic-looking "whalebone." The Four Winds Craft Guild on Straight Wharf has a particularly striking selection of these baskets, priced at $800 and up, and various jewelers in town carry versions of them—miniaturized in gold and silver—at equally distinctive prices. Both the post office and the Athenaeum Library are on Federal Street, two short blocks north of Main Street. The Athenaeum is worth a visit on architectural merit alone, but you will also find current newspapers and periodicals there. The movie theater is on South Water Street just north of Main Street. Nantucket Ship Chandlery on Old South Wharf carries marine hardware, including difficult-to-find items and an impressive selection of accessories and supplies. The Chandlery will arrange overnight shipment of parts not on hand.

For complete reprovisioning, a full-sized grocery store is at the head of Nantucket Boat Basin on Salem Street (with an ATM and public phones outside). Nantucket All Serve (508-228-8170 or VHF Channel 69) will bring out a grocery order to your boat for a delivery charge. All Serve also makes morning coffee, muffin and newspaper deliveries and evening seafood dinner deliveries. All Serve will also deliver fresh water-tank refills and make arrangements for engine, rigging and sail repairs, diving services, laundry and propane refills.

There is an excellent retail seafood store just inland of the steamboat wharf on Broad Street. Straight Wharf Fish Store, next to the bandstand, also has a fine fresh-catch selection. Bartlett's Ocean View Farm, at the corner of Main and Federal streets, trucks in fresh Nantucket-grown produce for street-side sale daily (except Sunday), 9 a.m. to 1 p.m. Nantucket Gourmet (India Street, just west of Federal Street) has a small deli counter with prepackaged delicacies ("saffron risotto with truffle butter and baby onions," for example). Murray's Beverages on lower Main Street has an ample supply of wine, spirits, gourmet nibbles, premium cigars and Cisco Brewer's local micro, Whale's Tale Pale Ale.

Nantucket's restaurants are numerous and varied. For casual food and drink with a harbor view, you can take your pick on Straight Wharf and Old South Wharf, including The Ropewalk (508-228-8886), overlooking the docks of the basin. A short walk through the village broadens these possibilities almost endlessly. The Brotherhood of Thieves (23 Broad St., 508-228-2551) serves up a robust atmosphere along with casual food and live entertainment nightly—frequented by the college set. Up the scale a bit, Woodbox Inn (36 Fair St., 508-228-0587) also serves a tantalizing breakfast menu and traditional American-style dinners in a beautiful old-inn setting (circa 1709). The Boarding House and the Pearl (12 Federal St., 508-228-9622) make the choices of exquisite entrees and extras doubly difficult. Le Languedoc Inn & Bistro (24 Broad St., 508-228-2552), though moderately priced, offers excellent continental cuisine in a quiet, intimate setting. 21 Federal (508-228-2121) has a stellar wine list to accompany dishes such as "sautéed halibut with foie gras butter" and "pasta with thyme-saffron and smoked tomato sauces with crabmeat-stuffed shrimp."

The Chanticleer in Sciasconset (9 New St., 508-257-4499) is well worth the taxi ride for those who seek one of the most sophisticated menus and finest dining experiences in New England, with a truly extraordinary wine cellar to match. Either lunch or dinner here is likely to be the season's highlight experience. For lighter fare and a far more modest price, also in Siasconset, try the 'Sconset Café (8 Main St., 508-257-4008).

Traveling around the island is best done by bicycle—your own or one rented at one of the four bike rental companies in the downtown area. Young's Bicycle Shop has been in business on Steamboat Wharf since 1931, currently renting bicycles, cars, jeeps and SUV's (508-228-1151).

ADDITIONAL RESOURCES:

- Nantucket Net, **www.nantucket.net**
- Nantucket Island Chamber of Commerce, **www.nantucketchamber.org**

NEARBY GOLF COURSES:
Miacomet Golf Club, 12 W. Miacomet Road, Nantucket, MA 02554, 508-325-0333, **www.miacometgolf.com**

NEARBY MEDICAL FACILITIES:
Nantucket Cottage Hospital, 7 S. Prospect St. Nantucket, MA 02554, 508-228-1200

Cruising Options

Mariners who chose to leave the Islands to head for Cape Cod Bay will not be disappointed. Here are the charming ports of Plymouth, Marblehead and Gloucester, among others. ■

Low tide on the island of Nantucket off the coast of Massachusetts.

Section Contents

Cape Cod Bay to Boston	383
Massachusetts Bay to Portsmouth	406
Kittery to Cape Small	431
Sequin Island to Pemaquid Point	451
Muscongus Bay to Rockland	467
Penobscot Bay to Eastport	482

MAINE
Eastport
Bangor
Bucks Harbor
Belfast
Bar Harbor
Camden
Southwest Harbor
Frenchman Bay
Rockport
Mt. Desert Island
Rockland
Isle au Haut
Bath
Penobscot Bay
Freeport
Muscongus Bay
Yarmouth
Falmouth
Portland
Casco Bay
Boothbay Harbor
Cape Elizabeth
Saco
Kennebunkport
York Village
Kittery
Portsmouth
Isles of Shoals
NEW HAMPSHIRE
Hampton
Gulf of Maine
Newburyport
Cape Ann
Gloucester
Marblehead
Massachusetts Bay
Boston
Weymouth
Provincetown
Plymouth
MASSACHUSETTS
Cape Cod Bay
Atlantic Ocean

N

WWW.WATERWAYGUIDE.COM

Planning

- Tide Tables 521
- GPS Waypoints 532

Above Cape Cod

Maine Tourism

The passage through or around the crooked elbow of Cape Cod marks a major step for most coastal cruising plans—and the entrance into an endless mariner's paradise. WATERWAY GUIDE covers the waters from Cape Cod Bay to eastern Maine in the following six chapters.

From the northeastern entrance of the Cape Cod Canal, WATERWAY GUIDE travels around Cape Cod Bay, and then clockwise up the coast of Massachusetts to Boston Harbor. From there, we cover the glorious North Shore, home for a great number of sailors and sailing vessels of all sizes at Marblehead, Manchester and Gloucester. Around Cape Ann, the mariner faces the open waters of the Gulf of Maine and New Hampshire, with the prominent harbors of Portsmouth, Kittery and York, and the remote Isles of Shoals. In Maine, WATERWAY GUIDE explores the bays and marinas from York all the way up the coast to Eastport, at the Canadian border. This comprehensive coverage includes the bays and islands along the way as well as the amenities and favorite haunts available to the cruising mariner.

Maritime Heritage

The cold waters north and east of Cape Cod are the birthplace of much of America's maritime heritage. Every harbor and almost every ledge carries a piece of American history or a legend of the sea. Cruising these waters gives the modern-day sailor a strong feeling of sea tradition. The fastest sailing ships the world has ever known sailed out of these ports—the great clipper ships *Flying Cloud, Sovereign of the Seas* and *Lightning,* among others. And what are considered the most seaworthy and able sailing vessels ever built, the huge Gloucester fishing schooners, made their fame and fortune fishing the Grand Banks in the dead of winter. They were designed and built along the river banks near Cape Ann. And, of course, there is always the *Mayflower,* a replica of which is now berthed at Plymouth.

To cruise "above the Cape" is to venture farther away from civilization and the recreational boating crowds. Self-sufficiency and competent seamanship become more important. The water is colder, the fog is thicker and the ledges are crueler in the swells of the open ocean. The sea here can be less forgiving to carelessness and inexperience than any other waters covered in WATERWAY GUIDE. There are no barrier islands offering an "inside passage" and protection from the sweep of the sea.

Tides

The rise and fall of the tide is an important factor in each day's plans, especially as you voyage farther east. Ten-foot tides are not unusual in these parts, and WATERWAY GUIDE mentions tidal conditions in each section. Keep in mind that all harbors are available to even the deepest-draft vessels at high tide, but that same tide can put you high and dry where hours earlier there was plenty of water underneath the keel. Furthermore, that ledge at the mouth of the harbor, clearly visible as you enter at low water, might be submerged and dangerous when you leave. Tidal currents are less predictable than they are below Cape Cod and, in fact, are less of a factor for the navigator, except in river mouths.

Distances—Mass. Waters

This table provides both point-to-point and cumulative distances from the Cape Cod Canal and from Boston. All measurements are given in approximate nautical miles.

LOCATION	BETWEEN POINTS	CUMULATIVE
EAST FROM CAPE COD CANAL		
Cape Cod Canal	0	0
Barnstable	10	10
Sesuit Harbor	7	17
Wellfleet	12	29
Provincetown	25	54
NORTH FROM CAPE COD CANAL		
Cape Cod Canal	0	0
Plymouth	20	20
Duxbury	2	22
Scituate	18	40
Cohasset	6	46
Boston	15	61
NORTH FROM BOSTON		
Boston	0	0
Marblehead	19	19
Salem	5	24
Beverly	1	25
Manchester	6	31
Gloucester	5	36
Rockport	17	53
Essex	8	61
Newburyport	16	77
Rye	15	92
Portsmouth	6	98
Isles of Shoals (offshore)	7	105

Cruising Conditions

A skipper whose ambitions exceed his abilities, whose schedule requires a daily quota of miles regardless of the weather and whose gear cannot hold up to rigorous use, can make things rough on himself and his crew. A voyage in these waters warrants considerable preparation and flexibility. A journey from one harbor to another will probably involve a stretch of open water, so skipper, crew and vessel must be prepared for the challenge. The water is markedly colder than the water below the Cape, and the vessel's water supply and hull will feel much cooler as a result. Most cruising boats have a small heating stove to warm up the cabin on cool mornings. Swimming is a more venturesome exercise, and an accidental swim must be considered a matter of life or death, because hypothermia is a risk even in the summer.

Fog can be a factor on any day (especially in June and July) even if it "burns off" by mid-morning and leaves a clear, warm day. The skipper making his way through "a pea-souper" for the first time is likely to take his navigational skills more seriously forever after. Fog is usually accompanied by calm waters and light winds, but beware the "smoky sou'wester." During this condition, a stiff breeze builds up rough seas that break on the ledges and obscure the sounds of bells and gongs. And if the fog remains heavy, obscuring islands, buoys and other boats, it is advisable to stay put in the harbor.

Dockage

Finding a slip every night can be very difficult for the itinerant mariner. Below Cape Ann, slips and full-service marinas are readily available, but they fill up rapidly in the peak season. If you require dockside services to load or unload provisions or crew, or for shore power, plan to arrive at your chosen harbor early in the afternoon. Most marinas will not reserve space until you are within VHF radio range, so get in early.

Moorings are a pleasant alternative in New England waters. Almost all harbors have moorings for transients, which are normally maintained by local yacht clubs, nearby marinas or by the towns themselves. Charges are usually about $25 to $35 per mooring per night (somewhat less in Maine), and may include launch service, shoreside amenities such as showers and phones and a dinghy dock. The mooring buoys sometimes indicate their availability, their charge per night or their weight. If the buoy is not marked, do not pick it up until authorized to do so by the harbormaster or the launch operator.

Anchoring is de rigueur in New England waters, and most boats carry a big hook ready to heave over the side. In the rocky harbors of Maine, a fisherman anchor (also called a yachtsman) will hold where a burying type (a plow or Danforth) will not. Buoy these anchors though, in case they snag a fluke under a rock ledge.

Equipment

Almost all cruising vessels now take advantage of some form of electronic aid to navigation, particularly GPS (Global Positioning System) receivers and radar. Though a few (very few) hearty traditionalists continue to rely on the bare minimum—compass and watch—for dead reckoning, the prevalence of fog, swift tidal currents, increased boat traffic and widespread availability of reliable electronics now encourage most skippers and their insurance carriers to adopt a more sophisticated (and safer) approach. Today most recreational vessels venturing any distance in New England waters, especially those headed "Down East," will carry an impressive array of electronic gear. Still most important among them, in addition to GPS, are a good VHF radio for weather reports and communications, a calibrated compass and up-to-date charts.

In addition, cruising boats should carry high-mounted radar reflectors and a neoprene wet suit for the crew's most able swimmer in the event of a prop's fouling among the ever-present lobster pot warps. Serious Maine cruisers may even go to the extreme of caging their props to prevent repeated entanglements. ■

Distances—Down East

This table provides point-to-point mileage for the Maine coast. All distances are given in approximate nautical miles.

LOCATION	MILES
SAND COAST	
Kittery	0
York Harbor	11
Wells Harbor	14
Kennebunk River	5
Cape Porpoise Harbor	5
Biddeford/Saco	15
CASCO BAY	
Portland Head Light	19
Falmouth Foreside	7
Yarmouth	8
South Freeport	8
Potts Harbor, Harpswell Neck (from Portland Light)	11
Mackerel Cove, Bailey Island	6
SEGUIN ISLAND TO MUSCONGUS BAY	
Seguin Island	15
Bath, Kennebec River	12
Ebencock Harbor, Sheepscot River (from Seguin Island)	8
Boothbay Harbor (from Seguin Island)	10
Christmas Cove, Damariscotta River	6
Pemaquid Point	4
Monhegan Island	9
Friendship (from Pemaquid Point)	12
PENOBSCOT BAY	
Rockland (from Pemaquid Point)	31
Rockport	6
Camden	5
Dark Harbor, Isleboro Island	7
Belfast	11
Castine (from Rockland)	22
Stonington, Deer Isle (from Rockland)	20
Carvers Harbor, Vinalhaven (from Rockland)	13
Isle au Haut	11
MOUNT DESERT/FRENCHMAN BAY	
Southwest/Northeast Harbors	28
Bar Harbor	12
Winter Harbor	6
EAST OF SCHOODIC POINT	
Petit Manan Island (from Bar Harbor)	17
Jonesport	17
Machiasport	20
Cutler	13
West Quoddy Head	15
Lubec	3
Eastport	3

Cape Cod Bay to Boston

CHARTS 13236, 13246, 13249, 13250, 13251, 13253, 13267, 13269, 13270, 13272, 13274

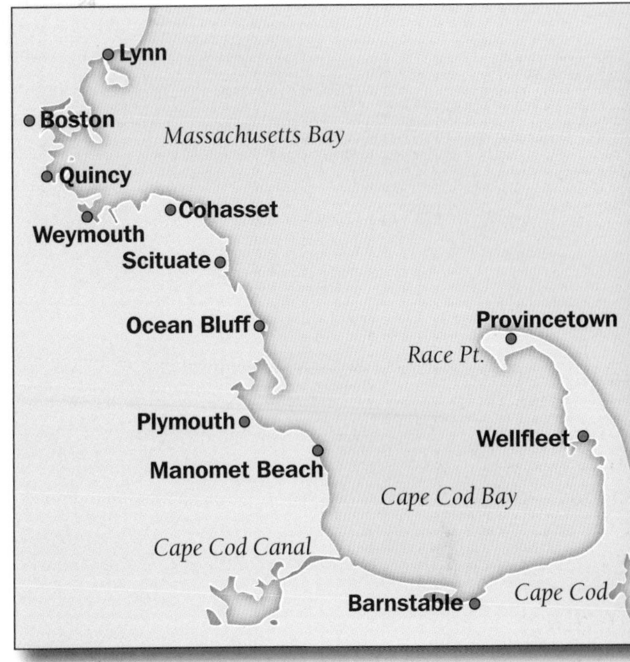

MASSACHUSETTS WATERS

Cape Cod is a peninsula that forms the eastern end of Massachusetts. It extends out easterly 31 miles from the mainland, and then turns 25 miles northward. In contrast to the resort atmosphere on the other side of the Cape Cod "hook," the ambience on Cape Cod Bay is quiet and relaxed. Even the weather cooperates. The boisterous southwester that creates heavy seas in Buzzards Bay can become a pleasant offshore wind on Cape Cod Bay. North of Plymouth, flats, shoals, ledges and rocks appear, big headlands and capes thrust outward and harbors are spaced far apart.

From the eastern end of Cape Cod Canal, many boats choose the long offshore run. They head directly for Cape Ann, then for Portland Harbor's large navigational buoy (which replaced the old lightship) and on to Seguin or Monhegan Island. Along the way northeastward, they might put in at Isles of Shoals or Portsmouth Harbor.

Most boats cruise the coast to explore the lovely ports from Plymouth to Boston, Marblehead and Gloucester, and then on to Portsmouth and the beginning of the Maine coast.

In these pages, Waterway Guide covers the Cape Cod Canal east around the inside of the hook to Provincetown. Then starting up the western shore of Cape Cod Bay, beginning at Plymouth, Waterway Guide harbor-hops into Massachusetts Bay and Boston.

CAPE COD BAY

Cape Cod Canal

Heavily traveled, well-marked and attractive, the (toll-free) Cape Cod Canal cuts across the neck of Cape Cod from Buzzards Bay to Cape Cod Bay, saving boats from the long and arduous 135-mile trip through Nantucket Shoals and around Cape Cod to reach Boston, MA, or Maine.

The canal opened in 1914. It was 15 feet deep and 100 feet wide, and accidents were frequent. During both World Wars, the canal was heavily used to avoid attack by German U-boats that lurked in offshore waters. In 1942, the steamship *Stephen R Jones* ran aground and sank in the shallow canal and traffic had to be rerouted around the dangerous waters off Cape Cod. As a result, the *SS Alexander Macomb* was torpedoed and sunk, with a loss of 10 lives. The wreck of the *Stephen R Jones* was then quickly removed with the help of 17 tons of dynamite. The modern-day version is the world's widest sea-level canal, with a channel width of 480 feet. Its average depth is now 32 feet. Accidents today are far less frequent.

NAVIGATION: Use Charts 13246, 13229 and 13236. The canal is able to handle vessels up to 825 feet long. Any vessel longer than 65 feet must contact the Marine Traffic Controller (508-759-4431 or VHF Channel 13) before entering the canal and must obey the three sets of traffic lights. Any delay on your part requires a second clearance to continue.

The seven-mile-long land cut can be almost clear of fog when both Buzzards and Cape Cod bays are thick with it. Once inside the confines of the canal, the 10-mile-long trip from Cedar Point on Great Neck to Cape Cod Bay is scenic and well-protected from the weather. However, the reverse passage south of Cedar Point, headed into Buzzards Bay, can be brutal, particularly when the ebb tide bound for Buzzards Bay is fueled by a piping southwesterly wind. That combination can challenge even adequately powered boats and moderately strong stomachs.

Despite the width and depth of the canal, tidal range conflict between the Cape Cod Bay end (9 feet) and the

Looking north over the Cape Cod Canal. (Not to be used for navigation.) WATERWAY GUIDE PHOTOGRAPHY

Buzzards Bay side (4 feet) remains strong, creating currents of about 3.5 knots on the eastward-setting flood and 4 to 6 knots on the ebb. Give careful attention to the tide and tidal current charts and make a very conservative estimate of the time you will need to pass both through the canal and beyond, in order to allow for the effects of a foul-setting tide.

For example, an ebbing tide will considerably slow eastbound mariners to the east of the traffic light and control tower at the tip of Wings Neck. Westbound, an entrance into the canal from Cape Cod Bay at slack water prior to a flood tide will result in favorable current well down Buzzards Bay. For the eastbound cruiser, however, the current is not as concentrated in Cape Cod Bay after a transit of the canal.

Even though commercial traffic is heavy on the canal, you should have no difficulties if you pick tide and weather carefully, proceed cautiously in what is typically a 4- or 5-knot current and stick to the right side of the channel, as if driving on a highway. Vessels traveling with the current have right of way. The U.S. Army Corps of Engineers also cautions that the canal is a No-Wake Zone; boaters must observe a 10-mph speed limit, yet complete their transit within 2.5 hours. This last requirement makes it particularly important to calculate your speed-versus-tide requirements with some care. All boats must be under power, as sailing through the canal is not permitted; neither are turning around, fishing or anchoring. Finally, as you transit the canal, monitor VHF Channel 13 for communications from the Corps of Engineers and be ready to alert them to emergency situations. Should you require assistance, contact the Marine Traffic Controller on VHF channels 13, 14 or 16, or by telephone at 508-759-4431 extension 500.

Anyone who transits the Cape Cod Canal will likely recognize the campus of the Massachusetts Maritime Academy at Taylor Point. Its training ship, the *T.S. Kennedy*, at 540 feet in length, dominates the west end of the canal. Both the academy and ship are available for tours at no charge. Call 508-830-5000 for more information.

Two fixed highway bridges cross the canal, both with 135-foot fixed vertical clearances. The single railroad lift bridge, crossing the canal east-northeast of Taylor Point, is virtually always open except during the occasional passage of a train to or from Cape Cod or for maintenance. Closed vertical clearance is a mere 7 feet, so very few vessels will clear the bridge during a closure. If running with a strong, favorable current, look well ahead to assure passage under the bridge, as turning at the last minute may not be an option. The bridge operator sounds two long blasts before lowering the bridge. It takes approximately 2.5 minutes to raise or lower it. If the bridge is lowered during periods of decreased visibility, the bridge operator will signal four short blasts every two minutes.

Prominent at the east end of the canal is the stack from the power plant on the southern bank near the boat basin where larger vessels must wait for permission to transit the canal.

Dockage: The Sandwich Marina, operated by the Town of Sandwich, has constructed extensive floating piers throughout the harbor. Arrange in advance to rent slip space from the marina if you wish to lie over at the eastern end of the canal. Transient reservations can be made online at their Web site: www.sandwichmarina.com. This marina is the best layover port for visiting Sandwich, whose own harbor a mile east of the canal on Cape Cod Bay is unsuitable for cruising boats. The marina also features modern showers and bathrooms and a very convenient fuel dock, which is open from 7 a.m. to 8 p.m. during the season. From the Sandwich Marina, you can walk a quarter mile to a 24-hour supermarket, banks with ATMs, a marine supply store, hardware store, liquor store, pharmacy, health clinic, optometrist, post office and a variety of shops. An excellent restaurant specializing in seafood, The Aqua Grille (508-888-8889), is right across the road from the marina. Sandwich, the oldest town on Cape Cod, has numerous attractions to tempt cruisers into a longer stay, including the Nye Homestead, dating to 1685 and holding exhibits of 17th-century living; the Dexter Grist Mill, a working mill dating to the 17th century; and the Sandwich Glass Museum (508-888-0251), a unique look at glass production in the 19th century, especially glass bead work. The Heritage Museum and Gardens (508-888-3300) exhibits the most important collection of American antique automobiles in the United States and a 1912 carousel. By the way, Sandwich was also the hometown of children's author Thornton W. Burgess, who wrote about Peter Cottontail and the Old Briar Patch.

Anchorage: Good anchorage lies at the western end of the canal, inside the pilings just below the Maritime Academy on Taylor's Point. Anchor on the eastern side of the channel, in 10 to 20 feet of water.

Important note: Cruisers may no longer anchor in the tiny "Harbor of Refuge," a dredged pocket of deep water at the eastern (Cape Cod Bay) end of the canal. The charted commercial pilings opposite the entrance to the Harbor of Refuge are reserved for barge traffic, which can arrive at any time, and recreational boats are banned from using these pilings. Video monitors will pick you up immediately, and a Coast Guard boat will arrive quickly to ask you, in no uncertain terms, to move along.

ADDITIONAL RESOURCES:

- An online telecam is updated every 30 minutes from sunrise to sunset at **www.telecamsystems.com/capecodcanal**
- Weather for the canal: (508-759-5991) or **www.weather.gov/forecasts/graphical/sectors/massachusetts.php#tabs**
- Navigational Regulations at **www.nae.usace.army.mil/recreati/ccc/navigation/navreg.htm**

Barnstable

MA RI

Barnstable is the largest community on Cape Cod. It is made up of seven villages: Barnstable, Centerville, Cotuit, Hyannis (including Hyannis Port), Marston Mills, Osterville and West Barnstable.

The town was named after Barnstaple, Devon, England. The first settlers were farmers, but fishing and salt soon became major industries. Before the arrival of the railroads towards the end of the 1800s, there were as many as 800 ships harbored there.

Barnstable is about 70 miles southeast of Boston, which made it a popular summer location for prominent 19th-century Bostonians. Some of the most famous people to have summered in Barnstable included Presidents Ulysses S. Grant and Grover Cleveland, and, of course, the Kennedys. Among the more recent notable residents are the late Judy Garland, Kurt Vonnegut, Tom Hamilton (bassist for Aerosmith) and Larry Page (co-founder of Google). Given its location, its beaches, its quaint shops and the possibility of bumping into some famous folks, it is no wonder that tourists come in droves to the Barnstable area during the summertime.

NAVIGATION: Use Charts 13246 and 13250. Go 10 miles east along the beaches and sand dunes east of Cape Cod Canal and you come to Barnstable. From a distance you will be able to see a lighted radio tower in Barnstable, the tower of a former lighthouse on the south side of Beach Point, and farther in the distance, a spire from a Yarmouth church.

The harbor is small, and charts indicate an approach depth of 7 feet (though this is reportedly disputable). A whale-watch boat reportedly helps keep the channel open. Entry to Barnstable Harbor should not be attempted in periods of high winds or seas. The constantly shifting channel is tricky and the prevailing currents tend to set a vessel outside the channel. There are rocks and ledges on the south side of the harbor, some of which are unmarked. Rocks near the channel that leads to the yacht club are marked but can be mistaken for the channel entrance to Maraspin Creek. It is a good idea to radio ahead to the municipal marina for some local knowledge before entering.

Dockage: Barnstable's municipal marina has an occasional slip available for transients with reported depths of 3 to 6 feet. Call the harbormaster at 508-790-6273 or on VHF Channel 16 for slip availability and local knowledge on channel depths. Availability is an issue, as there are long waiting lists to use the marinas and moorings.

Anchorage: The channel approaching Barnstable widens after rounding flashing red buoy "8" and good holding can be found in 8 to 25 feet of water. Watch out for the charted cable area extending southward from Beach Point. Be aware of the tide state and your swinging radius and remember that the mean tide range is 9.5 feet. Tides flood southward and ebb northward at an average of 1.3 knots. Outgoing fishermen and whale watchers can create morning noise and rocking.

Sesuit Harbor, East Dennis

NAVIGATION: Use Chart 13250. East of Barnstable, this harbor has the easiest entry on Cape Cod Bay's southern shore. The breakwater-protected entry channel is short and comparatively straight, but does have a tendency to shoal. It is periodically dredged to 6-foot depths, but exercise proper caution and watch the depth sounder. It might

Sandwich to Provincetown, MA

SANDWICH TO PROVINCETOWN		Largest Vessel Accommodated	VHF Channel Monitored	Transient Berths / Total Berths	Approach / Dockside Depth (reported)	Floating Docks	Gas / Diesel	Groceries, Ice, Marine Supplies, Snacks	Repairs: Hull, Engine, Propeller	Lift (tonnage), Crane, Rail	1=110V, 2=220V, B=Both, Max Amps	Laundry, Pool, Showers	Pump-Out Station	Nearby: Grocery Store, Motel, Restaurant
		Dockage					Supplies		Services					
1. Sandwich Marina/East Boat Basin WiFi	508-833-0808	100	09/16	25/180	15/9	F	GD	IMS			B/50	S	P	GMR
2. Barnstable Marine Services	508-362-3811	45		1/45	3/5	F	GD	IMS	HEP	L20	B/50	S		GMR
3. Barnstable Harbor Marina	508-790-6273	40	16/09	3/88	4/5	F					1/30		P	GMR
4. Mattakeese Wharf Restaurant	508-362-4511			2/3		F								GMR
5. Millway Marina Inc.	508-362-4904	35	09/78	0/50	7/7		G	I	HEP					GR
6. Dennis Yacht Club	508-385-3741	30			5/5					PRIVATE				
7. Northside Marina	508-385-3936	85	07	/120	6/6	F	GD	IMS	E	L25	B/30	S	P	GMR
8. Dennis Municipal Marina	508-385-5555	60	16/09	5/268	6/8	F					1/30	S		GMR
9. Town of Wellfleet Marina	508-349-0320	55	16/09	6/200	10/6	F	GD	IMS			B/30	S	P	GMR
10. Flyer's Boat Shop & Rentals ☐ WiFi	508-487-0898	95	/11	/50	25/12	F		GIM	E	L3,R		LS	P	GMR
11. Provincetown Marina	508-487-0571	65	09	20/50	20/13	F	GD	I			B/50		P	GMR

Corresponding chart(s) not to be used for navigation. ☐ Internet Access WiFi Wireless Internet Access

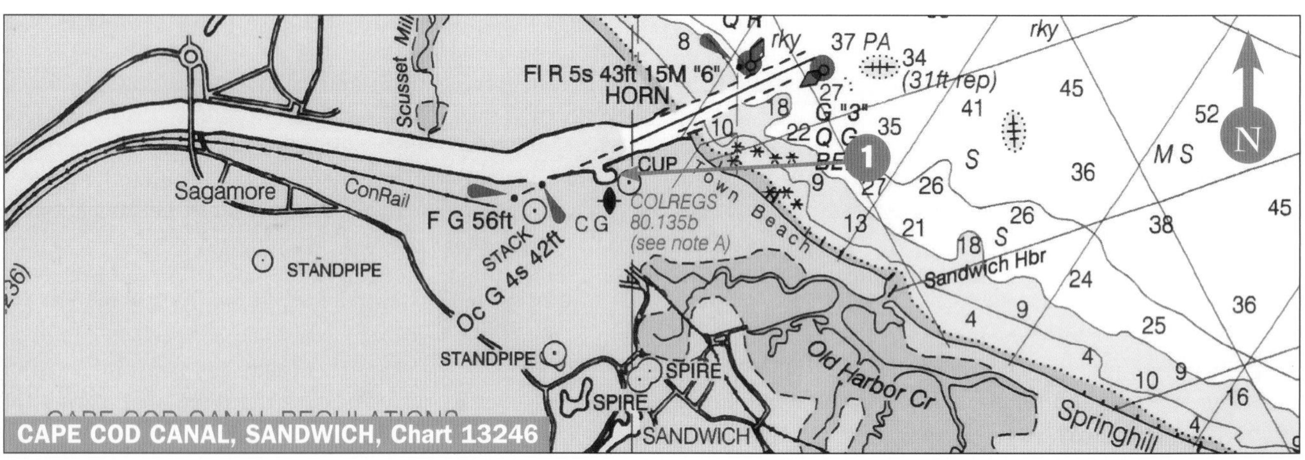

CAPE COD CANAL, SANDWICH, Chart 13246

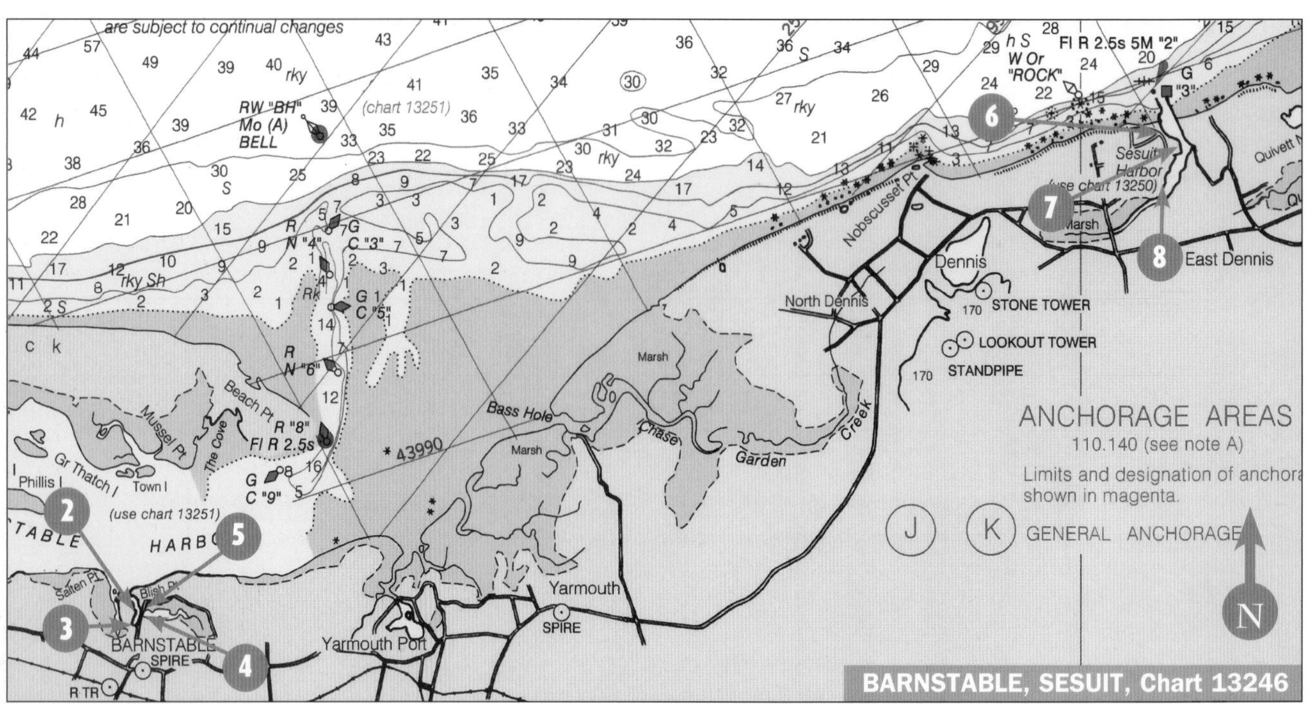

BARNSTABLE, SESUIT, Chart 13246

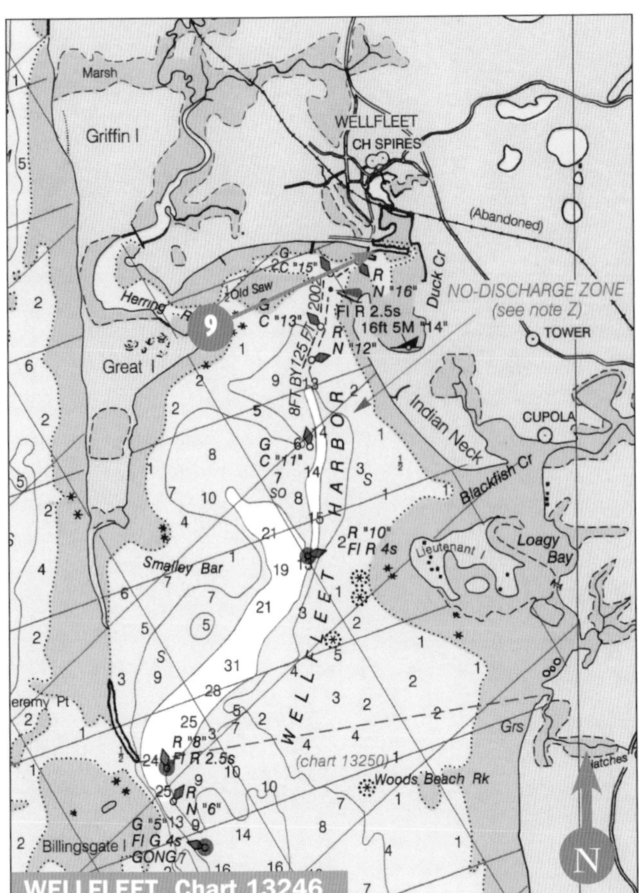

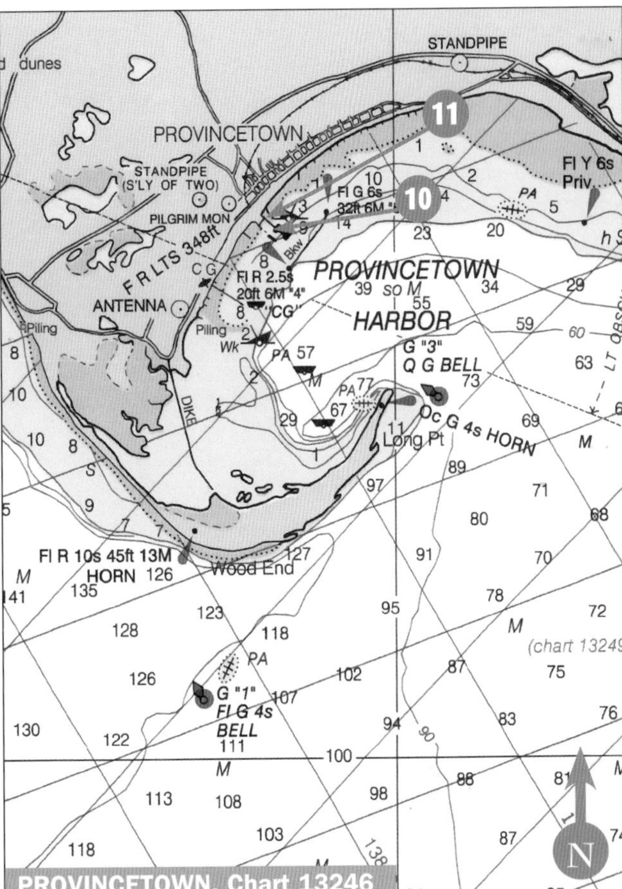

be a good idea to ask for local knowledge before entering. Please note that there is a 4 mph speed limit.

Dockage: With a yacht club and marinas, the harbor is an excellent base from which to do some sightseeing in the nearby villages. Northside Marina, a full-service yard, has limited transient dockage. Call ahead to check availability. The town of East Dennis provides provisioning possibilities, restaurants and other services. The Dennis Municipal Marina normally has transient dockage available. The Sesuit Cafe (508-685-6134), next to the Northside Marina, is casual, inexpensive, popular with the locals and the food is very good.

Anchorage: There is no anchoring in the harbor.

Wellfleet

Once second only to Gloucester as a cod and mackerel fishing port, Wellfleet is a quiet summer resort nestled among dunes, ocean and moors. Located about halfway up the "hook," the town has pretty white churches, high green hills, sleepy rural streets, lovely old houses and a tidy village straight out of Colonial America. Here Marconi built his first wireless station in 1901 and sent the first trans-Atlantic telegram in 1903. This section of Cape Cod is a walker's paradise. Explore the Cape Cod National Seashore beaches or the Audubon Society Wellfleet Bay Wildlife Sanctuary nearby.

NAVIGATION: Use Charts 13250 and 13246. The protected harbor, about 26 miles east of the Cape Cod Canal, has a five-mile-long, shoal-littered entry east of Billingsgate Shoal and Island. The latter qualifies as an island only at low water. Good fishing for striped bass can be had around the island. The channel shifts continually, and buoys are moved to mark the best water.

Looking toward Wellfleet Harbor, you will see a couple of church spires and the fire lookout tower located in South Wellfleet. The Wellfleet breakwater light sits upon a skeleton-like tower to starboard as you enter. The channel and anchorage basin are dredged with depths ranging from 7 to 10 feet with shoaling to about 1 foot along the southern edge.

Dockage: The harbor contains a large town marina and mooring basin behind Shirttail Point. Both harbor and the holding ground have been improved by recent dredging. Tidal range is 10 feet. Wellfleet Marine maintains 13 guest moorings. The town marina offers slips at floating concrete docks, a harbormaster's office, showers and 194 moorings. On the public wharf is a well-placed launching ramp. A second ramp nearby is also available. Wellfleet Bay Wildlife Sanctuary offers views of marsh and pine forests, with wildlife tours daily. Information and guidebooks are available at the sanctuary office (open daily 8:30 a.m. to 5 p.m.). You can also anchor off the sanctuary.

Anchorage: There are several anchorage areas near Wellfleet. In settled weather, there is good mud bottom north of Smalley Bar. Watch for the shoal marked by green "11"

Looking north over Plymouth Harbor. (Not to be used for navigation.)

and keep the 10-foot tidal range in mind. The depths will range from 10 to 20 feet. You will be somewhat exposed to westerly winds.

Probably the best overall anchorage is in the inner harbor off the town wharf. Pay attention in the channel between the inner and outer harbors; it can get narrow in spots. There are shoals on both sides, so keep an eye on the buoys.

To the south of Billingsgate Shoal there is a good anchorage in 12 to 42 feet. The shoal will serve as a natural breakwater from north winds and seas.

Wellfleet is adjacent to the Cape Cod National Seashore, which offers excellent birding, hiking, swimming and surfing. Located about four miles from Wellfleet Marina (508-349-6055), the Beachcomber Restaurant is in the National Seashore area and has excellent seafood offerings. Closer to the Marina is Winslow's Tavern (508-349-6450) and The Bookstore & Restaurant (508-349-3154), which has been serving books and meals for over 40 years. A market and gourmet shop are within easy walking distance. Seaman's Bank on Route 6 offers a 24-hour ATM. Fresh seafood is available from a number of markets in this seaside town.

Provincetown

In Provincetown, mariners will find a flourishing artists' colony, a thriving gay community, a working fishing fleet and—in the summer months—an army of tourists. On the north end of Cape Cod, Provincetown has one of the best harbors on the Atlantic coast.

NAVIGATION: Use Chart 13249. For Provincetown, use Boston tide tables. For high tide, add 16 minutes; for low tide, add 18 minutes. The big, wide harbor, more than a mile from Long Point to the town dock, is easy to enter under almost any condition. Be careful, though: Boats are always on the move, and floating nets, fish traps and moorings abound.

Dockage: Provincetown Marina, situated just seaward of the town landing, is accommodating to visitors. The marina has about 30 slips for transients and has a large field of rental moorings, with launch service included. The marina monitors VHF Channel 09 and offers launch service on the hour until 11 p.m. to both moored and anchored boats. Here you will find restrooms, coin-operated showers, bag ice and fuel. The shops on Commercial Street are a short walk from the docks. The Masthead Resort, also monitoring VHF, offers beachfront shore accommodations, along with moorings and launch service.

Anchorage: The mooring field, available for vessels up to 40 feet in length, now completely fills the area behind the breakwater and extends to the southwest past the breakwater to past the Coast Guard station. The remaining anchoring areas are southwest of the mooring field and northeast of the breakwater; both places are exposed to east winds. Inside the breakwater, anchoring is reported to be poor, due to the soft bottom and debris in the area. Anchoring is prohibited in the 100-yard-wide fairway and around the piers.

GOIN' ASHORE:

PROVINCETOWN, MA

Provincetown contains a heady mixture of cultures—sidewalk artists, actors, tourists, summer residents and the people who live here year-round, notably fishermen. Old elm trees and Colonial houses still have the traditional Cape Cod look. These days, art schools and art shows, souvenir shops and tourist attractions fill the narrow streets. You can rent a bicycle, horse, car or beach buggy to get away to the fine beaches. The Provincetown Heritage Museum is at the corner of Center and Commercial streets. For information, call 508-487-7098. Four boats leave MacMillan Wharf daily to go whale-watching.

From the town landing, the variety of restaurants and fast-food establishments virtually assaults the cruising visitor. The Lobster Pot (508-487-0842), about a block and a half to the east of the docks, offers lobster and a number of other choices, as well as a great harbor view from its second-story deck. Even closer is the Surf Club (508-487-1367), well regarded for lighter fare. Angel Foods (508-487-6666) is a terrific deli and bakery on the East End. Favorite spots on the waterfront include The Red Inn (15 Commercial St., 508-487-7334), serving tasty meals in a spectacular setting; Fanizzi's Restaurant By The Sea (539 Commercial St., 508-487-1964), featuring Northern-Italian specialties; Devon's (401 1/2 Commercial St., 508-487-4773), featuring modern American fine dining; and Lorraine's (463 Commercial St., 508-487-6074), for Mexican and seafood.

A walk along "P-town's" inimitable main drag will turn up just about any desired commodity or service. You will find an excellent bakery, a large marine supply house, an Army-Navy store and bookstores alongside jewelry and trinket shops. A supermarket is several blocks farther afield—you will need directions to get there. But do not ask for directions to a laundry—Provincetown does not have one.

Far Land Provisions (508-487-0045) provides a concierge delivery service of fine foods and wines, as well as prepared items. Visitors can go to their Web site (www.farlandprovisions.com) and place an order, with instructions for delivery to a mooring. Shopping in the store is also a treat; it stands at the corner of Bradford and Conwell streets.

Despite the shortage of mundane amenities, Provincetown makes a wonderful stop because of its vibrant arts scene, variety of restaurants and crazy, colorful nightlife. Like Key West, it has an edgy, edge of the world feel.

ADDITIONAL RESOURCES:

- Provincetown Banner, **www.provincetown.com**

NEARBY GOLF COURSES:
Highland Golf Links, 10 Highland Road, Truro, MA 02666, 508-487-9201

NEARBY MEDICAL FACILITIES:
Cape Cod Hospital, 27 Park St., Hyannis, MA 02601, 508-771-1800

Plymouth, Duxbury

NAVIGATION: Use Chart 13253. For Plymouth, use Boston tide tables. For high tide, add 4 minutes; for low tide, add 18 minutes. About 20 miles northwest, up Cape Cod Bay from the east end of the Cape Cod Canal, is the historic town of Plymouth. Entry to its big, breakwatered and protected harbor begins inside the long finger of Gurnet Point's high bare cliff with its white lighthouse. From the outset, you will have to negotiate around shore-to-shore lobster traps and fishermen in skiffs.

The wide channel, southeast of Gurnet Point, to Duxbury Pier (locally known as "Bug Light") is well-marked. But the outgoing tidal rip across the channel and shallow Brown's Bank to the south can present quite a challenge to inbound craft under sail. The red nun buoy "8," located southwest of Duxbury Pier, marks the entrance to Plymouth Harbor Channel, which rounds the banks off the point of Plymouth Beach. It then parallels the beach in a southeasterly direction for about a mile to flashing green four-second light "17." There, the channel takes a sharp turn to starboard for another well-marked run past the breakwater to the inner harbor. All of the navigational aids in this area have been renumbered, and several have been relocated from their indicated positions on the chart.

Dockage and Moorings: Upon entering the inner harbor, the Greek Revival monument protecting what remains of Plymouth Rock (after souvenir hunters did their utmost) lies dead ahead. The unmistakable hull and rig of Mayflower II comes into full view as well. Plymouth Yacht Club is prominently located on the knoll to port, followed immediately by the extensive facilities of Brewer Plymouth Marine. The Town Wharf is located at the northwestern corner of the inner harbor, at the end of the marked channel. Plymouth Yacht Club, founded in 1890 and one of the oldest yacht clubs in America, offers visiting cruisers a temporary membership, which makes available the use of a mooring and access to the club's showers and restaurant (daily, April through Labor Day, and fall weekends thereafter). Launch service is available for an additional fee; contact the club on VHF Channel 08.

Brewer Plymouth Marine is a full-service boatyard and marina with deep-draft transient slips available on floating docks. The yard has two lifts (the largest at 60 tons), mechanics on duty, complete repair and fabrication shops and easy access to both gasoline and diesel fuel. There are showers, laundry machines and a well-regarded restaurant on-site. The Town Wharf at the end of the harbor channel carries 11-foot depths at the fuel dock, which pumps both diesel and gasoline. There is dinghy dockage here as well. All transient moorings are now handled by the Plymouth Yacht Club, and the moorings are first-come, first-served. The yacht club dockmaster (508-747-0473 or VHF Channel 08) will help you locate a mooring.

Anchorage: Anchoring is prohibited in the inner harbor, which is filled with commercial craft and private moorings. However, excellent anchorage is available in the blind channel running parallel to the Plymouth Harbor Channel

Plymouth, Duxbury, Green Harbor, MA

PLYMOUTH, DUXBURY, GREEN HARBOR		Largest Vessel Accommodated	VHF Channel Monitored	Transient Berths / Total Berths	Approach / Dockside Depth (reported)	Floating Docks	Gas / Diesel	Groceries, Ice, Marine Supplies, Snacks	Repairs: Hull, Engine, Propeller	Lift (tonnage), Crane, Rail	1=110V, 2=220V, B=Both, Max Amps	Laundry, Pool, Showers	Pump-Out Station	Nearby: Grocery Store, Motel, Restaurant
		Dockage					Supplies		Services					
1. Plymouth Yacht Club	508-746-7207	50	08		12/12			I		PRIVATE				GMR
2. Brewer Plymouth Marine (Internet Access, Wireless Internet Access)	**508-746-4500**	**150**	**09/72**	**25/100**	**10/10**	**F**	**GD**	**IM**	**HEP**	**L60,C**	**B/50**	**LS**	**P**	**GMR**
3. Plymouth Town Wharf	508-747-6193	110	16		11/11		GD	I						GMR
4. Bayside Marine	781-934-0561		08		8/6		G	IM	HE					MR
5. Duxbury Town Pier	781-934-2866	50	16	MOORINGS	8/8					HARBOR POLICE			P	R
6. Long Point Marine	781-934-5302	60	16/09					M	HEP	L35,C	1/30			
7. Taylor Marine	781-837-9617	45		4/140	6/6	F	GD	I	E	L12,C2	1/30	S	P	GR
8. Green Harbor Marina	781-837-1181	55	65	20/180	8/8	F	G	IM	HEP	L25	B/50	S		GMR
9. Marshfield Town Dock-Green Harbor	781-834-5541	50	16/09	4/	5/5		GD						P	GR

Corresponding chart(s) not to be used for navigation. Internet Access Wireless Internet Access

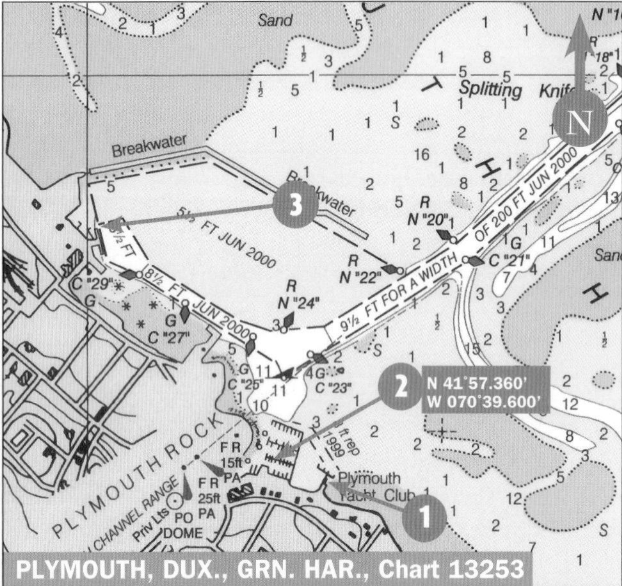

PLYMOUTH, DUX., GRN. HAR., Chart 13253

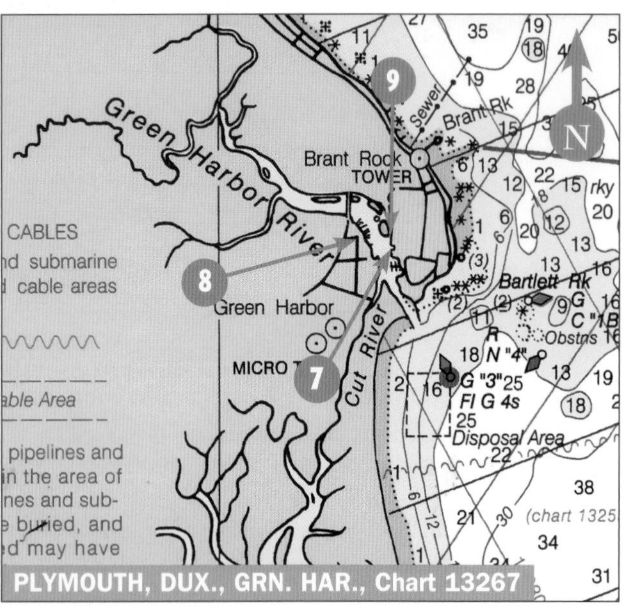

PLYMOUTH, DUX., GRN. HAR., Chart 13267

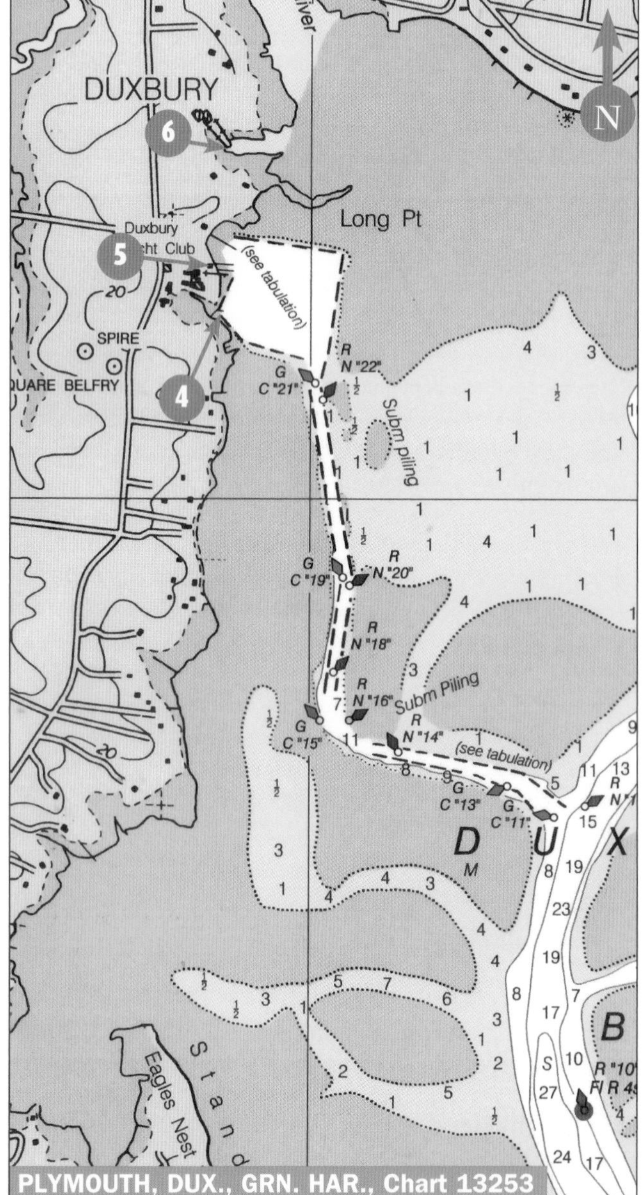

PLYMOUTH, DUX., GRN. HAR., Chart 13253

as it runs west, nearly perpendicular to Plymouth Beach. You can set a hook firmly in the mud with 7- to 15-foot depths (mean low water) along this half-mile-long tail of protected water. But the area of sufficient depth is relatively narrow, arguing for a check of actual depths in relation to the chart and tide table (with an 8- to 9-foot tidal range in this area).

The Cowyard, north of Plymouth Beach, also provides excellent anchorage possibilities, particularly to the west of Saquish Head or west of Clarks Island, where the Pilgrims first anchored. Depths are highly variable in the Cowyard—check specific locations carefully against charted depths and actual soundings. The chart makes it appear that additional anchorage may be plentiful in Goose Point Channel, but such is not the case—this area has silted so substantially that boats attempting to anchor here are likely to be left high and dry at low tide.

GOIN' ASHORE:

PLYMOUTH, MA

Wherever you tie up, Plymouth's contemporary village amenities are but a short walk away. Modest restaurants run the gamut from standard American fare (try the All-American Diner, especially for breakfast, 508-747-4763), cafes and delis, to Italian and Mexican. Fresh seafood is the main feature in several spots near the Town Wharf. The 14 Union Dockside Bar and Grill (508-747-4503) is located on-site at Brewer Plymouth Marine. The Plymouth Rock Trolley (774-454-8121) offers narrated tours stopping at major attractions numerous other locations for a daily fee. There are antiques shops and boutiques aplenty, restored 18th-century houses (including half a dozen you may visit) and the Pilgrim Hall Museum (508-746-1620). One of the very oldest in the country, the museum contains an impressive collection of Pilgrim lore and possessions (Miles Standish's swords, for example).

Not to be missed are Plimoth Plantation (the spelling serves to differentiate the museum from the original Plymouth Colony or Plantation and the present town of Plymouth) and *Mayflower II* (508-746-1622), which open the door to a faithful reproduction of the colonists' 17th-century existence and the ship that brought them. Plimoth Plantation, reconstructed inland of the original site, is only a short taxi ride away. Once inside the plantation's 1622 fort, "villagers" reenact the daily lives of their original counterparts as they tend gardens, cook food over open fires and make their own furniture, baskets and pottery. The houses are appealingly rustic and well-thatched, but cramped, dark and short of creature comforts on close inspection. The *Mayflower II* (built in Plymouth, England, in 1956, to reproduce an English merchantman of the early 1600s) makes a similar impression. How 102 passengers, plus a crew of 25, could have made their way across the Atlantic Ocean in this crude 90-foot vessel challenges credulity.

ADDITIONAL RESOURCES:

- Destination Plymouth, **www.visit-plymouth.com**

NEARBY GOLF COURSES:
Crosswinds Golf Club, 424 Long Pond Road, Plymouth, MA 02360, 508-830-1199, **www.crosswindsgolf.com**

NEARBY MEDICAL FACILITIES:
Jordan Hospital, 275 Sandwich St., Plymouth, MA 02360, 508-746-2000

Duxbury

Miles Standish founded this Colonial town early in Massachusetts' history. Though traditional clapboard housing stock of the period remains, Duxbury today bustles with summer resort and tourist traffic flocking to the contemporary shops and restaurants. The harbor is well-protected and visiting cruisers are welcomed, but available space is tight and approach depths are skimpy at low tide for those drawing 5 feet or more.

NAVIGATION: Use Chart 13253. Duxbury Bay is a big, shallow body of water with a fairly straight channel northeast from Duxbury Pier Lighthouse. The channel tends to silt in, however, and current conditions should be checked out with locals on approach. Privately maintained channel buoys mark the encroaching shoal at the southern tip of the Cowyard's long bar, and a half mile west at the mouth of the Jones River, north of The Nummet. At privately owned Clarks Island, the channel divides. The local-marked right branch follows the west side of Clarks Island to a fixed bridge (5-foot vertical clearance) three miles north. A protected anchorage is located north of the island. The main channel, well-buoyed into Duxbury Harbor, turns to the northwest. The channel's project depth (sometimes dredged by the U.S. Army Corps of Engineers) is 8 feet, but the area is shoal-prone, reducing the optimal depth significantly between dredging projects.

Dockage: No dockage is available for transients visiting Duxbury. The town controls the assignment of moorings; contact the harbormaster on VHF Channel 16.

Anchorage: In addition to the Cowyard, there is good holding north of Clarks Island. Any reliable anchorage is a substantial distance from Duxbury itself.

Green Harbor River

NAVIGATION: Use Chart 13253. Just five miles north of Gurnet Point, Green Harbor River, home to many charter and recreational fishing boats, is good to know about in an emergency. Flashing green bell buoy "3" has been set 600 yards southeast of the jettied entrance at the north end of long curving Duxbury Beach. The Corps of Engineers periodically dredges here to maintain project depths of 6 feet, but depths frequently shoal to just 4 feet. Shoaling is a recurrent problem along this stretch, so be sure to exercise caution and obtain local knowledge. Many local fishermen do not enter or leave within 90 minutes either side of low

New Inlet, Scituate, MA

NEW INLET, SCITUATE		Largest Vessel Accommodated	VHF Channel Monitored	Transient Berths / Total Berths	Approach / Dockside Depth (reported)	Floating Docks	Gas / Diesel	Groceries, Ice, Marine Supplies, Snacks	Repairs: Hull, Engine, Propeller	Lift (tonnage), Crane, Rail	1=110V, 2=220V, B=Both, Max Amps	Laundry, Pool, Showers	Pump-Out Station	Nearby: Grocery Store, Motel, Restaurant
		Dockage					Supplies				Services			
1. Scituate Harbor Yacht Club (WiFi)	781-545-9804	50	09	/5	10/10	F	GD	IS			1/50	S		GMR
2. Satuit Boat Club	781-545-9752	50	09	15/15	8/8			I			1/30	S		GMR
3. Scituate Harbor Marina (Internet)	781-545-2165	70	09	5/90	12/10	F	GD	IS			B/50	S		GMR
4. Scituate Launch/Waterline Moorings (Internet) (WiFi)	781-545-4154	50	16/09		12/10		GD	GIM	HEP			LS	P	GMR
5. Mill Wharf Marina	781-545-3333	40	09	/70	6/8	F	GD				B/50			GMR
6. Cole Parkway Marina	781-545-2130	44	16/09	10/180	10/8	F	GD	I			1/30	LS	P	GMR

Corresponding chart(s) not to be used for navigation. ☐ Internet Access (WiFi) Wireless Internet Access

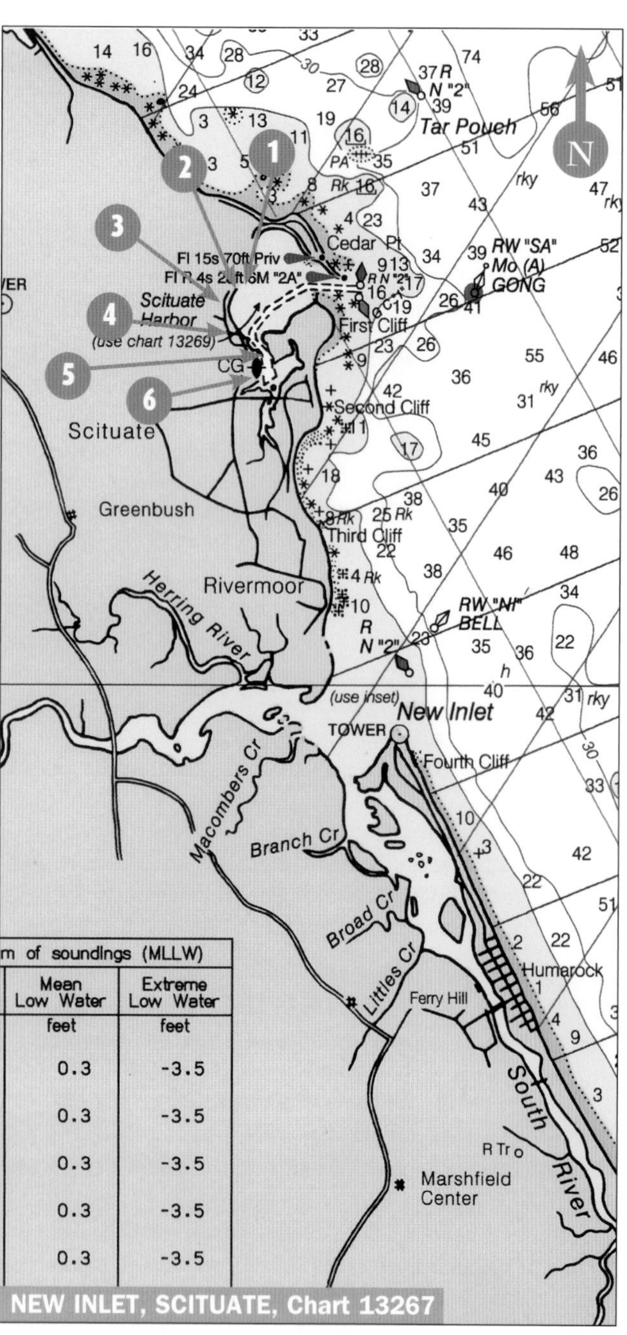

NEW INLET, SCITUATE, Chart 13267

tide. After passing red nun buoy "6" to starboard, head for flashing red "8" sited on the end of a jetty off Blackman's Point. Stay in the center between that jetty and the one to the south as you enter the narrowest part of the channel. Watch for moored boats that may make this narrow passage even smaller.

Dockage: The two marinas inside Green Harbor offer slips, full repairs, fuel and a restaurant. Green Harbor Marina has transient slips on floating docks, a renovated bathhouse, a ship's store, and a fuel dock. Contact the marina on VHF Channel 65. The town of Brant Rock is a short walk away and offers supplies and an excellent beach.

New Inlet Harbors

Just north of Fourth Cliff, New Inlet—a storm-cut passage made at the turn of the century—leads to quiet, attractive rivers and some superb gunkholing. While the narrow entry is well-marked, strong currents run through, and waves will sometimes break across the entrance in heavy weather and block the passage. In settled weather on a rising tide, entry is far less problematic.

NAVIGATION: Use Chart 13267. Seek local knowledge before planning a cruise into this inlet, due to frequent changes in the channels. Southwest from the red-and-white bell buoy "NI" signaling the entrance from Massachusetts Bay, a string of nuns clearly marks the channel. Follow them closely and do not stray too far to port. Note that green can buoy "3" marks a large rock that is awash at low tide. Inside, at red nun buoy "8," the channel splits north to the Herring and the North rivers, and south to the South River, leading to Ferry Hill and Humarock. Be prepared to deal with major currents at all times except slack water.

The North and South rivers have become very popular for kayakers and canoeists. The North River, bearing to port from the sand spit, was once known as the "River of the Thousand Ships" because it supported more than a score of yards in the 17th and 18th centuries. Now it is a quiet channel marked by stakes, best used for exploration and enjoyment in shallow-draft boats. Controlling depth of the South River is 3 feet. The river has no markers, but dinghies and shoal-draft boats can go as far as the fixed bridge (11-foot vertical clearance).

Dockage: Past the sand spit to the northwest, private buoys guide the way through twists and turns of the Herring River to James Landing Marina, located about a mile inland in a secluded and beautiful tidal marsh. Controlling depth at mean low water is 3 feet. However, the 9-foot tidal range here makes it quite possible for boats of substantially greater draft to enter at half-tide or more. All fuels, propane refills, repairs and showers are available here, and the amenities of Scituate are only a short drive away.

Scituate

Scituate (sit'-u-it, from the Indian word "Satuit" or "cold spring") rings a small, snug harbor—one of the most accommodating on the East Coast for recreational boats. Seven to 9 feet deep and well-protected (except in the most violent nor'easter), it offers easy access to all manner of supplies and services.

NAVIGATION: Use Chart 13267. For Scituate Harbor, use Boston tide tables. For high tide, add 3 minutes; for low tide, subtract 1 minute. Scituate is easily entered between Cedar Point, with its operating lighthouse, and First Cliff. From the red-and-white Morse (A) gong buoy "SA," follow a course of 289 degrees magnetic to the mouth of the channel. A breakwater protects the well-marked basin and its many lobster pots. Scituate Harbor's entrance channel is well-marked, but stay to the center until well past the jetties. Channel depth is about 7 feet, but shoals are present on the outside edges.

Dockage: Two private marinas and a town-operated marina may have slips available by reservation or on a first-come, first-served basis. They fill early, so check with the harbormaster or call ahead.

Moorings: A sign reading "Welcome To Scituate" describes the spirit of this inviting town. Although it is a crowded harbor and anchoring is prohibited, there is usually a transient mooring available and the harbor and town are well worth a stop for a day or two. The Scituate Yacht Club has a few moorings, but most are privately owned. Call Scituate Launch "Cedar Point" (781-545-4154 or on VHF Channel 09) for advice. They supervise a large number of rental moorings and can often accommodate transients and provide launch service into town or to the many restaurants on the harbor.

The town of Scituate surrounds the harbor and offers a variety of restaurants to satisfy anybody's appetite, a movie theater, a supermarket, two hardware stores and a bowling alley.

Speed limit in the harbor is 6 mph and is strictly enforced, as is the No-Discharge law. The Scituate Launch operates a pump-out boat, available by calling on VHF Channel 09. The town offers a shower and bathroom facility, for a small fee, payable at the harbormaster's office.

GOIN' ASHORE: SCITUATE, MA

In the days of mushrooming malls well outside of town, Scituate remains a traditional but still-thriving seaside village with all shops and services intact.

The Village Market (71 Front St., 781-545-4986), a grocery Is about a block's walk southwest of the harbormaster's office at the foot of the docks. In the same direction, The Cleaning Corner (781-545-0066), a large laundry (full-service or coin-operated, your choice), is situated at 55 Cole Parway. Satuit Hardware (1 Cole Parkway, 781-545-8370) is stocked with particular concern for the boating community. Scituate Playhouse (immediately behind the harbormaster's office at 120 Front St., 781-545-0045) has two theaters offering first-run movies. A UPS drop box is located just across the street. Along the town's main thoroughfare, outlining the harbor, you will also find two banks, Larry's (traditional) Barbershop (84 Front St., 781-545-5054), Scituate Harbor Body Stop Inc. (131 Front St., 781-545-0303, hairstyling), the Front Street Book Shop (165 Front St., 781-545-5011), the Silent Chef (bakery and deli, 113 Front St., 781-545-6665), CVS Pharmacy (100 Front St., 781-545-0240) and Harborside Wine and Spirits (109 Front St., 781-545-0059).

Restaurants along Front Street are both unpretentious and well-regarded. Largest and most popular, The Mill Wharf Restaurant (150 Front St., 781-545-3999) has a large and varied menu (from seafood to sirloin, veggie stir fries to sizzling fajitas) at modest prices. Petit Paris Bistro (95 Front St., 781-545-6092) serves meals with a continental flair. Of historical interest are the Cudworth House, Lawson Tower and the Stockbridge Mill, which are all easily visited.

ADDITIONAL RESOURCES:

- Town of Scituate, **www.town.scituate.ma.us**
- Scituate Historical Society, **www.scituatehistoricalsociety.org**

NEARBY GOLF COURSES:
Widow's Walk Golf Course, 250 The Driftway, Scituate, MA 02066, 781-544-7777

Nearby Medical Facilities:
Pembroke Hospital, 199 Oak St., Pembroke, MA 02359, 781-829-7000

Cohasset

On the fringes of Boston, Cohasset is a popular, crowded harbor with a large local fleet and good anchorage. Ashore are a hospitable yacht club, town landings, good restaurants and good beaches. Of special note are the restaurants of The Cohasset Harbor Resort—Atlantica (781-383-0900) for fine dining and The Olde Salt House (781-383-2203) for casual outdoor dining.

NAVIGATION: Use Charts 13269 or 13270. Cohasset is not for deep-draft boats, and even skippers of shallow-draft boats must be alert to all hazards. Rocks appear wherever

Cohasset, MA

COHASSET		Largest Vessel Accommodated	VHF Channel Monitored	Transient Berths / Total Berths	Approach / Dockside Depth (reported)	Floating Docks	Gas / Diesel	Groceries, Ice, Marine Supplies, Snacks	Repairs: Hull, Engine, Propeller	Lift (tonnage), Crane, Rail	1=110V, 2=220V, B=Both, Max Amps	Laundry, Pool, Showers	Pump-Out Station	Nearby: Grocery Store, Motel, Restaurant
		Dockage						Supplies	Services					
1. Cohasset Harbormaster	781-383-0863	50	16	3/				I	HE	R			P	GMR
2. Cohasset Harbor Marina	781-383-1504	45		75/75	7/6	F			HP		B/30			GMR
3. Mill River Marine Railways	781-383-1207	70		2/2	6/10	F		M	HEP	R	1/50			MR
4. Cohasset Yacht Club	781-383-9633	45	10		6/6			I			1			

Corresponding chart(s) not to be used for navigation. Internet Access Wireless Internet Access

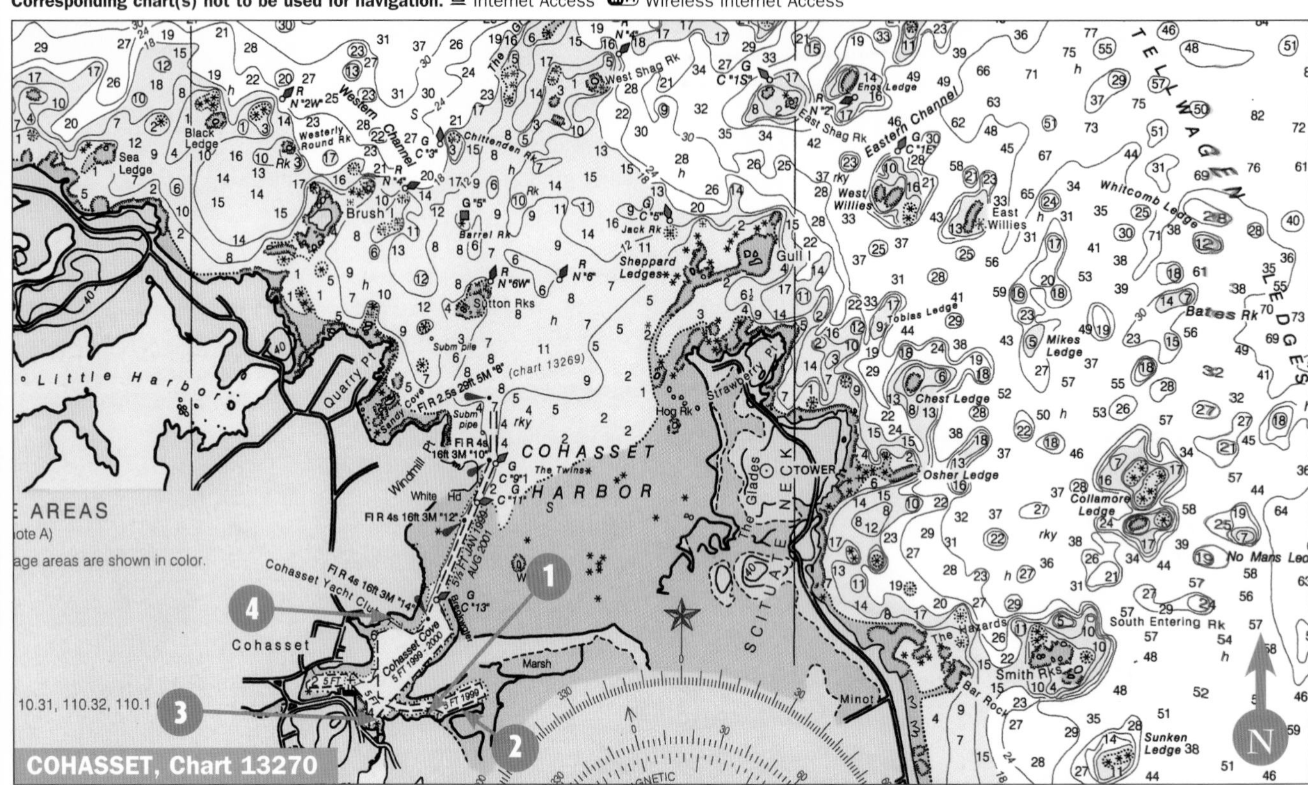

you look, with the channel shoaling to 4 feet at spots in the inner harbor. The entrance is narrow and calls for cautious navigation and slow speeds at all times.

Marking the entry on Massachusetts Bay is Minots Light, famous up and down the coast as the "I Love You Light," for its "one-four-three" flashing light. From here the approach is via any of three natural channels: Eastern Channel, The Gangway or Western Channel. All are marked and well-charted, threading between outlying rocks and ledges. These passages, like those found in Maine and on the northern shore of Long Island Sound, are somewhat difficult, but present no problem in clear weather.

Local authorities and the Coast Pilot disagree on channels. Local people like the wider Gangway Channel despite its unmarked rocks. The Coast Pilot prefers the narrower but deeper and clearer Eastern Channel. No one says much for Western Channel between Brush Ledge and Chittenden Rock. However, all agree that the best time to enter, especially if you draw more than 5 feet, is on a rising tide.

GREATER BOSTON

Unlike most big cities, Boston has within its harbor and immediate environs dozens of friendly yacht clubs, protected marinas, secluded anchorages, boatyards and facilities for recreational craft, many of which welcome cruising boats. Fascinating sightseeing is within easy distance of almost anywhere you dock. Nearby are historic towns and notable shore resorts to visit, as well as dozens of islands to investigate by dinghy.

Boston Harbor

NAVIGATION: Use Chart 13270. Use Boston tide tables. Red-and-white Morse (A) buoy "BG," located eight miles east-northeast of Deer Island, guides you into Boston Harbor.

Like all big-city harbors, Boston is crowded with commercial and recreational boats of all types. Freighters, tankers, trawlers and excursion boats vie with pleasure craft of all descriptions, from megayachts to day sailors, for command of the Inner Harbor waters—or to escape them for the Outer Harbor and beyond. The place hums with activity and nautical color. Yet "dirty" no longer describes this still-industrial harbor. The cleanup and rejuvenation efforts of the 1990s are evident everywhere, including in the water. Consequently, the porpoises and stripers have returned to the inner harbor, along with tall ships, submarines and the New York Yacht Club. This revitalization of the past decade is matched by enlargement or refit—in some cases, total reconstruction—of boating amenities throughout the harbor.

Beyond the crisscrossing of confusing wakes, the major hazard facing skippers is confusion in sorting out the numerous buoys and channels. Yet many side waters, notably Quincy and Dorchester bays, are relatively unmarked. Boston Harbor is much more difficult to navigate than New York Harbor. Even though you will discover that the numerous islands rarely look as you would expect them to from the charts, you should keep an up-to-date chart handy. The wide expanses of apparently "good" water are dotted with shoals, rocks and ledges, and while many of these obstructions are not marked, they are charted. The plethora of lights and buoys can be confusing; be sure to keep them sorted out in your mind. Also, keep a constant lookout astern, because the currents, which can run to 2.5 knots or more, can set you off course into very shallow water. If you go aground, no one can help—you simply have to wait for a high tide to lift you off.

The two main entrances to the harbor both have numerous, well-marked side channels feeding off in all directions. More southerly and frequently used by recreational craft is Nantasket Roads, giving direct access to a vast circle of bays, anchorages and rivers in the harbor's southern sector. The other, President Roads, is the main ship channel leading to the inner harbor and to northern parts of the outer harbor. Connecting the two are The Narrows and Nubble Channel.

Anchorage: With all its smaller bays and rivers, the Boston area has many anchorages. Some of these will be noted in the text below. You must keep the tidal range in mind when setting an anchor. The average rise and fall in the Boston Harbor area is 9.5 feet, and some high tides can be almost 12 feet above mean low water. An anchor rode of 50 feet in 10 feet of water (5:1) is woefully inadequate at high tide of 20 or 21 feet. Do not fail to consult the Boston tide tables when setting the anchor.

NANTASKET ROADS

NAVIGATION: Use Chart 13270. Enter Nantasket Roads between Point Allerton at the northern end of Nantasket Reach and Little Brewster Island, the site of the 102-foot-tall Boston Lighthouse. A short two miles west, turn south into Hull Gut, with its 2- to 3-knot currents, to go between Windmill Point and Peddocks Island into Hingham Bay with its various arms and islands. From the northeast corner of Hingham Bay, going clockwise, some anchorages worth knowing south of Nantasket Roads follow.

Hull Bay

Wide, well-marked Hull Bay has few obstructions and is perhaps the easiest of any Boston harbor to enter from Massachusetts Bay. Protected from all but westerlies, it has good anchorage in 8- to 10-foot depths, a hospitable yacht club and a marina that welcomes transient boats.

Anchorage: Allerton Harbor in its northeastern corner is small, shallow and crowded, but the inward channel is marked, and services for transients are available. A secure and scenic anchorage lies on the northern side of Bumkin Island in 8- to 10-foot depths. On approach, take care to avoid the submerged rock (2 feet below the surface at low tide), marked by a privately maintained buoy (a red barrel), located about 400 yards north/northeast of the western tip of the island.

Weir River

The buoyed channel passes around Worlds End and leads to Nantasket Beach, a favorite Boston retreat (excursion boats run here from Boston) with a big amusement park and a fine beach. The entrance channel leading to the public landing has a minimum depth of 5 feet.

Crow Point, Hingham Harbor

In this attractive stopover you will find a number of islands worth exploring. The channel leads past Crow Point's range lights into Hingham Harbor.

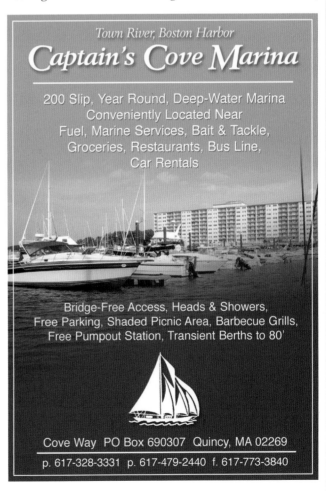

Dockage: Hingham Shipyard Marinas offers 500 slips at floating docks and 100 moorings with full marina services,

Weymouth Fore River, Hingham Bay, MA

WEYMOUTH FORE RIVER, HINGHAM BAY		Largest Vessel Accommodated	VHF Channel Monitored	Transient Berths / Total Berths	Approach / Dockside Depth (reported)	Floating Docks	Gas / Diesel	Groceries, Ice, Marine Supplies, Snacks	Repairs: Hull, Engine, Propeller	Lift (tonnage), Crane, Rail	1=110V, 2=220V, B=Both, Max Amps	Laundry, Pool, Showers	Pump-Out Station	Nearby: Grocery Store, Motel, Restaurant
		Dockage					Supplies		Services					
1. Hull Yacht Club (WiFi)	781-925-9739	45	71	MOORINGS	6/9			I				S		
2. Sunset Bay Marina	781-749-9855	30	10	6/7	7/5	F		IM					P	GMR
3. Hingham Yacht Club	781-749-9779	30			15/9		G	IS				S		
4. Hingham Shipyard Marinas (WiFi)	**781-749-6647**	**110**	**09**	**15/500**	**15/12**	**F**	**GD**	**GIMS**	**HEP**	**L35,C**	**B/50**	**LS**	**P**	**GMR**
5. R.N.R. Marine	781-740-1010		09					MS	HEP					GMR
6. Tern Harbor Marina	781-337-1964	100	09	10/140	15/10	F		IMS	HEP	L	50	S		GMR
7. Bay Pointe Marina	617-471-1777	150	09	/269	28/7	F	GD	I	HEP	L50	B/50	LS	P	R
8. Captain's Cove Marina	**617-328-3331**	**80**	**69**	**22/220**	**40/12**	**F**	**GD**	**I**			**B/50**	**S**	**P**	**GR**

Corresponding chart(s) not to be used for navigation. Internet Access (WiFi) Wireless Internet Access

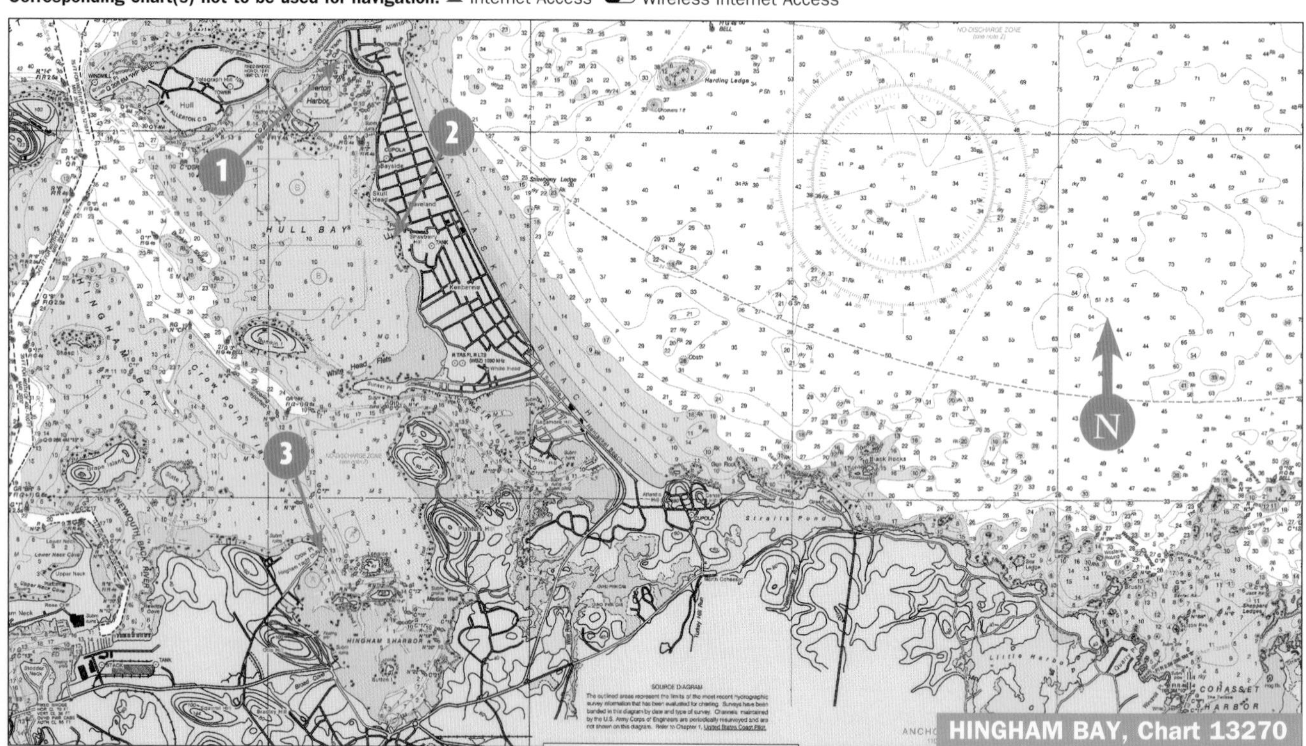

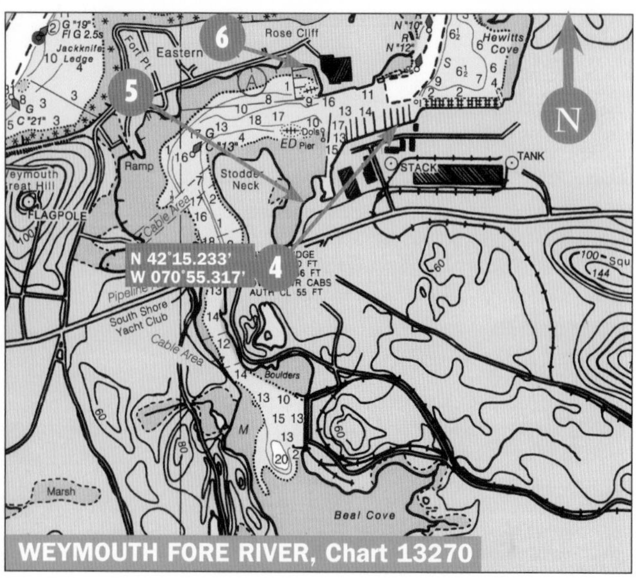

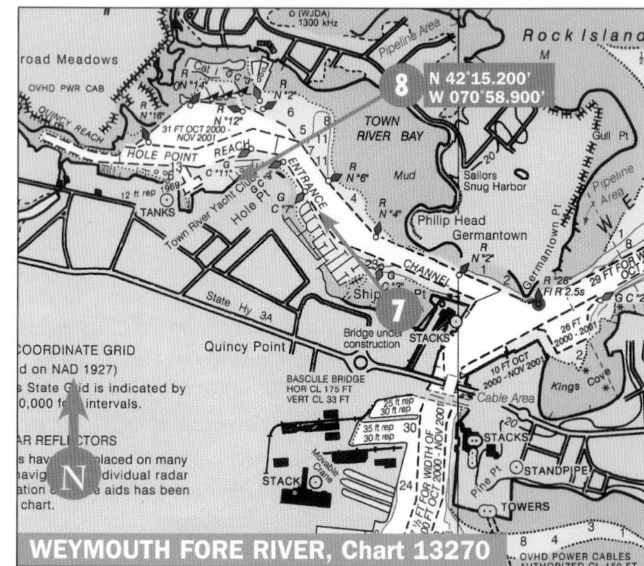

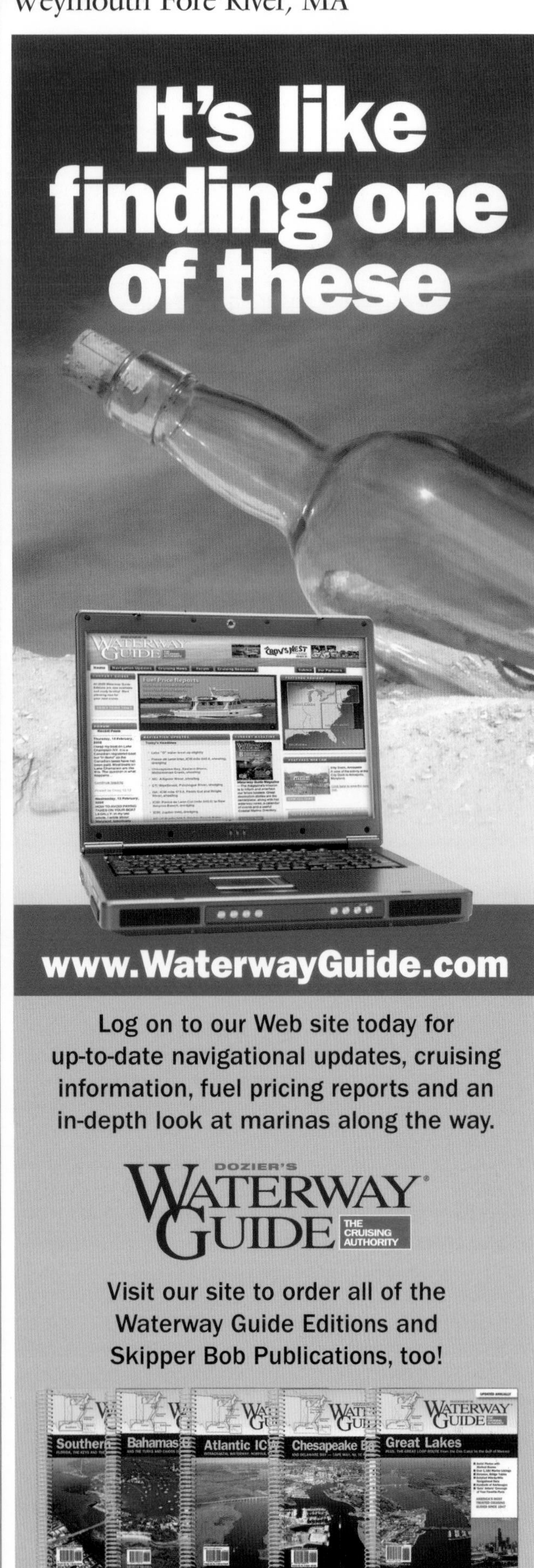

pump-out, diesel and gasoline. Hingham Shipyard is rapidly being converted into a destination marina. The marina is conveniently adjacent to the commuter ferry to downtown Boston as well as a ferry to the Boston Harbor Islands. The Boston Harbor Islands National Park are spectacular destinations for the recreational boater.

Anchorage: Hingham is a state harbor of refuge; several anchorage areas are available nearby.

Weymouth Back River

Midway between Weymouth and Hingham Harbor, this long, deep river offers both protection and a range of marine and other facilities.

Dockage: East of Stoddern Neck, on the north side of the channel, Tern Harbor Marina offers transient dockage with dockside water and electricity, but few other amenities are available within walking distance. Several restaurants are within easy walking distance, and a Super Stop and Shop is just two blocks away.

Weymouth Fore River

Wide and open to Germantown Point, the river has protected reaches that extend to East Braintree and Weymouth on the south. Upriver from the deep-draft channel, depths have been uncertain. Note restrictions: The bridge closes for weekday rush hours from 6:30 a.m. to 9 a.m. and 4:30 p.m. to 6:30 p.m.

Dockage: Turn northwest at Germantown Point and follow the entrance channel into Town River. Captain's Cove Marina lies up the reach past Hole Point. Captain's Cove offers transient slips, floating docks, gas and diesel fuel and a pump-out station.

Quincy Bay

Big and generally shallow, the bay has a number of yacht clubs along its shores.

Boston Harbor Islands National Park

The islands of outer Boston Harbor have long been a wonderful cruising ground; now enhanced by the development of the Islands and inclusion in the Boston Harbor Islands National Park. The Park service has placed moorings in six locations and built a 50-slip marina at Spectacle Island. Spectacle "grew" due to hundreds of tons of fill from the Big Dig project in Boston. The marina serves as a second transportation hub for the island ferries and has a restaurant on-site.

Reservations for marina slips and moorings can be made at 617-241-9640 for moorings and 617-645-0971 for marina slips.

Georges Island

On the northern edge of Nantasket Roads, this hub of the Boston Harbor Islands State Park system is accessible only by boat. Historic Fort Warren, built in 1689, offers a panoramic sweep of Boston Harbor. A wharf on the island's west side is best approached by dinghy.

Dockage and Anchorage: Best anchorage is north of the pier, but substantial weekend traffic and eddying currents through and around the islands keep the waters disturbed. The park also offers free day-use-only dockage on a first-come, first-served basis. Its pier has floating dock space to accommodate up to 20 boats, and boaters are asked to dock bow or stern to the float (no broadside docking). The Boston Harbor Islands National Recreation Area has approximately 50 rental moorings scattered among the islands. For reservations, contact the mooring manager on VHF Channel 09, by phone at 857-452-7221 or via e-mail at moorings@bosport.com. The calmest, most sheltered moorings (and anchorage) are on the west side of Peddocks Island.

Ashore, visitors can take a guided tour of the fort or explore the island on their own. Restrooms, picnic areas with grills and a snack bar are here. In addition, George's Island is the second hub of the water taxi service to five other islands in the harbor: Lovell's, Gallop's, Peddocks, Grape and Bumkin islands. These islands offer hiking areas, picnic trails and camping. They reserve their docks for off-loading people and supplies; boaters must anchor out, use one of the newly installed National Park Service moorings scattered throughout the islands or tie up at George's Island and take the water taxi to explore.

Little Brewster Island

Located on Little Brewster Island is the Boston Light (617-223-8666), the oldest light station in North America. Although boaters can view the light from offshore; it is not recommended to attempt a landing on the dock. Tours of the island and light begin at Fan Pier in South Boston and include a narrated history of Boston harbor and its lights as well as viewing of two other lighthouses.

PRESIDENT ROADS

Southwest of President Roads, the inner coves of Dorchester Bay and tidal reaches of the Neponset Bay are home to a number of yacht clubs and two large, full-service marinas.

Dockage: East of Squantum Point, Marina Bay on Boston Harbor is more of a self-contained yachting community than a marina. With some 685 berths, it is one of the largest marinas in the Northeast. Transient slips are usually available (though a call ahead is advisable), and easily approached in at least 12-foot depths (mean low water). On arrival, you will find five restaurants within a stroll of your slip, plus the Center Market (617-472-4499) with a take-out deli menu and basic groceries. In addition to restrooms, showers, coin-operated laundry machines and ice, you can access ATM, fax and express mailing services and haul-out for repairs (35-ton lift). Call a cab (Marina Bay Taxi, 617-472-4111) for rapid access to a pharmacy and complete re-provisioning possibilities at the nearby Super Stop & Shop, or a 15-minute ride to downtown Boston.

Adjacent Quincy, MA, offers multiple churches, hotels, interstate transportation and car rentals. Just west of the marina, the Marina Bay Beach Club (333 Victory Blvd., 617-689-0600) is a large and unusual nightclub, offering barbecue-style dining and live entertainment nightly during the season. In addition to the modern attractions, the Marina Bay area is steeped in history. The lightship Nantucket (617-821-6771) is permanently moored at Marina Bay and open for tours. During World War I, the nearby Victory Shipyard built a ship for the war effort in 45 days, a record still unequaled. A clock tower on the waterfront is a memorial to the Quincy losses in the Vietnam War. A fast ferry to Provincetown is available from Marina Bay.

West of Squantum Point, across the Neponset River, Norwood Marine is likely to have transient space as well as fuel and other amenities. The west side of the river holds a number of additional mooring possibilities for members of recognized yacht clubs: Dorchester Yacht Club, Savin Hill Yacht Club, Peninsula Yacht Club and Old Colony Yacht Club.

Boston's Inner Harbor

As you enter the Inner Harbor, downtown Boston's skyline fills the view to port. The huge and distinctive federal courthouse on the northeast elbow of South Boston serves as a sentinel beacon to the first of three excellent marinas that will take your lines for a berth in the center of the city's historic district.

Dockage: Directly across Fort Point Channel from the federal courthouse, the Marina at Rowe's Wharf is next to the ferry landing, under the massive arch of the hotel and condominium complex on the wharf. Accommodations can be made for vessels up to 135 feet. Showers, restrooms and laundry machines are next to the marina office, and there is a UPS box just outside. The Rowe's Wharf Water Taxi (617-406-8584) may be the most convenient transportation for you or your crew to Logan Airport. In this area of the harbor, a visitor will see a large fleet of daysailers that belong to the Boston Sailing Club, a major organization that promotes interest in boating.

The equivalent of a long city block farther north, just past the distinctive New England Aquarium on Central Wharf, Boston Waterboat Marina is tucked behind the north side of Long Wharf. The marina traces its heritage to the days when Boston's actual waterboat—tasked to tend oceangoing vessels moored in the harbor—once berthed here. Though enlarged and modernized, the marina still retains something of the salty air of its commercial past. Today its protected floating docks shelter a summertime mix of year-round liveaboards, long-term summer residents and transients in a relaxed atmosphere that seems incongruous with the busy city scene on land. The marina has restroom, showers and laundry facilities, but immediately accessible city amenities provide much more. Christopher Columbus Park at the foot of Long Wharf has an extraordinary play-scape for the younger set and a doggie park for canine crew. The unique shops and restaurants of Faneuil

Looking northwest over Boston's Inner Harbor. (Not to be used for navigation.)

Hall and Quincy Market are less than a block away. The New England Aquarium (617-973-5200), besides being a world-class attraction in its own right, has commercial parking for visitors, and the water shuttle (berthed on the south side of Long Wharf) will take you anyplace in the harbor.

On Commercial Wharf, the next to the north, Boston Yacht Haven is capable of handling virtually any boat up to and including megayachts (to 300 feet) at its state-of-the-art floating dock system. The marina boasts a splendid clubhouse, hotel and restaurant at the center of the complex. Telephone and cable TV connections and pump-out also are available. At the epicenter of Boston's Historic District, the Yacht Haven's full-service slips are in high demand, suggesting an advance reservation for assurance that a slip will be available on arrival.

East Boston

Across the harbor from the downtown waterfront is East Boston, bordering the property of Logan Airport. Just north of the airport property is a shipyard that appears to be inactive at times. There is a large marina and boatyard service facility adjacent to the shipyard, with docks well protected from passing ship wakes by stationary barges. In recent years, the facility has been operated by Boston Boatworks (617-561-9111) and has offered some dockage to transients. This yard also is your best bet for haul-out and repair in Boston Harbor. An easy 10-minute walk leads you to Maverick Station on the Blue Line of the Boston subway system.

Charlestown

From the Inner Harbor, a turn to port takes you into the mouth of the Charles River.

Dockage: On the east side of the decommissioned Navy Yard, steps from the final berthing of the USS Constitution, the World War II Destroyer Cassin Young and the Korean War Veterans Memorial, you will find Shipyard Quarters Marina on Pier Six and Pier Eight. The marina offers ample transient space for vessels of all sizes. Reservations are strongly suggested to guarantee space. Video cameras enable boaters to view their vessels online. Showers, restrooms and laundry are offered on both piers, along with complimentary wireless Internet service.

One of New England's favorite destinations, Tavern on the Water (617-242-8040), located on Pier Six, offers unequaled views and great dining for lunch and dinner. The adjacent water shuttle leaves every 15 minutes for Faneuil Hall and downtown.

Immediately east of Constitution Marina, its namesake, the *USS Constitution* ("Old Ironsides"), famed frigate of the War of 1812, has found its final berth in the Charle-

- The Best of Boston Just Off your Bow

Boston Inner Harbor

Constitution Marina
28 Constitution Road

Boston, MA 02129
617-241-9640 • Fax 617-242-3013
Email: Sebastian@bosport.com
www.constitutionmarina.com

Constitution Marina

- Boston Inner Harbor

Dockage Rate: $3.00 to $4.00/ft/day. Call for weekly, monthly, and special event rates.
Payment: Credit Card/Cash
Hours: 8am-8pm
Transient Slips/Total Slips: 265
VHF/Working: 69
MLW/LOA: 20'+/200'
Electric: 30/50/100 Amp
Pump-Out: Stationary & mobile
Fuel: Nearby, guest discounts
Repair: Yes
Restaurant/Miles: On premises & 200+/<1/4 mile
Pool: Yes
Haul-Out: Nearby
Head/Shower: Yes/Yes
Laundry: Yes
Internet Access: High-speed wireless
Cable: Yes
Special: The most protected docking on Boston Harbor! Located on the Historic Freedrom Trail. Concierge service, water taxi available, pool & deck.

Island Moorings Available

Spectacle Island Marina

- Boston Harbor Islands National Park

Dockage Rate: $20.00/boat/day (-30')
$30.00/boat/day (30'+) $1.75/ft/night (overnight)
Payment: Credit Card/Cash
Hours: Day 9am-6pm Night 5:30pm-10:30am
Transient Slips/Total Slips: 50/50
VHF/Working: 69
MLW/LOA: 7'/100'+
Electric: No
Pump-Out: Yes
Fuel: No
Head/Shower: Yes; day time only/No
Nearest Town/Miles: Boston/2 miles
Special: Spectacular views of Boston and surrounding islands. Located at the entrance to Boston Harbor. Part of the National Parks. Five miles of groomed walking trails. Two hills with gazebos and picnic tables. The highest elevation of any Boston Harbor Island. Conference facilities & museum. Volleyball & Two beaches. Convenient shuttle boat to Boston & other harbor islands.

Boston Harbor Islands National Park

Spectacle Island Marina
28 Constitution Road
Boston, MA 02129
857-452-7221 • Fax 617-242-3013
Email: cathy@bosport.com
www.constitutionmarina.com

Boston, South Boston, MA

BOSTON, SOUTH BOSTON		Largest Vessel Accommodated	VHF Channel Monitored	Transient Berths / Total Berths	Approach / Dockside Depth (reported)	Floating Docks	Gas / Diesel	Groceries, Ice, Marine Supplies, Snacks	Repairs: Hull, Engine, Propeller	Lift (tonnage), Crane, Rail	1=110V, 2=220V, B=Both, Max Amps	Laundry, Pool, Showers	Pump-Out Station	Nearby: Grocery Store, Motel, Restaurant
		Dockage					Supplies		Services					
1. Russo Marine 💻 WiFi	617-288-1000	60		20/150	17/17	F	GD	IM	HEP	L60	B/50			R
2. Old Colony Yacht Club	617-436-0513	46		6/	6/4			I			1/20			
3. Marina Bay on Boston Harbor 💻 WiFi	617-847-1800	210	10	100/685	14/12	F	GD	GIS	HEP	L35	B/100	LS	P	GMR
4. Dorchester Yacht Club	617-436-1002	40			6/6		G							R
5. Spectacle Island Marina	**857-452-7221**	**80**	**69**	**40/40**	**12/10**	**F**		**IS**						**R**
6. South Boston Yacht Club	617-268-6132	30			6/6		G	I						
7. Crystal Cove Marina	617-846-SAIL	70	10	10/118	6/6	F	GD	GI	HP	C15	B/30	LS		GMR
8. Marina at Rowes Wharf WiFi	617-748-5013	240	09	20/45	30/25	F		IS		R	B/100	LPS	P	GMR
9. Boston Yacht Haven 💻 WiFi	617-367-5050	300	09	15/75	25/25	F		I			B/100	LS	P	GMR
10. Boston Waterboat Marina	617-523-1027	160	09	12/36	32/14	F		I			B/100	LS	P	GMR
11. Constitution Marina 💻 WiFi	**617-241-9640**	**180**	**16/69**	**100/265**	**35/35**	**F**		**IS**	**HEP**		**B/100**	**LPS**	**P**	**GMR**
12. Shipyard Quarters Marina WiFi	617-242-2020	300	71	30/400	45/35	F		I			B/100	LS	P	GMR
13. Admiral's Hill Marina WiFi	617-889-4002	60	09	5/136	6/6	F	GD	IMS	HEP	L50	B/50	LS	P	GR

Corresponding chart(s) not to be used for navigation. 💻 Internet Access WiFi Wireless Internet Access

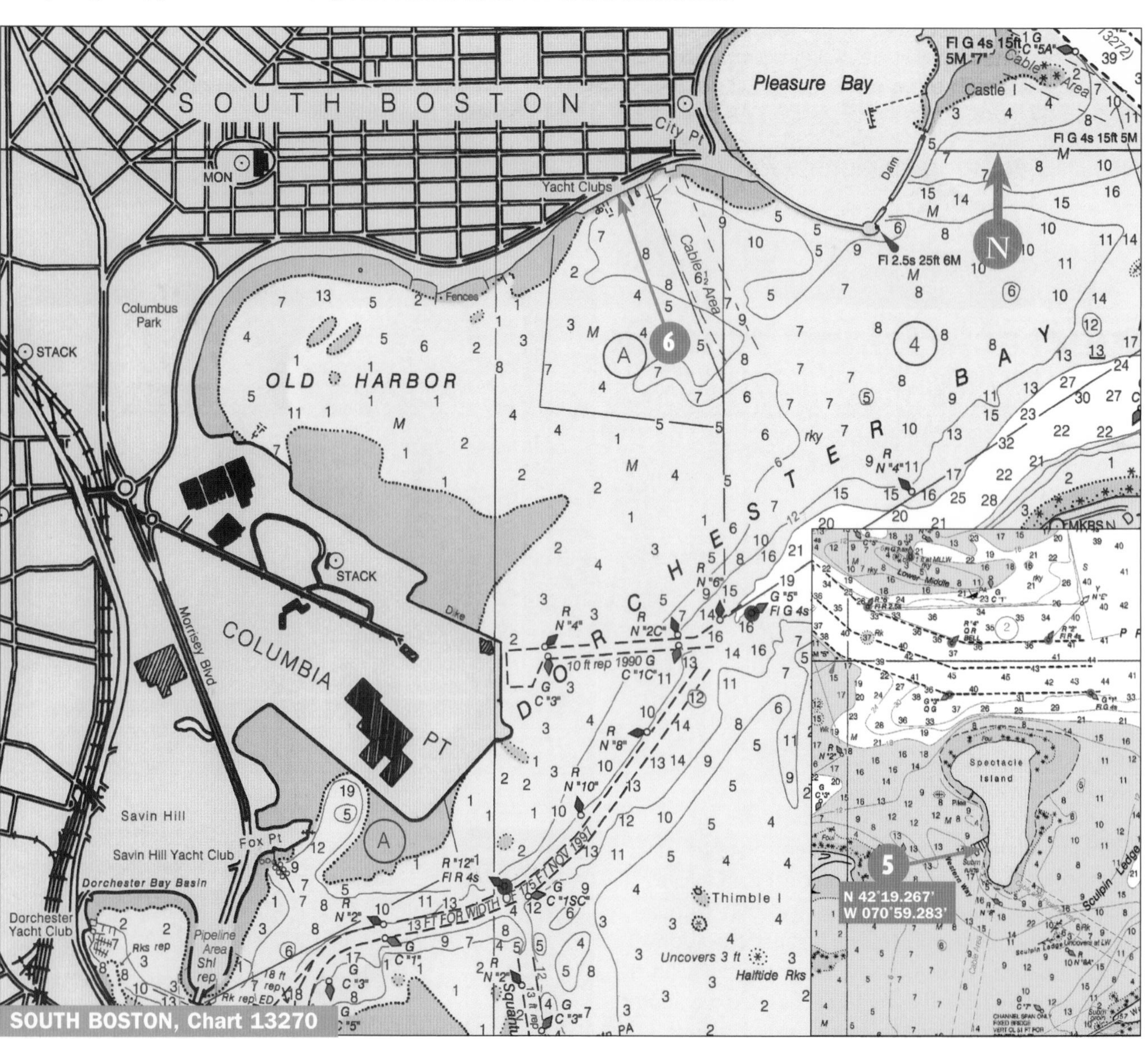

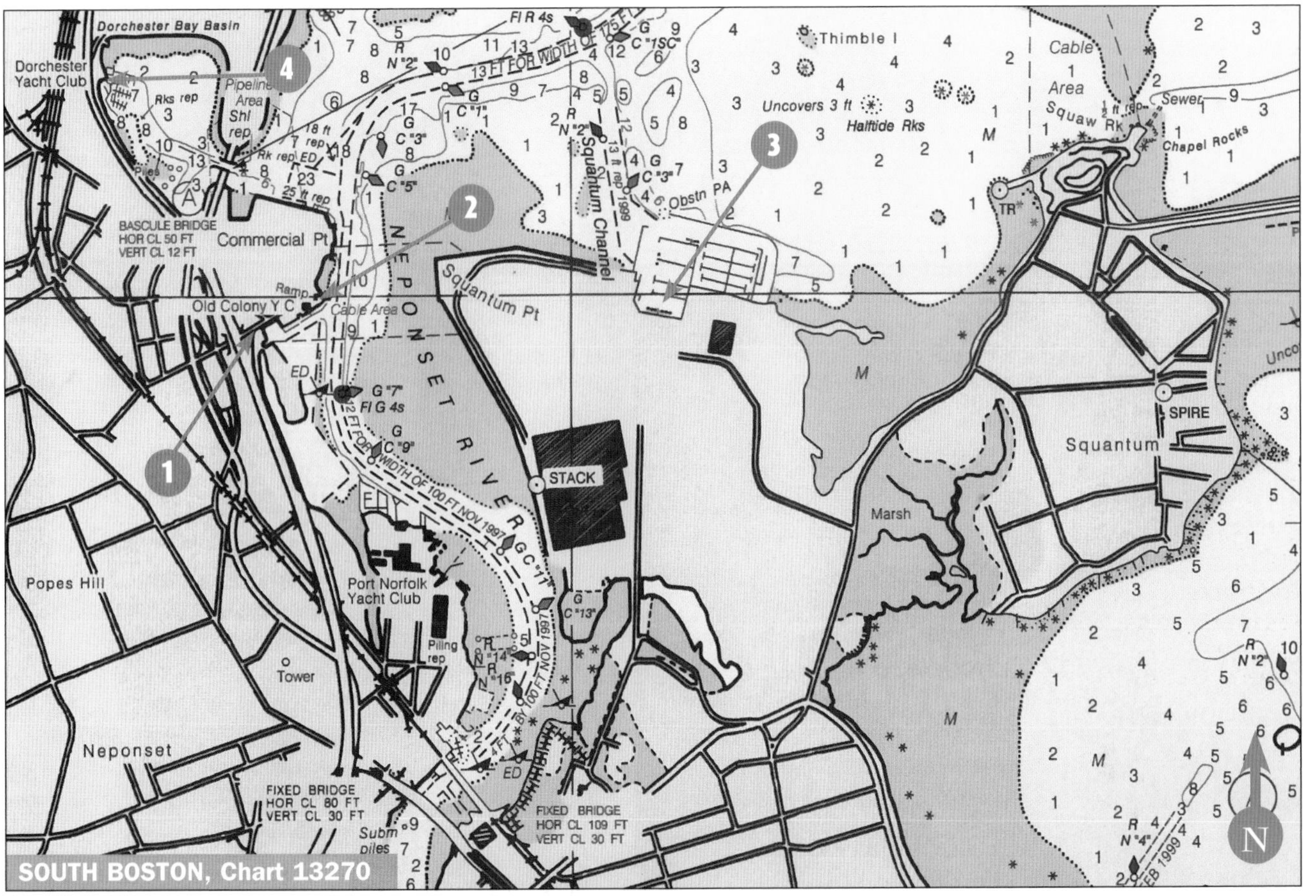

SOUTH BOSTON, Chart 13270

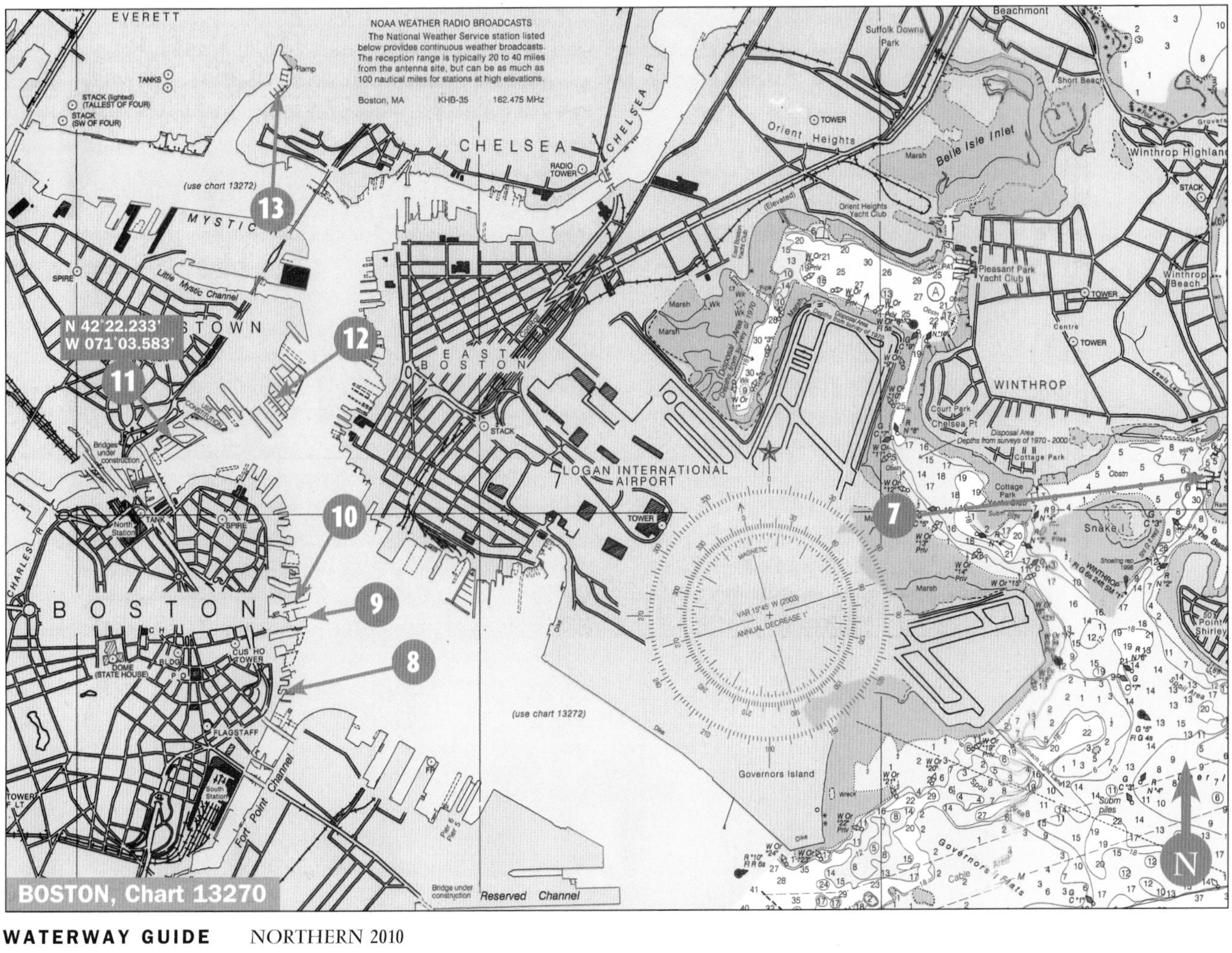

BOSTON, Chart 13270

NOAA WEATHER RADIO BROADCASTS

The National Weather Service station listed below provides continuous weather broadcasts. The reception range is typically 20 to 40 miles from the antenna site, but can be as much as 100 nautical miles for stations at high elevations.

Boston, MA KHB-35 162.475 MHz

N 42°22.233'
W 071°03.583'

stown Navy Yard (a.k.a., Boston Navy Yard and Boston Naval Shipyard), and is now maintained as a historic site by the National Park Service (617-242-5670).

On the north side of the river, just below the landmark Charlestown Bridge, Constitution Marina offers protected floating berths. Because of its proximity to downtown (either by foot or water taxi) and accessibility to a variety of amenities, the marina is home to about 100 liveaboards. There is usually ample transient space, though reservations are advised. Wireless Internet access is available at all slips. In addition to its dock complex, Constitution Marina operates Spectacle Island Marina and the island moorings program for the National Park Service. Moorings in the scenic outer harbor are rented to visitors. Restrooms, showers and laundry facilities are available at Constitution Marina's main building, and restaurants are within easy walking distance.

Of special note among the restaurants is the ancient Warren Tavern (2 Pleasant St., 617-241-8142). One of Robert B. Parker's characters in "Ceremony" (one of the series of Spenser detective novels, all set in and around Boston) says of the tavern: "It's in Charlestown, good place. Old. Food's good." The description has been apt for quite a while. It was a favorite of Paul Revere's, and George Washington at least once took "refreshments" here as well. The tavern was named in honor of Dr. Joseph Warren, an ardent American patriot who fell at the Battle of Bunker Hill, located just two blocks away.

GOIN' ASHORE: **BOSTON, MA**

Boston's attractions, historic landmarks and amenities are so numerous that they deserve a guidebook of their own. Fortunately, several are widely available in tourist shops around the harbor, but a good place to start, with an excellent map of major attractions and a free-guided tour, is the National Park Service booth at Faneuil Hall.

For those berthed next to the Historic District, access to reprovisioning and dining possibilities is immediate. Farm-fresh produce, along with a huge selection of specialty items, is on sale in the stalls and shops of Quincy Market (next to Faneuil Hall). An even larger selection of food items is offered a couple of blocks north at Haymarket. For basic groceries, deli items, newspapers or beverages, Christy's (in front of the New England Aquarium) is the most convenient. Restaurants in both waterfront hotels—Meritage (617-439-3995) in the Boston Harbor Hotel on Rowe's Wharf and Oceana (617-227-3838) in the Marriott Hotel on Long Wharf—receive praise for high-quality food and service. The Marriott receives especially high praise for its buffet breakfasts, served daily. Rudi's Resto Cafe (30 Rowe's Wharf, 617-459-4155) is also recommended for specialty pastries and coffees—outdoors when the weather is right.

For consistently excellent seafood, both Legal Sea Foods (617-523-0512) and the Barking Crab (617-426-2722) are easily reached on foot from any of the downtown marinas. In the North End, within reasonable walking distance from marinas on both sides of the Charles River, are dozens of Italian

Looking north over Nahant. (Not to be used for navigation.) WATERWAY GUIDE PHOTOGRAPHY

Lynn Harbor, MA

LYNN HARBOR		Largest Vessel Accommodated	VHF Channel Monitored	Transient Berths / Total Berths	Approach / Dockside Depth (reported)	Floating Docks	Gas / Diesel	Groceries, Ice, Marine Supplies, Snacks	Repairs: Hull, Engine, Propeller	Lift (tonnage), Crane, Rail	1=110V, 2=220V, B=Both, Max Amps	Laundry, Pool, Showers	Pump-Out Station	Nearby: Grocery Store, Motel, Restaurant
		Dockage					Supplies			Services				
1. Lynn Yacht Club	781-595-9825	50	09	2/50	12/8	F		I		L	1/30	S		R
2. Seaport Landing Marina	781-592-5821	65	16/09	20/200	20/15	F	GD	GIMS	HEP	L25	B/50	LS	P	GR
3. Lynn Municipal Pier	781-593-9850	200	16/09	10/10	20/20	F	COMMERCIAL ONLY				B			R

Corresponding chart(s) not to be used for navigation. Internet Access Wireless Internet Access

restaurants, plus a sprinkling of Irish pubs and untold numbers of interesting shops. If docked in Charlestown, try Paolo's Trattoria (251 Main St., 617-242-7229) for excellent contemporary Italian. They will deliver to Charlestown Marina.

For a guided circuit of the Historic District, a narrated trolley tour from Boston Upper Deck Tours (617-742-1440) is a good choice. For those with more specialized historical and cultural interests, Boston is home to the John F. Kennedy Library and Museum (617-514-1600); the magnificent art collection of the Isabella Stewart Gardner Museum, set in a reproduction of a 15th-century Venetian palace (617-566-1401); one of the world's greatest collections of American and European paintings at the Museum of Fine Arts (617-267-9300); the innumerable interactive exhibits of the Childrens Museum (300 Congress St., 617-426-8855); and the Boston Symphony Orchestra/Pops (617-266-1492).

Boston has long been a destination city for land-bound tourists. Now, with its newly cleaned harbor and refurbished marine facilities, it has clearly become a prime destination for cruising travelers as well.

ADDITIONAL RESOURCES:

- Greater Boston Convention and Visitors Bureau, **www.bostonusa.com**

NEARBY GOLF COURSES:
William Devine Golf Course At Franklin Park,
1 Circuit Drive, Dorchester, MA 02121, 617-265-4084

NEARBY MEDICAL FACILITIES:
Massachusetts General Hospital, 55 Fruit St.,
Boston, MA 02114, 617-726-2000

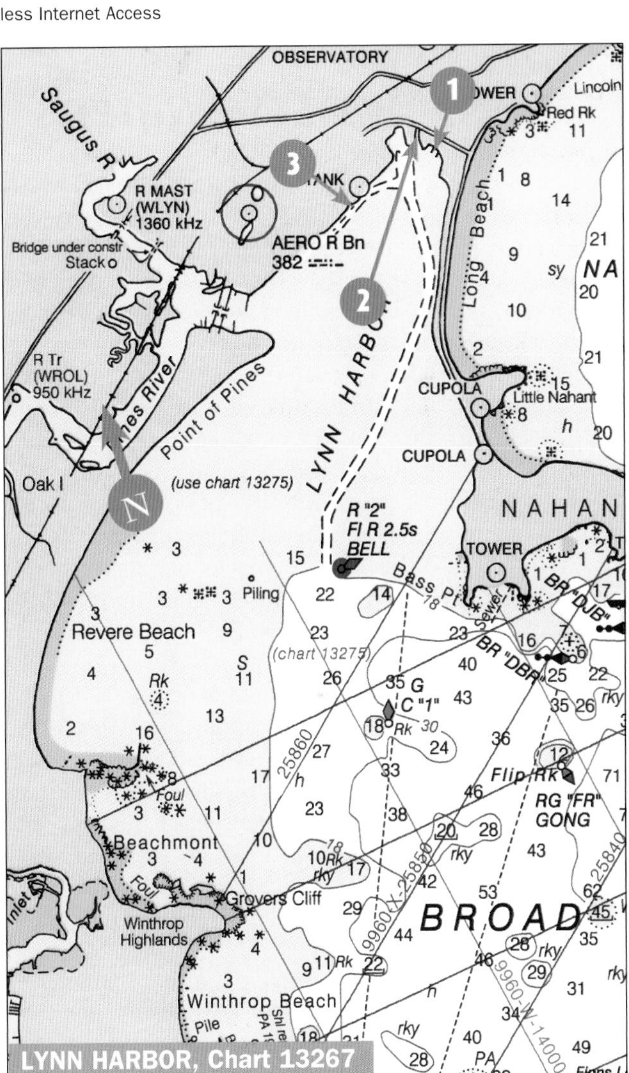

LYNN HARBOR, Chart 13267

BOSTON'S OUTER HARBOR

NAVIGATION: Use Chart 13270. From Boston Harbor, North Channel (preferred) and South Channel both lead from President Roads into big Broad Sound. Wide North Channel, marked by large, lighted sea buoys, is the primary thoroughfare for both big ships and recreational craft. South Channel is narrower, aids are smaller and ledges encroach.

From Finns Ledge at the northern end of North Channel, it is three miles to Bass Point on the southwestern tip of Nahant. Beyond Nahant are two narrow channels, one to marinas in Lynn, and the other to Point of Pines and Pines River. North Channel leads to Boston's North Shore.

Cruising Options

Just 12 miles northeast of Boston Harbor lies Salem Sound, lined by the harbors of Marblehead, Salem, Beverly and Manchester. Here, the mariner will find destinations rich in boating amenities and nautical heritage.

Massachusetts Bay to Portsmouth

CHARTS 13267, 13272, 13274, 13275, 13276, 13278, 13279, 13281, 13282, 13283, 13285, 13286

MASSACHUSETTS WATERS

Four fine, historic harbors—Marblehead, Salem, Beverly and Manchester—line Salem Sound, a four-mile-wide break in the shore located 12 miles northeast of Boston Harbor's entrance. Though all four began as commercial fishing centers, they have evolved into popular recreational harbors with dockage, moorings, marine businesses and a wealth of shoreside attractions.

Salem Sound's mouth is littered with islands, rocks and ledges, with three main channels threading through them. Strangers should be wary of trying to enter or leave in heavy weather or poor visibility. Good landmarks are on both sides of the sound: the tall lights on Bakers Island and Marblehead Neck; the five stacks of Salem's power plant; the radio tower opposite on Naugus Head; and the observation tower on Gales Point.

Salem Channel, the northernmost entrance, is the deep-draft passage used by commercial craft heading for Salem's terminals. It runs between Bakers and Great Misery islands, through Salem Sound, and then turns to the southeast to Salem Harbor. In the middle is Childrens Island Channel, which leads between Childrens and Eagle islands. Marblehead Channel, to the west, runs between Childrens Island and Marblehead Neck, then along the peninsula past mid-sound rocks and shoals to Salem Harbor.

Tidal range here averages 9 feet, and the tidal current has little force, except in Beverly Harbor, where it sets across the channel in several places.

Marblehead

Famous throughout the yachting world as the Yachting Capital of America, Marblehead was historically a fishing village. Even today, the harbor maintains a small fleet of lobster and fishing vessels. But more than ever, this is a home and layover port for cruising and racing boats from the world's most serious yachting circles.

The 12-meter *Nefertiti* was designed and built here; the Marblehead-Halifax race starts here on alternate years, and local races are virtually nonstop all summer. Some of the most elegant cruising vessels on the East Coast can be seen here, and a visit to Marblehead is not complete without a boat-lover's tour around the harbor. Lest you feel intimidated, this is also an accommodating and friendly port for cruisers arriving on something less than a classic 12-meter.

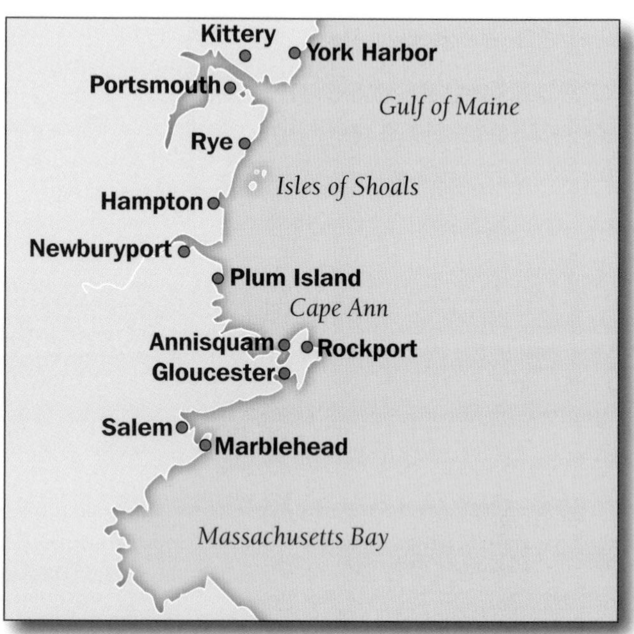

NAVIGATION: Use Chart 13274. The harbor is well-protected in all directions except the northeast. Indeed, many vessels have fetched up on the causeway beach at the head of the harbor during a three-day nor'easter. If the wind veers toward that direction, seek shelter elsewhere.

Dockage and Moorings: Though anchoring in this busy harbor is no longer a realistic prospect, four yacht clubs, a full-service boatyard and the town of Marblehead are likely to have moorings available to visitors, either gratis or for a modest fee. Most of the remaining moorings in the harbor are privately owned and you must call one of the several listed yacht clubs to arrange for mooring based upon availability. Contact the Marblehead harbormaster (VHF Channel 16 or telephone 781-631-2386) for availability of transient dock space and for assistance on your approach.

Marblehead, MA

MARBLEHEAD		Largest Vessel Accommodated	VHF Channel Monitored	Transient Berths / Total Berths	Approach / Dockside Depth (reported)	Floating Docks	Gas / Diesel	Groceries, Ice, Marine Supplies, Snacks	Repairs: Hull, Engine, Propeller	Lift (tonnage), Crane, Rail	1=110V, 2=220V, B=Both, Max Amps	Laundry, Pool, Showers	Pump-Out Station	Nearby: Grocery Store, Motel, Restaurant
		Dockage					Supplies		Services					
1. Corinthian Yacht Club	781-631-0005	100	69		10/7	F					1/30	LPS		GMR
2. Eastern Yacht Club	781-631-1400			PRIVATE CLUB										
3. Dolphin Yacht Club	781-631-8000		68	MOORINGS	20/8					RECIPROCAL		S		R
4. Boston Yacht Club	781-631-3100	80	68	MOORINGS	20/20		GD	I				S	P	GMR
5. Marblehead Harbormaster	781-631-2386	100	16		22/15	F					B/100	LS	P	GR
6. Lynn Marine Supply	**781-631-1305**		**09**					**M**						**R**
7. The Landing Restaurant	781-639-1878	60		3/12	25/15	F								R
8. Marblehead Trading Co.	781-639-0029	100		4/	30/17	F	GD	IM	HEP	CR	B/100			GMR

Corresponding chart(s) not to be used for navigation. Internet Access Wireless Internet Access

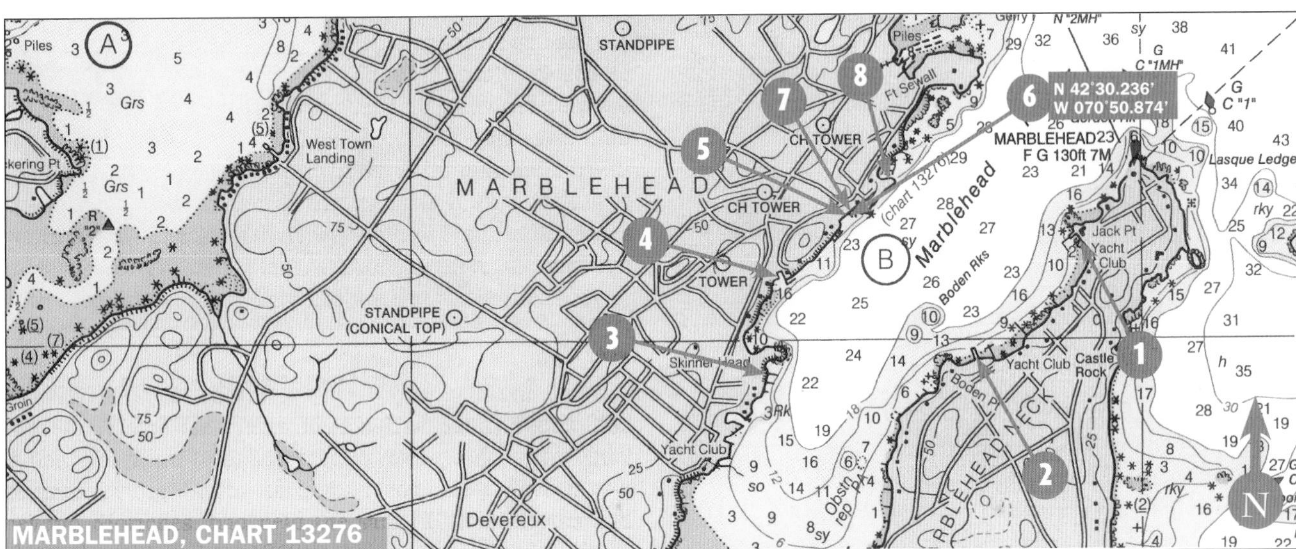

After entry, to starboard, about halfway down the length of the harbor, the Marblehead Trading Company (781-639-0029) is a compact but complete boatyard with major lift capacity and a marine supply store, The Forepeak Ship's Chandlery (89 Front St., 781-631-7184). Several courtesy moorings are normally available here, though there is no launch service. The Marblehead Town (Philip T. Clark) Landing is immediately ahead, with a large dinghy dock and additional floating docks for loading and unloading (30-minute limit). Public restrooms, phones, trash barrels and limited parking are just above the dock.

Lynn Marine Supply, a traditional ship's chandlery, (65 Front St., 781-631-1395), is handy to this location, with charts, hardware and all manner of nautical supplies. Open at 8 a.m. daily, the store closes at 5 p.m. on Sunday, 6 p.m. on Saturday and 7 p.m. Monday through Friday.

Farther west, still to starboard, the Boston Yacht Club is as elegant as it is famous. The impressive, multi-story clubhouse even has rooms to let to members of other recognized clubs. Visiting yachtsmen, as guests of the club, may request a rental mooring, available on a first-come, first-served basis, including launch service and use of the club's restrooms and showers. Lunch and dinner are served daily (outside grill during summer weekends and Wednesday nights). Still farther west, the Dolphin Yacht Club also may have moorings and launch service available, as may the Marblehead Yacht Club, Corinthian Yacht Club and the Eastern Yacht Club, all on the south side of the harbor.

Looking west over Marblehead Harbor. (Not to be used for navigation.) WATERWAY GUIDE PHOTOGRAPHY

GOIN' ASHORE: **MARBLEHEAD, MA**

Along the waterfront and for several blocks inland, 18th-century buildings—both modest and luxurious, residential and ancient-commercial—please the senses at every turn. Echoes of the Colonial, Revolutionary and Federal periods abound: the three-story Georgian "double" mansion of Greenleaf and Robert Hooper (c. 1728 and 1747); Saint Michael's Church, built by American shipwrights in 1714; the Town House of 1727, where Marbleheaders mustered for wars from the French and Indian to the Spanish-American; Fort Sewall (c. 1747), built on the original defense works erected by early settlers in 1644; the Lafayette House (c. 1731), so named because a corner had to be cut off its lower floor so that the Marquis de Lafayette's carriage could pass; the Elbridge Gerry birthplace (c. 1742), original home of the famed signer of the Declaration of Independence and inventor of politically inspired mal apportionment of voting districts ("gerrymandering"); the home (c. 1762) of Gen. John Glover, the first Marine general, who evacuated George Washington's troops from Long Island, carried them across the Delaware River and led the advance on Trenton; and many others.

Claims by nearby Beverly notwithstanding, Marblehead has been termed "the birthplace of the American Navy" because of the number of ships and men from Marblehead that were involved in the fledging Navy of Revolutionary War times. The prosperity of Marblehead was seriously affected by the losses of men, ships and commerce during the war years and the town was slow to recover.

In addition, modern amenities await the visitor. Nautical supplies can be found at Lynn Marine Supply (65 Front St.). Front and center on the waterfront, two popular restaurants flank the Philip T. Clark Landing. To the east, the Landing Pub Restaurant (81 Front St., 781-639-1266), serving lunch Monday through Saturday, Sunday brunch, dinner daily, has fresh-catch seafood, pastas, flowing suds and an unparalleled view of harbor activities. To the west, the Driftwood Restaurant (63 Front St., 781-631-1145) is open from 5:30 a.m. until 2 p.m. to serve a hearty breakfast and, later in the day, for seafood plates and sandwich lunches. The Barnacle (141 Front St., 781-631-4236), a few blocks east of the landing, serves steaks and seafood in a casual waterfront setting. Crosbyís Market (118 Washington St., a block north of the landing via State Street, 781-631-1741) is stocked with a full line of groceries, a huge deli selection, bakery items, bag-your-own nuts, grains, granola, beer and wine.

The contemporary village of Marblehead is several blocks north of the waterfront and most of a mile west. Most shops, restaurants and other services are located along Atlantic Avenue. There you will find two pharmacies; Fruit of the Four Seasons (34 Atlantic Ave., 781-631-9784) for fresh fruits and vegetables, Cafe Appassionato's (12 Atlantic Ave., 781-639-4236) special-roast coffees; and Fleet National Bank with an ATM. The Sand Bar Grille (259 Washington St., 781-631-1687, open daily), according to locals, has a great salad bar and is a top value for large portions from a varied menu (raw bar 3 p.m. to 6 p.m. daily).

Looking northeast over Salem Harbor. (Not to be used for navigation.) WATERWAY GUIDE PHOTOGRAPHY

Music lovers have two reasons to visit Marblehead in the summer: Symphony By The Sea (978-745-4955) is a series of classical performances in Abbott Hall (188 Washington St.) and the Marblehead Summer Jazz Festival conducts a series of concerts at the Unitarian Universalist Church on Mugford Street during the season. Visitors to Marblehead on the Fourth of July are treated to arts and crafts exhibits at The Marblehead Festival of Arts and the Harbour Illumination, in which hundreds of volunteers hold flares around the harbor, followed by incredible fireworks. A great way to stretch your legs is to follow the free walking tour of the town. You can download a free walking tour of Historic Marblehead at www.visitmarblehead.com or at the Chamber office at 62 Pleasant St. (781-631-2868).

ADDITIONAL RESOURCES:

- Marblehead Travel Guide, **www.visitmarblehead.com**

NEARBY GOLF COURSES:
Kelley Greens Golf Course, 1 Willow Road, Nahant, MA 01908, 781-581-0840, **www.kelleygreens.com**

NEARBY MEDICAL FACILITIES:
Lydia Pinkham Memorial Clinic, 250 Derby St., Salem, MA 01970, 978-744-3288

Salem

For a few years around the turn of the 18th century, Salem was truly America's trading capital and crossroads of the world. Daring sea captains and undaunted investors launched voyages that would open up the lucrative eastern trade to New England. Vessels laden with cod, rum, shingles and other products plied angry waters around Cape Horn and Cape of Good Hope to exchange their goods for exotic spices and other luxuries, returning (when disaster was averted) to reap vast profits. By 1800, Salem was the sixth largest city in America and the richest per capita. Salem sent out so many merchant ships that many foreigners assumed that the port must have been an independent nation.

Although those days are gone, the aura of that time persists in the grand homes and government houses that marked the era and in a few remaining wharves memorializing the many that once stretched their arms toward returning ships from the Orient. Salem's Marine National Historic Site (the nation's oldest), numerous intriguing museums, fashionable period homes, points of interest, restaurants and boating amenities are within easy walking distance of this premier harbor. The harbor itself is home port to a multi-million-dollar replica of the 171-foot *Friendship*, a world-ranging square-rigged trading ship, originally launched in 1797.

Salem, Beverly, MA

SALEM, BEVERLY		Largest Vessel Accommodated	VHF Channel Monitored	Transient Berths / Total Berths	Approach / Dockside Depth (reported)	Floating Docks	Gas / Diesel	Groceries, Ice, Marine Supplies, Snacks	Repairs: Hull, Engine, Propeller	Lift (tonnage), Crane, Rail	1=110V, 2=220V, B=Both, Max Amps	Laundry, Pool, Showers	Pump-Out Station	Nearby: Grocery Store, Motel, Restaurant
		Dockage					Supplies		Services					
1. Hawthorne Cove Marina	**978-740-9890**	**65**	**09**	**10/110**	**15/6**	**F**		**IM**	**HEP**	**L35**	**B/50**	**LS**		**GMR**
2. H&H Propeller Shop Inc. (OFF-WATER)	978-744-3806								P					
3. Pickering Wharf Marina (Internet Access) (WiFi)	**978-744-2727**	**120**	**09**	**10/100**	**8/8**	**F**		**GIS**			**1/50**	**LS**		**GMR**
4. Salem Water Taxi Inc.	**978-745-6070**	**65**	**68**	**10/120**	**12/10**			**I**				**LS**		**GMR**
5. Palmer's Cove Yacht Club	978-744-9722	40		PRIVATE							B/30	S		GMR
6. Fred J. Dion Yacht Yard Inc. (Internet Access)	**978-744-0844**	**100**	**09**	**6/20**	**10/8**	**F**		**M**	**HE**	**L50,C35**	**1/30**	**S**		**GMR**
7. Jubilee Yacht Club	978-922-9611	50	78	MOORINGS	35/7	F	GD	I			1	S		R
8. Tuck Point Marina	978-922-4631	150	7A/68	6/53	35/25					L	B/50	LPS		GMR
9. Beverly Port Marina Inc. (Internet Access) (WiFi)	978-232-3300	150	79	50/300	28/28	F	GD	GIMS	HEP	L35	B/50	LS		GMR
10. Danversport Yacht Club Inc.	978-774-8644	55	09	5/300	8/8	F	G	IS	HEP	L50,C	B/50	LPS	P	GMR
11. Liberty Marina	978-774-5105	50	09	12/180	12/8	F		I	HEP	L35	1/50	LS		MR

Corresponding chart(s) not to be used for navigation. (Internet Access icon) Internet Access (WiFi icon) Wireless Internet Access

NAVIGATION: Use Chart 13274. For Salem Harbor, use Boston tide tables. For high tide, subtract 2 minutes; for low tide, subtract 5 minutes. From Marblehead, follow the South Channel (Marblehead Channel), leaving Grays Rock to starboard, and pass directly between green daybeacon "1" and red nun buoy "2." As you continue, keep red nun buoy "4" and Triangle Rocks well to starboard, and then leave red nun buoy "6" and the Aquivitae rocks to starboard. Coming from the north or east, enter Salem Channel between Bakers and Great Misery islands, and then follow the well-marked, deepwater ship channel into Salem Harbor. The lighted stacks (aptly charted "STACKS") of the New England Power Plant on Salem Neck can be seen many miles out to sea.

Dockage and Moorings: A secure mooring for vessels up to 65 feet in length is easily at hand in Salem with a call to Salem Water Taxi. Just hail "Salem Water Taxi" (978-745-6070 or VHF Channel 68) on approach. As part of the mooring fee, Salem Water Taxi provides access to shower, restroom and laundry facilities at its shoreside location. Hawthorne Cove Marina has the first transient docks encountered on entry, to starboard just past the electric company's huge stacks. The marina's old-style showers and restrooms are clean and comfortable, as are its new-style floating docks and finger piers. Laundry facilities are available, and the marina's 35-ton lift facilitates repairs. Amenities at Hawthorne Cove Marina include complimentary newspapers and free coffee and donuts on Sunday morning.

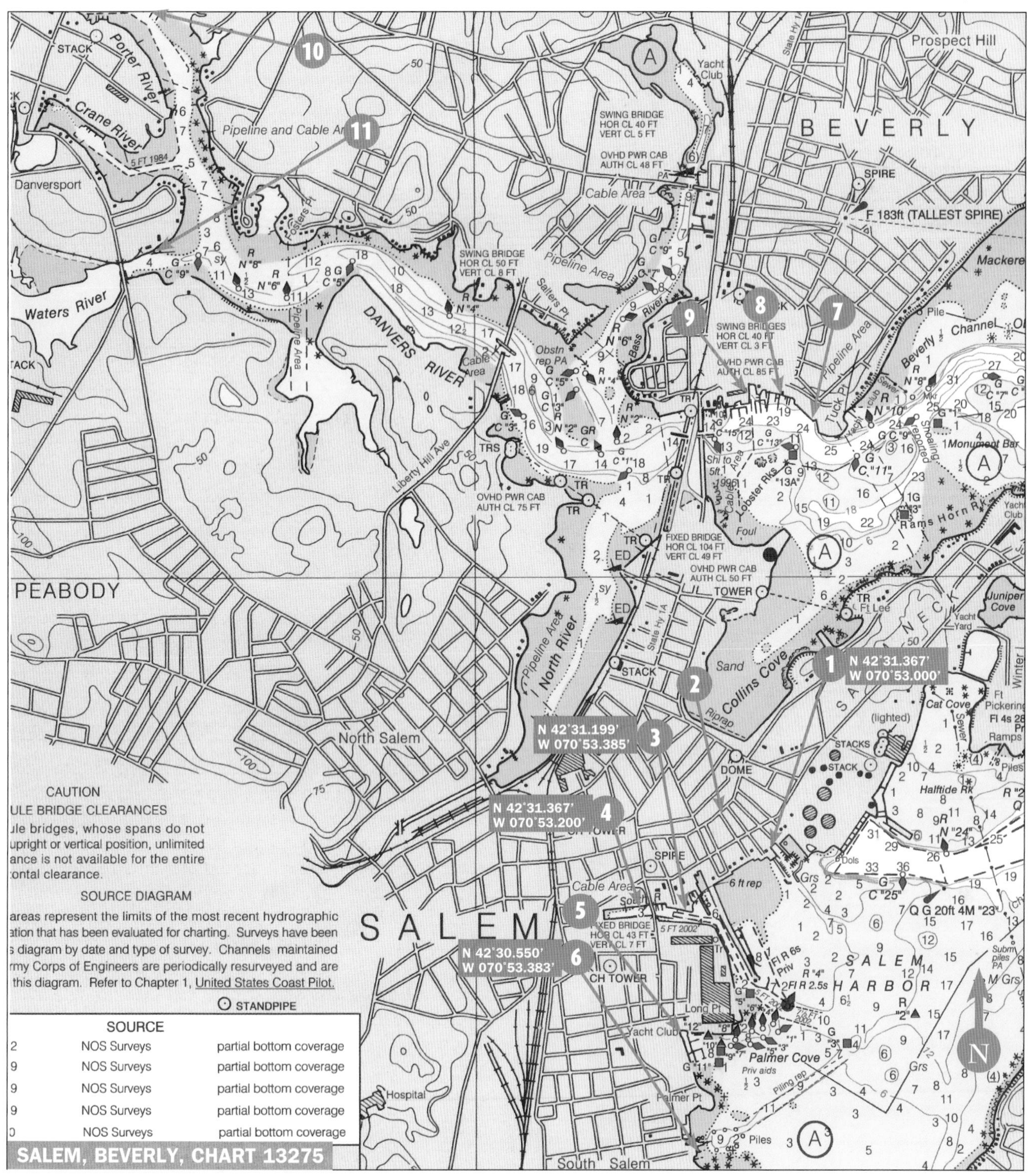

Pickering Wharf Marina, located inside the ample protection of Derby Wharf, is central to an array of shops and restaurants in the mini-mall on Pickering Wharf. Because of its convenient access and central location, a berth here is in demand during the summer; advance reservations are highly recommended. Transient moorings also may be rented from the marina. Modern restrooms, showers and laundry facilities are available at the dock house.

At the head of the harbor, Fred J. Dion Yacht Yard can handle virtually any yacht refitting or rebuilding requirement. The yard has a 50-ton lift, 100-ton railway and a substantial stock room/ship's store. North Sails is located on-site. Transient dock space is usually available for vessels up to 120 feet at easy-access docks. Guest moorings are likely to be open as well. To reach Dion's, travel west-southwest for about 100 yards to the individual pilings marking the deep channel into the yard's dredged turning basin. Call on VHF Channel 09 for availability and directions.

Other mooring services are available through Salem Water Taxi. The harbormaster (978-741-0098 of VHF Channel 09) can assist with any mooring requests. Salem

is the U.S. Customs Port of Entry for the region, and Customs maintains a dock for incoming vessels.

The town of Salem requires a closed head (No-Discharge) and offers free pump-out services at moorings. Call Salem Pump-out on VHF Channel 09.

GOIN' ASHORE: **SALEM, MA**

The best place to begin a visit to Salem may also be the easiest—on the head of Derby Wharf, at the U.S. Park Service Orientation Center for the Maritime National Historic Site, where there are illustrated touring guides and materials about the waterfront and adjacent village. The Peabody Essex Museum of Salem (150 Essex St., 978-745-9500), open all year since 1824, is a treasure for sailing history buffs, containing ancient logs of intrepid captains, more than 700 ship models, ancient instruments, extensive China trade items, scrimshaw and a collection of ship's figureheads. The Essex Institute (132 Essex St., open all year) houses museums within a museum—seven historically significant homes, each authentically furnished and decorated with the treasures of Salem's various historic eras. The Park Service Visitors Center next to the Peabody Essex Museum regularly shows an excellent cinematic overview of the town's mercantile, commercial and seafaring history. Nathaniel Hawthorne's birthplace, the famed House of Seven Gables, (c. 1668, 54 Turner St., 978-744-0991), is three blocks east of Derby Wharf, with tours daily between 9 a.m. and 6 p.m. You can visit the Witch Dungeon Museum (16 Lynde St., 978-741-3570) to take a dungeon tour and see a reenactment of the famed 1692 witch trials, adapted from original transcripts and performed by professional actors. Also, among the many beautifully restored and furnished period houses, regularly open to the public for a small fee, is The Witch House, (c. 1642, 310 Essex St., 978-744-8815).

On Essex Street, tucked in among the historic sites, are the Salem Five Cents Savings Bank (210 Essex St., 978-745-5555), a CVS Pharmacy (200 Essex St., 978-744-2224) and some blocks west, the Salem Public Library (370 Essex St., 978-744-0860), which has public computers with Internet access. The post office is a couple of blocks south of Essex Street at the corner of Norman and Margin streets. Gourmet Fare on Pickering Wharf (73 Warf St., 978-745-9190) sells fresh-baked and ready-to-bake pies, breads and "chocaholic" cookies. The Bunghole Liquor Store (978-744-2251) is a block away at 204 Derby St. Some 14 restaurants are within a two-block radius of Pickering Wharf alone. Standouts include the Lyceum Bar and Grill (43 Church St., 978-745-7665), considered the town's finest and priciest; the Grapevine Restaurant at 26 Congress St. on Pickering Wharf (978-745-9335); In a Pig's Eye Restaurant (148 Derby St., 978-741-4436), with fantastic lunches at reasonable prices (Mexican nights, Monday and Tuesday); Caffe Graziani (133 Washington St., 978-741-4282) is billed as "the family place" and is well known for its Italian specialties; and the Red Raven (75 Congress St., 978-745-8558), with "funky but fantastic food."

ADDITIONAL RESOURCES:

- Destination Salem, **www.salem.org**
- Salem Chamber of Commerce, 978-744-0004, **www.salemchamber.org**

NEARBY GOLF COURSES:
Olde Salem Greens Golf Course, Wilson Street, Salem, MA 01970, 978-744-2149

NEARBY MEDICAL FACILITIES:
Lydia Pinkham Memorial Clinic, 250 Derby St., Salem, MA 01970, 978-744-3288

Beverly Harbor. (Not to be used for navigation.) WATERWAY GUIDE PHOTOGRAPHY

Beverly

Dubbed "Birthplace of the American Navy," in honor of the schooner *Hannah* (though neighboring Marblehead often argues the designation), first naval vessel commissioned by Gen. George Washington, Beverly Harbor today has few reminders of its historic past.

NAVIGATION: Use Chart 13275. A 5-foot-deep shoal is reported near the old Route 1A Bridge (49-foot fixed vertical clearance) across the Danvers River between Beverly and Salem. Contact the Beverly harbormaster for more details at 978-921-6059. Though winding and sometimes narrow, the harbor channel is deep, well-marked and flanked to starboard on entry, at Tuck Point and beyond, with several marine facilities. The entire length of the Danvers River is a No-Wake Zone.

Dockage and Moorings: Jubilee Yacht Club has moorings for members of clubs with reciprocal arrangements, including launch service and use of the lounge, showers and restrooms. Restaurants are within walking distance.

Farther west, Beverly Port Marina rents slips at its deepwater floating docks. Telephone and TV hookups are available dockside, and you can take on gasoline or diesel fuel. The yard can handle boats up to 50 feet and has haul-out capability and a service shop.

Still farther along, next to the bridge, Glover Wharf Marina has transient space at its floating docks, and showers and restrooms at the dock house. Beyond a small pizzeria and a seafood outlet, other services within walking distance are in short supply.

Manchester-by-the-Sea

NAVIGATION: Use Charts 13274 and 13275. Cruising the six miles from Beverly to Manchester, you will find good water close to shore for a waterside view of the elegant estate and summer homes at Prides Crossing and Beverly Farms. The entrance to Manchester's crowded but unhurried harbor is graced by the Manchester Yacht Club's beautiful Victorian gazebo perched on a promontory near the entrance in front of its refined clubhouse. The channel is straight and well-marked, but a bit shallow. Boats drawing more than 5 feet are advised to arrive on a rising tide. The harbor, above Proctor Point, is virtually landlocked, affording excellent protection, and the village, though small and picturesque, is surprisingly accommodating to cruising visitors.

Dockage and Moorings: Beautiful, traditional and quiet, Manchester Yacht Club is virtually unchanged since its founding over a century ago. No dock space is available, but visiting yachtsmen may be able to use the mooring of a member off cruising.

At the inner harbor, to port, Crocker's Boat Yard is a family-owned and -operated traditional working yard. A few transient moorings are likely to be open here.

Manchester-By-The-Sea, MA

MANCHESTER		Largest Vessel Accommodated	VHF Channel Monitored	Transient Berths / Total Berths	Approach / Dockside Depth (reported)	Floating Docks	Gas / Diesel	Groceries, Ice, Marine Supplies, Snacks	Repairs: Hull, Engine, Propeller	Lift (tonnage), Crane, Rail	1=110V, 2=220V, B=Both, Max Amps	Laundry, Pool, Showers	Pump-Out Station	Nearby: Grocery Store, Motel, Restaurant
		Dockage					Supplies		Services					
1. Crocker's Boat Yard	978-526-1971	60	78A	2/16	7/7	F		M	HEP	L30,C	1/30			GMR
2. Manchester Marine Corp.	978-526-7911	45	72	6/47	9/7	F	GD	I	HEP	L30,C	B/50	S	P	GMR
3. Manchester Town Dock	978-526-7832				6/6			GIM		L	B/30	L		R

Corresponding chart(s) not to be used for navigation. Internet Access Wireless Internet Access

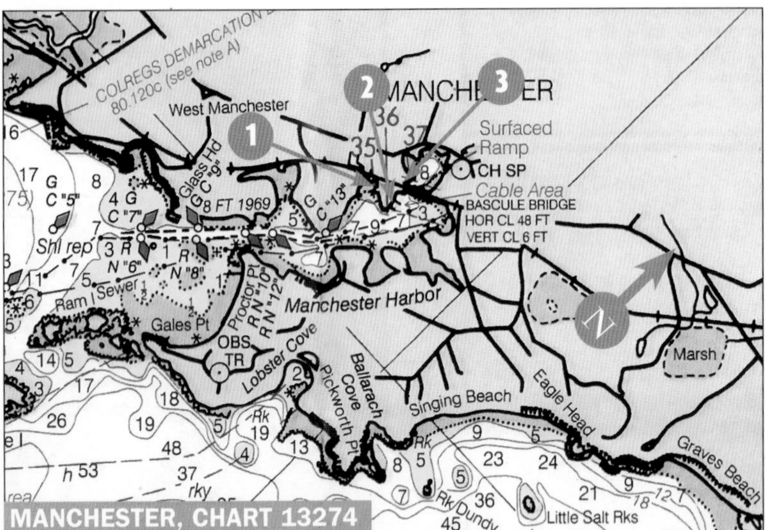

MANCHESTER, CHART 13274

Next door, Manchester Marine Corp. is another full-service operation that can handle substantial yachts. Transient floating dock space normally is available here, as are guest moorings with launch service. Since this is a popular place on summer weekends, it is a good idea to call ahead. Short-term tie-ups (15 minutes) are possible at the nearby Manchester Town Dock (6-foot depths).

GOIN' ASHORE: MANCHESTER-BY-THE-SEA, MA

Beautifully kept clapboard homes quietly line the narrow, shaded streets in this charming New

Looking north over Manchester-by-the-sea. (Not to be used for navigation.) WATERWAY GUIDE PHOTOGRAPHY

Looking southwest over Gloucester Harbor. (Not to be used for navigation.) WATERWAY GUIDE PHOTOGRAPHY

England village. Commercial establishments are sprinkled along the road tracing the head of the harbor. Supermarket-sized Crosby's Marketplace (3 Summer St., 978-526-4444) is stocked with all the basics and many specialty items. The Sunshine Laundry (7 Summer St., 978-526-4921) offers both self- and drop-off service. Beverly National Bank (11 Summer St., 978-526-9151) has an ATM. There is a sizable hardware store, a barbershop, gift shops and a family-style coffee shop and restaurant. A large public library is just up the hill overlooking the harbor. Visitors can use the Internet access at the library one time, for up to one hour. Singing Beach, said to be an excellent swimming spot, is but a short walk from the boatyards.

ADDITIONAL RESOURCES:

Town of Manchester-by-the-Sea, **www.manchester.ma.us**

NEARBY GOLF COURSES:
Cape Ann Golf Course, 99 John Wise Ave., Essex, MA 01929, 978-768-7544

NEARBY MEDICAL FACILITIES:
Beverly Hospital, 85 Herrick St., Beverly, MA 01915, 978-922-3000, **www.beverlyhospital.org**

Great Misery Island, Little Misery Island

Blocking the mouth of Manchester Bay, these nearly-joined scenic gems offer quiet refuge from the crowded harbors of the Salem Sound area, although weekend day-trippers are becoming increasingly numerous. Still, the holding is good, either in the small bight on the north side of Great Misery Island or in the tiny bay leading to the unnavigable cut between the two islands. A number of private or local yacht club moorings are often available at either location. The islands are largely open, and their accessible beaches invite exploration by dinghy. No services are available on the islands.

Northward Bound

NAVIGATION: Use Chart 13274. Leaving Manchester, yachts heading for Gloucester should stay at least a mile offshore. Do not be tempted to follow the lobster boats working closer inshore; they know where the ledges are, but you probably don't. About halfway to Gloucester is tiny Magnolia Harbor, a summer resort village with a landing, and an anchorage with poor holding ground in southerly exposure. At low tide, there are areas with 6-foot depths, charted but unmarked, that narrow the entrances to Magnolia Harbor. The approach from the west has fewer obstructions.

Gloucester

For three centuries the name Gloucester has been synonymous with fishermen and their boats. Now an important recreational boat harbor, Gloucester offers several protected anchorages, repairs for any size boat, restaurants with docks and an active summer community.

Gloucester, Annisquam River, Blynman Canal, MA

GLOUCESTER, ANNISQUAM R., BLYNMAN CANAL		Largest Vessel Accommodated	VHF Channel Monitored	Transient Berths / Total Berths	Approach / Dockside Depth (reported)	Floating Docks	Gas / Diesel	Groceries, Ice, Marine Supplies, Snacks	Repairs: Hull, Engine, Propeller	Lift (tonnage), Crane, Rail	1=110V, 2=220V, B=Both, Max Amps	Laundry, Pool, Showers	Pump-Out Station	Nearby: Grocery Store, Motel, Restaurant
		Dockage					Supplies		Services					
1. Enos Marine/Pier 7 Marina (Internet Access) (Wireless Internet Access)	978-281-1935	70	07	4/40	15/10	F		IMS	HEP	C5	1/50	S	P	GMR
2. Brown's Yacht Yard	978-281-3200	70	09/19	10/20	14/12	F	GD	IM	HE	L35	B/50	S		GMR
3. Beacon Marine Basin Inc.	978-283-2380	100		1/50	15/15	F	GD	M	HP		1/50			GMR
4. North Shore Sport Fisherman Dock	978-283-6880	46		2/16	12/8	F	GD	I			B/30	S		GR
5. Studio Restaurant	978-283-4123	111		8/8	9/9	F					1/30	S		GMR
6. Cape Ann Marina Resort	978-283-2116	120	10	5+/250	8/6	F	GD	IM	HEP	L100,C	B/50	LPS	P	GMR
7. Gloucester Marine Inc.	978-283-2828	40		1/100	10/20	F		IM	HP	C	1/30	S		GR
8. Annisquam Yacht Club	978-283-4507	50	68		6/6			I				S		GR
9. Lobster Cove Marina	978-772-6500	40	09/72	8/30	9/9		G	GIS			B/50			GR

Corresponding chart(s) not to be used for navigation. Internet Access Wireless Internet Access

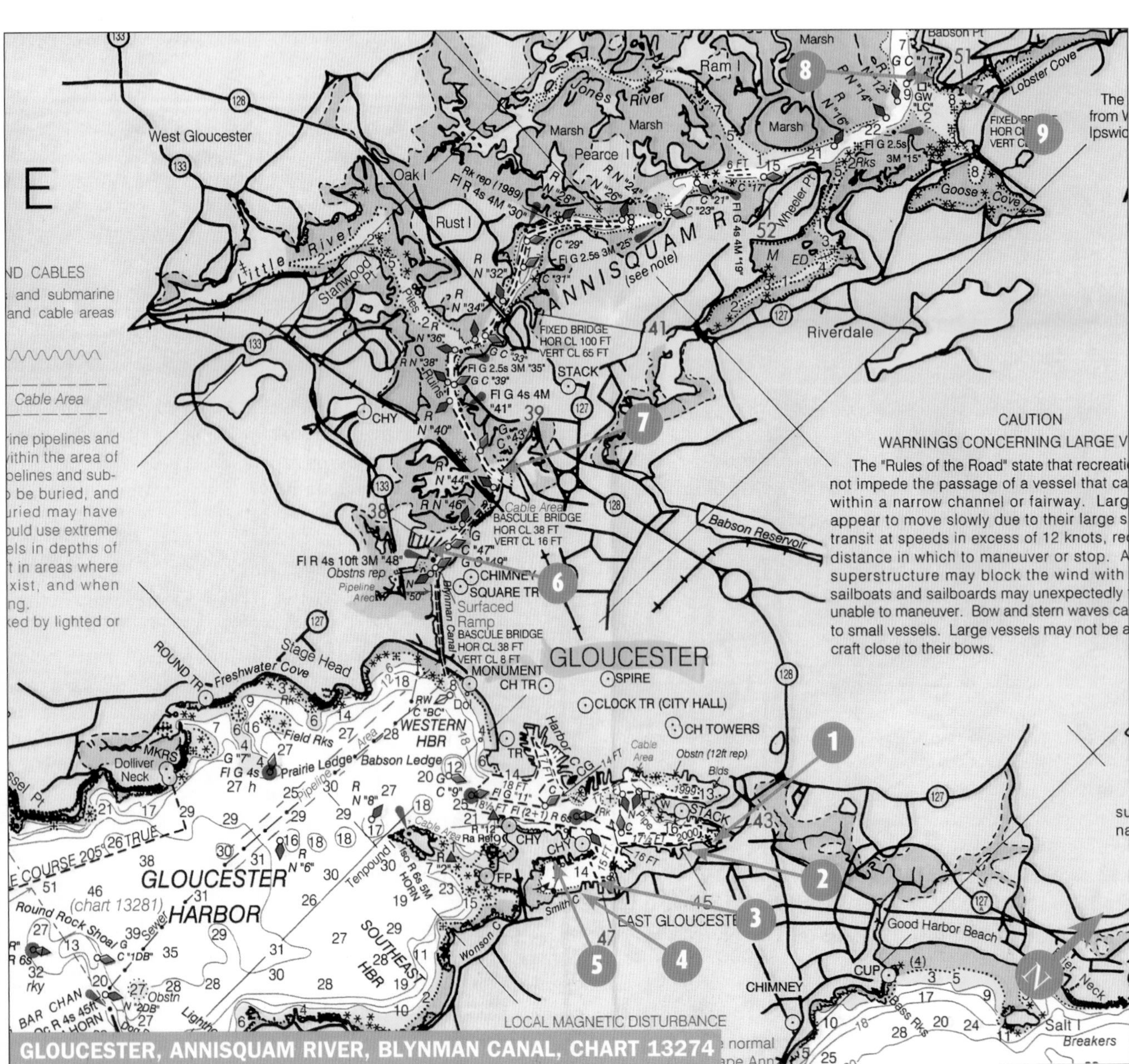

On the western shore near the entrance is Normans Woe Rock, of Longfellow's famous poem, "Wreck of the Hesperus."

Entering the big circular harbor from the sea, you look upon green hills dotted with houses, lighthouses and the old town's towers. West of Tenpound Island, named for what it cost to buy it from the Indians, is semicircular Western Harbor, head of the outer harbor. On the shore, just east of the entrance to Blynman Canal, the Fisherman's Memorial statue looks out to sea. Each Memorial Day, flowers, thrown from the bronze monument, float out to sea for the fishermen who never returned. Gloucester was one of the land-based settings for Sebastian Junger's book about a local fishing boat, the *Andrea Gail*, titled "The Perfect Storm," which later went on to become a blockbuster movie.

Anchorage and Moorings: For a harbor of the size and historic seafaring renown of Gloucester, surprisingly few marine facilities are open to cruising visitors. The harbor has the look and feel of a dedicated fishing port, yet the glory days of the commercial fleet have long since passed. There is anchorage space aplenty, though the harbor's considerable fetch and open access to prevailing southwesterlies makes a spot behind the breakwater at Eastern Point the best choice. Even so, you are almost certain to roll with the surge in this otherwise attractive location.

The Eastern Point Yacht Club is located southwest of Lighthouse Cove and will provide reciprocal amenities to cruisers with a yacht club affiliation, when available. Rental moorings here include launch service to and from the restaurant and bar at the cove's edge. Few other services are available.

Farther up the harbor, it is also possible to anchor in the lee of Tenpound Island. However, abrupt wind shifts accompanying the passage of summer fronts may suggest the far greater protection of Smith Cove behind Rocky Neck.

Unfortunately, this area has become increasingly crowded with resident-owned moorings, a fact which, combined with a 9-foot tidal range, makes finding a spot with adequate swing room more difficult than in the past.

Madfish Grille (77 Rocky Neck Ave., 781-281-4554) on Rocky Neck (reminiscent of a rustic Maine art colony) can accommodate a limited number of transients at its docks; call ahead to check availability. The Rocky Neck is lined with art galleries and studios and can provide a very enjoyable afternoon ashore, as well as good dining in casual settings. At the head of the harbor, to starboard, Brown's Yacht Yard has three transient moorings, including access to the yard's rustic but clean shower and restroom facilities.

There is no launch service, but dinghy tie-ups are permitted at the yard's service dock. The town also maintains a dozen transient moorings; for information about dockage, contact the Gloucester harbormaster at 978-282-3012 or VHF Channel 09. Avoid the moorings in Southeast Harbor if the wind is southeast to southwest and above 10 knots.

From the shelter of the Smith Cove marinas or from the town moorings, there is plenty to see and do in Gloucester. The Rocky Neck Art Colony is worth a day browsing the studios and shops, as well as a great place to catch a shore meal. The aforementioned Madfish Grille is great for lunch or dinner; The Studio Restaurant (51 Rocky Neck Ave., 781-283-4123), at 51 Rocky Neck Ave., has indoor and outdoor seating and can accommodate yachts up to 115 feet in length. Moving off the Neck, stop at the Cape Ann Chamber of Commerce (33 Commercial St. #5, 978-283-1601) for a walking map and information on the Saltwater Trolley.

Blynman Canal, Annisquam River

NAVIGATION: Use Chart 13274. From the northwestern end of the Gloucester outer harbor, Blynman Canal leads into the Annisquam River and makes a good foul-weather (and picturesque fair-weather) alternative to the offshore run around Cape Ann. The canal has a narrow, hidden entrance, which is all but invisible until you are lined up with it. A fast-operating bascule bridge with an 8-foot closed vertical clearance crosses the entrance to the canal. Stand well off until you are sure the opening is clear. The current runs fast, and the narrow confines of the draw provide no room for passing. If your boat's draft is 5 feet or more, you must navigate the canal on a rising or high tide. The controlling depth is 7 feet from Western Harbor to the B&M Railroad Bridge, and then shallows to 5-foot depths beyond.

Beyond the bridge at the entrance, the route turns to starboard. Past the bend, the canal is straight for three-tenths of a mile to a railroad bascule bridge with a 16-foot closed vertical clearance (usually open unless a train is approaching). Use extreme caution just past the bridge in the blind 90-degree turn to port. Currents are strong and can reverse direction unexpectedly.

A half mile farther, the channel turns sharply to starboard and goes under the 65-foot fixed vertical clearance bridge into the Annisquam River. Chart 13274 shows shoaling to zero depth in the vicinity of red nun buoy "24." Between red nun buoy "26" and green can buoy "23," use the east half of the channel.

Dockage: On the Annisquam River and Blynman Canal are four marinas, a boatyard and a yacht club. Between the bridges on the canal lies Cape Ann Marina Resort, a full-service marina, hotel and service yard. Amenities include floating docks, fuel, laundry, pumpout and a complimentary River Sunset cruise for slip holders in the summer.

Nearby is Stage Fork Park, which offers beaches, tennis, food concessions and good fun. Near the north end of the river is the resort of Annisquam, from which you can see the beaches and dunes of Ipswich Bay.

Just south of the town is Lobster Cove, a small, crowded, but sheltered harbor. The Annisquam Yacht

Looking northwest over the Blynman Canal and Annisquam River. (Not to be used for navigation.) WATERWAY GUIDE PHOTOGRAPHY

Club is here, as well as Lobster Cove Marina, an excellent store with supplies and a restaurant. The shoal at the northern river entrance is difficult to cross in a heavy sea. The best time to pass it is on a rising tide.

Moorings: North of the railroad bridge is a cove dredged to allow boats with 7-foot drafts. A club here offers slips, moorings (marked by private markers) and a restaurant, but no fuel.

Several yellow mooring buoys belonging to the Annisquam Yacht Club are between red nun buoy "14" and green can buoy "11." The charge includes a mooring and use of the launch service. Contact the yacht club on VHF Channel 68. You can anchor between the moored boats, but be careful not to bump them.

Rockport

MA RI

NAVIGATION: Use Chart 13274. Use Portland tide tables. For high tide, add 6 minutes; for low tide, add 6 minutes. Several small harbors break the coastline of Cape Ann, but Rockport is the one to visit. Located at the southwestern end of Sandy Bay, it is protected by two outer and two inner breakwaters but is still open to strong northeasterly and easterly winds. The bay's southern entrance, between Straitsmouth Island and Avery Ledge, is narrow and rocky, but the northern entrance is wide, deep and easy to navigate.

Anchorage and Moorings: Rockport Harbor itself consists of an outer basin and two inner basins divided by the town wharf. Controlling depth is 7 feet. Larger boats stop at Gloucester and visit overland. The harbor is not large and has no guest moorings. In summer, especially on weekends, visitors have little chance of getting a slip or mooring inside. However, the harbormaster (978-546-9589 or VHF channels 09 or 16) can sometimes arrange for a mooring or berth. Most likely you will be directed outside to an anchorage off the church (charted as "CH SP") in the cove north of town and south of Sandy Bay Ledge. In less than ideal conditions, it is not the most comfortable anchorage, but you can dinghy ashore and visit the town.

GOIN' ASHORE: ROCKPORT, MA

Rockport is one of the foremost art centers on the East Coast. The fisherman's shack here has been the subject of so many paintings that it is known throughout the art world as Motif 1. The lobster trap buoys that adorn the shack honor a local lobstermen who have passed away. Actually, the original shack burned down years ago and another was constructed on the same site. It looks the same except for a coat of dark red paint. (The original was faded.)

The waterfront is lined with galleries, shops and studios. Some of the best-known professional artists in the country live, work and teach here. Courses of a few days to several weeks are offered all summer. You will find fine restaurants, craft and gift shops and historic sites, as well as supplies. History buffs will enjoy a visit to the Sandy Bay Historical Society (40 King St.,

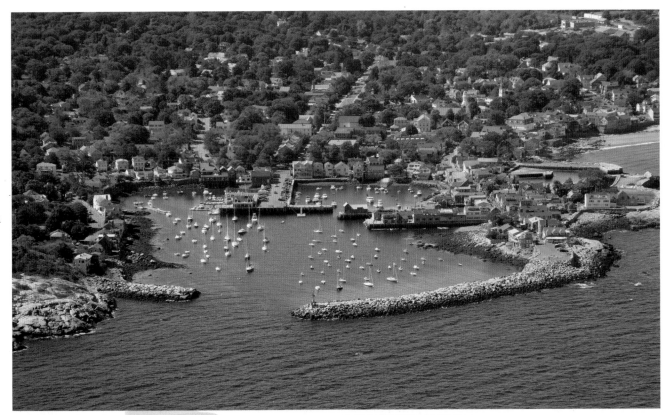

Looking southwest over Rockport Harbor. (Not to be used for navigation.) WATERWAY GUIDE PHOTOGRAPHY

978-546-9533) for an overview of North Shore history. Thacher Island (south of Rockport) affords a unique view of lighthouse history. The north and south towers on Thacher Island are the only operating twin lighthouses in America. The Thacher Island Association maintains two moorings for visiting boats; call 617-599-2590 for reservations and information. Once moored, you may row ashore to the ramp maintained by the association. Ashore you can climb the North Tower for views from Maine to Boston, hike and explore the trails covering the 50-acre island and visit the various buildings of the light station.

ADDITIONAL RESOURCES:

- Rockport Travel Guide, **www.rockportusa.com**

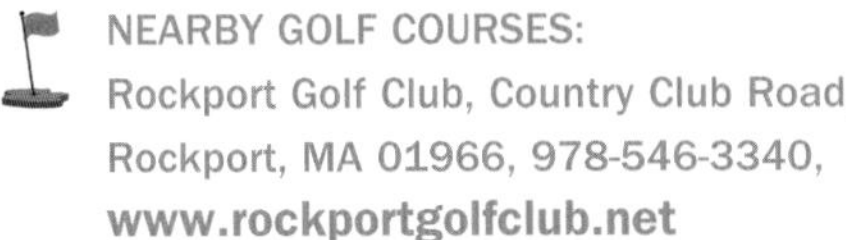

NEARBY GOLF COURSES:
Rockport Golf Club, Country Club Road, Rockport, MA 01966, 978-546-3340, **www.rockportgolfclub.net**

NEARBY MEDICAL FACILITIES:
Health Care Services, 272 Washington St., Gloucester, MA 01930, 978-281-8610

Coastal Ports

North of Cape Ann, where the Annisquam River enters Ipswich Bay with its famous clam beds, you have to go offshore again. You will encounter a few attractive harbors along this sandy coast, but enter all of them carefully. Shoals change constantly.

Essex

In the southwest corner of Ipswich Bay is the entrance to Colonial Essex, with its well-preserved houses, excellent seafood restaurants (many dockside) and facilities for boats up to 40 feet. The village is a short walk from the waterfront. Many of the great Gloucester schooners were built here, and the yard that built them still stands at the head of the shallow, winding river. Ashore, in an old schoolhouse at 66 Main St., is the Essex Shipbuilding Museum (978-768-7541), which contains photographs and artifacts from the great days of Essex shipbuilding. The extensive history includes the *Evelina M. Goulart*, originally built in 1927 and now on display while being rebuilt.

NAVIGATION: Use Chart 12374. The entrance from Ipswich Bay shifts constantly, and the aids to navigation (not charted) shift to match. In heavy weather, seas across the bar might make the entry impassable. Controlling depth to the town, about four narrow, shallow meandering miles upriver, is 4 feet, and the river bottom is all mud.

Anchorage: Entry and passage of Essex River are best made at half tide or better; the mean tidal range is about 9 feet. If, after exploring the river, conditions for leaving Essex Bay are bad, head for the protected anchorage in the lee of Castle Neck. While there are no amenities, this is a comfortable place to wait out the weather before crossing the bar back into Ipswich Bay. Be careful, though, as depths shallow quickly as you move west into the anchorage.

Essex River, MA

ESSEX RIVER		Largest Vessel Accommodated	VHF Channel Monitored	Transient Berths / Total Berths	Approach / Dockside Depth (reported)	Floating Docks	Gas / Diesel	Groceries, Ice, Marine Supplies, Snacks	Repairs: Hull, Engine, Propeller	Lift (tonnage), Crane, Rail	1=110V, 2=220V, B=Both, Max Amps	Laundry, Pool, Showers	Pump-Out Station	Nearby: Grocery Store, Motel, Restaurant
		Dockage					Supplies		Services					
1. Essex Marina	978-768-6833	34	16	0/85	4/4	F		IS	EP		B/30	S		GMR
2. Perkins Marine	978-768-7145	24		/96	4/4	F	G	IM	HEP	L25	1/30			MR
3. Pike Marine	978-768-7161	29		/70	1/4	F		IM	HEP	L10				MR

Corresponding chart(s) not to be used for navigation. Internet Access Wireless Internet Access

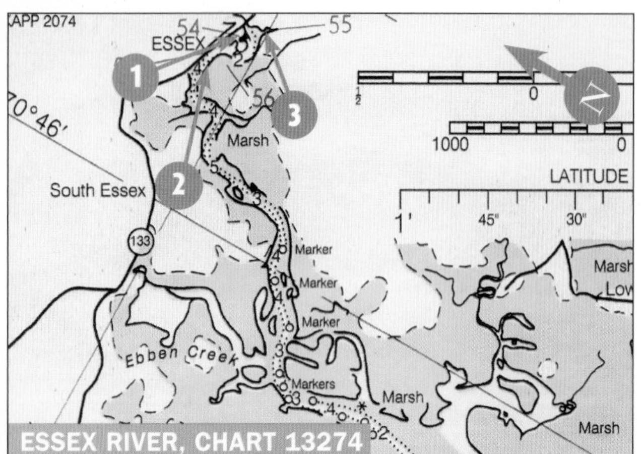

ESSEX RIVER, CHART 13274

Plum Island Sound

This sound is the juncture for the rivers and streams making in from the west and north between Castle Neck and Newburyport. It lies behind Plum Island's barrier strip, home to a wildlife refuge where you might see native and migrating wildfowl. This area also is favored by shell collectors who find whelks, periwinkles, slipper shells and blue mussels along the narrow sandy beach. The sound and its northern extension, Plum Island River, make a 10-mile link between Ipswich and Newburyport, but the river is suitable only for dinghies.

NAVIGATION: Use Chart 13274. The pass from Ipswich Bay to Plum Island Sound goes over a bar that can be dan-

Looking north over the Essex River. (Not to be used for navigation.) WATERWAY GUIDE PHOTOGRAPHY

Merrimack River entrance at Plum Island. (Not to be used for navigation.) WATERWAY GUIDE PHOTOGRAPHY

gerous in bad weather. The bottom can change considerably after a storm; use local knowledge.

Inside the sound, the Ipswich River winds nearly three miles west to Ipswich. Ipswich has perhaps the largest concentration of 17th-century houses in any American town. Where the river feeds into the sound, tidal rips give a false impression that the water is shallower than the charted 4 feet.

Heading up Plum Island Sound, leave Bass Rock well to starboard (honor red nun buoy "10" and green can buoy "11" strictly). It marks the end of a ledge making out from the tip of Plum Island. From here north, the sound makes an S-curve in and around low-lying dunes, then past a series of subsidiary streams that branch off helter-skelter.

Satellite rivers, working northward, are Eagle Hill and Rowley rivers and the incredibly pretty Parker River.

Newburyport

Newburyport is the smallest city in the state and one of the oldest, having been founded in 1635. The city boasts some finest examples of Colonial and Federal-era architecture in the nation, reminders of the days when its ships sailed around the world. Some of the most famous clipper ships in history were built here. Currently, the harbor is host to cruising boats and a sportfishing fleet. Transient vessels have easy access to its renovated downtown.

NAVIGATION: Use Chart 13274. Use Portland tide tables. For high tide, add 31 minutes; for low tide, add 1 hour 11 minutes. Newburyport Harbor has a well-marked and jettied inlet entrance with strong currents. Depths of 12 feet are reportedly available at low water, but check before entering if in doubt. As you approach the Merrimack River entrance, call the Coast Guard for the latest information. A diamond white daybeacon with an orange reflecting border and quick-flashing white light has been set inside the entrance. The words on the sign say Rough Bar, and when the light is flashing, that is what it means. The Coast Guard does not promise that the bar is safe when the light is not flashing, but does warn that only experienced skippers should try to cross the bar when it is flashing. The sign is maintained through the boating season from April 1 to Oct. 31. (Note that the sign is not readily apparent when you are entering the Merrimack River; it is much more visible when you are leaving.) Inside, the water is smooth, though the current is strong for some distance upriver.

Boating amenities are both above and below the bridges at Newburyport. The first bridge (35-foot closed vertical clearance), opens on signal between 6 a.m. and 10 p.m. from May to October, and between 8 a.m. and 5 p.m. from November to April. At other times the bridge opens with one-hour prior notice to the bridge tender. Just beyond the highway bridge is a railroad swing bridge with 13-foot closed vertical clearance. It is usually open. No-Wake speed limits are strictly enforced here.

Dockage: Newburyport Harbor Marina welcomes transients and offers gas and diesel fuel, floating docks, laundry services and a pump-out station. Windward Yacht Yard also has transient slips available and offers floating docks, marine supplies and gas and diesel fuel. Hilton's

Newburyport, MA

NEWBURYPORT		Largest Vessel Accommodated	VHF Channel Monitored	Transient Berths / Total Berths	Approach / Dockside Depth (reported)	Floating Docks	Gas / Diesel	Groceries, Ice, Marine Supplies, Snacks	Repairs: Hull, Engine, Propeller	Lift (tonnage), Crane, Rail	1=110V, 2=220V, B=Both, Max Amps	Laundry, Pool, Showers	Pump-Out Station	Nearby: Grocery Store, Motel, Restaurant
		Dockage					Supplies		Services					
1. Rings Island Marina	978-465-0307	45		5/100	15/12	F		IM	HEP		B/30	S	P	MR
2. Newburyport Harbor Marina WiFi	**978-462-3990**	**150**	**09/71**	**24/70**	**12/12**	**F**	**GD**	**GIMS**	**HEP**	**L85,C22**	**B/100**	**LS**	**P**	**MR**
3. Newburyport Central Waterfront Park	978-462-3746	125	12	40/28	12/22	F	GD	GIM	HP			L	P	MR
4. Hilton's Marina WiFi	**978-462-3990**	80	09/71	**/65**	**12/12**	F	**GD**	**I**	HEP	L85,C22	B/50	LS	P	MR
5. Windward Yacht Yard Internet WiFi	**978-462-6500**	**80**	**09/71**	**6/150**	**15/15**	**F**	**GD**	**IMS**	**HEP**	**L85,C25**	**B/100**	**LS**	**P**	**GMR**
6. Bridge Marina	978-462-2274	100					GD	IMS		L40				R
7. Cove Marina WiFi	978-462-4998	60	10	2/142	15/15				E		1/50	LS		GMR
8. Newburyport Yacht Club	978-463-9911	55	09/71	5/200	30/10	F			HP	LC	1/30	PS		GMR
9. Newburyport Boat Basin	**978-465-9110**	**60**	**09/71**	**10/225**	**12/12**	**F**		**IMS**	**HEP**		**B/50**	**S**	**P**	**GMR**
10. Merri-Mar Yacht Basin Inc.	978-465-3022	100	16/09	10/50	20/15	F		GIMS	HP	L35,C	B/50		P	GMR

Corresponding chart(s) not to be used for navigation. Internet Access WiFi Wireless Internet Access

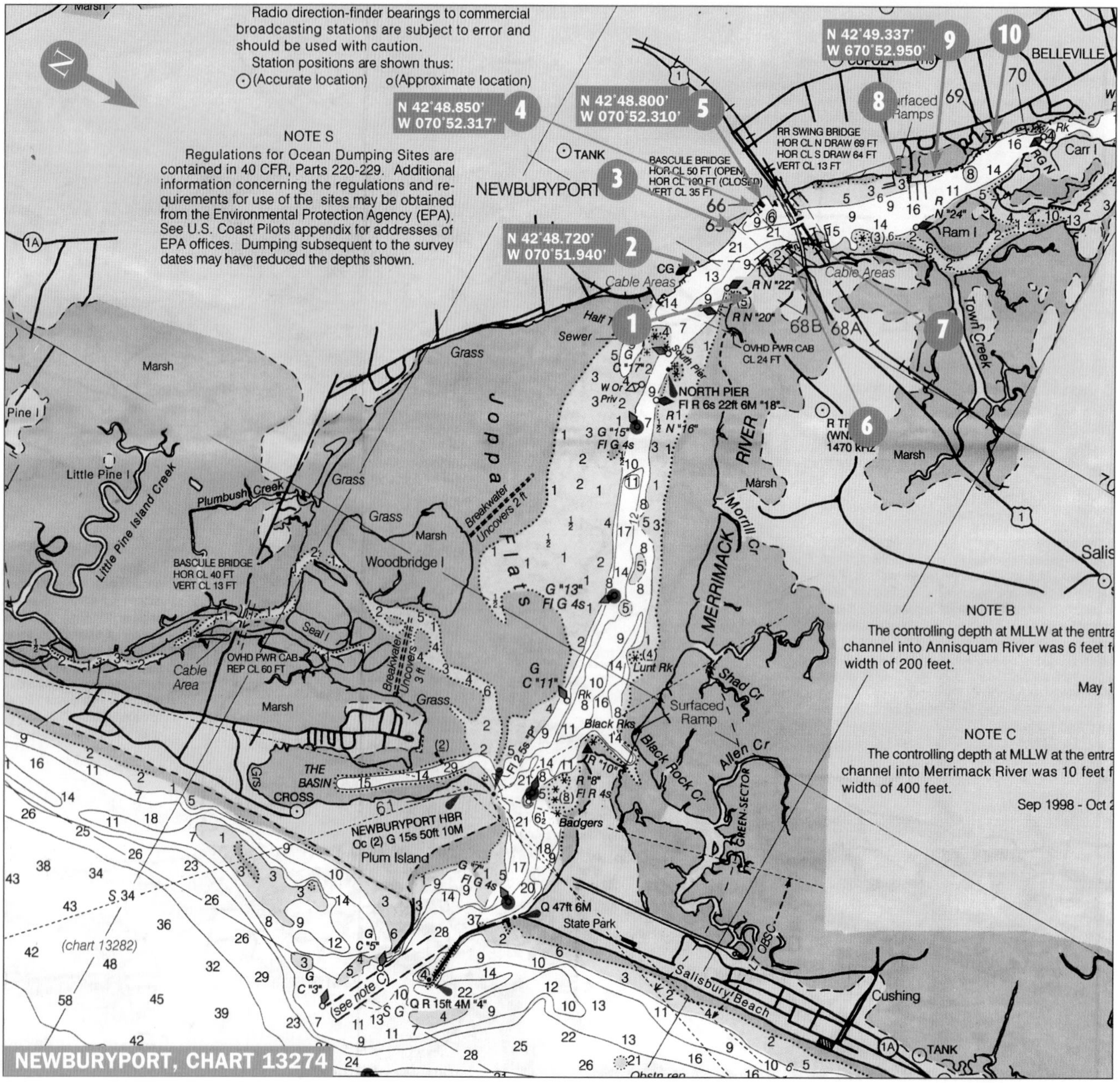

Radio direction-finder bearings to commercial broadcasting stations are subject to error and should be used with caution.
Station positions are shown thus:
⊙(Accurate location) o(Approximate location)

NOTE S
Regulations for Ocean Dumping Sites are contained in 40 CFR, Parts 220-229. Additional information concerning the regulations and requirements for use of the sites may be obtained from the Environmental Protection Agency (EPA). See U.S. Coast Pilots appendix for addresses of EPA offices. Dumping subsequent to the survey dates may have reduced the depths shown.

4 N 42°48.850' W 070°52.317'

5 N 42°48.800' W 070°52.310'

2 N 42°48.720' W 070°51.940'

9 N 42°49.337' W 070°52.950'

BASCULE BRIDGE
HOR CL 50 FT (OPEN)
HOR CL 100 FT (CLOSED)
VERT CL 35 FT

RR SWING BRIDGE
HOR CL N DRAW 69 FT
HOR CL S DRAW 64 FT
VERT CL 13 FT

NORTH PIER
Fl R 6s 22ft 6M "18"

NEWBURYPORT HBR
Oc (2) G 15s 50ft 10M

NOTE B
The controlling depth at MLLW at the entra channel into Annisquam River was 6 feet f width of 200 feet.
May 1

NOTE C
The controlling depth at MLLW at the entra channel into Merrimack River was 10 feet f width of 400 feet.
Sep 1998 - Oct 2

NEWBURYPORT, CHART 13274

Looking east over Newburyport. (Not to be used for navigation.) WATERWAY GUIDE PHOTOGRAPHY

Marina has gas and diesel fuel available. Newburyport Boat Basin is a full-service yacht yard and brokerage with an outboard mechanic on duty.

The Newburyport Central Waterfront Park lets transient mariners tie up overnight or rent a guest mooring. Electric and water connections have been added and public restrooms are nearby. The riverfront boardwalk is a great place to stroll and plan your visit to the town.

GOIN' ASHORE: NEWBURYPORT, MA

This classic New England coastal village offers historical interest, shopping and dining adventures. The Custom House Maritime Museum (25 Water St., 978-462-8681) and the Cushing House Museum (978-462-2681) at 98 High St. are both worth an afternoon visit. Dining opportunities include Joseph's Winter Street Café (24 Winter St., 978-462-1188) and Aquatini (27 State St., 978-463-8266), both serving excellent meals. The Starboard Galley Restaurant (55 Water St., 978-462-1326) is close to the river and good for casual dining. Birdwatchers, fishermen and nature lovers will enjoy a day at Plum Island. The Parker River National Wildlife Refuge, a 4,688-acre area that is home to more than 800 species of birds, plants and animals, covers the center of Plum Island (978-465-5753). In late July and August, there are complimentary Friday night concerts on the Newburyport waterfront.

ADDITIONAL RESOURCES:

- Greater Newburyport Chamber of Commerce, **www.newburyportchamber.org**

NEARBY GOLF COURSES:

Evergreen Valley Golf Course, 18 Boyd Drive, Newburyport, MA 01950, 978-463-8600, **www.evergreenvalleygolf.com**

NEARBY MEDICAL FACILITIES:

Anna Jaques Hospital, 25 Highland Ave., Newburyport, MA 01950, 978-463-1000, **www.ajh.org**

NEW HAMPSHIRE WATERS

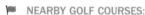

The New Hampshire coast to Portsmouth is all beach—a popular resort area with three harbors. The first, Hampton Harbor, has a dredged, jettied entry surrounded by rocks, party fishing boats, lots of recreational craft, a big, sheltered, full-service marina, excellent swimming, restaurants and amusements. Maintenance dredging attempts are made to keep depths at 8 feet, with a 7-foot shoal upstream. Next is tiny Rye Harbor (Chart 13283), which is also jettied. Favor the north jetty when entering. Neither Hampton nor Rye are often visited by cruisers, who prefer to stop farther up the coast at Portsmouth or the Isles of Shoals.

Isles of Shoals

Capt. John Smith charted this group of islets and ledges in 1614. Taken by their wind-swept beauty, he also attempted to name them in his honor, but the earlier name given the isles by itinerant fishermen is the one that stuck. Ancient tales—of pirate silver, noble lightkeepers, licentious fishwives, drowned and frozen sailors, famous summer tourists and murder most foul—hang almost as heavily about these islands as the frequent summer fogs. Despite their popularity with weekenders out of Portsmouth and distance cruisers stopping over during the trek to or from Maine, all of them are privately owned, and only one, Smuttynose Island (technically across the Maine line), is particularly hospitable to visitors.

NAVIGATION: Use Chart 13274. For Isles of Shoals, Gosport Harbor, use Portland tide tables. For high tide, add 2 minutes; for low tide, subtract 2 minutes.When approaching from the south, look for the south side of Anderson Ledge. On first approach, this can be somewhat confusing, as the ledge is identified on various NOAA chart reproductions, but the marker is not. A current chart shows a spindle on the ledge in addition to the nun buoy south of it. Steer between the Anderson Ledge nun buoy and the lighthouse on the eastern end of White Island, bearing west of the entrance to Gosport Harbor. From the north, give Duck Island and surrounding rocks and ledges a wide berth, heading for the western side of Appledore Island.

Anchorage and Moorings: Gosport Harbor has served visiting mariners for almost 400 years, but it has done so with a sustained reputation for poor holding and scant protection. To offset this difficulty, private parties from the mainland have established moorings of convenience here; local tradition has it that they are yours for the taking on a first-come, first-served basis (no guarantees on condition). But there are plenty of moorings, except on peak summer weekends. If the wind is up from the northwest, Gosport Harbor is not the place to be. At that point, cruisers either avoid the Isles of Shoals altogether, or take shelter in the eastern crotch formed by the southwestern side of Smuttynose Island and the causeway leading from there to Cedar Island.

GOIN' ASHORE: ISLES OF SHOALS, NH

At Smuttynose Island, you should negotiate dinghy passage into Haley Cove and land on an obliging rock adjacent to the island's two evident fishing cottages. There you will likely be met (during the summer months) by a volunteer "ranger" who will lend you a booklet describing a "self-guided walking tour" of this pleasant and historic spot.

The Haley House, next to the ranger's cottage, has been faithfully restored by annual visitor John MacKenzie who says, simply, "I saw it, and it needed redoin'." On a clear day, the views are gorgeous from almost every aspect of this easily traversed ocean jewel.

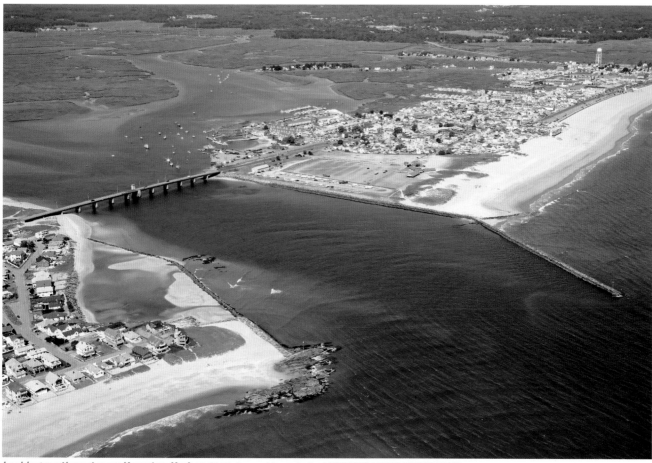

Looking northwest over Hampton Harbor. (Not to be used for navigation.) WATERWAY GUIDE PHOTOGRAPHY

Looking northwest over Rye Harbor. (Not to be used for navigation.) WATERWAY GUIDE PHOTOGRAPHY

New Castle Island

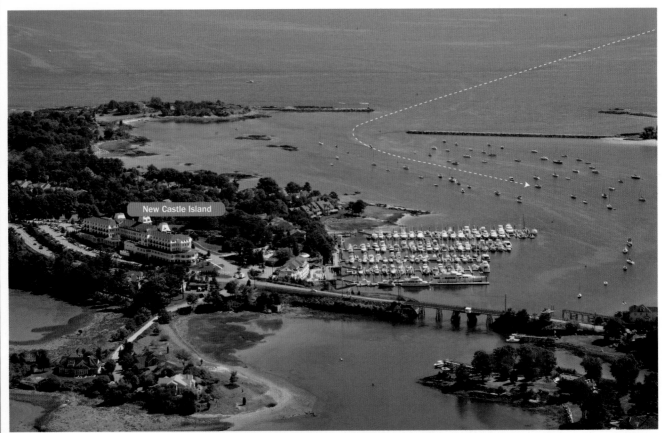

Looking southeast over Little Harbor. (Not to be used for navigation.) WATERWAY GUIDE PHOTOGRAPHY

New Hampshire Coastal Pumpout Stations

All waters within three miles of the New Hampshire shoreline and the Isles of Shoals are part of the coastal No Discharge Area. Tidal and estuarine waters, including all bays and rivers to the tidal dams, are incorporated in the No Discharge Area. All boat sewage discharges (including treated sewage) are prohibited.

Marinas charge $5 or less per pumpout.

George's Marina, Dover
Location: Cocheco River Phone: (603) 742-9089

Little Bay Boating Club, Dover
Location: Little Bay, Phone: (603) 749-9282, VHF: 9

Great Bay Marine, Newington
Location: Little Bay, Phone: (603) 436-5299, VHF: 68

Wentworth by the Sea Marina, New Castle
Location: Little Harbor, Phone: (603) 433-5050, VHF: 71

Hampton River Marina, Hampton
Location: Hampton Harbor, Phone: (603) 929-1422, VHF: 11

▲ Mobile Pumpout Boat
Location: coastal New Hampshire and up to Cape Neddick, Maine. Available May through November. Please call for an appointment,(603) 670-5130, VHF 9
Pumpout boat charges $10 per pumpout

Coastal pumpout facilities and the mobile pumpout boat are cooperative efforts between the New Hampshire Department of Environmental Services and the U.S. Fish and Wildlife Services's Clean Vessel Act grant program.

ATTENTION ALL NEW HAMPSHIRE BOATERS: PLEASE KEEP OUR WATER CLEAN - USE PUMPOUT STATIONS!

If you have questions concerning these facilities or the New Hampshire Clean Vessel Act program, please contact the NH CVA Coordinator:
P.O.Box 95, Concord, NH 03302-0095
(603) 271-8803 • watershed@des.nh.gov

http://des.nh.gov/organization/divisions/water/wmb/cva/index.htm

At less than high tide, Smuttynose Island is connected to tiny Malaga Island, the one place around where seagoing pets can find a relief station. Smuttynose Island is also connected via a rock breakwater to barren Cedar Island, immediately to the south. The Foyes, who own and live on Cedar Island during the summer, do not encourage landings, but they do serve delicious and reasonably priced lobster rolls from their weathered but accessible dock. You can order cooked lobsters there as well.

Star Island, on the south (New Hampshire) side of Gosport Harbor, provides the green but treeless setting for a stately and impressive religious compound, centering on what was once the Star Island Hotel. Now owned by the non-profit Star Island Corporation, the island's grounds and some buildings are devoted to religious and educational conferences and are open only on a limited basis to boating visitors, and then according to a substantial (though reasonable) list of "imperative" do's and don'ts. Dinghy tie-ups are forbidden at the island's docks. Monday through Friday (10 a.m. to 8 p.m.), you may land crew members (no dogs), but then you must stand off until they return from a tour. Actual guided tours begin at 1:15 p.m. daily at the east end of the main building porch. Check in at the reception desk for a copy of the corporation's map and guidelines. Also in the main building, you will find a gift store, snack bar and library.

Appledore Island (north of Smuttynose Island) also tolerates visits from the general public (sans pets), though most of the island's acres (also Duck Island farther north) have been designated Critical Natural Areas of the state of Maine and are off limits. All buildings are off limits as well. Appledore Island is a leasehold of Cornell University and has been given over to summer teaching and research activities of the Shoals Marine Laboratory. Beyond a nature walk along Rookery Trail and views of remarkably pleasant seascapes, the primary attraction here is the re-creation of Celia Thaxter's Garden of 1893. A landing may be made at the laboratory's dock on Babb's Cove on the west side of the island.

ADDITIONAL RESOURCES:

- Isles of Shoals History, **http://seacoastnh.com/shoals/history.html**

NEARBY GOLF COURSES:

Pease Golf Course, 200 Grafton Drive, Portsmouth, NH 03801, 603-433-1331, **www.peasedev.org**

NEARBY MEDICAL FACILITIES:

Portsmouth Regional Hospital, 333 Borthwick Ave., Portsmouth, NH 03801, 603-436-5110

Portsmouth

NAVIGATION: Use Charts 13274 and 13283. Use Portland tide tables. For high tide, add 22 minutes; for low tide, add 17 minutes. New Hampshire's seaport since the 17th century, Portsmouth Harbor is where the state meets Maine on the Piscataqua River. The well-marked deepwater entry, designed for the passage of large ships (the U.S. Navy has a base here), is easy to navigate under the right conditions. At full flow, however, the river develops currents as fierce as any on the East Coast, whistling along at 4 knots under the Interstate 95 Bridge on an average tide. To minimize excitement, check the tide and current tables to coordinate comings and goings with slack water and minimal flows.

Dockage and Moorings: Portsmouth operates a limited docking facility in Prescott Park, right on the waterfront and seaward of the first bridge on entry. Transient stays are limited to 72 hours, but the combination of swift currents and high wakes is unlikely to encourage a lengthy tie-up at the town dock. The advantage is its location in the heart of downtown.

The Marina at Harbour Place is also within walking distance of downtown Portsmouth, and offers seasonal and transient docking. Call ahead for availability.

Wentworth by the Sea Marina offers full protection, fuel and full amenities surrounding its floating docks in Little Harbor. Visitors here have access to the marina's heated pool, tennis courts and concierge services, in addition to restrooms, showers, laundry facilities and restaurants. Wentworth by the Sea is one of the most complete marinas that a cruiser will visit. Some additional amenities include complimentary wireless Internet and phone hookups, courtesy vehicles, car rentals on-site, a choice of restaurants and a newly established trolley service to historic Portsmouth.

Portsmouth, NH

PORTSMOUTH		Largest Vessel Accommodated	VHF Channel Monitored	Transient Berths / Total Berths	Approach / Dockside Depth (reported)	Floating Docks	Gas / Diesel	Groceries, Ice, Marine Supplies, Snacks	Repairs: Hull, Engine, Propeller	Lift (tonnage), Crane, Rail	1=110V, 2=220V, B=Both, Max Amps	Laundry, Pool, Showers	Pump-Out Station	Nearby: Grocery Store, Motel, Restaurant
		Dockage					Supplies		Services					
1. **Wentworth by the Sea Marina**	**603-433-5050**	**250**	**16/68**	**100/170**	**10/10**	**F**	**GD**	**IMS**			**B/100**	**LPS**	**P**	**GMR**
2. Portsmouth Yacht Club	603-436-9877	40	09/72	/26	20/15		GD				1/30	S		GMR
3. Portsmouth Public Launch Ramp	603-431-2000													
4. Prescott Park Municipal Dock	603-431-8478	55	09	8/10	40/18	F					1/30			R
5. **Marina at Harbour Place** (Wireless Internet Access)	**603-436-0915**	**150**			**35/18**	**F**					**B/50**	**LS**	**P**	
6. Great Bay Marine Inc.	603-436-5299	65	68	/120	30/8	F	GD	IM	HEP	LC	50	LS	P	MR

Corresponding chart(s) not to be used for navigation. Internet Access · Wireless Internet Access

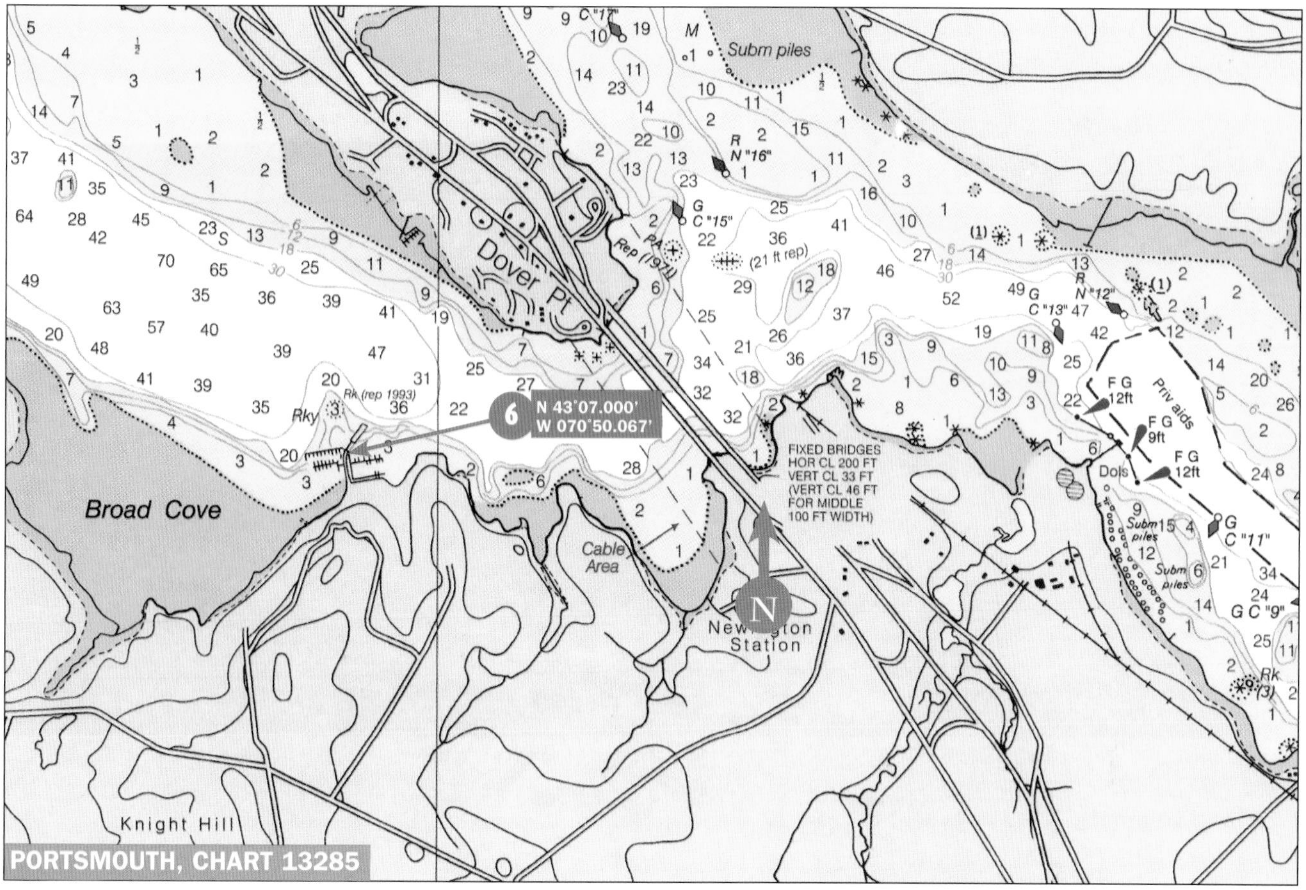

PORTSMOUTH, CHART 13285

Portsmouth Yacht Club, on New Castle Island, welcomes transients at their moorings (if available) for a rental fee, including access to the club's showers and restrooms. The club has guest moorings in front of its facility and across the Piscataqua River at Pepperell Cove, a long dinghy ride from the club. Fuel and ice are also available, and the clubhouse is open to visitors as long as the manager or members are present. Launch service usually operates until sundown, or those managing their own boat-to-dock-to-transport can use the club's dinghy landing. For a trip to town, a ride or taxi will be needed.

Anchorage: Numerous state moorings are maintained in Little Harbor (adjacent to Wentworth's docks) for lease to local residents. At any given time, half a dozen of these moorings are likely to be vacant and may be picked up by overnight visitors with the caveat that an uninvited guest should be prepared to leave if the rightful leaseholder returns.

One of the best anchorages along the New Hampshire shore, Little Harbor, between Jaffrey Point on New Castle Island and Frost Point on the mainland, offers good protection. Currents run swiftly with the tide, but the area is protected by a breakwater, and holding is good in 7- to 12-foot depths (mean low water) with an approximate 9-foot tidal range. Another popular anchorage is found in Pepperell Cove, across the river in Maine. Anchor west of the yacht club's mooring field in good holding ground. In addition, a special anchorage area is located on the north side of New Castle Island.

Looking east over New Castle Island at Portsmouth Harbor. (Not to be used for navigation.) WATERWAY GUIDE PHOTOGRAPHY

GOIN' ASHORE: **PORTSMOUTH, NH**

Among New England seaports, Portsmouth is more accessible to visitors and probably has more of its historic architecture intact than any other. Dozens of 17th-, 18th- and 19th-century homes, churches, shops and pubs were spared the city fire of 1813 and the wrecking crews of more recent times. Although the town is laced with historic houses inviting inspection (for example: the Warner House, c. 1716, and the John Paul Jones House, c. 1758), Strawbery Banke Museumís (14 Hancock St., 603-433-1100) collection of more than 30 such structures, recreating their exact look and feel during specific periods of the past four centuries, is not to be missed. The museum office is located just west of the waterfront, behind Prescott Park and the Public Gardens. It is open daily from 10 a.m. to 5 p.m. Beyond the Strawbery Banke area, the amenities of downtown Portsmouth are comparable to those of a considerably larger city. Within a few blocksí walk from the waterfront, you will encounter several banks, a music hall, churches, antiques stores, at least five bookstores and lots of interesting shopsóeven a cat loverís gift store. Portsmouth has more than 30 downtown restaurants serving everything from ethnic foods, to seafood, pizza and barbecue. There are the usual seafood eateries scattered along the waterfront; for something different, you might try Japanese cuisine at Sakura Japanese Restaurant (40 Pleasant St., 603-431-2721) or Breaking New Grounds (14 Market Square, 603-436-9555), which offers an array of coffees and breakfast and lunch items at the heart of city activities. If moored in Pepperell Cove, a short walk to Fort McClary State Park is worth the trip.

ADDITIONAL RESOURCES:

- Greater Portsmouth Chamber of Commerce, 603-436-3988, **www.portsmouthchamber.org**

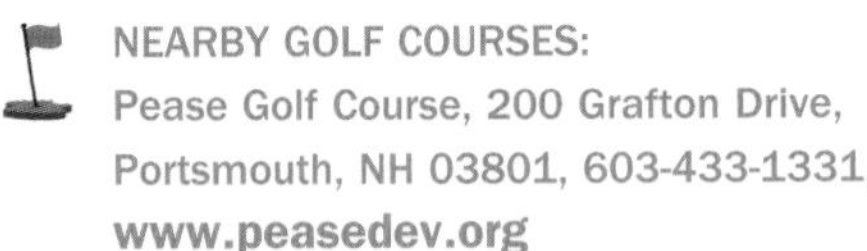

NEARBY GOLF COURSES:
Pease Golf Course, 200 Grafton Drive, Portsmouth, NH 03801, 603-433-1331, **www.peasedev.org**

NEARBY MEDICAL FACILITIES:
Portsmouth Regional Hospital, 333 Borthwick Ave., Portsmouth, NH 03801, 603-436-5110

Upriver on the Piscataqua

NAVIGATION: Use Charts 13283 and 13285. West of New Castle Island the Piscataqua River leaves Portsmouth Harbor to start its winding northward course up into rural New Hampshire. Pleasant communities with considerable yachting activity line the banks. Currents run strong—almost 4 knots on the ebb. About five miles upstream, a fixed bridge (46-foot vertical clearance) crosses from Dover Point to Newington Station. Here the river forks. On the western branch, Little Bay and its tributary streams, including scenic Great Bay, offer good anchorages and fascinating exploration.

Dockage: Great Bay Marine is a full-service facility with 128 slips on floating docks, 72 moorings, fuel, pump-out, Wireless Internet access at its slips, a ship's store and a popular on-site restaurant. It boasts one of the largest dry storage yards in the region.

Cruising Options

Ahead, to the north and east, lie the fabulous cruising grounds of the Maine coast. Spectacular scenery and a unique culture make Maine an unforgettable destination. ■

Kittery to Cape Small

CHARTS 13274, 13278, 13283, 13286, 13287, 13288, 13290, 13292

THE GULF OF MAINE

Boasting some of the world's most spectacular scenery, Maine offers a truly memorable cruising ground. As you cruise east, seafaring conditions become bigger and bolder with the landscape. The tidal range increases to more than 10 feet; the range between day and night temperatures widens; fog grows thicker and lasts longer; and the carpet of lobster-pot buoys, perhaps Maine's worst hazard, grows ever thicker.

Kittery, in the southwestern corner of Maine, to Eastport, in the northeast, measures about 250 miles of straight coastline. But perhaps 10 times that distance in bays, inlets, rivers and island shores lies in between. The glaciers that carved this rugged landscape, receding some 12,000 years ago, caused the sea to rise and drown much of the land. The character of the coast divides into about one-fifth beach and four-fifths rocky shoreline.

Throughout the length of the coast, the prevailing winds in summer are from the southwest. So while you may be cruising "up" on the chart, you are sailing downwind, eastward along the coast: hence, the phrase "Down East".

Just as in other beautiful areas, the number of boats cruising in Maine has increased. To take advantage of limited dock space, reservations are strongly advised. Many marinas, villages and yacht clubs also offer moorings on a first-come, first-served basis. Call ahead on VHF Channel 09 to confirm with the dockmaster or harbormaster.

Kittery

Maine's first port, on the Piscataqua River, is entered through New Hampshire's Portsmouth Harbor (see the "Massachusetts Bay to Portsmouth" chapter). Kittery, settled in 1622, is one of Maine's oldest towns, with many reminders of its maritime and Colonial history. The *Ranger*, first vessel to fly the Stars and Stripes, was launched from here in 1777. The blockhouse and parapets of old Fort McClary, now a memorial park, are landmarks on Kittery Point. Many Colonial homes are open to the public. The Lady Pepperell House, a 1760 Georgian mansion that is now privately owned, is only open to the public a few days during the year. Lady Pepperell was the widow of the first American to be knighted by the British Crown.

NAVIGATION: Use Chart 13283. Here at Portsmouth Harbor you get your first taste of Down East tides. The tidal range of 10 feet creates currents that drag buoys under; be sure to allow extra scope when anchoring. If you go up the Piscataqua River, do so at slack water to avoid the 3-knot currents through tricky stretches of navigation.

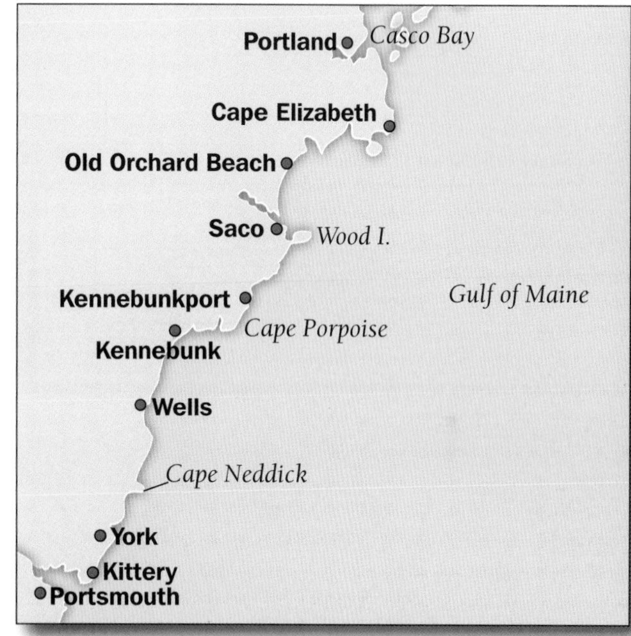

Dockage: Kittery Point Yacht Yard (207-439-9582) is a full-service facility with well-protected moorings and some dock space at the opening to Spruce Creek where reservations required. Here you can arrange for virtually any repair or for a ride into Kittery or Portsmouth.

While the town pier at the head of Pepperell Cove permits short-term tie-ups, other facilities in the cove are scarce. Cap'n Simeon's Galley (207-439-3655, 90 Pepperell Road) is a large, rather upscale seafood restaurant. Frisbee's Super Market (207-439-0014, 88 Pepperell Road), an old-fashioned grocery and sundry store (the oldest grocery in the U.S. run by the same family) is up to most reprovisioning requirements. The tiny Kittery Post Office is across the road from Frisbee's.

Anchorage and Moorings: For the best anchorage in the Piscataqua River, turn west off the 52-foot Portsmouth Harbor Lighthouse on Fort Point, and after a half mile, turn north into the mouth of Spruce Creek, and then westward again to Back Channel. Pay close attention to green can buoys "5" and "7," leaving both to port going upriver. Green can buoy "7" appears to be closer to the right-hand shore than the left.

Except when winds funnel in from due south, Pepperell Cove, north of Fort Point, beyond Fishing Island, has room to anchor in good holding, west of the mooring field.

Piscataqua River, York River, ME

PISCATAQUA RIVER, YORK RIVER		Largest Vessel Accommodated	VHF Channel Monitored	Transient Berths / Total Berths	Approach / Dockside Depth (reported)	Floating Docks	Gas / Diesel	Groceries, Ice, Marine Supplies, Snacks	Repairs: Hull, Engine, Propeller	Lift (tonnage), Crane, Rail	1=110V, 2=220V, B=Both, Max Amps	Laundry, Pool, Showers	Pump-Out Station	Nearby: Grocery Store, Motel, Restaurant
		Dockage					Supplies		Services					
1. Patten's Yacht Yard	207-439-3967	85	09						HP		B/50			
2. Badger's Island Marina 🖳	207-439-3810	90		1/27	65/6	F		I	HEP	L20,C,R	1/30	LS	P	GMR
3. Kittery Point Yacht Yard	207-439-9582	90	71	12/43	35/22	F		IM	HP	L70	B/50	S		GR
4. Kittery Point Wharf	207-439-0912	40	16/09	9/11				GIM	HEP	L40	B		P	GR
5. York Harbor Marine Service	207-363-3602	100	09	/50	8/8	F	GD	IM	HEP	R	B/50	LS		MR
6. Donnell's Marina	207-363-4308	131		6/6	10/10	F					B/100			GR

Corresponding chart(s) not to be used for navigation. 🖳 Internet Access (WiFi) Wireless Internet Access

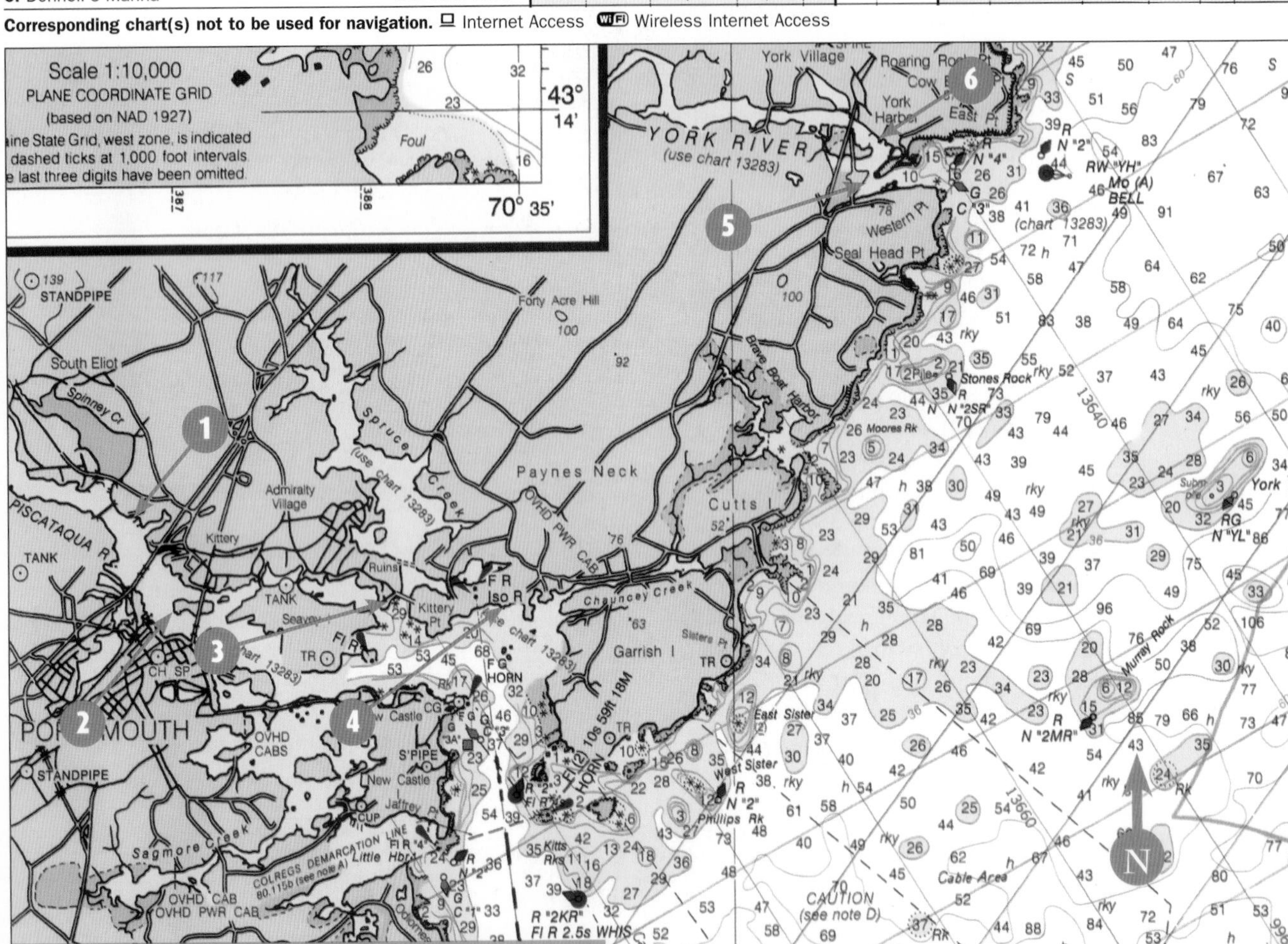

PISCATAQUA RIVER, YORK RIVER, Chart 13286

You can also rent a mooring from the friendly Portsmouth Yacht Club (603-436-9877), with launch service in season, (contact on VHF Channel 09 or 78), or from Frisbee's Market, although this requires a walk to the market. Frisbee's does not monitor the VHF.

York Harbor

NAVIGATION: Use Chart 13283. From Kitts Rock outside Portsmouth Harbor, it is about six miles north to popular, landlocked York Harbor, one of the coast's noted hurricane holes. Currents run strong in the narrow, winding channel causing surges and boils. Heed the markers, especially at the U-turn around Stage Neck, a half mile in from the entrance. Above Bragdon Island, a fixed bridge with a 15-foot vertical clearance limits exploration of the river, although there is ample water for at least a mile above the bridge for exploring and anchorage for those who can clear the bridge.

In the inner harbor, with its high, green shores, the current eases. Some moorings are available, but the northern and southern anchorages have shoaled substantially. Check locally for the best anchoring depths and use heavy tackle, as the current can run to 4.5 knots.

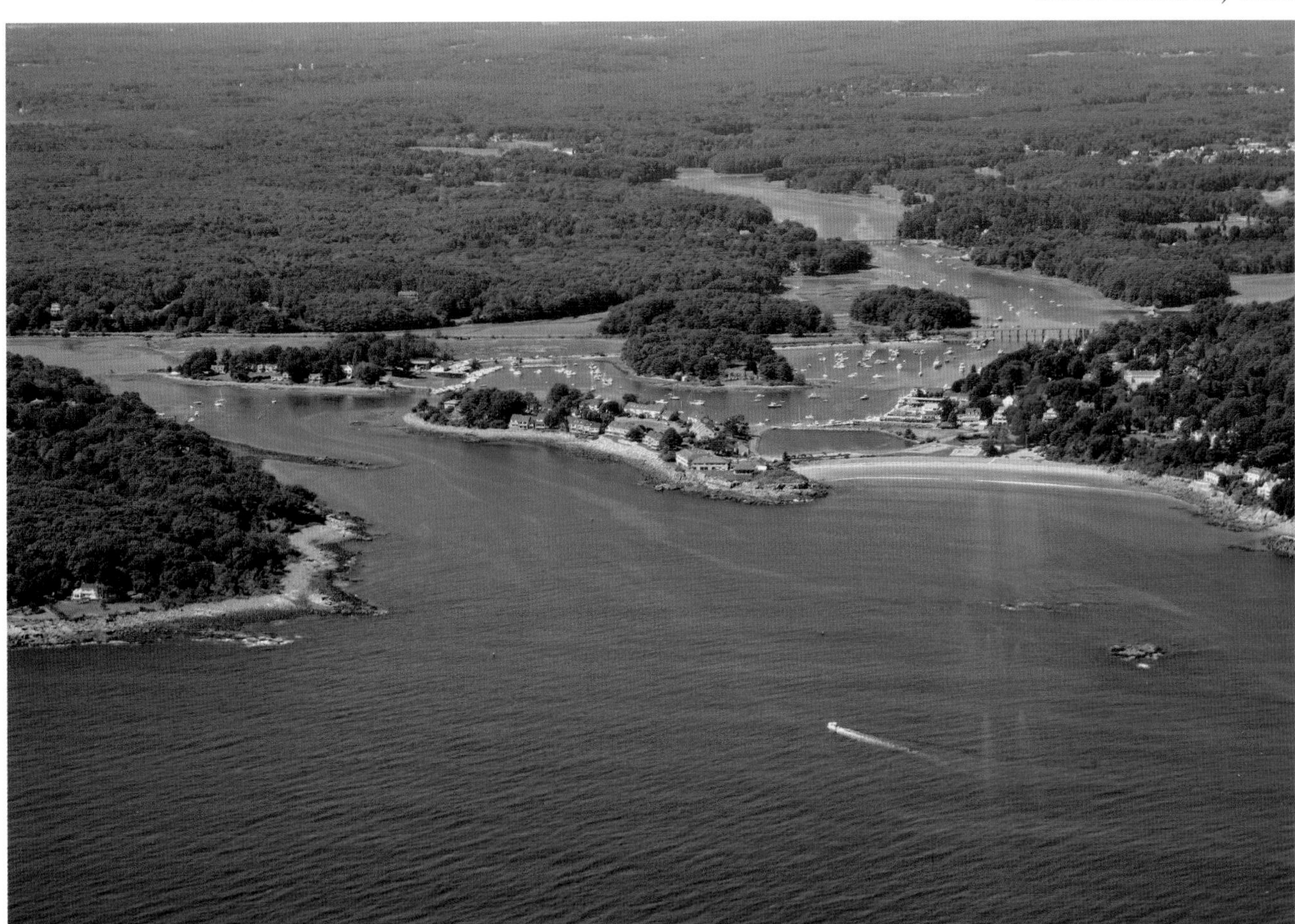

Looking west over York Harbor. (Not to be used for navigation.) WATERWAY GUIDE PHOTOGRAPHY

York is a busy harbor with typical summer resort activity—deep-sea fishing cruises, a water carnival and yacht club races three times a week. Ashore you find a Maine Colonial village (www.oldyork.org). Its best-known attraction is the Old Gaol, (207-363-4974, 207 York St.) built in 1719. The jail, now a museum, is thought to be the oldest English stone public building still in use in this country. Near the Old Gaol is the Emerson-Wilcox House, used alternately as a general store, post office and tavern where Post Road travelers stopped for rest, food and drink. The Old Gaol and the Emerson-Wilcox House are open daily June to mid-October from 10:00 a.m. to 5 p.m., and closed Sundays. Several York County towns provide trolley service up and down the coast from south of York Beaches to Kennebunkport. Visit www.shorelinexplorer.com or call 207-324-5762, extension 2932.

Dockage: York Harbor Marine Service is just inside Stage Neck, on the protected side of Harris Island. Ordinarily, a slip with electricity is available at this small, full-service yard, as are gas, diesel fuel, ice, some marine supplies and most repairs. It is about a mile's walk to the village from this location.

The town dock is somewhat closer to town, located to seaward of the low-clearance (15-foot) fixed bridge at the head of the harbor. There is an ample dinghy landing here, and you can dispose of your trash at the barrel on the dock.

The Stage Neck Inn (207-363-3850, 8 Stage Neck Road) is recommended for a memorable meal with an eagle's eye view of the harbor entrance. Every Saturday (9-1) and Tuesday (2-5:30) from early June until early October, there is a wonderful farmer's market in the back lot of the Greater York Region Visitors Center (info@yorkme.org, 207-363-4422, 1 Stonewall Lane) that is only a short walk from the town dock.

Anchorage: With the expansion of the mooring field, anchorage is more difficult, yet you should still be able to find a spot in depths ranging from 8 to 20 feet in a mud bottom. Ask the harbormaster for permission.

Cape Neddick Harbor

Behind the jutting promontory of Cape Neddick, small Cape Neddick Harbor offers emergency shelter for small boats. It is poorly marked and unprotected from any wind from the north or east. In a prevailing southwesterly, seek shelter in the unnamed cove between Cape Neddick proper and Barn Point. There are no aids to navigation in this area, but water depth is charted at 10 to 12 feet at low water well into the cove. Be aware of the shoals south of, and extending from, Barn Point. Cape Neddick is best known for the very picturesque Nubble Light (officially the Cape Neddick Light Station), which was built in 1879. It flashes three seconds on and three seconds off and its beacon is visible 13 miles out to sea in good visibility.

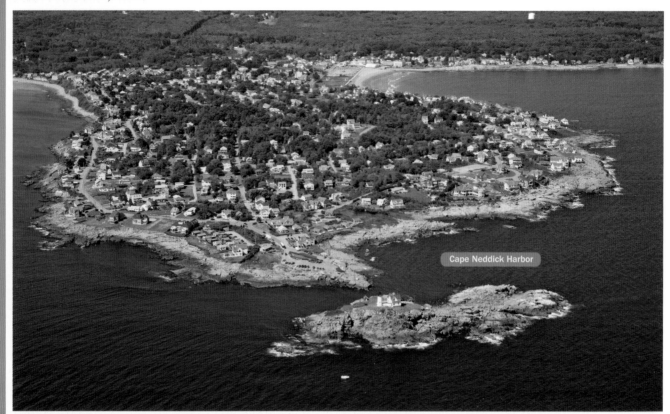

Looking northwest over Cape Neddick and the Nubble Lighthouse. (Not to be used for navigation.) WATERWAY GUIDE PHOTOGRAPHY

Perkins Cove

Perkins Cove is small, shallow, busy with lobster boats and popular with car-borne tourists in search of the archetypal Maine fishing village. In this case, the actual village, Ogunquit, is landlocked several miles from its harbor. Cruising vessels often enter the tiny harbor during settled weather for a brief tie-up in an emergency. Passage into Perkins Cove for all but low-clearance vessels will require an accomplice on the bridge to push the button there for a lift; hail the Perkins Cove Harbormaster on VHF Channel 16 for assistance.

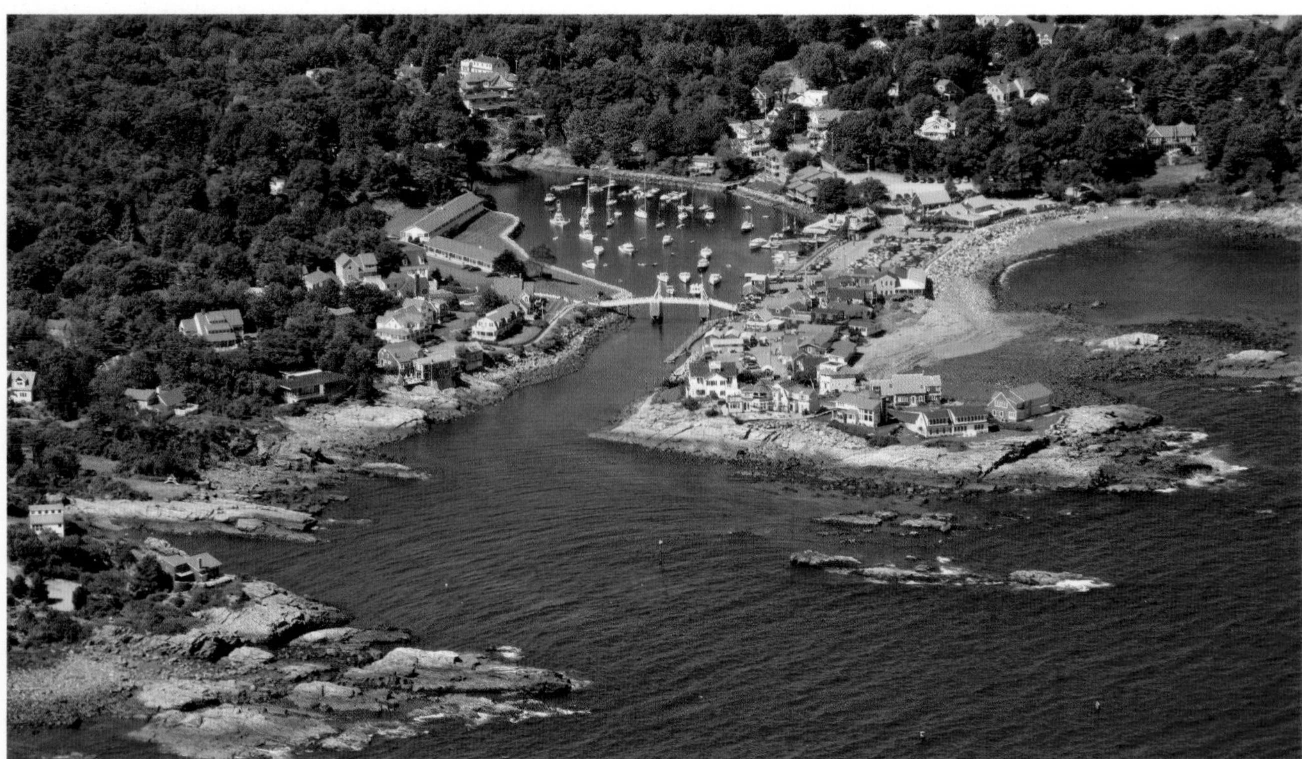

Perkins Cove in Ogunquit. (Not to be used for navigation.) WATERWAY GUIDE PHOTOGRAPHY

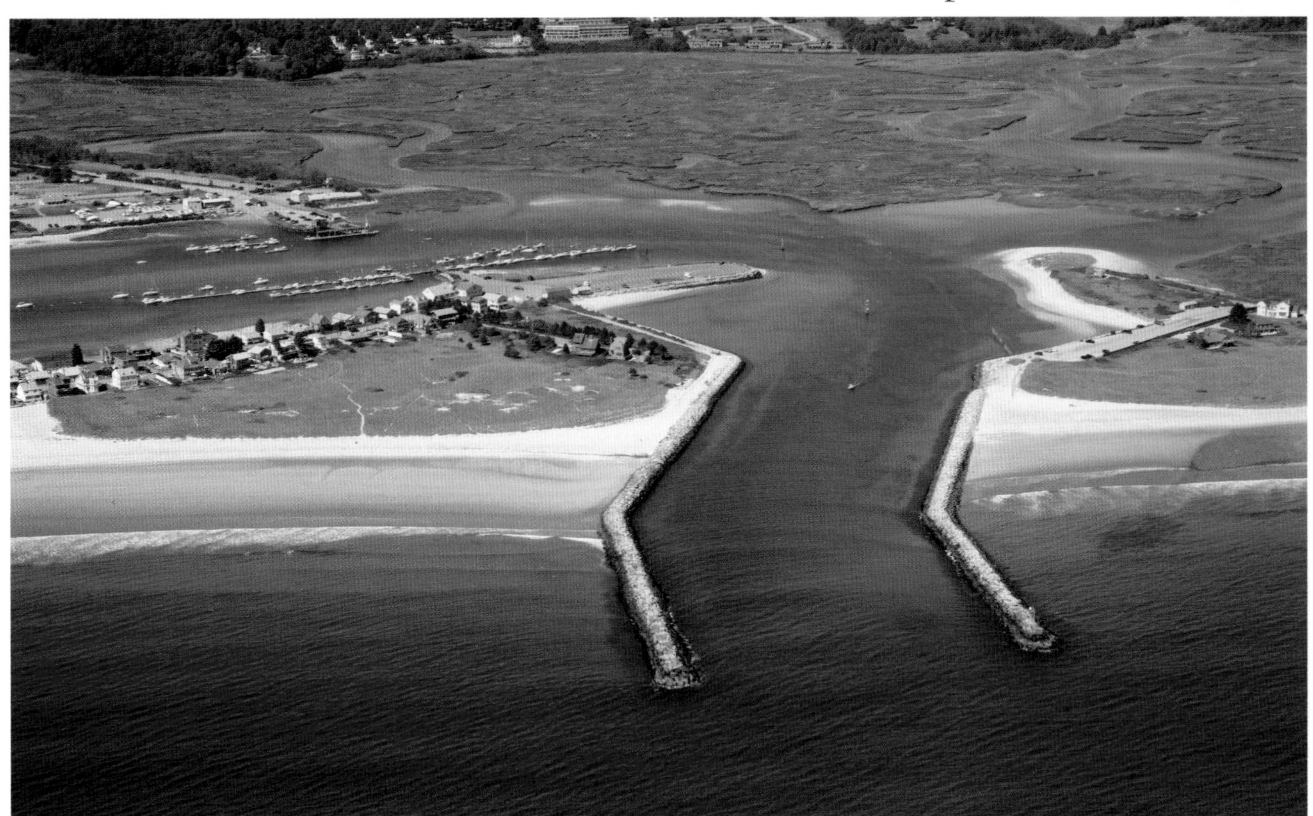

Use local knowledge to enter Wells Harbor. (Not to be used for navigation.) WATERWAY GUIDE PHOTOGRAPHY

Dockage: Thirty-minute dockage is permitted (immediately seaward of the unique lift bridge guarding the cove) against floating docks along the seawall to starboard.

Anchorage: No anchorage is available in the cove itself, though in conditions of necessity, as the bridge sign says, there are guest moorings for emergencies only—for a fee.

Wells Harbor

Wells Harbor, five miles up the coast and about 10 miles on a direct line from Cape Neddick, is accessed by a channel that was dredged in June 2004 to a depth of 6 feet at mean low water.

Dockage: Wells Harbor has a town dock and limited accommodations for transient boats with shoal draft. The harbor itself was dredged in 2001 and a new mooring plan was installed. The harbor can now moor 150 boats with lengths up to 44 feet. The harbormaster can be reached at 207-646-3236 for information on channel depth and availability of slips and moorings.

You are allowed to pick up and drop off crew from the public dock. The village of Wells, with its antique-car museum, is less than a mile away. Visitors to Wells can enjoy the nearby National Estuarine Research Reserve (207-646-1555, 342 Laudholm Farm Road) and the Rachel Carson Wildlife Refuge (207-646-9226, 321 Port Road) for nature hikes, photography and bird-watching. Wells Beach has good swimming and bi-weekly lobster bakes. Anchoring is inadvisable because of a lack of room. Most services (groceries, banks, etc.) are available on the Route 1 corridor in the town of Wells Beach.

Kennebunkport

NAVIGATION: Use Chart 13286. Use Portland tide tables. For high tide, add 7 minutes; for low tide, add 5 minutes. The Kennebunk River has been dredged to a controlling depth of 5 feet, and the entrance is well-protected by substantial breakwaters on either side. The preferred approach is to leave flashing green bell buoy "1" to port, honoring green can buoy "3" in the same manner before entering the river; favor the jetty to starboard on entry.

An approach can also be made from the southwest, between black-and-white "F" and green-and-white "O," located approximately in the middle of the fairly extensive rocky ledge charted as Fishing Rock. The river is best negotiated at half-tide flood or better, at which point there will be plenty of water, and wave action at the mouth will be subdued. Entrance during peak ebb can be downright nasty when the river's tidal current meets ocean swells driven by prevailing southwesterlies and powerful craft of all descriptions determined to beat the shallows of low-slack water.

At dead low, particularly when there's a less than average tide, several spots upstream will challenge keels of over 3.5 feet. Beyond the jetties, the river is well-marked. However, moored working boats (often aimed in the most improbable directions) are likely to obscure buoys ahead, thereby camouflaging the desired course along the winding, narrow channel. A new visitor to the area should stay to mid-channel, especially giving room to red

Kennebunkport, ME

KENNEBUNKPORT		Largest Vessel Accommodated	VHF Channel Monitored	Transient Berths / Total Berths	Approach / Dockside Depth (reported)	Floating Docks	Gas / Diesel	Groceries, Ice, Marine Supplies, Snacks	Repairs: Hull, Engine, Propeller	Lift (tonnage), Crane, Rail	1=110V, 2=220V, B=Both, Max Amps	Laundry, Pool, Showers	Pump-Out Station	Nearby: Grocery Store, Motel, Restaurant
		Dockage					Supplies		Services					
1. Chicks Marina (Internet Access) (Wireless Internet Access)	**207-967-2782**	**153**	**09/68**	**15/50**	**6/7**	**F**	**GD**	**IM**	**HEP**		**B/100**	**LS**	**P**	**GMR**
2. Kennebunkport Marina	207-967-3411	38	09	8/41	6/6	F		IM	HEP		B/50	LS	P	MR
3. Performance Marine	207-967-5550	70	16	/22	6/4	F	GD	GIM	HP	L	B/50	LS		GMR
4. Yachtsman Marina	207-967-2511	120	09/68	/64	6/7	F	GD				B/50			MR

Corresponding chart(s) not to be used for navigation. Internet Access, Wireless Internet Access

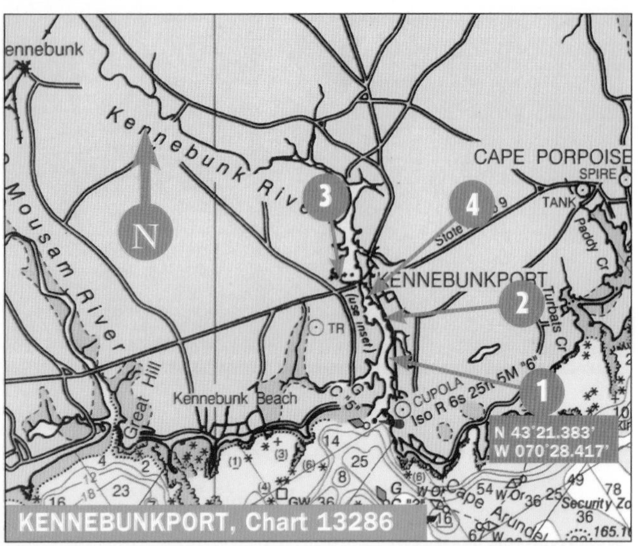

KENNEBUNKPORT, Chart 13286

nun buoy "8." The river takes a bend to starboard and it is easy to get swept into the buoy. Note that the swing bridge carrying state Highway 9 (5-foot closed vertical clearance) across the river no longer opens.

Dockage: As you power up the Kennebunk River, the first marina you will see to starboard (they are all to starboard) is the Nonantum Hotel, (207-967-4050) with slips, primarily for seasonal rental. Chicks Marina, about 300 yards farther along, is a full-service facility with a hospitable welcome for visiting yachts.

Chicks Marina is associated with Yachtsman Marina (still another 100 yards upriver); between the two of them you should find accommodations in a quiet, comfortable setting with a pastoral scene across the narrow river. Floating docks at both of these marinas, along with attentive dockhands, make landings and departures easy

Looking north over the entrance to the Kennebunk River. (Not to be used for navigation.) WATERWAY GUIDE PHOTOGRAPHY

whatever the current. You will find complete electric, TV and water hookups at all slips, excellent showers and restrooms, a laundry room, a fuel dock (at both marinas) and a boat supply shop. Additional amenities include grills and sundecks, concierge service and wireless Internet access. Anchoring is not possible anywhere on the river.

GOIN' ASHORE:
KENNEBUNKPORT, ME

Quaint and accessible, Kennebunkport has become one of Maine's most popular tourist magnets, all the more so because of the town's most famous summer residents, former presidents George Herbert Walker Bush and George W. Bush. Indeed, some of the town's best restaurants are identified by the line, "George Bush goes there a lot." Kennebunkport is also justly famous for its maritime heritage and its extraordinary 19th-century architecture, a veritable treasure trove of Colonial- and Federal-era sea captain's homes that are worth the short journey up the Kennebunk River. For example, the amazingly ornate and intricate Wedding Cake House (c. 1826) (207-985-4802) is unforgettable and is one of the most photographed Gothic Revival Style buildings in the U.S.). No visit to Kennebunkport is complete without stopping at The Seashore Trolley Museum (207-967-2712, 195 Log Cabin Road), started in 1939 and currently the largest railroad museum in the world. For a small fee, you can train to be a motorman and drive one of the antique streetcars around their two mile track.

Kennebunkport is also an excellent place to reprovision or to enjoy a fine meal out. The Dock Square area, just east of the swing bridge and about a half mile north of the marinas, has a general market, gourmet shop, bank, pharmacy, well-stocked bookstore, decoy shop, outdoor and imported clothing stores and several interesting galleries. Alisson's Restaurant (207-967-4841, 11 Dock Sq.), overlooking Dock Square, is popular with tourists and locals. Arundel Wharf Restaurant (207-967-3444, 43 Ocean Ave.), one or two blocks north of the marinas, serves a superb lobster stew, with moderate prices and a harbor view. The Landing Restaurant and Hotel (866-967-4221, 21 Ocean Ave.) is oriented toward the sea in both its decor and menu—indoor or outdoor dining with a water view.

Other notable standouts include the White Barn Inn (207-967-2321, 37 Beach Road) for upscale dining, which has earned the AAA five diamond award (a jacket is required for men but tie is optional), and Mabel's Lobster Claw (207-967-2562, 124 Ocean Ave.), casual and a short walk south of the marinas.

ADDITIONAL RESOURCES:

- Kennebunkport Business Association, **www.kennebunkport.org**

NEARBY GOLF COURSES:
Cape Arundel Golf Club, 1447 Old River Road, Kennebunkport, ME 04046, 207-967-3494, **www.capearundelgolfclub.com**

NEARBY MEDICAL FACILITIES:
Southern Maine Medical Center, 72 Main St., Kennebunk, ME 04043, 207-467-6999

Cape Porpoise Harbor

NAVIGATION: Use Chart 13286. A deepwater commercial lobsterman's harbor with an easy, straight entrance, Cape Porpoise Harbor offers the only full protection between Portsmouth and Portland for boats drawing up to 8 feet. Bell and whistle buoys and a horn and light on Goat Island make the harbor easy to find, even in fog. The main problem upon entering is dodging the lobster-pot buoys.

Anchorage: Cape Porpoise is a fishing harbor seldom visited by recreational boats. Few services are available here, but you can anchor in good holding ground anywhere off the channel if you allow for the tidal range. A public dock offers dinghy floats, a phone, a dumpster and a take-out restaurant where you can get ice. Water, gasoline and diesel fuel are available, but tie-ups at the dock can be difficult. There are no slips or moorings.

To Cape Elizabeth

The seaside resort towns between Cape Porpoise and Cape Elizabeth do not have good harbors, but there are several places to find shelter.

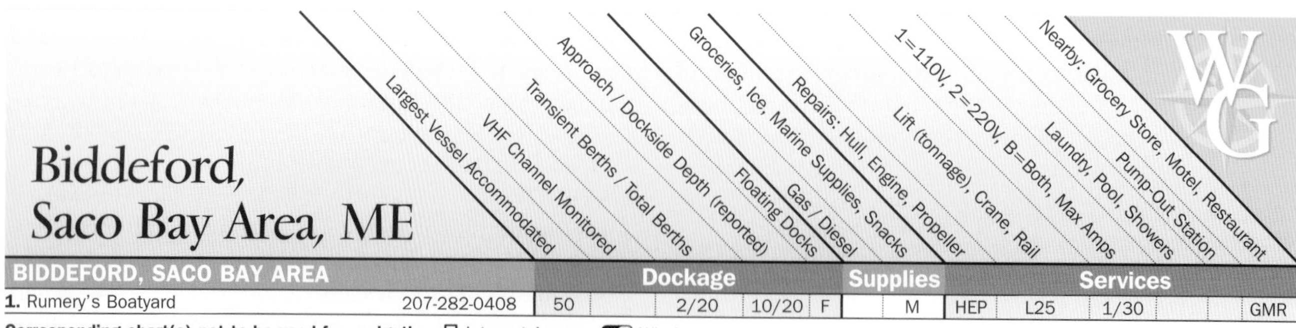

Biddeford, Saco Bay Area, ME

BIDDEFORD, SACO BAY AREA		Largest Vessel Accommodated	VHF Channel Monitored	Transient Berths / Total Berths	Approach / Dockside Depth (reported)	Floating Docks	Gas / Diesel	Groceries, Ice, Marine Supplies, Snacks	Repairs: Hull, Engine, Propeller	Lift (tonnage), Crane, Rail	1=110V, 2=220V, B=Both, Max Amps	Laundry, Pool, Showers	Pump-Out Station	Nearby: Grocery Store, Motel, Restaurant
		Dockage						Supplies		Services				
1. Rumery's Boatyard	207-282-0408	50		2/20	10/20	F		M	HEP	L25	1/30			GMR

Corresponding chart(s) not to be used for navigation. Internet Access Wireless Internet Access

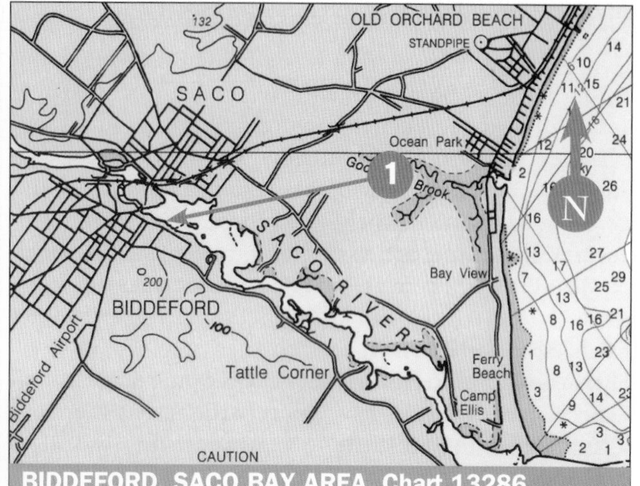

BIDDEFORD, SACO BAY AREA, Chart 13286

Biddeford Pool

Anchorage: Protected by Wood Island and surrounding ledges, Wood Island Harbor, just outside Biddeford Pool, is a good anchorage in most conditions; the pool itself is almost entirely landlocked, though tiny at low water. The anchorage is best approached from the north, leaving both Wood Island and green can "1" (marking the entrance to the Saco River) to port and passing between the westernmost ledge of Wood Island and the distinctive stone monument on Stage Island. Best anchorage will be found in 8 to 15 feet of water (mean low water); check depths carefully outside the increasingly large mooring field. The Biddeford Pool Yacht Club (207-282-0485, 14 Yates St.) offers guest moorings, as available. The fee includes use of showers, two round-trip launch rides and use of the mooring itself. Call on VHF Channels 09 or 68.

Ram Island

Wood Island Harbor

Looking east over the entrance to the Saco River. (Not to be used for navigation.) WATERWAY GUIDE PHOTOGRAPHY

Ashore is a small grocery store, F.O. Goldthwaite (207-284-8872, 3 Lester B Orcutt Blvd.), for basic provisions and newspapers. Also nearby are the post office and Pool Lobster Co. (207-284-5000, 3 Lester B. Orcutt Blvd.) with lobster rolls, fried foods and hot coffee. This is a pretty spot with ample space to walk along rock-bound coastal scenery and to watch the tidal workings of the pool.

Saco River

NAVIGATION: Use Chart 13286. The twin towns of Biddeford and Saco—curiously ignored during southern Maine's coastal revival of the 1980s—lie on either side of the Saco River about four miles upstream. The Saco River was dredged to 8 feet a few years ago but has now shoaled to 6 feet. If you need more than 5-foot depths, call ahead for the latest local information before attempting passage

Dockage: If you need repairs, Rumery's Boatyard in Biddeford can handle them.

Cape Elizabeth

Anchorage: A breakwater connecting Cape Elizabeth and Richmond Island creates two anchorages. The western one is Richmond Island Harbor, with protection from the northwest through the northeast. Seal Cove, on the eastern side of the breakwater, is better in the prevailing southwesterly winds. Note that there are charted but unmarked rocks in Seal Cove. As you approach the anchorage northeast of the breakwater, stay close to the shore of Richmond Island. Neither anchorage is free of surge.

Casco Bay

Twenty miles by twelve miles, Casco Bay makes the transition from the beach coast to the rocky coast of Maine. Long necks (as peninsulas are known hereabouts) divide the large bay into many smaller ones, with cross cuts forming the islands. An abundance of rock ledges requires careful navigation at all times, although most of the channels are well-marked. The water is deep enough for most cruising boats. WATERWAY GUIDE covers the mainland to the north and east from Portland to South Freeport, then cuts eastward to long Harpswell Neck with Orrs and Bailey islands, and then to New Meadows River and Cape Small.

Portland

As Maine's largest city, Portland has a long, colorful history and is still an active seaport for oceangoing vessels. Today it is also a major port of call for cruising yachts. Portland has transformed once-moldering waterfront warehouses and piers with an imaginative reconstruction of historic buildings, tasteful new buildings, shops and enterprises designed to attract modern commerce and low-density tourism. A large portion of the waterfront formerly occupied by Bath Iron Works is in transition, with facilities for cruise ships and visiting boaters of all types as the focus. Cruising visitors will find well-appointed marinas and fully stocked marine supply and equipment stores.

NAVIGATION: Use Charts 13288 and 13292. Use Portland tide tables. Portland is announced well to seaward by the red-and-white "P" light buoy (five miles east-southeast of Cape Elizabeth) with horn, Morse (A), whistle and RACON (- -), and the ship channel leading into the harbor is clearly marked. Monitor a continuous position here, nonetheless; keel-grinding obstructions abound outside the channel, which first slants to starboard and then hooks sharply to port. This circumstance alone would present no particular problem, but the fog here can drop quickly. Keep a sharp lookout for commercial traffic, inter-island ferries and numerous other vessels, including the fast-running ferry to Nova Scotia, that frequent this busy channel.

Dockage and Moorings: Immediately upon passing the lighthouse, just beyond the jetty extending from Spring Point, you will encounter Spring Point Marina, which has dockage on the South Portland side of the harbor for all but the largest vessels. To enter, after passing the lighthouse, head directly for the tall masts of the boats at the dock, and call VHF Channel 09 for docking instructions. The marina, featuring slips with 9-foot depths, also manages transient slips next door at Breakwater Marina. Gasoline and diesel fuel, ice, marine supplies, showers, restrooms, laundry machines, major repair capabilities and a restaurant all are available here.

Beyond Spring Point, the Fore River creates the inner harbor, dividing Portland from its far less developed sibling, South Portland. On the Portland side of the harbor, Portland Yacht Services (580 Fore St.) is a full-service boatyard and marina that rents space at its deepwater floating docks and transient dinghy dockage for those anchored out. In addition to ice, water, restrooms, showers and pump-out, the yard has a wide range of repair capabilities and on-site marine specialists, including Yale Cordage Inc., New England Fiberglass (207-773-3537) and Sea-Tow (207-772-6724). Hamilton Marine (207-774-1772, 100 Fore St.), the largest marine supply store north of Boston, is nearby.

With immediate access to the city's attractions, DiMillo's Old Port Marina may have a few slips (no moorings) available on its wood-barrier-protected docks. Electricity costs extra. Given the swift currents that run through the dock area, it may be advisable to time docking with slack water. DiMillo's is best known for its landmark, DiMillo's Floating Restaurant (207-772-2216, 28 Long Wharf) a huge and handsomely re-outfitted ferryboat, which serves well-prepared seafood at moderate prices. Gowen Marine (farther down from DiMillo's) can facilitate just about any repair imaginable with its 150-ton lift and full-service repair facilities. Across Commercial Street is the Old Port district, full of shops and restaurants too numerous to mention.

The Maine Yacht Center (100 Kensington St.), somewhat removed from downtown Portland, is well-positioned for finding restaurants and provisions. On the South Portland side of the harbor, past the abandoned lighthouse tower on entry from the outer harbor, Sunset Marina has more than 150 slips with depths of 6 to 14 feet at low water.

Portland, Falmouth, South Freeport, ME

PORTLAND, FALMOUTH, SOUTH FREEPORT		Largest Vessel Accommodated	VHF Channel Monitored	Transient Berths / Total Berths	Approach / Dockside Depth (reported)	Floating Docks	Gas / Diesel	Groceries, Ice, Marine Supplies, Snacks	Repairs: Hull, Engine, Propeller	Lift (tonnage), Crane, Rail	1=110V, 2=220V, B=Both, Max Amps	Laundry, Pool, Showers	Pump-Out Station	Nearby: Grocery Store, Motel, Restaurant
		Dockage					Supplies		Services					
1. Spring Point Marina (WiFi)	207-767-3254	200	09	30/275	10/8	F	GD	IMS	HEP	L35	B/100	LS	P	GMR
2. Breakwater Marina	207-799-2817	45	09	/125	7/7	F	GD	GIMS	HEP	L	B/50	LS	P	R
3. Sunset Marina	207-767-4729	200	16/09	20/150	30/14	F	GD	GIMS	HP	R	B/50	LS	P	GR
4. Centerboard Yacht Club	207-799-7084	40			7/5			GI			1	S		R
5. Portland Yacht Services Inc.	207-774-1067	200	09	15/204	35/35	F			HP		1/50	LS	P	GMR
6. Gowen Marine	**207-773-1761**	**100**			**27/27**	**F**		**M**	**HEP**	**L150**	**B/50**			**GMR**
7. Chartroom at Chase, Leavitt & Co.	207-772-6383		LIFE RAFT SERVICE STATION						M					GMR
8. DiMillo's Old Port Marina & Yacht Sales (Internet) (WiFi)	**207-773-7632**	**250**	**09/71**	**20/130**	**50/25**	**F**	**GD**	**IS**	**EP**		**B/100**	**LS**	**P**	**GMR**
9. South Port Marine (WiFi)	**207-799-8191**	**150**	**16/78**	**20/170**	**8/13**	**F**	**GD**	**GIMS**	**HEP**	**L,C**	**B/100**	**LS**	**P**	**GMR**
10. Maine Yacht Center (Internet) (WiFi)	**207-842-9000**	**120**	**09**	**15/80**	**15/15**	**F**	**GD**	**GIMS**	**HEP**	**L,R**	**B/100**	**LS**	**P**	**GMR**
11. Handy Boat Service (Internet)	**207-781-5110**	**125**	**09**	**35/40**	**15/**	**F**	**GD**	**IM**	**HP**	**L**	**1/30**		**P**	**GMR**
12. Portland Yacht Club	207-781-9820	70	68		25/6	F		I			1/15	LS		GR
13. Yankee Marina and Boatyard Inc.	**207-846-4326**	**50**	**16/09**	**4/110**	**7/7**	**F**		**IM**	**HEP**	**L60**	**B/50**	**S**	**P**	**GMR**
14. East Coast Yacht Sales	207-846-4545	60		1/8	/7			IM			1			R
15. Yarmouth Boat Yard	207-846-9050	40	09	2/150	6/6	F		M	HP		1/30			R
16. Harraseeket Yacht Club	207-865-4949				20/10				CALL AHEAD					
17. Strouts Point Wharf Co. (Internet)	207-865-3899	100	16/09	2/108	20/18	F	G	IMS	HEP	L25	B/50	S	P	GMR
18. Ring's Marine Services Inc.	207-865-6143	100	16/09		18/18			M	HEP					GR
19. Brewer South Freeport Marine (Internet) (WiFi)	**207-865-3181**	**150**	**09**	**5/100**	**16/12**	**F**	**GD**	**IM**	**HEP**	**L35**	**B/50**	**LS**	**P**	**GMR**
20. Vessel Services Inc.	207-772-5718	125	16/19	1/1	/15		D	IM						GMR

Corresponding chart(s) not to be used for navigation. (Internet) Internet Access (WiFi) Wireless Internet Access

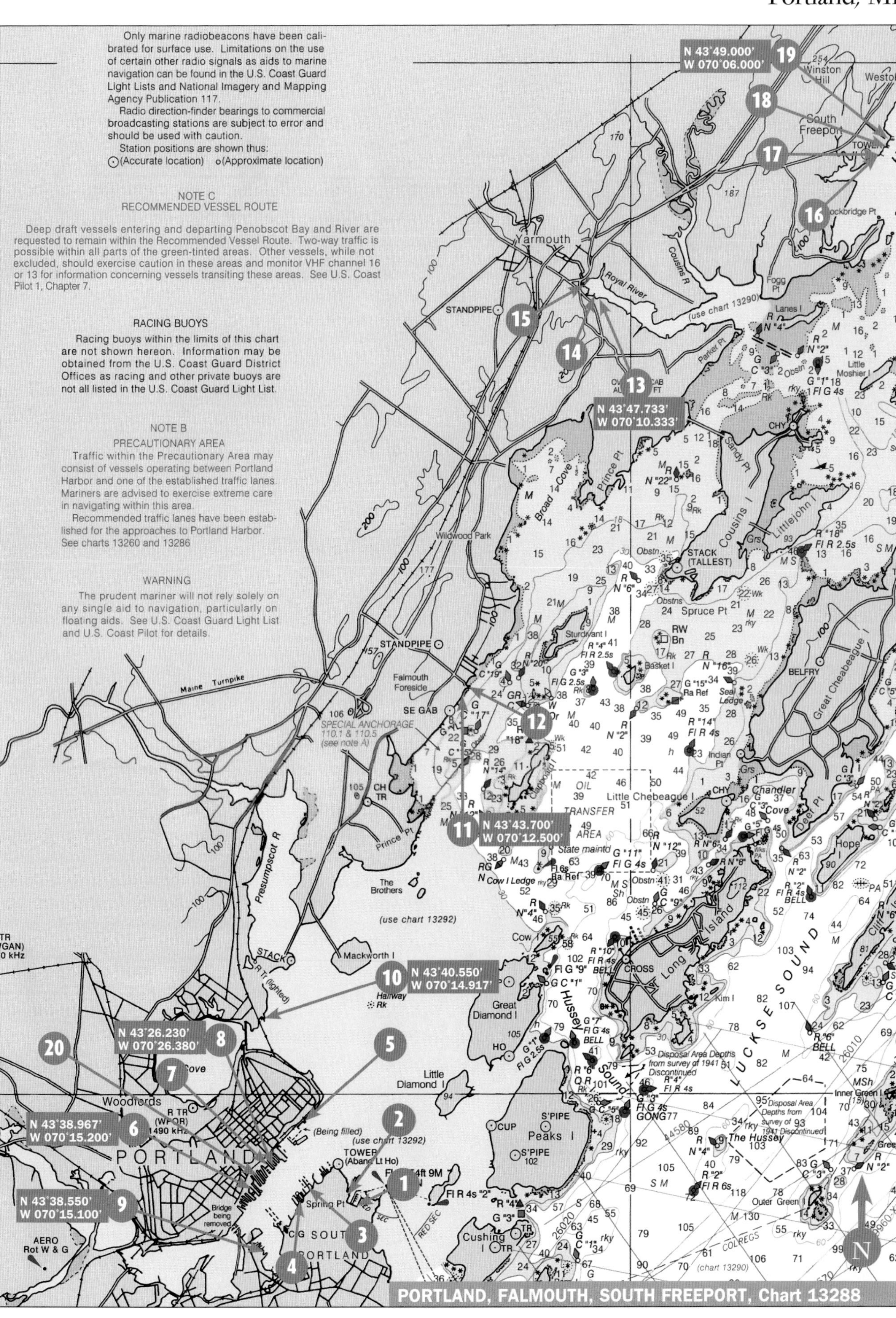
Only marine radiobeacons have been calibrated for surface use. Limitations on the use of certain other radio signals as aids to marine navigation can be found in the U.S. Coast Guard Light Lists and National Imagery and Mapping Agency Publication 117.
Radio direction-finder bearings to commercial broadcasting stations are subject to error and should be used with caution.
Station positions are shown thus:
(Accurate location) (Approximate location)
NOTE C
RECOMMENDED VESSEL ROUTE
Deep draft vessels entering and departing Penobscot Bay and River are requested to remain within the Recommended Vessel Route. Two-way traffic is possible within all parts of the green-tinted areas. Other vessels, while not excluded, should exercise caution in these areas and monitor VHF channel 16 or 13 for information concerning vessels transiting these areas. See U.S. Coast Pilot 1, Chapter 7.
RACING BUOYS
Racing buoys within the limits of this chart are not shown hereon. Information may be obtained from the U.S. Coast Guard District Offices as racing and other private buoys are not all listed in the U.S. Coast Guard Light List.
NOTE B
PRECAUTIONARY AREA
Traffic within the Precautionary Area may consist of vessels operating between Portland Harbor and one of the established traffic lanes. Mariners are advised to exercise extreme care in navigating within this area.
Recommended traffic lanes have been established for the approaches to Portland Harbor. See charts 13260 and 13286
WARNING
The prudent mariner will not rely solely on any single aid to navigation, particularly on floating aids. See U.S. Coast Guard Light List and U.S. Coast Pilot for details.
N 43°49.000' W 070°06.000'
19
18
17
16
15
14
13
N 43°47.733' W 070°10.333'
12
11
N 43°43.700' W 070°12.500'
10
N 43°40.550' W 070°14.917'
8
N 43°26.230' W 070°26.380'
20
7
5
6
N 43°38.967' W 070°15.200'
2
1
9
N 43°38.550' W 070°15.100'
3
4
Winston Hill
Weston
South Freeport
Yarmouth
Royal River
Cousins R
(use chart 13290)
Lanes I
Little Moshier I
Fogg Pt
Parker Pt
STANDPIPE
Broad Cove
Prince Pt
Sandy Pt
Cousins I
Littlejohn I
STACK (TALLEST)
Spruce Pt
Wildwood Park
Sturdivant I
Basket I
Seal Ledge
BELFRY
Great Chebeague
Maine Turnpike
Falmouth Foreside
SE GAB
SPECIAL ANCHORAGE 110.1 & 110.5 (see note A)
CH TR
Clapboard I
OIL TRANSFER AREA
State maintd
Little Chebeague I
Indian Pt
Chandler Cove
Deer Pt
Hope I
Presumpscot R
Prince Pt
The Brothers
Cow I Ledge
(use chart 13292)
Cow I
Long Island
LUCKSE SOUND
Hussey Sound
STACK
Mackworth I
Halfway Rk
Great Diamond I
CROSS
Kim I
Disposal Area Depths from survey of 1941 Discontinued
Cliff Isl
Cove
Woodfords
Little Diamond I
R TR (WPOR) 1490 kHz
PORTLAND
(Being filled)
(use chart 13292)
TOWER (Aband Lt Ho)
CUP
S'PIPE
Peaks I
S'PIPE 102
Disposal Area Depths from survey of 1941 Discontinued
The Hussey
Inner Green I
Outer Green I
Spring Pt
Bridge being removed
CG
SOUTH PORTLAND
AERO Rot W & G
RED SEC
Cushing I
TR
COLREGS
(chart 13290)
N
PORTLAND, FALMOUTH, SOUTH FREEPORT, Chart 13288

Joseph R. Melanson of www.Skypic.com

Looking northeast over Portland Harbor and the islands of Casco Bay. (Not to be used for navigation.)

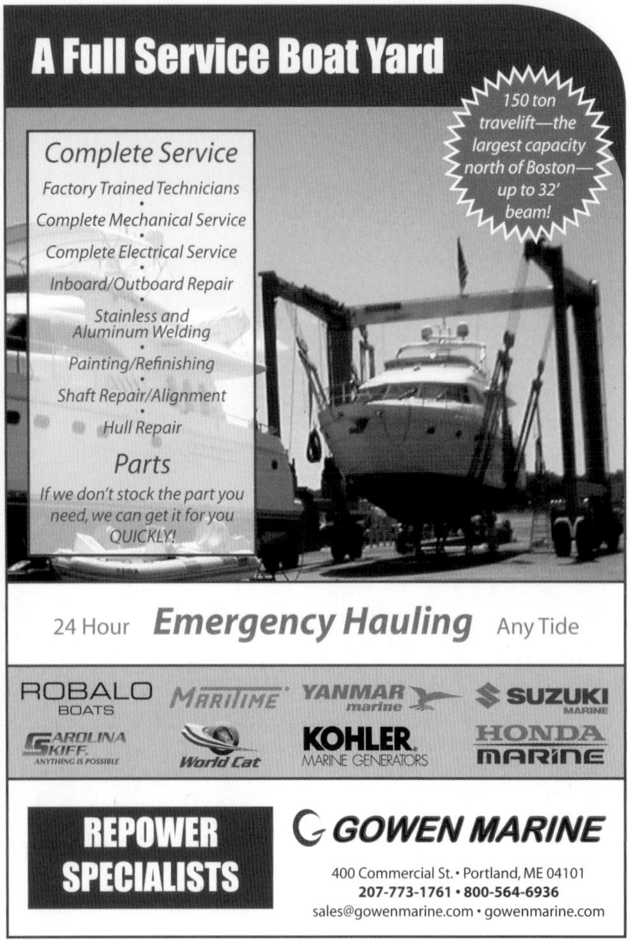

The Saltwater Grille Restaurant (207-799-5400, 231 Front St.) is located next door to the marina. Also next door, Centerboard Yacht Club (207-799-7084, 271 Front St.) ,is accommodating to visiting yachts. Moorings are available in 5-foot depths for a modest facilities fee, which includes launch service and use of the club's showers, excellent water, low-priced ice and a public phone.

Water-taxi service to the Portland side via the club's launch is possible at reasonable rates when a lull in ordinary business permits. Limited anchorage space may be available east of the club's mooring field, and there is a dinghy dock in front of the clubhouse. At the far end of the inner harbor, South Port Marine has deepwater dockage. Showers, laundry machines, ice and marine supplies are available, as are hull and engine repairs. The Mill Creek Shopping Center (two supermarkets, a hardware store and other shops and restaurants) is within walking distance.

GOIN' ASHORE:
PORTLAND, ME

Portland is clearly a city that has escaped the drive to modernization, which has made urban American centers all but unrecognizable to those whose memories span more than 20 years. A walk along Commercial Street (the waterfront boulevard), through the preserved and restored downtown grid, reveals interesting shops, pubs and restaurants. The Chartroom at Chase, Leavitt and Co. (on Dana Street just off Commercial Street, 207-772-6383) has an impressive

array of major marine appliances, equipment and hardware, and one of the most complete retail offerings of U.S. and Canadian charts anywhere. West on Commercial Street, Adams Marine Center (14 Ocean St., 207-772-2781) offers marine products at somewhat less than full list price. There are several ATM locations within an easy walk from the waterfront. Portland Museum of Art (7 Congress Square, 207-775-6148) is Maine's largest, where works of Homer and Wyeth share space with the impressionist masters. Next door is The Children's Museum of Maine (142 Free St, 207-828-1234), with interactive exhibits for the youngsters in the crew. Just down the street is an L.L. Bean outlet (207-772-5100). Portland Symphony Orchestra (20 Myrtle St., 207-842-0800) performs at Merrill Auditorium and plays pops as well as classical. You can also catch a performance of the Portland Players (420 Cottage Road, South Portland, 207-799-7337).

Reprovisioning and restaurant possibilities are nearly limitless. The Portland Greengrocer (211 Commercial St., 207-761-9232) has an outstanding produce selection, as well as gourmet deli items. The rapidly expanding Public Market House (28 Monument Square on Congress St., 207-228-2056) now replaces the old Portland Public Market. Public Market House is open Mon.-Sat. 8 a.m. to 7 p.m. and Sun. 10 to 5 and is a wonderful place to find cheeses from Maine farms, fresh cut flowers, sandwiches on fresh baked breads and beer from Maine microbreweries. To reprovision for a serious cruise Down East, a good one-stop possibility is the Mill Creek Shopping Center, located in South Portland just off Route 77 (Ocean Street), a short distance south of the Fore River Bridge.

For dining in the Old Port district (just behind Commercial Street), Street & Company (33 Wharf St., 207-775-0887) is strictly seafood—casual, intimate and widely regarded as the city's best; reservations are a must. Walter's Café (15 Exchange St., 207-871-9258) is the local favorite for nouvelle cuisine. The Twenty Milk Street Restaurant (Regency Hotel 20 Milk St., 207-774-4200) is far above what you would expect from a hotel restaurant. Thailand Restaurant (29 Wharf St., 207-775-7141) serves modestly priced Thai food. Hi Bombay (1 Pleasant St., 207-772-8767) is an excellent Indian Restaurant. If you have a yen for pub food, Gritty McDuff's (396 Fore St., 207-772-2739) brews its own beer to go with hearty servings—try the shepherd's pie. Old Port Tavern (11 Moulton St., 207-774-0444) serves mainstream food in a pub atmosphere. Fore Street Restaurant (288 Fore St., 207-775-2717) serves modern American cuisine with a commitment to the freshest ingredients—sometimes the evening's menu is not compiled until late in the afternoon. Standard Baking Company (75 Commercial Ave., 207-773-2112), bakes fresh bread and pastries daily. For a great Irish pub meal, try Ri Ra (72 Commercial Street, 207-761-4446) near DiMillo's. Breakfast is best at Becky's Diner (390 Commercial St., 207-773-7070), which opens early at 4:30 a.m. for the fishermen.

ADDITIONAL RESOURCES:

■ Portland's Downtown District, **www.portlandmaine.com**

NEARBY GOLF COURSES:
Riverside Municipal Golf Course, 1158 Riverside St., Portland, ME 04103, 207-797-3524

NEARBY MEDICAL FACILITIES:
Mercy Hospital, 144 State St., Portland, ME 04101, 207-879-3000

Falmouth Foreside

About five miles north of Portland, the suburb of Falmouth Foreside is the yachting center of Casco Bay. Protected by Prince Point to the southwest (there is also another Prince Point to the north on Broad Cove) and Clapboard Island to the east, Falmouth Foreside is easily accessible from Bigelow Bight via the well-marked channel through Hussey Sound or north from Portland through a wide, unobstructed passage. The dense forest of masts between Clapboard Island and the mainland guides the way.

Dockage and Moorings: As you approach the mooring field, Handy Boat Service can guide you to an affordable mooring (with launch service) and take care of your fuel needs, including compressed natural gas (no propane) and repair work. No shower or laundry facilities are available here, though there is a sailmaker on premises and, upstairs from Handy Boat's office, is a large chandlery and nautical clothing store. Downstairs, the Falmouth Sea Grill (207-781-5658, 215 Foreside Road) serves full-menu lunches and dinners (also early-bird specials) with an outstanding harbor view. The Hallett family has been involved with Handy Boat for 34 years and knows how to do it right. Next door, Portland Yacht Club has moorings (with launch service) available on a reciprocal basis to members of recognized clubs. For a modest facilities fee, you can take advantage of the club's amenities, including showers, coin-operated laundry and, in summer, lunch and dinner service.

Provisioning the Boat, a surprisingly complete, small supermarket, hardware and sundries store, is nearby. Or, for major reprovisioning, you may want to hire a cab for the trip to Portland. Sailing visitors arriving in early August can see, or participate in, the Monhegan Island Race, which has been run annually for most of the 20th century and continues today.

Yarmouth

NAVIGATION: Use Chart 13290. A side trip up the Royal River is well worth the two-mile dog-leg passage through the tidal flats to visit the quaint fishing village at the head of navigation. The narrow (typically no more than 50 feet wide) channel will carry 7-foot depths at low water and, unlike much of Maine, has a forgiving mud bottom if a mistake is made. Begin the Royal River approach channel at flashing green buoy "1" and take care not to miss succeeding nun and can buoys on the way upriver.

Dockage: On the southerly side of the river, within walking distance of village amenities, both Yankee Marina and Boatyard Inc. and Yarmouth Boatyard offer substantial marine repair services and a limited number of transient slips. Unfortunately, however, there is neither a mooring field nor anchorage anywhere along the channel. Lower Falls Landing, an office and retail complex offers yacht brokerage, marine insurance, Maine Cottage Furniture and a bookstore.

Looking southeast over Yarmouth and the Royal River (Not to be used for navigation.) WATERWAY GUIDE PHOTOGRAPHY

South Freeport

One of the most accommodating yacht harbors in Maine, South Freeport, on the Harraseeket River, is large, completely protected and relatively easy to enter. Full yacht services are readily had on arrival and, better yet for inveterate shoppers among the crew, nearby Freeport—just a courtesy car ride away—has the most amazing collection of retail outlet stores anywhere.

NAVIGATION: Use Chart 13290. Use Portland tide tables. For high tide, add 12 minutes; for low tide, add 10 minutes. Given the number of small islands, rock outcrops and ledges in upper Casco Bay, the best approach for first-timers to the harbor is via Broad Sound, east of Jewell Island.

From the west end of Whaleboat Island, follow the series of nun and can buoys leading to the opening of the Harraseeket River. In poor visibility, check your depths to maintain 25 feet of water so as to skirt the east edge of Crab Ledge and Crab Island on approach. The harbor entry is made between Stockbridge Point to the west of the channel and Pound of Tea Island, the islet southwest of Moore Point. Depths drop quickly north of green can buoy "7," so it is best to keep the can relatively close to port while rounding Pound of Tea Island into the deep harbor beyond.

Dockage: South Freeport Harbor has two full-service marinas and a mooring rental company to serve the visiting yachtsman. Strout's Point Wharf is the first marina to port on entering the mooring field. Sometimes you can find a vacant slip on their floating docks, and always gasoline and diesel at their fuel dock. Strout's has both a ship's store and lift to support its service and repair operations.

Just farther along, also to port, Brewer South Freeport Marina usually has a few transient slips available at its modern docks, gasoline and diesel at the fuel dock and the capability to handle nearly any marine repair need. Brewer also has a modern restroom/shower/laundry building for its guests. A recent expansion and reconfiguration of the docks has resulted in a larger marina with excellent slips, docks and equipment. Both marinas have transient moorings for rent, as does Rings Marine Service Inc. (monitoring VHF Channels 09 and 16). Despite the harbor's large size, only a small area has depths suitable for mooring (virtually all filled with the resident fleet). No anchoring is permitted. On particularly busy weekends, when accommodations are tight, you may want to call the harbormaster for assistance on VHF Channel 09 or 16.

GOIN' ASHORE:

SOUTH FREEPORT, ME, FREEPORT, ME

For all but the needs of the boat and minimalist requirements of the crew, going ashore at South Freeport really means a ride to the outlet shopping and other temptations of Freeport proper, a couple of miles distant. Without venturing far, directly between the marinas, in fact, Harraseeket Lobster

Looking north over South Freeport and the Harraseeket River. (Not to be used for navigation.) WATERWAY GUIDE PHOTOGRAPHY

(207-865-3535, Main Street) has some of the tastiest fresh seafood (window service) anywhere in Maine, with rustic indoor dining or covered picnic tables on the premises. The popularity of this place guarantees a considerable wait at prime time. The Village Market (207-865-4230, S Freeport Road) is walking distance from Brewer's Marina and offers sandwiches, pastries and basic supplies. A U.S. Post Office is next door.

De rigueur in this harbor is a tour of L.L. Bean's famed sporting goods and apparel store in Freeport (open 24 hours a day, 365 days a year, telephone 207-865-4761, 1 Casco St.). For those who wish to skip the 3 mile walk, a taxi cost under $10. The Freeport shopping district has become a thriving shopper's Mecca with dozens of top-of-the-line outlets, including Banana Republic (207-865-0559, 39 Main St.), Burberry (207-865-4400, 42 Main St.), J. Crew (207-865-3180, 10 Bow St.), Jones New York (207-865-3158, 58 Main St.), Rockport (207-865-1228, 31 Main St.), Nautica (207-865-1860, 15 Bow St.), Ralph Lauren (207-865-4176, 76 Main St.) and others, plus many small specialty shops. You will find restaurants to suit virtually every taste, from Cantonese to Corsican. For well-prepared standard American fare in a Colonial setting, try Jameson Tavern (115 Main St., next door to L.L. Bean, 207-865-4196). Discriminating locals recommend the Harraseeket Inn (162 Main St., 207-865-9377) for the best dining in town.

ADDITIONAL RESOURCES:

- Experience Freeport, **www.freeportusa.com**

NEARBY GOLF COURSES:
Freeport Country Club, 2 Old County Road, Freeport, ME 04032, 207-865-0711

NEARBY MEDICAL FACILITIES:
Hospital Parkview, 329 Maine St., Brunswick, ME 04011, 207-729-1641

Potts Harbor

Located in a bight at the south end of Harpswell Neck, Potts Harbor has long been favored by cruising skippers.

NAVIGATION: Use Chart 13288. The preferred approach to Potts Harbor is from the southwest through Broad Sound, with a turn to starboard to negotiate the channel between Upper Flag Island and Horse Island. In good light, the crooked though well-marked channel leading in from Merriconeag Sound is also usable.

Anchorage: The anchorage basin is well-protected by surrounding islets and ledges, yet offers matchless long-distance views of Casco Bay's archipelago scattered to the southwest. Dolphin Marina at Basin Point rents moorings, including launch service that responds to VHF Channel 09 or to a boat horn (8 a.m. to 7 p.m. daily). Otherwise there is room to anchor in 25 to 35 feet of water in good holding outside the mooring field. There is usually ample dinghy room inside the marina's inner float (paralleling the shore), though at low tide you will want to tilt your motor to avoid damaging a

Looking north over Potts Harbor (Not to be used for navigation.) WATERWAY GUIDE PHOTOGRAPHY

prop on the shallow rocks guarding the approach to the dinghy area.

Ashore, the Dolphin Restaurant (207-833-6000, 515 Basin Point Road) at the head of the dock serves hearty, stick-to-your-arteries breakfasts and, later, a whole new experience in lobster stews. Lobstermen and locals mix amicably with visiting cruisers and Bowdoin College (Brunswick, ME) professors. You can get ice here; a few supplies and repair services are available; and there is a phone on the outside north wall of the restaurant. Excellent reprovisioning is possible in Brunswick, but the distance is greater (about 20 minutes by car) than may appear on your chart. Enterprise Rent-A-Car (800-736-8222) will deliver a rental vehicle without extra charge.

Jewell Island

This deserted island, close to the direct route across Casco Bay, is a prime example of what mariners expect to find in Maine. The island has a secure anchorage on its western side. If you plan to stay overnight, get in by early afternoon because the harbor is always popular.

NAVIGATION: Use Chart 13288. Approaching from the west, use red bell buoy "6" off Cliff Island as a target; follow the western contour of Jewell Island and avoid the ledges to the south of the charted old wharf. Give a wide berth to the marks as you round to starboard, so that you can look straight into the protected harbor between Jewell Island and Little Jewell Island.

Approaching from the east, round the nun off Drunkers Ledges, then run toward West Brown Cow (bell "BS" is on the starboard hand and Cliff Island dead ahead) until you are abeam of the northern tip of Jewell Island.

Anchorage: Favor Jewell Island's western shore slightly for anchorage, with an eye to needed swinging room with the turn of the tide. Little Jewell Island is ideal, though boats with substantial keels anchor as far down as the pilings near the head of the harbor.

GOIN' ASHORE:

JEWELL ISLAND, ME

At the southern end of the island, a multi-storied World War II observation tower (the taller of two) may be climbed via internal concrete stairs for dazzling, panoramic views of virtually the entire bay. The nearby shorter tower is connected to extensive fortifications (also laid in heavy concrete) underground magazines and cannon emplacements, which beg for investigation. A dark, dripping labyrinth of underground passageways, conned chambers and blind alleys both fascinate and perplex. There is danger in these damp tunnels, however—uncovered manholes and ordnance shafts gape darkly for the unsuspecting explorer. A flashlight is a must, and this is no place to send unaccompanied youngsters or to explore alone. Even without the moldering bunker, the paths through the re-grown woods delight the senses, and abandoned structures cast a lingering spell from another time. Peace and beauty now dwell where war was once prepared. Jewell is an island truly worthy of its name.

Potts Harbor, New Meadows, ME

POTTS HARBOR, NEW MEADOWS		Largest Vessel Accommodated	VHF Channel Monitored	Transient Berths / Total Berths	Approach / Dockside Depth (reported)	Floating Docks	Gas / Diesel	Groceries, Ice, Marine Supplies, Snacks	Repairs: Hull, Engine, Propeller	Lift (tonnage), Crane, Rail	1=110V, 2=220V, B=Both, Max Amps	Laundry, Pool, Showers	Pump-Out Station	Nearby: Grocery Store, Motel, Restaurant
		Dockage					Supplies		Services					
1. Dolphin Marina & Restaurant	207-833-5343	75	09	6/6	40/15	F	GD	I	HP		1/30		P	GMR
2. Cook's Lobster House	207-833-2818	100		/20	15/8	F	GD	IMS			B/50			GMR
3. Sebasco Harbor Resort	207-389-1161	75	09	25/25	20/6	F	G	IS				LPS	P	GMR
4. Great Island Boat Yard	207-729-1639	60	09	5/65	12/12		GD	IMS	HEP	L12,C	1/30	S	P	
5. Paul's Marina	207-729-3067	32	09		6/6		G	GIMS		C20			P	
6. New Meadows Marina	207-443-6277	40		6/80	7/6	F	G	IM	EP	C	1/20	S	P	GMR

Corresponding chart(s) not to be used for navigation. Internet Access Wireless Internet Access

Peaks Island

Dockage and Moorings: To the southwest of Jewell Island lies Peaks Island. The marina on the western side of the island offers slips, moorings, fuel and water. You can drop the hook anywhere inside the moorings. The water is deep and holding is good in mud. The city of Portland is a lovely sight from across the bay. The Casco Bay ferry (207-774-7871) runs to Portland every hour and rates vary based upon seasonal date and the marina has a water taxi that operates 24 hours a day; it will take you anywhere in the bay area. Along the main street, you will find Hannigan's Island Market (207-766-2351, 76 Island Ave.), restaurants and public telephones. Island Tours (207-766-5514, www.islandtours.home.att.net) offers a unique golf cart tour of the island and is closed on Mondays.

Great Chebeague Island

NAVIGATION: Use Chart 13288. This island, larger than either Peaks or Jewell islands, lies a bit to the north. Best approach is from the south. Keep well over toward Little John Island, leaving flashing red buoy "18" to starboard before turning toward Chebeague. You can use the big, white Chebeague Island Inn building as a range—simply head right for it.

Anchorage and Moorings: Best anchorage is found off the stone pier in about 10 feet. Keep outside the moorings, because it gets shallow as you get close to the pier. Holding is good in mud. The inn also has a pair of moorings if you get there early enough and care to use one. Ashore are a market, phones and a take-out restaurant where you can buy ice. You can dinghy to the ferry float and tie up there to go into town. The Chebeague Island Inn (207-846-5155, 6 South Road) offers three meals a day and tea on Wednesday afternoon. They will also prepare a box lunch to take with you if you are hiking around the island.

Cliff Island

NAVIGATION: Use Chart 13288. Lying in Luckse Sound between Great Chebeague and Jewell islands is irregularly shaped Cliff Island. Enter the southwestern corner of the island, which brings you into Fisherman's Cove, a small port with fuel, ice and groceries. This is a good place to fill up, since Jewell Island has no facilities. There is no place to anchor, but the gas dock owns a few moorings.

Orrs Island

Anchorage: This big, lobster-shaped island has a good anchorage in Reed Cove, about halfway up the island, and in Beals Cove, across Merriconeag Sound from Harpswell Harbor. The Orr's-Bailey Yacht Club, (207-833-7312, 26 Osbourne Row) on the southwestern end of the island, has four guest moorings, water at the float and a dumpster. The fee is $20 and should be placed in the box at the top of the ramp or given to the dock attendant. The Salt Cod Café (207-833-6210, 1894 Harpswell Islands Road) is next to the cribwork bridge and Cook's Lobster House (207-833-2818, Garrison Cove Road) is across the bridge. At the northern tip of Bailey Island, near the Orrs Island Bridge, the lobster pound and restaurant has limited moorings and float berths. The Orrs/Bailey Island Bridge, the only cribwork bridge in the world, is a national landmark.

Mackerel Cove

NAVIGATION: Use Chart 13288. Mackerel Cove itself, the major harbor on Bailey Island, is easy to enter, with a lighted buoy marking its mouth. Although the chart shows a rock near the head of the cove, and the Coast Pilot says that it uncovers about 2 feet, local reports say that there is no obstruction.

Dockage and Moorings: You will find little anchoring room, but a full-service marina has several moorings for rent along with dockside space. Next to the marina in this picturesque traditional fishing village is a seafood restaurant.

Quahog Bay

NAVIGATION: UUse Chart 13288. This scenic area is well worth a visit. The approach is straightforward. With Yarmouth Island on your right, run along the bay, passing Pole Island on your left with Center Island ahead. For dockage and marina services, continue north into Orr's Cove to Great Island Boat Yard.

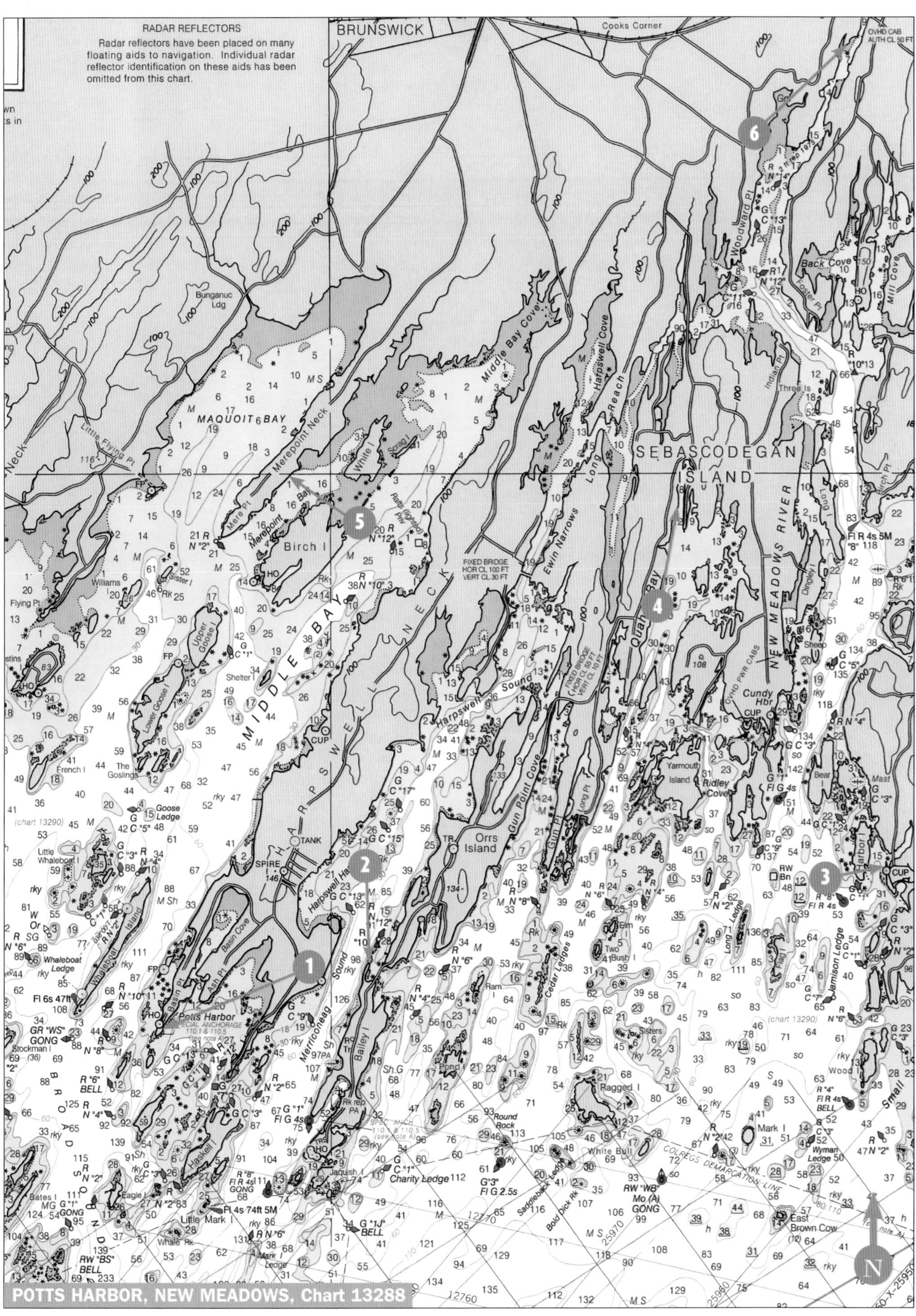
RADAR REFLECTORS
Radar reflectors have been placed on many floating aids to navigation. Individual radar reflector identification on these aids has been omitted from this chart.
BRUNSWICK
Cooks Corner
Bunganuc Ldg
MAQUOIT BAY
Little Flying Pt
Merepoint Neck
Mere Pt
Merepoint Bay
Birch I
White I
Scrag I
Middle Bay Cove
MIDDLE BAY
HARPSWELL NECK
Harpswell Cove
Long Reach
Ewin Narrows
Harpswell Sound
Orrs Island
Gun Point Cove
Long Pt
SEBASCODEGAN ISLAND
Quahog Bay
NEW MEADOWS RIVER
Woodward Pt
Back Cove
Foster Pt
Mill Cove
Indian Pt
Three Is
Long I
Birch Pt
Dingley I
Sheep I
Cundy Hbr
Yarmouth Island
Ridley Cove
Bear I
Harbor I
Flying Pt
Williams I
Sister I
Upper Goose I
Lower Goose I
Shelter I
French I
The Goslings
Goose Ledge
Little Whaleboat I
Whaleboat Island
Whaleboat Ledge
Basin Cove
Basin Pt
Ash Pt
Potts Harbor
Harpswell Hbr
Merriconeag Sound
Bailey I
Stockman I
BROAD SOUND
Haskell I
Eagle I
Bates I
Little Mark I
Whale Rk
Mark I Ledge
Jaquish I
Charity Ledge
Ram I
Cedar Ledges
Two Bush I
Elm I
Long Ledge
Rag I
Jamison Ledge
Round Rock
Ragged I
Sisters
White Bull
Saddleback Ledge
Bold Dick Rk
Mark I
East Brown Cow
Wyman Ledge
Wood I
COLREGS DEMARCATION LINE
FIXED BRIDGE HOR CL 100 FT VERT CL 30 FT
OVHD PWR CABS
RW "WB" Mo (A) GONG
RW "BS" BELL
GR "WS" GONG
POTTS HARBOR, NEW MEADOWS, Chart 13288
1
2
3
4
5
6

Dockage: Great Island is a full-service marina and boatyard with 66 slips, 40 moorings, fuel and pump-out. The fuel dock has 5 feet of water at low tide. Indoor or outside winter storage is available, along with repairs of any type. This is a safe and convenient place to leave the boat for a few weeks, or the whole winter, before continuing a Down East cruise.

Anchorage: Turn to the east after passing Pole Island, and you will be in 14-foot depths and ready to drop the hook. Holding is excellent. In this beautiful spot, you might catch sight of an acrobatic seal. The area abounds in other good anchorages. If you go into Orr's Cove, there is good holding south of the mooring field.

New Meadows River

NAVIGATION: Use Chart 13288. Easternmost of Casco Bay's long inlets, the New Meadows offers a choice of well-equipped harbors and some of the bay's best anchorages. Sebasco Harbor, near the mouth on the right bank, east of Harbor Island, has a marked entrance channel. Stay midway between the buoys to avoid rocky ledges on either side. Note that flashing red buoy "8" marks the New Meadows River and will be left to port when entering Sebasco Harbor.

Anchorage and Moorings: Moorings are available, as are good anchorages, and an elaborate lodge and resort at Sebasco Harbor welcome boat-weary travelers. The Sebasco Harbor Resort offers moorings with launch service, showers, laundry and on-site restaurants. The CUP symbol on current charts is the cupola on the top of the resort hotel. Hail on VHF Channel 09 for docking assistance or mooring assignment.

Cundy Harbor

Across the New Meadows River is the quintessential Maine fishing village of Cundys Harbor. There are no moorings available, but anchoring is possible in 20 feet of water. Go ashore to visit Watson's General Store (207-725-7794, Cundy's Harbor Road) or to buy freshly caught lobster at Hawkes Lobster (207-721-0472, 117 Cundy's Harbor Road).

The Basin

NAVIGATION: Use Chart 13288. This idyllic spot is a favored anchorage of many Down East cruisers. To get in, head northward up the New Meadows River about two miles beyond Sebasco Harbor. Watch for the house on the northern shore, and head for it once it is in view. Stay in mid-channel until you are inside the basin. As you round the southern tip of the peninsula, you may encounter water depths of 7 feet at low tide.

Anchorage: Sitting peacefully at anchor in 15 to 20 feet with good holding, you will swear you were on a lake in the White Mountains.

Cape Small

At West Point, on the northern shore of Small Point Harbor just northwest of Cape Small, are fuel docks, fish wharves, a general store and a nearby post office.

Anchorage: Some shelter can be found in Small Point Harbor, just north of Cape Small, and in the lee of Wood Island and Little Wood Island. Depths are 23 to 30 feet with a gravel bottom.

Cruising Options

Ahead lies more of the Maine coast. The many deep bays and rivers along this section beg for exploration. ■

WATERWAY GUIDE is always open to your observations from the helm. E-mail your comments on any navigation information in the guide to: editor@waterwayguide.com.

WATERWAY GUIDE advertising sponsors play a vital role in bringing you the most trusted and well-respected cruising guide in the country. Without our advertising sponsors, we simply couldn't produce the top-notch publication now resting in your hands. Next time you stop in for a peaceful night's rest, let them know where you found them—WATERWAY GUIDE, The Cruising Authority.

Seguin Island to Pemaquid Point

CHARTS 13288, 13290, 13295, 13296, 13297, 13298, 13301

THE GULF OF MAINE

The 17 miles of coastline between Cape Small and Pemaquid Point epitomize the rugged scenery that has made Maine famous. Above the tidal range, spruce and cedar trees cover the land, and nearly all the dozens of bays, rivers and guts one encounters are navigable.

Traveling east, there are five big waterways: the Kennebec River, Sheepscot Bay, Boothbay Harbor, the Damariscotta River and Johns Bay. There are two basic itineraries for cruising this section of Maine—running the outer shores and islands for a fast trip, or exploring the deep bays and rivers that wind in a more north/south direction. You can go from one to another frequently, depending on weather conditions and how fast you want to travel. The inside passages might look calm, but they can test your piloting skills with their tidal and river currents.

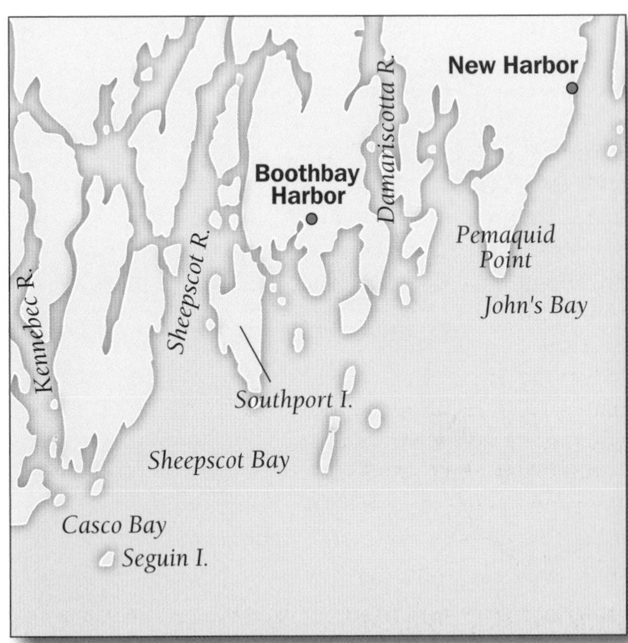

Kennebec River and Sasanoa River

NAVIGATION: Use Charts 13288, 13295 and 13293. Yachts heading east toward Maine, and westbound craft returning from Down East, are usually glad to see the turtle shape of Seguin Island in the distance. With its lighthouse perched on a high ridge, Seguin presents a conspicuous mark. Passages in this area should never be attempted in fog—the hazard is a local magnetic disturbance of up to eight degrees for a one-mile radius around Ellingwood Rock, off the northern tip of Seguin Island. In today's world of GPS, this is not as much of an issue, but be aware and pay close attention to possible differences between GPS readings and a magnetic compass.

Another danger is the strong current from the Kennebec River and the floating debris it brings downstream. In fog, stay south of Seguin Island, whose horn (atop 180-foot-tall Seguin Island Light) will help your dead reckoning. At this

Looking northwest over Seguin Island. Note the anchorage with protection from prevailing westerlies.
(Not to be used for navigation.)
WATERWAY GUIDE PHOTOGRAPHY

Bath, ME

BATH		Largest Vessel Accommodated	VHF Channel Monitored	Transient Berths / Total Berths	Approach / Dockside Depth (reported)	Floating Docks	Gas / Diesel	Groceries, Ice, Marine Supplies, Snacks	Repairs: Hull, Engine, Propeller	Lift (tonnage), Crane, Rail	1=110V, 2=220V, B=Both, Max Amps	Laundry, Pool, Showers	Pump-Out Station	Nearby: Grocery Store, Motel, Restaurant
		Dockage					Supplies		Services					
1. Maine Maritime Museum 💻	207-443-1316	225			25/20	F					B/100	LS		GMR
2. Kennebec Tavern & Marina 💻	207-442-9636													R

Corresponding chart(s) not to be used for navigation. 💻 Internet Access WiFi Wireless Internet Access

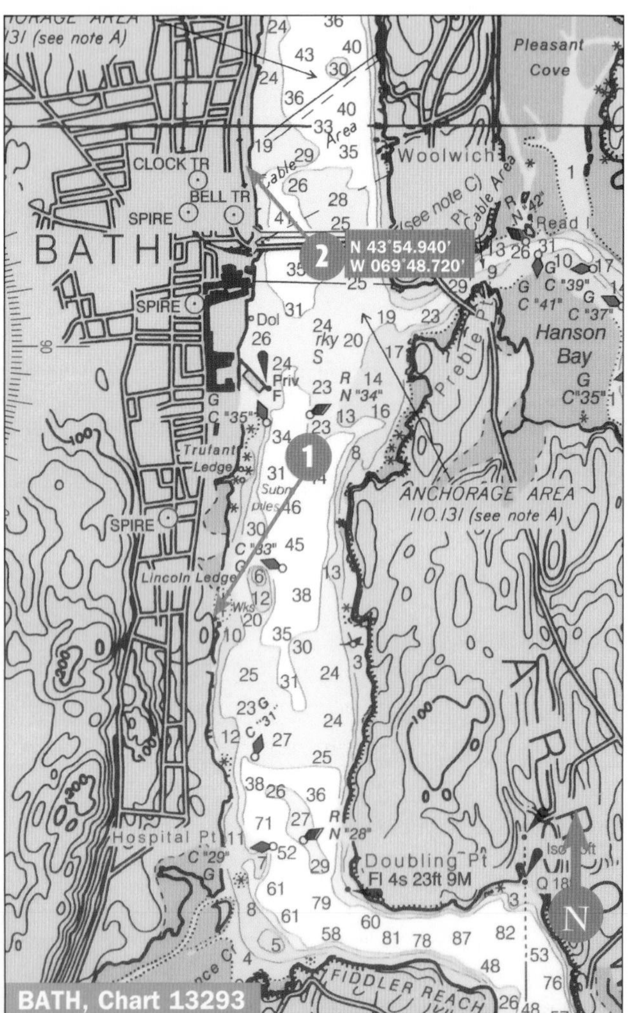

BATH, Chart 13293

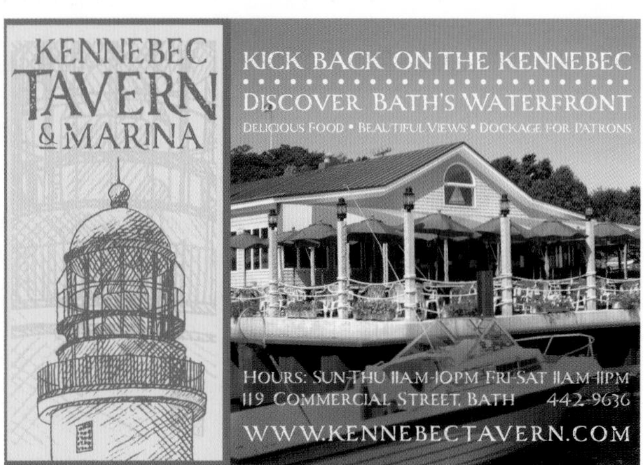

point, lay a course for The Cuckolds off Cape Newagen to the north-northeast.

A long mile north of Seguin Island, the mouth of the Kennebec River invites you to explore the lower reaches of this historically famous and splendid waterway. Use Chart 13295, as well as the appropriate tide and tidal current tables. Sailing directions warn that a strong southwesterly wind against an ebbing tide might produce confused sea conditions as one approaches the mouth of the river but, with sufficient power, careful navigation will soon bring the well-found yacht into calmer water to port off Fort Popham. Obviously, the best time to enter the river is at slack water or on a rising- tide. Anchor in the nearest cove, or if you are lucky, pick up a mooring for an hour.

Kennebec River

Deserted Fort Popham (207-389-1335), built to repel invaders at the onset of the Civil War, is worth an inspection. Its guns never fired a shot. The massive stone structure is a good example of an expensive 19th-century boondoggle. Popham Beach provides an excellent recreational sea-bathing area for an energetic crew. Filming for the Kevin Costner movie "Message In A Bottle" occurred here. A small grocery and a quick-lunch store are nearby.

From Popham, yachts often follow a fair tide past the hills on the Phippsburg side to port and the salt marshes to starboard. If you have a line with lure or bait on board, you might find it worthwhile to try for a bluefish. These lonely marshes and grassy meadows supplied salt hay used by early settlers. The meadows also produce mosquitoes. The expanse of waving meadow grass gives the impression that little has changed ecologically for several centuries.

As the Kennebec River twists north, groups of houses such as Center Phippsburg introduce signs of civilization. North of Lee Island, the river narrows, but beyond the dogleg at Winnegance Creek, the channel widens again as one approaches Bath. Depending on wind and tide, you might see boats anchored in the creek.

Bath

The upper Kennebec River is more placid than its mouth and provides ample opportunity for explorations. It is navigable for 40 miles to Maine's capital, Augusta. Bath, one of the country's leading shipbuilding centers, is 10 miles up the river. The famous Bath Iron Works builds top-of-the-line naval vessels, as well as commercial ships, and it turned out the America's Cup defender *Ranger* in 1938, considered the fastest sloop ever built. Wooden ship-building lives on, as well, at the Maine Maritime Museum, (243 Washington St.) open year-round, seven days a week, from 9:30 a.m. to 5 p.m., except for Thanksgiving, Christmas and New Year's Day. Visitors can see boats being built and restored in the boat shop. Overnight moorings are usually available, as is alongside dockage for larger yachts and other vessels. For more information, call the museum at 207-443-1316.

NAVIGATION: Use Chart 13293. Note that the lift bridge crossing the Kennebec River between Bath and Woolwich (10-foot closed vertical clearance) is closed between 6:30 a.m. and 7:30 a.m. and between 3:45 p.m. and 4:45 p.m. North beyond the Carlton Bridge, downtown Bath features fine-looking 18th-century houses, a few restaurants and a renovated theater. Moorings are available, but anchoring presents no problem. In addition to the museum, Bath is a quaint "big town, small city" kind of place and very interesting to visit.

Fine dining is available and some recommendations include Beale Street Barbeque (215 Water St., 207-442-9514) for Memphis-style barbecue and other delights. Brackett's Market (185 Front St., 207-443-2012) is a locally owned full-service grocery with added services like ATM, copying, a floral shop and a bakery. The Patten Free Library (33 Summer St., 207-443-5141) offers complimentary wireless Internet access to visitors. A cab ride away is the Bath shopping center.

Kennebec Tavern & Marina is a good stop, with dockage for patrons, on the north side of the bridge.

Waterfront Park (Commercial St.) is the focus point for visiting boaters. The Bath Farmer's Market takes place here on Saturdays 8:30 to 12 p.m. from May through October. The Bath Heritage Days are a town-wide four-day celebration over the 4th of July. A public launching ramp is at the northern end of the town; near Waterfront Park.

You can visit old towns on the upper reaches of the river, such as Brunswick, Gardiner and the state capital, Augusta, but one of the real advantages of going up the river to Bath is the opportunity to sail down the Sasanoa River to Boothbay Harbor. The Sasanoa River is a historic waterway. Years ago, Champlain explored it, pulling his boats up the river from Boothbay to Bath. To run this winding passage is a delight, but keep in mind several important cautions:

- Before you pass under the bridge at Woolwich, be sure you have Chart 13293.
- Keep close watch on the series of channel buoys. After passing Mill Point into Hockomock Bay, honor all marks as you make a gradual sweep to port. There is little room for error here. As you round the north end of Castle Island, leave green can buoy "7" to starboard, and then turn downriver toward Lower Hell Gate. If you are transiting on a rising tide, expect strong head currents in this short section.
- While the state of the tide is not easily predictable,plan to start when the tide at Boothbay is at low water.
- Both Hell Gates, especially Lower Hell Gate, will probably require full power—hence the sailor's auxiliary engine should be trustworthy.
- The tidal current at Goose Rocks Passage looks worse than it really is.
- There is a good marina at Robinhood.
- After you pass MacMahan Island, buoys lead to Townsend Gut and on to Boothbay.

Sheepscot Bay and River

Big, easy-to-enter Sheepscot Bay leads into the Sheepscot River, with deep channels, tree-lined shores, craggy rocks and small, Down East towns. In the early 17th century, Champlain sailed the Sheepscot River thinking he was on the St. Lawrence River.

NAVIGATION: Use Chart 13293. Cape Harbor, at the eastern entrance to the bay between Cape Island and Cape Newagen, is attractive, convenient to open water and easily entered from the west via a marked channel. You can approach from the east but the passage is shallow and calls for local knowledge.

Five Islands

NAVIGATION: Use Chart 13293. A few miles up Sheepscot Bay to port heading upriver, Five Islands Harbor has secure protection, fuel, a great seafood outlet and a rustic view. More accessible than it appears on the chart, the harbor may be entered with plenty of depth from the east or north.

Moorings: Several moorings (Styrofoam floats, well-marked) are available courtesy of the Five Islands Yacht Club (no clubhouse, just good-spirited members). Otherwise, 20 moorings are rented by Sheepscot Bay Boat Co. Anchoring is not advisable here. Sheepscot Bay Boat Co. permits short-term dinghy tie-ups for loading and unloading at its substantial dinghy landing and, although this is primarily a small-boat facility, there is turning room and ample depth (10 feet at mean low water) for craft in the 30- to 40-foot range to take on gas or diesel at its fuel dock. Patrons can off-load trash at the boat company's barrel, but the drinking water is unsatisfactory here (brackish throughout this end of the island).

High on the town wharf next door, Georgetown Fisherman's Co-op (207-371-2950) is plainly visible and attracts a crowd—both for its superb fresh seafood and for the passing show of work and recreational boats plying the waters below. Live lobsters are packed to go, or you can order them cooked to taste—also fresh-steamed crabs, clams, mussels and corn. Local mariners stream in here from miles around. You can tie up for 30 minutes at the fair-sized dinghy dock next to the town wharf, and there

Sheepscot Bay, Knubble Bay, ME

SHEEPSCOT BAY, KNUBBLE BAY		Largest Vessel Accommodated	VHF Channel Monitored	Transient Berths / Total Berths	Approach / Dockside Depth (reported)	Floating Docks	Gas / Diesel	Groceries, Ice, Marine Supplies, Snacks	Repairs: Hull, Engine, Propeller	Lift (tonnage), Crane, Rail	1=110V, 2=220V, B=Both, Max Amps	Laundry, Pool, Showers	Pump-Out Station	Nearby: Grocery Store, Motel, Restaurant
		Dockage					**Supplies**		**Services**					
1. Sheepscot Bay Boat Co.	207-371-2442	30	09		10/9	F	GD	M	HEP	C				R
2. Boothbay Region Boatyard	**207-633-2970**	**80**	**09**	**5/40**	**15/8**	**F**	**GD**	**IMS**	**HEP**	**L50**	**B/50**	**LS**	**P**	**GMR**
3. Robinhood Marine Center ☐	**207-371-2525**	**65**	**09**	**15/15**	**70/10**	**F**	**GD**	**IMS**	**HEP**	**L55,C18**	**B/50**	**LS**	**P**	**R**
4. The Eddy Marina	207-882-7776	45	16	Moorings	/21	F	GD	IMS				S		MR
5. Wiscasset Town Dock	207-882-8200	250			20/10	F								GMR
6. Wiscasset Yacht Club	207-882-9275	30			20/6						1/20	S		

Corresponding chart(s) not to be used for navigation. ☐ Internet Access (WiFi) Wireless Internet Access

SHEEPSCOT BAY, KNUBBLE BAY, Chart 13293

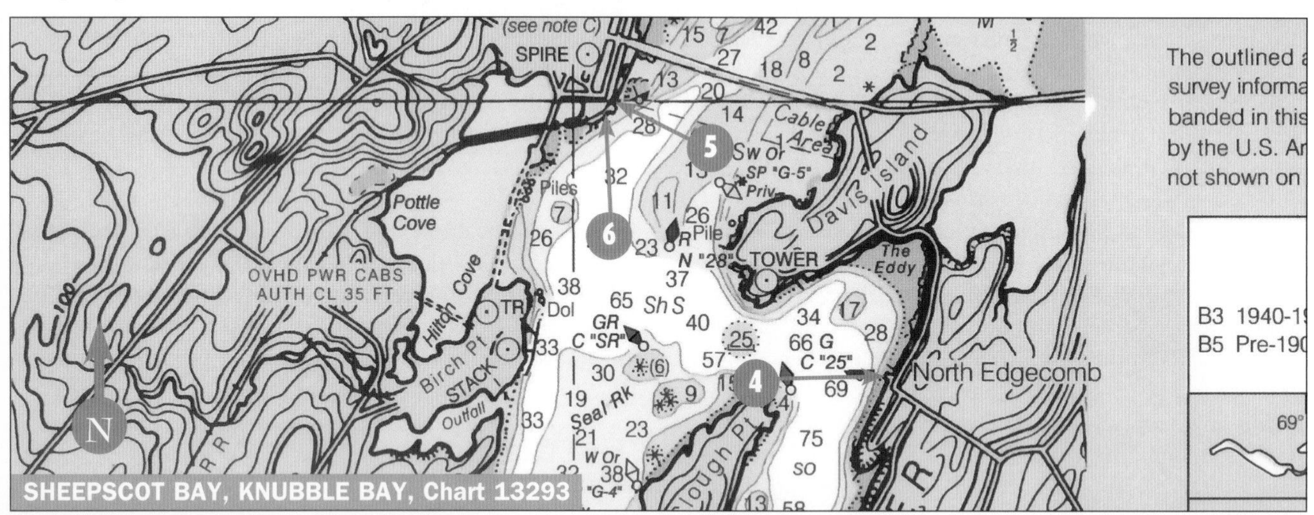

SHEEPSCOT BAY, KNUBBLE BAY, Chart 13293

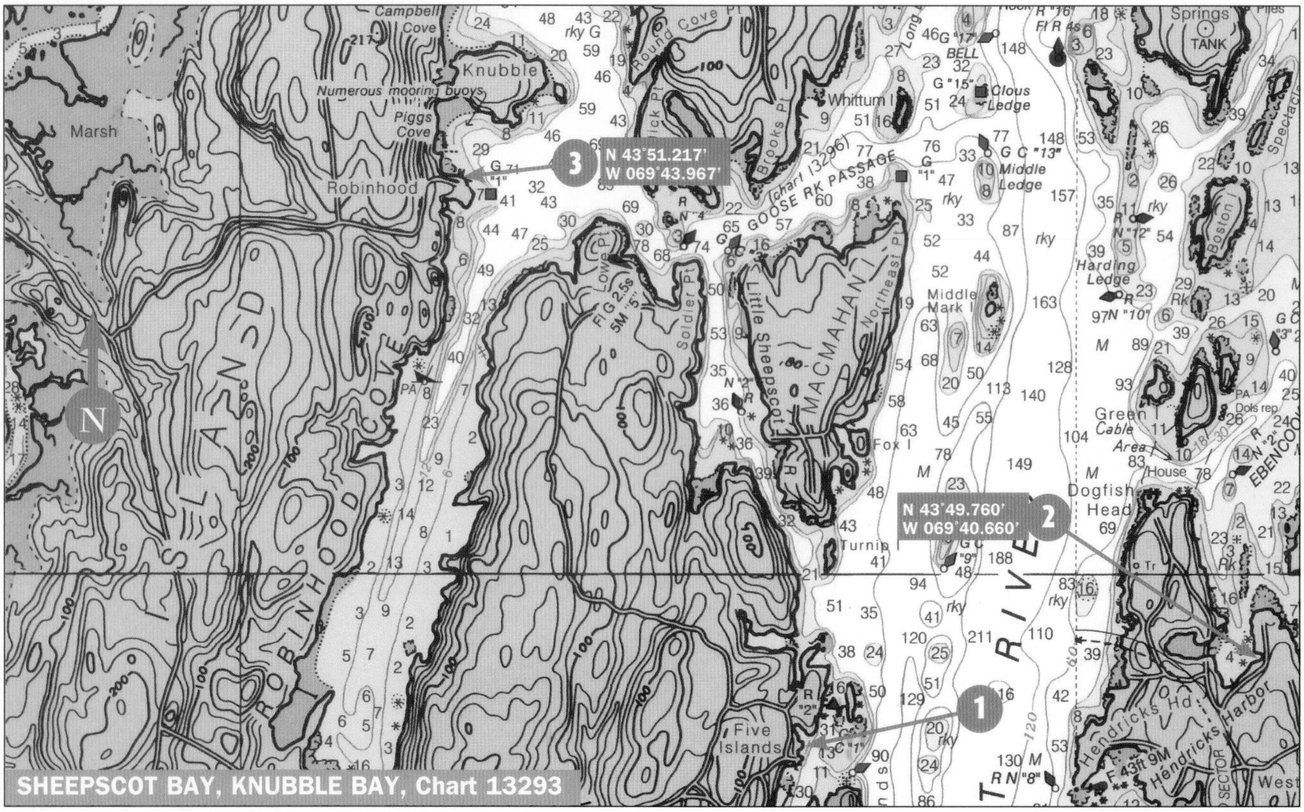

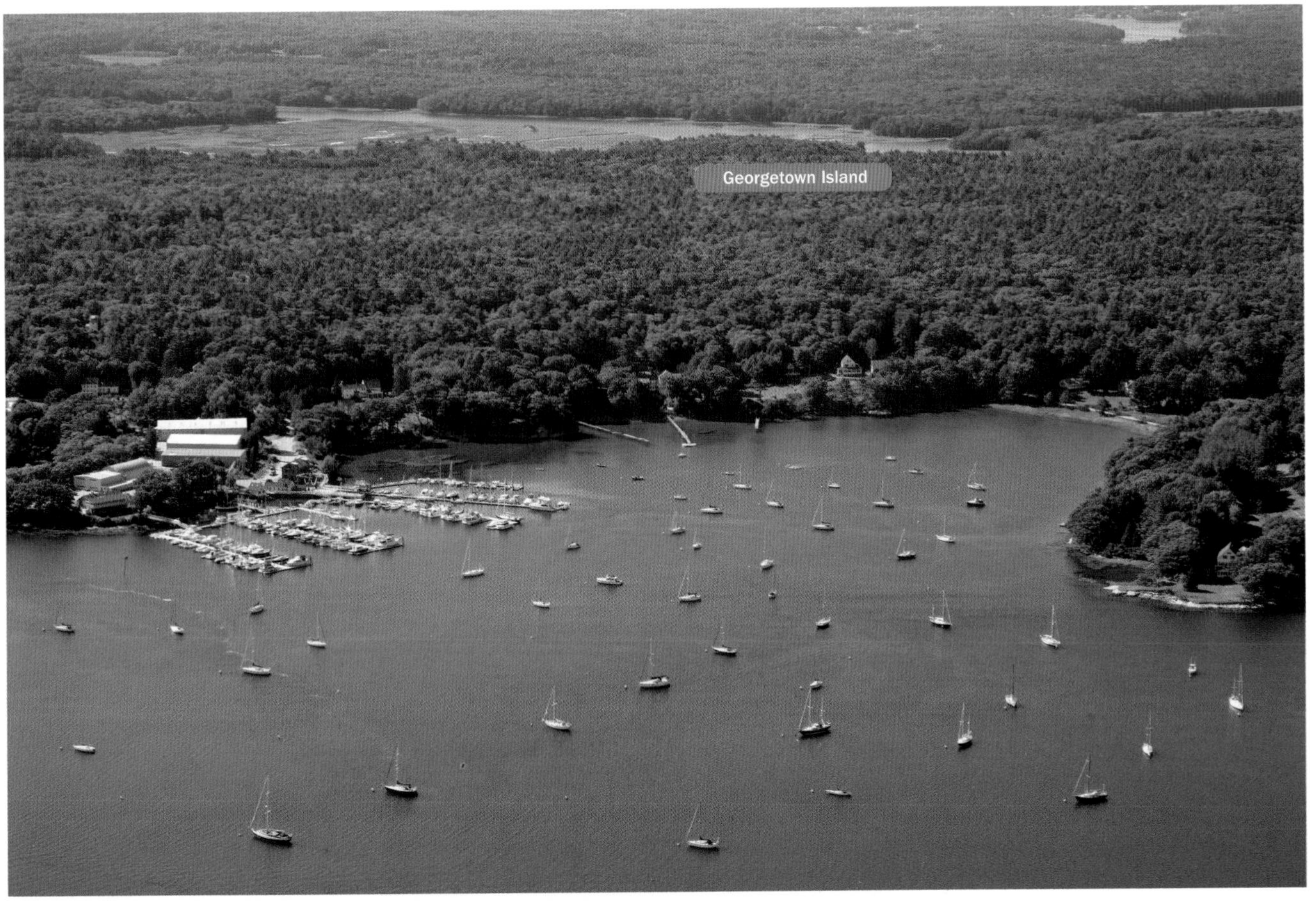

Georgetown Island

Looking northwest over Robinhood Cove. (Not to be used for navigation.) WATERWAY GUIDE PHOTOGRAPHY

are picnic tables on the docks above. Unfortunately, no other supplies are to be found here.

Robinhood Cove

NAVIGATION: Use Chart 13293. Accessible either through the Little Sheepscot River (easiest from Five Islands) or from the east through Goose Rock Passage, the cove is both a perfectly sheltered retreat from the elements and part of an intricate connective system with the Kennebec River. Using either passage for entry, easiest and safest transit is made during slack water to avoid the considerable effects of ripping tidal currents.

Dockage: As you reach the western mouth of Goose Rock Passage, Robinhood Marine Center will be visible immediately ahead. There you can find both slips and moorings for transients, showers, laundry, all fuels and major lift and repair services. The Osprey Restaurant (207-371-2530, 258 Robinhood Road), within walking distance, is said to be excellent.

Ebencook Harbor

NAVIGATION: Use Chart 13293. The river's first large harbor, on the northwestern shoulder of Southport Island, Ebencook Harbor is big, protected and easy to enter in any weather.

Dockage: Boothbay Region Boatyard is found at the southwest corner of Ebencook Harbor and offers transient accommodations, all fuels, restrooms, showers and a laundry.

Anchorage: Ebencook Harbor offers good anchorage in a choice of sheltered coves. East of Dogfish Head is a good area to drop the hook, but watch your depth, be aware of the tide state and check the chart for cable crossing areas before setting the anchor.

Wiscasset

NAVIGATION: Use Chart 13293. Use Portland tide tables. For high tide, add 16 minutes; for low tide, add 4 minutes. For nine more island-studded miles to the U.S. Route 1 Bridge at Wiscasset (four miles south of the limit to navigation at Sheepscot), the river is deep, well-marked and attractive. Look for the measured mile with shore ranges on the eastern bank at Barters Island to the east.

Dockage and Moorings: Several courtesy moorings are available on a first-come, first-served basis in front of Wiscasset Town Landing. The Town Landing's floats offer the only dockage—with a three-hour maximum. Water is available for refills and there are restrooms on the wharf, open daybreak until 10 p.m. A coin-operated pump-out service is located here as well.

Wiscasset Yacht Club, (207-882-4058, 2 Water St.) just south of the Town Landing, may have overnight dockage at its floats to accommodate members of reciprocating clubs. There is plenty of depth at the club's floats and hot water for showering inside. Though slips and moorings are few in number, there is ample anchorage with secure holding east of the town's mooring field in 12 to 20 feet of water. Tidal currents run swiftly on both ebb and flow, which should encourage setting a secure hook, tested in both directions.

GOIN' ASHORE: WISCASSET, ME

Once a major port of entry for goods from England (until the War of 1812), and revived briefly as a commercial harbor during the 19th century, Wiscasset is once again a thriving village, today more given to tourism than trade. Buildings and gardens from the town's heyday are now major attractions for history buffs. Locals refer to Wiscasset as "the prettiest village in Maine." Kingsbury House (1763, oldest in the town) at Federal and Washington Sts., Lilac Cottage (1789 or earlier) at Washington and Main Sts., Castle Tucker (1807) at High and Lee streets is an authentic Victorian house containing no reproductions, the Nickels-Sortwell House (1807) at Main and Federal streets, the Wiscasset Academy (1807) at Hodge and Warren Sts.(now home to the Maine Art Gallery), the 1869 Customs House (1869 to 1870) at Water, Fore and Middle streets and a variety of classic gardens are open to the public. Many of the town's private homes are also old and well restored. Restaurants in Wiscasset are simple but accommodating. You will find the world's best lobster rolls at Red's Eats (207-882-6128, 41 Water St. at Main St.) and well worth any wait in line to order. (Red's Eats is featured in a PBS documentary on sandwiches). Continental cuisine can be found at LeGarage (207-882-5409, 15 Water St.), which was originally

Joseph R. Melanson of www.Skypic.com

Looking east over Boothbay Harbor. (Not to be used for navigation.)

used as a garage in the early 20th Century. The Wiscasset Library, (207-882-7161, 21 High St.), offers public Internet access and is open Tuesday through Friday, 10 a.m. to 5 p.m. on Wednesdays open to 7 p.m.

ADDITIONAL RESOURCES:

NEARBY GOLF COURSES:
Boothbay Country Club, 33 Country Club Road, Boothbay, ME 04537, 207-633-6085

NEARBY MEDICAL FACILITIES:
Miles Memorial Hospital, 35 Miles St., Damariscotta, ME 04543, 207-563-1234

Boothbay Harbor

A summer resort with natural beauty, an easy entrance and many shore attractions, Boothbay Harbor has ample yacht amenities available on all but the busiest of holiday weekends.

NAVIGATION: Use Chart 13293. Use Portland tide tables. For high tide, subtract 6 minutes; for low tide, subtract 8 minutes. Boothbay Harbor is deep and access is easy from any direction, in any weather. The Cuckolds' 59-foot-tall lighthouse and radio beacon (continuous on 320 kHz) simplify entrance in thick weather or at night. This harbor can be crowded, so reservations for a slip are essential, especially on weekends. An unusual footbridge, built in 1900, spans the inner harbor, saving visitors and residents from the long walk around. It is occasionally washed out by ice, but is always rebuilt.

Dockage: The easiest access to shoreside amenities in this resort town is found in the northeastern cove, or inner harbor, of Boothbay Harbor. Excellent full-service marinas crowd along the eastern and western edges of the inner harbor. Most offer both moorings and transient slips, but it is best to call ahead (VHF Channel 09 or by phone) for a reservation.

First to starboard on entering the inner harbor, Carousel Marina's modern facilities include numerous transient berths at floating docks, rental moorings, all fuels at an easy-access dock [including on-premises compressed natural gas (CNG), excellent restroom and shower facilities, coin-operated laundry, snack bar, ship's store, wireless Internet access, courtesy car and the Whale's Tale Restaurant (207-633-6644, 125 Atlantic Ave.). If you are anchored out or on a mooring, for a small fee you can come into a slip for a wash down.

Brown's Wharf, just beyond, is a family-run marina, motel and restaurant, in business for more than 50 years. Flowers run riot at Brown's (even the pilings sprout them), and there are more than 40 floating-dock slips with water, electricity and cable TV in clear view of the boating action, but beyond the traffic noise from town. Brown's also has 15 moorings and coin-operated showers. Brown's Wharf Restaurant (207-633-5440, 121 Atlantic Ave.) serves breakfast and dinner. Two shopping trolleys leave from this location on a regular basis.

Boothbay Harbor, ME

Boothbay Harbor. (Not to be used for navigation.) WATERWAY GUIDE PHOTOGRAPHY

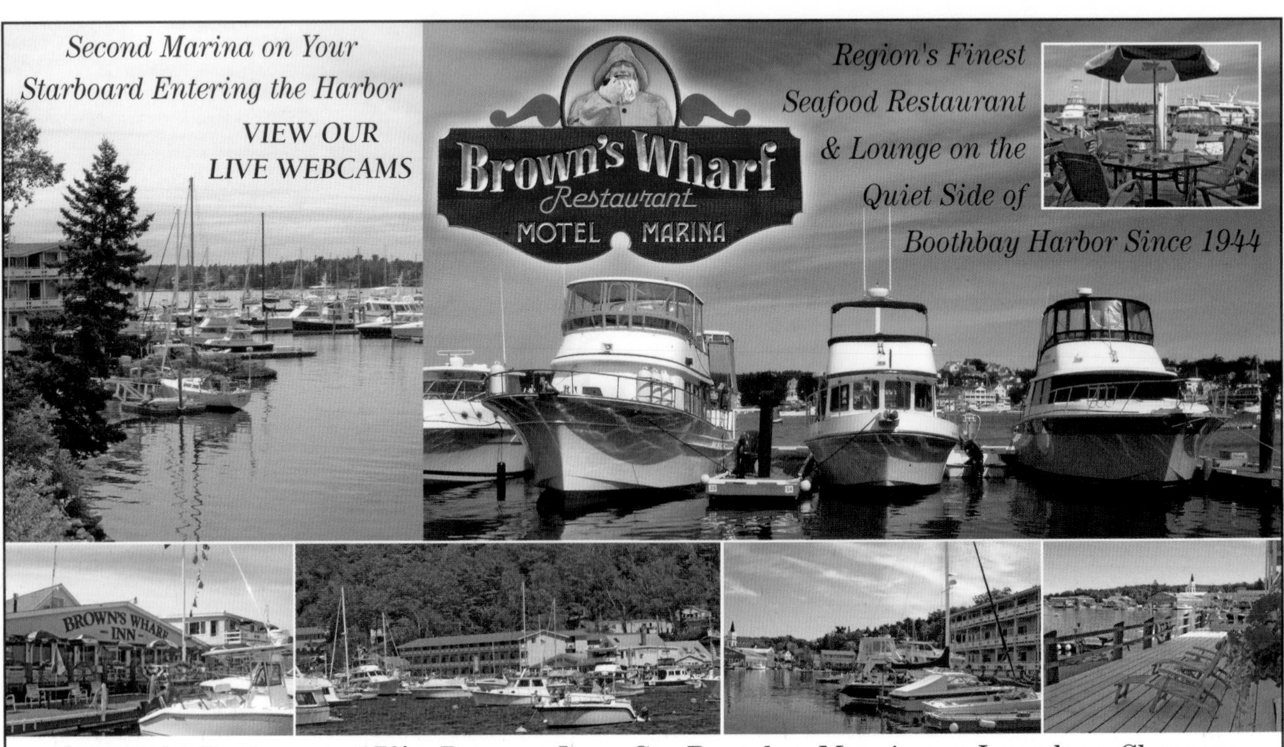

Boothbay Harbor, ME

BOOTHBAY HARBOR		Largest Vessel Accommodated	VHF Channel Monitored	Transient Berths / Total Berths	Approach / Dockside Depth (reported)	Floating Docks	Gas / Diesel	Groceries, Ice, Marine Supplies, Snacks	Repairs: Hull, Engine, Propeller	Lift (tonnage), Crane, Rail	1=110V, 2=220V, B=Both, Max Amps	Laundry, Pool, Showers	Pump-Out Station	Nearby: Grocery Store, Motel, Restaurant
		Dockage					Supplies		Services					
1. Carousel Marina (Internet Access) (Wireless Internet Access)	**207-633-2922**	**180**	**09**	**15/50**	**30/30**	**F**	**GD**	**GIM**	**EP**		**B/100**	**LS**	**P**	**GMR**
2. Brown's Wharf Marina (Internet Access) (Wireless Internet Access)	**207-633-5440**	**175**	**09**	**15/40**	**25/25**	**F**		**IS**			**B/50**	**LS**	**P**	**GMR**
3. Cap'n Fish's Motel & Marina (Wireless Internet Access)	207-633-6605	100	16	3/	15/10	F		IS			1			MR
4. Rocktide Inn	207-633-4455	45		5/5	8/5									GMR
5. Boothbay Harbor Marina (Internet Access) (Wireless Internet Access)	**207-633-6003**	**150**	**09/68**	**30/40**	**20/12**	**F**		**GI**			**B/50**	**LS**	**P**	**GMR**
6. Fisherman's Wharf Inn	207-633-5090	60			15/15			GIM						R
7. Tugboat Inn & Marina (Internet Access)	**207-633-4434**	**100**	**16/09**	**12/30**	**15/10**	**F**		**IS**			**B/50**	**LS**	**P**	**GMR**
8. Boothbay Harbor Shipyard	207-633-3171	100	09	Moorings	25/9			M		R				MR
9. Wotton's Wharf (Internet Access) (Wireless Internet Access)	207-633-7440	350	09		16/16	F	GD	IMS	HEP	LC	B/100	LS	P	GMR
10. Signal Point Marina	207-633-6920	40			25/15		GD	GI			B/50	LS		R
11. Boothbay Harbor Yacht Club (Internet Access)	207-633-5750	65	09	15/75	20/15	F		I				LS		MR

Corresponding chart(s) not to be used for navigation. (Internet Access icon) Internet Access (WiFi icon) Wireless Internet Access

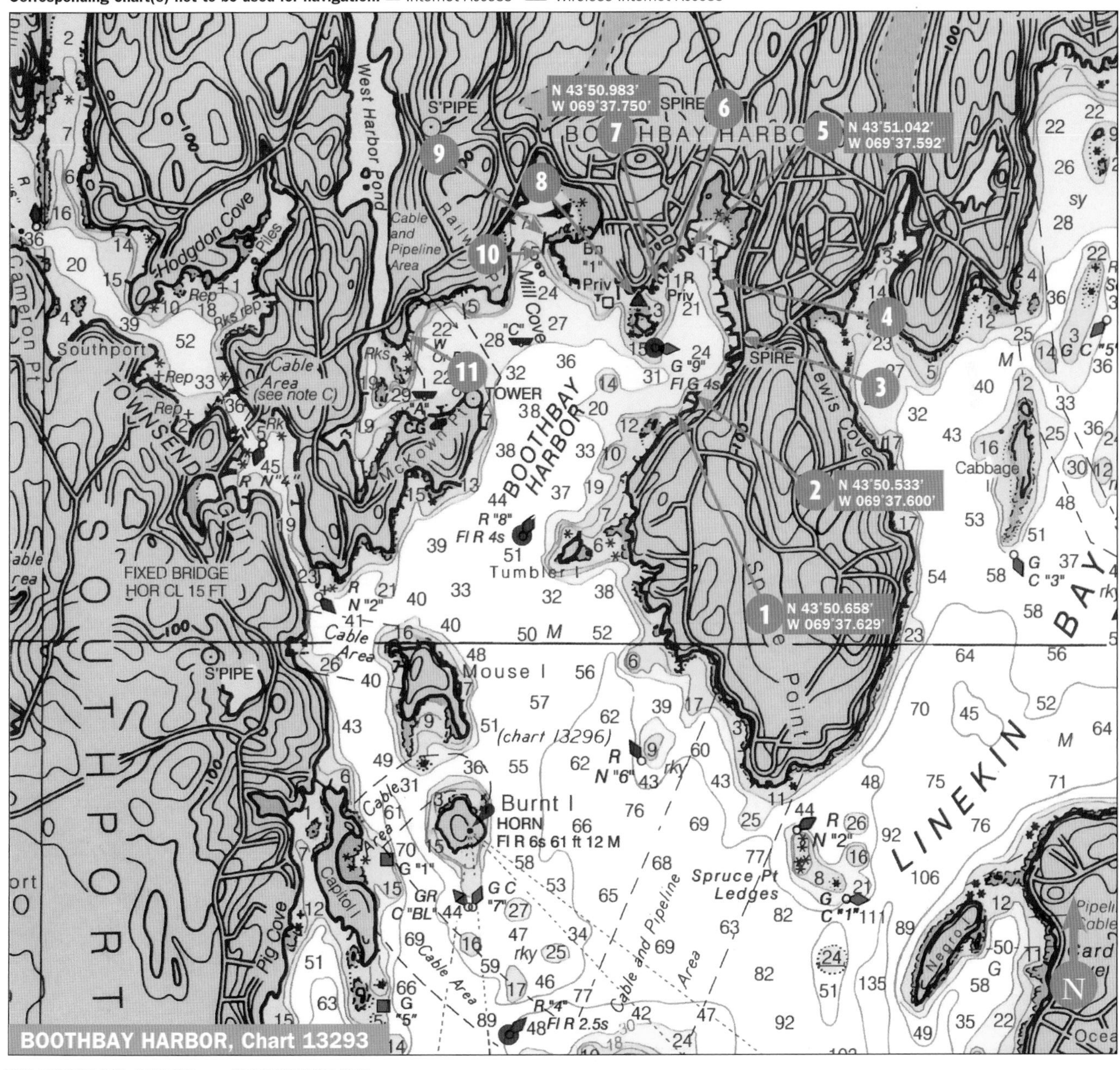

To port, on the village side, Boothbay Harbor Marina offers 500 feet of transient dockage, handling vessels of up to 100 feet, at the doorstep of the village center. The marina has gated and locked floating docks, showers, laundry, public telephone, ice and a full-service restaurant. Also near the town dock, the Tugboat Inn and Marina has substantial updated floating docks for transients with dockside cable TV, 15 rental moorings and modern, coin-operated showers and laundry (open 24 hours). Both marinas on the west side of the harbor offer immediate walking access to shops and restaurants.

Wotton's Wharf, affiliated with the Boothbay Region Boatyard, offers floating docks, wireless Internet access, fuel, shore amenities and repair service.

Anchorage and Moorings: On the western side of the main harbor area, Boothbay Harbor Yacht Club maintains a large number of moorings, some of which may be available for visiting yachtsmen. The club is identifiable by the BHYC sign on its roof and by its visible amenities, including tennis courts. The BHYC launch monitors VHF Channel 09 or responds to three blasts on the horn. Anchorage is possible in this general area, with 17- to 26-foot depths protected by McKown Point. If continuing east from Boothbay, note that the best course in good weather is to leave Squirrel Island to starboard, then cruise through the Fisherman's passage to the red-and-white Morse (A) bell buoy "HL" off the mouth of the Damariscotta River.

GOIN' ASHORE:

BOOTHBAY HARBOR, ME

This easily approached and scenic bay has a maritime history dating from the 15th century. Some say that authenticated Viking relics push the first dates of European exploration and fishing expeditions back centuries earlier. While maritime traditions are honored here, it is the more modern attractions and cool seaside summer weather that draw thousands of vacationers, both by land and by sea, each season. Though the center of activity is in Boothbay Harbor, all the significant islands protecting this classic bay are populated during the summer months.

On the western side of the footbridge, Boothbay Harbor's resort village has numerous shops, offering fudge and cotton candy, souvenirs, curios and antiques. You might also want to visit the nine-pin miniature bowling alley, multiple galleries displaying works by local artists, a yarn shop or Sherman's Books and Stationery (207-633-7262, 5 Commercial St.). A bank (with weather-protected 24-hour ATM) is located at center harbor on McKown Street. North of the town dock (Fisherman's Wharf), you will find well-stocked Grover's Hardware (207-633-2694, 59 Townsend Ave.). Village Market (207-633-0944, 24 Commercial Ave.), also just a few paces from the town dock, sells groceries, deli items, fresh meats and beer and wine. More complete reprovisioning will require a visit to the shopping center about a half mile north of town, home to a large Hannaford Supermarket (207-633-6465, 180

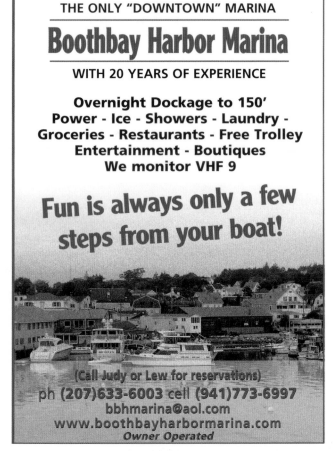

Townsend Ave.), bank and coin-operated laundry. The town's convenient shopping trolley leaves for this shopping center from the PICK-UP SOON sign at McKown and Oak streets.

Restaurants on the western side of the harbor include the Chowder House Boat Bar & Outdoor Grille (207-633-5761, 22 Granary Way) at the water's edge, strong on seafood, salads, sandwiches and light fare, with a splendid harbor view. Try some lobster pie at Kaler's Crab & Lobster House (207-633-5839, 48 Commercial St.) where you can visit their touch tank or sign up to go out with Dan the Lobsterman to pull and bait traps with him. The Blue Moon Café (207-633-2220), at 54 Commercial, is popular. In the footbridge area, choose between Pier One Pizza & Pub (207-633-5586, 15 Warf St.), Bridge Street Café (207-633-7447, 4 Bridge St.) or Andrew's Harborside Restaurant (207-633-4074, 12 Bridge St.). East of the footbridge, a dinghy trip for dinner at the Lobstermen's Co-op (207-633-4900, 15 Atlantic Ave.) is not to be missed. Picnic tables and open-air conviviality set the mood; the food is strictly fresh, relatively inexpensive and prepared to order. Next door, Brown's Wharf Restaurant (207-633-5440, 121 Atlantic Ave.) has a seafood restaurant, complete with outsized models of classic ships and workboats and the Old Salt Shed Lounge, still seeping brine from timbers dating from Boothbay's earliest settlement. The Whale's Tale Restaurant (207-633-6644, 125 Atlantic Ave.) at Carousel Marina dishes out hearty portions of piquant pastas, succulent seafood, novel chicken dishes, Black Angus steak and prime rib. A special treat is a visit to the Carousel Theatre and Supper Club (207-633-5297) 196 Townsend Avenue, where a good dinner is combined with a cabaret show; your waiter will be one of the performers.

Daily during the summer, sloops and a host of other classic hulls and rigs add interest to a harbor already bursting with boating color. Cap'n Fish (www.mainewhales.com; 207-633-3244,) offers up Whale Watching, Puffin Nature Cruises, Lobster Trap Hauling and Seal Watch scenic boat tours to name just a few choices. Boothbay has events and activities seemingly nonstop throughout the season. Some other special weekends include the Fisherman's Festival in early May, kicking off the visitor's season, Windjammer Days in late June, a nearly fifty-year-old festival that culminates with the unforgettable sight of the majestic Windjammer Ships sailing parade into the harbor and the Boothbay Boat Builder's Festival in early August.

ADDITIONAL RESOURCES:

- Boothbay Harbor Region Chamber of Commerce, **www.boothbayharbor.com**

NEARBY GOLF COURSES:
Boothbay Country Club, 33 Country Club Road, Boothbay, ME 04537, 207-633-6085

NEARBY MEDICAL FACILITIES:
St Andrews Hospital, 6 Saint Andrews Lane, Boothbay Harbor, ME 04538, 207-633-2121

Damariscove Island

NAVIGATION: Use Chart 13293. The approach to Damariscove Harbor is more straightforward than it might appear, especially when you look at waves broken by the reef known as The Motions. The reef is located to port of an entrance barely revealed by the sharp cliffs cascading into the narrow slot of a harbor. Several warnings are in order. First, stay well inside Bantam Rock, really a cluster of rocks extending toward the island from red bell buoy "2BR," located about a mile to the southwest of the harbor entrance. Second, keeping the red-and-white gong buoy "TM" (The Motions) to port, set a course for the center of the harbor opening and maintain enough power to overcome any following seas. Finally, once abeam of the western tip of the harbor entrance, correct course to favor that side (port) slightly, as a submerged boulder is to starboard.

Anchorage: You can anchor in soft mud, beginning just past the abandoned Coast Guard Station (now privately owned) to port. To allow adequate scope while preventing grounding during the tide swing at low water, both fore and aft anchors are well advised. It is also possible for a boat or two to set a careful hook in the inner harbor beyond the channel's choke point and abeam of the Nature Conservancy's hut, also to port. Since swing room is quite limited, and there is almost always a lobster car and boat nearby, nighttime fenders are in order. During settled weather, it is possible to anchor at the north end of the island at Bar Cove Beach, then row in for a landing on the pebbled beach below the island's freshwater pond. The cove is sheltered from the surge produced by prevailing southwesterlies, but is open to the northeast. Wherever you anchor, the Nature Conservancy asks that you check in with them before hiking ashore indiscriminately.

GOIN' ASHORE:
DAMARISCOVE ISLAND, ME

If year-round fishing villages count, Damariscove Island was unquestionably the earliest permanent European colony in the New World—permanent, that is, until the last resident family moved to the mainland in 1939. The *Mayflower* stopped at the island to barter for provisions en route to Massachusetts Bay in 1620, returning early the following year to beg additional supplies from the hearty Damariscove fishermen for the beleaguered Plymouth Colony settlers. Now all that remains are abandoned farmsteads, the boarded-up former Coast Guard station and a rustic Nature Conservancy hut.

Since 1966, the island has been owned and supervised during the summer by the Nature Conservancy. Title has recently been passed to the Boothbay Region Land Trust (207-633-4818). This windswept tribute to nature's capacity for austere beauty whispers of the Hebrides and of lost Viking outposts. Reportedly, the largest eider-duck colonies in the United States nest here, along with their nemesis, the great black-backed gull. Common yellowthroats, yellow warblers, catbirds and Savannah sparrows also nest here in abundance. The mile-and-a-half walk along the Pond Loop Trail traverses rocky shore, coastal tundra, salt marsh, freshwater pond and upland meadow. Passage here during mid-summer's wildflower profusion is certain to carve a lasting memory. To add interest to your walk, be sure to pick up the Nature Conservancy's free "Damariscove Island Natural History Trail Guide" at the Conservancy's rustic museum and nature center just north of the landing. The delicate natural beauty of the island argues for strict observance of the Conservancy's rules: no fires or camping, and the northern end of the island is off limits for the protection of nesting eider ducks until mid-August.

ADDITIONAL RESOURCES:

- Boothbay Region Land Trust, (207-633-4818) **www.bbrlt.org**

Linekin Bay

NAVIGATION: Use Chart 13293. In contrast to Boothbay Harbor, Linekin Bay, just east of Spruce Point, is quiet, noncommercial and nearly deserted. Entrance to Linekin Bay is an easy matter through the wide, deep passage between bold and wooded Negro Island (off the west side of Ocean Point) and green can buoy "1."

Moorings: The highlight of Linekin Bay, in addition to excellent protection in an easterly or southeasterly blow, is the renowned P.E. Luke Yard. Marine engineering buffs will relish a free tour of Luke's private museum of the company's colorful history in the world of traditional boatbuilding and ocean yacht racing. Though now out of the boatbuilding business, Luke's still has an extensive repair trade and manufactures heavy three-piece storm anchors, ingenious automatic feathering props and soapstone marine fireplaces. Luke's has heavy-duty moorings available out front (east of red nun buoy "4").

Anchorage: An often-overlooked anchorage is Lewis Cove, on the western side of Linekin Bay. The Linekin Bay Resort dominates the northern edge of the cove and the remainder of the shore is dotted by homes. There is excellent holding and good protection in 23 feet of water. More daring cruisers can pass the exposed rocks in the northern end of the cove to port and find anchorage in 14-foot depths. Remember the tidal range when adjusting the scope on your anchor.

Inside Passage to Bath

NAVIGATION: Use Chart 13293. One of Maine's most exciting and beautiful cruises, the 11-mile "back door passage" from Boothbay Harbor to Bath is narrow and winding, with currents that can tow buoys under. Those who do not draw more than 7 feet and can clear a 51-foot vertical clearance fixed bridge will find the trip well worth the effort. The route winds past remote coves, deeply-notched shores and green islands. Make the passage on a rising tide, and remember that tight spots call for careful navigation.

Townsend Gut

NAVIGATION: Use Chart 13293. From Boothbay Harbor, pass north of Mouse Island into twisting, confined Townsend Gut, leaving red nun buoy "2" at the entrance

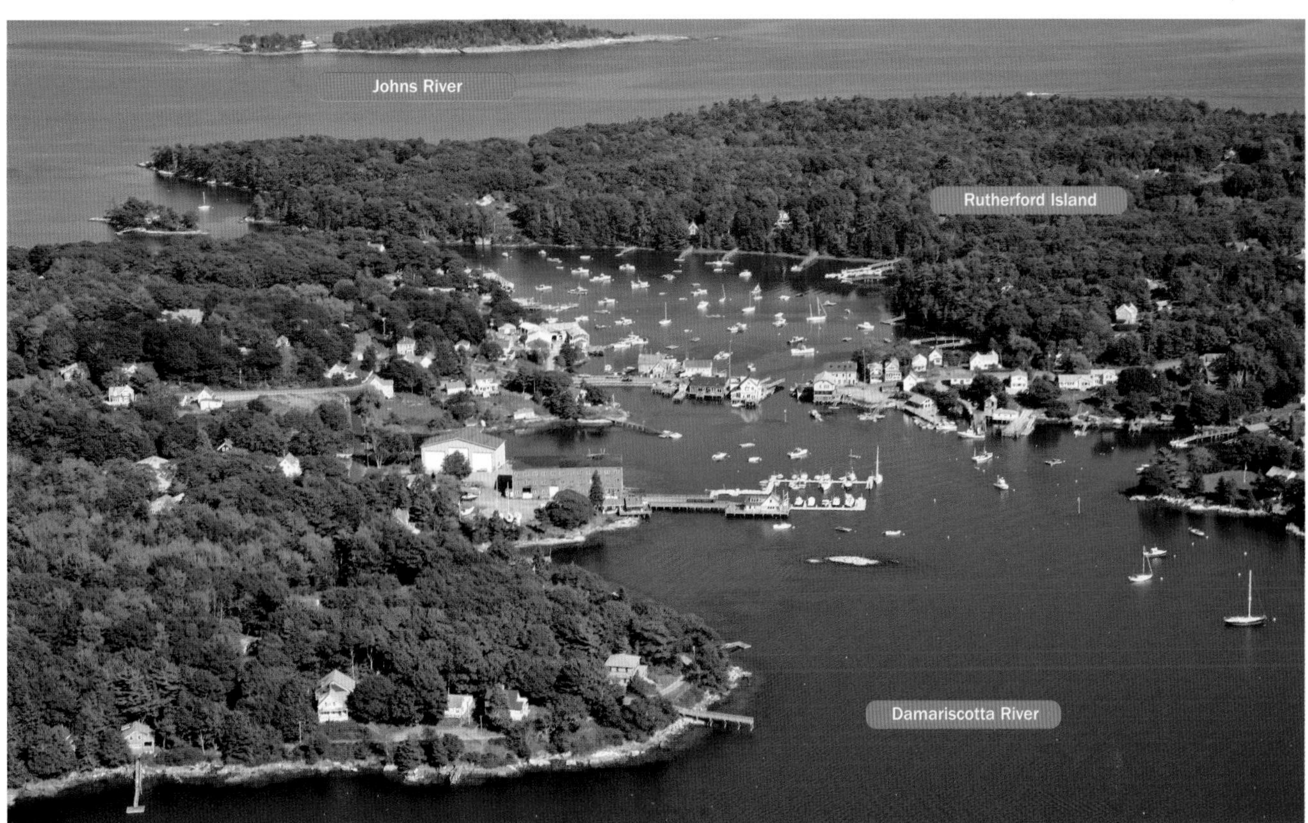

Looking east over South Bristol. The channel is called The Gut. (Not to be used for navigation.) WATERWAY GUIDE PHOTOGRAPHY

to starboard. Favor the bold western shore until the waters widen. Then stay to mid-channel to avoid the 5-foot-deep rock to starboard and go through the fast-operating swing bridge (10-foot closed vertical clearance). Currents run swiftly through here. From this point, pass between Cameron Point's flashing green "7" and red nun buoy "6" marking Indiantown Island ledge to starboard, one of the tightest squeezes of the cruise. In Ebencook Harbor Passage, leave green markers to starboard, red to port.

Goose Rock Passage

NAVIGATION: Use Charts 13293 and 13296. Across the Sheepscot River, entered north of MacMahan Island, is Goose Rock Passage, another winding, narrow, rocky channel. Here, leave green markers to port, red to starboard. Again, currents can drag aids to navigation under in this area. The passage opens into Knubble Bay, and then heads north through Lower Hell Gate, aptly named for currents up to 9 knots near the rocks toward the upper end called The Boilers. As you emerge into Hockomock Bay, keep the green buoys close to port. The first one, green can buoy "5," is frequently dragged under water. The channel twists between Hockomock Point and Mill Point and winds through Upper Hell Gate, only 60 yards wide. Just north of Upper Hell Gate, be especially careful going past dangerous Carleton Ledge—it is charted but unmarked. The route enters the Kennebec River at Sasanoa Point, where a fixed bridge has a vertical clearance of 51 feet. The town of Bath is right across the river.

Damariscotta River

Around Linekin Neck from Boothbay Harbor (use well-marked Fisherman Island Passage), the Damariscotta River is about a century removed from its more active neighbor to the west. One of Maine's most beautiful rivers, it flows past 15 miles of wooded islands, hidden coves, jagged rock outcroppings and high, green bluffs.

NAVIGATION: Use Chart 13293. Once plied by commercial schooners, the river's lazily winding channel is easy to navigate. You will pass harbors with sophisticated attractions, good food and two small but important shipbuilding villages. At the head of the river are two Colonial cities that once served as ports of entry. The tidal range here is 9 feet, so it is advisable to travel on a fair tide.

Christmas Cove

NAVIGATION: Use Chart 13293. Close to the river entrance, about a mile north of thickly wooded Inner Heron Island, Christmas Cove has an easy entrance, perfect protection with many moorings, a handsome shoreline and magnificent views. After passing red nun buoy "4," north of Inner Heron Island, head for the center of the harbor entrance, leaving Foster Point (and red-over-green nun buoy "FP") to port. Inside the harbor, look for green daybeacon "3" and red daybeacon "2," and pass between them without getting close to either.

Anchorage and Moorings: It might be difficult to anchor in the cove because of the densely packed moorings. Also, lobster buoys are thick in the harbor. The marina here offers a generous dinghy dock. Moorings are usu-

Damariscotta River, ME

DAMARISCOTTA RIVER		Largest Vessel Accommodated	VHF Channel Monitored	Transient Berths / Total Berths	Approach / Dockside Depth (reported)	Floating Docks	Gas / Diesel	Groceries, Ice, Marine Supplies, Snacks	Repairs: Hull, Engine, Propeller	Lift (tonnage), Crane, Rail	1=110V, 2=220V, B=Both, Max Amps	Laundry, Pool, Showers	Pump-Out Station	Nearby: Grocery Store, Motel, Restaurant
		Dockage					Supplies		Services					
1. Coveside Inn-Marina	207-644-8282	90	16	12/12	14/14	F	GD	IM			B/50	S		MR
2. Lobsterman's Wharf Restaurant & Inn	207-633-5481	50			12/18				RESTAURANT					R
3. Ocean Point Marina 🖳	207-633-0773	150	16/09	8/70	35/15	F	GD	IMS	HEP	L35	B/50	LS	P	GMR
4. Gamage Shipyard 🖳	207-644-8181	55	16	3/30	10/10	F	GD	IM	HEP	L25	B/50	S		G
5. South Bristol Fisherman's Co-op	207-644-8224	50			6/6		GD	IM						
6. Colonial Pemaquid State Historic Site	207-677-2423	60			10/7									R
7. Pemaquid Fisherman's Co-op	207-677-2801	50			4/4		GD							GR
8. Riverside Boat Co.	207-563-3398	40		MOORINGS				IS	H	R		L		R

Corresponding chart(s) not to be used for navigation. 🖳 Internet Access (WiFi) Wireless Internet Access

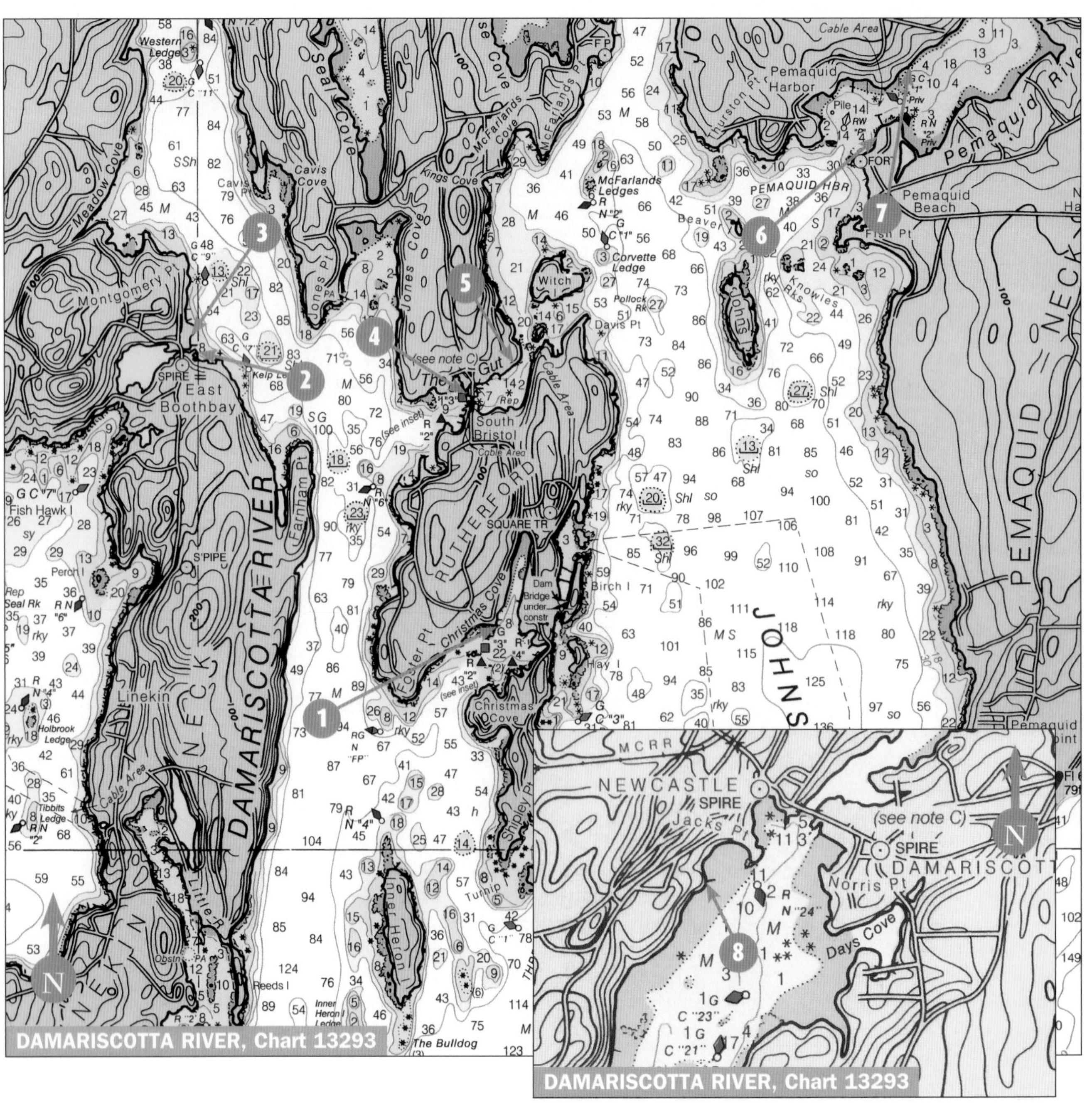

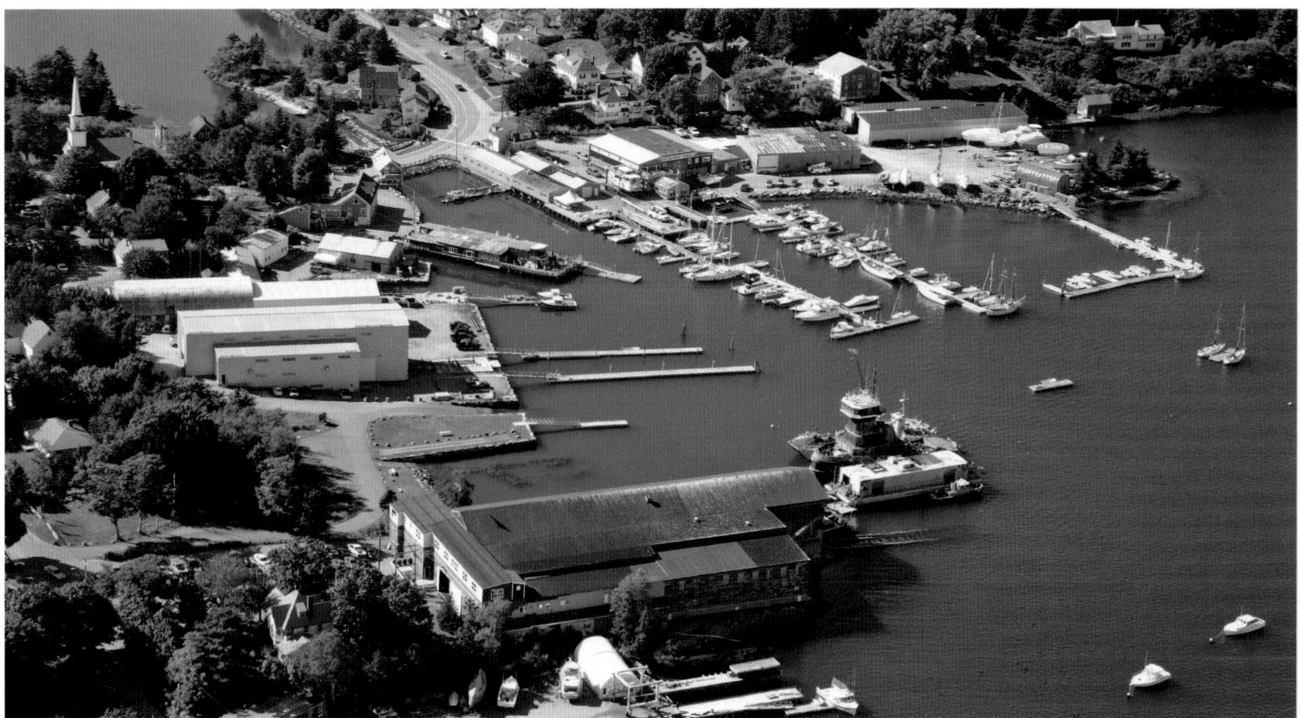

Looking northeast over East Boothbay. (Not to be used for navigation.) WATERWAY GUIDE PHOTOGRAPHY

ally available from Coveside Marina; hail "The Admiral" on VHF Channel 16 or 09 for a mooring assignment or to inquire about a slip.

East Boothbay

Dockage: This small boatbuilding village clusters along the mooring-filled cove on the west side of the river. Ocean Point Marina (formerly C&B Marina) is easily spotted because of its prominent sheds and long fuel dock paralleling the river to port. Gasoline, diesel fuel and reasonably priced transient slips on floating docks, with access to 30-amp power, showers, restrooms and a coin-operated laundry are available. The marina has a 35-ton lift, repair shops and mechanics for almost any needed repairs and an accessible pump-out station. The area's only commercial rapid-response rescue and towing operation, SeaTow, is located just upriver.

East Boothbay's post office is roadside, at the head of the dock. Immediately to the south, Lobsterman's Wharf (207-633-3443, 224 Ocean Point Road) serves lunch and dinner from a long list of moderately priced fish and lobster entrees (also pastas, salads and sandwiches). Courtesy dockage is available for patrons just below the bar and riverside dining deck. At the East Boothbay General Store (207-633-7800, 255 Ocean Point Road), two blocks south of the harbor on the road to Ocean Point, fresh pastries, newspapers and Green Mountain coffee draw an eager breakfast crowd. The store also stocks some dry goods, dairy and deli items and a limited variety of sodas, beers and wines.

Upriver to Damariscotta

NAVIGATION: Use Chart 13293. For Damariscotta, use Portland tide tables. For high tide, subtract 9 minutes; for low tide, subtract 10 minutes. Until the river reaches the twin villages of Damariscotta and Newcastle, 13 miles from the open ocean, it offers only beautiful scenery and an unlimited choice of peaceful anchorages. River currents run rapidly (up to 5 knots on the ebb), and the upper two miles of the river are winding and narrow, though reasonably well-marked. Those with limited cruising experience in such waters should seek local knowledge before making the trip.

Dockage and Moorings: Just south of Montgomery Point (north of green can buoy "7") is Ocean Point Marina, which offers transient berths, pump-out, all fuels, laundry, showers and a lift to facilitate repairs. Farther upriver at the head of navigation, below a fixed 5-foot vertical clearance bridge, Riverside Boat Co., on the Newcastle side, has fuels and can facilitate most repairs for boats under 40 feet. Across the river, at the resort town of Damariscotta, there is usually ample anchorage room in front of the town dock (out of the intense current). Ask the harbormaster if a mooring is available. Front floats of the town dock are reserved for short-term, courtesy dockage (up to two hours), and there is an ample dinghy dock. Schooner Landing Restaurant (207-563-7447, 40 Main St.), built over the water at the main channel, has facing docks on the channel that can accommodate substantial vessels. The current is pushed to high velocity here with the restriction of the channel just south of the bridge, making docking a genuine challenge.

GOIN' ASHORE: DAMARISCOTTA, ME

Damariscotta offers a considerable range of services on Main Street, half a block off the harbor front. Next to the post

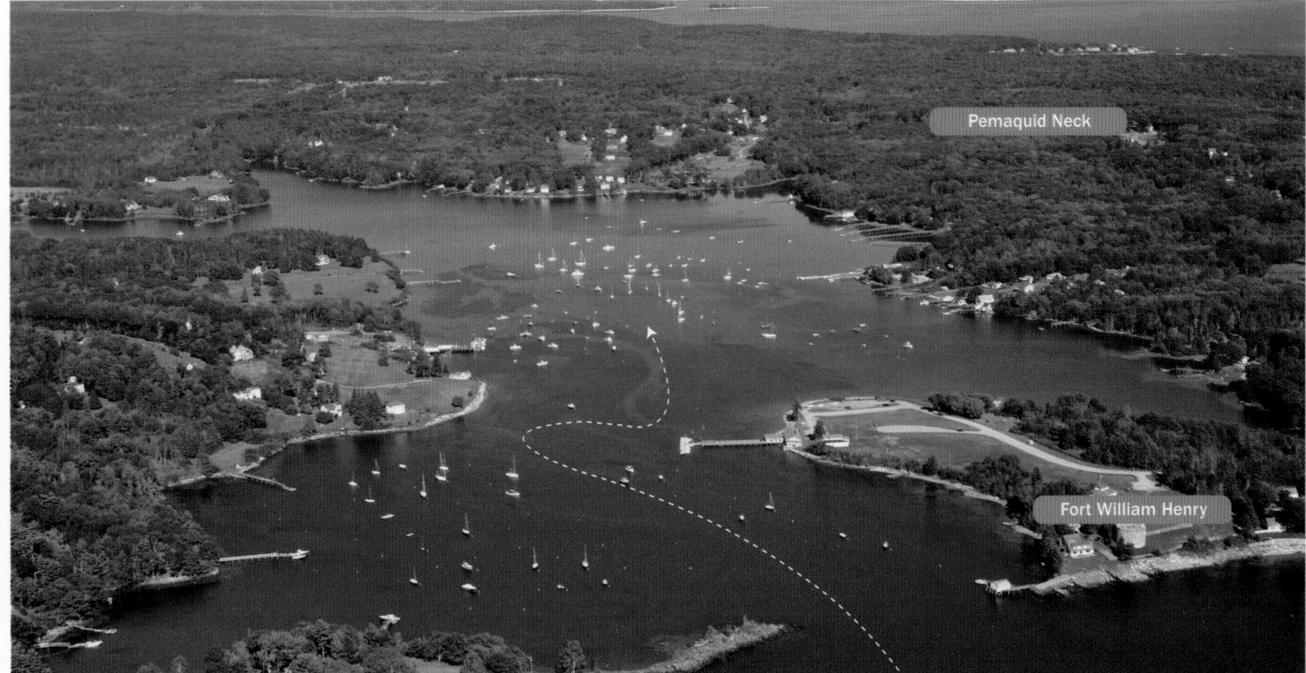

Looking east over Pemaquid Harbor. (Not to be used for navigation.) WATERWAY GUIDE PHOTOGRAPHY

office, Waltz Rexall Pharmacy (207-563-3128, 167 Main St.) has regional newspapers, the Concord Trailways bus stop and an old-fashioned soda fountain. Belknaps True Value Hardware (207-563-3095, 423 Main St.) is nearby, as are a Rite Aid Pharmacy (207-563-3506, 365 Main St.) and a bevy of gift and crafts shops. The Maine Coast Book Shop and Café (207-563-3207, 158 Main St.) sells out-of-town newspapers, including the New York Times, and serves specialty beverages. Maine Coast Photo & Digital (207-563-2111, 136 Main St.) offers same-day film processing. For dining, the Salt Bay Cafe (207-563-3302, 88 Main St.) serves interesting sandwiches and a full dinner menu at modest prices. The Breakfast Place (207-563-5434, Main St., 7 a.m. to 1 p.m.) serves just what you would expect, and the Schooner Landing (207-563-7447, 40 Main St.) at the docks is just fine for casual light eating, a brew and a view. For lobsters and seafood, try the Fisherman's Catch Seafood Market (207-563-5888, 49 Main St.). King Eider's Pub (207-563-6008, 2 Elm St.) is good for casual dining and the Damariscotta River Grill (207-563-2992, 155 Main St.) is a local favorite. In addition, numerous historic houses and churches enhance the town's appeal.

ADDITIONAL RESOURCES:

- Damariscotta Region Chamber of Commerce, **www.damariscottaregion.com**

NEARBY GOLF COURSES:
Wawenock Country Club, 685 State Route 129, Walpole, ME 04573, 207-563-3938

NEARBY MEDICAL FACILITIES:
Miles Memorial Hospital, 5 Miles St. Damariscotta, ME 04543, 207-563-1234

Johns Bay

NAVIGATION: Use Chart 13293. A number of routes lead into deep and open Johns Bay. You can sail around Thrumcap Island, then to the north between it and Pemaquid Ledge; or you can follow the deep, narrow Thread of Life, a fascinating buoyed thoroughfare north of Thrumcap Island, which runs between Thread of Life ledges and Turnip Island. Or, for perhaps the most interesting route of all, travel The Gut, a shortcut from the Damariscotta River, running through the lift bridge at South Bristol. The wooded, rocky shores make this an especially beautiful trip. Keep a sharp eye out for lobster-pot buoys here.

Pemaquid Harbor

Three miles up Johns Bay, on the eastern shore, this circular harbor is a pleasant stopover. Ashore you can get a fine dinner at the Pemaquid Fisherman's Co-op's Harbor View Restaurant (207-677-2642, off Pemaquid Harbor Road). Visit reconstructed Colonial Pemaquid State Historic Site Fort William Henry (207-677-2433) and from its parapets gaze at a splendid view of the bay, Pemaquid River and Johns Island. On a warm day, the swimming is excellent on crescent-shaped Pemaquid Beach.

Anchorage: Cross the river from Pemaquid Harbor, pass between Corvette and McFarlands ledges and anchor northwest of Witch Island in 20 to 28 feet of water. Watch for possible lobster traps when you swing with the tide.

Cruising Options

Leaving the beauty of the rivers, the cruiser will likely want to continue Down East to explore the ports between Muscongus and Rockland. Round Pond, Port Clyde and Tenants Harbor are in the following chapter. ■

Muscongus Bay to Rockland

CHARTS 13301, 13302, 13303, 13305, 13307

THE GULF OF MAINE

The powerful light at Pemaquid Point, high atop a rugged rock ledge, is a Maine landmark. The rolling seas that crash onto this prominent cape are a well-known phenomenon to the fishermen who live and work here.

Muscongus Bay, just east of Pemaquid Point, is 12 miles across at its mouth. It is an ill-defined bay, divided into several waterways: Muscongus Sound, Medomak River, Meduncook River and St. George River.

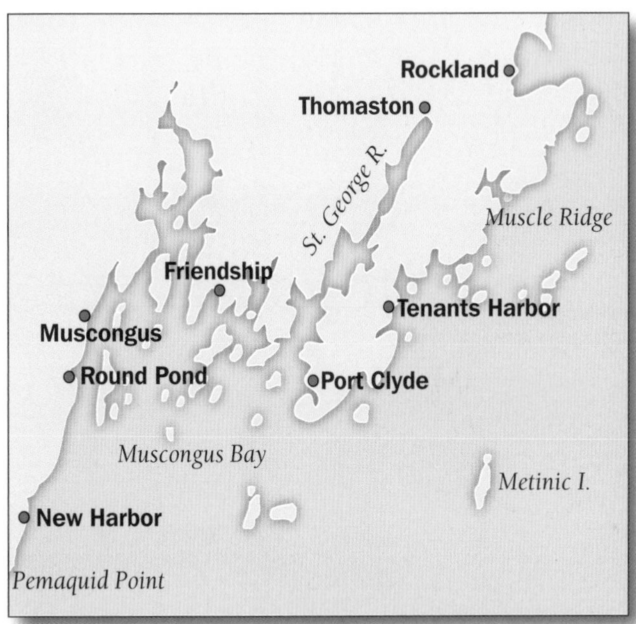

New Harbor

New Harbor, the first shelter on Pemaquid Neck, is one of the most picturesque spots in Maine. Being a fisherman's port, however, its seining and lobster boats regularly disturb the early morning quiet. Do not count on fuel being available to transients; New Harbor fishermen have first priority.

NAVIGATION: Use Chart 13288. For New Harbor, Muscongus Bay, use Portland tide tables. For high tide, subtract 10 minutes; for low tide, subtract 8 minutes. When entering New Harbor, follow the chart and buoys precisely. One of the overlapping shoals extends to the northeast from the southern bank, and the other reaches out from the northern shore almost halfway across the entry. The latter is marked by red nun buoy "4." The channel makes an S-curve around the ledges, south of the buoy, and then passes north of a daybeacon inside.

The local lobster docks, Shaw's Fish and Lobster Warf (207-677-2200, 129 Maine Route 32), will serve you a shore dinner at waterside, and the Gosnold Arms Inn and Restaurant (207-677-3727, 146 Maine Route 32), just across the road from the harbor, has a good restaurant. Contact the New Harbor Co-op (207-677-2791) or Shaw's Fish and Lobster Wharf; either might also assist in a mooring for the night. You can bring the dinghy to a landing at the western end of the harbor (but only at high tide) and

Looking north over New Harbor. (Not to be used for navigation.)
WATERWAY GUIDE PHOTOGRAPHY

Bremen, Round Pond, ME

NEW HARBOR, FRIENDSHIP		Largest Vessel Accommodated	VHF Channel Monitored	Transient Berths / Total Berths	Approach / Dockside Depth (reported)	Floating Docks	Gas / Diesel	Groceries, Ice, Marine Supplies, Snacks	Repairs: Hull, Engine, Propeller	Lift (tonnage), Crane, Rail	1=110V, 2=220V, B=Both, Max Amps	Laundry, Pool, Showers	Pump-Out Station	Nearby: Grocery Store, Motel, Restaurant
		Dockage					Supplies		Services					
1. Padebco Custom Boats	207-529-5106	50	BOATYARD STORAGE							HP	L20			R
2. Muscongus Bay Lobster Co.	207-529-5528				9/9		GD	GIM						R
3. Broad Cove Marine 🖳	207-529-5186	42	09	4/16	/6	F	GD	GIM	HE			L	P	

Corresponding chart(s) not to be used for navigation. 🖳 Internet Access (WiFi) Wireless Internet Access

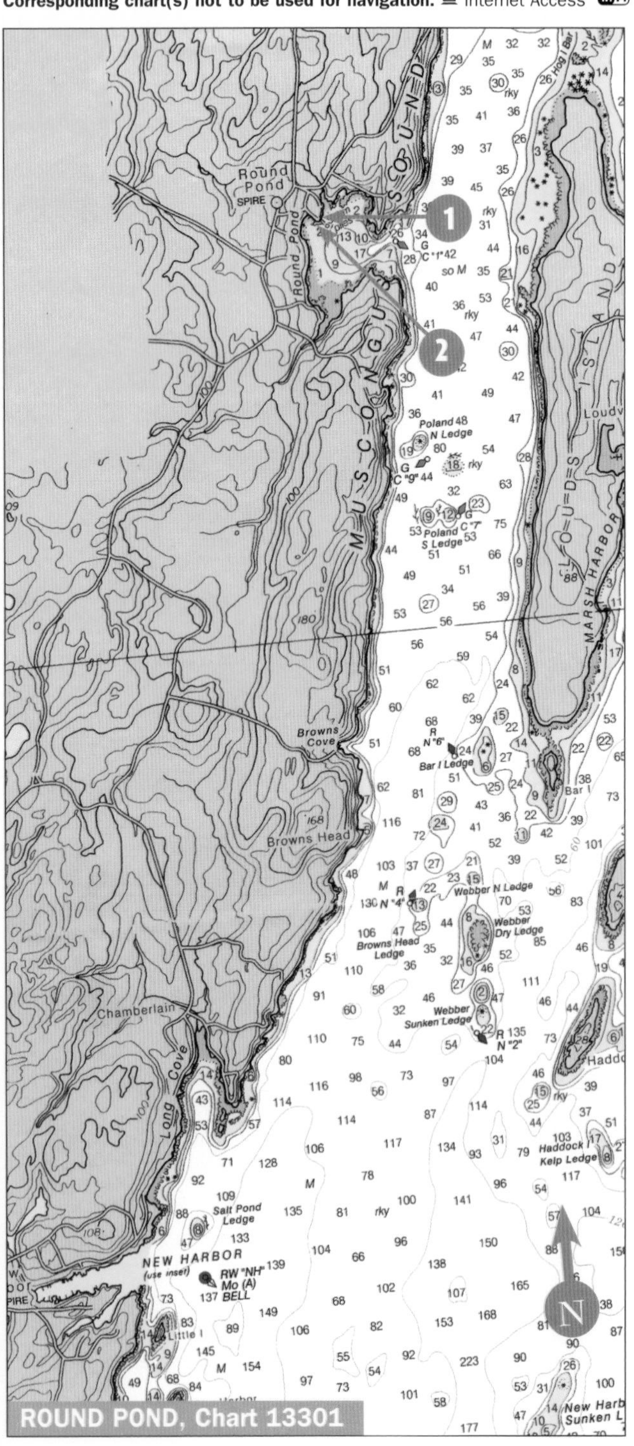
ROUND POND, Chart 13301

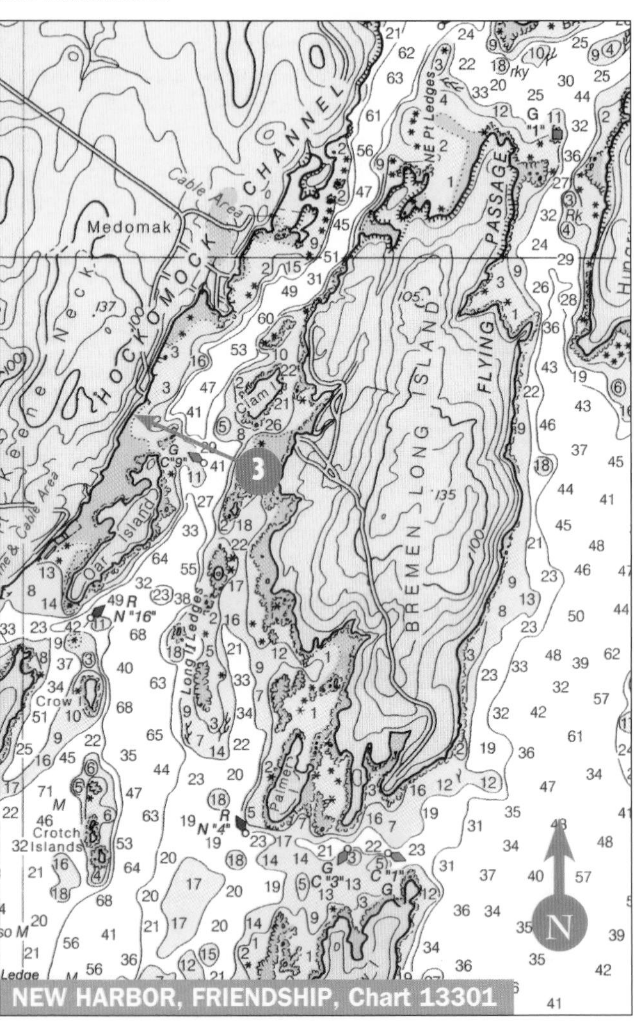
NEW HARBOR, FRIENDSHIP, Chart 13301

walk to a well-stocked grocery store, Ce Reilly and Son (207-677-2321, 2576 Bristol Road). The popular Samoset Restaurant (207-677-6771, 2477 Bristol Road) is nearby.

Round Pond

Once an active shipbuilding, quarrying and cargo port, Round Pond is now most active in the lobster trade and home to a considerable number of cruising vessels.

NAVIGATION: Use Chart 13288. For Round Pond, use Portland tide tables. For high tide, add 6 minutes; for low tide, add 14 minutes. On approaching Round Pond, heading north in Muscongus Sound, the best practice is to

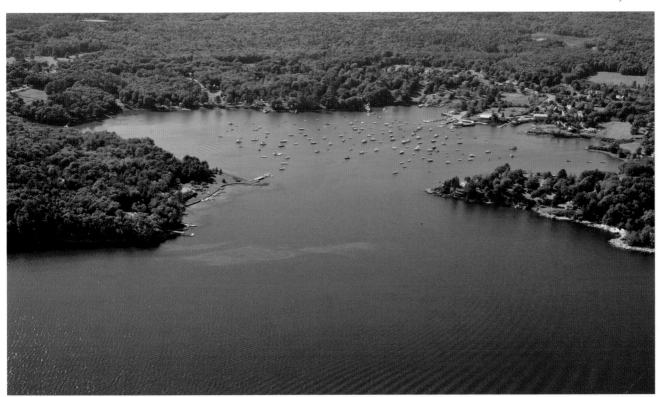

Looking northwest over Round Pond. (Not to be used for navigation.) WATERWAY GUIDE PHOTOGRAPHY

honor the marks precisely. Green can buoy "9," southeast of Poland North Ledge (just awash at low tide), must be strictly observed. Look for the small red house as a landmark for the Round Pond entry channel. Lobster pots are thickly placed throughout this area, in the harbor channel as well as the sound itself.

Moorings: Mooring balls dot Round Pond's harbor with little room left for an anchorage that will escape the bottom at low tide. But a vacant mooring is almost always available. Simply tie up and await the harbormaster's launch (usually about dinner time) to collect the fee. The town dock, with some dinghy space (you may have to crawl over a boat or two), is just to the right of the paved boat ramp. Immediately farther right, the Muscongus Bay Lobster Company (207-529-5528, 28 Landing Road) dock has gasoline, diesel fuel and fresh lobsters at the head of the dock.

A mile and a half north of Round Pond is the little harbor of Muscongus, with a small marina whose obliging owner rents a few moorings to transients and sells gas (no diesel) as well as live or boiled lobsters and steamer clams. You can picnic and dig your own clams in nearby coves. Prior to harvesting shellfish in Maine, check with local authorities on the status of licensing and "red tide" closures.

A mile and a half farther north of Muscongus Harbor, on the west side of Hockomock Channel, is Broad Cove Marine Services (BCMS). Located inside the northwest end of Oar Island, BCMS offers gas, diesel, water and ice and lobsters and clams, either live or cooked. Moorings are usually available and can be reserved on VHF Channel 09.

GOIN' ASHORE:
ROUND POND, ME

Ashore, the casual but delightful Anchor Inn (207-529-5584, highly visible to the right of the town dock) is a favorite with summer residents and natives alike, specializing in crab and lobster. Nearby, the Granite Hill Store (207-529-5864, Back Shore Rd.) is an old-fashioned country store with plenty of handmade (Maine) woolens, kitchen implements and other odds and ends. There is an interesting book selection upstairs. King Row Market, (207-529-5380, 1414 St. Route 32) in the center of the small village has groceries, frozen meats, camping and fishing equipment and videos. The post office is about half a mile south of the village center. There is no marina or chandlery in the area, but Padebco Boat Yard (builders of fine power vessels at the floating wharf farthest north of the town dock) is helpful with supplies and services for boats experiencing mechanical problems.

ADDITIONAL RESOURCES:

- The Inn at Round Pond, **www.theinnatroundpond.com**

NEARBY GOLF COURSES:
Wawenock Country Club, 685 State Route 129, Walpole, ME 04573, 207-563-3938

NEARBY MEDICAL FACILITIES:
Miles Memorial Hospital, 35 Miles St., Damariscotta, ME 04543, 207-563-1234

Friendship Harbor, ME

Looking north over Friendship Harbor. (Not to be used for navigation.) WATERWAY GUIDE PHOTOGRAPHY

Waldoboro

NAVIGATION: Use Chart 13288 and 13301. The run up the Medomak River to Waldoboro is relatively simple and well-marked, but it is best made on a rising tide or by dinghy. The river gets shoal and narrow in the upper reaches, where controlling depth is less than 4 feet. Follow Hockomock Channel. It looks narrow but has fewer obstructions than the water east of Bremen Long Island.

Friendship

About midway across Muscongus Bay on the Meduncook River is Friendship, birthplace of the Friendship sloop, originally designed for fishing and lobstering and now in demand as a recreational craft. A peaceful little lobstering town, Friendship has a good, easy-to-enter harbor and an anchorage protected in all but southwesterly winds. Fuel, a few moorings and limited repairs are available, and groceries can be had a mile away from the waterfront.

A launching ramp is at the eastern end of the harbor, about 100 yards west of the public wharf. Lobstermen sell their catches at an adjacent wharf between 2 p.m. and 3 p.m. Note that Friendship Sloop Days, featuring the popular Friendship Sloop Regatta, no longer take place in Friendship, but in Rockland to provide more sailing room.

Anchorage: Working outward from Friendship, the cruiser finds several secure anchorages and a number of picturesque offshore island communities seldom visited except by smack boats that come to pick up herring and lobsters. Remote and peaceful, these spots have no amenities and few visitors.

Try Hatchet Cove, just west of Friendship, or Friendship Long Island, where the best anchorage is located in a small cove on the northeastern end of the island. Follow the band of deep water to the charted 15-foot-deep spot and anchor a boat length to the west in 10- to 12-foot depths. Avoid the nearby larger cove which has several ledges covered at high tide.

Anchoring also is possible among boats in the cove lying between Friendship Island and Cranberry Island. Harbor Island is private property, but yachts anchor in the cove.

St. George River

NAVIGATION: Use Charts 13288 and 13301. Heading east from Friendship to the St. George River, honor the mark off Garrison Island (red nun buoy "6") and work through the maze of lobster-pot buoys to the next buoy, red "4." A long shoal extends east from Morse Island, marked by green can buoy "3." From there, round green can buoy "3" to starboard, and then head southwest for red nun "2" off the end of Gay Island. Continue past Gay Island, leaving the southern tip well to port, and then look for green can buoy "1" marking Goose Rock Ledge. Steer northeast, leaving that mark well to port, and then work your way up the St. George River. The St. George River can be quite full of lobster traps—especially from July through September.

Anchorage: Among the several attractive coves nearby are Pleasant Point Gut and Maple Juice Cove on the west side, and Turkey Cove on the east. All provide protection and easy entrance but have no yacht facilities.

St. George River, ME

ST. GEORGE RIVER		Largest Vessel Accommodated	VHF Channel Monitored	Transient Berths / Total Berths	Approach / Dockside Depth (reported)	Floating Docks	Gas / Diesel	Groceries, Ice, Marine Supplies, Snacks	Repairs: Hull, Engine, Propeller	Lift (tonnage), Crane, Rail	1=110V, 2=220V, B=Both, Max Amps	Laundry, Pool, Showers	Pump-Out Station	Nearby: Grocery Store, Motel, Restaurant
		Dockage					Supplies		Services					
1. Thomaston Town Landing	207-354-6107	70		/3	7/8			IM						GR
2. Lyman-Morse Boat Building	207-354-6904	150		6/20	12/10	F		M	HE	L110,C80	B/50	LS	P	GR
3. Jeff's Marine Service	207-354-8777	35		5/20	8/9			M	HEP		1/30			GMR

Corresponding chart(s) not to be used for navigation. Internet Access Wireless Internet Access

ST. GEORGE RIVER, Chart 13301

Thomaston

Several easy, attractive miles farther upriver at the head of navigation is historic Thomaston, where large, beautiful vessels are still built as they have been for decades.

Moorings: Lyman-Morse Boatbuilding Co. has a long, easy-access, floating face dock and overnight moorings, but no showers or restrooms. The yard also has extensive lift and repair facilities. It is best to call ahead for availability.

GOIN' ASHORE: THOMASTON, ME

The town's commercial services are arranged along Main Street (U.S. Route 1), about two-tenths of a mile north of the docks. Thomaston Grocery (207-354-2583, 193 Main St.) stocks dry goods, veggies, meats, beer, wine and "Bodacious Breads" from Waldoboro, ME. Within a block are several churches, Camden National Bank (207-354-2541, 188 Main St.), Bank of America (800-432-1000, 189 Main St.), Bank North (207-354-8751, 173 Main St.), a coin-operated laundry and dry cleaners, a hairdresser, Creative Images Hair Salon (207-354-2755, 175 Main St.), and the Personal Book Shop (207-354-8058, 78 Main St.) with plenty of marine books, classics, children's books and cards.

Looking northwest over Thomaston. (Not to be used for navigation.) WATERWAY GUIDE PHOTOGRAPHY

Looking northeast over Port Clyde. (Not to be used for navigation.) WATERWAY GUIDE PHOTOGRAPHY

The Thomaston Cafe and Bakery, the only restaurant nearby, (207-354-8589, 154 Main St.), is open Monday through Saturday, 7 a.m. to 2 p.m. and serves breakfast, soups, salads, sandwiches and espresso.

Several blocks west, Maine State Prison Showroom (207-354-9237, U.S. Route 1) sells crafts produced by inmates of the Maine State Prison, which used to dominate the landscape of Thomaston. Built in 1823, the prison was eventually destroyed, but the shop remains a great place to shop for model ships, handmade furniture and other items. The major tourist attraction is the restored Montpelier, The General Henry Knox Museum (207-354-8062, corner of U.S. Route 1 and Maine Route 131), home of Gen. Henry Knox, fellow campaigner of George Washington and the nation's first Secretary of War.

ADDITIONAL RESOURCES:

- Town of Thomaston, **www.town.thomaston.me.us**

NEARBY GOLF COURSES:
Rockland Golf Club, 606 Old County Road, Rockland, ME 04841, 207-594-9322, **www.rocklandgolf.com**

NEARBY MEDICAL FACILITIES:
Penobscot Bay Medical Center, 6 Glen Cove Drive, Rockport, ME 04856, 207-596-8000

Port Clyde

Once called Herring Gut, Port Clyde lies between Marshall Point and Hupper Island, close to the west/east route, east of the entrance to the St. George River. Widely used by fishermen and coasters as a harbor of refuge, it is home port of the Monhegan Island mail and passenger boat. It is always busy with lobster boats. It has a deep anchorage, town dock, fuel, and guest moorings for rent. The Port Clyde General Store (207-785-4496) offers a deli and the atmosphere of a bygone era. Near the ferry dock, the Dip Net restaurant (207-372-6307) for casual and delicious dining and local conversation on the wharf provides a great view of the harbor. A short stroll up the hill, an ice cream parlor scoops up refreshing treats. Art galleries abound.

NAVIGATION: Use Chart 13288 and 13301. Port Clyde's northern entrance, between Hupper Island and a ledge off Hupper Point, is tricky, so you might find the southern entrance easier.

Moorings: Ask about moorings at the Port Clyde General Store wharf, where you can also get groceries. A convenient launching ramp is nearby.

Georges Islands

Between Benner and Allen islands, you can anchor in the protected channel harbor, following the tradition set by English explorer George Waymouth in 1605. In this seemingly remote fishing outpost, you can feel like you have arrived Down East. The few structures are ramshackle but businesslike, and the docks are mounted on stripped fir tree polls at an impressive height. The tidal currents also mean business here.

Allen Island is privately owned and is developed only to the extent of an attractive house, barn and outbuilding complex for an experimental sheep ranching operation. (No dogs are allowed on Allen Island.) Lobstering activity starts well before dawn on Benner Island, with harrumphing engines joining the bleating of the lambs in this otherwise idyllic setting.

Anchorage: Directly to the east, Burnt Island provides good protection from the prevailing southwesterlies in a scallop-like harbor fashioned by Burnt Island's northern beach and Little Burnt Island to the northwest. The holding is good here in sand, but this location is quite exposed to winds shifting east and north.

Monhegan

ME

Long a favorite retreat for artists and writers, Monhegan Island is far enough off the beaten path to remain relatively undisturbed by tourism and commercial development. Though it is only nine miles southwest of the ferry landing in Port Clyde and little more than a dozen miles from the moorings at Tenants Harbor, the island never seems to attract more than a few sailors and a scattering of rough-clad day hikers who quickly blend in with the island's fishermen and summer-resident painters. They disappear along the island's 17 miles of mapped trails to imposing outlooks and quiet glens, or they are off to visit the rustic studios of some 20 professional artists who regularly display their works here. The tranquil beauty of the place, both natural and man-made, has a haunting quality that begs an early return. Entertainment is so exclusively intrinsic to the island itself that the sign over a local store's newspaper rack reads: "If You Cannot Enjoy the Natural Beauty of this Place Without the New York Times, the Boat Leaves at 12:30 and 4:30. Have a Happy Crossing."

NAVIGATION: Use Chart 13288. Use Portland tide tables. For high tide, subtract 13 minutes; for low tide, subtract 9 minutes. The island is easily approached from any direction with relatively few obstructions. From sea, Monhegan's powerful light (flashing every 15 seconds, 178 feet above sea level) is visible for many miles and is an important landmark for those making overnight crossings from southern New England or farther south.

Monhegan Light, supplemented by the radio beacon and horn on immediately-adjacent Manana Island, will guide you directly into the open entrance of Monhegan Harbor. From Sheepscot Bay to the west or from Muscongus Bay to the north, care must be taken to avoid the shallow ledges surrounding Duck Rocks (south of flashing green bell buoy "5"). Harbor entry can be made from the south between Monhegan and Manana islands.

Anchorage and Moorings: Tie-ups at the town dock are possible for up to 30 minutes, but your vessel must be attended. Stand clear for the arrival or departure of the daily ferries. (Typically, they arrive late morning and depart in the afternoon.) You may dispose of trash in the dumpster on the dock, though separation of bottles and cans is required, and you should expect a per-bag charge. It may be possible to purchase diesel fuel, but there is no piped water here.

For an overnight stay, it is best to arrange for a mooring from the harbormaster, who is usually available at the fish shack next to Fish Beach (second beach down from the town dock). You can try to hail him on VHF Channel 19A. One of the private moorings off the town beach may be available without charge or at a small fee. Otherwise, after the ferryboats have left for the day, visitors may tie up on any of their four heavy-tackle mooring balls (north of the town dock) until the next day's ferry arrivals.

Anchoring is not recommended in the harbor's deceptive mix of sand and rocks. It looks secure but is not—anchored boats regularly are dragged away by swift tidal currents. In settled weather, locals suggest that a hook can be set securely in Deadman's Cove. This location requires deepwater scope and a strong pulling arm for the dinghy. It is possible to tether a dinghy to the town pier next to the vertical ladder, but the rapid rise and fall of a substantial tide makes landing here undesirable for a visit of more than a few minutes. The better alternative is at Fish Beach (second sandy beach south of the town dock). Even here, a long dinghy tether secured to a location above the high-water mark will be required.

GOIN' ASHORE:

MONHEGAN ISLAND, ME

Monhegan is the most famous island in Maine, due to the art of George Bellows, Edward Hopper, Rockwell Kent, Jamie Wyeth and many others who have been drawn to paint its dramatic cliffs, which are the highest on the New England coast. About 70 residents live here year-round. The island's summer population is tenfold that of the winter. Located 10 miles off the coast, Monhegan is 1.4 miles long and .7 miles wide. The wildlife sanctuary hosting more than 600 varieties of wildflowers and 200 species of bird and a peaceful stretch of spruce and moss called Cathedral Woods make Monhegan attractive to naturalists and hikers. Its 17 miles of trails and awe-inspiring walks, inns, shops, an artists' colony, museum and swimming beach provide much to do.

Aside from exceptional hiking, viewing of rustic fishing sheds and studio-browsing ashore, few amenities are available. The Monhegan Associates Trail Map, available for a small charge at the inns and most shops, is invaluable for those hoping to sort out the island's maze of marked and highly scenic trails. After leaving the studio-dotted main road, a walk along the island's rocky perimeter will almost as inevitably turn up flocks of eiders as it will breathtaking seascapes. The Monhegan Museum (1 Lighthouse Way), preserving artifacts

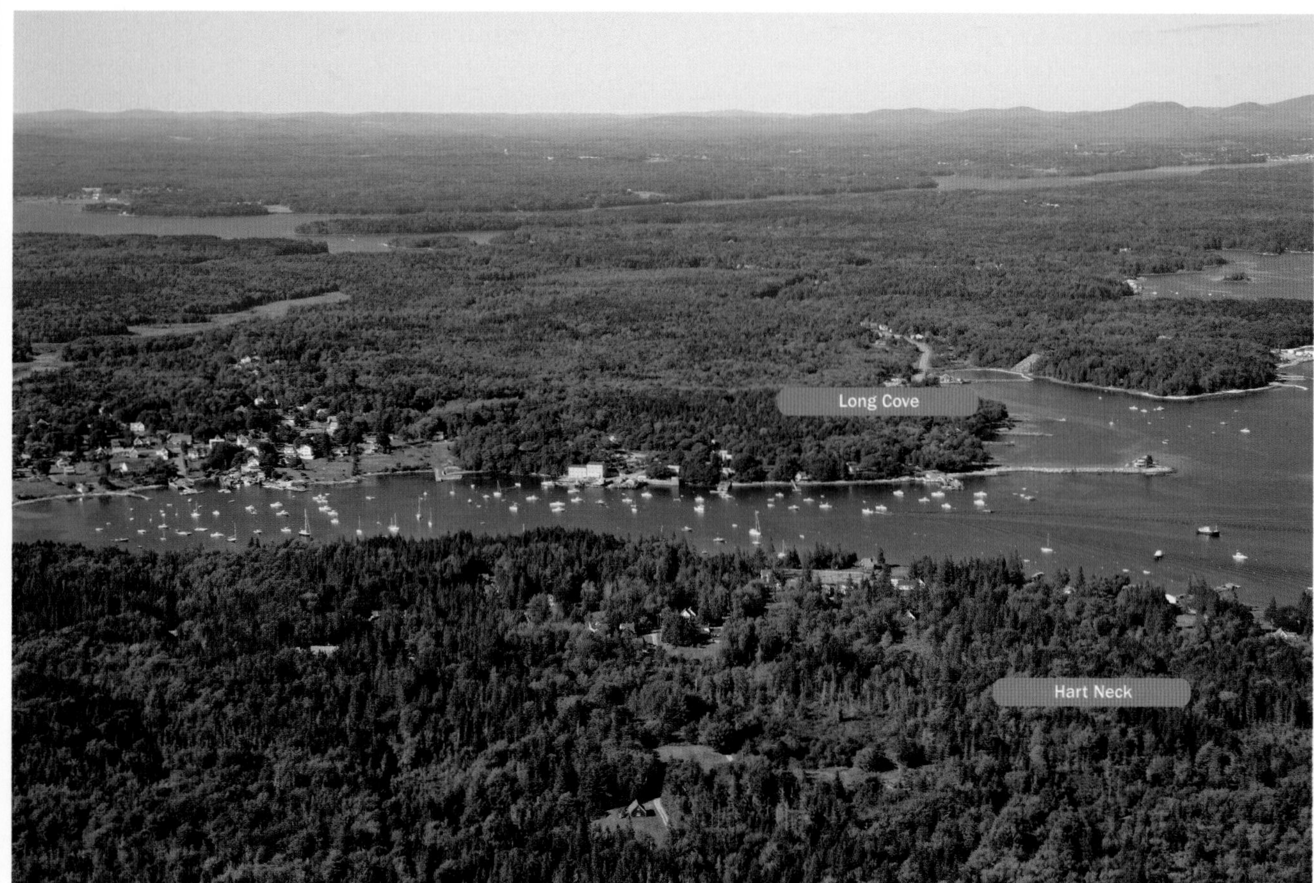

Looking north over Tenants Harbor. (Not to be used for navigation.) WATERWAY GUIDE PHOTOGRAPHY

and memorabilia from the island's unique history, is located in the lightkeeper's house overlooking the harbor. It is open daily July 1 through Aug. 31 from 11:30 a.m. to 3:30 p.m. From June 23 through June 30 and then from Sept. 1 through Sept. 30 it is only open from 11:30 a.m. to 2:30 p.m.

Monhegan Store, at the heart of the village, is a grocery store that also sells sandwiches, soup, beer and wine. Black Duck Emporium at village center next to the post office, is known for its daily baked goods, espresso, cappuccino and teas. Fish House Fish, on Fish Beach just off Main Street, has fresh fish, lobster, stews, chowders and lobster rolls. Carina, behind the Island Inn, carries groceries and take out breakfast and lunch.

A memorable escape from the galley may be found at the Island Inn (207-596-0371), perched above the town pier for a commanding view of the harbor and Manana Island. Monhegan regulars come often for old-fashioned, American-style elegance of both food and service for breakfast, lunch and dinner. The Barnacle Café and Bakery (on the pier below) serves fresh-brewed specialty coffees and espresso, a small deli selection and diet-busting mounds of fresh-baked sweet goods. The Trailing Yew (207-596-0440) also receives kind words for its simple, old fashioned and rustic home cooked meals served at large communal tables. The Monhegan House (207-594-7983) serves delightful, modestly priced country breakfasts in an antique setting.

Monhegan Island residents are dedicated to the preservation of their island environment and are especially concerned about the hazard of fire. As a result, most areas outside the village, including the rocks and cliffs, are restricted—off limits to smoking and outdoor fires.

ADDITIONAL RESOURCES:

- Monhegan Commons, **www.monhegan.com**

Tenants Harbor

North and east of Monhegan Island, the mouth of Penobscot Bay welcomes waterborne pilgrims to this sailor's mecca. Though exposed to an easterly blow, Tenants Harbor is the first of several fine shelters on the course ascending the bay.

NAVIGATION: Use Chart 13302. Use Portland tide tables. For high tide, subtract 11 minutes; for low tide, subtract 11 minutes. About four miles up the coast, Tenants is a good refuge in fog or heavy weather, and its approach is well-marked and unobstructed. An unusual-looking abandoned lighthouse and attendant buildings mark the approach at the end of Southern Island. If approaching after dark, look for the illuminated flag on the tall flagpole. The nearby flashing green bell buoy "1" should be left to port as you enter the wide mouth of the harbor. The harbor entrance is deep, with no obstructions on the straight course down the center of the harbor channel. Nevertheless, watch carefully to negotiate the minefield of brightly colored and closely spaced lobster buoys and toggles throughout the channel.

Tenants Harbor to Spruce Head, ME

TENANTS HARBOR TO SPRUCE HEAD		Largest Vessel Accommodated	VHF Channel Monitored	Transient Berths / Total Berths	Approach / Dockside Depth (reported)	Floating Docks	Gas / Diesel	Groceries, Ice, Marine Supplies, Snacks	Repairs: Hull, Engine, Propeller	Lift (tonnage), Crane, Rail	1=110V, 2=220V, B=Both, Max Amps	Laundry, Pool, Showers	Pump-Out Station	Nearby: Grocery Store, Motel, Restaurant
		Dockage					Supplies		Services					
1. Cod End Market, Cookhouse & Dock	207-372-6782	50	16/09		10/5		GD	IMS				LS		GMR
2. Tenants Harbor Town Dock	207-372-6363	40	16/09	MOORINGS	15/3									GMR
3. Spruce Head Marine	207-594-7545	38	16					G	HEP	L20,C15	1/20			GMR

Corresponding chart(s) not to be used for navigation. Internet Access Wireless Internet Access

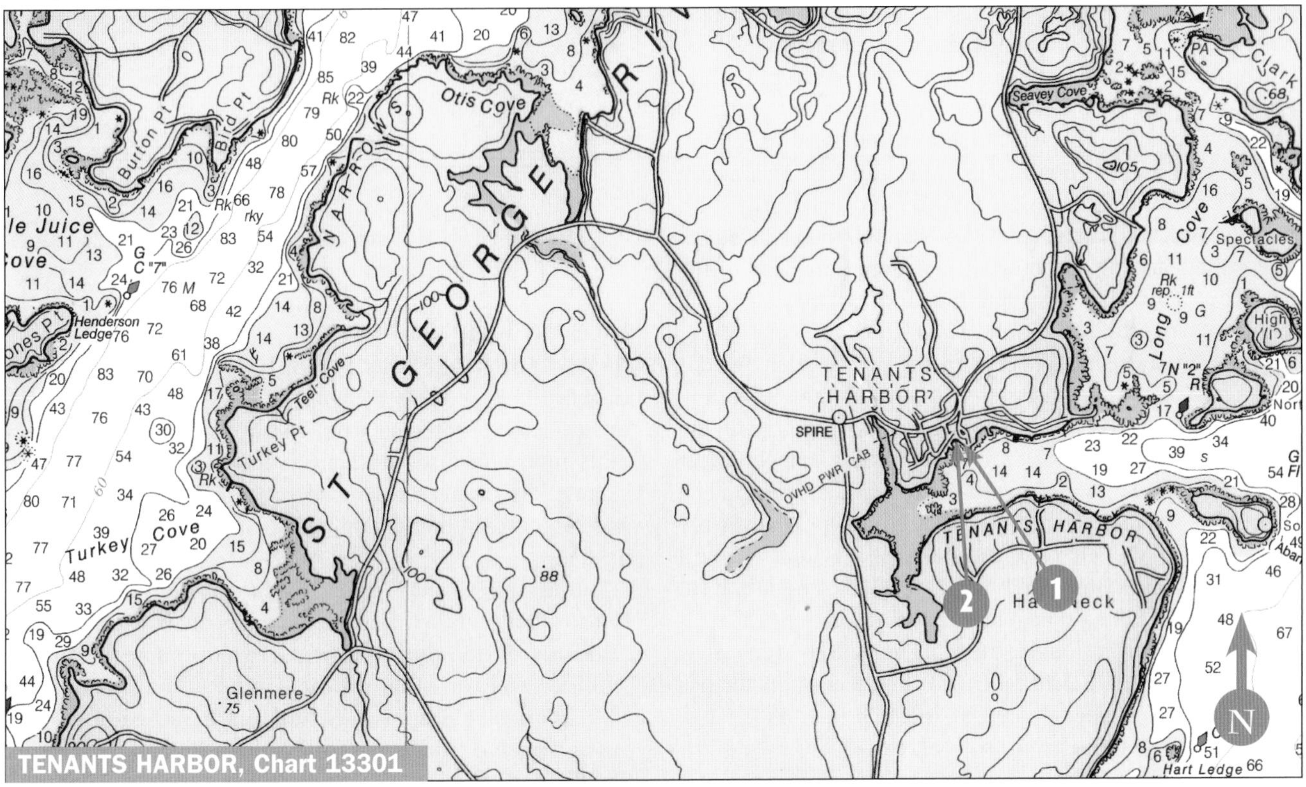

TENANTS HARBOR, Chart 13301

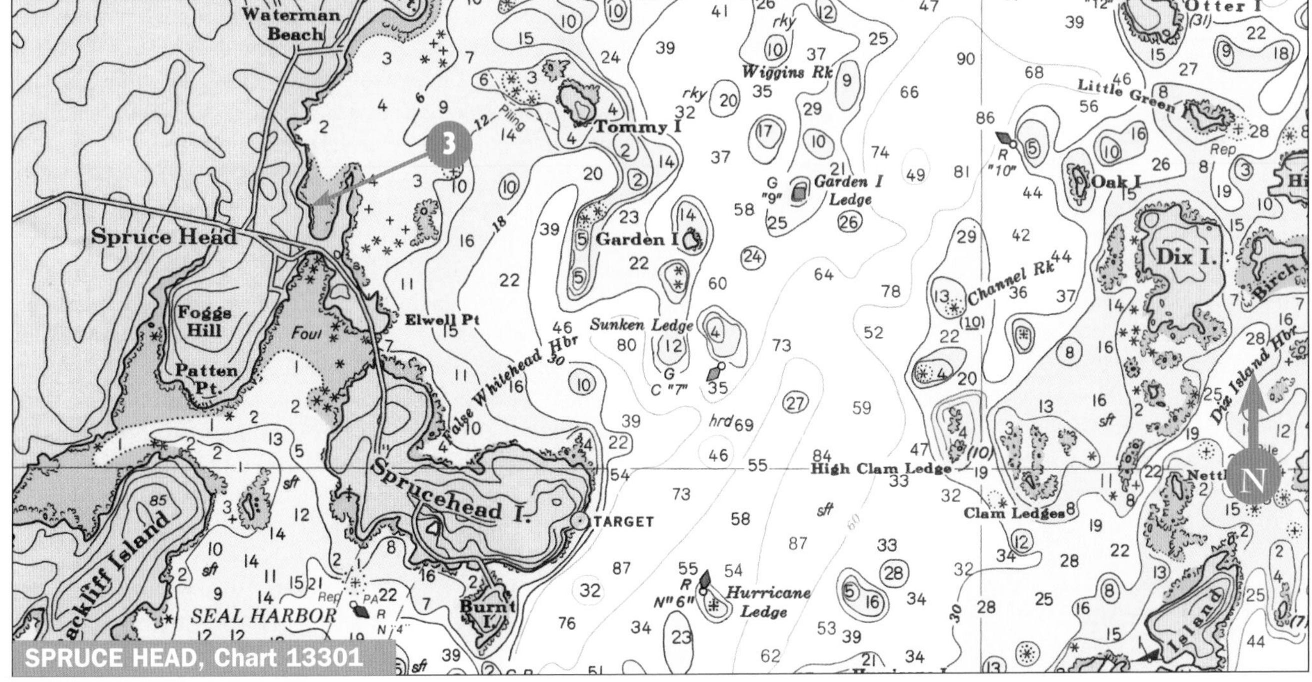

SPRUCE HEAD, Chart 13301

Anchorage and Moorings: It has been reported that anchoring is no longer allowed in Tenants Harbor, whether by law or because of the proliferation of moorings. Boats may anchor in the outer harbor, however, in the charted 13-foot area on the south side, inshore from Southern Island.

Numerous moorings are available in the inner harbor, with additional room to set a secure hook outside the mooring fleet. Another anchorage is found in Long Cove, just north of red nun "2" marking the channel west of Northern Island, though it is open to the southwest and has a ledge at the entrance. Long Cove has been known to accommodate over 70 vessels during yacht club cruises with plenty of room for more. These anchorages are a distance from village amenities. The northwestern branch of Long Cove offers 16 feet of water between the Spectacles and the mainland. You will sometimes see local fishermen exiting this area through a channel north of Spectacles, but this channel is not well marked and used only with thorough local knowledge of the channel and tidal range. The public landing and dinghy dock are at the head of the harbor to starboard, just past the Cod End Market dock and floats on the same side. Gas, diesel, ice and other supplies are available adjacent to the public wharf, and a motel and restaurants are right nearby. The town landing is a U-shaped affair with plenty of dinghy room inside the "U," leaving the face dock for larger vessels. Expect 4 feet of water here at low tide with a 9-foot tidal range. (The town also services trash barrels placed at the head of the dock ramp.) Witham's moorings look like rentals—round and white with a blue band marked RENTAL and a helpful pick-up wand. The other rental moorings may be difficult to distinguish from lobster buoys. The yellow-green ones marked COD END RENTAL are just that; Art's Lobster has red buoys for boaters, not the lobsters. Colors change somewhat with the seasons, so look closely to distinguish the rental moorings from the pot markers.

GOIN' ASHORE:

TENANTS HARBOR, ME

You will find most of the basics in this quaint and pleasant village, plus a few delightful extras. One of the Cod End rental moorings can be picked up without charge for a short visit to the superb seafood market of the same name. Cod End's fresh crabmeat, made-to-order lobster rolls and Maine-style blueberry pies are savored for their taste and reasonable prices. Cod End's dock, which carries 4-foot depths at low tide (with a 9-foot tidal range), offers diesel fuel and gasoline, clean freshwater and ice. Cod End Market (207-372-6782) will deliver cooked food to your boat in the evening on order; be sure to tip the driver. They can also arrange for mechanical services.

The clapboard-elegant East Wind Inn (800-241-VIEW) next door has a wrap-around porch for easy rocking with a harbor panorama. Breakfast and dinner are served to accompany the view. At the top of the gentle rise above the public landing, turn right on the Tenants Harbor's Main Street for a block's walk to Hall's Market (207-372-6311, 16 Main St.). This old-fashioned country store offers a surprisingly good selection of fresh fruits, veggies and meats, general groceries, ice, beer and wine. Farther along (just beyond the post office), the Schoolhouse Bakery (207-372-9608, 21 River Road) doubles as a coffee shop, serving soups, sandwiches, breads, pastries and beverages. Farmer's Restaurant (207-372-6111), the post office and a laundry are just up the street.

ADDITIONAL RESOURCES:

- Cod End (Tenants Harbor), **www.codend.com**

NEARBY GOLF COURSES:
Rockland Golf Club, 606 Old County Road,
Rockland, ME 04841, 207-594-9322,
www.rocklandgolf.com

NEARBY MEDICAL FACILITIES:
Penobscot Bay Medical Center, 6 Glen Cove Drive,
Rockport, ME 04856, 207-596-8200

Muscle Ridge Channel

NAVIGATION: Use Chart 13301. Northeast of Tenants Harbor, Muscle Ridge Channel offers an inside passage to Rockland. Protected from the open sea by a string of outlying islands, it is studded with well-marked rocks and ledges that should present no problem in good visibility, and numerous bights and coves provide shelter when needed.

Along the western shore is large, well-marked Seal Harbor, between Whitehead and Sprucehead islands. Two cans, one on the northern side (red nun buoy "4") of the entrance and the other on the southern (green can buoy "3"), mark shoal spots. A third mark (an unnumbered green-over-red can) is passable on either hand.

On the eastern side of Muscle Ridge Channel, High and Dix islands provide good anchorage and shelter from the prevailing southwesterlies. The entrance is straightforward from the channel between red nun buoy "10" and red daybeacon "12." Pilot a center course between Oak Island to starboard and Little Green Island to port.

Anchorage: Anchorage between Dix and High islands in depths from 8 to 20 feet at mean low water will provide protection from all but northwesterly winds and offer ready access to both these fascinating spots. In the late 19th century, as many as 2,000 quarrymen worked here, but today their houses, which numbered more than 100, as well as the opera house, are gone. The private association that now owns Dix Island permits cruising visitors ashore but prohibits littering, fires or camping and swimming in the quarries. This is a favorite anchorage for the pulling boats from Hurricane Island Outdoor Adventures.

Rockland

Rockland's large, open, easy-access harbor is ringed by all the services that one would expect from a maritime county seat with a population of 8,000. The city enjoys being known as a recreational boating center, offering several marinas and more than 500 moorings. Still, if there is a serious blow rolling in, cruisers and any nearby commercial vessels head for more protected waters at the northern end of the bay or in Eggemoggin Reach.

ME

NAVIGATION: Use Chart 13302. Use Bar Harbor tide tables. For high tide, add 9 minutes; for low tide, add 6 minutes. Around the bold, jutting headland of Owls Head, with its picturesque lighthouse, is Rockland Harbor. Easily approached from any direction in virtually any weather, it is protected by a mile-long breakwater, yet it is wide open to a severe easterly blow. A five-second flashing light marks the end of the breakwater, to starboard on entry, with a horn mounted on a 39-foot tower. Fully half a mile south, green can "1" marks the port side.

Dockage and Moorings: For a town mooring (almost always available), call the Rockland harbormaster on VHF Channel 09 or by phone at 207-594-0312. Beggar's Wharf also has moorings to offer. You can reach them by calling 207-594-8500. Moorings are available as well from Maples Moorings (207-594-2891). The harbormaster's office is now located in the former chamber of commerce office at the end of the pier. It sits in the middle of the waterfront park left of the Coast Guard station. Showers, restrooms and information on special events and local services are available at the harbormaster's building. The harbormaster can also give you details of the town-run launch service, and there is ample parking ashore to accommodate a crew change.

A new deep-water marina, Trident Yacht Basin, offers a courtesy vehicle and two restaurants on-site. Journey's End Marina is located front and center in the harbor, just north and west of the Coast Guard station, and about a quarter mile due east of Main Street. This is a full-service facility with haul-out and repair capabilities, all fuels, ample transient space on its modern floating docks and amenities including saunas. Knight Marine Service is next to the ferry terminal in Lermond Cove. Gasoline and diesel fuel can be pumped at the marina's accessible dock, and the berths here are well-protected by the breakwater. Knight's also has haul-out and substantial repair capability. The Landings Restaurant and Marina, just east of the public landing (and upwind of the fish pier), is also a full-service operation with floating docks, fuels and a popular restaurant.

Anchorage: As in many popular harbors, the number of moorings has increased, but ample anchorage room is generally available in any of the designated anchorage areas. The best anchorage is located in the extreme northern or southern ends of the harbor. Note that there is a cable area immediately behind the breakwater; avoid anchoring in this area. Watch for shallows, and consider the possibility of 10-foot tides. Here, in the absence of fog, superb views of the Camden Hills to the north are guaranteed.

GOIN' ASHORE:

ROCKLAND, ME

Along Main Street or in the immediate vicinity, you will find a bank with ATM, numerous restaurants, a complete hardware store, a marine supplies outlet and a variety of clothing stores. A Hannaford grocery store (207-594-2173, 75 Maverick St.) is about a mile from Knight Marine Service and the ferry terminal (where you can purchase New York and Boston newspapers from vending machines) and a Shaw's Supermarket (207-594-8615) is in the Harbor Plaza mall area about two miles from downtown. The mall area also has an office supply store, Radio Shack (207-594-7008, 235 Camden St.), Home Depot (207-594-6401 270 Camden St.) and more. East of the downtown area, Good Tern Food Co-op (207-594-8822, 750 Main St.) is a great place for organic groceries. Sage Market (207-594-5776, 410 Main St.) is a good source for wines and cheeses.

The large and accommodating Navigator Inn (207-594-2131, 520 Main St.) is also located in this area. Recommended restaurants near the waterfront are: Second Read (207-594-4123, open daily, 328 Main St. Suite 102) for gourmet coffees, sandwiches, pastas and lots of books, new, used and rare; Rockland Cafe (207-596-7556, 441 Main St.), with a large, varied menu and modest prices; Black Bull Tavern (207-593-9060, 420 Main St.), with reasonable prices for seafood, chicken and chops and a lively bar scene; the Landings Restaurant and Lounge (207-596-6563) directly on the harbor overlooking the water), for casual dining with dockage and fuel; the Water Works (207-596-2753, 7 Lindsay St.), with pub fare and microbrews; and the Brown Bag (207-596-6372, 606 Main St.), serving soups and sandwiches (hot and cold), vegetarian dishes and baked goods. Convenient for breakfast and lunch is The Brass Compass (207-596-5960, 305 Main St.).

On the opposite corner is The Park Street Grille (207-594-4944, 279 Main St. #7), serving dinner with a southwestern flair. Two blocks north on Main Street is the Atlantic Baking Company (207-596-0505, 351 Main St.), a great source of excellent breads and pastries as well as soups, sandwiches and salads at their tables or to take out. Suzuki's Sushi Bar (207-596-7447, 419 Main St.) has opened in the center of downtown near Amalfi (207-596-0012, 421 Main St.), another good bet for dinner. Directly across the street from the harbormaster's office is Rock City Coffee Roasters (207-594-5688, 254 Main St.), offering a cup or pound of freshly roasted, ground and brewed coffee. A short taxi drive away is Primo (207-596-0770, 2 S. Main St.), considered one of the finest dining experiences in Maine. Cruisers who want to enjoy a night ashore can choose from many bed and breakfasts or hotels. One great place is the Berry Manor Inn (207-596-7696, 81 Talbot Ave.), a classic Victorian mansion.

Highly recommended is a jaunt along Harbor Walk (see a map from the chamber of commerce), a public footpath hugging Rockland's historic waterfront, providing beautiful harbor vistas. Every July, the harbor fills with traditional Maine windjammers, competing in the Great Schooner Race from New Haven to Rockland. Rockland also boasts three fine museums. The Farnsworth Art Museum (207-596-5789,

Looking north over Rockland. (Not to be used for navigation.) WATERWAY GUIDE PHOTOGRAPHY

16 Museum St.) holds an extensive Andrew Wyeth collection, as well as American art and a large library. The Owls Head Transportation Museum (207-594-4418, three miles west of Rockland on Route 73 in Owl's Head, ME), has a unique collection of classic aircraft and automobiles in working condition. On Park Street, just off Main Street, are the Maine Lighthouse Museum (207-594-3301, 1 Park Drive), the chamber of commerce offices and the visitors center. There is a large branch of Keybank (207-594-8456, 331 Main St.) for ATM or other banking needs. The Strand Theater at 345 Main St. is an elegantly restored showplace that offers films and live acts throughout the year. Call 207-594-0070 for schedule.

Every summer in Rockland is filled with special events, starting with the Rockland North Atlantic Blues Festival in July; Friendship Sloop Days (207-596-0376), a nearly 50-year homecoming and regatta race with sloop races, is followed by the Maine Lobster Festival on the first weekend in August; and the Maine Boats, Homes and Harbors Boat Show, the only in water boat show in the state, on the second weekend in August.

ADDITIONAL RESOURCES:

- City of Rockland, **www.ci.rockland.me.us**

NEARBY GOLF COURSES:
Rockland Golf Club, 606 Old County Road, Rockland, ME 04841, 207-594-9322, **www.rocklandgolf.com**

Rockland, ME

ROCKLAND		Largest Vessel Accommodated	VHF Channel Monitored	Transient Berths / Total Berths	Approach / Dockside Depth (reported)	Floating Docks	Gas / Diesel	Groceries, Ice, Marine Supplies, Snacks	Repairs: Hull, Engine, Propeller	Lift (tonnage), Crane, Rail	1=110V, 2=220V, B=Both, Max Amps	Laundry, Pool, Showers	Pump-Out Station	Nearby: Grocery Store, Motel, Restaurant
		Dockage					Supplies		Services					
1. Trident Yacht Basin (Internet Access, Wireless Internet Access)	**207-236-8100**	**175**	**16**	**10/20**	**15/13**	**F**		**IS**	**HEP**		**B/300**	**LS**	**P**	**GMR**
2. Rockland Public Landing (Internet Access, Wireless Internet Access)	207-594-0314	95	16/09	15/15	12/10	F		I			B/50	LS	P	GMR
3. The Landings Restaurant & Marina (Internet Access, Wireless Internet Access)	207-596-6573	200	09/16	12/72	VARIES	F	GD	IM			100	LS	P	GMR
4. Hamilton Marine	207-594-8181	MARINE SUPPLIES						M						R
5. Journey's End Marina (Internet Access)	207-594-4444	220	09/18	10/70	20/14	F	GD	IM	HEP	L50,C30	B/100	S	P	GMR
6. Beggar's Wharf (Internet Access, Wireless Internet Access)	207-594-8500	150	09/16	MOORINGS			I				LS			
7. Knight Marine Service	207-594-7216	82	09	10/11	12/12	F	GD	GIM	HEP	L35	1/30	LS		GMR

Corresponding chart(s) not to be used for navigation. Internet Access · Wireless Internet Access

ROCKLAND, Chart 13305

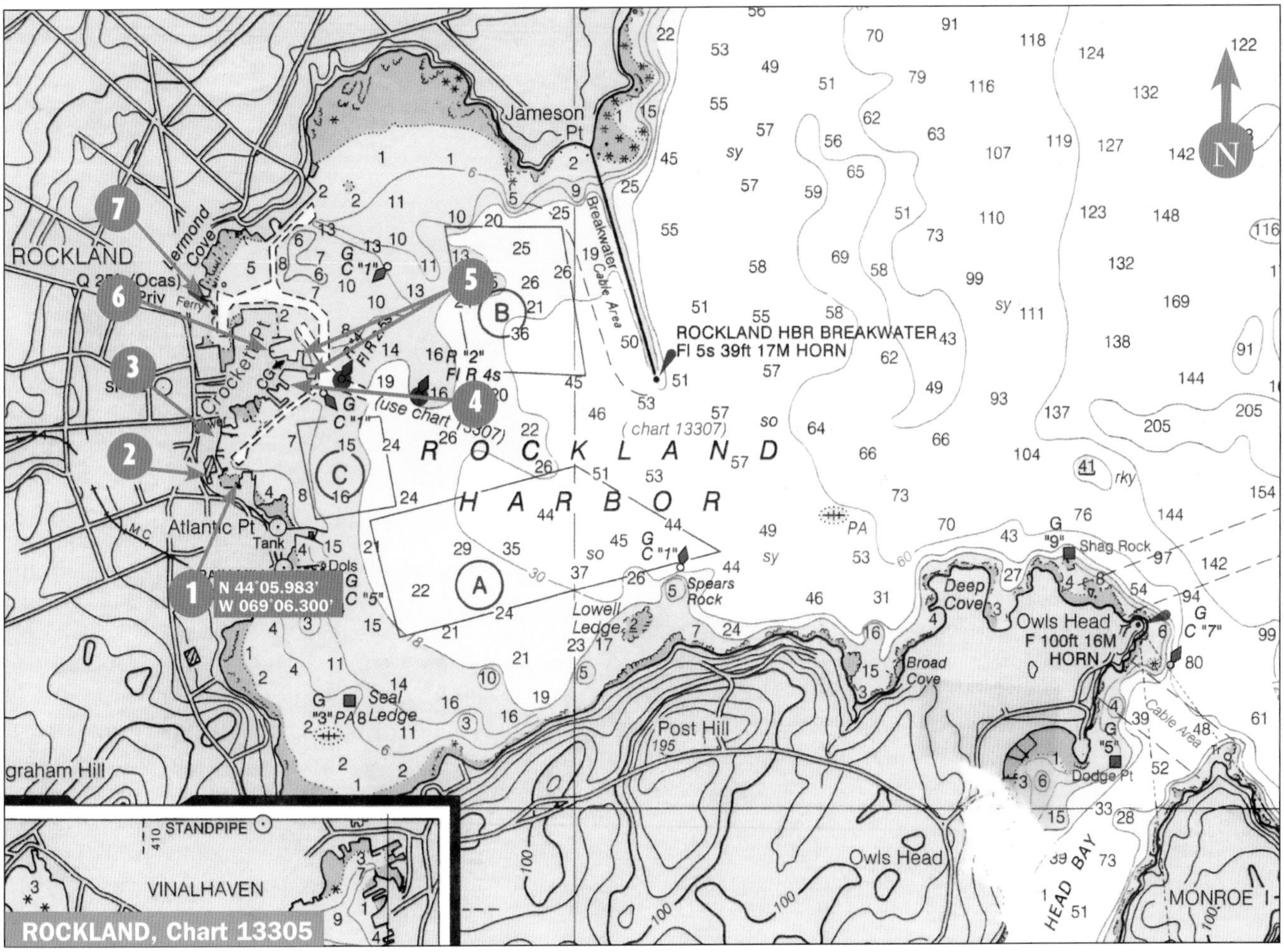

NEARBY MEDICAL FACILITIES:
Penobscot Bay Medical Center, 6 Glen Cove Drive, Rockport, ME 04856, 207-596-8200

Cruising Options

The last leg of this Down East tour takes the adventuresome boater from Rockport to Eastport, and includes some of the most pristine and breathtaking scenery in America. In the case of this Maine cruise, the best was truly saved for last. ■

Waterway Guide is always open to your observations from the helm. E-mail your comments on any navigation information in the guide to: editor@waterwayguide.com.

Waterway Guide advertising sponsors play a vital role in bringing you the most trusted and well-respected cruising guide in the country. Without our advertising sponsors, we simply couldn't produce the top-notch publication now resting in your hands. Next time you stop in for a peaceful night's rest, let them know where you found them—Waterway Guide, The Cruising Authority.

Penobscot Bay to Eastport

CHARTS 13302, 13303, 13307, 13308, 13312, 13313, 13315, 13316, 13318, 13321, 13322, 13323, 13324, 13325, 13326, 13392, 13394, 13396, 13398

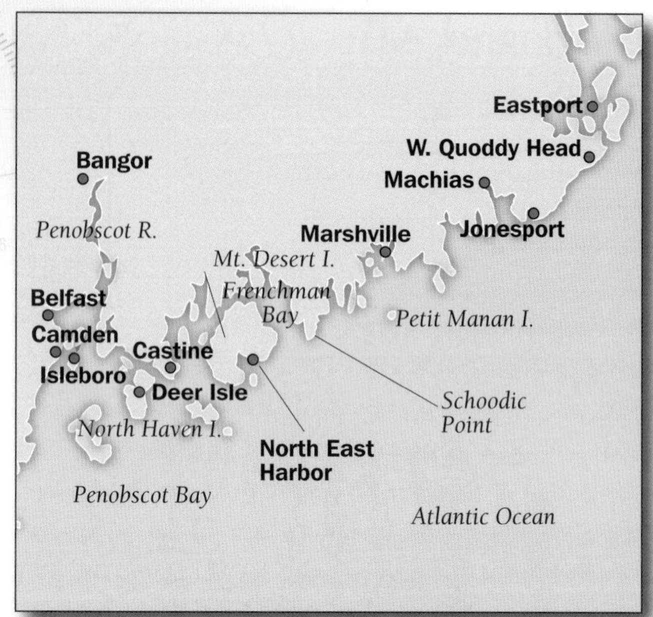

THE GULF OF MAINE

Fifteen miles south of Vinalhaven Island, the imposing 90-foot lighthouse on Matinicus Rock guides offshore mariners into Penobscot Bay. The largest of Maine's coastal indentations, Penobscot Bay is 20 miles wide and nearly 30 miles long, the watery basin of a steep-sided chalice rimmed by Camden Hills and Mount Battie to the west and Blue Hill and Mount Cadillac to the east. An archipelago of large and small islands—dominated by Islesboro to the north and Vinalhaven to the south—separates East and West Penobscot Bays. Deer Isle and Isle au Haut mark the archipelago's eastern boundary.

Penobscot Bay has bold shores of multi-colored granite, pine and spruce-covered islands, fine fishing, lobster buoys in abundance, good berry picking, patches of sandy beach, many harbors (shelter is never far away) and numerous rocks and ledges constantly pounded by thundering tides. Although Penobscot Bay is well-charted, cruising calls for careful navigation and alert watch for the effects of swift tidal currents and rapidly descending fogs. All your navigational equipment—GPS, radar, compass and charts—will come into play, as will fog horn and bell. Navigation must be precise, and buoys must be strictly followed. West Penobscot Bay, lying between the mainland and the islands, has few offshore rocks and ledges and is easy to navigate in the absence of fog.

Matinicus Island

NAVIGATION: Use Chart 13302. For Matinicus Harbor, use Bar Harbor tide tables. For high tide, add 5 minutes; for low tide, subtract 27 minutes. Because of numerous islets and ledges surrounding the entrance, Matinicus Harbor is best approached in fair weather and good visibility. From the north, stand east of Zypher Rock, marked by flashing green buoy "5," No Mans Land, The Barrel (just awash, charted but not marked by a navigational aid) and Harbor Ledge (immediately north of the red-and-green entrance bell buoy). From the south, leave Ragged Island and its surrounding islets to the west, making passage toward the entrance bell just west of West Black Ledge. Leave the south end of Wheaton Island well to port because of the submerged rocks there.

Anchorage: As you enter the harbor, limited anchorage (room only for a few boats) is located just inside the lee of Wheaton Island to port. The moorings situated farther to port, in the crotch between Wheaton Island and Matinicus Island, are attached to the bottom via a series of underwater cables, which will foul an anchor. Reportedly, one or two of these moorings may be available for overnight rental; ask around at wharf side. Do not attempt to claim the apparently empty area in the center of the harbor—Indian Ledge looms menacingly near the surface at low water.

Additional calm-weather anchorage is available in Old Cove, just south of the main harbor. Entrance to Old Cove is unencumbered (except for the rocky ledge stringing southward of Wheaton Island), and holding is secure in sand with 15-foot depths at mean low water. Enter the cove at dead center, making certain to clear the cut between Wheaton and Matinicus islands with enough distance to accommodate adequate rode scope so as not to block the channel. Intrepid (and substantial) lobster boats blast through this narrow and not altogether deep passage frequently, often at night, on any tide. This and the ocean swells will make certain that you are rocked asleep (or awake). However, the cut is convenient for a dinghy trip to the state wharf inside the main harbor. Simply keep to the Matinicus shore on entry to avoid the shallows on the Wheaton side and the center harbor reef. Tie the dinghy up to the side of the steel ladder on the state wharf, allowing enough painter length for the 9-foot tidal range and space for transport boats that also make the ladder their destination.

Looking north over Rockport. (Not to be used for navigation.) WATERWAY GUIDE PHOTOGRAPHY

GOIN' ASHORE:

MATINICUS ISLAND, ME

The quintessential offshore Maine fishing and farming community, Matinicus Island is not well organized for tourists and visiting cruisers. It is perhaps because of this that the island is such a special place to visit. Here the stylistic Down East tall-timbered waterfront is matched by classic New England farmsteads ashore, some still delivering summer produce to the semi-weekly farmers markets (check signs ashore for times and locations). On a clear day, a leisurely walk around the island's level roadways offers 19th-century vistas and profound seascapes at every turn.

ADDITIONAL RESOURCES:

- Matinicus Island Vacations, **www.matinicusisland.com**

Ragged Island (Criehaven)

No longer populated year-round, Ragged Island epitomizes a remote Maine fishing outpost. Only a few handfuls of hardy lobstermen maintain their summer base camps here, preferring the remoteness of the place and the still-excellent lobster grounds. Their harbor on the northwest side of the island is accessible and secure from the prevailing southerly swells.

Do not stray out of the mooring field, as the edges of the harbor are littered with ledges which only bare near low tide. Anchorage is impossible on the harbor's solid granite bottom, but you may be able to secure a vacant mooring; ask one of the lobstermen or ask ashore during a brief tie-up. Boats over 40 feet are well advised to bypass this narrow, crowded harbor. There are no stores, phones or other amenities here.

Rockport

Built on the hills surrounding this sock-shaped harbor five miles north of Rockland, protected yet commodious Rockport has become a cruising favorite.

NAVIGATION: Use Chart 13302. Use Bar Harbor tide tables. For high tide, add 9 minutes; for low tide, subtract 6 minutes. Rockport Harbor is easy to enter, deep almost to the shore and free of ledges and boulders. The exception is Porterfield Ledge at the center of the entrance, marked by a great pillar of granite blocks topped by a green-and-white daybeacon. The harbor is protected by all but southerly winds and has a friendly boat club, full-service marina, public landing and attractive restaurant.

Porterfield Ledge, the only obstruction to harbor entry, is unlit and is revealed at low water. Note that the ledge extends farther west than might appear on the large-scale chart. Take care, upon entering from the north and east, not to cut corners when rounding Indian Island. A submerged reef extends to the south of the island; the flashing red six-second light at Lowell Rock should be left to starboard.

Anchorage and Moorings: You can anchor if space is available south of the mooring field, but this location will require long dinghy rides for services ashore. The

Rockport, ME

Rockport Boat Club has a float for temporary tie-ups, but it only accommodates 2-foot drafts at low tide. Rockport Marine has 10 feet of water at its fuel dock at low tide and offers a few slips and moorings for transients. Since the marina does not monitor the radio or provide launch service, pick up a mooring pennant from one of the numbered white buoys, then dinghy in to complete your arrangements. There is ample dinghy space behind the marina's fuel dock. Showers are available, but bring your own towel. Public phones are located in the parking area. The Sail Loft Restaurant, formerly in the space above the boatyard, is no longer in operation.

The Rockport Marine Park on the northwestern side of the inner harbor, just to port of the boat club, has two large floats with 6 feet of water at low tide to accommodate crew changes, trips to replenish the larder and refilling of water tanks. If space permits, overnight tie-ups are sometimes possible. Contact the harbormaster on VHF Channel 16 for availability. Parking space is just ashore of these floats and to the left, with additional parking to the right, past the picnic tables and across the footbridge over the stream leading into the harbor. Here, it is difficult not to notice the lime kilns that were commercially critical to the area a century ago. You may also see the diminutive wood-fired locomotive that hauled lime and cordwood to the kilns.

Short distances west of the marine park are two specialty stores that stock gourmet items, quality groceries, desserts and baked goods. A pizzeria is nearby and The Helm Restaurant (207-236-4337) on Route 1 is a pleasant 20-minute walk from the harbor.

GOIN' ASHORE:

ROCKPORT, ME

Rockport has long been a summer colony for artists and musicians, with historic houses, art galleries, shops, a public library, park and a chilly beach. Yet commercial facilities are few. Apart from the marina, restaurant, a small luncheonette and several gift shops and galleries uphill from the marina and west of the marine park, more serious shopping will require a trip of several miles to Camden. Basic reprovisioning is possible at Hildenon's IGA (35 Railroad Ave., 978-546-2844) about a mile from the marina. A good spot for fresh lobster, other seafood or Black Angus beef is Bayview Lobsters (207-236-2005) at 1 Bayview Landing.

What Rockport lacks in commercial activity, it makes up in traditional maritime offerings. Rockport is home port to the 70-foot windjammer *Timberwind*, which miraculously negotiates a regular passage through the field of moorings to its berth just south of the public floats. On Friday nights, the Camden schooners often anchor in the harbor before returning home the next day.

ADDITIONAL RESOURCES:

- Town of Rockport, **www.town.rockport.me.us**

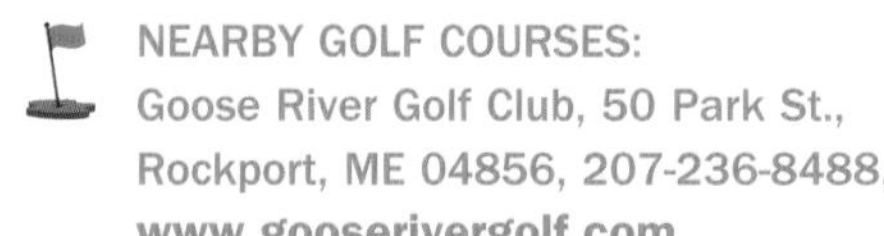

NEARBY GOLF COURSES:
Goose River Golf Club, 50 Park St., Rockport, ME 04856, 207-236-8488, **www.gooserivergolf.com**

NEARBY MEDICAL FACILITIES:
Penobscot Bay Medical Center, 6 Glen Cove Drive, Rockport, ME 04856, 207-569-8200

Robinson Rock

Lying just two miles due east of the abandoned lighthouse still guarding the eastern end of Rockport Harbor, Robinson Rock has no landing, no beacon and no amenities. What it does have are seals. A close review of the chart clearly shows Robinson Rock and its nearby neighbors stretching to the north and east, making it possible for cruisers and commercial seal-watching vessels to move in for a close view of the aquatic animals. But do not expect a rollicking display—the harbor seals' idea of a good time seems to be enjoying the fresh air and sunshine on these rocks and rolling over occasionally for a great yawn. Two-and-a-half miles to the northeast, many more seals are usually in search of sunshine on Mouse Island and on the rocky ledges stretching southward toward Goose Island.

Camden

At the foot of Mount Battie, Camden is one of Maine's busiest and best-equipped harbors. This resort town suffers from bumper-to-bumper traffic ashore all summer. The harbor is full of boats, including the coastal schooner fleet that offers week-long cruises of the spectacular Maine coast. In town you can shop, restock the ship's stores, visit a hilltop library or climb Mount Battie for an incomparable view of all of Penobscot Bay.

NAVIGATION: Use Chart 13302. Camden Harbor is marked by red bell buoy "2," located about 600 yards from the accessible southeastern entrance. As you approach from the south, The Graves, marked by flashing green gong buoy "13," may be left to either side; in poor visibility, however, it is best to pass east of this shoal.

Upon entering the harbor, Curtis Island, identified by a fixed green light atop a 52-foot flashing green (occulting) lighthouse, should be left to the south and west. The northeastern approach is marked by the red-and-white bell buoy "CH," located just less than a half mile east/northeast off Northeast Point, which is identified by 20-foot flashing red "2." Green daybeacon "3" warns of the Inner Ledges to port.

Dockage and Moorings: Newcomers to Camden Harbor can be assisted with dockage and mooring needs by contacting the Harbormaster, Camden Yacht Club or Wayfarer Marine. The Harbormaster monitors VHF Channel 16 or can be reached at 207-236-7969; Camden Yacht Club monitors VHF Channel 68 and Wayfarer Marine is available on VHF Channel 71. During July and August, cruisers are advised to call in advance to reserve dockage.

Camden, ME

CAMDEN		Largest Vessel Accommodated	VHF Channel Monitored	Transient Berths / Total Berths	Approach / Dockside Depth (reported)	Floating Docks	Gas / Diesel	Groceries, Ice, Marine Supplies, Snacks	Repairs: Hull, Engine, Propeller	Lift (tonnage), Crane, Rail	1=110V, 2=220V, B=Both, Max Amps	Laundry, Pool, Showers	Pump-Out Station	Nearby: Grocery Store, Motel, Restaurant
		Dockage					Supplies		Services					
1. Rockport Marine Inc.	207-236-9651	105		5/5	20/10	F	GD	I	HEP	L50,C	B/50			GMR
2. Camden Yacht Club	207-236-3014	50	68		12/8									GMR
3. Willey Wharf	207-236-3256	100		1/7	10/10	F	GD				B/100	S		GMR
4. Camden Town Docks	207-236-7969	160	16	10/	10/10	F					1/50			GMR
5. Wayfarer Marine Corp. 🖳 WiFi	207-236-4378	100	71	18/49	12/14	F	GD	GIMS	HEP	L110,C	B/50	LS	P	GMR

Corresponding chart(s) not to be used for navigation. 🖳 Internet Access WiFi Wireless Internet Access

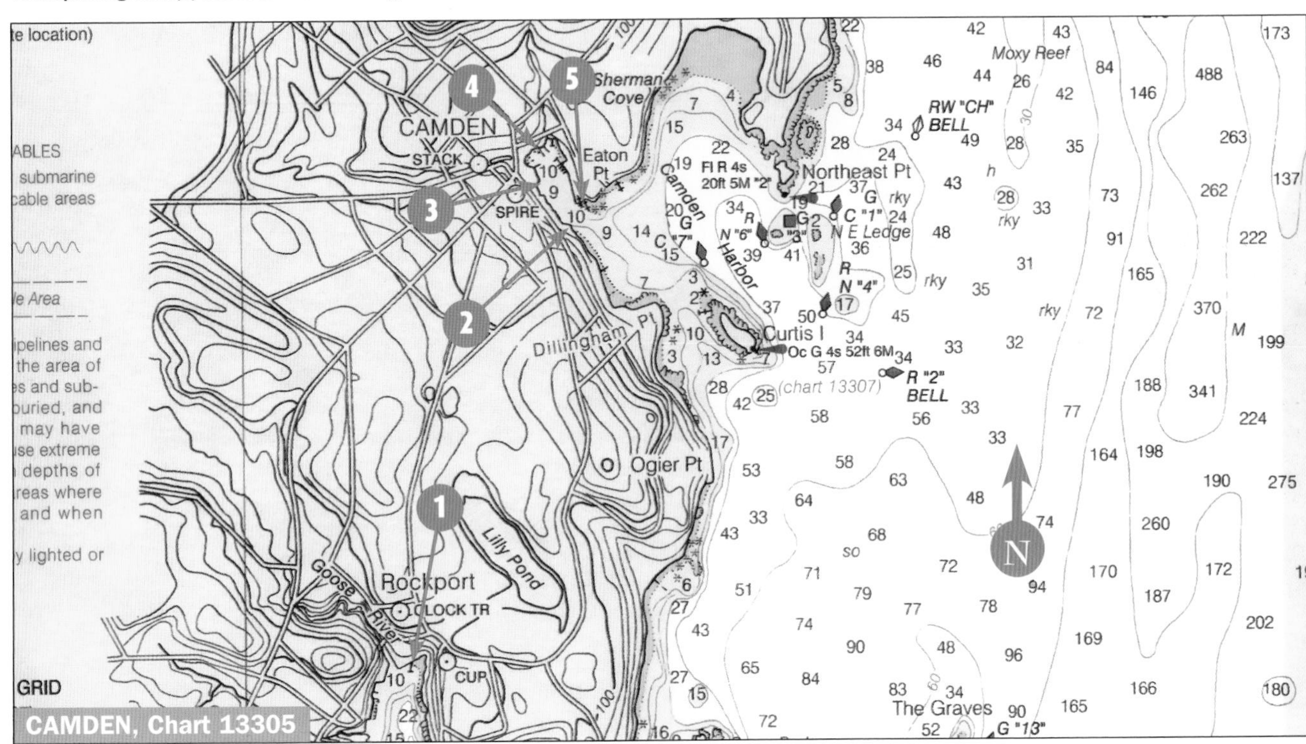

CAMDEN, Chart 13305

The town docks, which offer the easiest access to shoreside shopping, have 15-, 30- and 50-amp service.

Across the harbor, Wayfarer Marine has a large number of guest moorings and a few deepwater slips. Located on Eaton Point, this fully equipped marina and boatyard has complete rigging, carpentry, engine and electronic shops, along with heavy lifting and moving equipment or haul-outs. You can purchase both gasoline and diesel at the fuel dock. They also have a pump-out station on the fuel dock. There are restrooms, showers and laundry facilities and a launch service for customers.

Immediately across from Wayfarer Marine, on the town side of the harbor, Wiley Wharf has 140 feet of dock space with limited access to both gasoline and diesel fuel. Wiley's has one guest float in the inner harbor and a few transient moorings in the outer harbor.

Camden Yacht Club has inner floats and outer harbor moorings. Transients are welcome at the club's dock for short 20-minute tie-ups for crew changes and to take on water or drop off trash. The club also provides harbor launch services.

Anchorage: The only anchorage available in Camden is in Sherman Cove, the northern bight of Camden Harbor, in 7 to 22 feet of water at low tide. There is usually plenty of room to anchor here, but watch out for the numerous boats on long anchor rodes that accommodate a 10-foot tidal range.

GOIN' ASHORE: CAMDEN, ME

For a map, area guidebook and calendar of events, stop at the Chamber of Commerce, located in the cedar shake building just inland of the town landing. A half-block inland from the chamber at the corner of Elm and Bayview streets, French and Brawn Marketplace (207-236-3361, the closest grocery store), has a full-service deli, custom-cut meats, seafood, baked goods and fresh produce. Within yards of French and Brawn are two banks with ATMs. Half a mile south, at 83 Elm St., is Reny's

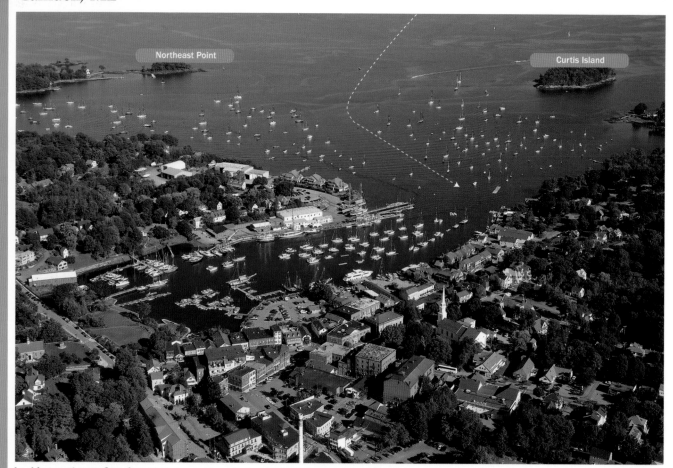

Looking east over Camden. (Not to be used for navigation.) WATERWAY GUIDE PHOTOGRAPHY

Department Store, which carries a full line of discount-priced child and adult clothing. Hannaford Supermarket (145 Elm St.), a full-scale grocery, is a mile south of downtown. Camden has two second-hand bookstores: Stone Soup (35 Main St., 207-763-3354) and ABCD Books (23 Bay View St., 207-236-3903). The Owl and Turtle (32 Washington St., 207-236-4769), named Maine's best independent bookstore, is located in the Knox Mill, about a block from French and Brawn Marketplace, at the corner of Washington and Mechanic streets. It has thousands of titles as well as a complete line of cruising guides and charts for New England waters.

Casual restaurants near the harbor include Cappy's Chowder House (207-236-2254, 1 Main St.)—busy and family oriented; Atlantica Gallery and Grille (207-236-6011, 1 Bayview Landing)—native seafood, beverages and homemade pastries; Bayview Lobsters (207-236-2005, Bayview Landing)—Angus beef and local seafood and lobsters; Peter Ott's (207-236-4032, 16 Bayview St.); Waterfront Restaurant (207-236-3747, 40 Bay View St.) and Frogwater Café (207-236-8998, 31 Elm St.)—small and friendly, with vegetarian specialties, meats, seafood and pasta. Fitzpatrick's Café (207-236-2041) at Bay View Landing comes well recommended. For European-style dining featuring fresh Maine ingredients, try Francine Bistro Café (207-230-0083) at 55 Chestnut St.

ADDITIONAL RESOURCES:

- Camden-Rockport-Lincolnville Chamber of Commerce, **www.camdenme.org**

NEARBY GOLF COURSES:
Goose River Golf Club, 50 Park St.,
Rockport, ME 04856, 207-236-8488,
www.gooserivergolf.com

NEARBY MEDICAL FACILITIES:
Penobscot Bay Medical Center, 6 Glen Cove Drive,
Rockport, ME 04856, 207-596-8200

Above Camden

North of Camden, the steep shore is broken by few harbors. You can take a ferry from Lincolnville to Islesboro in midbay. A convenient launching ramp is adjacent to the ferry dock. The harbor, charted as Ducktrap Harbor, is open to the south, but tenable in calm weather. Lincolnville Beach has a post office, small grocery and several good restaurants. Chez Michel (2532 Atlantic Hwy., 207-789-5600) is worth a stop for bouillabaisse, fresh lobster dishes and pasta. Whale's Tooth Restaurant and Pub (2531 Atlantic Hwy., 207-789-5200) has good food and unbeatable views from its outside dining area.

Saturday Cove, about nine miles northeast from Camden, is protected except from the east. Northport, farther north, is good in a southwester and also has a yacht club and golf course. Although there is no defined harbor, you may safely anchor in 23-foot depths just east of Browns Head near the mouth of Little River.

Belfast

The name means "good anchorage," and Belfast is a refurbished recreational port with several recreational-boat amenities. The entrance to Belfast Harbor is marked by Steels Ledge Monument Light, which makes a good radar target. You can anchor off the entrance to the river west of Steels Ledge in 19- to 28-foot depths.

The Belfast waterfront has undergone a renaissance in the last few years. There is now a town dock, which offers 25 slips on floating docks that are all available to transients, as well as rental moorings. Contact the harbormaster on VHF Channel 09 for a slip or mooring assignment. A classic motor cruiser makes several trips per day to Castine as well as sightseeing trips in the area.

The downtown business district is revitalized with several good restaurants and stores, including the Belfast Cooperative (123 High St., 207-338-2532), a full-service market featuring organic and homegrown items and a cafe. Darby's (155 High St., 207-338-2339) has been a local favorite for years. Rollie's Bar and Grill (207-338-4502) at 37 Main Street is a great stop for burgers and other casual food. Nearby, Scoops (207-338-3350) offers ice cream, crepes, specialty coffees and other sweet delights. The house special is the "Bombe," 28 scoops of ice cream and all the toppings you can handle.

Although the town has burned twice, several historic buildings remain, including First Church, which has a Paul Revere bell in the belfry. On the third Saturday in July, the town holds a big parade and what residents claim is the world's biggest chicken barbecue, followed by a fireworks display in the shoreside city park. Later in the summer, an August street fair attracts artists, craftspeople and antiques swappers.

Custom boatbuilder French and Webb (207-338-6706) is located in buildings bordering the waterfront park and welcomes visitors. The craftsmanship is the finest that Maine has to offer. The Belfast Free Library (207-338-3884), 106 High St., is open to the public every day except Sunday. Public access computers are available.

Early July in Belfast is time for the Maine Celtic Celebration featuring food, dance, highland games and vendors/exhibitors of all kinds.

Searsport

Four miles northeast of Belfast, the expansive, wide-open harbor of Searsport offers no obstructions on approach and easy shore access. This ancient home to ship captains and flourishing maritime industries is today dominated by a recreational small-boat fleet, including serious anglers.

Anchorage and Moorings: The anchorage and mooring field for recreational boats is to port on approaching the wide, scalloped harbor. Oil tankers, potato reefers and other large commercial ships dominate a more protected refuge in Long Cove, beyond Mack Point east of the village.

As you approach the recreational fleet, check in with the Searsport harbormaster (monitoring VHF Channels 09, 10, 71 and 78A) to inquire about the availability of a mooring or for current anchoring instructions. The town mooring (#1, attached to a large granite block) may be available, or possibly the museum's large mooring ball (#55, hooked to a 10-ton block) will be unclaimed. Otherwise, you will likely be anchoring outside the mooring field in 23- to 32-foot depths at mean low water with a 9-foot tidal range. Prevailing southwesterlies are tempered by Islesboro Island, yet it is often quite breezy in the afternoon. The accompanying seesaw action of waves over a long fetch regularly sends boats on insufficient scope drifting into the mooring field even though the holding is good; make sure your anchor is well set.

The town dock complex (periodically dredged to a 4-foot low-water depth) makes it possible for smaller vessels and those working with the tide to tie up for two- to four-hour periods on one of the inner docks. Water, electricity and trash disposal are available. For most visitors, it will be more convenient to pull a tender up to one of the floating dinghy landings (note signs with rules for each dock) inside the L-shaped outer dock for the walk to town.

GOIN' ASHORE: SEARSPORT, ME

Searsport's Main Street (U.S. Route 1) is about a quarter mile due north from the docks. There, within a few blocks, you will locate a well-stocked hardware store; the town post office; two banks; a pharmacy; and a bookstore with many used volumes. The Penobscot Marine Museum (5 Church St., 207-548-2529) is farther along to the east at the end of the business district. The museum's evolving collection of marine paintings, treasures brought home from abroad by local ships years ago, restored 19th-century buildings and re-creations of Searsport life in a bygone era are almost certain to appeal. About a mile farther east on U.S. 1, Hamilton Marine Inc. (155 E. Main St., 207-548-6302), the largest marine supply store north of Boston, has marine supplies, gear, equipment, books and charts. This family-run operation will special-order parts for rapid delivery. On the east side of town, near Hamilton Marine, is The Rhumb Line Restaurant (200 E. Main St., 207-548-2600), serving dinner only, but an excellent choice for fine dining.

ADDITIONAL RESOURCES:

- Searsport Business and Visitors Guide, **www.searsportme.net**

NEARBY GOLF COURSES:
Searsport Pines Golf Course, 240 Mt. Ephraim Road, Searsport, ME 04974, 207-548-2854, **www.searsportpines.com**

NEARBY MEDICAL FACILITIES:
Waldo County General Hospital, 118 Northport Ave., Belfast, ME 04915, 207-338-2500

Looking north over Bucksport. (Not to be used for navigation.) WATERWAY GUIDE PHOTOGRAPHY

Penobscot River

Another of Maine's mighty rivers, flowing from deep within the interior, the Penobscot River was the embattled boundary between the English and the French in Colonial times. During the hectic logging years of the 19th century, it became the major artery for the flow of vast quantities of timber. The Penobscot River has significant currents; be sure to make your transit with a favorable tide.

NAVIGATION: Use Charts 13302 and 13309. The Penobscot River is navigable for 25 miles to Bangor, but the current flows swiftly at its mouth and must be entered on a rising tide. Past Fort Point Cove, the river narrows over the four miles to Bucksport, and then widens out at Frankfort Flats, another two miles up the river. Heavy commercial traffic makes night running tricky. A public observatory in the western tower offers a tremendous view of Penobscot Bay and the surrounding area. For boaters, this will involve anchoring or mooring in Bucksport and walking or getting a taxi to the bridge. A combined trip to the bridge and Fort Knox Park makes a great outing. Contact Bucksport Chamber of Commerce for information about Ft. Knox and the Bridge/Observatory at 207-469-6818.

Anchorage and Moorings: If you anchor, make sure you are solidly hooked. Much of the bottom, covered with sawdust from lumbering days, has poor holding. Across from Bucksport is Fort Knox Park, with its granite fortress and picnic grounds. Fort Knox was built in the 1840s to defend against a feared third British invasion (following the Revolutionary War and the War of 1812), which never occurred.

Bucksport, a paper mill town, has a few moorings and a floating dock for temporary use just beyond the high fixed bridge. Shops are handy downtown, and the old railroad station has been converted into a historical museum. The head of navigation is less than four miles farther upriver, at Winterport, offering berths, repairs and storage. Bucksport has improved its waterfront with a walkway along much of the town as well as park areas.

Winterport

The 19th-century town of Winterport is an interesting stop on a cruise up the Penobscot. Winterport Marina (207-223-8885) has improved and enlarged its facility, offering 1,000 feet of dock space with water, electricity, haul-out capabilities and fuel. The downtown area is less than a mile away and has many old homes, shops and a small museum.

Bangor

Once the world's largest lumber port, Bangor is about 12 miles upstream from Winterport. For years, the upper reaches of the Penobscot River near Bangor were congested with commercial traffic, polluted with waste from lumber and paper mills and offered no amenities for recreational boats. But that picture has changed. The river has undergone a clean-up, and the neighboring towns of Bangor and Hampden have worked together to develop 11 acres as a

Penobscot River, ME

PENOBSCOT RIVER		Largest Vessel Accommodated	VHF Channel Monitored	Transient Berths / Total Berths	Approach / Dockside Depth (reported)	Floating Docks	Gas / Diesel	Groceries, Ice, Marine Supplies, Snacks	Repairs: Hull, Engine, Propeller	Lift (tonnage), Crane, Rail	1=110V, 2=220V, B=Both, Max Amps	Laundry, Pool, Showers	Pump-Out Station	Nearby: Grocery Store, Motel, Restaurant
		Dockage					Supplies		Services					
1. Belfast City Landing (Internet Access) (Wireless Internet Access)	207-338-1142	160	16/09	25/25	15/13	F	GD	I			B/100	LS	P	GMR
2. Belfast Boatyard	207-338-5098	75	16	2/20	16/10			M	HP		1/30			GMR
3. Searsport Public Landing	207-548-2722	60	16	/3	11/4.5	F		GIM			1/	L		R
4. Bucksport Public Dock (Wireless Internet Access)	207-469-7241	220	16/09		16/15	F								GMR
5. Bucksport Marina	207-989-5840	110	09	6/58	19/6	F	G	IM			2/50	LS	P	GMR
6. Turtle Head Marina Inc. (Internet Access)	207-941-8619	55	16	20/65	30/8	F		IM	HEP	L25	1/30	S	P	
7. Bangor Landing Waterfront Park	207-947-5251	165	16/09	/30	16/15						1/50	S	P	GMR

Corresponding chart(s) not to be used for navigation. Internet Access Wireless Internet Access

PENOBSCOT RIVER, Chart 13309

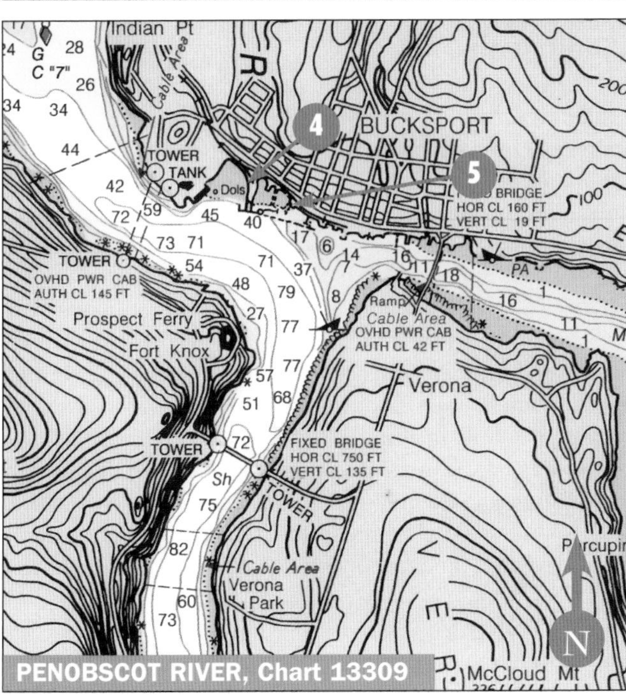

PENOBSCOT RIVER, Chart 13309

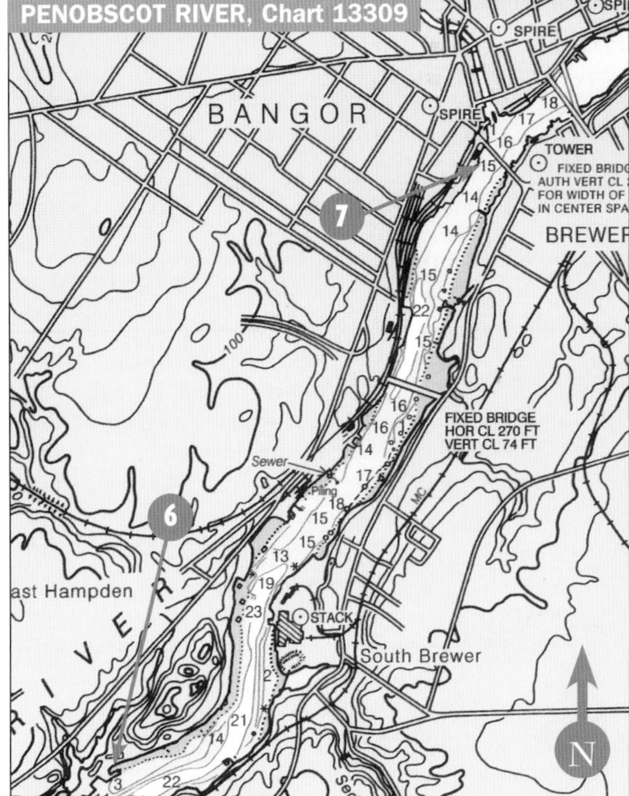

PENOBSCOT RIVER, Chart 13309

Dark Harbor, ME

DARK HARBOR		Largest Vessel Accommodated	VHF Channel Monitored	Transient Berths / Total Berths	Approach / Dockside Depth (reported)	Floating Docks	Gas / Diesel	Groceries, Ice, Marine Supplies, Snacks	Repairs: Hull, Engine, Propeller	Lift (tonnage), Crane, Rail	1=110V, 2=220V, B=Both, Max Amps	Laundry, Pool, Showers	Pump-Out Station	Nearby: Grocery Store, Motel, Restaurant
		Dockage					Supplies		Services					
1. Dark Harbor Boat Yard	207-734-2246	100	09	MOORINGS	14/6		GD	IMS	HEP	LCR	1/30	LS		

Corresponding chart(s) not to be used for navigation. Internet Access Wireless Internet Access

boating center with marina, restaurant, motel and chandlery. The completed project offers moorings and dockage. Bangor today is perhaps best known as the home of best-selling author Stephen King.

Islesboro

A fashionable resort, with grand old estates at Dark Harbor and a busy yachting community, big Islesboro is the heart of a group of islands cutting across Penobscot in mid-bay. The island has ferry service to Lincolnville on the mainland north of Camden.

NAVIGATION: Use Chart 13302. Gilkey Harbor is easily approached from either north or south. The lovely town of Dark Harbor is on its eastern end. The harbor is the hub of a through-passage along Islesboro's southern half, which is the most scenic route to northern Penobscot Bay. Remember, the nuns and cans switch sides at Thrumcap Island. Do not try Bracketts Channel, a privately marked southeastern entrance with ledges, unless you know it well.

Anchorage and Moorings: On the eastern side of Gilkey Harbor, Ames Cove is home to the Tarratine Yacht Club, which is more of a day-sailing than cruising club. No moorings are available here, but there is good holding in the cove, and the nearly 100-year-old clubhouse offers a pleasant visit. To the west, Cradle Cove, shielded by northerly necks of Seven Hundred Acre Island, affords excellent protection and good holding in 11- to 14-foot depths at low tide. The moorings in the cove are available from Dark Harbor Boat Yard, which also offers water, diesel fuel and gasoline at its floating dock.

On entry, mind the private stake-markers identifying the ledges on either side of the channel. Still, there is plenty of room to turn and maneuver. The yard has full repair capabilities, laundry machines, shower (bring your own soap and towel) and a ship's store with both block and cube ice. No other facilities are to be found, but the secluded sea vistas and foggy-forest smells along the island's meandering dirt roads are a double payback for a long walk. Good anchorage in 17- to 28-foot depths may be had in the cove just above Thrumcap Island. The moorings that once welcomed visiting yachts to the Islesboro Inn now are marked PRIVATE. The venerable inn is now a private summer home.

At the northern end of the through-passage, opposite Grindel Point, a mariner's park encompasses all of wild,

DARK HARBOR, Chart 13302

remote Warren Island. Accessible only by boat, not crowded and a regular port of call for the cruising schooners, the park has four free heavy moorings for cruising boats. A dock and float with 4-foot depths at low tide and picnic tables are available, as well as either a park shelter or tent space for camping. Mussels are available for the taking at low tide, and you will find walking paths on the island.

Vinalhaven

Southernmost of the larger islands in Penobscot Bay is Vinalhaven, with its ragged shoreline, satellite islands, scores of coves and anchorages and one major harbor with a remote, picturesque village. The eastern shore is full of gunkholes for exploring—deep indentations that may dry out at low tide.

Carvers Harbor

On the south shore of Vinalhaven, protected by Greens Island and numerous islets and ledges, Carvers Harbor is the island's most important commercial port. Though seemingly ample in size, the harbor is teeming with lobster boats, draggers, seiners, floats and tenders. The village, still displaying public remnants from its granite quarrying heyday (fountains, hitching posts and the like), is a good place to reprovision, dine out or arrange an emergency repair.

NAVIGATION: Use Chart 13305. For Vinalhaven, use Bar Harbor tide tables. For high tide, add 9 minutes; for low tide, add 10 minutes. Carvers Harbor may be approached

Vinalhaven, North Haven, ME

VINALHAVEN, NORTH HAVEN		Largest Vessel Accommodated	VHF Channel Monitored	Transient Berths / Total Berths	Approach / Dockside Depth (reported)	Floating Docks	Gas / Diesel	Groceries, Ice, Marine Supplies, Snacks	Repairs: Hull, Engine, Propeller	Lift (tonnage), Crane, Rail	1=110V, 2=220V, B=Both, Max Amps	Laundry, Pool, Showers	Pump-Out Station	Nearby: Grocery Store, Motel, Restaurant
		Dockage					Supplies		Services					
1. Hopkins Boat Yard	207-863-2551				16/8			M	HEP	L35	/100			GMR
2. Thayer's Y-Knot Boatyard	207-867-4701	50	16/09		4/4			M	HEP	LCR		S		GR
3. J.O. Brown & Son Inc.	207-867-4621	80	16	MOORINGS	15/8		GD	IM	HEP	L15	1/30	LS		GR

Corresponding chart(s) not to be used for navigation. Internet Access Wireless Internet Access

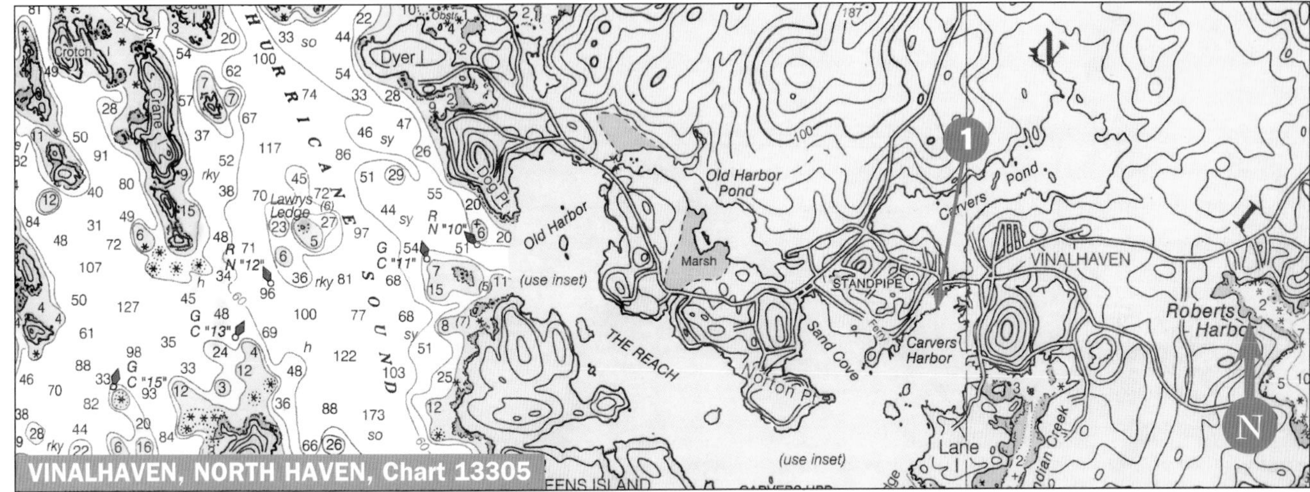

VINALHAVEN, NORTH HAVEN, Chart 13305

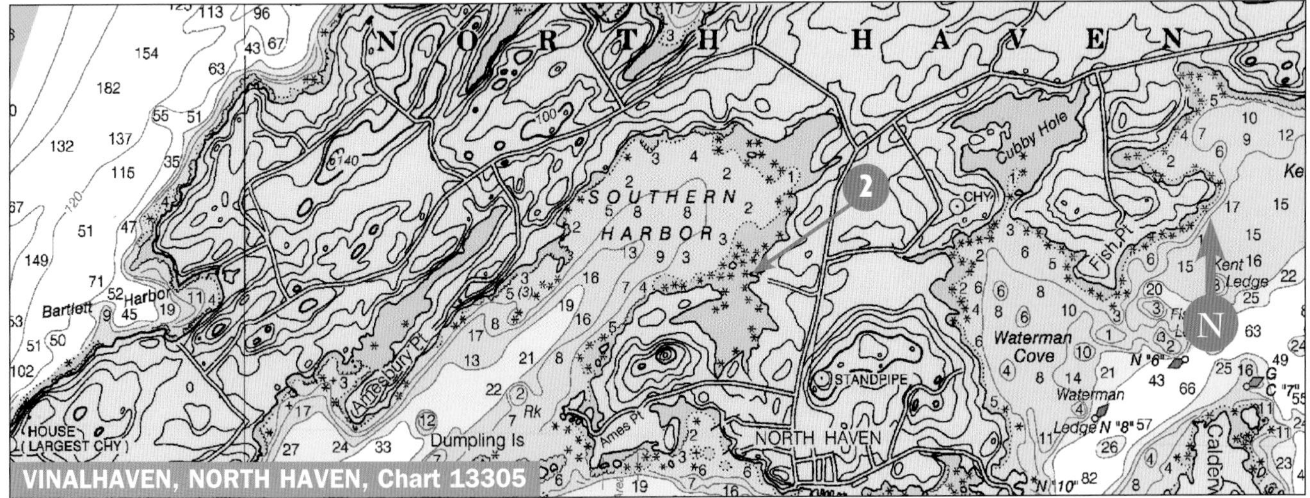

VINALHAVEN, NORTH HAVEN, Chart 13305

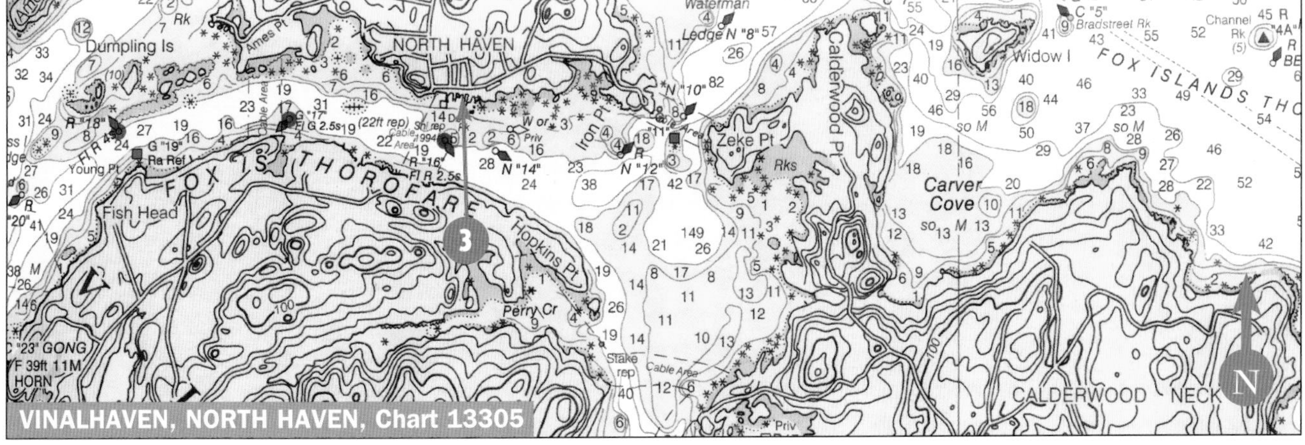

VINALHAVEN, NORTH HAVEN, Chart 13305

Looking north over Carvers Harbor on Vinalhaven Island. (Not to be used for navigation.) WATERWAY GUIDE PHOTOGRAPHY

via marked channels from either south or east, both entering the south end of The Reach between Folly Ledge and Green Ledge, the latter marked by 19-foot-high flashing red "2." The harbor also may be approached via The Reach from Hurricane Sound north of Greens Island, entering the northeastern end of The Reach between green can buoy "11" and red nun buoy "10." Despite well-placed navigation aids, none of these winding, rock- and ledge-strewn passages is the place to be in dense fog.

Anchorage and Moorings: The harbor will likely have a few moorings available for visiting cruisers, but they are hard to spot. Best to call Hopkins Boat Yard or Harbormaster Bob Hopkins (207-863-2551) for availability and location. There may be anchorage space in the southeastern end of the harbor, though swing room will be at a premium. The town-maintained dock at the extreme head of the harbor has ample space for a dinghy tie-up (two-hour limit). Trash barrels are located just above the landing at the town's breakwater.

GOIN' ASHORE:

CARVERS HARBOR, ME

From the town landing and parking lot, immediately across Main Street, Carver's Harbor Market (207-863-4319, almost a supermarket), has fresh vegetables, fruits, meats, fresh live lobsters, beer, wine and dry goods. The post office is next door. The Harbor Gawker (207-863-9365) serves fresh Maine lobster. West of the market on Main Street is the Paper Store (207-863-4826, out-of-town newspapers, current magazines and books of local interest); Key Bank; Vinalhaven Fuel (207-863-4441) propane tank exchanges, empties are taken to the mainland to be refilled); and Hopkins Boat Yard (207-863-2551) for most emergency repairs. Carvers Harbor is a great place to stretch the legs, seek out classic municipal watering troughs and other remnants of granite quarrying days and visit the Nature Conservancy preserve on Lane Island (walking south from the head of the harbor). The Vinalhaven Historical Society (207-863-4410), up the hill from town, is well worth a visit.

ADDITIONAL RESOURCES:

- Vinalhaven Chamber of Commerce, **www.vinalhaven.org**

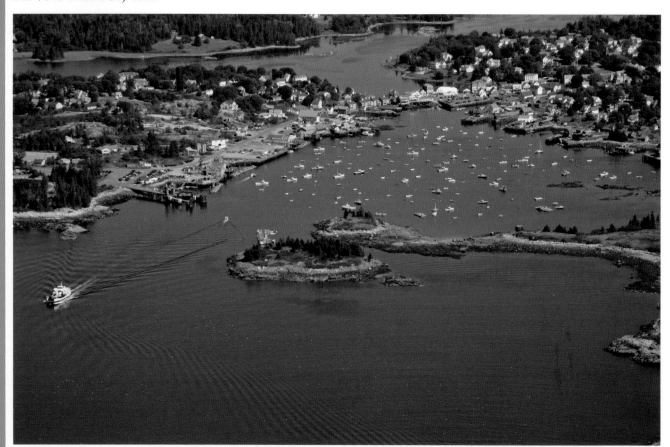

NEARBY GOLF COURSES:
Goose River Golf Club, 50 Park St., Rockport, ME 04856, 207-236-8488, **www.gooserivergolf.com**

NEARBY MEDICAL FACILITIES:
Penobscot Bay Medical Center, 6 Glen Cove Drive, Rockport, ME 04856, 207-596-8200

Hurricane Sound

Southwest of Vinalhaven, parallel strings of classic Maine islands form this delightful passage, with its remote harbors and scenic vistas. You can enter the sound from the south between Greens Island and Hurricane Island, keeping well clear of Deadman Ledge (charted, but unmarked) and the northerly running reefs to the east of Hurricane Island.

Hurricane Island

Moorings: Hurricane Island welcomes visiting mariners. Four guest moorings (marked by bright orange floats with pick-up toggles) are located on the east side of the island on a first-come, first-served basis (overnight or as a day stop). On approach, look out for the spindle-marked ledge fronting the east side of the island, which will block a straightforward run at the moorings. Or call ahead for instructions on VHF Channel 16. Stop at the rescue station or the main office above the mess hall to sign in and pick up a map of the island. To inquire in advance about visiting the island, call the Rockland office of Outward Bound at 207-594-5548.

GOIN' ASHORE:

HURRICANE ISLAND, ME

Home of the Outward Bound School, where students are given rigorous summer courses in survival, Hurricane Island (west of Greens Island in Hurricane Sound) was once the site of a thriving granite quarry business with a local population in excess of 1,000. The industry had a short life, lasting only from the mid-1870s until 1915, but in its heyday, island granite was used in the bridges and buildings of major cities, including the Metropolitan Museum of Art in New York City. The old granite quarry is now filled with water, providing Outward Bound with a convenient training obstacle.

The 2.5-mile path around the island winds through woods loaded with raspberry and blueberry bushes and field-pea vines to an oceanside granite ledge offering a magnificent view of island-dotted seascapes. The path continues past a summerhouse, cantilevered from a sheer cliff over a breathtaking view of the southern approach to Penobscot Bay. From there, it is a short walk to the Outward Bound School's rock-climbing and high-rope courses. When classes are in session, visitors may observe from a distance but are asked not to disturb the students' concentration. Smoking and fires are prohibited.

ADDITIONAL RESOURCES:

- Vinalhaven Chamber of Commerce, **www.vinalhaven.org**

NEARBY GOLF COURSES:
Goose River Golf Club, 50 Park St., Rockport, ME 04856, 207-236-8488, **www.gooserivergolf.com**

NEARBY MEDICAL FACILITIES:
Penobscot Bay Medical Center, 6 Glen Cove Drive, Rockport, ME 04856, 207-596-8200

Brimstone Island

Off the southeastern tip of Vinalhaven Island is magnificent Brimstone Island. All pure volcanic rock, the island has beaches of round black stones; on calm days you can land on the beaches on the north side. Brimstone Island is privately owned, so respect the property: no fires, no smoking and no litter. It is not suitable for an overnight anchorage.

White Islands

This truly beautiful cluster of windswept isles lies just northwest of Hurricane Island and is often the short-term home of Outward Bound students on their solos. In clear weather, you can enter the narrow anchorage with relative ease from the south between Big White Island to the west and Little White Island to the east. Holding is good in mud, but swing room is in short supply, and the combination of strong currents and emerging boulders in the tidal ebb might make a night there more memorable than you would like. Big White Island is easy to approach from the north by dinghy.

Cedar and Lawrys Islands

Just north of Crane Island, Cedar and Lawrys islands form a protected cove with easy access and good holding ground. The sheer rock faces of Cedar Island offer some of the cleanest and most delightful mussels in Maine.

Long Cove

At the northeastern end of Hurricane Sound, due east of Leadbetter Island, Long Cove forms a remote mini-fjord stretching for the better part of a mile into the interior of Vinalhaven Island. American eagles nest here, and their aerial presence offers a rare treat. Ospreys, too, are here in abundance. Their fishing acrobatics at the far end of the inner cove are a daily event.

NAVIGATION: Use Chart 13305. The entrance to Long Cove is marked by a great pile of granite tailings on the hill to the right of the channel and visible for some distance from the west. Enter the channel just north of Fiddlehead Island. The channel then turns left and narrows as it enters the inner anchorage, which might be overcrowded on a summer weekend.

Still, there is usually room to set a hook, with good holding in the protected location, by proceeding east to somewhat deeper water (25- to 30-foot depths at low water). Near the top of a rising tide, it is possible to cross the reef that (at low water) cuts off access to the far reaches of the cove. The water deepens appreciably beyond the reef with numerous pools of 20 to 30 feet at low tide, making good anchorage spots amid rustic surroundings. This remote setting is popular with Outward Bound instructors, who direct their charges to refreshing swims at daybreak after a night's rest on the oars of their longboats.

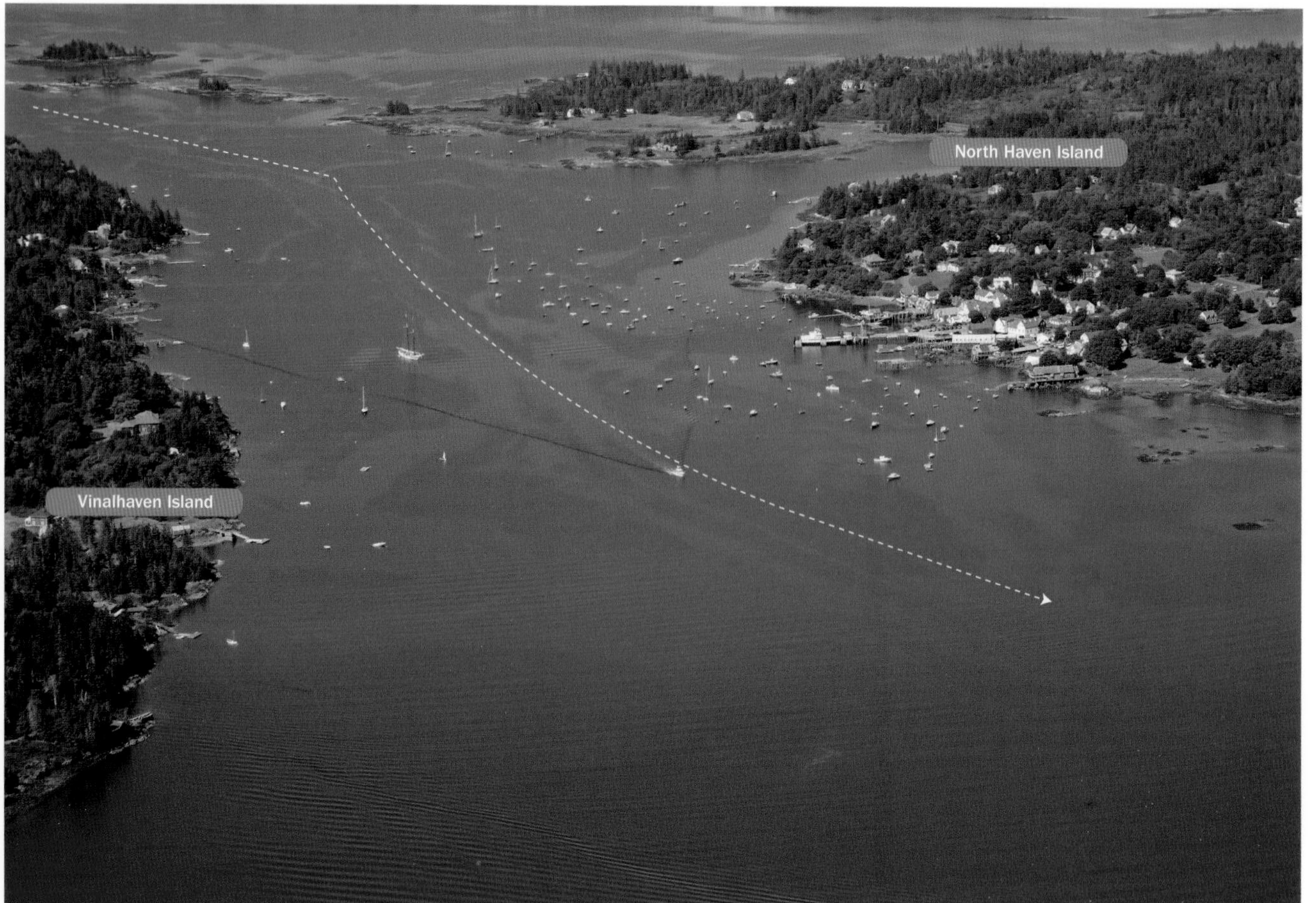

Looking west over Fox Islands Thorofare. (Not to be used for navigation.) WATERWAY GUIDE PHOTOGRAPHY

North Haven Island

The northern cap of the archipelago known as the Fox Islands (called after the abundant silver foxes seen by the first explorer here), North Haven Island with its various channels, coves and islets, offers exciting and scenic cruising. Excellent, uncluttered harbors are abundant, and an amazing variety of "one-off" (custom) and other classic cruising boats ply these waters. You will contend with obstructions, dense fog, swift currents and extreme tidal ranges. For the most part, the area is well charted and marked.

Pulpit Harbor

NAVIGATION: Use Chart 13305. On the northwestern shore of North Haven, guarded by pointed Pulpit Rock, is popular Pulpit Harbor. Do not be dismayed if you see a line of boats ahead of you turning in; there is plenty of room. Narrow coves fanning outward from the entrance provide abundant space. Entry is easy, though you might not think so until you get close enough to see the rock with the osprey nest. Enter between the rock and the eastern shore.

Anchorage: The harbor is well-protected, and anchorage is secure in mud, but you will have to cope with some kelp here. Latecomers will be obliged to anchor in more than 20 feet of water toward the center of the harbor at low tide.

At the eastern end of the harbor, a public float provides a dinghy dock and short-term tie-up space for moderate-sized boats to take on fresh water. A public phone is located just beyond the footbridge leading to shore.

Fox Islands Thorofare

NAVIGATION: Use Chart 13305. The most popular passage across Penobscot Bay, Fox Islands Thorofare runs between North Haven and Vinalhaven islands. It is about seven miles long and is well-marked, with obstructions clearly charted and buoyed. Note that the buoys lead from east to west. It has several snug anchorages, though holding can be poor over rock. You will find excellent harbors for rustic but secure anchorage both to the north and south of this beautiful channel.

Southern Harbor

NAVIGATION: Use Chart 13305. Entrance to this nearly two-mile-long bight is straightforward during clear weather in the relatively wide channel between Amesbury Point and the Dumpling Islands. Instead of entering the Fox Island Thorofare from the west, leave the Sugar Loaves and Calderwood Rock well to starboard, steering a course straight down the center of the channel between Amesbury Point and the easternmost outcropping of the Dumpling Islands.

Anchorage and Moorings: You can anchor in 10- to 17-foot depths at low water, with relatively secure holding in a soft mud bottom. Moorings are also available from Thayer's Y-Knot Boatyard (1 Main St., 207-867-4701). Southern Harbor is exposed to the prevailing southwesterlies, which can kick up some wave action at times.

North Haven

This quiet village is about halfway through Fox Islands Thorofare, centered on the ferry landing. The village and surrounding island countryside have long been a summer refuge for families from among the leading names of American industry, law and politics. Reprovisioning is no longer possible in the village, but you can dial the grocery (from a pay phone outside the ferry office) for a ride to a good-sized store about two miles away. Call North Haven Grocery at 207-867-2233.

On the water, just east of J. O. Brown and Son Boat Yard, is the Coal Wharf Restaurant (207-867-4739), dinners only, daily, with its own ample dinghy dock. The old village store has been reborn as a community center, with a coffee shop and activities for all ages, including plays and films.

Anchorage and Moorings: Anchorage is possible outside the mooring field adjacent to the village waterfront (giving the ferry approach a wide berth), but it is not recommended because of uncertain holding and rapid, bidirectional currents that scour this area. Fortunately, vacant rental moorings are almost always available for a modest fee. West of the obvious ferry landing (center village), moorings (marked NHC) may be rented from the local yacht club (North Haven Casino), with easy access to the club's dinghy dock. J.O. Brown and Son (rentals marked JOB) own all moorings east of the ferry landing. Pick one up and pay the fee in the antique yard office ashore. Brown's offers emergency hull, prop and engine repair services, a 15-ton lift, all fuels, an amazing assortment of spares and odd-lot parts and rapid availability of marine equipment and supplies from the mainland. You also can purchase live lobsters from Brown's tank. You cannot dispose of trash here or anywhere else on the island.

Perry Creek

Just south of Fox Islands Thorofare, tucked behind Hopkins Point (less than a mile southwest of North Haven as the crow flies), Perry Creek offers a series of small, pastoral and well-protected anchorages. Homes hug the shoreline, and their private moorings dot the harbor.

NAVIGATION: Use Chart 13305. Proceeding south from the Thorofare, enter at the center of the channel between the small island off the tip of Hopkins Point to port and the shore to starboard. At high tide, submerged ledges extending from both north and south will not be visible; centering on the channel is critical. Once fully past the small island at the entrance to starboard, favor the shore to port to avoid a 4-foot-deep spot at low tide.

Anchorage: Anchor west of the cable area marked on the chart in 8- to 12-foot depths at low water. The holding is good in mud, but keep to the center of the creek when anchoring at high tide to avoid ending up with more than an anchor on the bottom. A falling tide reveals muddy banks gradually sloping toward the center.

Seal Cove

Easier to enter than Perry Creek, Seal Cove is less picturesque and more exposed when the wind veers to the north. Pick a spot southwest of the cable area indicated on the chart, and north of the small island located near the western shore of the cove. Holding is good in 13-foot depths at low tide.

Kent Cove

Fully exposed to the south, Kent Cove is less favored than other harbors in this region. Yet it is easily accessible, and anchorage is secure in the northeastern bight of the cove, between Indian Point and the island off the western shore.

Carver Cove

This cove is easily entered from either west or east of Widow Island, which straddles the Fox Islands Thorofare. Best anchorage is found at the mouth of the cove's extension at its south end in 8- to 13-foot depths at low tide. Holding is good in mud, with good protection from prevailing southerlies. When the wind backs to the northeast or north, however, this is not the place to be. Wildlife is abundant here.

Winter Harbor (Vinalhaven Island)

One of the most rustic and unspoiled anchorages on Vinalhaven Island, Winter Harbor is relatively easy to enter and well-protected from every direction save the northeast.

NAVIGATION: Use Chart 13305. Enter south of Calderwood Neck, north of Bluff Head and the Hen Islands. Steer a center-channel course to avoid the entrance's 2-foot-deep spot near the Calderwood Neck side. Otherwise, passage is unencumbered and the scenery is unsurpassed.

Anchorage: During the height of the summer cruising season, there are likely to be several boats anchored in the center of this beautiful sea finger, yet anchorage is less than certain here. More secure holding is reported on the Penobscot Island side of the harbor, in 8- to 10-foot depths at mean low water, just northeast of the two small islets immediately across from the unmistakable 163-foot sheer rock bluff on the Calderwood Neck side of the harbor. Beware of the charted, but unmarked 2-foot-deep spot in the middle of the way, just beyond the bluff. The harbor is passable by small boat for almost two miles into the interior of Vinalhaven as it becomes the Mill River.

Seal Bay

In some eyes, the anchorages of Seal Bay surpass even those of Winter Harbor in their unspoiled scenic beauty and secluded charm.

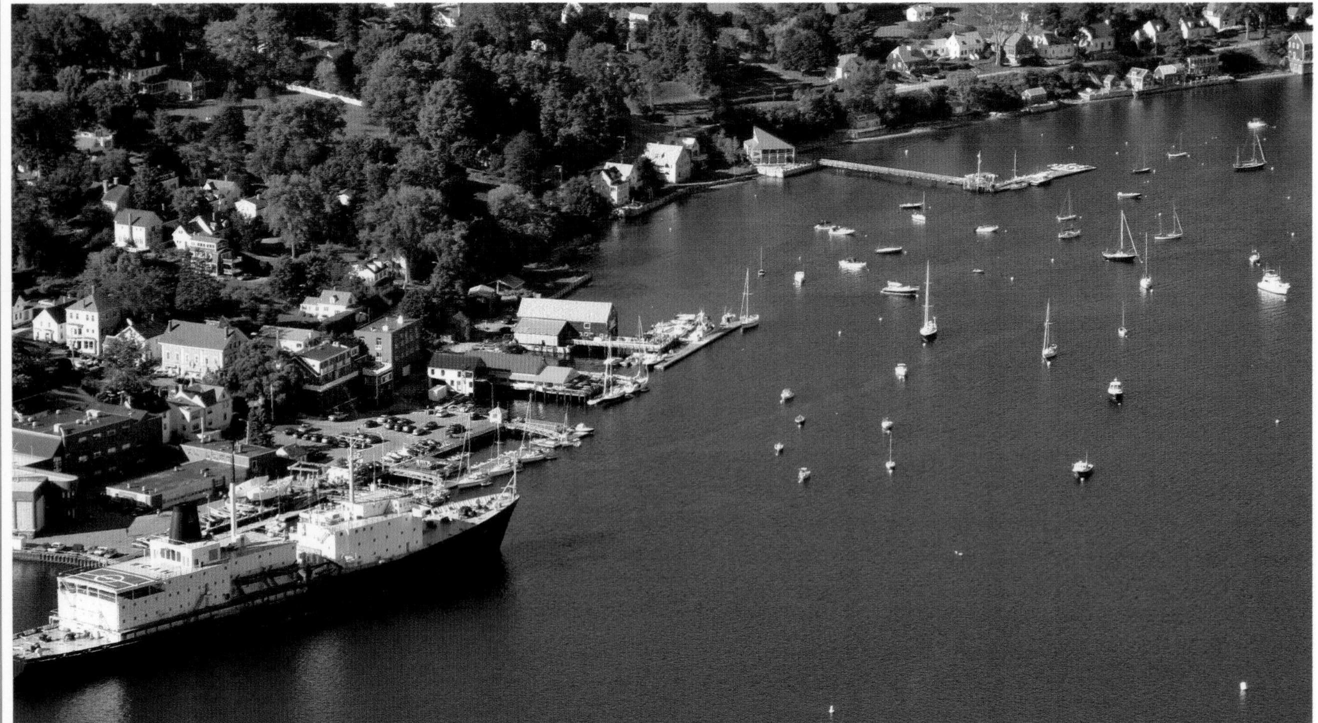

Looking north over Castine. (Not to be used for navigation.) WATERWAY GUIDE PHOTOGRAPHY

NAVIGATION: Use Chart 13305. Entering from East Penobscot Bay on the same course as taken to Winter Harbor, steer center-channel just past the westernmost of the two Hen Islands, and then take an abrupt turn to port along the bold shore of the western Hen Island. Obstructions along the eastern end of Penobscot Island are still visible at high water and are relatively bold. Using Chart 13305 on a clear day, work your way around the east end of Penobscot Island, looking out for the locally placed slender stakes that mark hazardous rocks.

Anchorage: Your reward for this effort will be a serene and thoroughly protected anchorage in good holding between the northern ends of Burnt Island and Hay Island in 7- to 10-foot depths (mean low water). Additional good anchorage is found in about 10 feet of water at the southeast end of the bay. Approach on a mid-tide or better to avoid several low spots reported on the path to this location. Thick-blooded locals favor the sandy beach on Hay Island for swimming and sunbathing.

Castine

At the head of East Penobscot Bay, off the northern end of Islesboro, the bluffs of Dice Head guard the entrance to the Bagaduce River and Castine, site of Fort George, a British stronghold during the American Revolution.

Anchorage: The holding ground is poor off Castine, where depths of the Bagaduce River run to 12 fathoms, and swift tidal currents scour the bottom. A secure anchorage can be found, however, to the south. The closest anchorage to town, out of the main current, is the area just west of Hospital Island, or more protected Smith Cove. The most attractive shelter under bold, forested shores is well inside, southeast of Sheep Island. When heading for these anchorages, be careful of the buoyed Middle Ground rock in mid-harbor. It comes clear out of the water with spring tides.

Most interesting of Castine's anchorages is Holbrook Harbor, unnamed on the chart, and entered from East Penobscot Bay between Nautilus Island and Holbrook Island. (Stay clear of the buoyed mid-channel rock in the entrance.) An alternate entrance to Holbrook Harbor is between Cape Rosier on the south and Holbrook and Ram Island (known locally as "Rain") on the north side.

Approximately four nautical miles south of Cape Rosier, one of the prettiest anchorages in upper Penobscot Bay is formed by an unspoiled cluster of spruce-capped islets between Great Spruce Head Island to the west and Butter Island to the east. The area is known as the Barred Islands. If you are entering the lagoon-like bay formed by these islands for the first time, it is best to enter from the northwest at below half-tide, after running southeasterly past green can "1A" off Great Spruce Head Island. Favor the northernmost of the islands, Escargot, since it is bold, while a reef extends to the north from Little Barred Island on the southern side of the harbor entrance. Anchorage to the southeast of Little Barred Island affords good holding, with protection offered by a sandbar and rocks that block the prevailing southwesterlies. The ospreys provide constant entertainment as they fish for their dinner here.

Moorings: Friendly Castine Yacht Club has two guest moorings for boats of up to 35 feet. It might also be possible to lie alongside the club's dock on a space-available basis for an overnight fee. Inside, showers are available for a small fee. Dennett's Wharf and Eaton's Boatyard also offer rental moorings and might have space for an overnight stay alongside their docks. Dennett's Wharf has floating docks, an excellent restaurant and a great waterfront bar.

Castine, Bucks Harbor, ME

CASTINE, BUCKS HARBOR		Largest Vessel Accommodated	VHF Channel Monitored	Transient Berths / Total Berths	Approach / Dockside Depth (reported)	Floating Docks	Gas / Diesel	Groceries, Ice, Marine Supplies, Snacks	Repairs: Hull, Engine, Propeller	Lift (tonnage), Crane, Rail	1=110V, 2=220V, B=Both, Max Amps	Laundry, Pool, Showers	Pump-Out Station	Nearby: Grocery Store, Motel, Restaurant
		Dockage					Supplies		Services					
1. Castine Town Dock	207-266-7711	140	09/16		60/25						/50			GMR
2. Eaton's Boat Yard	207-326-8579	200	09/16	6/6	50/13	F	GD	IM	HEP		B/100	S		GMR
3. Seal Cove Boatyard Inc.	207-326-4422	60	09/16	MOORINGS	8/8	F		M	HEP	L35,C14,R	1/30			
4. Buck's Harbor Marine	207-326-8839	110	16/09	MOORINGS	28/20	F	GD	IMS		C	1/30	LS		GR

Corresponding chart(s) not to be used for navigation. Internet Access Wireless Internet Access

CASTINE, BUCKS HARBOR, Chart 13309

GOIN' ASHORE: CASTINE, ME

Castine is an active summer resort, though it is more reserved and far less hectic than Camden. Dominating the harbor is the *State of Maine*, the 13,000-ton, 500-foot-long training ship of the Maine Maritime Academy, which offers undergraduate and graduate degrees in engineering, transportation and management. Both the vessel and the Academy are open to visitors (800-464-6565).

During its highly contested early days, Castine changed hands 25 times among the English, French, Dutch, Spanish and American colonists. The town is rich with reminders of its exciting past. Paul Revere ruined his military career in an ill-fated attempt to capture Fort George from the British in 1779. The fort is open to the public. The entire town is on the National Historic Register. Your best bet is to pick up a copy of "A Walking Tour of Castine" from any merchant. The Castine Historical Society (207-326-4118), open Tuesday to Sunday from July 1st through Labor Day, houses a permanent exhibit on the ill-fated Penobscot expedition of 1779 and seasonal exhibits on various aspects of Castine's rich history.

A number of cruising amenities are available here. On Water Street just past Main Street, the T&C Grocery (207-326-4818) has basic provisions, including fresh fish, meat and spirits. On the waterside, north of Main Street, Four Flags (207-326-8526) offers gift items. On Sea Street, directly on the harbor, Dennett's Wharf (207-326-9045) features a lobster pound, open-air dining and an airy indoor restaurant. On Main Street, above Water Street, the Castine Inn (207-326-4365) has extraordinary gardens and is considered the choice for elegant dining in town. Across the street, the Pentagoet Inn was formerly the Maine Maritime Academy. The dining room at The Pentagoet Inn is open to the public for dinner seven days a week and is a culinary treat. Call Jack or Julie at 207-326-8616.

ADDITIONAL RESOURCES:

- Town of Castine, **www.castine.me.us**

NEARBY GOLF COURSES:
Castine Golf Club, Battle Avenue, Castine, ME 04421, 207-326-8844, **www.castinegolfclub.com**

NEARBY MEDICAL FACILITIES:
Waldo County General Hospital, 118 Northport Ave., Belfast, ME 04915, 207-338-2500

Eggemoggin Reach

NAVIGATION: Use Chart 13309. This broad and well-marked route is northernmost of the sheltered inside passages that join Penobscot Bay to Jericho Bay. It runs southeast between the mainland and the Deer Isles. The passage offers dozens of enticing islets and coves, some with yacht facilities and boatbuilding establishments. It is called a reach because the prevailing southwesterlies usually blow across the length of the channel, allowing wind-driven vessels to sail on a reach, whether eastbound or westbound.

Horseshoe Cove

NAVIGATION: Use Chart 13309. Difficult to enter, but protected and a richly rewarding Down East experience is Horseshoe Cove, nearly hidden at the western entrance to Eggemoggin Reach. Northwest of Thrumcap Island, about a quarter mile off the point marked "Horseshoe Cove" on the chart, is a privately maintained "daybeacon" (a red plastic jerry can on a stake) that is a critical find for a stranger to the area. It marks the end of a shoal extending from the point. Do not cut it off, lest you end up at low water on the exposed ledges with the seals. Follow a course centering between the red marker to starboard and the small island off the shore to port. Immediately after entry, a slight turn to starboard will align your passage directly down the center of the relatively narrow channel ahead. About a half mile from the entrance, two closely spaced green spar buoys indicate an unseen twist in the channel. Favor these buoys and leave them close to port. Shortly thereafter, a small red daybeacon to starboard indicates a rounded rock exposed at low tide.

Anchorage and Moorings: The Seal Cove Boatyard maintains several moorings in this area and immediately to the north. Visit the boatyard in your dinghy, not your boat. Passage above the moorings looks easy, but most boats will not successfully negotiate the submerged boulders without a pilot. No swing room for anchorage is available in the mooring area, but anchorage is possible south of the green spar buoys in more than 20 feet of water. This place is well-protected and extraordinarily beautiful. The *pièce de résistance* is a tidal float trip by dinghy (preferably an inflatable one) up the winding, two-mile "river" that makes up this cove to the shallow tidal basin at its head. The trip should begin with the tapering of the flood, about an hour before slack tide. Returning on the ebb and waiting for the tide change will come more slowly than your ascent on the rapids of the flood, so count on needing about three hours for this adventure.

Orcutt Harbor

NAVIGATION: Use Chart 13309. Over Long Mountain, directly to the east of Horseshoe Cove, Orcutt Harbor is easy to enter and reasonably well-protected at its far reaches. Its character is somewhat suburban, with many well-trimmed lawns reaching its edges. Favor the starboard side upon entry to avoid a 5-foot-deep spot off the western shore. Another 5-foot-deep rock, about two-thirds of the way along the bight, is identified on the chart. The area has good holding in mud in 7- to 20-foot depths in the upper harbor. No amenities are available.

Bucks Harbor

Long incorrectly designated on the chart as "Buck Harbor," (named after former Maine Gov. Jonathan Buck) because government chart makers refused to accept the "S," it is now correctly identified. Whatever the name, this harbor has been a special favorite of the cruising fraternity for many years. Located at the western mouth of Eggemoggin Reach and protected by tiny Harbor Island, are an active yacht club, marina and other facilities that welcome visiting yachts.

Buck's Harbor Marine sits on a granite dock that dates back to the days when schooners lay alongside to load the giant stones that built many of New York City's skyscrapers and bridges. A British blockading frigate stood guard in this harbor during the War of 1812, and President Franklin Delano Roosevelt came ashore on the pier to buy an ice cream cone on his way to meet Winston Churchill in Newfoundland, as the United States entered World War II.

NAVIGATION: Use Chart 13309. Easily approached on either side of Harbor Island from red-and-white Morse (A) bell buoy "EG" at the mouth of Eggemoggin Reach to the south, the inner harbor is unobstructed (save for submerged Harbor Ledge, marked by a green can).

Anchorage and Moorings: Except when a visit coincides with a touring yacht club or power squadron, a mooring is almost always available. The harbor affords ample anchorage with secure holding at the eastern end, outside the mooring fields, making it a favorite spot for touring schooners. Buck's Harbor Yacht Club (BHYC) maintains two guest moorings (marked BHYC), and it is possible to tie up briefly at the club's floating dock in ample depths. Fresh water (for fill-ups only) is piped to the dock, and there are restrooms (no showers) in BHYC's rustic clubhouse. A public phone is on the porch. Just east of the yacht club, Buck's Harbor Marine rents a number of transient moorings. The marina consists of a series of floats attached to a large granite facing pier, offering gasoline and diesel, water and a dinghy landing (behind the floating docks). Above the pier are restrooms, showers and a small store with basic marine supplies, daily newspapers, used books, fresh crabmeat and a public telephone.

Provisions can be obtained at the top of the rise (from the yacht club) at Buck's Harbor Market (207-326-8683), stocking all the basics and limited fresh meats, seafood, locally grown produce, European-style breads, coffee, sodas, beer and wine and the New York Times. The lunch counter serves one of the best haddock sandwiches on the coast of Maine. A seasonal restaurant in the rear of the store is a great dinner choice. Across from the yacht club, Herrick's Landing welcomes diners in an attractive setting with exceptional harbor views. It also provides guest moorings for its customers on request and has a dinghy dock just west of the yacht club.

Benjamin River

In the pastoral stretch of green fields, gently rolling land, tiny towns and impressive "pine orchards," Benjamin River enters the Eggemoggin Reach from the north at the village of West Brooklin.

NAVIGATION: Use Chart 13316. Entry is easiest at low tide, when it is possible to see the channel ledge extending from the eastern shore and all but blocking access to the inner harbor. Incoming yachts must favor the western shore as it curves to the northwest until reaching the 50-foot-deep pool inside.

Anchorage and Moorings: Moorings are available here from Benjamin River Marine, and anchorage is possible along the eastern side in mud with 7- to 18-foot depths at low tide. No fuel is available, and services are limited.

Center Harbor

Farther down Eggemoggin Reach, tucked in behind Chatto Island, Center Harbor is dominated by Brooklin Boatyard at its eastern end, specializing in the construction and reconstruction of wooden boats of all sizes. In 1998, the yard wowed the traditional boating world with the launch of its 76-foot W-class cutter, *Wild Horses*, designed by the late Joel White. Because of this wooden boat orientation and the specialized maintenance services provided here, many owners of traditional boats make Center Harbor their home port. Classic lines, shapes and styles (flawlessly restored) encourage a stop for closer review.

Moorings: This is easily done by picking up one of Brooklin Boat Yard's lobster-buoy-shaped moorings. The Center Harbor Yacht Club may also have a guest mooring available. However, this small-boat (Beetle Cats, mostly) sailing club has few other facilities for visitors. After a leisurely tour of the wooden fleet, you can tie up a dinghy behind the Boat Yard's float for a walk to town. It is also possible to dock briefly here (with 4- to 5-foot depths at low tide) to take on water, off-load trash or use the pay phone; no fuels are available.

The village of Brooklin is about two-tenths of a mile up the rise from the docks to the main road, then to the right about a mile farther. The old-fashioned Brooklin General Store (207-359-8817), with basic groceries, household goods, some clothing, beer and wine, is located right at the crossroads. It also has a good selection of fresh fish and live lobsters and will deliver your purchases—and you—to the docks on request; remember to tip accordingly. Across the road, the tiny Morning Moon Cafe (207-359-2373) is open 7 a.m. to 2 p.m. daily, serving dinner some evenings. The town's public library sits across the way on the other side. Just a few paces farther east, the Marine Environmental Research Institute (207-374-2135, open daily during the summer) has an eco-gift shop and sponsors an active summer lecture series and local nature tours. The post office is west of the village center, and there is a public phone outside. The Brooklin Inn (207-359-2777) is a delightful spot for dinner and will provide transportation to and from your boat.

GOIN' ASHORE:
WOODENBOAT SCHOOL

The WoodenBoat School and WoodenBoat Magazine headquarters (207-359-4651) are located in the large white-washed-brick complex just north of the Babson Islands. During the summer months, the school offers courses in traditional and contemporary boat construction, as well as related skills such as marine surveying and celestial navigation. Visitors are

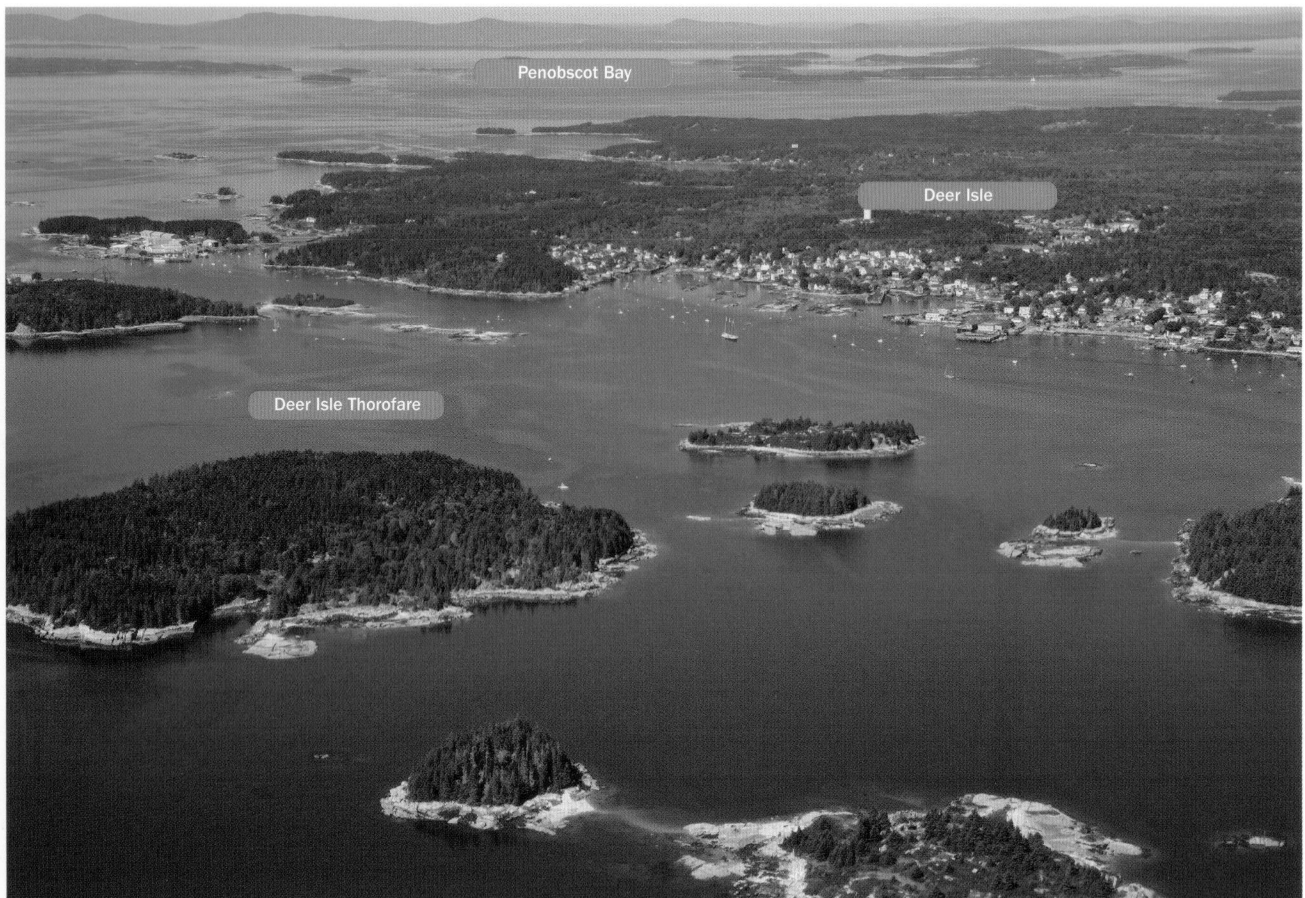

Looking over the islands of Merchants Row and the town of Stonington. (Not to be used for navigation.) WATERWAY GUIDE PHOTOGRAPHY

welcomed to this friendly place. Anchorage is available south of the school's dock in 10 to 11 feet of water at low tide in good holding. Or just pick up one of the school's guest moorings and check in with the dockmaster to be sure that there is no conflict with a reservation. The school's large dinghy dock will accommodate your landing, and the main facilities are but a short walk past the boathouse at the foot of the dock. The WoodenBoat shop is open during the day so that you can locate missing back issues and specialty items.

ADDITIONAL RESOURCES:

- The WoodenBoat School, **www.thewoodenboatschool.com**

Naskeag Harbor

Just behind Hog Island, near the eastern end of Eggemoggin Reach, beautiful Naskeag Harbor provides adequate protection in most conditions.

Anchorage: Best anchorage is found close to the north of Hog Island, avoiding The Triangles, a rocky ledge farther still to the north of the island. You can drop the hook in 14 to 16 feet of water at low tide.

Deer Isle and Merchant Row

The large summer resort island of Deer Isle is the southern edge of Eggemoggin Reach. The Rainbow Bridge, mentioned in Steinbeck's "Travels with Charlie," joins it to the mainland. Harbors on the western side of Deer Isle include Burnt Cove and its lobster village of West Deer Isle; Sylvester Cove, with a hospitable yacht club, guest moorings and anchorage among the fleet south of Dunham Point; and long, narrow Northwest Harbor, north of Dunham Point, with the best anchorage in the center. The head of the harbor dries at low tide and is open to northwest winds.

Deer Island Thorofare

Narrow and well-marked, the Deer Island Thorofare at the southern end of the island threads between rocky outcroppings and tiny islands and past protected coves and scenic anchorages. Two of Deer Isle's best protected harbors are Southeast Harbor, at the Thorofare's eastern entrance, and Webb Cove, just northwest of Grog Island and unmarked Grog Ledge. To enter Webb Cove, favor the western shore, giving Channel Rock and other ledges to the northeast a wide berth. Crotch Island, on the western end of the Thorofare, is the source of famous Deer Island granite and still is an active quarry. Here you can sight the gantry used to lift granite blocks for loading on a barge. For the last few years, the owners of Crotch Island have been constructing an amazing stone building on the waterfront; the building is visible from the Thorofare.

Anchorage: Scenic summer anchorages are due east of the northern end of Camp Island in 11 to 17 feet of water, and west of the southern end of Bold Island next door. The lengthy slot west of Hells Half Acre and between Bold

Island and Devil Island is also a gorgeous anchorage, with good holding in depths from 11 to 22 feet at mean low water. A dinghy trip to state-owned and uninhabited Hell's Half Acre is a must for a walk around this diminutive but beautiful spot. Camping is permitted here, but build fires below the high-water mark.

Stonington

This town of white houses sits on the side of a hill sloping down to the harbor. The inhabitants once depended on granite quarries and sardine canneries, but now derive their living mainly from lobster pounds and summer visitors. Shore accommodations and restaurants are available, as is a major boatyard with repair services. There is also a country club nearby. Draggers, fishing smacks, yachts, an excursion boat, a ferry and fishermen all make Stonington their home port, giving harbor and town an appealing blend of these diverse elements. A town dock sits between the commercial fishing piers. Nearly a mile west of the village center, Billings Diesel & Marine Service is located on Moose Island and offers fuel, slip space, transient moorings, towing, repairs and marine supplies. Make arrangements for whatever you need here before closing time at 3:30 p.m.

Merchant Row

The southernmost passage between East Penobscot Bay and Jericho Bay, this route lies between Isle au Haut and Stonington. Merchant Row is wider and deeper than Deer Island Thorofare, easy to navigate (all major obstructions are buoyed), and hemmed in by islands ranging in size from a single big rock to mile-long Merchant Island.

Anchorage: Merchant Row consists of protected, uninhabited islands providing many anchorages. Opportunities abound to go ashore for beachcombing or blueberry picking, and it is never too crowded to find a private anchorage. McGlathery Island is a particularly favored spot. Best anchorages are in the cove on the north side of the island in 21-foot depths at low tide or in the slot between McGlathery and Round Island just to the west in 8- to 10-foot depths at low water. McGlathery Island is a nature preserve, and its beaches, cliffs and woods beg to be explored. On Wreck Island, just west of McGlathery, you may see evidence of sheep grazing, brought from the mainland for the summer season.

Isle au Haut

This heavily wooded island, named in 1604 by Samuel de Champlain, is 550 feet high. Pronounced "I'll a hoe," it is mostly wilderness, has a few trails, one main road and town, fishing settlements, a few year-round residents and some summer people. Its only connection to the outside world is the Stonington mail/passenger boat.

The village of Isle au Haut, on the east side of the Thorofare opposite Kimball Island, has a store, small school, church, community center and town wharf. At the northern end of the Thorofare is the summer community of Point Lookout. The Island Store Association, in the village, offers an excellent variety of goods for reprovisioning, featuring fresh fish and produce, beer, wine and ice. Call in advance orders to 207-335-5211.

Moores Harbor and Head Harbor both look inviting on the chart but are wide open to the prevailing southwesterly winds. Duck Harbor on the northern side of Duck Harbor Mountain is a gunkhole praised by many skippers. When entering, leave the ledge to port.

In settled weather, the anchorage in Marsh Cove at the west end of the Thorofare is attractive.

Blue Hill Bay

About 14 miles long, Blue Hill Bay has few obstructions, numerous coves and wooded islands and dramatic scenery on all sides. This mostly uninhabited area derives its name from the rounded mountain that towers over it to the northwest. The evergreen trees on the mountain take on a bluish cast from a distance.

Anchorage: Just North of Casco Passage, there is a wonderful anchorage on the southeastern side of Pond Island. The anchorage is well-protected from the prevailing southwesterlies, and you can anchor off the rocky beach in 13 to 18 feet. Remember the tidal range in this area is 9 to 12 feet. Farther north, the Pond Island Passage connects Blue Hill Bay with Herrick Bay, a wide, deep area with anchorages west of Flye Point. Herrick Bay is not buoyed, but it is accurately charted and safe to enter and anchor in 11 to 15 feet.

E. Penobscot Bay, Blue Hill Bay, ME

EAST PENOBSCOT BAY, BLUE HILL BAY		Largest Vessel Accommodated	VHF Channel Monitored	Transient Berths / Total Berths	Approach / Dockside Depth (reported)	Floating Docks	Gas / Diesel	Groceries, Ice, Marine Supplies, Snacks	Repairs: Hull, Engine, Propeller	Lift (tonnage), Crane, Rail	1=110V, 2=220V, B=Both, Max Amps	Laundry, Pool, Showers	Pump-Out Station	Nearby: Grocery Store, Motel, Restaurant
		Dockage					Supplies		Services					
1. Center Harbor Yacht Club	207-359-8868	40			17/4				CALL AHEAD					
2. Brooklin Boat Yard	207-359-2236	70		3/	7/5	F		M	HEP	L70,C				GMR
3. Billings Diesel & Marine Service Inc.	**207-367-2328**	**160**	**16**	**20/25**	**20/10**	**F**	**GD**	**IM**	**HEP**	**L35,C,R**	**B/100**	**LS**	**P**	**GMR**
4. Raynes Marine 💻	207-374-2877	50		MOORINGS				M	HEP				P	GMR
5. Kollegewidgwok Yacht Club	207-374-5581	50	68		2/7	F	GD							GMR
6. Webbers Cove Boatyard	207-374-2841	48			14/3			M	HP					

Corresponding chart(s) not to be used for navigation. 💻 Internet Access (WiFi) Wireless Internet Access

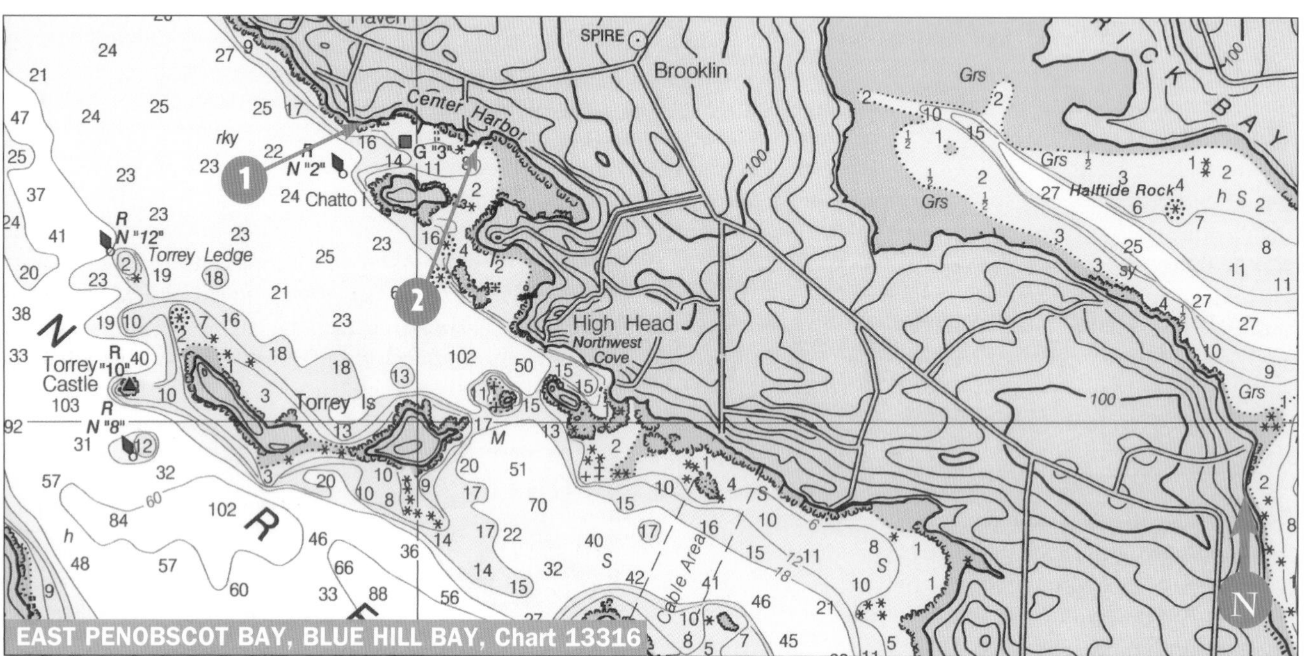

EAST PENOBSCOT BAY, BLUE HILL BAY, Chart 13316

EAST PENOBSCOT BAY, BLUE HILL BAY, Chart 13305

EAST PENOBSCOT BAY, BLUE HILL BAY, Chart 13316

Swans Island

This large island has three small villages and two secure harbors, both easily accessible if charted obstructions and buoys are observed. Though the island attracts a swelling summer population, it has avoided the distasteful clutter of modern tourism and still boasts a serious fishing and lobstering economy.

Burnt Coat Harbor

NAVIGATION: Use Chart 13313. Burnt Coat Harbor on the south shore is long, narrow and well-protected and serves as home port for two small villages. Enter south of green can "3" off Gooseberry Ledge and pass between green gong buoy "5" off the tip of Hockamock Head and red daybeacon "4" north of Harbor Island, turning to port for anchorage outside the mooring field in 20 to 35 feet of water at low tide. You also can enter and exit through the narrow but well-marked channel between Harbor Island and Stanley Point.

Anchorage and Moorings: Anchorage is possible north of Harbor Point but can be uncomfortable because of its greater vulnerability to ocean swells. Closer to the village of Swans Island on the western shore, heavy-tackle rental moorings (brightly painted lobster floats) are available from Swan's Island Boat House Gifts and Take Out (207-526-4201). Diesel fuel is available at Fishermen's Cooperative, though recreational boats are asked to fuel up before 1 p.m. to make room for returning lobster boats. Kent's Wharf, just north of the Boat House, offers fuel, water and a little bit of everything else. You can contact them on VHF Channel 68. There is no alcohol on this dry island; even brown bags are out of bounds at the restaurant. The general store in Minturn has closed after struggling for several years to remain in business, leaving the island with no source for provisioning. Approximately half a mile north of the Fishermen's Co-op, the harbor shallows appreciably, making even a grocery run by dinghy tide-dependent. There are no taxis on the island, but locals are obliging, often offering a ride, and the market will deliver. At Minturn, you can have a freshwater swim at Quarry Pond. If a sandy, secluded ocean beach is your preference, ask for directions. Three are within walking distance of the harbor.

Mackerel Cove

NAVIGATION: Use Chart 13313. Picturesque Mackerel Cove, on the north shore, is entered from York Narrows between Orono and Round islands to the north and Swan Island shore on the south. One caution: Midway between the tip of Roderick Head and green can "3" (off the ferry landing), an enormous ledge presents a considerable hazard to navigation since it is submerged at high tide. During high water, give this visible ledge a very wide berth at slow speed, watching the depth sounder.

Anchorage: Large enough to accommodate a flotilla of cruising boats, Mackerel Cove has two favored anchorage spots, one on either side of Roderick Head in the southwest corner of the cove. The only improved landing in Mackerel Cove is found near the ferry dock on the east side of the cove, where it is also quite possible to set a hook, preferably well south of the ferry's comings and goings from Bass Harbor on Mount Desert Island. There are more private moorings in Mackerel Cove than previously, and it is possible to pick up a vacant one if you are prepared to move should the owner appear.

Buckle Harbor

Anchorage: An enchanting anchorage is located at Buckle Island, just south of York Narrows at the northwest corner of Swans Island. Enter Buckle Harbor between green cans

"7" and "5" of York Narrows to reach a secure anchorage with good holding that easily accommodates a dozen boats. A tour of the island paths is a primeval must—wild strawberries growing atop granite boulders, seascape cameos through mossy vistas, the door of a long-vanished cabin framing a nearly hidden pathway in the mist, the scolding of an invisible squirrel or a doe venturing out to a seaside meadow as your dinghy departs.

Marshall and Long Islands

Southwest of Swans Island, Marshall Island has another fine sandy beach and a good anchorage in Sand Cove. Southeast of Swans Island is the former pirate's hide-out of Long Island, which is high, wooded and round, not "long" at all. As you pass south toward Long Island, you will see floating pens that hold salmon, between Placentia and Black islands. Placentia Island was wholly owned by a couple of physicists who retreated to the island and lived a semi-hermit lifestyle from the late 1940s to the 1980s, rowing their four-oar dory into Bass Harbor for monthly shopping trips. The Nature Conservancy now owns the island. There is no safe place to anchor and go ashore.

Lunt Harbor

NAVIGATION: Use Chart 13312. Frenchboro, the tiny hamlet at Lunt Harbor, is surely the mind's-eye vision of what a classic out-island Maine fishing village should look like. The harbor is fortified against all winds but the craftiest northeasterlies, and even those are partially blocked by Harbor Island at its mouth. Easily accessible, Lunt Harbor may be approached from the west, using green bell buoy "1" as a guide to the channel between Harbor Island and the northwestern shoulder of Long Island. About a third of the way along Harbor Island, a hard turn to starboard will take you into the open mouth of the harbor. From the east, the red-and-white Morse (A) gong buoy "LI" aids the passage south/southwest below Crow Island and Harbor Island for an almost straight course into the harbor.

Anchorage and Moorings: Anchorage is no longer possible amid the mooring field now carpeting the harbor. Anchorage outside the harbor south of Harbor Island is exposed to ocean swells and is likely to be uncomfortable. For security, it is best to pick up one of Lunt's moorings, row in for a tie-up behind the face dock and lobster cars and pay the fee at the deli take-out window. Lunt's Deli's lobster rolls and steamed lobsters are tasty enough to attract day-trippers from Mount Desert Island. Perched on a side hill at the head of the harbor (beyond a variety of picturesque but precarious lobstering sheds, docks and equipment), the island's small museum captures the spirit of a seafaring past. The attached lending library will lend books to visitors on the promise to mail them back. Now that the island's general store has closed, the only other signs of commerce are the tiny Frenchboro Post Office, attached to a local lobsterman's house, and a minuscule T-shirt shop. The local postmistress is a fountain of local lore and good humor.

GOIN' ASHORE: LONG ISLAND, ME

Long Island is popular both as a quaint end-of-the-line stop and as a great place to stretch out cramped sea legs on a trip farther east. Roads on both sides of the harbor are paved, but intriguing dirt roads and trails lead off in several directions. One interesting walk begins at the head of the harbor where a narrow dirt road departs the pavement southward, undulating pleasantly to the granite-bound south shore. A walk east along the rocks picks up a well-worn path with a circle back through an ancient fir-fringed bog where orchids bloom every July and the canary-like songs of abundant white-winged crossbills trill throughout the summer. Kids of all ages will thrill at a close encounter with the tame deer that appear frequently. Before exploring, you should wisely invest 50 cents in an island trail map at the museum.

On the east side of Long Island, Eastern Cove is as remote and unspoiled as it is beautiful. Open only to the northeast, the cove is protected from the south and east by Richs Head and the main island to the north and west. Holding is good and exploration of the long-abandoned farmsteads ashore is well worthwhile. Lunt Harbor is about an hour's woodland walk away.

Blue Hill

Nestled in a rustic setting, fully protected against winds from any quarter, yet convenient to reprovisioning, shopping and good restaurants, Blue Hill is everything a cruising destination should be.

NAVIGATION: Use Chart 13312. For Blue Hill Harbor, use Bar Harbor tide tables. For high tide, add 9 minutes; for low tide, add 11 minutes. Blue Hill's inner harbor is most easily approached on a due-north course from a position off Sand Point on Blue Hill Neck. Shallow ledges guard the entrance, making it necessary to carefully observe the entrance buoys. The second flagpole (west of Sculpin Point and identified on the Blue Hill Harbor chart) will be visible long before the channel cans come into view and should be used for a bearing on approach.

Dockage: On the east side of the inner harbor, moorings are usually available for a modest facilities fee from the Kollegewidgwok (pronounced "College-widge'-wok") Yacht Club. Look for KYC markings on the floats or call the club's launch tender (VHF Channel 09) for assistance. The club provides tie-up space for your dinghy, restrooms (no showers), access to a public phone and a comfortable clubhouse with harbor view. There is ample depth at the club's fuel dock to refill both fuel and water tanks, and you can buy ice here as well.

Anchorage: The inner harbor's combination of an 11-foot-plus tidal range and a densely packed mooring field makes an attempt to anchor on the easterly side of the harbor ill advised. From the club, it is a scenic 1.7-mile walk to the village. Above half-tide, you can take your dinghy west across the inner harbor to the town dock and dinghy dock at the harbor's northwestern

Looking northwest over Blue Hill Harbor. (Not to be used for navigation.) WATERWAY GUIDE PHOTOGRAPHY

head, just across from the Blue Hill Memorial Hospital. Below half-tide, the dock is left high and dry for some distance.

The west side of the inner harbor also has plenty of anchorage space in 14- to 27-foot depths. If setting the hook, it is best to wait for low tide when the limits to safe anchorage will be more apparent. There is good holding here on a mud bottom.

GOIN' ASHORE: BLUE HILL, ME

This classic New England town appears to reawaken each late spring with the return of its summer residents and the reopening of winter-dormant businesses and restaurants. The area also has become something of a magnet for artists, artisans and musicians who display their talents in a variety of shops, shows and performances. The town is a bit spread out for those on foot, but it is altogether possible to reprovision, sightsee and have an excellent meal here with an eye to the tide for trips to and from the boat.

The walk from the inner harbor landing to Merrill & Hinckley Store (207-374-2821) would be worth it even if you could not reprovision there. But you can, with a reasonable supply of groceries, including fresh fruits and vegetables, meats and fish. The market also serves as the town liquor store. There are several antiques stores, craft shops, a complete hardware store, pharmacy, post office, library and two banks (with ATMs).

A short walk up the hill, toward the yacht club, the Pantry Restaurant (207-374-2229) fixes delicious breakfasts and lunches. The Vinery (Main Street, 207-374-2441, open for dinner Wed.-Sun.) serves well-presented American fare in an early-1800s house in three separate dining areas, each with a fireplace. Fish Net Seafood Restaurant (207-374-5240) on Main Street serves some of the freshest takeout seafood available. Arborvine (Main Street, 207-374-2119) sets the standard for excellent dinner cuisine; reservations are strongly suggested. At the other end of the village, the Blue Hill Food Co-op (207-374-2165) is a natural food store that offers lunch in a café in the rear of the store.

ADDITIONAL RESOURCES:

- Blue Hill Peninsula, **www.bluehillme.com**

NEARBY GOLF COURSES:
Bar Harbor Golf Course, 51 Jordan River Road, Trenton, ME 04605, 207-667-7505, **www.barharborgolfcourse.com**

NEARBY MEDICAL FACILITIES:
Blue Hill Memorial Hospital, Water Street, Blue Hill, ME 04614-0823, 207-374-2836

Union River Bay

Cruising sailors seldom use this bay because its narrow north/south orientation makes sailing difficult in the prevailing summer southerlies, but this spot is very inviting for travelers who value their privacy.

Anchorage: There are two well-protected anchorages: Mill Cove and Patten Bay. The latter is within walking distance of the grocery store in Surry. Ellsworth, up the Union River, has a delightful Main Street of shops and restaurants.

Mount Desert Island, ME

MOUNT DESERT ISLAND		Largest Vessel Accommodated	VHF Channel Monitored	Transient Berths / Total Berths	Approach / Dockside Depth (reported)	Floating Docks	Gas / Diesel	Groceries, Ice, Marine Supplies, Snacks	Repairs: Hull, Engine, Propeller	Lift (tonnage), Crane, Rail	1=110V, 2=220V, B=Both, Max Amps	Laundry, Pool, Showers	Pump-Out Station	Nearby: Grocery Store, Motel, Restaurant
		Dockage					Supplies		Services					
1. F.W. Thurston Co.	207-244-3320	50	WHOLESALE SEAFOOD		7/7	F	GD	M			B			
2. Morris Yachts Bass Harbor	207-244-5511	60	09	10/10	25/10	F	D	I	HEP	L35,C	B/50	LS		GMR
3. The Hinckley Co.	207-244-5572	150	09/16		30/25	F	D	IM	HEP	L160,C	B/50	LS	P	GMR
4. Islesford Dock Restaurant	207-244-7494	50		5/10	15/10	F	GD	GIMS						GMR
5. Dysart's Great Harbor Marina (Internet Access, Wireless Internet Access)	**207-244-0117**	**180**	**09**	**50/135**	**18/12**	**F**	**D**	**GIMS**	**HEP**		**B/100**	**LPS**	**P**	**GMR**
6. Southwest Boat Marine Services	207-244-5525	120	09	5/24	25/14	F		M	HP		B/50		P	GMR
7. Beal's Lobster Pier	207-244-3202	100	16/88	MOORINGS	15/10	F	GD	IMS						GR
8. Claremont Hotel	800-244-5036	40		MOORINGS	30/7					CALL AHEAD				GMR
9. Clifton Dock	207-276-5308	70	09		20/20		GD	IM						
10. Northeast Harbor Marina	207-276-5737	160	09	10/52	10/10	F					B/100	S	P	GMR
11. Morris Service Northeast Harbor (Wireless Internet Access)	207-276-5300	60	09	12/18	6/6			GIMS	HEP	L25,C	B/50	LS		GMR
12. Bar Harbor Municipal Pier (Wireless Internet Access)	207-288-5571	185	09/68	8/8	16/11	F					B/100			GMR
13. Harbor Side Hotel & Marina (Internet Access)	207-288-5033	120		8/8	8/8							PS		GMR
14. Holiday Inn Bar Harbor (Internet Access)	207-288-9723	200		10/	15/12	F		GIS			B/100	LPS		MR

Corresponding chart(s) not to be used for navigation. Internet Access · Wireless Internet Access

Looking north over Bass Harbor. (Not to be used for navigation.) WATERWAY GUIDE PHOTOGRAPHY

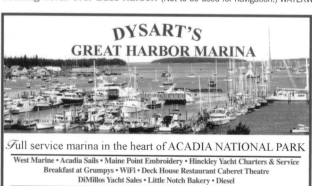

A recent dredging project resulted in minimum depths of 5 feet to the town landing and anchorage area. Be aware of possible strong currents, especially in rainy weather. A dam above Ellsworth controls the river current and level.

Mount Desert Island

Samuel de Champlain named this large magnificent island L'Isle de Monts Desert when he visited in 1604. Debate continues about whether the accent should be placed on the first syllable for the bare, desert-like mountaintops or on the second syllable for the French meaning, deserted. Most people pronounce it like the treat that it is—the icing on the cake, the dessert to the fine repast of Maine cruising.

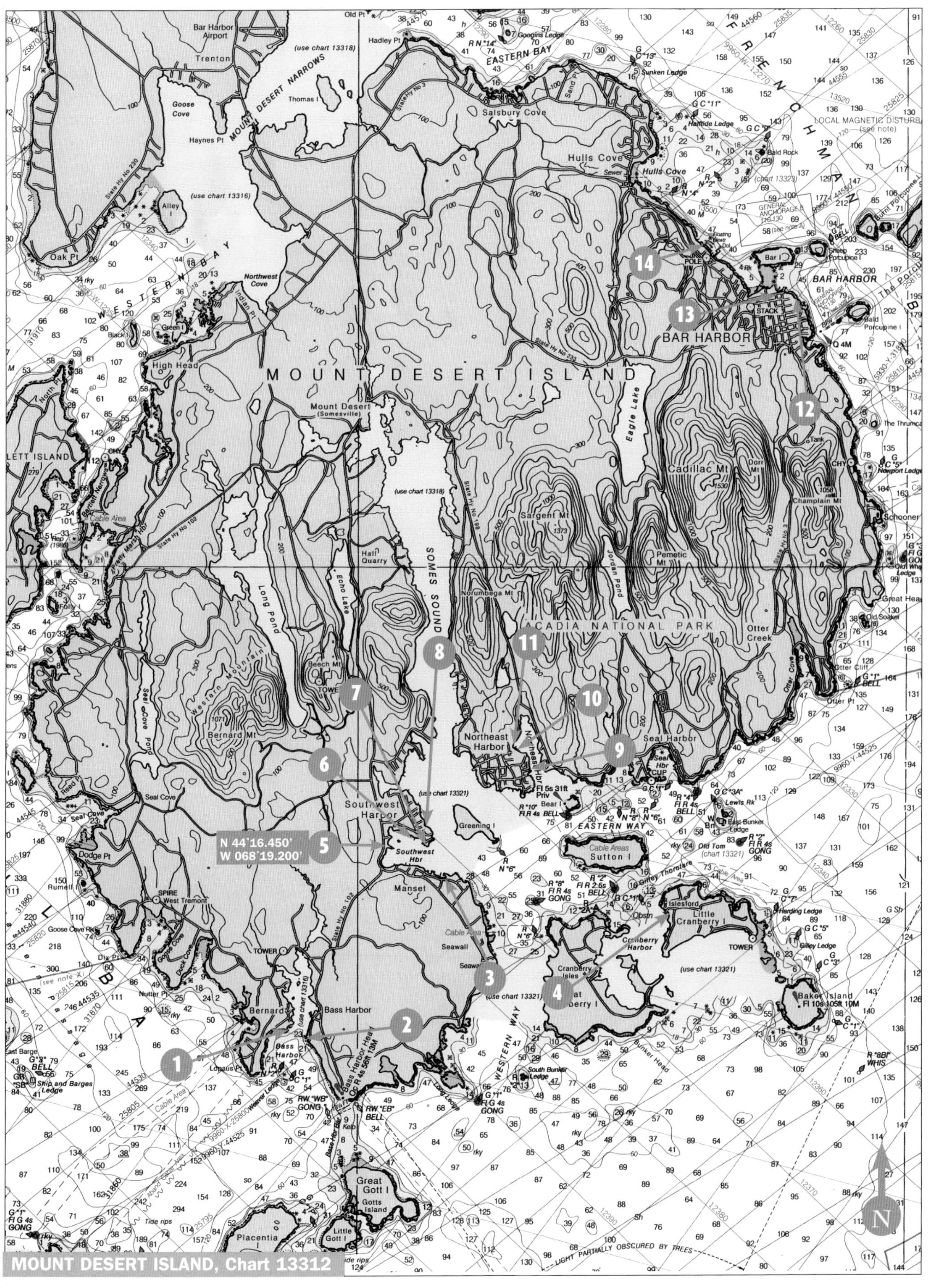

MOUNT DESERT ISLAND, Chart 13312

Order Waterway Guides online at www.WaterwayGuide.com or call toll-free 800-233-3359

Southwest Harbor, ME

WATERWAY GUIDE's coverage of this area moves counterclockwise from the northernmost bay. Cruisers are finding a new, free Island Explorer shuttle bus service particularly convenient for picking up and dropping off crew. It is provided by Friends of Acadia and L.L. Bean and connects all the Acadia National Park destinations, villages and cruising harbors of Mount Desert: Bar Harbor, Northeast Harbor, Somes Sound and Bass Harbor, as well as the airport.

Western Bay

Anchorage: In the northwest corner of Mount Desert, Western Bay has two good anchorages, Northwest Cove and Goose Cove. The shallow narrows and the fixed bridge prevent circumnavigation of Mount Desert.

Pretty Marsh Harbor, halfway down Mount Desert and northeast of Hardwood Island, is easy to enter, past grassy Folly Island. The harbor is well-protected and scenic. Just north of Pretty Marsh Harbor is Bartlett Narrows, which runs between Mount Desert Island and Bartlett Island. There is a municipal landing at the Narrows, but no services except for a trash dumpster. It is possible to anchor in Great Cove on the east side of Bartlett Island. Seal Cove, south of Pretty Marsh, is open to westerlies. Hardwood Island is privately owned.

Bass Harbor

Bass Harbor, in the southwestern corner of the island, just off Blue Hill Bay, is southernmost of the fabulous isle's yacht harbors. A lovely port in the shadow of Mount Desert's hills, Bass Harbor has a substantial lobster fleet, a ferry to Swans Island, good anchorage in the inner harbor and facilities in the inner and outer harbors.

In recent years, Bass Harbor has become popular with cruisers seeking serenity and scenery. Restaurants and bed and breakfasts dot the shore of the harbor, which is flanked by the cozy communities of Bass Harbor on the east and Bernard on the west.

On the Bass Harbor side, The Seafood Ketch (207-244-7463) does a great job for lunch and dinner. Just opposite the Maine State Ferry Terminal is Mainely Delights (207-244-3656), a great seasonal choice for lunch or dinner with seating inside and on the porch.

NAVIGATION: Use Chart 13318. The entrance is easy. Pass either side of Weaver Ledge (marked by two buoys) into the outer harbor (open to the south). Here on the eastern shore are the ferry slips, a full-service boatyard owned by Morris Yachts, the town dock and the village of Bass Harbor. The Morris Yachts facility (207-244-5509 or VHF Channel 09) offers moorings and repairs of all kinds. Visitors will find showers, a laundry, a well-stocked supply room and plenty of friendly faces.

The well-buoyed inner harbor offers complete protection, a fuel dock near the entry at Thurston's Wharf, a marina and, on the western shore, the charming old community of Bernard. The Tremont Harbormaster (207-244-4564) oversees all activities in the harbor. Prominent on the Bernard shore is the yellow roof of Thurston's Lobster Pound (207-244-7600), a great place for a real Maine lobster dinner. There is limited room for anchoring, but usually a vacant mooring can be found. On approaching the innermost area of the harbor, be alert for red nun buoy "6," which can be obscured by moored boats and is deceptively close to the shore. Leave it to starboard on entering the inner harbor, and then turn into the mooring pool. The town of Tremont is negotiating with the U.S. Army Corps of Engineers to allow dredging in order to enlarge the mooring area, but improvement is probably several years away.

Southwest Harbor

NAVIGATION: Use Chart 13318. For Southwest Harbor, use Bar Harbor tide tables. For high tide, add 0 minutes; for low tide, subtract 27 minutes. Entering Western Way between Great Cranberry Island and the mainland of Mount Desert, Southwest Harbor opens up to the east, and is frequently used by large commercial vessels and recreational boats. The harbor has a large mooring field; contact the harbormaster on VHF Channel 09 to reserve a mooring. The town maintains a public dinghy dock on the north side of the harbor. Anchoring is no longer allowed in the harbor, but good holding can be found between the Southwest Harbor shore and Greening Island, north of the harbor proper and beyond the Coast Guard station. Anchorage is best nearer Greening Island. This does, however, create a lengthy dinghy ride to shore access at the town dock.

Dockage and Moorings: The Hinckley Company's well known yacht yard and ship's store are on the south shore at Manset. There you will have easy access to water, gasoline and diesel fuels. The yard has extensive lift and repair capabilities. Rental moorings usually are available, including restrooms, showers and coin-operated laundry. You can secure your dinghy at the extensive floating dock east of the yard's main pier.

Manset Yacht Services is a J-Boat dealer and offers service to sailors. The Manset town dock has a dinghy tie-up and is convenient to the Bella Mare Restaurant (48 Shore Road, 207-244-9144), serving Northern Italian fare. XYZ Restaurant (80 Seawall Road, 207-244-5221), a very popular Mexican spot known for delicious margaritas and authentic Mexican fare, is located a short walk up the hill and across Manset Road. Dysart's Great Harbor Marina, at the head of the harbor, accommodates visiting yachts and crews at its floating docks and ashore, with numerous amenities. The Deck House Restaurant and Cabaret Theatre (207-244-5044), previously located in Bass Harbor, is now in Southwest Harbor on the premises of Dysart's Great Harbor Marina, providing popular dinner theater performances by college students who also wait tables. Dysart's Great Harbor Marina also is the site of Acadia Sails (207-244-5722), West Side Grill and Salad Bar restaurant (207-244-5959), a West Marine store (207-244-0300) and Maine Point (207-244-7787), a maker of fender covers and fleece products. Groceries, laundry, ice and marine supplies are available here.

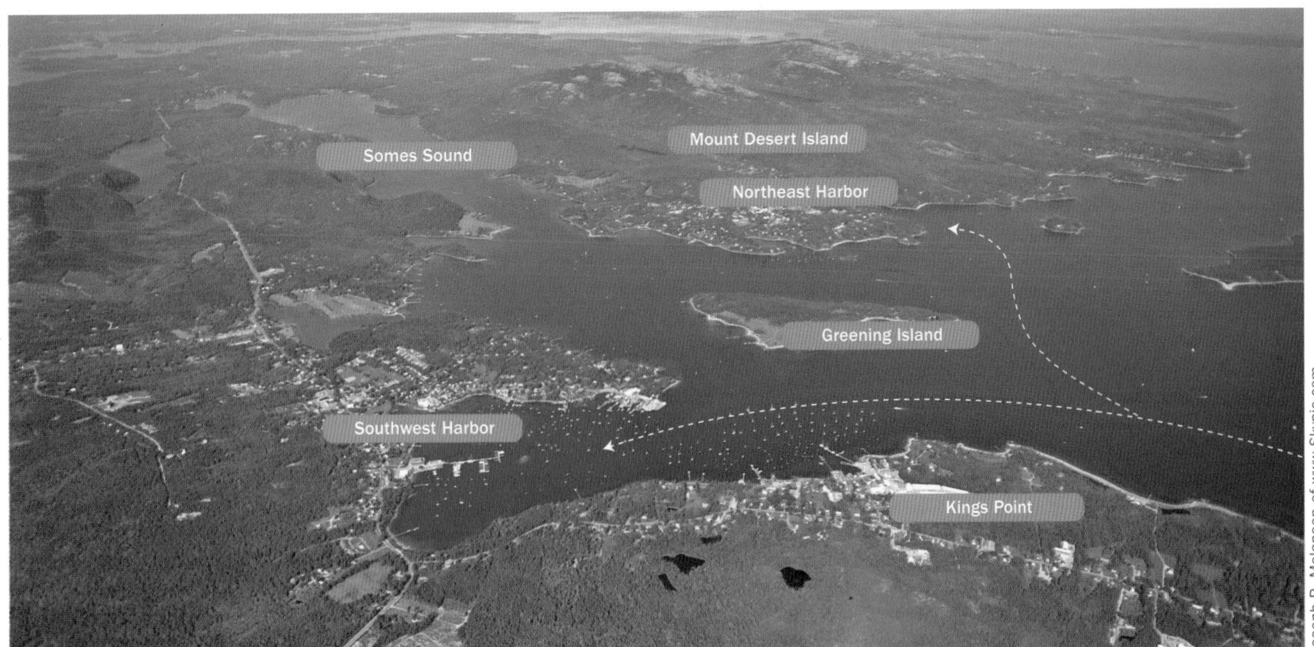

Looking north over Southwest Harbor, Greening Island and Northeast Harbor. (Not to be used for navigation.)

Looking northwest over Southwest Harbor. (Not to be used for navigation.) WATERWAY GUIDE PHOTOGRAPHY

Nearby, Southwest Boat has large lift and marine railway capacity to facilitate repairs for recreational and commercial vessels. Beal's Lobster Pier, next to the Coast Guard station, rents slips and moorings and also has gasoline and diesel fuel at its floats. Lobsters may be purchased—crawling or ready to eat. Next to Beal's are two excellent independent service facilities: Downeast Diesel and Marine (207-244-5145) for mechanical repairs and DNW Marine Services (207-244-3490) for electrical and electronic service and installation. In the village at the harbor head you will find Sawyer's Market (207-244-3315), selling groceries, meats, fresh vegetables, fresh breads and Sawyer's Specialties (207-244-3317), a purveyor of fine wines and other delicacies.

Sips (207-244-4550) is a new tapas and wine bar just behind Sawyer's Specialties on 4 Clark Point Road. Other candidates for an evening of fine dining are Red Sky (207-244-0476, 14 Clark Point Road) and Fiddler's Green (207-244-9416, 411 Main St. near the Marina). Across Main Street from Sawyer's, you will find a well-stocked hardware store. Carroll Drug Store (207-244-5588) is here, as well as two full-service banks complete with ATMs, several restaurants and the Liquor Locker (207-244-3788), with an excellent selection of liquor, beers and wines. Birders and wood carvers will want to visit the Wendell Gilley Museum (207-244-7555) with its distinctive collection of bird and waterfowl carvings and its demonstrations and workshops.

Looking northwest over Somes Sound. (Not to be used for navigation.) WATERWAY GUIDE PHOTOGRAPHY

Somes Sound

Considered the only true fjord in North America (outside Alaska), Somes Sound begins its dramatic six-mile cleavage into the heart of Mount Desert Island at the busy channel off Clark Point, the tip of the peninsula that separates Southwest Harbor from the sound. Throughout most of the sound's length, steep hills of 600- and 800-foot heights plummet directly to the water's edge and beyond. In the background, mountains of substantially greater size add grandeur to an awe-inspiring landscape and seascape. Those under sail will find the sound reminiscent of lake sailing—whistling winds abating almost instantly to a dead calm, rapid wind shifts and reversals of 180 degrees. Part way along, Valley Cove attracts adventuresome crews with the promise of accessible paths to the summits of the sheer cliffs above for stunning views. The water is deep in the cove—90 feet or more within short distances of shore.

Moorings: Located about two-thirds of the distance from Clark Point to Somes Harbor on the west side of the sound, John M. Williams Co. rents a few transient moorings and can make or facilitate engine, hull and rigging repairs. Directly across the sound, Bar Harbor Boating offers mooring rentals, sells ice and can make repairs.

Somes Harbor

Just a short walk from this snug harbor, Somesville's white-washed clapboard houses and vintage public buildings are bordered by garlands of brilliant flowers, encouraging visitors to stretch their legs in search of Kodak moments in both directions from the head of the harbor.

NAVIGATION: Use Chart 13318. Somes Harbor is entered west of Myrtle Ledge through the deep but narrow passage between the green can and Bar Island (owned by the state of Maine and open for exploration).

Anchorage and Moorings: Numerous private moorings dot the harbor, yet you will still find adequate swing room, with 20-foot depths at low water and good holding, just north of Bar Island. Several moorings are likely to be vacant, though there is no one to manage their use while their owners are away. On the west side of the harbor, Somesville Landing Corp. maintains a substantial floating dock and ramp to accommodate dinghies (those with motors outside the long float; those without, inside).

Somesville

A short walk from the landing is the village, strung out along a seasonally busy two-lane state highway. Turn left at the highway, and you will soon arrive at Port in a Storm Bookstore (1112 Main St., 207-244-4114)—likely one of the largest in Maine. The Library Association building next door is tiny by comparison. Across the street, the Mount Desert Historical Society Museum is tucked behind a flower-ringed pond crossed by the Thaddeus Shepley Somes Bow Bridge, which fairly begs to be photographed. Farther south, A.V. Higgins Store (207-244-5401) no longer carries groceries, but does sell fresh-brewed Green Mountain coffee, baked goods, gifts and antiques. Turn right on the highway from the harbor road, and the third-of-a-mile walk produces basic commercial amenities. On The Run (207-244-5504) stocks groceries, including various deli items (and prepared sandwiches), frozen veggies, fruits, soft drinks, beer, wine, spirits and regional newspapers. You can have your propane tank filled here, and there are FedEx and UPS drop stations. Directly across the road, Union Trust has an ATM and there is a post office.

Cranberry Islands

Just two to three miles southwest of Southwest Harbor, the Cranberry Islands seem at once remote yet accessible and familiar. Combining a mix of working lobstermen, long-term summer residents, artists and artisans, these islands are both interesting and friendly places to visit. Though the namesake cranberry bogs have long been drained, these islands still excel for pleasant walks with seascape backdrops of Mount Desert.

Great Cranberry Island

Great Cranberry Island, the largest of the group, is home to some 50 families year-round and a much expanded summer population.

NAVIGATION: Use Chart 13318. The approach to Spurling Cove, on the north side of the island, is open and straightforward; the few outlying obstructions are well-marked.

Anchorage and Moorings : Though wide open to the north and northwest, anchorage is possible outside the cove's mooring field in 15- to 25-foot depths, and there is a dinghy float at the (west) public dock. Moorings are available from Island Woodworking, and you can take on water, gas or diesel at its dock (east of the town dock). If weather conditions preclude anchoring off Great Cranberry, consider taking a mooring in Northeast Harbor and riding one of the regular ferries to the island from Northeast Harbor.

GOIN' ASHORE: GREAT CRANBERRY ISLAND, ME

Along the parking lot next to the town dock is the Cranberry General Store (207-244-0622) for groceries, ice, soda, sandwiches and desserts. Just one-half mile up Cranberry Road, with views of water on both sides and past lovely old ship captains' homes, is Cranberry House with Hitty's Cafe (207-244-7845), serving lunch and ice cream treats. Cranberry House hosts the Preble-Marr Museum, which documents the island's varied history from Indian days, ship building and the influx of wealthy "Rusticators" to the present. There is also a cultural center for classes, concerts and exhibitions. Behind the museum is a lovely public trail (about one mile) through the woods to Whistlers Cove on the Western Way. A short walk farther brings you to the Whales Rib Gift Shop run by Polly Bunker and featuring many local crafts and artwork.

ADDITIONAL RESOURCES:

- The Cranberry Isles, **www.cranberryisles.com**

Little Cranberry Island

Little Cranberry Island is smaller, yet attracts a greater number of visitors by boat. Perhaps this is because the number of shoreside attractions is greater and the woodsy walks, though just as appealing, are shorter. The vibrant community of Islesford—some 400 in the summer, pared down to about 80 in the winter—seems to affect those who visit with a yen to return, for years to come.

NAVIGATION: Use Chart 13318. Little Cranberry Island is as easily accessed as its sister island to the west—simply steer north of red bell buoy "2," marking Spurling Rock, and enter Haddock Cove, leaving green cans "1" and "3" to port.

Anchorage and Moorings: Little Cranberry Yacht Club maintains two courtesy guest moorings—orange, marked LCYC—or if these are taken, Islesford Dock (left of the prominent ferry landing) can direct you to a rental mooring. Anchorage is possible outside the mooring area, but the bottom here (even more so toward the head of the harbor) is covered with thick grass and often kelp. Setting a hook securely enough to handle relatively swift currents of reversing tides may require several tries. The crowded dinghy dock alongside the ferry landing requires some ingenuity and agility to negotiate the cross-tender tie-ups for passage ashore. Stay clear of the face dock, which is regularly taken over by the inter-island ferry from Northeast Harbor.

GOIN' ASHORE: LITTLE CRANBERRY ISLAND, ME

Left of the ferry dock, the Lobstermen's Co-op sells fresh live lobsters. One pier to the left, the over-water Islesford Dock Restaurant (207-244-7494) serves brunch, lunch and dinner in a homey and convivial atmosphere (mid-June through September). The Islesford Dock is a local gathering place and something of a destination point for locals "in the know" from Mount Desert. Just inland of the dock and to the left, the National Park Service maintains the tiny but fascinating Islesford Museum, which displays well-presented artifacts and pictures of traditional Maine island life. The Neighborhood House and Library has a remarkable children's collection and houses Julia's Garden—sculpted cedar fencing enclosing a must-see collection of local mosses, plants and flowers.

ADDITIONAL RESOURCES:

- The Cranberry Isles, **www.cranberryisles.com**
- Little Cranberry Island/Islesford/Maine/USA, **www.islesford.com**

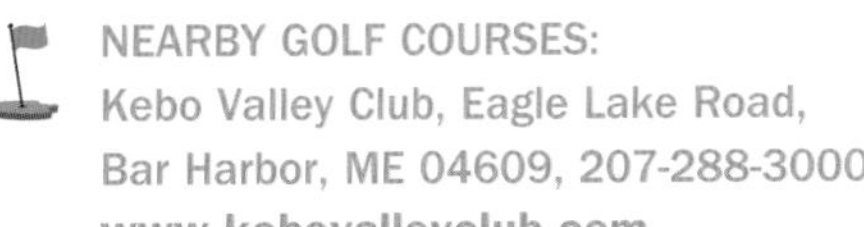

NEARBY GOLF COURSES:
Kebo Valley Club, Eagle Lake Road,
Bar Harbor, ME 04609, 207-288-3000,
www.kebovalleyclub.com

NEARBY MEDICAL FACILITIES:
Mount Desert Island Hospital, 10 Wayman Lane,
Bar Harbor, ME 04609, 207-288-5081

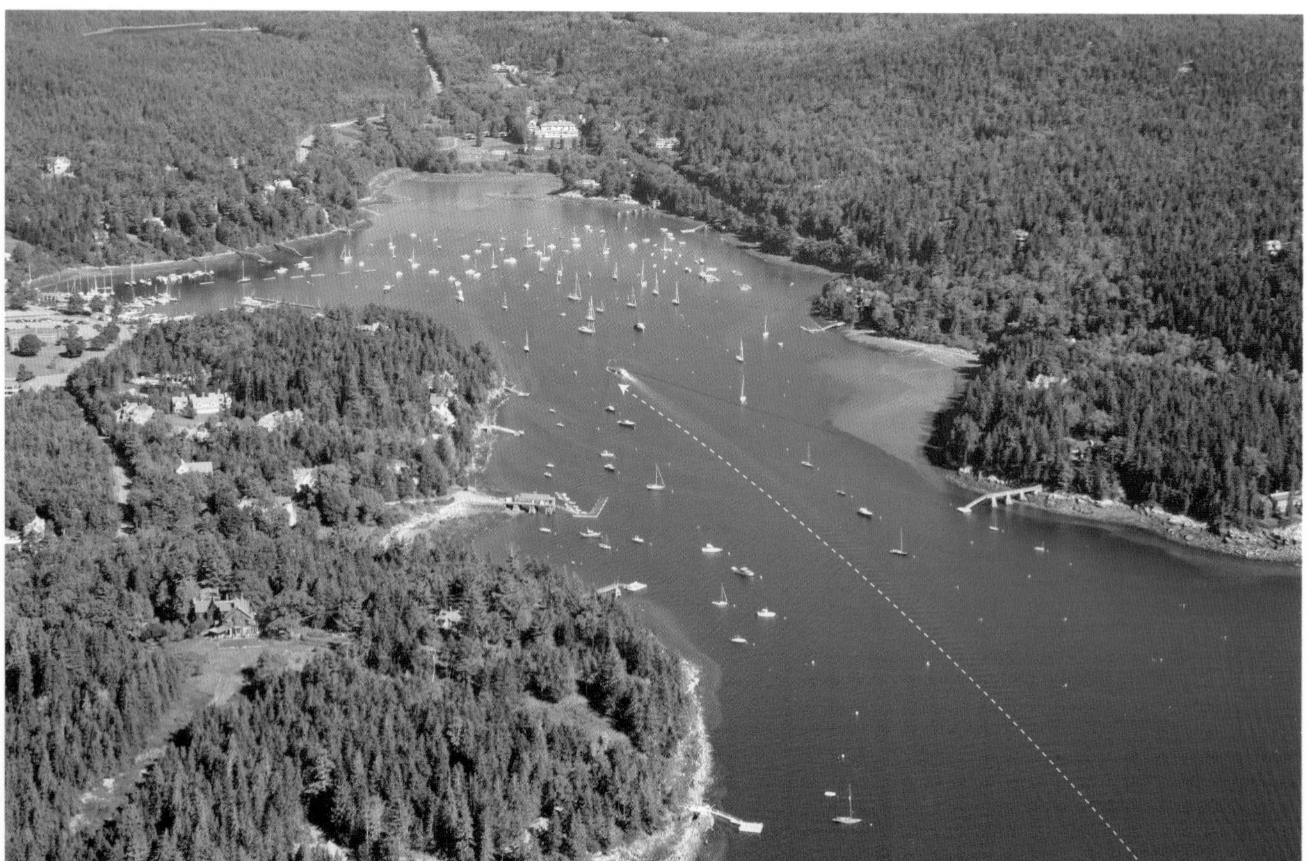

Looking north over Northeast Harbor. (Not to be used for navigation.) WATERWAY GUIDE PHOTOGRAPHY

Northeast Harbor

NAVIGATION: Use Chart 13318. Northeast Harbor is a landlocked bight, easily entered from the south. Its only obstruction is a rock located about 500 yards directly off the center of the harbor's mouth, marked by green can buoy "1" to the east and red nun buoy "2" to the west. The rock may be passed on either side if you take care to observe the red-right-returning rule for the eastern passage around the rock, and south and west of Bear Island and red nun buoys "2A," "4" and "6."

Dockage and Moorings: Morris Service's new yard in Northeast Harbor is more than just a service yard, offering dockage, complete repair capabilities, shore power and showers, along with haul-out service. Just inside the harbor entrance to port, Clifton Dock Corp. offers mooring rentals and an easily accessible deepwater dock with gasoline, diesel, block and bag ice and a few supplies. Northeast Harbor Marina Docks dominates the western cove of the harbor with some 70 slips.

The harbormaster can be reached on VHF Channel 09 or by calling 207-276-5737. The harbormaster assigns spaces through advance reservations or, during the season, from a waiting list. You should call ahead to be recorded on the harbormaster's list, then pick up an available mooring from among the harbor's large field of rentals. At 9:30 a.m. and 2:30 p.m. each day, available dock space is offered to those on the waiting list via VHF Channel 09. A percentage of the moorings in the inner harbor have been converted to a two-point mooring, anchoring a float. Cruisers traveling in company can request both sides of the same float. In any event, the moorings are a relatively easy ride by tender from the ample dinghy dock at the municipal pier. Public phones and restrooms are next to the harbormaster's office. Nearby to the right, the Yachtsmen's Building, operated by the chamber of commerce, provides tourism information, a reading room with current newspapers and five-minute showers for a small fee (bring your own soap and towel). Wireless Internet service is available from the chamber of commerce during business hours.

GOIN' ASHORE:
NORTHEAST HARBOR, ME

Well-organized but always seemingly filled to capacity, Northeast Harbor plays host to nearly every conceivable recreational vessel. The village is upscale but quaint, and most of the shops are located nearby on Main Street. Sea Princess Cruises (207-276-5352), providing mail and passenger service to the Cranberry Islands, is based here, as is *Sunbeam V*, which provides religious services to the out islands. Various tour boats also are docked here for whale-watching tours and naturalists' excursions. The Thuya Gardens (207-276-3727) are permanently moored to the hill on the northeastern side of the harbor and are a botanist's and a gardener's delight. Although the rugged appeal of mountainous Acadia National Park is close by, this community is primarily oriented toward the sea.

Main Street offers excellent reprovisioning opportunities. Pine Tree Market and Liquors (121 Main St., 207-276-3335) will deliver to the town dock. You can make arrangements with MDI Water Taxi (207-244-7312) to transport both you and your provisions from dockside to boat. To the right on Main Street, you will find The Holmes Store (114 Main St., 207-276-3273), offering all the proper clothing for Down East yachting, the Shirt Off Your Back Laundry (1 Main St., 207-276-5611), the post office, a bank and F.T. Brown Hardware and Marine (106 Main St., 207-276-3329), one of the largest retail chandleries in Maine. You will also find a gift and wine specialties shop, bookstore, coin-operated laundry, newspaper and stationery store and several attractive galleries and boutiques.

On the east side of Main Street, Main Street Variety (120 Main St., 207-276-3225) has some groceries, beer and wine, gas pumps and bicycles for rent down the alley. The biggest and brightest restaurant is said to be Main Sail (10 Huntington Road, 207-276-3383), attached to the Kimball Terrace Inn, to the left of the town dock. On Sea Street, the Docksider Restaurant (207-276-3965) is casual, with a full menu (including lobster and ice cream) and a take-out window.

McGrath Variety Store (207-276-5548) is the village center for video rentals and newspapers, including the New York Times and Boston Globe and has a coffee, espresso and galato bar. There are two full-service banks with ATMs. The Northeast Harbor Library (1 Joy Road, 207-276-3333), which underwent a complete overhaul, is now open, offering complete library services with computers for Internet access.

ADDITIONAL RESOURCES:

Mount Desert Chamber of Commerce, **www.mountdesertchamber.org**

NEARBY GOLF COURSES:
Kebo Valley Club, Eagle Lake Road, Bar Harbor, ME 04609, 207-288-3000, **www.kebovalleyclub.com**

NEARBY MEDICAL FACILITIES:
Mount Desert Island Hospital, 10 Wayman Lane, Bar Harbor, ME 04609, 207-288-5081

Seal Harbor

On the southern shore of Mount Desert, on Eastern Way, is Seal Harbor, surrounded by impressive summer houses. There is no dockage, but a dinghy landing is located at the town dock, and a broad and sandy beach is at the head of the harbor. Anchoring is no longer a good prospect here, since private moorings have taken over most of the available space; you might be able to make arrangements with the harbormaster for an overnight stay at a vacant mooring. Expect a rolling night here due to surge from the east. No other services are available in this residential setting, except for a restaurant and gas station with a few groceries and supplies.

Frenchman Bay

Four miles wide, 10 miles long and easy to navigate, Frenchman Bay offers dramatic views of Mount Desert and the bluffs of the Schoodic Peninsula to the east. A group of islands with deep channels between them cuts across the bay about halfway up, creating shelter for the upper bay. It is a spectacular run up the bay along sea-washed cliffs, past Thunder Hole (where you can hear the surf crashing against the rocks at the right tidal stage), Sand Beach (behind Old Soaker) and great inland mountains.

Bar Harbor

Once famous for the huge "cottages" of its wealthy summer residents, Bar Harbor is now best known as Acadia National Park's primary tourist center. A disastrous fire in 1947 leveled much of the town, ending a way of life. But the legacy of the "cottage people"—their gifts of vast tracts of land to create the national park—ensured the beginning of a different but vibrant new era. Located on the east side of Mount Desert, under the imposing summits of Cadillac, Dorr and Champlain mountains, the town attracts throngs of hikers, climbers and kayakers, as well as sedentary vacationers and motorists. Surprisingly few arrive by water. An exception to this rule is the recent increase in visits by cruise ships. Be aware that you might share the harbor and channel with a 1,000-foot cruise liner.

NAVIGATION: Use Chart 13318. Use Bar Harbor tide tables. Bar Harbor is easily approached from the south on either side of Egg Rock, identified by a red five-second flashing light and horn on a 64-foot tower. The harbor is open to the east and can be entered through any of the deep channels between the Porcupine Islands. A breakwater extends to the west from Bald Porcupine Island, marked by a white daybeacon at its western end. Entry also may be made between the daybeacon and the mainland. The breakwater will be submerged at high water, but do not attempt to cross it.

Anchorage and Moorings: Anchorage is possible outside the mooring area just east of the municipal pier. Unfortunately, the holding ground is poor, and the relatively open harbor can become quite rough even in a moderate blow. Leaving an anchored boat unattended here is not recommended. A better idea, especially when reprovisioning or changing crews, is to take one of the usually available town moorings.

You can reach the harbormaster on VHF Channel 09; pay the fee at the office at the foot of the dock. The town's large dinghy dock is located on the western side of the pier. Dockage is unlikely to be available, but it might be possible to tie up for a brief period at the floats on the eastern side of the pier while you load, unload or replenish your water supply. Frenchman Bay Boating Co., just west of the town dock, has ice, Texaco diesel and gasoline. The major pier about a mile west of the town center is the between-trips berth of *The Cat*, the enormous catamaran car ferry running from Bar Harbor to Yarmouth, Nova Scotia. Adjacent to *The Cat*, the Bar Harbor Regency Hotel and Marina offers floating

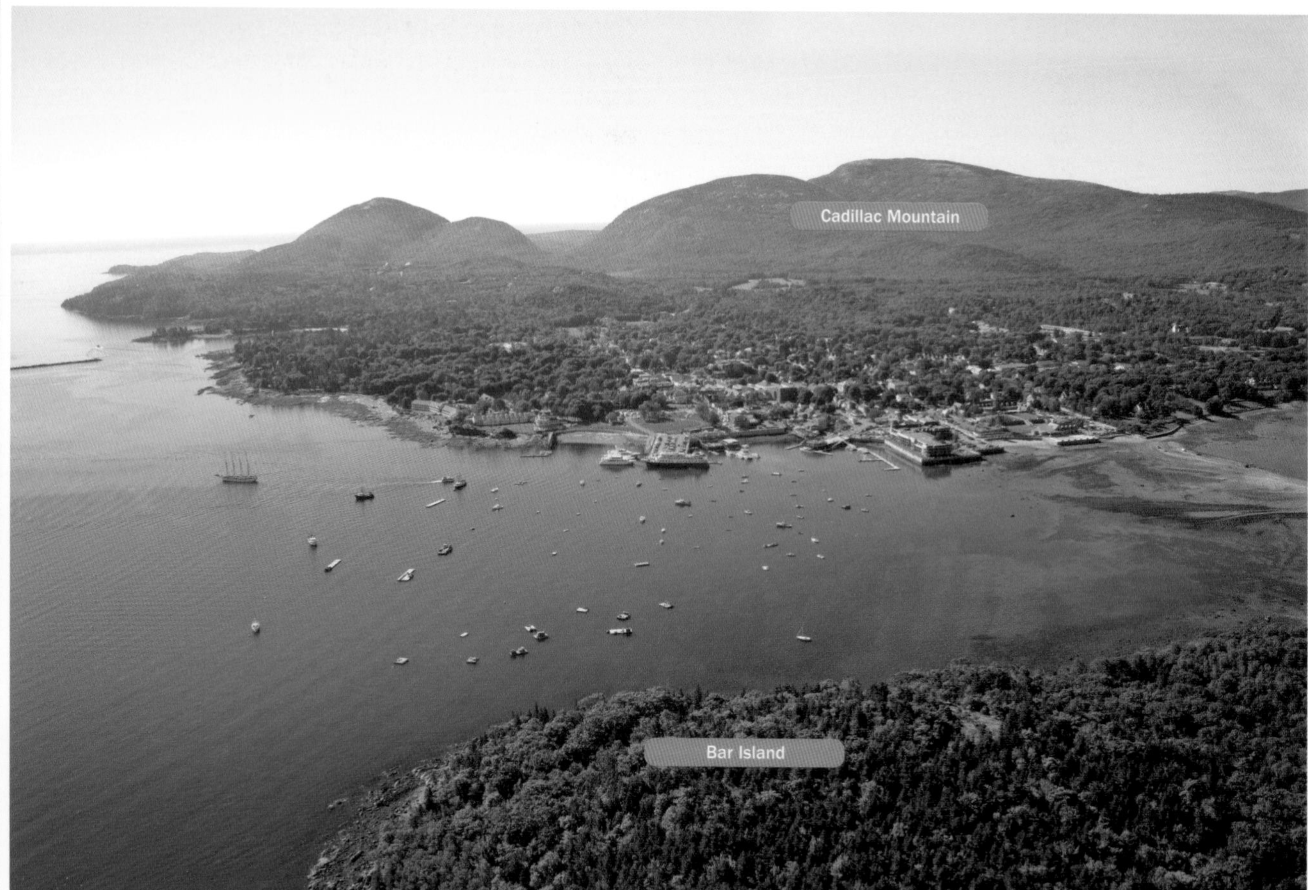

Looking south over Bar Harbor. (Not to be used for navigation.) WATERWAY GUIDE PHOTOGRAPHY

concrete docks with access to the resort's attractive pool, exercise room and showers. Two restaurants are on the premises, but access to other services will require about a mile's walk or taxi ride to the village center.

GOIN' ASHORE: BAR HARBOR, ME

Main Street (beginning just to the right of the Municipal Pier) and Cottage Street (beginning a block up Main Street) offer interesting browsing and reprovisioning opportunities. Walking up the hill on Main Street, you'll find Sherman's Book and Stationery (56 Main St., 207-288-3161) on the left, with nautical guides, nature books and NOAA charts for Maine. Farther along are two banks with ATMs, a drugstore, and JH Butterfield Co.'s gourmet grocery and wine store (152 Main St., 207-288-3386).

The Criterion Theatre (35 Cottage St., 207-288-3441) is an art deco masterpiece, which has more than 900 seats and runs two movies every night. There is now a second theater, Reel Pizza Cinerama (33 Kennebec Place, 207-288-3828), just off the village green.

Acadia Bike and Coastal Kayak Rentals (48 Cottage St., 207-288-9605), Cadillac Mountain Sports (26 Cottage St., 207-288-4532) and a large Rite Aid drugstore (207-288-2222) all are located along Cottage Street. About half a mile away on Cottage Street is Hannaford Supermarket and Pharmacy (86 Cottage St., 207-288-5680), the only fully stocked grocery store within reasonable walking distance.

Dinner reservations are advisable at most restaurants to avoid a long wait. On Main Street, Poor Boy's Gourmet (300 Main St., 207-288-4148) deserves high marks for well-prepared meals at reasonable prices and for a clever wine list. Parkside on the Green (185 Main St., 207-288-3700) seems (but is not) entirely al fresco, offering colorful views of the passing scene. McKay's Public House (207-288-2002) at 231 Main offers "elevated pub fare" and is highly recommended. On Cottage Street, Island Chowder House (38 Cottage St., 207-288-4905) serves seafood fast, and Rosalie's Pizza and Italian Restaurant (46 Cottage St., 207-288-5666) offers Italian specialties and beer on tap. Pizza connoisseurs will find it worthwhile to make the trek down Cottage Street to Rosalie's, located on the left. Near the municipal pier, Duffy's Quarterdeck (1 Main St., 207-288-1161) specializes in seafood with a harbor view. The most elegant waterfront dining is to be found at the Bar Harbor Inn (1 Newport Dr., 207-288-3351), which has its own dock just east of the town pier. Stewman's Lobster Pound (207-288-9723), at the Bar Harbor Regency Marina, serves Down East favorites, while fine dining on a more formal note is available at the Edenfield Restaurant (207-288-9723) there. Of special note is the funky Café This Way (207-288-4483) on 14 Mount Desert St.

ADDITIONAL RESOURCES:

- Bar Harbor Chamber of Commerce, **www.barharborinfo.com**

NEARBY GOLF COURSES:
Kebo Valley Club, Eagle Lake Road,
Bar Harbor, ME 04609, 207-288-3000,
www.kebovalleyclub.com

NEARBY MEDICAL FACILITIES:
Mount Desert Island Hospital, 10 Wayman Lane,
Bar Harbor, ME 04609, 207-288-5801

Sorrento

One of the most beautiful and well-protected harbors on the coast, Sorrento is at the tip of Waukeeg Neck. The Sorrento Yacht Club maintains a floating dock for dinghies and permits brief big-boat tie-ups for water or phone calls. Anchorage protection is excellent. There is a guest mooring with a wooden tag that identifies it as a memorial to a yachtsman who has passed on to Fiddler's Green.

Winter Harbor

A cruise across the bay from Mount Desert leaves the tourist crush in its wake. The harbor—three harbors, really—is (are) unobstructed and easy to enter, even in fog. Each harbor has a landing with a floating dock, though ease of access to the village varies.

Anchorage and Moorings: On entering the outer harbor through the marked channel between Grindstone Neck and Ned Island, a turn to port will quickly reveal the distinctive clubhouse of the Winter Harbor Yacht Club on the west shore of Sand Cove. Protection is only fair in this cove; your boat will pitch a bit here when the wind is up. But the yacht club's moorings are up to the task, and there is plenty of anchorage room with excellent holding on either end of the mooring field. Launch and trash disposal services are included with the club's mooring fee, and showers are available in the clubhouse basement for a small fee. There are no other facilities on Sand Cove, and the village is about a mile's walk to the right. Another mile's trek on the dirt road left from the clubhouse will take you to pleasant outlooks over the pink granite shore at the southern tip of Grindstone Neck.

Local fishermen have wisely claimed virtually all of the Inner Harbor, which offers the harbor's overall best protection. There is no room to anchor, but it may be possible to secure a vacant mooring; ask a lobsterman. Winter Harbor Co-op has a dock and float with both gasoline and diesel fuel. It may be possible to rent dock space with electricity here. The village is but a few blocks away from the landing.

Henry Cove, a straight shot in from the outer harbor, is the most exposed of the three coves, but is relatively convenient to town. Winter Harbor Marina, located on the east side of the cove, maintains several rental moorings and may have dock space with water and electricity at its floats (depths to 6 feet at low water).

In center village, J.M. Garrish's Store (207-963-2727) serves breakfast, tasty light (and reasonable) lunches and ice cream. Across the street is the Winter Harbor Five and Dime Store (207-963-7927). The post office is about half a mile east on Main Street, and the sizable IGA market is across the street, particularly convenient to Winter Harbor Marina.

In August, Winter Harbor puts on its Annual Lobster Festival, which includes a lobster dinner, parade and booths offering homemade foods and local crafts. The main event of the day is a "serious" lobster boat race, most of whose participants appear to end up in Bar Harbor for an after-race recap and other activities.

East of Schoodic Point

Beyond Mount Desert and Schoodic Point lies a green, lonesome land of ragged islands, rocky reaches, swift Bay of Fundy currents and ever-increasing tidal stages. An exciting, even dangerous coast, this is an area for the experienced skipper or the wary neophyte, not for the afternoon sailor in a small powerboat or low-powered auxiliary.

On this coast, the best guidebook is experience and vigilance. You will need practical navigational know-how, a thorough oceangoing knowledge of your boat and how she acts under all weather conditions, and enough mechanical ability to make repairs as needed. Between Winter Harbor and Eastport, more than 60 miles away, there are no lifts and few mechanics. Despite such daunting observations, the ragged island outposts to the east bear silent witness to an increasing parade of recreational craft under sail and power each summer, as intrepid skippers seek the solitude and pleasure of a near-wilderness experience.

All vessels should have a depth sounder, a VHF radio, GPS or LORAN (though you are likely to encounter signal disturbances near the naval communications center at Cutler) and a stable dinghy. A cabin heater is often welcome to dry out during foggy spells and to warm up on chilly evenings. The best time for cruising extends from mid-July to late August, although many skippers enjoy the clear, cool weather of early September.

From Schoodic Point east, tidal range increases rapidly. Sixteen feet is normal for U.S. waters (easterly storms add a fathom), and in the Bay of Fundy the tidal difference reaches 60 feet. Obviously, such tidal changes produce powerful currents of widely varying set. No graphs or sets of tables help much, and current predictions are impossible.

Between Schoodic Point and the U.S./Canadian border (which bisects Quoddy Roads) lie a few dozen islands and ports where fuel is available. Few have fresh water in quantity; fewer still have dockside electricity. However, most offer excellent mechanical services.

In general, fuel ports lie well up the reaches, so allow for a fairly lengthy inshore run when fuel gets low. Some of the sources, passing east, are Prospect Harbor, Corea Harbor, Cape Split, Beals Island, Jonesport, Bucks Harbor, Cutler, the deep cove in Bailey's Mistake and, of course, Eastport and Lubec. These are working ports, not yachting centers. Most have no facilities other than small lobstermen's docks. Make your stay at dockside as brief as possible and get out on a mooring for the night. The exception is Eastport, which has developed a 50-slip marina with lighted floating docks and friendly service. Cruisers can

Hancock Point, Sorrento, ME

HANCOCK POINT, SORRENTO		Largest Vessel Accommodated	VHF Channel Monitored	Transient Berths / Total Berths	Approach / Dockside Depth (reported)	Floating Docks	Gas / Diesel	Groceries, Ice, Marine Supplies, Snacks	Repairs: Hull, Engine, Propeller	Lift (tonnage), Crane, Rail	1=110V, 2=220V, B=Both, Max Amps	Laundry, Pool, Showers	Pump-Out Station	Nearby: Grocery Store, Motel, Restaurant
		Dockage					Supplies		Services					
1. Hancock Point Dock	207-422-3393			MOORINGS										M
2. Sorrento Town Dock	207-422-6549	80	09	/8							1/20			

Corresponding chart(s) not to be used for navigation. Internet Access Wireless Internet Access

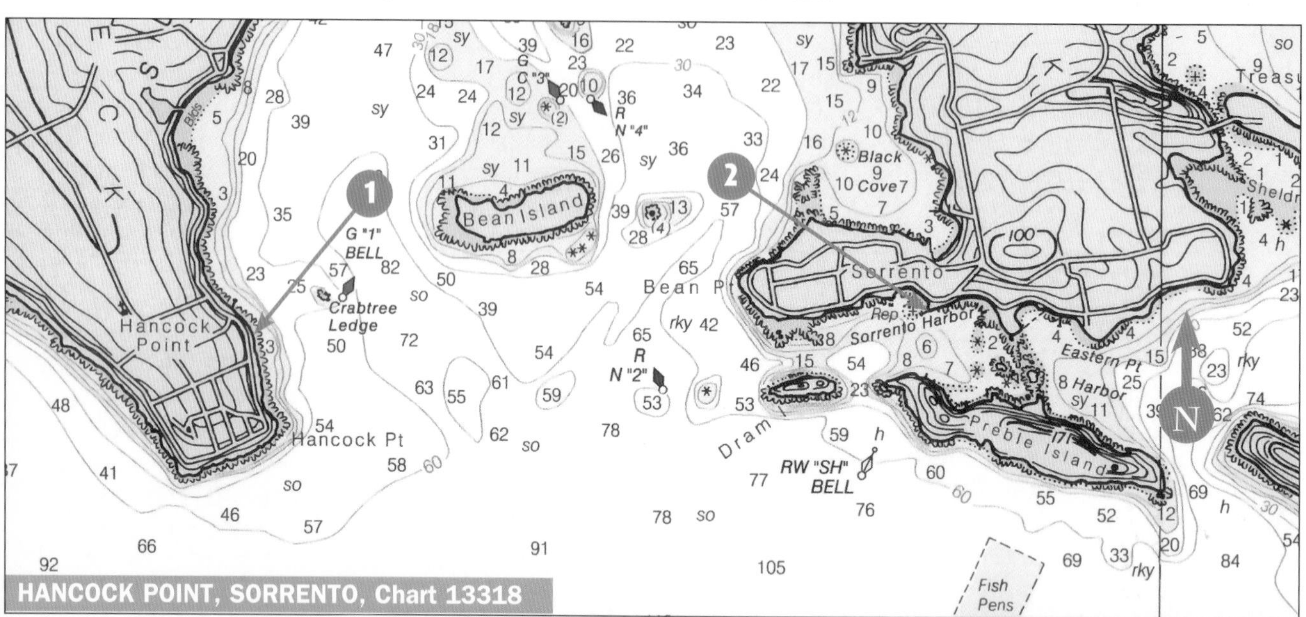

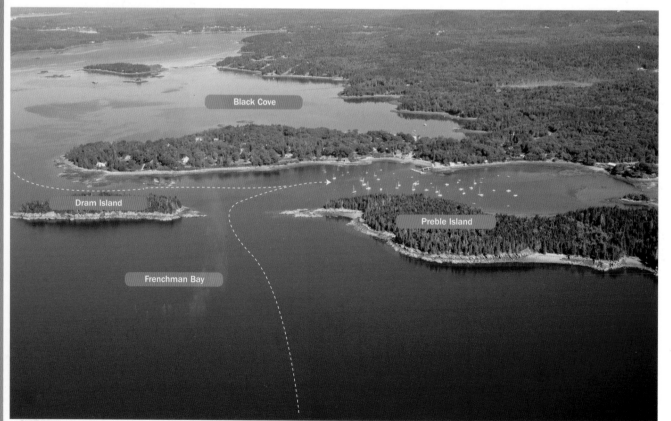

Looking north over Sorrento. (Not to be used for navigation.) WATERWAY GUIDE PHOTOGRAPHY

Winter Harbor, ME

WINTER HARBOR		Largest Vessel Accommodated	VHF Channel Monitored	Transient Berths / Total Berths	Approach / Dockside Depth (reported)	Floating Docks	Gas / Diesel	Groceries, Ice, Marine Supplies, Snacks	Repairs: Hull, Engine, Propeller	Lift (tonnage), Crane, Rail	1=110V, 2=220V, B=Both, Max Amps	Laundry, Pool, Showers	Pump-Out Station	Nearby: Grocery Store, Motel, Restaurant
		Dockage					Supplies		Services					
1. Winter Harbor Marine Inc.	207-963-7449	100	16/09		35/25		GD	GIMS	HEP		B	LS	P	GMR
2. Winter Harbor Yacht Club	207-963-2275		16/09		50/20			I				S		

Corresponding chart(s) not to be used for navigation. Internet Access Wireless Internet Access

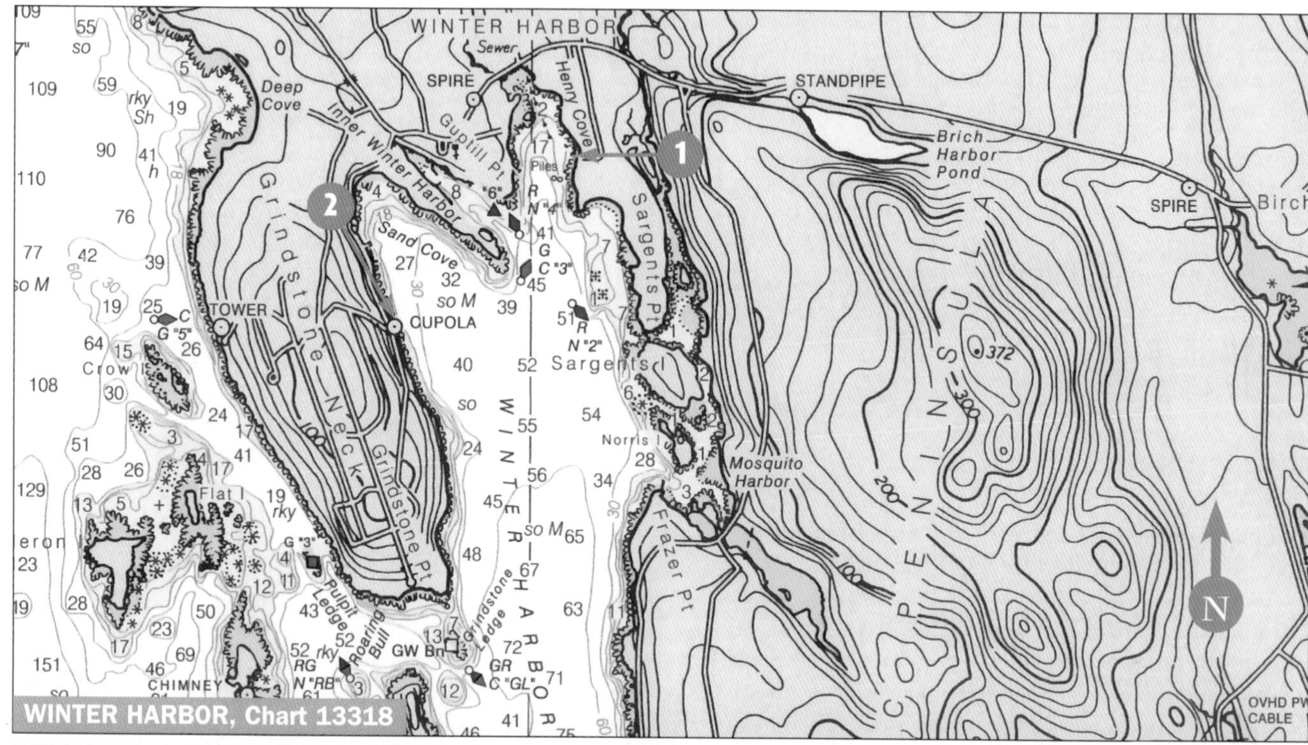

Looking northwest over Winter Harbor and Henry Cove. (Not to be used for navigation.) WATERWAY GUIDE PHOTOGRAPHY

Jonesport, ME

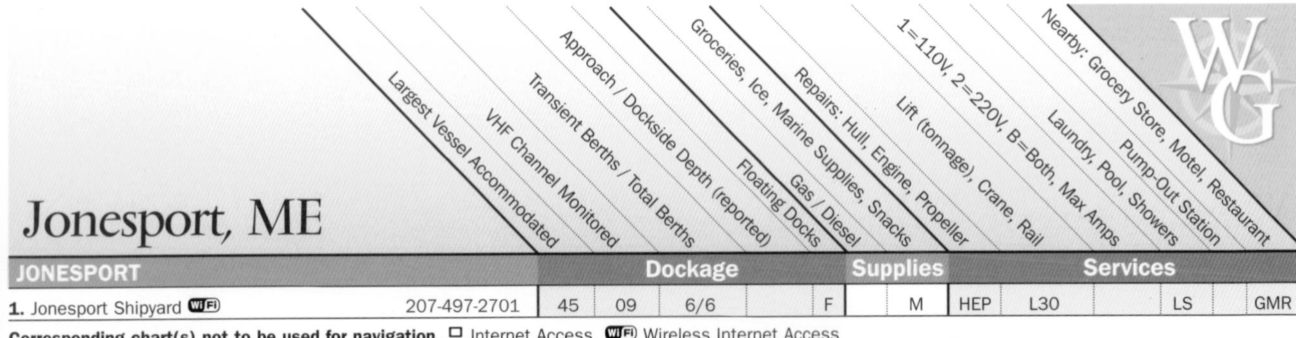

JONESPORT		Largest Vessel Accommodated	VHF Channel Monitored	Transient Berths / Total Berths	Approach / Dockside Depth (reported)	Floating Docks	Gas / Diesel	Groceries, Ice, Marine Supplies, Snacks	Repairs: Hull, Engine, Propeller	Lift (tonnage), Crane, Rail	1=110V, 2=220V, B=Both, Max Amps	Laundry, Pool, Showers	Pump-Out Station	Nearby: Grocery Store, Motel, Restaurant
		Dockage						Supplies	Services					
1. Jonesport Shipyard (WiFi)	207-497-2701	45	09	6/6		F		M	HEP	L30		LS		GMR

Corresponding chart(s) not to be used for navigation. Internet Access (WiFi) Wireless Internet Access

tie up at no charge for several hours if shopping or dining. The town dock recently added 120 feet of new pier.

Schoodic Point to Campobello

The fixed highway bridge usually dictates the choice between going offshore or running the coast with its 39-foot fixed vertical clearance at Jonesport. The coaster who runs outside the islands and headlands, and works the sea buoys, has a comparatively easy but less interesting run than the vessel cruising the reaches and thoroughfares. The former faces the usual blue water sea and weather problems, while the latter follows stretches of coast where carpets of lobster-pot buoys intermingle with small islands and ledges crowded with sunbathing seals. The route has hazards that make piloting a challenge even to the experienced cruising mariner.

Alongshore Run

NAVIGATION: Use Charts 13318 and 13324. When Schoodic Head and the island disappear into the fog astern, some harbors of a different stripe lie ahead. As long as the wind is fair and seas are moderate, do not let fog interfere with your cruising plans. Fog is simply a fact of life here. Avoid searching for silent buoys (cans or nuns) unless you have radar.

Corea

This traditional Down East lobstering village delivers prime material for scores of Maine postcards. The high, tide-permissive wharves, piled with lobster traps, floats and gear make it clear that this harbor is all business—no cushy marina berths here. Coming ashore is likely to mean a muddy slog, followed by a 25-foot climb up a slippery ladder. Fresh lobsters can be bought from the Lobster Co-op, but little else is available.

NAVIGATION: Use Chart 13325. Approach Corea from the south, using the red-and-white "CE" whistle south of Western Island as a guide. From there, set a course along Western Island's bold western shore, then trace the contour of the shore halfway along the northern side of the island at a distance of about 150 to 200 yards before turning northward toward the cliffs, just east of the narrow Corea Harbor entrance. A radar reflector on a stake marks a rock located out from the western side, urging a course that hugs the eastern side of the entrance until you reach the Lobster Co-op dock.

Moorings: An orange mooring ball is in the narrow channel just in front of the co-op's dock, which you can use for a short transaction, but vessels of more than 30 feet will soon have to move to make room for unloading lobster boats. Ask about the availability of a mooring in the inner harbor for a longer stay.

A walk through this quaint village is well worth climbing the ladder. The town's sole grocery store has closed, but the post office is still open. Also open during the season is an unnamed family restaurant across from the white church visible from the harbor. The crab and lobster rolls are delicious (and inexpensive), as are the freshly baked bread, blueberry pies and muffins. But other amenities, such as ice and groceries, can no longer be had from anywhere closer than Birch Harbor, several miles to the west.

Looking north over Corea Harbor and Goluldsboro Bay. (Not to be used for navigation.) WATERWAY GUIDE PHOTOGRAPHY

Additional Anchorage: East of Petit Manan are many islands in Western Bay such as Trafton and Flint—also Cape Split Harbor—which are highly regarded as secure anchorages. If your mast is short enough (less than 39 feet), sail Moosabec Reach to Jonesport via Beals Island Bridge. A state pier, launching ramp, fuel, ice and provisions make this sardine and lobster town an important place on the coast. The B.S. Look Wharf sells fresh fish and scallops at the large building that looks like a warehouse, a short walk from the state pier and float. Do not try to dock at the Look Wharf. The tidal range at Jonesport is impressive, as is the speed of ebb and flood currents.

Eastern Bay

NAVIGATION: Use Chart 13325. This island-studded bay lies partly enclosed between Great Wass Island on the west side and Head Harbor and Steele Harbor islands on the east. In clear weather, Eastern Bay is an intricate but generally well-buoyed puzzle for pilots with Chart 13326. In fog, it becomes a worrisome place when landmarks and navigational aids are obscured. Fortunately, a reliable foghorn is mounted on the lighthouse (flashing 30-second light at 72 feet in elevation) at what is known as Moose Peak, showing the way into the deep passage of Main Channel Way east of Mistake and Knight islands. Do not attempt to enter the false channel between these two islands. High tide gives the appearance of a channel here, but a barely submerged rock ledge bars the way.

Anchorage: Having entered Main Channel Way, west of Steel Harbor Island, make a turn to port around the northern end of Knight Island, which will lead to a well-protected anchorage between Mistake Island and Water Island in 10 to 15 feet at low tide. There is room for half a dozen boats here, but be wary of kelp that can foul your anchor, and of shoaling that occurs on the western side of Mistake Island. From here, a short dinghy ride into the cut between Knight and Mistake islands will bring you to an abandoned Coast Guard boathouse and ramp. Here, a wooden boardwalk leads through the scrub and the abundant blueberry and raspberry bushes on the way to the lighthouse on Moose Peak. (Be ready for a piercing blast from the foghorn if light conditions weaken.) The lightkeeper's house is gone, but the scenery and views rank among the most stunning in Maine. Seals usually can be seen on the ledges below and, often, eagles in the skies above.

Eastern Bay has numerous other anchorages, particularly along the east and north shores of Great Wass Island. The most important of these, both for the beauty of its setting and hurricane hole protection, is in Mud Hole, a mile-long cleft in the east side of Great Wass Island, northwest of the northern tip of Knight Island. Entry and departure are most safely made on a rising tide, half tide or higher, skirting the south side of the harbor entrance to avoid a grass-covered shoal that blocks the north side. Reports are that the submerged remains of an old weir obstruct the area about an eighth of a mile outside the entrance to port (on entry). You will want to skirt that location before heading toward the south side of the harbor entry to work your way in. In settled weather, good anchorage can be made outside Mud Hole in about 35 feet of water to permit exploration by dinghy. Once inside, however, there is protection in any weather with excellent holding in (no surprise) mud, with 10 feet of water at low tide. Most of Great Wass Island is owned by the Nature Conservancy, which maintains hiking trails. Park your dinghy at a likely landing spot on the south side of Mud Hole (keeping in mind the 10-foot tidal range when tying off the painter) and scramble up the bank for about 50 yards to reach the unmistakable trail above. In a two-hour summer walk through the spruce forests, along the boreal bogs and out to the granite beaches, you will undoubtedly observe dozens of types of mosses and lichens, a variety of mushrooms, bell flowers, beach irises and possibly unusual plants such as the baked-apple berry and dragon's mouth orchid. American eagles do not nest on the island, but they are frequent visitors, as are numerous songbirds, including the palm warbler, which nests here.

Chandler Bay

Anchorage: Privately owned Roque Island has a large outer harbor with a deservedly famous beach. Secure anchorage is easy in sand or mud here in 10 to 16 feet of water at low tide and located only a short ride from a dinghy landing on the beach. The entire island is posted as a wildlife stronghold, and a sign prominently posted by the Roque Island Gardner Homestead Corp. denies access beyond the beach itself, except to those with written permission from the island's owners. The owners request that you do not enter the southern half of the mile-long beach, which is reserved for the Gardner family. Despite these restrictions, the area is worth a stop because of its extraordinary beauty. Bald eagles are almost inevitably sighted here, and Seal Ledge on the eastern side of the harbor is still appropriately named. Lakeman Harbor, formed by Marsh, Bar and Lakeman islands at the southeastern end of Roque Island, offers a protected inner harbor with secure holding in 7 to 8 feet of water at low tide. On the northern side of Roque Island, Shorey Cove is protected from the prevailing southwesterlies and offers good holding in 7 to 11 feet of water, with pleasant views of the Gardner houses, barns and docks. Public use of the dock is prohibited. The rock "Rep" in the center of the channel west of Great Spruce Island is reportedly not to be found by either depth sounder or keel.

Cutler, marked by the Little River Island light and horn, is closer to open water than many of the villages along this coast, yet is a secure anchorage except in a piping nor'easter. Cutler is a good point of departure for the Canadian Maritime Provinces and is frequently a gathering place for club cruises rallying for an international passage. A few moorings might be available, but most boats anchor here in soft mud. In a blow, dragging anchors are commonplace. You can land a dinghy on the dark beach in front of the village's cluster of houses, though you should make provision for the Fundy-influenced 13-foot tides. You can also make a landing farther down the harbor at the float at the end of the Little River Lobster Co. dock. Just tie your dinghy to the dock and carefully climb the wooden ladder marked with a sign that says, PASS AT YOUR OWN RISK. The Village Grocery is a short distance to the right of a landing at either spot, selling basic provisions and bag ice and serving breakfast or lunch in the small diner at the rear of the store. A public phone is outside. A couple of blocks past the Village Grocery and to the left is a second grocery store and luncheonette, complete with pool table and television, and the post office. To the left of the lobster company's wharf, it is a short walk to The Lodge, where showers are available, with towel, for a fee. Across the street, the town office and library has a marine hatchery that you can visit when someone is there to let you in.

GOIN' ASHORE:

MACHIAS SEAL ISLAND, ME

Cutler also is a frequent jumping-off place for a visit to Machias Seal Island, 10 miles to the southeast. There is only one reason to visit this 15-acre, barren and often fog-shrouded outcrop—the extraordinary bird life. Machias Seal Island is the spring and summer home of 3,500 to 4,500 puffins, an estimated 900 razorbill hawks and several other species of sea birds, including Arctic terns and petrels. Until mid-August annually (in recent years longer), these nesting birds fill the sea and air for a mile around the island. A sail along this rocky outcrop, even if only for an hour or so, will be more than worth the detour. Clown-like puffins will buzz the boat, seemingly oblivious to the gesturing humans on deck as they go about the serious business of gathering herring from the teeming waters below. This is fortunate because it is quite difficult to land on the island, and only 30 people per day are allowed ashore during the nesting period. You can hail the Canadian rangers on the island (VHF Channel 19) for current status and permission.

On even the calmest day, ocean swells make for a daunting landing on the slippery granite rocks virtually everywhere along the island's shore. Just to make matters more interesting, the best place to secure a foothold to clamber ashore (in the lee of the 82-foot lighthouse) has a steel marine railway that can do serious damage to an inflatable. (It is for this reason that the area's professional guides cover their heavy metal tenders in thick fiberglass.) Anchorage—on kelp-covered rocks—is difficult as well, making a fouled set and dragging anchor a near certainty. The more secure way to visit the birds ashore will be to arrange a trip with one of the guides who make tours of the island. For example, John Norton of Jonesport, ME (207-497-5933), has been taking groups here (along with his father, who started the business in 1940) all of his life. He is knowledgeable and colorful and will get you on and off the island in one piece.

ADDITIONAL RESOURCES:

- Puffin Tours of Machias Seal Island, **www.machiassealisland.com**

Lubec, Eastport, ME

LUBEC, EASTPORT		Largest Vessel Accommodated	VHF Channel Monitored	Transient Berths / Total Berths	Approach / Dockside Depth (reported)	Floating Docks	Gas / Diesel	Groceries, Ice, Marine Supplies, Snacks	Repairs: Hull, Engine, Propeller	Lift (tonnage), Crane, Rail	1=110V, 2=220V, B=Both, Max Amps	Laundry, Pool, Showers	Pump-Out Station	Nearby: Grocery Store, Motel, Restaurant
		Dockage						Supplies		Services				
1. Eastport Breakwater/City Dock	207-853-4614	100	16/09	20/50	40/8	F	GD	GIMS		L50	1/30	L		GMR

Corresponding chart(s) not to be used for navigation. Internet Access Wireless Internet Access

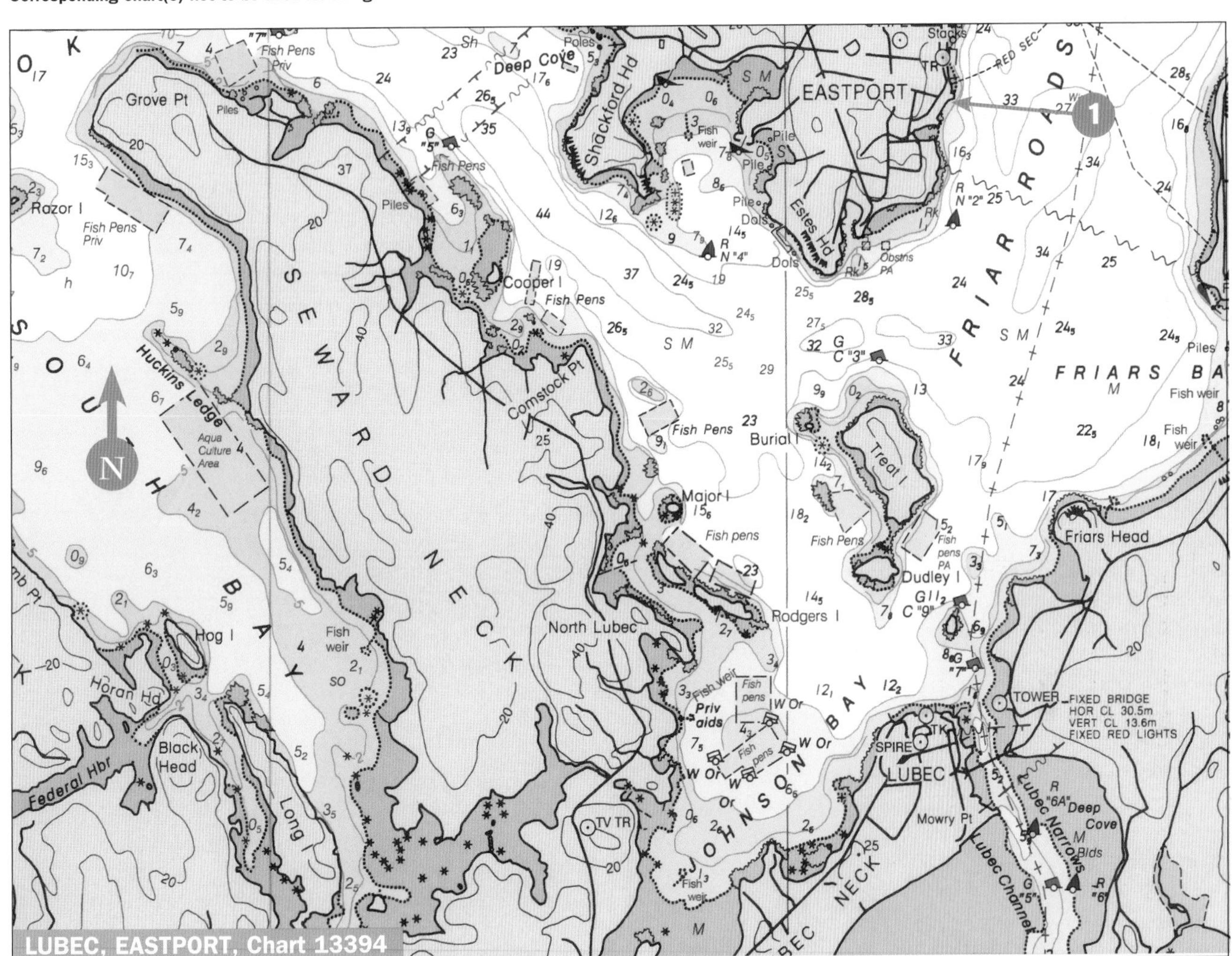

LUBEC, EASTPORT, Chart 13394

Lubec

A day's sail east of Cutler will bring you to West Quoddy Head, the easternmost point of land in the United States. Around the corner from the barber-pole lighthouse, Lubec Channel leads to the town of Lubec and eventually to Eastport. Lubec is located on the narrows of the same name, separating Maine from Canada.

NAVIGATION: Use Chart 13325. The town of Lubec is located beyond the International Bridge at the narrows. High water offers a vertical clearance of 47 feet. If you are determined to take this route, plan to reach the bridge at low water slack (which lasts five to 15 minutes) or at the early stage of the flood. Incoming currents become swift here (up to 6 knots), and the outgoing even more so (as swift as 8 knots). The passage is quite narrow, and long-tethered Coast Guard buoys might appear to be off-station at low water. (As a result, many locals advise in favor of the longer passage around East Quoddy Head on Campobello Island through Head Harbor Passage and Friar Roads.)

Moorings: You can take a taxi to Campobello Island, where the former home of Franklin and Eleanor Roosevelt is open to the public. Fuel trucks can deliver to the marina, and several grocery stores are located in the area.

Eastport

Dockage and Moorings: Forty miles by highway from Lubec, but only three miles by water, Eastport is a better layover choice. Boats can tie up out of the tidal current at the substantial L-shaped wharf and breakwater. A berth might be available at the floats on the northern and western sides of this manmade harbor, but space is usually at a premium here, and turning room is scarce. The best bet for vessels over 25 feet is to raft up at the end of one of the lines of fishing boats tied to the harbor's eastern breakwater. Access to the harbor is to the left of the large concrete dolphin in the center of the entrance. The mooring lines of the fishing boats, tied to the bollard atop the dolphin, usually rule out entry to the right of the dolphin. The wharf just south of the enclosed harbor provides additional dock space. In either location, many amenities are close at hand. Moose Island Marine is located immediately at the end of the short road leading from the breakwater to Water Street. An impressive range of parts and supplies is available there, and specialty items can be ordered quickly. Repair services include a certified radar technician on staff. Nearby, the state of Maine has installed a 60-ton haul-out facility.

The large gray stone building just to the left of the harbor houses the post office on the upper level and the U.S. Customs office below (by far the easiest place in these waters to check back into the United States after a trip to Canada). The IGA grocery across the street from the post office provides all items necessary for major reprovisioning. East of the harbor, the Cannery Wharf Restaurants at Stinson's Wharf offer an alternative both for dockage (in a quieter and less crowded setting) and for dining. Blue Iris Restaurant (207-853-2440) is located at 31 Water St. The Happy Crab (35 Water St., 207-853-9400), a sports bar and grille, is a lively spot year-round. Bank Square Pizza and Deli (34 Water St., 207-853-2709) is a good choice for a more casual meal.

Cruising Options

At the Canadian border, mariners may choose to head for superb cruising opportunities in the Maritime Provinces or to retrace steps homeward. A third alternative, before heading south and without checking in and out of Canada, is to experience the beauty and extraordinary riptides (6-foot dancing waters and dinghy-sized whirlpools) of a day cruise along the international border in Passamaquoddy Bay and up the lower reaches of the St. Croix River. ■

WATERWAY GUIDE is always open to your observations from the helm. E-mail your comments on any navigation information in the guide to: editor@waterwayguide.com.

WATERWAY GUIDE advertising sponsors play a vital role in bringing you the most trusted and well-respected cruising guide in the country. Without our advertising sponsors, we simply couldn't produce the top-notch publication now resting in your hands. Next time you stop in for a peaceful night's rest, let them know where you found them—WATERWAY GUIDE, The Cruising Authority.

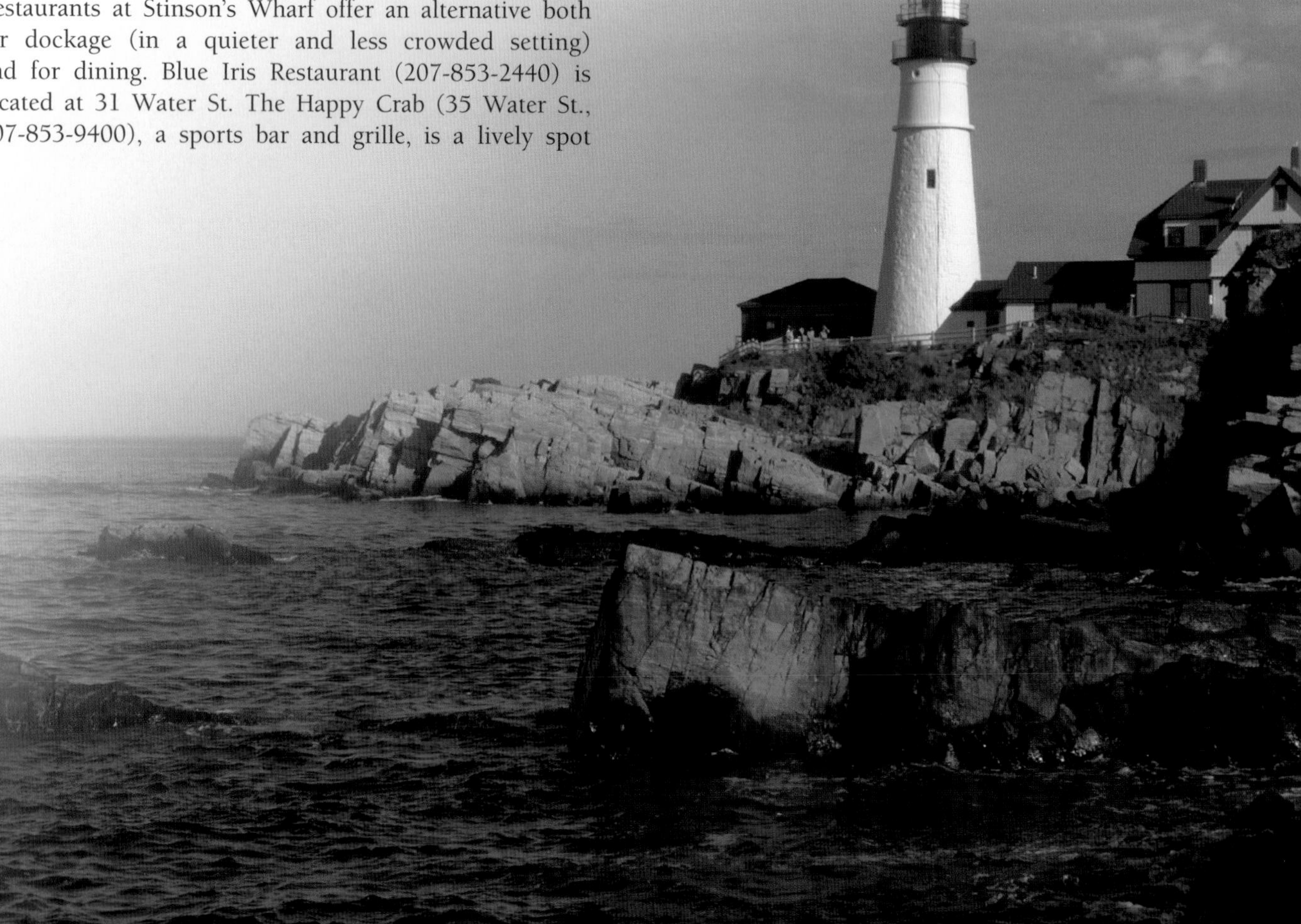

Portland Head Light is just one of the many lighthouses in Maine. ©ISTOCKPHOTO/EASYBUY4U

Atlantic City, New Jersey, 2010

Times and Heights of High and Low Waters

March

Day	Time (h m)	ft	cm	Time (h m)	ft	cm	Time (h m)	ft	cm	Time (h m)	ft	cm
1 M	0122	-1.1	-34	0736	5.1	155	0153*	-1.1	-34	0804*	4.9	149
2 Tu	0214	-1.0	-30	0824	4.9	149	0239*	-1.0	-30	0852*	4.9	149
3 W	0306	-0.9	-27	0911	4.6	140	0325*	-0.7	-21	0941*	4.8	146
4 Th	0359	-0.6	-18	1000	4.1	125	0412*	-0.4	-12	1031*	4.6	140
5 F	0453	-0.2	-6	1051	3.7	113	0501*	-0.1	-3	1124*	4.3	131
6 Sa	0551	0.2	6	1147	3.3	101	0556*	0.3	9			
7 Su ◑	1223	4.0	122	0654	0.5	15	1250*	3.0	91	0656*	0.6	18
8 M	0127	3.8	116	0801	0.6	18	0200*	2.9	88	0800*	0.7	21
9 Tu	0232	3.8	116	0904	0.7	21	0307*	2.9	88	0903*	0.7	21
10 W	0332	3.8	116	1001	0.6	18	0404*	3.0	91	1000*	0.6	18
11 Th	0424	3.9	119	1048	0.5	15	0452*	3.2	98	1049*	0.4	12
12 F	0509	4.1	125	1129	0.3	9	0533*	3.5	107	1133*	0.3	9
13 Sa	0549	4.2	128	1205*	0.1	3	0611*	3.7	113			
14 Su	1214	0.1	3	0726	4.2	128	0138*	0.0	0	0746*	3.9	119
15 M ●	0152	0.0	0	0802	4.2	128	0209*	0.0	0	0819*	4.1	125
16 Tu	0229	0.0	0	0836	4.2	128	0240*	-0.1	-3	0852*	4.2	128
17 W	0305	0.0	0	0909	4.0	122	0310*	-0.1	-3	0924*	4.3	131
18 Th	0342	0.0	0	0942	3.9	119	0342*	0.0	0	0957*	4.4	134
19 F	0421	0.1	3	1017	3.7	113	0417*	0.1	3	1033*	4.4	134
20 Sa	0504	0.2	6	1055	3.5	107	0457*	0.2	6	1116*	4.3	131
21 Su	0554	0.4	12	1141	3.3	101	0544*	0.3	9			
22 M	1207	4.3	131	0653	0.5	15	1239*	3.1	94	0643*	0.4	12
23 Tu ◐	0110	4.2	128	0800	0.5	15	0151*	3.1	94	0752*	0.4	12
24 W	0223	4.2	128	0910	0.4	12	0310*	3.2	98	0907*	0.3	9
25 Th	0337	4.4	134	1014	0.2	6	0421*	3.6	110	1018*	0.1	3
26 F	0444	4.5	137	1112	-0.1	-3	0522*	4.0	122	1122*	-0.3	-9
27 Sa	0543	4.7	143	1205*	-0.4	-12	0617*	4.5	137			
28 Su	1221	-0.5	-15	0637	4.9	149	1253*	-0.7	-21	0707*	4.8	146
29 M	0116	-0.8	-24	0727	4.9	149	0140*	-0.8	-24	0755*	5.1	155
30 Tu ○	0208	-0.9	-27	0816	4.8	146	0226*	-0.8	-24	0842*	5.2	158
31 W	0259	-0.8	-24	0903	4.6	140	0310*	-0.6	-18	0927*	5.2	158

April

Day	Time (h m)	ft	cm	Time (h m)	ft	cm	Time (h m)	ft	cm	Time (h m)	ft	cm
1 Th	0349	-0.6	-18	0950	4.3	131	0355*	-0.4	-12	1013*	5.0	152
2 F	0439	-0.4	-12	1037	4.0	122	0441*	-0.1	-3	1101*	4.8	146
3 Sa	0530	0.0	0	1126	3.6	110	0530*	0.3	9	1150*	4.4	134
4 Su	0624	0.3	9	1220*	3.3	101	0622*	0.6	18			
5 M	1245	4.1	125	0722	0.6	18	0120*	3.1	94	0720*	0.8	24
6 Tu ◑	0145	3.9	119	0823	0.7	21	0226*	3.0	91	0824*	1.0	30
7 W	0248	3.8	116	0923	0.8	24	0330*	3.0	91	0928*	1.0	30
8 Th	0348	3.7	113	1016	0.7	21	0426*	3.2	98	1026*	0.9	27
9 F	0442	3.8	116	1103	0.6	18	0515*	3.5	107	1117*	0.7	21
10 Sa	0529	3.9	119	1143	0.5	15	0557*	3.7	113			
11 Su	1203	0.5	15	0612	4.0	122	1220*	0.3	9	0635*	4.0	122
12 M	1246	0.3	9	0652	4.0	122	1254*	0.2	6	0711*	4.3	131
13 Tu	0126	0.1	3	0730	4.0	122	0128*	0.1	3	0746*	4.5	137
14 W ●	0205	0.0	0	0807	4.0	122	0201*	0.0	0	0821*	4.7	143
15 Th	0244	0.0	0	0843	3.9	119	0236*	0.0	0	0856*	4.8	146
16 F	0324	0.0	0	0920	3.8	116	0313*	0.0	0	0933*	4.8	146
17 Sa	0406	0.0	0	1000	3.7	113	0353*	0.1	3	1014*	4.8	146
18 Su	0453	0.1	3	1044	3.5	107	0439*	0.2	6	1101*	4.7	143
19 M	0544	0.2	6	1136	3.4	104	0532*	0.3	9	1154*	4.6	140
20 Tu	0642	0.3	9	1237*	3.4	104	0634*	0.4	12			
21 W ◐	1257	4.5	137	0745	0.3	9	0148*	3.4	104	0744*	0.5	15
22 Th	0206	4.4	134	0848	0.2	6	0259*	3.6	110	0857*	0.4	12
23 F	0316	4.4	134	0949	0.1	3	0405*	4.0	122	1007*	0.2	6
24 Sa	0422	4.4	134	1045	-0.1	-3	0504*	4.4	134	1110*	-0.1	-3
25 Su	0521	4.4	134	1137	-0.3	-9	0557*	4.8	146			
26 M	1209	-0.3	-9	0616	4.5	137	1226*	-0.4	-12	0647*	5.1	155
27 Tu	0103	-0.5	-15	0707	4.4	134	0113*	-0.5	-15	0734*	5.3	162
28 W ○	0154	-0.6	-18	0756	4.3	131	0159*	-0.4	-12	0820*	5.3	162
29 Th	0243	-0.5	-15	0843	4.2	128	0244*	-0.3	-9	0904*	5.3	162
30 F	0331	-0.4	-12	0929	4.0	122	0329*	-0.1	-3	0949*	5.1	155

May

Day	Time (h m)	ft	cm	Time (h m)	ft	cm	Time (h m)	ft	cm	Time (h m)	ft	cm
1 Sa	0419	-0.2	-6	1016	3.8	116	0414*	0.2	6	1033*	4.8	146
2 Su	0507	0.1	3	1103	3.5	107	0500*	0.5	15	1120*	4.5	137
3 M	0557	0.3	9	1153	3.3	101	0549*	0.7	21			
4 Tu	1209	4.2	128	0648	0.6	18	1247*	3.2	98	0643*	1.0	30
5 W	0102	4.0	122	0740	0.7	21	0146*	3.2	98	0743*	1.1	34
6 Th ◑	0158	3.8	116	0832	0.8	24	0244*	3.2	98	0844*	1.1	34
7 F	0255	3.7	113	0922	0.8	24	0339*	3.4	104	0944*	1.0	30
8 Sa	0350	3.7	113	1007	0.7	21	0429*	3.7	113	1038*	0.9	27
9 Su	0441	3.7	113	1049	0.6	18	0514*	3.9	119	1128*	0.7	21
10 M	0528	3.7	113	1129	0.4	12	0555*	4.2	128			
11 Tu	1214	0.5	15	0612	3.7	113	1207*	0.3	9	0634*	4.5	137
12 W	1258	0.3	9	0655	3.7	113	1246*	0.2	6	0713*	4.8	146
13 Th	0141	0.1	3	0737	3.8	116	0126*	0.1	3	0752*	5.0	152
14 F ●	0223	0.0	0	0819	3.8	116	0207*	0.0	0	0833*	5.1	155
15 Sa	0307	-0.1	-3	0902	3.7	113	0251*	0.0	0	0916*	5.1	155
16 Su	0353	-0.1	-3	0948	3.7	113	0338*	0.0	0	1001*	5.1	155
17 M	0442	-0.1	-3	1038	3.7	113	0429*	0.1	3	1051*	5.0	152
18 Tu	0534	0.0	0	1133	3.7	113	0526*	0.2	6	1145*	4.8	146
19 W	0629	0.0	0	1234*	3.7	113	0629*	0.3	9			
20 Th ◐	1245	4.6	140	0726	0.0	0	0139*	3.8	116	0737*	0.4	12
21 F	0149	4.4	134	0824	0.0	0	0244*	4.1	125	0846*	0.4	12
22 Sa	0255	4.2	128	0921	0.0	0	0346*	4.3	131	0954*	0.3	9
23 Su	0359	4.1	125	1017	-0.1	-3	0444*	4.6	140	1057*	0.1	3
24 M	0500	4.1	125	1109	-0.1	-3	0538*	4.9	149	1155*	0.0	0
25 Tu	0556	4.0	122	1200*	-0.2	-6	0627*	5.1	155			
26 W	1249	-0.2	-6	0649	4.0	122	1248*	-0.2	-6	0715*	5.2	158
27 Th ○	0140	-0.2	-6	0738	3.9	119	0135*	-0.1	-3	0800*	5.2	158
28 F	0228	-0.2	-6	0825	3.8	116	0220*	0.0	0	0843*	5.1	155
29 Sa	0314	-0.1	-3	0910	3.7	113	0305*	0.2	6	0926*	5.0	152
30 Su	0359	0.0	0	0955	3.6	110	0349*	0.4	12	1008*	4.8	146
31 M	0443	0.1	3	1039	3.5	107	0433*	0.6	18	1051*	4.6	140

June

Day	Time (h m)	ft	cm	Time (h m)	ft	cm	Time (h m)	ft	cm	Time (h m)	ft	cm
1 Tu	0527	0.3	9	1125	3.4	104	0518*	0.8	24	1134*	4.3	131
2 W	0610	0.5	15	1212*	3.4	104	0606*	0.9	27			
3 Th	1220	4.1	125	0654	0.6	18	0102*	3.4	104	0659*	1.1	34
4 F ◑	0108	3.8	116	0737	0.7	21	0154*	3.4	104	0756*	1.1	34
5 Sa	0159	3.6	110	0821	0.7	21	0246*	3.6	110	0856*	1.1	34
6 Su	0252	3.5	107	0906	0.7	21	0337*	3.8	116	0954*	1.0	30
7 M	0347	3.4	104	0950	0.6	18	0425*	4.1	125	1048*	0.8	24
8 Tu	0440	3.4	104	1036	0.5	15	0512*	4.4	134	1140*	0.6	18
9 W	0531	3.4	104	1122	0.3	9	0557*	4.7	143			
10 Th	1228	0.4	12	0621	3.5	107	1208*	0.2	6	0642*	4.9	149
11 F	0116	0.1	3	0709	3.6	110	1256*	0.0	0	0728*	5.2	158
12 Sa ●	0203	-0.1	-3	0757	3.7	113	0144*	-0.1	-3	0814*	5.3	162
13 Su	0250	-0.2	-6	0845	3.8	116	0234*	-0.2	-6	0901*	5.4	165
14 M	0338	-0.3	-9	0935	3.9	119	0326*	-0.2	-6	0950*	5.4	165
15 Tu	0427	-0.3	-9	1028	4.0	122	0420*	-0.1	-3	1040*	5.2	158
16 W	0517	-0.3	-9	1123	4.1	125	0518*	0.0	0	1133*	5.0	152
17 Th	0609	-0.3	-9	1221*	4.2	128	0620*	0.2	6			
18 F	1230	4.7	143	0702	-0.2	-6	0121*	4.3	131	0725*	0.3	9
19 Sa ◐	0130	4.3	131	0757	-0.1	-3	0223*	4.4	134	0833*	0.4	12
20 Su	0233	4.0	122	0854	0.0	0	0325*	4.6	140	0939*	0.4	12
21 M	0338	3.8	116	0950	0.1	3	0424*	4.7	143	1043*	0.3	9
22 Tu	0441	3.7	113	1045	0.1	3	0519*	4.9	149	1142*	0.2	6
23 W	0539	3.6	110	1138	0.1	3	0610*	5.0	152			
24 Th	1236	0.1	3	0633	3.6	110	1228*	0.1	3	0658*	5.0	152
25 F	0126	0.1	3	0722	3.6	110	0115*	0.2	6	0742*	5.0	152
26 Sa ○	0211	0.0	0	0808	3.6	110	0200*	0.2	6	0824*	5.0	152
27 Su	0255	0.1	3	0851	3.7	113	0243*	0.3	9	0904*	4.9	149
28 M	0336	0.1	3	0932	3.6	110	0325*	0.4	12	0944*	4.8	146
29 Tu	0415	0.2	6	1012	3.6	110	0406*	0.5	15	1022*	4.6	140
30 W	0452	0.3	9	1053	3.6	110	0448*	0.7	21	1100*	4.4	134

July

Day	Time (h m)	ft	cm	Time (h m)	ft	cm	Time (h m)	ft	cm	Time (h m)	ft	cm
1 Th	0529	0.4	12	1133	3.6	110	0531*	0.9	27	1139*	4.1	125
2 F	0605	0.5	15	1216*	3.6	110	0617*	1.0	30			
3 Sa	1220	3.9	119	0642	0.6	18	0101*	3.7	113	0709*	1.1	34
4 Su ◑	0105	3.6	110	0722	0.7	21	0149*	3.8	116	0807*	1.1	34
5 M	0155	3.4	104	0806	0.7	21	0241*	3.9	119	0907*	1.1	34
6 Tu	0252	3.3	101	0855	0.6	18	0336*	4.2	128	1008*	1.0	30
7 W	0353	3.2	98	0949	0.5	15	0430*	4.4	134	1106*	0.7	21
8 Th	0453	3.3	101	1044	0.4	12	0524*	4.7	143			
9 F	1200	0.5	15	0550	3.5	107	1139	0.2	6	0616*	5.1	155
10 Sa	1251	0.2	6	0644	3.7	113	1233*	-0.1	-3	0706*	5.3	162
11 Su ●	0141	-0.1	-3	0737	3.9	119	0127*	-0.2	-6	0756*	5.5	168
12 M	0229	-0.3	-9	0828	4.1	125	0220*	-0.4	-12	0845*	5.6	171
13 Tu	0317	-0.5	-15	0919	4.3	131	0314*	-0.4	-12	0934*	5.5	168
14 W	0405	-0.6	-18	1011	4.5	137	0409*	-0.3	-9	1025*	5.3	162
15 Th	0453	-0.5	-15	1104	4.6	140	0507*	-0.2	-6	1116*	5.0	152
16 F	0543	-0.4	-12	1200*	4.6	140	0607*	0.1	3			
17 Sa	1211	4.6	140	0635	-0.2	-6	1258*	4.6	140	0710*	0.3	9
18 Su ◐	0109	4.2	128	0730	0.0	0	0159*	4.6	140	0816*	0.5	15
19 M	0212	3.8	116	0827	0.2	6	0301*	4.6	140	0923*	0.6	18
20 Tu	0319	3.6	110	0926	0.3	9	0403*	4.7	143	1028*	0.6	18
21 W	0425	3.5	107	1024	0.4	12	0501*	4.7	143	1127*	0.5	15
22 Th	0525	3.4	104	1120	0.4	12	0553*	4.8	146			
23 F	1220	0.4	12	0618	3.5	107	1211*	0.4	12	0640*	4.8	146
24 Sa	0108	0.3	9	0705	3.6	110	1258*	0.4	12	0723*	4.9	149
25 Su	0151	0.3	9	0748	3.7	113	0142*	0.4	12	0803*	4.9	149
26 M ○	0230	0.2	6	0828	3.8	116	0223*	0.4	12	0841*	4.9	149
27 Tu	0306	0.2	6	0905	3.9	119	0302*	0.4	12	0917*	4.8	146
28 W	0341	0.2	6	0942	3.9	119	0340*	0.5	15	0952*	4.6	140
29 Th	0414	0.3	9	1018	3.9	119	0419*	0.6	18	1027*	4.4	134
30 F	0445	0.4	12	1053	3.9	119	0458*	0.8	24	1102*	4.1	125
31 Sa	0517	0.5	15	1130	4.0	122	0540*	0.9	27	1138*	3.9	119

August

Day	Time (h m)	ft	cm	Time (h m)	ft	cm	Time (h m)	ft	cm	Time (h m)	ft	cm
1 Su	0551	0.6	18	1210*	4.0	122	0628*	1.1	34			
2 M	1219	3.6	110	0630	0.7	21	1256*	4.0	122	0723*	1.2	37
3 Tu ◑	0107	3.4	104	0716	0.7	21	0149*	4.1	125	0826*	1.2	37
4 W	0206	3.3	101	0811	0.7	21	0251*	4.3	131	0932*	1.0	30
5 Th	0315	3.2	98	0912	0.6	18	0354*	4.5	137	1035*	0.8	24
6 F	0424	3.4	104	1016	0.4	12	0455*	4.8	146	1133*	0.5	15
7 Sa	0526	3.6	110	1118	0.2	6	0552*	5.2	158			
8 Su	1226	0.1	3	0623	3.9	119	1216*	-0.1	-3	0646*	5.4	165
9 M	0116	-0.2	-6	0717	4.3	131	0112*	-0.3	-9	0737*	5.6	171
10 Tu ●	0204	-0.4	-12	0808	4.6	140	0207*	-0.5	-15	0826*	5.7	174
11 W	0251	-0.6	-18	0858	4.9	149	0301*	-0.5	-15	0915*	5.5	168
12 Th	0338	-0.6	-18	0949	5.1	155	0355*	-0.4	-12	1005*	5.3	162
13 F	0426	-0.5	-15	1040	5.1	155	0451*	-0.2	-6	1056*	4.9	149
14 Sa	0515	-0.3	-9	1134	5.0	152	0549*	0.0	0	1150*	4.5	137
15 Su	0606	0.0	0	1231*	4.9	149	0651*	0.3	9			
16 M ◐	1248	4.0	122	0701	0.3	9	0131*	4.7	143	0756*	0.6	18
17 Tu	0152	3.7	113	0801	0.5	15	0236*	4.6	140	0904*	0.8	24
18 W	0301	3.5	107	0904	0.7	21	0340*	4.5	137	1009*	0.8	24
19 Th	0409	3.4	104	1005	0.8	24	0440*	4.6	140	1108*	0.7	21
20 F	0509	3.5	107	1103	0.7	21	0533*	4.6	140	1159*	0.6	18
21 Sa	0600	3.6	110	1154	0.7	21	0619*	4.7	143			
22 Su	1243	0.5	15	0644	3.8	116	1239*	0.6	18	0700*	4.8	146
23 M	0122	0.4	12	0723	3.9	119	0121*	0.5	15	0737*	4.8	146
24 Tu ○	0158	0.4	12	0800	4.1	125	0200*	0.4	12	0813*	4.8	146
25 W	0231	0.3	9	0835	4.2	128	0238*	0.4	12	0848*	4.7	143
26 Th	0302	0.3	9	0909	4.3	131	0315*	0.5	15	0922*	4.5	137
27 F	0332	0.4	12	0942	4.3	131	0352*	0.6	18	0955*	4.3	131
28 Sa	0402	0.5	15	1014	4.4	134	0429*	0.7	21	1028*	4.1	125
29 Su	0433	0.6	18	1049	4.3	131	0510*	0.9	27	1103*	3.8	116
30 M	0507	0.7	21	1127	4.3	131	0556*	1.0	30	1143*	3.6	110
31 Tu	0548	0.8	24	1213*	4.3	131	0651*	1.1	34			

September

Day	Time (h m)	ft	cm	Time (h m)	ft	cm	Time (h m)	ft	cm	Time (h m)	ft	cm
1 W ◑	1232	3.4	104	0638	0.8	24	0109*	4.4	134	0755*	1.1	34
2 Th	0136	3.3	101	0739	0.8	24	0216*	4.4	134	0904*	1.0	30
3 F	0251	3.3	101	0848	0.7	21	0326*	4.6	140	1008*	0.8	24
4 Sa	0404	3.6	110	0958	0.5	15	0431*	4.9	149	1107*	0.5	15
5 Su	0507	3.9	119	1102	0.2	6	0530*	5.2	158			
6 M	1200	0.1	3	0604	4.4	134	1202*	-0.1	-3	0625*	5.4	165
7 Tu	1249	-0.2	-6	0656	4.8	146	1259*	-0.4	-12	0716*	5.5	168
8 W ●	0136	-0.5	-15	0746	5.2	158	0153*	-0.5	-15	0806*	5.5	168
9 Th	0223	-0.6	-18	0835	5.4	165	0246*	-0.6	-18	0854*	5.3	162
10 F	0309	-0.6	-18	0924	5.5	168	0339*	-0.5	-15	0944*	5.1	155
11 Sa	0356	-0.4	-12	1014	5.5	168	0434*	-0.2	-6	1034*	4.7	143
12 Su	0445	-0.1	-3	1106	5.3	162	0530*	0.1	3	1128*	4.3	131
13 M	0537	0.2	6	1201*	5.0	152	0630*	0.4	12			
14 Tu	1226	3.9	119	0633	0.6	18	0101*	4.7	143	0733*	0.7	21
15 W ◐	0131	3.6	110	0734	0.8	24	0206*	4.5	137	0839*	0.9	27
16 Th	0241	3.4	104	0840	1.0	30	0311*	4.4	134	0943*	0.9	27
17 F	0348	3.4	104	0943	1.0	30	0412*	4.4	134	1040*	0.9	27
18 Sa	0446	3.6	110	1041	1.0	30	0504*	4.4	134	1128*	0.8	24
19 Su	0534	3.7	113	1131	0.8	24	0549*	4.5	137			
20 M	1209	0.6	18	0616	4.0	122	1216*	0.7	21	0630*	4.6	140
21 Tu	1246	0.5	15	0653	4.2	128	1257*	0.6	18	0707*	4.6	140
22 W	0119	0.4	12	0729	4.4	134	0136*	0.5	15	0743*	4.6	140
23 Th ○	0151	0.4	12	0803	4.5	137	0214*	0.4	12	0818*	4.5	137
24 F	0222	0.4	12	0835	4.6	140	0251*	0.4	12	0852*	4.3	131
25 Sa	0252	0.4	12	0908	4.7	143	0328*	0.5	15	0926*	4.1	125
26 Su	0323	0.5	15	0940	4.7	143	0406*	0.6	18	1000*	3.9	119
27 M	0356	0.6	18	1015	4.7	143	0447*	0.8	24	1036*	3.7	113
28 Tu	0434	0.7	21	1055	4.6	140	0534*	0.9	27	1120*	3.5	107
29 W	0519	0.8	24	1143	4.6	140	0630*	1.0	30			
30 Th	1214	3.4	104	0614	0.8	24	1242*	4.5	137	0733*	1.0	30

October

Day	Time (h m)	ft	cm	Time (h m)	ft	cm	Time (h m)	ft	cm	Time (h m)	ft	cm
1 F ◑	0122	3.4	104	0720	0.9	27	0150*	4.5	137	0840*	0.8	24
2 Sa	0238	3.5	107	0833	0.8	24	0302*	4.6	140	0943*	0.6	18
3 Su	0349	3.8	116	0944	0.5	15	0408*	4.8	146	1040*	0.3	9
4 M	0450	4.2	128	1049	0.2	6	0508*	5.0	152	1132*	0.0	0
5 Tu	0545	4.7	143	1149	-0.1	-3	0603*	5.1	155			
6 W	1221	-0.3	-9	0636	5.2	158	1245*	-0.4	-12	0655*	5.2	158
7 Th ●	0108	-0.5	-15	0725	5.5	168	0139*	-0.5	-15	0745*	5.1	155
8 F	0155	-0.5	-15	0813	5.7	174	0231*	-0.5	-15	0834*	4.9	149
9 Sa	0241	-0.5	-15	0901	5.7	174	0323*	-0.4	-12	0923*	4.7	143
10 Su	0329	-0.3	-9	0949	5.6	171	0415*	-0.2	-6	1013*	4.3	131
11 M	0417	0.0	0	1039	5.3	162	0509*	0.1	3	1106*	4.0	122
12 Tu	0508	0.4	12	1132	5.0	152	0606*	0.4	12			
13 W	1203	3.7	113	0604	0.7	21	1229*	4.6	140	0706*	0.7	21
14 Th ◐	0106	3.5	107	0704	1.0	30	0130*	4.4	134	0807*	0.9	27
15 F	0213	3.4	104	0809	1.1	34	0233*	4.2	128	0907*	0.9	27
16 Sa	0317	3.4	104	0913	1.1	34	0332*	4.1	125	1000*	0.9	27
17 Su	0413	3.6	110	1011	1.1	34	0425*	4.1	125	1046*	0.8	24
18 M	0500	3.8	116	1102	0.9	27	0511*	4.2	128	1127*	0.6	18
19 Tu	0541	4.0	122	1148	0.7	21	0554*	4.2	128			
20 W	1203	0.5	15	0619	4.3	131	1231*	0.6	18	0633*	4.2	128
21 Th	1237	0.4	12	0655	4.5	137	0111*	0.4	12	0711*	4.2	128
22 F	0110	0.3	9	0730	4.7	143	0150*	0.4	12	0748*	4.1	125
23 Sa ○	0143	0.3	9	0804	4.8	146	0228*	0.3	9	0824*	4.0	122
24 Su	0216	0.3	9	0838	4.9	149	0307*	0.3	9	0901*	3.9	119
25 M	0251	0.3	9	0914	4.9	149	0347*	0.4	12	0939*	3.7	113
26 Tu	0329	0.4	12	0952	4.9	149	0431*	0.5	15	1020*	3.6	110
27 W	0412	0.5	15	1036	4.8	146	0520*	0.5	15	1108*	3.5	107
28 Th	0502	0.6	18	1126	4.7	143	0614*	0.6	18			
29 F	1206	3.4	104	0601	0.7	21	1224*	4.6	140	0714*	0.6	18
30 Sa ◑	0114	3.5	107	0709	0.7	21	0130*	4.5	137	0816*	0.5	15
31 Su	0225	3.7	113	0821	0.6	18	0239*	4.5	137	0915*	0.3	9

November

Day	Time (h m)	ft	cm	Time (h m)	ft	cm	Time (h m)	ft	cm	Time (h m)	ft	cm
1 M	0332	4.0	122	0932	0.4	12	0345*	4.5	137	1011*	0.0	0
2 Tu	0431	4.4	134	1037	0.2	6	0446*	4.5	137	1104*	-0.2	-6
3 W	0526	4.9	149	1137	-0.1	-3	0543*	4.6	140	1154*	-0.4	-12
4 Th	0617	5.2	158	1233*	-0.3	-9	0636*	4.6	140			
5 F	1243	-0.5	-15	0706	5.5	168	0126*	-0.5	-15	0726*	4.5	137
6 Sa ●	0130	-0.5	-15	0753	5.6	171	0217*	-0.5	-15	0816*	4.4	134
7 Su	0117	-0.4	-12	0740	5.5	168	0207*	-0.4	-12	0804*	4.2	128
8 M	0204	-0.2	-6	0827	5.4	165	0257*	-0.2	-6	0853*	3.9	119
9 Tu	0252	0.1	3	0914	5.1	155	0348*	0.0	0	0943*	3.7	113
10 W	0341	0.4	12	1003	4.8	146	0439*	0.3	9	1036*	3.5	107
11 Th	0433	0.6	18	1054	4.5	137	0532*	0.5	15	1133*	3.3	101
12 F	0529	0.9	27	1148	4.2	128	0626*	0.6	18			
13 Sa ◐	1233	3.3	101	0630	1.0	30	1244*	3.9	119	0719*	0.7	21
14 Su	0132	3.3	101	0731	1.1	34	0141*	3.8	116	0809*	0.7	21
15 M	0227	3.5	107	0831	1.0	30	0235*	3.7	113	0854*	0.7	21
16 Tu	0317	3.7	113	0926	0.9	27	0326*	3.7	113	0936*	0.6	18
17 W	0401	3.9	119	1016	0.7	21	0413*	3.6	110	1015*	0.4	12
18 Th	0442	4.2	128	1101	0.5	15	0457*	3.7	113	1053*	0.3	9
19 F	0521	4.5	137	1144	0.4	12	0539*	3.7	113	1130*	0.2	6
20 Sa	0559	4.7	143	1225*	0.2	6	0620*	3.7	113			
21 Su ○	1208	0.1	3	0637	4.8	146	0106*	0.1	3	0700*	3.6	110
22 M	1247	0.0	0	0715	4.9	149	0148*	0.0	0	0741*	3.6	110
23 Tu	0128	0.0	0	0755	5.0	152	0231*	0.0	0	0823*	3.6	110
24 W	0212	0.0	0	0837	5.0	152	0317*	0.0	0	0909*	3.5	107
25 Th	0300	0.1	3	0923	4.9	149	0405*	0.0	0	1001*	3.5	107
26 F	0353	0.2	6	1013	4.7	143	0457*	0.0	0	1058*	3.5	107
27 Sa	0453	0.3	9	1109	4.5	137	0552*	0.0	0			
28 Su ◑	1201	3.6	110	0559	0.4	12	1211*	4.3	131	0649*	0.0	0
29 M	0107	3.8	116	0709	0.4	12	0116*	4.1	125	0747*	-0.1	-3
30 Tu	0211	4.1	125	0819	0.3	9	0223*	4.0	122	0843*	-0.2	-6

December

Day	Time (h m)	ft	cm	Time (h m)	ft	cm	Time (h m)	ft	cm	Time (h m)	ft	cm
1 W	0312	4.5	137	0924	0.1	3	0326*	3.9	119	0938*	-0.3	-9
2 Th	0408	4.8	146	1025	-0.1	-3	0425*	3.9	119	1031*	-0.4	-12
3 F	0500	5.0	152	1122	-0.3	-9	0520*	3.9	119	1121*	-0.4	-12
4 Sa	0550	5.2	158	1214*	-0.4	-12	0612*	3.9	119			
5 Su ●	1210	-0.4	-12	0637	5.2	158	0104*	-0.5	-15	0701*	3.8	116
6 M	1258	-0.4	-12	0723	5.2	158	0152*	-0.4	-12	0748*	3.7	113
7 Tu	0145	-0.2	-6	0808	5.0	152	0239*	-0.3	-9	0834*	3.6	110
8 W	0230	0.0	0	0852	4.8	146	0324*	-0.2	-6	0920*	3.5	107
9 Th	0316	0.2	6	0935	4.6	140	0409*	0.0	0	1006*	3.3	101
10 F	0403	0.4	12	1019	4.3	131	0454*	0.2	6	1054*	3.2	98
11 Sa	0451	0.6	18	1104	4.0	122	0538*	0.4	12	1144*	3.2	98
12 Su	0544	0.8	24	1152	3.7	113	0623*	0.5	15			
13 M ◐	1237	3.2	98	0642	0.9	27	1244*	3.4	104	0708*	0.5	15
14 Tu	0131	3.3	101	0742	0.9	27	0138*	3.3	101	0753*	0.5	15
15 W	0224	3.5	107	0841	0.9	27	0234*	3.1	94	0839*	0.5	15
16 Th	0314	3.7	113	0937	0.7	21	0328*	3.1	94	0924*	0.4	12
17 F	0401	4.0	122	1028	0.5	15	0419*	3.1	94	1009*	0.2	6
18 Sa	0446	4.3	131	1116	0.3	9	0507*	3.2	98	1054*	0.0	0
19 Su	0529	4.5	137	1201*	0.1	3	0553*	3.3	101	1139*	-0.1	-3
20 M	0612	4.8	146	1245*	-0.1	-3	0638*	3.4	104			
21 Tu ○	1225	-0.3	-9	0655	4.9	149	0129*	-0.3	-9	0723*	3.5	107
22 W	0111	-0.4	-12	0739	5.0	152	0213*	-0.4	-12	0809*	3.6	110
23 Th	0200	-0.4	-12	0824	5.0	152	0259*	-0.5	-15	0857*	3.7	113
24 F	0250	-0.4	-12	0911	4.9	149	0346*	-0.5	-15	0948*	3.8	116
25 Sa	0345	-0.3	-9	1000	4.7	143	0435*	-0.5	-15	1043*	3.8	116
26 Su	0443	-0.1	-3	1053	4.4	134	0526*	-0.4	-12	1142*	3.9	119
27 M	0547	0.0	0	1151	4.1	125	0621*	-0.4	-12			
28 Tu ◑	1244	4.0	122	0654	0.1	3	1254*	3.8	116	0718*	-0.3	-9
29 W	0148	4.2	128	0804	0.1	3	0201*	3.5	107	0817*	-0.2	-6
30 Th	0251	4.3	131	0911	0.1	3	0309*	3.4	104	0915*	-0.2	-6
31 F	0351	4.5	137	1014	-0.1	-3	0412*	3.3	101	1012*	-0.3	-9

Heights are referred to mean lower low water which is the chart datum of soundings. All times are local. Daylight Saving Time has been used when needed.

Sandy Hook, New Jersey, 2010

Times and Heights of High and Low Waters

March

Day	Time (h m)	Height (ft)	Height (cm)	Day	Time (h m)	Height (ft)	Height (cm)
1 M	0122	-1.1	-34	16 Tu	0229	0.0	0
	0736	5.1	155		0836	4.2	128
	0153*	-1.1	-34		0240*	-0.1	-3
	0804*	4.9	149		0852*	4.2	128
2 Tu	0214	-1.0	-30	17 W	0305	0.0	0
	0824	4.9	149		0909	4.0	122
	0239*	-1.0	-30		0310*	-0.1	-3
	0852*	4.9	149		0924*	4.3	131
3 W	0306	-0.9	-27	18 Th	0342	0.0	0
	0911	4.6	140		0942	3.9	119
	0325*	-0.7	-21		0342*	0.0	0
	0941*	4.8	146		0957*	4.4	134
4 Th	0359	-0.6	-18	19 F	0421	0.1	3
	1000	4.1	125		1017	3.7	113
	0412*	-0.4	-12		0417*	0.1	3
	1031*	4.6	140		1033*	4.4	134
5 F	0453	-0.2	-6	20 Sa	0504	0.2	6
	1051	3.7	113		1055	3.5	107
	0501*	-0.1	-3		0457*	0.2	6
	1124*	4.3	131		1116*	4.3	131
6 Sa	0551	0.2	6	21 Su	0554	0.4	12
	1147	3.3	101		1141	3.3	101
	0556*	0.3	9		0544*	0.3	9
7 Su ◑	1223	4.0	122	22 M	1207	4.3	131
	0654	0.5	15		0653	0.5	15
	1250*	3.0	91		1239*	3.1	94
	0656*	0.6	18		0643*	0.4	12
8 M	0127	3.8	116	23 Tu ◐	0110	4.2	128
	0801	0.6	18		0800	0.5	15
	0200*	2.9	88		0151*	3.1	94
	0800*	0.7	21		0752*	0.4	12
9 Tu	0232	3.8	116	24 W	0223	4.2	128
	0904	0.7	21		0910	0.4	12
	0307*	2.9	88		0310*	3.2	98
	0903*	0.7	21		0907*	0.3	9
10 W	0332	3.8	116	25 Th	0337	4.4	134
	1001	0.6	18		1014	0.2	6
	0404*	3.0	91		0421*	3.6	110
	1000*	0.6	18		1018*	0.1	3
11 Th	0424	3.9	119	26 F	0444	4.5	137
	1048	0.5	15		1112	-0.1	-3
	0452*	3.2	98		0522*	4.0	122
	1049*	0.4	12		1122*	-0.3	-9
12 F	0509	4.1	125	27 Sa	0543	4.7	143
	1129	0.3	9		1205*	-0.4	-12
	0533*	3.5	107		0617*	4.5	137
	1133*	0.3	9				
13 Sa	0549	4.2	128	28 Su	1221	-0.5	-15
	1205*	0.1	3		0637	4.9	149
	0611*	3.7	113		1253*	-0.7	-21
					0707*	4.8	146
14 Su	1214	0.1	3	29 M	0116	-0.8	-24
	0726	4.2	128		0727	4.9	149
	0138*	0.0	0		0140*	-0.8	-24
	0746*	3.9	119		0755*	5.1	155
15 M ●	0152	0.0	0	30 Tu ○	0208	-0.9	-27
	0802	4.2	128		0816	4.8	146
	0209*	0.0	0		0226*	-0.8	-24
	0819*	4.1	125		0842*	5.2	158
				31 W	0259	-0.8	-24
					0903	4.6	140
					0310*	-0.6	-18
					0927*	5.2	158

April

Day	Time (h m)	Height (ft)	Height (cm)	Day	Time (h m)	Height (ft)	Height (cm)
1 Th	0349	-0.6	-18	16 F	0324	0.0	0
	0950	4.3	131		0920	3.8	116
	0355*	-0.4	-12		0313*	0.0	0
	1013*	5.0	152		0933*	4.8	146
2 F	0439	-0.4	-12	17 Sa	0406	0.0	0
	1037	4.0	122		1000	3.7	113
	0441*	-0.1	-3		0353*	0.1	3
	1101*	4.8	146		1014*	4.8	146
3 Sa	0530	0.0	0	18 Su	0453	0.1	3
	1126	3.6	110		1044	3.5	107
	0530*	0.3	9		0439*	0.2	6
	1150*	4.4	134		1101*	4.7	143
4 Su	0624	0.3	9	19 M	0544	0.2	6
	1220*	3.3	101		1136	3.4	104
	0622*	0.6	18		0532*	0.3	9
					1154*	4.6	140
5 M	1245	4.1	125	20 Tu	0642	0.3	9
	0722	0.6	18		1237*	3.4	104
	0120*	3.1	94		0634*	0.4	12
	0720*	0.8	24				
6 Tu ◑	0145	3.9	119	21 W ◐	1257	4.5	137
	0823	0.7	21		0745	0.3	9
	0226*	3.0	91		0148*	3.4	104
	0824*	1.0	30		0744*	0.5	15
7 W	0248	3.8	116	22 Th	0206	4.4	134
	0923	0.8	24		0848	0.2	6
	0330*	3.0	91		0259*	3.6	110
	0928*	1.0	30		0857*	0.4	12
8 Th	0348	3.7	113	23 F	0316	4.4	134
	1016	0.7	21		0949	0.1	3
	0426*	3.2	98		0405*	4.0	122
	1026*	0.9	27		1007*	0.2	6
9 F	0442	3.8	116	24 Sa	0422	4.4	134
	1103	0.6	18		1045	-0.1	-3
	0515*	3.5	107		0504*	4.4	134
	1117*	0.7	21		1110*	-0.1	-3
10 Sa	0529	3.9	119	25 Su	0521	4.4	134
	1143	0.5	15		1137	-0.3	-9
	0557*	3.7	113		0557*	4.8	146
11 Su	1203	0.5	15	26 M	1209	-0.3	-9
	0612	4.0	122		0616	4.5	137
	1220*	0.3	9		1226*	-0.4	-12
	0635*	4.0	122		0647*	5.1	155
12 M	1246	0.3	9	27 Tu	0103	-0.5	-15
	0652	4.0	122		0707	4.4	134
	1254*	0.2	6		0113*	-0.5	-15
	0711*	4.3	131		0734*	5.3	162
13 Tu	0126	0.1	3	28 W ○	0154	-0.6	-18
	0730	4.0	122		0756	4.3	131
	0128*	0.1	3		0159*	-0.4	-12
	0746*	4.5	137		0820*	5.3	162
14 W ●	0205	0.0	0	29 Th	0243	-0.5	-15
	0807	4.0	122		0843	4.2	128
	0201*	0.0	0		0244*	-0.3	-9
	0821*	4.7	143		0904*	5.3	162
15 Th	0244	0.0	0	30 F	0331	-0.4	-12
	0843	3.9	119		0929	4.0	122
	0236*	0.0	0		0329*	-0.1	-3
	0856*	4.8	146		0949*	5.1	155

May

Day	Time (h m)	Height (ft)	Height (cm)	Day	Time (h m)	Height (ft)	Height (cm)
1 Sa	0419	-0.2	-6	16 Su	0353	-0.1	-3
	1016	3.8	116		0948	3.7	113
	0414*	0.2	6		0338*	0.0	0
	1033*	4.8	146		1001*	5.1	155
2 Su	0507	0.1	3	17 M	0442	-0.1	-3
	1103	3.5	107		1038	3.7	113
	0500*	0.5	15		0429*	0.1	3
	1120*	4.5	137		1051*	5.0	152
3 M	0557	0.3	9	18 Tu	0534	0.0	0
	1153	3.3	101		1133	3.7	113
	0549*	0.7	21		0526*	0.2	6
					1145*	4.8	146
4 Tu	1209	4.2	128	19 W	0629	0.0	0
	0648	0.6	18		1234*	3.7	113
	1247*	3.2	98		0629*	0.3	9
	0643*	1.0	30				
5 W	0102	4.0	122	20 Th ◐	1245	4.6	140
	0740	0.7	21		0726	0.0	0
	0146*	3.2	98		0139*	3.8	116
	0743*	1.1	34		0737*	0.4	12
6 Th ◑	0158	3.8	116	21 F	0149	4.4	134
	0832	0.8	24		0824	0.0	0
	0244*	3.2	98		0244*	4.1	125
	0844*	1.1	34		0846*	0.4	12
7 F	0255	3.7	113	22 Sa	0255	4.2	128
	0922	0.8	24		0921	0.0	0
	0339*	3.4	104		0346*	4.3	131
	0944*	1.0	30		0954*	0.3	9
8 Sa	0350	3.7	113	23 Su	0359	4.1	125
	1007	0.7	21		1017	-0.1	-3
	0429*	3.7	113		0444*	4.6	140
	1038*	0.9	27		1057*	0.1	3
9 Su	0441	3.7	113	24 M	0500	4.1	125
	1049	0.6	18		1109	-0.1	-3
	0514*	3.9	119		0538*	4.9	149
	1128*	0.7	21		1155*	0.0	0
10 M	0528	3.7	113	25 Tu	0556	4.0	122
	1129	0.4	12		1200*	-0.2	-6
	0555*	4.2	128		0627*	5.1	155
11 Tu	1214	0.5	15	26 W	1249	-0.2	-6
	0612	3.7	113		0649	4.0	122
	1207*	0.3	9		1248*	-0.2	-6
	0634*	4.5	137		0715*	5.2	158
12 W	1258	0.3	9	27 Th ○	0140	-0.2	-6
	0655	3.7	113		0738	3.9	119
	1246*	0.2	6		0135*	-0.1	-3
	0713*	4.8	146		0800*	5.2	158
13 Th	0141	0.1	3	28 F	0228	-0.2	-6
	0737	3.8	116		0825	3.8	116
	0126*	0.1	3		0220*	0.0	0
	0752*	5.0	152		0843*	5.1	155
14 F ●	0223	0.0	0	29 Sa	0314	-0.1	-3
	0819	3.8	116		0910	3.7	113
	0207*	0.0	0		0305*	0.2	6
	0833*	5.1	155		0926*	5.0	152
15 Sa	0307	-0.1	-3	30 Su	0359	0.0	0
	0902	3.7	113		0955	3.6	110
	0251*	0.0	0		0349*	0.4	12
	0916*	5.1	155		1008*	4.8	146
				31 M	0443	0.1	3
					1039	3.5	107
					0433*	0.6	18
					1051*	4.6	140

June

Day	Time (h m)	Height (ft)	Height (cm)	Day	Time (h m)	Height (ft)	Height (cm)
1 Tu	0527	0.3	9	16 W	0517	-0.3	-9
	1125	3.4	104		1123	4.1	125
	0518*	0.8	24		0518*	0.0	0
	1134*	4.3	131		1133*	5.0	152
2 W	0610	0.5	15	17 Th	0609	-0.3	-9
	1212*	3.4	104		1221*	4.2	128
	0606*	0.9	27		0620*	0.2	6
3 Th	1220	4.1	125	18 F	1230	4.7	143
	0654	0.6	18		0702	-0.2	-6
	0102*	3.4	104		0121*	4.3	131
	0659*	1.1	34		0725*	0.3	9
4 F ◑	0108	3.8	116	19 Sa ◐	0130	4.3	131
	0737	0.7	21		0757	-0.1	-3
	0154*	3.4	104		0223*	4.4	134
	0756*	1.1	34		0833*	0.4	12
5 Sa	0159	3.6	110	20 Su	0233	4.0	122
	0821	0.7	21		0854	0.0	0
	0246*	3.6	110		0325*	4.6	140
	0856*	1.1	34		0939*	0.4	12
6 Su	0252	3.5	107	21 M	0338	3.8	116
	0906	0.7	21		0950	0.1	3
	0337*	3.8	116		0424*	4.7	143
	0954*	1.0	30		1043*	0.3	9
7 M	0347	3.4	104	22 Tu	0441	3.7	113
	0950	0.6	18		1045	0.1	3
	0425*	4.1	125		0519*	4.9	149
	1048*	0.8	24		1142*	0.2	6
8 Tu	0440	3.4	104	23 W	0539	3.6	110
	1036	0.5	15		1138	0.1	3
	0512*	4.4	134		0610*	5.0	152
	1140*	0.6	18				
9 W	0531	3.4	104	24 Th	1236	0.1	3
	1122	0.3	9		0633	3.6	110
	0557*	4.7	143		1228*	0.1	3
					0658*	5.0	152
10 Th	1228	0.4	12	25 F	0126	0.1	3
	0621	3.5	107		0722	3.6	110
	1208*	0.2	6		0115*	0.2	6
	0642*	4.9	149		0742*	5.0	152
11 F	0116	0.1	3	26 Sa ○	0211	0.0	0
	0709	3.6	110		0808	3.6	110
	1256*	0.0	0		0200*	0.2	6
	0728*	5.2	158		0824*	5.0	152
12 Sa ●	0203	-0.1	-3	27 Su	0255	0.1	3
	0757	3.7	113		0851	3.7	113
	0144*	-0.1	-3		0243*	0.3	9
	0814*	5.3	162		0904*	4.9	149
13 Su	0250	-0.2	-6	28 M	0336	0.1	3
	0845	3.8	116		0932	3.6	110
	0234*	-0.2	-6		0325*	0.4	12
	0901*	5.4	165		0944*	4.8	146
14 M	0338	-0.3	-9	29 Tu	0415	0.2	6
	0935	3.9	119		1012	3.6	110
	0326*	-0.2	-6		0406*	0.5	15
	0950*	5.4	165		1022*	4.6	140
15 Tu	0427	-0.3	-9	30 W	0452	0.3	9
	1028	4.0	122		1053	3.6	110
	0420*	-0.1	-3		0448*	0.7	21
	1040*	5.2	158		1100*	4.4	134

July

Day	Time (h m)	Height (ft)	Height (cm)	Day	Time (h m)	Height (ft)	Height (cm)
1 Th	0529	0.4	12	16 F	0543	-0.4	-12
	1133	3.6	110		1200*	4.6	140
	0531*	0.9	27		0607*	0.1	3
	1139*	4.1	125				
2 F	0605	0.5	15	17 Sa	1211	4.6	140
	1216*	3.6	110		0635	-0.2	-6
	0617*	1.0	30		1258*	4.6	140
					0710*	0.3	9
3 Sa	1220	3.9	119	18 Su ◐	0109	4.2	128
	0642	0.6	18		0730	0.0	0
	0101*	3.7	113		0159*	4.6	140
	0709*	1.1	34		0816*	0.5	15
4 Su ◑	0105	3.6	110	19 M	0212	3.8	116
	0722	0.7	21		0827	0.2	6
	0149*	3.8	116		0301*	4.6	140
	0807*	1.1	34		0923*	0.6	18
5 M	0155	3.4	104	20 Tu	0319	3.6	110
	0806	0.7	21		0926	0.3	9
	0241*	3.9	119		0403*	4.7	143
	0907*	1.1	34		1028*	0.6	18
6 Tu	0252	3.3	101	21 W	0425	3.5	107
	0855	0.6	18		1024	0.4	12
	0336*	4.2	128		0501*	4.7	143
	1008*	1.0	30		1127*	0.5	15
7 W	0353	3.2	98	22 Th	0525	3.4	104
	0949	0.5	15		1120	0.4	12
	0430*	4.4	134		0553*	4.8	146
	1106*	0.7	21				
8 Th	0453	3.3	101	23 F	1220	0.4	12
	1044	0.4	12		0618	3.5	107
	0524*	4.7	143		1211*	0.4	12
					0640*	4.8	146
9 F	1200	0.5	15	24 Sa	0108	0.3	9
	0550	3.5	107		0705	3.6	110
	1139	0.2	6		1258*	0.4	12
	0616*	5.1	155		0723*	4.9	149
10 Sa	1251	0.2	6	25 Su	0151	0.3	9
	0644	3.7	113		0748	3.7	113
	1233*	-0.1	-3		0142*	0.4	12
	0706*	5.3	162		0803*	4.9	149
11 Su ●	0141	-0.1	-3	26 M ○	0230	0.2	6
	0737	3.9	119		0828	3.8	116
	0127*	-0.2	-6		0223*	0.4	12
	0756*	5.5	168		0841*	4.9	149
12 M	0229	-0.3	-9	27 Tu	0306	0.2	6
	0828	4.1	125		0905	3.9	119
	0220*	-0.4	-12		0302*	0.4	12
	0845*	5.6	171		0917*	4.8	146
13 Tu	0317	-0.5	-15	28 W	0341	0.2	6
	0919	4.3	131		0942	3.9	119
	0314*	-0.4	-12		0340*	0.5	15
	0934*	5.5	168		0952*	4.6	140
14 W	0405	-0.6	-18	29 Th	0414	0.3	9
	1011	4.5	137		1018	3.9	119
	0409*	-0.3	-9		0419*	0.6	18
	1025*	5.3	162		1027*	4.4	134
15 Th	0453	-0.5	-15	30 F	0445	0.4	12
	1104	4.6	140		1053	3.9	119
	0507*	-0.2	-6		0458*	0.8	24
	1116*	5.0	152		1102*	4.1	125
				31 Sa	0517	0.5	15
					1130	4.0	122
					0540*	0.9	27
					1138*	3.9	119

August

Day	Time (h m)	Height (ft)	Height (cm)	Day	Time (h m)	Height (ft)	Height (cm)
1 Su	0551	0.6	18	16 M ◐	1248	4.0	122
	1210*	4.0	122		0701	0.3	9
	0628*	1.1	34		0131*	4.7	143
					0756*	0.6	18
2 M	1219	3.6	110	17 Tu	0152	3.7	113
	0630	0.7	21		0801	0.5	15
	1256*	4.0	122		0236*	4.6	140
	0723*	1.2	37		0904*	0.8	24
3 Tu ◑	0107	3.4	104	18 W	0301	3.5	107
	0716	0.7	21		0904	0.7	21
	0149*	4.1	125		0340*	4.5	137
	0826*	1.2	37		1009*	0.8	24
4 W	0206	3.3	101	19 Th	0409	3.4	104
	0811	0.7	21		1005	0.8	24
	0251*	4.3	131		0440*	4.6	140
	0932*	1.0	30		1108*	0.7	21
5 Th	0315	3.2	98	20 F	0509	3.5	107
	0912	0.6	18		1103	0.7	21
	0354*	4.5	137		0533*	4.6	140
	1035*	0.8	24		1159*	0.6	18
6 F	0424	3.4	104	21 Sa	0600	3.6	110
	1016	0.4	12		1154	0.7	21
	0455*	4.8	146		0619*	4.7	143
	1133*	0.5	15				
7 Sa	0526	3.6	110	22 Su	1243	0.5	15
	1118	0.2	6		0644	3.8	116
	0552*	5.2	158		1239*	0.6	18
					0700*	4.8	146
8 Su	1226	0.1	3	23 M	0122	0.4	12
	0623	3.9	119		0723	3.9	119
	1216*	-0.1	-3		0121*	0.5	15
	0646*	5.4	165		0737*	4.8	146
9 M	0116	-0.2	-6	24 Tu ○	0158	0.4	12
	0717	4.3	131		0800	4.1	125
	0112*	-0.3	-9		0200*	0.4	12
	0737*	5.6	171		0813*	4.8	146
10 Tu ●	0204	-0.4	-12	25 W	0231	0.3	9
	0808	4.6	140		0835	4.2	128
	0207*	-0.5	-15		0238*	0.4	12
	0826*	5.7	174		0848*	4.7	143
11 W	0251	-0.6	-18	26 Th	0302	0.3	9
	0858	4.9	149		0909	4.3	131
	0301*	-0.5	-15		0315*	0.5	15
	0915*	5.5	168		0922*	4.5	137
12 Th	0338	-0.6	-18	27 F	0332	0.4	12
	0949	5.1	155		0942	4.3	131
	0355*	-0.4	-12		0352*	0.6	18
	1005*	5.3	162		0955*	4.3	131
13 F	0426	-0.5	-15	28 Sa	0402	0.5	15
	1040	5.1	155		1014	4.4	134
	0451*	-0.2	-6		0429*	0.7	21
	1056*	4.9	149		1028*	4.1	125
14 Sa	0515	-0.3	-9	29 Su	0433	0.6	18
	1134	5.0	152		1049	4.3	131
	0549*	0.0	0		0510*	0.9	27
	1150*	4.5	137		1103*	3.8	116
15 Su	0606	0.0	0	30 M	0507	0.7	21
	1231*	4.9	149		1127	4.3	131
	0651*	0.3	9		0556*	1.0	30
					1143*	3.6	110
				31 Tu	0548	0.8	24
					1213*	4.3	131
					0651*	1.1	34

September

Day	Time (h m)	Height (ft)	Height (cm)	Day	Time (h m)	Height (ft)	Height (cm)
1 W ◑	1232	3.4	104	16 Th	0241	3.4	104
	0638	0.8	24		0840	1.0	30
	0109*	4.4	134		0311*	4.4	134
	0755*	1.1	34		0943*	0.9	27
2 Th	0136	3.3	101	17 F	0348	3.4	104
	0739	0.8	24		0943	1.0	30
	0216*	4.4	134		0412*	4.4	134
	0904*	1.0	30		1040*	0.9	27
3 F	0251	3.3	101	18 Sa	0446	3.6	110
	0848	0.7	21		1041	1.0	30
	0326*	4.6	140		0504*	4.4	134
	1008*	0.8	24		1128*	0.8	24
4 Sa	0404	3.6	110	19 Su	0534	3.7	113
	0958	0.5	15		1131	0.8	24
	0431*	4.9	149		0549*	4.5	137
	1107*	0.5	15				
5 Su	0507	3.9	119	20 M	1209	0.6	18
	1102	0.2	6		0616	4.0	122
	0530*	5.2	158		1216*	0.7	21
					0630*	4.6	140
6 M	1200	0.1	3	21 Tu	1246	0.5	15
	0604	4.4	134		0653	4.2	128
	1202*	-0.1	-3		1257*	0.6	18
	0625*	5.4	165		0707*	4.6	140
7 Tu	1249	-0.2	-6	22 W	0119	0.4	12
	0656	4.8	146		0729	4.4	134
	1259*	-0.4	-12		0136*	0.5	15
	0716*	5.5	168		0743*	4.6	140
8 W ●	0136	-0.5	-15	23 Th ○	0151	0.4	12
	0746	5.2	158		0803	4.5	137
	0153*	-0.5	-15		0214*	0.4	12
	0806*	5.5	168		0818*	4.5	137
9 Th	0223	-0.6	-18	24 F	0222	0.4	12
	0835	5.4	165		0835	4.6	140
	0246*	-0.6	-18		0251*	0.4	12
	0854*	5.3	162		0852*	4.3	131
10 F	0309	-0.6	-18	25 Sa	0252	0.4	12
	0924	5.5	168		0908	4.7	143
	0339*	-0.5	-15		0328*	0.5	15
	0944*	5.1	155		0926*	4.1	125
11 Sa	0356	-0.4	-12	26 Su	0323	0.5	15
	1014	5.5	168		0940	4.7	143
	0434*	-0.2	-6		0406*	0.6	18
	1034*	4.7	143		1000*	3.9	119
12 Su	0445	-0.1	-3	27 M	0356	0.6	18
	1106	5.3	162		1015	4.7	143
	0530*	0.1	3		0447*	0.8	24
	1128*	4.3	131		1036*	3.7	113
13 M	0537	0.2	6	28 Tu	0434	0.7	21
	1201*	5.0	152		1055	4.6	140
	0630*	0.4	12		0534*	0.9	27
					1120*	3.5	107
14 Tu	1226	3.9	119	29 W	0519	0.8	24
	0633	0.6	18		1143	4.6	140
	0101*	4.7	143		0630*	1.0	30
	0733*	0.7	21				
15 W ◐	0131	3.6	110	30 Th	1214	3.4	104
	0734	0.8	24		0614	0.8	24
	0206*	4.5	137		1242*	4.5	137
	0839*	0.9	27		0733*	1.0	30

October

Day	Time (h m)	Height (ft)	Height (cm)	Day	Time (h m)	Height (ft)	Height (cm)
1 F ◑	0122	3.4	104	16 Sa	0317	3.4	104
	0720	0.9	27		0913	1.1	34
	0150*	4.5	137		0332*	4.1	125
	0840*	0.8	24		1000*	0.9	27
2 Sa	0238	3.5	107	17 Su	0413	3.6	110
	0833	0.8	24		1011	1.1	34
	0302*	4.6	140		0425*	4.1	125
	0943*	0.6	18		1046*	0.8	24
3 Su	0349	3.8	116	18 M	0500	3.8	116
	0944	0.5	15		1102	0.9	27
	0408*	4.8	146		0511*	4.2	128
	1040*	0.3	9		1127*	0.6	18
4 M	0450	4.2	128	19 Tu	0541	4.0	122
	1049	0.2	6		1148	0.7	21
	0508*	5.0	152		0554*	4.2	128
	1132*	0.0	0				
5 Tu	0545	4.7	143	20 W	1203	0.5	15
	1149	-0.1	-3		0619	4.3	131
	0603*	5.1	155		1231*	0.6	18
					0633*	4.2	128
6 W	1221	-0.3	-9	21 Th	1237	0.4	12
	0636	5.2	158		0655	4.5	137
	1245*	-0.4	-12		0111*	0.4	12
	0655*	5.2	158		0711*	4.2	128
7 Th ●	0108	-0.5	-15	22 F	0110	0.3	9
	0725	5.5	168		0730	4.7	143
	0139*	-0.5	-15		0150*	0.4	12
	0745*	5.1	155		0748*	4.1	125
8 F	0155	-0.5	-15	23 Sa ○	0143	0.3	9
	0813	5.7	174		0804	4.8	146
	0231*	-0.5	-15		0228*	0.3	9
	0834*	4.9	149		0824*	4.0	122
9 Sa	0241	-0.5	-15	24 Su	0216	0.3	9
	0901	5.7	174		0838	4.9	149
	0323*	-0.4	-12		0307*	0.3	9
	0923*	4.7	143		0901*	3.9	119
10 Su	0329	-0.3	-9	25 M	0251	0.3	9
	0949	5.6	171		0914	4.9	149
	0415*	-0.2	-6		0347*	0.4	12
	1013*	4.3	131		0939*	3.7	113
11 M	0417	0.0	0	26 Tu	0329	0.4	12
	1039	5.3	162		0952	4.9	149
	0509*	0.1	3		0431*	0.5	15
	1106*	4.0	122		1020*	3.6	110
12 Tu	0508	0.4	12	27 W	0412	0.5	15
	1132	5.0	152		1036	4.8	146
	0606*	0.4	12		0520*	0.5	15
					1108*	3.5	107
13 W	1203	3.7	113	28 Th	0502	0.6	18
	0604	0.7	21		1126	4.7	143
	1229*	4.6	140		0614*	0.6	18
	0706*	0.7	21				
14 Th ◐	0106	3.5	107	29 F	1206	3.4	104
	0704	1.0	30		0601	0.7	21
	0130*	4.4	134		1224*	4.6	140
	0807*	0.9	27		0714*	0.6	18
15 F	0213	3.4	104	30 Sa ◑	0114	3.5	107
	0809	1.1	34		0709	0.7	21
	0233*	4.2	128		0130*	4.5	137
	0907*	0.9	27		0816*	0.5	15
				31 Su	0225	3.7	113
					0821	0.6	18
					0239*	4.5	137
					0915*	0.3	9

November

Day	Time (h m)	Height (ft)	Height (cm)	Day	Time (h m)	Height (ft)	Height (cm)
1 M	0332	4.0	122	16 Tu	0317	3.7	113
	0932	0.4	12		0926	0.9	27
	0345*	4.5	137		0326*	3.7	113
	1011*	0.0	0		0936*	0.6	18
2 Tu	0431	4.4	134	17 W	0401	3.9	119
	1037	0.2	6		1016	0.7	21
	0446*	4.5	137		0413*	3.6	110
	1104*	-0.2	-6		1015*	0.4	12
3 W	0526	4.9	149	18 Th	0442	4.2	128
	1137	-0.1	-3		1101	0.5	15
	0543*	4.6	140		0457*	3.7	113
	1154*	-0.4	-12		1053*	0.3	9
4 Th	0617	5.2	158	19 F	0521	4.5	137
	1233*	-0.3	-9		1144	0.4	12
	0636*	4.6	140		0539*	3.7	113
					1130*	0.2	6
5 F	1243	-0.5	-15	20 Sa	0559	4.7	143
	0706	5.5	168		1225*	0.2	6
	0126*	-0.5	-15		0620*	3.7	113
	0726*	4.5	137				
6 Sa ●	0130	-0.5	-15	21 Su ○	1208	0.1	3
	0753	5.6	171		0637	4.8	146
	0217*	-0.5	-15		0106*	0.1	3
	0816*	4.4	134		0700*	3.6	110
7 Su	0117	-0.4	-12	22 M	1247	0.0	0
	0740	5.5	168		0715	4.9	149
	0207*	-0.4	-12		0148*	0.0	0
	0804*	4.2	128		0741*	3.6	110
8 M	0204	-0.2	-6	23 Tu	0128	0.0	0
	0827	5.4	165		0755	5.0	152
	0257*	-0.2	-6		0231*	0.0	0
	0853*	3.9	119		0823*	3.6	110
9 Tu	0252	0.1	3	24 W	0212	0.0	0
	0914	5.1	155		0837	5.0	152
	0348*	0.0	0		0317*	0.0	0
	0943*	3.7	113		0909*	3.5	107
10 W	0341	0.4	12	25 Th	0300	0.1	3
	1003	4.8	146		0923	4.9	149
	0439*	0.3	9		0405*	0.0	0
	1036*	3.5	107		1001*	3.5	107
11 Th	0433	0.6	18	26 F	0353	0.2	6
	1054	4.5	137		1013	4.7	143
	0532*	0.5	15		0457*	0.0	0
	1133*	3.3	101		1058*	3.5	107
12 F	0529	0.9	27	27 Sa	0453	0.3	9
	1148	4.2	128		1109	4.5	137
	0626*	0.6	18		0552*	0.0	0
13 Sa ◐	1233	3.3	101	28 Su ◑	1201	3.6	110
	0630	1.0	30		0559	0.4	12
	1244*	3.9	119		1211*	4.3	131
	0719*	0.7	21		0649*	0.0	0
14 Su	0132	3.3	101	29 M	0107	3.8	116
	0731	1.1	34		0709	0.4	12
	0141*	3.8	116		0116*	4.1	125
	0809*	0.7	21		0747*	-0.1	-3
15 M	0227	3.5	107	30 Tu	0211	4.1	125
	0831	1.0	30		0819	0.3	9
	0235*	3.7	113		0223*	4.0	122
	0854*	0.7	21		0843*	-0.2	-6

December

Day	Time (h m)	Height (ft)	Height (cm)	Day	Time (h m)	Height (ft)	Height (cm)
1 W	0312	4.5	137	16 Th	0314	3.7	113
	0924	0.1	3		0937	0.7	21
	0326*	3.9	119		0328*	3.1	94
	0938*	-0.3	-9		0924*	0.4	12
2 Th	0408	4.8	146	17 F	0401	4.0	122
	1025	-0.1	-3		1028	0.5	15
	0425*	3.9	119		0419*	3.1	94
	1031*	-0.4	-12		1009*	0.2	6
3 F	0500	5.0	152	18 Sa	0446	4.3	131
	1122	-0.3	-9		1116	0.3	9
	0520*	3.9	119		0507*	3.2	98
	1121*	-0.4	-12		1054*	0.0	0
4 Sa	0550	5.2	158	19 Su	0529	4.5	137
	1214*	-0.4	-12		1201*	0.1	3
	0612*	3.9	119		0553*	3.3	101
					1139*	-0.1	-3
5 Su ●	1210	-0.4	-12	20 M	0612	4.8	146
	0637	5.2	158		1245*	-0.1	-3
	0104*	-0.5	-15		0638*	3.4	104
	0701*	3.8	116				
6 M	1258	-0.4	-12	21 Tu ○	1225	-0.3	-9
	0723	5.2	158		0655	4.9	149
	0152*	-0.4	-12		0129*	-0.3	-9
	0748*	3.7	113		0723*	3.5	107
7 Tu	0145	-0.2	-6	22 W	0111	-0.4	-12
	0808	5.0	152		0739	5.0	152
	0239*	-0.3	-9		0213*	-0.4	-12
	0834*	3.6	110		0809*	3.6	110
8 W	0230	0.0	0	23 Th	0200	-0.4	-12
	0852	4.8	146		0824	5.0	152
	0324*	-0.2	-6		0259*	-0.5	-15
	0920*	3.5	107		0857*	3.7	113
9 Th	0316	0.2	6	24 F	0250	-0.4	-12
	0935	4.6	140		0911	4.9	149
	0409*	0.0	0		0346*	-0.5	-15
	1006*	3.3	101		0948*	3.8	116
10 F	0403	0.4	12	25 Sa	0345	-0.3	-9
	1019	4.3	131		1000	4.7	143
	0454*	0.2	6		0435*	-0.5	-15
	1054*	3.2	98		1043*	3.8	116
11 Sa	0451	0.6	18	26 Su	0443	-0.1	-3
	1104	4.0	122		1053	4.4	134
	0538*	0.4	12		0526*	-0.4	-12
	1144*	3.2	98		1142*	3.9	119
12 Su	0544	0.8	24	27 M	0547	0.0	0
	1152	3.7	113		1151	4.1	125
	0623*	0.5	15		0621*	-0.4	-12
13 M ◐	1237	3.2	98	28 Tu ◑	1244	4.0	122
	0642	0.9	27		0654	0.1	3
	1244*	3.4	104		1254*	3.8	116
	0708*	0.5	15		0718*	-0.3	-9
14 Tu	0131	3.3	101	29 W	0148	4.2	128
	0742	0.9	27		0804	0.1	3
	0138*	3.3	101		0201*	3.5	107
	0753*	0.5	15		0817*	-0.2	-6
15 W	0224	3.5	107	30 Th	0251	4.3	131
	0841	0.9	27		0911	0.1	3
	0234*	3.1	94		0309*	3.4	104
	0839*	0.5	15		0915*	-0.2	-6
				31 F	0351	4.5	137
					1014	-0.1	-3
					0412*	3.3	101
					1012*	-0.3	-9

Heights are referred to mean lower low water which is the chart datum of soundings. All times are local. Daylight Saving Time has been used when needed.

New York (The Battery), New York, 2010

Times and Heights of High and Low Waters

March

Day	Time (h m)	ft	cm	Time (h m)	ft	cm	Time (h m)	ft	cm	Time (h m)	ft	cm
1 M	0225	-1.1	-34	0823	5.6	171	0254*	-1.2	-37	0853*	5.6	171
2 Tu	0316	-1.1	-34	0912	5.4	165	0339*	-1.1	-34	0943*	5.6	171
3 W	0405	-0.9	-27	1004	5.1	155	0423*	-0.8	-24	1034*	5.4	165
4 Th	0454	-0.6	-18	1058	4.7	143	0509*	-0.4	-12	1127*	5.2	158
5 F	0547	-0.2	-6	1153	4.4	134	0559*	0.1	3			
6 Sa	1220	4.9	149	0645	0.3	9	1249*	4.1	125	0657*	0.5	15
7 Su ◑	0113	4.6	140	0750	0.6	18	0145*	3.8	116	0803*	0.8	24
8 M	0210	4.3	131	0854	0.7	21	0246*	3.7	113	0907*	0.9	27
9 Tu	0311	4.2	128	0953	0.7	21	0349*	3.6	110	1005*	0.9	27
10 W	0414	4.2	128	1044	0.6	18	0450*	3.8	116	1056*	0.7	21
11 Th	0511	4.3	131	1130	0.4	12	0542*	4.0	122	1144*	0.6	18
12 F	0600	4.5	137	1213*	0.3	9	0626*	4.3	131			
13 Sa	1229	0.4	12	0642	4.6	140	1254*	0.1	3	0705*	4.5	137
14 Su	0112	0.2	6	0819	4.7	143	0232*	0.0	0	0839*	4.7	143
15 M ●	0253	0.1	3	0854	4.7	143	0309*	-0.1	-3	0910*	4.8	146
16 Tu	0333	0.0	0	0927	4.6	140	0343*	-0.1	-3	0937*	4.8	146
17 W	0411	0.0	0	0959	4.5	137	0415*	0.0	0	1003*	4.9	149
18 Th	0447	0.0	0	1031	4.4	134	0444*	0.1	3	1030*	4.9	149
19 F	0523	0.1	3	1107	4.2	128	0514*	0.2	6	1106*	4.9	149
20 Sa	0601	0.3	9	1151	4.1	125	0547*	0.4	12	1151*	4.8	146
21 Su	0647	0.5	15	1243*	4.0	122	0629*	0.5	15			
22 M	1245	4.7	143	0754	0.7	21	0141*	3.9	119	0732*	0.7	21
23 Tu ◐	0147	4.7	143	0912	0.7	21	0245*	3.9	119	0908*	0.8	24
24 W	0255	4.7	143	1020	0.5	15	0355*	4.1	125	1026*	0.5	15
25 Th	0410	4.7	143	1119	0.2	6	0506*	4.4	134	1130*	0.2	6
26 F	0525	4.9	149	1212*	-0.2	-6	0611*	4.8	146			
27 Sa	1228	-0.2	-6	0630	5.1	155	0103*	-0.5	-15	0706*	5.3	162
28 Su	0124	-0.5	-15	0726	5.3	162	0153*	-0.7	-21	0756*	5.6	171
29 M	0217	-0.7	-21	0816	5.4	165	0241*	-0.8	-24	0843*	5.9	180
30 Tu ○	0309	-0.9	-27	0904	5.4	165	0327*	-0.8	-24	0929*	5.9	180
31 W	0358	-0.9	-27	0953	5.2	158	0413*	-0.6	-18	1016*	5.8	177

April

Day	Time (h m)	ft	cm	Time (h m)	ft	cm	Time (h m)	ft	cm	Time (h m)	ft	cm
1 Th	0446	-0.7	-21	1043	4.9	149	0457*	-0.3	-9	1105*	5.6	171
2 F	0533	-0.4	-12	1137	4.6	140	0541*	0.1	3	1156*	5.3	162
3 Sa	0622	0.0	0	1232*	4.4	134	0629*	0.5	15			
4 Su	1249	4.9	149	0715	0.4	12	0127*	4.1	125	0723*	0.9	27
5 M	0142	4.6	140	0815	0.7	21	0221*	3.9	119	0827*	1.2	37
6 Tu ◑	0236	4.4	134	0917	0.9	27	0317*	3.9	119	0933*	1.3	40
7 W	0332	4.2	128	1015	0.9	27	0415*	3.9	119	1033*	1.2	37
8 Th	0432	4.1	125	1106	0.8	24	0512*	4.0	122	1126*	1.0	30
9 F	0530	4.2	128	1151	0.7	21	0605*	4.2	128			
10 Sa	1213	0.8	24	0622	4.3	131	1233*	0.5	15	0650*	4.5	137
11 Su	1259	0.6	18	0707	4.4	134	0113*	0.4	12	0729*	4.8	146
12 M	0143	0.4	12	0746	4.5	137	0153*	0.3	9	0803*	5.0	152
13 Tu	0226	0.2	6	0823	4.6	140	0231*	0.2	6	0833*	5.1	155
14 W ●	0308	0.1	3	0858	4.6	140	0308*	0.2	6	0901*	5.3	162
15 Th	0349	0.0	0	0932	4.5	137	0344*	0.2	6	0929*	5.3	162
16 F	0429	0.0	0	1009	4.4	134	0420*	0.2	6	1003*	5.3	162
17 Sa	0509	0.0	0	1052	4.3	131	0457*	0.3	9	1045*	5.2	158
18 Su	0552	0.2	6	1143	4.2	128	0537*	0.4	12	1136*	5.1	155
19 M	0641	0.3	9	1240*	4.2	128	0627*	0.6	18			
20 Tu	1236	5.0	152	0742	0.5	15	0140*	4.2	128	0736*	0.8	24
21 W ◐	0140	4.9	149	0851	0.5	15	0241*	4.3	131	0859*	0.8	24
22 Th	0246	4.8	146	0956	0.3	9	0344*	4.5	137	1012*	0.6	18
23 F	0354	4.8	146	1053	0.1	3	0449*	4.8	146	1115*	0.3	9
24 Sa	0504	4.8	146	1146	-0.1	-3	0550*	5.2	158			
25 Su	1212	0.0	0	0609	4.9	149	1236*	-0.3	-9	0645*	5.6	171
26 M	0107	-0.3	-9	0706	5.0	152	0126*	-0.4	-12	0735*	5.9	180
27 Tu	0200	-0.5	-15	0757	5.1	155	0214*	-0.4	-12	0821*	6.0	183
28 W ○	0251	-0.6	-18	0846	5.0	152	0302*	-0.3	-9	0906*	6.0	183
29 Th	0340	-0.6	-18	0934	4.9	149	0348*	-0.2	-6	0951*	5.8	177
30 F	0427	-0.4	-12	1024	4.7	143	0432*	0.1	3	1038*	5.6	171

May

Day	Time (h m)	ft	cm	Time (h m)	ft	cm	Time (h m)	ft	cm	Time (h m)	ft	cm
1 Sa	0513	-0.2	-6	1116	4.5	137	0516*	0.4	12	1127*	5.3	162
2 Su	0558	0.1	3	1210*	4.3	131	0601*	0.8	24			
3 M	1219	4.9	149	0646	0.4	12	0103*	4.2	128	0650*	1.1	34
4 Tu	0110	4.7	143	0738	0.7	21	0155*	4.1	125	0748*	1.3	40
5 W	0200	4.4	134	0834	0.9	27	0245*	4.1	125	0853*	1.5	46
6 Th ◑	0251	4.3	131	0930	0.9	27	0335*	4.1	125	0955*	1.4	43
7 F	0343	4.1	125	1021	0.9	27	0427*	4.2	128	1050*	1.3	40
8 Sa	0438	4.1	125	1106	0.8	24	0518*	4.4	134	1139*	1.0	30
9 Su	0533	4.1	125	1148	0.7	21	0605*	4.6	140			
10 M	1226	0.8	24	0623	4.2	128	1229*	0.6	18	0646*	4.9	149
11 Tu	0112	0.6	18	0709	4.3	131	0110*	0.5	15	0722*	5.1	155
12 W	0158	0.3	9	0750	4.4	134	0152*	0.4	12	0755*	5.4	165
13 Th	0243	0.1	3	0829	4.4	134	0234*	0.3	9	0829*	5.5	168
14 F ●	0327	0.0	0	0909	4.5	137	0318*	0.2	6	0905*	5.6	171
15 Sa	0411	-0.1	-3	0952	4.5	137	0401*	0.2	6	0946*	5.6	171
16 Su	0455	-0.1	-3	1041	4.5	137	0446*	0.2	6	1035*	5.5	168
17 M	0541	-0.1	-3	1137	4.5	137	0533*	0.3	9	1132*	5.4	165
18 Tu	0631	0.0	0	1236*	4.5	137	0628*	0.5	15			
19 W	1234	5.2	158	0727	0.1	3	0134*	4.6	140	0734*	0.6	18
20 Th ◐	0135	5.1	155	0828	0.2	6	0231*	4.8	146	0847*	0.7	21
21 F	0235	4.9	149	0929	0.1	3	0329*	5.0	152	0957*	0.6	18
22 Sa	0337	4.8	146	1026	0.0	0	0428*	5.2	158	1059*	0.4	12
23 Su	0442	4.7	143	1119	0.0	0	0528*	5.4	165	1156*	0.2	6
24 M	0547	4.6	140	1210*	-0.1	-3	0623*	5.6	171			
25 Tu	1250	0.0	0	0646	4.6	140	0100*	-0.1	-3	0714*	5.8	177
26 W	0143	-0.2	-6	0740	4.7	143	0149*	0.0	0	0801*	5.9	180
27 Th ○	0233	-0.3	-9	0829	4.7	143	0238*	0.1	3	0845*	5.8	177
28 F	0322	-0.3	-9	0917	4.6	140	0325*	0.2	6	0929*	5.7	174
29 Sa	0407	-0.2	-6	1005	4.5	137	0410*	0.4	12	1014*	5.4	165
30 Su	0451	-0.1	-3	1055	4.4	134	0453*	0.6	18	1101*	5.2	158
31 M	0533	0.1	3	1146	4.3	131	0536*	0.8	24	1149*	4.9	149

June

Day	Time (h m)	ft	cm	Time (h m)	ft	cm	Time (h m)	ft	cm	Time (h m)	ft	cm
1 Tu	0616	0.3	9	1236*	4.2	128	0619*	1.1	34			
2 W	1237	4.7	143	0659	0.6	18	0124*	4.2	128	0708*	1.3	40
3 Th	0123	4.5	137	0746	0.7	21	0208*	4.2	128	0807*	1.5	46
4 F ◑	0208	4.3	131	0836	0.9	27	0252*	4.2	128	0910*	1.5	46
5 Sa	0253	4.1	125	0927	0.9	27	0335*	4.3	131	1009*	1.4	43
6 Su	0341	4.0	122	1015	0.9	27	0421*	4.5	137	1103*	1.2	37
7 M	0435	3.9	119	1100	0.8	24	0507*	4.7	143	1152*	0.9	27
8 Tu	0532	3.9	119	1144	0.7	21	0554*	4.9	149			
9 W	1240	0.7	21	0627	4.0	122	1229*	0.6	18	0639*	5.2	158
10 Th	0129	0.4	12	0716	4.2	128	0117*	0.4	12	0721*	5.4	165
11 F	0217	0.1	3	0802	4.4	134	0206*	0.3	9	0804*	5.7	174
12 Sa ●	0305	-0.1	-3	0847	4.5	137	0256*	0.1	3	0848*	5.8	177
13 Su	0352	-0.3	-9	0935	4.6	140	0345*	0.0	0	0936*	5.8	177
14 M	0438	-0.4	-12	1028	4.7	143	0435*	0.0	0	1028*	5.7	174
15 Tu	0525	-0.4	-12	1125	4.8	146	0526*	0.1	3	1126*	5.6	171
16 W	0613	-0.4	-12	1223*	4.9	149	0621*	0.2	6			
17 Th	1226	5.4	165	0705	-0.2	-6	0120*	5.0	152	0723*	0.4	12
18 F	0124	5.2	158	0802	-0.1	-3	0214*	5.2	158	0831*	0.5	15
19 Sa ◐	0221	4.9	149	0901	0.0	0	0309*	5.2	158	0938*	0.5	15
20 Su	0319	4.6	140	0959	0.1	3	0406*	5.3	162	1041*	0.4	12
21 M	0422	4.4	134	1054	0.1	3	0504*	5.4	165	1139*	0.3	9
22 Tu	0527	4.3	131	1146	0.2	6	0602*	5.5	168			
23 W	1233	0.2	6	0629	4.3	131	1238*	0.2	6	0655*	5.5	168
24 Th	0125	0.1	3	0724	4.4	134	0128*	0.3	9	0743*	5.6	171
25 F	0215	0.0	0	0813	4.4	134	0217*	0.4	12	0828*	5.5	168
26 Sa ○	0302	0.0	0	0900	4.5	137	0304*	0.4	12	0911*	5.5	168
27 Su	0346	-0.1	-3	0945	4.5	137	0348*	0.5	15	0953*	5.3	162
28 M	0427	0.0	0	1031	4.4	134	0430*	0.6	18	1035*	5.1	155
29 Tu	0506	0.1	3	1117	4.4	134	0511*	0.8	24	1118*	4.9	149
30 W	0544	0.2	6	1203*	4.4	134	0550*	0.9	27			

July

Day	Time (h m)	ft	cm	Time (h m)	ft	cm	Time (h m)	ft	cm	Time (h m)	ft	cm
1 Th	1201	4.7	143	0620	0.4	12	1246*	4.3	131	0632*	1.1	34
2 F	1243	4.5	137	0656	0.6	18	0126*	4.3	131	0719*	1.3	40
3 Sa	0123	4.3	131	0733	0.8	24	0203*	4.4	134	0819*	1.4	43
4 Su ◑	0204	4.1	125	0818	0.9	27	0239*	4.4	134	0924*	1.4	43
5 M	0248	3.9	119	0911	1.0	30	0319*	4.6	140	1024*	1.3	40
6 Tu	0339	3.8	116	1008	0.9	27	0406*	4.7	143	1118*	1.0	30
7 W	0440	3.8	116	1102	0.8	24	0501*	4.9	149			
8 Th	1210	0.7	21	0545	3.9	119	1155	0.6	18	0559*	5.2	158
9 F	0101	0.4	12	0645	4.1	125	1249*	0.4	12	0654*	5.5	168
10 Sa	0152	0.1	3	0737	4.4	134	0143*	0.2	6	0745*	5.7	174
11 Su ●	0242	-0.2	-6	0827	4.7	143	0237*	0.0	0	0834*	5.9	180
12 M	0330	-0.5	-15	0917	4.9	149	0330*	-0.2	-6	0924*	6.0	183
13 Tu	0417	-0.7	-21	1010	5.1	155	0422*	-0.3	-9	1017*	5.9	180
14 W	0504	-0.7	-21	1105	5.3	162	0514*	-0.2	-6	1113*	5.7	174
15 Th	0551	-0.6	-18	1202*	5.4	165	0607*	0.0	0			
16 F	1210	5.4	165	0640	-0.4	-12	1258*	5.4	165	0706*	0.2	6
17 Sa	0107	5.1	155	0733	-0.2	-6	0152*	5.4	165	0811*	0.4	12
18 Su ◐	0204	4.8	146	0831	0.1	3	0246*	5.4	165	0918*	0.6	18
19 M	0302	4.5	137	0932	0.3	9	0342*	5.3	162	1022*	0.6	18
20 Tu	0403	4.2	128	1031	0.4	12	0441*	5.2	158	1120*	0.5	15
21 W	0509	4.1	125	1126	0.5	15	0542*	5.2	158			
22 Th	1214	0.4	12	0613	4.1	125	1218*	0.5	15	0637*	5.2	158
23 F	0105	0.3	9	0708	4.3	131	0108*	0.5	15	0726*	5.3	162
24 Sa	0153	0.2	6	0756	4.4	134	0156*	0.5	15	0810*	5.3	162
25 Su	0238	0.1	3	0840	4.5	137	0242*	0.5	15	0851*	5.3	162
26 M ○	0320	0.1	3	0921	4.6	140	0326*	0.5	15	0929*	5.3	162
27 Tu	0359	0.1	3	1002	4.6	140	0406*	0.6	18	1007*	5.1	155
28 W	0435	0.1	3	1042	4.6	140	0445*	0.7	21	1045*	4.9	149
29 Th	0509	0.2	6	1121	4.6	140	0522*	0.8	24	1123*	4.7	143
30 F	0540	0.4	12	1159	4.5	137	0559*	1.0	30			
31 Sa	1201	4.5	137	0608	0.6	18	1233*	4.5	137	0638*	1.2	37

August

Day	Time (h m)	ft	cm	Time (h m)	ft	cm	Time (h m)	ft	cm	Time (h m)	ft	cm
1 Su	1239	4.2	128	0634	0.7	21	0106*	4.5	137	0727*	1.3	40
2 M	0119	4.1	125	0707	0.9	27	0142*	4.6	140	0836*	1.4	43
3 Tu ◑	0204	3.9	119	0756	1.0	30	0225*	4.7	143	0946*	1.3	40
4 W	0257	3.8	116	0914	1.0	30	0317*	4.8	146	1047*	1.1	34
5 Th	0401	3.8	116	1028	0.9	27	0420*	5.0	152	1142*	0.8	24
6 F	0513	4.0	122	1130	0.7	21	0529*	5.2	158			
7 Sa	1235	0.4	12	0619	4.3	131	1228*	0.4	12	0632*	5.5	168
8 Su	0126	0.0	0	0716	4.7	143	0125*	0.1	3	0728*	5.8	177
9 M	0217	-0.3	-9	0807	5.1	155	0220*	-0.2	-6	0819*	6.0	183
10 Tu ●	0305	-0.6	-18	0857	5.4	165	0314*	-0.4	-12	0909*	6.1	186
11 W	0352	-0.8	-24	0948	5.6	171	0406*	-0.5	-15	1000*	6.0	183
12 Th	0439	-0.8	-24	1040	5.7	174	0458*	-0.4	-12	1053*	5.7	174
13 F	0525	-0.7	-21	1135	5.8	177	0550*	-0.2	-6	1150*	5.4	165
14 Sa	0612	-0.4	-12	1231*	5.7	174	0646*	0.1	3			
15 Su	1248	5.0	152	0704	0.0	0	0126*	5.5	168	0748*	0.4	12
16 M ◐	0146	4.6	140	0802	0.4	12	0221*	5.4	165	0855*	0.7	21
17 Tu	0244	4.3	131	0906	0.7	21	0318*	5.2	158	1000*	0.7	21
18 W	0346	4.1	125	1009	0.8	24	0418*	5.0	152	1059*	0.7	21
19 Th	0451	4.1	125	1106	0.9	27	0520*	5.0	152	1153*	0.6	18
20 F	0554	4.1	125	1159	0.8	24	0617*	5.0	152			
21 Sa	1241	0.5	15	0648	4.3	131	1248*	0.7	21	0706*	5.1	155
22 Su	0126	0.4	12	0735	4.5	137	0134*	0.6	18	0748*	5.2	158
23 M	0209	0.3	9	0816	4.7	143	0219*	0.6	18	0827*	5.2	158
24 Tu ○	0249	0.2	6	0854	4.8	146	0301*	0.5	15	0903*	5.2	158
25 W	0326	0.2	6	0929	4.9	149	0341*	0.5	15	0938*	5.1	155
26 Th	0401	0.2	6	1003	4.9	149	0420*	0.6	18	1012*	4.9	149
27 F	0433	0.3	9	1034	4.9	149	0456*	0.7	21	1045*	4.7	143
28 Sa	0502	0.4	12	1103	4.8	146	0532*	0.8	24	1120*	4.4	134
29 Su	0527	0.6	18	1132	4.8	146	0607*	1.0	30	1158*	4.2	128
30 M	0553	0.8	24	1208*	4.8	146	0648*	1.2	37			
31 Tu	1242	4.1	125	0626	0.9	27	1252*	4.8	146	0752*	1.3	40

September

Day	Time (h m)	ft	cm	Time (h m)	ft	cm	Time (h m)	ft	cm	Time (h m)	ft	cm
1 W ◑	0134	3.9	119	0715	1.1	34	0145*	4.8	146	0912*	1.3	40
2 Th	0232	3.9	119	0836	1.1	34	0245*	4.9	149	1019*	1.1	34
3 F	0339	4.0	122	1007	1.0	30	0353*	5.0	152	1117*	0.7	21
4 Sa	0451	4.2	128	1113	0.7	21	0506*	5.2	158			
5 Su	1210	0.3	9	0558	4.6	140	1212*	0.3	9	0613*	5.5	168
6 M	0100	-0.1	-3	0655	5.1	155	0109*	0.0	0	0710*	5.8	177
7 Tu	0150	-0.4	-12	0747	5.5	168	0203*	-0.3	-9	0801*	6.0	183
8 W ●	0238	-0.7	-21	0835	5.9	180	0257*	-0.5	-15	0850*	6.0	183
9 Th	0325	-0.8	-24	0924	6.1	186	0349*	-0.6	-18	0940*	5.8	177
10 F	0412	-0.8	-24	1014	6.1	186	0440*	-0.5	-15	1032*	5.5	168
11 Sa	0458	-0.5	-15	1106	6.0	183	0531*	-0.3	-9	1129*	5.2	158
12 Su	0544	-0.2	-6	1202*	5.8	177	0624*	0.1	3			
13 M	1228	4.8	146	0635	0.2	6	1258*	5.5	168	0723*	0.5	15
14 Tu	0127	4.5	137	0732	0.7	21	0155*	5.2	158	0828*	0.8	24
15 W ◐	0226	4.3	131	0838	1.0	30	0252*	5.0	152	0934*	0.9	27
16 Th	0326	4.1	125	0944	1.1	34	0351*	4.8	146	1034*	0.9	27
17 F	0428	4.1	125	1044	1.1	34	0452*	4.7	143	1126*	0.8	24
18 Sa	0529	4.2	128	1137	1.0	30	0548*	4.8	146			
19 Su	1212	0.6	18	0622	4.4	134	1224*	0.9	27	0638*	4.9	149
20 M	1254	0.5	15	0707	4.6	140	0110*	0.7	21	0720*	5.0	152
21 Tu	0134	0.4	12	0747	4.9	149	0153*	0.6	18	0759*	5.0	152
22 W	0213	0.3	9	0822	5.0	152	0235*	0.5	15	0835*	5.0	152
23 Th ○	0250	0.2	6	0855	5.1	155	0316*	0.4	12	0908*	4.9	149
24 F	0325	0.3	9	0924	5.2	158	0355*	0.4	12	0941*	4.8	146
25 Sa	0357	0.3	9	0950	5.1	155	0432*	0.5	15	1013*	4.6	140
26 Su	0427	0.5	15	1015	5.1	155	0509*	0.6	18	1047*	4.4	134
27 M	0455	0.6	18	1046	5.0	152	0546*	0.8	24	1128*	4.2	128
28 Tu	0526	0.7	21	1127	5.0	152	0628*	0.9	27			
29 W	1219	4.0	122	0604	0.9	27	1220*	4.9	149	0728*	1.1	34
30 Th	0118	4.0	122	0656	1.1	34	0121*	4.9	149	0845*	1.1	34

October

Day	Time (h m)	ft	cm	Time (h m)	ft	cm	Time (h m)	ft	cm	Time (h m)	ft	cm
1 F ◑	0220	4.0	122	0824	1.1	34	0226*	4.9	149	0953*	0.9	27
2 Sa	0326	4.2	128	0952	1.0	30	0335*	5.0	152	1052*	0.6	18
3 Su	0434	4.5	137	1059	0.6	18	0447*	5.1	155	1144*	0.2	6
4 M	0538	4.9	149	1157	0.2	6	0553*	5.4	165			
5 Tu	1234	-0.2	-6	0635	5.4	165	1253*	-0.1	-3	0650*	5.5	168
6 W	0123	-0.5	-15	0726	5.8	177	0147*	-0.4	-12	0742*	5.7	174
7 Th ●	0211	-0.6	-18	0813	6.1	186	0240*	-0.6	-18	0832*	5.6	171
8 F	0259	-0.7	-21	0900	6.3	192	0332*	-0.6	-18	0921*	5.5	168
9 Sa	0346	-0.6	-18	0948	6.2	189	0422*	-0.5	-15	1012*	5.2	158
10 Su	0432	-0.3	-9	1038	6.0	183	0511*	-0.3	-9	1108*	4.9	149
11 M	0519	0.0	0	1133	5.7	174	0602*	0.0	0			
12 Tu	1207	4.6	140	0608	0.4	12	1230*	5.3	162	0656*	0.4	12
13 W	0107	4.4	134	0703	0.9	27	0127*	5.0	152	0757*	0.7	21
14 Th ◐	0204	4.2	128	0806	1.2	37	0223*	4.8	146	0900*	0.9	27
15 F	0301	4.1	125	0914	1.3	40	0318*	4.6	140	0959*	0.9	27
16 Sa	0359	4.1	125	1015	1.3	40	0415*	4.5	137	1051*	0.8	24
17 Su	0455	4.2	128	1109	1.1	34	0510*	4.5	137	1136*	0.7	21
18 M	0548	4.4	134	1157	0.9	27	0602*	4.5	137			
19 Tu	1217	0.5	15	0634	4.7	143	1242*	0.7	21	0647*	4.6	140
20 W	1256	0.4	12	0713	4.9	149	0125*	0.6	18	0728*	4.7	143
21 Th	0135	0.3	9	0748	5.1	155	0208*	0.4	12	0805*	4.7	143
22 F	0212	0.3	9	0820	5.2	158	0250*	0.3	9	0840*	4.6	140
23 Sa ○	0249	0.3	9	0848	5.3	162	0331*	0.2	6	0914*	4.5	137
24 Su	0325	0.3	9	0914	5.3	162	0411*	0.2	6	0947*	4.4	134
25 M	0400	0.4	12	0943	5.3	162	0450*	0.3	9	1025*	4.3	131
26 Tu	0434	0.5	15	1020	5.2	158	0531*	0.4	12	1111*	4.1	125
27 W	0512	0.6	18	1106	5.1	155	0617*	0.6	18			
28 Th	1208	4.1	125	0555	0.7	21	1204*	5.0	152	0713*	0.7	21
29 F	0110	4.1	125	0654	0.9	27	0108*	4.9	149	0820*	0.7	21
30 Sa ◑	0211	4.2	128	0817	0.9	27	0213*	4.9	149	0926*	0.5	15
31 Su	0313	4.4	134	0937	0.8	24	0319*	4.9	149	1025*	0.3	9

November

Day	Time (h m)	ft	cm	Time (h m)	ft	cm	Time (h m)	ft	cm	Time (h m)	ft	cm
1 M	0415	4.7	143	1043	0.5	15	0426*	4.9	149	1118*	0.0	0
2 Tu	0517	5.1	155	1142	0.1	3	0532*	5.0	152			
3 W	1208	-0.3	-9	0614	5.5	168	1238*	-0.2	-6	0631*	5.1	155
4 Th	1257	-0.5	-15	0706	5.8	177	0131*	-0.4	-12	0725*	5.1	155
5 F	0146	-0.6	-18	0754	6.1	186	0224*	-0.6	-18	0815*	5.1	155
6 Sa ●	0234	-0.6	-18	0840	6.1	186	0315*	-0.6	-18	0904*	5.0	152
7 Su	0222	-0.4	-12	0826	6.0	183	0304*	-0.6	-18	0855*	4.8	146
8 M	0309	-0.2	-6	0915	5.7	174	0352*	-0.4	-12	0948*	4.6	140
9 Tu	0356	0.1	3	1006	5.4	165	0439*	-0.1	-3	1045*	4.4	134
10 W	0443	0.4	12	1101	5.1	155	0528*	0.2	6	1142*	4.2	128
11 Th	0533	0.8	24	1155	4.8	146	0621*	0.5	15			
12 F	1237	4.1	125	0630	1.1	34	1248*	4.5	137	0718*	0.7	21
13 Sa ◐	0129	4.0	122	0734	1.3	40	0139*	4.3	131	0815*	0.8	24
14 Su	0221	4.0	122	0838	1.3	40	0231*	4.2	128	0907*	0.7	21
15 M	0313	4.1	125	0934	1.2	37	0324*	4.1	125	0953*	0.6	18
16 Tu	0404	4.2	128	1024	1.0	30	0417*	4.1	125	1035*	0.5	15
17 W	0452	4.5	137	1111	0.7	21	0508*	4.1	125	1116*	0.4	12
18 Th	0534	4.7	143	1156	0.5	15	0554*	4.2	128	1156*	0.3	9
19 F	0612	4.9	149	1241*	0.3	9	0635*	4.2	128			
20 Sa	1236	0.2	6	0646	5.1	155	0125*	0.1	3	0713*	4.3	131
21 Su ○	0117	0.2	6	0717	5.2	158	0208*	0.0	0	0750*	4.3	131
22 M	0158	0.1	3	0750	5.3	162	0251*	-0.1	-3	0828*	4.2	128
23 Tu	0239	0.1	3	0825	5.3	162	0333*	-0.1	-3	0911*	4.2	128
24 W	0321	0.1	3	0908	5.3	162	0417*	-0.1	-3	1001*	4.2	128
25 Th	0405	0.2	6	0958	5.1	155	0503*	0.0	0	1059*	4.2	128
26 F	0454	0.3	9	1057	5.0	152	0555*	0.1	3	1159*	4.2	128
27 Sa	0553	0.4	12	1159	4.9	149	0653*	0.1	3			
28 Su ◑	1257	4.4	134	0706	0.5	15	0100*	4.7	143	0756*	0.1	3
29 M	0155	4.6	140	0820	0.5	15	0201*	4.6	140	0856*	-0.1	-3
30 Tu	0254	4.8	146	0927	0.3	9	0305*	4.5	137	0951*	-0.2	-6

December

Day	Time (h m)	ft	cm	Time (h m)	ft	cm	Time (h m)	ft	cm	Time (h m)	ft	cm
1 W	0354	5.0	152	1027	0.0	0	0412*	4.4	134	1043*	-0.3	-9
2 Th	0453	5.3	162	1122	-0.2	-6	0514*	4.5	137	1134*	-0.4	-12
3 F	0547	5.5	168	1216*	-0.4	-12	0611*	4.5	137			
4 Sa	1224	-0.5	-15	0637	5.7	174	0108*	-0.6	-18	0702*	4.6	140
5 Su ●	0114	-0.4	-12	0724	5.7	174	0158*	-0.6	-18	0751*	4.5	137
6 M	0203	-0.4	-12	0809	5.6	171	0246*	-0.6	-18	0839*	4.5	137
7 Tu	0250	-0.2	-6	0855	5.4	165	0331*	-0.5	-15	0929*	4.3	131
8 W	0335	0.0	0	0943	5.1	155	0415*	-0.3	-9	1020*	4.2	128
9 Th	0419	0.2	6	1032	4.9	149	0458*	-0.1	-3	1112*	4.0	122
10 F	0503	0.5	15	1121	4.6	140	0542*	0.2	6			
11 Sa	1202	4.0	122	0551	0.8	24	1209*	4.3	131	0629*	0.4	12
12 Su	1250	3.9	119	0647	1.0	30	1255*	4.1	125	0720*	0.6	18
13 M ◐	0136	3.9	119	0750	1.1	34	0142*	3.9	119	0812*	0.7	21
14 Tu	0222	3.9	119	0852	1.1	34	0231*	3.7	113	0902*	0.7	21
15 W	0309	4.0	122	0947	0.9	27	0325*	3.6	110	0949*	0.6	18
16 Th	0359	4.2	128	1038	0.7	21	0422*	3.6	110	1033*	0.5	15
17 F	0447	4.4	134	1126	0.5	15	0516*	3.7	113	1118*	0.3	9
18 Sa	0532	4.6	140	1212*	0.2	6	0605*	3.8	116			
19 Su	1203	0.2	6	0614	4.9	149	1259*	0.0	0	0648*	4.0	122
20 M	1249	0.0	0	0653	5.1	155	0145*	-0.2	-6	0729*	4.1	125
21 Tu ○	0136	-0.2	-6	0733	5.3	162	0230*	-0.4	-12	0812*	4.2	128
22 W	0223	-0.3	-9	0815	5.3	162	0315*	-0.6	-18	0857*	4.3	131
23 Th	0310	-0.4	-12	0901	5.3	162	0359*	-0.6	-18	0948*	4.4	134
24 F	0357	-0.4	-12	0952	5.2	158	0444*	-0.6	-18	1044*	4.4	134
25 Sa	0448	-0.2	-6	1048	5.0	152	0532*	-0.5	-15	1141*	4.5	137
26 Su	0544	-0.1	-3	1146	4.8	146	0625*	-0.4	-12			
27 M	1237	4.6	140	0650	0.1	3	1245*	4.6	140	0725*	-0.3	-9
28 Tu ◑	0133	4.7	143	0801	0.2	6	0144*	4.3	131	0826*	-0.2	-6
29 W	0231	4.8	146	0909	0.1	3	0246*	4.1	125	0925*	-0.2	-6
30 Th	0331	4.9	149	1010	0.0	0	0354*	4.0	122	1021*	-0.2	-6
31 F	0434	5.0	152	1107	-0.2	-6	0500*	4.0	122	1115*	-0.3	-9

Heights are referred to mean lower low water which is the chart datum of soundings. All times are local. Daylight Saving Time has been used when needed.

Bridgeport, Connecticut, 2010

Times and Heights of High and Low Waters

March

Day	Time (h m)	ft	cm	Day	Time (h m)	ft	cm
1 M	0522	-1.3	-40	16 Tu	1211	7.1	216
	1129	7.9	241		0628	-0.1	-3
	0545*	-1.2	-37		1233*	6.8	207
	1152*	8.2	250		0637*	0.1	3
2 Tu	0613	-1.3	-40	17 W	1245	7.2	219
	1218*	7.7	235		0704	-0.1	-3
	0631*	-1.0	-30		0109*	6.7	204
					0712*	0.2	6
3 W	1239	8.2	250	18 Th	0118	7.2	219
	0703	-1.1	-34		0741	-0.1	-3
	0107*	7.4	226		0147*	6.6	201
	0718*	-0.7	-21		0748*	0.3	9
4 Th	0128	8.0	244	19 F	0154	7.2	219
	0754	-0.8	-24		0821	-0.1	-3
	0157*	7.0	213		0226*	6.5	198
	0807*	-0.3	-9		0827*	0.4	12
5 F	0217	7.6	232	20 Sa	0233	7.2	219
	0847	-0.3	-9		0904	0.0	0
	0250*	6.6	201		0310*	6.3	192
	0859*	0.2	6		0911*	0.6	18
6 Sa	0311	7.1	216	21 Su	0318	7.0	213
	0942	0.1	3		0954	0.2	6
	0346*	6.2	189		0400*	6.1	186
	0956*	0.6	18		1003*	0.8	24
7 Su ◑	0408	6.7	204	22 M	0411	6.9	210
	1042	0.5	15		1051	0.4	12
	0446*	5.9	180		0457*	6.0	183
	1058*	1.0	30		1102*	0.9	27
8 M	0510	6.3	192	23 Tu ◐	0513	6.8	207
	1144	0.8	24		1155	0.5	15
	0549*	5.7	174		0601*	6.0	183
9 Tu	1202	1.1	34	24 W	1209	0.8	24
	0614	6.1	186		0621	6.8	207
	1245*	0.8	24		0101*	0.4	12
	0651*	5.8	177		0706*	6.2	189
10 W	0104	1.0	30	25 Th	0118	0.6	18
	0715	6.1	186		0730	6.9	210
	0141*	0.8	24		0204*	0.2	6
	0747*	6.0	183		0809*	6.6	201
11 Th	0200	0.9	27	26 F	0224	0.2	6
	0810	6.3	192		0834	7.1	216
	0230*	0.6	18		0302*	-0.1	-3
	0836*	6.2	189		0908*	7.1	216
12 F	0249	0.6	18	27 Sa	0325	-0.2	-6
	0858	6.4	195		0934	7.4	226
	0313*	0.4	12		0355*	-0.4	-12
	0920*	6.5	198		1002*	7.6	232
13 Sa	0333	0.4	12	28 Su	0422	-0.7	-21
	0940	6.6	201		1029	7.6	232
	0351*	0.3	9		0445*	-0.7	-21
	1000*	6.8	207		1052*	8.1	247
14 Su	0513	0.2	6	29 M	0515	-1.0	-30
	1120	6.7	204		1120	7.7	235
	0528*	0.2	6		0533*	-0.8	-24
	1136*	7.0	213		1141*	8.4	256
15 M ●	0551	0.0	0	30 Tu ○	0605	-1.1	-34
	1157	6.7	204		1209*	7.7	235
	0602*	0.1	3		0620*	-0.7	-21
				31 W	1227	8.4	256
					0653	-1.1	-34
					1257*	7.5	229
					0706*	-0.5	-15

April

Day	Time (h m)	ft	cm	Day	Time (h m)	ft	cm
1 Th	0114	8.3	253	16 F	1250	7.5	229
	0741	-0.9	-27		0719	-0.2	-6
	0145*	7.3	223		0125*	6.7	204
	0752*	-0.2	-6		0724*	0.5	15
2 F	0201	8.0	244	17 Sa	0129	7.5	229
	0829	-0.5	-15		0802	-0.2	-6
	0234*	7.0	213		0208*	6.7	204
	0840*	0.2	6		0807*	0.6	18
3 Sa	0249	7.5	229	18 Su	0213	7.5	229
	0919	-0.1	-3		0848	-0.1	-3
	0324*	6.6	201		0254*	6.6	201
	0931*	0.6	18		0855*	0.7	21
4 Su	0340	7.1	216	19 M	0302	7.3	223
	1011	0.3	9		0939	0.1	3
	0417*	6.3	192		0346*	6.5	198
	1025*	0.9	27		0950*	0.8	24
5 M	0435	6.6	201	20 Tu	0357	7.2	219
	1106	0.7	21		1036	0.2	6
	0513*	6.0	183		0443*	6.4	195
	1124*	1.2	37		1051*	0.8	24
6 Tu ◑	0534	6.3	192	21 W ◐	0459	7.0	213
	1204*	1.0	30		1136	0.3	9
	0612*	5.9	180		0544*	6.5	198
					1157*	0.8	24
7 W	1226	1.3	40	22 Th	0605	6.9	210
	0636	6.1	186		1238*	0.3	9
	0101*	1.1	34		0647*	6.8	207
	0711*	6.0	183				
8 Th	0127	1.3	40	23 F	0105	0.5	15
	0736	6.0	183		0712	6.9	210
	0156*	1.0	30		0139*	0.2	6
	0807*	6.2	189		0748*	7.1	216
9 F	0224	1.1	34	24 Sa	0209	0.2	6
	0832	6.1	186		0815	7.0	213
	0245*	0.9	27		0236*	0.0	0
	0857*	6.5	198		0845*	7.6	232
10 Sa	0315	0.8	24	25 Su	0310	-0.2	-6
	0921	6.2	189		0915	7.1	216
	0330*	0.8	24		0329*	-0.1	-3
	0942*	6.8	207		0939*	7.9	241
11 Su	0401	0.5	15	26 M	0406	-0.5	-15
	1006	6.4	195		1010	7.3	223
	0411*	0.6	18		0420*	-0.2	-6
	1023*	7.0	213		1029*	8.2	250
12 M	0443	0.3	9	27 Tu	0458	-0.7	-21
	1048	6.5	198		1101	7.3	223
	0450*	0.5	15		0509*	-0.2	-6
	1101*	7.2	219		1118*	8.3	253
13 Tu	0522	0.1	3	28 W ○	0547	-0.8	-24
	1128	6.7	204		1150	7.3	223
	0528*	0.4	12		0556*	-0.2	-6
	1137*	7.4	226				
14 W ●	0601	-0.1	-3	29 Th	1204	8.3	253
	1207*	6.7	204		0634	-0.7	-21
	0606*	0.4	12		1238*	7.2	219
					0642*	0.0	0
15 Th	1213	7.5	229	30 F	1250	8.1	247
	0639	-0.2	-6		0720	-0.5	-15
	1245*	6.8	207		0124*	7.1	216
	0644*	0.4	12		0728*	0.3	9

May

Day	Time (h m)	ft	cm	Day	Time (h m)	ft	cm
1 Sa	0136	7.8	238	16 Su	0111	7.8	238
	0806	-0.2	-6		0746	-0.3	-9
	0211*	6.9	210		0152*	6.9	210
	0815*	0.5	15		0752*	0.5	15
2 Su	0223	7.4	226	17 M	0159	7.7	235
	0852	0.1	3		0834	-0.2	-6
	0258*	6.6	201		0240*	6.9	210
	0903*	0.8	24		0844*	0.5	15
3 M	0311	7.0	213	18 Tu	0250	7.6	232
	0939	0.5	15		0926	-0.1	-3
	0347*	6.4	195		0333*	6.9	210
	0955*	1.1	34		0940*	0.6	18
4 Tu	0402	6.6	201	19 W	0346	7.4	226
	1029	0.8	24		1020	0.0	0
	0439*	6.3	192		0429*	7.0	213
	1049*	1.3	40		1041*	0.6	18
5 W	0457	6.3	192	20 Th ◐	0446	7.2	219
	1120	1.0	30		1117	0.1	3
	0533*	6.2	189		0527*	7.1	216
	1147*	1.4	43		1145*	0.5	15
6 Th ◑	0553	6.1	186	21 F	0549	7.0	213
	1212*	1.1	34		1215*	0.2	6
	0627*	6.3	192		0627*	7.3	223
7 F	1245	1.3	40	22 Sa	1250	0.4	12
	0650	6.0	183		0653	6.9	210
	0104*	1.1	34		0113*	0.2	6
	0720*	6.5	198		0726*	7.5	229
8 Sa	0141	1.2	37	23 Su	0153	0.2	6
	0746	6.0	183		0755	6.8	207
	0154*	1.1	34		0210*	0.2	6
	0810*	6.7	204		0823*	7.8	238
9 Su	0234	1.0	30	24 M	0253	0.0	0
	0838	6.1	186		0855	6.8	207
	0242*	1.0	30		0305*	0.2	6
	0857*	6.9	210		0917*	8.0	244
10 M	0322	0.7	21	25 Tu	0349	-0.2	-6
	0927	6.2	189		0951	6.9	210
	0327*	0.9	27		0357*	0.2	6
	0941*	7.1	216		1008*	8.1	247
11 Tu	0408	0.4	12	26 W	0441	-0.4	-12
	1013	6.4	195		1043	6.9	210
	0411*	0.8	24		0447*	0.3	9
	1023*	7.3	223		1057*	8.1	247
12 W	0451	0.2	6	27 Th ○	0529	-0.4	-12
	1056	6.5	198		1132	7.0	213
	0454*	0.7	21		0535*	0.3	9
	1103*	7.5	229		1144*	8.0	244
13 Th	0533	-0.1	-3	28 F	0616	-0.3	-9
	1139	6.7	204		1219*	6.9	210
	0536*	0.6	18		0622*	0.4	12
	1144*	7.7	235				
14 F ●	0616	-0.2	-6	29 Sa	1229	7.8	238
	1222*	6.8	207		0700	-0.2	-6
	0619*	0.5	15		0104*	6.9	210
					0707*	0.6	18
15 Sa	1226	7.8	238	30 Su	0114	7.6	232
	0700	-0.3	-9		0743	0.0	0
	0106*	6.8	207		0148*	6.8	207
	0704*	0.5	15		0752*	0.7	21
				31 M	0159	7.3	223
					0825	0.2	6
					0232*	6.7	204
					0837*	0.9	27

June

Day	Time (h m)	ft	cm	Day	Time (h m)	ft	cm
1 Tu	0244	7.0	213	16 W	0238	7.9	241
	0908	0.5	15		0908	-0.4	-12
	0317*	6.6	201		0316*	7.4	226
	0924*	1.1	34		0929*	0.2	6
2 W	0330	6.7	204	17 Th	0333	7.6	232
	0951	0.7	21		1000	-0.3	-9
	0403*	6.6	201		0411*	7.5	229
	1014*	1.2	37		1028*	0.2	6
3 Th	0419	6.4	195	18 F	0431	7.3	223
	1036	0.8	24		1054	-0.1	-3
	0451*	6.6	201		0507*	7.6	232
	1106*	1.3	40		1130*	0.3	9
4 F ◑	0509	6.2	189	19 Sa ◐	0531	7.0	213
	1123	1.0	30		1150	0.1	3
	0540*	6.6	201		0604*	7.7	235
5 Sa	1200	1.3	40	20 Su	1233	0.3	9
	0603	6.0	183		0633	6.7	204
	1212*	1.1	34		1248*	0.3	9
	0630*	6.7	204		0703*	7.7	235
6 Su	1255	1.2	37	21 M	0135	0.2	6
	0657	5.9	180		0735	6.6	201
	0102*	1.1	34		0146*	0.4	12
	0720*	6.8	207		0800*	7.7	235
7 M	0149	1.0	30	22 Tu	0235	0.1	3
	0751	5.9	180		0835	6.5	198
	0152*	1.1	34		0242*	0.5	15
	0809*	6.9	210		0856*	7.7	235
8 Tu	0241	0.8	24	23 W	0331	0.1	3
	0844	6.0	183		0932	6.5	198
	0242*	1.1	34		0337*	0.6	18
	0858*	7.1	216		0949*	7.7	235
9 W	0331	0.5	15	24 Th	0424	0.0	0
	0935	6.2	189		1025	6.6	201
	0332*	0.9	27		0429*	0.6	18
	0945*	7.3	223		1039*	7.7	235
10 Th	0419	0.2	6	25 F	0512	0.0	0
	1024	6.4	195		1114	6.7	204
	0421*	0.8	24		0517*	0.6	18
	1031*	7.6	232		1126*	7.6	232
11 F	0506	0.0	0	26 Sa ○	0557	0.0	0
	1111	6.6	201		1200*	6.7	204
	0509*	0.6	18		0603*	0.7	21
	1118*	7.8	238				
12 Sa ●	0553	-0.3	-9	27 Su	1211	7.5	229
	1158	6.8	207		0639	0.1	3
	0557*	0.4	12		1243*	6.8	207
					0646*	0.7	21
13 Su	1206	7.9	241	28 M	1253	7.4	226
	0641	-0.4	-12		0718	0.2	6
	1246*	7.0	213		0124*	6.8	207
	0647*	0.3	9		0729*	0.8	24
14 M	1255	8.0	244	29 Tu	0135	7.2	219
	0729	-0.5	-15		0757	0.3	9
	0134*	7.2	219		0205*	6.8	207
	0738*	0.2	6		0811*	0.8	24
15 Tu	0145	8.0	244	30 W	0216	7.0	213
	0818	-0.5	-15		0835	0.4	12
	0224*	7.3	223		0245*	6.8	207
	0832*	0.2	6		0854*	0.9	27

July

Day	Time (h m)	ft	cm	Day	Time (h m)	ft	cm
1 Th	0258	6.7	204	16 F	0316	7.7	235
	0914	0.6	18		0936	-0.4	-12
	0326*	6.8	207		0348*	8.0	244
	0938*	1.0	30		1010*	0.0	0
2 F	0342	6.5	198	17 Sa	0412	7.3	223
	0954	0.7	21		1029	-0.1	-3
	0409*	6.8	207		0443*	7.9	241
	1026*	1.1	34		1110*	0.1	3
3 Sa	0428	6.2	189	18 Su ◐	0510	6.9	210
	1037	0.9	27		1125	0.2	6
	0454*	6.8	207		0540*	7.7	235
	1116*	1.1	34				
4 Su ◑	0517	6.0	183	19 M	1212	0.3	9
	1123	1.0	30		0612	6.6	201
	0541*	6.8	207		1224*	0.5	15
					0639*	7.6	232
5 M	1209	1.1	34	20 Tu	0115	0.4	12
	0610	5.9	180		0715	6.4	195
	1213*	1.1	34		0124*	0.7	21
	0631*	6.8	207		0739*	7.4	226
6 Tu	0104	1.0	30	21 W	0216	0.4	12
	0706	5.9	180		0816	6.3	192
	0107*	1.2	37		0224*	0.8	24
	0723*	6.9	210		0838*	7.4	226
7 W	0200	0.9	27	22 Th	0313	0.4	12
	0803	5.9	180		0914	6.4	195
	0202*	1.1	34		0320*	0.8	24
	0817*	7.1	216		0933*	7.3	223
8 Th	0255	0.6	18	23 F	0405	0.3	9
	0859	6.1	186		1007	6.5	198
	0257*	1.0	30		0412*	0.8	24
	0911*	7.3	223		1023*	7.3	223
9 F	0349	0.3	9	24 Sa	0452	0.3	9
	0953	6.4	195		1055	6.6	201
	0352*	0.7	21		0500*	0.7	21
	1004*	7.6	232		1109*	7.3	223
10 Sa	0441	0.0	0	25 Su	0535	0.3	9
	1044	6.7	204		1138	6.7	204
	0445*	0.5	15		0544*	0.7	21
	1056*	7.9	241		1151*	7.3	223
11 Su ●	0531	-0.3	-9	26 M ○	0614	0.2	6
	1135	7.0	213		1218*	6.9	210
	0537*	0.2	6		0625*	0.7	21
	1148*	8.1	247				
12 M	0619	-0.6	-18	27 Tu	1231	7.2	219
	1224*	7.3	223		0650	0.3	9
	0630*	-0.1	-3		1257*	6.9	210
					0704*	0.7	21
13 Tu	1238	8.2	250	28 W	0110	7.1	216
	0708	-0.7	-21		0726	0.3	9
	0113*	7.6	232		0134*	7.0	213
	0723*	-0.2	-6		0743*	0.7	21
14 W	0130	8.2	250	29 Th	0148	7.0	213
	0756	-0.7	-21		0801	0.4	12
	0204*	7.8	238		0211*	7.0	213
	0817*	-0.3	-9		0823*	0.7	21
15 Th	0222	8.0	244	30 F	0227	6.8	207
	0846	-0.6	-18		0836	0.5	15
	0255*	8.0	244		0248*	7.0	213
	0913*	-0.2	-6		0904*	0.8	24
				31 Sa	0307	6.6	201
					0914	0.7	21
					0327*	7.0	213
					0947*	0.9	27

August

Day	Time (h m)	ft	cm	Day	Time (h m)	ft	cm
1 Su	0350	6.3	192	16 M ◐	0448	6.8	207
	0955	0.9	27		1100	0.4	12
	0409*	6.9	210		0515*	7.6	232
	1035*	1.0	30		1149*	0.4	12
2 M	0437	6.1	186	17 Tu	0550	6.5	198
	1040	1.0	30		1201*	0.8	24
	0455*	6.9	210		0616*	7.3	223
	1127*	1.0	30				
3 Tu ◑	0530	6.0	183	18 W	1252	0.6	18
	1132	1.2	37		0653	6.3	192
	0547*	6.9	210		0103*	1.0	30
					0718*	7.1	216
4 W	1224	1.0	30	19 Th	0153	0.7	21
	0627	5.9	180		0755	6.3	192
	1229*	1.2	37		0205*	1.0	30
	0644*	6.9	210		0818*	7.0	213
5 Th	0125	0.9	27	20 F	0251	0.7	21
	0728	6.0	183		0853	6.4	195
	0129*	1.2	37		0302*	1.0	30
	0744*	7.1	216		0914*	7.0	213
6 F	0224	0.6	18	21 Sa	0342	0.6	18
	0827	6.2	189		0945	6.5	198
	0230*	0.9	27		0354*	0.9	27
	0844*	7.4	226		1003*	7.1	216
7 Sa	0321	0.3	9	22 Su	0427	0.5	15
	0924	6.5	198		1030	6.7	204
	0328*	0.6	18		0439*	0.7	21
	0941*	7.7	235		1048*	7.1	216
8 Su	0415	-0.1	-3	23 M	0507	0.4	12
	1018	6.9	210		1112	6.9	210
	0424*	0.2	6		0521*	0.6	18
	1036*	8.0	244		1128*	7.2	219
9 M	0506	-0.4	-12	24 Tu ○	0544	0.4	12
	1110	7.4	226		1150	7.1	216
	0519*	-0.2	-6		0600*	0.5	15
	1128*	8.2	250				
10 Tu ●	0555	-0.7	-21	25 W	1206	7.1	216
	1200*	7.8	238		0618	0.4	12
	0612*	-0.5	-15		1226*	7.2	219
					0638*	0.5	15
11 W	1220	8.3	253	26 Th	1243	7.1	216
	0643	-0.8	-24		0652	0.4	12
	1249*	8.2	250		0101*	7.2	219
	0705*	-0.6	-18		0715*	0.5	15
12 Th	0111	8.2	250	27 F	0120	6.9	210
	0731	-0.8	-24		0726	0.5	15
	0139*	8.3	253		0136*	7.2	219
	0758*	-0.6	-18		0752*	0.5	15
13 F	0202	8.0	244	28 Sa	0157	6.8	207
	0819	-0.6	-18		0801	0.6	18
	0229*	8.4	256		0211*	7.2	219
	0852*	-0.4	-12		0831*	0.6	18
14 Sa	0255	7.6	232	29 Su	0235	6.6	201
	0910	-0.3	-9		0838	0.8	24
	0322*	8.2	250		0248*	7.1	216
	0949*	-0.2	-6		0913*	0.7	21
15 Su	0350	7.2	219	30 M	0317	6.4	195
	1003	0.0	0		0919	1.0	30
	0416*	7.9	241		0329*	7.0	213
	1047*	0.1	3		1000*	0.8	24
				31 Tu	0404	6.2	189
					1006	1.1	34
					0417*	6.9	210
					1053*	0.9	27

September

Day	Time (h m)	ft	cm	Day	Time (h m)	ft	cm
1 W ◑	0458	6.1	186	16 Th	1224	0.9	27
	1100	1.3	40		0628	6.3	192
	0512*	6.9	210		1240*	1.2	37
	1153*	1.0	30		0653*	6.8	207
2 Th	0557	6.0	183	17 F	0125	0.9	27
	1201*	1.3	40		0729	6.3	192
	0614*	6.9	210		0142*	1.2	37
					0754*	6.7	204
3 F	1256	0.9	27	18 Sa	0221	0.9	27
	0700	6.1	186		0826	6.4	195
	0105*	1.1	34		0239*	1.0	30
	0719*	7.1	216		0849*	6.8	207
4 Sa	0158	0.6	18	19 Su	0310	0.8	24
	0801	6.4	195		0916	6.7	204
	0209*	0.8	24		0329*	0.9	27
	0822*	7.4	226		0937*	6.9	210
5 Su	0256	0.3	9	20 M	0354	0.7	21
	0859	6.9	210		1000	6.9	210
	0309*	0.4	12		0414*	0.7	21
	0921*	7.7	235		1021*	6.9	210
6 M	0350	-0.1	-3	21 Tu	0433	0.6	18
	0954	7.4	226		1040	7.1	216
	0406*	-0.1	-3		0455*	0.5	15
	1016*	8.0	244		1101*	7.0	213
7 Tu	0440	-0.4	-12	22 W	0509	0.5	15
	1045	7.9	241		1118	7.3	223
	0501*	-0.5	-15		0533*	0.4	12
	1109*	8.2	250		1139*	7.0	213
8 W ●	0529	-0.7	-21	23 Th ○	0544	0.5	15
	1135	8.3	253		1153	7.4	226
	0554*	-0.8	-24		0610*	0.3	9
9 Th	1200	8.2	250	24 F	1216	7.0	213
	0616	-0.7	-21		0619	0.5	15
	1224*	8.6	262		1227*	7.4	226
	0645*	-0.8	-24		0647*	0.3	9
10 F	1250	8.1	247	25 Sa	1252	6.9	210
	0704	-0.7	-21		0654	0.6	18
	0113*	8.6	262		0102*	7.4	226
	0737*	-0.8	-24		0724*	0.3	9
11 Sa	0140	7.8	238	26 Su	0129	6.8	207
	0752	-0.4	-12		0730	0.7	21
	0203*	8.5	259		0137*	7.3	223
	0830*	-0.5	-15		0803*	0.4	12
12 Su	0232	7.4	226	27 M	0209	6.6	201
	0843	-0.1	-3		0808	0.9	27
	0254*	8.2	250		0215*	7.2	219
	0924*	-0.1	-3		0845*	0.5	15
13 M	0326	7.1	216	28 Tu	0251	6.4	195
	0937	0.3	9		0851	1.0	30
	0349*	7.7	235		0258*	7.1	216
	1021*	0.3	9		0933*	0.7	21
14 Tu	0424	6.7	204	29 W	0339	6.3	192
	1035	0.7	21		0940	1.2	37
	0447*	7.3	223		0349*	7.0	213
	1122*	0.6	18		1028*	0.8	24
15 W ◐	0525	6.4	195	30 Th	0434	6.2	189
	1136	1.0	30		1037	1.2	37
	0550*	7.0	213		0447*	6.9	210
					1129*	0.8	24

October

Day	Time (h m)	ft	cm	Day	Time (h m)	ft	cm
1 F ◑	0534	6.2	189	16 Sa	1247	1.0	30
	1141	1.2	37		0655	6.3	192
	0552*	7.0	213		0111*	1.2	37
					0720*	6.4	195
2 Sa	1232	0.7	21	17 Su	0141	1.0	30
	0637	6.4	195		0750	6.5	198
	1248*	1.0	30		0207*	1.1	34
	0658*	7.1	216		0814*	6.4	195
3 Su	0133	0.5	15	18 M	0229	0.9	27
	0739	6.7	204		0839	6.7	204
	0152*	0.6	18		0258*	0.9	27
	0802*	7.3	223		0903*	6.5	198
4 M	0230	0.2	6	19 Tu	0313	0.8	24
	0836	7.2	219		0924	7.0	213
	0253*	0.1	3		0343*	0.6	18
	0901*	7.6	232		0948*	6.6	201
5 Tu	0323	-0.1	-3	20 W	0354	0.7	21
	0930	7.8	238		1005	7.2	219
	0350*	-0.3	-9		0425*	0.4	12
	0956*	7.8	238		1030*	6.7	204
6 W	0414	-0.4	-12	21 Th	0432	0.6	18
	1021	8.3	253		1043	7.3	223
	0444*	-0.7	-21		0504*	0.3	9
	1049*	7.9	241		1109*	6.7	204
7 Th ●	0502	-0.6	-18	22 F	0510	0.6	18
	1111	8.6	262		1120	7.4	226
	0535*	-0.9	-27		0542*	0.2	6
	1139*	7.9	241		1148*	6.8	207
8 F	0550	-0.6	-18	23 Sa ○	0547	0.6	18
	1159	8.7	265		1155	7.4	226
	0626*	-0.9	-27		0620*	0.1	3
9 Sa	1229	7.8	238	24 Su	1226	6.7	204
	0638	-0.4	-12		0624	0.6	18
	1247*	8.6	262		1231*	7.4	226
	0716*	-0.8	-24		0659*	0.1	3
10 Su	0119	7.5	229	25 M	0105	6.7	204
	0727	-0.2	-6		0703	0.7	21
	0137*	8.3	253		0109*	7.4	226
	0806*	-0.4	-12		0740*	0.2	6
11 M	0210	7.2	219	26 Tu	0146	6.6	201
	0817	0.2	6		0745	0.8	24
	0227*	7.9	241		0151*	7.3	223
	0859*	-0.1	-3		0825*	0.2	6
12 Tu	0302	6.9	210	27 W	0231	6.5	198
	0910	0.6	18		0831	0.9	27
	0321*	7.5	229		0237*	7.2	219
	0953*	0.4	12		0914*	0.4	12
13 W	0357	6.6	201	28 Th	0320	6.4	195
	1007	0.9	27		0923	1.0	30
	0418*	7.0	213		0330*	7.1	216
	1050*	0.7	21		1009*	0.5	15
14 Th ◐	0456	6.3	192	29 F	0415	6.3	192
	1108	1.2	37		1022	1.0	30
	0519*	6.7	204		0430*	7.0	213
	1149*	0.9	27		1108*	0.5	15
15 F	0556	6.3	192	30 Sa ◑	0515	6.4	195
	1211*	1.3	40		1126	0.9	27
	0620*	6.5	198		0534*	6.9	210
				31 Su	1208	0.4	12
					0616	6.7	204
					1232*	0.7	21
					0639*	6.9	210

November

Day	Time (h m)	ft	cm	Day	Time (h m)	ft	cm
1 M	0107	0.3	9	16 Tu	1241	1.0	30
	0716	7.1	216		0656	6.6	201
	0137*	0.3	9		0119*	0.8	24
	0742*	7.0	213		0723*	6.1	186
2 Tu	0204	0.1	3	17 W	0128	0.9	27
	0813	7.5	229		0742	6.8	207
	0237*	-0.1	-3		0207*	0.6	18
	0842*	7.2	219		0811*	6.2	189
3 W	0258	-0.1	-3	18 Th	0212	0.8	24
	0908	8.0	244		0826	7.0	213
	0334*	-0.5	-15		0252*	0.4	12
	0938*	7.3	223		0856*	6.3	192
4 Th	0349	-0.3	-9	19 F	0255	0.7	21
	0959	8.3	253		0907	7.2	219
	0427*	-0.7	-21		0334*	0.2	6
	1030*	7.4	226		0939*	6.4	195
5 F	0439	-0.4	-12	20 Sa	0337	0.6	18
	1049	8.5	259		0947	7.3	223
	0518*	-0.9	-27		0415*	0.0	0
	1121*	7.4	226		1021*	6.5	198
6 Sa ●	0528	-0.3	-9	21 Su ○	0418	0.5	15
	1137	8.5	259		1027	7.4	226
	0608*	-0.8	-24		0456*	-0.1	-3
					1102*	6.6	201
7 Su	1210	7.3	223	22 M	0459	0.5	15
	0516	-0.2	-6		1107	7.4	226
	1126	8.3	253		0538*	-0.2	-6
	0556*	-0.7	-21		1144*	6.6	201
	1159*	7.2	219				
8 M	0604	0.0	0	23 Tu	0542	0.5	15
	1214*	8.0	244		1149	7.4	226
	0644*	-0.4	-12		0622*	-0.2	-6
9 Tu	1247	7.0	213	24 W	1227	6.6	201
	0654	0.3	9		0627	0.5	15
	0103*	7.6	232		1234*	7.4	226
	0733*	0.0	0		0708*	-0.2	-6
10 W	0137	6.7	204	25 Th	0113	6.6	201
	0745	0.6	18		0716	0.5	15
	0154*	7.2	219		0123*	7.3	223
	0823*	0.3	9		0757*	-0.1	-3
11 Th	0229	6.5	198	26 F	0203	6.6	201
	0838	0.9	27		0810	0.5	15
	0247*	6.8	207		0216*	7.2	219
	0914*	0.6	18		0850*	0.0	0
12 F	0322	6.3	192	27 Sa	0257	6.7	204
	0934	1.1	34		0908	0.5	15
	0342*	6.4	195		0314*	7.0	213
	1007*	0.9	27		0945*	0.1	3
13 Sa ◐	0417	6.2	189	28 Su ◑	0354	6.8	207
	1033	1.2	37		1011	0.5	15
	0440*	6.2	189		0416*	6.8	207
	1100*	1.0	30		1043*	0.1	3
14 Su	0512	6.3	192	29 M	0454	7.0	213
	1131	1.2	37		1116	0.3	9
	0537*	6.0	183		0519*	6.7	204
	1152*	1.0	30		1141*	0.1	3
15 M	0605	6.4	195	30 Tu	0553	7.3	223
	1227*	1.0	30		1220*	0.1	3
	0632*	6.0	183		0623*	6.6	201

December

Day	Time (h m)	ft	cm	Day	Time (h m)	ft	cm
1 W	1239	0.0	0	16 Th	1239	0.9	27
	0651	7.5	229		0656	6.5	198
	0121*	-0.2	-6		0127*	0.6	18
	0723*	6.7	204		0731*	5.7	174
2 Th	0134	0.0	0	17 F	0130	0.9	27
	0747	7.8	238		0745	6.7	204
	0219*	-0.5	-15		0216*	0.4	12
	0821*	6.8	207		0821*	5.9	180
3 F	0228	-0.1	-3	18 Sa	0218	0.7	21
	0840	8.0	244		0832	6.8	207
	0313*	-0.6	-18		0303*	0.1	3
	0914*	6.8	207		0908*	6.1	186
4 Sa	0320	-0.2	-6	19 Su	0306	0.6	18
	0931	8.0	244		0917	7.0	213
	0403*	-0.7	-21		0349*	-0.1	-3
	1005*	6.9	210		0954*	6.3	192
5 Su ●	0410	-0.1	-3	20 M	0352	0.4	12
	1020	8.0	244		1002	7.3	223
	0451*	-0.7	-21		0433*	-0.3	-9
	1054*	6.9	210		1038*	6.5	198
6 M	0458	-0.1	-3	21 Tu ○	0438	0.2	6
	1108	7.8	238		1046	7.4	226
	0538*	-0.6	-18		0518*	-0.5	-15
	1140*	6.8	207		1123*	6.6	201
7 Tu	0546	0.1	3	22 W	0524	0.0	0
	1154	7.6	232		1132	7.6	232
	0623*	-0.4	-12		0603*	-0.6	-18
8 W	1226	6.7	204	23 Th	1208	6.8	207
	0632	0.2	6		0612	-0.1	-3
	1240*	7.3	223		1219*	7.6	232
	0707*	-0.1	-3		0650*	-0.7	-21
9 Th	0111	6.6	201	24 F	1255	6.9	210
	0719	0.4	12		0702	-0.1	-3
	0126*	6.9	210		0109*	7.5	229
	0751*	0.1	3		0737*	-0.6	-18
10 F	0157	6.5	198	25 Sa	0144	7.0	213
	0807	0.6	18		0756	-0.1	-3
	0214*	6.6	201		0201*	7.3	223
	0835*	0.4	12		0828*	-0.5	-15
11 Sa	0244	6.4	195	26 Su	0236	7.1	216
	0857	0.8	24		0853	-0.1	-3
	0303*	6.3	192		0257*	7.0	213
	0921*	0.6	18		0920*	-0.3	-9
12 Su	0333	6.3	192	27 M	0331	7.2	219
	0949	1.0	30		0954	0.0	0
	0354*	6.0	183		0356*	6.7	204
	1008*	0.8	24		1016*	-0.2	-6
13 M ◐	0423	6.3	192	28 Tu ◑	0429	7.2	219
	1044	1.0	30		1058	0.0	0
	0448*	5.7	174		0459*	6.4	195
	1057*	0.9	27		1115*	0.0	0
14 Tu	0515	6.3	192	29 W	0529	7.2	219
	1140	1.0	30		1202*	-0.1	-3
	0543*	5.6	171		0603*	6.2	189
	1148*	1.0	30				
15 W	0606	6.4	195	30 Th	1215	0.1	3
	1234*	0.8	24		0629	7.3	223
	0638*	5.6	171		0105*	-0.2	-6
					0706*	6.2	189
				31 F	0115	0.1	3
					0729	7.4	226
					0204*	-0.3	-9
					0805*	6.3	192

Heights are referred to mean lower low water which is the chart datum of soundings. All times are local. Daylight Saving Time has been used when needed.

New London, Connecticut, 2010

Times and Heights of High and Low Waters

March

Day	Time (h m)	Height (ft)	Height (cm)
1 M	0337	-0.7	-21
	0927	3.1	94
	0359*	-0.6	-18
	0950*	3.3	101
2 Tu	0429	-0.7	-21
	1016	2.9	88
	0445*	-0.5	-15
	1040*	3.3	101
3 W	0522	-0.6	-18
	1106	2.7	82
	0534*	-0.3	-9
	1132*	3.3	101
4 Th	0617	-0.4	-12
	1157	2.5	76
	0626*	-0.1	-3
5 F	1224	3.1	94
	0714	-0.2	-6
	1251*	2.3	70
	0722*	0.1	3
6 Sa	0120	2.9	88
	0814	0.0	0
	0148*	2.1	64
	0823*	0.3	9
7 Su ◑	0221	2.6	79
	0915	0.2	6
	0253*	2.0	61
	0926*	0.5	15
8 M	0329	2.5	76
	1015	0.3	9
	0403*	1.9	58
	1029*	0.5	15
9 Tu	0437	2.4	73
	1112	0.3	9
	0507*	2.0	61
	1129*	0.5	15
10 W	0537	2.4	73
	1205*	0.3	9
	0600*	2.2	67
11 Th	1224	0.4	12
	0626	2.5	76
	1251*	0.3	9
	0645*	2.3	70
12 F	0112	0.3	9
	0708	2.5	76
	0132*	0.2	6
	0725*	2.5	76
13 Sa	0153	0.2	6
	0747	2.5	76
	0208*	0.2	6
	0804*	2.6	79
14 Su	0332	0.1	3
	0925	2.5	76
	0342*	0.1	3
	0942*	2.7	82
15 M ●	0409	0.0	0
	1002	2.5	76
	0415*	0.1	3
	1019*	2.8	85
16 Tu	0446	0.0	0
	1040	2.5	76
	0449*	0.1	3
	1055*	2.9	88
17 W	0525	-0.1	-3
	1117	2.5	76
	0524*	0.1	3
	1130*	2.9	88
18 Th	0606	-0.1	-3
	1155	2.4	73
	0600*	0.2	6
19 F	1205	2.9	88
	0651	0.0	0
	1234*	2.3	70
	0641*	0.3	9
20 Sa	1242	2.9	88
	0741	0.0	0
	0115*	2.2	67
	0728*	0.4	12
21 Su	0125	2.8	85
	0836	0.1	3
	0202*	2.1	64
	0825*	0.5	15
22 M	0218	2.8	85
	0935	0.1	3
	0259*	2.1	64
	0928*	0.5	15
23 Tu ◐	0325	2.7	82
	1033	0.1	3
	0406*	2.1	64
	1034*	0.4	12
24 W	0440	2.7	82
	1131	0.1	3
	0515*	2.2	67
	1139*	0.3	9
25 Th	0549	2.8	85
	1227*	0.0	0
	0617*	2.5	76
26 F	1242	0.1	3
	0648	2.9	88
	0121*	-0.1	-3
	0711*	2.8	85
27 Sa	0142	-0.2	-6
	0740	3.0	91
	0212*	-0.3	-9
	0801*	3.1	94
28 Su	0239	-0.4	-12
	0829	3.0	91
	0300*	-0.4	-12
	0849*	3.3	101
29 M	0332	-0.5	-15
	0917	3.0	91
	0347*	-0.4	-12
	0937*	3.5	107
30 Tu ○	0422	-0.6	-18
	1006	2.9	88
	0433*	-0.4	-12
	1026*	3.5	107
31 W	0512	-0.6	-18
	1054	2.8	85
	0519*	-0.2	-6
	1115*	3.5	107

April

Day	Time (h m)	Height (ft)	Height (cm)
1 Th	0602	-0.4	-12
	1144	2.6	79
	0607*	0.0	0
2 F	1205	3.3	101
	0653	-0.3	-9
	1235*	2.5	76
	0658*	0.2	6
3 Sa	1256	3.1	94
	0747	0.0	0
	0127*	2.4	73
	0754*	0.4	12
4 Su	0150	2.9	88
	0843	0.2	6
	0222*	2.3	70
	0855*	0.6	18
5 M	0248	2.7	82
	0940	0.3	9
	0322*	2.2	67
	0957*	0.7	21
6 Tu ◑	0352	2.5	76
	1036	0.4	12
	0427*	2.2	67
	1059*	0.7	21
7 W	0458	2.4	73
	1130	0.5	15
	0531*	2.3	70
	1158*	0.6	18
8 Th	0559	2.4	73
	1220*	0.5	15
	0626*	2.4	73
9 F	1252	0.6	18
	0650	2.4	73
	0105*	0.5	15
	0712*	2.6	79
10 Sa	0140	0.5	15
	0734	2.4	73
	0147*	0.4	12
	0754*	2.7	82
11 Su	0224	0.3	9
	0815	2.4	73
	0226*	0.4	12
	0832*	2.9	88
12 M	0304	0.2	6
	0854	2.5	76
	0303*	0.3	9
	0909*	3.0	91
13 Tu	0343	0.1	3
	0932	2.5	76
	0339*	0.3	9
	0945*	3.1	94
14 W ●	0421	0.0	0
	1011	2.5	76
	0416*	0.3	9
	1021*	3.1	94
15 Th	0501	-0.1	-3
	1050	2.5	76
	0453*	0.3	9
	1057*	3.1	94
16 F	0544	-0.1	-3
	1131	2.4	73
	0534*	0.4	12
	1136*	3.1	94
17 Sa	0630	-0.1	-3
	1213*	2.4	73
	0618*	0.4	12
18 Su	1218	3.1	94
	0721	0.0	0
	1258*	2.3	70
	0710*	0.5	15
19 M	0107	3.1	94
	0815	0.0	0
	0149*	2.3	70
	0811*	0.5	15
20 Tu	0203	3.0	91
	0912	0.1	3
	0246*	2.3	70
	0916*	0.5	15
21 W ◐	0308	2.9	88
	1009	0.1	3
	0351*	2.4	73
	1022*	0.4	12
22 Th	0418	2.8	85
	1105	0.1	3
	0457*	2.6	79
	1126*	0.3	9
23 F	0526	2.8	85
	1159	0.1	3
	0558*	2.9	88
24 Sa	1229	0.1	3
	0626	2.8	85
	1252*	0.0	0
	0652*	3.1	94
25 Su	0129	-0.1	-3
	0719	2.8	85
	0144*	-0.1	-3
	0742*	3.4	104
26 M	0225	-0.2	-6
	0809	2.7	82
	0234*	-0.1	-3
	0829*	3.5	107
27 Tu	0318	-0.3	-9
	0857	2.7	82
	0322*	-0.1	-3
	0916*	3.6	110
28 W ○	0407	-0.4	-12
	0945	2.7	82
	0409*	0.0	0
	1003*	3.6	110
29 Th	0455	-0.4	-12
	1034	2.6	79
	0456*	0.1	3
	1051*	3.5	107
30 F	0542	-0.3	-9
	1123	2.6	79
	0544*	0.2	6
	1140*	3.3	101

May

Day	Time (h m)	Height (ft)	Height (cm)
1 Sa	0629	-0.1	-3
	1213*	2.5	76
	0633*	0.4	12
2 Su	1230	3.2	98
	0719	0.1	3
	0104*	2.5	76
	0727*	0.6	18
3 M	0122	2.9	88
	0810	0.3	9
	0156*	2.4	73
	0824*	0.7	21
4 Tu	0216	2.7	82
	0902	0.4	12
	0252*	2.4	73
	0924*	0.8	24
5 W	0313	2.5	76
	0953	0.5	15
	0351*	2.4	73
	1023*	0.8	24
6 Th ◑	0413	2.4	73
	1042	0.6	18
	0451*	2.5	76
	1119*	0.8	24
7 F	0512	2.3	70
	1129	0.6	18
	0546*	2.6	79
8 Sa	1212	0.7	21
	0606	2.3	70
	1213*	0.6	18
	0635*	2.8	85
9 Su	0102	0.6	18
	0655	2.3	70
	1257*	0.6	18
	0718*	2.9	88
10 M	0148	0.4	12
	0739	2.3	70
	0139*	0.5	15
	0757*	3.0	91
11 Tu	0232	0.3	9
	0820	2.4	73
	0221*	0.5	15
	0834*	3.1	94
12 W	0314	0.1	3
	0900	2.4	73
	0303*	0.5	15
	0911*	3.2	98
13 Th	0356	0.0	0
	0941	2.4	73
	0344*	0.4	12
	0949*	3.3	101
14 F ●	0439	-0.1	-3
	1023	2.5	76
	0427*	0.4	12
	1030*	3.4	104
15 Sa	0523	-0.2	-6
	1107	2.5	76
	0513*	0.4	12
	1114*	3.4	104
16 Su	0611	-0.2	-6
	1154	2.5	76
	0602*	0.4	12
17 M	1203	3.3	101
	0701	-0.1	-3
	1244*	2.5	76
	0658*	0.4	12
18 Tu	1256	3.2	98
	0754	-0.1	-3
	0137*	2.6	79
	0800*	0.4	12
19 W	0151	3.1	94
	0849	0.0	0
	0234*	2.7	82
	0905*	0.4	12
20 Th ◐	0251	2.9	88
	0944	0.0	0
	0335*	2.8	85
	1010*	0.4	12
21 F	0356	2.8	85
	1038	0.1	3
	0438*	3.0	91
	1113*	0.3	9
22 Sa	0501	2.6	79
	1132	0.1	3
	0538*	3.1	94
23 Su	1215	0.2	6
	0603	2.6	79
	1225*	0.1	3
	0633*	3.3	101
24 M	0115	0.1	3
	0659	2.5	76
	0118*	0.2	6
	0723*	3.5	107
25 Tu	0211	-0.1	-3
	0750	2.5	76
	0211*	0.2	6
	0811*	3.5	107
26 W	0303	-0.1	-3
	0839	2.5	76
	0301*	0.2	6
	0857*	3.5	107
27 Th ○	0351	-0.2	-6
	0926	2.5	76
	0349*	0.3	9
	0943*	3.5	107
28 F	0437	-0.1	-3
	1014	2.5	76
	0436*	0.3	9
	1030*	3.4	104
29 Sa	0521	-0.1	-3
	1102	2.6	79
	0523*	0.4	12
	1118*	3.3	101
30 Su	0605	0.0	0
	1151	2.6	79
	0610*	0.5	15
31 M	1207	3.1	94
	0650	0.2	6
	1240*	2.6	79
	0659*	0.6	18

June

Day	Time (h m)	Height (ft)	Height (cm)
1 Tu	1255	2.9	88
	0735	0.3	9
	0130*	2.6	79
	0752*	0.7	21
2 W	0144	2.8	85
	0821	0.4	12
	0221*	2.6	79
	0848*	0.8	24
3 Th	0234	2.6	79
	0907	0.5	15
	0314*	2.6	79
	0943*	0.8	24
4 F ◑	0327	2.4	73
	0953	0.6	18
	0408*	2.7	82
	1037*	0.8	24
5 Sa	0423	2.3	70
	1037	0.6	18
	0503*	2.8	85
	1130*	0.7	21
6 Su	0519	2.2	67
	1121	0.7	21
	0553*	2.9	88
7 M	1221	0.6	18
	0612	2.2	67
	1207*	0.7	21
	0638*	3.0	91
8 Tu	0110	0.5	15
	0700	2.2	67
	1253*	0.6	18
	0720*	3.1	94
9 W	0158	0.3	9
	0745	2.3	70
	0141*	0.6	18
	0800*	3.2	98
10 Th	0245	0.2	6
	0827	2.3	70
	0229*	0.5	15
	0840*	3.3	101
11 F	0331	0.0	0
	0911	2.4	73
	0317*	0.4	12
	0922*	3.4	104
12 Sa ●	0416	-0.1	-3
	0956	2.5	76
	0406*	0.3	9
	1008*	3.5	107
13 Su	0502	-0.2	-6
	1044	2.6	79
	0456*	0.2	6
	1057*	3.5	107
14 M	0550	-0.3	-9
	1134	2.7	82
	0548*	0.2	6
	1149*	3.5	107
15 Tu	0639	-0.2	-6
	1227*	2.8	85
	0645*	0.2	6
16 W	1241	3.3	101
	0730	-0.2	-6
	0121*	2.9	88
	0747*	0.3	9
17 Th	0136	3.1	94
	0823	-0.1	-3
	0217*	3.0	91
	0851*	0.3	9
18 F	0232	2.9	88
	0917	0.0	0
	0315*	3.1	94
	0955*	0.3	9
19 Sa ◐	0333	2.7	82
	1011	0.1	3
	0417*	3.2	98
	1058*	0.3	9
20 Su	0438	2.5	76
	1106	0.2	6
	0517*	3.3	101
21 M	1200	0.2	6
	0542	2.4	73
	1201*	0.3	9
	0615*	3.3	101
22 Tu	1259	0.2	6
	0641	2.3	70
	1257*	0.3	9
	0707*	3.4	104
23 W	0155	0.1	3
	0734	2.3	70
	0152*	0.4	12
	0756*	3.4	104
24 Th	0247	0.1	3
	0823	2.4	73
	0244*	0.4	12
	0842*	3.4	104
25 F	0334	0.0	0
	0909	2.4	73
	0333*	0.4	12
	0927*	3.3	101
26 Sa ○	0418	0.1	3
	0955	2.5	76
	0419*	0.4	12
	1012*	3.2	98
27 Su	0459	0.1	3
	1041	2.6	79
	0502*	0.5	15
	1057*	3.1	94
28 M	0539	0.1	3
	1127	2.6	79
	0546*	0.5	15
	1142*	3.0	91
29 Tu	0618	0.2	6
	1214*	2.7	82
	0631*	0.6	18
30 W	1227	2.9	88
	0658	0.3	9
	0100*	2.7	82
	0719*	0.7	21

July

Day	Time (h m)	Height (ft)	Height (cm)
1 Th	0111	2.8	85
	0739	0.4	12
	0147*	2.8	85
	0810*	0.7	21
2 F	0156	2.6	79
	0821	0.5	15
	0235*	2.8	85
	0903*	0.8	24
3 Sa	0243	2.4	73
	0904	0.6	18
	0324*	2.8	85
	0956*	0.8	24
4 Su ◑	0334	2.3	70
	0948	0.6	18
	0415*	2.8	85
	1048*	0.7	21
5 M	0430	2.2	67
	1034	0.7	21
	0507*	2.9	88
	1141*	0.6	18
6 Tu	0527	2.1	64
	1122	0.7	21
	0557*	3.0	91
7 W	1233	0.5	15
	0621	2.2	67
	1214*	0.7	21
	0644*	3.1	94
8 Th	0125	0.3	9
	0710	2.2	67
	0107*	0.6	18
	0729*	3.2	98
9 F	0216	0.2	6
	0756	2.3	70
	0201*	0.5	15
	0814*	3.4	104
10 Sa	0305	0.0	0
	0842	2.5	76
	0255*	0.3	9
	0900*	3.5	107
11 Su ●	0352	-0.2	-6
	0929	2.6	79
	0347*	0.2	6
	0949*	3.6	110
12 M	0439	-0.3	-9
	1019	2.8	85
	0440*	0.0	0
	1039*	3.6	110
13 Tu	0526	-0.3	-9
	1111	3.0	91
	0534*	0.0	0
	1131*	3.5	107
14 W	0613	-0.3	-9
	1205*	3.1	94
	0631*	0.0	0
15 Th	1223	3.3	101
	0703	-0.3	-9
	1259*	3.2	98
	0731*	0.1	3
16 F	0116	3.1	94
	0755	-0.1	-3
	0154*	3.3	101
	0833*	0.1	3
17 Sa	0211	2.8	85
	0850	0.0	0
	0252*	3.3	101
	0937*	0.2	6
18 Su ◐	0310	2.6	79
	0946	0.2	6
	0353*	3.3	101
	1039*	0.3	9
19 M	0415	2.4	73
	1043	0.3	9
	0456*	3.2	98
	1141*	0.3	9
20 Tu	0523	2.3	70
	1141	0.4	12
	0557*	3.2	98
21 W	1241	0.3	9
	0625	2.2	67
	1240*	0.5	15
	0653*	3.2	98
22 Th	0137	0.3	9
	0720	2.3	70
	0137*	0.5	15
	0743*	3.2	98
23 F	0229	0.2	6
	0807	2.4	73
	0229*	0.5	15
	0828*	3.2	98
24 Sa	0314	0.2	6
	0851	2.5	76
	0317*	0.5	15
	0911*	3.1	94
25 Su	0355	0.2	6
	0934	2.6	79
	0400*	0.5	15
	0953*	3.1	94
26 M ○	0432	0.2	6
	1017	2.7	82
	0441*	0.5	15
	1034*	3.0	91
27 Tu	0508	0.2	6
	1101	2.8	85
	0522*	0.5	15
	1116*	3.0	91
28 W	0544	0.3	9
	1144	2.8	85
	0603*	0.5	15
	1157*	2.8	85
29 Th	0619	0.3	9
	1228*	2.9	88
	0647*	0.6	18
30 F	1239	2.7	82
	0656	0.4	12
	0110*	2.9	88
	0734*	0.6	18
31 Sa	0120	2.6	79
	0736	0.5	15
	0153*	2.9	88
	0824*	0.7	21

August

Day	Time (h m)	Height (ft)	Height (cm)
1 Su	0203	2.4	73
	0818	0.6	18
	0237*	2.8	85
	0917*	0.7	21
2 M	0250	2.3	70
	0904	0.7	21
	0325*	2.8	85
	1011*	0.7	21
3 Tu ◑	0344	2.2	67
	0954	0.8	24
	0419*	2.9	88
	1106*	0.6	18
4 W	0445	2.1	64
	1048	0.7	21
	0516*	2.9	88
5 Th	1201	0.5	15
	0544	2.2	67
	1144	0.7	21
	0612*	3.1	94
6 F	1255	0.3	9
	0638	2.3	70
	1242*	0.5	15
	0703*	3.3	101
7 Sa	0148	0.2	6
	0728	2.5	76
	0140*	0.4	12
	0752*	3.4	104
8 Su	0238	0.0	0
	0816	2.7	82
	0237*	0.2	6
	0840*	3.5	107
9 M	0326	-0.2	-6
	0905	2.9	88
	0331*	0.0	0
	0928*	3.6	110
10 Tu ●	0412	-0.3	-9
	0955	3.1	94
	0425*	-0.2	-6
	1018*	3.5	107
11 W	0458	-0.4	-12
	1046	3.3	101
	0518*	-0.2	-6
	1109*	3.4	104
12 Th	0545	-0.3	-9
	1139	3.5	107
	0614*	-0.2	-6
13 F	1201	3.2	98
	0634	-0.2	-6
	1233*	3.5	107
	0712*	-0.1	-3
14 Sa	1254	3.0	91
	0726	-0.1	-3
	0128*	3.5	107
	0812*	0.1	3
15 Su	0149	2.7	82
	0822	0.1	3
	0225*	3.4	104
	0915*	0.2	6
16 M ◐	0248	2.5	76
	0922	0.3	9
	0327*	3.2	98
	1018*	0.3	9
17 Tu	0353	2.3	70
	1023	0.5	15
	0433*	3.1	94
	1119*	0.4	12
18 W	0503	2.3	70
	1124	0.6	18
	0539*	3.0	91
19 Th	1219	0.4	12
	0609	2.3	70
	1225*	0.6	18
	0638*	3.0	91
20 F	0115	0.4	12
	0704	2.4	73
	0122*	0.6	18
	0728*	3.0	91
21 Sa	0204	0.4	12
	0749	2.5	76
	0213*	0.5	15
	0811*	3.0	91
22 Su	0248	0.4	12
	0831	2.6	79
	0259*	0.5	15
	0851*	3.0	91
23 M	0326	0.3	9
	0911	2.7	82
	0340*	0.4	12
	0930*	3.0	91
24 Tu ○	0401	0.3	9
	0951	2.8	85
	0419*	0.4	12
	1009*	2.9	88
25 W	0434	0.3	9
	1031	2.9	88
	0457*	0.4	12
	1048*	2.9	88
26 Th	0507	0.3	9
	1112	3.0	91
	0536*	0.4	12
	1127*	2.8	85
27 F	0541	0.4	12
	1152	3.0	91
	0617*	0.4	12
28 Sa	1207	2.7	82
	0616	0.5	15
	1231*	3.0	91
	0701*	0.5	15
29 Su	1247	2.5	76
	0654	0.6	18
	0110*	2.9	88
	0750*	0.5	15
30 M	0129	2.4	73
	0737	0.7	21
	0150*	2.9	88
	0843*	0.6	18
31 Tu	0214	2.3	70
	0828	0.8	24
	0237*	2.9	88
	0939*	0.6	18

September

Day	Time (h m)	Height (ft)	Height (cm)
1 W ◑	0307	2.2	67
	0924	0.8	24
	0335*	2.9	88
	1036*	0.5	15
2 Th	0410	2.2	67
	1024	0.8	24
	0441*	2.9	88
	1132*	0.5	15
3 F	0514	2.3	70
	1124	0.7	21
	0544*	3.1	94
4 Sa	1227	0.3	9
	0612	2.4	73
	1225*	0.5	15
	0640*	3.2	98
5 Su	0119	0.2	6
	0704	2.7	82
	0124*	0.3	9
	0731*	3.4	104
6 M	0210	0.0	0
	0753	3.0	91
	0221*	0.0	0
	0819*	3.4	104
7 Tu	0258	-0.2	-6
	0842	3.3	101
	0316*	-0.2	-6
	0907*	3.4	104
8 W ●	0344	-0.3	-9
	0931	3.5	107
	0409*	-0.3	-9
	0955*	3.4	104
9 Th	0430	-0.3	-9
	1021	3.7	113
	0502*	-0.3	-9
	1046*	3.2	98
10 F	0517	-0.2	-6
	1113	3.7	113
	0555*	-0.3	-9
	1137*	3.0	91
11 Sa	0606	-0.1	-3
	1206*	3.7	113
	0651*	-0.1	-3
12 Su	1230	2.9	88
	0659	0.1	3
	0100*	3.5	107
	0749*	0.1	3
13 M	0126	2.6	79
	0756	0.3	9
	0157*	3.3	101
	0850*	0.2	6
14 Tu	0225	2.5	76
	0858	0.5	15
	0259*	3.1	94
	0952*	0.4	12
15 W ◐	0330	2.3	70
	1002	0.6	18
	0406*	2.9	88
	1053*	0.5	15
16 Th	0439	2.3	70
	1105	0.7	21
	0514*	2.9	88
	1150*	0.5	15
17 F	0546	2.4	73
	1206*	0.7	21
	0615*	2.8	85
18 Sa	1244	0.5	15
	0641	2.5	76
	0102*	0.6	18
	0705*	2.8	85
19 Su	0131	0.5	15
	0725	2.6	79
	0152*	0.6	18
	0747*	2.8	85
20 M	0213	0.5	15
	0806	2.8	85
	0236*	0.5	15
	0826*	2.8	85
21 Tu	0250	0.4	12
	0844	2.9	88
	0316*	0.4	12
	0903*	2.8	85
22 W	0324	0.4	12
	0922	3.0	91
	0354*	0.3	9
	0941*	2.8	85
23 Th ○	0358	0.4	12
	1000	3.1	94
	0431*	0.3	9
	1019*	2.7	82
24 F	0431	0.4	12
	1037	3.1	94
	0509*	0.3	9
	1058*	2.7	82
25 Sa	0505	0.5	15
	1115	3.1	94
	0549*	0.3	9
	1138*	2.6	79
26 Su	0541	0.5	15
	1152	3.1	94
	0633*	0.3	9
27 M	1218	2.5	76
	0620	0.6	18
	1230*	3.0	91
	0721*	0.4	12
28 Tu	0100	2.4	73
	0706	0.7	21
	0111*	3.0	91
	0815*	0.4	12
29 W	0147	2.3	70
	0800	0.8	24
	0201*	2.9	88
	0912*	0.5	15
30 Th	0241	2.3	70
	0903	0.8	24
	0302*	2.9	88
	1009*	0.4	12

October

Day	Time (h m)	Height (ft)	Height (cm)
1 F ◑	0344	2.3	70
	1007	0.7	21
	0412*	2.9	88
	1105*	0.4	12
2 Sa	0450	2.4	73
	1109	0.6	18
	0519*	3.0	91
	1159*	0.3	9
3 Su	0550	2.6	79
	1211*	0.4	12
	0617*	3.1	94
4 M	1251	0.1	3
	0644	2.9	88
	0110*	0.1	3
	0709*	3.2	98
5 Tu	0141	0.0	0
	0733	3.3	101
	0208*	-0.1	-3
	0758*	3.2	98
6 W	0229	-0.1	-3
	0820	3.5	107
	0302*	-0.3	-9
	0846*	3.2	98
7 Th ●	0317	-0.2	-6
	0908	3.7	113
	0354*	-0.4	-12
	0934*	3.1	94
8 F	0404	-0.2	-6
	0957	3.8	116
	0445*	-0.4	-12
	1023*	3.0	91
9 Sa	0451	-0.1	-3
	1047	3.8	116
	0536*	-0.3	-9
	1115*	2.9	88
10 Su	0541	0.0	0
	1140	3.7	113
	0629*	-0.1	-3
11 M	1208	2.7	82
	0633	0.2	6
	1234*	3.5	107
	0724*	0.1	3
12 Tu	0103	2.6	79
	0730	0.4	12
	0130*	3.2	98
	0822*	0.3	9
13 W	0200	2.5	76
	0833	0.6	18
	0229*	3.0	91
	0921*	0.4	12
14 Th ◐	0302	2.4	73
	0937	0.7	21
	0333*	2.8	85
	1019*	0.5	15
15 F	0408	2.4	73
	1040	0.7	21
	0439*	2.7	82
	1114*	0.6	18
16 Sa	0513	2.4	73
	1139	0.7	21
	0540*	2.6	79
17 Su	1204	0.6	18
	0609	2.6	79
	1234*	0.7	21
	0631*	2.6	79
18 M	1249	0.6	18
	0655	2.7	82
	0124*	0.6	18
	0715*	2.6	79
19 Tu	0131	0.5	15
	0736	2.9	88
	0208*	0.5	15
	0756*	2.6	79
20 W	0209	0.5	15
	0815	3.0	91
	0248*	0.4	12
	0834*	2.6	79
21 Th	0246	0.5	15
	0852	3.1	94
	0327*	0.3	9
	0912*	2.6	79
22 F	0321	0.4	12
	0928	3.2	98
	0405*	0.2	6
	0951*	2.6	79
23 Sa ○	0357	0.4	12
	1004	3.2	98
	0444*	0.1	3
	1030*	2.5	76
24 Su	0434	0.5	15
	1041	3.2	98
	0525*	0.1	3
	1111*	2.5	76
25 M	0512	0.5	15
	1118	3.1	94
	0609*	0.1	3
	1153*	2.4	73
26 Tu	0555	0.6	18
	1159	3.1	94
	0658*	0.2	6
27 W	1237	2.4	73
	0644	0.6	18
	1246*	3.1	94
	0751*	0.2	6
28 Th	0126	2.3	70
	0742	0.7	21
	0138*	3.0	91
	0847*	0.3	9
29 F	0221	2.3	70
	0847	0.6	18
	0239*	2.9	88
	0943*	0.2	6
30 Sa ◑	0323	2.4	73
	0952	0.6	18
	0346*	2.8	85
	1038*	0.2	6
31 Su	0428	2.6	79
	1056	0.4	12
	0453*	2.8	85
	1130*	0.1	3

November

Day	Time (h m)	Height (ft)	Height (cm)
1 M	0529	2.8	85
	1157	0.2	6
	0554*	2.8	85
2 Tu	1222	0.0	0
	0624	3.1	94
	1257*	0.0	0
	0648*	2.8	85
3 W	0113	0.0	0
	0714	3.4	104
	0154*	-0.2	-6
	0738*	2.8	85
4 Th	0203	-0.1	-3
	0802	3.6	110
	0248*	-0.3	-9
	0826*	2.8	85
5 F	0253	-0.1	-3
	0849	3.7	113
	0339*	-0.4	-12
	0914*	2.8	85
6 Sa ●	0341	-0.1	-3
	0937	3.7	113
	0429*	-0.4	-12
	1003*	2.7	82
7 Su	0330	0.0	0
	0926	3.6	110
	0417*	-0.3	-9
	0954*	2.7	82
8 M	0419	0.1	3
	1017	3.5	107
	0507*	-0.2	-6
	1046*	2.6	79
9 Tu	0510	0.2	6
	1109	3.3	101
	0557*	0.0	0
	1139*	2.5	76
10 W	0605	0.4	12
	1202*	3.0	91
	0651*	0.2	6
11 Th	1234	2.4	73
	0704	0.6	18
	1257*	2.8	85
	0745*	0.3	9
12 F	0131	2.4	73
	0805	0.7	21
	0155*	2.6	79
	0838*	0.4	12
13 Sa ◐	0231	2.4	73
	0906	0.7	21
	0255*	2.4	73
	0929*	0.5	15
14 Su	0332	2.5	76
	1004	0.7	21
	0354*	2.3	70
	1017*	0.5	15
15 M	0429	2.6	79
	1058	0.6	18
	0450*	2.3	70
	1101*	0.5	15
16 Tu	0519	2.7	82
	1148	0.5	15
	0539*	2.3	70
	1144*	0.5	15
17 W	0603	2.8	85
	1234*	0.4	12
	0623*	2.3	70
18 Th	1226	0.5	15
	0643	3.0	91
	0117*	0.3	9
	0704*	2.3	70
19 F	0106	0.5	15
	0721	3.0	91
	0158*	0.1	3
	0744*	2.3	70
20 Sa	0147	0.4	12
	0758	3.1	94
	0239*	0.0	0
	0823*	2.4	73
21 Su ○	0227	0.4	12
	0835	3.1	94
	0320*	-0.1	-3
	0904*	2.4	73
22 M	0308	0.3	9
	0913	3.2	98
	0402*	-0.1	-3
	0945*	2.4	73
23 Tu	0351	0.3	9
	0955	3.2	98
	0447*	-0.1	-3
	1030*	2.4	73
24 W	0437	0.3	9
	1040	3.1	94
	0535*	-0.1	-3
	1117*	2.4	73
25 Th	0529	0.3	9
	1128	3.1	94
	0626*	-0.1	-3
26 F	1208	2.4	73
	0627	0.4	12
	1221*	3.0	91
	0720*	0.0	0
27 Sa	0103	2.5	76
	0731	0.4	12
	0118*	2.8	85
	0815*	0.0	0
28 Su ◑	0202	2.6	79
	0837	0.3	9
	0220*	2.7	82
	0909*	0.0	0
29 M	0305	2.7	82
	0941	0.2	6
	0326*	2.5	76
	1002*	0.0	0
30 Tu	0407	2.9	88
	1043	0.1	3
	0430*	2.4	73
	1055*	0.0	0

December

Day	Time (h m)	Height (ft)	Height (cm)
1 W	0504	3.1	94
	1143	-0.1	-3
	0529*	2.4	73
	1149*	0.0	0
2 Th	0557	3.3	101
	1241*	-0.2	-6
	0621*	2.4	73
3 F	1242	-0.1	-3
	0646	3.4	104
	0135*	-0.3	-9
	0711*	2.4	73
4 Sa	0134	-0.1	-3
	0734	3.5	107
	0225*	-0.4	-12
	0759*	2.4	73
5 Su ●	0225	-0.1	-3
	0821	3.4	104
	0313*	-0.4	-12
	0846*	2.5	76
6 M	0313	0.0	0
	0909	3.3	101
	0359*	-0.3	-9
	0935*	2.5	76
7 Tu	0401	0.0	0
	0957	3.2	98
	0444*	-0.2	-6
	1025*	2.5	76
8 W	0449	0.2	6
	1046	3.0	91
	0529*	-0.1	-3
	1115*	2.4	73
9 Th	0539	0.3	9
	1135	2.8	85
	0616*	0.1	3
10 F	1205	2.4	73
	0632	0.4	12
	1224*	2.6	79
	0703*	0.2	6
11 Sa	1257	2.4	73
	0728	0.5	15
	0115*	2.4	73
	0751*	0.3	9
12 Su	0151	2.4	73
	0825	0.6	18
	0208*	2.2	67
	0838*	0.4	12
13 M ◐	0247	2.4	73
	0922	0.6	18
	0304*	2.1	64
	0925*	0.5	15
14 Tu	0344	2.5	76
	1016	0.5	15
	0403*	2.0	61
	1010*	0.5	15
15 W	0438	2.6	79
	1107	0.5	15
	0458*	2.0	61
	1056*	0.5	15
16 Th	0527	2.7	82
	1157	0.3	9
	0548*	2.0	61
	1142*	0.5	15
17 F	0611	2.8	85
	1244*	0.2	6
	0633*	2.1	64
18 Sa	1229	0.4	12
	0651	2.9	88
	0129*	0.0	0
	0715*	2.1	64
19 Su	0115	0.3	9
	0731	3.0	91
	0213*	-0.1	-3
	0756*	2.2	67
20 M	0201	0.2	6
	0811	3.1	94
	0256*	-0.3	-9
	0838*	2.3	70
21 Tu ○	0247	0.1	3
	0852	3.1	94
	0340*	-0.4	-12
	0921*	2.3	70
22 W	0333	0.0	0
	0936	3.2	98
	0425*	-0.4	-12
	1007*	2.4	73
23 Th	0422	0.0	0
	1023	3.1	94
	0511*	-0.4	-12
	1056*	2.5	76
24 F	0515	0.0	0
	1112	3.0	91
	0600*	-0.4	-12
	1147*	2.6	79
25 Sa	0613	0.0	0
	1203*	2.9	88
	0651*	-0.3	-9
26 Su	1241	2.7	82
	0715	0.0	0
	1257*	2.7	82
	0745*	-0.2	-6
27 M	0138	2.8	85
	0820	0.0	0
	0156*	2.4	73
	0840*	-0.1	-3
28 Tu ◑	0239	2.8	85
	0924	0.0	0
	0301*	2.2	67
	0935*	-0.1	-3
29 W	0343	2.9	88
	1027	0.0	0
	0408*	2.1	64
	1032*	0.0	0
30 Th	0445	3.0	91
	1128	-0.1	-3
	0512*	2.1	64
	1129*	0.0	0
31 F	0543	3.1	94
	1227*	-0.2	-6
	0608*	2.1	64

Heights are referred to mean lower low water which is the chart datum of soundings. All times are local. Daylight Saving Time has been used when needed.

TIDE TABLES

Montauk, Fort Pond Bay, New York, 2010

Times and Heights of High and Low Waters

March

Day	Time (h m)	Height (ft)	Height (cm)	Day	Time (h m)	Height (ft)	Height (cm)
1 M	0314 0900 0334* 0923*	-0.8 2.5 -0.7 2.9	-24 76 -21 88	16 Tu	0423 1014 0423* 1032*	-0.1 2.0 0.0 2.4	-3 61 0 73
2 Tu	0407 0949 0420* 1014*	-0.7 2.4 -0.6 2.9	-21 73 -18 88	17 W	0503 1053 0458* 1109*	-0.1 2.0 0.1 2.4	-3 61 3 73
3 W	0501 1039 0509* 1106*	-0.6 2.2 -0.4 2.8	-18 67 -12 85	18 Th	0546 1131 0534* 1144*	-0.1 1.9 0.2 2.4	-3 58 6 73
4 Th	0557 1129 0601* 1158*	-0.4 2.0 -0.2 2.6	-12 61 -6 79	19 F	0632 1209* 0613*	0.0 1.8 0.3	0 55 9
5 F	0657 1221* 0659*	-0.2 1.8 0.1	-6 55 3	20 Sa	1221 0725 1250* 0659*	2.3 0.1 1.7 0.4	70 3 52 12
6 Sa	1253 0759 0116* 0802*	2.4 0.0 1.6 0.3	73 0 49 9	21 Su	0102 0822 0135* 0758*	2.3 0.1 1.6 0.4	70 3 49 12
7 Su ◑	0153 0902 0217* 0907*	2.1 0.2 1.5 0.4	64 6 46 12	22 M	0152 0921 0229* 0905*	2.2 0.2 1.6 0.5	67 6 49 15
8 M	0301 1004 0326* 1011*	2.0 0.3 1.4 0.4	61 9 43 12	23 Tu ◐	0256 1020 0334* 1013*	2.2 0.1 1.6 0.4	67 3 49 12
9 Tu	0412 1102 0435* 1112*	1.9 0.3 1.5 0.4	58 9 46 12	24 W	0409 1116 0443* 1117*	2.2 0.1 1.8 0.2	67 3 55 6
10 W	0514 1153 0532*	1.9 0.3 1.6	58 9 49	25 Th	0519 1209* 0547*	2.3 0.0 2.0	70 0 61
11 Th	1205 0602 1235* 0618*	0.4 1.9 0.3 1.8	12 58 9 55	26 F	1220 0619 0100* 0642*	0.0 2.4 -0.2 2.3	0 73 -6 70
12 F	1250 0643 0110* 0659*	0.3 2.0 0.2 1.9	9 61 6 58	27 Sa	0119 0712 0149* 0733*	-0.2 2.5 -0.3 2.7	-6 76 -9 82
13 Sa	0129 0721 0144* 0738*	0.2 2.0 0.1 2.1	6 61 3 64	28 Su	0216 0802 0236* 0822*	-0.4 2.5 -0.4 2.9	-12 76 -12 88
14 Su	0307 0858 0316* 0917*	0.1 2.1 0.0 2.2	3 64 0 67	29 M	0310 0850 0322* 0911*	-0.6 2.5 -0.4 3.1	-18 76 -12 94
15 M ●	0345 0936 0349* 0955*	0.0 2.1 0.0 2.3	0 64 0 70	30 Tu ○	0401 0938 0407* 1000*	-0.6 2.4 -0.4 3.2	-18 73 -12 98
				31 W	0451 1027 0453* 1050*	-0.6 2.3 -0.3 3.1	-18 70 -9 94

April

Day	Time (h m)	Height (ft)	Height (cm)	Day	Time (h m)	Height (ft)	Height (cm)
1 Th	0542 1116 0541* 1140*	-0.4 2.2 -0.1 3.0	-12 67 -3 91	16 F	0524 1104 0506* 1114*	-0.1 2.0 0.3 2.7	-3 61 9 82
2 F	0634 1207* 0632*	-0.2 2.1 0.1	-6 64 3	17 Sa	0611 1146 0549* 1156*	0.0 2.0 0.4 2.6	0 61 12 79
3 Sa	1232 0730 1258* 0730*	2.7 0.0 1.9 0.4	82 0 58 12	18 Su	0704 1232* 0642*	0.0 1.9 0.5	0 58 15
4 Su	0125 0829 0152* 0834*	2.5 0.2 1.8 0.5	76 6 55 15	19 M	1243 0800 0121* 0746*	2.6 0.1 1.9 0.5	79 3 58 15
5 M	0222 0928 0251* 0939*	2.2 0.3 1.7 0.6	67 9 52 18	20 Tu	0136 0858 0218* 0855*	2.5 0.1 1.9 0.5	76 3 58 15
6 Tu ◑	0325 1025 0357* 1043*	2.0 0.4 1.7 0.7	61 12 52 21	21 W ◐	0238 0954 0321* 1002*	2.4 0.1 2.0 0.4	73 3 61 12
7 W	0432 1118 0504* 1141*	1.9 0.5 1.7 0.6	58 15 52 18	22 Th	0345 1048 0426* 1107*	2.3 0.1 2.1 0.3	70 3 64 9
8 Th	0534 1204* 0602*	1.9 0.5 1.9	58 15 58	23 F	0453 1140 0528*	2.3 0.0 2.4	70 0 73
9 F	1234 0626 1245* 0648*	0.6 1.9 0.5 2.1	18 58 15 64	24 Sa	1209 0555 1231* 0623*	0.1 2.3 0.0 2.7	3 70 0 82
10 Sa	0120 0709 0122* 0729*	0.5 1.9 0.4 2.2	15 58 12 67	25 Su	0108 0649 0120* 0714*	-0.1 2.3 -0.1 3.0	-3 70 -3 91
11 Su	0201 0748 0158* 0807*	0.3 2.0 0.3 2.4	9 61 9 73	26 M	0204 0740 0208* 0802*	-0.2 2.3 -0.1 3.1	-6 70 -3 94
12 M	0240 0826 0234* 0844*	0.2 2.0 0.3 2.5	6 61 9 76	27 Tu	0257 0828 0255* 0850*	-0.3 2.3 -0.1 3.2	-9 70 -3 98
13 Tu	0319 0904 0311* 0921*	0.1 2.0 0.2 2.6	3 61 6 79	28 W ○	0346 0916 0342* 0938*	-0.4 2.2 -0.1 3.2	-12 67 -3 98
14 W ●	0359 0943 0348* 0958*	0.0 2.1 0.2 2.7	0 64 6 82	29 Th	0434 1005 0429* 1027*	-0.3 2.2 0.0 3.1	-9 67 0 94
15 Th	0440 1023 0426* 1035*	-0.1 2.0 0.2 2.7	-3 61 6 82	30 F	0522 1055 0516* 1117*	-0.2 2.1 0.2 2.9	-6 64 6 88

May

Day	Time (h m)	Height (ft)	Height (cm)	Day	Time (h m)	Height (ft)	Height (cm)
1 Sa	0611 1145 0607*	-0.1 2.1 0.4	-3 64 12	16 Su	0552 1126 0534* 1139*	-0.1 2.1 0.3 2.9	-3 64 9 88
2 Su	1207 0703 1237* 0702*	2.7 0.1 2.0 0.5	82 3 61 15	17 M	0643 1216* 0631*	-0.1 2.1 0.4	-3 64 12
3 M	1259 0756 0130* 0803*	2.5 0.3 1.9 0.7	76 9 58 21	18 Tu	1230 0738 0109* 0736*	2.8 0.0 2.1 0.4	85 0 64 12
4 Tu	0152 0850 0225* 0906*	2.3 0.4 1.9 0.8	70 12 58 24	19 W	0123 0833 0205* 0844*	2.6 0.0 2.2 0.4	79 0 67 12
5 W	0247 0941 0325* 1007*	2.1 0.5 1.9 0.8	64 15 58 24	20 Th ◐	0220 0927 0305* 0951*	2.5 0.0 2.3 0.4	76 0 70 12
6 Th ◑	0346 1028 0427* 1103*	1.9 0.5 2.0 0.8	58 15 61 24	21 F	0322 1020 0408* 1055*	2.3 0.1 2.5 0.3	70 3 76 9
7 F	0446 1110 0523* 1155*	1.9 0.6 2.1 0.7	58 18 64 21	22 Sa	0427 1111 0508* 1157*	2.1 0.1 2.7 0.2	64 3 82 6
8 Sa	0540 1151 0612*	1.8 0.5 2.3	55 15 70	23 Su	0529 1202* 0604*	2.0 0.1 2.9	61 3 88
9 Su	1242 0628 1230* 0654*	0.6 1.8 0.5 2.4	18 55 15 73	24 M	1256 0626 1253* 0656*	0.0 2.0 0.1 3.0	0 61 3 91
10 M	0127 0710 0110* 0733*	0.4 1.9 0.4 2.6	12 58 12 79	25 Tu	0152 0718 0144* 0744*	-0.1 2.0 0.1 3.1	-3 61 3 94
11 Tu	0210 0750 0151* 0810*	0.3 1.9 0.4 2.7	9 58 12 82	26 W	0243 0807 0234* 0831*	-0.1 2.0 0.1 3.1	-3 61 3 94
12 W	0252 0830 0233* 0847*	0.1 2.0 0.3 2.8	3 61 9 85	27 Th ○	0332 0856 0322* 0919*	-0.2 2.1 0.2 3.1	-6 64 6 94
13 Th	0334 0911 0315* 0926*	0.0 2.0 0.3 2.9	0 61 9 88	28 F	0418 0944 0409* 1007*	-0.1 2.1 0.2 3.0	-3 64 6 91
14 F ●	0418 0953 0359* 1007*	-0.1 2.0 0.3 2.9	-3 61 9 88	29 Sa	0503 1034 0455* 1055*	-0.1 2.1 0.3 2.8	-3 64 9 85
15 Sa	0503 1038 0444* 1051*	-0.1 2.1 0.3 2.9	-3 64 9 88	30 Su	0548 1124 0543* 1144*	0.0 2.1 0.5 2.7	0 64 15 82
				31 M	0634 1215* 0634*	0.1 2.1 0.6	3 64 18

June

Day	Time (h m)	Height (ft)	Height (cm)	Day	Time (h m)	Height (ft)	Height (cm)
1 Tu	1232 0720 0106* 0730*	2.5 0.3 2.0 0.7	76 9 61 21	16 W	1215 0711 1252* 0724*	2.8 -0.2 2.4 0.2	85 -6 73 6
2 W	0121 0807 0157* 0829*	2.3 0.4 2.0 0.8	70 12 61 24	17 Th	0107 0804 0148* 0831*	2.6 -0.1 2.5 0.3	79 -3 76 9
3 Th	0210 0853 0251* 0927*	2.1 0.4 2.1 0.8	64 12 64 24	18 F	0201 0858 0245* 0937*	2.4 -0.1 2.6 0.3	73 -3 79 9
4 F ◑	0301 0936 0346* 1022*	1.9 0.5 2.1 0.8	58 15 64 24	19 Sa ◐	0259 0951 0346* 1041*	2.2 0.0 2.7 0.2	67 0 82 6
5 Sa	0355 1018 0440* 1113*	1.8 0.5 2.2 0.7	55 15 67 21	20 Su	0401 1044 0447* 1143*	2.0 0.1 2.8 0.2	61 3 85 6
6 Su	0450 1059 0530*	1.7 0.5 2.3	52 15 70	21 M	0505 1138 0546*	1.8 0.2 2.8	55 6 85
7 M	1203 0542 1141 0616*	0.6 1.7 0.5 2.5	18 52 15 76	22 Tu	1242 0605 1232* 0640*	0.2 1.8 0.2 2.9	6 55 6 88
8 Tu	1251 0629 1225* 0657*	0.5 1.7 0.5 2.6	15 52 15 79	23 W	0138 0659 0126* 0729*	0.1 1.8 0.3 2.9	3 55 9 88
9 W	0137 0713 0112* 0737*	0.3 1.8 0.4 2.7	9 55 12 82	24 Th	0229 0750 0217* 0816*	0.1 1.9 0.3 2.9	3 58 9 88
10 Th	0224 0756 0159* 0817*	0.1 1.9 0.3 2.9	3 58 9 88	25 F	0316 0838 0306* 0902*	0.0 1.9 0.3 2.8	0 58 9 85
11 F	0309 0839 0248* 0859*	0.0 2.0 0.2 3.0	0 61 6 91	26 Sa ○	0359 0925 0352* 0948*	0.0 2.0 0.4 2.8	0 61 12 85
12 Sa ●	0355 0925 0337* 0945*	-0.2 2.0 0.2 3.0	-6 61 6 91	27 Su	0441 1014 0436* 1034*	0.0 2.0 0.4 2.7	0 61 12 82
13 Su	0442 1014 0428* 1033*	-0.2 2.1 0.1 3.0	-6 64 3 91	28 M	0521 1102 0520* 1120*	0.1 2.1 0.5 2.6	3 64 15 79
14 M	0530 1106 0522* 1123*	-0.3 2.2 0.1 3.0	-9 67 3 91	29 Tu	0601 1150 0606*	0.2 2.1 0.5	6 64 15
15 Tu	0620 1159 0620*	-0.2 2.3 0.2	-6 70 6	30 W	1205 0641 1238* 0657*	2.5 0.2 2.2 0.6	76 6 67 18

July

Day	Time (h m)	Height (ft)	Height (cm)	Day	Time (h m)	Height (ft)	Height (cm)
1 Th	1249 0722 0125* 0751*	2.3 0.3 2.2 0.7	70 9 67 21	16 F	1247 0733 0125* 0814*	2.6 -0.2 2.8 0.1	79 -6 85 3
2 F	0133 0804 0213* 0846*	2.1 0.4 2.2 0.7	64 12 67 21	17 Sa	0140 0828 0222* 0919*	2.3 0.0 2.8 0.2	70 0 85 6
3 Sa	0218 0846 0302* 0941*	1.9 0.5 2.2 0.7	58 15 67 21	18 Su ◐	0236 0924 0322* 1023*	2.1 0.1 2.8 0.3	64 3 85 9
4 Su ◑	0306 0928 0353* 1034*	1.8 0.5 2.2 0.7	55 15 67 21	19 M	0337 1021 0425* 1126*	1.9 0.2 2.7 0.3	58 6 82 9
5 M	0359 1012 0445* 1125*	1.7 0.6 2.3 0.6	52 18 70 18	20 Tu	0443 1119 0529*	1.7 0.3 2.7	52 9 82
6 Tu	0454 1058 0535*	1.6 0.6 2.4	49 18 73	21 W	1226 0547 1216* 0626*	0.3 1.7 0.4 2.7	9 52 12 82
7 W	1216 0547 1147 0621*	0.5 1.7 0.5 2.6	15 52 15 79	22 Th	0123 0644 0113* 0717*	0.3 1.8 0.4 2.7	9 55 12 82
8 Th	0106 0637 1239* 0706*	0.3 1.7 0.4 2.7	9 52 12 82	23 F	0213 0735 0205* 0803*	0.2 1.8 0.4 2.7	6 55 12 82
9 F	0156 0724 0133* 0751*	0.1 1.9 0.3 2.9	3 58 9 88	24 Sa	0257 0821 0252* 0846*	0.2 1.9 0.4 2.7	6 58 12 82
10 Sa	0244 0811 0227* 0837*	0.0 2.0 0.1 3.0	0 61 3 91	25 Su	0337 0906 0335* 0928*	0.2 2.0 0.4 2.6	6 61 12 79
11 Su ●	0331 0900 0320* 0924*	-0.2 2.2 0.0 3.1	-6 67 0 94	26 M ○	0413 0951 0415* 1010*	0.2 2.1 0.4 2.6	6 64 12 79
12 M	0418 0951 0414* 1014*	-0.3 2.3 -0.1 3.1	-9 70 -3 94	27 Tu	0448 1037 0456* 1053*	0.2 2.2 0.4 2.5	6 67 12 76
13 Tu	0505 1043 0509* 1104*	-0.4 2.5 -0.1 3.0	-12 76 -3 91	28 W	0523 1122 0539* 1135*	0.2 2.3 0.5 2.4	6 70 15 73
14 W	0552 1137 0607* 1155*	-0.4 2.7 0.0 2.8	-12 82 0 85	29 Th	0559 1206* 0625*	0.3 2.3 0.5	9 70 15
15 Th	0642 1231* 0709*	-0.3 2.8 0.0	-9 85 0	30 F	1217 0636 1249* 0715*	2.3 0.4 2.4 0.6	70 12 73 18
				31 Sa	1258 0715 0132* 0808*	2.1 0.5 2.3 0.6	64 15 70 18

August

Day	Time (h m)	Height (ft)	Height (cm)	Day	Time (h m)	Height (ft)	Height (cm)
1 Su	0139 0757 0216* 0903*	1.9 0.6 2.3 0.7	58 18 70 21	16 M ◐	0213 0859 0257* 1002*	2.0 0.3 2.8 0.3	61 9 85 9
2 M	0222 0843 0303* 0958*	1.8 0.6 2.3 0.6	55 18 70 18	17 Tu	0314 1001 0403* 1106*	1.9 0.5 2.6 0.4	58 15 79 12
3 Tu ◑	0311 0932 0356* 1052*	1.7 0.7 2.3 0.6	52 21 70 18	18 W	0422 1104 0511*	1.8 0.5 2.5	55 15 76
4 W	0409 1025 0453* 1145*	1.7 0.7 2.4 0.5	52 21 73 15	19 Th	1206 0531 1204* 0613*	0.5 1.8 0.6 2.5	15 55 18 76
5 Th	0509 1120 0548*	1.7 0.6 2.6	52 18 79	20 F	0102 0631 0101* 0703*	0.5 1.9 0.6 2.5	15 58 18 76
6 F	1238 0606 1217* 0639*	0.3 1.8 0.4 2.8	9 55 12 85	21 Sa	0150 0720 0152* 0746*	0.4 2.0 0.6 2.5	12 61 18 76
7 Sa	0129 0657 0114* 0728*	0.2 2.0 0.3 2.9	6 61 9 88	22 Su	0231 0803 0235* 0825*	0.4 2.1 0.5 2.5	12 64 15 76
8 Su	0218 0747 0211* 0815*	0.0 2.2 0.1 3.1	0 67 3 94	23 M	0306 0844 0315* 0904*	0.4 2.3 0.5 2.5	12 70 15 76
9 M	0305 0837 0306* 0903*	-0.2 2.5 -0.1 3.1	-6 76 -3 94	24 Tu ○	0339 0926 0353* 0944*	0.3 2.4 0.4 2.5	9 73 12 76
10 Tu ●	0350 0927 0400* 0952*	-0.3 2.7 -0.2 3.1	-9 82 -6 94	25 W	0411 1007 0432* 1024*	0.3 2.5 0.4 2.5	9 76 12 76
11 W	0436 1019 0455* 1042*	-0.4 2.9 -0.2 2.9	-12 88 -6 88	26 Th	0443 1049 0512* 1104*	0.3 2.5 0.4 2.4	9 76 12 73
12 Th	0522 1112 0551* 1133*	-0.3 3.1 -0.2 2.8	-9 94 -6 85	27 F	0517 1130 0555* 1144*	0.4 2.6 0.4 2.3	12 79 12 70
13 F	0610 1206* 0651*	-0.2 3.1 -0.1	-6 94 -3	28 Sa	0552 1210* 0642*	0.5 2.5 0.5	15 76 15
14 Sa	1225 0702 0100* 0754*	2.5 -0.1 3.1 0.1	76 -3 94 3	29 Su	1224 0629 1250* 0734*	2.1 0.6 2.5 0.6	64 18 76 18
15 Su	0117 0759 0156* 0858*	2.3 0.1 3.0 0.2	70 3 91 6	30 M	0104 0712 0130* 0830*	2.0 0.7 2.4 0.6	61 21 73 18
				31 Tu	0146 0802 0214* 0927*	1.9 0.8 2.4 0.6	58 24 73 18

September

Day	Time (h m)	Height (ft)	Height (cm)	Day	Time (h m)	Height (ft)	Height (cm)
1 W ◑	0235 0901 0309* 1023*	1.8 0.8 2.4 0.6	55 24 73 18	16 Th	0402 1048 0447* 1139*	1.9 0.7 2.4 0.6	58 21 73 18
2 Th	0335 1002 0415* 1118*	1.7 0.8 2.5 0.5	52 24 76 15	17 F	0513 1149 0550*	1.9 0.7 2.4	58 21 73
3 F	0440 1102 0518*	1.8 0.6 2.6	55 18 79	18 Sa	1232 0613 1245* 0640*	0.6 2.0 0.7 2.4	18 61 21 73
4 Sa	1211 0541 1202* 0614*	0.4 2.0 0.5 2.8	12 61 15 85	19 Su	0116 0700 0132* 0721*	0.6 2.2 0.6 2.4	18 67 18 73
5 Su	0101 0635 0100* 0705*	0.2 2.3 0.2 2.9	6 70 6 88	20 M	0153 0740 0214* 0759*	0.5 2.3 0.6 2.4	15 70 18 73
6 M	0149 0726 0157* 0753*	0.0 2.6 0.0 3.0	0 79 0 91	21 Tu	0227 0819 0252* 0837*	0.5 2.5 0.5 2.4	15 76 15 73
7 Tu	0235 0815 0253* 0841*	-0.1 2.9 -0.2 3.0	-3 88 -6 91	22 W	0259 0857 0329* 0914*	0.4 2.6 0.4 2.4	12 79 12 73
8 W ●	0321 0904 0346* 0930*	-0.2 3.1 -0.3 2.9	-6 94 -9 88	23 Th ○	0331 0936 0407* 0953*	0.4 2.7 0.3 2.4	12 82 9 73
9 Th	0406 0955 0440* 1019*	-0.3 3.3 -0.3 2.8	-9 101 -9 85	24 F	0404 1015 0446* 1033*	0.4 2.7 0.3 2.3	12 82 9 70
10 F	0452 1047 0534* 1110*	-0.2 3.4 -0.2 2.6	-6 104 -6 79	25 Sa	0438 1053 0528* 1113*	0.4 2.7 0.3 2.2	12 82 9 67
11 Sa	0540 1140 0631*	-0.1 3.3 -0.1	-3 101 -3	26 Su	0514 1132 0614* 1153*	0.5 2.7 0.4 2.1	15 82 12 64
12 Su	1202 0633 1234* 0731*	2.5 0.1 3.2 0.1	76 3 98 3	27 M	0552 1210* 0705*	0.6 2.6 0.5	18 79 15
13 M	1255 0731 0130* 0834*	2.3 0.3 3.0 0.3	70 9 91 9	28 Tu	1235 0636 1250* 0801*	2.0 0.7 2.5 0.5	61 21 76 15
14 Tu	0151 0836 0231* 0938*	2.1 0.5 2.7 0.5	64 15 82 15	29 W	0119 0733 0137* 0900*	1.9 0.8 2.5 0.5	58 24 76 15
15 W ◐	0253 0942 0337* 1041*	1.9 0.7 2.5 0.5	58 21 76 15	30 Th	0211 0840 0235* 0957*	1.8 0.8 2.5 0.5	55 24 76 15

October

Day	Time (h m)	Height (ft)	Height (cm)	Day	Time (h m)	Height (ft)	Height (cm)
1 F ◑	0312 0946 0343* 1051*	1.9 0.8 2.5 0.4	58 24 76 12	16 Sa	0445 1125 0513* 1150*	2.0 0.8 2.1 0.6	61 24 64 18
2 Sa	0419 1049 0450* 1142*	2.0 0.6 2.6 0.3	61 18 79 9	17 Su	0545 1219* 0605*	2.1 0.7 2.1	64 21 64
3 Su	0521 1150 0549*	2.2 0.4 2.6	67 12 79	18 M	1231 0632 0105* 0649*	0.6 2.3 0.6 2.1	18 70 18 64
4 M	1231 0615 1248* 0642*	0.2 2.5 0.2 2.7	6 76 6 82	19 Tu	0107 0712 0147* 0728*	0.5 2.4 0.5 2.1	15 73 15 64
5 Tu	0119 0705 0145* 0731*	0.0 2.9 0.0 2.8	0 88 0 85	20 W	0142 0750 0225* 0806*	0.5 2.6 0.4 2.1	15 79 12 64
6 W	0205 0754 0240* 0819*	-0.1 3.2 -0.2 2.7	-3 98 -6 82	21 Th	0216 0827 0303* 0844*	0.4 2.7 0.3 2.2	12 82 9 67
7 Th ●	0252 0842 0332* 0907*	-0.2 3.4 -0.3 2.7	-6 104 -9 82	22 F	0252 0905 0341* 0923*	0.4 2.7 0.2 2.2	12 82 6 67
8 F	0338 0932 0424* 0956*	-0.2 3.5 -0.3 2.6	-6 107 -9 79	23 Sa ○	0328 0942 0421* 1002*	0.4 2.8 0.2 2.1	12 85 6 64
9 Sa	0425 1023 0516* 1047*	-0.1 3.5 -0.2 2.5	-3 107 -6 76	24 Su	0405 1020 0504* 1043*	0.4 2.7 0.2 2.1	12 82 6 64
10 Su	0514 1115 0609* 1139*	0.0 3.3 -0.1 2.3	0 101 -3 70	25 M	0444 1058 0550* 1126*	0.4 2.7 0.2 2.0	12 82 6 61
11 M	0606 1209* 0706*	0.2 3.1 0.1	6 94 3	26 Tu	0525 1139 0641*	0.5 2.6 0.2	15 79 6
12 Tu	1233 0705 0104* 0807*	2.2 0.4 2.8 0.3	67 12 85 9	27 W	1211 0614 1224* 0736*	1.9 0.6 2.6 0.3	58 18 79 9
13 W	0129 0811 0203* 0909*	2.0 0.6 2.6 0.5	61 18 79 15	28 Th	0100 0715 0114* 0833*	1.9 0.7 2.5 0.3	58 21 76 9
14 Th ◐	0230 0919 0305* 1008*	1.9 0.7 2.4 0.5	58 21 73 15	29 F	0154 0825 0211* 0929*	1.9 0.7 2.4 0.3	58 21 73 9
15 F	0337 1025 0411* 1102*	1.9 0.8 2.2 0.6	58 24 67 18	30 Sa ◑	0254 0933 0315* 1022*	1.9 0.6 2.4 0.2	58 18 73 6
				31 Su	0358 1037 0421* 1112*	2.1 0.4 2.3 0.1	64 12 70 3

November

Day	Time (h m)	Height (ft)	Height (cm)	Day	Time (h m)	Height (ft)	Height (cm)
1 M	0459 1138 0523*	2.4 0.2 2.3	73 6 70	16 Tu	0456 1130 0510* 1118*	2.2 0.5 1.8 0.4	67 15 55 12
2 Tu	1201 0555 1237* 0618*	0.0 2.7 0.0 2.3	0 82 0 70	17 W	0540 1214* 0554* 1156*	2.3 0.4 1.8 0.4	70 12 55 12
3 W	1250 0646 0133* 0709*	0.0 3.0 -0.2 2.3	0 91 -6 70	18 Th	0620 1255* 0634*	2.4 0.2 1.8	73 6 55
4 Th	0138 0735 0227* 0758*	-0.1 3.2 -0.3 2.3	-3 98 -9 70	19 F	1236 0658 0135* 0713*	0.3 2.5 0.1 1.8	9 76 3 55
5 F	0226 0823 0318* 0846*	-0.2 3.3 -0.4 2.3	-6 101 -12 70	20 Sa	0116 0735 0216* 0753*	0.3 2.6 0.0 1.9	9 79 0 58
6 Sa ●	0314 0912 0408* 0935*	-0.2 3.3 -0.4 2.3	-6 101 -12 70	21 Su ○	0157 0813 0258* 0833*	0.2 2.6 -0.1 1.9	6 79 -3 58
7 Su	0302 0902 0357* 0926*	-0.1 3.2 -0.3 2.2	-3 98 -9 67	22 M	0239 0852 0342* 0916*	0.2 2.7 -0.1 1.9	6 82 -3 58
8 M	0352 0953 0448* 1018*	0.0 3.1 -0.2 2.1	0 94 -6 64	23 Tu	0322 0933 0428* 1002*	0.2 2.7 -0.1 1.9	6 82 -3 58
9 Tu	0444 1046 0541* 1112*	0.2 2.9 0.0 2.0	6 88 0 61	24 W	0409 1018 0518* 1051*	0.2 2.6 -0.1 1.9	6 79 -3 58
10 W	0540 1139 0636*	0.4 2.6 0.2	12 79 6	25 Th	0501 1105 0610* 1142*	0.3 2.6 -0.1 1.9	9 79 -3 58
11 Th	1207 0642 1233* 0732*	1.9 0.5 2.4 0.3	58 15 73 9	26 F	0603 1155 0704*	0.3 2.4 -0.1	9 73 -3
12 F	0104 0748 0128* 0826*	1.9 0.6 2.1 0.4	58 18 64 12	27 Sa	1236 0710 1249* 0758*	1.9 0.3 2.3 -0.1	58 9 70 -3
13 Sa ◐	0205 0851 0227* 0916*	1.9 0.7 2.0 0.4	58 21 61 12	28 Su ◑	0133 0818 0149* 0851*	2.0 0.3 2.1 -0.1	61 9 64 -3
14 Su	0307 0950 0326* 1000*	1.9 0.7 1.8 0.5	58 21 55 15	29 M	0234 0923 0252* 0942*	2.2 0.2 2.0 -0.1	67 6 61 -3
15 M	0406 1043 0422* 1040*	2.0 0.6 1.8 0.5	61 18 55 15	30 Tu	0336 1025 0356* 1033*	2.4 0.0 1.9 -0.1	73 0 58 -3

December

Day	Time (h m)	Height (ft)	Height (cm)	Day	Time (h m)	Height (ft)	Height (cm)
1 W	0434 1124 0455* 1124*	2.6 -0.1 1.8 -0.1	79 -3 55 -3	16 Th	0504 1137 0516* 1114*	2.1 0.2 1.4 0.3	64 6 43 9
2 Th	0528 1221* 0549*	2.8 -0.3 1.9	85 -9 58	17 F	0548 1223* 0601* 1159*	2.2 0.1 1.5 0.2	67 3 46 6
3 F	1216 0619 0115* 0639*	-0.2 2.9 -0.4 1.9	-6 88 -12 58	18 Sa	0629 0107* 0643*	2.3 0.0 1.6	70 0 49
4 Sa	0107 0708 0205* 0728*	-0.2 3.0 -0.4 1.9	-6 91 -12 58	19 Su	1245 0708 0151* 0724*	0.1 2.4 -0.2 1.6	3 73 -6 49
5 Su ●	0157 0756 0253* 0817*	-0.2 2.9 -0.4 1.9	-6 88 -12 58	20 M	0132 0748 0235* 0807*	0.0 2.5 -0.3 1.7	0 76 -9 52
6 M	0246 0845 0340* 0907*	-0.2 2.9 -0.4 1.9	-6 88 -12 58	21 Tu ○	0218 0829 0320* 0852*	-0.1 2.6 -0.4 1.8	-3 79 -12 55
7 Tu	0334 0934 0426* 0958*	-0.1 2.7 -0.3 1.9	-3 82 -9 58	22 W	0306 0913 0405* 0940*	-0.2 2.6 -0.5 1.9	-6 79 -15 58
8 W	0423 1023 0513* 1049*	0.0 2.5 -0.2 1.9	0 76 -6 58	23 Th	0356 0959 0452* 1030*	-0.2 2.6 -0.5 1.9	-6 79 -15 58
9 Th	0515 1112 0600* 1141*	0.2 2.4 0.0 1.8	6 73 0 55	24 F	0450 1047 0541* 1121*	-0.2 2.5 -0.5 2.0	-6 76 -15 61
10 F	0610 1201* 0649*	0.3 2.1 0.1	9 64 3	25 Sa	0550 1137 0633*	-0.1 2.3 -0.4	-3 70 -12
11 Sa	1233 0709 1250* 0736*	1.8 0.4 1.9 0.2	55 12 58 6	26 Su	1214 0655 1228* 0725*	2.1 -0.1 2.1 -0.3	64 -3 64 -9
12 Su	0127 0809 0142* 0822*	1.8 0.5 1.7 0.3	55 15 52 9	27 M	0110 0801 0124* 0819*	2.2 -0.1 1.9 -0.3	67 -3 58 -9
13 M ◐	0223 0907 0236* 0905*	1.8 0.5 1.5 0.3	55 15 46 9	28 Tu ◑	0209 0906 0225* 0914*	2.3 -0.1 1.7 -0.2	70 -3 52 -6
14 Tu	0320 1000 0333* 0947*	1.9 0.4 1.4 0.3	58 12 43 9	29 W	0312 1009 0330* 1009*	2.3 -0.2 1.5 -0.2	70 -6 46 -6
15 W	0415 1050 0427* 1030*	2.0 0.3 1.4 0.3	61 9 43 9	30 Th	0415 1110 0434* 1105*	2.4 -0.2 1.5 -0.2	73 -6 46 -6
				31 F	0513 1208* 0533*	2.5 -0.3 1.5	76 -9 46

Heights are referred to mean lower low water which is the chart datum of soundings. All times are local. Daylight Saving Time has been used when needed.

TIDE TABLES

Newport, Rhode Island, 2010

Times and Heights of High and Low Waters

March

Day	Time (h m)	Height (ft)	Height (cm)
1 M	0123 0758 0147* 0822*	-1.0 4.4 -0.9 4.7	-30 134 -27 143
2 Tu	0213 0847 0226* 0911*	-1.0 4.2 -0.8 4.6	-30 128 -24 140
3 W	0300 0936 0305* 1002*	-0.8 4.0 -0.7 4.4	-24 122 -21 134
4 Th	0346 1026 0344* 1053*	-0.5 3.7 -0.4 4.1	-15 113 -12 125
5 F	0431 1118 0424* 1147*	-0.2 3.3 -0.1 3.7	-6 101 -3 113
6 Sa	0521 1211* 0510*	0.2 3.0 0.2	6 91 6
7 Su ◑	1243 0630 0107* 0605*	3.3 0.5 2.7 0.5	101 15 82 15
8 M	0143 0836 0208* 0726*	3.0 0.7 2.6 0.7	91 21 79 21
9 Tu	0250 0939 0313* 0909*	2.9 0.7 2.6 0.7	88 21 79 21
10 W	0357 1019 0415* 1009*	2.8 0.6 2.7 0.5	85 18 82 15
11 Th	0453 1050 0508* 1053*	2.9 0.4 2.9 0.3	88 12 88 9
12 F	0539 1119 0551* 1134*	3.1 0.3 3.2 0.2	94 9 98 6
13 Sa	0617 1151 0628*	3.2 0.1 3.4	98 3 104
14 Su	1213 0751 0124* 0802*	0.0 3.3 -0.1 3.6	0 101 -3 110
15 M ●	0152 0824 0157* 0834*	-0.1 3.4 -0.2 3.7	-3 104 -6 113
16 Tu	0228 0857 0230* 0907*	-0.2 3.4 -0.2 3.8	-6 104 -6 116
17 W	0303 0931 0302* 0941*	-0.2 3.4 -0.2 3.8	-6 104 -6 116
18 Th	0337 1009 0334* 1019*	-0.2 3.3 -0.2 3.7	-6 101 -6 113
19 F	0410 1050 0407* 1100*	-0.1 3.2 -0.2 3.6	-3 98 -6 110
20 Sa	0446 1135 0444* 1148*	0.0 3.0 -0.1 3.6	0 91 -3 110
21 Su	0528 1225* 0528*	0.2 2.9 0.0	6 88 0
22 M	1241 0620 0120* 0622*	3.5 0.4 2.9 0.1	107 12 88 3
23 Tu ◐	0140 0735 0221* 0731*	3.4 0.5 2.9 0.2	104 15 88 6
24 W	0245 0924 0326* 0857*	3.4 0.4 3.1 0.2	104 12 94 6
25 Th	0355 1034 0433* 1020*	3.5 0.2 3.4 0.0	107 6 104 0
26 F	0503 1123 0535* 1127*	3.7 -0.1 3.8 -0.3	113 -3 116 -9
27 Sa	0605 1207* 0632*	3.9 -0.3 4.3	119 -9 131
28 Su	1225 0659 1249* 0723*	-0.6 4.1 -0.5 4.6	-18 125 -15 140
29 M	0119 0749 0131* 0812*	-0.7 4.2 -0.7 4.8	-21 128 -21 146
30 Tu ○	0209 0837 0212* 0900*	-0.8 4.2 -0.7 4.9	-24 128 -21 149
31 W	0256 0925 0253* 0948*	-0.7 4.1 -0.6 4.7	-21 125 -18 143

April

Day	Time (h m)	Height (ft)	Height (cm)
1 Th	0340 1013 0332* 1037*	-0.6 3.9 -0.4 4.4	-18 119 -12 134
2 F	0422 1102 0412* 1127*	-0.3 3.6 -0.2 4.1	-9 110 -6 125
3 Sa	0504 1152 0453*	0.0 3.3 0.1	0 101 3
4 Su	1219 0548 1244* 0538*	3.7 0.3 3.0 0.4	113 9 91 12
5 M	0113 0641 0138* 0631*	3.3 0.6 2.8 0.7	101 18 85 21
6 Tu ◑	0209 0801 0235* 0746*	3.0 0.8 2.7 0.9	91 24 82 27
7 W	0310 0932 0336* 0937*	2.8 0.8 2.8 0.9	85 24 85 27
8 Th	0413 1020 0436* 1044*	2.7 0.7 2.9 0.7	82 21 88 21
9 F	0511 1057 0529* 1130*	2.8 0.5 3.1 0.5	85 15 94 15
10 Sa	0559 1132 0614*	2.9 0.4 3.4	88 12 104
11 Su	1210 0639 1207* 0652*	0.3 3.1 0.2 3.6	9 94 6 110
12 M	1249 0716 1243* 0727*	0.1 3.2 0.0 3.8	3 98 0 116
13 Tu	0128 0751 0118* 0801*	0.0 3.4 -0.1 3.9	0 104 -3 119
14 W ●	0206 0827 0154* 0837*	-0.1 3.4 -0.1 4.0	-3 104 -3 122
15 Th	0243 0905 0229* 0914*	-0.1 3.4 -0.2 4.1	-3 104 -6 125
16 F	0319 0946 0305* 0956*	-0.1 3.4 -0.1 4.1	-3 104 -3 125
17 Sa	0356 1030 0344* 1042*	-0.1 3.3 -0.1 4.0	-3 101 -3 122
18 Su	0435 1119 0425* 1133*	0.1 3.2 0.0 3.9	3 98 0 119
19 M	0520 1212* 0513*	0.2 3.2 0.1	6 98 3
20 Tu	1228 0613 0109* 0610*	3.8 0.4 3.2 0.2	116 12 98 6
21 W ◐	0127 0725 0208* 0723*	3.7 0.4 3.3 0.4	113 12 101 12
22 Th	0230 0858 0310* 0854*	3.6 0.4 3.5 0.3	110 12 107 9
23 F	0335 1003 0413* 1019*	3.6 0.2 3.8 0.1	110 6 116 3
24 Sa	0441 1051 0514* 1122*	3.6 0.0 4.1 -0.1	110 0 125 -3
25 Su	0542 1133 0611*	3.7 -0.2 4.5	113 -6 137
26 M	1216 0638 1215* 0703*	-0.3 3.8 -0.3 4.7	-9 116 -9 143
27 Tu	0106 0728 1256* 0752*	-0.4 3.9 -0.4 4.8	-12 119 -12 146
28 W ○	0154 0816 0138* 0839*	-0.4 3.9 -0.4 4.8	-12 119 -12 146
29 Th	0238 0903 0220* 0926*	-0.4 3.9 -0.3 4.6	-12 119 -9 140
30 F	0320 0951 0302* 1013*	-0.3 3.7 -0.2 4.3	-9 113 -6 131

May

Day	Time (h m)	Height (ft)	Height (cm)
1 Sa	0400 1039 0344* 1102*	-0.1 3.5 0.0 4.0	-3 107 0 122
2 Su	0440 1128 0427* 1151*	0.1 3.3 0.3 3.6	3 101 9 110
3 M	0521 1218* 0513*	0.4 3.1 0.5	12 94 15
4 Tu	1241 0606 0108* 0605*	3.3 0.6 3.0 0.8	101 18 91 24
5 W	0131 0700 0159* 0711*	3.0 0.7 3.0 0.9	91 21 91 27
6 Th ◑	0222 0806 0252* 0844*	2.8 0.8 3.0 1.0	85 24 91 30
7 F	0315 0909 0345* 1002*	2.7 0.7 3.1 0.9	82 21 94 27
8 Sa	0410 0958 0437* 1054*	2.7 0.6 3.2 0.7	82 18 98 21
9 Su	0503 1041 0525* 1137*	2.8 0.4 3.4 0.5	85 12 104 15
10 M	0551 1121 0608*	2.9 0.3 3.7	88 9 113
11 Tu	1219 0634 1200* 0649*	0.3 3.1 0.1 3.9	9 94 3 119
12 W	0100 0716 1239* 0729*	0.1 3.3 0.0 4.1	3 101 0 125
13 Th	0142 0757 0119* 0810*	0.0 3.4 -0.1 4.3	0 104 -3 131
14 F ●	0224 0840 0200* 0853*	-0.1 3.5 -0.1 4.3	-3 107 -3 131
15 Sa	0306 0926 0243* 0939*	-0.1 3.5 -0.2 4.4	-3 107 -6 134
16 Su	0349 1014 0327* 1028*	-0.1 3.5 -0.1 4.3	-3 107 -3 131
17 M	0432 1106 0415* 1121*	0.0 3.5 0.0 4.2	0 107 0 128
18 Tu	0517 1200* 0507*	0.1 3.6 0.1	3 110 3
19 W	1217 0609 1256* 0607*	4.0 0.2 3.6 0.3	122 6 110 9
20 Th ◐	0114 0710 0153* 0721*	3.8 0.3 3.8 0.4	116 9 116 12
21 F	0213 0822 0252* 0857*	3.7 0.2 3.9 0.4	113 6 119 12
22 Sa	0314 0926 0352* 1018*	3.5 0.2 4.1 0.3	107 6 125 9
23 Su	0417 1016 0453* 1117*	3.5 0.1 4.3 0.1	107 3 131 3
24 M	0519 1100 0551*	3.5 0.0 4.4	107 0 134
25 Tu	1208 0616 1143 0644*	0.0 3.6 -0.1 4.6	0 110 -3 140
26 W	1255 0708 1225* 0734*	0.0 3.6 -0.1 4.6	0 110 -3 140
27 Th ○	0140 0757 0108* 0821*	-0.1 3.6 -0.1 4.6	-3 110 -3 140
28 F	0222 0843 0152* 0907*	0.0 3.6 0.0 4.4	0 110 0 134
29 Sa	0301 0930 0237* 0952*	0.0 3.6 0.1 4.2	0 110 3 128
30 Su	0339 1016 0321* 1037*	0.1 3.5 0.2 3.9	3 107 6 119
31 M	0416 1102 0406* 1122*	0.2 3.4 0.4 3.6	6 104 12 110

June

Day	Time (h m)	Height (ft)	Height (cm)
1 Tu	0454 1149 0451*	0.3 3.3 0.5	9 101 15
2 W	1207 0534 1235* 0540*	3.3 0.4 3.2 0.7	101 12 98 21
3 Th	1250 0617 0119* 0637*	3.1 0.5 3.2 0.9	94 15 98 27
4 F ◑	0134 0706 0204* 0747*	2.9 0.6 3.2 1.0	88 18 98 30
5 Sa	0218 0801 0249* 0907*	2.8 0.6 3.2 1.0	85 18 98 30
6 Su	0307 0857 0338* 1009*	2.7 0.6 3.3 0.8	82 18 101 24
7 M	0401 0947 0429* 1100*	2.8 0.5 3.5 0.6	85 15 107 18
8 Tu	0457 1034 0521* 1146*	2.9 0.3 3.7 0.5	88 9 113 15
9 W	0551 1118 0611*	3.0 0.2 3.9	91 6 119
10 Th	1232 0642 1203* 0700*	0.3 3.2 0.0 4.2	9 98 0 128
11 F	0119 0730 1249* 0747*	0.1 3.4 -0.1 4.4	3 104 -3 134
12 Sa ●	0207 0818 0137* 0835*	0.0 3.6 -0.2 4.5	0 110 -6 137
13 Su	0254 0907 0226* 0924*	-0.1 3.7 -0.2 4.6	-3 113 -6 140
14 M	0340 0957 0317* 1015*	-0.2 3.8 -0.2 4.5	-6 116 -6 137
15 Tu	0423 1050 0409* 1108*	-0.2 3.9 -0.1 4.4	-6 119 -3 134
16 W	0507 1144 0504*	-0.1 4.0 0.0	-3 122 0
17 Th	1202 0553 1239* 0604*	4.2 -0.1 4.1 0.2	128 -3 125 6
18 F	1258 0644 0135* 0718*	3.9 0.0 4.1 0.4	119 0 125 12
19 Sa ◐	0154 0742 0232* 0853*	3.7 0.1 4.2 0.5	113 3 128 15
20 Su	0252 0845 0331* 1013*	3.5 0.2 4.2 0.4	107 6 128 12
21 M	0353 0942 0432* 1112*	3.3 0.2 4.2 0.4	101 6 128 12
22 Tu	0456 1031 0532*	3.2 0.2 4.2	98 6 128
23 W	1203 0555 1116 0627*	0.3 3.3 0.2 4.3	9 101 6 131
24 Th	1248 0650 1201* 0718*	0.3 3.3 0.2 4.3	9 101 6 131
25 F	0130 0739 1246* 0804*	0.3 3.4 0.2 4.3	9 104 6 131
26 Sa ○	0207 0824 0131* 0848*	0.2 3.5 0.2 4.2	6 107 6 128
27 Su	0242 0908 0217* 0930*	0.2 3.5 0.2 4.0	6 107 6 122
28 M	0316 0951 0303* 1011*	0.2 3.5 0.3 3.8	6 107 9 116
29 Tu	0350 1034 0347* 1051*	0.2 3.5 0.4 3.6	6 107 12 110
30 W	0425 1115 0431* 1131*	0.2 3.4 0.5 3.4	6 104 15 104

July

Day	Time (h m)	Height (ft)	Height (cm)
1 Th	0501 1156 0514*	0.3 3.4 0.6	9 104 18
2 F	1209 0538 1236* 0601*	3.2 0.4 3.3 0.8	98 12 101 24
3 Sa	1249 0618 0116* 0655*	3.0 0.4 3.3 0.9	91 12 101 27
4 Su ◑	0131 0703 0158* 0801*	2.9 0.5 3.3 1.0	88 15 101 30
5 M	0217 0755 0245* 0917*	2.8 0.5 3.4 0.9	85 15 104 27
6 Tu	0311 0852 0339* 1022*	2.8 0.5 3.5 0.8	85 15 107 24
7 W	0410 0948 0438* 1116*	2.8 0.4 3.7 0.6	85 12 113 18
8 Th	0513 1041 0538*	3.0 0.2 3.9	91 6 119
9 F	1208 0612 1133 0635*	0.4 3.2 0.0 4.2	12 98 0 128
10 Sa	1258 0706 1226* 0727*	0.1 3.5 -0.2 4.5	3 107 -6 137
11 Su ●	0148 0757 0120* 0817*	-0.1 3.8 -0.3 4.7	-3 116 -9 143
12 M	0235 0847 0215* 0908*	-0.2 4.1 -0.4 4.8	-6 125 -12 146
13 Tu	0320 0938 0309* 0958*	-0.4 4.3 -0.4 4.7	-12 131 -12 143
14 W	0402 1030 0403* 1051*	-0.4 4.4 -0.3 4.5	-12 134 -9 137
15 Th	0444 1124 0458* 1144*	-0.4 4.5 -0.1 4.3	-12 137 -3 131
16 F	0526 1218* 0555*	-0.2 4.5 0.1	-6 137 3
17 Sa	1238 0611 0113* 0704*	4.0 -0.1 4.4 0.4	122 -3 134 12
18 Su ◐	0133 0703 0210* 0841*	3.6 0.1 4.2 0.5	110 3 128 15
19 M	0230 0803 0309* 1005*	3.4 0.3 4.1 0.6	104 9 125 18
20 Tu	0330 0910 0411* 1107*	3.2 0.4 4.0 0.6	98 12 122 18
21 W	0434 1010 0514* 1158*	3.1 0.5 3.9 0.6	94 15 119 18
22 Th	0537 1101 0612*	3.1 0.5 4.0	94 15 122
23 F	1241 0632 1147 0703*	0.5 3.2 0.4 4.0	15 98 12 122
24 Sa	0115 0721 1232* 0747*	0.5 3.4 0.4 4.0	15 104 12 122
25 Su	0145 0804 0118* 0828*	0.4 3.5 0.3 4.0	12 107 9 122
26 M ○	0215 0845 0203* 0906*	0.3 3.6 0.3 3.9	9 110 9 119
27 Tu	0246 0924 0246* 0943*	0.2 3.6 0.3 3.8	6 110 9 116
28 W	0319 1002 0328* 1019*	0.2 3.7 0.3 3.6	6 113 9 110
29 Th	0352 1038 0408* 1054*	0.1 3.6 0.4 3.4	3 110 12 104
30 F	0425 1115 0446* 1131*	0.2 3.6 0.5 3.3	6 110 15 101
31 Sa	0459 1152 0526*	0.3 3.5 0.7	9 107 21

August

Day	Time (h m)	Height (ft)	Height (cm)
1 Su	1210 0534 1232* 0609*	3.1 0.3 3.4 0.8	94 9 104 24
2 M	1253 0614 0115* 0703*	3.0 0.4 3.4 0.9	91 12 104 27
3 Tu ◑	0141 0702 0204* 0819*	2.9 0.5 3.5 1.0	88 15 107 30
4 W	0235 0802 0301* 0947*	2.8 0.5 3.5 0.9	85 15 107 27
5 Th	0337 0908 0405* 1053*	2.9 0.4 3.7 0.7	88 12 113 21
6 F	0443 1013 0511* 1146*	3.0 0.3 4.0 0.4	91 9 122 12
7 Sa	0546 1113 0613*	3.4 0.0 4.3	104 0 131
8 Su	1235 0643 1211* 0708*	0.1 3.8 -0.2 4.6	3 116 -6 140
9 M	0122 0736 0108* 0759*	-0.1 4.2 -0.4 4.8	-3 128 -12 146
10 Tu ●	0207 0827 0204* 0849*	-0.4 4.5 -0.5 4.8	-12 137 -15 146
11 W	0250 0917 0259* 0939*	-0.5 4.7 -0.5 4.7	-15 143 -15 143
12 Th	0332 1008 0352* 1030*	-0.5 4.8 -0.4 4.5	-15 146 -12 137
13 F	0413 1101 0444* 1122*	-0.5 4.8 -0.2 4.2	-15 146 -6 128
14 Sa	0454 1154 0537*	-0.3 4.7 0.1	-9 143 3
15 Su	1215 0538 1249* 0639*	3.9 -0.1 4.4 0.4	119 -3 134 12
16 M ◐	0110 0626 0146* 0819*	3.6 0.2 4.1 0.7	110 6 125 21
17 Tu	0208 0724 0247* 0954*	3.3 0.5 3.9 0.8	101 15 119 24
18 W	0309 0840 0351* 1056*	3.1 0.7 3.7 0.8	94 21 113 24
19 Th	0414 1002 0456* 1144*	3.0 0.7 3.7 0.7	91 21 113 21
20 F	0517 1059 0555*	3.1 0.7 3.7	94 21 113
21 Sa	1220 0613 1144 0644*	0.7 3.2 0.6 3.7	21 98 18 113
22 Su	1246 0700 1226* 0726*	0.6 3.4 0.5 3.8	18 104 15 116
23 M	0111 0741 0107* 0804*	0.4 3.6 0.4 3.8	12 110 12 116
24 Tu ○	0140 0818 0148* 0838*	0.3 3.8 0.3 3.8	9 116 9 116
25 W	0212 0853 0228* 0912*	0.2 3.8 0.3 3.7	6 116 9 113
26 Th	0244 0927 0307* 0945*	0.1 3.9 0.3 3.6	3 119 9 110
27 F	0317 1000 0343* 1020*	0.1 3.8 0.3 3.5	3 116 9 107
28 Sa	0350 1035 0418* 1057*	0.2 3.7 0.4 3.4	6 113 12 104
29 Su	0422 1112 0454* 1138*	0.2 3.7 0.6 3.2	6 113 18 98
30 M	0456 1154 0533*	0.3 3.6 0.7	9 110 21
31 Tu	1223 0535 1241* 0622*	3.1 0.4 3.6 0.9	94 12 110 27

September

Day	Time (h m)	Height (ft)	Height (cm)
1 W ◑	0114 0622 0134* 0733*	3.0 0.5 3.6 1.0	91 15 110 30
2 Th	0211 0723 0234* 0919*	2.9 0.6 3.6 0.9	88 18 110 27
3 F	0313 0839 0341* 1032*	3.0 0.5 3.8 0.7	91 15 116 21
4 Sa	0420 0954 0449* 1123*	3.2 0.3 4.0 0.4	98 9 122 12
5 Su	0524 1101 0552*	3.6 0.0 4.3	110 0 131
6 M	1207 0622 1200* 0647*	0.1 4.1 -0.2 4.5	3 125 -6 137
7 Tu	1250 0715 1257* 0739*	-0.2 4.6 -0.4 4.7	-6 140 -12 143
8 W ●	0133 0805 0152* 0828*	-0.4 4.9 -0.6 4.7	-12 149 -18 143
9 Th	0216 0855 0244* 0917*	-0.6 5.1 -0.6 4.7	-18 155 -18 143
10 F	0258 0945 0335* 1007*	-0.6 5.1 -0.4 4.4	-18 155 -12 134
11 Sa	0340 1036 0424* 1059*	-0.5 5.0 -0.2 4.1	-15 152 -6 125
12 Su	0422 1129 0514* 1152*	-0.2 4.7 0.1 3.8	-6 143 3 116
13 M	0505 1225* 0609*	0.1 4.3 0.5	3 131 15
14 Tu	1248 0551 0122* 0737*	3.5 0.4 4.0 0.8	107 12 122 24
15 W ◐	0145 0648 0223* 0931*	3.2 0.7 3.7 0.9	98 21 113 27
16 Th	0246 0809 0327* 1031*	3.1 0.9 3.5 0.9	94 27 107 27
17 F	0350 1005 0431* 1113*	3.0 0.9 3.4 0.8	91 27 104 24
18 Sa	0453 1059 0529* 1141*	3.1 0.8 3.4 0.7	94 24 104 21
19 Su	0547 1138 0618*	3.3 0.7 3.5	101 21 107
20 M	1205 0633 1215* 0658*	0.6 3.5 0.5 3.6	18 107 15 110
21 Tu	1231 0712 1252* 0734*	0.4 3.8 0.4 3.6	12 116 12 110
22 W	0102 0747 0129* 0807*	0.3 3.9 0.3 3.7	9 119 9 113
23 Th ○	0135 0820 0207* 0840*	0.1 4.0 0.2 3.7	3 122 6 113
24 F	0209 0852 0244* 0913*	0.1 4.0 0.2 3.6	3 122 6 110
25 Sa	0242 0925 0319* 0949*	0.1 4.0 0.3 3.5	3 122 9 107
26 Su	0315 1001 0354* 1028*	0.1 3.9 0.4 3.4	3 119 12 104
27 M	0349 1040 0429* 1112*	0.2 3.8 0.5 3.2	6 116 15 98
28 Tu	0425 1126 0508*	0.3 3.8 0.7	9 116 21
29 W	1201 0505 1217* 0557*	3.1 0.4 3.7 0.8	94 12 113 24
30 Th	1255 0555 0114* 0706*	3.0 0.5 3.7 0.9	91 15 113 27

October

Day	Time (h m)	Height (ft)	Height (cm)
1 F ◑	0153 0659 0215* 0854*	3.1 0.6 3.7 0.8	94 18 113 24
2 Sa	0256 0821 0321* 1007*	3.2 0.6 3.7 0.6	98 18 113 18
3 Su	0400 0945 0427* 1054*	3.5 0.4 3.9 0.3	107 12 119 9
4 M	0503 1053 0530* 1136*	3.9 0.1 4.1 0.0	119 3 125 0
5 Tu	0601 1151 0626*	4.4 -0.2 4.3	134 -6 131
6 W	1218 0654 1245* 0718*	-0.3 4.8 -0.4 4.5	-9 146 -12 137
7 Th ●	0100 0744 0137* 0807*	-0.5 5.1 -0.5 4.5	-15 155 -15 137
8 F	0143 0833 0228* 0856*	-0.6 5.2 -0.5 4.4	-18 158 -15 134
9 Sa	0226 0922 0316* 0945*	-0.5 5.1 -0.4 4.2	-15 155 -12 128
10 Su	0309 1013 0403* 1036*	-0.4 4.9 -0.1 3.9	-12 149 -3 119
11 M	0351 1105 0449* 1129*	-0.2 4.5 0.2 3.6	-6 137 6 110
12 Tu	0435 1200* 0538*	0.1 4.1 0.5	3 125 15
13 W	1224 0522 1256* 0640*	3.4 0.5 3.8 0.8	104 15 116 24
14 Th ◐	0121 0616 0154* 0833*	3.2 0.8 3.5 0.9	98 24 107 27
15 F	0219 0732 0254* 0942*	3.0 1.0 3.2 0.9	91 30 98 27
16 Sa	0319 0940 0355* 1021*	3.0 1.0 3.1 0.8	91 30 94 24
17 Su	0418 1038 0452* 1050*	3.1 0.9 3.1 0.7	94 27 94 21
18 M	0512 1117 0541* 1118*	3.3 0.7 3.2 0.5	101 21 98 15
19 Tu	0558 1153 0622* 1150*	3.5 0.5 3.3 0.4	107 15 101 12
20 W	0638 1229* 0659*	3.7 0.4 3.4	113 12 104
21 Th	1223 0713 0106* 0734*	0.2 3.9 0.2 3.5	6 119 6 107
22 F	1258 0747 0144* 0809*	0.1 4.0 0.2 3.5	3 122 6 107
23 Sa ○	0134 0821 0222* 0845*	0.0 4.1 0.1 3.5	0 125 3 107
24 Su	0210 0856 0259* 0924*	0.0 4.1 0.2 3.5	0 125 6 107
25 M	0246 0935 0336* 1006*	0.0 4.0 0.2 3.4	0 122 6 104
26 Tu	0323 1018 0414* 1053*	0.1 4.0 0.3 3.2	3 122 9 98
27 W	0402 1107 0456* 1145*	0.2 3.9 0.5 3.2	6 119 15 98
28 Th	0447 1201* 0545*	0.3 3.8 0.6	9 116 18
29 F	1240 0540 1258* 0649*	3.2 0.4 3.7 0.6	98 12 113 18
30 Sa ◑	0138 0646 0158* 0816*	3.3 0.5 3.7 0.6	101 15 113 18
31 Su	0238 0811 0301* 0931*	3.5 0.5 3.7 0.4	107 15 113 12

November

Day	Time (h m)	Height (ft)	Height (cm)
1 M	0340 0940 0405* 1021*	3.7 0.3 3.7 0.1	113 9 113 3
2 Tu	0441 1048 0507* 1104*	4.1 0.1 3.8 -0.1	125 3 116 -3
3 W	0539 1143 0604* 1147*	4.5 -0.2 4.0 -0.3	137 -6 122 -9
4 Th	0634 1234* 0657*	4.8 -0.3 4.1	146 -9 125
5 F	1229 0725 0124* 0747*	-0.5 4.9 -0.4 4.1	-15 149 -12 125
6 Sa ●	0113 0814 0212* 0836*	-0.5 5.0 -0.4 4.0	-15 152 -12 122
7 Su	0157 0802 0158* 0824*	-0.5 4.8 -0.3 3.9	-15 146 -9 119
8 M	0141 0852 0242* 0914*	-0.3 4.6 -0.1 3.7	-9 140 -3 113
9 Tu	0225 0942 0325* 1005*	-0.1 4.3 0.1 3.5	-3 131 3 107
10 W	0310 1034 0408* 1058*	0.1 3.9 0.4 3.3	3 119 12 101
11 Th	0356 1127 0455* 1151*	0.4 3.5 0.6 3.1	12 107 18 94
12 F	0448 1219* 0550*	0.7 3.2 0.7	21 98 21
13 Sa ◐	1245 0553 0112* 0657*	3.0 0.9 3.0 0.8	91 27 91 24
14 Su	0138 0729 0206* 0800*	3.0 0.9 2.9 0.7	91 27 88 21
15 M	0232 0853 0259* 0848*	3.1 0.8 2.8 0.6	94 24 85 18
16 Tu	0325 0942 0350* 0928*	3.2 0.7 2.8 0.4	98 21 85 12
17 W	0414 1023 0437* 1007*	3.3 0.5 2.9 0.3	101 15 88 9
18 Th	0457 1102 0520* 1045*	3.5 0.4 3.1 0.1	107 12 94 3
19 F	0537 1142 0600* 1123*	3.7 0.2 3.2 0.0	113 6 98 0
20 Sa	0615 1222* 0639*	3.9 0.1 3.3	119 3 101
21 Su ○	1202 0653 0103* 0720*	-0.1 4.0 0.0 3.4	-3 122 0 104
22 M	1242 0733 0144* 0802*	-0.2 4.1 0.0 3.4	-6 125 0 104
23 Tu	0122 0816 0225* 0848*	-0.2 4.1 0.0 3.4	-6 125 0 104
24 W	0205 0903 0306* 0937*	-0.2 4.1 0.0 3.3	-6 125 0 101
25 Th	0249 0953 0348* 1030*	-0.1 4.0 0.1 3.4	-3 122 3 104
26 F	0338 1047 0434* 1124*	0.0 3.9 0.2 3.4	0 119 6 104
27 Sa	0433 1143 0528*	0.1 3.7 0.2	3 113 6
28 Su ◑	1221 0538 1241* 0634*	3.5 0.3 3.6 0.2	107 9 110 6
29 M	0119 0702 0140* 0745*	3.7 0.3 3.5 0.1	113 9 107 3
30 Tu	0218 0834 0242* 0844*	3.8 0.2 3.4 0.0	116 6 104 0

December

Day	Time (h m)	Height (ft)	Height (cm)
1 W	0320 0943 0344* 0934*	4.0 0.1 3.4 -0.2	122 3 104 -6
2 Th	0420 1038 0444* 1020*	4.3 -0.1 3.5 -0.3	131 -3 107 -9
3 F	0516 1127 0539* 1105*	4.4 -0.2 3.6 -0.4	134 -6 110 -12
4 Sa	0609 1215* 0630* 1149*	4.5 -0.2 3.6 -0.4	137 -6 110 -12
5 Su ●	0658 0100* 0718*	4.5 -0.2 3.6	137 -6 110
6 M	1235 0746 0143* 0806*	-0.4 4.4 -0.2 3.6	-12 134 -6 110
7 Tu	0120 0833 0223* 0853*	-0.3 4.2 -0.1 3.5	-9 128 -3 107
8 W	0205 0920 0301* 0941*	-0.2 3.9 0.0 3.3	-6 119 0 101
9 Th	0250 1006 0338* 1028*	0.0 3.6 0.1 3.2	0 110 3 98
10 F	0335 1053 0417* 1116*	0.2 3.3 0.2 3.1	6 101 6 94
11 Sa	0422 1139 0458*	0.4 3.1 0.4	12 94 12
12 Su	1203 0515 1224* 0545*	3.0 0.6 2.8 0.4	91 18 85 12
13 M ◐	1249 0620 0110* 0640*	3.0 0.7 2.6 0.5	91 21 79 15
14 Tu	0136 0743 0157* 0739*	2.9 0.8 2.5 0.5	88 24 76 15
15 W	0225 0854 0249* 0833*	3.0 0.7 2.5 0.4	91 21 76 12
16 Th	0317 0947 0344* 0922*	3.1 0.5 2.6 0.2	94 15 79 6
17 F	0410 1033 0437* 1007*	3.2 0.4 2.7 0.1	98 12 82 3
18 Sa	0459 1118 0526* 1051*	3.4 0.2 2.9 -0.1	104 6 88 -3
19 Su	0545 1203* 0612* 1135*	3.7 0.0 3.1 -0.2	113 0 94 -6
20 M	0630 1248* 0657*	3.9 -0.1 3.3	119 -3 101
21 Tu ○	1220 0715 0132* 0743*	-0.4 4.1 -0.2 3.4	-12 125 -6 104
22 W	0106 0801 0214* 0830*	-0.5 4.2 -0.3 3.5	-15 128 -9 107
23 Th	0154 0849 0255* 0920*	-0.5 4.2 -0.4 3.6	-15 128 -12 110
24 F	0243 0939 0335* 1012*	-0.5 4.1 -0.3 3.7	-15 125 -9 113
25 Sa	0333 1031 0417* 1105*	-0.4 3.9 -0.3 3.7	-12 119 -9 113
26 Su	0427 1125 0503*	-0.2 3.7 -0.2	-6 113 -6
27 M	1200 0529 1221* 0556*	3.8 0.0 3.5 -0.1	116 0 107 -3
28 Tu ◑	1257 0649 0118* 0659*	3.8 0.2 3.3 -0.1	116 6 101 -3
29 W	0156 0827 0219* 0807*	3.8 0.2 3.1 -0.1	116 6 94 -3
30 Th	0259 0940 0323* 0908*	3.8 0.1 3.0 -0.1	116 3 91 -3
31 F	0402 1038 0425* 1000*	3.9 0.0 3.1 -0.2	119 0 94 -6

Heights are referred to mean lower low water which is the chart datum of soundings. All times are local. Daylight Saving Time has been used when needed.

Nantucket, Massachusetts, 2010

Times and Heights of High and Low Waters

March

Day	Time (h m)	Height (ft)	Height (cm)
1 M	1202 0547 1229* 0616*	3.5 -0.6 3.7 -0.5	107 -18 113 -15
2 Tu	1253 0643 0123* 0705*	3.7 -0.6 3.6 -0.4	113 -18 110 -12
3 W	0144 0738 0218* 0754*	3.8 -0.6 3.4 -0.3	116 -18 104 -9
4 Th	0235 0834 0313* 0844*	3.8 -0.5 3.2 -0.1	116 -15 98 -3
5 F	0328 0931 0409* 0936*	3.8 -0.3 2.9 0.1	116 -9 88 3
6 Sa	0421 1030 0506* 1031*	3.6 -0.1 2.7 0.3	110 -3 82 9
7 Su ◑	0517 1130 0606* 1128*	3.5 0.0 2.6 0.5	107 0 79 15
8 M	0615 1232* 0706*	3.3 0.2 2.5	101 6 76
9 Tu	1227 0714 0132* 0805*	0.5 3.2 0.3 2.4	15 98 9 73
10 W	0126 0812 0227* 0859*	0.6 3.2 0.3 2.5	18 98 9 76
11 Th	0222 0905 0315* 0945*	0.6 3.1 0.3 2.5	18 94 9 76
12 F	0313 0953 0357* 1025*	0.5 3.1 0.4 2.6	15 94 12 79
13 Sa	0400 1037 0435* 1100*	0.4 3.0 0.4 2.7	12 91 12 82
14 Su	0543 1217* 0610*	0.3 3.0 0.4	9 91 12
15 M ●	1235 0624 1256* 0644*	2.9 0.3 3.0 0.4	88 9 91 12
16 Tu	0110 0704 0136* 0718*	3.0 0.2 2.9 0.4	91 6 88 12
17 W	0146 0744 0216* 0752*	3.1 0.1 2.9 0.4	94 3 88 12
18 Th	0223 0824 0257* 0829*	3.2 0.0 2.8 0.4	98 0 85 12
19 F	0302 0907 0340* 0907*	3.3 0.0 2.7 0.4	101 0 82 12
20 Sa	0344 0953 0426* 0950*	3.3 0.0 2.6 0.4	101 0 79 12
21 Su	0430 1042 0515* 1038*	3.4 0.0 2.5 0.4	104 0 76 12
22 M	0521 1136 0608* 1132*	3.4 0.0 2.5 0.4	104 0 76 12
23 Tu ◐	0616 1233* 0704*	3.5 0.0 2.5	107 0 76
24 W	1231 0716 0132* 0802*	0.3 3.5 0.0 2.6	9 107 0 79
25 Th	0134 0818 0230* 0901*	0.2 3.5 -0.1 2.8	6 107 -3 85
26 F	0238 0920 0326* 0958*	0.1 3.6 -0.2 3.0	3 110 -6 91
27 Sa	0341 1022 0420* 1054*	-0.1 3.6 -0.2 3.3	-3 110 -6 101
28 Su	0441 1122 0511* 1147*	-0.3 3.5 -0.3 3.5	-9 107 -9 107
29 M	0539 1219* 0600*	-0.5 3.5 -0.3	-15 107 -9
30 Tu ○	1238 0634 0115* 0649*	3.7 -0.6 3.4 -0.2	113 -18 104 -6
31 W	0128 0728 0209* 0737*	3.9 -0.6 3.3 -0.2	119 -18 101 -6

April

Day	Time (h m)	Height (ft)	Height (cm)
1 Th	0218 0821 0302* 0826*	3.9 -0.6 3.1 0.0	119 -18 94 0
2 F	0307 0914 0354* 0916*	3.9 -0.5 3.0 0.1	119 -15 91 3
3 Sa	0358 1007 0447* 1008*	3.7 -0.3 2.8 0.3	113 -9 85 9
4 Su	0449 1102 0540* 1101*	3.6 -0.1 2.7 0.4	110 -3 82 12
5 M	0543 1158 0633* 1158*	3.4 0.1 2.6 0.6	104 3 79 18
6 Tu ◑	0637 1254* 0727*	3.2 0.2 2.5	98 6 76
7 W	1256 0733 0150* 0820*	0.6 3.1 0.3 2.5	18 94 9 76
8 Th	0156 0829 0242* 0910*	0.6 3.0 0.4 2.6	18 91 12 79
9 F	0252 0923 0329* 0955*	0.6 2.9 0.5 2.7	18 88 15 82
10 Sa	0345 1014 0411* 1037*	0.5 2.9 0.5 2.8	15 88 15 85
11 Su	0433 1101 0450* 1116*	0.4 2.8 0.5 3.0	12 85 15 91
12 M	0517 1145 0527* 1154*	0.3 2.8 0.5 3.1	9 85 15 94
13 Tu	0558 1228* 0603*	0.2 2.8 0.5	6 85 15
14 W ●	1232 0639 0110* 0639*	3.2 0.1 2.7 0.5	98 3 82 15
15 Th	0111 0719 0153* 0716*	3.3 0.0 2.7 0.5	101 0 82 15
16 F	0151 0801 0236* 0756*	3.4 -0.1 2.7 0.4	104 -3 82 12
17 Sa	0233 0845 0321* 0839*	3.5 -0.2 2.7 0.4	107 -6 82 12
18 Su	0318 0932 0408* 0926*	3.6 -0.2 2.6 0.4	110 -6 79 12
19 M	0408 1022 0459* 1018*	3.6 -0.2 2.6 0.4	110 -6 79 12
20 Tu	0501 1116 0552* 1116*	3.6 -0.1 2.7 0.3	110 -3 82 9
21 W ◐	0559 1211* 0648*	3.6 -0.1 2.8	110 -3 85
22 Th	1218 0700 0108* 0745*	0.3 3.5 -0.1 2.9	9 107 -3 88
23 F	0123 0802 0205* 0843*	0.2 3.4 -0.1 3.1	6 104 -3 94
24 Sa	0228 0906 0300* 0939*	0.0 3.3 -0.1 3.4	0 101 -3 104
25 Su	0331 1008 0353* 1033*	-0.1 3.3 -0.1 3.6	-3 101 -3 110
26 M	0431 1109 0444* 1125*	-0.3 3.2 -0.1 3.8	-9 98 -3 116
27 Tu	0528 1207* 0534*	-0.4 3.1 0.0	-12 94 0
28 W ○	1216 0622 0102* 0623*	3.9 -0.5 3.0 0.0	119 -15 91 0
29 Th	0105 0713 0155* 0711*	3.9 -0.5 3.0 0.1	119 -15 91 3
30 F	0153 0803 0245* 0800*	3.9 -0.5 2.9 0.2	119 -15 88 6

May

Day	Time (h m)	Height (ft)	Height (cm)
1 Sa	0241 0853 0334* 0849*	3.8 -0.3 2.8 0.3	116 -9 85 9
2 Su	0329 0942 0422* 0939*	3.7 -0.2 2.7 0.5	113 -6 82 15
3 M	0418 1032 0509* 1031*	3.5 0.0 2.7 0.6	107 0 82 18
4 Tu	0507 1123 0557* 1126*	3.3 0.1 2.6 0.6	101 3 79 18
5 W	0558 1213* 0645*	3.2 0.3 2.7	98 9 82
6 Th ◑	1223 0650 0103* 0733*	0.7 3.0 0.4 2.7	21 91 12 82
7 F	0120 0743 0152* 0820*	0.7 2.9 0.5 2.8	21 88 15 85
8 Sa	0217 0837 0237* 0905*	0.6 2.8 0.5 2.9	18 85 15 88
9 Su	0311 0929 0320* 0949*	0.5 2.7 0.6 3.1	15 82 18 94
10 M	0400 1020 0401* 1031*	0.4 2.6 0.6 3.2	12 79 18 98
11 Tu	0445 1109 0441* 1113*	0.3 2.6 0.6 3.3	9 79 18 101
12 W	0529 1156 0521* 1155*	0.1 2.6 0.6 3.5	3 79 18 107
13 Th	0611 1241* 0601*	0.0 2.6 0.5	0 79 15
14 F ●	1237 0654 0127* 0643*	3.6 -0.1 2.6 0.5	110 -3 79 15
15 Sa	0122 0738 0214* 0728*	3.7 -0.2 2.7 0.4	113 -6 82 12
16 Su	0209 0825 0301* 0816*	3.8 -0.3 2.7 0.3	116 -9 82 9
17 M	0258 0913 0351* 0908*	3.8 -0.3 2.8 0.3	116 -9 85 9
18 Tu	0351 1003 0443* 1004*	3.8 -0.3 2.9 0.3	116 -9 88 9
19 W	0447 1056 0536* 1104*	3.7 -0.2 3.0 0.3	113 -6 91 9
20 Th ◐	0545 1150 0632*	3.6 -0.2 3.1	110 -6 94
21 F	1208 0646 1245* 0728*	0.2 3.4 -0.1 3.3	6 104 -3 101
22 Sa	0114 0748 0140* 0824*	0.1 3.3 0.0 3.5	3 101 0 107
23 Su	0219 0852 0234* 0919*	0.0 3.1 0.0 3.7	0 94 0 113
24 M	0322 0956 0327* 1014*	-0.1 3.0 0.1 3.8	-3 91 3 116
25 Tu	0421 1058 0420* 1106*	-0.2 2.9 0.2 3.9	-6 88 6 119
26 W	0516 1156 0510* 1157*	-0.3 2.9 0.2 3.9	-9 88 6 119
27 Th ○	0608 1250* 0559*	-0.3 2.8 0.3	-9 85 9
28 F	1245 0657 0140* 0648*	3.9 -0.3 2.8 0.4	119 -9 85 12
29 Sa	0132 0745 0227* 0735*	3.8 -0.2 2.7 0.4	116 -6 82 12
30 Su	0217 0831 0311* 0823*	3.7 -0.1 2.7 0.5	113 -3 82 15
31 M	0302 0916 0353* 0911*	3.6 0.0 2.7 0.6	110 0 82 18

June

Day	Time (h m)	Height (ft)	Height (cm)
1 Tu	0347 1001 0436* 1001*	3.5 0.1 2.7 0.6	107 3 82 18
2 W	0433 1046 0519* 1053*	3.3 0.2 2.8 0.7	101 6 85 21
3 Th	0520 1131 0603* 1147*	3.1 0.3 2.8 0.7	94 9 85 21
4 F ◑	0609 1216* 0647*	3.0 0.4 2.9	91 12 88
5 Sa	1242 0700 0101* 0732*	0.7 2.8 0.5 3.0	21 85 15 91
6 Su	0138 0752 0145* 0818*	0.7 2.7 0.6 3.1	21 82 18 94
7 M	0231 0845 0229* 0903*	0.6 2.6 0.7 3.3	18 79 21 101
8 Tu	0322 0938 0313* 0948*	0.4 2.5 0.7 3.4	12 76 21 104
9 W	0410 1030 0357* 1034*	0.3 2.5 0.6 3.6	9 76 18 110
10 Th	0457 1121 0442* 1121*	0.2 2.5 0.6 3.7	6 76 18 113
11 F	0543 1210* 0528*	0.0 2.6 0.5	0 79 15
12 Sa ●	1209 0629 0100* 0615*	3.9 -0.1 2.7 0.4	119 -3 82 12
13 Su	1258 0716 0149* 0705*	4.0 -0.2 2.8 0.3	122 -6 85 9
14 M	0149 0803 0239* 0758*	4.0 -0.3 2.9 0.2	122 -9 88 6
15 Tu	0242 0852 0331* 0853*	4.0 -0.4 3.0 0.2	122 -12 91 6
16 W	0336 0943 0423* 0951*	4.0 -0.3 3.2 0.1	122 -9 98 3
17 Th	0433 1034 0517* 1053*	3.8 -0.3 3.4 0.1	116 -9 104 3
18 F	0531 1126 0612* 1157*	3.6 -0.2 3.5 0.1	110 -6 107 3
19 Sa ◐	0632 1220* 0708*	3.4 0.0 3.7	104 0 113
20 Su	0103 0735 0115* 0804*	0.1 3.1 0.1 3.8	3 94 3 116
21 M	0208 0840 0210* 0901*	0.1 3.0 0.2 3.9	3 91 6 119
22 Tu	0311 0944 0305* 0956*	0.0 2.8 0.3 3.9	0 85 9 119
23 W	0410 1047 0358* 1050*	0.0 2.7 0.4 3.9	0 82 12 119
24 Th	0504 1145 0450* 1141*	0.0 2.7 0.5 3.9	0 82 15 119
25 F	0554 1237* 0539*	0.0 2.7 0.5	0 82 15
26 Sa ○	1228 0640 0123* 0627*	3.8 0.0 2.7 0.5	116 0 82 15
27 Su	0113 0724 0204* 0713*	3.7 0.0 2.7 0.6	113 0 82 18
28 M	0155 0806 0243* 0759*	3.6 0.1 2.7 0.6	110 3 82 18
29 Tu	0236 0847 0321* 0845*	3.5 0.2 2.8 0.6	107 6 85 18
30 W	0318 0927 0359* 0932*	3.4 0.2 2.9 0.7	104 6 88 21

July

Day	Time (h m)	Height (ft)	Height (cm)
1 Th	0401 1008 0439* 1020*	3.3 0.3 2.9 0.7	101 9 88 21
2 F	0445 1048 0521* 1111*	3.1 0.4 3.0 0.7	94 12 91 21
3 Sa	0532 1130 0604*	3.0 0.5 3.1	91 15 94
4 Su ◑	1203 0621 1212* 0648*	0.7 2.8 0.6 3.2	21 85 18 98
5 M	1256 0712 1256* 0734*	0.6 2.7 0.7 3.3	18 82 21 101
6 Tu	0149 0805 0142* 0821*	0.6 2.6 0.7 3.4	18 79 21 104
7 W	0242 0858 0229* 0910*	0.5 2.5 0.7 3.6	15 76 21 110
8 Th	0334 0952 0318* 1000*	0.3 2.5 0.6 3.7	9 76 18 113
9 F	0424 1046 0409* 1052*	0.2 2.6 0.5 3.9	6 79 15 119
10 Sa	0514 1139 0500* 1144*	0.0 2.7 0.4 4.0	0 82 12 122
11 Su ●	0603 1231* 0553*	-0.1 2.8 0.2	-3 85 6
12 M	1237 0651 0123* 0647*	4.1 -0.2 3.0 0.1	125 -6 91 3
13 Tu	0131 0740 0214* 0742*	4.2 -0.3 3.2 0.0	128 -9 98 0
14 W	0226 0829 0307* 0839*	4.1 -0.3 3.4 0.0	125 -9 104 0
15 Th	0321 0918 0400* 0939*	4.0 -0.3 3.6 -0.1	122 -9 110 -3
16 F	0419 1009 0454* 1040*	3.8 -0.2 3.7 0.0	116 -6 113 0
17 Sa	0517 1102 0549* 1143*	3.5 -0.1 3.9 0.0	107 -3 119 0
18 Su ◐	0618 1156 0645*	3.3 0.1 3.9	101 3 119
19 M	1248 0721 1252* 0743*	0.1 3.0 0.3 3.9	3 91 9 119
20 Tu	0153 0826 0149* 0842*	0.1 2.9 0.4 3.9	3 88 12 119
21 W	0256 0931 0245* 0939*	0.1 2.8 0.5 3.8	3 85 15 116
22 Th	0355 1033 0340* 1034*	0.2 2.7 0.6 3.8	6 82 18 116
23 F	0449 1129 0432* 1125*	0.2 2.7 0.6 3.7	6 82 18 113
24 Sa	0537 1217* 0521*	0.2 2.7 0.6	6 82 18
25 Su	1211 0620 1258* 0608*	3.7 0.2 2.7 0.6	113 6 82 18
26 M ○	1253 0700 0135* 0652*	3.6 0.3 2.8 0.6	110 9 85 18
27 Tu	0132 0738 0209* 0736*	3.5 0.3 2.8 0.6	107 9 85 18
28 W	0211 0815 0244* 0819*	3.4 0.3 2.9 0.6	104 9 88 18
29 Th	0250 0851 0321* 0904*	3.3 0.4 3.0 0.6	101 12 91 18
30 F	0332 0929 0359* 0949*	3.2 0.5 3.1 0.6	98 15 94 18
31 Sa	0415 1006 0439* 1036*	3.1 0.5 3.2 0.6	94 15 98 18

August

Day	Time (h m)	Height (ft)	Height (cm)
1 Su	0500 1046 0522* 1125*	2.9 0.6 3.3 0.6	88 18 101 18
2 M	0548 1127 0607*	2.8 0.7 3.4	85 21 104
3 Tu ◑	1216 0638 1212* 0654*	0.6 2.7 0.7 3.4	18 82 21 104
4 W	0110 0730 0101* 0744*	0.5 2.6 0.7 3.6	15 79 21 110
5 Th	0205 0824 0153* 0837*	0.4 2.6 0.7 3.7	12 79 21 113
6 F	0300 0920 0248* 0932*	0.3 2.6 0.6 3.8	9 79 18 116
7 Sa	0353 1015 0343* 1027*	0.2 2.7 0.4 4.0	6 82 12 122
8 Su	0445 1109 0439* 1123*	0.0 2.9 0.2 4.1	0 88 6 125
9 M	0535 1203* 0535*	-0.1 3.1 0.0	-3 94 0
10 Tu ●	1219 0625 1255* 0632*	4.2 -0.2 3.3 -0.1	128 -6 101 -3
11 W	0114 0713 0148* 0728*	4.1 -0.3 3.6 -0.2	125 -9 110 -6
12 Th	0210 0802 0240* 0825*	4.0 -0.3 3.8 -0.3	122 -9 116 -9
13 F	0306 0852 0333* 0924*	3.9 -0.2 3.9 -0.2	119 -6 119 -6
14 Sa	0403 0943 0427* 1024*	3.6 -0.1 4.0 -0.2	110 -3 122 -6
15 Su	0502 1036 0523* 1126*	3.4 0.1 4.0 0.0	104 3 122 0
16 M ◐	0602 1131 0621*	3.2 0.3 4.0	98 9 122
17 Tu	1229 0705 1229* 0720*	0.1 3.0 0.4 3.9	3 91 12 119
18 W	0133 0809 0128* 0820*	0.2 2.8 0.6 3.8	6 85 18 116
19 Th	0236 0912 0227* 0920*	0.3 2.8 0.6 3.7	9 85 18 113
20 F	0335 1012 0323* 1016*	0.3 2.7 0.7 3.6	9 82 21 110
21 Sa	0426 1104 0416* 1106*	0.4 2.8 0.7 3.6	12 85 21 110
22 Su	0512 1148 0504* 1150*	0.4 2.8 0.7 3.5	12 85 21 107
23 M	0552 1225* 0549*	0.4 2.9 0.6	12 88 18
24 Tu ○	1230 0629 1258* 0632*	3.4 0.5 2.9 0.6	104 15 88 18
25 W	0108 0704 0131* 0714*	3.3 0.5 3.0 0.5	101 15 91 15
26 Th	0146 0739 0206* 0755*	3.3 0.5 3.1 0.5	101 15 94 15
27 F	0225 0814 0242* 0836*	3.2 0.6 3.2 0.5	98 18 98 15
28 Sa	0305 0849 0320* 0919*	3.1 0.6 3.3 0.5	94 18 101 15
29 Su	0348 0926 0400* 1003*	3.0 0.7 3.3 0.5	91 21 101 15
30 M	0432 1005 0443* 1051*	2.9 0.7 3.4 0.5	88 21 104 15
31 Tu	0520 1048 0529* 1142*	2.8 0.8 3.5 0.5	85 24 107 15

September

Day	Time (h m)	Height (ft)	Height (cm)
1 W ◑	0609 1136 0619*	2.7 0.8 3.5	82 24 107
2 Th	1236 0702 1228* 0713*	0.4 2.6 0.7 3.6	12 79 21 110
3 F	0132 0757 0126* 0810*	0.4 2.7 0.6 3.7	12 82 18 113
4 Sa	0229 0853 0225* 0908*	0.3 2.8 0.5 3.8	9 85 15 116
5 Su	0324 0949 0325* 1007*	0.2 2.9 0.3 3.9	6 88 9 119
6 M	0416 1043 0424* 1104*	0.0 3.2 0.1 4.0	0 98 3 122
7 Tu	0507 1136 0521*	-0.1 3.4 -0.1	-3 104 -3
8 W ●	1202 0557 1229* 0618*	4.0 -0.2 3.7 -0.3	122 -6 113 -9
9 Th	1258 0645 0121* 0714*	3.9 -0.2 3.9 -0.4	119 -6 119 -12
10 F	0154 0735 0213* 0810*	3.8 -0.1 4.1 -0.4	116 -3 125 -12
11 Sa	0250 0824 0306* 0907*	3.6 0.0 4.2 -0.4	110 0 128 -12
12 Su	0347 0916 0400* 1004*	3.4 0.1 4.1 -0.2	104 3 125 -6
13 M	0444 1009 0456* 1104*	3.2 0.3 4.0 -0.1	98 9 122 -3
14 Tu	0543 1105 0553*	3.1 0.4 3.9	94 12 119
15 W ◐	1205 0644 1204* 0653*	0.1 2.9 0.6 3.7	3 88 18 113
16 Th	0107 0745 0105* 0754*	0.3 2.8 0.7 3.6	9 85 21 110
17 F	0208 0845 0206* 0853*	0.4 2.8 0.7 3.5	12 85 21 107
18 Sa	0304 0940 0304* 0948*	0.5 2.8 0.7 3.4	15 85 21 104
19 Su	0354 1028 0357* 1038*	0.5 2.9 0.7 3.3	15 88 21 101
20 M	0437 1109 0445* 1123*	0.5 3.0 0.6 3.3	15 91 18 101
21 Tu	0516 1144 0529*	0.6 3.0 0.5	18 91 15
22 W	1203 0551 1218* 0611*	3.2 0.6 3.1 0.5	98 18 94 15
23 Th ○	1242 0626 1252* 0651*	3.1 0.6 3.2 0.4	94 18 98 12
24 F	0121 0701 0128* 0730*	3.1 0.7 3.3 0.3	94 21 101 9
25 Sa	0200 0735 0204* 0810*	3.0 0.7 3.4 0.3	91 21 104 9
26 Su	0241 0811 0243* 0851*	2.9 0.7 3.4 0.3	88 21 104 9
27 M	0324 0849 0325* 0935*	2.8 0.7 3.5 0.3	85 21 107 9
28 Tu	0409 0930 0409* 1022*	2.8 0.7 3.5 0.3	85 21 107 9
29 W	0456 1016 0458* 1113*	2.7 0.7 3.6 0.3	82 21 110 9
30 Th	0547 1108 0551*	2.7 0.7 3.6	82 21 110

October

Day	Time (h m)	Height (ft)	Height (cm)
1 F ◑	1207 0640 1205* 0648*	0.3 2.7 0.7 3.6	9 82 21 110
2 Sa	0104 0735 0106* 0748*	0.3 2.8 0.6 3.7	9 85 18 113
3 Su	0200 0831 0209* 0848*	0.2 3.0 0.4 3.7	6 91 12 113
4 M	0255 0926 0311* 0949*	0.1 3.2 0.2 3.7	3 98 6 113
5 Tu	0348 1020 0411* 1048*	0.0 3.5 -0.1 3.7	0 107 -3 113
6 W	0439 1113 0509* 1146*	0.0 3.8 -0.3 3.6	0 116 -9 110
7 Th ●	0529 1204* 0605*	-0.1 4.0 -0.4	-3 122 -12
8 F	1243 0618 1256* 0700*	3.6 -0.1 4.2 -0.5	110 -3 128 -15
9 Sa	0139 0708 0147* 0754*	3.5 0.0 4.2 -0.5	107 0 128 -15
10 Su	0234 0758 0240* 0848*	3.3 0.1 4.2 -0.4	101 3 128 -12
11 M	0329 0850 0333* 0943*	3.2 0.3 4.1 -0.2	98 9 125 -6
12 Tu	0424 0943 0427* 1039*	3.1 0.4 3.9 0.0	94 12 119 0
13 W	0520 1039 0523* 1136*	3.0 0.6 3.7 0.1	91 18 113 3
14 Th ◐	0617 1137 0621*	2.9 0.7 3.5	88 21 107
15 F	1234 0713 1238* 0718*	0.3 2.8 0.8 3.4	9 85 24 104
16 Sa	0130 0808 0140* 0816*	0.4 2.9 0.8 3.2	12 88 24 98
17 Su	0223 0858 0238* 0910*	0.5 2.9 0.7 3.1	15 88 21 94
18 M	0311 0943 0332* 1001*	0.6 3.0 0.7 3.0	18 91 21 91
19 Tu	0354 1023 0421* 1048*	0.6 3.1 0.6 3.0	18 94 18 91
20 W	0433 1101 0505* 1132*	0.7 3.2 0.5 2.9	21 98 15 88
21 Th	0510 1138 0546*	0.7 3.3 0.4	21 101 12
22 F	1213 0546 1214* 0626*	2.9 0.7 3.4 0.3	88 21 104 9
23 Sa ○	1254 0622 1252* 0705*	2.8 0.7 3.5 0.2	85 21 107 6
24 Su	0136 0659 0131* 0745*	2.8 0.7 3.6 0.1	85 21 110 3
25 M	0218 0737 0212* 0826*	2.8 0.7 3.6 0.1	85 21 110 3
26 Tu	0301 0818 0256* 0911*	2.7 0.7 3.6 0.1	82 21 110 3
27 W	0347 0902 0343* 0958*	2.7 0.7 3.7 0.1	82 21 113 3
28 Th	0436 0952 0435* 1049*	2.7 0.6 3.6 0.1	82 18 110 3
29 F	0527 1047 0530* 1142*	2.8 0.6 3.6 0.1	85 18 110 3
30 Sa ◑	0620 1148 0629*	2.9 0.5 3.6	88 15 110
31 Su	1237 0715 1252* 0730*	0.1 3.0 0.4 3.5	3 91 12 107

November

Day	Time (h m)	Height (ft)	Height (cm)
1 M	0133 0811 0157* 0832*	0.1 3.3 0.3 3.4	3 101 9 104
2 Tu	0227 0905 0300* 0934*	0.1 3.5 0.1 3.4	3 107 3 104
3 W	0320 0959 0401* 1035*	0.1 3.8 -0.2 3.3	3 116 -6 101
4 Th	0412 1052 0458* 1134*	0.0 4.0 -0.3 3.3	0 122 -9 101
5 F	0503 1144 0553*	0.1 4.2 -0.5	3 128 -15
6 Sa ●	1231 0553 1235* 0646*	3.2 0.1 4.2 -0.5	98 3 128 -15
7 Su	0125 0544 1226* 0638*	3.1 0.2 4.2 -0.5	94 6 128 -15
8 M	0118 0634 0116* 0729*	3.1 0.2 4.1 -0.4	94 6 125 -12
9 Tu	0210 0725 0207* 0820*	3.0 0.4 4.0 -0.2	91 12 122 -6
10 W	0301 0817 0259* 0911*	2.9 0.5 3.8 0.0	88 15 116 0
11 Th	0352 0911 0350* 1003*	2.9 0.6 3.6 0.1	88 18 110 3
12 F	0443 1007 0443* 1055*	2.8 0.7 3.3 0.3	85 21 101 9
13 Sa ◐	0533 1106 0537* 1146*	2.9 0.8 3.2 0.4	88 24 98 12
14 Su	0622 1206* 0631*	2.9 0.8 3.0	88 24 91
15 M	1235 0709 0105* 0725*	0.5 3.0 0.7 2.9	15 91 21 88
16 Tu	0122 0753 0200* 0817*	0.6 3.1 0.6 2.8	18 94 18 85
17 W	0206 0836 0250* 0908*	0.7 3.2 0.5 2.7	21 98 15 82
18 Th	0248 0917 0335* 0956*	0.7 3.3 0.4 2.7	21 101 12 82
19 F	0327 0958 0418* 1041*	0.7 3.4 0.3 2.6	21 104 9 79
20 Sa	0406 1039 0459* 1125*	0.7 3.5 0.2 2.6	21 107 6 79
21 Su ○	0445 1120 0539*	0.7 3.6 0.1	21 110 3
22 M	1209 0525 1203* 0621*	2.6 0.6 3.7 0.0	79 18 113 0
23 Tu	1253 0607 1247* 0704*	2.7 0.6 3.8 -0.1	82 18 116 -3
24 W	0139 0652 0134* 0749*	2.7 0.5 3.8 -0.1	82 15 116 -3
25 Th	0226 0741 0223* 0836*	2.7 0.5 3.8 -0.1	82 15 116 -3
26 F	0315 0834 0316* 0926*	2.8 0.4 3.7 -0.1	85 12 113 -3
27 Sa	0407 0932 0413* 1018*	3.0 0.4 3.6 -0.1	91 12 110 -3
28 Su ◑	0500 1035 0512* 1111*	3.1 0.3 3.4 0.0	94 9 104 0
29 M	0555 1140 0614*	3.3 0.2 3.3	101 6 101
30 Tu	1206 0650 1246* 0717*	0.0 3.5 0.1 3.1	0 107 3 94

December

Day	Time (h m)	Height (ft)	Height (cm)
1 W	0101 0746 0150* 0821*	0.1 3.7 0.0 3.0	3 113 0 91
2 Th	0155 0841 0250* 0924*	0.1 3.9 -0.2 2.9	3 119 -6 88
3 F	0249 0935 0348* 1024*	0.1 4.0 -0.3 2.9	3 122 -9 88
4 Sa	0341 1028 0441* 1120*	0.2 4.1 -0.4 2.9	6 125 -12 88
5 Su ●	0433 1119 0532*	0.2 4.1 -0.4	6 125 -12
6 M	1213 0523 1208* 0621*	2.9 0.3 4.0 -0.3	88 9 122 -9
7 Tu	0102 0612 1257* 0709*	2.8 0.3 3.9 -0.2	85 9 119 -6
8 W	0149 0702 0144* 0755*	2.8 0.4 3.8 -0.1	85 12 116 -3
9 Th	0235 0751 0230* 0841*	2.8 0.5 3.6 0.0	85 15 110 0
10 F	0319 0842 0317* 0927*	2.8 0.6 3.4 0.1	85 18 104 3
11 Sa	0403 0935 0405* 1013*	2.8 0.6 3.2 0.3	85 18 98 9
12 Su	0448 1030 0454* 1059*	2.9 0.7 3.0 0.4	88 21 91 12
13 M ◐	0532 1127 0545* 1145*	3.0 0.7 2.8 0.5	91 21 85 15
14 Tu	0618 1224* 0638*	3.0 0.6 2.6	91 18 79
15 W	1231 0704 0120* 0732*	0.6 3.1 0.6 2.5	18 94 18 76
16 Th	0116 0750 0212* 0825*	0.7 3.2 0.5 2.5	21 98 15 76
17 F	0200 0835 0300* 0917*	0.7 3.3 0.4 2.4	21 101 12 73
18 Sa	0244 0921 0345* 1006*	0.7 3.5 0.2 2.5	21 107 6 76
19 Su	0328 1006 0429* 1054*	0.6 3.6 0.1 2.5	18 110 3 76
20 M	0411 1052 0512* 1140*	0.6 3.7 0.0 2.5	18 113 0 76
21 Tu ○	0456 1138 0556*	0.4 3.8 -0.2	12 116 -6
22 W	1227 0543 1226* 0641*	2.6 0.3 3.9 -0.2	79 9 119 -6
23 Th	0114 0633 0115* 0726*	2.8 0.2 3.9 -0.3	85 6 119 -9
24 F	0202 0725 0207* 0814*	2.9 0.2 3.8 -0.3	88 6 116 -9
25 Sa	0252 0821 0301* 0902*	3.1 0.1 3.7 -0.3	94 3 113 -9
26 Su	0344 0920 0358* 0953*	3.2 0.1 3.5 -0.2	98 3 107 -6
27 M	0438 1022 0457* 1046*	3.4 0.1 3.3 -0.1	104 3 101 -3
28 Tu ◑	0533 1127 0600* 1141*	3.6 0.0 3.1 0.0	110 0 94 0
29 W	0629 1233* 0704*	3.7 0.0 2.9	113 0 88
30 Th	1237 0727 0138* 0810*	0.1 3.8 -0.1 2.8	3 116 -3 85
31 F	0134 0825 0239* 0914*	0.2 3.9 -0.1 2.7	6 119 -3 82

Heights are referred to mean lower low water which is the chart datum of soundings. All times are local. Daylight Saving Time has been used when needed.

Boston, Massachusetts, 2010

Times and Heights of High and Low Waters

March

Day	Time (h m)	ft	cm	Time (h m)	ft	cm	Time (h m)	ft	cm	Time (h m)	ft	cm
1 M	0509	-1.6	-49	1124	11.8	360	0537*	-1.8	-55	1150*	11.5	351
2 Tu	0601	-1.8	-55	1215*	11.6	354	0624*	-1.6	-49			
3 W	1238	11.6	354	0651	-1.7	-52	0105*	11.2	341	0712*	-1.2	-37
4 Th	0126	11.4	347	0742	-1.3	-40	0156*	10.5	320	0800*	-0.6	-18
5 F	0215	11.0	335	0834	-0.8	-24	0249*	9.8	299	0850*	0.1	3
6 Sa	0307	10.5	320	0929	-0.1	-3	0344*	9.1	277	0943*	0.9	27
7 Su ◑	0402	9.9	302	1027	0.6	18	0444*	8.5	259	1040*	1.5	46
8 M	0501	9.4	287	1129	1.0	30	0547*	8.1	247	1141*	1.8	55
9 Tu	0604	9.1	277	1234*	1.3	40	0652*	8.0	244			
10 W	1244	1.9	58	0707	9.0	274	0136*	1.3	40	0751*	8.1	247
11 Th	0143	1.8	55	0805	9.1	277	0229*	1.1	34	0843*	8.4	256
12 F	0236	1.5	46	0855	9.3	283	0314*	0.9	27	0927*	8.7	265
13 Sa	0322	1.1	34	0940	9.5	290	0352*	0.7	21	1006*	9.1	277
14 Su	0504	0.8	24	1120	9.7	296	0528*	0.5	15	1141*	9.4	287
15 M ●	0543	0.5	15	1158	9.8	299	0603*	0.4	12			
16 Tu	1216	9.7	296	0621	0.2	6	1234*	9.8	299	0639*	0.3	9
17 W	1249	9.9	302	0659	0.0	0	0111*	9.7	296	0715*	0.4	12
18 Th	0124	10.0	305	0738	0.0	0	0149*	9.6	293	0752*	0.5	15
19 F	0200	10.1	308	0818	0.0	0	0228*	9.4	287	0831*	0.6	18
20 Sa	0239	10.1	308	0902	0.1	3	0311*	9.1	277	0914*	0.8	24
21 Su	0322	10.1	308	0949	0.2	6	0359*	8.8	268	1002*	1.1	34
22 M	0411	10.0	305	1042	0.4	12	0452*	8.6	262	1056*	1.2	37
23 Tu ◐	0507	9.9	302	1140	0.5	15	0552*	8.6	262	1156*	1.3	40
24 W	0609	9.9	302	1242*	0.4	12	0656*	8.7	265			
25 Th	0100	1.1	34	0715	10.1	308	0145*	0.2	6	0800*	9.1	277
26 F	0205	0.6	18	0820	10.4	317	0245*	-0.2	-6	0900*	9.7	296
27 Sa	0307	0.0	0	0922	10.7	326	0342*	-0.6	-18	0956*	10.4	317
28 Su	0405	-0.7	-21	1020	11.1	338	0434*	-1.0	-30	1048*	11.1	338
29 M	0500	-1.2	-37	1115	11.3	344	0524*	-1.2	-37	1138*	11.5	351
30 Tu ○	0552	-1.6	-49	1206*	11.3	344	0612*	-1.2	-37			
31 W	1226	11.7	357	0642	-1.7	-52	1256*	11.1	338	0659*	-0.9	-27

April

Day	Time (h m)	ft	cm	Time (h m)	ft	cm	Time (h m)	ft	cm	Time (h m)	ft	cm
1 Th	0112	11.7	357	0731	-1.6	-49	0145*	10.7	326	0746*	-0.5	-15
2 F	0159	11.4	347	0820	-1.1	-34	0235*	10.2	311	0834*	0.0	0
3 Sa	0247	10.9	332	0909	-0.6	-18	0325*	9.6	293	0923*	0.7	21
4 Su	0336	10.3	314	1001	0.1	3	0417*	9.0	274	1014*	1.2	37
5 M	0429	9.8	299	1055	0.7	21	0513*	8.5	259	1109*	1.7	52
6 Tu ◑	0526	9.3	283	1152	1.2	37	0612*	8.2	250			
7 W	1207	2.0	61	0626	8.9	271	1252*	1.5	46	0711*	8.2	250
8 Th	0107	2.1	64	0727	8.8	268	0150*	1.6	49	0808*	8.3	253
9 F	0206	1.9	58	0824	8.9	271	0242*	1.5	46	0859*	8.6	262
10 Sa	0300	1.6	49	0917	9.0	274	0328*	1.3	40	0944*	9.0	274
11 Su	0348	1.2	37	1004	9.2	280	0410*	1.1	34	1025*	9.4	287
12 M	0432	0.8	24	1047	9.4	287	0449*	0.9	27	1103*	9.7	296
13 Tu	0513	0.4	12	1127	9.5	290	0527*	0.8	24	1139*	10.1	308
14 W ●	0553	0.1	3	1207*	9.6	293	0606*	0.7	21			
15 Th	1216	10.3	314	0633	-0.2	-6	1246*	9.6	293	0644*	0.6	18
16 F	1253	10.5	320	0714	-0.3	-9	0126*	9.6	293	0725*	0.6	18
17 Sa	0132	10.6	323	0756	-0.3	-9	0208*	9.4	287	0807*	0.7	21
18 Su	0215	10.6	323	0842	-0.3	-9	0253*	9.3	283	0853*	0.8	24
19 M	0301	10.5	320	0931	-0.1	-3	0343*	9.1	277	0944*	1.0	30
20 Tu	0353	10.4	317	1024	0.0	0	0438*	9.1	277	1040*	1.1	34
21 W ◐	0451	10.2	311	1121	0.2	6	0537*	9.1	277	1141*	1.1	34
22 Th	0553	10.1	308	1221*	0.2	6	0638*	9.4	287			
23 F	1245	0.9	27	0658	10.1	308	0122*	0.1	3	0739*	9.8	299
24 Sa	0149	0.5	15	0803	10.2	311	0221*	0.0	0	0838*	10.3	314
25 Su	0250	-0.1	-3	0905	10.4	317	0317*	-0.2	-6	0933*	10.8	329
26 M	0348	-0.6	-18	1003	10.5	320	0410*	-0.4	-12	1025*	11.3	344
27 Tu	0443	-1.0	-30	1058	10.6	323	0500*	-0.4	-12	1114*	11.5	351
28 W ○	0534	-1.3	-40	1149	10.6	323	0548*	-0.3	-9			
29 Th	1202	11.6	354	0623	-1.3	-40	1238*	10.4	317	0635*	-0.1	-3
30 F	1248	11.5	351	0711	-1.1	-34	0126*	10.1	308	0722*	0.2	6

May

Day	Time (h m)	ft	cm	Time (h m)	ft	cm	Time (h m)	ft	cm	Time (h m)	ft	cm
1 Sa	0134	11.2	341	0758	-0.7	-21	0213*	9.7	296	0808*	0.6	18
2 Su	0220	10.7	326	0845	-0.2	-6	0301*	9.3	283	0856*	1.1	34
3 M	0308	10.2	311	0933	0.3	9	0350*	9.0	274	0945*	1.5	46
4 Tu	0358	9.7	296	1022	0.8	24	0441*	8.7	265	1037*	1.8	55
5 W	0450	9.3	283	1114	1.2	37	0533*	8.5	259	1131*	2.0	61
6 Th ◑	0545	9.0	274	1206*	1.5	46	0627*	8.5	259			
7 F	1228	2.1	64	0642	8.8	268	1259*	1.6	49	0719*	8.6	262
8 Sa	0124	1.9	58	0738	8.7	265	0150*	1.6	49	0809*	8.9	271
9 Su	0218	1.7	52	0831	8.8	268	0238*	1.6	49	0855*	9.2	280
10 M	0308	1.3	40	0922	8.9	271	0324*	1.4	43	0939*	9.6	293
11 Tu	0355	0.8	24	1009	9.1	277	0407*	1.2	37	1021*	10.0	305
12 W	0440	0.4	12	1053	9.2	280	0450*	1.1	34	1102*	10.3	314
13 Th	0524	0.0	0	1137	9.4	287	0533*	0.9	27	1143*	10.6	323
14 F ●	0607	-0.3	-9	1220*	9.5	290	0616*	0.7	21			
15 Sa	1225	10.9	332	0651	-0.5	-15	0104*	9.6	293	0700*	0.7	21
16 Su	0109	11.0	335	0737	-0.7	-21	0150*	9.6	293	0747*	0.6	18
17 M	0156	11.1	338	0824	-0.7	-21	0239*	9.6	293	0837*	0.6	18
18 Tu	0246	11.0	335	0915	-0.6	-18	0330*	9.6	293	0930*	0.7	21
19 W	0340	10.8	329	1007	-0.4	-12	0424*	9.7	296	1027*	0.7	21
20 Th ◐	0438	10.5	320	1103	-0.2	-6	0521*	9.8	299	1127*	0.7	21
21 F	0539	10.3	314	1200*	0.0	0	0620*	10.0	305			
22 Sa	1230	0.5	15	0642	10.0	305	1258*	0.1	3	0718*	10.3	314
23 Su	0133	0.3	9	0746	9.9	302	0156*	0.2	6	0815*	10.7	326
24 M	0234	-0.1	-3	0848	9.8	299	0252*	0.2	6	0910*	10.9	332
25 Tu	0332	-0.4	-12	0946	9.8	299	0346*	0.3	9	1003*	11.1	338
26 W	0427	-0.6	-18	1042	9.8	299	0437*	0.3	9	1053*	11.2	341
27 Th ○	0518	-0.7	-21	1133	9.8	299	0526*	0.4	12	1141*	11.2	341
28 F	0606	-0.7	-21	1222*	9.7	296	0613*	0.6	18			
29 Sa	1227	11.0	335	0652	-0.5	-15	0108*	9.6	293	0659*	0.8	24
30 Su	0112	10.8	329	0737	-0.3	-9	0153*	9.4	287	0744*	1.0	30
31 M	0156	10.5	320	0821	0.0	0	0237*	9.2	280	0830*	1.3	40

June

Day	Time (h m)	ft	cm	Time (h m)	ft	cm	Time (h m)	ft	cm	Time (h m)	ft	cm
1 Tu	0241	10.1	308	0905	0.4	12	0321*	9.0	274	0916*	1.5	46
2 W	0328	9.8	299	0949	0.7	21	0407*	8.9	271	1004*	1.7	52
3 Th	0415	9.4	287	1035	1.1	34	0454*	8.9	271	1054*	1.8	55
4 F ◑	0505	9.1	277	1122	1.3	40	0541*	8.9	271	1147*	1.9	58
5 Sa	0557	8.8	268	1210*	1.5	46	0630*	9.0	274			
6 Su	1240	1.8	55	0651	8.6	262	1259*	1.6	49	0718*	9.2	280
7 M	0134	1.6	49	0744	8.5	259	0149*	1.7	52	0806*	9.4	287
8 Tu	0227	1.3	40	0837	8.6	262	0238*	1.6	49	0853*	9.8	299
9 W	0317	0.9	27	0929	8.7	265	0326*	1.4	43	0940*	10.1	308
10 Th	0406	0.4	12	1018	8.9	271	0414*	1.2	37	1026*	10.5	320
11 F	0454	-0.1	-3	1107	9.2	280	0502*	0.9	27	1113*	10.9	332
12 Sa ●	0542	-0.5	-15	1155	9.4	287	0550*	0.6	18			
13 Su	1201	11.2	341	0629	-0.8	-24	1243*	9.7	296	0639*	0.4	12
14 M	1249	11.4	347	0717	-1.0	-30	0132*	9.9	302	0729*	0.2	6
15 Tu	0140	11.5	351	0807	-1.1	-34	0222*	10.1	308	0821*	0.1	3
16 W	0232	11.4	347	0857	-1.0	-30	0314*	10.3	314	0915*	0.1	3
17 Th	0327	11.1	338	0949	-0.8	-24	0407*	10.4	317	1012*	0.1	3
18 F	0424	10.7	326	1042	-0.5	-15	0502*	10.5	320	1111*	0.2	6
19 Sa ◐	0524	10.3	314	1137	-0.1	-3	0558*	10.6	323			
20 Su	1213	0.2	6	0625	9.8	299	1234*	0.2	6	0656*	10.6	323
21 M	0115	0.2	6	0728	9.5	290	0132*	0.5	15	0753*	10.7	326
22 Tu	0217	0.1	3	0831	9.3	283	0229*	0.7	21	0850*	10.7	326
23 W	0316	0.0	0	0931	9.2	280	0324*	0.9	27	0944*	10.7	326
24 Th	0412	-0.1	-3	1027	9.2	280	0417*	0.9	27	1035*	10.7	326
25 F	0503	-0.2	-6	1118	9.2	280	0506*	1.0	30	1123*	10.7	326
26 Sa ○	0550	-0.2	-6	1205*	9.2	280	0553*	1.0	30			
27 Su	1209	10.6	323	0633	-0.1	-3	1249*	9.2	280	0638*	1.0	30
28 M	1252	10.5	320	0715	0.0	0	0130*	9.2	280	0721*	1.1	34
29 Tu	0134	10.3	314	0755	0.2	6	0210*	9.2	280	0804*	1.2	37
30 W	0215	10.0	305	0835	0.4	12	0250*	9.2	280	0847*	1.3	40

July

Day	Time (h m)	ft	cm	Time (h m)	ft	cm	Time (h m)	ft	cm	Time (h m)	ft	cm
1 Th	0258	9.8	299	0915	0.6	18	0331*	9.2	280	0932*	1.4	43
2 F	0341	9.4	287	0956	0.9	27	0413*	9.2	280	1018*	1.5	46
3 Sa	0427	9.1	277	1039	1.2	37	0457*	9.2	280	1107*	1.6	49
4 Su ◑	0516	8.8	268	1125	1.4	43	0542*	9.2	280	1158*	1.6	49
5 M	0607	8.5	259	1213*	1.6	49	0630*	9.4	287			
6 Tu	1251	1.5	46	0700	8.4	256	0104*	1.7	52	0720*	9.6	293
7 W	0146	1.2	37	0755	8.4	256	0156*	1.6	49	0811*	9.9	302
8 Th	0241	0.8	24	0851	8.5	259	0249*	1.4	43	0903*	10.2	311
9 F	0334	0.4	12	0945	8.8	268	0342*	1.1	34	0955*	10.7	326
10 Sa	0426	-0.2	-6	1038	9.2	280	0435*	0.7	21	1047*	11.2	341
11 Su ●	0517	-0.7	-21	1130	9.6	293	0527*	0.2	6	1139*	11.5	351
12 M	0607	-1.1	-34	1220*	10.0	305	0619*	-0.2	-6			
13 Tu	1231	11.8	360	0656	-1.4	-43	0111*	10.4	317	0711*	-0.5	-15
14 W	0123	11.8	360	0746	-1.5	-46	0201*	10.8	329	0804*	-0.6	-18
15 Th	0216	11.6	354	0836	-1.4	-43	0252*	10.9	332	0858*	-0.6	-18
16 F	0311	11.2	341	0926	-1.0	-30	0344*	11.0	335	0954*	-0.5	-15
17 Sa	0407	10.7	326	1019	-0.6	-18	0438*	10.9	332	1052*	-0.3	-9
18 Su ◐	0506	10.1	308	1113	0.0	0	0534*	10.8	329	1153*	0.0	0
19 M	0607	9.5	290	1210*	0.5	15	0632*	10.6	323			
20 Tu	1256	0.2	6	0710	9.1	277	0108*	0.9	27	0731*	10.4	317
21 W	0159	0.4	12	0814	8.8	268	0208*	1.2	37	0831*	10.3	314
22 Th	0300	0.4	12	0916	8.7	265	0305*	1.3	40	0927*	10.3	314
23 F	0357	0.4	12	1012	8.8	268	0359*	1.3	40	1020*	10.3	314
24 Sa	0447	0.3	9	1102	8.9	271	0448*	1.2	37	1107*	10.3	314
25 Su	0531	0.3	9	1146	9.0	274	0534*	1.1	34	1151*	10.3	314
26 M ○	0612	0.2	6	1226*	9.1	277	0616*	1.0	30			
27 Tu	1231	10.2	311	0649	0.3	9	0103*	9.2	280	0657*	1.0	30
28 W	0110	10.1	308	0726	0.3	9	0140*	9.3	283	0738*	0.9	27
29 Th	0149	9.9	302	0803	0.4	12	0216*	9.4	287	0818*	1.0	30
30 F	0228	9.7	296	0840	0.6	18	0254*	9.4	287	0900*	1.0	30
31 Sa	0309	9.4	287	0919	0.9	27	0333*	9.4	287	0943*	1.1	34

August

Day	Time (h m)	ft	cm	Time (h m)	ft	cm	Time (h m)	ft	cm	Time (h m)	ft	cm
1 Su	0352	9.1	277	1000	1.1	34	0414*	9.4	287	1029*	1.2	37
2 M	0438	8.7	265	1044	1.4	43	0459*	9.4	287	1119*	1.3	40
3 Tu ◑	0528	8.5	259	1132	1.6	49	0547*	9.5	290			
4 W	1213	1.3	40	0622	8.3	253	1225*	1.7	52	0640*	9.6	293
5 Th	0110	1.1	34	0719	8.3	253	0121*	1.6	49	0736*	9.9	302
6 F	0208	0.8	24	0818	8.5	259	0218*	1.3	40	0833*	10.3	314
7 Sa	0305	0.3	9	0916	8.9	271	0316*	0.9	27	0930*	10.8	329
8 Su	0400	-0.3	-9	1012	9.4	287	0412*	0.3	9	1025*	11.3	344
9 M	0453	-0.9	-27	1105	10.0	305	0506*	-0.3	-9	1120*	11.7	357
10 Tu ●	0543	-1.3	-40	1156	10.6	323	0559*	-0.8	-24			
11 W	1213	11.9	363	0633	-1.6	-49	1246*	11.1	338	0652*	-1.1	-34
12 Th	0106	11.9	363	0722	-1.6	-49	0136*	11.4	347	0745*	-1.3	-40
13 F	0158	11.6	354	0811	-1.4	-43	0226*	11.5	351	0838*	-1.2	-37
14 Sa	0252	11.1	338	0901	-1.0	-30	0318*	11.4	347	0933*	-0.9	-27
15 Su	0347	10.5	320	0953	-0.4	-12	0411*	11.1	338	1030*	-0.4	-12
16 M ◐	0445	9.8	299	1047	0.3	9	0508*	10.7	326	1130*	0.1	3
17 Tu	0547	9.2	280	1145	0.9	27	0607*	10.3	314			
18 W	1233	0.5	15	0651	8.8	268	1245*	1.3	40	0709*	10.0	305
19 Th	0138	0.7	21	0755	8.6	262	0147*	1.5	46	0811*	9.8	299
20 F	0241	0.8	24	0857	8.5	259	0246*	1.6	49	0909*	9.8	299
21 Sa	0337	0.8	24	0952	8.7	265	0340*	1.4	43	1001*	9.9	302
22 Su	0425	0.7	21	1039	8.9	271	0429*	1.2	37	1048*	10.0	305
23 M	0507	0.6	18	1120	9.1	277	0512*	1.0	30	1129*	10.0	305
24 Tu ○	0544	0.5	15	1157	9.3	283	0553*	0.8	24			
25 W	1208	10.0	305	0619	0.5	15	1232*	9.5	290	0632*	0.7	21
26 Th	1245	10.0	305	0654	0.5	15	0107*	9.6	293	0711*	0.6	18
27 F	0122	9.8	299	0730	0.6	18	0141*	9.7	296	0749*	0.6	18
28 Sa	0200	9.6	293	0806	0.7	21	0217*	9.7	296	0829*	0.7	21
29 Su	0239	9.3	283	0844	0.9	27	0255*	9.7	296	0911*	0.8	24
30 M	0321	9.0	274	0925	1.2	37	0335*	9.7	296	0956*	0.9	27
31 Tu	0406	8.7	265	1009	1.4	43	0420*	9.6	293	1046*	1.0	30

September

Day	Time (h m)	ft	cm	Time (h m)	ft	cm	Time (h m)	ft	cm	Time (h m)	ft	cm
1 W ◑	0456	8.5	259	1058	1.6	49	0511*	9.6	293	1141*	1.1	34
2 Th	0551	8.3	253	1153	1.6	49	0607*	9.7	296			
3 F	1239	0.9	27	0651	8.4	256	1253*	1.5	46	0707*	10.0	305
4 Sa	0140	0.6	18	0751	8.7	265	0154*	1.2	37	0808*	10.4	317
5 Su	0239	0.1	3	0851	9.2	280	0254*	0.6	18	0908*	10.8	329
6 M	0335	-0.4	-12	0947	9.9	302	0352*	-0.1	-3	1006*	11.3	344
7 Tu	0428	-0.9	-27	1040	10.6	323	0447*	-0.8	-24	1101*	11.6	354
8 W ●	0518	-1.3	-40	1131	11.2	341	0541*	-1.3	-40	1154*	11.8	360
9 Th	0608	-1.5	-46	1221*	11.7	357	0633*	-1.6	-49			
10 F	1247	11.7	357	0657	-1.4	-43	0110*	11.9	363	0725*	-1.7	-52
11 Sa	0139	11.4	347	0746	-1.1	-34	0159*	11.8	360	0817*	-1.4	-43
12 Su	0232	10.8	329	0835	-0.6	-18	0250*	11.5	351	0911*	-1.0	-30
13 M	0326	10.2	311	0927	0.0	0	0343*	11.0	335	1006*	-0.4	-12
14 Tu	0423	9.6	293	1021	0.7	21	0440*	10.5	320	1105*	0.2	6
15 W ◐	0523	9.0	274	1119	1.3	40	0540*	10.0	305			
16 Th	1207	0.7	21	0627	8.6	262	1220*	1.7	52	0643*	9.6	293
17 F	0111	1.0	30	0730	8.5	259	0122*	1.8	55	0745*	9.4	287
18 Sa	0213	1.1	34	0830	8.5	259	0223*	1.7	52	0844*	9.4	287
19 Su	0307	1.1	34	0922	8.7	265	0317*	1.5	46	0935*	9.5	290
20 M	0353	1.0	30	1007	9.0	274	0404*	1.2	37	1021*	9.7	296
21 Tu	0433	0.8	24	1047	9.3	283	0447*	0.9	27	1102*	9.7	296
22 W	0510	0.7	21	1123	9.6	293	0527*	0.6	18	1141*	9.8	299
23 Th ○	0546	0.7	21	1158	9.8	299	0605*	0.4	12			
24 F	1218	9.7	296	0621	0.7	21	1232*	10.0	305	0643*	0.3	9
25 Sa	1255	9.6	293	0657	0.8	24	0107*	10.0	305	0722*	0.3	9
26 Su	0133	9.4	287	0734	0.9	27	0143*	10.0	305	0802*	0.3	9
27 M	0212	9.2	280	0813	1.1	34	0221*	10.0	305	0844*	0.4	12
28 Tu	0254	9.0	274	0855	1.3	40	0303*	9.9	302	0929*	0.6	18
29 W	0340	8.8	268	0941	1.4	43	0350*	9.9	302	1019*	0.7	21
30 Th	0431	8.6	262	1032	1.6	49	0443*	9.8	299	1115*	0.8	24

October

Day	Time (h m)	ft	cm	Time (h m)	ft	cm	Time (h m)	ft	cm	Time (h m)	ft	cm
1 F ◑	0528	8.6	262	1130	1.6	49	0542*	9.9	302			
2 Sa	1214	0.7	21	0628	8.7	265	1232*	1.4	43	0645*	10.0	305
3 Su	0114	0.4	12	0729	9.2	280	0134*	0.9	27	0748*	10.3	314
4 M	0213	0.0	0	0828	9.8	299	0236*	0.3	9	0849*	10.7	326
5 Tu	0309	-0.4	-12	0923	10.5	320	0334*	-0.4	-12	0947*	11.0	335
6 W	0402	-0.8	-24	1016	11.1	338	0429*	-1.1	-34	1043*	11.2	341
7 Th ●	0453	-1.0	-30	1106	11.7	357	0523*	-1.5	-46	1136*	11.3	344
8 F	0543	-1.1	-34	1156	12.0	366	0614*	-1.8	-55			
9 Sa	1228	11.2	341	0632	-0.9	-27	1244*	12.0	366	0705*	-1.7	-52
10 Su	0119	10.9	332	0720	-0.6	-18	0133*	11.8	360	0756*	-1.4	-43
11 M	0211	10.4	317	0810	-0.1	-3	0223*	11.4	347	0847*	-0.9	-27
12 Tu	0304	9.9	302	0901	0.5	15	0316*	10.8	329	0941*	-0.2	-6
13 W	0359	9.3	283	0954	1.0	30	0410*	10.2	311	1036*	0.4	12
14 Th ◐	0456	8.9	271	1050	1.5	46	0508*	9.7	296	1134*	0.9	27
15 F	0556	8.6	262	1150	1.9	58	0609*	9.3	283			
16 Sa	1234	1.2	37	0655	8.5	259	1251*	2.0	61	0710*	9.1	277
17 Su	0132	1.4	43	0752	8.6	262	0150*	1.8	55	0808*	9.1	277
18 M	0225	1.4	43	0842	8.9	271	0244*	1.6	49	0900*	9.1	277
19 Tu	0311	1.3	40	0927	9.2	280	0333*	1.2	37	0947*	9.2	280
20 W	0353	1.1	34	1008	9.5	290	0417*	0.8	24	1030*	9.4	287
21 Th	0432	1.0	30	1046	9.8	299	0458*	0.5	15	1111*	9.4	287
22 F	0510	0.9	27	1122	10.0	305	0537*	0.3	9	1150*	9.4	287
23 Sa ○	0548	0.9	27	1158	10.2	311	0616*	0.1	3			
24 Su	1229	9.4	287	0626	0.9	27	1235*	10.3	314	0656*	0.0	0
25 M	0108	9.3	283	0705	1.0	30	0113*	10.4	317	0737*	0.0	0
26 Tu	0149	9.2	280	0747	1.0	30	0154*	10.4	317	0821*	0.0	0
27 W	0233	9.0	274	0831	1.1	34	0238*	10.3	314	0908*	0.1	3
28 Th	0320	8.9	271	0919	1.2	37	0328*	10.2	311	0958*	0.2	6
29 F	0412	8.9	271	1013	1.3	40	0423*	10.1	308	1053*	0.3	9
30 Sa ◑	0508	9.0	274	1111	1.3	40	0522*	10.0	305	1150*	0.3	9
31 Su	0607	9.2	280	1214*	1.0	30	0625*	10.0	305			

November

Day	Time (h m)	ft	cm	Time (h m)	ft	cm	Time (h m)	ft	cm	Time (h m)	ft	cm
1 M	1249	0.2	6	0707	9.7	296	0117*	0.6	18	0729*	10.1	308
2 Tu	0148	0.0	0	0805	10.2	311	0218*	0.1	3	0831*	10.3	314
3 W	0244	-0.2	-6	0900	10.8	329	0317*	-0.6	-18	0930*	10.4	317
4 Th	0338	-0.4	-12	0953	11.4	347	0413*	-1.1	-34	1026*	10.6	323
5 F	0430	-0.5	-15	1044	11.7	357	0506*	-1.4	-43	1120*	10.6	323
6 Sa ●	0520	-0.5	-15	1134	11.9	363	0557*	-1.6	-49			
7 Su	1211	10.5	320	0509	-0.4	-12	1122	11.8	360	0547*	-1.5	-46
8 M	1201	10.3	314	0558	-0.1	-3	1211*	11.5	351	0636*	-1.1	-34
9 Tu	1251	9.9	302	0646	0.3	9	1259*	11.1	338	0725*	-0.7	-21
10 W	0141	9.6	293	0735	0.7	21	0149*	10.6	323	0814*	-0.1	-3
11 Th	0232	9.2	280	0826	1.2	37	0240*	10.0	305	0905*	0.4	12
12 F	0324	8.9	271	0919	1.6	49	0333*	9.5	290	0957*	0.9	27
13 Sa ◐	0418	8.6	262	1014	1.8	55	0429*	9.1	277	1050*	1.3	40
14 Su	0511	8.6	262	1112	1.9	58	0526*	8.8	268	1143*	1.5	46
15 M	0604	8.7	265	1209*	1.9	58	0623*	8.7	265			
16 Tu	1234	1.5	46	0654	8.9	271	0104*	1.6	49	0717*	8.7	265
17 W	0123	1.5	46	0741	9.2	280	0155*	1.3	40	0808*	8.7	265
18 Th	0208	1.4	43	0825	9.5	290	0242*	0.9	27	0855*	8.8	268
19 F	0252	1.3	40	0907	9.8	299	0326*	0.5	15	0939*	9.0	274
20 Sa	0334	1.2	37	0947	10.1	308	0409*	0.2	6	1022*	9.1	277
21 Su ○	0416	1.0	30	1027	10.4	317	0451*	-0.1	-3	1104*	9.2	280
22 M	0457	0.9	27	1107	10.6	323	0533*	-0.3	-9	1146*	9.2	280
23 Tu	0540	0.8	24	1149	10.7	326	0616*	-0.5	-15			
24 W	1229	9.3	283	0624	0.7	21	1233*	10.8	329	0701*	-0.5	-15
25 Th	0114	9.3	283	0711	0.7	21	0120*	10.7	326	0749*	-0.5	-15
26 F	0202	9.3	283	0802	0.7	21	0211*	10.6	323	0839*	-0.4	-12
27 Sa	0254	9.4	287	0856	0.7	21	0306*	10.3	314	0931*	-0.2	-6
28 Su ◑	0349	9.6	293	0954	0.7	21	0405*	10.1	308	1027*	-0.1	-3
29 M	0446	9.8	299	1056	0.6	18	0507*	9.9	302	1124*	0.1	3
30 Tu	0544	10.1	308	1159	0.3	9	0611*	9.7	296			

December

Day	Time (h m)	ft	cm	Time (h m)	ft	cm	Time (h m)	ft	cm	Time (h m)	ft	cm
1 W	1223	0.1	3	0642	10.5	320	0101*	-0.1	-3	0714*	9.7	296
2 Th	0120	0.1	3	0739	10.9	332	0202*	-0.5	-15	0815*	9.7	296
3 F	0216	0.1	3	0833	11.2	341	0258*	-0.8	-24	0912*	9.8	299
4 Sa	0309	0.0	0	0926	11.4	347	0352*	-1.1	-34	1006*	9.8	299
5 Su ●	0401	0.0	0	1016	11.4	347	0442*	-1.1	-34	1057*	9.8	299
6 M	0450	0.1	3	1105	11.3	344	0530*	-1.1	-34	1145*	9.7	296
7 Tu	0538	0.2	6	1152	11.1	338	0617*	-0.8	-24			
8 W	1232	9.5	290	0624	0.5	15	1237*	10.8	329	0702*	-0.5	-15
9 Th	0117	9.3	283	0711	0.7	21	0123*	10.4	317	0746*	-0.1	-3
10 F	0203	9.1	277	0758	1.0	30	0209*	9.9	302	0831*	0.3	9
11 Sa	0248	9.0	274	0846	1.3	40	0257*	9.4	287	0917*	0.7	21
12 Su	0335	8.8	268	0936	1.6	49	0347*	9.0	274	1004*	1.1	34
13 M ◐	0423	8.8	268	1029	1.7	52	0440*	8.6	262	1052*	1.4	43
14 Tu	0512	8.8	268	1123	1.7	52	0534*	8.3	253	1142*	1.6	49
15 W	0602	8.9	271	1218*	1.6	49	0629*	8.2	250			
16 Th	1233	1.7	52	0652	9.1	277	0113*	1.4	43	0724*	8.2	250
17 F	0123	1.6	49	0740	9.4	287	0204*	1.0	30	0816*	8.3	253
18 Sa	0212	1.5	46	0827	9.7	296	0253*	0.6	18	0906*	8.5	259
19 Su	0259	1.3	40	0913	10.1	308	0340*	0.1	3	0953*	8.8	268
20 M	0346	1.0	30	0958	10.5	320	0425*	-0.3	-9	1038*	9.0	274
21 Tu ○	0432	0.7	21	1043	10.8	329	0510*	-0.7	-21	1123*	9.3	283
22 W	0518	0.4	12	1129	11.1	338	0556*	-1.0	-30			
23 Th	1209	9.6	293	0605	0.1	3	1216*	11.2	341	0642*	-1.1	-34
24 F	1255	9.8	299	0654	0.0	0	0104*	11.1	338	0729*	-1.1	-34
25 Sa	0143	10.0	305	0745	-0.1	-3	0155*	10.9	332	0818*	-1.0	-30
26 Su	0233	10.1	308	0839	-0.1	-3	0250*	10.6	323	0909*	-0.7	-21
27 M	0326	10.2	311	0937	0.0	0	0347*	10.1	308	1003*	-0.3	-9
28 Tu ◑	0422	10.3	314	1037	0.0	0	0449*	9.6	293	1059*	0.0	0
29 W	0520	10.4	317	1140	0.0	0	0553*	9.3	283	1158*	0.3	9
30 Th	0619	10.4	317	1244*	0.0	0	0658*	9.1	277			
31 F	1258	0.5	15	0719	10.5	320	0147*	-0.2	-6	0802*	9.0	274

Heights are referred to mean lower low water which is the chart datum of soundings. All times are local. Daylight Saving Time has been used when needed.

Portland, Casco Bay, Maine, 2010

Times and Heights of High and Low Waters

March

Day	Time (h m)	Height (ft)	Height (cm)
1 M	0458	–1.5	–46
	1113	11.3	344
	0526*	–1.7	–52
	1140*	11.1	338
2 Tu	0550	–1.7	–52
	1204*	11.1	338
	0614*	–1.5	–46
3 W	1228	11.1	338
	0641	–1.6	–49
	1255*	10.7	326
	0701*	–1.1	–34
4 Th	0116	10.9	332
	0733	–1.3	–40
	0147*	10.1	308
	0750*	–0.5	–15
5 F	0206	10.5	320
	0827	–0.7	–21
	0242*	9.3	283
	0842*	0.2	6
6 Sa	0258	10.0	305
	0924	–0.1	–3
	0339*	8.7	265
	0937*	0.9	27
7 Su	0355	9.4	287
	1026	0.4	12
	0442*	8.1	247
	1038*	1.4	43
8 M	0457	8.9	271
	1131	0.8	24
	0548*	7.8	238
	1144*	1.7	52
9 Tu	0603	8.7	265
	1237*	1.0	30
	0653*	7.7	235
10 W	1249	1.8	55
	0706	8.6	262
	0137*	1.0	30
	0751*	7.9	241
11 Th	0148	1.6	49
	0803	8.8	268
	0228*	0.9	27
	0841*	8.1	247
12 F	0239	1.3	40
	0853	9.0	274
	0313*	0.7	21
	0924*	8.4	256
13 Sa	0323	1.0	30
	0936	9.1	277
	0351*	0.5	15
	1001*	8.8	268
14 Su	0503	0.7	21
	1114	9.3	283
	0525*	0.4	12
	1135*	9.0	274
15 M	0539	0.4	12
	1150	9.3	283
	0557*	0.4	12
16 Tu	1206	9.3	283
	0613	0.2	6
	1224*	9.3	283
	0627*	0.4	12
17 W	1237	9.5	290
	0646	0.1	3
	1257*	9.2	280
	0658*	0.4	12
18 Th	0108	9.6	293
	0721	0.0	0
	0132*	9.1	277
	0731*	0.5	15
19 F	0142	9.7	296
	0758	0.0	0
	0210*	8.9	271
	0807*	0.6	18
20 Sa	0219	9.7	296
	0840	0.1	3
	0251*	8.6	262
	0849*	0.8	24
21 Su	0302	9.7	296
	0926	0.2	6
	0339*	8.4	256
	0936*	1.0	30
22 M	0350	9.6	293
	1019	0.3	9
	0433*	8.2	250
	1030*	1.2	37
23 Tu	0447	9.5	290
	1119	0.4	12
	0535*	8.1	247
	1133*	1.2	37
24 W	0551	9.5	290
	1225*	0.4	12
	0643*	8.3	253
25 Th	1242	1.1	34
	0700	9.6	293
	0132*	0.2	6
	0750*	8.7	265
26 F	0151	0.7	21
	0809	9.9	302
	0235*	–0.2	–6
	0852*	9.3	283
27 Sa	0257	0.1	3
	0913	10.3	314
	0333*	–0.6	–18
	0949*	10.0	305
28 Su	0356	–0.6	–18
	1012	10.6	323
	0426*	–1.0	–30
	1040*	10.7	326
29 M	0451	–1.2	–37
	1106	10.8	329
	0515*	–1.2	–37
	1129*	11.1	338
30 Tu	0543	–1.6	–49
	1158	10.8	329
	0603*	–1.1	–34
31 W	1216	11.3	344
	0633	–1.7	–52
	1247*	10.6	323
	0649*	–0.9	–27

April

Day	Time (h m)	Height (ft)	Height (cm)
1 Th	0103	11.2	341
	0722	–1.5	–46
	0137*	10.2	311
	0736*	–0.4	–12
2 F	0149	10.9	332
	0812	–1.1	–34
	0227*	9.7	296
	0824*	0.1	3
3 Sa	0237	10.5	320
	0903	–0.6	–18
	0318*	9.1	277
	0914*	0.7	21
4 Su	0327	9.9	302
	0956	0.1	3
	0413*	8.6	262
	1007*	1.3	40
5 M	0421	9.3	283
	1053	0.6	18
	0511*	8.1	247
	1105*	1.7	52
6 Tu	0520	8.8	268
	1153	1.0	30
	0611*	7.9	241
7 W	1208	2.0	61
	0623	8.5	259
	1254*	1.3	40
	0712*	7.8	238
8 Th	0111	2.0	61
	0725	8.4	256
	0152*	1.3	40
	0808*	8.0	244
9 F	0210	1.8	55
	0823	8.5	259
	0244*	1.3	40
	0858*	8.3	253
10 Sa	0303	1.5	46
	0914	8.6	262
	0329*	1.1	34
	0942*	8.6	262
11 Su	0349	1.1	34
	1000	8.8	268
	0408*	1.0	30
	1020*	9.0	274
12 M	0430	0.7	21
	1041	9.0	274
	0444*	0.8	24
	1055*	9.4	287
13 Tu	0508	0.4	12
	1119	9.1	277
	0518*	0.7	21
	1129*	9.6	293
14 W	0544	0.1	3
	1156	9.1	277
	0551*	0.7	21
15 Th	1202	9.9	302
	0620	–0.1	–3
	1232*	9.1	277
	0626*	0.7	21
16 F	1237	10.1	308
	0657	–0.2	–6
	0110*	9.0	274
	0703*	0.7	21
17 Sa	0114	10.2	311
	0737	–0.3	–9
	0151*	9.0	274
	0744*	0.8	24
18 Su	0155	10.2	311
	0821	–0.2	–6
	0236*	8.8	268
	0829*	0.9	27
19 M	0242	10.1	308
	0910	–0.1	–3
	0326*	8.7	265
	0920*	1.0	30
20 Tu	0334	10.0	305
	1004	0.0	0
	0422*	8.7	265
	1018*	1.1	34
21 W	0433	9.8	299
	1103	0.1	3
	0523*	8.7	265
	1122*	1.1	34
22 Th	0537	9.7	296
	1207*	0.2	6
	0627*	8.9	271
23 F	1230	0.9	27
	0646	9.7	296
	0110*	0.1	3
	0731*	9.3	283
24 Sa	0139	0.5	15
	0754	9.8	299
	0212*	–0.1	–3
	0831*	9.9	302
25 Su	0243	0.0	0
	0858	9.9	302
	0309*	–0.3	–9
	0927*	10.4	317
26 M	0343	–0.6	–18
	0956	10.1	308
	0402*	–0.4	–12
	1018*	10.9	332
27 Tu	0437	–1.0	–30
	1051	10.2	311
	0452*	–0.4	–12
	1107*	11.2	341
28 W	0528	–1.3	–40
	1142	10.1	308
	0540*	–0.3	–9
	1154*	11.2	341
29 Th	0617	–1.3	–40
	1231*	10.0	305
	0626*	–0.1	–3
30 F	1239	11.1	338
	0705	–1.1	–34
	0119*	9.7	296
	0712*	0.3	9

May

Day	Time (h m)	Height (ft)	Height (cm)
1 Sa	0125	10.7	326
	0752	–0.7	–21
	0207*	9.3	283
	0759*	0.7	21
2 Su	0211	10.3	314
	0839	–0.3	–9
	0255*	8.9	271
	0847*	1.1	34
3 M	0258	9.8	299
	0928	0.2	6
	0345*	8.6	262
	0937*	1.5	46
4 Tu	0348	9.3	283
	1018	0.7	21
	0437*	8.3	253
	1030*	1.8	55
5 W	0442	8.9	271
	1111	1.1	34
	0530*	8.1	247
	1127*	2.0	61
6 Th	0538	8.6	262
	1204*	1.3	40
	0624*	8.1	247
7 F	1226	2.0	61
	0636	8.4	256
	1257*	1.5	46
	0716*	8.3	253
8 Sa	0124	1.9	58
	0733	8.3	253
	0148*	1.5	46
	0806*	8.5	259
9 Su	0218	1.6	49
	0826	8.3	253
	0234*	1.5	46
	0851*	8.9	271
10 M	0307	1.3	40
	0916	8.4	256
	0317*	1.4	43
	0933*	9.2	280
11 Tu	0352	0.9	27
	1002	8.6	262
	0357*	1.2	37
	1012*	9.6	293
12 W	0434	0.5	15
	1044	8.7	265
	0436*	1.1	34
	1050*	9.9	302
13 Th	0514	0.1	3
	1126	8.9	271
	0516*	0.9	27
	1129*	10.2	311
14 F	0554	–0.2	–6
	1207*	9.0	274
	0556*	0.8	24
15 Sa	1209	10.5	320
	0636	–0.4	–12
	1250*	9.1	277
	0639*	0.7	21
16 Su	1252	10.6	323
	0720	–0.6	–18
	0135*	9.1	277
	0725*	0.7	21
17 M	0138	10.7	326
	0807	–0.6	–18
	0223*	9.2	280
	0815*	0.7	21
18 Tu	0229	10.6	323
	0858	–0.5	–15
	0316*	9.2	280
	0910*	0.8	24
19 W	0323	10.4	317
	0952	–0.4	–12
	0411*	9.3	283
	1009*	0.8	24
20 Th	0423	10.1	308
	1049	–0.2	–6
	0510*	9.4	287
	1112*	0.8	24
21 F	0526	9.9	302
	1148	–0.1	–3
	0611*	9.6	293
22 Sa	1219	0.6	18
	0632	9.6	293
	1248*	0.1	3
	0711*	9.9	302
23 Su	0126	0.4	12
	0738	9.5	290
	0148*	0.2	6
	0810*	10.3	314
24 M	0230	0.0	0
	0842	9.5	290
	0245*	0.2	6
	0906*	10.6	323
25 Tu	0329	–0.4	–12
	0942	9.5	290
	0340*	0.3	9
	0958*	10.8	329
26 W	0423	–0.6	–18
	1037	9.5	290
	0431*	0.3	9
	1048*	10.9	332
27 Th	0514	–0.8	–24
	1128	9.4	287
	0520*	0.4	12
	1135*	10.8	329
28 F	0602	–0.7	–21
	1216*	9.4	287
	0606*	0.6	18
29 Sa	1220	10.7	326
	0648	–0.6	–18
	0102*	9.2	280
	0652*	0.8	24
30 Su	0104	10.4	317
	0732	–0.3	–9
	0147*	9.0	274
	0736*	1.1	34
31 M	0148	10.1	308
	0816	0.0	0
	0231*	8.8	268
	0821*	1.3	40

June

Day	Time (h m)	Height (ft)	Height (cm)
1 Tu	0232	9.7	296
	0859	0.3	9
	0315*	8.6	262
	0907*	1.6	49
2 W	0317	9.4	287
	0943	0.7	21
	0400*	8.5	259
	0955*	1.7	52
3 Th	0404	9.0	274
	1027	1.0	30
	0446*	8.5	259
	1045*	1.9	58
4 F	0453	8.7	265
	1113	1.2	37
	0533*	8.5	259
	1138*	1.9	58
5 Sa	0545	8.4	256
	1159	1.4	43
	0621*	8.6	262
6 Su	1232	1.8	55
	0639	8.2	250
	1247*	1.6	49
	0709*	8.8	268
7 M	0127	1.7	52
	0733	8.1	247
	0135*	1.6	49
	0756*	9.0	274
8 Tu	0220	1.4	43
	0827	8.1	247
	0223*	1.6	49
	0842*	9.3	283
9 W	0310	1.0	30
	0919	8.2	250
	0310*	1.4	43
	0928*	9.7	296
10 Th	0357	0.5	15
	1008	8.4	256
	0357*	1.2	37
	1013*	10.1	308
11 F	0443	0.1	3
	1055	8.7	265
	0443*	1.0	30
	1059*	10.5	320
12 Sa	0529	–0.4	–12
	1142	9.0	274
	0531*	0.7	21
	1146*	10.8	329
13 Su	0615	–0.7	–21
	1230*	9.2	280
	0619*	0.5	15
14 M	1234	11.0	335
	0703	–0.9	–27
	0118*	9.5	290
	0710*	0.3	9
15 Tu	0124	11.1	338
	0752	–1.0	–30
	0209*	9.7	296
	0803*	0.2	6
16 W	0217	11.0	335
	0843	–1.0	–30
	0301*	9.8	299
	0859*	0.2	6
17 Th	0313	10.7	326
	0936	–0.8	–24
	0356*	10.0	305
	0958*	0.2	6
18 F	0411	10.3	314
	1030	–0.5	–15
	0452*	10.1	308
	1100*	0.3	9
19 Sa	0512	9.9	302
	1127	–0.2	–6
	0550*	10.1	308
20 Su	1205	0.3	9
	0616	9.5	290
	1226*	0.2	6
	0649*	10.2	311
21 M	0111	0.2	6
	0722	9.1	277
	0125*	0.5	15
	0748*	10.3	314
22 Tu	0215	0.1	3
	0827	8.9	271
	0224*	0.7	21
	0846*	10.4	317
23 W	0315	–0.1	–3
	0928	8.9	271
	0321*	0.8	24
	0941*	10.4	317
24 Th	0410	–0.2	–6
	1024	8.9	271
	0414*	0.9	27
	1032*	10.4	317
25 F	0501	–0.3	–9
	1115	8.9	271
	0503*	0.9	27
	1119*	10.4	317
26 Sa	0548	–0.2	–6
	1201*	8.9	271
	0549*	1.0	30
27 Su	1203	10.3	314
	0631	–0.2	–6
	1244*	8.9	271
	0632*	1.1	34
28 M	1245	10.1	308
	0712	0.0	0
	0125*	8.8	268
	0714*	1.1	34
29 Tu	0125	9.9	302
	0751	0.2	6
	0204*	8.8	268
	0755*	1.2	37
30 W	0205	9.7	296
	0828	0.4	12
	0243*	8.7	265
	0836*	1.4	43

July

Day	Time (h m)	Height (ft)	Height (cm)
1 Th	0246	9.4	287
	0906	0.6	18
	0322*	8.7	265
	0919*	1.5	46
2 F	0328	9.0	274
	0944	0.8	24
	0402*	8.7	265
	1004*	1.6	49
3 Sa	0411	8.7	265
	1024	1.1	34
	0443*	8.8	268
	1051*	1.6	49
4 Su	0458	8.4	256
	1106	1.3	40
	0527*	8.8	268
	1142*	1.6	49
5 M	0549	8.1	247
	1152	1.5	46
	0614*	8.9	271
6 Tu	1236	1.5	46
	0643	7.9	241
	1242*	1.6	49
	0704*	9.1	277
7 W	0132	1.3	40
	0740	7.9	241
	0135*	1.6	49
	0756*	9.4	287
8 Th	0228	0.9	27
	0837	8.0	244
	0229*	1.4	43
	0849*	9.8	299
9 F	0322	0.5	15
	0933	8.3	253
	0323*	1.1	34
	0942*	10.3	314
10 Sa	0415	–0.1	–3
	1027	8.7	265
	0416*	0.7	21
	1034*	10.7	326
11 Su	0505	–0.6	–18
	1118	9.1	277
	0509*	0.3	9
	1126*	11.1	338
12 M	0554	–1.0	–30
	1208*	9.6	293
	0601*	0.0	0
13 Tu	1218	11.4	347
	0644	–1.3	–40
	1258*	10.0	305
	0654*	–0.3	–9
14 W	0110	11.4	347
	0733	–1.4	–43
	0149*	10.3	314
	0749*	–0.5	–15
15 Th	0203	11.2	341
	0823	–1.3	–40
	0241*	10.5	320
	0845*	–0.5	–15
16 F	0258	10.8	329
	0915	–1.0	–30
	0334*	10.5	320
	0943*	–0.3	–9
17 Sa	0356	10.3	314
	1008	–0.6	–18
	0429*	10.5	320
	1044*	–0.2	–6
18 Su	0456	9.7	296
	1104	–0.1	–3
	0527*	10.4	317
	1148*	0.1	3
19 M	0600	9.2	280
	1203*	0.4	12
	0626*	10.2	311
20 Tu	1253	0.2	6
	0706	8.8	268
	0104*	0.8	24
	0728*	10.0	305
21 W	0158	0.3	9
	0811	8.5	259
	0206*	1.1	34
	0828*	9.9	302
22 Th	0300	0.3	9
	0913	8.5	259
	0305*	1.2	37
	0925*	9.9	302
23 F	0356	0.2	6
	1009	8.5	259
	0359*	1.2	37
	1017*	10.0	305
24 Sa	0446	0.1	3
	1058	8.6	262
	0448*	1.1	34
	1104*	10.0	305
25 Su	0530	0.1	3
	1142	8.7	265
	0532*	1.0	30
	1146*	9.9	302
26 M	0610	0.1	3
	1221*	8.8	268
	0612*	1.0	30
27 Tu	1225	9.9	302
	0647	0.2	6
	1258*	8.8	268
	0651*	1.0	30
28 W	0102	9.7	296
	0721	0.3	9
	0133*	8.9	271
	0728*	1.0	30
29 Th	0138	9.5	290
	0755	0.4	12
	0207*	8.9	271
	0806*	1.0	30
30 F	0215	9.3	283
	0828	0.6	18
	0242*	9.0	274
	0845*	1.1	34
31 Sa	0253	9.0	274
	0903	0.8	24
	0318*	9.0	274
	0925*	1.2	37

August

Day	Time (h m)	Height (ft)	Height (cm)
1 Su	0334	8.7	265
	0940	1.0	30
	0357*	9.0	274
	1010*	1.3	40
2 M	0418	8.3	253
	1021	1.2	37
	0440*	9.0	274
	1058*	1.3	40
3 Tu	0507	8.1	247
	1107	1.4	43
	0527*	9.1	277
	1152*	1.3	40
4 W	0601	7.9	241
	1159	1.5	46
	0621*	9.2	280
5 Th	1251	1.1	34
	0701	7.9	241
	1256*	1.5	46
	0718*	9.5	290
6 F	0152	0.8	24
	0803	8.0	244
	0157*	1.3	40
	0818*	9.8	299
7 Sa	0252	0.4	12
	0903	8.4	256
	0257*	0.9	27
	0917*	10.3	314
8 Su	0348	–0.2	–6
	1000	8.9	271
	0355*	0.4	12
	1013*	10.8	329
9 M	0441	–0.8	–24
	1054	9.5	290
	0450*	–0.2	–6
	1108*	11.3	344
10 Tu	0532	–1.2	–37
	1145	10.1	308
	0545*	–0.7	–21
11 W	1201	11.5	351
	0621	–1.5	–46
	1235*	10.6	323
	0638*	–1.0	–30
12 Th	1253	11.5	351
	0710	–1.5	–46
	0125*	10.9	332
	0732*	–1.1	–34
13 F	0147	11.2	341
	0800	–1.3	–40
	0216*	11.0	335
	0827*	–1.0	–30
14 Sa	0241	10.7	326
	0851	–0.9	–27
	0308*	10.9	332
	0924*	–0.8	–24
15 Su	0338	10.1	308
	0944	–0.4	–12
	0403*	10.6	323
	1023*	–0.4	–12
16 M	0437	9.5	290
	1040	0.2	6
	0501*	10.3	314
	1126*	0.0	0
17 Tu	0541	8.9	271
	1140	0.8	24
	0602*	9.9	302
18 W	1232	0.4	12
	0647	8.5	259
	1243*	1.2	37
	0706*	9.6	293
19 Th	0138	0.6	18
	0753	8.3	253
	0147*	1.4	43
	0809*	9.5	290
20 F	0240	0.6	18
	0854	8.3	253
	0248*	1.4	43
	0907*	9.5	290
21 Sa	0335	0.6	18
	0948	8.4	256
	0342*	1.3	40
	0959*	9.6	293
22 Su	0424	0.5	15
	1035	8.6	262
	0429*	1.1	34
	1044*	9.7	296
23 M	0506	0.4	12
	1116	8.8	268
	0511*	0.9	27
	1125*	9.7	296
24 Tu	0543	0.4	12
	1152	8.9	271
	0550*	0.8	24
25 W	1202	9.7	296
	0617	0.4	12
	1226*	9.1	277
	0626*	0.7	21
26 Th	1237	9.6	293
	0648	0.5	15
	1258*	9.2	280
	0701*	0.7	21
27 F	0111	9.4	287
	0719	0.6	18
	0129*	9.2	280
	0736*	0.7	21
28 Sa	0146	9.2	280
	0751	0.7	21
	0202*	9.3	283
	0812*	0.7	21
29 Su	0222	8.9	271
	0825	0.9	27
	0237*	9.3	283
	0851*	0.8	24
30 M	0301	8.6	262
	0902	1.1	34
	0316*	9.2	280
	0934*	0.9	27
31 Tu	0345	8.3	253
	0944	1.3	40
	0400*	9.2	280
	1023*	1.0	30

September

Day	Time (h m)	Height (ft)	Height (cm)
1 W	0434	8.1	247
	1032	1.5	46
	0450*	9.2	280
	1117*	1.0	30
2 Th	0530	8.0	244
	1127	1.5	46
	0547*	9.3	283
3 F	1218	0.9	27
	0632	8.0	244
	1229*	1.4	43
	0650*	9.5	290
4 Sa	0122	0.7	21
	0736	8.3	253
	0134*	1.1	34
	0754*	9.9	302
5 Su	0225	0.2	6
	0839	8.8	268
	0237*	0.6	18
	0856*	10.3	314
6 M	0323	–0.3	–9
	0936	9.4	287
	0337*	0.0	0
	0955*	10.8	329
7 Tu	0417	–0.8	–24
	1030	10.1	308
	0434*	–0.7	–21
	1050*	11.2	341
8 W	0507	–1.2	–37
	1121	10.7	326
	0528*	–1.2	–37
	1143*	11.4	347
9 Th	0556	–1.4	–43
	1210*	11.2	341
	0621*	–1.5	–46
10 F	1236	11.3	344
	0645	–1.3	–40
	1259*	11.4	347
	0713*	–1.5	–46
11 Sa	0128	10.9	332
	0734	–1.0	–30
	0149*	11.3	344
	0807*	–1.3	–40
12 Su	0222	10.4	317
	0825	–0.5	–15
	0241*	11.0	335
	0902*	–0.9	–27
13 M	0318	9.8	299
	0918	0.1	3
	0335*	10.5	320
	1000*	–0.4	–12
14 Tu	0416	9.2	280
	1014	0.7	21
	0433*	10.0	305
	1102*	0.2	6
15 W	0519	8.7	265
	1116	1.2	37
	0535*	9.5	290
16 Th	1207	0.6	18
	0624	8.3	253
	1220*	1.5	46
	0640*	9.2	280
17 F	0112	0.9	27
	0728	8.2	250
	0125*	1.6	49
	0744*	9.1	277
18 Sa	0212	0.9	27
	0827	8.3	253
	0225*	1.5	46
	0842*	9.1	277
19 Su	0306	0.9	27
	0919	8.5	259
	0318*	1.3	40
	0933*	9.2	280
20 M	0353	0.8	24
	1004	8.7	265
	0405*	1.0	30
	1018*	9.3	283
21 Tu	0433	0.7	21
	1043	9.0	274
	0446*	0.8	24
	1058*	9.4	287
22 W	0509	0.6	18
	1118	9.2	280
	0524*	0.6	18
	1135*	9.4	287
23 Th	0541	0.6	18
	1150	9.4	287
	0559*	0.5	15
24 F	1210	9.3	283
	0612	0.7	21
	1222*	9.5	290
	0633*	0.4	12
25 Sa	1244	9.2	280
	0643	0.8	24
	1253*	9.5	290
	0707*	0.4	12
26 Su	0118	9.0	274
	0716	0.9	27
	0126*	9.6	293
	0743*	0.4	12
27 M	0155	8.8	268
	0751	1.1	34
	0202*	9.6	293
	0822*	0.5	15
28 Tu	0235	8.6	262
	0831	1.2	37
	0243*	9.5	290
	0906*	0.6	18
29 W	0320	8.4	256
	0915	1.4	43
	0329*	9.5	290
	0956*	0.7	21
30 Th	0410	8.2	250
	1007	1.5	46
	0423*	9.4	287
	1052*	0.7	21

October

Day	Time (h m)	Height (ft)	Height (cm)
1 F	0508	8.2	250
	1105	1.5	46
	0523*	9.4	287
	1154*	0.7	21
2 Sa	0611	8.3	253
	1210*	1.3	40
	0628*	9.6	293
3 Su	1258	0.5	15
	0715	8.7	265
	0117*	0.9	27
	0735*	9.8	299
4 M	0200	0.1	3
	0817	9.3	283
	0222*	0.3	9
	0838*	10.2	311
5 Tu	0258	–0.3	–9
	0914	10.0	305
	0322*	–0.3	–9
	0938*	10.6	323
6 W	0352	–0.7	–21
	1007	10.6	323
	0419*	–1.0	–30
	1034*	10.8	329
7 Th	0443	–1.0	–30
	1057	11.2	341
	0512*	–1.4	–43
	1127*	10.9	332
8 F	0532	–1.0	–30
	1146	11.5	351
	0604*	–1.7	–52
9 Sa	1219	10.8	329
	0621	–0.9	–27
	1234*	11.5	351
	0655*	–1.6	–49
10 Su	0110	10.5	320
	0710	–0.5	–15
	0123*	11.3	344
	0747*	–1.3	–40
11 M	0202	10.0	305
	0800	0.0	0
	0214*	10.9	332
	0840*	–0.8	–24
12 Tu	0256	9.5	290
	0852	0.5	15
	0307*	10.3	314
	0935*	–0.2	–6
13 W	0353	9.0	274
	0948	1.0	30
	0403*	9.8	299
	1034*	0.4	12
14 Th	0452	8.5	259
	1048	1.5	46
	0504*	9.3	283
	1135*	0.8	24
15 F	0553	8.3	253
	1151	1.7	52
	0607*	8.9	271
16 Sa	1236	1.1	34
	0654	8.2	250
	1254*	1.8	55
	0709*	8.7	265
17 Su	0134	1.2	37
	0750	8.3	253
	0153*	1.6	49
	0807*	8.7	265
18 M	0226	1.2	37
	0840	8.5	259
	0247*	1.4	43
	0858*	8.8	268
19 Tu	0312	1.1	34
	0924	8.8	268
	0334*	1.1	34
	0945*	8.9	271
20 W	0353	1.0	30
	1004	9.1	277
	0416*	0.8	24
	1026*	9.0	274
21 Th	0429	1.0	30
	1040	9.4	287
	0454*	0.5	15
	1105*	9.0	274
22 F	0503	0.9	27
	1114	9.6	293
	0530*	0.3	9
	1142*	9.0	274
23 Sa	0536	0.9	27
	1146	9.8	299
	0605*	0.2	6
24 Su	1217	9.0	274
	0610	1.0	30
	1220*	9.9	302
	0641*	0.1	3
25 M	1254	8.9	271
	0645	1.0	30
	1256*	9.9	302
	0719*	0.1	3
26 Tu	0132	8.8	268
	0724	1.1	34
	0135*	9.9	302
	0800*	0.1	3
27 W	0214	8.6	262
	0807	1.1	34
	0219*	9.9	302
	0846*	0.2	6
28 Th	0301	8.6	262
	0855	1.2	37
	0308*	9.8	299
	0937*	0.3	9
29 F	0354	8.5	259
	0949	1.3	40
	0404*	9.7	296
	1033*	0.3	9
30 Sa	0451	8.6	262
	1050	1.2	37
	0505*	9.6	293
	1133*	0.4	12
31 Su	0553	8.8	268
	1155	1.0	30
	0611*	9.6	293

November

Day	Time (h m)	Height (ft)	Height (cm)
1 M	1235	0.3	9
	0655	9.2	280
	0103*	0.7	21
	0718*	9.7	296
2 Tu	0136	0.1	3
	0755	9.8	299
	0208*	0.1	3
	0822*	9.8	299
3 W	0234	–0.2	–6
	0852	10.4	317
	0309*	–0.5	–15
	0923*	10.1	308
4 Th	0329	–0.4	–12
	0945	10.9	332
	0405*	–1.0	–30
	1019*	10.2	311
5 F	0421	–0.5	–15
	1036	11.3	344
	0458*	–1.4	–43
	1112*	10.3	314
6 Sa	0511	–0.5	–15
	1125	11.4	347
	0549*	–1.5	–46
7 Su	1204	10.2	311
	0459	–0.3	–9
	1113	11.4	347
	0539*	–1.4	–43
	1154*	9.9	302
8 M	0548	0.0	0
	1201*	11.1	338
	0628*	–1.1	–34
9 Tu	1244	9.6	293
	0637	0.4	12
	1250*	10.6	323
	0718*	–0.6	–18
10 W	0134	9.2	280
	0727	0.8	24
	0140*	10.1	308
	0809*	–0.1	–3
11 Th	0226	8.8	268
	0819	1.2	37
	0232*	9.6	293
	0901*	0.4	12
12 F	0319	8.5	259
	0914	1.6	49
	0327*	9.1	277
	0955*	0.9	27
13 Sa	0414	8.3	253
	1013	1.8	55
	0424*	8.7	265
	1050*	1.2	37
14 Su	0509	8.3	253
	1113	1.8	55
	0523*	8.4	256
	1143*	1.4	43
15 M	0602	8.3	253
	1211*	1.7	52
	0620*	8.3	253
16 Tu	1235	1.5	46
	0652	8.5	259
	0106*	1.5	46
	0715*	8.3	253
17 W	0122	1.4	43
	0738	8.8	268
	0156*	1.2	37
	0805*	8.3	253
18 Th	0206	1.4	43
	0820	9.1	277
	0241*	0.8	24
	0851*	8.5	259
19 F	0246	1.3	40
	0900	9.4	287
	0322*	0.5	15
	0933*	8.6	262
20 Sa	0324	1.2	37
	0937	9.7	296
	0401*	0.2	6
	1013*	8.7	265
21 Su	0402	1.1	34
	1014	9.9	302
	0439*	0.0	0
	1052*	8.8	268
22 M	0440	1.0	30
	1052	10.1	308
	0518*	–0.2	–6
	1131*	8.8	268
23 Tu	0520	0.9	27
	1132	10.3	314
	0559*	–0.3	–9
24 W	1213	8.9	271
	0603	0.8	24
	1215*	10.3	314
	0642*	–0.4	–12
25 Th	1257	8.9	271
	0649	0.8	24
	0102*	10.3	314
	0729*	–0.4	–12
26 F	0146	8.9	271
	0740	0.8	24
	0153*	10.1	308
	0820*	–0.3	–9
27 Sa	0238	9.0	274
	0836	0.8	24
	0249*	9.9	302
	0914*	–0.1	–3
28 Su	0334	9.2	280
	0936	0.8	24
	0350*	9.7	296
	1012*	0.0	0
29 M	0433	9.4	287
	1042	0.6	18
	0454*	9.4	287
	1111*	0.1	3
30 Tu	0534	9.7	296
	1149	0.4	12
	0601*	9.3	283

December

Day	Time (h m)	Height (ft)	Height (cm)
1 W	1212	0.1	3
	0634	10.0	305
	1254*	0.0	0
	0707*	9.3	283
2 Th	0112	0.1	3
	0732	10.4	317
	0156*	–0.5	–15
	0810*	9.4	287
3 F	0209	0.1	3
	0827	10.7	326
	0254*	–0.8	–24
	0908*	9.5	290
4 Sa	0303	0.1	3
	0920	11.0	335
	0347*	–1.1	–34
	1001*	9.5	290
5 Su	0354	0.1	3
	1009	11.0	335
	0437*	–1.2	–37
	1051*	9.5	290
6 M	0443	0.1	3
	1057	10.9	332
	0525*	–1.1	–34
	1139*	9.4	287
7 Tu	0530	0.3	9
	1143	10.7	326
	0611*	–0.8	–24
8 W	1225	9.2	280
	0616	0.5	15
	1229*	10.3	314
	0656*	–0.5	–15
9 Th	0110	9.0	274
	0703	0.8	24
	0114*	9.9	302
	0740*	–0.1	–3
10 F	0156	8.8	268
	0749	1.1	34
	0200*	9.5	290
	0825*	0.4	12
11 Sa	0241	8.6	262
	0838	1.4	43
	0248*	9.0	274
	0910*	0.7	21
12 Su	0328	8.4	256
	0929	1.6	49
	0338*	8.6	262
	0957*	1.1	34
13 M	0416	8.4	256
	1023	1.7	52
	0431*	8.2	250
	1045*	1.4	43
14 Tu	0505	8.4	256
	1119	1.7	52
	0527*	7.9	241
	1134*	1.6	49
15 W	0555	8.5	259
	1216*	1.6	49
	0623*	7.8	238
16 Th	1224	1.7	52
	0644	8.7	265
	0110*	1.3	40
	0719*	7.8	238
17 F	0114	1.6	49
	0732	8.9	271
	0201*	1.0	30
	0811*	7.9	241
18 Sa	0201	1.5	46
	0818	9.3	283
	0247*	0.6	18
	0859*	8.1	247
19 Su	0246	1.3	40
	0902	9.6	293
	0331*	0.2	6
	0944*	8.4	256
20 M	0330	1.0	30
	0945	10.0	305
	0414*	–0.2	–6
	1027*	8.7	265
21 Tu	0414	0.7	21
	1029	10.4	317
	0456*	–0.6	–18
	1110*	8.9	271
22 W	0459	0.5	15
	1113	10.6	323
	0540*	–0.8	–24
	1154*	9.2	280
23 Th	0545	0.2	6
	1159	10.7	326
	0625*	–1.0	–30
24 F	1240	9.4	287
	0634	0.1	3
	1248*	10.7	326
	0712*	–1.0	–30
25 Sa	0128	9.6	293
	0726	0.0	0
	0140*	10.5	320
	0801*	–0.9	–27
26 Su	0219	9.7	296
	0822	0.0	0
	0235*	10.1	308
	0854*	–0.6	–18
27 M	0313	9.8	299
	0922	0.1	3
	0334*	9.7	296
	0949*	–0.3	–9
28 Tu	0411	9.9	302
	1026	0.1	3
	0438*	9.2	280
	1048*	0.1	3
29 W	0511	9.9	302
	1133	0.1	3
	0546*	8.9	271
	1149*	0.4	12
30 Th	0613	10.0	305
	1240*	0.0	0
	0654*	8.7	265
31 F	1252	0.5	15
	0714	10.1	308
	0145*	–0.3	–9
	0759*	8.7	265

Heights are referred to mean lower low water which is the chart datum of soundings. All times are local. Daylight Saving Time has been used when needed.

TIDE TABLES

Bar Harbor, Maine, 2010

Times and Heights of High and Low Waters

March

Day	Time (h m)	Height (ft)	Height (cm)
1 M	0443	−1.6	−49
	1054	13.3	405
	0509*	−1.8	−55
	1120*	13.0	396
2 Tu	0533	−1.8	−55
	1144	13.1	399
	0557*	−1.6	−49
3 W	1208	13.0	396
	0624	−1.7	−52
	1235*	12.6	384
	0645*	−1.1	−34
4 Th	1256	12.8	390
	0716	−1.3	−40
	0126*	11.9	363
	0734*	−0.4	−12
5 F	0146	12.3	375
	0809	−0.7	−21
	0220*	11.1	338
	0826*	0.3	9
6 Sa	0239	11.6	354
	0905	0.0	0
	0317*	10.3	314
	0922*	1.1	34
7 Su ◑	0336	11.0	335
	1006	0.6	18
	0418*	9.6	293
	1023*	1.7	52
8 M	0438	10.4	317
	1109	1.1	34
	0523*	9.2	280
	1128*	2.0	61
9 Tu	0542	10.1	308
	1213*	1.3	40
	0627*	9.1	277
10 W	1231	2.1	64
	0645	10.1	308
	0113*	1.3	40
	0725*	9.3	283
11 Th	0130	1.8	55
	0742	10.2	311
	0205*	1.1	34
	0816*	9.6	293
12 F	0221	1.5	46
	0831	10.5	320
	0251*	0.8	24
	0900*	10.0	305
13 Sa	0306	1.1	34
	0915	10.7	326
	0331*	0.6	18
	0939*	10.4	317
14 Su	0446	0.8	24
	1054	10.9	332
	0507*	0.5	15
	1114*	10.7	326
15 M ●	0523	0.5	15
	1130	11.0	335
	0541*	0.4	12
	1146*	10.9	332
16 Tu	0558	0.3	9
	1204*	11.0	335
	0612*	0.4	12
17 W	1218	11.1	338
	0632	0.2	6
	1238*	10.9	332
	0644*	0.5	15
18 Th	1250	11.2	341
	0706	0.2	6
	0113*	10.7	326
	0716*	0.7	21
19 F	0124	11.3	344
	0742	0.2	6
	0150*	10.5	320
	0752*	0.9	27
20 Sa	0201	11.2	341
	0822	0.2	6
	0231*	10.2	311
	0832*	1.1	34
21 Su	0243	11.2	341
	0908	0.4	12
	0318*	10.0	305
	0919*	1.3	40
22 M	0333	11.0	335
	1000	0.5	15
	0412*	9.7	296
	1014*	1.5	46
23 Tu ◐	0430	10.9	332
	1101	0.6	18
	0514*	9.6	293
	1118*	1.6	49
24 W	0535	10.9	332
	1207*	0.6	18
	0621*	9.8	299
25 Th	1228	1.4	43
	0644	11.1	338
	0115*	0.3	9
	0729*	10.2	311
26 F	0137	0.9	27
	0752	11.4	347
	0218*	−0.1	−3
	0831*	10.9	332
27 Sa	0242	0.1	3
	0855	11.9	363
	0316*	−0.6	−18
	0928*	11.7	357
28 Su	0341	−0.6	−18
	0953	12.4	378
	0409*	−1.0	−30
	1020*	12.4	378
29 M	0435	−1.3	−40
	1046	12.6	384
	0459*	−1.3	−40
	1109*	12.9	393
30 Tu ○	0526	−1.7	−52
	1137	12.7	387
	0547*	−1.3	−40
	1157*	13.1	399
31 W	0616	−1.8	−55
	1227*	12.4	378
	0634*	−1.0	−30

April

Day	Time (h m)	Height (ft)	Height (cm)
1 Th	1243	13.0	396
	0705	−1.6	−49
	0115*	12.0	366
	0720*	−0.5	−15
2 F	0130	12.6	384
	0754	−1.2	−37
	0205*	11.4	347
	0809*	0.1	3
3 Sa	0219	12.1	369
	0844	−0.6	−18
	0256*	10.7	326
	0859*	0.8	24
4 Su	0309	11.4	347
	0937	0.1	3
	0349*	10.1	308
	0953*	1.4	43
5 M	0403	10.7	326
	1033	0.7	21
	0446*	9.5	290
	1051*	1.9	58
6 Tu ◑	0502	10.2	311
	1132	1.2	37
	0546*	9.2	280
	1152*	2.2	67
7 W	0604	9.9	302
	1232*	1.5	46
	0647*	9.2	280
8 Th	1254	2.2	67
	0705	9.8	299
	0130*	1.5	46
	0743*	9.3	283
9 F	0152	1.9	58
	0802	9.8	299
	0222*	1.4	43
	0834*	9.6	293
10 Sa	0245	1.6	49
	0853	10.0	305
	0309*	1.2	37
	0919*	10.1	308
11 Su	0331	1.2	37
	0939	10.2	311
	0350*	1.0	30
	0959*	10.5	320
12 M	0413	0.7	21
	1020	10.4	317
	0428*	0.9	27
	1035*	10.8	329
13 Tu	0452	0.4	12
	1059	10.6	323
	0504*	0.8	24
	1110*	11.1	338
14 W ●	0528	0.1	3
	1135	10.7	326
	0538*	0.7	21
	1144*	11.4	347
15 Th	0604	−0.1	−3
	1212*	10.7	326
	0612*	0.7	21
16 F	1219	11.5	351
	0641	−0.2	−6
	1249*	10.6	323
	0649*	0.8	24
17 Sa	1256	11.6	354
	0720	−0.3	−9
	0130*	10.5	320
	0729*	0.9	27
18 Su	0138	11.6	354
	0804	−0.2	−6
	0214*	10.4	317
	0814*	1.0	30
19 M	0224	11.5	351
	0852	−0.1	−3
	0304*	10.2	311
	0905*	1.2	37
20 Tu	0317	11.4	347
	0946	0.1	3
	0400*	10.1	308
	1003*	1.3	40
21 W ◐	0416	11.2	341
	1046	0.2	6
	0501*	10.2	311
	1108*	1.2	37
22 Th	0521	11.1	338
	1150	0.2	6
	0606*	10.4	317
23 F	1217	1.0	30
	0629	11.1	338
	1254*	0.1	3
	0710*	10.8	329
24 Sa	0124	0.5	15
	0736	11.2	341
	0155*	−0.1	−3
	0810*	11.4	347
25 Su	0228	−0.1	−3
	0838	11.5	351
	0253*	−0.3	−9
	0906*	12.0	366
26 M	0326	−0.7	−21
	0936	11.7	357
	0346*	−0.5	−15
	0959*	12.5	381
27 Tu	0420	−1.2	−37
	1030	11.9	363
	0437*	−0.6	−18
	1048*	12.8	390
28 W ○	0510	−1.5	−46
	1121	11.8	360
	0525*	−0.5	−15
	1135*	12.8	390
29 Th	0559	−1.5	−46
	1209*	11.7	357
	0612*	−0.2	−6
30 F	1221	12.6	384
	0646	−1.3	−40
	1257*	11.3	344
	0658*	0.2	6

May

Day	Time (h m)	Height (ft)	Height (cm)
1 Sa	0107	12.3	375
	0733	−0.9	−27
	0144*	10.9	332
	0745*	0.7	21
2 Su	0153	11.7	357
	0820	−0.3	−9
	0232*	10.4	317
	0833*	1.1	34
3 M	0241	11.2	341
	0909	0.2	6
	0321*	10.0	305
	0923*	1.6	49
4 Tu	0331	10.6	323
	0959	0.7	21
	0413*	9.6	293
	1017*	1.9	58
5 W	0424	10.2	311
	1052	1.2	37
	0506*	9.4	287
	1113*	2.1	64
6 Th ◑	0520	9.8	299
	1145	1.4	43
	0600*	9.4	287
7 F	1211	2.1	64
	0617	9.6	293
	1238*	1.6	49
	0653*	9.5	290
8 Sa	0107	2.0	61
	0713	9.5	290
	0129*	1.6	49
	0743*	9.8	299
9 Su	0200	1.7	52
	0807	9.6	293
	0217*	1.5	46
	0830*	10.1	308
10 M	0250	1.3	40
	0856	9.7	296
	0302*	1.4	43
	0913*	10.5	320
11 Tu	0335	0.8	24
	0941	9.9	302
	0344*	1.2	37
	0953*	10.9	332
12 W	0417	0.4	12
	1024	10.1	308
	0424*	1.1	34
	1032*	11.3	344
13 Th	0457	0.0	0
	1105	10.3	314
	0503*	0.9	27
	1111*	11.6	354
14 F ●	0537	−0.3	−9
	1146	10.5	320
	0543*	0.8	24
	1152*	11.9	363
15 Sa	0619	−0.5	−15
	1228*	10.6	323
	0625*	0.7	21
16 Su	1235	12.0	366
	0702	−0.7	−21
	0113*	10.6	323
	0711*	0.7	21
17 M	0121	12.1	369
	0749	−0.7	−21
	0201*	10.7	326
	0801*	0.7	21
18 Tu	0211	12.0	366
	0840	−0.6	−18
	0253*	10.7	326
	0855*	0.8	24
19 W	0306	11.8	360
	0934	−0.5	−15
	0349*	10.7	326
	0955*	0.8	24
20 Th ◐	0406	11.5	351
	1032	−0.3	−9
	0448*	10.9	332
	1059*	0.7	21
21 F	0509	11.2	341
	1132	−0.1	−3
	0549*	11.1	338
22 Sa	1204	0.5	15
	0614	11.0	335
	1233*	0.0	0
	0650*	11.4	347
23 Su	0110	0.2	6
	0719	10.9	332
	0132*	0.1	3
	0749*	11.7	357
24 M	0212	−0.2	−6
	0822	10.9	332
	0230*	0.1	3
	0846*	12.0	366
25 Tu	0310	−0.6	−18
	0920	11.0	335
	0325*	0.1	3
	0939*	12.3	375
26 W	0405	−0.9	−27
	1015	11.0	335
	0417*	0.2	6
	1029*	12.4	378
27 Th ○	0455	−1.0	−30
	1106	11.0	335
	0506*	0.3	9
	1116*	12.3	375
28 F	0543	−1.0	−30
	1154	10.9	332
	0553*	0.5	15
29 Sa	1202	12.1	369
	0629	−0.8	−24
	1239*	10.7	326
	0638*	0.7	21
30 Su	1246	11.8	360
	0713	−0.5	−15
	0124*	10.5	320
	0723*	1.0	30
31 M	0130	11.5	351
	0757	−0.1	−3
	0208*	10.2	311
	0807*	1.3	40

June

Day	Time (h m)	Height (ft)	Height (cm)
1 Tu	0214	11.1	338
	0840	0.3	9
	0252*	10.0	305
	0854*	1.5	46
2 W	0300	10.6	323
	0925	0.6	18
	0337*	9.8	299
	0941*	1.8	55
3 Th	0347	10.2	311
	1010	1.0	30
	0423*	9.7	296
	1031*	1.9	58
4 F ◑	0436	9.9	302
	1056	1.3	40
	0511*	9.7	296
	1124*	1.9	58
5 Sa	0527	9.6	293
	1144	1.5	46
	0559*	9.8	299
6 Su	1217	1.9	58
	0621	9.4	287
	1232*	1.7	52
	0648*	10.0	305
7 M	0111	1.7	52
	0715	9.3	283
	0122*	1.7	52
	0736*	10.2	311
8 Tu	0203	1.3	40
	0808	9.3	283
	0210*	1.7	52
	0824*	10.6	323
9 W	0252	0.9	27
	0859	9.5	290
	0258*	1.5	46
	0910*	11.0	335
10 Th	0340	0.4	12
	0947	9.8	299
	0345*	1.3	40
	0956*	11.4	347
11 F	0426	0.0	0
	1034	10.1	308
	0431*	1.0	30
	1042*	11.9	363
12 Sa ●	0511	−0.5	−15
	1121	10.5	320
	0517*	0.7	21
	1128*	12.2	372
13 Su	0558	−0.9	−27
	1208*	10.8	329
	0605*	0.5	15
14 M	1216	12.5	381
	0645	−1.1	−34
	1256*	11.0	335
	0656*	0.3	9
15 Tu	0107	12.5	381
	0734	−1.2	−37
	0146*	11.2	341
	0749*	0.1	3
16 W	0159	12.4	378
	0825	−1.1	−34
	0239*	11.4	347
	0844*	0.1	3
17 Th	0255	12.2	372
	0918	−0.9	−27
	0334*	11.5	351
	0944*	0.1	3
18 F	0353	11.8	360
	1014	−0.6	−18
	0430*	11.6	354
	1045*	0.1	3
19 Sa ◐	0454	11.3	344
	1111	−0.3	−9
	0529*	11.6	354
	1149*	0.1	3
20 Su	0557	10.9	332
	1210*	0.1	3
	0629*	11.7	357
21 M	1253	0.1	3
	0702	10.6	323
	0110*	0.4	12
	0728*	11.7	357
22 Tu	0156	−0.1	−3
	0805	10.4	317
	0210*	0.6	18
	0826*	11.8	360
23 W	0255	−0.2	−6
	0905	10.3	314
	0307*	0.7	21
	0921*	11.8	360
24 Th	0350	−0.4	−12
	1001	10.4	317
	0400*	0.8	24
	1012*	11.9	363
25 F	0441	−0.4	−12
	1051	10.4	317
	0449*	0.8	24
	1100*	11.8	360
26 Sa ○	0527	−0.4	−12
	1138	10.4	317
	0536*	0.9	27
	1144*	11.7	357
27 Su	0611	−0.3	−9
	1221*	10.4	317
	0619*	1.0	30
28 M	1227	11.5	351
	0652	−0.2	−6
	0102*	10.3	314
	0701*	1.1	34
29 Tu	0107	11.3	344
	0731	0.0	0
	0141*	10.2	311
	0742*	1.2	37
30 W	0148	11.0	335
	0810	0.3	9
	0220*	10.2	311
	0823*	1.3	40

July

Day	Time (h m)	Height (ft)	Height (cm)
1 Th	0228	10.7	326
	0849	0.6	18
	0300*	10.1	308
	0906*	1.5	46
2 F	0310	10.3	314
	0928	0.9	27
	0340*	10.1	308
	0950*	1.6	49
3 Sa	0354	10.0	305
	1009	1.2	37
	0422*	10.1	308
	1037*	1.7	52
4 Su ◑	0440	9.6	293
	1052	1.4	43
	0507*	10.1	308
	1127*	1.7	52
5 M	0530	9.3	283
	1138	1.7	52
	0555*	10.2	311
6 Tu	1220	1.6	49
	0624	9.1	277
	1228*	1.8	55
	0645*	10.4	317
7 W	0115	1.3	40
	0721	9.1	277
	0121*	1.8	55
	0738*	10.7	326
8 Th	0211	1.0	30
	0818	9.3	283
	0216*	1.6	49
	0832*	11.1	338
9 F	0305	0.4	12
	0913	9.7	296
	0310*	1.3	40
	0925*	11.6	354
10 Sa	0357	−0.1	−3
	1006	10.2	311
	0403*	0.8	24
	1017*	12.1	369
11 Su ●	0447	−0.7	−21
	1057	10.7	326
	0456*	0.3	9
	1108*	12.6	384
12 M	0536	−1.2	−37
	1146	11.2	341
	0547*	−0.1	−3
13 Tu	1200	12.9	393
	0626	−1.5	−46
	1236*	11.6	354
	0640*	−0.4	−12
14 W	1251	13.0	396
	0715	−1.6	−49
	0127*	11.9	363
	0734*	−0.6	−18
15 Th	0144	12.8	390
	0806	−1.5	−46
	0219*	12.1	369
	0829*	−0.6	−18
16 F	0239	12.4	378
	0858	−1.1	−34
	0312*	12.1	369
	0927*	−0.5	−15
17 Sa	0336	11.8	360
	0952	−0.7	−21
	0408*	12.1	369
	1027*	−0.3	−9
18 Su ◐	0436	11.2	341
	1048	−0.1	−3
	0506*	11.9	363
	1130*	−0.1	−3
19 M	0539	10.6	323
	1148	0.4	12
	0606*	11.6	354
20 Tu	1234	0.1	3
	0644	10.2	311
	1249*	0.8	24
	0707*	11.5	351
21 W	0138	0.2	6
	0748	9.9	302
	0151*	1.1	34
	0808*	11.4	347
22 Th	0238	0.2	6
	0849	9.9	302
	0250*	1.2	37
	0905*	11.3	344
23 F	0334	0.1	3
	0945	10.0	305
	0344*	1.1	34
	0957*	11.4	347
24 Sa	0424	0.0	0
	1034	10.1	308
	0433*	1.1	34
	1044*	11.4	347
25 Su	0509	0.0	0
	1118	10.2	311
	0518*	1.0	30
	1126*	11.4	347
26 M ○	0550	0.0	0
	1158	10.3	314
	0558*	0.9	27
27 Tu	1206	11.3	344
	0627	0.0	0
	1235*	10.4	317
	0637*	0.9	27
28 W	1243	11.2	341
	0703	0.2	6
	0111*	10.4	317
	0715*	1.0	30
29 Th	0120	11.0	335
	0738	0.4	12
	0146*	10.4	317
	0752*	1.0	30
30 F	0157	10.7	326
	0812	0.6	18
	0221*	10.4	317
	0830*	1.1	34
31 Sa	0235	10.3	314
	0847	0.9	27
	0258*	10.4	317
	0911*	1.2	37

August

Day	Time (h m)	Height (ft)	Height (cm)
1 Su	0315	10.0	305
	0925	1.2	37
	0337*	10.4	317
	0954*	1.3	40
2 M	0359	9.6	293
	1006	1.4	43
	0420*	10.3	314
	1042*	1.4	43
3 Tu ◑	0447	9.3	283
	1052	1.7	52
	0508*	10.4	317
	1135*	1.4	43
4 W	0542	9.2	280
	1144	1.8	55
	0602*	10.5	320
5 Th	1234	1.2	37
	0641	9.1	277
	1242*	1.8	55
	0701*	10.7	326
6 F	0135	0.9	27
	0743	9.4	287
	0143*	1.5	46
	0801*	11.2	341
7 Sa	0234	0.4	12
	0843	9.8	299
	0244*	1.1	34
	0900*	11.7	357
8 Su	0330	−0.3	−9
	0940	10.5	320
	0341*	0.4	12
	0956*	12.3	375
9 M	0423	−0.9	−27
	1033	11.2	341
	0436*	−0.2	−6
	1050*	12.8	390
10 Tu ●	0514	−1.4	−43
	1124	11.8	360
	0530*	−0.8	−24
	1142*	13.1	399
11 W	0603	−1.7	−52
	1214*	12.3	375
	0623*	−1.2	−37
12 Th	1234	13.1	399
	0652	−1.7	−52
	0104*	12.6	384
	0716*	−1.3	−40
13 F	0127	12.9	393
	0742	−1.5	−46
	0155*	12.7	387
	0810*	−1.2	−37
14 Sa	0221	12.4	378
	0834	−1.0	−30
	0247*	12.6	384
	0907*	−0.9	−27
15 Su	0317	11.7	357
	0927	−0.4	−12
	0342*	12.2	372
	1006*	−0.5	−15
16 M ◐	0416	11.0	335
	1024	0.2	6
	0440*	11.8	360
	1108*	0.0	0
17 Tu	0519	10.3	314
	1125	0.8	24
	0542*	11.3	344
18 W	1212	0.4	12
	0624	9.9	302
	1229*	1.3	40
	0646*	11.0	335
19 Th	0117	0.6	18
	0729	9.6	293
	0132*	1.5	46
	0748*	10.9	332
20 F	0218	0.6	18
	0830	9.7	296
	0232*	1.4	43
	0846*	10.9	332
21 Sa	0313	0.5	15
	0924	9.8	299
	0326*	1.3	40
	0937*	11.0	335
22 Su	0401	0.4	12
	1011	10.1	308
	0413*	1.1	34
	1023*	11.1	338
23 M	0444	0.3	9
	1053	10.3	314
	0456*	0.9	27
	1104*	11.2	341
24 Tu ○	0523	0.2	6
	1130	10.5	320
	0535*	0.7	21
	1142*	11.2	341
25 W	0558	0.2	6
	1205*	10.6	323
	0611*	0.6	18
26 Th	1217	11.0	335
	0631	0.4	12
	1237*	10.7	326
	0646*	0.6	18
27 F	1252	10.8	329
	0703	0.5	15
	0110*	10.7	326
	0721*	0.7	21
28 Sa	0127	10.6	323
	0735	0.8	24
	0143*	10.7	326
	0757*	0.8	24
29 Su	0203	10.3	314
	0809	1.0	30
	0218*	10.7	326
	0835*	0.9	27
30 M	0241	10.0	305
	0846	1.3	40
	0257*	10.6	323
	0917*	1.0	30
31 Tu	0324	9.7	296
	0927	1.5	46
	0341*	10.5	320
	1005*	1.1	34

September

Day	Time (h m)	Height (ft)	Height (cm)
1 W ◑	0413	9.4	287
	1015	1.7	52
	0432*	10.5	320
	1100*	1.2	37
2 Th	0510	9.3	283
	1111	1.8	55
	0529*	10.6	323
3 F	1202	1.0	30
	0612	9.3	283
	1214*	1.7	52
	0632*	10.8	329
4 Sa	0106	0.7	21
	0717	9.6	293
	0120*	1.3	40
	0737*	11.2	341
5 Su	0208	0.2	6
	0819	10.2	311
	0224*	0.7	21
	0839*	11.8	360
6 M	0306	−0.4	−12
	0916	11.0	335
	0323*	0.0	0
	0937*	12.4	378
7 Tu	0359	−1.0	−30
	1009	11.8	360
	0419*	−0.8	−24
	1031*	12.8	390
8 W ●	0450	−1.4	−43
	1100	12.5	381
	0512*	−1.4	−43
	1124*	13.1	399
9 Th	0539	−1.6	−49
	1150	12.9	393
	0604*	−1.7	−52
10 F	1216	13.0	396
	0628	−1.6	−49
	1239*	13.1	399
	0656*	−1.8	−55
11 Sa	0107	12.6	384
	0717	−1.2	−37
	0129*	13.0	396
	0749*	−1.5	−46
12 Su	0200	12.0	366
	0808	−0.7	−21
	0221*	12.6	384
	0844*	−1.0	−30
13 M	0255	11.3	344
	0902	0.0	0
	0315*	12.1	369
	0942*	−0.4	−12
14 Tu	0354	10.6	323
	0959	0.7	21
	0413*	11.5	351
	1043*	0.2	6
15 W ◐	0456	10.0	305
	1101	1.3	40
	0516*	10.9	332
	1147*	0.6	18
16 Th	0600	9.6	293
	1205*	1.6	49
	0620*	10.6	323
17 F	1250	0.9	27
	0704	9.5	290
	0109*	1.7	52
	0723*	10.4	317
18 Sa	0150	0.9	27
	0803	9.6	293
	0208*	1.6	49
	0820*	10.5	320
19 Su	0243	0.9	27
	0855	9.8	299
	0301*	1.3	40
	0911*	10.6	323
20 M	0331	0.7	21
	0940	10.1	308
	0347*	1.0	30
	0956*	10.8	329
21 Tu	0412	0.6	18
	1021	10.4	317
	0429*	0.7	21
	1037*	10.9	332
22 W	0450	0.5	15
	1057	10.7	326
	0507*	0.5	15
	1114*	10.9	332
23 Th ○	0524	0.5	15
	1130	10.9	332
	0543*	0.4	12
	1149*	10.8	329
24 F	0557	0.6	18
	1203*	11.0	335
	0617*	0.3	9
25 Sa	1224	10.6	323
	0629	0.7	21
	1235*	11.0	335
	0652*	0.4	12
26 Su	1258	10.4	317
	0701	0.9	27
	0108*	11.0	335
	0727*	0.4	12
27 M	0134	10.2	311
	0736	1.2	37
	0144*	11.0	335
	0806*	0.5	15
28 Tu	0214	9.9	302
	0814	1.4	43
	0225*	10.9	332
	0849*	0.7	21
29 W	0258	9.7	296
	0858	1.6	49
	0311*	10.8	329
	0939*	0.8	24
30 Th	0349	9.5	290
	0950	1.7	52
	0405*	10.7	326
	1035*	0.8	24

October

Day	Time (h m)	Height (ft)	Height (cm)
1 F ◑	0447	9.5	290
	1050	1.7	52
	0506*	10.7	326
	1138*	0.8	24
2 Sa	0551	9.7	296
	1156	1.5	46
	0612*	10.9	332
3 Su	1242	0.5	15
	0655	10.1	308
	0103*	1.1	34
	0718*	11.2	341
4 M	0144	0.1	3
	0757	10.7	326
	0208*	0.4	12
	0821*	11.7	357
5 Tu	0242	−0.4	−12
	0854	11.5	351
	0307*	−0.4	−12
	0919*	12.2	372
6 W	0335	−0.9	−27
	0947	12.3	375
	0403*	−1.2	−37
	1014*	12.5	381
7 Th ●	0426	−1.2	−37
	1037	12.9	393
	0456*	−1.7	−52
	1106*	12.6	384
8 F	0516	−1.3	−40
	1127	13.2	402
	0547*	−1.9	−58
	1158*	12.5	381
9 Sa	0604	−1.1	−34
	1215*	13.2	402
	0637*	−1.8	−55
10 Su	1248	12.1	369
	0653	−0.7	−21
	0104*	13.0	396
	0729*	−1.5	−46
11 M	0140	11.6	354
	0744	−0.1	−3
	0155*	12.4	378
	0821*	−0.9	−27
12 Tu	0233	11.0	335
	0837	0.5	15
	0248*	11.8	360
	0917*	−0.3	−9
13 W	0329	10.3	314
	0933	1.1	34
	0345*	11.1	338
	1015*	0.4	12
14 Th ◐	0428	9.9	302
	1033	1.6	49
	0445*	10.6	323
	1115*	0.8	24
15 F	0529	9.5	290
	1135	1.8	55
	0547*	10.2	311
16 Sa	1215	1.1	34
	0630	9.5	290
	1237*	1.9	58
	0648*	10.0	305
17 Su	0112	1.2	37
	0726	9.6	293
	0135*	1.7	52
	0745*	10.0	305
18 M	0204	1.2	37
	0817	9.9	302
	0228*	1.4	43
	0836*	10.2	311
19 Tu	0251	1.1	34
	0902	10.2	311
	0315*	1.0	30
	0923*	10.3	314
20 W	0333	1.0	30
	0943	10.5	320
	0358*	0.7	21
	1005*	10.4	317
21 Th	0412	0.9	27
	1020	10.9	332
	0437*	0.4	12
	1044*	10.5	320
22 F	0448	0.8	24
	1055	11.1	338
	0514*	0.2	6
	1120*	10.5	320
23 Sa ○	0522	0.9	27
	1129	11.2	341
	0549*	0.1	3
	1156*	10.4	317
24 Su	0556	0.9	27
	1203*	11.3	344
	0625*	0.1	3
25 M	1233	10.3	314
	0631	1.0	30
	1238*	11.3	344
	0702*	0.1	3
26 Tu	0111	10.2	311
	0709	1.2	37
	0118*	11.3	344
	0743*	0.1	3
27 W	0153	10.1	308
	0751	1.3	40
	0201*	11.2	341
	0829*	0.2	6
28 Th	0240	9.9	302
	0839	1.4	43
	0251*	11.1	338
	0920*	0.3	9
29 F	0332	9.9	302
	0934	1.5	46
	0347*	11.0	335
	1016*	0.4	12
30 Sa ◑	0431	10.0	305
	1035	1.4	43
	0448*	10.9	332
	1117*	0.4	12
31 Su	0532	10.2	311
	1142	1.2	37
	0554*	11.0	335

November

Day	Time (h m)	Height (ft)	Height (cm)
1 M	1219	0.3	9
	0635	10.7	326
	1249*	0.7	21
	0700*	11.1	338
2 Tu	0120	0.0	0
	0735	11.3	344
	0153*	0.1	3
	0803*	11.4	347
3 W	0218	−0.3	−9
	0832	11.9	363
	0252*	−0.6	−18
	0903*	11.7	357
4 Th	0313	−0.5	−15
	0926	12.5	381
	0348*	−1.2	−37
	0958*	11.9	363
5 F	0405	−0.7	−21
	1017	12.9	393
	0441*	−1.6	−49
	1051*	11.9	363
6 Sa ●	0455	−0.7	−21
	1107	13.1	399
	0531*	−1.7	−52
	1142*	11.8	360
7 Su	0444	−0.5	−15
	1055	13.0	396
	0520*	−1.6	−49
	1131*	11.6	354
8 M	0533	−0.2	−6
	1143	12.7	387
	0610*	−1.2	−37
9 Tu	1221	11.1	338
	0622	0.3	9
	1232*	12.2	372
	0659*	−0.7	−21
10 W	0111	10.7	326
	0712	0.8	24
	0122*	11.6	354
	0750*	−0.1	−3
11 Th	0203	10.2	311
	0805	1.3	40
	0214*	11.0	335
	0842*	0.4	12
12 F	0256	9.8	299
	0900	1.7	52
	0309*	10.4	317
	0936*	0.9	27
13 Sa ◐	0351	9.6	293
	0958	1.9	58
	0406*	10.0	305
	1030*	1.2	37
14 Su	0445	9.5	290
	1056	2.0	61
	0503*	9.7	296
	1124*	1.4	43
15 M	0539	9.6	293
	1153	1.8	55
	0600*	9.6	293
16 Tu	1216	1.5	46
	0629	9.9	302
	1247*	1.6	49
	0653*	9.6	293
17 W	0104	1.5	46
	0717	10.2	311
	0136*	1.2	37
	0743*	9.7	296
18 Th	0149	1.4	43
	0800	10.5	320
	0222*	0.9	27
	0829*	9.9	302
19 F	0231	1.3	40
	0841	10.8	329
	0304*	0.5	15
	0911*	10.0	305
20 Sa	0311	1.2	37
	0919	11.1	338
	0344*	0.2	6
	0951*	10.1	308
21 Su ○	0349	1.1	34
	0957	11.4	347
	0423*	0.0	0
	1030*	10.2	311
22 M	0427	1.0	30
	1035	11.6	354
	0501*	−0.2	−6
	1110*	10.3	314
23 Tu	0506	1.0	30
	1115	11.7	357
	0542*	−0.3	−9
	1151*	10.4	317
24 W	0548	0.9	27
	1158	11.8	360
	0625*	−0.4	−12
25 Th	1236	10.4	317
	0634	0.9	27
	1245*	11.7	357
	0712*	−0.3	−9
26 F	0124	10.4	317
	0725	0.9	27
	0136*	11.6	354
	0803*	−0.2	−6
27 Sa	0217	10.5	320
	0821	0.9	27
	0232*	11.4	347
	0858*	−0.1	−3
28 Su ◑	0313	10.7	326
	0922	0.9	27
	0333*	11.1	338
	0956*	0.0	0
29 M	0413	10.9	332
	1027	0.7	21
	0437*	11.0	335
	1056*	0.1	3
30 Tu	0514	11.2	341
	1133	0.4	12
	0543*	10.9	332
	1157*	0.2	6

December

Day	Time (h m)	Height (ft)	Height (cm)
1 W	0614	11.6	354
	1237*	0.0	0
	0647*	10.9	332
2 Th	1257	0.1	3
	0713	12.0	366
	0138*	−0.5	−15
	0748*	11.0	335
3 F	0154	0.0	0
	0808	12.4	378
	0235*	−0.9	−27
	0845*	11.1	338
4 Sa	0248	0.0	0
	0901	12.6	384
	0328*	−1.2	−37
	0939*	11.2	341
5 Su ●	0339	0.0	0
	0951	12.7	387
	0418*	−1.3	−40
	1029*	11.2	341
6 M	0428	0.1	3
	1039	12.6	384
	0506*	−1.2	−37
	1116*	11.1	338
7 Tu	0516	0.3	9
	1125	12.3	375
	0552*	−0.9	−27
8 W	1202	10.8	329
	0602	0.6	18
	1211*	11.9	363
	0637*	−0.5	−15
9 Th	1248	10.5	320
	0648	0.9	27
	1257*	11.5	351
	0722*	0.0	0
10 F	0133	10.3	314
	0735	1.2	37
	0143*	10.9	332
	0807*	0.4	12
11 Sa	0219	10.0	305
	0824	1.5	46
	0230*	10.4	317
	0853*	0.9	27
12 Su	0306	9.8	299
	0914	1.7	52
	0320*	10.0	305
	0940*	1.2	37
13 M ◐	0354	9.7	296
	1008	1.9	58
	0413*	9.6	293
	1029*	1.5	46
14 Tu	0444	9.7	296
	1103	1.9	58
	0507*	9.3	283
	1119*	1.8	55
15 W	0535	9.8	299
	1158	1.8	55
	0603*	9.2	280
16 Th	1210	1.9	58
	0625	10.0	305
	1251*	1.5	46
	0657*	9.2	280
17 F	0100	1.9	58
	0713	10.3	314
	0142*	1.2	37
	0748*	9.3	283
18 Sa	0148	1.7	52
	0800	10.7	326
	0229*	0.7	21
	0836*	9.6	293
19 Su	0234	1.5	46
	0845	11.1	338
	0314*	0.3	9
	0921*	9.9	302
20 M	0318	1.2	37
	0928	11.5	351
	0357*	−0.1	−3
	1005*	10.2	311
21 Tu ○	0401	0.9	27
	1012	11.9	363
	0439*	−0.5	−15
	1048*	10.5	320
22 W	0445	0.6	18
	1056	12.2	372
	0523*	−0.8	−24
	1132*	10.8	329
23 Th	0531	0.4	12
	1142	12.4	378
	0608*	−0.9	−27
24 F	1218	11.1	338
	0620	0.2	6
	1230*	12.3	375
	0655*	−0.9	−27
25 Sa	0107	11.3	344
	0711	0.1	3
	0122*	12.1	369
	0745*	−0.8	−24
26 Su	0158	11.4	347
	0807	0.1	3
	0217*	11.8	360
	0838*	−0.5	−15
27 M	0253	11.5	351
	0907	0.2	6
	0316*	11.3	344
	0934*	−0.2	−6
28 Tu ◑	0351	11.5	351
	1010	0.2	6
	0419*	10.9	332
	1033*	0.2	6
29 W	0451	11.5	351
	1116	0.2	6
	0525*	10.5	320
	1135*	0.5	15
30 Th	0553	11.6	354
	1222*	0.0	0
	0632*	10.4	317
31 F	1238	0.6	18
	0655	11.8	360
	0125*	−0.2	−6
	0736*	10.4	317

Heights are referred to mean lower low water which is the chart datum of soundings. All times are local. Daylight Saving Time has been used when needed.

GPS Waypoints

The following list provides selected waypoints for the waters covered in this book. The latitude/longitude readings are taken from government light lists and must be checked against the appropriate chart and light list for accuracy. Some waypoints listed here are lighthouses and should not be approached too closely as they may be on land, in shallow water or on top of a reef. Many buoys must be approached with caution as they are often located near shallows or obstructions. The positions of every aid to navigation should be updated using the appropriate Coast Guard Local Notice to Mariners, which are available online at www.navcen.uscg.gov/lnm.

At 0400 UTC on May 2, 2000, the Selective Availability (SA) signal degradation of GPS signals was turned off by order of President Clinton. With SA turned on, users could expect GPS positions to fall within 100 meters of a correct position, 95 percent of the time. Now, with the SA degradation turned off, users should expect to obtain accuracy to within 20 meters or closer.

The U.S. Coast Guard will continue to provide Differential GPS (DGPS) correction signals for those who need accuracy of 10 meters or less. Most GPS units need the addition of a separate receiver to receive DGPS broadcasts.

Prudent mariners will not rely solely on these waypoints to navigate. Every available navigational tool should be used at all times to determine your vessel's position.

C&D Canal to Cape May

LOCATION	LAT	LON
1. Junction Lighted Bell Buoy CD	N 39°33.867'	W 075°33.300'
2. Ship John Shoal Light (on shoal)	N 39°18.317'	W 075°22.600'
3. Elbow of Cross Ledge Light	N 39°10.933	W 075°16.100'
4. Miah Maull Shoal Light (on shoal)	N 39°07.600'	W 075°12.600'
5. Fourteen Foot Bank Light	N 39°02.900'	W 075°10.933'
6. Brandywine Shoal Light (on shoal)	N 38°59.167'	W 075°06.783'
7. Brown Shoal Light	N 38°55.333'	W 075°06.050'
8. Cape May Canal W. Ent. S. Jetty Light 10	N 38°57.967'	W 074°58.033'

Cape May to Sandy Hook

LOCATION	LAT	LON
1. Cape May Inlet West Jetty Light 5	N°38 56.200'	W 074°51.917'
2. Great Egg Harbor Inlet Otr. Lgtd. Whst. B. GE	N°39 16.233'	W 074°31.933'
3. Absecon Inlet Breakwater Light 7	N°39 21.833'	W 074°24.433'
4. Little Egg Inlet Outer Lighted Whistle B. LE	N°39 26.800'	W 074°17.367'
5. Barnegat Lighted Whistle Buoy B1	N°39 44.483'	W 074°03.850'
6. Manasquan Inlet Light 3	N°40 00.170'	W 074°01.917'

New York Harbor

LOCATION	LAT	LON
1. Ambrose Light	N 40°27.000'	W 073°48.000'
2. Junction Lighted Buoy TC	N 40°28.400'	W 074°02.300'
3. Atlantic Highlands Breakwater Light	N 40°25.117'	W 074°01.167'
4. Great Kills Light	N 40°31.300'	W 074°07.900'
5. Coney Island Light	N 40°34.600'	W 074°00.700'
6. Romer Shoal Light	N 40°30.800'	W 074°00.800'

South Shore of Long Island

LOCATION	LAT	LON
1. Rockaway Inlet Lighted Bell Buoy 2	N 40°31.767'	W 073°56.383'
2. Jones Inlet Light	N 40°34.383'	W 073°34.533'
3. Fire Island Light	N 40°37.950'	W 073°13.117'
4. Moriches Inlet Approach Breakwater Light 2	N 40°45.800'	W 072°45.183'
5. Shinnecock Inlet Approach Lgtd. Whst. B. SH	N 40°49.000'	W 072°28.600'
6. Montauk Point Lighted Whistle Buoy MP	N 41°01.800'	W 071°45.700'

Long Island Sound, North Shore

LOCATION	LAT	LON
1. Chimney Sweeps Lighted Buoy 1	N 40°51.750'	W 073°46.783'
2. Hen and Chickens South Lighted Buoy 2	N 40°54.200'	W 073°44.400'
3. Great Captain Rocks Lighted Buoy 2	N 40°58.950'	W 073°39.067'
4. Great Captain Island Light	N 40°58.900'	W 073°37.400'
5. Twenty-Six Foot Spot Lighted Bell Buoy 32A	N 40°58.100'	W 073°32.800'
6. Stamford Harbor West Breakwater Light 3	N 41°00.900'	W 073°32.800'
7. Greens Ledge Light 4	N 44°17.417'	W 068°49.700'
8. Cable and Anchor Reef Lighted Bell B. 28C	N 41°00.550'	W 073°25.133'
9. Bridgeport Harbor Ch. Appr. Lgtd. Whst. B. BH	N 41°06.233'	W 073°11.733'
10. Middle Ground Light	N 41°03.583'	W 073°06.083'
11. Stratford Point Light	N 41°09.117'	W 073°06.200'
12. New Haven Harbor Lighted Whistle B. NH	N 41°12.100'	W 072°53.800'
13. Branford Reef Light	N 41°13.300'	W 072°48.300'
14. Goose Island Lighted Bell Buoy 10GI	N 41°12.100'	W 072°40.500'
15. Guilford Harbor Lighted Bell Buoy 4	N 41°15.000'	W 072°39.200'
16. Long Sand Shoal W. End Ltd. Gong B. W	N 41°13.583'	W 072°27.600'
17. Saybrook Breakwater Light	N 41°15.800'	W 072°20.567'
18. Long Sand Shoal East End Buoy E	N 41°15.800'	W 072°19.350'
19. Bartlett Reef Light	N 41°16.467'	W 072°08.233'
20. New London Channel Lighted Buoy 1	N 41°17.600'	W 072°04.800'
21. Seaflower Reef Light	N 41°17.767'	W 072°01.983'
22. North Dumpling Light	N 41°17.300'	W 072°01.200'
23. Latimer Reef Light	N 41°18.300'	W 071°56.000'
24. Inner Reef North Buoy 5	N 41°14.533'	W 072°46.050'

Long Island Sound, South Shore

LOCATION	LAT	LON
1. Stepping Stones Light	N 40°49.467'	W 073°46.483'
2. Hart Island Light 46	N 40°50.700'	W 073°46.000'
3. Plum Point Lighted Buoy 1	N 40°49.933'	W 073°43.717'
4. Gangway Rock Light 27A	N 40°51.483'	W 073°44.750'
5. Execution Rocks Light	N 40°52.683'	W 073°44.267'
6. Glen Cove Breakwater Light 5	N 40°51.700'	W 073°39.600'
7. Cold Spring Harbor Light	N 40°54.800'	W 073°29.600
8. Eaton's Neck Light	N 40°57.233'	W 073°23.717'
9. Port Jefferson Appr. Lighted Whistle Buoy PJ	N 40°59.300'	W 073°06.400'
10. Mattituck Inlet Breakwater Light MI	N 41°00.917'	W 072°33.667'
11. Orient Point Light	N 41°09.800'	W 072°13.400'
12. Valiant Rock Lighted Whistle Buoy 11	N 41°13.767'	W 072°04.000'
13. Race Rock Light	N 41°14.617'	W 072°02.817'
14. Gardiners Island Lighted Gong Buoy 1GI	N 41°09.000'	W 072°08.900'
15. Gardiners Bay S. Ent. Lighted Bell Buoy S	N 41°02.200'	W 072°03.100'
16. Threemile Harbor Ent. Lighted Bell Buoy TM	N 41°02.700'	W 072°11.300'
17. Montauk Harbor Ent. Lighted Bell Buoy M	N 41°05.100'	W 071°56.400'

Rhode Island

LOCATION	LAT	LON
1. Watch Hill Lighted Bell Buoy 2	N 41°17.983'	W 071°51.667'
2. Great Salt Pond Entrance Bell Buoy 2	N 41°12.100'	W 071°35.700'
3. Block Island N. Reef Lighted Bell Buoy 1BI	N 41°15.500'	W 071°34.600'
4. Point Judith Lighted Whistle Buoy 2	N 41°18.500'	W 071°28.300'
5. Narragansett Bay Ent. Lighted Whistle B. NB	N 41°23.000'	W 071°23.400'
6. Beavertail Light	N 41°26.967'	W 071°23.983'
7. Brenton Point Lighted Whistle Buoy 2	N 41°25.900'	W 071°21.800'
8. Sakonnet River Ent. Lighted Whistle B. SR	N 41°25.700'	W 071°13.400'

Buzzards Bay

LOCATION	LAT	LON
1. Buzzards Bay Entrance Light	N 41°23.800'	W 071°02.017'
2. Westport Harbor Entrance Light 7	N 41°30.400'	W 071°05.300'
3. Padanaram Breakwater Light 8	N 41°34.450'	W 070°56.350'
4. Phinney Rock Lighted Buoy DP	N 41°33.100'	W 070°53.000'
5. Butler Flats Light	N 41°36.200'	W 070°53.700'
6. New Bedford West Barrier Light	N 41°37.617'	W 070°54.367'
7. Dumpling Rocks Light 7	N 41°32.300'	W 070°55.283'
8. Ned Point Light	N 41°39.050'	W 070°47.733'
9. Sippican Harbor Lighted Buoy 2	N 41°39.700'	W 070°43.600'
10. Cleveland East Ledge Light	N 41°37.850'	W 070°41.650'
11. Quisset Harbor Entrance Lighted Buoy 2	N 41°32.600'	W 070°40.000'
12. Lone Rock Lighted Buoy	N 41°27.650'	W 070°51.150'
13. Cuttyhunk East Ent. Lighted Bell Buoy CH	N 41°26.600'	W 070°53.400'
14. Cuttyhunk West Entrance Buoy 1W	N 41°26.700'	W 070°55.500'

Cape Cod's South Shore, Vineyard Sound, Nantucket Sound

LOCATION	LAT	LON
1. Coffin Rock Lighted Buoy 1	N 41°30.700'	W 070°39.700'
2. Falmouth Inner Harbor Light 1	N 41°32.517'	W 070°36.500'
3. Hyannis Harbor Appr. Lighted Bell Buoy HH	N 41°36.000'	W 070°17.200'
4. Chatham Roads Bell Buoy 3	N 41°38.300	W 070°02.900'
5. Vineyard Sound Ent. Ltd. Whistle Buoy 32	N 41°22.100'	W 070°57.400'
6. Quicks Hole Entrance Ltd. Bell Buoy 1	N 41°25.800'	W 070°50.400'
7. Tarpaulin Cove Light	N 41°28.133'	W 070°45.450'
8. West Chop Light	N 41°28.850'	W 070°35.983'
9. East Chop Light	N 41°28.217'	W 070°34.050'
10. Edgartown Light	N 41°23.450'	W 070°30.183'
11. Cape Poge Light	N 41°25.167'	W 070°27.133'
12. Nantucket Bar Lighted Bell Buoy NB	N 41°19.000'	W 070°06.200'
13. Brant Point Light	N 41°17.400'	W 070°05.417'

Cape Cod Bay to Boston

LOCATION	LAT	LON
1. Cape Cod Canal Appr. Lighted Bell Buoy CC	N 41°48.900'	W 070°27.600'
2. Billingsgate Shoal Lighted Bell Buoy 1	N 41°48.800'	W 070°05.417'
3. Long Point Shoal Lighted Bell Buoy 3	N 42°02.000'	W 070°09.700'
4. Plymouth Bay Channel Lighted Buoy 3	N 41°59.700'	W 070°36.100'
5. Scituate Approach Lighted Gong Buoy SA	N 42°12.100'	W 070°41.900'
6. Nantasket Roads Channel Lighted Bell B. 3	N 42°19.100'	W 070°52.800'
7. Boston Lighted Whistle Buoy B	N 42°22.700	W 070°47.000'
8. Boston South Channel Entrance Buoy 1	N 42°21.900'	W 070°53.800'
9. Boston North Chan. Ent. Lighted Whistle B. NC	N 42°22.500'	W 070°54.300'

Massachusetts Bay to Portsmouth

LOCATION	LAT	LON
1. Tinkers Rock Gong Buoy TR	N 42°28.900'	W 070°48.900'
2. Marblehead Harbor Buoy 1MH	N 42°30.500'	W 070°50.000'
3. Salem Channel Buoy 3	N 42°31.100'	W 070°45.100'
4. Eastern Point Lighted Whistle Buoy 2	N 42°34.200'	W 070°39.800'
5. Annisquam River Ent. Lighted Bell Buoy AR	N 42°40.400'	W 070°41.000'
6. Essex Bay Entrance Lighted Bell Buoy 1	N 42°40.800'	W 070°42.300'
7. Merrimack River Ent. Lighted Whistle B. MR	N 42°48.600'	W 070°47.100'
8. Rye Harbor Ent. Lighted Whistle Buoy RH	N 42°59.600'	W 070°43.800'
9. Wood Island Lighted Buoy 2	N 43°27.400'	W 070°19.700'
10. Isles of Shoals Bell Buoy IS	N 42°58.900'	W 070°37.400'

Kittery to Portland

LOCATION	LAT	LON
1. York Harbor Lighted Bell Buoy YH	N 43°07.800'	W 070°37.000'
2. Perkins Cove Lighted Bell Buoy PC	N 43°14.400'	W 070°34.200'
3. Cape Porpoise Lighted Whistle Buoy CP	N 43°20.300'	W 070°23.600'
4. Wood Island Light	N 43°27.400'	W 070°19.700'
5. Portland Lighted Horn Buoy P	N 43°31.600'	W 070°05.500'
6. Portland Head Light	N 43°37.400'	W 070°12.500'

Casco Bay to Penobscot Bay

LOCATION	LAT	LON
1. Halfway Rock Light	N 43°39.350'	W 070°02.200'
2. Little Mark Island Monument Light	N 43°42.533'	W 070°01.867
3. Fuller Rock Light	N 43°41.750'	W 069°50.017'
4. Pond Island Light	N 43°44.400'	W 069°46.200'
5. Sheepscot River Ent. Lighted Bell Buoy 2SR	N 43°45.600'	W 069°41.200'
6. Seguin Light	N 43°42.500'	W 069°45.500'
7. Burnt Island Light	N 43°49.500'	W 069°38.400'
8. The Cuckolds Light	N 43°46.800'	W 069°39.000'
9. Ram Island Light	N 43°48.233'	W 069°35.950'
10. Manana Island Lighted Whistle Buoy 14M	N 43°45.300'	W 069°22.500'
11. Pemaquid Point Light	N 43°50.200'	W 069°30.350'
12. Marshall Point Lighted Whistle Buoy MP	N 43°55.300'	W 069°10.900'
13. Two Bush Ledge Lighted Bell Buoy 5TB	N 43°56.783'	W 069°04.917'
14. Tenants Harbor App. Lighted Bell Buoy 1	N 43°57.700'	W 069°10.900'
15. Whitehead Light	N 43°58.717'	W 069°07.450'
16. W. Penobscot Bay Ent. Lighted Gong B. PA	N 44°01.100'	W 069°00.300'
17. Matinicus Island Lighted Bell Buoy 9MI	N 43°53.100'	W 068°52.867'

Penobscot Bay to West Quoddy Head

LOCATION	LAT	LON
1. Brown Cow Ledge Whistle Buoy 2BC	N 44°06.733'	W 068°43.850'
2. Isle Au Haut Light	N 44°03.900'	W 068°39.100'
3. Saddleback Ledge Light	N 44°00.900'	W 068°43.600'
4. Burnt Coat Harbor Ent. Whistle Buoy BC	N 44°05.017'	W 068°26.233'
5. Long Island Lighted Gong Buoy LI	N 44°08.300'	W 068°20.500'
6. Long Ledge Lighted Gong Buoy 1	N 44°13.267'	W 068°17.783'
7. Frenchman Bay S. App. Lighted Whistle B. FBS	N 44°09.600'	W 068°08.800'
8. Great Duck Island Light	N 44°08.500'	W 068°14.700'
9. Mount Desert Rock Light	N 43°58.100'	W 068°07.700'
10. Schoodic Lighted Bell Buoy 2S	N 44°19.100'	W 068°02.100'
11. Southeast Rock Lighted Whistle Buoy 6A	N 44°19.800'	W 067°48.600'
12. Seahorse Lighted Bell Buoy 2SR	N 44°25.700'	W 067°38.500'
13. Moose Peak Light	N 44°28.500'	W 067°31.900'
14. Libby Island Light	N 44°34.100'	W 067°22.000'
15. Little River Daybeacon 1	N 44°39.050'	W 067°11.533'
16. West Quoddy Head Bell Buoy WQ	N 44°48.900'	W 066°57.000'

Extended Cruising

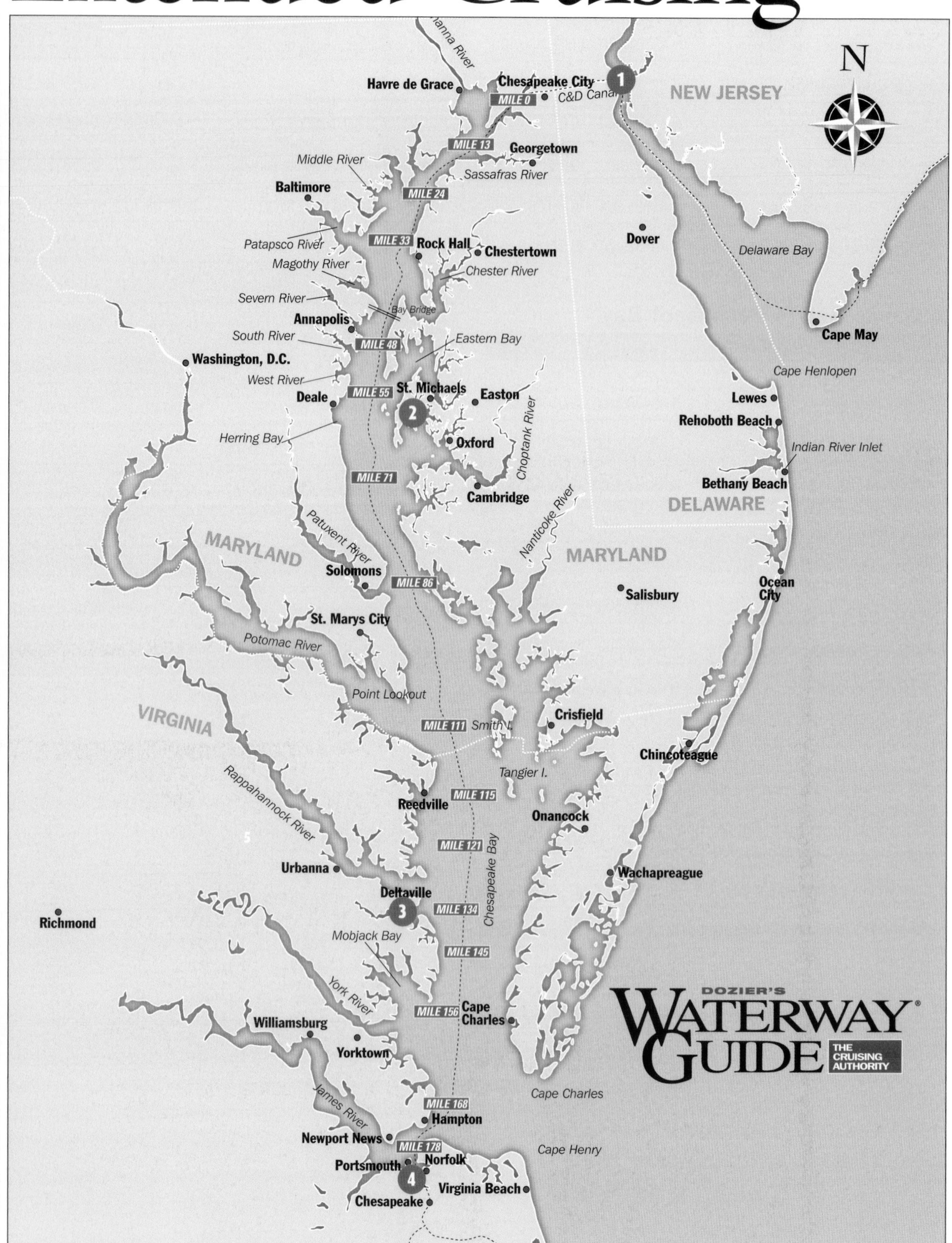

For detailed navigational information, charts, and extensive marina coverage see WATERWAY GUIDE, 2010 Chesapeake Bay Edition. Purchase online: www.waterwayguide.com or call 800-233-3359.

Chesapeake Bay Marinas

1. **Summit North**
   Bear, DE 302-836-1800

2. **St. Michaels Marina**
   St. Michaels, MD 800-678-8980

3. **Dozier Yachting Centers**
   Deltaville, VA 804-776-6711

4. **Tidewater Yacht Agency**
   Portsmouth, VA 757-393-2525

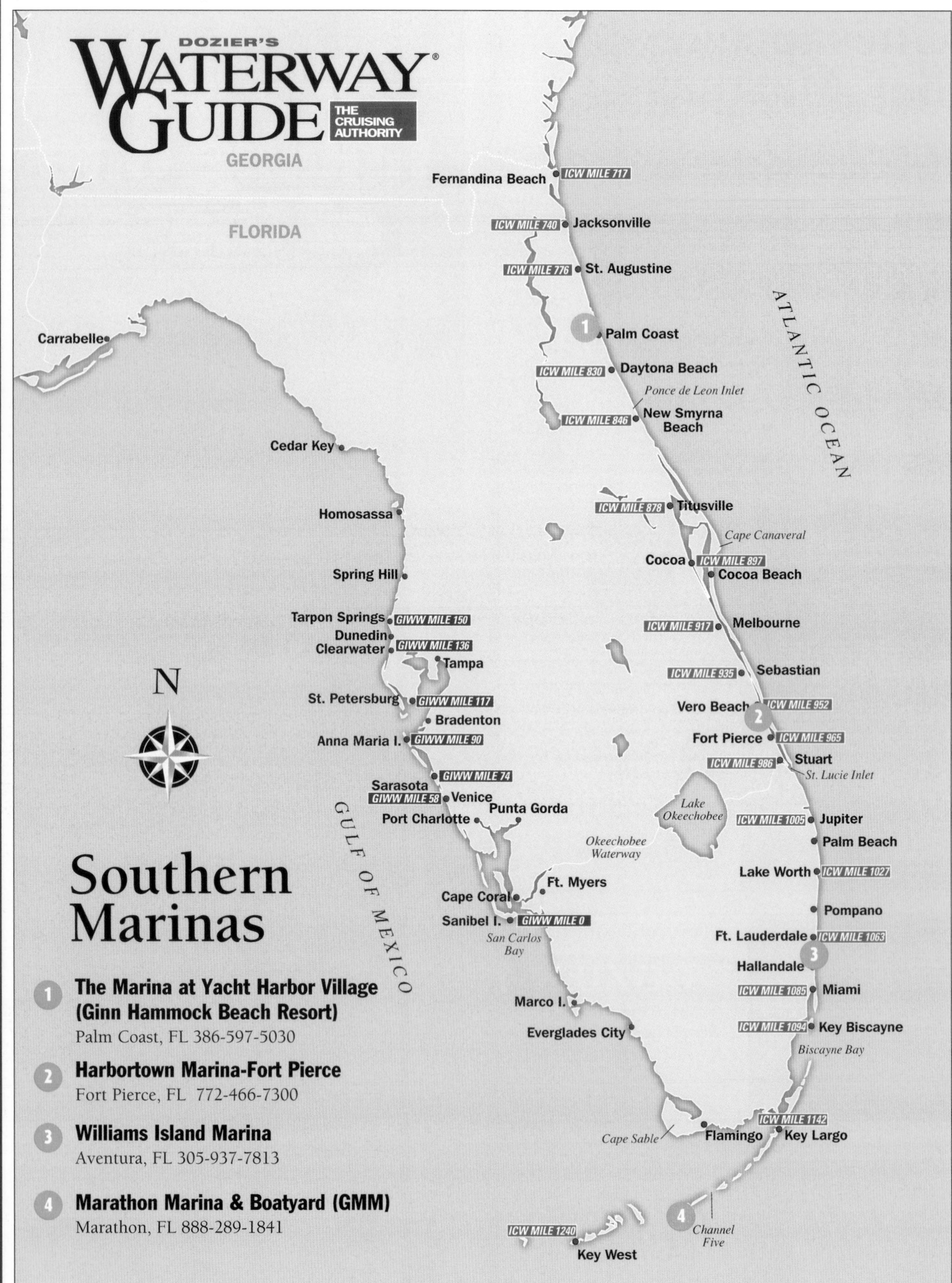

Southern Marinas

1. **The Marina at Yacht Harbor Village (Ginn Hammock Beach Resort)**
   Palm Coast, FL 386-597-5030
2. **Harbortown Marina-Fort Pierce**
   Fort Pierce, FL 772-466-7300
3. **Williams Island Marina**
   Aventura, FL 305-937-7813
4. **Marathon Marina & Boatyard (GMM)**
   Marathon, FL 888-289-1841

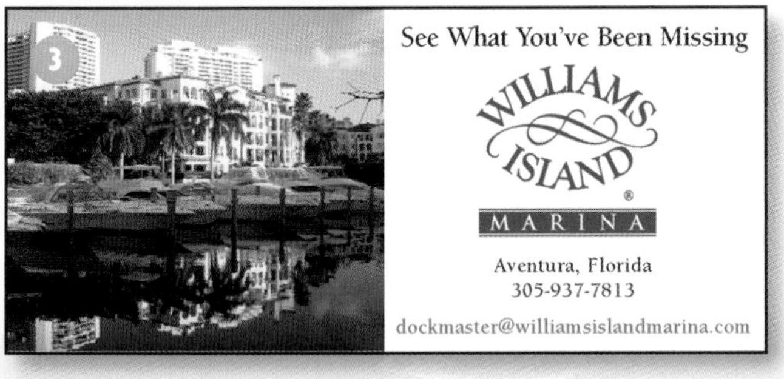

For detailed navigational information, charts, and extensive marina coverage see WATERWAY GUIDE, 2010 Southern Edition. Purchase online: www.waterwayguide.com or call 800-233-3359.

Advertising Sponsor/Marina Index

(Advertising Sponsors/Marinas are listed in bold.)

3 Mile Harbor Boatyard, 279, 280
79th Street Boat Basin, 104, 106

A

A Market - Newport, 314
A. C. Wescoat Co., 58
A.P.'s Inlet Marina, 80
Ace Insurance, Inside Front Cover
Admiral's Cove, The Club at, 3
Admiral's Hill Marina, 402
Advanced Tracking & Monitoring Services, 541
America's Great Loop Cruisers' Association (AGLCA), 18
Al Grovers High & Dry Marina, 137
Albany Yacht Club, 122
Aldo's Place, 295
Aldrich Boatyard, 154
All Island Marine, 134
All Seasons Marina, 54
All Seasons Marine, 100
Allen Harbor Marine Service, Inc., 362
Allen Harbor Yacht Club, 362
Alpine Boat Basin, 106
Amity Harbor Marine, 143
Anchorage Yacht Club Condominium, 143
Andrew's Marina at Harper's Landing, 215
Andy's Barnegat Boat Basin, 68
Angel's Marina, 308
Annisquam Yacht Club, 416
Apponaug Harbor Marina, 308
Aqualights, 5
Arnold's Yacht Basin, 76
Arrow Yacht Club, 129
Athens on the Hudson, 120
Atlantic Cruising Club, 5
Atlantic Highlands Municipal Harbor, 83
Atlantic Highlands Yacht Club, 83
Atlantis Yacht Club, 90
Avalon Anchorage Marina, 52
Avalon Pointe Marina Inc., 52
Avondale Boat Yard, 238

B

B & E Marine, A Virtual Boat Corp., 52
Back Eddy Restaurant, The, 334
Badger's Island Marina, 432
Bahrs Landing, 90
Bangor Landing Waterfront Park, 487
Bannister's Wharf, 312, 315
Bar Harbor Municipal Pier, 504
Barden's Boat Yard Inc., 341
Barnstable Harbor Marina, 386
Barnstable Marine Services, 386
Barrington Yacht Club, 320
Bass River Marina, 360
Bay Club Marina-Ocean City, 54
Bay Marina Inc., 308
Bay Pointe Marina, 396
Bay Shore Yacht Club, 146
Bayside Marine, 390
Baywood Marina, 76
Beach Haven Yacht Club Marina, 62, 63, 64
Beacon Marine Basin Inc., 416
Beacon Point Marine, 176
Beal's Lobster Pier, 504
Beaver Dam Marina, 150
Before the Bridge Restaurant, 154
Beggar's Wharf, 479
Belfast Boatyard, 487
Belfast City Landing, 487
Belle Vue Yachting Center, 298, 299, 302
Belmar Marina, 79,80, 81
Between the Bridges North, 208
Between the Bridges South, 208
Beverly Port Marina Inc., 410
Beverly Yacht Club, 341
Billings Diesel & Marine Service Inc., 499, 500
Billington Cove Marina, 301
Bismore Park, 360
Black Dog Wharf, The, 368
Block Island Boat Basin, 295
Block Island Harbormaster, 295
Blue Point Marina, 147
Blue Water Yacht Club, 138
Bluewater Books, 328
Boat Max at Minneford Marina, 160
Boathouse Restaurant and Marina Deck, 52
Boats Inc., 221
Boatworks, Inc 182
Boothbay Harbor Marina, 459, 460
Boothbay Harbor Shipyard, 459
Boothbay Harbor Yacht Club, 459
Boothbay Region Boatyard, 454, 456
Boston Waterboat Marina, 402
Boston Yacht Club, 407
Boston Yacht Haven, 402
Branford Landing Marina, 194
Branford Yacht Club, 194
Breakwater Marina, 440
Bree-Zee-Lee Yacht Basin, 44
Brennan Boat Company & Marina, 76
Brenton Cove Moorings, 312
Brewer Bruce and Johnson Marina - West, 194, 196
Brewer Bruce and Johnson Marina, 194, 196
Brewer Capri Marina at Inspiration Wharf, 241, 242, 243
Brewer Capri Marina East, 241, 242, 243
Brewer Capri Marina West, 241, 242, 243
Brewer Cove Haven Marina, 323
Brewer Dauntless Marina, 208, 211
Brewer Dauntless Shipyard and Marina, 208, 211
Brewer Deep River Marina, 213, 215
Brewer Ferry Point Marina, 208, 210
Brewer Fiddler's Cove Marina, 344, 348
Brewer Greenwich Bay Marina North A, 308, 310
Brewer Greenwich Bay Marina North B, 308, 310
Brewer Greenwich Bay Marina, 308, 309
Brewer Pilots Point Marina East, 199, 200
Brewer Pilots Point Marina North, 199, 200
Brewer Pilots Point Marina South, 199, 200
Brewer Plymouth Marine, 390
Brewer Post Road Boat Yard, 169
Brewer Sakonnet Marina, 327, 326
Brewer South Freeport Marine, 440
Brewer Stirling Harbor Marina, 270, 268
Brewer Stratford Marina, 189, 190
Brewer Wickford Cove Marina, 304, 306
Brewer Yacht Haven Marina, 176, 179
Brewer Yacht Yard at Cowesett, 308, 309
Brewer Yacht Yard at Glen Cove, 246, 247
Brewer Yacht Yard at Greenport, 267, 270
Brewer Yacht Yard at Mystic, 230, 232
Brewer Yacht Yards, Inside Back Cover & Flap
Brick Cove Marina, 270
Bridge Marina, Bayville, NY, 249
Bridge Marina, Salisbury, MA, 422
Brielle Marine Basin, 77
Brielle Yacht Club & Sandbar Restaurant, 77
Bristol Marine, 320
Bristol Yacht Club, 320
Brittania Yachting Center, 257
Broad Cove Marine Service, 468
Brooklin Boat Yard, 500
Brooklyn Marine, 100
Brown & Howard Marina, 311, 312, 315
Brown's Boat Works, 190
Brown's Boat Yard, 194
Brown's Wharf Marina, 457, 458, 459
Brown's Yacht Yard, 416
Bry's Marine, 80
Buck's Harbor Marine, 495
Bucksport Marina, 487
Bucksport Public Dock, 487
Burnett's Marina, 146
Burr Bros. Boats Inc., 341
Burr's Marina, 224

C

Camden Town Docks, 483
Camden Yacht Club, 483
Camp Marine Services, 52
Canyon Club Resort Marina, 43, 44, 47
Cape Ann Marina Resort, 416
Cape Cod Shipbuilding Co., 341
Cape May 43,
Cape May Marine, 44
Capital District Marina, 122
Cap'n Fish's Motel & Marina, 459

Captain Andy's Fishing Center, 54
Captain J.J. O'Connell Co., 324
Captain's Cove Marina, Highlands, NJ, 90
Captain's Cove Marina, Quincy, MA, 395, 396, 398
Captain's Cove Seaport, 187
Captain's Inn, 68
Captree State Park Marina, 144
Carousel Marina, 457, 459, 461
Carriage House Marina, 90
Carver Boat Sales, 77
Casey's Marina, 312
Cassidy's Marina, 76
Castaways Yacht Club, 165, 166, 167
Castine Town Dock, 495
Castleton Boat Club, 122
Catskill Marina, 119, 120, 121
Catskill Yacht Club, 120
Cay Electronics 310,
Cedar Cove Marina, 72
Cedar Creek Sailing Center/ Marina, 71
Cedar Island Marina, 199, 200, 201
Cedar Marina Inc., 187
Cedar Point Yacht Club, 185
Center Harbor Yacht Club, 500
Centerboard Yacht Club, 440
Centerport Yacht Club, 257
Certified Marine Service, 116
Champlin's Marina, Hotel and Resort, 295
Channel Club Marina, 90
Charles Point Marina, 112
Chartroom at Chase, Leavitt & Co., 440
Chestnut Neck Boat Yard, 58
Chicks Marina, 436, 437
Chrisholm Marina, 215
City Island Yacht Club, 165
City Island Yacht Sales, 165
City Point Yacht Club, 192
Claremont Hotel, 504
Clark Boat Yard & Marine Works, LLC, 317
Clark's Landing Marina Bar & Grill, 77
Claudio's Marina, Restaurant and Clam Bar, 270
Clifton Dock, 504
Club at Admiral's Cove, The 3
Cobalt Marine, 215
Cod End Market, Cookhouse & Dock, 475
Coecles Harbor Marina and Boatyard, 270
Coeymans Landing Marina, 120
Cohasset Harbor Marina, 394
Cohasset Harbormaster, 394
Cohasset Yacht Club, 394
Cole Parkway Marina, 392
Colonial Pemaquid State Historic Site, 464
Colonial Shores Resort and Marina, 154
Commodore Bay Marina, 52
Compass Rose Marine Supply, 255
Compo Yacht Basin, 185
Comstock Boat Works, 76
Conanicut Marine Services Inc., 317
Concordia Company Inc., 336
Coneys Marine, 255
Connors and O'Brien Marina, 238
Consolidated Yachts Inc., 165
Constitution Marina, 401, 402, 404
Cook's Lobster House, 448
Corey Yacht Docks, 356, 357
Corinthian Yacht Club of Cape May, 44
Corinthian Yacht Club, 407
Cornwall Yacht Club, 116
Cortland Yacht Club, 112
Cotuit Town Wharf, 356
Cove Marina, 422
Coveside Inn-Marina, 464
Coxsackie Yacht Club, 120
Cozy Cove Marina, 72
Crocker's Boat Yard, 414
Crocker's Boatyard Inc., 224
Crosby Yacht Yard Inc., 356
Crow's Nest Marina, 134
Crystal Cove Marina, 402
Crystal Point Yacht Club, 77
Custom Navigation Systems, 199
Cutchogue Harbor Marina Inc., 289
Cuttyhunk Marina, 366

D

Dale's Marina, Sanzari Companies, 76
Damar, Ltd./Midway Marina, 215
Danford's Marina and Inn, 261, 262
Danversport Yacht Club Inc., 410
Dark Harbor Boat Yard, 488
David Beaton & Sons, 76
David S. Dunavan Visitors Dock, 182
Davis & Tripp Inc., 336
Davis Park Marina, 144
Davison's Metro Power Center, 134
DELEMAR Greenwich Harbor, 176
Delmarine, 138
Dennis Municipal Marina, 386
Dennis Yacht Club, 386
Derecktor Shipyards, 169
Derecktor Shipyards, 187
Dering Harbor Marina, 270
Diamond Cove Marina, 284
Dickson's Marine, 150
Digital Yachts, 450
Dillon's Creek Marina, 72
DiMillo's Old Port Marina & Yacht Sales, 439, 440, 443
Dockside Marina, 368
Dodson Boatyard, 235
Dolphin Marina & Restaurant, 448
Dolphin Yacht Club, 407
Donnell's Marina, 432
Dorchester Yacht Club, 402
Doug Westin's Boat Shop, 147
Dozier's Port Urbanna Marina, 539
Dozier's Regatta Point Yachting Center, 539
Dutch Harbor Boat Yard, 317
Dutch Wharf Boat Yard and Marina Inc., 194
Duxbury Town Pier, 390
Dysart's Great Harbor Marina, 504, 506

E

Earl's Marina & Comorant Marine, 339
East Coast Yacht Sales, 440
East Creek Marina, 288
East End Yacht Club, 187
East Greenwich Yacht Club, 308
East Hampton Marina, 279
East Hampton Point Marina & Boatyard, 279
East Hampton Town Dock, 279
Eastern Marine, 62
Eastern Yacht Club, 407
Eastport Breakwater/ City Dock, 519
Eaton's Boat Yard, 495
Eddy Marina, The, 454
Edgartown Harbor, 368
Edgartown Yacht Club, 368
Edgewater Marina, 106
Edgewood Yacht Club, 323
Edwards Boatyard Inc., 356
EM Falmouth, dba East Marine, 353
Empire Point Marina, 134
Engines Inc., 58
Englewood Boat Basin, 106
Enos Marine/Pier 7 Marina, 416
Escape Harbor Marina, 62
Essex Boat Works Inc., 208
Essex Island Marina, 208
Essex Marina, 420
Essex Yacht Club, 208

F

F.L.Tripp & Sons Inc., 334
F.W. Thurston Co., 504
Fair Haven Yacht Works, 90
Fairhaven Shipyard Companies North Yard, 336, 337, 338
Fairhaven Shipyard Companies South Yard, 336, 337, 338
Falmouth Marine & Yachting Center, 353
Falmouth Town Marina, 353
Fayerweather Boat Yard, 187
Fayerweather Yacht Club, 187
Fire Island Pines Marina, 144
Fisherman's Wharf Inn, 459
Fishers Island Mobil, 227
Fishers Island Yacht Club Marina, 227, 228
Flagship Marina, 190
Florida Bow Thrusters, 552
Flyer's Boat Shop & Rentals, 386
Flying Bridge Restaurant, 353
Flynn's Marina & Restaurant, 144
Forked River State Marina, 68
Forsberg's Boat Works, 76
Fort Rachel Marine Service Inc., 230
Forty 1° North, 312
Frank & Dick's Bait, Tackle Food & Fuel, 144
Frank Hall Boat Yard, 238
Frank M. Weeks Yacht Yard, 150
Fred Chall Marine, 137
Fred J. Dion Yacht Yard Inc., 410, 412
Front Street Marina, 116

G

G&R Marine Repair Service, 165
Gales Ferry Marina, 224
Gamage Shipyard, 464
Garden State Yacht Sales & Marina, 77
Gardiner's Marina, 278, 279, 280
Gateway Marina, Brooklyn, NY 100
Gateway Marina, Highlands, NJ 90
Gilchrist Restaurant, 58
Glen Cove Marina, 245, 246, 247
Gloucester Marine Inc., 416
Goat Island Marina, 312, 315, 316
Gold Star Battalion/Coneys Marine, 255
Goldsmith's Boat Shop, 270
Gone Fishing Marina, 284
Goodsell Point Marina, 194
Gowen Marine, 439, 440, 442
Graef Boat Yard, 54
Grant Boat Works, 68
Grassy Sound Marina, 52
Great Bay Marina, 58
Great Bay Marine Inc., 428
Great Island Boat Yard, 448
Great Peconic Bay Marina, 288
Green Cove Marina, 76
Green Harbor Marina, 390
Green Pond Marina, 356

Greenhaven Marina, 238
Greenport Mitchell Park Marina, 269, 270
Greenport Yacht and Ship Co., 270
Greenwich Cove Marina, 308
Grey Lady Marine, 376
Guilford Boat Yards Inc., 194
Guilford Yacht Club, 194
Gulfway Marine Service, 242
Gus Marine, 138
Guy Lombardo Marina, 137
Gwenmor Marina Inc., 230

H

H&H Propeller Shop Inc., 410
H&M Powles Marina, 249
Hagler's Marina, 62
Half Moon Bay Marina, 112, 113
Halsey's Marina, 278, 279, 280
Hamilton Marine, 479
Hampton Boat Works, 154
Hampton Shipyard, 154
Hampton Watercraft & Marine, 154, 289
Hancock Point Dock, 514
Handy Boat Service, 440, 444
Harbor Hill Marina, 221
Harbor House Marina, 176, 177, 179
Harbor Island Municipal Marina, 169
Harbor Light Marina, 308
Harbor Marina, 278, 279
Harbor One Marina, 205, 207
Harbor Park Marina/ Dockhouse Deli, 176
Harbor Side Hotel & Marina, 504
Harbor View Marina, 44
Harborside Marina, 199
Harbortown Marina - Ft. Pierce, 541
Harbour Cove Marina, 54
Harbourside Lobstermania, 308
Harlem Yacht Club, 165
Harraseeket Yacht Club, 440
Harry's Marine Repair, 199
Harry's Starcrest Marina, 52
Haverstraw Marina, 112
Hawthorne Cove Marina, 410
Hays Haven Marina Inc., 215
Hempstead Harbour Yacht Club, 246
Hempstead Town Marina East, 136
Hempstead Town Marina West, 136
Herreshoff Marine Museum, 320, 321
Hidden Cove Marina Inc., 276
Hidden Harbor Marina, 143
Hideaway Marina, 116
Hilton's Marina, 421, 422, 423
Hinch Marina, 44
Hinckley Co., The, 504
Hinckley Company's Little Harbor Marine, The, 319
Hinckley Yacht Services, 76
Hingham Shipyard Marinas, 395, 396, 397
Hingham Yacht Club, 396
Historic Gardner's Basin, 58
Hobby Lobby Marine, 72
Hochstrasser's Marina, 62
Holiday Harbor Marina, 68, 69
Holiday Inn Bar Harbor, 504
Hopkins Boat Yard, 489
Hop-O-Nose Marina, 120
Hudson Power Boat Assoc., 120
Hudson River Maritime Museum, 116
Huguenot Yacht Club, 165
Hull Yacht Club, 396
Hunt Yachts, 319
Huntington Town Dock, 255
Huntington Yacht Club, 255
Hyannis Marina/Tugboats Restaurant, 358, 359, 360
Hyannis Yacht Club, 360
Hyde Park Marina/Brass Anchor Restaurant, 116

I

Ida Lewis Yacht Club, 312
Imperial Yacht Club Inc., 165
Indian Cove Restaurant & Marina, 154, 289
Indian Neck Yacht Club, 194
Innspot on the Bay, 154
Irwin Marine, 90
Island Boatyard and Marina, The, 270
Island Cove Marina, 208
Island Heights Yacht Club, 72
Island View Marina, 150
Islander Boat Center, 143
Islesford Dock Restaurant, 504

J

J.O. Brown & Son Inc., 489
Jack Baker's Lobster Shanty & Wharfside, 77
Jack's Marine, 270
Jackson's Marina, 154, 289
Jamestown Boat Yard, 317
Jeff's Marine Service, 471
Jeff's Yacht Haven, 116
Jersey Shore Marina, 76
Johnson Brothers Boat Works, 76
Johnson's Boatyard, 304
Jonesport Shipyard, 518
Journey's End Marina, 479
Jubilee Yacht Club, 410
Julius Petersen Boat Yard, 111

K

Kadey Krogen Yachts, Outside Back Flap
Kammerman's Atlantic City Marina, 57, 58
Karl Tank Shipyard, 143
Kennebec Tavern & Marina, 452, 453
Kennebunkport Marina, 436
Keyport Marine Basin, 87
Kingman Yacht Center, 343, 344, 347
Kingston Municipal Marina, 116
Kittery Point Wharf, 432
Kittery Point Yacht Yard, 432
Knickerbocker Yacht Club, 242
Knight Marine Service, 479
Knutson Marine, 255
Knutson's Yacht Haven Marina, 255
Kollegewidgwok Yacht Club, 500

L

La Sala Boat Yard, 143
Landfall Navigation, 16
Landing Restaurant, The, 407
Landings Restaurant & Marina, The, 479
Land's End Motel & Marina, 147
Lanoka Harbor Marina, 71
Larchmont Yacht Club, 169
Larry's Lighthouse Marina, 288
Laurel Harbor Marina, 71
Lavallette Yacht Club, 72
Leeward Cove South, 150
Lentze Marina Inc., 87
Leonardo State Marina, 83
Liberty Harbor Marina and Dry Dock Inc., 106
Liberty Landing Marina, 106
Liberty Marina, 410
Lighthouse Marina, 68
Lighthouse Point Marina, 72
Lighthouse Pointe Marina, 52
Lincoln Harbor Yacht Club, 106, 109
Little Egg Harbor Yacht Club, 62
Lobster Cove Marina & Market, 416
Lobster House Restaurant, The, 43, 44, 48, 49
Lobster Inn, The, 154
Lobsterman's Wharf Restaurant & Inn, 464
Lockwood Boat Works, 86, 87, 89
Long Cove Marina, 301
Long Island Maritime Museum, 147
Long Island Yacht Club, 143
Long Island Yacht Sales, 146
Long Island Yacht Services, 255
Long Key Marina, 68
Long Point Marine, 390
Louie's Oyster Bar & Grille, 242
Lou's Boat Basin LLC, 187
Lou's Boat Basin, 116
Lyman-Morse Boat Building, 471
Lynch's Marina, 119
Lynn Marine Supply, 407
Lynn Municipal Pier, 405
Lynn Yacht Club, 405

M

MacDonald Yacht Rigging, 176
MacDougalls' Cape Cod Marine Service, 352, 353, 354
Maciel Marine, 368
Mad Max Marina, 368, 373
Maidstone Harbor Marina, 279
Maine Maritime Museum, 452
Maine Yacht Center, 439, 440
Mako Marine, 137
Mamaroneck Beach and Yacht Club, 169
Manchester Marine Corp., 414
Manchester Town Dock, 414
Manhasset Bay Marina/La Motta's Restaurant, 242
Manhasset Bay Yacht Club, 242
Mansion Marina, 98
Mantoloking Yacht Club, 76
Marathon Marina & Boatyard, 541
Marblehead Harbormaster, 407
Marblehead Trading Co., 407
Marina at American Wharf, The, 224
Marina at Barnegat Light, The, 68
Marina at Hammock Beach, 541
Marina at Harbour Place, 427, 428, 429
Marina at Rowes Wharf, 402
Marina at Tall Oaks, The, 68
Marina at the Dock, 190
Marina at Vanderbilt's Wharf, 147
Marina Bay Docking, 301
Marina Bay on Boston Harbor, 402
Marina Life, 125
Marina on the Bay, 90
Marine Basin Marina, 100
Marine Max Mid-Atlantic Marina, 77
Mariner's Cove Marine, 154, 289
Mariner's Harbor, 116
Mariner's Marina, 68
Maritech Marine Electronics, 176
Marshfield Town Dock-Green Harbor, 390
Marshview Marina LLC, 199
Martha's Vineyard Shipyard, 368
Mason's Island Marina, 230
Mattakeese Wharf Restaurant, 386

Matt-A-Mar Marina, 264
Mattapoisett Boatyard Inc., 339
Mattituck Inlet Marina and Shipyard Inc., 264
McMichael Rushmore Yard, 169
McMichael Yacht Yard, 169
Menemsha Harbor, 368
Menemsha Texaco Service, 368
Mentor Marine, 76
Mermaid's Cove Marina, 76
Merri-Mar Yacht Basin Inc., 422
Metedeconk Marina, 76
Metedeconk River Yacht Club, 76
Metro Marine, 129
Miamogue Yacht Club, 187
Middlesex Yacht Club, 215
Middletown - Harbor Park, 215
Milford Boat Works, 190
Milford Landing, 190
Milford Yacht Club, 190
Mill Creek Marina, 276
Mill Dam Marina, 255
Mill River Marine Railways, 394
Mill Wharf Marina, 392
Millway Marina Inc., 386
Milt's Marina @ TWS Restaurant, 308
Minisceongo Yacht Club, 112
Minmar Marine & Boat Sales, 52
Minneford Marina, 163, 165
Miss Chris Marina, 44
Modern Yachts Inc, 154, 289
Molly Pitcher Inn/Marina, 90, 92
Montauk Lake Club and Marina, 281, 282, 284
Montauk Marine Basin, 284
Montauk Yacht Club Resort & Marina, 282, 283, 284
Monument Beach Marina, 344
Mooring, The, 137
Morgan Marina, 87
Morris Service Northeast Harbor, 504
Morris Yachts Bass Harbor, 504
Morrison's Beach Haven Marina, 62
Mt. Sinai Yacht Club, 262
Muscongus Bay Lobster Co., 468
Mystic Downtown Marina, 230
Mystic River Marina, 230
Mystic Seaport Museum and Docks, 230, 233, 234
Mystic Shipyard, 230, 231, 232

N

Nacote Creek Marina, 58
Nantucket Boat Basin, 376, 377
Nantucket Moorings, 376
Nantucket Ship Chandlery Corp., 376
Nantucket Yacht Club, 376
Nature Conservancy, The, 351
Nauticus Marina, 356
Navesink Marina, 90
NE Boatworks at East Passage Yachting Center, 319
Nelson Marine Basin and Sailing Center, 72
New Bedford Yacht Club, 336
New Hamburg Yacht Club, 116
New Hampshire Dept. of Environment, 426
New Haven Yacht Club, 192
New London Waterfront Park, 224
New Meadows Marina, 448
New Rochelle Municipal Marina, 165, 167, 168
New Suffolk Shipyard, 289
New York Athletic Club, 165
New York Sailing Center & Yacht Club, 165
New York Skyports Marina, 129
Newburyport Boat Basin, 421, 422, 423
Newburyport Central Waterfront Park, 422
Newburyport Harbor Marina, 421, 422, 423
Newburyport Yacht Club, 422
Newport Harbor Hotel & Marina, 312, 314, 315
Newport Marina, 104, 105, 106
Newport Marina, 312
Newport Onshore Marina, 312
Newport Restoration Foundation, 312
Newport Shipyard, 312
Newport Yacht Club, 312
Newport Yachting Center Marina, 312
Nichols Great Kill Park Marine, 98
Nichols Yacht Yard Inc., 169
Nicoll's Point Marina, 147
Noank Shipyard, 230
Noank Village Boatyard, 229, 230
North Cove Marina, 106
North Cove Yacht Club, 205
North Hempstead Town Dock, 242
North Marine, 353
North Shore Sport Fisherman Dock, 416
North Shore Yacht Club, 242
Northeast Harbor Marina, 504
Northport Village Dock, 257
Northport Yacht Club, 257
Northside Marina, 386
Norton's Shipyard & Marina Inc., 308
Norwalk Cove Marina Inc., 181, 182
Norwalk Yacht Club, 182
Norwest Marine, Pawcatuck, CT, 238
Norwest Marine, Norwalk, Ct, 182

O

Oak Bluffs Marina, Martha's Vineyard, 368
Oak Leaf Marina Inc., 208, 210
Oakdale Yacht Service, 147
Oakland's Restaurant & Marina, 154
Ocean Beach Marina Central, 71
Ocean Beach Marina, 72
Ocean Gate Yacht Basin, 72
Ocean Marine, 137
Ocean Outboard, 138
Ocean Point Marina, 464
Oceanic Marina, 90
Oceanport Landing, 90
Offshore East Marina, 208
Old Colony Yacht Club, 402
Old Lyme Dock Co., 208
Old Lyme Marina Inc., 208
Old Man's Boatyard, 262
Oldport Marine Services, 312
Onset Bay Marina, 344
Orient by the Sea Marina & Restaurant, 270
Outboard Barn, 143
Outboard Service of Al Grovers, 137
Outermost Harbor Marine, 363
Oyster Bay Marine Center, 247, 249
Oyster Bend Marina, 182
Oyster Harbors Marine, 356
Oyster Point Hotel/Marina, 90, 92
Oyster Point Marina, 192
Oyster River Boat Yard, 363

P

Padebco Custom Boats, 468
Palmer Point Marina and Ship's Store, 176
Palmer's Cove Yacht Club, 410
Pantaenius, Back Cover
Parker's Boatyard Inc., 344
Patsy's Bay Marina, 112
Patten Point Yacht Club, 90
Patten's Yacht Yard, 432
Paul's Marina, 448
Pawtuxet Cove Marina, 323
Payne's Dock, 295
Pease Boat Works & Marine Railway, 363
Peconic Marina, 289
Peekskill Yacht Club, 112
Pemaquid Fisherman's Co-op, 464
Penny Bridge Marine, 112
Pequonnock Yacht Club Inc., 187
Performance Marine, 436
Perkins Marine, 420
Peterson's Riviera Inn & Marina, 77
Petzold's Marine Center, 215
Pickering Wharf Marina, 410
Pier 37, 353
Pier 47 Marina, 52
Pier 65 Marina, 238
Pier 76 Marina, 199
Pier One Marina, Restaurant & Motel, 72
Pike Marine, 420
Pine Island Marina, 224
Pirate Cove Marina, 327
Pirates Cove Marine Inc., 227
Pleasant Street Wharf Inc., 304
Pleasure Bay Yacht Basin, 90
Plymouth Town Wharf, 390
Plymouth Yacht Club, 390
Point at Key Harbor Marina, LLC, The, 68
Point Independence Yacht Club, 344
Point Judith Marina, 298, 299, 302
Polychron Marina, 165
Ponaug Marina, 308
Ponquoge Marina, 154
Pootatuck Yacht Club, 190
Pope's Island Marina, 336
Port Clinton Marina, 199
Port Edgewood, 323
Port Imperial Marina, 106
Port Jefferson Town Marina, 262
Port Milford Marina, 190
Port Niantic, 221
Port of Egypt Marine, 270
Port Sheepshead Marina, 100
Port Washington Yacht Club, 242
Portland Boat Works Inc., 215
Portland Riverside Marina, 215
Portland Yacht Club, 440
Portland Yacht Services, 440
Portsmouth Public Launch Ramp, 428
Portsmouth Yacht Club, 428
Poughkeepsie Yacht Club, 116
Prescott Park Municipal Dock, 428
Pridwin Hotel, The, 270
Provincetown Marina, 386

Q

Quantum Sails Long Island Sound, 242
Quissett Harbor Boat Yard, 350

R

R.N.R. Marine, 396
Ragged Rock Marina, 208
Ralph's Fishing Station, 262
Ram Point Marina, 301
Ram's Head Inn, 270
Raynes Marine, 500
Remsenburg Marina, 150
Rex Marine Center, 182
Rhode Island Yacht Club, 323

Rick's Marina, 68
Rings Island Marina, 422
Ring's Marine Services Inc., 440
Riverbank Marina, 72
Riverside Boat Co., 464
Riverview Marine Services Inc., 120
Riverview Restaurant, The, 147
Robert Moses State Park Boat Basin, 144
Robinhood Marine Center, 454, 455, 456
Rockland Public Landing, 479
Rockport Marine Inc., 483
Rocktide Inn, 459
Rondout Yacht Basin, 116
Roseman's Boat Yard, 44
Rowayton Yacht Club, 182
Rudy's Tackle Barn, 172
Rumery's Boatyard, 438
Russo Marine, 402
Ryders Cove Boat Yard, 363

S

S.T. Preston and Son, 270
Sag Harbor Cove East, 276
Sag Harbor Cove West, 276
Sag Harbor Yacht Club, 274, 275, 276
Sag Harbor Yacht Yard, 276
Sagamore Yacht Club, 249
Sailor's Haven Marina, 144
Sakonnet Point Marina, 327
Salem Water Taxi Inc., 410, 412
Saltaire Marina, 134
Samalot Marine, 112
Sandwich Marina/East Boat Basin, 386
Saquatucket Municipal Marina, 362
Satuit Boat Club, 392
Saugerties Marina, 119
Saybrook Point Inn & Marina, 205, 206
Schooner Island Marina, 52
Schooner Restaurant, 137
Scituate Harbor Marina, 392
Scituate Harbor Yacht Club, 392
Scituate Launch/Waterline Moorings, 392
Sea Fuels Marine, 336
Sea View Marina, 144
Sea Village Marina, 54
Seaboard Marine, 87
Seaborn Marina, 146
Seal Cove Boatyard Inc., 495
Seaport Inn & Marina, 336
Seaport Landing Marina, 405
Seaport Marine, 230
Searsport Public Landing, 487
Seaside Park Yacht Club, 72
Seaview Harbor Marina, 54
Seaweed Yacht Club, 112
Sebasco Harbor Resort, 448
Senator Frank S. Farley State Marina, 58
Setauket Yacht Club Inc., 262
Seymour's Boat Yard, 257
Shady Harbor Marina & Water's Edge Restaurant, 120
Shagwong Marina, 279
Shark River Hills Marina, 80
Shark River Yacht Club Inc., 80
Shattemuc Yacht Club, 111
Shaw's Boat Yard Inc., 324
Sheepscot Bay Boat Co., 454
Sheepshead Bay Yacht Club, 100
Shelter Harbor Marina, 62
Shelter Island Yacht Club, 270
Sheltered Cove Marina, 62
Shennecossett Yacht Club, 224
Sherry & Joe Cores Best Boat Works, 154
Shinnecock Canal Marina, 1 54, 289
Ship Ashore Marina, 276
Ship Shops Inc., 360
Shipyard Quarters Marina, 402
Shongut Marine, 172
Signal Point Marina, 459
Silly Lily Fishing Station, 150
Silver Cloud Harbor Marina, 68
Silver Spring Marine, 301
Smuggler's Cove Marina, 295
Smugglers Cove, 52
Snapper Inn Waterfront Restaurant, 147
Snug Harbor Marina, Wakefield, RI, 299
Snug Harbor Marina, Montauk, NY, 284
Somers Point Marina, 54
Somerset Marine Inc., 324
Sorrento Town Dock, 516
South Boston Yacht Club, 402
South Bristol Fisherman's Co-op, 464
South Jersey Marina, 43, 44, 45
South Minneford Yacht Club, 165
South Port Marine, 440, 442, 444
Southwest Boat Marine Services, 504
Southwick's Marina, 62
Southwinds Harbour Marina, 68
Spectacle Island Marina, 401, 402, 404
Spellman's Marine, 154
Spencer's Bayside Marina, 68
Spencer's Marina, 190
Spicer's Noank Marina, 230
Spring Point Marina, 440
Sprite Island Yacht Club, 182
Spruce Head Marine, 475
St. Brendan's Isle, 20
St. Michaels Marina, 539
Stage Harbor Marine, 363
Stamford Landing Marina, 176
Standish Boat Yard, 327
Stanley's Boat Yard Inc., 320
Star Island Yacht Club and Marina, 284, 285
Steamboat Inn, 230
Stelter Marine Sales, 165
Stone Cove Marina, 301
Stone Harbor Marina, 52
Stonington Harbor Yacht Club, 235
Stony Brook Yacht Club, 259
Stony Point Bay Marina & Yacht Club, 112
Striper Marina Inc., 320
Strong's Marine LLC, 264
Strouts Point Wharf Co., 440
Studio Restaurant, 416
Stuyvesant Yacht Club, 165
Suffolk Marine Center, 143
Summit North Marina, 539
Sun-Dek Marina, 150
Sunset Bay Marina & Anchorage, 19
Sunset Bay Marina, 396
Sunset Harbor Marina, 148, 149, 150
Sunset Marina, South Portland, ME, 440
Sunset Marina, Brant Beach, NJ, 76
Surfside 3 at Chelsea Piers, 106
Surfside 3 Marina, 143
Surfside 3 West Hampton, 153
Surfside Marina, 90
Swansea Marina, 324
Switlik , 1

T

Tabat Marine, 150
Table 28 Restaurant, 308
Tarrytown Marina, 111
Taunton Yacht Club, 324
Taylor Marine, 390
Taylor's Point Marina, 344
Ted & Sons Forked River Marina, 68
Tenants Harbor Town Dock, 475
Tern Harbor Marina, 396
Thames Harbor Inn and Marina, 224
Thamesport Marina, 224
Thayer's Y-Knot Boatyard, 489
Thomaston Town Landing, 471
Thompson Marine & Engine, 54
Three Bells Marina, 221
Tide Mill Yacht Basin, 172
Tide's End Marina, 68
Tidewater Yacht Agency, 539
Tisbury Wharf Company, 368
Tom's Point Marina, 242
Tom's River Yacht Club, 72
Torches Marina, 116
Total Marina at Seaview Inc., 80
Total Marine, 182
Town of Wellfleet Marina, 386
Townsend Manor Marina, 269, 268, 270
Townsend's Marina, 68
Travelers Marine Engine Co., 137
Trawler Fest 269,
Treasure Cove Resort Marina, 288
Treasure Island Marina, 138
Triangle Sea Sales, 270
Trident Yacht Basin, 477, 478, 479
Trixie's Landing, 71
Troy Dock, 122
Tuck Point Marina, 410
Tuckerton Marine, 62
Tugboat Inn & Marina, 459, 460
Turtle Head Marina Inc., 487
Twenty Water Street Restaurant, 308
Two Mile Landing Marina, 44

U

Uihlein Marina and Boat Rentals, 284
Urie's Waterfront Restaurant, 52
Utsch's Marina, 43, 44, 48, 49

V

Van Schaick Island Marina, 122
Vessel Services, Inc., 440
Viking Boatyard, 112
Viking Marina, 238
Viking Yachting Center, 58
Vikings Marina, 87
Village of Sag Harbor Dock, 276
Vineyard Haven Marina, 368
Vineyard Haven Town Dock, 368
Vinings Marine Group, 2
Von Dohn Brothers, 106

W

Wantaugh Park Marina, 138
Warwick Cove Marina, 308
Washington Irving Boat Club, 111
Watch Hill Boat Yard, 238
Watch Hill Docks, 235
Watch Hill National Seashore Marina, 144
Waterfront at Sag Harbor, The, 274, 276
Wayfarer Marine Corp., 483
Webbers Cove Boatyard, 500
Wehrlen Bros Marina, 76
Wentworth by the Sea Marina, 427, 428
West Cove Marine, 192
West Falmouth Dock & Harbor, 350
West Harbor Yacht Service, 165
West Sayville Boat Basin, 147

West Shore Marina, 116
West Shore Marina, 255
West Wind Marina LLC, 312
Westerly Marina, 111
Westerly Yacht Club, 238
Westhampton Bath and Tennis Hotel and Marina, 153
Westhampton Beach Municipal Yacht Basin, 153
Westlake Fishing Lodge and Marina, 284
Westport Yacht Club, 334
Wethersfield Cove Yacht Club, 215
Whaleneck Marina, 138
Whaler's Cove Yacht Club, 249
Wharf Marina Inc., 308
White Water Marine Service, 150
White's Hudson River Marina, 116
Wickford Marina, 304, 305, 306
Wickford Shipyard Inc., 304
Wickford Yacht Club, 304
Wilbert's Marina, 68
Willey Wharf, 483
Williams Island Marina, 541
Willis Marine Center, 255
Wilson Cove Marina, 182
Wilson Cove Yacht Club, 182
Windswept Marina, 150
Windward Yacht Yard, 421, 422, 423
Winter Harbor Marine Inc., 515
Winter Harbor Yacht Club, 515
Wiscasset Town Dock, 454
Wiscasset Yacht Club, 454
Woods Hole Boat Sales, 353
Woods Hole Marine, 350
Woods Hole Yacht Club, 350
World's Fair Marina, 129, 130
Wotton's Wharf, 459
Wright Island Marina, 165

Y

Yachtsman Marina, 436
Yachtsmen's Cove, 137
Yankee Boatyard and Marina, 215
Yankee Marina and Boatyard Inc., 440, 444
Yarmouth Boat Yard, 440
York Harbor Marine Service, 432

Z

Zecco Marina, 341
Zuback's Marine, 87

Goin' Ashore Index

Atlantic City, NJ, 60
Atlantic Highlands, NJ, 85
Bar Harbor, ME, 512
Blue Hill, ME, 503
Boothbay Harbor, ME, 460
Boston, MA, 404
Branford, CT, 196
Bridgeport, CT, 188
Bristol. RI, 321
Camden, ME, 483
Cape May, NY, 45
Carvers Harbor, ME, 490
Castine, ME, 496
Chester, CT, 216
City Island, NY, 164
Clinton, CT, 200
Cold Spring Harbor, NY, 252
Cuttyhunk, MA, 365
Damariscotta, ME, 465
Damariscove Island, ME, 462
East Haddam, CT, 217
East Hampton, NY, 280
Edgartown, MA, 374
Essex, CT, 211
Fairhaven, MA, 338
Falmouth, MA, 352
Fire Island, NY, 144
Fishers Island, NY 228
Freeport, ME, 445
Galilee, RI, 300
Great Cranberry Island, ME, 509
Great Kills, NY, 98
Greenport, NY, 269
Greenwich, CT, 175
Groton, CT, 224
Guilford, CT, 198
Hartford, CT, 218
Huntington, NY, 254
Hurricane Island, ME, 491
Hyannis, MA, 358
Isles of Shoals, NH, 424
Jamestown, RI, 318
Jewell Island, ME, 447
Jones Beach, NY, 140
Kennebunkport, ME, 437
Larchmont, NY, 169
Little Cranberry Island, ME, 509
Long Island, ME, 502
Machias Seal Island, ME, 518
Manchester-By-the-Sea, 413
Manhasset Bay, NY, 244
Marblehead, MA, 408
Marion, MA, 342
Matinicus Island, ME, 481
Mattapoisett, MA, 340
Mattituck, NY, 265
Monhegan Island, ME, 473
Montauk, NY, 286
Mount Sinai, NY, 263
Mystic Seaport Museum, 234
Mystic Village, CT, 232
Nantucket, MA, 378
New Bedford, MA, 338
New Haven, CT, 192
New London, CT, 223
New Rochelle, NY, 168
Newburyport, MA, 421
Newport, RI, 310
Niantic, CT, 222
Noank, CT, 229
Northeast Harbor, ME, 510
Northport, NY, 256
Norwalk, CT, 182
Oak Bluffs, MA, 372
Old Harbor, RI, 296
Old Saybrook, CT, 208
Onset, MA, 345
Orient, NY, 267
Oyster Bay, NY, 248
Padanaram, MA, 335
Plymouth, MA, 391
Port Jefferson, NY, 261
Portland, ME, 442
Portsmouth, NH, 427
Provincetown, MA, 389
Riverhead, NY, 288
Rockland, ME, 477
Rockport, MA, 418
Rockport, ME, 482
Round Pond, ME, 469
Sag Harbor, NY, 276
Salem, MA, 411
Scituate, MA, 393
Searsport, ME, 485
Shelter Island, NY, 273
South Freeport, ME, 445
South Street Seaport Museum, 127
Stamford, CT, 179
Staten Island, NY, 98
Stoney Brook, NY, 259
Stoney Creek, CT, 197
Stonington Borough, CT, 237
Stratford, CT, 189
Tenants Harbor, ME, 476
The Thimble Islands, CT, 197
Thomaston, ME, 471
Vineyard Haven, MA, 370
Watch Hill, RI, 237
Westbrook, CT, 202
Westport, CT, 184
Westport, MA, 334
Wickford, RI, 306
Wiscasset, ME, 456
Woodenboat School, 497
Woods Hole, MA, 350

Subject Index

(Navigation text page numbers are in bold)

A

Absecon Inlet, 42, 56, 57, 60
Acadia National Park, 506
Acoaxet, 332
Acushnet River, 338, 340
Albany, 65, 94, 96, 97, 106, 110, 118, 122, **123**,124
Alder Island, 136
Aldo, 294, 295
Allegheny Rock, 370
Allen Harbor, 307, **361**, 362
Allen Island, 473
Allerton Harbor, 395
Ames Cove, 488
Amesbury Point, 492
Amityville, 95, 132, 138, 140, 141, 142
Anderson Ledge, 424
Annisquam River, 416, **417**, 418, 419
Appledore Island, 424, 426
Apponagansett Bay, 335
Apponaug, 292, 293, 307-**309**
Aquidneck Island, 310, 318, 326
Arnold Neck, 309
Asharoken Beach, 258
Atlantic Beach, 135
Atlantic City, 42, 43, 47, 50-52, 55-56, **57**-60, 65, 67, 69, 78
Atlantic Highlands, **84**, 93
Avalon Beach, 52
Avery Ledge, 418
Avondale, 238, 239

B

Babson Islands, 497
Babylon, **142**, 143, 146
Back Channel, 212, 431
Back River, 346
Bagaduce River, 494
Bailey Island, 382, 448
Bailey Rock, 168
Bakers Island, 406
Bald Porcupine Island, 511
Baldwin Bay, 138
Bangor, 380, 381, 480, **486**-488
Bantam Rock, 462
Bar Cove Beach, 462
Bar Harbor, 380-382, 477, 480, 481, 488, 502-504, 506, 508, 509, **511**-513
Bar Island, 508, 512
Barker Point, 241, 245
Barn Point, 433
Barnegat Bay, 42-47, 50-65, 66-80
Barnegat Inlet, 42, **66**-69
Barnstable, 330, 331, 381, 383, **385**, 386
Barred Islands, 494
Barren Island, 99
Barters Island, 456
Bartlett Reef, 220
Basin Point, 280, 446
Bass Harbor, 501, 502, 504, **506**
Bass Point, 405
Bass River, 61, 330, 352, 360, 361
Bass Rock, 421
Bassetts Island, 346, 347
Battery Park, **104**, 126
Battery, The, **103**
Bay of Fundy, 513
Bayonne, 100, 103, 104
Bayport, 148
Bayview, 482-484
Bayville, 247, 251
Beach Haven Inlet, 63
Beach Island, 63, 64, 67, 302
Beals Cove, 448
Beals Island, 513
Bear Island, 510
Bear Mountain, 110, **114**, 115
Beaufort Point, 168
Beaverdam Creek, 74, 149
Beavertail Point, 303, 310
Belfast, 380-382, 480, **485**, 487, 496
Bellmore, 138
Bellport Bay, 149
Belmar, 79
Benjamin River, 497
Beverly, 341, 342, 381, 405, 406, 408, 410-**412**, 413-415
Biddeford, 382, **438**, 439
Big White Island, 491
Bigelow Bight, 444
Billingsgate Shoal, 388
Biltmore Shores, 140
Birch Harbor, 516
Bird Island, 330
Bird Rock, 194
Black Point, 220
Black Rock Harbor, 185-188
Black Rock, 185-188
Block Island, 95, 157, 158, 159, 199, 220, 223, 238, 266, 267, 282, 286, 290-292, **293**-300, 302, 316
Blood Ditch Cut, 61
Blue Hill Bay, **499**, 500, 501, 506
Blue Hill, 480, 500-**503**, 506
Blue Point, 147, 148, 150
Bluff Head, 493
Bluff Point, 184, 256, 357
Blyn Rock, 194
Blynman Canal, 416, **417**, 418
Bold Island, 498
Boothbay Harbor, 380-382, 451, 453, **457**-463
Boston Harbor, 381, **394**, 395, 398-402, 404, 405
Boston, 170, 171, 198, 200, 202, 203, 208, 210, 222, 223, 294, 316, 332, 334, 345, 352, 355, 358, 361, 371, 373, 376, 380-390, 392-**399**, 404-405, 406, 407, 410, 419, 439, 477, 478, 485, 511
Bracketts Channel, 488
Branch Channel, 247
Branford River, 194, 196
Branford, 158, 159, 188, 189, 191, **192**, 194-198
Brant Point, 375, 376
Brant Rock, 392
Bremen Long Island, 470
Brenton Cove, 311, 312, **314**-316
Bricktown, 73
Bridgehampton, 156, 266, 286
Bridgeport, 158, 159, 174, 175, **186**-188, 191, 194, 196, 200, 247, 253, 256, 258, 260, 261, 263, 264
Brielle, 65, 74, 75, 77
Brien, 238
Brimstone Island, 491
Bristol, 292, 293, 302, 303, 320, **321**-324, 463, 464, 466, 468
Broad Channel, 100
Broad Cove Marine, 468, 469
Broad Creek Channel, 138
Broad Sound, 405, 445
Broadwater Cove, 287
Brockport, 140
Brockway Island, 212
Bronx, 96, 97, 126, 127, 130, 163, 164, 168
Brookhaven, 146, 149 263
Brooklin, 497, 500
Brooklyn, 94-97, 100, 102, 103, 126, 128, 131, 240
Brooks Point, 227
Browns River, 148
Brush Ledge, 394
Bucks Harbor, 496
Bucksport, 486, 487
Bug Light, 389
Bull Island, 367
Bullhead Bay, 290
Bullock Cove, 322
Burgess Point, 344, 345
Burnt Coat Harbor, 501
Burnt Cove, 498
Burnt Island, 473, 494
Butter Island, 494
Buttermilk Channel, 94, 103
Buzzards Bay, 297, 330-336, 338-342, 344-351, 352, 364, 365, 367, 383, 384
Byram Harbor, 174
Byram River, 171, 173, 174

C

Calderwood Neck, 493
Calf Islands, 174
Calf Pasture Point, 181, 182, 307
Calves Island, 210, 211
Camden Harbor, 482, 483
Camden, 380-382, 471, 477, 480, **482**-484, 488, 496
Cameron Point, 463
Camp Island, 498
Campobello Island, 519
Canapitsit Channel, 364
Cape Ann, 380-382, 406, 415-419
Cape Cod Bay, 330, 331, 345, 346, 380, 381, 383-385, 389
Cape Cod Canal, 345, **383**
Cape Elizabeth, 380, 381, 431, 437, 439
Cape Harbor, 453
Cape Henlopen, 50
Cape Island Creek, 43
Cape May Harbor, 42, 43, 46, 47
Cape May Point, 50
Cape May, **42**-47, 50-65, 67
Cape Neddick Harbor, **433**-435
Cape Newagen, 452
Cape of Good Hope, 409
Cape Poge Bay, 374
Cape Porpoise Harbor, 382
Cape Rosier, 494
Cape Small, 380, 431-450, 451
Captain Islands, 174, 178
Captree Island, 141, 142, 143
Carvers Harbor, 382, **488**-490
Casco Bay, 380-382, 431, 439, 442, 444-448
Castine, 382, 480, 485, **494**-496
Castle Hill, 310, 312
Castle Neck, 419
Cataumet Rock, 348
Catskill, 114, 115, 118, **119**, 120, 121, 123
Cedar Creek, 70, 71, 186
Cedar Neck, 371
Cedar Point, 184, 185, 276, 345, 383, 393
Cedar Tree Point, 309
Center Harbor, 497
Center Island, 448
Centerport Harbor, 253, 254, 256
Centre Island, 247, 248
Champagne Island, 52
Champlin, 294-296, 300, 306
Chandler Bay, 518
Chappaquiddick, 330, 331, 373, 374
Charles Island, 191
Charles River, 400, 404
Charlestown, 292, 293, **400**, 404, 405

Chatham Roads, 362
Chatham, 330, 331, 352, **361**-363
Chester Creek Bar, 212, 213
Chester Creek, 212, 213
Chester, 158-162, 164, 166-168, 170-173, 174, 212, **213**, 216, 217
Chickens Ledge, 169
Chimon Island, 182
Chocomount Cove, 227
Christmas Cove, 382, **463**
City Island, 158-162, **163**-173
Clam Creek, 57, 60
Clapboard Island, 444
Clark Point, 507, 508
Clarks Island, 391
Clason Point, 130
Clermont, 118
Cleveland Ledge Channel, 342
Cliff Island, 447, 448
Clinton, 158, 159, 161, 189, 192, 197, **199**, 200, 202
Coast Guard, 42, 45, 46, 52, 57, 60, 61, 67, 69, 75, 78, 93, 102, 103, 106, 126, 135, 141, 149, 152, 153, 156, 170, 223, 225, 226, 238, 253, 258, 282, 293, 300, 318, 332, 346, 351, 366, 368, 378, 385, 388, 421, 462, 477, 506, 507, 517, 519
Cockenoe Island, 182, 184
Coecles Harbor, 270-**272**, 273
Coeymans, 120, 123
Cohasset, 381, 383, **393**, 394
Cold Spring Harbor, 158, 239, 240-242, 244, 246-249, 251, **252**
Cole River, 324
College Point, 128, 130
Columbia, 128
Compo Beach, 184
Conanicut, 292, 293, 303, 305, 310, 316-318
Concordia, 335, 336
Coney Island, 94-97, 99, **100**, 101, 132, 133
Conimicut Point, 322
Conklin Island, 69
Connecticut River, 158, 203, **204**-214, 216, 218, 219, 220
Connetquot River, 148
Conscience Point, 290
Contents, 96, 158, 292, 331, 380
Converse Point, 340
Cooper Bluff, 251
Copiague, 142, 143
Corea Harbor, **516**, 517
Corey Creek, 287
Cormorant Point, 157
Corson Inlet, 52
Cos Cob, **177**, 178
Cotuit, 330, 331, 352, 355-358, 385
Cove Harbor, 179
Cow Cove, 296
Cowesett, 309
Coxsackie, 120, 121
Crab Island, 445
Cradle Cove, 488
Cranberry Island, 470, 506, 509
Crane Island, 491
Crane Neck Point, 258
Crescent Beach, 182, 297
Crookes Point, 95, 98
Cross Lake, 124
Croton Point, 113
Crow Island, 336, 338
Crow Point, 395
Curtis Island, 482, 484
Customs, 63, 274, 275, 411, 456, 520
Cutchogue, 265, 287, 289
Cutler, 382, 513, 518, 519
Cuttyhunk, 329, 330-332, 336, 364, **365**-367

D

Damariscotta River, 382, 451, 460, **463**, 464, 466
Damariscove Island, 461, **462**
Danvers River, 412, 413
Dark Harbor, 382, 488
Davenport Neck, 166, 167
Davids Island, 163, 166
Dead Horse Bay, 99
Dead Neck, 355, 357, 358
Deadman Ledge, 491
Deep River, 204, 212, **213**-215, 398
Deer Island, 394, 498, 499
Deer Island Thorofare, 498
Delancey Point, 169
Delaware River, 408
Dering Harbor, 270-273
Devil Island, 52, 499
Devils Island, 52
Devon, 189, **190**, 282, 385, 389
Dice Head, 494
Dix Island, 476
Doanes Creek, 361
Dodson, 235-237
Dorchester Bay, 399
Dorchester, 395, 399, 402, 405
Double Creek Channel, 67, 69
Double Creek, 67, 69
Duck Harbor, 499
Duck Island Harbor, 253, 256, **258**
Duck Island, 200, 203, 253, 256, 258, 424, 426
Duck Point, 168
Duck Rocks, 473
Dumpling Rocks, 335
Dunham Point, 498
Dutch Island, **303**, 304
Duxbury, 381, 389-**391**
Dyer Island, 318

E

Eagle Hill, 421
East Bay, 138, 303, 322
East Chop, 370, 371
East Creek, 287, 288
East Greenwich, 307
East Haddam, 203, 204, 210, 216, **217**
East Hampton, 156, 266, 274, 275, 277-**280**, 281
East Harbor, 227, 318
East Point, 156
East River, 93-96, 102, 103, 124, **126**-131, 162, 163, 198, 240
East Rockaway, 95, 99, **132**-135
Eastchester Bay, 162
Easter Point, 226
Eastern Bay, 517
Eastern Cove, 502
Eastern Point, 417
Eastport, 153, 380-382, 431, 479, 480-482, 484-486, 488-**519**, 520
Eaton, 483, 494, 495
Eatons Neck, 253, 256, 258
Echo Bay, 166-168
Edgartown Harbor, 368, 373, 375
Edgartown, 330, 331, 353, 364, 367, 368, 372, **373**-375
Edgewood, 322, 323
Eel Pond, 348, 349, 351, 355
Egg Island, 358
Egg Rock, 511
Eggemoggin Reach, 477, **496**-498
Elizabeth Islands, 330, 331, **364**, 366, 367
Ellingwood Rock, 451
Ellis Island, 103, 104
Ellis Reef, 235
Endeavor Shoal, 282
Enders Island, 235
Erie Canal, 93, 103, 123, 124
Essex River, 420
Essex, 158-160, 203, 204, 208-210, **211**-213, 412, 415, 419, 420
Eustasia Island, 212, 213
Execution Rocks, 95, 160, 245

F

Fair Harbor, 143
Fairhaven, 330-332, 335, 336, 338, 339
Falkner Island, 198
Fall River, 292, 293, 303, 322, 324, 335
Falmouth, 330-332, 348-351, 352-354, 364, 367, 380-382, 440, 441, **444**
False Hook Channel, 80
Ferry Point, 130, 210
Fields Point, 322
Finns Ledge, 405
Fire Island, 95, **133**-135, 141, **142**-146, 148, 149, 152, 153
Fire Island Inlet, 134
First Point, 378
Fishers Island, 160, 220, **226**-228, 235
Fishing Island, 431
Fishing Rock, 435
Fishtail, 94, 156, 157, 158, 252, 266-274, 276-282, 284-286, 288, 290
Five Foot Rock, 194
Five Islands, 144, **453**, 456
Fivemile River, 180
Flanders Bay, 287, 288, 290
Flat Creek, 140
Flat Neck Point, 178
Flint Point, 328
Flushing Bay, 128-130
Fogland Harbor, 328
Fogland Point, 328
Folly Island, 506
Folly Ledge, 490
Fore River, 396, 398, 439
Forked River, 67-68, **69**-70
Fort Adams, 310, 311, 314, 316
Fort Barton, 326
Fort George, 494, 496
Fort Hill, 213
Fort Knox, 486
Fort McClary, 430, 431
Fort Point Channel, 399
Fort Point, 399, 431, 486
Fort Pond Bay, 282
Fort Popham, 452
Fort Schuyler, 130
Fort Sewall, 408
Fort Totten, 130, 240
Fort Wadsworth, 102
Fort William Henry, 466
Foundry Cove, 115
Fourfoot Rocks, 173
Fox Island, 305, **492**
Foxwoods, 222, 226
Frankfort, 486
Freeport Creek, 138
Freeport, 95-97, 132, 137, 138, 380, 382, 439-441, 445, 446
Frenchboro, 502
Frenchman Bay, 380-382, 511, 514
Friendship, 470
Frost Point, 429
Fulton Landing, 126

G

Gales Ferry, 224, 226
Gales Point, 406
Galilee, 292, 293, 298, **300**
Galloway, 342
Gangway Channel, 394
Gangway Rock, 245
Gansett Point, 348
Gardiners Bay, 265, 266
Gardiners Island, 266, 282
Gardner Island, 302
Gardners Neck, 324
Garrison Island, 470
Garvies Point, 247

Gay Head, 330, 331, 364, 367, 374
George Washington Bridge, 110
Georges Islands, 472
Georges Rock, 184
Germantown Point, 398
Gerritsen Inlet, 99
Gibraltar, 115
Gildersleeves Island, 218
Gilgo Beach, 141
Gilkey Harbor, 488
Gin Beach, 282
Gleason Point, 272
Glen Cove, 160, 245-247, 472, 476, 479, 482, 484, 490, 491
Glen Island, 166-169
Gloucester, 379, 380, 381, 383, 387, 406, **415**-419
Goat Island, 311, 315, 316, 437
Goats Neck, 367
Goodsell, 194, 196
Goose Cove, 506
Goose Creek, 141
Goose Island, 167, 168, 228, 482
Goose Point, 391
Goose Rock Passage, 456, 463
Goose Rocks, 196, 453
Gooseberry Neck, 330-332
Gosport Harbor, 424, 426
Gould Island, 326
Government Publications, 328
Governors Island, 96, 97, 103, 126
Grass Island, 142, 178, 217
Grassy Bay, 100
Grassy Point, 95, 114
Gravesend Bay, 100
Grays Rock, 410
Great Bay, 58, 60, **61**, 428, 430
Great Cove, 148, 506
Great Cranberry Island, 509
Great Egg, 42, 54-57
Great Gunn, 152
Great Harbor, 174, 277, 348, 349, 389, 506
Great Hog Neck, 287
Great Island, 300, 333, 448, 450
Great Kills, **89**, 95, 97-99
Great Ledge, 349
Great Peconic Bay, 135, 155-157, 266, 287, 288, 290
Great Salt Pond, 292, **293**-297
Great Schooner Race, 477
Great South Bay, 132, 135, 141, 142, 146, 148, 149
Great South Bay, 96, 97
Great Spruce Island, 518
Great Wass Island, 517
Green Harbor, 391
Green Pond, 352, **354**-356
Greenport, 158, 159, 265, 266, **267**-272, 277
Greens Island, 490, 491
Greens Ledge, 180
Greenwich, **174**, 175-177
Greenwich Bay, 292, 293, 303, 307-310
Greenwich Cove, 178, 308, 309
Grindel Point, 488
Grindstone Neck, 513
Griswold Island, 220
Grog Island, 498
Groton, 204, 220, **223**-226, 228, 229
Guilford, 160, 188, 189, 194, 196-**198**, 200
Gull Island, 52, 228, 364
Gull Point, 318
Gull Pond, 269
Gurnet Point, 389, 391

H

Haddock Cove, 509
Hadley, 349, **367**
Haley Cove, 424
Half Moon, 113, 245
Halfmile Rock, 332
Hallets Point, 95,128
Hamburg Cove, 204, **212**
Hammersmith, 310, 312
Hampden, 486
Hampton Bays, 96, 97, 157
Hampton Harbor, 381, 425
Harbor Islands, 397-401, 517
Harbor Ledge, 179, 497
Harbor Point, 175, 266, 501
Harding Beach, 362
Hardwood Island, 506
Harlem River, 95, 110, 126, **128**
Harpswell Neck, 382, 439, 446, 447
Harraseeket River, 445, 446
Harris Island, 433
Hart Cove, 153
Hart Island, 162, 163, 166
Hartford, 204, 212, **218**, 219
Harwich Port, 352, **361**, 362
Hashamomuck Pond, 271
Hatchett Reef, 220
Haunts Creek, 138
Haverstraw Bay, 112, 113
Hay Island, 494
Haywater Cove, 287
Head Harbor, 499, 517, 519
Hebrides, 462
Hell Gate, 94, 95, 126-**128**, 130, 131, 163, 453, 463
Hempstead Bay, 132
Hempstead Harbor, 158-160, 162, 240, **245**-247
Hen Cove, 347
Hen Islands, 493, 494
Henry Cove, 513, 515
Hereford Inlet, 42, 51, 52
Herring Gut, 472
Herring Island, 74
Hewlett Point, 241
High Island, 197
Highlands, 93, 355
Hingham, 395-398
Hitchcock Rock, 178
Hitchcock, 178, 188
Hockamock Head, 501
Hockomock Bay, 453, 463
Hockomock Channel, 469
Hog Creek Point, 282
Hog Island, **135**, 136, 321, 344, 346, 498
Hog Neck, 287, 344, 345
Holbrook Harbor, 494
Holding Tanks, 258, 333
Homeland Security, 93, 126
Hopkins Point, 493
Horse Island, 446
Horse Neck, 310
Horseneck Point, 332, 333
Horseshoe Cove, 496
Horseshoe Shoal, 376
Horton Point, 265
Hospital Cove, 347
Hospital Island, 494
Houghtaling Island, 123
Housatonic River, 189
Howard Beach, 100
Howells Point, 149
Huckleberry Island, 168
Hudson Canal, 110
Hudson River Valley, 110
Hudson River, 93-105, **106**-124, 126-128
Huguenot, 165, 167
Hull Bay, 395
Hull Gut, 395
Humarock, 392
Hummock Point, 328
Huntington Bay, 158-161, 180, 252, **253**-265
Huntington, 158-161, 180, 223, 251, 252, 253, **254**-265, 511
Hupper Island, 472
Hupper Point, 472
Hurricane Island, 476, 490, **491**
Hurricane Sound, 490, 491
Hussey Sound, 444
Hyannis, 330, 331, 352, **358**, 360, 361, 385, 389
Hyde Park, 97, 116, 118

I

Indian Harbor, 160, 174, 175, 177
Indian Island, 481
Indian Point, 102, 114, 493
Indiantown Island, 463
Ingram Thorofare, 52
Inland Sea, 159
Inner Heron Island, 463
Iona Island, 114, 115
Ipswich Bay, 417-420
Irvington, 110
Island Creek, 43, 100, 140
Isles of Shoals, 380, 381, 383, 406, **424**, 426, 427
Islesboro, 480, 484, 485, **488**, 494
Islesford, 504, 509

J

Jacob Riis Beach, 99
Jamaica Bay, 96, 97, **99**, 100, 133
James Landing, 393
Jamestown, 302, 304, 314, **316**-318, 322
Jericho Bay, 496, 499
Jersey City, 93, 96, 97, 103-105
Jessup Neck, 273, 287
Jewell Island, 445, **447**, 448
Johns Bay, 451, 466
Johns Island, 466
Johnsons Creek, 188
Jones Beach, 95, **133**, 138, **140**, 141
Jones Inlet, 133, 141
Jones River, 391
Jonesport, 382, 480, 513, 516-518
Joshua Cove, 196

K

Katama Bay, 330, 373
Kelsey Point, 199, 200
Kennebec River, 382, 451, **452**, 453, 463
Kennebunk River, 435-437
Kennebunkport, 380, 381, 431, 433, **435**-437
Kent Cove, 493
Kettle Creek, 71
Key Bank, 490
Kickamuit River, 323
Kill Van Kull 88
Kimball Island, 499
Kingman, 347
Kings Point, 131, 166, 240, 241, 507
Kingston, 94, 96, 97, 110, 115, 116, **118**, 119, 307
Kittery, **431**, 432
Kitts Rock, 432
Knight Island, 517
Knubble Bay, 454
Knutson, 255
Kollegewidgwok, 500, 502

L

Lagoon Pond, 371
Lake Champlain, 93, 103, 124
Lake Erie, 93, 124
Lake Montauk, 282, 285
Lake Ontario, 124
Lake Wyandannee, 282
Lane Island, 490
Larchmont, 158-160, **168**-170
Lavallette, 71, 72
Lawrence Point, 128
Lee River, 324
Leeds Pond, 241, 244
Lermond Cove, 477
Lewis Bay, 358, 360
Liberty Island, 102, 103
Lincolnville, 484, 488
Lindenhurst, 142

Linekin Bay, 457, **462**
Little Barred Island, 494
Little Bay, 430
Little Beach, 373
Little Brewster Island, 395, 399
Little Burnt Island, 473
Little Cranberry Island, 509
Little Eel River, 358
Little Egg Harbor, 61-63
Little Green Island, 476
Little Harbor, 319, 342, 348, 354, 426, 429, 430
Little Jewell Island, 447
Little Neck, 130, 158, 160, **240**-242, 244-248, 251, 252, 256
Little Peconic Bay, 266, 286
Little Ram Island, 273
Little River Island, 518
Little Sheepscot River, 456
Lloyd Harbor, 161, **253**
Lloyd Neck, 253
Lobster Cove, 416, 417
Locust Point, 162
Long Beach Island, 63, 64, 67
Long Beach Point, 267, 342
Long Cove, 301, 474, 476, 485, **491**
Long Creek, 138
Long Island, ME, 502
Long Island Sound, 93, 94, 96, 97, 124, 126-131, 133, 142, 158-163, 166, 169, 170, 173, 174, 178-180, 182, 184, 186, 188, 191, 194, 197, 199, 200, 204, 206, 207, 210, 212, 220, 227, 236, 237, 239, 240-243, 245-247, 251, 252, 253, 258, 260, 266, 282, 287, 291, 297, 394
Long Point, 70, 224, 228, 229, 307, 388, 390
Long Rock, 220
Long Sand Shoal, 203
Lowell Rock, 481
Lubec, 382, 513, **519**
Luckse Sound, 448
Ludlam Bay, 52
Lunt Harbor, 502
Lynde Point, 204
Lyndhurst, 110
Lynn, 383, 404, 405, 407, 408

M

Machias Seal Island, 518
Maciel, 368, 371
Mack Point, 485
Mackerel Cove, 448, **501**
MacMahan Island, 453
Magnolia Harbor, 415
Maidstone Harbor, 279, 280
Maine Island, 447, 509
Majors Point, 272
Malaga Island, 424
Mamaroneck, 160, 162, 169, **170**,171, 245
Manahawkin Bay, 64
Manana Island, 473
Manasquan River, 65, 74, 75, 78
Manasquan, 42, 46, 65, 66-70, 72-74, **75**-80
Manchester Bay, 415
Manchester, 381, 405, **413**-415
Manhasset Bay, 160, 239, **241**-245
Manhattan, 60, 93, 94, 96, 97, 100, 102-106, 108-110, 126-128, 130, 131, 175, 270
Manresa Island, 180
Manset, 506
Mantoloking, 65, 66, **73**, 74, 76, 77
Maple Juice Cove, 470
Marblehead, 379, 380, 381, 383, 405, **406**-410, 412
Margate City, 56, 57
Marina Bay, 301, 302, 399, 402
Marion, 270, 330-332, 340-**342**
Marlboro, 118
Marlborough, 312
Martha's Vineyard, 367
Marshelder Channel, 61
Mashnee Island, 346
Mashomack Point, 274
Mason, 229, 230, 232, 235
Massachusetts Bay, 380, 381, 383, 392, 394, 395, 406-416, 418-430, 431, 462
Massapequa, 96, 97, 140
Massasoit, 323
Mastic Beach, 142, 149
Matinicus, **480**, 481
Mattapoisett, 330, 331, 338-**340**
Mattituck, 160, 161, 253, 260, 263, **264**-266, 287
McGlathery Island, 499
McKown, 457, 460, 461
Medomak River, 467, 470
Meduncook River, 467, 470
Meetinghouse Creek, 287
Megansett, 344, 348
Menauhant, 355
Menemsha, 330, 331, **367**, 368
Menunketesuck River, 200
Menunketesuck, 200
Merchant Island, 499
Merrick, 138
Merriconeag Sound, 446, 448
Merrimack River, 421
Metedeconk River, 73-76
Metedeconk River, 73-76
Miamogue, 187
Miamogue, 287
Mianus River, 177
Middle Bay, 138
Middle Flats, 373
Middletown, 215, 217, 218
Middletown, 314, 318, 322
Milburn Creek, 138
Mile Harbor, 266, 277-282, 286
Milford, 158, 159,189-**191**
Mill Cove, 306, 457, 503
Mill Creek, 271, 273, 276, 287, 442, 443
Mill Neck, 248, 251
Mill Point, 453
Mill Pond, 240
Mill Pond, 362
Mill Rock, 127, 128
Mill Rock, 208
Milton Harbor, 169, **171**
Mistake Island, 517
Mitchell River, 362
Monhegan, 382, 383, 444, 472, **473**, 474
Monomoy Island, 362
Montauk, 94-97, 132, 153, 157, 158-160, 222, 224, 225, 228, 266, 267, 277, 281, **282**, 284-286, 290, 293
Monument Beach, 344, 346
Moore Point, 445, 446
Moores Harbor, 499
Moosabec Reach, 517
Moose Island, 499, 520
Moriches, 95-97, 134, **135**, 142, 149-153, 156
Moriches Bay, 149
Morris Canal, 104, 106
Morris Cove, 192
Morris Island, 362
Mosquito Cove, 246
Mount Desert, 382, 501, 502, **504**-509, 511, 513
Mount Hope, 291, 303, **323**-326
Mount Misery, 260, 261
Mount Sinai, 160, 262, **263**, 264
Mouse Island, 218, 228, 482
Mud Creek, 138, 148, 287
Mud Hole, 517, 518
Mullica River, 58, 61
Murphy Point, 232
Muscle Ridge, 476
Muscongus Bay, 380-382, 467-479
Mystic Seaport Museum, 229, **232**-234
Mystic, 158-161, 199, 219, 220, 222, 228-231, **232**-235, 237, 282

N

Nahant, 404, 405, 409
Nantasket, 395
Nantucket, 186, 306, 329, 330-332, 336, 345, 351, 352, 355, 358, 362, 364, **375**-379, 383
Napatree Beach, 237
Napeague Bay, 282
Narragansett Bay, 237, 239, 291, 292, 297, 298, 300, 302, 303-322, 324-329, 332
Narrow Bay, 149
Naskeag Harbor, 498
Nassau Point, 287
Naugus Head, 406
Naushon, 332, 351, **367**
Nautilus Island, 494
Navesink, **91**, 93
Ned Island, 513
Ned Point, 340
Negro Island, 462
Nells Island, 189
Neponset River, 399
Neptune Island, 167, 168
New Bedford Harbor, **335**
New Castle Island, 426, 427, 429, 430
New Gretna, 61
New Hamburg, 116, 118
New Harbor, 293, 294, 296, 297, 451, **467**, 468
New Haven, 158-160, 188, 189, **191**-194, 196, 198, 204, 477
New Inlet Harbors, 392
New London, 158-161, 205, 211, 220, 222, **223**-226, 229, 265, 266, 267, 270, 277, 282, 287, 296
New Meadows River, 439, **450**
New Rochelle, 158-160, 162, 165, **166**-168, 170
New Suffolk, 287, 289
New York Bay, 93-102, 104-108, 110, 112, 114-118, 120-124
Newark, 60, 96, 97, 102, 105
Newburgh, 96, 97, 115, 118
Newburyport, 380, 381, 406, 419-**421**, 423-424, 465
Newfoundland, 178, 497
Newington, 430
Newport Harbor, **310**, 315, 318
Newport, 104, 105, 199, 237, 245, 291-293, 303, 304, **310**-316, 318, 321, 322, 326, 328, 329, 332, 336, 340, 342, 364, 512
Newtown Creek, 128
Niantic, 158, 159, 169, 219, **220**-239
Noank, **228**-230, 232
Nonamesset Island, 367
North Bay, 357
North Cove, 104, 106, 126, 204, 205, 208, 210-212
North Haven, 493
North Haven Peninsula, 271-273
North Hempstead, 241, 242
North Neck, 374, 110, 392
Northeast Harbor, 504, 506, 507, 509, **510**, 511
Northport, 160, 171, 253, 254, **256**-258, 263, 484, 485, 496
Norton Point, 95, 97
Norwalk, 158-160, 174, **180**-182, 184
Norwich, 220, 224-226
Nott Island, 211, 439, 511
Noyack Bay, **273**, 287
Nubble Channel, 395
Nummy Island, 51
Nyack, 96, 97, 113

O
Oak Beach, 141, 144
Oak Bluffs, 330, 331, 352, 364, 367, 368, **371**-374
Oak Island, 142, 144, 476
Oak Neck, 247, 249, 251
Oakdale, 147, 148
Oakland, 154, 309
Oar Island, 469
Ocean City, 52, **54**-56, 65
Offshore Islands, 174, 188, 330
Ogunquit, 434
Old Harbor, 292, 293, **296**, 297
Old Lyme, 210
Old Port, 294, 312, 373, 439, 443
Old Saybrook, 158, 159, 203, 204, **205**-208, 210
Oldport, 312, 314, 316
Olympia, 238
Onset, 330-332, **342**, 344, 345, 452
Orchard Beach, 164, 242, 243, 431
Orcutt Harbor, 496
Orient, 124, 158-161, 220, 253, 265, 266, **267**, 270-272, 409
Orowoc Creek, 148
Orrs, 439, 448
Osprey Beach, 223
Ossining, 111, **113**
Osterville, 330, 331, 352, **355**-358, 385
Owls Head, 477, 478
Oyster Bay, 138, 139, 158-161, 239, 240, **247**-252, 253
Oyster Creek Channel, 67, 69

P
Padanaram, 330, 332, **335**, 336
Paerdegat Basin, 100
Parker River, 421, 424
Patchogue, 142, 146, **148**-150, 152, 200, 202
Patience Island, 310
Patten Bay, 503
Pawcatuck River, 237-239
Peaks Island, 448
Peck Bay, 55
Peconic Bay, 135, 155-157, 265, 266, 286-290
Peddocks Island, 395, 399
Peekskill, 112, 114
Pemaquid River, **466**
Penataquit Creek, 148
Penobscot Bay, 380-382, 472, 474, 476, 478, 479, 480-512, 514-520
Penobscot River, 486
Pepperell Cove, 427, 429, 430, 431
Perkins Cove, **434**
Perry Creek, 493
Philadelphia, 50, 56, 60
Phillips Point, 156
Phinneys Harbor, 330, 346
Piermont, 110
Pigs Reef, 332
Pine Island, 166, 223, 224
Pine Neck, 156
Piscataqua River, 427, 430, 431, 432
Plato Island, 302
Pleasant Bay, 330, 362
Pleasant Point Gut, 470
Pleasure Bay, 400
Plum Gut, 158, 160, 253, 254, 256, 258-265, **266**, 274, 278, 286
Plum Island River, 420
Plum Island, 265, 266
Plum Island, 406, 419-421, 424
Plum Point, 161, 241, 244, 247, 248
Plymouth Beach, 388, 391
Plymouth Rock, **389**, 391
Plymouth, 379, 380, 381, 383, 388-391, 462
Pocasset, 323, 330-332, 346, 347, 352
Point Allerton, 395
Point Gammon, 361
Point Isabella, 357
Point Judith, 291-296, **297**-302, 303
Point Lookout, 133, 135, 136, 499
Point Pleasant, 66, 73, **74**, 75, 78
Pole Island, 448, 450
Ponquogue Point, 156
Popasquash, 321
Popes Island, 336, 338
Popham, 452
Porcupine Islands, 511
Port Chester, 158-162, 164, 166-168, 170, 171,**172**-174
Port Clyde, 467, **472**, 473
Port Edgewood, 323
Port Ewen, 118
Port Imperial, 106
Port Jefferson, 158-161, 189, 253, 258, **260**-264
Port Washington, 96, 97, 160, 240, **241**-245
Portland (CT), 204, 207, 215, **218**
Portland (ME), 380-383, 418, 421, 424, 427, 435, 437, **439**-445, 448, 456, 457, 465, 467, 468, 473, 474, 520
Portsmouth, 103, 322, 328, 335, 380, 381, 383, 406, 408-426, **427**-430, 431, 432, 437
Pot Island, 197
Potowomut Neck, 307
Potter Cove, 318
Potts Harbor, 382, **446**-449
Poughkeepsie, 96, 97, 110, 116-**118**
Prescott, 427, 428, 430
Prince Cove, 357
Prince Point, 444
Proctor Point, 413
Prospect Harbor, 513
Providence, 291-293, 303, 306, 309, 310, **322**, 323
Provincetown, 361, 380, 381, 383, 386, 387, **388**, 389, 399
Prudence Island, 318
Pulpit Harbor, 492

Q
Quahog Bay, 448
Quantuck Bay, 156
Queens, 126, 130, 240
Quicks Hole, 330, 331, 364
Quincy, 383, 395, 398-400, 404
Quissett Harbor, 330, 348, 350
Quogue, 154, 156, 258

R
Ragged Island, 480, **481**, 513
Ram Island, 229, 235, 272, 273, 438, 494
Raritan Bay, **86**, 93, 96, 97
Red Brook Harbor, 347, 348
Red Creek, 290
Red Rock, 178
Reed Cove, 448
Reel Point, 272
Reynolds Channel, 135, 136
Richmond Creek, 287
Richmond Island, 439
Rikers Island, 128, 131
Rings Island, 422, 423
Risley Channel, 55, 56
Riverhead, 142
Riverhead, 265, 266, 287, 288, 290
Robinhood Cove, 455, **456**
Robins Island, 287
Robinson Rock, 482
Robinsons Hole, 364
Rock Harbor, 185-188, 330, 331
Rockaway Beach, 99
Rockaway Inlet, 99, **133**
Rockland, 114, 380-382, 466, 467-472, 474, 475, **476**-479, 481, 491
Rockport, 380-382, 406, **418**, 419, 446, 472, 476, 479, **481**-484, 490, 491
Rocky Neck, 415, 417
Rocky Point, 247, 264
Roderick Head, 501
Rodman Neck, 163
Rome Point, 305
Rondout Creek, 118
Roosevelt Island, 102, 126-128, 131
Roque Island, 518
Round Island, 499
Round Pond, 467-**469**
Round Rock, 307
Rowayton, 174, 180, 182
Royal River, 444, 445
Rules of the Road, 93
Rumstick Neck, 322
Rye, 162, 171, 172, 245, 381, 406, 424, 425

S
Sachem Head, 196, 197
Sachuest Cove, 328
Saco River, 438, **439**
Sag Harbor, 96, 97, 158, 159, 271, 272, **274**-278
Sakonnet, 291-293, 302, 303, 326-**328**, 329
Salem Channel, 406, 410
Salem, 379, 381, 405, 406, 408, **409**-413, 415
Salmon River, 217
Salt Pond, 292-297, 300
Saltaire, 134, 143
Salty Brine Beach, 300
Sammys Beach, 278
Sampsons Island, 357
Sand Beach, 511
Sand Hill Cove, 298, 300
Sand Point, 502
Sands Point, 241, 245
Sandwich, 346, 367, 384-386, 391, 408
Sandy Bay, 418
Sandy Hook, 63, 67, 70, 73, 75, 78-80, **84**, 93, 95-97, 99, 100, 131, 133, 142, 148, 149, 156
Saquatucket Harbor, 361
Sasanoa River, 451, 453
Sasco Hill Beach, 185
Saugatuck River, 184, 185
Saugerties, 97, 110, **118**, 119
Saughkonet, 326
Saybrook, 158-161, 203, 204-208, 210, 211
Sayville, 147, 148
Schoodic Head, 516
Schoolhouse Creek, 287
Scituate, 381, 383, 392, **393**
Sconset, 184, 379
Scow Creek, 138
Scraggy Neck, 346-348
Sculpin Point, 502, 503
Sea Dog Creek, 136, 138
Seaford Creek, 140
Seal Bay, 493
Seal Cove, 439, 493, 495, 496, 506
Seal Island, 156, 518
Seamans Creek, 140
Seapuit River, 355, 358
Searsport, **485**, 487
Seatuck Cove, 149, 153
Sebasco Harbor, 448, 450
Sebonac Creek, 290
Sedge Island, 278
Seekonk River, 323
Seguin Island, 382, 451-466
Selden Creek, **212**
Sesuit Harbor, 381, **385**
Setauket, 96, 97, 261-**263**
Sewell Point, 50

Seymour Rock, 184
Shad Island, 61
Shark River, 75, **78**-80
Sheep Island, 494
Sheepscot Bay, 451, 453, 454, 463, 473
Sheepshead Bay, 97, **99**, 100
Shell Beach, 272
Shell Island, 318
Shelter Island, 96, 97, 266, 267, 270, **271**-274, 286, 287
Sherman Cove, 483
Shinnecock Bay, 94, **135**, 154, 155, **156**, 157
Ship Rock, 170, 171
Shippan Point, 178, 179
Shirttail Point, 387
Short Beach, 136, 141, 171, 188, 189
Siasconset, 330, 331, 379
Silver Bay, 71
Singing Beach, 415
Sippican, 330, 331, 340, 342
Sissy Cove, 69
Sloop Channel, 133, 136, 138, 141
Smith Cove, 222
Smith Cove, 271, 272, 417, 494
Smith Creek, 156
Smith Island, 180
Smith Point, 149
Smithtown Bay, 158, 159, 258
Smugglers Cove, 52
Smuttynose Island, 424, 426
Snow Rock, 340
Snug Harbor, 99, 241, 284, 298-300, 302, 336, 508
Somers Point, 54, 55
Somes Sound, 506-**508**
Somesville, 508
Sorrento, 513, 514
South Beach, 362, 374
South Freeport, 382, 439-441, **445**, 446
South River, 392
Southport, **185**
South Street Seaport Museum, 127
Southampton, 156, 274, 275, 281, 286, 290
Southeast Harbor, 168, 417, 498
Southern Harbor, 493
Southern Island, 474, 476
Southold Bay, 270, 271
Southwest Harbor, **506**-509
Southwest Ledge, 347
Southwick, 62
Speonk, 149, 153
Spray Beach, 63
Spring Point, 439, 440
Spruce Creek, 431
Spruce Point, 457, 462
Spurling Cove, 509
Spuyten Duyvil, 110
Squeteague Harbor, 348
St. Charles, 263, 264
St. George River, 467, **470**-472
St. Lawrence River, 453
Stage Harbor, 330, **361**-363
Stage Island, 438
Stamford, 158-161, 174, 176, **178**-179, 247
Stanley Point, 501
Star Island, 282, 284, 285, 426
Staten Island, 93, 94, 97-100, 102, 103, 126
Steel Harbor Island, 517
Stirling Basin, 267-269
Stockbridge Point, 445, 446
Stone Harbor, 52
Stone Island, 200
Stonington (CT), 158, 159, 220, 232, 234, 235, **236**, 237,
Stonington (ME), 382, 498, **499**
Stony Brook, 160, 258, **259**, 260
Stony Point, 110, 112-114
Straitsmouth Island, 418
Stratford, 158-161, 188, **189**-196, 198-200, 202, 203
Strawbery Banke, 430
Success Rock, 245
Suffolk County, 253, 256, 286-288
Suffolk County, 94
Sugar Reef, 239
Sungic Point, 272
Sunset Lake, 51
Surf City, 62, 63
Swan Creek, 148
Swan Island, 501
Swan River, 148
Swift Creek, 138
Sylvester Cove, 498

T

Tarpaulin Cove, 367
Tarrytown, 95-97, 106, 111, **113**
Taunton River, 326
Tenants Harbor, 466, 467, **474**-476
Tenpound Island, 415, 417
Thames River, 223, 225, 226
Thimble Islands, 188, 196, 197
Thomaston, 471, **472**
Three Mile Harbor, 266, **277**-282, 286
Throgs Neck, 126, 130, 131, 160, 162, 240
Thrumcap Island, 466, 488, 496
Thuya Gardens, 510
Tiana Bay, 156
Tices Shoal, 69
Tinkers Point, 263
Tisbury, 370, 371
Tiverton, 292, 293, 303, 323, **326**, 328
Tobay Beach, 141
Tobys Island, 346
Toms River, 66, 69, **70**-73
Tottenville, 99
Tow Island, 61
Townsend, 68, 250, 268, 270, 453, 460-**462**
Travers Island, 168
Trenton, 408, 503
Trout Pond, 274, 287
Troy, 94, 96, 97, 106, 110, 122-**124**
Try Hatchet Cove, 470
Tuck Point, 410, 413
Tuckernuck Shoal, 376
Tuckerton, 62, 63
Turkey Cove, 470
Turnip Island, 466
Tuthill Cove, 153
Tweed Island, 177
Twin Rivers, 97
Twomile Rock, 332
Twotree Island Channel, 220
Tyler Point, 322

U

Udalls Mill Pond, 240
Umbrella Rock, 168
Uncatena Island, 367
Union River Bay, 503

V

Valley Cove, 508
Ventnor City, 57, 65
Vinalhaven, 382, 480, **488**-493
Vineyard Haven, 330-332, 352, 364, 367, **368**, 370-375

W

Waites Wharf, 315
Wakefield, 292, 293, 298, 301, **302**
Waldoboro, **470**, 471
Wampanoag, 323
Wamphassuc Point, 235
Wantagh, 138, 140, 141
Waquoit Bay, 330, **355**
Wardells Neck, 74
Wards Island, 127, 128
Wareham, 341, **342**, 345
Waretown, 68, 69
Warren Island, 488
Warren River, 322
Warwick, 292, 293, 303, 307, 308, **309**, 310
Washburn Island, 355
Watch Hill, **237**, 238
Watchogue Creek, 148
Water Island, 517
Webb Cove, 498
Weehawken, 106, 108, 109
Weir River, 395
Wellfleet, 383, **387**
Wells Harbor, 435
Wentworth, 427, 429
Wepawaug River, 191
Westbrook, 158, 159, 188, 189-**200**, 202, 203, 212
Westchester, 113, 129, 130, 166, 170, 173
Westcott Cove, 179
Western Bay, 506, 517
Western Channel, 131, 212, 394
Westhampton, 95, 152, **153**, 156
West Point, 115
Westport (CT), **184**, 185
Westport (MA), **333**-335
Wethersfield Cove, 215
Weymouth, 380, 381, 383, 396, **398**
Whale Rock, 228, 303, 364, 365
Whaleboat Island, 445
Wheaton Island, 480
White Island, 424, 491
White Rock, 235
Wianno Beach, 355
Wickford, 292, 293, 302, 303, **304**-307
Wickham Creek, 287
Wicopesset, 239
Widow Island, 493
Wildwood, 50
Willets Point, 130, 240
Willow Point, 232
Wilson Cove, 180, 182
Wincoma Point, 253
Windmill Point, 395
Windsor Locks, 219
Wings Neck, 345, 346, 384
Winnegance Creek, 452
Winter Harbor, 382, **493**, 494, **513**, 515
Winterport, 486
Wiscasset, 454, **456**, 457
Wood Island Harbor, 438
Wood Island, 438, 450
Woodcleft Canal, 138
Woodenboat School, 497, 498
Woods Hole, 330-332, **348**-351, 352, 353, 364, 367
Woodsburgh, 135
Wright Island, 165, 167
Wychmere Harbor, 330, **361**
Wyeth, 473, 478

Y

Yarmouth, 330, 331, 361, 380-382, 385, 440, **444**, 445, 448, 511
Yonkers, 96, 97, 110
York Harbor, 432
York Narrows, 501, 502

Z

Zypher Rock, 480

SUBJECT INDEX

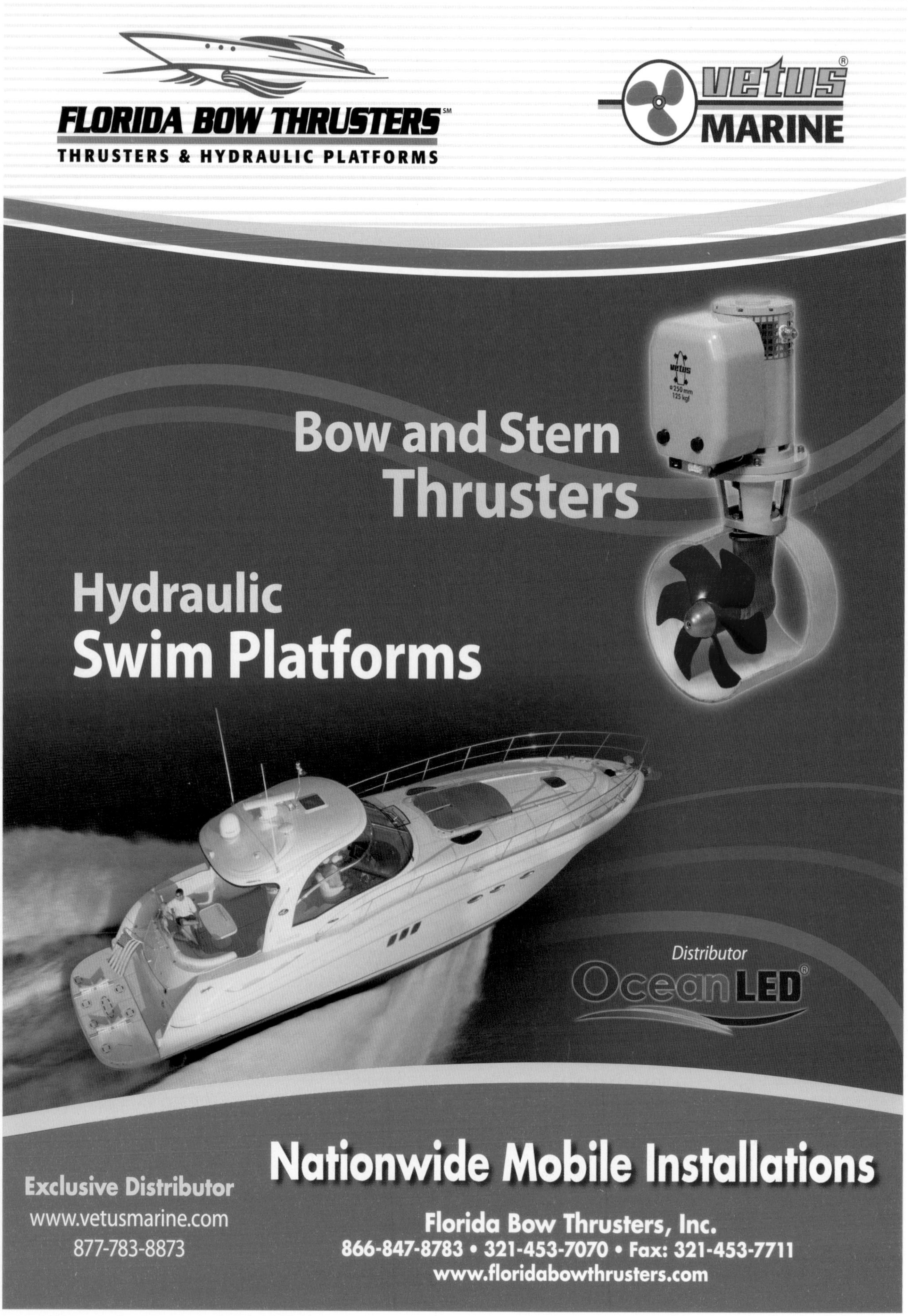

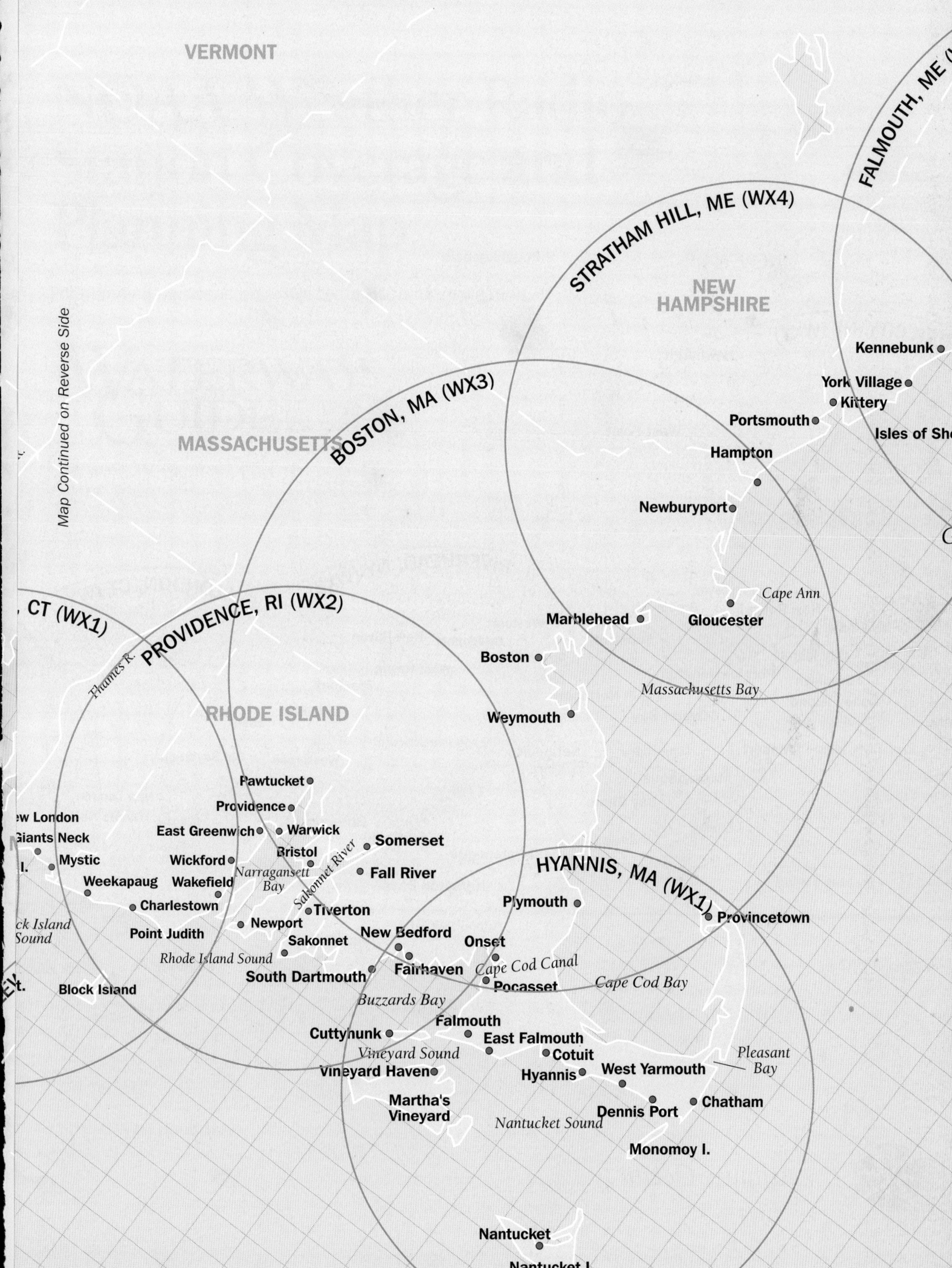

Map Continued on Reverse Side

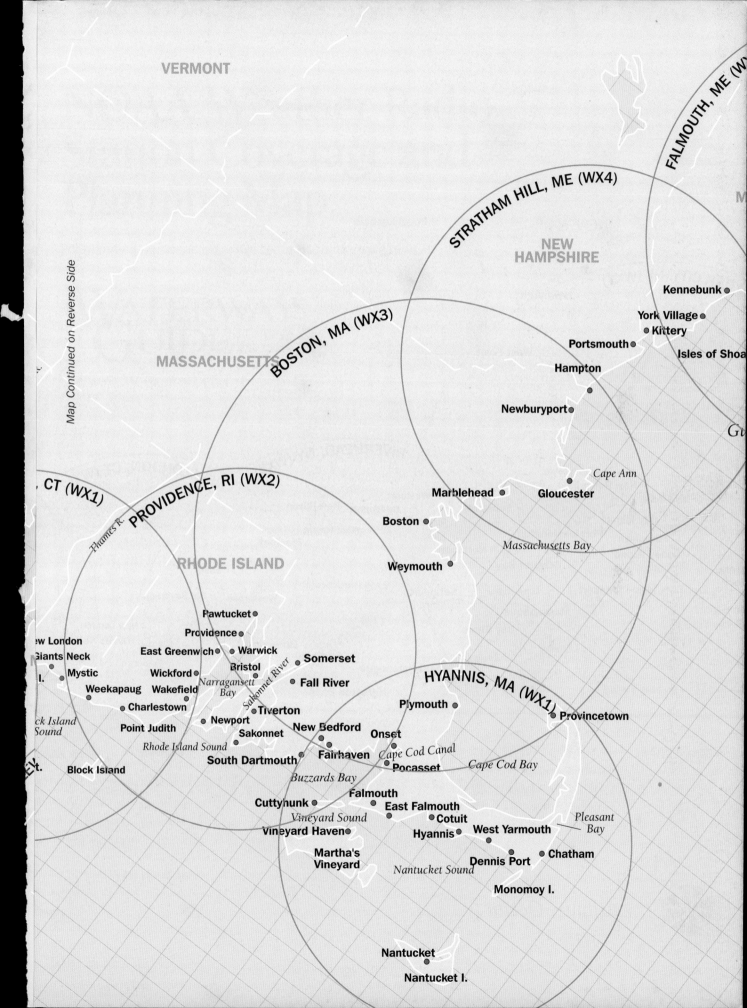

X1)
DRESDEN, ME (WX3)
ELLSWORTH, ME (WX2)
Bangor
Belfast
AINE
Yarmouth
Freeport
Bath
Waldoboro
Camden
Falmouth
Portland
Casco Bay
Rockport
Penobscot Bay
Rockland
Saco
Cape Elizabeth
Bar Harbor
Boothbay Harbor
Muscongus Bay
Mt. Desert Island
Southwest Harbor
Frenchman Bay
Isle au Haut
ls
lf of Maine
N

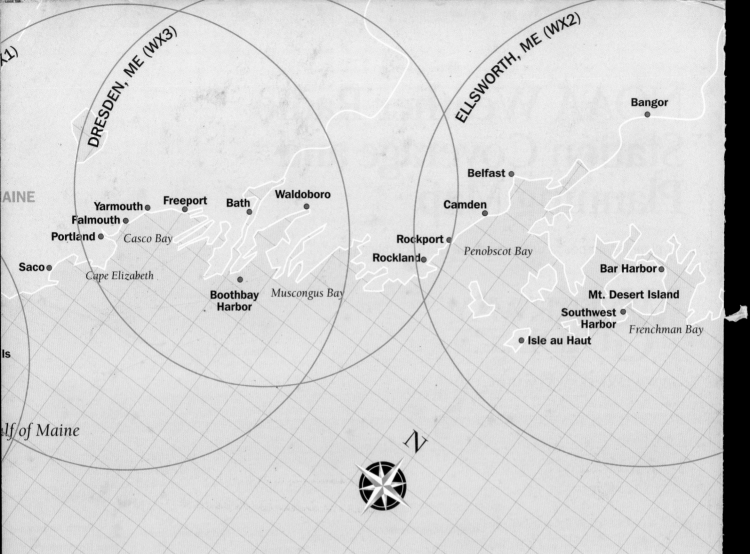

NOAA Weather Radio Station Coverage and Planning Map

For planning purposes only. Not to be used for navigation.

WWW.WATERWAYGUIDE.COM